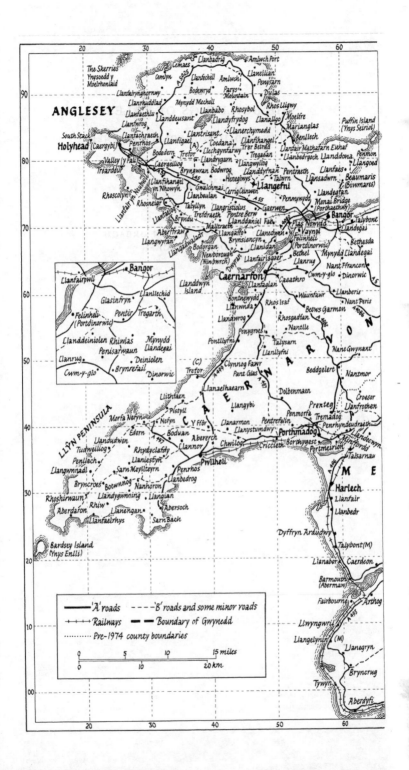

THE BUILDINGS OF WALES

FOUNDING EDITOR: NIKOLAUS PEVSNER

GWYNEDD

RICHARD HASLAM, JULIAN ORBACH
AND ADAM VOELCKER

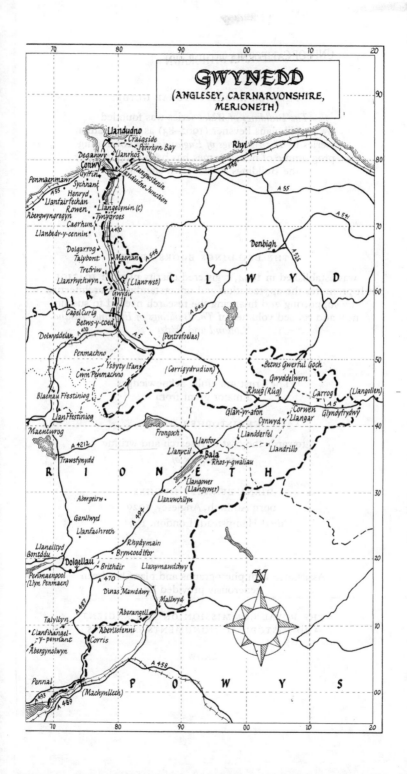

PEVSNER ARCHITECTURAL GUIDES

The Buildings of Wales series was founded
by Sir Nikolaus Pevsner (1902–83) as a companion
series to *The Buildings of England*. The continuing
programme of new volumes has been supported by
the Buildings Books Trust since 1994

THE BUILDINGS BOOKS TRUST

was established in 1994, registered charity number 1042101.
It promotes the appreciation and understanding of architecture
by supporting and financing the research needed to sustain
new and revised volumes of *The Buildings of England, Ireland,
Scotland* and *Wales*

The Trust gratefully acknowledges
a major grant from

CHRISTOPHER WADE

towards the cost of research and writing
in memory of

DIANA BENNETT HUGHES
born Amlwch, Anglesey, 1929
died Hampstead, London, 1991

Assistance with photographs and plans has been
generously provided by

THE ROYAL COMMISSION ON THE ANCIENT
AND HISTORICAL MONUMENTS OF WALES

CADW

Gwynedd

ANGLESEY, CAERNARVONSHIRE
AND MERIONETH

BY

RICHARD HASLAM

JULIAN ORBACH

AND

ADAM VOELCKER

WITH CONTRIBUTIONS BY

JUDITH ALFREY

DAVID GWYN

JOHN KENYON

AND

FRANCES LYNCH

THE BUILDINGS OF WALES

YALE UNIVERSITY PRESS
NEW HAVEN AND LONDON

YALE UNIVERSITY PRESS
NEW HAVEN AND LONDON
302 Temple Street, New Haven CT 06511
47 Bedford Square, London WC1B 3DP
www.pevsner.co.uk
www.lookingatbuildings.org.uk
www.yalebooks.co.uk
www.yalebooks.com
for
THE BUILDINGS BOOKS TRUST

Published by Yale University Press 2009
2 4 6 8 10 9 7 5 3 1

ISBN 978 0 300 14169 6

Printed in China
through World Print
Set in Monotype Plantin

Gratefully dedicated to

THE HISTORICAL SOCIETIES OF WALES
whose members and publications are a vital resource
and inspiration

and
in memory of

CHARLOTTE HASLAM
whose writing career began at Plas Brondanw,
then flowered at the Landmark Trust
and whom good buildings
made happy

CONTENTS

CONTENTS

LIST OF TEXT FIGURES AND MAPS

Every effort has been made to contact or trace all copyright holders. The publishers will be glad to make good any errors or omissions brought to our attention in future editions.

MAPS

PHOTOGRAPHIC ACKNOWLEDGEMENTS

A special debt is owed to the Royal Commission on the Ancient and Historical Monuments of Wales and its photographer Iain Wright for providing most of the photographs for this volume. (*www.rcahmw.gov.uk*).

All images are Crown Copyright © Royal Commission on the Ancient and Historical Monuments of Wales, with the exception of the following:

Cadw, Welsh Assembly Government (Crown Copyright): 2, 5, 6, 7, 8, 19, 21, 24, 25, 26, 27, 28, 29, 30, 31, 32, 47, 52, 53
Greta Hughes: 97
National Trust Photographic Library/Matthew Antrobus: 45
National Trust Photographic Library/Michael Caldwell: 80
National Trust Photographic Library/Andreas von Einsiedel: 78
Julian Orbach: 85, 89
Alex Ramsay: 115
John Rowlands (*www.pixaerial.co.uk*): 120
Adam Voelcker: 58, 59, 60

MAP REFERENCES

The numbers printed in italic type in the margin against the place names in the gazetteer of the book indicate the position of the place in question on the index map (pp. ii–iii), which is divided into sections by the 10-kilometre reference lines of the National Grid. The reference given here omits the two initial letters which in a full grid reference refer to the 100-kilometre squares into which the area is divided. The first number indicates the *western* boundary, and the third the *southern* boundary, of the 10-kilometre square in which the place in question is situated. For example, Aberffraw (reference 3569) will be found in the 10-kilometre square bounded by grid lines 30 (on the *west*) and 40, and 60 (on the *south*) and 70; Tywyn (reference 5801) in the square bounded by the grid lines 50 (on the *west*) and 60, and 00 (on the *south*) and 10.

The map contains all those places, whether towns, villages, or isolated buildings, which are the subject of separate entries in the text.

FOREWORD

This final volume of the *Buildings of Wales* was begun by Richard Haslam, joined in 2006 by Julian Orbach and Adam Voelcker. The rough division of work has been that Richard Haslam wrote draft texts for the region and final text for Anglesey, Adam Voelcker wrote the final text for Caernarvonshire and Julian Orbach for Merioneth, with entries on major country houses and the four principal Caernarvonshire towns by Richard Haslam. In practice the process has been much more mixed, Adam Voelcker making contributions to western Merioneth and to the accounts of Bangor and Caernarfon, and Julian Orbach to chapels, some country houses and to the accounts of Conwy and Llandudno. Specialist authors have also contributed text: Frances Lynch the entries on prehistoric and Roman sites as well as the introduction chapter on these periods, John Kenyon all the castle entries as well as the introduction chapter, while David Gwyn wrote the chapter on industrial archaeology and contributed draft text for the gazetteer. In addition, Judith Alfrey has written the introduction chapter on vernacular houses and farm buildings.

Particular thanks are due to the many owners and occupiers of houses who generously allowed us to view their homes and gave us valuable information. It should be firmly stated that mention of a building in the text does not in any way imply that it is open to the public. We are also grateful to the incumbents, ministers, chapel secretaries and churchwardens for help with churches and chapels.

Research in the London archives of the RIBA, particularly the volumes of *The Builder* and *Building News* and other architectural periodicals, was undertaken by Karen Evans, who also looked at the church-building papers of the Incorporated Church Building Society at Lambeth Palace. The authors used the archives of the National Library of Wales, Aberystwyth, and the four county record offices at Caernarfon, Dolgellau, Llandudno and Llangefni, and thanks are due to the archivists and staff at all of these. The staff of the Royal Commission on the Ancient and Historical Monuments of Wales, in Aberystwyth, contributed unstintingly, both personal comments and research assistance. Particular thanks must go to the successive Secretaries, Peter Smith, Peter White and Peter Wakelin, and to the Commission's photographer Iain Wright whose talent illuminates the illustrations of this volume.

The Gwynedd Archaeological Trust has assisted on much more than archaeology, David Longley and Andrew Davidson particularly on the churches, David Gwyn on industrial sites. The historic buildings section at Cadw provided listed building information and advice whenever requested. Particular thanks are due to Judith Alfrey for discussing individual buildings and looking over text with consistent and scholarly dedication. The Snowdonia National Park Authority and the County Councils of Gwynedd, Ynys Môn, Conwy and Denbighshire have all given assistance generally through their conservation officers, as has Liz Green at the National Trust regional office.

Persons to whom we would like to give special thanks include a group whose advice across many fields has been both specialist and general: Margaret Dunn, Peter Howell, Thomas Lloyd, David McLees, Robert Scourfield, Richard Suggett, Phil Thomas. Specialist advice has come from Tim Palmer, Jana Horák and John Davies (building stones); Olwen Jenkins (chapels); John Morgan Guy and Matthew Saunders (churches); Frances Voelcker (landscape introduction and Tremadog); Malcolm Seaborne (schools); Geoffrey Fisher (sculpture); Alan Brooks, Peter Cormack and Michael Kerney (stained glass). Matthew Craske (Henry Cheere) and John Kenworthy-Browne (Joseph Nollekens) have advised on particular sculptors; for particular sites, Marion Barter (Bangor University), Edmund Douglas-Pennant (Penrhyn Castle), Robin Grove-White (Plas Coch), Bettina Harden (Nanhoron), Katie Lench (Vaynol), Robin Llywelyn (Portmeirion), Donald Moore (Caerdeon), Kenneth Powell (Our Lady and St Winefride, Amlwch), David Robinson (Cymer Abbey), and Peter Welford (Gwydir Castle); for particular architects, Mrs Pam Phillips (Herbert North), members of the Morris family (O. Morris Roberts and Griffith Morris), Andy Foster (Birmingham architects), and Clare Hartwell (Manchester architects); and for particular towns, Iwan Bryn Williams (Bala), David Price (Bangor), and the Rev. Neil Fairlamb, Michael Burkham and Richard Hayman (Beaumaris). Architects who gave information on their own work include Bill Davies (Bowen Dann Davies), Graeme Hughes (Gwynedd County schools), Maredudd ab Iestyn, John Madin and Gruffydd Price. And much is owed to the late Mrs C. S. Haslam.

In memoriam thanks are due to Dr Ian Allan, a magpie of a collector of facts about buildings and architects in North Wales and author of an unpublished thesis on Herbert North.

The project was undertaken by the Buildings Books Trust under Simon Jenkins and the Trust Secretary Gavin Watson. The book was edited by Simon Bradley at Yale University Press and seen through production by Sophie Kullmann.

In spite of all this help, gaps and mistakes will surely remain. Corrections and supplementary information will be welcomed by the authors and publisher and will be incorporated in a subsequent reprint or edition.

INTRODUCTION

THE THREE COUNTIES

The ancient counties of Anglesey, Caernarvonshire and Merioneth roughly correspond to the North Wales principality of Gwynedd before the English conquest of 1283. As constituted in the post-conquest settlement they lasted until the late C20 boundary changes, since when modern borders and names have changed several times. The two mainland counties are now divided between the local authorities of Gwynedd (western Caernarvonshire and most of Merioneth), Conwy (eastern Caernarvonshire) and Denbighshire (five communities of NE Merioneth around Corwen).

The mainland LANDSCAPES are among the most beautiful in Britain and tend to make the buildings seem trivial in comparison. A contour map shows that almost a third of the area is above 1,000 ft (300 metres). Unlike the more rounded uplands and plateaus elsewhere in Wales, the high ground of CAERNAR-VONSHIRE is jagged, dramatic, 'horrid' and 'sublime' in the terms of the Romantics. The hard rocks (chiefly dolerites and rhyolites) yield neither simple access routes, sweet soil for cultivation, nor easy building stone. On the fringes of the mountainous core are different landscapes. The Llŷn peninsula is a softer land more like Cornwall, edged by sandy coves and rocky cliffs. The Creud-dyn peninsula in the NE, cut off by the Penmaenmawr headland, has a famously mild climate (resulting in the suburban sprawl of Llandudno), but the underlying geology of grey limestone and red sandstone gives it a texture unlike the rest of the county. Some historical subdivision names for the county are still current: three of the *cantref* names, Arfon (the NW montains, Caernarfon and Bangor), Arllechwedd (the NE mountains, Conwy), and Llŷn (the SW peninsula); and of the smaller commote names, Eifionydd (between Porthmadog and Pwllheli), Nant Conwy (the Conwy valley) and Creuddyn (the Llandudno peninsula).

MERIONETH, mostly upland rising to mountain, can be spectacularly rocky in the Rhinogs and the great mass of Cader Idris, but is characteristically broader, with some of the loveliest valleys. The lakes at Bala and Talyllyn fill broad glacial valleys with mountains to each side, the four estuaries are each the foreground to beautiful hills, with placid pastureland inland on the Dwyryd and Dysynni, and wooded ravines with waterfalls towards the headwaters of the Mawddach and its tributaries Cain

and Eden. The county is historically subdivided into the
commotes of Ardudwy (the NW), Edeirnion (NE), Mawddwy
(Mallwyd and Dinas Mawddwy), Penllyn (around Bala Lake),
Talybont (Tywyn to Dolgellau) and Ystumanner (SW).

ANGLESEY is quite different, an island of rolling country rising
to rock at the N. The outcrops mostly do not reach 650 ft (200
metres); the highest point is Holyhead Mountain on Holy Island.
There are no rivers of significance but the Malltraeth Marsh, a
fenland, cuts a broad swathe up from the S coast. The island's
rich soils grew grain in large fields, for which it has been known
since early medieval times as Mam Cymru, the mother of Wales.
There were windmills – almost unknown on the mainland – in
quantity, to process the grain. Settlements on Anglesey are more
concentrated.

There is great variation of climate. Mediterranean flora
flourish at Portmeirion, Llandudno, and on Anglesey's Menai
Riviera, while just behind the dark mountains loom, cut by the
five deep gorges of Snowdonia, with sombre forestry conifers,
curly sessile oak, purple heather, escarpments and scree, and
hidden cold lakes.

As with most of West Wales there is a scarcity of nucleated
settlements, this being a country of small farms and smaller
holdings. In industrial times quarrymen settled on tiny encroachments on the commons in the face of enclosures by landlords.
While there are ancient nucleated villages such as Llanfechell
(A), Aberdaron (C) and Dinas Mawddwy (M), most clustered
settlements have grown much more recently, close to extractive
industrial sites, at key points on transport routes and, not entirely
recently, at tourist locations. The pattern of landholding with
several very large landed estates has created a small number of
recognizable 'estate villages' and a large number of estate farms,
generally with C19 buildings. The ancient farming practice of
transhumance, moving livestock in the summer from main holdings on low ground to common grazing on uplands, is reflected
in the many house names with *hendre* (old settlement) or *hafod*
(summer house).

The difficulty of access has meant that the North West has
remained a bastion of Welsh culture and language, still spoken
by over two-thirds of the population. In settlements less influenced by tourism and immigration it can be the first language of
over 80 per cent. While it is easy to imagine this sparsely populated region a place out of time, little touched, it has been altered
by successive waves of habitation and exploitation since earliest
times, as the prehistoric, British and Roman forts and burial
places, the mines and quarries and the harbours and quays testify.

Exploitation of the landscape for metals appears to have begun
in prehistoric times, for copper, lead and gold. From the late C18
the character of Anglesey was changed by the copper mines of
Parys Mountain, followed in Caernarvonshire and Merioneth in
the C19 by the mining of slate. These extractive industries
required concentrated workforces, sophisticated processing facilities, roads, tramways and railways, changing much more than

the immediate extraction sites. Facilities for shipping slate developed at Port Penrhyn (Bangor), Port Dinorwic (Y Felinheli), Caernarfon (first the Seiont quayside, then the Victoria Dock), Porthmadog and Aberdyfi. The extraction of slate and copper has all but ceased, leaving the typical intriguing scars. No single employment has followed to fill the gap and the exporting ports are mostly used for holiday boating. The principal modern harbour is Holyhead, protected artificially by the Great Breakwater.

All three counties are predominately rural, and towns are mostly small. In Anglesey Holyhead is by far the largest, with over 11,000 inhabitants in 2001. In Caernarvonshire, Llandudno outstrips the older ones with 20,000, although Bangor has 10,000 students to add to its population of 14,000. The other main town, Caernarfon, has some 9,000 inhabitants. Merioneth, sparsely populated, saw the numbers in slate-quarrying Blaenau Ffestiniog rise to nearly 12,000 in the early C20, now just under 5,000; Dolgellau, Barmouth and Bala have populations in descending order from 3,000 to 2,000.

GEOLOGY AND BUILDING MATERIALS

Stone and Slate

The rocks of Gwynedd are unequalled for variety in Wales, except perhaps on the NW tip of Pembrokeshire. Most of those in North Wales are pre- or Lower Palaeozoic, with the sequence of Precambrian, Cambrian and Ordovician predominating in Gwynedd, bounded to the E and S by the younger Silurian strata which underlie most of Mid and NE Wales. These rocks produced hard, dark and unforgiving stone which was difficult to work, yet was so abundant that its undressed use was ubiquitous, giving Welsh buildings their typical rugged character. Dressed stone in medieval times mostly came from the Lower Carboniferous sandstones on either side of the Menai Strait, or more locally, e.g. Egryn (M).

The PRECAMBRIAN/CAMBRIAN rocks run in bands NE to SW, chiefly across Anglesey. Granite, hornfels and gneisses (Coedana Complex) outcrop across the centre of the island and as small outliers at Carmel Head, between Llanerchymedd and Bryngwran, and SE of Amlwch. Of the thick Monian Supergroup succession, only quartzite and serpentine were quarried, the former used for the harbour walls and breakwater at Holyhead in the early C19 and the latter as an ornamental stone. Serpentinite, or 'Mona Marble',* a late Precambrian/Cambrian rock outcropping in small areas on Holy Island and W of Llanfechell, produced red and green stone which could be highly polished and used decoratively, e.g. the drawing-room fireplace at Penrhyn Castle. Dark grey and greenish grey schists can be seen on

---

*Not to be confused with 'Anglesey Marble', a common name for the Carboniferous Limestone.

buildings in Menai Bridge. Bands of Precambrian occur on the mainland, especially between Bangor and Caernarfon, between Bethesda and the coast w of Penygroes (largely volcanic lavas, quartz-felsites, tuffs and grits), and at the NW extremity of Llŷn between Nefyn and Aberdaron (minor gneisses and plutonic igneous rocks). Coastal outcrops of a chaotic unit of the Monian Supergroup contain massive blocks of sandstone and volcanic rock but also blocks of red jasper, used in pieces of unparalleled size on the Norwich Union building, Piccadilly, London (1906–8).

CAMBRIAN rocks crop out in two main areas. The larger is the Harlech Dome, covering much of Merioneth and displaying the thickest succession of Cambrian rocks in Britain. The Rhinog Grits produced hard sandstones, grits and quartzitic boulders, seen commonly in field walls and farm buildings. Blue and purple slatey stone from the Llanbedr area was quarried, as was a softer green stone in the Barmouth area, seen in the town's Wesleyan chapel, and at the strikingly green Shire Hall at Dolgellau, 1825. Green stone in rough squared blocks characterizes C19 Dolgellau, e.g. the fine Eldon Row (1830). Egryn sandstone, a coarse stone predominantly buff in colour but also ochre, rusty and grey-green, was being quarried in the C12 along the Harlech to Barmouth coastline. Examples can be seen in church dressings, notably the s doorway at Llanaber, as well as at Harlech Castle and Cymer Abbey. Shales, mudstones and micaceous sandstones from the Dolgelley, Ffestiniog and Maentwrog beds (collectively known as the Lingula Flags) have produced hard but workable building stone. Dolgellau church, 1716, is of squared slatey stone. Much of Maentwrog is built of very long regular stone from the Gelli Grin quarry SW of the village. Some reach prodigious lengths, e.g. at the White Lion Inn, Trawsfynydd, where a single 23-ft (7-metre) stone spans almost the entire elevation.

The second area of Cambrian rock is along the N side of Snowdon, the result of the compression of mudstones. This area contains some of the best-known slate quarries. Penrhyn (Bethesda), Dinorwic (Llanberis) and Nantlle (E of Penygroes) all produced purple roofing slates and also slab suitable for walls and floors. A number of small quarries in the Talysarn area yielded green and multicoloured slates. The same rock crops out N of Snowdon at the Gallt-y-llan quarry near Nant Peris, one of the sources for the picturesque multicoloured slates *Herbert North* loved to use.

ORDOVICIAN rocks sweep in a vast semicircle around the Harlech Dome, with spurs N towards Penmaenmawr and W along the Llŷn peninsula. They display two distinct types: roofing slates like the Cambrian, and much harder rocks of volcanic origin. The main area of production was in and around Blaenau Ffestiniog. Further s, two superimposed veins, Narrow and Broad, run some 18 miles from the coast near Aberdyfi through Abergynolwyn, Corris and Aberllefenni to Dinas Mawddwy. These also yielded grey slates for roofing, but were better known for slabs and sills. Aberllefenni was the last worked, its slate used to clad

Trawsfynydd Power Station. Quarry offcuts are widely used in Corris and Abergynolwyn buildings. The hard volcanic rocks are responsible for all the larger mountain blocks, such as Yr Eifl (The Rivals) and the isolated hills of Llŷn, Snowdonia, Arenig Fawr, Rhobell Fawr, Aran Mawddwy and the Cadair Idris ridge. The small mountain above Trefor (C) yields a grey granite used chiefly for setts, and granite from Graig Lwyd, Penmaenmawr, was exploited in the Neolithic period for stone axes which found their way as far as Land's End and Scotland. The quarries today produce ballast for railways. Outcrops of rhyolitic tuff s of Peny-groes provided ready-made lintels and 'through' stones, usually hexagonal in cross-section due to the columnar formation.

Rocks from the SILURIAN period are absent in Gwynedd except at the E and S fringes. A band runs on the W side of the Conwy river between Conwy and Llanrwst and reappears around Corwen and Bala, continuing SW as far as the Dyfi estuary. Grits and flags predominate and can be seen at Conwy Castle, built of the rock on which it sits.

The DEVONIAN (Old Red Sandstone) succession, likewise mostly absent, makes a surprise appearance in Anglesey in a narrow band extending S almost to Llangefni from Dulas Bay. The pinnacles and parapets of Llaneilian church may be of this material, which would have provided a useful source of dressed stone had it been more plentiful. CARBONIFEROUS Limestone occurs on the two Ormes Heads on the Creuddyn peninsula (Llandudno), the Vaynol promontory SW of Bangor, and on Anglesey: the E tip around Penmon, a band N of the Menai Strait opposite Caernarfon, and a larger area tapering SW to Bodorgan from Moelfre and Red Wharf Bay. These were an important source of building stone from the earliest times: the massive stones at Din Lligwy (Rhos Lligwy) are Romano-British, and p. 219 Caernarfon and Beaumaris castles were built of the dense, light grey material, as were Penrhyn Castle and the two Anglesey bridges in the C19. The stone was exported, e.g. for Birmingham Town Hall, where recent renovation has required matching stone from Moelfre. Carboniferous sandstones and grits from Anglesey and Arfon were used as freestone, and pink-brown sandstone from Moel-y-don on the Menai Strait was used for the distinctive bands of Caernarfon Castle's outermost walls.

For younger IMPORTED STONE, Gwynedd was dependent on NE Wales and England: e.g. Cefn-y-fedw sandstone (Millstone Grit) from Flintshire and Denbighshire, and strong yellow Cefn quartzitic sandstone (Coal Measures) from the Wrexham area. Red Kinnerton sandstone (Permo-Triassic) was used for dressings at Conwy Castle and is seen in towns such as Bangor and Betws-y-coed. Triassic sandstones from the Runcorn and Chester areas, also red, were favoured by *John Douglas* and his followers: *Beckett*'s St Saviour, Llandudno is entirely of this hand-some material. Grinshill, a pale Triassic stone from the Shrews-bury area, has a long history of use, and occasionally stone from more distant regions was imported, such as the Ancaster limestone at St Mary, Betws-y-coed, and the yellow stone of

Christ Church, Llanfairfechan, brought from Lancashire along with its architect.

Roofing Materials

THATCH (reed rather than straw) was the predominant roofing material before slate, but very few thatch roofs survive. SLATE QUARRYING before the mid to late C18 was small-scale, the slates usually thick and rough and in a variety of widths and lengths, put to visual advantage by laying in diminishing courses. As production grew, the sizes were regularized, starting with Odds and Doubles at the small end and rising through the ranks of female aristocracy with Ladies, Countesses, Marchionesses, Duchesses and Princesses. The thinnest slates were categorized as Best, the thickest as Third quality. Regular-coursed slating became prevalent. Today the range has been drastically reduced and mechanization has replaced hand-dressing. Welsh slate is threatened by imports sometimes indistinguishable from the native type. Clay and concrete TILES are uncommon, especially within the Snowdonia National Park where their use is discouraged. Red plain tiles appear on late C19 and Edwardian buildings, imitating the materials of Kent and Sussex.

Brick and Terracotta

Pre-industrial BRICK is very rare. The wings added to Bodwrdda, Aberdaron (C) in 1621 are surprising both for the early date and the westerly location. (Sir Richard Clough introduced brick in 1567 to the Vale of Clwyd, drawing inspiration from his residence at Antwerp.) Brick was used in 1687 for the chimneys and upper gables at Llannerch, Llannor (C). In the 1720s–30s red bricks made apparently on site were used for facings at Peniarth, Llanegryn (M), and similarly at Plas Gwyn, Pentraeth (A) in the 1740s. The White Lion Hotel at Bala (M), 1759, is brick-fronted. From the mid C19 there were small-scale brick pits in the Conwy valley and on Anglesey at Traeth Dulas, Dulas. Bricks were made later on Anglesey at Holyhead, Cemaes and Porth Wen 97 (Llanbadrig), where the Hoffmann kilns and chimneys still stand on the beach. The Seiont brickworks, Caernarfon (closed in 2008), produced the distinctive yellow brick that typifies the northern edge of the town. By the end of the century yellow and red bricks were very widely imported from Buckley and Ruabon in NE Wales and can be seen all over the region. The houses at the West End, Pwllheli (C), built from 1894, are of yellow Ruabon brick brought in on the Cambrian Railway.

TERRACOTTA is also an import of the late C19 and early C20, probably mostly from the works of J. C. Edwards of Ruabon. John Douglas used red terracotta at the Castle Hotel, Conwy, p. 71 and fitted tall fancy chimney pots to Glangwna, Caeathro (C). Moriah chapel, Llanbedr (M) displays a honey-coloured terracotta for its entire elevation, and the early C20 Merioneth county schools use it extensively. COADE STONE is used exceptionally on the gateway to Tremadog church (C), c. 1811.

Timber

TIMBER construction has a long history in western Wales despite the predominance of stone. Timber-framed buildings are recorded in illustrations in several towns and survive in Conwy and Beaumaris. The upper Dee valley (Edeirnion) is within the NE Wales zone of timber building. Oak trees were grown even in inhospitable areas for structural timber and fittings (*see* Vernacular, p. 40) until replaced in the later C18 by pine imported from the Baltic and Quebec. After the Second World War wooden houses from Sweden were put up by several local authorities, though many have been over-clad since. More recently home-grown hardwoods have been promoted in the interests of sustainability. Buildings with token areas of oak, larch or cedar boarding have become fashionable; the Galeri arts centre, Caernarfon, is entirely clad in boarding.

Wall Finishes

LIME RENDERS and LIMEWASH covered most stone buildings, usually for weather protection. Gruffudd ap Cynan's limewashed churches on Anglesey 'glittered like stars in the firmament'. Castles may have had a similar treatment, though the dark bands of Caernarfon's walls must have been intended for show. SLATE CLADDING is oddly not common – Totnes in Devon has more slate-clad houses lining its streets than, say, Caernarfon. A finish obtained by pressing small pieces of stone into wet mortar is a local C19 to C20 technique in Caernarvonshire and Anglesey. Cement-based PEBBLEDASH is all too common; Aberffraw (A) is an example of a spoilt village. With the increased awareness of building conservation and the growing availability of lime products, this trend may be reversing.

Other Materials

CLAY walling (called CLOM in Welsh) was widespread in Llŷn (*see* Vernacular, p. 40)*. Some foundries made IRON building components. Iron windows probably from Machynlleth can be found around Corris (M) and in Aberdyfi and Corris churches. The windows at Britannia Place, Porthmadog (C) were probably from the nearby foundry and most of the iron components in the Quarry Workshops, Dinorwic (C) were made on-site, including the attractive latticed windows. Chapel gallery columns may have been made locally, but later in the C19 could be imported from specialist makers such as *Macfarlane* in Glasgow or *Coalbrookdale*,

---

* Clough Williams-Ellis wrote a delightful book about clay construction in 1916 but makes no mention of Wales.

whose names appear on balconies, gateways and the cast-iron arcades of Llandudno. Iron staircase railings made by *William Hazledine* of Shrewsbury appear in country houses *c.* 1800. On a much larger scale he made the iron for *Telford*'s Waterloo Bridge, Betws-y-coed (C), 1815–16, and the chains for his suspension bridges at Menai Bridge (A) and Conwy (C). For the iron railway bridges by *Robert Stephenson* at the same crossings *see* p. 61.

CONCRETE makes one surprising early appearance, on the Dinas Mawddwy (M) estate of Sir Edmund Buckley, in the late 1860s: first for garden walls, then farm buildings, and finally a hotel, 1870–3. Much later examples include the demolished West End Hotel, Pwllheli (C), 1896, and the peculiar Plas Dolydd, Sychnant (C), *c.* 1922, of blocks cast with broken stone to give a rubble effect, with mass concrete roofs, presumably reinforced. The Catholic churches in Amlwch (A) and Porthmadog (C), built in the 1930s by the Italian engineer *Giuseppe Rinvolucri*, are radical essays in reinforced concrete, the former a particularly elegant parabolic building. *Clough Williams-Ellis*'s buildings often incorporate concrete in an *ad hoc* way; Morannedd Café, Criccieth (C) is more explicit (1948). Stone-faced blocks were experimented with in the Porthmadog and Harlech areas by a local builder *Hughie Thomas* in conjunction with the architects *O. Morris Roberts & Son* and *Griffith Morris*. Plas Nantcol, Llanbedr (M), by the latter in 1955, and the HSBC bank in Trawsfynydd (M) are examples.

PREHISTORIC AND ROMAN GWYNEDD

BY FRANCES LYNCH

The central geographical feature of Gwynedd, the great mountain range of Snowdonia, does not feature prominently in the early history of settlement. More important are the lowland areas which surround it, particularly Anglesey, for long the main agricultural producer for the region, and to a lesser extent the Llŷn peninsula with its open southern shore. This area looks across Cardigan Bay to the coastal belt of Ardudwy and the Mawddach estuary, another major centre of prehistoric occupation, and one which, through the Wnion and Dee valleys, had contacts with peoples to the E and S. Edeirnion, the valley of the Dee between Bala and Corwen, is a nodal point in communications, and there is a concentration of monuments in this fertile oasis. Another enclosed and sheltered area of considerable fertility is the Conwy valley; here, too, there was a notable concentration of settlement from the Neolithic period (4500–2300 B.C.) onwards, especially where the valley broadens out near Rowen. In the Bronze Age (2300–800 B.C.) the higher ground of Arllechwedd and Rhinogydd was penetrated, and in the Roman period there is evidence for agriculture at surprisingly high altitudes, but the central massifs of Snowdon and Arenig were never extensively settled by early man.

The earliest evidence belongs to the MESOLITHIC PERIOD
(10,000–4500 B.C.) when the ice had retreated and small bands
of hunters were active in thick deciduous woodland which spread
with the increasing warmth of climate. They also exploited the
wildfowl, fish and shellfish of the coastal belt, which was then
wider, for the sea level was a good deal lower than today.
Surviving occupation sites in Gwynedd are mostly coastal,
perhaps originally some distance from the shore: at Aberdaron
(C) on the tip of Llŷn, on Bardsey (C) and at Trwyn Du,
Aberffraw (A), where a date c. 8000 B.C. has been obtained for
the manufacture of the characteristically small arrow tips of the
period. Occasional finds of such flint tools have come from caves
in the Great Orme headland (and most notably a decorated horse
jaw from Kendrick's Cave there), as from many South Welsh
caves, and evidence is emerging of camps in the upper reaches
of the Lledr valley, also in Conwy.

Although we imagine that these hunting bands were small and
isolated, there is evidence to suggest that they understood the
special properties of certain rocks, which they exchanged over
quite large distances. When the first farmers occupied the area,
these rocks were exploited on a much larger scale to provide polished stone axes necessary to clear woodland. Gwynedd can
boast two notable centres for large-scale production. Graig
Lwyd, Penmaenmawr (C), one of the largest 'factories', exported
its products across England to Yorkshire, Kent and especially
Wiltshire. The other centre, on Mynydd Rhiw on the end of Llŷn
(C), was smaller, but is important as one of the few sites where
the stone was actually mined from pits. Elsewhere suitable rock
was picked up from screes, or quarried. The rock was roughly
worked to shape at the factory sites, finished by polishing elsewhere, and, when complete, traded away. Evidence for this trade
occurs early in the fourth millennium, but it seems to have
reached its greatest expansion towards the end of the Neolithic
period, when farming had extended into all areas of the country.

The origin of the first farmers in Gwynedd is uncertain, but
they undoubtedly maintained close links with Ireland, and the
Irish Sea is likely to have been their means of access (travel eastwards, through tree-choked valleys and mountains, would have
been difficult). Their elegant, undecorated pottery, their rectangular wooden houses of which three have been excavated, two at
Llandegai (C) and one at Trefignath, Holyhead (A), and many
of their stone tombs are similar to those in Ireland and in
Pembrokeshire and SW England.

Since evidence of wooden houses is rare, it is the distribution
of the huge stone TOMBS of the period which gives the fullest
picture of the extent of earlier Neolithic settlement. These 'megalithic' tombs were the communal burial places of farming communities over many centuries and must also have been the focus
of their religious activity. They reflect a tradition widespread in
western Europe at this time, although the architectural details of
the chambers and the cairns which covered them vary from place
to place. In the coastal area of Ardudwy, the Llŷn peninsula and

the Conwy valley, the dominant style is that of the portal dolmen, a single chamber with tall entrance stones and a high closing slab between, covered by a capstone often of staggering size. These tombs, even in decay, represent some of the most exciting early structures to be seen anywhere in Britain, for the casual skill with which the large stones are balanced still defies engineers' analysis. These tombs are closely comparable to many in SE Ireland, and excavations at Dyffryn Ardudwy (M) suggested that the style was established in Wales during the earlier Neolithic. Later on, new ideas on tomb building, with several chambers in one neatly walled cairn, entered the region from the SE, reflected in the tombs of Carneddau Hengwm, Talybont (M) and Ystum Cegid Isaf, Criccieth (C). Even more distinctively 'Severn–Cotswold' in design is Capel Garmon (Clwyd), whose siting above the Conwy valley is related to tracks from the Berwyns which lead eventually to the homeland of tombs in this style, in Breconshire and the Cotswolds.

Twenty megalithic tombs survive in Anglesey and there were originally more, suggesting that this was the most densely populated region of Gwynedd during the Neolithic, as throughout most of prehistory. However, no one style is dominant, and it is difficult to devise a relative chronology. A group of passage graves with short passages, such as Bodowyr (Llangaffo) and Tŷ Newydd (Llanfaelog), and the first chamber at Trefignath (Holy-p. 138 head) may be among the earliest. Excavations at Trefignath, where two box-like chambers similar to some in Scotland were added over several hundred years from 4000 B.C., have confirmed that these tombs may be of more than one period. The island also contains tombs unlike those elsewhere, such as Pant-y-saer (Llanfair Mathafarn Eithaf) and Bryn yr Hen Bobl (Llanedwen; a rare example of a chamber covered by its original cairn), which are a strange mixture of styles.

The best-known tombs on Anglesey are likely to be amongst the latest. The cruciform passage grave, Barclodiad-y-gawres (Llanfaelog), is related to the Boyne tombs in Ireland and, like p. 163 them, is decorated with abstract carvings, while the famous 7, 8 passage grave at Bryn Celli Ddu (Llanddaniel Fab) was built over a henge monument, a type of open-air sanctuary which we may guess to have been somewhat inimical to the enclosed ritual of the stone tombs. That the henge was covered by the megalithic tomb suggests that this monument represents the resurgence of an earlier tradition.

The later Neolithic HENGE is far more characteristic of southern England. However, two of these circular embanked monuments were built at Llandegai (C), and excavation suggested that their builders were involved with the axe trade, an activity which must have been a channel through which new ideas were passed.

The builders of the later of the Llandegai henges used Beaker pottery, a distinctive ceramic style whose appearance in Britain *c.* 2900 B.C. seems to herald a number of technological and social changes. These were traditionally explained as the results of immigration or invasion, by warriors from the mouth of the

Rhine (where the closest analogues to the British beakers are found). Such an 'event' is now doubted, but the period during which this pottery was popular certainly saw important new trends, notably the introduction of metalworking, and a greater individuality and bellicosity in a society which was becoming more sharply stratified. The succeeding Bronze Age, with its individual burials, private possessions and martial status symbols, seems a far cry from the anonymous communality of the more peaceful Neolithic.

Beaker pottery is most frequently found in CIST BURIALS, beneath small round barrows or cairns, accompanying a crouched inhumation often with other possessions. Several such graves have been found in Gwynedd, mostly in Anglesey but also in the Conwy valley and near Clynnog Fawr (C). That they contain the later styles of pottery (long-necked beakers) suggests that the new ideas that this style of burial represents came from areas in England where the earlier forms are more plentiful.

In many parts of Britain the individual grave beneath the ROUND BARROW becomes the standard burial monument of the Bronze Age. In Gwynedd, though the round barrow or cairn became dominant, the older tradition of multiple burials survived in a new form: Early Bronze Age cremations are placed individually in urns, buried in groups under one barrow. Thus a single monument may be considered a cemetery rather than an individual grave. The excavation record is good in Anglesey, where several Early Bronze Age graves (dating from c. 2000 B.C.) have been studied. They reveal a great variety in pottery styles; a fairly high standard of living, judging by the availability of imported amber and jet beads; and a lack of concern with weapons, which elsewhere rank high as symbols of status. Round cairns are to be seen in many upland areas, especially the moorland above Penmaenmawr (C), the higher ground of Ardudwy, the N and W slopes of Cader Idris and the ridges of Edeirnion (all M), but modern excavation has been less extensive in those areas. Bronze Age monuments of any kind are surprisingly rare in the Llŷn peninsula, but some barrows have been revealed by air photography.

Alongside burial cairns we also find the more enigmatic monuments of the Early Bronze Age, the ring cairns, stone circles, standing stones and alignments. These are often built close to groups of burials, as at Penmaenmawr (C), where the famous Druids' Circle forms the centre. It is assumed that they had some function connected with the power of the dead, and also perhaps with the worship of sky deities. RING CAIRNS consist of low stone banks, sometimes containing cremated human burials, or simply pits filled with charcoal. STONE CIRCLES, rings of small upright stones, have less connection with burial, and excavation has provided disappointingly little information about their role. There are other combinations of cairn and circle: the KERB CIRCLE, in which a contiguous ring of upright stones surrounds a low stone platform, or the CAIRN CIRCLE, in which a ring of tall stones rises from within a solid mass of stone. These more interesting

elaborations of the common heap of stones may be seen in
several parts of the region, notably Ardudwy, Edeirnion and
Arllechwedd.

Some STANDING STONES in Gwynedd have connections with
burials, but most are strung out along the mountain tracks which
cross the high moorland. It has been argued that they were set
up as markers, but on the best-defined tracks, through Bwlch-y-
ddeufaen, Rowen (C), from Llanbedr to Trawsfynydd (M), and
along the northern slopes of Cader Idris (M), they tend to occur
on the lower stretches and fail the traveller on the more open
wastes. Thus they may be considered memorials (of individuals
or of events) rather than way-markers. In the same way, cairns
and circles are strung out along tracks where many people must
have passed, and today these make the most rewarding archaeological walks.

Everyday Bronze Age activities are chronicled in Wales by
chance finds of tools and weapons of bronze. From these we may
postulate the distribution of population, the growth in prosperity and the fluctuating fortunes of centres of manufacture. In
Gwynedd it is particularly interesting to see the waxing and
waning of Irish influences and those from the South East,
together with occasional stimulus from Continental centres of
manufacture, and, for a significant period at the beginning of the
Middle Bronze Age, the rise of a local school of metalworking
known as the Acton Park Complex. The background of the
earliest metalworking is largely Irish, but moulds have been found
which indicate that axes and spearheads were even then being
made in the area. Radiocarbon dates reveal that local ores were
exploited as early as c. 2500 B.C. On the Great Orme, Llandudno
(C), visitors can enter the narrow galleries of the Bronze Age
MINES; similar mines at Parys Mountain (A) remain inaccessible to the public.

During the ascendancy of the Acton Park Complex
(1600–1400 B.C.) the design of axe-heads was the most advanced
in the country, and products are found as far afield as North
Germany and Holland. Later Bronze Age metalworking in North
Wales was very conservative and rather derivative, mainly
following 'English' styles.

The record of BRONZE AGE SETTLEMENT in Wales is meagre;
no houses have been positively identified, though some of the
undated ROUND STONE HUTS in the area may belong to this
period. Round huts, isolated or in groups associated with walls
and small paddocks, are frequent in the hills and even survive in
the agricultural lands of Anglesey. Modern excavation and radiocarbon dating have shown that these farms were established
much earlier than the Roman period, and often continued into
the 'Dark Ages'. The record of three so-called hut settlements
excavated at Graeanog, Pant Glas (C), demonstrates this longer
chronology, having been founded c. 200 B.C. and continuing in
occupation into the late C4 A.D.

One distinctive type of HUT SETTLEMENT – the 'concentric
circle', a single large round house surrounded by a circular

enclosure – previously believed to be post-Roman – has now been conclusively dated to the Iron Age by excavations at Moel Goedog (Harlech) and nearby Moel-y-gerddi, Merioneth. More recent excavations at Sarn Meyllteyrn on Llŷn have hinted at a Bronze Age origin for the type, which is particularly characteristic of Merioneth and South Caernarvonshire.

Work on HILLTOP SETTLEMENTS may eventually fill some of the Bronze Age vacuum, for radiocarbon dating is showing that man was beginning to occupy strategic high ground long before the Iron Age. Although recent excavations in many parts of Britain show that palisades were being erected around such settlements during the later Bronze Age, early dates have not yet been obtained in Gwynedd. The fluidity of these chronologies is one reason why the idea of any 'invasion' at the beginning of the Iron Age (c. 800 B.C.) is now seriously questioned. The appearance of iron-making, however, must indicate Continental stimulus. The gradual adoption of iron is increasingly being recognized among metalworking debris of the Late Bronze Age. In North Wales such early evidence is not yet known, but a local IRON-SMELTING INDUSTRY based on bog ores was well established in Merioneth in the later Iron Age, both in hill-forts e.g. Bryn-y-castell (Llan Ffestiniog) and at undefended settlements e.g. Crawcwellt (Trawsfynydd).

The defended hilltops are usually seen as refuges within which local chieftains and their followers could withstand cattle-raiding attacks, and eventually, and less successfully, the invading Roman army. Many of the stone-walled FORTS of Gwynedd seem best suited to this purpose, being too bleak and uncomfortable in our eyes for prolonged occupation; yet some of the most exposed have clear indications of permanent stone houses clustering inside and must have held surprisingly large populations. They must therefore have played a peaceful role as well, as social and economic centres controlling surrounding territories of farmland and grazing. The best-known of these hill-forts in Gwynedd is p. 386 9 Tre'r Ceiri, Llanaelhaearn (C), where both stone ramparts and huts are well preserved; a similar situation may be recognized at Conwy Mountain, Garn Fadryn (Llaniestyn) and Garn Boduan (Boduan), and at the now-destroyed site on Penmaenmawr (all C). Excavation has tended to concentrate on military aspects, sectioning ramparts and uncovering entrances to elucidate the history of the defences, which were often refurbished, remodelled or enlarged through several centuries. These military aspects are clearly demonstrated by the ankle-breaking carpet of short vertical stones ('*chevaux de frise*') outside the gates of Pen-y-gaer, Llanbedr-y-cennin (C). Most of the Gwynedd hill-forts are defended by thick stone walls, and some also have rock-cut ditches. A few, e.g. Dinas Dinlle (Llandwrog, C) and Dinas Dinorwig (Llanddeiniolen, C), have multiple earthen banks and very wide, deep ditches. At the latter site this rather 'foreign'-looking arrangement superseded a simpler stone-walled fort. In Anglesey and along the N coast of Llŷn there are several PROMONTORY FORTS, where the sea provides the real protection and defences are concentrated on the narrow neck.

The important role played by fighting, serious or ritualized, is further illustrated by the discovery of masses of rapiers in the lake near Beddgelert (C) and of paper-thin bronze shields in mountain bogs on Moel Siabod and at Gwern Einion, offerings to the water gods within. The tradition of depositing valuables in lakes or pools survived into the Iron Age, and even beyond. The religious nature of these finds is explained by classical writers describing the customs of the European Celts. The large mass of war gear, spears, swords, shields and chariots dredged up from Llyn Cerrig Bach, Llanfair yn Neubwll (A), seems to have accumulated over a long time, and some offerings appear to have come from distant regions, perhaps indicating a shrine of more than local significance. The latest pieces with Belgic connections may be linked to the presence of refugees from the South East, driven westward by the advancing Roman power.

The ROMANS arrived in full strength in North Wales in the years 60–78 A.D., when Segontium (Caernarfon) was chosen as the main base for the area, which it remained until the early C5. Roman power relied upon an efficient system of roads and intermediate small forts and repair and victualling stations. The fort at Caerhun (C) was the Conwy crossing on the road from the legionary centre at Chester. Caergai (Llanuwchllyn, M) was part of the route SW towards Brithdir and Pennal (M) and was linked to the large, remote fort at Tomen-y-mur, Trawsfynydd (M), with its parade ground, amphitheatre and practice camps, indicating the perennial need to keep troops occupied.

Several forts in the S parts of the region were abandoned in the second half of the C2, suggesting that the area was well pacified by then, an impression confirmed by the number of prosperous NATIVE FARMS. On the lower slopes the round-houses are substantial and are grouped into homesteads, often within acres of terraced fields, like those still to be seen around the two farms at Caerau, Pant Glas (C). Recent excavation at nearby Graeanog has shown that cereal crops were grown, and metalworking in iron and bronze was also carried out on these farms, but pottery and some domestic luxuries were bought in at Roman centres such as Segontium. The design of homesteads varies: some rather haphazard with curvilinear enclosing walls and isolated huts; some tightly clustered with huts or rooms opening onto a central yard; yet others with straight, formal enclosure walls and carefully balanced buildings in the interior. The best-known is Din Lligwy, Rhos Lligwy (A), which has lean-to workshops against the wall and two big round-houses built with meticulous care. It is tempting to see these larger well-organized farms as the equivalent of the southern English villa, less formally Roman but equally a product of the Pax Romana. Elsewhere in Anglesey, notably at Tŷ Mawr (Holyhead), the huts give the impression of a straggling village rather than a centrally controlled settlement. Unfortunately we can know nothing of the social organization of the native population during the later

p. 219
10

Holyhead, Tŷ Mawr Hut Circles.
Reconstruction drawing

Roman occupation, but radiocarbon dates suggest that part of the Tŷ Mawr settlement, in origin Iron Age or even Late Bronze Age, continued in use up to the c6.

The final years of Roman rule were unsettled. The Imperial title was continually disputed and the frontiers of the Empire were under increasing pressure. In Gwynedd the threat came from the w. What was probably the last Roman public building to be constructed was a coastal base against the marauding Irish at Holyhead (A). Their raids may have caused the reoccupation of hill-forts, for at many sites, e.g. Parciau, Llanallgo (A), late stone huts may be seen within the defences. At Dinas Emrys above Beddgelert (C) excavation suggested that the hilltop fortress is entirely post-Roman. Datable finds from the c5–c6 are rare, but MEMORIALS beside the Roman roads show that this efficient network, at least, survived the withdrawal in the early c5, and a silver brooch and amethyst ring from stone huts in Anglesey suggest that many older farms may have been occupied by people of some standing who perhaps yearned for a return of Roman governance and security, as the c6 stones from Penmachno (C) so movingly reveal (*see* Early Christian Gwynedd, p. 18).

THE MEDIEVAL HISTORICAL BACKGROUND

The post-Roman history of Gwynedd legendarily begins with the departure of Magnus Maximus (Macsen Wledig) in 383 and the abandonment of Britain in 410. Irish raids had begun before this

and may be the reason for the invitation to a branch of the Vota-
dini of the Firth of Forth under Cunedda to move to North
Wales, c. 440. Cunedda's sons founded Welsh kingdoms including Gwynedd, which extended from Anglesey to the Conwy.
Recorded history of the c6 to the c9 is primarily of the church.
Maelgwn Fawr (†549), king of Gwynedd, installed both St
p. 128 Deiniol in Bangor and St Cybi in Holyhead. Deiniol was consecrated bishop in 546, the first territorial bishopric in Britain.
Monastic settlements called *clasau* were established by powerful
religious figures, the extent of their influence traceable through
church dedications. Dedications to Deiniol and Cybi spread
down into Ceredigion. The *clas* of St Cadfan at Tywyn (M) had
widespread influence in the c6, as did that of St Seiriol at
p. 206 Penmon (A), and, in the c7, that of St Beuno at Clynnog Fawr
(C). The smaller *llan* sites indicate settlements of individual
saints, some of which achieved longer renown through medieval
pilgrimage, like that of Derfel at Llandderfel (M). The Padrig of
Llanbadrig (A) is reputedly the Patrick of Ireland.

Physical evidence for secular or religious sites is almost entirely
lacking. One excavated settlement at Glyn, Llanbedrgoch (A)
proved to have been occupied from the c6 to the c10, its wooden
houses burnt by Vikings. Little has been found at Aberffraw (A),
seat of Maelgwn and his successors until 1283.

Wars are recorded more precisely than periods of calm.
Cadfan, called 'rex sapientissimus' on his stone at Llangadwaladr (A), died c. 625. Saxons from Northumbria attacked Cadfan's
son Cadwallon on Puffin Island (A) in 629 and in the c7 severed
the link with and then eliminated the British kingdoms of Northern England and Scotland. Cadwallon, briefly and devastatingly
successful, killed Edwin of Northumbria near Doncaster in 633,
but was himself killed in 634. He was the last British king to campaign in England. The name of his son Cadwaladr (†c. 664) lived
on as a potent myth into Tudor times as the once and future king
of a reunited Britain. Saxon expansion slowed and stopped on
the borders of Wales in the c8. Rhodri Mawr, king 844–77, briefly
united Gwynedd territories down to South Wales, and in 856
checked the Vikings, already established on Man, the Scottish
islands and the Irish coast. The two centuries before the arrival
of the Normans saw power ebb and flow between Gwynedd
and Deheubarth, the kingdoms of the North and South.
Rhodri's grandson, Hywel the Good (†950) of Deheubarth
unified Wales apart from Glamorgan and Gwent, his great
achievement the codification of Welsh law. Viking attacks,
resumed from Dublin and Man, were devastating but did not
result in permanent settlement. In the c11 Gruffudd ap Llywelyn
briefly united Wales but over-reached himself in intervening in
English affairs and was killed after defeat by Harold Godwinson,
1063. Dynastic disarray plagued Gwynedd and most of
Wales when William of Normandy defeated Harold in 1066
and continued until 1081 when Gruffudd ap Cynan (†1137)
and Rhys ap Tewdwr emerged respectively in Gwynedd and
Deheubarth.

The allocation of border lands to William's baronial followers threatened Gwynedd early. After Gruffudd ap Cynan was taken prisoner in 1081 by Hugh, Earl of Chester, and Edeirnion was overrun with Powys, it seemed that all Wales would fall. But final conquest took another two hundred years. Gruffudd escaped in 1094, and in 1098 the Norman earls were defeated in Anglesey through the intervention of the Norsemen of Dublin and Norway. From 1100 Henry I and his successors preferred control from afar to the risks of invasion. Gruffudd was able to extend the lands of Gwynedd through Meirionnydd to the Dyfi in 1123, establishing the boundaries that broadly remain.*

Gruffudd's son Owain (Owain Gwynedd), 1137–70, was the last to be called king of Gwynedd; his successors would be princes of North Wales. Llywelyn ap Iorwerth (Llywelyn the Great) established himself from 1200 as ruler of Wales, taking homage from Powys and Deheubarth and raiding far into the territories of the barons of the Marches. Dynastic marriages with Joan, daughter of King John, and of members of his family with the marcher lords secured his gains. He built castles to ring Gwynedd at Castell y Bere (Llanfihangel y Pennant, M), Dolbadarn (Llanberis, C), Dolwyddelan, Criccieth and Deganwy, and encouraged the Cistercians to found abbeys at Cymer (Llanelltyd, M) and Aberconwy (Conwy, C).

After Llywelyn's death in 1240 Henry III reasserted sovereignty with a destructive campaign against Dafydd ap Llywelyn (†1246). The divided inheritance of Dafydd was reunited under Llywelyn ap Gruffudd (Llywelyn the Last) in 1255. Llywelyn secured overlordship of most of independent Wales and some of the marcher lordships and was styled Prince of Wales, a title Henry III acknowledged in 1267. This apogee of independent Wales lasted a brief ten years before Edward I began the wars that would extinguish it. Edward's huge campaign of 1277 restricted Llywelyn to Gwynedd, symbolized by encircling castles from Aberystwyth to Flint. The final war of 1282 began outside Gwynedd but soon drew Llywelyn in. Edward's armed response was overwhelming and Llywelyn was killed near Builth.

Three imposing castles within Gwynedd, at Caernarfon, Conwy and Harlech, anchored Edward's conquest. By the Statute of Rhuddlan, 1284, Gwynedd was divided into the counties of Anglesey, Caernarvonshire and Merioneth, under English sheriffs and ruled from Caernarfon Castle. The courts of Llywelyn were demolished, his halls symbolically re-erected in Caernarfon and Harlech castles, and Aberconwy Abbey, burial place of his family, removed to another site. After Wales rose up in 1294–5 under Madog ap Llywelyn, another fortress, Beaumaris, was added, to control Anglesey. The new walled towns at Caernarfon, Conwy and Beaumaris were reserved for colonists.

---

*Eastern Merioneth remained in dispute with the princes of Powys, a distinction reflected in present-day diocesan boundaries, Bangor taking all Gwynedd but the disputed area, Penllyn and Edeirnion, is with St Asaph.

The separation of the English in the towns from the Welsh in the countryside diminished in the C14, particularly after the Black Death. Welshmen fought in English wars, and carved effigies attest to the rise of gentry families e.g. at Penmynydd (A), Dolgellau (M) and Llanuwchllyn (M). National aspirations in the later C14 centred on Owain Lawgoch, last of the Gwynedd royal house, assassinated in France in 1378, and then on Owain Glyndŵr, also of princely descent. Glyndŵr initiated the greatest of Welsh uprisings in 1400, campaigning across Wales and into England, capturing castles such as Harlech, and negotiating as a sovereign prince with France, which supplied a fleet to attack Caernarfon in 1403 and an army in 1405. The uprising slowed in 1406 and was mostly over by 1408 when Harlech was retaken, but the destruction was such as to reduce crown income for decades.

In the C15 Welsh gentry families such as those of Penrhyn and Gwydir began to be drawn into the national arena, though English families associated with royal government such as the Stanleys in Anglesey were still more powerful. In 1468 Harlech became the last Lancastrian stronghold to surrender during the Wars of the Roses, wars through which a minor Anglesey gentry family, the Tudors of Penmynydd, came to lead the Lancastrian cause and take the throne in 1485.

EARLY CHRISTIAN GWYNEDD

The evidence for the C5 and C6 is principally in INSCRIBED STONES. These are mostly in Latin, without the Irish Ogam incisions found in SW Wales.* Typically they are grave markers, giving the name as in CUNOGISI HIC IACET, at Llanfaelog (A). Often there is a parent's name, occasionally other detail; at Llangefni (A) a second wife; at Penmachno and Llanaelhaearn (C) places of origin. Occasionally more enigmatic information is given, such as the HOMO PLANUS from Trawsfynydd (M) and the MONEDO RIGI from Llanaber (M) for which 'plain man' and 'king of the mountains' have been advanced as translations. The long ebb of Roman influence is also felt in titles: two at Penmachno refer to a magistrate and a consul, the Aberdaron stones (C) identify priests as 'presbyter' and the Llangian one (C) a doctor as 'medicus'. Exceptionally, historical figures are identified in the C7 stones at Llansadwrn (A) to St Sadwrn and his wife and at Llangadwaladr (A) identifying Catamus as king (assumed to be Cadfan †c. 625, grandfather of Cadwaladr who presumably put up the memorial). The former has lettering in debased Roman capitals characteristic of the C5–C7, the latter is in Hibernian minuscules characteristic of the late C7 and after. The most interesting later stone is that of the C8 at Tywyn (M), lettered in large minuscules on four sides recognizably in Welsh, the earliest record of the language.

*A single Ogam stone is known from NW Wales, at Llystyn Gwyn, Pant Glas (C).

Tywyn, St Cadfan, inscribed stone.
Engraving, C19

INSCRIBED CROSSES are rare on the earlier stones; one is at Penmachno. Later stones inscribed just with crosses are relatively common built into church walls. Their positioning is not always significant, many having been brought in for safekeeping in the C19. The ornament on the HIGH CROSSES of Penmon (A) identifies them as C9 to C11, with typical Celtic interlace and frets on the larger cross. The bolder interlaced rings (ring-chain) of the back of the smaller cross have been linked to Manx stones at Kirk Michael and Kirk Oswald. Similar ring-chain occurs on

FONTS at Pistyll (C) and Llangristiolus (A), but the latter also
has rough arcading of a Norman Romanesque type found also
15, 17 at Heneglwys, Llanbeulan, and Llanbadrig (all A) which may
indicate a C12 date for them all.

11   The numerous CIRCULAR CHURCHYARDS so often associated
with local saints, as at Llanbabo (A), are identified probably
rightly with early foundations, but there is little excavated
evidence to support accurate dating, just as there is none to date
the HOLY WELLS associated with particular saints.

MEDIEVAL CHURCHES AND MONUMENTS

Churches up to 1282

The ROMANESQUE architecture of Gwynedd reflects the wish of
the native rulers to emulate the architecture of the Holy Roman
Empire. During this high period of Welsh independence, the old
clas foundations were brought under the stricter regime of the
new monastic orders and many churches were built (or rebuilt).
Bangor Cathedral was rebuilt in 1120 with an apsed E end (rebuilt
square in the English fashion in the early C13). All that survives
of this period is a buttress and a blocked round-headed window
in the presbytery S wall, and short lengths of wall in the S
transept. The important church at Tywyn (M), possibly the
largest apart from Bangor, was aisled with a crossing tower. It
12 retains its C12 nave with plain round-headed arcades on fat cylindrical piers, and small clerestory windows. Also outstanding is
p. 206 the early to mid-C12 church at Penmon (A): the nave walls and
S door with carved tympanum, the crossing with its pyramidal-
roof tower and arches with typical chevron and chequer-board
billet mouldings, and the S transept with its blind arcading. The
not so typical grotesque capitals of the crossing W arch, and
the S door tympanum, surely show Celtic influence, even more
obvious at the re-set chancel arch at Aberffraw (A). Pyramid-
roofed towers feature also on the *clas* churches on Puffin Island
13 (A), now a ruin, and Llaneilian (A). C12 fabric is found in many
other churches, e.g. chevron-carved stones, *in situ* or re-set,
at Holyhead, Penmynydd and Llanbabo, and round-headed
windows and chancel arches at Llanfairynghornwy, Llanfechell
and Llangeinwen (all A). Aberdaron (C) has a fine W doorway of
the late C12, of three bold plain orders.

     The TRANSITIONAL period is linked to the coming of the
Cistercians, who brought the pointed arch, and an architecture
of restraint relying on beautiful proportions rather than elaborate
detail. Little survives of the abbey at Aberconwy, founded in the
late C12; the W wall (now Conwy parish church) has a fine triplet
of lancets as well as a W door perhaps moved from the former
19 chapter house. Cymer Abbey (M), early C13, has very similar E
lancets, and the contemporary Augustinian priory church of
Beddgelert (C) has a two-bay N arcade and an exceptionally tall
and elegant group of three E lancets, considered by Hughes and
North the finest architectural feature in Snowdonia. At Penmon

Llanelltyd, Cymer Abbey.
Engraving by S. and N. Buck, 1742

little remains of this period in the church (the C13 chancel was rebuilt in the C19) but the refectory block survives, its dormitory lit by a tall W lancet. Although some C13 fabric survives at Bangor Cathedral, much of the E end was rebuilt in the early C16, and later by *Sir G. G. Scott*. 35

Surviving EARLY GOTHIC features elsewhere include pointed doorways, e.g. the blocked roll-moulded N door at Llangadwaladr (A), with fluted imposts, the triple lancet E windows at Llanfrothen (M) and Llaniestyn (C), and pointed chancel arches, the best at Llangristiolus (A). The earlier, square chancels of the C12 were often lengthened or rebuilt, e.g. Llanfechell (A) and Aberdaron (C). The finest C13 church is Llanaber (M). Here the arcade piers are still cylindrical but the arches have become 20 pointed. The capitals show a variety of foliage of evolving degrees of stiffness. The S doorway of four orders of triple shafts and foliage capitals must rank as one of the most exquisite church features in Gwynedd.

Churches from 1282 to the Sixteenth Century

The Edwardian conquest brought churches to the new borough towns. The old abbey church at Conwy (C), now parochial, was rebuilt and extended, starting with the nave and aisles, parts of the chancel and the tower. Slightly later, the fine S transept was added, its superior workmanship contrasting with the native work. Typical of the new DECORATED style are the transept's continuously moulded arches and its two E windows, one intersecting, the other reticulated. At Caernarfon, the garrison chapel, St Mary's, *c.* 1307, has early C14 arcades. The old parish church of St Peblig has the chancel and S transept of the C14, the re-set window in the later N chapel good Dec work: two trefoil-head lights below a split-cusped trefoil. Much of Beaumaris church (A) is of this date, with identical windows. Beaumaris Castle chapel is purely English too, with a rare stone vault and cusped blind arcading. There is Dec work at Newborough (A): its unusually long church (because extended in the late C15) was built *c.* 1303 for the population of Llanfaes, who were transferred here when Beaumaris became the chief town. It has a fine reticulated E window.

The most notable work of this period was the rebuilding of Aberconwy Abbey at Maenan (C) to make way for the new town of Conwy. The minimal remains, mostly stonework reused elsewhere, suggest a building of quality. Of churches not in the borough towns, Bangor Cathedral was clearly influenced by the Edwardian masons. The crossing and transepts were rebuilt c. 1300 (and again in the C19), and the aisles too. The present nave and arcades are an early C16 replacement. Elsewhere, the influence of the English masons is less, and there is very little C14 work in Merioneth at all. Most church building was on Anglesey, where we see English details executed, more roughly, by local masons. One form of cusped window, with a pair of horizontal mouchettes above a single light, is found only on the island, at Tregaean, Rhodogeidio (Llanerchymedd), Llanbabo and Llandrygarn. There are pointed doorways with continuous rounded mouldings at Llanfair Mathafarn Eithaf, Trefdraeth and Bodedern.

The Black Death must have halted building activity in the mid C14, and in the early years of the C15 Owain Glyndŵr's revolt caused widespread damage. However, in the late C14 and early C15 churches were rebuilt at Penmynydd, Llandyfrydog and Llanddyfnan (all A). Penmynydd, c. 1400, with an early C15 porch and chapel, is a fine example, little altered. Llandyfrydog, of surprisingly square plan, has a chancel arch with two hollow-chamfered orders dying into the responds, without capitals. At Trefdraeth and Llanfair Mathafarn Eithaf (both A) the early C15 windows are almost identical, their cusped lights below curvilinear tracery.

The accession to the throne in 1485 of Henry Tudor, grandson of Owain Tudor of Penmynydd, brought prosperity to Wales, closer ties with England, and a second renaissance in church building. Fine PERPENDICULAR work was carried out at the major churches, and hardly a church elsewhere was left unaffected. The lead seems to have been from Bangor, where under Richard Kyffin, Dean c. 1480–1502, and Bishop Skevington, 1509–33, the nave arcades and W tower were rebuilt. Outstanding Perp work is at Clynnog Fawr (C): chancel and transepts c. 1480, nave and porch c. 1500, W tower and chapel c. 1520. Holyhead (A) shows a similar development over the same period. During these fifty golden years, some churches were almost entirely rebuilt, e.g. Llaneilian (A), Dolwyddelan (C), Llandderfel (M). Many saw enlargement for growing populations. CHANCELS were rebuilt, e.g. Beaumaris (A), and chapels or transepts added, e.g. Caerhun (C), Llandudwen (C) or Trewalchmai (A). At Llanfairynghornwy (A), the late C15 chancel was extended with a S chapel of equal length in the early C16. Second NAVES or AISLES were often added alongside the original, e.g. Aberffraw (A), Abererch, Llanrhychwyn (C). In one remarkable instance, Llangwnnadl (C), two were added, 1520 and *c.* 1530. The ARCADES are usually four-centred, either with continuous mouldings, as at Llanengan and Llangwnnadl (C) or with capitals, as at Aberdaron and Abererch (C). Good Perp WINDOWS and DOORWAYS can be seen in numerous churches, big and small. Clynnog Fawr (C) has a variety of large windows with Tudor heads of different shapes. Llanengan and Llangwnnadl have fine E windows, so does Llangristiolus (A), where the window is almost too big to fit. Doorways with flat hoods and decorated spandrels are common, at Bangor and Clynnog Fawr and in small remote churches like Bodwrog (A). Llanddyfnan (A) has a surprisingly grand S doorway, with remarkably intact canopied niches above and at each side. The S doorway at Holyhead (A) is set in a wall carved with blind tracery and 44 containing the Trinity within a canopied niche. Many TOWERS were built, including the W one at Bangor Cathedral, 1532, that appears to have been begun at a grander scale than achieved. They are mostly plain, with battlements and smallish belfry lights.

The majority of church ROOFS were built or rebuilt at this time. The most common type is the oak arch-braced collar-beam truss, usually with cusped raking struts, and supporting large purlins laid flat (often with cusped or plain wind-braces). Another roof type, more common in bigger churches, is shallower: either of camber-beam construction, perhaps incorporating hammerbeams, e.g. Holyhead (A) and Clynnog Fawr (C), or king- and queenposts, e.g. Llangelynin (M). The shallow roofs were covered with lead rather than slate and hidden behind embattled parapets, sometimes embellished as at Holyhead. The barrel ceiling common in South Wales is rare in Gwynedd except as a canopy or celure over the sanctuary. They were usually painted, though few of these survive, e.g. at Gyffin (C) and 38 Talyllyn (M). It is possible that the roofs at Caerhun (C) and the S transept at Llanbeblig (Caernarfon, C), of close-spaced arch-braced collar-beam trusses, were originally ceiled.

Fittings and Monuments

FONTS possibly of the C13 survive at Llanfor (M) and Gyffin (C). The octagonal one at Llanaber with carving on all the faces looks forward to those of the C15. There are fine C15 octagonal fonts at Bangor Cathedral and Conwy, both with intricate carving and open-traceried panels to the shafts. At Llanengan and Llangwnnadl (C) the bowls are carved less busily than the early C15 types. There are excellent late C15 to early C16 SCREENS in Caernarvonshire and Merioneth (but very few in Anglesey). The best, e.g. at Llanegryn (M) and Llanengan (C), retain their 37 lofts. Llanegryn is a remarkable (and probably late) example of the Welsh type, with three square-headed bays each side of the central opening, a panelled and bossed coving, and intricately carved loft parapets. The S aisle screen at Llanengan is similar, perhaps from the same school of woodcarvers. The English style

of screen is best seen at Conwy (though the loft no longer
survives), altogether less heavy, with pointed and traceried
openings below fan-vaulted coving. The screen at Clynnog Fawr
(C) is of English influence too, but much renewed. At Llaneilian
(A) the plain balustraded loft survives, above a boarded coving
and a screen of close-centred uprights each side of the doorway.
Fine STALLS and BENCH ENDS remain at Llaneilian (A), Aber-
erch, Conwy and Llanengan (C). There are carved MISERI-
CORDS at Clynnog Fawr and Abererch (C), the best probably at
Beaumaris (A), with figures from everyday life lovingly depicted.
C14 FLOOR TILES can be seen in the presbytery and choir of
Bangor Cathedral, and re-set on the sanctuary s wall at Conwy
(C). Wall PAINTINGS, much overpainted but the earliest possibly C14, survive at Llangar (M). The figures in the painted celure
at Gyffin (C) are a rare survival. Fragments of C15 GLASS survive
at Llanbedrog, Penmorfa (C), Penmon and Trefdraeth (A). In
the s aisle E window at Llanrhychwyn (C) there is beautifully
drawn York-type yellow-stain glass of *c.* 1460. The similar glass at
Llanfechell (A) is less well drawn. At Beaumaris (A) there
are fragments of *c.* 1500 in the chancel, mostly yellow-stain.
At Llangadwaladr (A), late C15 fragments re-set in mid-C19 glass
have excellent detail, the bones of Christ showing as in an X-ray
and the unusual eyes, like those of a cat. Two finely drawn chancel
windows at Gwyddelwern (M), *c.* 1500, show German influence.

A distinct North Wales school of SCULPTURE appears in the
mid C13. The earliest MONUMENT is the coffin-lid of Princess
Joan at Beaumaris (A), *c.* 1237. It shows just head and shoulders
above floriate decoration derived from E.E. stiff-leaf. From the
same school may be the coffin-lid with expanded-arm cross at
Llanfair-yn-y-cwmwd (Dwyran, A) and gravestones at Amlwch
and Llanfechell (A), where the coarse-grained stone dictated
plain, bold carving rather than the more elaborate foliage pattern.
In the early C13 four-circle crosses became popular, e.g. the slabs
at St Tudno, Llandudno (C) showing Celtic influence. At Conwy
(C) are slab memorials with foliate crosses of the C14.

As sculptors gained confidence their work became more three-
dimensional, and EFFIGIES grew in popularity: of priests,
e.g. Corwen (M), or knights, e.g. Dolgellau, Llanuwchllyn and
Tywyn (all M), mid-C14, where we see the first appearance in
North Wales of plate armour. The Black Death probably stopped
such things, but the discovery of a very fine-grained pale grey
sandstone in Flintshire around 1380 brought a monopoly to a
single workshop there. Three remarkable memorials from it can
be seen at Bangor Cathedral (C), Llaniestyn and Llanbabo (both
A). All are finely carved in very low relief and were donated by
Gruffudd ap Gwilym when he moved to Anglesey from
Flintshire. His mother Eva is commemorated on the Bangor slab;
St Iestyn and King Pabo, Early Christian saints, on the other two.
Effigies at Betws-y-coed (C) and Llanuwchllyn (M), dated 1395,
are probably from the same workshop, as are late C14 examples
at Newborough (A) and Ysbyty Ifan (C). By *c.* 1400, however,
alabaster from England was becoming available and the North

Wales school died. Good ALABASTER TOMBS datable to the late
C15 can be seen at Penmynydd, Beaumaris (both A) and
Llandegai (C), each with double effigies.

The 'Mostyn Christ' in Bangor Cathedral is a rare example of   40
a pre-Reformation BOUND ROOD, depicting in oak an exhausted
Christ awaiting death. Much cruder, but a rare survival, is St
Derfel's horse at Llandderfel (M). Early C16 BRASSES can be
seen at Beaumaris and Dolwyddelan (C).

CASTLES
BY JOHN R. KENYON

To gain an understanding of the development of the castle in
Britain, both the military and the domestic aspects, the student
can do no better than to examine those of Gwynedd; not only
the remains of earthwork mottes and ringworks, and the great
Edwardian castles, but also the strongholds built by the Welsh,
notably by Llywelyn ap Iorwerth (Llywelyn the Great †1240) and
his grandson, Llywelyn ap Gruffudd (Llywelyn the Last †1282).
Taken together, these provide a wondrous array of castle planning and building styles, and a reminder that in terms of more
domestic aspects, such as chapel interiors, fine windows and
general accommodation, castles should not be neglected in any
overview of medieval architecture.

Early Castles

Whilst it is not possible to state categorically whether some of
the EARTH-AND-TIMBER CASTLES were built by a Norman or a
Welsh lord, the Welsh chronicles and the location of some sites
are of some help. Generally speaking, the larger mottes tend to
be those built by the Normans. Whatever the origin of many of
these early sites, several were at one time or another in the hands
of the Welsh, often having been taken by force and occupied,
rather than destroyed. Nor should native-built castles be necessarily seen as a means of combating Norman incursions; some
represent internal political aspirations of Welsh lords, which did
not always accord with the views of their fellow countrymen. A
number of the first Norman castles in Gwynedd, in the late C11
and C12, appear to have been deliberately located within the
administrative unit of a Welsh lord, the commote. Examples
include the MOTTES at Abergwyngregyn (C) and Bala (M), and
the now destroyed motte at Caernarfon. It is hard to assign a
pattern for the distribution of the early castles built by the Welsh.
Few if any are associated with the historic centres or courts
(*llysoedd*), and it has been argued that the pattern reflects more
the control of territorial boundaries and lines of communication.
Again, in the C13 the distribution of the majority of the newly
built native Welsh castles does not reflect the location of the
llysoedd, apart from Deganwy (C), and both strategic and political

reasons may again have been influential here, and it is worth noting that these castles played an important role in internal political problems, with both Llywelyns housing various family members as prisoners.

The particularly fine Norman motte on Anglesey, Castell Aberlleiniog, Llangoed, was built as part of the short-lived late CII Norman incursion across North Wales. The small motte at Dolbenmaen (C) may have been Welsh-built. We are on firmer ground with Cymer (M), the earliest surviving Welsh castle for which we have a date (1116), and also Castell Cynfal (Bryncrug, M), raised before 1147 by Cadwaldr ap Gruffudd ap Cynan, only to be destroyed by his nephews. The small mound of Tomen Las, near Pennal (M), may be the castle of 1156 built by Rhys ap Gruffudd (the Lord Rhys), whose centre of power lay to the S, in Deheubarth. The large motte built within the Roman fort at Tomen-y-mur (Trawsfynydd, M) may have been raised during one of the Norman campaigns across North Wales, in the reign of either William II or Henry I.

Castle RINGWORKS are not common in North Wales, nor were they a form of castle particularly favoured by the Welsh. However, examples can be seen at Penucha'r Llan, Llanfor (M), and Tomen Fawr, Llanystumdwy (C).

Although not securely dated, it is generally accepted that the first MASONRY TOWERS built in Gwynedd were those at the small Welsh strongholds at Dinas Emrys (Beddgelert, C) and Tomen Castell (Dolwyddelan, C), just E of the C13 castle of Dolwyddelan. In his account of Archbishop Baldwin's journey through Wales in 1188, Gerald of Wales mentions two recent castles. One is associated with Castell Aber Iâ, a rocky knoll that had a tower on it until much of the masonry was used in building the house now the hotel at Portmeirion (M) in the C19. The second is thought to be the stronghold represented by the dry-stone wall on the highest point of the Garn Fadryn (Llaniestyn, C) in the Llŷn peninsula. A site with long historical associations is Deganwy (C), but here the fragmentary remains, both Welsh and English, date from the C13. At Castell Prysor (Trawsfynydd, M) the castle stands on a stone-revetted rocky knoll, and traces of walling can be seen; the date of this enigmatic site is unknown, apart from a late C13 reference, and it could have been constructed earlier in the C13 or even in the late C12.

MASONRY CASTLES of a more recognizable form begin to be built by Llywelyn the Great, notably at Castell y Bere (Llanfihangel y Pennant, M), Criccieth, Dolbadarn and p. 364 Dolwyddelan (all C), whilst the very ruinous Castell Carndochan (Llanuwchllyn, M) is probably another of his works. There is no secure dating evidence for the foundation of these, apart from the reference in 1221 to Llywelyn having taken the *cantref* of Meirionnydd from his son, who had started to build a castle there. This is thought to be Castell y Bere, commanding the Dysynni valley on the southern border of Gwynedd. The sculptural decoration discovered when the castle was excavated in the mid C19 has affinities with English work, even if the masons were more local, and this link with the Welsh Marches is seen in more spectacular fashion at Criccieth and Dolbadarn.

The finest part of Criccieth (C) is the twin-towered GATE- 23 HOUSE. Though a smaller example can be seen at Castell Dinas Brân in Denbighshire, this is the only Welsh example on a par with what was being built in England and the Welsh Marches from the late C12, and English influence is therefore suspected.

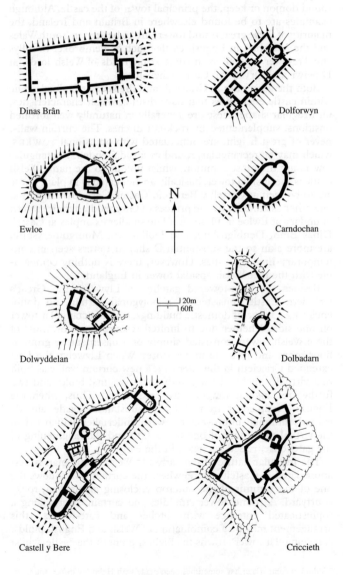

Comparative plans of native Welsh castles.

The link here is that one of Llywelyn's daughters had married John le Scot, nephew of Earl Ranulph of Chester, and Ranulph, soon after 1220, had built the formidable castle of Beeston in the middle of the Cheshire Plain, close to the border. The gatehouse at Criccieth bears a strong resemblance to the inner gatehouse at Beeston, and there are also similarities with the gatehouse into Henry III's new castle of Montgomery, under construction from 1223. The main feature that survives at Dolbadarn (C) is the round donjon or keep, the principal tower of the castle. Although examples are to be found elsewhere in Britain and Ireland, the majority of these great round towers are to be seen in South Wales and the Marches, in English castles such as Pembroke, Bronllys and Tretower, as well as in some strongholds of Welsh lords, at Dinefwr and Dryslwyn, Carmarthenshire.

p. 392

p. 349

Both the gatehouse at Criccieth and the keep at Dolbadarn lie within castle enclosures that have distinct Welsh characteristics. Of irregular shape, these are generally in naturally well-fortified positions, supplemented by rock-cut ditches. The curtain walls, never of great height, are punctuated with occasional TOWERS, which may be rectangular, round or apsidal-ended. Rectangular towers are the most common, whilst unique to the native Welsh castle is the apsidal tower, basically an elongated D in plan. These are to be seen at Castell y Bere and Castell Carndochan, and at one other castle built by the princes of Gwynedd on their eastern boundary at Ewloe in Flintshire. The smaller examples at Castell Dinas Brân, Denbighshire, and Dolforwyn, Montgomeryshire, are more akin to the substantial D-shaped towers seen in contemporary English castles. However, there is nothing comparable with the true Welsh apsidal tower in England.*

Besides the twin-towered gatehouse, Llywelyn the Great's Criccieth Castle consisted of a polygonal curtain, no doubt enclosing a range of domestic buildings, with a rectangular tower on one side. Whether due to limited resources or not, most of these Welsh towers consisted simply of a basement or ground-floor room and just one upper storey. When Llywelyn the Last extended Criccieth in the later c13, a new curtain wall was built that virtually enclosed his grandfather's original build, and two further rectangular towers were constructed. Thus, when the English occupied it from 1283, a substantial castle already existed, although improvements were undertaken which led to the virtual rebuilding of one tower (SE) and the heightening of the gatehouse, raised yet again in the early c14.

The irregular nature of the early c13 Welsh castle plan is best appreciated at Castell y Bere, where the curtain wall follows the line of the summit of the outcrop enclosing an uneven, rocky courtyard. A round tower straddles the curtain, overlooking a sophisticated entrance with ditches and gate-towers (this arrangement may be a combination of Welsh and English build). A rectangular tower crowns the highest point of the castle, whilst

---

*Although comparison has sometimes been made with Helmsley in Yorkshire, any link here is coincidental.

a third type of tower, apsidal-ended, dominates the opposite end of the courtyard. At the southern end of the castle lies a second apsidal tower, which when first built may have been detached from the rest, later to be linked after the castle had been taken by the English in 1283. There is no doubt that the N and S apsidal towers at Castell y Bere were well-appointed buildings, the fine stone carving in the N tower indicating a hall, or chapel, on the upper floor. Both towers are unusual in that they have ground-floor entrances, with an external doorway on the first floor of the N tower.

The Edwardian Castles

The EDWARDIAN CASTLES of North Wales, particularly those in Gwynedd, represent one of the finest architectural achievements of the Middle Ages anywhere in Europe. Since 1986 Beaumaris, Caernarfon, Conwy and Harlech have been on the World Heritage List, together with the Caernarfon and Conwy town walls. By their nature they cannot compare with the great medieval ecclesiastical monuments as works of art, but when a number of factors are considered, the castles of Edward I should be seen as pre-eminent works of medieval architecture. First, Conwy, Caernarfon and Harlech were begun as soon as the English took control, indicating the presence of skilled planners and architects. Faced with the need to build almost immediately in unfamiliar territory, the plans were drawn up superbly to take into account the varying topography, although Caernarfon and Conwy are not so dissimilar in arrangement, and all are situated ideally for waterborne access.*

25-32

The second factor is the truly remarkable administrative system that enabled the king's clerical staff and chief masons to implement the plans, providing a workforce that included, amongst others, masons, carpenters and ditch-cutters from all over England. It was also a workforce that, on the whole, was paid regularly, men and materials for the Gwynedd castles costing the Crown over £46,000 by 1304, with expenditure at Caernarfon and Beaumaris coming to over £10,500 from 1304 to c. 1330. Thirdly, although local stone formed the core of the castles, much had to be transported in, mainly by sea, especially the finer ashlar for framing doorways and windows, and also such items as glass and metalwork; the accounts bear witness to the steady stream of men and materials. These three factors enabled Conwy – both castle and town walls – and Harlech to be completed to all intents and purposes in under ten years; whilst at Beaumaris, which like Caernarfon was never finished, the core of the castle much as we see it today was raised in the first two building seasons (1295–6).

p. 33

p. 30

*The English would have been familiar to some extent with North Wales and Henry III's castle of Deganwy would have had a clear view of the Conwy estuary. Indeed Edward I was at Deganwy at the end of the war of 1277 concluded by the Treaty of Aberconwy.

Beaumaris Castle, view from the north.
Engraving by S. and N. Buck, 1742

Finally, and not least, there is the architecture itself. The four
great castles are the finest expressions of military might in
Britain, with massive towers commanding short stretches of
27   curtain wall, and great gatehouses at Beaumaris, Caernarfon and
Harlech. The GATEHOUSES were not only planned to be impreg-
nable, each with an entrance passage that could be secured by a
number of two-leaved doors and portcullis, with arrowslits in the
side walls and murder holes in the roof, but on the upper floors
were suites of fine chambers. Their design was anticipated at the
de Clare castles of Tonbridge, Kent, and Caerphilly, Glamorgan.
Another comparable Edwardian example is that at St Briavels in
Gloucestershire, built in 1292. The gatehouses at Caernarfon,
although unfinished, differ from the more standard late C13 form
at Beaumaris and Harlech. Here both the King's Gate and the
Queen's Gate have twin towers that flank gate passages, but it is
in the inner sections of the two gatehouse complexes that we see
a greater level of sophistication envisaged in the original design.
On the SW side of the rear of the King's Gate a vaulted passage
would lead into the lower ward, protected by a door, portcullis
and drawbridge, and it is logical to suggest that something similar
must have been planned for the approach to the upper ward. The
outer passage, therefore, must have led into a lobby or open
courtyard, with a doorway on either side leading into the two
wards. Something similar, but less sophisticated, was planned for
the Queen's Gate, where at the rear of the gate passage those
entering the upper ward would have passed through a lobby and
into a short passage with portcullis and doorway. The gatehouse
built from 1282 at Denbigh Castle by Henry de Lacy, Earl of
Lincoln, gives an idea of what was intended at Caernarfon, for
here a triple-towered gatehouse framed a lobby, on one side of
which a defended passage led into the interior of the castle.

    The careful DOMESTIC PLANNING seen in these gatehouses
was carried into other areas of the castles. Caernarfon is a
p. 290 veritable fortress-palace, with chambers lit by fine two-light
windows with seats in the embrasures, hooded fireplaces, easy

access to latrines, and in some cases small chapels. Thus a series
of well-appointed chambers were provided in the polygonal
towers that line the enceinte, the greatest being the Eagle Tower.
One disappointing aspect is the kitchen range, which is on a
ridiculously small scale for such a large castle, although
evidence indicates that a larger building was envisaged
originally. The towers at the other three castles were on a par with
Caernarfon, the latrine arrangement at Beaumaris being but one
of a series of notable features. At Conwy the inner ward houses
a small, compact unit intended as the residence for Edward I p. 329
and Queen Eleanor, arguably the best example of medieval royal
accommodation to have come down to us largely unaltered.

The provision for the care of souls was met by a number of
CHAPELS. Often the only indication that a room was designed
for this purpose is the remains of a piscina, and possibly a sedile.
Both at Caernarfon and Harlech a chapel lay over the entrance
passage of the main gatehouse, the latter having two small
chapels, one above the other, on the first and second floors. These
were designed for the use of those residing in the gatehouse, for
at Harlech the main chapel is in the inner ward. Small chapels
are located in some of the mural towers at Caernarfon, but on
the analogy with the other castles, there must have been a larger
chapel in one of the wards, now lost, perhaps never completed.
The finest chapels are at Conwy and Beaumaris. The range in
the outer ward at Conwy that included the great hall had, at the p. 326
E end, a chapel with slight evidence for a handsome three-light
glazed window. What remains of this chapel pales into
insignificance compared to that provided for the king and queen
in the Chapel Tower at the NE corner of the inner ward at Conwy.
The main floor forms a circular nave for this chapel royal, with
the semi-hexagonal chancel built into the thickness of the tower,
the two areas possibly divided by a rood screen. Two chambers
flank the chapel, the larger of which would have been the sacristy.
An even finer chapel was built at Beaumaris. This shares with
that at Conwy the provision of a small upper window through
which the Mass could be observed from a small mezzanine
chamber, there being two examples at Beaumaris. Entrance into
the chapel there was through a pair of trefoil-headed doorways,
and five lancet windows lit the rib-vaulted interior; below each
one of these is a panel into which is set a blind arcade with trefoil
heads.

Coupled with the construction of the castles at Caernarfon and
Conwy are two of the most outstanding medieval TOWN
WALLS, largely cleared of modern accretions and conserved in 26, 28
the later C20. The defences of the borough at Conwy are
especially remarkable, with three twin-towered gatehouses and
twenty-one mural towers still standing, various sections still
retaining battlements, whilst at Caernarfon two twin-towered
gate-houses punctuate a circuit that has a mere eight towers.
A town wall planned for Beaumaris from the outset was not fully
implemented until the early C15, and has been demolished.

We have many names in the accounts of those responsible for the construction of the Edwardian castles, or different aspects thereof, the details of which were drawn together by the late Arnold Taylor in *The History of the King's Works*, 1963, and numerous other publications. The Savoyard *Master James of St George* is the man associated most closely with the works, and although the precise nature of his role has recently been called into question (that he was more administrator than architect), it is still generally accepted that the man whose position as Master of the King's Works in Wales was confirmed for life in 1284 played a pivotal role. Master James arrived in Wales from Savoy to work on the castles built following the war of 1277, such as Flint and Rhuddlan in Flintshire, and there is no doubt that he was an architect who also had great organizational abilities. The responsibility for the actual design of the castles built from 1283 may not have been his, however; Edward I as 'patron' would have been heavily involved at the initial stage. (In this capacity it is interesting to note the instructions to Master James, after he had moved from Wales to Scotland in 1298, for the construction of fortifications at Linlithgow in 1302: Edward I specified the design on which he was to work, including a twin-towered gatehouse.) Besides being involved with the king's four great Welsh castles, Master James was also associated with works undertaken at Castell y Bere, Criccieth and Dolwyddelan.

The ties between England and Savoy (now divided between France, Switzerland and Italy) came through Edward I's mother, Eleanor of Provence, and many Savoyards were to be found in the court of Henry III. Before Edward returned from crusade in 1274 he had stayed with Count Philip of Savoy, and amongst the men who played a leading role in the conquest of Wales was Sir Otto de Grandison, who led the army that took Castell y Bere, then proceeding to Harlech to establish the castle there. Another was Sir John de Bonvillars, who was to die at the siege of Dryslwyn in South Wales in 1287.

Other names that stand out in building the castles include *Walter of Hereford*, who was sent to oversee the repair of both castle and town walls at Caernarfon following the uprising of 1294–5, and to complete the castle as designed. *Henry of Oxford*, master carpenter, was present at Conwy from the start, building accommodation for king and queen. Later, in 1286, he was being paid for the completion of the carpentry in the hall in the outer ward, and for work on the royal lodgings in the inner ward, including a staircase. The master engineer *Richard of Chester* had a long career in the employment of the king and within the earldom of Chester, starting at Flint in 1277, and is named in the records for Caernarfon and Conwy, and in preparations for the construction of Beaumaris.

Taylor was able to trace a number of other Savoyards employed on the castles besides James of St George. Much has been made of the SAVOYARD INFLUENCE on the design of the Edwardian castles, although design is perhaps too strong a word.

What cannot be disputed is that there are aspects in construction and finished detail that can be better paralleled in Savoy than in England. There is no need to look to Savoy for the origin of the great towers and gatehouses, as there are enough earlier parallels in England and Wales. However, the use of inclined or helicoidal scaffolding, evident from the putlogs at Beaumaris, Conway and Harlech, has been taken as one example of Savoyard technique. Another is the triple finials that capped the merlons of Conwy, although in most cases only stubs remain. Slight evidence of this decorative device survives at Harlech, where we have the names of several Savoyards. Here the most remarkable link with Savoy is the range of windows on the w face of the gatehouse and on the N and s sides of the top storey. These mirror closely a number of windows in the Count of Savoy's castle of Chillon. Successive constables of Harlech were from Savoy – Sir John de Bonvillars in 1285, his wife Agnes from his death in 1287, then Master James himself in 1290–3.

Castles after the Mid-Fourteenth Century

Little architectural development happened in North Wales from the mid-c14. The works at Beaumaris and Conwy continued into the opening decades of the c14, but ended leaving the castles unfinished, Beaumaris in particular. The immediate approach to the entrance at Harlech was enhanced in 1323–4 with a fixed bridge set between two towers, with a wooden drawbridge at either end. At Beaumaris the sw section of the outer curtain wall was reinforced with a series of arches at some date, possibly after the inspection of the North Wales castles by William de Emeldon

Harlech Castle.
Engraving by J.S. Cotman, early c19

in 1343. His survey highlights the poor state of the castle largely
due to the towers being unfinished; a section of curtain wall is
described as ruinous. There is evidence for minor works undertaken at Dolwyddelan by Maredudd ab Ieuan, ancestor of the
Wynns of Gwydir, in the late C15.

The most significant event in the CONSERVATION of the
castles came when the Deputy Constable of Caernarfon Castle,
Sir Llewelyn Turner, began repair and renewal in the 1870s,
chronicled in a booklet in 1902. His works included the renewal
of battlements, the flooring and the roofing of the Queen's Tower,
and the completion of the upper storey of the Well Tower. Other
works, such as flooring many of the other towers, were undertaken in time for the investiture of the Prince of Wales in 1911.
The passing of most of the castles and town walls into state care
in the C20 began a long programme of conservation, of both
Welsh and English castles, and in some restoration such as the
new treads for newel stairs.

MEDIEVAL TOWNS

There were infant towns before the Edwardian conquest at
Pwllheli and Nefyn (C), and a substantial one at Llanfaes (A)
outside the Friary, that might lay claim to being the chief town
of princely Gwynedd. The conquest established fortified towns
at Caernarfon, Conwy and Beaumaris on a scale not previously
seen in Wales. Unwalled towns were founded around other castles
such as Harlech (M) and Castell y Bere (Llanfihangel y Pennant,
M), the one barely successful, the other failing completely, and
Criccieth (C). In Merioneth, Bala and Dinas Mawddwy were C14
English foundations, and it is certain that some tiny settlement
occurred at Tywyn. Dolgellau's birth and early growth are
unrecorded. In Anglesey, the Welsh population of Llanfaes, dispossessed with the construction of Beaumaris, were moved to a
new town, Newborough, in 1303. At Bangor, as at St Davids in
the SW, the built area around the cathedral remained minimal
long after the medieval period.

One medieval STONE HOUSE survives in a town, Tŷ Gwyn,
Barmouth (M), of the mid C15. Not strictly a town house as it
predates any town here, it may have been connected with coastal
trade or defence. It has a single-room plan: basement, ground
floor and first-floor hall. Despite its tiny scale an encomiastic
poem to its builder, Gruffudd Fychan of Corsygedol, by Tudur
Penllyn (†c. 1485), compares it to the largest towers at Caernarfon and Harlech, to 'Bwrlai' (Burleigh House?) and to the buildings of London, Calais, Bristol, Bath and Troy. Early C19 views
show numerous TIMBER-FRAMED late medieval buildings in
Conwy and some in Caernarfon. In Conwy, Aberconwy House,
early C15, must stand for what has gone. With a jettied timber
upper storey over a stone basement, it is akin to Northern
European merchants' houses. The ground floor was probably
commercial, under a first-floor hall. One other, badly damaged,

timber house survives in Conwy and another in Castle Street, Beaumaris. Cwrt Plas-yn-dre, Dolgellau (M), a late C15 town house with a spere-truss, was dismantled in the late C19 and partially re-erected at Newtown, Powys, and Henblas, Beaumaris, a large timber-framed complex, was recorded before demolition in 1870.

CHURCHES AND MONUMENTS,
LATER C16 AND C17

Post-Reformation church work in Gwynedd is mostly the PRIVATE CHAPELS built by landowners, either as church additions or on their estates. Examples of the former are the Vaynol Chapel at Llanbeblig church, Caernarfon, presumably built for the tomb of William Griffith †1587, that at Dolwyddelan (C), c. 1590, for Robert Wynn of Plas Mawr, Conwy, and that at Llanddwywe (bont, M), 1615, for the Vaughans of Corsygedol. An example of the latter is the Vaynol estate chapel (Felinheli, C), 1596, a plain chamber, the windows with arched lights in threes and fours. Llanddwywe has its own external door, as did the chapel at Llanbeblig. The retrograde S chapel at Llangadwaladr church (A), built 1661 by Hugh Owen of 64 Bodowen, has two big Perp windows, harking back to former times. It also has its own door, with an ornate keystone and hood.

Transepts were added at Llanfaglan and Llanaelhaearn (C) in 1600 and 1622 respectively. The enchanting E end at Nant Peris (C) evolved during the C16 and C17 to a cross plan with chapels in the NE and SE angles. Mallwyd (M) has a C17 character, Dr John Davies having added the chancel in 1624 with uncusped tracery to the E window. The boarded timber bell-tower and porch are dated 1640–1.

The exquisite estate chapels at Rûg (M) and Gwydir (C) demonstrate the liturgical and architectural concerns of the time. Both are unremarkable externally but have sumptuous INTERIORS. At Rûg, built in 1637 by Col. William Salusbury, the 65 interior is both medieval and Renaissance. Here are painted canopied pews each side of the altar, guilloche-moulded panelling, unusual carved shaped bench ends, and an ornate roof in the medieval style covered in rose-trail painting. Gwydir Uchaf chapel, built in 1673 by Sir Richard Wynn, is High Church with a Jacobean flavour, the painted ceiling a provincial Baroque. The 62 seating is arranged collegiate-fashion, with pulpit and desk on the S wall, the communion table surrounded on three sides by turned-baluster rails, and a W gallery. The iconography of the 63 ceiling – the Trinity and Last Trump amid angels and clouds – hints at a Catholicism latent in the Wynns of Gwydir.

As for FITTINGS, the translation of the Bible into Welsh in 1588 and the shift from ritual to the spoken word made the PULPIT the focus. There are unusual examples at Llangoed (A), 1622, and Llanfihangel Din Silwy (Llanddona, A), 1628, probably by the same carver. Both hexagonal, they taper towards the base and are carved with floral and geometrical patterns in panels framed by rails enriched with vines, dolphins and sunflowers. Many pulpits have been made up of reused pieces, e.g. Trefriw and St Michael, Betws-y-coed (C). There are good early C17 Laudian COMMUNION RAILS at Llanrhychwyn (C), 1636; at Llangelynin (C) they are later C17 of barley-twist type. The few surviving BOX PEWS are mostly C18 or early C19, though reused C17 panels survive in several churches. The reassembled box pew at Llanfaethlu (A) has a grand three-bay pilastered back containing shields and the date 1635. Handsome C17 COMMUNION TABLES survive, often hidden by their coverings, e.g. Llanengan (C), Holyhead and Rhos Lligwy (A). There are earlier C17 FONTS at Betws Garmon (C), 1614, and Llanfaethlu (A), 1640, with bold lettering. A tiny marble bowl of 1651 at Dolgellau dates from the time of the Puritan vicar, John Ellis, oddly copied in stone at Llanelltyd (M) 1689. There are post-Restoration fonts at Holyhead (A) and Llanddeiniolen (C). A very late example of the medieval type of SCREEN is in the Vaughan Chapel at Llanddwywe (Talybont, M), 1620. The most remarkable GLASS is the imported set of C16 windows from Louvain, Belgium, at Llanwenllwyfo (Dulas, A), mostly of *c.* 1520 (three are late C16 and *c.* 1600). There are C16 and early C17 heraldic fragments at Beaumaris (A).

The finest of Elizabethan MONUMENTS is the Griffiths tomb with double alabaster effigies at Llanbeblig (Caernarfon), the figures realistic and the ornament Renaissance. An unusual stone table tomb with a semicircular hood appears in Gwynedd as in Clwyd, the earliest to Robert Wynn of Plas Mawr at Conwy *c.* 1600, the latest at Llandrillo (M), early C18. Others are at Clynnog Fawr (C), Llanfaethlu (A) and Beaumaris. Wall memorials of the early C17 are often charming but naïve, with the deceased kneeling at a prayer-desk and children kneeling behind, e.g. Llanwnda (C), Clynnog Fawr (C) and Llanddwywe (Talybont, M). The early C17 Wynn memorial at Dolwyddelan (C) is of painted plaster, with three shields divided by columns. Classical-to-Baroque detail begins to replace Jacobean as in the tablet to Thomas Caesar (†1632) at Beaumaris (A). The alabaster and marble memorial to Archbishop John Williams (†1650) at Llandegai (C) shows him kneeling at a prayer-desk in a surround of Corinthian capitals and broken segmental pediment. The Owen memorial at Llangadwaladr (A), *c.* 1660, is similar, two kneeling figures in Ionic niches.

Good BRASSES are at Llanwenllwyfo (Dulas, A); Clynnog Fawr (C), early C17 with kneeling figures; and Llanddeiniolen (C), later C17, with conventional emblems of mortality. WOOD was not much used for monuments, but Bryncroes (C) has late C17 painted oak panels to the Trygarn family. There are early C16 and mid-C17 Flemish WOODCARVINGS at Bangor Cathedral, and an early C16 TRIPTYCH, also Flemish.

PAINTINGS, particularly painted texts, may survive beneath limewash in many churches. Examples of the C16 and C17 are at Llangar (M), Llangelynin (C) and Llangelynin (M).

At Llangelynin (M) and Llangar are images of Death as a skeleton, these possibly late C17 to C18.

COUNTRY HOUSES c. 1400–1700

The absence of houses datable before the C15 across Wales has been attributed to the ferocity of the Glyndŵr uprising and its suppression, but replacement of inconvenient structures on the same site must also be an element. Hafoty, Llansadwrn (A) may have begun as a late C14 cruck-framed hall. High-status C15–C16 HALLS are known to have existed at Penrhyn, Llandegai (C) and Plas Newydd, Llanedwen (A), before their C18 reconstructions, the latter having a chapel at right angles, and the encomia of poets record hospitality at many another C15 hall. One surviving hall, that of the former abbot's lodgings at Cymer Abbey, Llanelltyd (M), ring-dated to 1441, proves to be small, though its 25-ft (8-metre) roof-span is the broadest in Merioneth, and diminutive scale must have been typical of most gentry halls. The grandest of these small halls, at Plas Uchaf (Cynwyd, M), Penarth Fawr (Llanarmon, C) and Egryn (Talybont, M) each has a single spere or aisle truss, at Plas Uchaf ring-dated to 1435 and combined with cruck-trusses, at Egryn ring-dated to 1510. The other small halls, mostly of the C16, generally with a single decorated truss, are mentioned in the Vernacular section.

The great halls of Cochwillan (Tal-y-bont, Bangor, C), and Gloddaeth (Llanrhos, C), to a much more ambitious scale, span the end of the medieval period, and it seems likely that the Hall of Meredith at Gwydir (C) does also. Gloddaeth and Cochwillan have hammerbeam roofs of great richness, testimony to the rise of Welsh families after the Tudor revolution. It may be that the present first-floor hall at Gwydir represents a C15 hall floored in the mid C16, but the rather plain roof has not been ring-dated. The adjacent Solar Tower with its extraordinary four storeys appears to be of c. 1500, altered through the C16. Such a storeyed house, perhaps referring back to defensive keeps, is unparalleled in Wales. The fact that the two were not linked suggests a high-status example of the unit system common across the area (see p. 43). Small C16 halls appear across Merioneth and Caernarvonshire but hardly at all in Anglesey and not at all in Ceredigion to the s, in the former probably because replaced later, in the latter because of relative poverty. Chimneys were generally inserted in the C16, but Cochwillan and Gloddaeth had fireplaces from the beginning. Extensive use of timber framing is suggested by Buckler's 1810 views of the subsidiary ranges at Gwydir, datable to the mid C16, but no house in the region keeps this type of display.

A different order of architectural display appears in the reign of Elizabeth, originating, it would seem, in mercantile contacts with London and the Low Countries. The characteristic STEPPED GABLES were introduced to North Wales in Denbighshire by Sir Richard Clough in 1567, and these appear with pedimented mullion-and-transom windows and polyhedron

⁵³ finials at Plas Mawr, Conwy, 1576–85, and a little later on at Plas
⁴⁸ Coch, Llanedwen (A). The window type is seen over the porch
at Corsygedol, Talybont (M), 1593, and at Talyllyn (A), 1597.
Ceilings of ornately moulded beams in three tiers – main,
subsidiary, and joists – can be found at Corsygedol, in the
inserted floor in the Hall of Meredith, Gwydir, and at Maes-y-
castell, Caerhun (C). Particularly exuberant PLASTERWORK of
^{52, 54} the late C16 is at Plas Mawr, Conwy, and Maenan Hall (C), 1582,
and the crude vigour of the Plas Mawr caryatids was equalled in
the lost 'Caesars' chimneypiece at Gwydir Castle. Imported in
the C20 from Emral Hall, Flintshire, the early C17 Hercules
⁵⁶ ceiling in the Town Hall, Portmeirion (M), combines classical
scenes with Jacobean strapwork.*

The Renaissance influence in this plasterwork and carved
detail may also be seen in formal SYMMETRIES at Plas Mawr,
both the main house, 1576–80 and the gatehouse, 1585. But this
is exceptional. Sir John Wynn's Gwydir Uchaf (C), of 1604,
known from one view of 1684, was wholly symmetrical, a Renaissance pleasure villa, but the details are impossible to recover. Typically, as at Dolaugwyn, Bryncrug (M), the mullion-and-transom
windows and stepped gables of Plas Mawr are present but the
elevation is asymmetrical, the original house of 1620 with off-
centre porch-tower, the big cross-wing and side stair-tower added
in 1656. Similar asymmetries are at Plas Talhenbont, Llanystumdwy (C), 1606, Bodysgallen, Llanrhos (A), 1620, and
Castellmarch, Abersoch (C), 1625–9. By contrast Plas Berw,
⁵⁰ Pentre Berw (A), 1615, and Glyn Cywarch, Talsarnau (M), 1616,
have near-regular fronts, and at Bodwrdda, Aberdaron (C), the
extraordinary refronting in brick in 1621 included also the
addition of wings to make a formal N front to the C16 stone
house. The central hall typical of Renaissance planning appears
very early at Plas Berw, 1615, but is not general until the next
^{p. 337} century. Plas Mawr, Conwy, 1576, with a service room between
hall and parlour, may be a prototype.

The transition to stone cross-windows might be expected in
the late C17 but houses of this type are exceptional. Mullion-and-
transom-windowed additions were made at Vaynol, Y Felinheli
(C), in the 1660s. The regular five-bay front with cross-windows
and stepped end gables at Caerberllan, Llanfihangel y Pennant
(M) is clearly transitional to the regular façades of the C18, but
the date is uncertain: dated 1590 and 1755, the front actually
looks late C17. Benar, Penmachno (C), 1693, has a plain five-bay
front. Both are already a world away from the irregular fronts of
Rhiwaedog, Rhos-y-gwaliau (M), dated 1664, or of Parc, Croesor
⁴⁹ (M), 1671, and the unit-system agglomeration of such as Dduallt,
Maentwrog (M) and Plas Newydd, Minffordd (M).

If the C17 Renaissance house of the Jonesian kind is absent
from the region, so also are INTERIORS of the same period. There
are none of the rich Restoration interiors of the type of Powis

---

*The enthusiasm for HERALDRY shown at Plas Mawr continues well into the C17,
as at Glyn Cywarch, 1638–9, and Glyn, Llanbedrgoch (A), 1644.

Castle, nor any of the typical late C17 heavy plaster ceilings. The
dining room at Gwydir Castle, re-fitted with its panelling brought
back from New York, is the exception: the single finest C17
room to survive, but a hybrid combining the spiral columns of
Counter-Reformation Italy with panelling patterns of Jacobean
type. If pre-Civil War, the provenance must be directly from the
Court, where Sir Richard Wynn was treasurer to the queen. The
spiral columns of St Mary, Oxford, 1637, were by *Nicholas Stone*,
whom Wynn employed for a plaque in Llanrwst church, making
such rapid transmission less implausible. Otherwise domestic
Jacobean and Stuart woodwork is rare. The staircases at Castellmarch and Vaynol have heavy newels and turned balusters, that
at Wern (Caeathro, C) has flat balusters. At the end of the
century typical bolection moulding and spiral balusters appear
at Pengwern, Llan Ffestiniog (M), *c.* 1693. Spiral balusters are
also on the gallery and staircase at Gloddaeth. Caerau
(Llanfairynghornwy, A) has a fine bolection-moulded panelled
room of the late C17 and heavy turned balusters.

Bodfel, Llannor (C), three-storey and cruciform, is suggested
as a possible GATEHOUSE to an unbuilt C17 mansion, to a scale
paralleled only at Plas Mawr. The two-storey embattled gatehouse at Madryn, Llandudwen (C), survives the mansion it
fronted, its date probably earlier C17. Smaller gatehouses, symmetrical about a central gable, survive at Cefnamwlch,
Tudweiliog (C), 1607, Corsygedol, Talybont (M), 1630, and at 55
Rhiwaedog, Rhos-y-gwaliau (M). Two large DOVECOTES at
Penmon and Parciau, Marianglas (A), probably both early C17, 57
are the best survivors of the type in the region.

Remnants of early GARDENS are discernible at a number of
sites. At Bodysgallen the terraced gardens may be early C17, the

Talybont, Corsygedol, gatehouse.
Engraving, early C19

largest sunk with a viewing gallery above. At Gwydir, the Dutch
garden with its fountain basin is probably C17, but that on the
other side with its Renaissance arch is late C16. At Corsygedol
and Pengwern the lines of C17 layouts may be discerned.

VERNACULAR HOUSES AND FARM
BUILDINGS

BY JUDITH ALFREY

Gwynedd has no single signature in vernacular building, reflecting its diverse topography and historical development. The most
obvious division is between upland and lowland, with the massif
of Snowdonia and its intervening valleys sharply distinct from the
coastal plains of Llŷn and Anglesey. The chronology of survival,
as well as the types and style of building, are quite different in
these differing zones.

Across the whole area, stone dominates the vernacular building stock, though masking in some respects and in some locali-
ties the use of other materials. One of the earliest references to
CRUCK CONSTRUCTION in Britain comes from Merioneth
(Harlech, 1305), and a well-developed tradition of working in
timber is suggested by the sophisticated carpentry displayed in
churches and domestic buildings alike, from the C15 at least.
Aspects of this are clearly derived from articulate principles of
timber construction – the box-framed aisle trusses at Penarth
Fawr, Llanarmon (C) and Egryn, Talybont (M), for example, or
54   the crucks at Maenan (C), Hafod Ysbyty, Llan Ffestiniog (M)
and Gorllwyn-uchaf, Prenteg (C). All these are now associated
with an external structure of stone. Early ROOFS also exhibit
carpentry of a high order: the hammerbeam roofs of Gloddaeth,
47   Llanrhos (C) or Cochwillan, Tal-y-bont (C) are exceptional, but
there are numerous fine display-timber roofs even in houses of
lesser status. External TIMBER FRAMING is rare, though it may
once have been more widespread, especially in town buildings.
The majority of surviving examples show its early combination
45   with stone, as at Aberconwy House, Conwy (C) or Tŷ Mawr,
Gwyddelwern (M).

At the other end of the scale, a diminishing number of EARTH
or CLOM buildings have survived. These are generally cottages or
farm buildings, and unlikely to be earlier than c. 1800. They are
concentrated in the Rhoshirwaun area of Llŷn, where good
building stone was scarce, but it is clear from the documentary
record that the use of earth was more widespread, even within
the stony mountain massif – at Dinas Mawddwy, for example.
Other examples may yet come to light.

But it is undoubtedly STONE that contributes most to the
vernacular signature of the county. It exhibits considerable local
variation in use, linked in the first place to the complexities
of geology. The Cambrian grits of the Harlech Dome are
characteristically hard and difficult to dress; used in distinctive
large blocks, they were not always limewashed (though the use

of lime was once more common even here). The slates and shales that encircle the Dome were more tractable but worked in smaller and often rougher blocks, often demanding a limewash or render finish. Similarly, limewash or render was generally used with the Anglesey schists, which were highly irregular and hard to dress. The use of lime was itself susceptible to architectural treatment, e.g. in its judicious use to give emphasis to a façade or distinguish house from farm building. It could be a form of display, as examples of conspicuously white houses suggest.

There is both a chronology and a social hierarchy visible in the treatment of stone. Fine variations in technique denoted subtle differences in resources, status and building use: there is often a distinction between domestic and agricultural buildings, with dry-stone walling derived from field clearance largely now confined to field cowhouses (though once also characteristic of poorer dwellings). Developments in stoneworking technique permitting a neater finish encouraged the abandonment of limewashing, and the taste for exposed stonework was widespread after c. 1860, when the popularity of e.g. a rock-faced finish brought greater uniformity.

SLATE has become the dominant roofing material, and exceptions are rare. Again, there are considerable variations in type and use; small graded slates were superseded in many areas by the evenly cut slates of the industrial age. Small slates bedded in mortar and grouted are still characteristic of the coastal plains of Llŷn and Anglesey. Instances of thatch have been recorded but rarely survive, though its use has been recently occasionally revived.

Some domestic buildings from the C15 survive, but they are rare. Thereafter there is a good chronological profile across the county, though richest in the mountain areas. In the coastal lowlands, some exceptional survivals indicate early prosperity, e.g. Hafoty and Penarth Fawr, but here the vernacular character is overwhelmingly that of the C19. In the uplands, the constraints of topography most restricted agricultural improvement, and the shifting focus of C19 investment and settlement with industrial development fostered survival of early buildings. Thus in the fringes of Snowdonia and the valleys that cut into the massif small numbers of houses survive from the later C15, with a good sequence from the mid C16 onwards. The status and quality of many of these, even in what now appear intractable and isolated locations such as Hafod Ysbyty, Pengwern and Cae Canol Mawr (all in Llan Ffestiniog, M), or Nantpasgan Fawr, Llandecwyn (M), are clear evidence of shifting cultural and economic geographies.

The earliest houses offer only a glimpse of social organization, but from the mid C16 a clearer pattern is discernable, as a gentry class emerged in the years following the Acts of Union (1536 and 1543) and small estates were established or consolidated. A series of important vernacular country houses, such as Gwydir, Corsygedol, and Bodwrdda, is ample testimony to the growing ambitions, standing and fortunes of this class by the early C17,

but there are many others of slightly lesser status. From the late
C16, houses associated with relatively modest farms have also survived in significant numbers, but it is not until the later C18
that a fuller social landscape is expressed in surviving
buildings.

In parallel with this visible social structure was a ramifying
architectural language. The earliest surviving dwellings (from the
later C15 to the second quarter of the C16) are HALL-HOUSES,
displaying remarkable conformity of plan: a hall with open
hearth, between an inner (or 'upper') unit beyond the dais
partition, and an outer (or 'lower') unit below the cross-passage.
Examples include Hafoty and Penarth Fawr, also Egryn
(Talybont, M), Trefadog (Llanfaethlu, A), Coed-y-ffynnon
(Penmachno, C), and Cefn Caer (Pennal, M). Adaptations
springing from the insertion of an upper floor within the hall and
differing locations for inserted fireplaces from the later C16
resulted in greater diversification of plan.

From the mid C16 a distinctive regional vernacular also began
to emerge, as for example Bryn-yr-odyn (Llan Ffestiniog, M),
Uwchlaw'r Coed (Llanbedr, M), and Llannerch-y-felin (Rowen,
C). The SNOWDONIA HOUSE is characteristically storeyed, with
end chimneys, and a compact plan. It retains some of the

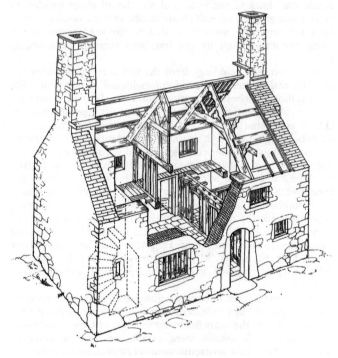

Typical Snowdonia house.
Reconstructed cut-away drawing

divisions characteristic of its predecessor the hall-house, having a hall and cross-passage with opposed doorways, but compressing parlour and service room together beyond the cross-passage, dispensing with an inner unit beyond the hall, and introducing a heated chamber on the first floor. At first, the staircase was likely to have been a winding mural stair alongside the stack, but the plan-form readily accommodated a central staircase as centralized planning (and carpentry staircases) became fashionable in the C17. The earliest examples also retain the tradition of display carpentry, in enriched upper chamber roofs, e.g. Cae Glas, Croesor (M), 1548. This highly consistent regional style suggests a class with a distinct identity, and its distribution across the whole of Gwynedd points to a social rather than a strictly geographical foundation. The plan-type proved remarkably enduring, adopted for small houses and cottages well into the C19.

Houses may also reveal detail about household arrangement: Gwynedd is rich in examples of the UNIT SYSTEM, in which two (sometimes more) houses are adjacent on the same holding. It is generally assumed that the secondary house was established for the widow of the preceding generation, and the different status is often indicated in the architectural language adopted for each house. At Llanfair-isaf, Llanfair (M) and Llwyndu, Llanaber (M) a seemingly earlier architectural form based on the open hall is adopted for the secondary house. In other examples, the requirement for multiple households took more complex and innovative architectural forms, e.g. Parc (Croesor, M), Plas Newydd (Minffordd, M) and Dduallt (Maentwrog, M). Perhaps a lingering survival of this practice is the double farms that exist here and there across the area, e.g. Cwm Cloch, Beddgelert (C).

It is more difficult to reconstruct a coherent architectural identity in the coastal lowlands, where fewer early buildings

Unit-system house (Minffordd, Plas Newydd).
Drawing

survive, but here too, by the C18, the dominant plan was a central-entry house with gable-end chimneys, e.g. Trygarn, Sarn Meyllteyrn (C). It was only a short step to the vernacular Georgian which so dominated regional building in the C19, and which, playing on a minute set of variations, gave architectural demarcation to almost an entire society.

By *c.* 1800, social and economic changes brought another class to the fore: the rapid growth of slate-quarrying and mineral mining sustained a large smallholding class, whose COTTAGES are a distinctive part of the landscape of northern Snowdonia especially. Some were tolerated by landowners needing a labour force; others were set down as encroachments on common land, forming a distinctive settlement pattern, e.g. at Rhosgadfan and Garndolbenmaen (Dolbenmaen), often on intractable land. Further W, too, on Llŷn, common and waste lands and even road-sides were colonized – the settlement pattern is clear at Garn Fadryn (Llaniestyn), Mynytho (Botwnnog) and above Nefyn, and on a smaller scale, but with some exceptionally well-preserved small buildings at Mynydd Rhiw (Rhiw). The scale of these buildings varied with acreage. Where the size of holding justified it, there might be diminutive farm buildings associated with the house. Some of these display the resourcefulness of the vernacular – the domed pigsty for example is an occasional feature, e.g. Frondeg (Rhiw) – but the surviving dwellings themselves are for the most part well-built and, whilst small, far from rudimentary. In architectural terms, these cottages represent scaled-down versions of their larger neighbours: a near-central doorway with service room (or rooms) or perhaps a parlour to one side, and a kitchen to the other. The extent to which they aspired to politer architectural models is indicated in the occasional presence of a false chimney. The *croglofft* is an interesting measure of economy, giving a partial upper floor alongside an open hall.

The chronology of survival for FARM BUILDINGS is less complete, and intact farmstead groups are rare before the C19. As a result, a whole picture of the pre-industrial farming economy is p. 188 elusive. Though stock-rearing dominated, the early corn BARNS that survive even in the uplands indicate that mixed farming was important, e.g. Penybryn and Hafod-dwyryd (both Penmachno, C). The high quality of many of these is testimony to their status within the farmstead, e.g. Corsygedol (Talybont, M). Although the transhumance described by Thomas Pennant in the late C18 has left little direct architectural trace, the strength of a tradition of dispersed grazing supported by isolated COWHOUSES (widely called field barns) is clearly displayed throughout the uplands, especially in Merioneth. Some of these incorporate crucks, hinting at an early date. Their siting – often close to the *ffridd* wall – is intimately connected to the particular geography of land use characteristic of upland farms. The distinctive open-sided upland HAY BARN made its appearance in the early C19, one symptom of agricultural improvement. Some were constructed using vast monoliths of slate, nicely demonstrating the

connections between agriculture and industry, e.g. Tan-y-bwlch
Home Farm, Maentwrog (M).

It is, however, in the intact FARMSTEAD GROUPS of the lowlands that agricultural improvement after c. 1800 is most apparent, e.g. Llwydiarth Esgob, Llanerchymedd (A). Some bear the
signature of the estates that were significant patrons of building
in this period, investing wealth derived from industry in the
agricultural economy. It is on estate farms that the tightest
planning is found; the Penrhyn and Newborough estates
were particularly prolific builders of farms, which once again
delineate a clear hierarchy in scale, e.g. Tŷ'n-yr-hendre and
Glan-y-môr-isaf (Talybont, Bangor, C) and Coetmor (Bethesda,
C). This building programme culminated in the remarkable
series of double farmyards built by the Newborough estate on
Bardsey Island (C) in the 1870s.

In some respects, the estates continued to foster a vernacular
tradition: the numerous cottages built for slate workers on the
Penrhyn estate are tightly planned in multiples and make use of
quarried and sawn slate, but they resemble their vernacular precursors in form and scale. It was only towards the end of the C19
that radically different vocabularies of building were introduced.

COUNTRY HOUSES c. 1700–1830

Progressive GEORGIAN ARCHITECTURE touched the region
rarely. The quiet flow of the first half of the C18 is characterized
in Anglesey by a series of low two-storey end-chimney houses of
between five and eight bays, as at Henblas, Llangristiolus, c. 1700,
Plas Llanddyfnan, 1709, and Plas Llanedwen, with typical central
stairs and bolection-moulded panelled rooms. Their equivalents
in the other two counties are rarer, and generally altered.
Garthmaelan (Dolgellau, M) is taller than the Anglesey type,
earlier C18, the stair framed in a fluted double arch, and
Llanfendigaid, Llangelynin (M), 1745, has a regular seven-bay
front and fielded panelling of mid-C18 type. Brynodol,
Tudweiliog (C), 1743, is similar.

Tros-y-marian (Llangoed, A) has a seven-bay s front with
centre gable, probably mid-C18, making a DOUBLE-PILE house
back-to-back with the C17 N range, the double pile proving a
simple way of enlarging an earlier house. The late arrival of this
plan-type in the region is remarkable, not at all in the C17 and
generally by addition before the mid C18. Medieval Plas Newydd
(Llanedwen, A) was doubled in width in 1751–5. At Peniarth,
Llanegryn (M), the outbuilding of 1727 has Queen Anne   74
cambered-headed windows while the mansion, refaced in the
1730s, is pedimented and windowed in an up-to-date Palladian
way, and of double-pile plan. The confusion of stonework and
interior details here leaves the sequence to a double-pile
uncertain, but it was probably achieved in the 1730s. That both
are of red brick in a country of stone is particularly remarkable.
Red brick is also used on the only other surviving high-quality

75   PALLADIAN house, Plas Gwyn, Pentraeth (A), 1754. Contemporary pedimented houses, both demolished, were Hengwrt,
Llanelltyd (M), 1754, and Ynysmaengwyn, Bryncrug (M), 1758,
the former three-storey, the latter two. At all of these the double-
pile plan gave a broad entrance hall opening on to a staircase.
   A series of small three-bay pedimented houses around
Dolgellau seemingly pays homage to Hengwrt: Tŷ'n-y-coed,
Caerdeon, 1756, Tŷ'n Celyn, Llanelltyd, 1773, and some in Dolgellau town. Larger and rather cruder is Dolrhyd, Dolgellau,
c. 1763, five bays with blank roundels under the eaves, its plain
simplicities echoed in the little Apollo, or meeting room, that
William Vaughan built in front. Inside the Apollo, however, the
plasterwork is an exuberant display of Neoclassical motifs of
c. 1770, undisciplined perhaps, but unparalleled in Wales.
   In the 1770s the pace of construction changed with new
wealth, largely from copper and slate. Baron Hill, Beaumaris (A),
p. 112   as rebuilt in 1776–9 by *Samuel Wyatt*, was a tall three-and-a-half-
storey house with a domed bow and half-octagonal side bays,
a bravura piece of metropolitan house-planning. *John Cooper*
of Beaumaris who worked here went on to design Bodorgan,
1779–84, and to begin re-casing Plas Newydd, 1783–6, for the
other two leading families of the island. Both houses have a
central bow, that at Plas Newydd re-casing work of 1751–3.
78   This mid-C18 work at Plas Newydd is significant because it
was GOTHIC, with battlements and ecclesiastical quatrefoils,
partly in a stuccoed timber frame: a folly of the Horace Walpole
era, apparently designed by Sir Nicholas Bayly, the owner.
Caught between medieval and martial are the two genuine forts
designed by *Thomas Wynn*, Lord Newborough, on his Glynllifon
estate, Llandwrog (C): Fort Williamsburg, c. 1761, and the more
82   picturesque Fort Belan, c. 1775. At Penrhyn, Llandegai (C), the
medieval house was remodelled in symmetrical Gothic from 1782
by *Samuel Wyatt*, a short-lived house most remarkable for being
clad in yellow imitation brick (mathematical tiles). Cooper's work
at Plas Newydd was followed in 1795–8 by that of *James Wyatt*
and *Joseph Potter*, more wholeheartedly Gothic, the pointed
windows of the centre very like Samuel's work at Penrhyn. The
interiors of the hall and central room, Gothic-vaulted in painted
timber and stucco, ostensibly by Potter, are so close to Wyatt's
emerging Gothic style as to be almost certainly by him. *Benjamin
Wyatt* built two picturesque Gothic buildings in the 1790s in the
Ogwen valley for Lady Penrhyn. Ogwen Bank (demolished) had
a round corner tower with large traceried windows; Penisarnant,
Nant Ffrancon (C), a villa with dairy, is hipped with veranda and
pointed windows. Its slate-slab cladding gives the effect of lined
ashlar.
   The taste for the castellated seen at Plas Newydd, seemingly
perfect for the rugged landscapes of the region, left only modest
other examples of the type. The embattled refacing of Rhiwlas
(Llanfor, M) in 1809 has not survived, although the rather better
gate arch there by *Thomas Rickman*, 1813, remains. The plain
symmetrical front with towers at Arthog Hall (M) dates probably

from the 1820s. By that time such mild castellation was being ousted by the gables, occasionally Tudor, generally bargeboarded, that became the ruling style for the seaside and mountain villa, encouraged by the many pattern books of the era. An early example is Craig-y-don, Llandegfan (A), *c.* 1830. Interesting in their sensitivity to the past are the additions to Gwydir Castle, 1828, by *Charles Barry*, reusing old stone and windows from demolished parts of the house.

After *John Cooper's* Baron Hill and Bodorgan, the next group of CLASSICAL HOUSES are probably all by *Joseph Bromfield* of Shrewsbury, spanning the turn of the century and the shift from the Adam and Wyatt-style cubic box to the Nash-style low-lying VILLA with deep-eaved roof. Nannau, Llanfachreth (M), completed 1795, is square with parapets, only the narrow centre bay elaborated, with Wyatt-style tripartite windows. Rhug (M), 1799, is more ambitious, with a severe Neoclassical portico without pediment. The garden front has a central bow. Caerynwch, Brithdir (M), 1801–4, and Nanhoron (C), 1803, are villa-like, with deep-eaved roofs and tall lower windows onto gardens. The iron veranda at Nanhoron is added but fits absolutely in the integration of the Georgian country house into its garden setting, and verandas typify early C19 villas generally. Sir Richard Colt Hoare's possibly self-designed Fach-ddeiliog, Llangower (M), *c.* 1801, has a single bow-fronted reception room flanked by bedrooms opening onto verandas, a gentleman's retreat from which to contemplate lake and mountain, with even the services banished. Less extreme is Sir Watkin Williams-Wynn's Glan-llyn, Llanuwchllyn (M), on the same lake and of similar date, which has the bedroom storey diminished to attic-like proportions above French windows onto the view. Rhagatt, Carrog (M), 1819–20, is similar.

The most spectacular Georgian house is the most anomalous. Penrhyn Castle, Llandegai (C), on which *Thomas Hopper* was probably first consulted in 1819–20, stands almost unparalleled as a huge country house disguised as a Norman castle. Hopper had already essayed at Gosford Castle, Armagh, begun 1820, the dramatic and broken silhouette that suggests a spreading medieval castle entirely built *c.* 1100, but at Penrhyn the scale is much larger. The consistent and overwhelming Romanesque interiors of the late 1820s and 1830s show the motifs of Norman churches applied to every aspect of design. One other Neo-Norman house, Bryn Bras Castle, Llanrug (C), has a turreted phase of 1830–2 and turns more wholeheartedly Norman after 1832, the detail good enough to suggest *Hopper*.

The larger estates began building ESTATE HOUSING in the early C19. Most of this is Victorian, but the most extensive, on the Nannau estate, Llanfachreth (M), dates from *c.* 1805–40. The cottages span the Picturesque from the simply pretty, as in the columned verandas in Llanfachreth village, 1812, through the miniature (Tŷ'n-y-llwyn, 1812, Gelli, 1814), to the pattern-book Tudor of Efail Fach *c.* 1820, Hywel Sele Lodge and Bryn-teg, 1839. The patterns are those of P. F. Robinson's *Rural Architecture*, 1822,

Penrhyn Castle, Grand Hall.
Engraving by G. Hawkins, 1846

stripped of much of the pretty detail. Nannau has an
uncomfortable Tudor LODGE and gate arch combined.
The castellated Port Lodge at Penrhyn Castle of 1819–20 and
the slightly later Neo-Norman Grand Lodge are much more
accomplished.

VICARAGES are rarely earlier than the late C18. The one at
Mallwyd (M) reputedly dates from 1611, and its present simple
form accords with a survey of 1730. Llanfigael (A) is late C18, by
John Cooper, with tripartite windows. The hipped roof and three-
bay front appear regularly in the early C19, as at Llanfor (M),
1814, to plans by a local man. Llandderfel (M), 1826, is unusually large, cruciform and hipped, and the plans for the 1860
remodelling of Llanengan (C) record the handsome pedimented
original of *c.* 1805. *Thomas Jones* of Chester signs plans for
Tudor-style vicarages in the 1830s at Llanfaelog (A) and
Llanfachraeth (A).

GEORGIAN CHURCHES AND MONUMENTS

Few NEW CHURCHES were built during the Georgian period. They are generally plain from limitations of budget and hard stone. Dolgellau (M), 1716–27, has big arched windows and an apsed end, but comparison with Whitchurch, Shropshire, of similar type, shows how much was sacrificed to intractable stone. Boduan (C), 1765, since remodelled, is cruciform, and had arched windows probably glazed in cast iron, and simple gable pediments. Amlwch (A), 1800, probably by *James Wyatt*, is the one church of architectural scale, with a big balustraded w tower against a broad dentilled pediment. Towers were added at Llandegfan and Llanfaes (A), 1811, and Llangefni (A) was rebuilt in Georgian Gothic, 1824, with Y-tracery and an embattled tower. Tremadog (C) is another essay in Georgian Gothic, *c.* 1811, for William Madocks's new town. It has a tower and spire of surprising complexity for the time, the detail all in cement. Sir R. W. Vaughan of Nannau rebuilt Llanfachreth (M) in a simple round-arched style in 1820, of which the tower and possibly the spire survive. St David, Barmouth (M), 1830, by *Edward Haycock* of Shrewsbury, is in a formulaic Perp Gothic, still novel to the region, and Aberdyfi (M), 1837, is similar if simpler, with pointed windows and tower.

Fittings and Monuments

Typical of Georgian fittings are the BOX PEWS, panelled plainly and often jostling for space in a cluttered whitewashed interior where the communion table remains elusive. There are fine box pews at Llanfaglan (C): oak for the squire (in front of the pulpit and enriched with decoration), pine for the plain people. Llangelynin (M) has open benches of Shaker-like simplicity, with names and dates, as does cynhaearn, Pentrefelin (C), 1832. The crowded layout at Llangar (M) is particularly interesting: box pews along the N wall, some carved and made up of C17 panels; open benches along the S wall, either side of the pulpit; the box pew for the rector's family against the railed sanctuary. Llanfigael (A), 1841, shows how late these interiors continued. Two-decker PULPITS can be seen at Llanfaglan (C), dated 1767 with the simplest of sounding boards, Llanfigael (A), and Penllech (C), where there is a delightful carved sun on the sounding-board soffit. Three-decker arrangements – pulpit, reading desk and clerk's desk – are at Llangwyllog (A), Llangar (M), and Ynyscynhaearn (C), where each level is served by an elegant curved staircase. At Bodwrog (A) a plain pulpit at one side of the E window is matched by a reading desk at the other. A rare example of a choir MUSIC STAND is at Llangar, *c.* 1715. BOARDS for the Lord's Prayer etc. can be seen at many of the above, often in Welsh and painted on wood, or metal in the earlier C19.

MONUMENTS by local makers begin to give way to those from English border towns and even London. *Robert Wynne* of Ruthin made the early C18 alabaster cartouche at Penmorfa (C) to the

Royalist soldier Sir John Owen †1666, and possibly the lively Bulkeley memorial at Llanwnda (C), *c.* 1708. London sculptors include *Sir Henry Cheere*, who did early work in the 1730s at Llanfachreth (M) and Tywyn (M), and perhaps the memorial to Sir Thomas Wynn (†1749) in Llandwrog (C). *Joseph Nollekens* made two elegant marble monuments for the Wynn family at Boduan, †1754 and †1773, the later one a fine Neoclassical sarcophagus, and at Llandwrog the large monument with reading female to the Bodvels of Bodfan, †1731–60. The numerous unsigned Baroque memorials include good works like the portrait relief at Llanfaes (A) of Henry Whyte †1728, and the Griffith monument at Llanfaethlu (A). *Van der Hagen* of Shrewsbury has later C18 works in Merioneth, at Corwen and Llanddwywe (Talybont), characterized by good portraits. He may have done the lovely Edwards monument at Pennal (M) with its four portrait reliefs. There are minor later C18 memorials by *Benjamin Bromfield* of Liverpool at Conwy (C) characterized by coloured marbles. Unusually fine urns among so many are on unsigned memorials at Boduan (C) and Corwen (M). *Sir Richard Westmacott* produced Gwynedd's finest Neoclassical monument, 1820, to the 1st Lord Penrhyn, a Roman rustic couple admiring his encomium. Westmacott also did the memorial to the 7th Viscount Bulkeley (†1822) at Beaumaris (A), with his bust mourned by his wife, comforted by Faith. By the early C19 numerous firms were making marble memorials: *Franceys & Spence* of Liverpool and *Carline* of Shrewsbury pre-eminent, with several London firms. Those by *Spence* at Llandwrog (C) and the one by *Ternouth* at Beaumaris are more accomplished works than the routine assemblages of urns or Neo-Greek detail.

TOWNS FROM THE C16 TO *c.* 1830

Caernarfon, Conwy and Beaumaris prospered as trading ports in the C16, and Caernarfon as an administrative centre. In all three the principal families built within the walled towns while the castles fell to decay. Henblas, Beaumaris, became the principal seat of the Bulkeleys, erstwhile Constables of the castle, until they moved to Baron Hill in 1618. The late C16 Plas Mawr, the palace of Robert Wynn in Conwy, and its demolished namesake in Caernarfon represent a new departure for Wales, the equivalent of the TOWN HOUSES of European merchant princes, although neither owner was wealthy primarily from trade. They were town houses in that entry was directly from the street and there were minimal gardens. Buckler's 1810 view of Caernarfon shows the Plas Mawr there rearing above low timber-framed houses. Almost nothing survives of the substantial C16 or C17 buildings in Caernarfon, although elements may remain in altered buildings. At Conwy, similarly early C19 views show numerous timber-framed houses, almost all gone. Speed's maps of Beaumaris and Caernarfon, 1610, show well-filled streets within the walled towns, at Beaumaris the walls already partly removed.

CARNARVON, NORTH WALES.

THE ROYAL HOTEL,
(LATE UXBRIDGE ARMS,)

Caernarfon, Celtic Royal Hotel.
Engraving, late C19

The Civil War affected Harlech, Beaumaris and Conwy castles, but its effect on towns was small. None retains major C17 urban structures, although a small court house of 1614 and grammar school of 1603 survive in part at Beaumaris. The George and Dragon in Castle Street here is an encased timber frame dated 1610, and several other houses including the Bull's Head and No. 10 Castle Street have C17 origins. At Bala the long main street had C17 town houses, now replaced, but the big hipped-roofed late C17 Bull's Head testifies to the importance of the main road. At Dolgellau the court house in Queen's Square reputedly dates from 1606, and although rebuilt in the C18, the walls and massive floor beams may be early C17. Otherwise only the bridge can be reliably dated to the C17.

Before the late C18 there was little urban development, and the towns were generally characterized as ill-built by passing visitors. Modern INNS then appeared both in the towns and on the main roads. The White Lion at Bala, 1759, is modern in its use of brick. The hotel at Corwen (M) is also mid-C18. The Eagle and Child at Holyhead dates from 1784, the demolished Penrhyn Arms Hotel, Bangor, from 1799, and the Royal Hotel, Caernarfon, is early C19. With the completion in the 1820s of *Telford*'s 267-mile road from London to Holyhead the towns along its route prospered and new settlements appeared. Roadside hotels were the beginnings of Betws-y-coed, Beddgelert and Bethesda. The George Hotel at Bangor was consequent on the ferry across the Strait, and the mid-C19 Victoria Hotel at Menai Bridge opposite consequent on Telford's bridge. The stimulus of tourism revitalized Beaumaris, with its handsome Bulkeley Hotel dating from 1835.

Georgian TERRACED HOUSES come late and in small quantities. Bangor has a short early C19 terrace on the approach from the NE, Caernarfon a long brick terrace overlooking Castle Square, and Dolgellau has Eldon Row of 1830 in the centre, a charming marriage of the polite with the massive stones of the area. The finest terrace was built for tourism, Victoria Terrace,

Beaumaris, by *Hansom & Welch*, 1832–3, in grey Anglesey ashlar
91   with a pedimented centrepiece disguising the way in which the
row is angled for different views. William Madocks's planned
town at Tremadog (C), 1805–12, has its tiny T-plan centred on
the town hall and hotel, and simple two-storey rows in the square
and three streets. Madocks's second new town, Porthmadog, of
the 1820s, has no such formal plan, being intended primarily as
a port for the export of slate.

Late Georgian PUBLIC BUILDINGS include modest town halls
at Bala and Beaumaris, late C18, and Pwllheli, early C19, and
even more modest market halls at Bangor, 1831, and Caernarfon, 1832. Dolgellau's pedimented Shire Hall, 1825 by *Edward
Haycock*, is the best Georgian public building of the
region, with the possible exception of the Gaol at Beaumaris,
90   1828–9, by *Hansom & Welch*, with its superb limestone masonry.
A neat classical group is the cluster of Customs buildings and
commemorative arch at Holyhead, 1823–4, by *Telford* and
Thomas Harrison, which mark the beginning of the road to
London.

Pigot's *Directory* of 1828–9 gives POPULATION FIGURES from
the 1821 census. Caernarfon had nearly 6,000 inhabitants, far
more than Holyhead with 4,000 and Bangor with 3,500. Beaumaris and Dolgellau had just over 2,000, Corwen just under,
while Bala, Barmouth, Pwllheli and Conwy each had just over
1,000. The surprises are the 2,500 at Llangefni and 2,400 at
Tywyn, but both figures are inflated by hinterlands, including the
industrial Parys Mountain and its rapidly growing port at
Amlwch in the one case and the mines and resort of Aberdyfi in
the other. Neither has much Georgian architecture to show, while
Dolgellau and Barmouth, growing on the manufacture and
export of woollen cloth, have substantial Late Georgian houses.
Barmouth, which the *Directory* calls 'much frequented', was
beginning to show the impact of tourism, and tourist trade is
mentioned at Tywyn and Aberdyfi, exemplified at the latter by
some semi-detached lodging houses of the 1820s or 1830s.
Beaumaris was the most successful early C19 resort, as shown by
its buildings. The particularly notable expansions of Bangor, from
just 93 houses in the 1790s, and of Caernarfon, were due to slate,
and the impact of industry on the towns closest to mining sites
would be seen not in grand terraces but small tenements, of
which those of Bangor and Caernarfon became notorious in the
cholera epidemics of the 1840s.

INDUSTRIAL GWYNEDD

BY DAVID GWYN

The industrial economy of Gwynedd was dominated from the
late C18 to the mid C20 by the quarrying of slate, although mining
for copper and to a lesser extent for ironstone, gold, manganese
and lead assumed importance at various periods. Not only did
the quarries and mines grow to a gigantic size, they also called

into being distinctive industrial communities – towns like Bethesda (C) and Blaenau Ffestiniog (M), villages like Deiniolen, Talysarn (C) and Corris (M) – and efficient transport links connecting mines and quarries in the hinterland with navigable water. Smaller-scale industries such as textiles developed at the same time, and the C20 saw the construction of large-scale power-generating sites.

Mineral Extraction: Metals

Mineral extraction in Gwynedd stretches back to Roman and Prehistoric times, and there was mining for copper and lead in the Middle Ages. The immediate boost to COPPER MINING came with the increasing use from 1761 of copper sheathing for naval vessels. Cornish ores, smelted in Swansea and worked up in Birmingham or Bristol, had been usurping the place of German ores since the beginning of the C18. Before long, ores from Gwynedd were also making their way to Swansea. Drws-y-coed mine (Nantlle, C) was active from 1761 in the hands of Cornish adventurers, copper was also worked at Llanberis (C), and in 1764 the Macclesfield Company of Charles Roe leased the ancient but inactive mine on Parys Mountain (A). The discovery of low-grade ore near the surface, combined with the entrepreneurial skills of the lawyer Thomas Williams, led to Parys becoming the most productive copper-mining area in the world for a number of years, as well as producing by-products such as ochre and sulphur. Parys ores were also smelted at Amlwch, and further afield, at Ravenhead and Liverpool. By 1800 Thomas Williams was conducting half the copper industry of the kingdom. The glory days did not outlast the recession after Waterloo and deep mining effectively ceased at Parys in the 1880s. However, Parys's prosperity attracted investment in copper in mainland Gwynedd from the late C18. The Caernarvonshire copper mines continued to be worked and the copper mines on the Great Orme, Llandudno (C), enjoyed a temporary prosperity until the mid C19.

Further S, in Merioneth, copper working resumed in the C18 and more particularly after 1815, employing as many as 265 men as late as 1861 – more than Caernarvonshire.

The discovery of GOLD in 1844 led to the first Merioneth gold rush, four years before that in California, seven years before that in Australia. Gold was found at the defunct Vigra and Clogau mines (Bontddu) in 1859, yielding enormous dividends and leading to the second gold rush, of 1862. Two mines were maintained on a care-and-maintenance basis until the early C21.

LEAD MINING revived in the mid C19 with mines near Dinas Mawddwy and Llanfachreth (M), at Llanengan (C) on Llŷn and on the Gwydir estate N of Betws-y-coed (C). By the end of the century this last had become one of the most productive areas in the United Kingdom, outlasting the Van mine, N of Llanidloes, and outstripping the Cardiganshire lead field. Work went on until 1921 at Aberllyn and 1963 at Parc.

IRONSTONE has been extracted at a number of locations. The Tir Stent mine near Dolgellau (M) appears to have been at work by 1719, supplying the Quaker furnace at Dolgun. Mines were developed at Ystrad and Garreg Fawr, near Betws Garmon (C) in the C19 and early C20, where the workings resolve themselves into a rabbit-warren series of openings up the hillside.

Specific short-term needs caused mines to be opened or revived. MANGANESE, worked in Llŷn and Merioneth from the mid C19 to make bleach and glass, was increasingly used from the early C20 to harden steel, particularly armaments. The needs of heavy engineering in two world wars caused mines to be opened and worked intensively for short periods. Most of these mines are in fact long shallow trenches following an outcrop with a minimum of underground working. The adjacent Rhiw and Benallt mines on the Llŷn peninsula, the only deep manganese mines in Gwynedd, supplied two-thirds of Britain's output by 1906. Cae Coch IRON PYRITES mine in the Conwy valley, which had supplied pyrites to the Lancashire chemical industry since the 1790s, was taken over by the Government in 1917–19 and 1941–2.

Mineral Extraction: Slate and Stone

SLATE, quarried on a limited scale by the Romans, was being worked from the outcrops of the Ogwen valley (Bethesda, C) and Mynydd Cilgwyn (Nantlle, C) by the start of the second Christian millennium. Roofing slates have been found on the site of the pre-Conquest *llys* (royal court) at Rhosyr, Newborough (A). By the beginning of the C18 a small but flourishing export trade in ROOFING SLATES was supplying the burgeoning markets of Liverpool, London and Dublin, but not until the 1780s did the industry of NW Wales enter its capitalist phase. Richard Pennant (1st Lord Penrhyn from 1783), a Liverpool merchant whose immense fortune derived from sugar estates in Jamaica, reunited the ancient Penrhyn estate in the Ogwen valley and set about establishing control over the independent quarrymen. From 1801 a six-mile-long iron railway of 2-ft (60-cm.) gauge connected the workings to a new port (Port Penrhyn, Bangor). The quarry itself was rearranged in a series of regular ledges or galleries.

The example was not lost on other landowners and capitalists. The defining year for Dinorwic (C) was 1787 when several small workings in the parishes of Llanddeiniolen and Llanberis were leased by Thomas Assheton-Smith to Thomas Wright, Hugh Ellis and William Bridge. They concentrated their efforts around two existing quarries, discouraging the practice of open quarrying on the commons. In 1800 John Evans, a wily Caernarfon lawyer, secured a lease of the crown commons at Cilgwyn (Nantlle, C) and set about installing machinery – again, doing his best to stop independent quarrymen working elsewhere on the commons. The same year William Turner, an experienced slate quarryman from the Lake District, took over the Diffwys quarry in Blaenau

Ffestiniog (M). By the 1820s distinguished investors were involved in Blaenau quarries, which began to evolve into underground workings – Lord Palmerston at Rhiwbryfdir, and, briefly, Nathan Meyer Rothschild at Moelwyn. In the Nantlle area the earlier scattered workings were expanding, and equipping themselves with haulage equipment and railways.

First and last, well over 400 sites have produced slate within Gwynedd. Most were concentrated in four main areas. The Ogwen valley, dominated by the Penrhyn quarry (Bethesda), was the most productive, followed closely by Dinorwic. Here, the near-vertical veins of purple Cambrian slate and the topography of the quarries lent themselves to working in benches on the hillside. In the Nantlle valley, the same veins had to be worked in open pits. At Blaenau Ffestiniog (M), grey slate veins of the Ordovician period slant at approximately 30 degrees to the horizontal; here early C19 open workings had to give way to underground extraction, so that a Ffestiniog quarry is in fact a mine, resembling a honeycomb in cross-section. In the smaller Corris (M) group the vein inclines much more steeply, and has to be extracted from chambers that sometimes resemble a bottle in cross-section.

Though there were local variations in quarrying methods and techniques, many features are common to all. Slate quarrying is an extremely wasteful industry. Well over 90 per cent of the rock extracted is unworkable and has to be thrown away, creating massive SLATE TIPS which form remarkable landscape features in their own right, as well as providing vital evidence for earlier quarrying processes. Powered MILLS to saw raw blocks into architectural slabs are recorded at Rhyd-y-sarn near Ffestiniog from c. 1802, at Felin Fawr, Tregarth (C), serving Penrhyn quarry from 1803, and at Dinorwic from 1828, supplanting the hand-operated saws used since the late C17 for gravestones, etc. The production of thin ROOFING SLATES, however, has never been successfully mechanized, and still relies on the slate-makers' skill in wielding hammer and chisel to split the block in precisely the right place. From at least the late C18, this process was carried out in a crude three-sided roofed shelter called a *gwal*. From the 1850s, Ffestiniog led the way in building integrated mills in which powered circular saws cut the raw blocks, which then still had to be hand-split. Their edges were trimmed mechanically, by guillotine or rotating blade, or by the traditional slate-trimming knife. This method spread to Nantlle by the 1860s, though here and there the remains suggest that workers suspicious of the factory-style approach had to be placated by the construction of internal divisions which effectively formed interior *gwaliau*. With few exceptions, the mills are long, low buildings, quite unlike the multi-storey Lancashire cotton mill, and are as likely to have been built for water power as for steam.

A feature common to practically all slate quarries was their reliance on internal narrow-gauge RAILWAYS, nearly always to a nominal 2-ft gauge. These might be hand- or horse-operated, though larger quarries also used locomotives. Another distinctive feature was the extensive use of railed INCLINED PLANES to overcome differences in levels. Where the load favoured the direction of traffic, these were counterbalanced, full wagons pulling up the empties on a parallel track by means of a chain or rope passed around a horizontal drum at the summit. Where the load had to be raised, it might be counterweighted by a railed water tank, filled at the summit and emptied at the bottom, or wound by a steam engine or electric motor. These features were often carried on massive embankments built of slate waste, frequently the most visible elements in the quarry landscape.

Increasing levels of capitalization from the mid 1850s led to a boom in the quarry settlements together with the construction of many chapels. Investment peaked in 1863, and fell off rapidly after the financial crash of 1866. The year 1877 is usually identified as the end of the expansionist period of the slate industry, and though periods of mild prosperity continued, they alternated increasingly with ever-deeper depressions. One serious blow was the long-drawn-out strike at the Penrhyn quarries in 1900–3. These had grown to be among the largest excavations in the world, employing 3,000 men, who mostly lived in the village of Bethesda (C) at the foot of the quarry. Problems of nationality, politics, religion and language added a peculiar bitterness; Bethesda remains divided by the strike to this day. Slates were now being imported from Italy and the United States, and the tile market began to take over. The First World War dealt another heavy blow, and the depression of 1929–31 spelled the end for many operations. By the late 1960s, when former giants like Oakeley in Blaenau Ffestiniog, Dorothea in Nantlle and Dinorwic closed, it appeared that the industry was on its way to extinction. Since then, there has been a revival; McAlpine's purchase of Penrhyn quarry in 1964 ensured its future, and vigorous modernization at the remaining smaller quarries has meant that the industry survives into the C21. Penrhyn, the former Oakeley quarry in Blaenau Ffestiniog, and its neighbour Llechwedd quarry remain in production.

At Penmaenmawr (C) the GRANITE which had attracted Neolithic axe-makers began to be worked again for street setts from 1830. Sett-making has never been mechanized, and the stones were hammered into shape by workmen in three-sided stone-built sheds, built either in rows or facing away from each other to minimize the danger of chipped stone hitting fellow workers. Crushing mills for macadamized road surfaces and for railway ballast were erected in 1888–9, 1893 and 1902. An impressive network of inclines and contour railways moved the stone to the mills, jetties and mainline railway. The quarry is now worked for railway ballast and aggregate. Smaller granite quarries came into being at other coastal locations, e.g. Trefor (C), Nant Gwrtheyrn (Llithfaen, C) and Tonfannau (Llangelynin, M).

LIMESTONE has been quarried in both Anglesey and Caernarvonshire, for a variety of purposes. Around Penmon and

Red Wharf Bay, on the SE tip of Anglesey, extensive quarries were opened for lime fertilizer, architectural slabs ('Anglesey Marble'), steelworks flux and impermeable stone for construction work. Penmon limestone was used to build the Telford and Stephenson bridges over the Menai Strait, Liverpool docks and the Seaforth container terminal. Small quarries near Llangefni (A) fed two substantial banks of KILNS, visible from the A55 road, which produced field lime, and many smaller kilns survive in farmyards and around the Anglesey coast. Quarries on the Great and Little Orme near Llandudno (C) were used for building works and for cement manufacture as well as for field-lime production. Kilns were to be found at most of the small coastal inlets of Caernarvonshire and Merioneth.

Metal Works and Foundries

METAL PROCESSING was revived in the early modern period near Dolgellau. At Dôl-y-clochydd (Llanelltyd, M) a charcoal-fired BLAST FURNACE was established in the late C16. At Dolgun (Dolgellau) the remains of a furnace survive originally set up by Abraham Darby I of Coalbrookdale, in conjunction with the local Quaker community. This first went into blast in 1719. E of the Conwy (just in Clwyd) one of the last charcoal-fired water-blown blast furnaces was built at Bodnant in 1750 by the Kendall family who in 1779 made the transition to coke firing when they built Beaufort Furnace in Ebbw Vale, thereby setting the South Wales iron industry on its path to greatness. Nearby, at Dolgarrog (C), a modern ALUMINIUM rolling mill sustained the tradition of metal processing until closure in 2007. Rio Tinto Zinc's smelting works at Penrhos (A) remains the largest aluminium plant in the UK, built 1969–71. Raw materials shipped to Salt Island (Holyhead) are transported along a two-mile underground conveyor to the smelters. Reduction is carried out in carbon-lined steel vessels before the aluminium is cast. The product is taken away by rail.

The extractive industries and shipping trade of the C19 spawned a number of FOUNDRIES and IRONWORKS. The best-known was the versatile Union Ironworks on the Seiont river at Caernarfon, established c. 1839, which could turn out ships' boilers, locomotives, gas plant, sugar-boilers, ore-crushers and saw-tables. Other ironworks, at Valley (A), Menai Bridge, Bangor and Porthmadog (C), specialized in cast and wrought iron, but the move to steel production at the end of the C19 forced them to close or to serve a purely local clientèle.

Factories etc.

Mines and quarries also called for EXPLOSIVES FACTORIES, e.g. at Tyddyn Gadlys, Ganllwyd (M), established 1887–9 – a typical and well-preserved establishment, with the processes carried out in a series of small buildings to avoid explosions.

Cooke's explosives works at Penrhyndeudraeth (M), established 1865, was much larger; by the 1970s it supplied 90 per cent of the British coal industry. Closed in 1996, it has since been demolished.

German bombing from 1940 onwards led a number of ENGINEERING CONCERNS to relocate to Gwynedd. The North East Coast Aircraft Co. established a factory at Caernarfon as well as making use of slate mills at Dinorwic quarry (C), and Saunders-Roe, seaplane manufacturers, became established at Llanfaes (A). The Government's dirigiste approach to industrial recovery after the Second World War led to the creation of advanced FACTORIES such as the Ferodo plant at Parciau, near Caernarfon. Another major development was the Hotpoint factory at Llandudno Junction (C), designed by *S. Colwyn Foulkes*, but demolished 2000.

Textiles

The WOOL TRADE was centred on the S part of Gwynedd, where by the end of the C18 most weavers were within walking distance of a *pandy* (fulling mill). Merioneth was second only to Montgomeryshire for woollen manufacture, with principal centres at Dolgellau and Bala, but whereas Montgomeryshire produced flannel, Merioneth produced a hard web used for clothing slaves and soldiers. Developments in textile processing in Lancashire and elsewhere in England were echoed in Gwynedd. Existing *pandai* were enlarged to accommodate carding engines. Of new factories, the most substantial was constructed at Tremadog (C) by William Madocks in 1807. Smaller ventures, on the Conwy tributaries, at Llanrug (C) and near Dolgellau (M), were almost all water-powered.

Timber

The woodlands of the Conwy valley were being felled for timber in the aftermath of the Edwardian conquest, and were worked again from the late C17. Maentwrog oak was prized for shipbuilding; a timber SAWMILL was established at Rhyd-y-Sarn nearby, possibly before 1800, one of the very earliest in the United Kingdom (later adapted as a slate-slab mill). Small estate sawmills were constructed in the later C19.

Power Generation and Water Supply

WINDMILLS are recorded in Anglesey as early as 1303 and towers are still numerous there, the Llynon Mill (Llanddeusant, 1775–6) fully restored. The majority were tower mills, though some post mills are recorded. Most ground corn, though one ground ochre and other coloured earths to make paint, one powered a sawmill and some pumped mines and quarries. Caernarvonshire windmills were confined to the Creuddyn peninsula (Llandudno), Nantlle and Llŷn. More recently, extensive WIND FARMS have been erected in the N part of Anglesey.

The mountainous topography of Caernarvonshire and Merioneth made them ideally suited to WATER POWER. Anglesey,
though flatter, was a major corn-growing area, and made early
use of WATER MILLS. It is possible that water-powered corn
mills were introduced to Gwynedd by the Cistercians but
as yet no evidence has confirmed their existence before the
Edwardian conquest. INDUSTRIAL WATER WHEELS probably
date from no earlier than the English and Cornish influx to
the copper mines in the 1760s. By the early C19 they were
commonplace, powering rope-ways, inclines, stone-processing
machinery and foundry blowers. The largest in Gwynedd was
the iron suspension wheel installed at Dinorwic quarry workshops (Dinorwic, C), 1870. Water wheels were installed in
Gwynedd slate quarries as late as the 1920s; the last to operate,
at the Penrhyn quarry slab mill at Felin Fawr, Tregarth, only
went out of use in 1965. These water wheels were generally
coupled by gearing to the machines they turned, rather than
the lengthy flat-rod systems common in Cornwall. WATER
TURBINES were extensively used from the 1860s, and from at
least 1907 were manufactured locally, by Richard Edwards of
Llanuwchllyn (M), using castings from the Britannia Foundry in
Porthmadog (C).

From the end of the C19 water turbines were increasingly used
to power ELECTRICAL INSTALLATIONS. Commercial supply of
water-generated electricity began in Blaenau (M) in 1902. Moses
Kellow's pioneering work on alternating current systems in the
Croesor valley (M), operational from 1904, is reflected in the
establishment of the North Wales Power and Traction Co., whose
a.c. station at Cwm Dyli, Nant Gwynant, opened in 1906. After
1918 the company supplied electricity as far afield as the Crewe
works of the London & North Western Railway. In 1957–63 the
Central Electricity Generating Board built the world's first
PUMPED-STORAGE POWER STATION at Llŷn Ystradau (Tanygrisiau) near Blaenau Ffestiniog (M), whereby energy can be
stored as water in high-level reservoirs and re-converted within
seconds to electrical power. The Dinorwic pumped storage
scheme (C), designed by *James Williamson & Partners*, commissioned 1982, was then the second largest in the world. NUCLEAR
POWER STATIONS were constructed at Trawsfynydd (M),
1959–63 (closed 1994) and Wylfa (Cemaes, A), 1962–71.

A number of Gwynedd RESERVOIRS supply towns with
drinking water, including Llyn Celyn (Frongoch, M) from which
Liverpool draws water. The decision in 1957 to drown a small
village for this lake confirmed Wales's institutional weakness and
gave a considerable boost to Plaid Cymru.

Roads and Railways

Gwynedd's pre-industrial transport links were adequate for an
agricultural economy based on the sale of livestock in English
markets. Improvements came about in the C18–C19 to provide a
through route from London to Ireland, and sea outlets for the

burgeoning slate industry. The first major external investment
was the turnpike trust established in 1761 to build a road around
the bluff at Penmaenmawr (C), with funding from both the
Westminster and Dublin parliaments. After the Act of Union in
1800 Irish M.P.s clamoured for better roads to London.
Early schemes anticipated a route from a port on the Llŷn
peninsula, and *William Madocks*'s extensive improvements on the
Traeth Bach estuary were undertaken partly in the hope
that some of this traffic might be routed through his estate.
His project to construct a stone embankment nearly a mile long
across the mouth of the estuary, undertaken 1808–13, though it
ruined him, created a road of sorts to his model village of
Tremadog (C), whose two main arteries were known tellingly as
London Street and Dublin Street. But when *Telford*'s POST ROAD
came to be built in 1815–28 it started from Holyhead (A) and
ran further N and E. At Betws-y-coed (C) it spanned the Conwy
by an iron bridge cast at *William Hazledine*'s Plas Kynaston
foundry near Ruabon in 1816. Telford's heroic suspension bridge
over the Menai Strait was completed in 1826. His Conwy bridge
of 1825 was part of the route along the North Wales coast.

The return to road transport after the railway era is evident as
early as 1906, when 140 cars and charabancs entered Llandudno
(C) on the August Bank Holiday. The tunnels and arches of
1930–6 at Penmaenmawr (C) were the first major investment in
local roads since Telford. Further improvements have included
the Conwy tunnel, opened in 1991, the new A55 across Anglesey
and the reconstruction of Stephenson's Britannia Bridge for both
rail and road.

RAILWAYS came perhaps just before the end of the C18. They
had been a feature of the coalfields of South Wales since 1697,
and of Flintshire since 1740. One was a short system using
wooden rails in Llanberis copper mine (C), the other connected
Lord Penrhyn's port (Port Penrhyn, Bangor) on the mouth of the
Cegin with a chert mill near Llandegai (C). By 1801 this had
been extended the six miles up to his slate quarries. Penrhyn's
quarry railway set the pattern for early railways in Gwynedd, and
indirectly had a profound influence on railway construction
worldwide. Not only was it one of the earliest iron edge-railways
(where the flange is on the wheel and not the rail), but its 2-ft
(60-cm.) gauge made possible tight curves and sinuous contour
formations, with narrow cuttings and steep-sided stone-faced
causeways. In 1825 Thomas Assheton-Smith of Vaynol followed
Penrhyn's lead and built a railway from his Dinorwic quarries to
the coast. The Nantlle Railway (1828), Gwynedd's first public
railway, connecting the Nantlle quarries and mines with
the sea at Caernarfon, was built with the advice of *Robert
Stephenson Sen.** All these railways were horse-worked where they
did not use inclined planes. The Festiniog Railway (Minffordd,
M), opened 1836, was worked by horses upward and by gravity

*Brother of George and uncle of the more famous Robert.

downward. However, faced with increasing traffic and the threat from standard-gauge railways, between 1863 and 1872 the Festiniog took the tradition of the unimproved narrow-gauge railway into the age of passenger transport, steam traction and articulated locomotives and carriages, a model adopted worldwide.

The comparative cheapness of such NARROW-GAUGE RAILWAYS made them practical for developing countries or rural economies, and the sharp curves of the 2-ft gauge made them ideal for use in industry or by contractors. They also found imitators elsewhere in Gwynedd. Some established horse-operated railways were rebuilt and realigned for steam power. Other railways were built anew. The Talyllyn, serving Bryn Eglwys slate quarry, Abergynolwyn (M), and carrying passengers down to Tywyn, opened in 1866 and operated with minimum maintenance and renewal for eighty-four years. Less successful was the North Wales Narrow Gauge Railway (1877) from Dinas, near Caernarfon, down the Gwyrfai valley to the Moel Tryfan slate quarries. This led a hand-to-mouth existence, despite being reborn as the Welsh Highland Railway and extended to Porthmadog (C) with Government loans after the First World War, until it closed in 1937.

Gwynedd's narrow-gauge lines again led the way when amateur preservationists rescued the Talyllyn Railway from closure in 1950 and reopened the Festiniog in 1956. At the time of writing, the Festiniog Railway Co. is completing the rebuilding of the Welsh Highland to form what will be Britain's longest narrow-gauge railway. The 'Great Little Trains' now form a vital part of an economy based on tourism, and include two railways of unconventional type. The Snowdon Mountain Railway, Britain's only rack-and-pinion railway, has operated since 1896; the Great Orme Tramway (Llandudno, C), the only rope-hauled passenger tramway in Britain, has carried holidaymakers to the summit since 1903.

MAIN-LINE RAILWAYS reached Gwynedd in 1848, when the Chester–Bangor and Llanfair–Holyhead sections of the coastal mainline opened. *Robert Stephenson*'s Britannia Bridge, p. 62, 169 completed in 1850, united the two parts. Like his earlier Conwy bridge, it had masonry columns carrying wrought-iron tubes, a revolutionary technology which profoundly influenced bridge-building and marine engineering. Branch and cross-country lines constructed from the 1860s included the Cambrian Railway from Dovey Junction to Pwllheli, with its viaduct across the Mawddach at Barmouth, 1867. In 1879 the London & North Western Railway branch from Llandudno Junction reached Blaenau Ffestiniog, via an impressive bridge below Dolwyddelan and a two-and-a-half-mile-long tunnel under Moel Dyrnogydd.

Britannia Bridge, during construction.
Engraving, C19

Water Communications

The sea coast of Gwynedd and its long tidal rivers have meant
that waterborne transport has always been important, though
canals barely figure. Water gates and WHARVES were constructed
in association with the Edwardian castles, but otherwise the
creeks of Gwynedd were simply places where vessels could be
beached. Red Wharf Bay (A) preserves something of the character of these landing places with its cluster of houses along the
shore. Pwllheli (C) acquired harbour facilities by an Enclosure
Act of 1811, but otherwise quays and wharves were only built
where mineral exports became important, from the late C18
onwards. At Amlwch (A) an Act of 1793 empowered the 'enlargement, deepening, cleansing, improvement and regulation of the
harbour'. In the late C18 Lord Penrhyn transferred the export of
his slates from the mouth of the Ogwen to Port Penrhyn, a
specially built estate harbour at the mouth of the Cegin, a
mile to the w. Assheton-Smith began to ship Dinorwic slate
through his quay at Y Felinheli (C) from 1793, around which
in the following century the village of Port Dinorwic grew.

At Caernarfon, Acts of 1793 and 1809 authorized the improvement of navigation and established a harbour trust. Public quays were constructed or improved, served by the Nantlle Railway from 1828. This superseded the old method of shipping slate into lighters at the Foryd, a bay s of the town, for transfer into seagoing vessels anchored in the Menai Strait.

Similar developments were marked on the Traeth Mawr and the Traeth Bach. Ffestiniog slates had been carted down to wharves below Maentwrog (M), whence river vessels took them to Ynys Cyngar, an island between Borth-y-gest (C) and Morfa Bychan, for transfer to seagoing vessels. Madocks's embankment fortuitously created a deep-water harbour by the sluices, which from 1824 became the transhipment point. From 1836 the quarries had the option of using the Festiniog Railway to transport slates directly to Portmadoc, as the harbour came to be known (now Porthmadog, C). The most significant port within Merioneth was Aberdyfi, where some c17 and c18 harbour structures survive. A wharf and jetty were constructed for the Cambrian Railways in 1885 primarily for the export of slate.

Holyhead (A) was an exception, as the main shipping point for Ireland. Existing harbour facilities were substantially extended by *John Rennie*, 1811–21. To this period belongs the Admiralty pier. The lengthy breakwater of 1848–73, 7,860 ft (2,418 metres) long, effectively doubled the harbour capacity. In the 1990s a new terminal for the Irish catamaran service was built at Turkey Shore.

Modern Industry

NW Wales has by no means de-industrialized completely. Attempts in the c20 to broaden its economic base began with the hydro-schemes and aluminium plant at Dolgarrog (C) in the Conwy valley, followed by the pumped-storage schemes and nuclear power stations. However, it is now industrial heritage that brings much-needed revenue to former industrial communities; the Dinorwic quarry's massive Gilfach Ddu workshops and the nearby Vivian quarry reopened as a branch of the National Museum of Wales in 1970, and Llechwedd and the little Llanfair quarry near Harlech (M) also welcome visitors. Other industrial sites reopened as tourist attractions include the Sygun copper mine (Beddgelert, C) and the prehistoric mines on the Great Orme (Llandudno, C); the rich maritime heritage is commemorated in a number of museums.

VICTORIAN AND EDWARDIAN CHURCHES

New Churches

Churches in the Late Georgian tradition continued to be built into the Early Victorian period. A spate in the early 1840s perhaps took advantage of grants from the newly established Bangor

Diocesan Church Building Society, e.g. those by *Thomas Jones* of Chester at Llwyngwril (M) and Llangwstenin (C), and Blaenau Ffestiniog (M), those by *George Alexander* at Betws Garmon, Llanwnda and Penrhos (all C), and those by *John Welch* at Llanffinan and Brynsiencyn (A), and Aberdaron, Llandygwnning and Llandudno (C). There is something endearing in all of these, particularly the toy-like quality of Llandygwnning and the simple Romanesque detail of *Alexander*'s churches.

In 1841 a young London architect, *Henry Kennedy*, moved to North Wales to work on churches, remaining for fifty years mostly in the dominant position of Diocesan Architect. Llan Ffestiniog (M), 1843, and Llanllechid (C), 1844, were his first new churches, both Neo-Norman, the style briefly popular in the 1840s and locally boosted by Penrhyn Castle. Llanllechid is an improvement on the clumsy Ffestiniog church, but was disliked by the Ecclesiological Society, after which *Kennedy* designed in the Gothic style more acceptable to them. It is a rare exception to find a church untouched by Kennedy in Caernarvonshire and Anglesey, less so in Merioneth. Never outstanding, his work tends to wiry tracery detail. Where funds were available there were towers and spires as at Dulas (A), 1856 for Lady Dinorben, Deiniolen (C), 1857, for Thomas Assheton-Smith, and Llandwrog (C), 1858 for Lord Newborough. St James (now R.C.), Bangor, 1864–6, shows his qualities and defects, workmanlike Dec traceries but too much variety, and all a little thin.

By the late 1840s new churches were generally in the approved C13–C14 ENGLISH GOTHIC, but lack of funds and Kennedy's dominance make outstanding examples rare. The first Ecclesiologically 'correct' churches were perhaps the group by the Sheffield architects *Weightman & Hadfield*, Llanddeiniolen (C), 1843, and Llanfaes and Llangaffo (A), *c.* 1845. *Benjamin Ferrey*'s Bala (M), 1853–4, stands out, in an austere E.E. with a high broach spire. *Anthony Salvin*'s Christ Church, Caernarfon (C), 1855, is also E.E, richer in detail, the very good tower and spire added later. *G. G. Scott*'s little church at Tudweiliog (C), 1849, is decent conventional Dec as is Bryncoedifor (M), 1850–1, by an unknown hand. *Scott*'s Glan-yr-afon (M), 1863–4, shows what a leading Gothicist could achieve in a small country church, well-proportioned and beautifully fitted within. *E. B. Ferrey* designed several churches around the Bala Lake in the 1870s, of which Llanfor (M) with its saddleback tower is the best. The region was little touched by the national interest in CONTINENTAL GOTHIC originating *c.* 1850 with Ruskin and others, which experimented with structural polychromy and with North Italian or Early French styles (indeed, the significant experiments are in private houses and public buildings; *see* p. 69). The reason is probably the conservatism of patrons and of the Diocesan Architect.

The later C19 saw several large churches added to growing towns. *H. P. Horner*'s oddly spiky St Mary, Bangor (C), 1861–4, was joined by *Kennedy*'s St James, 1864–6, and *A. W. Blomfield*'s superb St David, 1887–8, formidable stone outside, dramatically

red brick inside. In Llandudno (C), *G. Felton*'s plodding Holy
Trinity, 1865–74, was joined by *J. O. Scott*'s high and elegant St
Paul, 1893. The best were by architects from outside Wales. *Alfred
Waterhouse* designed Penmaenmawr (C), with its subtly
polychrome brick interior, 1867; *Paley & Austin* of Lancaster
the massive St Mary, Betws-y-coed (C), 1872, and *J. O. Scott* 105
also designed Pwllheli (C), 1887. *John Douglas*'s St John,
Barmouth (M), 1889–95, is one of the best of its era, with its 106
monumental crossing tower. *Douglas* also designed fine churches
at Deganwy and Criccieth (C), and memorably rebuilt Maentwrog (M). Notable works by local architects include Llanberis
(C), 1884, by *Arthur Baker*, a Londoner who had settled in the
region after working for Scott, and Boduan (C), 1894, a
Romanesque remodelling of the Georgian cruciform church so
unlike *Kennedy* as to suggest the hand of his partner and successor, *P. S. Gregory*. The charming little church (1862) at
Caerdeon (M) is designed by an amateur, the *Rev. J. L. Petit*, its
unconventional rusticity in many ways the most original church
design of the mid C19.

Llanberis, St Padarn.
Engraving by Herbert Baker, 1885

Caerdeon links to the one nationally significant church of the region, at Brithdir (M), 1895–8, by *Henry Wilson*, in taking inspiration from the rocky landscape without recourse to conventional medieval detail. Brithdir is Wilson's masterpiece, and hence a masterpiece of the British Arts and Crafts movement, appropriately designed and built to Arts and Crafts principles, Wilson and his assistants involved not just in the design but in the making of the superb fittings. Such work necessarily stands alone but its spirit imbues the work, especially the radical but unbuilt church designs, of one of the young men who worked on it, *H. L. North*.

The lovely LYCHGATE of 1906 near Brithdir at Bryncoedifor (M) remains an Arts and Crafts mystery, its designer unknown. A few other lychgates may be mentioned. The surprisingly elaborate one at Llangian (C), 1863, may be by *Kennedy*. The delightful slate and timber gateway with clock at Maentwrog (M) is by *Douglas & Fordham*, 1897, and at Tywyn (M) is a stone gateway in understated Romanesque, 1908, the best of many by *Harold Hughes*.

The ROMAN CATHOLICS built one only major Gothic church in the C19, at Llandudno (C), 1893, by *Edmund Kirby*, with elegant Dec traceries in red stone.

Church Restorations

Almost all the churches of Gwynedd were restored by the Victorians. Many architects imposed an unjustified Gothic on interiors too simple for C19 taste. *R. G. Thomas* inserted several arches at Llanbeblig, Caernarfon (C), and *Kennedy* memorably thought Gothic tracery and arcades right for Wyatt's classical church at Amlwch (A). Kennedy's mark is overwhelming across Bangor Diocese. The most expensive work by far was *Scott*'s restoration of Bangor Cathedral, and the eastern end should be judged a successful and carefully considered piece of creative re-creation, undramatic because lacking the crossing tower and spire that Scott intended. At Conwy (C) he reinstated the clerestory, and he was careful at Holyhead (A), these works probably mostly by his assistant, *Arthur Baker*. Some restorations were all but rebuildings because the modest architectural detail of the original was not thought of interest. Photographs of Llanycil (M), show rough windows and a rough bellcote, none of which survived the works of 1880. *S. Pountney Smith* at Llandrillo (M) kept only the old tower, but as a base for his fancy (and good) octagonal top and spire. He restored Llandderfel nearby more carefully.

The careful approach, for which the Society for the Protection of Ancient Buildings was founded by William Morris in 1877, had early if rarely successful advocates. In 1846, the Rev. Henry Longueville Jones founded the Cambrian Archaeological Association which through its journal *Archaeologia Cambrensis* began immediately to call for the preservation of old churches, those at Llanidan (A), Nant Peris, Aberdaron and Llandudno (C) being

defended in the very first volume. When in 1847 Kennedy produced an over-radical scheme for Penmynydd (A), *Longueville
Jones* took the project in hand himself. And it seems that the antiquary W. W. E. Wynne of Peniarth took more than a detached
interest in the restorations in his domain, intervening for conservation at Llanegryn and Llanaber (M). *Kennedy* could be conservative; he worked with a relatively light hand at Abererch,
Caerhun and Criccieth (C).

The influence of the SPAB was felt directly in the rescue of
the roofless Llandanwg (M), 1884, and indirectly through the
career of *Harold Hughes*, SPAB member and Diocesan Surveyor
in the early C20. Hughes, a staunch member of the C.A.A. and
prolific contributor to its journal, repaired churches minimally
and sympathetically throughout Gwynedd including Bryncroes,
Clynnog Fawr and Llanrhychwyn (all C); Llangelynin and
Mallwyd (M); and Llaneilian (A). His first restoration was the
island church of Llangwyfan (A), 1891–3, repaired with Arthur
Baker, whose practice he continued. *Herbert North* was also
involved with repairs, but preferred reordering and designing fittings. The two influential (and charming) books on old churches
and houses in Snowdonia, by North and Hughes, contributed
hugely to understanding and appreciation of the architecture of
the region.

Fittings

The best VICTORIAN FITTINGS are those contemporary with
good churches, and generally designed by the architect. At
Douglas's Barmouth (1895) and Deganwy (C), 1899, funds were   106
sufficient to complete the interiors in style. The same was rarely
true of *Kennedy*'s churches except where his patrons were
wealthy, as at Deiniolen and Llandwrog (C). At the latter the
seating is arranged collegiate-style with intricate canopies and
there is a good wrought-iron screen. Scott's Glan-yr-afon (M)
has a splendid display of *Minton* tiles and G. E. *Street*'s Carrog
(M) good simple stalls. The richly carved pulpit at Bangor
Cathedral is by G. G. *Scott*, and the stalls completing his father's
work by J. O. *Scott*. There are High Victorian circular fonts of
quality by *Paley & Austin* at Betws-y-coed (1872) and by
Blomfield at St David, Bangor (1888–9), and the latter has a good
pulpit apparently of terracotta. J. O. *Scott*'s Llandudno church
has a rich marble font and alabaster pulpit, 1893. Unusual late
C19 fittings are at Llansadwrn (A), where the chancel was fitted
by *Demaine & Brierley* of York, 1895, made by *Shrigley & Hunt*,
including the reredos and altar canopy.

Brithdir (M) must be picked out for its exceptional ARTS AND   107
CRAFTS FITTINGS, comparable with those at similar masterpieces such as E. S. Prior's church at Roker, Sunderland (1906).
These were designed by *Henry Wilson*, who, as a metalworker,
had a close hand in making some himself, and were intended to
contrast with the plain, rugged exterior. They include the great
cast copper altar frontal of the Annunciation, the pulpit clad in

beaten copper, the lead font, based on a design by Lethaby and made by *Arthur Grove*, and the stalls with carved animals, also by Grove. Early C20 fittings include the reredos (and later screens) at St Seiriol, Penmaenmawr (C), by *W. D. Caröe*, 1907, the carved screen and mosaic pavement at Bryncoedifor (M), 1907, and the carved woodwork by the Austrian *Ferdinand Stuflesser* at the R.C. church, Barmouth (M), 1909. The organ case at Tywyn (M) by *C. E. Bateman*, 1911, is a good piece of late Gothic design.

Credit should also be given to local craftsmen, sometimes amateurs, who made fittings to glorify their churches. At Penmaenmawr (C) the organ screen is a delightful piece of communal carving by members of the congregation, 1902. *Constance Greaves* of Wern, Penmorfa, put her carving skills to use at Penmorfa, Tremadog and Porthmadog (C). The lovely Arts and Crafts reredos at Llanaber (M) was made by *John & Mary Batten*, 1911.

Monuments

The numerous Gothic wall memorials do not deserve special mention. The canopied chest tomb of the 1830s at Llandegfan (A) is a replica of the medieval original now at Bisham, Berkshire. The great sculptor John Gibson is commemorated by his bust by *Theed*, 1866, at Conwy. One delightful memorial is the family group on a brass at Pennal (M), *c.* 1855. The only major sculptural monument is the white marble memorial at Holyhead (A) with the effigy of W. O. Stanley between poised angels, an exceptional piece by *Hamo Thornycroft*, set behind a bronze screen, 1896–7. *Harold Hughes* designed a fine Celtic cross in the churchyard at Llansadwrn (A), *c.* 1900, Christian imagery one side and African wildlife on the other.

Stained Glass

The C19 stained-glass revival begins in Gwynedd at Penrhyn Castle, Llandegai (C), with work by *David Evans* (chapel *c.* 1833, drawing room *c.* 1837) and *Thomas Willement* (Great Hall, 1835). Evans had joined John Betton of Shrewsbury *c.* 1814 and restored medieval glass (mostly replacing it with accurate copies) as well as designing new windows, often copies of Old Master paintings. There are good examples at Bangor Cathedral, 1838, Llandegfan (A), 1830s, and at Heneglwys and Bodedern (A), of the 1840s. At Penmon (A), *Evans*'s S transept window is a skilful integration of a few late C15 fragments in a York-style imitation, *c.* 1855. *Charles Clutterbuck* made dark windows, often marred by technical faults with his enamels, e.g. Llanddeiniolen and Llanllechid (C), 1840s, and Llanedwen (A), 1850s. At Llanfechell (A) is a rare example of work by his son, *Charles Clutterbuck Jun.*, *c.* 1869.

C. A. Gibbs made a fine Good Samaritan window at Aberffraw (A), 1849, and *O'Connor*, a pupil of Willement in the 1820s, made the good E window at Glan-yr-afon (M), *c.* 1864. At Llandwrog (C) is an early work by *Clayton & Bell*, *c.* 1860, and Dolgellau,

Carrog and Corwen (all M) have good sets by them, 1864, 1867 and 1871–2. *Lavers, Barraud & Westlake* designed beautifully coloured windows at Llanfor (M), 1875. *Heaton, Butler & Bayne* made the six windows of Welsh saints at Dwygyfylchi (Penmaenmawr, C), 1889. Blomfield's St David, Bangor (C), is a rare example of a large church almost entirely glazed by one firm, a richly coloured set by *Mayer* of Munich. *Powells* of Whitefriars did work at numerous churches including the intriguing decorative glass of Islamic flavour at Bodewryd and Llanbadrig (A). At the latter, the chancel is lined with their blue glazed tiles, used also at Rhoscolyn (A). The E window by *J.-B. Capronnier* of Brussels at Cynwyd (M), 1870, exemplifies a taste for the very pictorial. There is glass by *C. E. Kempe* at Beaumaris, Llandegfan, Rhoscolyn (all A) and a set at St John, Barmouth (M). At Llanengan (C), *Kempe* glass has been re-set in Pace-style leadwork by *Donald Buttress*, c. 1980. Later work by *Hardman & Co.*, Pugin's favoured firm earlier in the century, can be seen at Holy Trinity, Llandudno (C), c. 1880. *Morris & Co.* could always be relied on for good coloration, beautiful landscapes and vegetation, and Pre-Raphaelite faces. The earliest, made the year after Morris's death, is the beautiful window in Holyhead (A), 1897, a pattern of lush foliage and fruit. There are later works of the firm, some reusing designs by *Edward Burne-Jones*, at Conwy, c. 1915, Rhoscolyn (A) and St Mary, Betws-y-coed (C), both 1919, Bethesda, 1922, and Abererch, 1935.

VICTORIAN AND EDWARDIAN GREATER HOUSES

The typical North Wales style for LARGER HOUSES after c. 1840 was gabled, between bargeboarded-cottage and Tudor, considered to convey both antiquity and rusticity. The larger examples were built for retiring or holiday-making clients, predominantly English, and often with wealth from the industrial towns. A tour of the Mawddach estuary, Merioneth, will give the picture (and could be repeated in Caernarvonshire and along the Menai Strait): Abergwynant (Penmaenpool), 1839, built for a Peninsular War general; Penmaenuchaf (Penmaenpool), 1860s, for a Bolton cotton manufacturer; Bryntirion (Bontddu), 1874, for a Lord Mayor of Birmingham; Tŷ'n-y-coed (Arthog), 1875, for a Rhondda coal-owner; and Garthangharad (Arthog), 1880s, for a Clerk of the Peace of Surrey.

The most extraordinary of Victorian seaside houses is Rhianfa, [92] Llandegfan (A), 1849–50, designed by *Lady Sarah Hay Williams* of Bodelwyddan with *Charles Verelst* as a Loire château with conical-roofed towers. Another seaside eccentric, the very picturesque Clock House, Barmouth (M), was achieved by steady agglomeration from 1844, each addition treated as a feature in its own right. The vein of self-designed eccentricity can be followed to the mountains. Pensychnant, Sychnant Pass (C), 1877–82, by the Oldham industrial architect *A. H. Stott*, with its Hansel-and-Gretel roofs, seems to have strayed from

central Europe. At Dolmelynllyn, Ganllwyd (M), the spiky
additions of the 1870s were by a professional, *George Williams*,
brother of the owner.

Not all major works were for incomers; fires in 1836 caused
the enormous rebuildings at two ancient seats, Baron Hill,
Beaumaris (A), 1838–43, for Sir Richard Bulkeley Williams-
Bulkeley, and Glynllifon, Llandwrog (C), 1836–46, for Lord
Newborough. Both emerged as very large stuccoed houses, the
one by *Henry Harrison*, ungainly Italianate, now ruined, the
other, by *Edward Haycock*, with a noble Neoclassical raised
portico. Another ancient Anglesey family rebuilt Henllys,
Llanfaes, in Elizabethan style, 1852–3, in fine grey local limestone, the architect unexpectedly *C. F. Hansom*, based in Bristol.
The widow of Lord Dinorben of the Anglesey copper mines had
Llysdulas (demolished), Dulas (A), built by *Benjamin Woodward*
of Dublin, 1856–8, one of the first High Victorian Gothic houses
in Britain, following Woodward's Oxford Museum and equally
imbued with the spirit of Ruskin. C. H. Wynn of the Newborough family celebrated his coming-of-age by doubling Rhug (M)
in 1880, to the detriment of the original, but incorporating a
magnificent conservatory-cum-ballroom, demolished now except
for some arcading. His architect was *Henry Kennedy*.

The High Victorian GOTHIC of Llysdulas is rare, apart from
Bryntirion (*see* above). Gothic windows appear with generally
Tudor detail on Plas Glyn-y-weddw, Llanbedrog (C), 1856, by
Henry Kennedy. The interior is unexpectedly dramatic with a
hammerbeamed stair hall with Gothic galleries and stained glass.
95 Tŷ'n-y-coed, Arthog (M), 1875, not especially Gothic outside,
contains supremely Gothic polychrome fireplaces and a stair hall
that have hints of William Burges's work at Cardiff Castle. The
very young *Edwin Seward* had just previously designed a very
similar polychrome staircase at Ely (now Insole) Court, Llandaff,
Cardiff. Bodlondeb, Conwy (C), by *T. M. Lockwood*, 1877, is
stone and Gothic with a distinctly gentle touch marking the
waning of the High Victorian, the influence being Richard
Norman Shaw and *W. E. Nesfield*, the latter having added to
Gloddaeth, Llanrhos (C), in 1876.

The classical style slid into ITALIANATE, sometimes with the
belvedere tower of Queen Victoria's Osborne House. The largest,
Noddfa, Penmaenmawr (C), a Gladstone family villa of the
late 1860s, is probably by *Cornelius Sherlock* of Liverpool.
The additions to Plas Llanfair, Llanfairisgaer (C), also 1860s,
have a thinner tower. Tre-ysgawen, Llanfihangel Tre'r Beirdd (A),
1882, by *R. G. Thomas* of Menai Bridge, symmetrical and without
a tower, is distinguished by good stonework, much better than
his earlier (and altered) Treborth Hall, Bangor, *c.* 1872.

OLD ENGLISH styles, Tudor to Elizabethan shading into the
fancy shapes of the Jacobeans, remained current through the
second half of the C19. The ogee-domed tower and Elizabethan
windows of Henllys reappear forty years later at Hengwrt Uchaf,
Rhydymain (M), 1894. Similarly mullioned-and-transomed
were *J. E. Gregan*'s Glyn Garth, Llandegfan (A), 1850, and

James Stevens's Plas yn Dinas, Dinas Mawddwy (M), 1864–7, both demolished. Better than both is Pale, Llandderfel (M), 1869–71, by *S. Pountney Smith*, for the railway engineer Henry Robertson. Subtle and varied asymmetries make for changing Picturesque groupings, the whole united by superb stonework. The additions to Plas Tan-y-bwlch, Maentwrog (M), 1869–71, for the Oakeleys, rich on Blaenau Ffestiniog slate, are step-gabled, perhaps in homage to Plas Mawr, Conwy, and its C17 followers. *John Douglas* may have been involved here; certainly he drew the genuine step-gabled C17 Dolaugwyn (Bryncrug, M) before designing Plas Mynach, Barmouth (M), 1882–3. *Douglas* designed two Caernarvonshire houses, Wern, Penmorfa, 1892, and Glangwna, Caeathro, 1893, for the quarry-owning Greaves family, the former with Jacobean gables, the latter with a great deal of half-timber. His additions to Gloddaeth, Llanrhos (C), 1889, are Elizabethan with half-timbering at the skyline. Douglas must be the influence for the large Caerhun Hall (C), 1895, with its stepped gables and the grey and red stone of Douglas's Gloddaeth additions and Barmouth church, the detail frenetic and entertaining. Llugwy (Pennal, M) also has a hint of Douglas, of similar coloured stones, the curved gables Jacobean.

HALF-TIMBERING as at Glangwna came early at Dolserau, Brithdir (M), 1864, but is more commonly Late Victorian to Edwardian and associated with holidays, especially fishing lodges. The valley through Ganllwyd (M) displays late C19 and early C20 examples, including the fishing hotel. It appears also on lodges of large houses, as those to Bodlondeb and Gloddaeth.

Caeathro, Glangwna Hall.
Engraving, C19

These are red-tiled and half-timbered in the consciously pretty Domestic Revival manner that Shaw and Nesfield unleashed, which also characterizes the suburbs of Llandudno just by Gloddaeth.

ESTATE COTTAGES of the Glynllifon and Penrhyn estates are to be found in Llandwrog, Llandegai and Abergwyngregyn (all C), generally variations of the gabled stone cottage. Some earlier ones of the 1840s for the Gwydir estate, at Trefriw and Betws-y-coed (C), hark back to the Picturesque, with circular chimneys and eaves on an array of stone brackets. At Tudweiliog (C) are Edwardian ones for Cefnamwlch, by *Grayson & Ould* of Liverpool, in garden-suburb mode.

By the end of the century the era of the large house had all but passed, and that of the VILLA, suburban or rural, arrived. The edges of all the towns display these, gabled generally, stone mostly, sometimes half-timbered at upper level, sometimes with hot red terracotta to draw attention. *Owen Williams*'s very red villa in Bangor, Bryn Afon, 1885, is one of the most elaborate. Villas around Dolgellau tend to the gabled in dark stone. John Douglas's work had many imitators, often of the worst aspects. The red terracotta windows of his Castle Hotel, Conwy, reappear all over the region, notably in Barmouth (M), while Cartref, Llanfaes (A) displays more Douglas motifs than seem credible or digestible on one house. Caernarfon villas show the local yellow brick, while Upper Bangor tends to a hard red brick. At Llandudno (C) the Mostyn estate architect *G. A. Humphreys* worked mostly in red brick and half-timber, though his own house, Ardwy Orme, 1895, and its neighbour are sophisticated Domestic Revival works, one in red sandstone, the other tile-hung.

The cult of simplicity associated with the ARTS AND CRAFTS MOVEMENT produced the best houses of the period 1895–1914. *H. L. North*'s hillside development, The Close, in his hometown of Llanfairfechan (C) began in 1899 with two houses, and he would add more until 1940. They and his own house Wern Isaf, 1900, demonstrate the ideas from which he hardly deviated in the next forty years: simple gabled elevations, white roughcast, and sweeping slate roofs. Cefn Isaf, Tŷ'n-y-groes (C), 1904–8, explores similar themes on a larger scale.

p. 437

Other houses worthy of mention fall into two categories. The first are smaller houses by local architects, notably *Richard Hall* of Bangor and *Joseph Owen* of Menai Bridge. Owen is particularly inventive, his houses with dramatic contrasts of scale, tiny oriels and sweeping gables: Doldir, Llangefni (A) and Carreg Lwyd, Menai Bridge, both 1913, are the best. Hall is less extreme, his Bronwydd near Bangor, 1905, predominantly roughcast with sweeping roofs, a feature of his vicarage at Brithdir (M), 1902–3. Avilion, Trearddur (A), 1910, has conical turrets, common to many seaside villas. *Clough Williams-Ellis*'s rectory at Pentrefelin (C), 1913, is subtly traditional with half-dormers, but planned as wings meeting at a curved porch. His work at his own house, Plas Brondanw, Llanfrothen (M) is sensitive to the C16–C17 fabric, set in the lovely gardens he began in 1908. The Orangery of 1912 evokes a rustic C18 style, not grandiose, in keeping with the sense of slow evolution of house and gardens.

The other category is of holiday retreats by outside architects. *George Walton*'s Wern Fawr, Harlech (M), 1908–10, reinterprets the Georgian into something quite strange through a vocabulary of massive masonry. Sadly the great music room added to the N has gone. Aberartro Hall, Llanbedr (M), by *C. E. Bateman* of Birmingham, 1907–12, one of the largest early C20 houses, is a relaxed and spreading interpretation of the Cotswold manor, the square-mullion windows showing the influence of C. F. A. Voysey. Voysey also inflenced the nearby Plas Gwynfryn, Llanbedr, *c.* 1910, by an unknown architect. Rhowniar, Aberdyfi (M), 1911–12, by *Oswald Milne*, has a vernacular Georgian flavour, colourwashed walls and sash windows. *Ralph Knott*'s remodelling of the interiors of Garthangharad, Arthog (M), 1911–12, created a white Queen Anne sequence within a Victorian gabled mansion. His lodges are pyramid-roofed, informally classical. Smaller pyramid lodges of 1914 are at Plas Newydd, Llanedwen (A).

TOWNS AND PUBLIC BUILDINGS *c.* 1830–1914

Travel and tourism continue the sequence of HOTELS begun with the Telford road to Holyhead. The Bulkeley Hotel at Beaumaris, *c.* 1835 by *Hansom & Welch*, indicates a new luxury. The Victoria Hotel, Menai Bridge (A) and the Bull Hotel, Llangefni (A), both of *c.* 1852, are contrastingly classical and Neo-Tudor. At the same time the railway brought the British Hotel to Bangor and the original terminus hotel to Holyhead, both 1851. The steady growth of older towns can be measured in modest suburban rings around the centres, and the rebuilding of commercial streets with generally three-storey houses with shops. The stucco Late Georgian manner characterizes most mid-C19 commercial building, with the stone tradition continuing in Dolgellau and Barmouth. Brick remains exceptional until the later C19. The conversion of private banks to Joint Stock Banks after the 1830s began to be reflected in ornate BANKING PREMISES in the mid C19. The first appeared in Bangor, the Neo-Jacobean Williams & Co. bank of 1849 by Sheffield architects and a fine Florentine palazzo of 1860 by *Henry Kennedy*.

PUBLIC BUILDINGS of the first Victorian years are few apart from the WORKHOUSES, built to very varied designs under the Poor Law Amendment Act of 1834. The best examples survive in Merioneth, at Bala, Corwen, Dolgellau and Minffordd. Those at Caernarfon and Bangor are altered for hospital use and that at Conwy demolished. The two Anglesey examples at Valley (demolished) and Llanerchymedd came very late. Around 1850 the buildings of local government begin in a small way with POLICE STATIONS, a series of small hipped ones on Anglesey (as at Brynsiencyn), an attractive round-arched one at Dolgellau (M), and a slightly Tudor one at Conwy (C), by *John Lloyd*, 1859.

Bangor railway station.
Engraving, 1848

Lloyd as County Architect designed the first county offices in
Caernarfon, 1853, dwarfed by the next ones of only a decade
later. The Stanley estate rather than the county was responsible
for the large Jacobean-gabled Market at Holyhead, 1855.

93   The County Hall, Caernarfon, 1863, by Lloyd's successor *John
Thomas*, is one of the best public buildings of its time in Wales,
with giant portico and wings on a scale sufficient to allow an
extended composition. It reflects great confidence in the prosperity of the time, largely founded on slate. Thomas designed the
contrastingly Gothic gaol behind in 1867.

MUNICIPAL BUILDINGS could not aspire as high as those of
a county. Conwy's Gothic Guildhall, 1863, is small, but Holyhead's Town Hall, 1875, also by *John Thomas*, is High Victorian
Gothic with considerable presence, unexpectedly in yellow brick.
Llangefni (A) has a Gothic town hall over a market, 1882, by
R. G. Thomas. Another notably High Victorian Gothic public
building is the former library (now Royal Town Council Office)
at Caernarfon by *Richard Owens*, 1884. Dolgellau's Market Hall
with assembly room above, 1870, by *W. H. Spaull*, has a sturdy
and styleless character, its arcades effectively Italian. The handsome Court House of the 1860s at Llangefni (A) is classical, its
heavy stonework appropriate to its function.

The architecture of RAILWAYS was never as spectacular as
their engineering achievements except in the case of *Francis
Thompson*, architect to the Chester & Holyhead Railway, to whom
the splendid architectural embellishments of the Britannia
88   Bridge (Llanfairpwll, A) and Conwy Tubular Bridge (C) are due,
as also the tunnel portals at Conwy and Bangor. Thompson's
Bangor station, 1848, typically Italianate in brick and stone,
survives with additions, but Conwy, with stepped gables to match
Plas Mawr, has gone. Small Thompson stations survive at Bodorgan (Llangadwaladr, A) and Valley (A), stuccoed with deep eaves
and a canopy between single-storey office wings. The Cambrian
Railways line coming up the coast from the s has brick stations
at Aberdyfi and Tywyn, and a stone one at Barmouth (all M) of
1867, possibly by the engineer *Benjamin Piercy*. The Llangollen

to Corwen line has two surviving stations, attractive stone gabled designs, at Glyndyfrdwy and Carrog (M), 1863–4, possibly by *S. Pountney Smith* of Shrewsbury. The continuation from Corwen to Bala and Dolgellau preserves a small gabled brick station at Llanuwchllyn (M), 1867. The line up the Mawddach to Dolgellau, 1865–8, also preserves one station, at Penmaenpool (M), 1879, in brick. The LNWR branched down the Conwy valley to Llanrwst in 1862 and Betws-y-coed in 1868, where the large station in stone and coloured brick was surely designed for the tourist trade. The LNWR station at Felinheli (C), 1874, is in coloured brick with big half-hips. The modest terminus of Sir Edmund Buckley's seven-mile Mowddwy Railway survives at Minllyn (Dinas Mawddwy, M), 1867.

SCHOOL BUILDINGS of the earlier and mid C19 are generally small, whether built by Anglicans (the National Schools) or Nonconformists (the British Schools). Two attractive buildings in adjoining Merioneth villages illustrate the early type with teacher's house and school under the same roof: the tiny church-school at Llanycil, 1838, looks like an estate cottage, and that built by the Williams-Wynn family at Llanuwchllyn, 1841, like a village house. The bleak British School in Blaenau Ffestiniog (M), 1849, was based on model plans devised by the Nonconformists' Committee of Council on Education. British Schools tended to be functionally adequate but unremarkable architecturally. More ambitious ones include Bala (M), 1854, by *Ebenezer Thomas*, slightly Tudor, Caernarfon by *John Lloyd*, 1858, large with Jacobean gables, and the very altered Pwllheli (C) by *Wehnert & Ashdown*, 1856. Corris, 1872 by *O. Morris Roberts*, is Gothic, i.e. more like the National Schools. These were often given to church architects and tended to a gabled Gothic-to-Tudor character, as at Llangefni (A), 1851, and Llandwrog (C), 1853, both by the Diocesan Architect *Henry Kennedy*, responsible for many schools, and Bala, by *Benjamin Ferrey*, 1872. A local man, *Hugh Jones*, was responsible for Llanengan (C), 1845, the big Jacobean gables almost overpowering the building. The collegiate style deemed appropriate for rebuilt grammar schools in English towns unexpectedly arrived in Bala in 1850, where Jesus College, Oxford, commissioned *Wigg & Pownall* of London to design the Grammar School with a diminutive Tudor great hall.

Most of the British schools were taken over by the new Board Schools when the 1870 Education Act brought in compulsory schooling. No new BOARD SCHOOLS are of particular interest – *Richard Owens* designed one in Gwyddelwern (M), and *O. Morris Roberts* two, in Llan Ffestiniog and Blaenau Ffestiniog (M), all weakly Gothic. Liberal and Nonconformist North Wales was enthusiastic to implement this Act and the Welsh Intermediate Education Act of 1889 (*see* p. 77).

Higher education was initially in religious hands and the few COLLEGES built were for training ministers or schoolteachers. St Mary's Training College, established by the Anglicans in Caernarfon in 1856 to train teachers, moved to new buildings in Bangor, by *R. Grierson*, 1893–4, in an economical Tudor style.

Much more ambitious was the Normal College, Bangor, founded by the British and Foreign School Society to train primary-school teachers. *John Barnett*'s building of 1858–62, in fine grey limestone, has the air of a Jacobean mansion with wings and central tower, set in grounds overlooking the Strait. Two colleges for training ministers were founded in Bala (M), of which the Calvinistic Methodist Bala College thrived, building a substantial Gothic range, 1865–7 by *W. H. Spaull* (the tower rebuilt in the 1890s), on a dominant slope outside the town.

p. 406   The most important URBAN DEVELOPMENT of the C19 was the rise of Llandudno from a small copper-mining settlement on the Great Orme to one of the more spectacular resorts of Britain. The overall control of the Mostyn estate and its agents helped the town to the unity that distinguishes it from the other North Wales resorts. The initial development was rapid after the Improvement Act of 1854, the grand plan by *Wehnert & Ashdown* being implemented in its main respects by the mid 1860s: the parade of stuccoed terraces facing the bay, and the principal commercial street, Mostyn Street, following the same curve just inland. Llandudno initially was a town of terraces, with villas only
3   on the slope of the Great Orme to the w. The seafront terraces and Mostyn Street date from the 1850s–80s, stucco prevailing, but in the 1890s under the estate architect *G. A. Humphreys* changing to brick and half-timbered villas. The Town Hall, a competition victory for *T. B. Silcock* of Bath, 1894, is an accomplished work in the revived Queen Anne style, the plan of the town oddly not allowing it the space it needs.

SEASIDE TERRACES of the late C19 appear in the smaller resorts such as Barmouth and Aberdyfi (both M), not stucco here but in the formidably hard stones of the region. Nearby Tywyn made a late attempt at holiday remodelling, impelled by the landowner, John Corbett of Ynysmaengwyn. One terrace of the 1890s was all that was built on the new promenade, but a stuccoed assembly room and a stone and yellow brick market remain of his endeavours in the town. Porthmadog and Pwllheli (both C) have later C19 stuccoed and stone terraces, the West End of Pwllheli developed in brick after 1894 by the Cardiff entrepreneur Solomon Andrews. His next attempt, on the Mawddach, at Arthog (M), left only three scattered terraces.

COMMERCIAL BUILDINGS of the late C19, as elsewhere in Britain, are characterized by imported building materials. Notable in Merioneth are the bricks and terracottas of Ruabon, as are those of Flintshire and Lancashire in Caernarvonshire. Edwardian brick and stone interlopers, disregarding the stucco, can be found in the central sections of Mostyn Street, Llandudno, generally interestingly designed, the authors unknown. The iron awnings, as characteristic of Mostyn Street as they are for example of Southport, Lancashire, seem to date from the late C19. An Edwardian row of commercial buildings is in Station Road, Llanfairfechan (C), 1905–8, by *Richard Hall*, varied in motifs and materials, and Stanley Street, Holyhead, has one good early C20 roughcast gabled building. Holyhead and Menai Bridge

have turn-of-the-century banks for the North & South Wales
Bank, possibly both by *Joseph Owen*, with undisciplined Baroque
motifs, and Pwillheli (C) one in good Queen Anne style by
Woolfall & Eccles.

LIBRARIES introduced an Edwardian stylistic wilfulness across
Britain. That at Bangor by *A. E. Dixon*, 1907, is low and domed
Edwardian Baroque; Llandudno's, of 1908–10, by *G. A.
Humphreys*, is grander but still Baroque, the circular galleried
vestibule clearly from the same root as the vestibule at Bangor.

Of other buildings of public amenity, *Rowland Lloyd Jones*
designed the Institute complex at Newborough (A), 1902–5, a
generous benefaction from the co-proprietor of the Dickens &
Jones store in London, where manorial half-timber and stone
were deemed appropriate. The hall at Cemaes (A), 1898, by
Richard Owens & Son had similar origins. Bangor's Post Office,
1909, by *W. Pott*, large because it housed County Court offices,
has an Edwardian Baroque flavour, as does *Humphreys*'s Post
Office, Llandudno, 1904, with giant columns in terracotta,
between bays with cupolas. His Mostyn Art Gallery next door,
1901–2, is more mixed, a flurry of oriels and arches with a slate
pyramid in the middle. The memorial clock tower at Llangefni
(A), by *Douglas & Minshull*, 1902, is an effective civic centrepiece,
where the one at Bangor, in red brick, 1887, is underscaled.

However, the principal public buildings of the turn of the C20
were those for education. From the late C19 a new impetus was
given to the building of SCHOOLS by the 1889 Welsh Intermediate Education Act and the Education Act of 1902. The 1902 Act
made education the responsibility of the new county councils,
giving the county architects a leading role, *Joseph Owen* in Anglesey, *Rowland Lloyd Jones* in Caernarvonshire and *Deakin &
Howard Jones* in Merioneth. The Intermediate schools in Holyhead, Llangefni, Pwllheli, Caernarfon and Tywyn are by the
county architects, but those at Dolgellau, by *T. M. Lockwood* of
Chester, at Blaenau Ffestiniog, by *Willink & Thicknesse* of Liverpool, and at Bala and Llangefni, both by *Harry Teather* of Cardiff,
are products of the competition system. Holyhead with its gables
and off-centre turret, and Tywyn, with its yellow and red gabled
centrepiece, are probably the best. A different effect, of antique
learning, was attempted for the relocated grammar school of
Bangor, the Friars School. Its buildings, by *John Douglas*, 1899,
Tudorbethan with a low tower, are similar to his grammar school
at Ruthin, Denbighshire, 1891.

The PRIMARY SCHOOLS designed after 1902 give a particular
stamp to rural Caernarvonshire and Merioneth (much less so in
Anglesey, where more often older schools were kept in use).
Rowland Lloyd Jones's schools are characterized by repeated half-
timbered gables above stepped windows, as at Llandudno Junction, 1907. *Deakin & Howard Jones* in Merioneth typically use
big rounded windows in terracotta surrounds, the smaller schools
of T-plan as at Carrog or Ganllwyd, the larger ones with repeated
gables as at Penrhyndeudraeth and Glyndyfrdwy. New ideas from
the Continent challenged the dominance of the C19 central-hall

schools. In 1911 the Caernarvonshire Education Committee erected two experimental schools based on 'OPEN-AIR' principles pioneered in Germany in 1904 and subsequently tried out by forward-looking education authorities in England. Sunny locations were chosen, often on the edges of towns and villages, and the buildings designed so that entire elevations could be opened up to let in fresh air. The two first schools, at Y Ffôr and Brynaerau (Pontllyfni, C) have been changed somewhat, but Betws-y-coed (C) survives, designed by *Rowland Lloyd Jones* in 1913 (built 1928). It has canted-recessed s windows which slide back fully, a marching corridor, and folding partitions between classrooms, each with its own fireplace – elements which permeated many of the later County Schools, even if not 'open-air' in name.

p. 247   The decision to site the UNIVERSITY COLLEGE of North Wales at Bangor changed the character of the town. The initial buildings of the late C19 are not special apart from the prettily detailed Queen Anne-style women's hall, 1897, by *Frank Bellis*, but the main buildings of 1907–11 by *Henry Hare* are one of the crowning achievements of early C20 British architecture. Hare's ability to group asymmetrically and compose formally takes the British Arts and Crafts movement into an area of monumentality rarely attempted. The massive and unadorned tower is the point around which the other elements circle: manorial gables in the smaller courtyard, Northern Renaissance formality in the hall and library. While it is regrettable that the main quadrangle was not completed to Hare's design, the completion as planned of the buildings overlooking the city achieves the unforgettable cathedral-cum-palace skyline. The interiors contain much remarkable craftsmanship in stone, metal, wood and plaster, particularly the Shankland Library, with woodwork in a free C17 style. Hare's other large work in Bangor, too little known, is his halls of residence for the Normal College, 1910, a formal grouping of steep-roofed blocks, Arts and Crafts manorial in detail, but arranged in heroic formality on a stepped site overlooking the Strait.

HOSPITAL buildings have no particular presence until the 1920s, but at Llandudno is a very lavish privately built convalescent home (North Wales Medical Centre) in park surroundings, 1902–4 by *E. B. I'Anson*, formally composed with canted wings.

PUBLIC SCULPTURE includes the statues at Bala of the Rev. Thomas Charles, 1875 by *William Davies*, in marble, and at Caernarfon of Sir Hugh Owen, 1887 by *J. Milo Griffith*, in bronze. More lively are the early C20 ones by *William Goscombe John*: T. E. Ellis M.P. at Bala, 1903, the Rev. Lewis Edwards at Bala College, 1911, and David Lloyd George at Caernarfon, 1921. His roadside Celtic cross at Corris (M) to Dr Hughes, 1905, reanimates a tired convention.

An aspect of the late C19 is the beginning of interest in the conservation and repair of the great castles and town walls, in which the dynamic Sir Llewelyn Turner at Caernarfon took the lead (*see* p. 34). However, his High Victorian interventions for the

Guildhall in the East Gate (Porth Mawr) and the Yacht Club in the West Gate (Porth yr Aur) show him a conservationist within the limits of the age.

NONCONFORMIST CHAPELS

NW Wales was the arena for several leading figures of C17 Dissent, and Merioneth was a heartland of the Quakers until persecution forced their migration to the Welsh Tract in Pennsylvania in the 1680s. The first Caernarvonshire Independent congregation met in Pwllheli (C) reputedly in Cromwellian times. Merioneth's early apostle was Hugh Owen of Llangelynin (1639–1700).

Anglican ministers who took the path of Methodism in the C18 included the Rev. Thomas Charles and the Rev. Simon Lloyd in Bala (M), where a Methodist society was formed in the 1740s. Their presence and that of John Evans (1723–1817) made Bala the centre of Calvinistic Methodism in North Wales well before the split from the Established church in 1811. Of the four main Welsh DENOMINATIONS Calvinistic Methodism was the most numerous in the region, followed by the Independents, followed by the Wesleyans (increased in certain areas by immigration of miners from Cornwall), and then the Baptists. The Baptists of Anglesey were strengthened by the ministry of Christmas Evans from 1802 to 1826, and the Calvinistic Methodists there by that of John Elias from 1811 to 1841, two of the three giants of Welsh preaching. English-speaking churches took root in tourist towns during the later C19, the Congregationalists equivalent to the Independents, the Presbyterians to the Calvinistic Methodists. Conversely Welsh Wesleyanism thrived in parallel with the main English-speaking church. Several small denominations existed without making any architectural impact. David Lloyd George, the future Prime Minister, was brought up by his uncle, pastor of the Scotch Baptist (Campbellite) church in Criccieth.

The bulk of CHAPELS of the C18 and early C19 were rebuilt in the later C19. The earliest surviving chapel building of any denomination is the wonderfully evocative Capel Newydd, 67 Nanhoron (C), 1770, barn-like, and still with its earthen floor and pews down the long wall. Cildwrn Baptist, Llangefni (A), p. 181 Christmas Evans's church, was founded in 1750 but the sequence of six subsequent dates causes confusion. Ebenezer Wesleyan, Caernarfon, 1826, by *John Lloyd*, stands out in Wales as a large urban chapel of the Georgian period, its ashlar front with Gothic detail. There are a few unaltered rural chapels. At Carmel Baptist, Aberdaron (C), the house and chapel are under one roof and may be mid-C19, the tiny scale evocative of sparse congregations from scattered farms. The rural chapels of Merioneth are typically single-roofed with the chapel house, as at Llanfachreth. Early ones are entered on the LONG WALL, later ones, or altered early ones, on the gable-end, as at Llidiardau, Llanycil (M), 1860. Ainon Baptist, Llanuwchllyn (M), 1840, however, is a single chapel of massive boulders with deep eaves.

Capel Isaf, Dolwyddelan (C), 1860, shows how late the long-wall type survived, with arched windows and outer doors. Salem, Llanbedr (M), 1850, also long-wall, has an extreme severity, four sash windows above a single door.

Early INTERIORS of crowded box pews survive rarely. Carmel and Salem are remarkably intact, the door at Carmel opening into the space between the banked box pews and the *sêt-fawr*. Good early galleries are at Cildwrn, panelled and five-sided. In general the pulpit and deacons' seat or *sêt-fawr* were replaced in the later C19 with more ample constructions in pitch pine rather than the painted deal of earlier woodwork.

HIPPED-ROOFED CHAPELS are intermediate between long-wall and gable-entry versions. Anglesey has a series from Capel y Drindod, Beaumaris, 1833, through to Aberffraw and the two at Penysarn, all of the 1860s, and generally plain. The temple portico at Tremadog (C), once thought to be part of the original building of 1808–11, was actually added in 1849. A unique enhancement, so apt to Madocks's little planned town as to suggest that it was intended from the beginning, it stands counter to the general lack of adornment before the 1860s.

The ornate architectural GABLE FRONT comes to the fore in the 1860s, as SPECIALIST CHAPEL ARCHITECTS begin to oust the local builder. The *Rev. Thomas Thomas* of Landore, Swansea, brought to NW Wales one of the finest of his giant-arched Italianate fronts as early as 1860, at Porthmadog (C), a composition that he repeated and others copied for the next thirty years. He followed Porthmadog with Amlwch Port (A), Penmaenmawr, Pwllheli (both C), and Caernarfon, all Italianate (1861–2). His Bala (M), 1866–7, varies the Italian detail, and Bethania at Bethesda (C), 1885, almost his last work, introduces a harder-edged North Italian. Thomas also designed in a simple lancet Gothic, as at Menai Bridge (A), 1867 and Llandderfel (M), 1868, and experimented with a mixed Tudor and Italian at Dolgellau (M), also 1868. Thomas's works were mostly for his Independent denomination.

Richard Owens of Liverpool was a native of Caernarvonshire, and the region is filled with his works, mostly for the Calvinistic Methodists. Owens's characteristic style is round-arched Italian with Gothic rose windows, doorcases and moulded detail, sometimes called Italo-Lombard. More than Thomas he repeated designs: the centrepiece arched window over a rose and three arched lights reappear at Gwyddelwern, Llandderfel and Carrog, all in Merioneth (1870–1). A larger version with outer windows in triangular-headed recesses appears at Dwyran (A) and Betws-y-coed (C). Owens was fully Gothic at Barmouth (M), 1878, and Castle Square, Caernarfon, 1882–3. He also had a varied Italian palette: the giant portico at Engedi, Caernarfon, 1867, the pilasters and pediments of Bethesda (C), 1874, and Gorffwysfa, Penrhyndeudraeth (M), 1880.

The other major chapel designers of the later C19 were *Owen Morris Roberts* of Porthmadog, *Richard Davies* of Bangor and *R. G. Thomas* of Menai Bridge. *Roberts* tended to an Italian style,

quite restrained at Hyfrydle, Holyhead (A), 1887, later overladen
with detail, as at Seion, Criccieth (C), Moreia, Llangefni (A), and   103
Garth, Porthmadog (C) of the later 1890s. *Davies*, mostly Italian,
as at Ebenezer, Dolgellau (M), 1880, could be impressively severe
with a touch of Romanesque, as at Trawsfynydd (M) and Tabernacl, Conwy (C), both 1885. His most remarkable work is the
half-round interior of Jerusalem, Bethesda (C), 1872–5, echoed   101
on smaller scale at Salem, Dolgellau, 1893–4. At Amlwch Port (A),
1900, he notably abandons the gable front for a square plan under   104
a deep hipped roof, the front rather eighteenth-century with
colonnade between pavilions. *R. G. Thomas* has a less defined per-
sonality; at Beaumaris, 1870, he is harshly Gothic, but at Menai
Bridge (A), 1888, he designed the most thoroughgoing Gothic
chapel of the region, where for once the money was not short.

Generally the ENGLISH CONGREGATIONS tended towards
the Gothic more than the Welsh, three showing in Llandudno
(C), the Congregational by *Joseph James* of London, 1857–67, the
Wesleyan, 1865, by *George Felton*, and the English Presbyterian,
1891, by *T. G. Williams* of Liverpool. *Richard Davies*'s two English
chapels at Bangor, 1875 and 1882, have the nave and chancel
form of the Anglicans. But *W. H. Spaull* of Oswestry was chosen
to rebuild Thomas Charles's church in Bala (M), 1867, the heart
of Welsh-speaking Calvinistic Methodism, in Gothic, albeit
without the Anglican plan and detail.

The INTERIORS of the late C19 chapels tend to richness,
pulpits enlarged to broad platforms, galleries panelled in contrasting wood or cast iron, and the pulpit backed by complex
plasterwork, or very large organs. *O. Morris Roberts* was particularly lavish in late interiors, with carved gallery panels and ceilings of multiple roundels.

The pace of building slowed at the turn of the C20, but the
variety becomes bewildering with the free styles of the
EDWARDIAN ERA. Tabernacle, Bangor, 1902–5, by *James Cubitt*,
now converted to flats, was the most interesting, a cruciform
church-like design with aisles, crossing tower and long chancel,
the chancel actually a hall. The style, very late Gothic of C16 type,
could not be more different to Cubitt's wholly Victorian Union
Chapel, Islington. *G. Dickens-Lewis*'s chapel at Trefriw (C) shows
Arts and Crafts freedom within the Gothic, well handled.
Late Gothic of a Perp to C17 kind characterizes the terracotta
traceries of numerous chapels of this period. The terracotta-faced
chapel at Llanbedr (M), 1913, by *O. Morris Roberts & Son*, has
cupola-topped turrets and mullioned windows in a cheerfully free
style, found with less exuberance at Pennal (M), 1908. Horeb,
Llanfairfechan (C), 1912, has an uneasy shouldered narrow front
against a tower of almost equal bulk, the windows mullion-and-
transom.

Roberts's firm in the 1890s had experimented with twin-
towered façades at Salem, Caernarfon, and at Bontnewydd (C),
the latter with domed tops. *G. A. Humphreys* designed the
splendid Seilo, Llandudno, 1905, in rich grey and red stone, the
twin towers with almost Baroque cupolas. Tabernacl, Holyhead

(A), 1913, has a pair of roughcast towers carrying domes. In Llandudno the Cardiff chapel specialist *W. Beddoe Rees* designed Ebeneser Chapel, 1908–9, as a neat Edwardian Baroque domed square building, like a library of the date. The circular interior has a plaster dome on thin iron columns.

The building of new chapels did not quite cease with the First World War. The large chapel of 1924 at Corris (M) by *O. Morris Roberts & Son* has tall Tudor windows. *Clough Williams-Ellis* designed the chapel at Llanystumdwy (C), 1936, as a neat rather colonial piece of village scenery, the hipped roof crowned by a cupola. Penuel, Bangor (C) by *B. Price Davies*, 1950, is in a stripped-down traditional, with long windows, central porch-tower and thin-coursed stonework.

By the later c20 chapels were beginning to close, often oppressed by the burden of maintenance. The sale of great numbers of smaller chapels for CONVERSION to houses has gone almost unrecorded. Among the larger ones, major losses have thus far been few, but many are closed, like Engedi, Caernarfon, or in uses that do not guarantee upkeep, like Caersalem, Barmouth (M), and not one has been satisfactorily reused retaining the interior.

THE TWENTIETH CENTURY AND AFTER

1918–1945

War memorials after 1918 often took the form of MEMORIAL HALLS, e.g. Criccieth (C), by *O. Morris Roberts & Son*, 1922, or HOSPITALS, as at Blaenau Ffestiniog (M), by *Clough Williams-Ellis*, 1924, and Dolgellau (M) by *Herbert North*, 1927–9. Ashlar CLOCK TOWER memorials appear across Anglesey, at Gwalchmai, Llanfairpwll, Llanfechell and Rhosneigr, and at Llandudno *S. Colwyn Foulkes* designed the soaring obelisk on the seafront. Good sculpture is rare. Holyhead has bronze reliefs by *L. F. Roslyn*.

Of COMMERCIAL ARCHITECTURE, the National Provincial BANKS of *Palmer & Holden* stand out: the Portland stone palazzo at Llandudno, 1920, the little Arts and Crafts gem in Criccieth (C), 1923, and the half-timbered one in Corwen (M), 1924. Two notable buildings by *S. Colwyn Foulkes* are the former Palace Cinema in Conwy (C), 1935, and the Manweb showroom in Llandudno Junction (C), 1938. The major CIVIC BUILDING proposed, *Sir Giles Gilbert Scott*'s 1939 design for the County Hall in Dolgellau (M), was not built.

Of interwar CHURCHES the two of the early 1930s by *Giuseppe Rinvolucri* stand out for their structural use of concrete: the extraordinary parabolic-arched R.C. church at Amlwch (A) and the less dynamic one at Porthmadog (C). *Herbert North* built the intimate University Chaplaincy chapel in Bangor (C), 1933. His masterpiece, the chapel at the former St Winifred's School, Llanfairfechan (C), *c.* 1930, was demolished in 1970.

C.O.P.E.C. Cottages, Bangor.

H.L.North, BA,MIBA, Arch.   Richard Owen, Builder

Bangor, Seiriol Road housing.
Engraving by Herbert North, early C20

The need to replace slum terraces in Bangor (C) led to a massive programme of HOUSING from 1929. Under *B. Price Davies*, the City Surveyor, the standard by-law house plan was adapted to the climate of North Wales (e.g. by separating front door and passage from the rooms). Several estates remain in the city. In Seiriol Road, Bangor, is good housing by *H. L. North* of similar purpose but built by a church-led group, 1927. A well-considered housing scheme in Penmaenmawr (C) for the granite quarry, of the later 1930s, shows that terraces need not be bland and featureless.

Herbert North added further HOUSES to his picturesque Close development in Llanfairfechan (C) and clients outside the village commissioned houses from him until his death in 1941, as did local developers, as in Deganwy (C), *c.* 1933. Almost contemporary with the Close was the first phase (1926–39) of Portmeirion (M), the Italianate fantasy village created by *Clough Williams-Ellis* in an idyllic cove on the Dwyryd estuary near Porthmadog. The pre-war phase, built light for economy and speed (render on timber often masquerading as stone), drew on Clough's Arts and Crafts training, at times becoming whimsical, even Surrealist. An oddity is Plas Dolydd, Sychnant (C), *c.* 1922, built almost entirely of concrete, by *A. H. Stott Jun.*

MODERNIST or International Style buildings are rare. Six experimental houses commissioned *c.* 1937 by Sir Michael Assheton-Smith for quarry-workers at Dinorwic (C), designed in the modern white aesthetic by *D. Pleydell-Bouverie*, have not survived. An exception is *Harry Weedon*'s remarkable Villa Marina at Craigside (C), 1936. Chevrons, nearby, is in the same white style though there is no record of Weedon being its architect. *Clough Williams-Ellis* was also not averse to breaking from historicism, as shown by his hotel restaurant at Portmeirion (M), 1930 and his exciting first proposal for the Conwy Falls café (Penmachno, C), 1938.

109

112, 114

1945–c. 1980

After the Second World War the reality of the region's poverty hit
home. The heyday of slate production was well past, and entire
quarry communities were without work. Not surprisingly, very
little new building was called for. Shortage of materials meant
that the Dolgellau County Offices, 1953, were largely built of
prefabricated aluminium. One post-war planning achievement
was the designation of the SNOWDONIA NATIONAL PARK,
1951, covering two-thirds of mainland Gwynedd, its controls
restricting most new development.

New CHURCHES were built at Penrhyn Bay (C), by *Rosier &
Whitestone* of Cheltenham, 1963, and at Penrhosgarnedd, Bangor,
1956, and Benllech (A), 1964 by *North & Padmore. Weightman &
Bullen* were responsible for the R.C. churches in Bethesda (C),
Llandudno Junction (C) and Tywyn (M); *S. Powell Bowen*
designed the R.C. church in Benllech (A), 1967. All these are
Modernist in different ways and reflect planning after the Second
Vatican Council, contrasting with the Romanesque R.C. church
in Dolgellau, designed by the parish priest with *M. T. Pritchard*,
1963–6.

Good Modernist SCHOOLS were built on Anglesey in the
1940s–50s by *Norman Squire Johnson*, County Architect,
e.g. Amlwch (the first Comprehensive School to be built in
Britain), Llangefni, and the primary school in Beaumaris.
BANGOR UNIVERSITY embarked on a programme of building
in the 1950s–60s, mostly by *Sir Percy Thomas*'s practices.
The Dudok-style Thoday building is perhaps the most memorable. A scheme that deserves mention is *David Roberts*'s (now
demolished) halls and refectory, Plas Gwyn, 1962, built when
architectural ideals counted more than cost. At Coleg Harlech
(M) *Colwyn Foulkes & Partners* built a high-rise tower of student
bedrooms, 1968, and the sub-Brutalist Theatr Harlech, 1973.

Not much good HOUSING was built in this period, but
S. Colwyn Foulkes's colourful estate in Beaumaris (A), 1950,
deserves a mention. A second, more classical phase of
Portmeirion began in 1954, completed *c.* 1975. *Clough Williams-
Ellis* continued to stray into Modernist mode occasionally, as at
the butterfly-plan Morannedd Café, Criccieth (C), 1948. *Alison
& Peter Smithson* designed an unbuilt house in 1960 for the
film-director Joseph Losey near Penrhyndeudraeth.

An important area of activity in the 1960s was POWER
GENERATION. Atomic power stations were commissioned at
Trawsfynydd (M) in 1963 and at Wylfa (A) in 1971. Both projects
involved careful consideration of the impact of the vast buildings
on the landscape, particularly Trawsfynydd in the National Park.
The landscape architect *Sylvia Crowe* was brought in to advise
Sir Basil Spence at Trawsfynydd and *Farmer & Dark* at Wylfa.
A third nuclear power station proposed at Edern (C) was
abandoned after protest. The pumped storage station at
Tanygrisiau, Blaenau Ffestiniog (M), the first in Britain, was
designed by *S. Colwyn Foulkes* in 1957–63.

Since 1980

The most important modern CIVIC BUILDING is Pencadlys
(Gwynedd County Hall), Caernarfon, built in the 1980s by
Gwynedd County Architects with guidance from *Dewi-Prys Thomas*.
This large complex succeeds in integrating itself in the heart of
the walled town, albeit in a style that is less successful. The
Library in Caernarfon, also by the *Gwynedd County Architects*,
1982, is more convincing. The reorganization of Gwynedd in
1996, when Anglesey and the Snowdonia National Park became
separate authorities, necessitated new offices for each. The
opportunity was missed in Llangefni but seized with vigour by
Dylan Roberts (of *Gwynedd County Architects*) with the new Park
office, Penrhyndeudraeth (M).

Buildings of a broadly CULTURAL nature, such as galleries,
museums and visitor centres, include a good ticket office and
shop at Conwy Castle by *Bowen Dann Davies*, 1989. The Galeri,
Caernarfon, by *Richard Murphy*, 2005, provides an interesting [119]
mix of workplace and culture, given handsome physical expression by a no-nonsense Modern aesthetic still new to North
Walians. The new hospital at Tremadog (C) by *Nightingale Associates*, 2008, is another high-quality building, perhaps as chal-
lenging architecturally, and demonstrating that hospitals need
not be dull and soulless. The Rural Life Centre, Llanfor (M), by
Dobson:Owen, 2008, is an imaginative combination of new and
existing agricultural structures. The new Snowdon summit building, by *Ray Hole Architects*, is due for completion late in 2008 and [120]
an extension to the Mostyn Art Gallery, Llandudno (C), by *Ellis
Williams Architects*, in 2009. Both promise to be of high quality.

No new CHURCHES have been built in this period, but many
underwent repair in the later C20, thanks to generous grants from
Cadw and the Heritage Lottery Fund. Others have been adapted
to provide meeting rooms, kitchen, lavatories etc., sometimes discreetly within an aisle or vestry, or more radically, e.g. Llanfaelog
(A), 2000, by *Adam & Frances Voelcker* and Bala (M), 2006–7, by
Roy Olsen.

Gwynedd County Architects built sensibly organized and attractive SCHOOLS through the late C20 and early C21, most of them
designed by *Graeme Hughes*, e.g. at Bangor, Caernarfon, Penygroes and Penrhyn Bay (C). The Postmodern primary school at
Penisa'r waun (C), by *Dilwyn Gray-Williams*, illustrates the stylistic freedom encouraged within the department. *Nicholas Hare
Architects* added good new UNIVERSITY BUILDINGS at Bangor.

The 1980s witnessed good and bad alike in HOUSING. Local
authority repair grants encouraged pebbledash and roughcast
claddings in a misguided attempt to reduce damp, and entire
streets, even villages, were transformed into drab grey barracks.
On the other hand, the decade marks the high point of one
notable practice, *Bowen Dann Davies*, designing in a distinct vernacular entirely suited to the Welsh landscape and climate. Good
housing schemes by them are Hafan Elan, Llanrug (C), 1981,
sheltered courtyards with a carefully considered sense of scale;

and a denser development, Twr Llewelyn, in the centre of Conwy
(C), 1985. Their best, and biggest, building is the outdoor
pursuits centre at Plas Menai, Llanfairisgaer (C), 1982; the courtyard of staff housing here is delightful, and a model for how
modern housing should be handled.

Good PRIVATE HOUSES in Gwynedd have usually been
designed by architects for themselves: *Gruffydd Price* in Llanbedr
(M), 1995, *Maredudd ab Iestyn* in Caernarfon, 2000, and *David
Wilkinson* near Nantmor (C), 2006. Cynefin, Llanegryn (M), by
Christopher Day and *Julian Bishop*, continues the ideas of
harmony with the land that Day explored in Pembrokeshire,
clothed in local stone and undulating slate roofs that follow the
hills. A Postmodern seaside house, built in 1982 in Pwllheli (C)
by two young architects influenced by Terry Farrell, now looks
dated.

INDUSTRIAL ESTATES and BUSINESS PARKS are mostly
indifferent, but some aspire to a better-quality environment.
Examples include the Snowdonia Business Park, Minffordd (M),
won by *Edmund Kirby Architects* of Liverpool through an architectural competition, and the large Parc Menai outside Bangor
with one or two well-designed units, e.g. Technium cast by
TACP, 2004. The Antur Waunfawr unit at the Cibyn industrial
estate outside Caernarfon, by *Selwyn Jones*, 2005, displays design
skill combined with an awareness of sustainability issues. Out-of-
town shopping areas continue to threaten town-centre businesses
and to spoil town approaches, but *Bowen Dann Davies* succeeded
in the 1980s in improving the quality of supermarkets with their
Co-op stores in Porthmadog and Caernarfon.

Improved ROAD links along the N coast in the 1980s, and later
across Anglesey to Holyhead, pushed affluence towards the
remoter regions of Gwynedd, even if this only manifested itself
in the form of second homes, marinas and tourist attractions.
Road improvement schemes within the National Park have
often been carried out sympathetically, with local stone used
for walls etc., e.g. on the A470 near Dolwyddelan (C). The
Conwy TUNNEL (C) was innovative in its construction, the first
immersed tube tunnel in Britain, 1991. Two Millennium pedestrian BRIDGES at Holyhead (A) and over the Dyfi near Corris
(M) show imagination even if they lack engineering flair.

As the first decade of the C21 comes to an end, the overall
trend appears to indicate no great changes. Conservation rather
than expansion remains the accepted policy, not surprising in a
region where landscape is of more consequence than buildings.
Conservation funding has consolidated the fabric and enhanced
the character of historic centres such as Caernarfon and
Dolgellau. Occasionally individual conservation projects boost
local regeneration, e.g. Plas Mawr, Conwy. Where expansion
takes place, it is a mixed blessing: out-of-town shopping steals
trade and life from the town centres, the expansion of seaside
resorts for tourists brings in trade but pushes out local
inhabitants. As issues of sustainability become crucial, the
sparsely populated region would seem ideal for the decentralized,

self-help, 'small is beautiful' way of life, but surprisingly few developments suggest this is the way forward.

FURTHER READING

The three counties of Gwynedd have between them a wealth of written material even from early times. Gerald of Wales, Giraldus Cambrensis, was one of the first to write about the region, in his *Itinerary through Wales*, 1188 (Penguin translation 1978). Thomas Pennant's *A Tour of Wales*, 1778 (with illustrations by Moses Griffith) and Richard Fenton's *Tours in Wales, 1804–13* (published 1917) both visit Gwynedd, and Samuel Lewis's *Topographical Dictionary of Wales*, 1833, covers each parish. Works more specifically about the counties are *A Description of Caernarvonshire, 1809–11*, by Edmund Hyde Hall (published 1952), and *The Heart of Northern Wales*, 1912, by W. B. Lowe. C. A. Gresham's *Eifionydd*, 1973, concentrates on the area around Porthmadog. c20 guides include the excellent *Companion Guide to North Wales*, 1975, by Elisabeth Beazley and Peter Howell, and the *Shell Guides*, to *North Wales*, by E. Beazley and L. Brett, and to *Mid-Western Wales*, by V. Rees, both 1971, with lovely black-and-white photographs which capture the spirit of the country perfectly. There are too many other photographic books to list, but those showing aerial surveys include *Wales from the Air* by C. Musson and *Snowdonia from the Air*, 1996, by P. Crew and C. Musson, both excellent for the photos as well as the text.

For GENERAL HISTORY, John Davies's *A History of Wales*, 1993, is a good starting point. A. D. Carr, *Medieval Anglesey*, 1982, and A. H. Dodd, *History of Caernarvonshire*, 1968, cover these counties fairly succinctly. Much fuller is the *History of Merioneth:* vol. 1, 1967, ed. E. G. Bowen and C. A. Gresham, and vol. 2, 2001, ed. J. B. Smith and L. B. Smith. *An Historical Atlas of Wales*, 1972, by W. Rees, and E. Price, *Atlas of Caernarvonshire*, 1976, cover some of the same ground, more graphically.

J. B. Hilling, *The Historic Architecture of Wales*, 1976, is a very readable introduction to the BUILDINGS. The *Royal Commission on Ancient and Historical Monuments in Wales* inventories for *Anglesey* (1937, rev. 1960) and for *Caernarvonshire* (3 vols, 1956, 1960, 1964) are essential sources up to and including the later medieval period, with valuable historical introductions. Less thorough and reliable is the *Merioneth* volume, 1921, but the chapters on castles, churches and houses in vol. 2 of the *History of Merioneth* compensate to a certain extent (*see* below). The prehistoric and Roman periods are well covered by Frances Lynch in *Gwynedd*, 1995, and *Prehistoric Anglesey*, 1991; by C. J. Arnold and J. L. Davies in *Roman and Early Medieval Wales*, 2000; and by Lynch, Aldhouse Green and Davies in *Prehistoric Wales*, 2000. *Early Medieval Settlements in Wales*, 1988, ed. N. Edwards and A. Lane, deals with the c4–c11, and two important works are devoted to early monuments: *The Early Christian Monuments of Wales*, 1950, by V. E. Nash-Williams, and *Medieval Stone Carving in North Wales*, 1968, by C. A. Gresham. P. Lord,

The Visual Culture of Wales: Medieval Vision, 2003, is an informed
and beautifully illustrated work on medieval Wales seen through
the eyes of its craftsmen.

In addition to the Cadw guides to individual CASTLES, there
are general works, e.g. *The King's Works in Wales, 1277–1330*, by A.
J. Taylor, 1974, and *The Castle in England and Wales*, 1988, by D.
J. Cathcart King. 'The Castles: A Study in Military Architecture'
by D. J. Cathcart King with J. Kenyon (Chapter 9 in *History of
Merioneth*, vol. 2) and R. Avent, *Castles of the Princes of Gwynedd*,
1983, are more specific to the region, as is E. Neaverson, *Medi-
aeval Castles in North Wales*, 1947. The latter is particularly useful
for building stone, and complements works on GEOLOGY such
as *The Geology of Anglesey*, vol. 2, by E. Greenly, 1919, and the
updated *British Regional Geology* volume on Wales, by M. F.
Howells, 2007. *Stones in Wales* is a collection of papers given at
the Welsh Stone Conference, 2002, ed. Malcolm Coulson.

There is abundant material on CHURCHES. General church
history is discussed by G. Williams in *The Welsh Church from Conquest to Reformation*, 1962, and *The Diocese of Bangor during Three
Centuries*, 1929, by A. I. Pryce. The Cistercians receive attention
in D. M. Robinson, *The Cistercians in Wales*, 2006, D. H. Williams,
The Welsh Cistercians, 2001, and J. B. Smith and L. A. S. Butler's
chapter on Cymer Abbey in the *History of Merioneth. The Welsh
Historic Churches Project*, funded by Cadw and carried out by
Andrew Davidson of Gwynedd Archaeological Trust, 1997, is a
thorough survey of every medieval church of note; see also
Davidson's chapter on churches in the *History of Merioneth*.
Further research on individual churches has been carried out by
the Trust as a result of excavations or building work. Excellent
reports by David Longley have been prepared for Penmon,
Llangelynin (M), Nant Peris etc. C12 churches are explored in
depth by M. Thurlby in *Romanesque Architecture and Sculpture in
Wales*, 2006. *Archaeologia Cambrensis*, the journal of the Cambrian Archaeological Association, covers all aspects of churches
from its foundation in 1846. In particular, Anglesey churches etc.
are described by the Rev. P. C. Ellis, 1847 onwards, and C15
screens and lofts by Crossley and Ridgway, 1945. Harold Hughes
was a prolific contributor; his delightful *The Old Churches of
Snowdonia*, 1924 (with Herbert North), was the fruit of bicycle
tours. The indefatigable Sir Stephen Glynne visited most of
Gwynedd's churches in the mid C19 and provides valuable information about them before alteration. His notes are reproduced
in *Arch. Camb.*, 1884–1901. For the alterations themselves, the
Incorporated Church Building Society records held at Lambeth
Palace are indispensable (available at *www.churchplansonline.org*).
Diocesan records are also kept at the Archives Department of
Bangor University and at the National Library of Wales, Aberys-
twyth. M. L. Clarke provides brief notes on C19 Anglesey
churches in the *Transactions of the Anglesey Antiquarian Society*,
and an account of C19 church building and restoration
in Caernarvonshire in the *Transactions of the Caernarvonshire
Historical Society*, both 1961. M. Lewis, *Stained Glass in North
Wales up to 1850*, 1970, is the only detailed work on the subject.

M. Harrison, *Victorian Stained Glass*, 1980, is a good general work. Most churches have guidebooks, many of dubious scholarship, but the booklets on Beddgelert, by A. Bott and M. Dunn, 2004, and Llangelynin (M), by S. K. Land, 2004, are excellent, as is the Cadw guide, *Rûg Chapel, Llangar Church, Gwydir Uchaf Chapel*, by W. Nigel Yates, 1993, revised edn, 2005. For Bangor Cathedral, valuable early sources are *Bangor Cathedral* by Storer, 1818, and Browne Willis's *Survey*, 1721. For SCULPTURE *see* R. Gunnis, *Dictionary of British Sculptors 1660–1851*, revised 1968 (3rd edn forthcoming).

For CHAPELS, A. Jones, *Welsh Chapels*, 1996, remains the standard work. The prolific career of the Rev. Thomas Thomas is explored by Stephen Hughes in *Arch. Camb.*, 2003. *Hanes Eglwysi Annibynol Cymru*, by Rees and Thomas, 1870–5, gives a history of every Independent or Congregational cause, with a fifth volume update in 1894. The Royal Commission and National Library database covers chapels across the whole of Wales, and D. Huw Owen, *Capeli Cymru*, 2005, offers a selection of the major ones.

M. Seaborne, *Schools in Wales*, 1992, is a readable account of SCHOOLS between 1500 and 1900. The buildings of Bangor University are well documented in *The University College of North Wales Bangor*, 1930, and M. L. Clarke, *An Architectural History and Guide*, 1966.

Peter Smith, *Houses of the Welsh Countryside*, 1978 (revised edn, 1988) is the most authoritative work on DOMESTIC ARCHITECTURE; also the author's chapter on houses *c.* 1415–*c.* 1642 in the *History of Merioneth*. Briefer but still useful is the summary of the subject in vol. 3 of the RCAHMW *Caernarvonshire* inventory. I. Peate, *The Welsh House*, 1944, recently updated and expanded, is still valuable. *The Old Cottages of Snowdonia* by Hughes and North, 1908, is erudite, charming and beautifully illustrated. There are few books about the larger houses; Penrhyn Castle and Plas Newydd are covered in National Trust guides and articles in *Country Life*, and Plas Mawr, Conwy, in the Cadw guide. T. Lloyd, *Lost Houses of Wales*, 1986 (2nd edn 1989), records the few losses. GARDENS of note are included in the Cadw *Register of Landscapes, Parks and Gardens for Conwy, Gwynedd and the Isle of Anglesey*, by E. Whittle, 1998.

VERNACULAR buildings are covered by J. Lowe in two slim books, *Welsh Industrial Workers' Housing* and *Welsh Country Workers' Housing*, both 1989, and more recently in a series of Cadw booklets which combine historical information with advice on care and conservation: *Small Rural Dwellings in Wales*, 2003, *Industrial Workers' Housing*, 2005, and *Traditional Agricultural Buildings*, 2006. The standard work on FARM BUILDINGS is E. Wiliam, *The Historic Farm Buildings of Wales*, 1986.

For INDUSTRIAL ARCHAEOLOGY, A. H. Dodd, *The Industrial Revolution in North Wales*, is a comprehensive overview, 1990, and D. Gwyn, *Gwynedd: Inheriting a Revolution*, 2006, provides a broad and immensely readable survey of the subject. J. Lindsay, *History of the North Wales Slate Industry*, 1974, and *Slate Quarrying in Wales*, 2006, and *Gazetteer of Slate Quarrying in Wales*, 2007, both by A. J. Richards, are just three of many on this subject.

P. Lord, *The Visual Culture of Wales: Industrial Society*, 1998, explores the industrialization of Wales through images.

The Towns of Medieval Wales, by I. Soulsby, 1983, gives an informative introduction to the older TOWNS of Gwynedd, most of which also have individual accounts of varying quality. Bangor Civic Society has an excellent website (*www.bangorcivicsociety.org*), listing sources of historical information for the city, reproducing some online. E. Beazley, *Madocks and the Wonder of Wales*, 1985, provides the best account of William Madocks's life and achievements in the Porthmadog area. For Portmeirion, Clough Williams-Ellis wrote *Portmeirion, the Place and its Meaning*, 1963. Pwllheli has a good history by L. Lloyd, 1991. R. Hayman writes about the architecture and development of Beaumaris in the C19 in *Arch. Camb.*, 2004. On Llandudno, the *Complete Guide*, by J. Williams, 1865, charts the town near its outset, and G. Hiller, *Your Obedient Servant*, 2003, traces its history through the Mostyn estate and its agents.

Among useful books on ROADS, BRIDGES and RAILWAYS are *The Drovers' Roads of Wales*, by F. Godwin and S. Toulson, 1978 (revised 1994), *Thomas Telford's Holyhead Road: the A5 in North Wales*, by J. Quartermaine, B. Trinder and R. Turner, 2003, and *The Chester & Holyhead Railway*, by P. E. Baughan, 1972. For contemporary accounts of the building of the Conwy and Anglesey bridges, there are *The Britannia and Conway Tubular Bridges*, by E. Clark, 1850, and *An Account of the Construction of the Britannia and Conway Tubular Bridges*, by Sir W. Fairbairn, 1849. More accessible and up-to-date are two excellent books by L. T. C. Rolt, *Thomas Telford*, 1958, and *George and Robert Stephenson*, 1960. Other bridges are covered by E. Jervoise, *The Ancient Bridges of Wales and Western England*, 1937.

Information on INDIVIDUAL ARCHITECTS can be found in H. M. Colvin, *Biographical Dictionary of English Architects 1600–1840*, 2008 (4th edn), the *Directory of British Architects 1834–1900* (British Architectural Library), 1993 (expanded edn, 2001, 2 vols, up to 1914), and A. S. Gray, *Edwardian Architecture, a Biographical Dictionary*, 1985. Monographs include *The Work of John Douglas*, by E. Hubbard, 1991, *George Walton: Designer and Architect*, by K. Moon, 1993, and *Clough Williams-Ellis* by R. Haslam, RIBA Monographs No. 2, 1996. The *Journal of the Merioneth Historical and Record Society* has two useful articles by Dr I. Allan, one on George Walton's work at Harlech (1985), the other on correspondence between Henry Wilson and the patron of Brithdir church (1979–80). Also on Herbert North, Allan's unpublished thesis, 1988, (and part of a chapter in *Wandering Architects*, by M. Drury, 2000). *Architect Errant* is Clough Williams-Ellis's account of himself, modest and delightful, 1971.

The counties' historical societies have published numerous articles in their journals, on a great variety of subjects: *Transactions of the Anglesey Antiquarian Society*, *Transactions of the Caernarvonshire Historical Society* and the *Journal of the Merioneth Historical and Record Society*.

ANGLESEY

The principal *llys*, or court, of the Princes of Gwynedd in the early Middle Ages was at this protected coastal site, with easy connections with other *llysoedd* on the Eifionydd and Merioneth coasts and in north Caernarvonshire. Its position has proved elusive; excavations N of the church at Maes Llywelyn in 1957, where stone remnants had been identified with the *llys* c. 1750, proved nothing, though a length of Roman ditch found in later excavations suggested that an auxiliary fort might underlie the village centre, perhaps explaining its later selection as a seat of government. The palace's principal timber hall was moved to Caernarfon Castle in 1317 by Edward II (cf. the Ystumgwern hall and Harlech Castle).

ST BEUNO (SH 353 658). The church connected with the royal seat and containing some of the most significant Romanesque work on the island. Two aisles, with a W bellcote between. Dec traceried windows (since renewed), S porch and N vestry all of 1868, by *Kennedy*. Externally the S doorway alone, of two chamfered orders with plain capitals, is late C13. However, on the inner face of the W wall of the S aisle is a reconstructed Romanesque arch appropriate to the W face of a chancel arch (and conceivably evidence of a cruciform plan as at Penmon). This was discovered in 1840 during a restoration by *Thomas Jones* of Chester. But Malcolm Thurlby, who links the work to St John's, Chester, favours the suggestion that this was the entry to a W tower, mentioned as long gone in 1833. Inner order of square section, with chevron mouldings; outer one of shafts with trumpet capitals, carrying an arch of twenty-five heads, apparently rams and bulls, under a hoodmould.

The church was rebuilt in the C16 when its plan became a wide rectangle by the insertion of two Tudor chancel arches and two nave ones, on octagonal piers with two hollow-chamfer orders (cf. Llanidan, Llangwyfan etc.). Of this date the six-bay aisle roofs. Trusses with cusped upper braces and lower braces carried on wall-posts on foliage-carved corbels. – FONT. Large octagonal C13 bowl, re-cut. – STAINED GLASS. E window, Feed my Sheep, and four others by *E. R. Suffling* of London. – N aisle E, Good Samaritan by *C. A. Gibbs*, 1849, with typical mid-C19 decorative panels. – MONUMENT.

s chancel window, Rev. Henry Morris of Llanfachraeth †1763, beautifully lettered.

SEION WESLEYAN CHAPEL. 1887 by *William Lloyd Jones* of Bangor. Bold two-storey chapel rising above the estuary just below Bodorgan Square. In unpainted cement, with steep pediment made more forceful by wide shoulders with urns, the detail loosely Italian. Continuous gallery on iron columns, the choir gallery and organ framed in a basket-arched recess.

CALVINISTIC METHODIST CHAPEL, Chapel Street. 1861. A hipped box with tall round-headed windows. Reordered 1905 with a rich latticed ceiling border. It faces a little yard, with chapel house and schoolroom on two other sides.

Aberffraw's small harbour was in use till the end of the C18 and its market continued into the C19. The old approach was by causeway across dunes, over the Ffraw by the elliptical-arched BRIDGE built in 1731 by Sir Arthur Owen of Bodowen, and up Bridge Street into BODORGAN SQUARE, the market. The square is irregular, sloping, the houses mostly altered with late C20 pebbledash and replaced windows, but nonetheless exceptional among generally linear villages. On CHURCH STREET, THE EAGLES, two cottages converted to a school in 1735 under the will of Sir Arthur Owen. Also two C18 stone cottages, Pendref, and behind No. 31 the diminutive TŶ BACH, unaltered and of a type which the island has almost completely lost; just 14 by 16 ft (4.3 by 4.9 metres) externally, of one storey, with a door between two windows, S. Further E, housing of 1959 by *Alex Gordon & Partners*.

TRWYN DU CAIRN, ½ m. S (SH 353 678). A small cairn excavated in the 1950s. The structure of the mound suggests the earliest Bronze Age. Surrounding kerb of upright stones, alternating high and low to produce almost a castellated effect, unfortunately now covered, though the taller stones break the surface around the circumference. The cairn was built over part of a Mesolithic flint-working site (*c.* 8000 B.C.), excavated in 1973 to prevent its erosion by the sea. Thousands of flint implements were found, but no evidence for houses or even light shelters around the hearths. N of the barrow, apparent foundations of round huts, probably Romano-British.

AMLWCH

A harbour recorded since the C16, in a creek no doubt long used by merchants. Houses and amenities grew up round the sheltered port (*see* Amlwch Port) and inland near the ancient church. A school founded in 1689 and sophisticated C17 memorials in the church tell of prosperity; the demolished *plas* had a C16 arch-braced roof. Amlwch's heyday came with the discovery of copper deposits in the Mona mine (1768) and the Parys mine (1775) and lasted till the 1840s. But much of the town actually dates from later, and its industrial structures have in their turn recently been largely removed.

St Eleth. By *James Wyatt*, 1800 (but planned from 1787), ⁶⁹
replacing the medieval church which had a w tower and
transepts. The commission presumably derived from Wyatt's
patron at Plas Newydd, Llanedwen, who contributed to the
cost of £2,500, as did the other part-owner of the Parys mine,
the Rev. Edward Hughes, and the manager Thomas Williams.
Local greenish rubble stone with grey ashlar dressings.
The sheer w tower has big single-arched belfry windows, ashlar
angle pilasters and balustrade. The nave, with similar angle
pilasters and a dentilled pediment, presages the design of a
thousand chapels. Egregious Gothic remodelling by *Kennedy
& O'Donoghue* in 1867 inserted Perpendicular window tracery,
redone in concrete in 1965 by *Edwin Cockshutt*, and replaced
Wyatt's galleried interior with Gothic arcades. But the interior
possesses considerable grace, being divided by three-bay
arcades of lofty octagonal Bath stone columns, the capitals
touched by a breath of classicism. E end divided into a
sanctuary and lateral chapels, the piers responding with extra
shafts on the N and S; high sanctuary arch, lower chapel ones
sprung from corbels.

In 1999–2000 another reordering, by *Adam & Frances
Voelcker*, brought new spaces at the w on two levels. A deep
gallery now contains the C19 ORGAN by *Bevington*. Beneath, a
dark baptistery opposite the entrance has a light-directing
copper canopy over the FONT of 1900. – STAINED GLASS. E
window, patterned 1860s glass. – MONUMENTS. Capt. David
Lloyd †1641, in a strapwork surround with heraldry above. –
Howell Lewis †1683, a fine elliptical swelling panel and
escutcheon, erected by his twelfth son. – Stephen Roose †1821,
tapering Grecian stele. White marble on black. – George Roose
†1856, Gothic aedicule framed by foliage-carved colonnettes.
– Thomas Lewis Prichard, killed in France. Tile mosaic of St
Louis, by *Powells,* 1916. – Rev. Thomas Prichard †1926, in
alabaster, with a chalice and the Host. – In the porch.
SEPULCHRAL SLAB, *c.* 1250–80, with a cross in relief with
trilobed foliage curling down its sides.

Our Lady Star of the Sea and St Winefride (R.C.), Bull
Bay Road. A piece of Italian architectural daring of the 1930s.
Its designer, *Giuseppe Rinvolucri*, came from an engineering
background in Piedmont, but was then living in Conwy. His
little team of builders constructed his innovative parabolic
vault in six months in 1935. From a gaunt stone basement
housing the church hall, begun in 1932, up which steps rise to
the (liturgical) w end, a soaring reinforced concrete and brick
vault was formed on six arches, expressed as ribs externally
and internally, with a conical apse. Three transverse bands of
glazing in geometric trefoils of white on blue. Five glass stars ¹¹⁵
(made in France) perforate the E wall round the apse. What
inspired this Futurist church, closer to Freyssinet's 1920s airship
hangars at Orly, Paris, than to Catholic church design, and so
unlike the conservatism of Anglesey building? In the apse,
mural PAINTING of Christ Crucified by *Gordon Wallace*, 1963.

Structural problems have led to (hopefully temporary) closure.

BETHESDA CALVINISTIC METHODIST CHAPEL, Bethesda Street. 1871, by *Richard Owens*. A large gable front in rubble with grey limestone dressings, in Owens's typical mix of Italian and Gothic. Stilted arched triplet with blind octofoils in the heads and long arched side windows. The heavy porch is an addition of 1905 by *Richard Davies*.

ENGLISH WESLEYAN CHAPEL, Wesley Street. Built for Cornish miners in 1832 by James Treweek, manager of the Mona mine. Stucco long-wall façade of three pointed windows and a door. Schoolroom and chapel house in line, r.

WESLEYAN CHAPEL, Wesley Street. 1909 by *W. F. Brindle*. Unpainted stucco, old-fashioned in its arched triplet and arched side windows, but made monumental by high parapets and a great rectangular plaque across the gable. The warehouse door cut through the façade is poignant.

SIR THOMAS JONES COUNTY SECONDARY SCHOOL, Pentrefelin. 1953. The largest and most striking of the post-war schools erected while *N. Squire Johnson* was County Architect. Architect in charge *Kenneth M. Raw*. It was the first purpose-built comprehensive school in Britain, named after the local doctor who first proposed that education on the island should be open to all. The central features of this large spreading school are a main hall approached by generous steps and a bare stone tower with a flush stone clock face and the proportions of a Cornish engine house. The link with pre-war civic building is clear.

PERAMBULATION

The central space is DINORBEN SQUARE, with the DINORBEN ARMS (the title given in 1831 to the Hughes family, owners of the Mona copper mine) opposite the churchyard. Five bays, stuccoed. Early Victorian, with Soaneian incised ornament to the piers of the porch (cf. the Bulkeley Arms, Beaumaris). Neo-Jacobean staircase. From the square radiate the main streets. In LÔN GLAS, off Queen Street, the main axis to the s, MAGISTRATES' COURT and COUNCIL OFFICES, Neo-Jacobean of 1902, like the building at Holyhead. MONA STREET, w, offers the most consistent streetscape with two- and three-storey houses, the Market Inn and some bank buildings; but it soon fades. Further on the r., MONA LODGE, scribed stucco pair of early C19 houses. Porches under a central gable, two-storey quoined wings; a stone coachhouse to the r. Beyond is Bethesda Chapel (*see* above). Bull Bay Road runs NW with the old NATIONAL SCHOOL of 1821 and the R.C. church. The school is between Grecian and Tudor, with Roman and Gothic lettering. The central entrance arch led originally to a two-storey block and with the girls' and boys' schoolrooms to either side, all with cyclopean cornices and low pyramidal

roofs. Surely a late product of the Wyatt connection? MARKET
STREET runs E, past the large hipped MEMORIAL HALL, r.,
1920s, the pedimented stucco forebuilding containing the Roll
of Honour. Further on, now WESLEY STREET, the English
Wesleyan Chapel above the pavement, l. and, closing the view
E, the disused Welsh Wesleyan Chapel, a piece of townscape
worth preserving.

FRONDEG, ½ m. SW. Stuccoed house on a hill overlooking the
town, c. 1828, belonging to the Parys Mountain mine manager.
Hipped roof, veranda with intersecting tracery windows at
each end. Embattled walls to yard behind and to the octagonal well-house.

BULL BAY/PORTH LLECHOG, 1 m. NW. A tiny length of Cornish
quay wall, presumably of c. 1800 as at Amlwch. Above, the Late
Victorian presence of the Bull Bay Hotel. An early C19 bathing
castle once stood on this shore with a two-storey gatehouse
and curtain walls screening a bath cut from the rock and filled
by the sea.

AMLWCH PORT/PORTH AMLWCH   4594

The most Welsh of ports, a narrow creek 500 ft long and 100 ft
wide (150 and 30 metres) at the entrance. Investment came after
the mid-C18 copper rush, much of the ore being bound for
Swansea and Lancashire. An Act of 1793 led to a Board of Harbour
Trustees constructing the harbour walls. Shipbuilding began in the
C19 and continued up to 1914 in yards either side of the harbour
mouth. By 1768 there were rows of houses here; these survivors
are among the oldest from an industrial context in Wales.

The quays on the W were begun in the C16. The main retaining
walls, and two breakwaters originally with a lighthouse on
each, are constructed Cornish-fashion with the stones on edge,
the wave-resisting technique used till the mid C19: presumably
an indication that the contractors had experience at Cornwall's
exposed ports. One C18 warehouse or ore bin (No. 8) in the
row of nine STORAGE BINS on the E quay; WATCH HOUSE of
1817, rebuilt 1853, with a segmental arched doorway. Of the
1790s the bases of conical SULPHUR KILNS. A second
BREAKWATER, 150 ft (46 metres) long, was constructed E of
the harbour in 1816 and given its own lighthouse in 1817; the
existing LIGHTHOUSE is of 1853. Harbour master's house of
this period; C19 LIMEKILN above.
  Surviving round the harbour, if fragmentarily, are the Mona
and Parys smelters; Hill's chemical works and incline; and a
brewery where an C18 warehouse stands. To the NE were the
SHIPYARD started by Nicholas Treweek from Cornwall c. 1850,
the SAIL LOFT of c. 1870 (now the heritage centre) and the
rock-cut DRY DOCK of c. 1880. On the ridge, W, MELIN-

Y-BORTH, a windmill of 1816 and seamark, its 160-ft (49-metre) brick tower the tallest in Anglesey.

CARMEL INDEPENDENT CHAPEL, Chapel Street. Disused. Enlarged 1861, the giant arch typical of the *Rev. Thomas Thomas*, who made this form his own from 1858 (cf. Salem Chapel, Porthmadog). The entablature and Doric pilasters are designed with some skill. To the l. a long schoolroom range, the further gable with a big lunette, early C20, and characterful.

104   PENIEL CALVINISTIC METHODIST CHAPEL, Llaneilian Road. A remarkably sophisticated design of 1900, by *Richard Davies*. The plan is square with a pyramid roof, the façade a confident reminiscence of a Neoclassical orangery, in unpainted stucco. Three-bay centre with arched windows between Doric columns, framed by pedimented pavilions each with a lunette over a pedimented porch. Interior without galleries. Radial seating. Boarded ceiling above an enriched plaster cove.

6176   BEAUMARIS/BIWMARES

Beaumaris was a new town created with the castle and immediately became the administrative centre of Anglesey. It replaced the adjoining Welsh town and port of Llanfaes. Like Caernarfon and Conwy, Beaumaris was designed as a walled town with a fortress supplied by sea. The Norman French name means beautiful marsh ('Beau Marais'). The borough charter was granted in 1296 and the town's walls, now vanished, were not built till after the Glyndŵr revolt in 1414. Beaumaris rapidly became a trading port and was the customs centre for NW Wales.

The natural advantages of Beaumaris prompted its re-creation as a resort. The road from the Porthaethwy (Menai Bridge) ferry was made in 1804–5 by Viscount Bulkeley in anticipation of a bridge being built, and Telford's Menai Bridge was completed in 1826. The castle was an attraction, but less so than Harlech or Caernarfon: 'too low to be a striking object', according to Richard Fenton in 1810. Sir Richard Bulkeley Williams-Bulkeley, nonetheless tidied the ruins. The first terrace was built in 1825, the hot baths in 1828, the gaol in 1829, the hotel *c.* 1835. Princess Victoria visited in 1832, for whom Victoria Terrace was named in 1833. Development after that was curtailed by the absence of a railway and the succession of Llangefni as county town in the 1880s, and Beaumaris remained a compact small town. While the town walls have all but disappeared, the medieval street grid survives; the judicial buildings and others left stranded by the change of status contribute to an unusual architectural entity on a small scale. The employment of the architects *Joseph Hansom* and *Edward Welch* of York on the major works of the late 1820s, and their use of the fine grey Penmon stone, give Beaumaris its special Late Georgian quality.

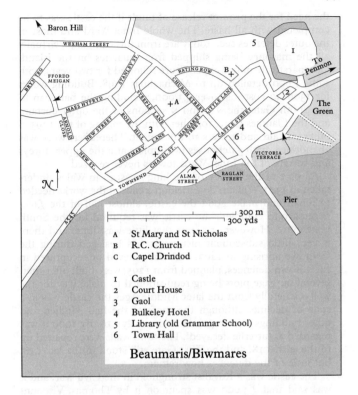

A   St Mary and St Nicholas
B   R.C. Church
C   Capel Drindod

1   Castle
2   Court House
3   Gaol
4   Bulkeley Hotel
5   Library (old Grammar School)
6   Town Hall

Beaumaris/Biwmares

BEAUMARIS CASTLE

This is the definitive concentric castle of the Middle Ages. p. 99
Although the last of the Edwardian castles in Wales to be built,
the speed with which it was erected, even to its present unfinished state, must mean that the design was already drawn up
well before 1295, awaiting implementation. It is known that
Edward I was in the prosperous Welsh borough of Llanfaes in
summer 1283, not far from the future site. The catalyst for the
castle's construction was the Welsh uprising of 1294, during
which the sheriff of Anglesey was seized and hanged.

The surviving accounts show that over £6,000 was spent in
the building season of 1295, monies being advanced to *James
of St George*, Master of the King's Works in Wales, from that
April. Enough of the castle was standing by July to allow the
king to stay in temporary accommodation within its walls. Over
£4,000 of expenditure was recorded for the following twelve
months, and the workforce in 1296 numbered over 2,500 men,
400 of them stonemasons. In February of that year Master
James and Walter of Winchester, clerk of works in Wales, wrote
at the request of the Exchequer detailing progress, emphasizing

the need for the prompt release of funds if the castle was to be completed with all haste. The whole Inner Ward and most of the outer defences seen today are from this campaign, virtually all the masonry being shipped from quarries on the island. Comparatively minor expenditure followed for two years, with some £600 detailed up to Michaelmas 1298. Building works for 1306–30 cost just over £3,000, including the barbican to the South Gate, the NW and N sections of the outer curtain, and the Llanfaes Gate, together with the raising of the 1295–6 outer curtain and towers to full height. Thereafter, work was abandoned, with gatehouses incomplete and the upper storeys and turrets of the Inner Ward towers never realized.

As part of the survey of the king's castles in Wales under-taken in 1343, William de Emeldon itemized the works needed to repair and make good the castle; almost half of the £684 necessary to complete the castle was required for the South Gatehouse. However, it seems that little was done, and there is very little subsequent history. It was besieged during the Glyndŵr uprising in 1403, and was relieved or recaptured in 1405. Town defences, planned from 1295, were built after that, several burgage plots being requisitioned to make way for the wall. Generally from the later Middle Ages the castle was in a state of decline, although the roofs of the hall, kitchen and other buildings were repaired in the early C16. By 1609 it was regarded as 'utterlie decayed'. The town walls were repaired up to the early C18, and the West Gate still stood in the late C18, but little of the defences now remain.

The castle was a Royalist stronghold in the Civil War, and it was said that £3,000 was spent on it by Thomas, Viscount Bulkeley. It surrendered in 1646, but was held again for the king in the abortive Anglesey uprising of 1648. Partial demolition may have followed the Restoration of 1660. In 1807 the 7th Viscount purchased the castle from the Crown. His successor laid out walks with shrubberies, and entertained Princess Victoria here at a Royal Eisteddfod in 1832. Following its transfer to state care in 1925, repairs and consolidation of the fabric began, and the moat was reinstated on three sides.

The level site in marshy terrain enabled the castle to be laid out on a regular plan where it could be supplied by sea and could use the tides to maintain the water level in the moat. The PLAN consists of a square Inner Ward with two large gatehouses and six mural towers, the two middle ones being D-shaped, the others circular and placed at the corners. A lower, outer, curtain surrounds the Inner Ward, giving the castle its concentric plan – a defence within a defence. It is the best surviving example of its type of all the Edwardian castles, the outer curtains at e.g. Harlech and Rhuddlan being more fragmentary. The multiple latrine arrangement throughout is just one extraordinary feature of this great stronghold.

The Outer Ward

Starting with the exterior of the OUTER CURTAIN, the main entrance was the Gate next the Sea, from which the foundations of the TOWN WALL run S before turning SW. Circular towers are distributed around the outer curtain, the largest at the NW and NE corners, with smaller examples of varying size at regular intervals. About 8 ft (2.4 metres) above moat level is a clear horizontal line that demarcates a change of masonry used in construction, and whilst the lower arrowslits in the towers of 1295–8 do not have a lintel, those at the upper levels and throughout the towers built after 1306 do have this feature.

On the NE side of the outer curtain stands the incomplete LLANFAES GATE, twin gate-towers lacking their fronts, and framing the entrance passage with slits opening onto it from the side chambers; the entrance also had a portcullis. The gate stands asymmetrically with the North Gatehouse of the Inner Ward. The stubs of the towers project irregularly, and were

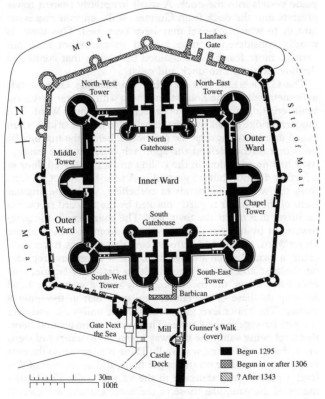

Beaumaris Castle.
Plan

squared off following the decision to abandon construction.
From within the castle the towers were entered from the rear,
with a mural stair in the W tower leading to the upper levels
and the curtain wall, whilst arches across the towers carried an
improvised wall-walk due to the unfinished nature of the gate.
A fine LATRINE with a grotesque head as the spout on the
E curtain is best seen from the park on this side.

Approaching the main entrance in the S side of the outer
curtain, the CASTLE DOCK lies on the r., framed between
foundations of the town wall and the flanking wall known as
GUNNERS WALK. In the outer curtain between the Gate next
the Sea and the flanking wall is a shoulder-arched doorway
through which goods could be transferred from ships into the
castle. Gunners Walk itself is at battlement level, enabling
archers to cover the dock and the moat to the E, evidence for
the outer revetment of which can be seen on the E side of the
flanking wall. Arrowslits are also set into the E and W walls of
the passage below. The platform at the S end of the Walk may
have held a small piece of artillery, or perhaps a beacon to
guide vessels into the dock. A small irregularly shaped tower
projects into the dock from Gunners Walk; an iron ring is set
into it, to which a vessel may have been tied. This tower is
usually considered to have housed an undershot mill, but
perhaps more feasibly it contained the sluices that controlled
the flow of water into dock and moat.

The GATE NEXT THE SEA, like the Llanfaes Gate, stands
asymmetrically to the South Gatehouse with its later barbican,
again creating a staggered approach to the Inner Ward. The
modern bridge passes over the drawbridge pit; the bridge when
raised fitted flush against the gatehouse, below the machicolations that further defend the approach. The entrance passage
itself had murder slots in the ceiling and a two-leaved door as
a further defence, but no portcullis. A spur-like turret projects
from the W tower on bands of corbelling, whilst the angular
form of the E tower is partly masked by the forward rectangular turret that meets the town wall. The chambers in the gate-
towers, lit by narrow slits, are entered from doorways in the
Outer Ward, corbels and a groove over that to the W tower indicating a former porch arrangement. The W tower has fireplaces
on the first and second floors, with a first-floor latrine, corbelled out above the moat, originally with a grotesque head
forming the base of the chute, similar to that in the outer E
curtain. The upper level gave access to the wall-walk, and over
the gate passage to the E tower. This tower has no ground floor,
this level being solid; the doorway opens on to a flight of steps
up to the first floor and wall-walk. There is a latrine on the first
floor, and a fireplace on the upper floor, and at the rear of this
level a passage and staircase to the SE wall-walk. The battlements of the gate, like those of the outer curtain, are carried
on a corbel table.

Within the OUTER WARD one appreciates the concentric
nature of the castle: the much larger Inner Ward towers rise

high above the outermost, even without their upper storeys and turrets. The WALL-WALK around the outer curtain, accessed from the outer gates and from the ground by stairs, has lost most of its crenellated battlements and arrowslits, but its supporting moulded corbel table remains. Steps also carry the wall-walk round the rear of the mural towers. Latrines are built into the curtain towards the s end of the e and w curtains, and also near the NW and NE corners of the ward. Accommodation was provided in the larger towers, at the NW and NE angles of the outer curtain, as indicated by a single fireplace and a private latrine for each tower. The sw section of the outer curtain was reinforced with internal arches, possibly following Emeldon's survey of 1343. An inspection of the numerous arrowslits in the walls, at two levels, and three levels in the towers, shows that many were blocked subsequently, date unknown.

The w outer curtain originally finished opposite the Inner Ward's MIDDLE TOWER. A stub of masonry on this tower marks the site of a temporary wall that linked the two curtains. The junction of the two phases of the outer curtain can also be seen just to the w of the North-East Tower, between the two nearest arrowslits. Examination of the Middle Tower and the two adjacent Inner Ward towers shows that most of the large rectangular two-light windows have been blocked. Unblocked windows can be seen in the gatehouses and the towers on the e side, but only in the SOUTH-EAST TOWER can one see a window complete with mullion. A final feature to note from the Outer Ward is the bellcote at the junction of CHAPEL TOWER with the inner curtain to its s.

The Inner Ward

The South Gatehouse was planned as the main entrance to the Inner Ward, but before it stands the BARBICAN, built *c.* 1306 to compensate for the unfinished gate and its lack of portcullises. In the barbican the ground level and battlements have cruciform arrowslits. Two gargoyle water spouts survive in the s wall. The two-centred-arched doorway has a semicircular rere-arch. Although the rear of the SOUTH GATE is almost at foundation level, from the surviving evidence, coupled with what can be seen in the more complete North Gate, its entrance passage was intended to have a chain of barriers: three two-leaf doors secured by drawbars, three portcullises, three series of murder slots in the passage roof, and arrowslits in the passage walls, with further slits in the faces of the towers. Doorways off the passage led to the rooms for guards and porters, and so on to both the front chambers and the newel staircases in the rear turrets. These turrets, most of the inner half of the gate, and the upper floors and battlements of the twin gate-towers were never built, although evidence for a building in the SE corner of the Inner Ward suggests that more of the e or rear wall of the gatehouse stood by the

Beaumaris Castle, south-east view.
Engraving by S. and N. Buck, 1742

early C14 than today. Fireplaces survive in the ground-floor chambers, whilst connecting doorways and hooded fireplaces can be seen at first-floor level.

p. 30

The NORTH GATEHOUSE also stands incomplete. Whilst a barbican was not built here to provide additional protection, there is evidence to show that the entrance passage was partly blocked. Although the twin D-shaped towers were built almost to full height, the rear half, with two floors of majestic windows flanked by the stair-turrets on battered bases, was only half finished. The passage was to have three double-leaf doors and three portcullises, as well as murder slots; arrowslits in deep embrasures cover the middle part, and slits also face N. Again, access to the ground-floor rooms was through doorways towards the rear of the passage, and the newel stairs in the turrets were reached from the ground-floor S chambers. These are lit from the Inner Ward by rectangular windows, those in the SW chamber smaller than that to the SE.

Access to the first floor was also provided from the Inner Ward, with an external timber stair leading to the westernmost of the five windows that sit above a moulded string course; this window has its sill set lower to allow for a doorway in the lower half. This fine range of windows has the jambs of the upper halves moulded in a different fashion to the lower, together with hoodmoulds and hollow-chamfered rere-arches; the E opening retains its transom. They lit what may have been intended as the king's personal hall, and were to be mirrored by a similar series lighting the royal accommodation on the floor above. The window bases and their seats here are still evident, as is the springing for the main arch that would have carried the upper floor. That there are two hooded fireplaces in the hall suggests that the room was to be subdivided. Doorways off the stair-turrets also gave access to the first and second floors.

There are two upper floors in each of the D-shaped towers, with a further two floors over the entrance passage, each with hooded fireplaces. Rectangular windows light the first-floor rooms, whilst the upper chambers have on the N side two-light trefoil-headed windows, as well as seats in the embrasures. A pent roof covered the N half of the gatehouse in its almost finished state, whilst the line of corbels in the first-floor hall took the wall-posts of a low-pitched roof.

The INNER WARD itself is almost featureless, but set into or built close to the curtain is an indication of what stood here formerly. In the NW corner are foundations of the kitchen, with a fireplace set into the curtain. There was access from this range to the North-West Tower and to the North Gatehouse through a first-floor doorway in the gate's W stair-turret. The area S of the kitchen may mark the site of the STABLES. Here in the face of the curtain can be seen inclined lines of putlog holes for the original scaffolding. A slight offset running the length of the curtain and the upper doorways in the towers indicates that the W range included a first floor. In the NE corner, in the angle of the E stair-turret and curtain, is an oven. In the inner face of the E curtain two fireplaces and the tooth-ings for a wall just S of the entrance to the Chapel Tower mark the site of a hall and chamber, perhaps intended as royal apart-ments, especially as they are placed close to the Chapel Tower. The rooms were set over a low basement lit or ventilated by an opening through the N wall. The creasing for the roof of a later building on the site of the hall cuts through one fireplace. In the SE corner of the ward the remains of wall plaster indicate that a further building stood here. At the top of the middle section of the E and W curtains are rounded projections set on corbels; these allow the wall-walk to pass round the rear of the Middle and Chapel towers and past a stair-turret.

All the mural towers and connecting curtain could be reached from the Inner Ward. The towers led to a continuous network of first-floor WALL PASSAGES, provided with air vents. The passages are roofed using flagstones creating a flat-shouldered vault, and have shouldered doorways throughout. Light is provided by slits in deep embrasures overlooking the Outer Ward. At several points the passages provide access to small mural chambers, perhaps to house the garrison or house-hold staff, and also to eight sets of latrines, at wall-walk and first-floor levels.

Enough of the MURAL TOWERS themselves survives to allow the internal arrangements to be appreciated, although only the Chapel Tower is floored and roofed. All were intended to have three floors, although little of the upper storeys was ever built. The round towers at the angles have circular basements with octagonal upper chambers. Sloping vents provided the only light and air to the basements, and access was via passages through shouldered doorways; circular stairs led to the upper floors. Stone diaphragm arches carried the first floors, except in the North-West Tower and the Chapel Tower, whilst the North-East Tower has a further arch to take the intended upper floor. The upper chambers were provided with hooded fire-places, and lit by two-light windows, seats being set in each embrasure.

The MIDDLE TOWER, D-shaped in plan, with semi-octagonal chambers, was furnished similarly to the angle towers. The
CHAPEL TOWER in the centre of the E curtain is the best surviving of all the towers. Set over a barrel-vaulted basement that
is entered from the courtyard, the chapel is remarkable in its
survival. The main entrance was through the arched upper
doorway set in the curtain wall, but within the domestic range
that we have seen was built against the curtain at this point.
Access to the chapel, adjacent lobbies and viewing chambers
was from a vestibule entered from the mural passage to the N
and S. Closing a series of wooden doors would have sealed off
the component parts of this complex – chapel, vestibule,
lobbies and viewing chambers – from the rest of the castle. The
chapel itself is entered through twin trefoil-headed doorways
with moulded shafts, capitals and bases, and has a ribbed vault
springing from semi-octagonal shafts. Set into five bays are
double-splayed lancet windows, below which runs a series of
panels, constituting a trefoil-headed blind arcade. High in each
N and S wall is a narrow opening to allow those in the viewing
chambers to observe the Mass, and another squint was cut in
the N wall. At the W end of the chapel is a pair of lights on
either side of the main doorway, and from the lobbies steps led
up to the viewing chambers, that on the N having a lockable
door. Also at the W end is an air vent running up to the wall-
walk, and an indication that a gallery was built over the chapel
entrance. Outside and visible from the Outer Ward is a small
corbelled feature on the S face of the tower, where it meets the
curtain wall; it has been suggested that this was the chapel's
bellcote. Enough remains of the upper storey to show that it
was intended to have a fireplace and a latrine, perhaps to
accommode a priest.

The WALL-WALK has lost virtually its entire battlemented
wall, with only a few merlons with arrowslits intact. Nevertheless, the staggered arrangement of the loops to provide
archers with different fields of fire is apparent. The remarkable
feature of the wall top is the eight pairs of latrines. A large pit,
originally scoured by the moat, serves each pair and those
below that lie off the mural passages. Each individual latrine
is divided from its neighbour by a rectangular ventilation shaft.
The latrines on the wall-walk were never roofed as intended,
and so their internal arrangement is clear to see. A flight of
steps leads down to each latrine, a doorway at the foot of them;
in some cases the remains of the iron door hinges remain, set
in lead. In the latrine itself the setting for the wooden seat can
be seen in the masonry.

The North Gatehouse could only be reached from the wall-
walks by a wooden bridge on each side. These could be with-
drawn in times of need, isolating the gate from the curtain wall.
A modern timber walkway is on the site of the W bridge.

The castle ticket office was replaced in 2005 for Cadw by
Robin Wolley.

TOWN WALLS. There is very little evidence for the borough
defences apart from the foundations at the Gate next the Sea.
The bank and ditch constructed *c.* 1407 have gone, as has most
of the wall, along with its towers and gates. It is known that
mural passages and latrines formed part of the C15 work.
A short stretch of curtain may remain as the side wall of a
property visible from the SW corner of the parish churchyard,
and no doubt much stone was used to build houses in modern
times, and also the gaol.

CHURCHES AND CHAPELS

SS MARY AND NICHOLAS. Anglesey's civic church for centuries,   34
containing notable funerary monuments. The citizens of the
new town petitioned for a church. As at Bala, Harlech and
Aberystwyth, where none was built, the larger entity remained
subordinate to the older parish, here Llandegfan. At first sight
a slightly wild example of Tudor post-Perpendicular, with
wriggling uncusped tracery and knobbly finials; but this a
reworking of an orderly C14 building. Chancel, aisled nave with
S porch and W tower. The last is of two builds, the lower storeys
of irregular limestone blocks, mostly grey, with two sturdy buttresses at each angle, door at the S, two trefoiled lancets above,
as also on the W and N. Bell-stage of plain ochre stonework,
part of work by *John Hall* of Bangor in 1825, but with the late
Perp sandstone battlements and finials carved with linked
chevrons re-set on top. S aisle of similarly mixed stonework,
two-light windows with Y-tracery and two Dec ones with interlacing ogee arches and trefoils. The peal of bells, six of 1819,
two added later, is the only full set on the island. The N aisle
has two similar windows and one simpler Dec pattern, and a
tall W window with Perp tracery in ochre stone. The N aisle
was raised in coarse brown ashlar by *Hall*, to allow for galleries
within (removed 1902, the outline of rectangular gallery lights
still visible), but capped with the sandstone embattled parapet.
The chancel was apparently lengthened by two bays in the late
Perp; buttresses with two set-offs, limestone battlements,
elegant finials set diagonally. Three-light windows with cusping
under elliptical heads. In the Tudor remodelling the nave walls
were heightened in the brown stone to form a taller clerestory
and a shallower roof, and so was the S aisle. Of this stage also
the uncusped E windows to chancel and aisles, of five and four
lights respectively; the former has tracery below and above a
transom and is designed with sub-arches and full-height mullions. Plain S porch of the same period, formerly with a room
above. Restored by *G. F. Bodley* in 1902.

INTERIOR. The C14 S doorway has a plain continuous
chamfer with hoodmould and headstops. Low tower doorway
of the same date. Chancel arch also low, apparently the survivor
of a more modest project; two continuous orders of Dec wave
mouldings, foliage stops. The nave arcades on the other hand

are conventionally lofty: four bays of octagonal piers with two orders of wave mouldings dying into the imposts. Hoodmoulds on all faces, headstops only on the N of the S aisle. S clerestory of five circular windows with quatrefoils, C14; on the N, mullioned clerestory windows of the C16, like the fine low-pitched roof with its carved foliate bosses. Bare stone walls, the plaster having been scraped off by *Bodley* who paved the sanctuary with chequerboard slabs.

FITTINGS. REREDOS, with angels carved in wood, of some refinement, early C20. – STALLS. Remains of late C15 or early C16 chancel fittings as elaborate as Conwy's, perhaps brought from Llanfaes Friary at the Dissolution. On each side eight seats along the wall and two on the returns, each with a MISERICORD (eight being replacements of 1902). The traceried ends of the stalls are cut down. Desks to match, still with poppyhead ends. – PISCINA, S aisle. Small, with ogee arch. – FONT. Early C20, in mottled grey polished Penmon limestone. Each of the eight faces sharply carved with different Neo-Dec traceries, a piece of sophistication worthy of *Bodley*. – ORGAN LOFT, nave W bay. A large confection in C20 Gothic. ORGAN with three towers on the C18 pattern by *John Collins* of Liverpool, 1807, but rebuilt in 1862 by *Kirkhead & Jardine*. – STAINED GLASS. E window, Crucifixion, a strong composition across five lights, by *Clayton & Bell*, 1921. – Chancel S, re-set medieval fragments including heads of some quality, and a window of 1923 by *J. C. Bewsey*. – S aisle: E, Nativity and two saints, richly drawn, by *Kempe*, 1904, and S, the Presentation, 1899, old-fashioned, and then Noah and Moses, *Kempe*, 1906. – N aisle: E, Annunciation with David and Isaiah, *Kempe*, 1906; S, Baptism and Suffer the Children, *Wailes & Strang*, 1900, and SS Peter and John, *Kempe*, 1909.

MONUMENTS. The finest group in Anglesey, notable for heraldry and lettering. – W end of N aisle, a large late medieval alabaster table tomb, very like that at Penmynydd (q.v.). Effigies of William Bulkeley (†c. 1490) and his wife Elen Gruffudd of Penrhyn, a base with eighteen saints or bishops under Perp canopies. He is in armour, his head on a helmet and his feet on a lion, and she in robes hanging in folds and with two dogs at her feet. – Chancel E wall. Margaret Jones of Castellmarch †1609. Alabaster aedicule with Renaissance motifs. – Dr Thomas Caesar †1632. Baroque motifs and heraldry. – Large slab to Sir Henry Sidney K.G. †1563, with five shields of arms. – Chancel N wall. Thomas, 7th Viscount Bulkeley †1822, who had paid for restoration. By *Richard Westmacott*. Roman bust on a half-column, his wife seated mourning beside it and comforted by a standing hooded figure of Faith. – Charlotte Williams Bulkeley †1829, by *John Ternouth*. Kneeling young woman in a classical shift. – Captain Hugh Williams, killed in Grenada in 1795. Low-relief sarcophagus. – Brasses to Richard and Elizabeth Bulkeley with their children, in a Gothic niche c. 1531. – Anne Owen †1604, heraldic engraved brass. – Large Gothic memorial to David

Hughes †1609, who endowed the Free Grammar School and
almshouses; erected 1819. – s aisle. Nicely lettered brass listing
the town charities, 1745. – Margaret Hughes †1697 in mottled
grey 'marble' with Ionic columns. – Owen Owen †1833,
surgeon to His Majesty's 6th Regiment of Foot, and family,
beneath a Gothic wreath. – Porch. Monumental stone COFFIN
with carved lid in which Princess Joan, daughter of King John
and wife of Llywelyn the Great (cf. Llanrwst, Clwyd), was
buried at Llanfaes Friary in 1237. The lid shows a female figure
in relief with a wimple on the head and the hands open on the
breast, all below that being formalized as a floriated stem; at
its base a serpent biting a wyvern. The handling not without
Romanesque traces; the inscription recording its recovery by
Viscount Bulkeley, 1808. – s of chancel, table tomb with a
semicircular stone hood, similar to ones at Llanfaethlu and
Conwy, early to mid-C17.

OUR LADY QUEEN OF MARTYRS (R.C.), Rating Row. 1908–9.
Arts and Crafts Gothic in dark green stone with sandstone
dressings. Nave and short chancel, a broad free Perp-style
window over the porch.

PUBLIC BUILDINGS

TOWN HALL, Castle Street. Completed 1785, for Viscount
Bulkeley. Plain, of five bays with low sandstone arches and
stuccoed upper storey. The ground floor was originally open
for a market. Upstairs assembly room and other rooms with
guilloche mouldings to the dado rails and doorcases. There was
a connecting door through to the Bulkeley Hotel for gentry
attending functions. Bronze plaque in Latin, 1818, recording a
visit by the Tsar's brother.

COURT HOUSE, facing the town gate to the castle. Built in 1614
by the Anglesey justices. Only two stone doorframes with cambered arches to the porch and courtroom give a clue to its
august origin, since its irregular, low, rendered exterior has
Gothick windows and a semi-octagonal bay on the castle side.
The model for the court itself was evidently the great hall of
a house; three arch-braced hammerbeam trusses. A celure
pierced with a small cupola for light over the arena of the trials,
where the fittings are early C19. A medievalizing cove of
honour, of the Jacobean build, partly covers the Judge's seat,
and the bressumer above it is carved as though this were the
dais of a hall. To one side of the public space, which is
separated from the court by fearsome Regency railings, is a
raised desk or pew for the mayor and bailiffs of Beaumaris,
with a tester like an C18 pulpit. The projection to the E with
the Gothick details was the Grand Jury Room. Coved ceiling
and a pretty Regency stone fireplace in the Greek style.

GAOL and HOUSE OF CORRECTION, Rose Hill. Of 1828–9, by 90
Hansom & Welch. It incorporates many of the innovations of
the Millbank Penitentiary, London, of 1812–21 according to
Simon Thurley: a remarkable initiative for a provincial centre.

It is notable as an early survival of a prison on a radial-wing plan, with instructive mid-Victorian improvements. Sheer outer curtain walls broken only by buttresses and the entrance range, of huge blocks, screened by bare and massive ironwork. The use of rusticated limestone blocks contrasting with ashlared window jambs and lintels looks Piranesian.

The plan was originally a T set in a square, with daunting stonework to the yards so formed. Three unchanged corridors meet at the lower level, divided by arches and iron barriers. Upstairs, under an octagonal glass cupola, the governor's office projects as a canted bay with three glazed windows at the meeting of the corridors, to allow a clear view of the upper floor. The chapel furnishings are later C19.

At the end of the entry axis is the NEW WING of 1867–8, by *Robert Griffiths* subtly easier to the eye and the mind; the cell doorways have rounded frames, the iron gates are a bit more generous, the iron stairs and balcony even have decorative elements. In one yard a TREADWHEEL for six men, installed 1867, now the only surviving example in a British prison. It served to raise water to roof tanks whence it ran to every cell. Infirmary on the upper level, with a fireplace. The prison closed in 1878 and is now a museum.

BEAUMARIS PIER. 600 ft (185 metres) long, with no architectural pretensions, giving a panorama of the E approaches to the Strait. The original of 1846 was lengthened in 1873, was much shortened and halved in width in the C20.

PERAMBULATION

The inlet which fed salt water into the castle moat has been obscured, and silting has driven the shore further S from its C13 line, thus forming the GREEN in front of the castle, described as a 'delightful promenade' in 1834. Leading from the castle, the low twelve-bay terrace is GREEN EDGE of 1824–5 by *John Hall* of Bangor, the first development by the Corporation in reconstructing the town as a resort. Central pediment on its plain roughcast front; canted bay on the r. end, facing E up the coast (the reading room of the Beaumaris Book Society?). The pretty trelliswork veranda is an addition. Next is the Corporation's much more ambitious VICTORIA TERRACE, completed 1833, by *Hansom & Welch*. The Bath-like proportions of this bold limestone group of ten houses set a marker for Beaumaris that was not to be repeated. Canted plan, adapted to its headland position: the E wing looks to the Great Orme, the W wing to views of the mountains, and the angle between them is resolved in a grand pedimented block. At the SW a segmental transition leads to a return side looking towards the Strait. Most houses have three bays with arched windows in linear rustication below and tall straight-headed ones above. The pedimental block has four bays and five pilasters with sunk panelling. Only No. 1 remains a single house, the rest are subdivided. Behind, a long MEWS.

Set back is a short row with CHAUNTRY HOUSE, a small house in the same Penmon stone, and GWYNFA, a gabled addition, 1860s. Then the garden front of the BULKELEY HOTEL (*see* Castle Street), *c.* 1835, by *Hansom & Welch*. Parts of the town walls were demolished to provide material for the project.

Further round to the w is a three-sided group of Baron Hill estate terraces backing onto Castle Street, filling the space between the hotel and the hot baths. Plans were made in the 1840s by *David Roberts* but the first houses were built as late as 1857. BULKELEY TERRACE, plain, hipped and three-storey, was partly built by 1861. The two short rows at right angles, RAGLAN STREET, r., and ALMA STREET, l., date from the 1850s. Just beyond is a castellated chimney, possibly the only surviving part of the HOT BATHS which *Hansom & Welch* may have designed in the late 1820s. Turning inland to Castle Street, the constriction of Bulkeley Terrace marks the site of the two-towered medieval West Gate.

CASTLE STREET is architecturally the finest in Anglesey, with buildings from the C15 onward, completely straight. The LIVERPOOL ARMS and BISHOPSGATE HOUSE just w are externally later C18. The former has a seven-bay front of sash windows, raised to three storeys in the mid C19, but a C17 staircase within. The latter, of five bays, has a central gable and a later C18 Chinese Chippendale staircase. Much of the rest of this broad and somewhat English street consists of pleasant modestly classical fronts, some lower ones C17 or C18, with many two-and-a-half or three-storey fronts of the mid C19. No. 32 is a reminder that Beaumaris was a town of timber buildings for centuries. Behind the diminutive herringbone timber frontage of its parlour block, the remnant of a hall of *c.* 1400. Within the GEORGE AND DRAGON is a timber-framed merchant's house dated 1610 with wall paintings in the upper hall including the mottoes NOSCE TE IPSUM and DEUS PROVIDEBIT. The exterior is early C19, altered. Further on, at the corner of Rating Row, the Bull's Head and No. 10, on the opposite corner, of C17 origin. THE BULL'S HEAD, with a bland façade of scribed stucco in two parts, has a rainwater head marked TIB 1766. The l. side looks C18 with an early C19 parapet to match the added three r. bays. No. 10 was Tŷ Mawr, later C17 as evidenced by the diagonally set end chimneys. Tall three-storey stuccoed front with Late Georgian sashes.

On the s side, the Town Hall (*see* above) and the BULKELEY HOTEL, the finest of its date in Wales. By *Hansom & Welch*, *c.* 1835. Tall limestone palazzo of five bays; the pedimented first-floor windows for the ballroom. Porch with square pillars with incised Soanean decoration, and coat of arms. Inside, a sub-Grecian stair to a half-landing that gave access to the Town Hall, and two flights back up to a landing and the arch to the ballroom. On the N side, at the w end, Nos. 2–4, a handsome Late Georgian pair for the Baron Hill estate. Brick, with triple sashes on the main floors; No. 4 stuccoed.

Turning N up RATING ROW, the three stone gables of the Bull's Head STABLES on the l., c. 1800. Central early C19 gateway with a wicket in its enormous wooden gate. The chimney over the gate draws smoke from the house to the N. Near the R.C. church, a SURGERY of 1996 by *Gwilym Evans* of *Ap Thomas Partnership*. LITTLE LANE runs W parallel to Castle Street to CHURCH STREET, the broad main cross-axis of the medieval town. Until 1869 Henblas stood on the W, the sprawling medieval house of the Bulkeley family. On the site, the harsh Gothic former ENGLISH PRESBYTERIAN CHAPEL, 1870, by *R. G. Thomas*, and the terraces of Margaret Street. On Church Street, to the S, half-concealed, the former WESLEYAN CHAPEL, 1859, altered 1896 and 1906, now shops. The painted panelled gallery on four sides survives. Opposite, shops around the open market, 1826, single-storey. Further up, opposite the church, a stepped three-storey group, of which No. 24, in fine limestone, is of c. 1830 by *Hansom & Welch*, all originally with integral shops. No. 26 much lower, a former inn; Nos. 28–30 later C18 with low gables and oriel windows.

MARGARET STREET, with late C19 terraces in red brick, leads to Steeple Lane, the start of the small streets outside the circuit of the walls. On the corner of CHAPEL STREET, the stuccoed Italianate former SEION INDEPENDENT CHAPEL, 1873, now a house, a good conversion retaining the ceiling. Further on, the hipped CAPEL Y DRINDOD (Calvinistic Methodist), probably of 1833–4, remodelled in 1873 and restored lavishly in 2007. Galleried interior, the gallery front in long and square panels. A return to STEEPLE LANE, climbing NW with the gaol walls, l., and an early C20 PARISH ROOM, r., at the back of the churchyard, opposite a former NATIONAL SCHOOL, dated 1816. A nameless street, sometimes called BUNKER'S HILL runs SW past the gaol (*see* above). Then, r., into Rose Hill, and l., into NEW STREET, where the FIRE STATION neatly occupies a gabled mullioned school of 1880, by *R. G. Thomas*. The high perimeter walls were of the C18 Anglesey Militia BARRACKS. NEW STREET runs back to Steeple Lane which curves NE to WEXHAM STREET. Nos. 2–10 are very attractive single-storey C18 cottages each with an attic dormer over the door. No. 30, W, dated 1772, is the earliest dated brick house in the town. STANLEY STREET, l., is entirely of red brick, c. 1850, opposed rows of paired two-storey houses with stone window frames and entries from arched passageways. A model housing scheme for the Baron Hill estate, flanking a former drive, marked at the Maes Hyfryd end by magnificent Cockerellesque gatepiers with urns. Facing the Wexham Street end, gatepiers and lodge of a disused drive to Baron Hill (*see* opposite).

MAES HYFRYD, exemplary housing by *S. Colwyn Foulkes*, 1950, consists of curved terraces with houses stepping both on plan and in height. A few original windows survive. On Iscoed, the COUNTY PRIMARY SCHOOL, by the County Architect, *N. Squire Johnson*, 1947. Long and low; white-rendered wings splayed each side of a brick tower.

Returning down Rating Row to the R.C. church, and turning l., the former GRAMMAR SCHOOL is by the modern library. Founded 1603. Rubble stone single-storey schoolroom with mullion-and-transom windows. Two-storey, two-bay house, r., with C18 windows and an added low stuccoed attic storey. Much restored in 1926, it survived as a secondary school until 1962. The old town pumps are reset outside. The lane runs on to Castle Street opposite the Court House (*see* above).

w of Chapel Street the curve of the bay is fronted by detached and paired houses, several dating from before Lord Bulkeley's coast road of 1805. The battered sea wall is partly of Cornish masonry. Facing SW, THE WEST END is a plain terrace of seven houses dated 1869. Along TOWNSEND, PORTH HIR is dated 1605, much altered. CLEIFIOG and the house to the E were the Custom House. HENDREF and LLWYNCELYN, a tall pair in grey Penmon stone, must date from the beginnings of the resort. TROS-YR-AFON, with C19 curving bay roofs and Gothic bargeboards, began as a C17 lobby-entry house, to which three houses were added to form a short row. THE BRYN, set back, is on a site marked on Speed's 1610 map. The 1712 plaque on the lodge may date the formal end-chimney house with a rear stair-tower. Speed's map also shows Briton's Mills in the Nant Meigan valley behind. Established as early as *c.* 1500, by Robert de Vieilleville, natural son of Henry VII. The hillside above the coast road covered by the C20 Cae Mair housing estate was sacrificed by the Baron Hill estate to save the castle meadows from compulsory purchase.

BARON HILL

High on the coastal slope above Beaumaris, ½ m. W, with panoramic views E and S. Ruins of a large Italianate mansion, largely rebuilt by *Henry Harrison* after a fire in 1836. Both house and park, of distinguished C18 design, were slowly remodelled on a larger scale till the 1860s and after, but damage while in military use in 1945 doomed the house. p. 112

The history of this important site is little recorded, but merits analysis. A stone house or lodge was built in 1618 by Sir Richard Bulkeley to accommodate Henry, Prince of Wales (whose favourite he was), on his progress to Ireland to act as viceroy; Sir Richard's Royalist son Thomas was created Viscount Bulkeley in 1644. Two successor houses encased this first house, and both have burned, so what remains of its high grey schist walls can be seen as the ruinous additions fall away. A painting shows the site *c.* 1700, and Samuel Wyatt's plans give the C17 form within the enlarged house (*see* below). The four-storey front, enclosed in a yard entered by a step-gabled archway and with a formal avenue, faced N, away from the Strait. It had a one-bay porch-tower between one-bay corner

Beaumaris, Baron Hill.
Engraving by Conrad Metz, 1779

towers, and a skyline with many chimneys. The 'old smoaky
hall', set longitudinally in the single-pile plan, had columnar
screens at either end and four niches in the long walls. An older
two-storey house to the W had become its service wing. Below
was a garden enclosed by brick walls.

The 7th Viscount Bulkeley, one of the few wealthy C18
Welshmen to visit Rome, commissioned *Samuel Wyatt* to
enlarge the house into a villa. His architectural assistant was
John Cooper (cf. Bodorgan and Plas Newydd, Llanedwen,
pp. 116, 152). This house, of 1776–9, is known from an engraving and from plans. A full-height bow with attic and shallow
dome was added on the side facing the Strait; lower octagonal
towers added either side created an effect (on a much smaller
scale) like the Dukes of Savoy's hunting lodge at Stupinigi,
near Turin. The bow was occupied by the dining room, one of
the lateral towers by the drawing room. The effect of theatri-
cality and excessive height (it had three storeys and an attic),
criticized in Evans's *Beauties of North Wales* in 1812, was
increased by balustraded parapets on the central block and
conical roofs on the wings.

The fire of 1836 burned this house back to the brickwork.
Rebuilding began promptly; the rainwater heads are dated
1838. The client was Sir Richard Bulkeley Williams-Bulkeley,
10th Bt (†1875), grandson of the second wife of the 6th
Viscount. What survives is largely of the florid Italian style popularized by Barry and Salvin. *Henry Harrison*'s S façade has

only two massively articulated storeys, the lower with channelled rustication; the N façade has many, oddly cramped, round-headed windows. Interior of fireproof construction with iron beams; full-height main staircase with a scrolly balustrade, designed 1843. A little of the elaborate and slightly French plasterwork still clings to the walls; but Baron Hill's ante-room with Corinthian pilasters, its saloon with columnar screen and carved mirror frames, and its dining room with rich plasterwork and semi-octagonal end, have become vanished dreams.

Other elements of the 7th Viscount Bulkeley's vision remain. He leased then bought Beaumaris Castle (of which his family had long held the post of Constable) from the Crown, and with the help of the landscape architect *William Emes* set about integrating house and castle (and the remains of the Franciscan friary of Llanfaes (q.v.), since lost) into a park of high quality. This has since been overlaid by C19 work near the house. To its W a broad Italianate PARTERRE, at a lower level to the balustraded TERRACE on the S of the house. This was extended by a long walk to meet the main downhill axis (connecting visually with the drive at the N at a lost Ionic balcony) at a circular FOUNTAIN BASIN. Spreading most of this distance, but at a higher level and hidden by trees, are the disproportionately vast SERVICE COURTYARDS and STABLES added to Wyatt's or Cooper's single yard facing N.

The origins of the PARK are obscure. *Emes*'s lost plan of *c.* 1780 survives in part in the long greensward sloping down from house to castle. This is crossed imperceptibly by the older road, E, as a result of its being sunk. In the landscape surviving clumps of oak, which with clumps of pine framed the house and shaded the deer. Of the *Wyatt* or *Cooper* period the small twin-towered Gothic stone EAST LODGE at the top of the park, and the low brick OCTAGON in paddocks NE of the house, where racehorses ferried from Chester were stabled.

The VICTORIAN PARK was laid out with a long drive connecting with the C19 road to Menai Bridge, W. The inclined rock-cut route includes a Picturesque BRIDGE with pylon buttresses and LODGE of *c.* 1840 over the Llansadwrn lane. Its entrance on the coast road was embellished with the GRAND LODGE (*see* Llandegfan).

OBELISK, 90 ft (28 metres) high, on the skyline above Llanfaes, *c.* 1880, in memory of Sir Richard Bulkeley Williams-Bulkeley. Architect unknown. It has a slightly hard quality characteristic of the engineering aspects of the Victorian park and garden.

BENLLECH 5282

Seaside resort. Some older buildings of *c.* 1900 on the main road, otherwise a combination of C20 housing for the retired, and holiday jumble. W of the main road, BREEZE HILL, a housing estate by *B. Hallwood Lingard & Associates*, 1959–66.

St Andrew. One of the few modern Anglican churches in
Gwynedd, by *North & Padmore*, 1964. Roughcast, with full-
height windows. A lofty bright interior, painted brick and a
zigzag section ceiling. PULPIT and DESK, plain boxes of grey
polished stone decorated with gilded braiding. Matching
PISCINA and tapering hexagonal FONT.

Our Lady of Lourdes (R.C.), Beach Road. By *S. Powell
Bowen*, 1967. Two roughcast and slated monopitch roofs rise
steeply for the altar spaces. Dramatic interior, quite low then
opening up above the sanctuary.

BETHEL *see* TREFDRAETH

BODEDERN

Almost a small town, noted in the C19 for woollen mills.
The centre terraces press on a narrow grid of streets, their
stonework hidden by modern render. E of the Crown Hotel, a
Doric aedicule with limestone columns shelters the WATER
PUMP, given in 1897 by the Stanleys of Penrhos. Four small
chapels: SOAR WESLEYAN, 1822, the birthplace of the break-
away Wesle Bach movement *c.* 1831, a simple long-wall chapel
with arched windows and chapel house in line; SARON
INDEPENDENT, 1880 and 1907, with Ionic columned porch and
a wheel window; TABERNACLE BAPTIST, 1829, altered 1857 and
1884; and GILGAL CALVINISTIC METHODIST, 1911. Just W,
below the church, are farmyards.

St Edern. Medieval. Built of the local blue-green stone with its
undulating bedding, and raised high in a square churchyard in
the tight context of the C19 townscape. The nave, though much
rebuilt with the old stones in 1871 by *Kennedy & O'Donoghue*,
is essentially C14 – see the N doorway with its continuous wave
mouldings. Many Perp improvements: S doorway in a boldly
moulded frame, porch with arch-braced trusses, two paired
cinquefoiled windows on the S, one on the W wall, two more
N. Chancel, N transept, W bellcote and S porch doorway with
detail of 1871; but the four-centred arched E window, with
three-light tracery and again boldly scooped outer and inner
reveals, is C15. The roofs of nave and chancel, close-set arched
braces as though for barrel ceilings, also make it likely that a
chancel was added in the C15. The continuously moulded
chancel arch and N transept arch are Victorian. – SANCTUARY
WOODWORK with Edwardian Wrenaissance carved foliage. –
W GALLERY with balustraded front dated 1771. – FONT,
medieval, octagonal, disused. – STAINED GLASS. E, Crucifixion, style of *David Evans*, *c.* 1849. Transept, Epiphany in a
Morrisian landscape, *c.* 1890, by *Mayer*. Window by *Celtic
Studios*, 1951. – In the transept, C6 INSCRIBED STONE, marked
ERGAGNI laterally from the top, the name also found in

Llansaint, Carms. – Other MONUMENTS. Chunky Grecian memorial to Lt William Wynn Jones of the Bengal Native Infantry †1835 by *H. Hopper* of London. – In the sanctuary, Neoclassical tablet to Elizabeth Jones †1839 by *C. M. Seddon* of Liverpool. Finely lettered slate tablet to Lt Morys Wynn Jones †1914.

PRESADDFED, 1 m. E. A C17 estate house, partly rebuilt by John Owen after 1712 (see the arms over the doorway), and externally remodelled in 1821 with Tudor hoodmoulds. Three generous bays and two storeys, with gables, built around a five-bay classical house. Originally there were two house units, the early C17 one, l., incorporated only in 1875. The more important unit, of 1685, retains a room with an old-fashioned strapwork plaster frieze. Staircase with paired twisted balusters and a handrail with a stepped profile underneath. Over the gate to the large walled GARDEN beside the house the evidence for the Renaissance garden layout in the inscription NIL TEMETE and the date 1618. The gardens are said to have been replanned in the early C20 by *Gertrude Jekyll*.

PRESADDFED BURIAL CHAMBER, just W (SH 348 809). Two groups of stones about 2 m. apart. The S one is standing, a polygonal chamber sufficiently intact to have sheltered an evicted family in the C18. The N group consists of one large standing stone with two others fallen beside it. No cairn survives. In view of the unexpected results of the excavation of Trefignath (Holyhead) it would be unwise to try to interpret these stones too precisely.

Not far away at Arfryn (SH 342 800) excavation revealed a large CEMETERY of simple inhumation graves surrounding a small wooden structure which may have been a shrine, one marked by the C6 stone now in the church.

BODEWRYD 4091

Church, Plas and dovecote together, 2½ m. SE of Cemaes.

ST MARY. Tiny rectangular, medieval, with W bellcote. Tudor three-light E window. N porch/transept in which the round-headed S doorway of *c.* 1500 has been re-set. Repairs by *Kennedy & O'Donoghue*, 1867, for the 3rd Lord Stanley. – STAINED GLASS. Late C19, by *Powells*. Decorative, containing Islamic motifs. – BRASS to Margaret Wynn †1723.

PLAS BODEWRYD, opposite the church, N. Large and irregular. White stucco, sashes. A late medieval core, with lateral fireplace, built by the Wynn family. Extended N and S, and a stair wing E, all late C17.

DOVECOTE on an eminence above the house, C18 square tower with four plain gables above the alighting shelf. Within, some 400 nest holes formed in brick.

STANDING STONES. One ¼ m. SE, SH 406 903, stands more than 13 ft (4 metres) high. Another is in a field 2 m. NNW near Burwen, SH 415 928.

BODFFORDD see HENEGLWYS

BODORGAN

The peninsula between the Aberffraw dunes and the Malltraeth sands.

BODORGAN HALL. In *c.* 1559 the then small estate of Bodorgan was leased to Richard Meyrick, when his brother became Bishop of Bangor. A survey by Lewis Morris in 1724–7 shows a centrally planned C17 house on a rectangular yard, approached from the sea by an avenue terminating at the shore in an ellipse. The present house ('different plans' by *John Wolfe* having been rejected) is a well-documented work of *John Cooper* of Beaumaris, 1779–84, with alterations of 1861 by *John Gibson.* The patron was Owen Putland Meyrick, whose family had inherited farms all over the island.

The original entry front has nine bays, the central three in a semicircular bow reached by paired curving steps. The sandstone for the ashlar astylar façade was quarried on the shore and erected by the mason *Samuel Forrest.* Cooper had just finished working on Samuel Wyatt's Baron Hill, Beaumaris (p. 111), and in plan and elevation, and in the layout of the service and estate buildings, Bodorgan is his most Wyatt-influenced project. It has a circular saloon between rectangular corner rooms, decorated with Neoclassical plaster friezes and Kilkenny marble fireplaces, and the main staircase in an apse. The C19 alterations introduced richer materials like scagliola columns and stained glass by *Thomas Baillie,* and replaced the small-paned windows with plate glass. At the same time the entrance was moved E and given paired Doric columns, while the drive to seaward was replaced with garden terraces.

Service yard arranged with a central corridor. Octagonal game larder. Circular dovecote.

STABLES. Of *c.* 1780 and of *c.* 1825, the COACHHOUSES of the second period.

LODGE. Late Georgian, square, with a central chimney, the pyramidal roof coming low over verandas on each side. It stands by a GATEWAY with concave wing walls ending in square piers capped with exquisitely flat stones. SARN LODGE is Victorian Tudor.

(HOME FARM. Large courtyard with accretions. Barn with dressed quoins and ashlar segmental arches. Cowhouses and cartsheds dating from the widespread farm improvements of the later C19.)

(BODOWEN, ½ m. SW. The seat of the Owen family, demolished in the C19. One wall of its courtyard stands, with a late C16 cambered arch with a pediment on semi-octagonal pilasters. Two other gateways survive, one the main entrance to the house reconstructed in 1652 and having the initials OHA. Raised terrace N of the courtyard.)

TWYN-Y-PARC PROMONTORY FORT (SH 370 650). A classic example, on a narrow, rocky finger of land pushing out into Malltraeth Bay and cut off at the narrow landward end by quite elaborate defences. The main defence is a huge inner rampart, still 16 ft (5 metres) high, running E–W between two creeks. The entrance must have been at the W end but the other side of the gateway has been lost to erosion. Outside this rampart is a much weaker one, which has a wide entrance where a rocky ridge provides a natural roadway into the fort. The only comfortable living site within the steep and rocky interior is likely to have been on the narrow strip of flat land just behind the great inner rampart, though no hut platforms can be seen there. Random excavations inside produced evidence for occupation during the Roman period, but like so many Anglesey hill-forts, it is likely that the promontory was first defended during later prehistory.

BODWROG

4078

ST TWROG (SH 401 776). Small rectangular church on a rocky outcrop. Bodwrog was a dependency of Holyhead, which must explain the surprisingly grand Perp E window with cusped panel tracery and elaborately cusped sanctuary S window. S and N doorways with elliptical and four-centred heads and carved spandrels, in casement-moulded frames. The Bulkeley bull's head over the S doorway. – Matching PULPIT and READING DESK in the sanctuary, each side of the E window; late C18 or early C19. – Simple painted BOX PEWS. – FONT. Small cylindrical tub of gritstone, of unknown date.

The church is isolated 1 m. NE of Gwalchmai, beyond BODWROG, one of the largest Baron Hill estate farms. The much altered Neo-Tudor twin-gabled farmhouse is dated 1840, the large farmyard with elliptical-arched barns and sheds 1832.

BRITANNIA BRIDGE see LLANFAIRPWLL

BRYNDU

3573

Between Llanfaelog and Tŷ Croes station. Mostly C20 but with two large windmill towers, both now houses, MELIN UCHAF, 1785, and MELIN-Y-BONT, 1825, the latter a combined wind and water mill. On the W approach, CYNLAS, dated 1902, an ornate villa with arched windows and a spired corner bay.

BRYNDU CALVINISTIC METHODIST CHAPEL. 1901. Said to
have cost £3,700, which seems high. A late example in
unpainted cement of the giant-arched façade popularized by
the Rev. Thomas Thomas in the 1860s (cf. Salem, Porthmadog). Rich Late Victorian interior, similar to Horeb at
Brynsiencyn: curved panelled gallery, timber-bordered ceiling
with elaborate plaster and good build-up from curved *sêt-fawr*
to platform pulpit with carved panels and finally to Corinthian
pilastered aedicule. John Elias preached his first Anglesey
sermon here in 1796. Forecourt RAILINGS from the *Black
Bridge Foundry*, Holyhead.

BRYNGWRAN

3578

Linear settlement on Telford's Holyhead Road. In the centre, the
IORWERTH ARMS, mid-C19 in green stone, three-bay with
fanlight.

HOLY TRINITY. 1841 by *John Lloyd* of Caernarfon, to replace
two medieval churches, Llechylched, 1 m. SW (SH 340 767) and
Holy Rood, Ceirchiog, ½ m. ESE (SH 361 769) (churchyards
still visible). Small, in green stone. Nave with W porch and
bellcote, short chancel. Square mullion-and-transom windows,
more school-like than church. Reordered 1867 by *Kennedy &
O'Donoghue*.

BRYNSIENCYN

4767

A long closely built main street, mostly C19 and later, from which
workers commuted weekly to the Dinorwic slate quarries across
the Strait. A few *croglofft* houses of the C18 survive. E of Horeb
chapel, DOLYDD, mid-C19 former police station with the typical
hipped roof and arched double chimney. Beyond the village,
towards the church, former NATIONAL SCHOOL, *c.* 1843, two
rooms and a porch, the master's house beside with gablets and
another porch. The area around appears to have been particularly
well settled in Romano-British times.

ST NIDAN, E of the village on the main road. A replacement for
Llanidan church (q.v.) by the shore, which fell into ruin in the
C18. Built 1839–43 for Lord Boston by *John Welch*, similar to
his church at Llandudno but bolder. Cruciform, the broad
gables with triple big lancets. Single lancets to the nave. W
tower, parapet originally gabled for a clock, but made top-
heavy with battlements in 1933, like a water tower. Quarter-
round additions for organ and vestry in the chancel angles.
Inside, four equal and bold crossing arches, and crowded
seating in the nave and W gallery, pre-Ecclesiological. – FONT,
from Llanidan church. C13, circular, sharply carved with an
interlacing fleur-de-lys design. – RELIQUARY, found buried

under the altar at Llanidan. Perhaps C16. Gabled arched stone
chest, the sides canted forward, the front cut away as a window
onto what it protected. – STAINED GLASS. E triplet, Faith,
Hope and Charity, by *Heaton, Butler & Bayne*, 1877. N triplet,
Ascension, *Shrigley & Hunt*, 1929. Outside, N, BUST of Sir Ellis
Ellis-Griffith M.P. †1926, in a wing collar, late C19.

HOREB CALVINISTIC METHODIST CHAPEL. 1883, by
O. Morris Roberts. A powerful winged façade in two tones of
grey stone with almost white rock-faced stone quoins. Broad
front with four arched windows over linked porches and stair
wings gabled at right angles. Elaborate woodwork, the pulpit
with arcaded panels, the U-plan gallery with varied panels,
some with tiny balusters. A rich arched plaster aedicule on the
back wall. Two-storey VESTRY, remodelled from the former
chapel of 1841.

GARN BURIAL MOUND, on the lane to Llanidan (SH 487 669).
A large round mound intact to a height of over 6 ft (almost
2 metres), on a sloping site overlooking the Strait, one of the
best examples on the island.*

CAER IDRIS, ½ m. NE of the church (SH 494 679). Very little
remains of this small hill-fort in the wood, the only multivallate
fort in Anglesey with close-set ramparts. A good deal of the
interior has been lost to quarrying and to the road, but the
entrance survives on the SE side. On the W side three ramparts,
on the E four. The ends are overlapped so that the entry zigzags
between them, although the gateways would seem to be fool-
ishly wide. Some large stones can be seen in the third rampart.

CAER LEB, ¾ m. NW (SH 473 674). An imposingly defended
native settlement of the C1–C3. The enclosure is straight-sided,
slightly bowed on the E, where the entrance is (other breaks in
the banks are modern). It was defended by two banks and by
two still very wet ditches. The outer bank has been flattened
on the N and E but the inner one remains to an imposing height
all round. Probably built more to impress than defend, for the
site is low-lying, overlooked by higher ground to the E. C19
excavation revealed some rectangular buildings against the E
rampart and a round hut in the centre, which produced
evidence of C3 occupation.

HUT CIRCLES. The remains of an open Romano-British 'village'
in the corner of the field just NE of Pont Sarn Las (SH 470
679). One round hut can be recognized as a circular hollow
and other foundations can just be made out. A straggling group
of huts, extending along the riverbank for almost ½ m., were
mostly removed by agricultural improvement in the 1870s.
There were several of these villages in the area, obviously a
prosperous place during the Roman period. It is interesting to
speculate on the social differences between these unenclosed
settlements and the enclosed homestead at Caer Leb.

---

*There were other Bronze Age burials (though their barrows are not recorded) in
similar situations, near Moel-y-don (Llanedwen) and on the Caernarvonshire shore.

CASTELL BRYN GWYN, 1 m. W (SH 465 670). A large embanked enclosure with a deep outer ditch, now filled in, with a confusing history. It may have begun as a later Neolithic 'Henge' monument, like Bryn Celli Ddu (Llanddaniel Fab, q.v.) but without the inner ring of stones. The remains of this first bank and ditch were reused, the ditch redug and the bank heightened more than once, during the Roman period and perhaps even by a band of marauding Vikings. There is an intriguing reference to 'King Olaf's Castle' somewhere near and this is the most likely site.

BRYNGWYN STANDING STONES, further W (SH 462 669). Two enormous monoliths in the field hedge, the largest in Anglesey. Early (and confused) references suggest that they are the remains of a huge circle of stones. However they may never have been more than a pair, like those at Plas Meilw, Holyhead. In the early C19 the thinner stone was incorporated into the end of a small cottage. Notches for the purlins can still be seen.

CAERGEILIOG
3279

One of the new villages clustered lineally on the new Holyhead road. The origin is marked by the octagonal TOLL HOUSE at the W end, one of five built by *Telford c.* 1820, two-storey with deep eaves and a central chimney. This one has a single-storey wing but lacks the iron veranda. The village demonstrates a greater variety of the local C19 house types than most of the A5 villages: single-storey houses placed at right angles to the road; two-storey mid-C19 terraces; and from the Late Victorian period Y FRON DEG, a tall house in a formal gated garden.

ST DAVID. 1920. Small Arts and Crafts-influenced church in green stone. Battered buttresses, Gothic porch and asymmetrical bellcote. – STAINED GLASS. E window *c.* 1920.

CAPEL COCH see LLANFIHANGEL TRE'R BEIRDD

CARMEL see LLECHGYNFARWY

CEMAES
3793

Of some size compared with others on the N coast, the attractive HARBOUR has two quays of Cornish mason-work and a breakwater of 1828–35, built by *Ishmael Jones* after storm damage, repaired 1889 and 1900. Modest houses back from the waterside, some of C18 origin, like TŶ'N CEFN, Glascoed Road, two-storey, two-chimneyed but measuring no more than 22 by 18 ft (7 by 5.5 metres) externally. The HIGH STREET running inland is a Victorian town in miniature, mostly two-storey terraces. In the centre, the VILLAGE HALL, 1898, by *Richard Owens &*

Son of Liverpool. With a clock tower in front, turning octagonal at the top. Main gable filled with patterned terracotta. It was a generous benefaction with a concert hall, news and smoking room, reading room and library, and keeper's house behind. At the main road, the church (*see* below), with Bethesda chapel out to the w. s of the road, the CEMAES BRICKWORKS, SH 373 931, with Hoffman kiln and a prominent chimney, built 1907, closed 1914. It was connected to the quay by a narrow-gauge railway. On the Llanfechell road MELIN CEMAES windmill.

ST PATRICK. *Kennedy & Rogers*, 1865, for the convenience of the town (the ancient church of Llanbadrig, q.v., being 1½ m. away). Grouped lancets in recessed panels with dentilated heads. Weak. Closely spaced scissor trusses in the nave, rounded type in the chancel. Stone addition N by *N. Squire Johnson*, 1980s. – STAINED GLASS. E window and another by *Powells*, 1911.

BETHEL CONGREGATIONAL CHAPEL, High Street. 1910. Small, with an entertaining tower in stucco and roughcast, topped by a slated pyramid.

BETHESDA CALVINISTIC METHODIST CHAPEL, Holyhead Road, SW of the town, 1860s. A typical hipped chapel in stucco with arched windows, minimal but pleasing in its orderliness. Four windows, the centre two short over a big arched doorway. School of 1894 behind.

WYLFA NUCLEAR POWER STATION, 1½ m. W. Plans were announced in 1961 to build a Magnox reactor on this otherwise protected coast, to be linked by pylon lines across North Wales' finest landscapes. It was built in 1962–71 by British Nuclear Design and Construction, the elevations by *Farmer & Dark*, landscaping by *Sylvia Crowe & Associates*. Twin gas-cooled reactors, then the largest in the world, housed in two cylindrical structures 180 ft (55 metres) high, sited N and S with a service complex beside them; the turbine house is 170 ft (52 metres) long. The huge mass of concrete is treated externally as narrow canted walls on a polyhedrous plan round each 96-ft (30-metre) pressure vessel. All elements rise to the same height – though the simplicity of the first concept has been diluted by additions. Water for cooling comes from intakes 500 ft (150 metres) offshore. The excavated material was used as artificial hills to screen the power station in some views from Cemaes to the E. From the W there is no hiding its dark-grey brooding bulk.

CEMLYN

3393

A scattered settlement around Cemlyn Bay on the N coast, a site considered for the Irish packet port but rejected in favour of Holyhead. A causeway of Cornish masonry leads to BRYN ABER on the W side, house of the pioneer aviator and birdwatcher Capt. Vivian Hewitt, who built the high windbreak walls as part of his

Cemlyn Bay bird reserve in 1939. Llanrhwydrys church is down a lane to the W, past TÝ'N LLAN, early C19.

ST RHWYDRYS, Llanrhwydrys (SH 322 932). Recently conserved small church in part of a circular *llan*. With Llanbabo, one of only two constructed with crucks to survive on the island. Short nave, with C12 S doorway of undressed voussoirs, and possibly C14 W bellcote. Comparatively long chancel, unusually with its original gable copings, to which an undatable N transept is added. The early C15 E window has two ogee lights and panel tracery, and angels holding shields as stops. If the Romanesque church consisted of the tiny nave, the chamfers and abaci of the tall pointed chancel arch date the remodelling to the C13. Is it then reasonable to assert that the crucks – two pairs in the chancel, one in the nave – are also C13? Each is crudely braced to form a pointed arch. All are buried in the stone walls except the N half of the E couple, exposed through opening up for the transept. Over the sanctuary a C19 celure. W GALLERY dated 1776. – FONT. C12, circular, with a band round the base. – Early C19 LYCHGATE.

PLAS CEMLYN, 1 m. E. A group of C16–C18 vernacular farm buildings and farm house, well conserved, which contrasts with so many structures around.

(GAFNAN/FELIN GAFNAN, 1½ m. E. Group of C18 and C19 stone-built mill buildings, on the seashore at Porth y Felin. C18 WATER MILL with C19 corn-milling machinery. Nearby C18 DRYING KILN now used as a cowshed. Opposite is the former MILLER'S HOUSE dating from the early C19, and remains of the earlier (C18) miller's house and shippons.)

4275

CERRIG CEINWEN

Isolated church on a lane W of Llangristiolus.

ST CEINWEN (SH 424 737). 1860, by *Kennedy & Rogers*. Plain lancet style with W bellcote. The inner lintel of the S door is a reused C12 slab incised with a four-petal cross in a circle, the arms billeted and the shaft cut with joggled joints. – FONT. C12, slightly tapering cylinder with five panels, four filled with interlace, crosses and knots. – CROSS-SHAFT. The upper part of a simple C9–C11 shaft incised with a four-leaf cross in a circle. – MEMORIAL. Morris Lloyd, Royalist, †1647.

ST CEINWEN'S WELL set into the rock S of the church.

4482

COEDANA

A roadside village SE of Llanerchymedd.

ST ANEU. In a mostly round *llan*. Rebuilt 1894 in mechanical C13 Gothic. – FONT, cylindrical, dated 1702.

Tŷ Hen Newydd, ½ m. N. Late C18 or early C19 geometrically planned model farm. Like the stable court at Henblas, Llangristiolus, but around five sides of an octagon, and much smaller. Central block with hayloft, elliptical-headed doorways in the canted sections, elliptical arches for cartsheds in the ends. On the diameter, a decorative building with an *œil de boeuf* and catslide roofs. What connects these extravagances? The three-bay farmhouse is conventionally Late Georgian.

DULAS

4890

The area N of Traeth Dulas, the estuary of the Goch, largely occupied by the Llysdulas estate. The settlement on the main road is called City Dulas. The Victorian church is reached by a lane running SE from Penysarn.

St Gwenllwyfo Old Church. In a circular *llan* NE of Llysdulas. Medieval, rectangular, now ruined and recently reduced to 5-ft (1.5-metre) walls. This historic parish church of Llanwenllwyfo was restored in the C18, the date of the lychgate arch towards the park of Llysdulas. The medieval roof collapsed in 1950, following abandonment in favour of the Victorian church.

St Gwenllwyfo (SH 477 893). A Victorian estate church with its needle spire rising over trees. One of *Kennedy*'s better works, built in 1856 for Lady Dinorben of Llysdulas (a big slate tablet shows she gave £936 towards the cost of £1,417). Long chancel and nave in lancet style. Narrow W tower and disproportionately tall masonry spire. – FONT. From the old church, retooled. Octagonal lobed bowl on a new base. – MONUMENTS. Gertrude, Lady Dinorben, †1871, by *Morris* of London. – Two carved mandorla-shaped marble tablets, to Sir Arundell Neave †1877, by *Morris*, and his wife Gwen †1916. – BRASS to Marcelie Lloyd †1607, daughter of David Lloyd of Llysdulas. She kneels with her husband Richard Williams between their three sons. Three lozenge-shaped HATCHMENTS, with the arms of Sir Arundell Neave, Lady Dinorben and Lord Dinorben. – STAINED GLASS. Sir Arundell Neave presented the outstanding panels of early C16 Flemish stained glass collected by his grandfather Sir Thomas Neave, inserted 1877. There are several series, including the E window tracery. The provenance of the latter is the memorial chapel of Pope Adrian VI of 1522, in the Carthusian monastery at Louvain (he was tutor to the Emperor Charles V, whose head appears in the cinquefoil). – E, the Crucifixion, in a Northern landscape, between Christ before Pilate and the Road to Calvary; in the lower tier Christ taken in the Garden, between the Adoration of the Magi and the Flight into Egypt. – Sanctuary S, Coronation of the Virgin with musician angels, above the naturalistic Noli Me Tangere in a farmyard setting. – Chancel S, Mystic Marriage of St Catherine, above Christ with Mary Magdalen. – Chancel N,

Lazarus raised from the Tomb, in front of a Flemish Renaissance castle, above the raising of Jairus's daughter. – Nave, six
windows to the E on N and S, New Testament scenes partly
based on drawings by *Bernard van Orley* and with a date 1522.
– Nave N, three panels of Old Testament scenes, *c.* 1600.

LLYSDULAS. Victorian LODGES surround the estate lavishly
developed by Gertrude, widow of W. L. Hughes, 1st Baron
Dinorben, on the profits of his Mona copper mine, Parys
Mountain. Her house by the Dublin firm of *Deane & Wood-
ward*, built 1856–8, fell derelict and was demolished in 1976.*
A new house was built on the site in 2005.

The Victorian house was built round a glazed arcaded court-
yard, incorporating older Elizabethan-style wings by another
architect. The designer was *Benjamin Woodward* just after his
Oxford Museum had brought to life the architectural theories
of Ruskin. Like the Museum it was significant for its Ruskinian
sculptural decoration of naturalistic birds, animals and foliage.
The carving was done by the Irish masons who worked on
Woodward's Kildare Street Club, Dublin, and the Ormond
Hall, Kilkenny Castle, including the famous *O'Shea* brothers.
The front had Venetian Gothic windows in pairs and triplets,
with pierced stone balconies. But for the use of fine stones for
columns round the two-storey covered courtyard, it could have
been a learned and grandiose rectory.

YNYS DULAS, ½ m. offshore. The tall TOWER on the island was
built in 1824 as a navigation beacon and refuge for those
shipwrecked.

4566   DWYRAN

Substantial village E of Newborough, across the Braint from the
old church of Llangeinwen.

ST CEINWEN, Llangeinwen, just W of the modern village. The
blocked plain Romanesque N doorway, unicameral nave and
chancel may all be C12; but harling obscures the walls and any
other evidence surviving repairs in 1812. Transeptal N chapel
added in restoration of 1838 by *John Lloyd* of Caernarfon.
W tower and Y-tracery windows of 1829. In the stumpy, angle-
buttressed tower, such windows appear on all three storeys.
Nave roof C14 (?). Further repairs in 1929 by *Harold Hughes*.
– FONT. *c.* 1200. Round bowl with roll moulding on the base.
Finely carved with fleurs-de-lys and palmettes in relief. –
EARLY CHRISTIAN SLABS. C7–C10 cross carved with spirals,
NW buttress. Two more on the SW buttress.

ST MARY (SH 447 668), Llanfair-yn-y-cwmwd, ½ m. NE of
Llangeinwen church. Small unicameral church of undeter-
minable date, rescued from dilapidation in the C18. – FONT.

* There was a C16–C17 house of the Lewis family here, already altered *c.* 1810.

Inconsistent with the island Romanesque fonts, this is oval but on a strangely carved rectangular base. The bowl has zigzag on the rim and crosses in relief on the sides, and the base band has a head at each corner and another head and two serpents on the sides between them, with other designs. – COFFIN LID. C13, with stiff-leaf tendrils carved round a cross.

DWYRAN CALVINISTIC METHODIST CHAPEL. 1867–9 by *Richard Owens* of Liverpool. A striking façade in deep green stone laid like crazy paving, with sandstone dressings, based on Owens's Tabernacle at Rhyl, Flints, of 1866, and in his 'Lombard' style. Tall round arched windows but a Gothic rose over a stilted triplet with Gothic capitals and a Gothic porch. Most notable the triangular heads to the recesses of the outer windows. – In the graveyard, MEMORIAL to John Owen Jones †1899, journalist campaigner for farm workers.

On the Menai Strait, 1½ m. SE, two small earlier C19 villas. TALGWYNEDD, Late Regency with a full-height bay, built for the Rev. R. R. Hughes, and, slightly later, PLAS PENRHYN, still classical but plain, with a three-window front facing the panorama.

GAERWEN

One of the linear villages on Telford's Holyhead road. Two ruined windmills, MELIN MAENGWYN and MELIN SCUTHAN. A low hill to the N, CAPEL EITHIN (SH 490 727) was excavated in the 1970s, revealing a Christian cemetery with 102 burials, and earlier Bronze Age cremation burials. The importance of this hilltop goes back to the Late Neolithic, when a huge, enigmatic wooden tower stood on the site.

ST MICHAEL. Replacing the medieval church of Llanfihangel Ysgeifiog. 1847–8, by *Kennedy*, improving on plans by an unknown amateur. Altered 1897 by *P. S. Gregory*. Buttressed nave with traceried double bellcote, short chancel. The Dec windows, containing older parts and the S door with hollow chamfer moulding, look reused probably from the old church. Cusped collar-trusses with big ogee braces on oversized corbels. Multi-foil W window. W gallery on octagonal stone columns. – STAINED GLASS. E window probably by *Clayton & Bell*, c. 1896. N window by *Celtic Studios*, 1984. – Gabled Gothic LYCHGATE. – Mid-Victorian former SCHOOL and master's house, E, probably also by *Kennedy*. Very steep roofs and a slate sundial in the S gable.

OLD CHURCH, 1 m. NNE (SN 478 734). Ruined medieval church of Llanfihangel Ysgeifiog, in a roundish *llan*. Roofless by the 1930s, though its chancel and C17 N chapel, added by Thomas Holland of Plas Berw, Pentre Berw, still stood.

GWALCHMAI

Gwalchmai Isaf is one of the linear villages along the Holyhead road in the former parish of Trewalchmai. A *Telford* octagonal TOLL HOUSE *c.* 1820 at the E end. The centre mostly Late Victorian, with a war memorial CLOCK TOWER, 1926, by *John Griffiths* (like the one at Rhosneigr) and MORIAH INDEPENDENT CHAPEL of 1892 and 1902. Gwalchmai Uchaf is slightly separated, to the SE.

ST MORHAIARN. In a small circular *llan* on a hill-crest. Unicameral chancel and nave, added W bellcote; NE chapel added *c.* 1500 or later. Three-light chancel window (removed from Heneglwys church in 1845) with renewed cusped Dec flowing tracery; chapel E window with uncusped panel tracery. S windows trefoiled and cusped under straight hoodmoulds; round-arched blocked S doorway with a deep label hood, C16. N doorway segmental-arched. In the N chapel the N chancel windows, re-set. Its two-bay arcade has an octagonal pier and semi-octagonal responds with baluster-like bases. Arches of Tudor profile; two hollow chamfers. The date 1674 on the E gable and in the S chancel window indicates some reconstruction. Roofs in both parts of the same type, with arch braces forming elliptical profiles, so of the early C16. Porch added and nave windows renewed by *Kennedy, c.* 1885. – FONT. Octagonal; C15? – MONUMENT. Richard Lewis †1725, a handsome Palladian design of grey-veined alabaster. Fluted pilasters set back, marble inscription slab set forward.
JERUSALEM CALVINISTIC METHODIST CHAPEL, Gwalchmai Uchaf. A hipped chapel of 1849, altered in 1925, the date of the façade embellishments. The interior may be of 1925, though the character is richly turn-of-the-century with semi-circular seating, arcaded curved *sêt-fawr*, ornate platform pulpit and curved gallery, all with floral carving and decoration.

HENEGLWYS

Dominated by the airfield to the W. The main settlement is Bodffordd to the N, centred on SARDIS INDEPENDENT CHAPEL, rebuilt 1895, and to the N, MELIN FROGWY, windmill tower.

ST LLWYDIAN. In a big, once round churchyard. Partly rebuilt by the *Rev. John Wynne Jones* in 1845 on the old unicameral plan, restored in 1896 by *P. S. Gregory*. From the reused features this was a C12 church rebuilt in the C14; now with a S porch and triple W bellcote. Two-light trefoiled and three-light cinquefoiled windows reused, but the E window is Victorian, the medieval original now at Gwalchmai. Pointed S and N doorways, the former with hollow and roll mouldings. Re-set above both are voussoir stones with lions' heads and

chevrons from a C12 Romanesque arch (cf. Aberffraw). On the
E wall, stones with a C12 billet ornament, and a human face.
– FONT. One of the finest Romanesque fonts on the island. [17]
Cylindrical, with a continuous arcade of columns and
depressed arches in relief; above these a band of flattened
Greek key ornament, and below, a band of lozenge ornament
more crudely done. – STOUP. Rectangular, also C12. –
INSCRIBED STONE. On a N window sill. The remaining part
reads FILIUS EV . . . NIMA REQUIES. . .

MONA FARM, 1 m. S. Built as a coaching inn at the halfway point
on Telford's Holyhead road, replacing Y Gwyndy, Llandrygarn,
on the old road.* Handsome Late Georgian, with a lower W
wing. Five bays, a fanlight over the central door. Attached
behind are two YARDS. The inn stands on the first, a very large
cobbled courtyard enclosed by ranges including lofted stables
and a five-bay coachhouse facing the back of the inn across the
short axis. Outer yard of the same dimensions but structurally
less complete. Is the whole impressive layout *Telford*'s, and the
date therefore 1818?

HOLYHEAD/CAERGYBI [2583]

The town on Holy Island has been the principal port for Ireland
since 1800. Rennie's harbour improvements began in 1810,
Telford's road from London was built from 1815 and Stephenson's railway from 1844. These have all but erased the pre-C19
character, but Holyhead was a port town long before. Jonathan
Swift sailed from here in 1727, and the government communication with Dublin was via Holyhead from the late C16. The
parish church testifies to medieval importance, continuing from
the early Christian monastery of St Cybi founded in the C5 or
C6 and built within the walls of a Roman coastal defence probably of the C4. The town is largely C19, the terraces, chapels and
other buildings mostly of the modest sub-classical type found
throughout the industrial expansion in NW Wales. Collectively
they form a weaker townscape than that at Dun Laoghaire (formerly Kingstown), the corresponding port on the Irish side.

ST CYBI

St Cybi, who founded churches bearing his name in Llŷn, the [p. 128]
Teifi valley and the Usk valley, is principally associated with Holy
Island. There is an echo of the Early Christian era in the presence
of two (or more) churches in one churchyard (cf. Meifod,
Powys). The name of the Eglwys-y-bedd, 'burial church',
attached to the fragmentary church S of the parish church recalls
the burial of founder-saints' distinct cells elsewhere. Here the
adoption of the Roman fort as a religious settlement seems to
have happened very early, possibly soon after the Romans

---

*The name Mona appears on all the cast-iron milestones.

withdrew in the late C4, and presumably under the patronage of the local ruler. By tradition it was Maelgwn Gwynedd who established the *clas* here (cf. Penmon). It continued unreformed on this remote island till the Dissolution – a situation paralleled at Bardsey Island and at Clynnog Fawr in Caernarvonshire. The remaining domestic buildings seem to have been demolished piecemeal in the last 200 years.

Small for a collegiate church, the plan of complex evolution though now largely Perp in style, rich in exterior carving and battlemented except at the E. C13 chancel rebuilt in the late C15, nave with late C15 clerestory, aisles and transepts, ornate early C16 S porch. W tower, with a pyramid roof behind battlements, possibly C17. The roofs were restored 1813–14. Restored by *Sir George Gilbert Scott*, 1877–9, and his assistant *Arthur Baker*, who designed the Stanley memorial chapel of 1896–7, this work carried out under *Harold Hughes*.

Chancel of local blue rubble stone, with lancet openings renewed in yellow sandstone and a three-light E window with cusped intersecting tracery. Angle buttresses added in 1896–7. The transepts of *c*. 1480, with parapets added *c*. 1520. S gable with heraldry for the patron (perhaps Lady Margaret Beaufort) and a mitred head between angels at the apex of the parapet. Handsome battlements of pink stone, crocketed finials, and a band of circled quatrefoils below. At the SW angle with the nave an octagonal stair-turret, the spire of 1877. N aisle of three bays, *c*. 1500, with big three-light Perp windows. Of *c*. 1520, the S aisle, its windows richly carved, and the flamboyant S porch, nearly as exotic as that at Holywell, Flints. Built of ashlar like the aisles, very large, with two tiers of unglazed traceried side windows. Shallow gable between complex angle buttresses each supporting three crocketed

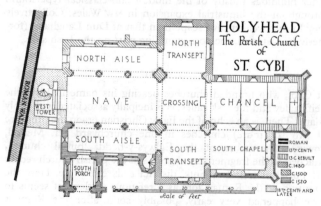

Holyhead, St Cybi.
Plan.

finials. Segmental-pointed doorway with a flat hoodmould. The much-panelled vaulting with a Tudor rose was installed by *Scott* on the original springers. Fine s doorway, with a plethora 44 of heraldry and beasts, the wall above lined with flowing tracery around a relief-carved figure. At the sides, canopied niches without their statues. s of the chancel, the Stanley Chapel, of dressed blue stone with big sandstone fleurons in the parapet and three crocketed statue niches in the gable. One reused C15 window, s.

INTERIOR. The cruciform plan of a *clas* church could survive in the crossing, where a C15 elliptical arch tells of the rebuilding of everything w of it. In the s arm some re-set Romanesque stonework with chevron carving. In the chancel the panelled timber barrel ceiling is part of the Victorian works. The w crossing arch, the two w arches of the transepts and the N arcade are all one medieval project, with low arches on two orders of shallow multiple mouldings with gargoyle heads or angels as stops; but the s transept arches are *Scott*'s. The s arcade loftier and more elegant in that its piers, set diagonally, have deeper hollows between the angle shafts; a peculiar detail in the way the piers return to the octagonal. The clerestory repaired by *Scott*, who renewed much of the low-pitched roofs; the nave roof with finely carved foliate bosses (the central one C19 with two birds, the Stanley arms).

FURNISHINGS. COMMUNION TABLE. Turned legs and apron of two segmented arches with a pendant. Mid-C17. – FONTS. Octagonal bowl renewed in 1662, with the names of the churchwardens. In the s chapel, circular C12 font with Romanesque saltires, from Llanfair yn Neubwll. – WALL PAINTING. A scrap with a Tudor rose on the E wall of the N transept, early C16. – ORGAN. By *Whiteley* of Chester, 1881, from Eaton Hall, Cheshire. In a handsome Victorian case with motifs as much Art Nouveau or Renaissance as Gothic. – Stone MORTAR with saltire decoration. – STALLS and PEWS, C19, reusing late medieval pieces. – ARMS of George III, w, 1817. – STAINED GLASS. E, 1883, *Kempe*. – N transept E, *Morris & Co.*, 1927. – s aisle s, *J. Jennings*, 1904, traditional. Chapel E, a lovely window of fruitful branches by *Morris & Co.*, 1896–7. Two other windows by the firm on the s, one of 1897, the other of 1921. – MONUMENTS. N aisle. Restrained Baroque memorial to John Owen of Penrhos †1712. – s transept. A group of Neoclassical tablets to Louisa Lloyd †1818, Jared Jackson †1802, William Vickers †1823. – Judith, Susannah and Jane Vickers, 1814, with columns and slate pyramid. – At the w a panel of Dutch tiles commemorating Dutch servicemen in the U.K. 1940–7. – s chapel. Monument to W. O. Stanley of Penrhos †1884. An exceptional piece of Late Victorian sculp- 72 ture by *Hamo Thornycroft*, who was passed the commission originally offered to *G. F. Watts*. Seen through a bronze arabesque screen, a white marble effigy on an Italian Renais-sance chest is set against a dark E wall between two angels with dramatically spread wings, offering a wreath and a torch.

EGLWYS-Y-BEDD (Capel Llan-y-gwyddel). The nave of a second medieval church in the same churchyard. Converted by Dr Edward Wynn as the town's first school after 1748. Exposed chancel arch (the chancel removed in the C17) with two orders of C14 wavy mouldings. At the W a C14 window with a C15 doorway below.

CAER GYBI ROMAN FORT. Enclosing the churchyard. Generally believed to belong to the reorganization of coastal defences under Count Theodosius, like the C4 fort at Cardiff. It is assumed that the base at Holyhead was set up to protect North Wales from Irish piracy. The enclosure wall has survived almost intact because in the C6 this piece of obsolete government property was given to St Cybi as a site for his hermitage or small monastery.

The plan is a rectangle of about 230 by 150 ft (71 by 46 metres), with round corner towers. No wall on the E, as originally the N and S walls continued down to the shore to protect the beached ships. The stump of the N extension can be seen on the NE tower. Only the NW TOWER survives in its original form, founded on rock and rising to 27 ft (8 metres) still. The W ones are partly encroached by houses, the SE one was rebuilt in the earlier C19 as part of Stanley House (*see* Perambulation). The WALL with its herringbone masonry and rampart walk is very well preserved, standing 13 ft (4 metres) high and 5 ft (1.5 metres) thick. The entrance in the S wall is original but the arches have been rebuilt; smaller modern doorway in the N wall. Such herringbone masonry occurs at other Roman sites like Caerleon, Caerwent and Calleva Atrebatum. The present E wall is C17, built on a retaining wall part of which (e.g. the relieving arch at the SE) is medieval. The NEW CHURCHYARD at quay level below is early C19, the ostentatious Jacobean gateway dated 1926.

OTHER CHURCHES AND CHAPELS

OUR LADY HELP OF CHRISTIANS (R.C.), at the foot of Market Street. 1965. A large formal square church, raised on a platform, with copper pyramid roof.

BETHEL BAPTIST CHAPEL, Edmund Street. 1895. Italianate front in stucco with panels of roughcast. Arched windows above, cambered heads below, a quartet in the centre. Twin pedimented porches, similar to those on Hyfrydle chapel.

EBENEZER CALVINISTIC METHODIST CHAPEL, Kingsland Road, 1 m. S. A weighty Baroque façade, of grey-green stone with orange dressings. Two storeys. Big dentilled pediment carried on first-floor pilasters that frame arched windows. Ground floor with piers and a small pediment. The stair wings have carved scrolls against the main chapel. It must date from the 1890s, possibly a refronting. The chapel of 1850 was enlarged in 1859–60.

HEBRON BAPTIST CHAPEL, Kingsland Road, 1 m. S. 1879 and 1902. Big roughcast and stucco two-storey front. Triple arched windows above a balustraded double doorway. The small-paned windows presumably of 1879.

HYFRYDLE CALVINISTIC METHODIST CHAPEL, Thomas Street. 1887–8 by *O. Morris Roberts* of Porthmadog. A well-handled stucco façade. Centre gable recessed between balustraded wings that clasp a pair of pedimented arched porches, giving three layers of recession. Arched upper windows and square heads below, gathered 2–3–2, the centre triplet under an arch. Galleried interior with ornate ceiling. Big platform pulpit in pine and maple on the back wall with later organ behind and, unusually, some STAINED GLASS, Christ the Shepherd, by *J. Wippell & Co.* of Exeter and in the gallery, South Stack lighthouse by *Maile & Son, c.* 1948. Forecourt RAILINGS made at the local *Black Bridge Foundry*.

MOUNT PLEASANT INDEPENDENT CHAPEL, Thomas Street. Now Elim Pentecostal Church. 1883 by *O. Morris Roberts*. A robust Italianate façade in stucco, apparently winged but only because the centre pedimental gable is inset a little, giving some oddities between the outer and centre quoin pilasters and the top cornices. The centre bay is recessed under a triangular head, a motif Roberts borrows from Richard Owens (cf. Dwyran) with an arched triplet over a big balustraded arched porch.

TABERNACL INDEPENDENT CHAPEL, Thomas Street. The cheerful façade of 1913 by *Owen & Thomas* was added to a chapel originally of 1823–4 by *Owen Lewis* of Llangefni, enlarged in 1856. Roughcast and stucco, theatrical with twin domed towers and a big rusticated lunette in the centre. Galleried interior, panelled ceiling with six ventilators. Organ by *Blackett & Howden*.

PUBLIC BUILDINGS

TOWN HALL, Newry Street. 1875 by *John Thomas* of Caernarfon. Striking High Victorian civic Gothic, in yellow brick with some black brick and sandstone enrichment. Symmetrical, two-storey with tall storey heights, central gable and big paired windows for the upper civic rooms. Behind, a hall for 900.

MARKET, Stanley Street. 1855, by *John Edwards*. Disused since 2006. Surprisingly large, Neo-Jacobean in greenish-blue stone with pinkish ashlar dressings. Triple-roofed with three broad shaped gables, the centre one taller with oriel and triple-arched entrance. Iron gates from the *Black Bridge Foundry*.

UCHELDRE CENTRE, Mill Bank. The chapel of the former R.C. Bon Sauveur convent, with TŶ'N PARC, the early C19 stuccoed house in whose grounds the convent was built in 1909. The other buildings were demolished in the 1980s, leaving the remarkable CHAPEL of 1937, by *R.M. Butler* of Dublin, as a community centre. Hiberno-Romanesque with a saddleback w tower and apsed E end, of green stone facing a concrete core. The originality is revealed within. A six-bay concrete tunnel vault with transverse ribs on half-shafts between clerestory windows; the arches of the side chapel interpenetrate the vault. Under the apse semi-dome a baldachino coloured as marble.

YSGOL UWCHRADD CAERGYBI. South Stack Road. The former COUNTY SCHOOL, 1909 by *Joseph Owen*, County Architect. A long range in Ruabon brick and brown sandstone, a series of gables, some with lunettes, the centre one paired with an octagonal tower. Across the road, s, the modern SECONDARY SCHOOL buildings, 1970s, two-storey, flat-roofed. In 1949 the two schools of Holyhead were amalgamated to become the first state school in Britain with 'comprehensive' admissions.

HOLYHEAD HARBOUR

The Buck engraving of 1742 shows no quay, just boats on the mud in the Inner Harbour. There was then little else apart from saltworks on Salt Island. With the Act of Union with Ireland in 1800 and the threat from France, development accelerated. The South Stack lighthouse was built in 1809, Salt Island was purchased and Rennie's harbour (now the Old Harbour) constructed 1810–17, in time for the opening of Telford's road to London and the first steam paddle-boats, introduced in 1819. The next stages were initiated by the railway in the 1840s. The 'Great Harbour of Refuge' was begun in 1847 with the enormous breakwater completed in 1873. Enhancements of 1875–80 for the London & North Western Railway included the new station and Station Hotel. In recent times, the drive-on car-ferry berth was added in 1965, the long pier for the aluminium works 1970, the container port 1972, and the remodelled passenger terminal and drive-on facilities for the giant jet-propelled catamarans in 1995–8. The harbour thus comprises several parts: the original inlet or Inner Harbour, the early C19 Old Harbour at its seaward end with most of its structures on Salt Island, regrettably inaccessible, and the huge Outer Harbour protected by the great breakwater.

The INNER HARBOUR is crossed by the dramatic bow-form stainless steel CELTIC GATEWAY BRIDGE by *Gifford & Partners*, erected in 2006 to re-establish connection from the port to the town centre. Its plan is inspired by a Celtic knot. The STATION, opened in 1851 by the Chester & Holyhead Railway, had buildings of 1857 by *Charles Verelst*. These were replaced by the LNWR in 1879–80 with a V-plan station of two glazed platforms either side of the harbour, linked by a four-storey hotel of red brick with yellow dressings, by *William Baker*, the company engineer. The two platforms, arrivals on the E and departures on the W, had impressive overall iron roofs. The hotel and W platform were demolished in 1979, but the E half survives, over 1,300 ft (400 metres) long, eighteen bays, the trusses of wrought-iron bars, which also frame the continuous ventilator. On the W, cast-iron brackets with leaf decoration spring from columns. In the yard by the station, the cast-iron CLOCK TURRET, 1878, originally on the quay.

N of the station is the new FERRY TERMINAL, by *Manser Associates*, 1995–6, and 2004 by *Ellis Williams Architects*, like a small airport with curving roofs. Further N, cleared areas for containers, partly on the site of the LNWR's 420-ft (129-metre) graving dock, infilled in 2001, and the modern fish dock. Around the corner, running N, the SOUTH PIER of 1810 by *John Rennie*, protecting the s side of the harbour entry.

On the W side of the Inner Harbour, rail tracks and then the MARINE YARD, begun in 1850 to service the ships and enlarged after the LNWR extended the NW shoreline with a new quay in 1863–6. The tightly grouped complex of WORKSHOPS is the most significant such survival in Wales. All are of stone with brick dressings and are top-lit in addition to the wall openings. The complex, inaccessible and largely disused, includes a fitting shop mostly of 1874 but with a pre-1850s building embedded, a smithy of 1852–9 at right angles to the quay, and a boiler shop in range with the SMITHY, at the Victoria Road end, pre-1874 enlarged in the 1880s. The BOILER SHOP has a deep eaves cornice and rubble piers, the tall openings allowing the boilers to be moved vertically. Six-bay interior with two travelling cranes. Nearby a BOILER ROOM and SAWMILL, pre-1874, the latter in green-grey rubble with ashlar voussoirs to tall openings. At right angles, four adjoining buildings aligned N–S, pre-1874, distinguished by two chimneys and black rubble window arches. They contained the iron foundry, coppersmithy and brass foundry. Next, the ERECTING SHOP, pre-1874, contiguous with the enlarged fitting shop. The GENERAL STORES, detached near the quay, also had workshops for upholsterers, polishers and sailmakers. To the N, on Pelham Quay, JOINERS' and CARPENTERS' SHOPS in red and black brick, erected before 1900 and before 1924 respectively.

SALT ISLAND beyond, linked by a short causeway, had a salt-works until the mid C18. *John Rennie*, commissioned with Capt. Joseph Huddart to review the route for the Irish mails in 1801, was instructed to improve the harbours at Holyhead and Howth in 1809. Work began in 1810. After Rennie's death in 1821, *Thomas Telford* completed the project, by 1828. A wooden jetty (demolished) was built in 1858 for Brunel's *Great Eastern*, which laid the transatlantic cable from here in 1866.

The QUAY WALL was built 1810–24, and the further wall on the isthmus was also finished by 1824. The ADMIRALTY PIER, almost 1,000 ft (300 metres) long, was completed by *Rennie;* the lighthouse, harbour office and custom house were erected to his designs by *Telford*, who added a graving dock in 1825–6. The LIGHTHOUSE, 1821, is 48 ft (15 metres) high with an iron gallery, the lantern head (the oldest in Wales) covered by a copper roof. The CUSTOMS HOUSE and HARBOUR OFFICE, 1823, were built together, of limestone, the one with a three-bay pilastered front, the other with a centre square clock tower with octagonal belfry. They adjoin the MEMORIAL ARCH, 1824, by *Thomas Harrison*, erected by public subscription to commemorate George IV's visit in 1821, and marking the end of the road from London. A small Doric gateway in 'Anglesey marble' from the Red Wharf quarry, Benllech, it has two unfluted columns *in antis*, a cornice and frieze. The inscription facing the town is in Welsh, that to the pier is in Latin. The original design was Egyptian in style.

The OUTER HARBOUR, or Great Harbour of Refuge, was proposed in 1846 by the engineer *J. M. Rendel* to allow large numbers of ships to take shelter. Rendel planned two enormous breakwaters, but the E one was too dangerous to build and only the W one was constructed, on an enormous scale, between 1847 and 1873. Rendel died in 1856, succeeded by *John Hawkshaw* with *G. F. Lyster* as assistant engineer. At 7,860 ft (2,418 metres) this is the longest breakwater in Britain, made of seven million tons of quartz rubble quarried from Holyhead Mountain and brought by broad-gauge railway built by the contractors *Joseph & Charles Rigby* of London. Faced in Moelfre limestone, it stands in up to 40 ft (12 metres) of water, rising 40 ft from the low-tide line and 250 ft (77 metres) wide at the base. A railway protected by a high W parapet with steps and refuges runs out to an ovoid platform intended for guns, around a square LIGHTHOUSE, 63 ft (19 metres) high, by *Hawkshaw*. At the landward end, BREAKWATER QUAY, stone-faced. The whole enterprise cost £125,000.

PERAMBULATION

Beginning from the foot of the slope, MARKET STREET joins VICTORIA ROAD at a small square. The WAR MEMORIAL, a granite cenotaph, has good bronze reliefs by *L. F. Roslyn*, 1923. It stands in front of the EAGLE AND CHILD INN, which began in 1784 serving the Irish packet, and has returned to its original name and function, having been the Royal Hotel after George IV's visit in 1821 and then houses when the Station Hotel below opened in 1878. Handsome stucco seven-bay façade with an added bay, l. Market Street ascends slowly to Market Square. On the l., COLEG MENAI occupies a good building of *c.* 1900, roughcast with four gables and leaded oriel windows. On the r. PORTH CELTAIDD, opening to the new footbridge (*see* Harbour above) with mosaic panels, 2006. At the top of the street, adjoining the churchyard entrance, STANLEY HOUSE, typical plain stucco of three storeys and three bays, *c.* 1810. From the churchyard its substantial C19 enlargement for the Stanley family can be seen, with stepped gables and mullioned windows to create an antiquity missing from the town. It is linked to the rebuilt SE tower of the Roman fort (p. 130). On the N side, the former NORTH & SOUTH WALES BANK, 1899, in red Ruabon brick and sandstone, with English Baroque detail wilfully misplaced. Good lettering.

STANLEY STREET runs N. A large commercial block on the l., dated 1906 and 1912, with three two-storey arches below and two more storeys above. At the N end of the street, on a platform, the Market (p. 131), and on the lower corner, the former NATIONAL PROVINCIAL BANK, c. 1900, sandstone ashlar with a little Arts and Crafts detail. Down BOSTON STREET, on Victoria Road, the former BETHEL WESLEYAN CHAPEL, now flats, a big two-storey stuccoed front of 1901. The original chapel was of 1808 by *Evan Roberts* of Denbigh. Stanley Street continues N with the MAGISTRATES' COURT, l., 1894, Neo-Jacobean like the one at Amlwch, in contrasting grey stones. NEWRY STREET then runs N with the Town Hall and ENGLISH BAPTIST CHAPEL, r., 1861, by *Charles Rigby*, the Breakwater contractor, and the ENGLISH PRESBYTERIAN CHURCH, l., 1891, by *Richard Davies*. Behind this the later C20 LIBRARY, two-storey, glass, the ground floor recessed.*

Newry Street continues to the NORTH FORESHORE, with the MARITIME MUSEUM, Jacobean-style, in a large mid-C19 former lifeboat house. Further w the modern MARINA and former TRINITY HOUSE DEPOT, built c. 1870 to service lighthouses. Beyond, PORTH-Y-FELIN, large stucco mansion (derelict 2006) built c. 1849 for the resident engineer *G. F. Dobson* by the contractor, *Charles Rigby*, possibly to *Dobson*'s design. Italianate with a pedimented centre and big three-sided bays to each end. Further on, of the same period, SOLDIER'S POINT, built by *Charles Rigby* for himself, weakly Gothic with a landscape of embattled walls.

Returning to Market Street, an excursion may be made up THOMAS STREET into an area of C19 stuccoed small terraces with numerous chapels. On Thomas Street, successively Mount Pleasant, Tabernacl and Hyfrydle chapels, with Bethel chapel off to the l. in Edmund Street, and the Ucheldre Centre above. The secondary school is beyond on SOUTH STACK ROAD, also some 1930s semi-detached Modern houses still with metal glazing and curved glass. Off to the s is GORS AVENUE, a suburb with Late Victorian middle-class villas culminating in AKAROA on the r., a splendid amalgam of Arts and Crafts motifs. At the end, the orderly row of SUNRISE TERRACE. South Stack Road runs w through Llaingoch to Holyhead Mountain (*see* below). Thomas Street runs NW as Porth-y-felin Road to the coast at the Breakwater (p. 134).

s of the town, Victoria Road runs s into KINGSLAND, a Victorian railway suburb with stuccoed three-storey houses more typical of the far side of the Irish sea. On KINGSLAND ROAD, l., Hebron chapel (p. 130), and on the r. in Tŷnpwll Road, STANLEY COTTAGES, six almshouses built c. 1866 by W. O. Stanley, with a shield re-set on a gable. Beyond Ebenezer chapel (p. 130), MILL ROAD runs SW to KINGSLAND WINDMILL, c. 1820. Four storeys, important for the preservation of almost all its machinery, though the cap and sails were removed in 1939.

E of the harbour, LONDON ROAD crosses the railway to BLACK BRIDGE, the area E of the Inner Harbour, industrialized from

---

*Tabernacl Newydd Chapel by the *Rev. Thomas Thomas*, 1867, has been demolished, as has his nearby Capel Armenia, 1886.

early on; site of the Black Bridge Foundry. Prominently overlooking the town, the large white stone OBELISK to Capt. J. M.
Skinner of Stanley House, captain of the mail packet, drowned
1832. Set on a high plinth and decorated with ships' prows,
inverted torches and an Egyptian winged sun. Near it a circular
PILLBOX in rubble stone with copings as if a garden building.
Two tiers of rifle loops. At the junction of Llanfawr Road a
group of Arts and Crafts houses: PLAS ALLTRAN, built 1891
as a doctor's home and surgery, together with four cottages
and a stable building. Along Llanfawr Road a PRIMARY
SCHOOL by *N. Squire Johnson*, 1959.

HOLYHEAD MOUNTAIN/MYNYDD TŴR

1½ m. W of the town. On the NE slope, the QUARRY from which
the huge quantity of stone for the Breakwater of 1847–73 was
taken. The line of the railway to the sea remains. Around the
quarry, FELIN NEWYDD, the stone-crushing house,
workmen's barracks, explosive stores and a large late C19 silica
brickworks with tall chimney.

On the summit (SH 219 829), CAER-Y-TŴR, an inhospitable
hill-fort. No evidence of construction date, but traditionally
assigned to the Iron Age. Most of the summit is rugged and
steep, and only in the E half could any hut platforms have been
contrived. However, a great deal of effort was put into enclosing the summit with a huge dry-built rampart, 11 ft (3.5
metres) wide and still 10 ft (3 metres) high in places. This is
not present on the S side where precipitous cliffs make it super-
fluous, but on the NE it snakes along the contours till it turns
in along a narrow gully at the NE corner to cover the narrow
entrance passage. The rampart flanks the other side of the
entrance and then runs off along the N side where it is less well
preserved. At one point the wall appears to have fallen inwards,
thought to be the result of deliberate destruction of the
defences, either by the Roman army or by later Irish raiders.

On the very summit, the square foundations of a Late
Roman SIGNAL STATION, built, presumably in association
with the fort by the shore (p. 130) to give warning of the
approach of enemy ships. Other possible sites along the coast
may have carried the message back to the main Roman base
at Chester. Remains of two CAIRNS near the summit, possibly
Bronze Age.

SOUTH STACK/YNYS LAWD

87 SOUTH STACK LIGHTHOUSE, 3 m. W. Dramatically sited on
cliffs, the lighthouse of 1809 was one of the first improvements
to navigation into the nascent port. The designer was the
architect-engineer *Daniel Alexander*, appointed surveyor to
Trinity House in 1807; the builder of the whole complex was
Joseph Nelson. Tower heightened 1874. Keepers' COTTAGES at
the foot, single-storey, long double-roofed range, the whole

complex enclosed in whitewashed walls. In 1828 Holy Island was linked to the main island by a suspension BRIDGE, protected by iron fencing of the design used by *Telford* on the Menai Strait bridge, so perhaps by him. Replaced 1843 and 1997.

ELLIN'S TOWER, S of the lighthouse. Built 1868 by W. O. Stanley as a summerhouse and look-out, named for his wife. Restored in the 1980s as a bird-watching centre.

TÝ MAWR HUT CIRCLES, ½ m. SE of the lighthouse (SH 210 820). Remains of a flourishing village perhaps founded in the Late Bronze Age (a hoard of bronze tools was found near the NE end), and surviving for over a thousand years. As late as the 1860s more than fifty huts could be seen straggling along the terraced hillside on either side of a meandering 'street'. The scattered, almost random, planning suggests that the individual houses may be of varying dates, and the contrast with enclosed settlements such as Din Lligwy (Rhos Lligwy) and Caer Leb (Brynsiencyn) implies that the social context was very different. The houses were set among cultivated fields; some of the terraces can be recognized on the slopes below. Copper slag in some huts showed that metalworking was carried on, though the level of prosperity was not high; only a few Roman coins were found in the largest house, and there was no fine Samian pottery. p. 15

Fifteen round-houses and five smaller rectangular buildings survive in two main groups, the one nearer the road being the better preserved. The round-houses, normally about 23 ft (7 metres) across, have evidence for hearths, stone seats, and mortars for grinding roots and vegetables. One of these can be seen set into the floor of the largest house. One house was subdivided, but normally they provided a single room covered by a conical roof of thatch or turf, with a wide doorway to let in light. The low thick walls, never much higher than they are now, are designed to take the thrust of the roof. In some cases this was designed like a wigwam, in others supported on central timbers. The small, semi-subterranean rectangular buildings were perhaps workshops or food stores.

Several houses were excavated in the 1870s by W. O. Stanley and in the 1980s there were further excavations in the NE group (through the gate). Radiocarbon dating revealed a long and complex history of the main farmstead. A single house was built, another added after 200 B.C., with an enclosed yard. The older house was partly demolished to make way for a granary raised on seven stones. By the C6 the buildings were probably ruined, but the surrounding fields were still being worked.

PLAS MEILW STANDING STONES, Penrhosfeilw, 2 m. SE (SH 227 809). A pair of very impressive stones only a few metres apart, supposedly at either end of a large cist grave which was opened in the C19. Such paired stones are unusual, but not unique.

GORSEDD GWLWM CAIRN, N of Penrhosfeilw (SH 227 816). Remains of a round cairn with a low kerb. Near the centre three stones on edge, perhaps the remains of a very large cist or small megalithic tomb.

TREFIGNATH BURIAL CHAMBER, 1½ m. SE of Holyhead (SH 259 805). Excavations in the late 1970s revealed not one 'long grave' but three separate chambers built in succession. The earliest seems to have been a chamber with a short passage facing N, perhaps set in a round cairn. This was followed by the central chamber, a simple rectangular box-like structure with relatively low portal stones (not unlike some in SW Scotland), entered from a narrow forecourt defined by dry-walling. Later another box-like chamber was built in this forecourt blocking access to the earlier tomb. This chamber has much higher portal stones and looks rather like the portal dolmens found in Caernarvonshire and Merioneth. However, it, too, has a narrow forecourt edged with dry-stone walling, an arrangement more typical of Severn–Cotswold tombs in SE Wales. Decorated pottery from this forecourt suggests the Late Neolithic period. The long cairn which covered the chambers was edged with neat dry-walling and was built in two stages. The junction, clearly visible on the S side, constitutes the best evidence in the field for the multi-period construction of a megalithic tomb. To the NW, a STANDING STONE (SH 253 808) now surrounded by industrial/business development.

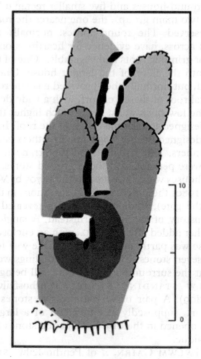

Trefignath burial chamber.
Plan

LLANALLGO

1 m. SW of Moelfre.

ST GALLGO (SH 502 851). Originally of *c*. 1500. Much rebuilt by *Kennedy* in 1892, when the short nave was perhaps length-ened and the interior brick-lined. Transepts, making an irregular cruciform plan. In the mid C19 a small addition opening into the nave from the W was used a baptistery. Big Perp E window with renewed tracery. S chancel and transept windows of two cusped lights under square labels, E transept windows of single cusped lights. N doorway also late Perp. Some old shallow arch-braced trusses in the nave, boarded elsewhere. – FITTINGS. 1934. Limed-oak sanctuary panelling, LECTERN, PULPIT etc. Arts and Crafts manner. – BELL. Late C13, inscribed Ave Maria Gracia Plena.

In the churchyard, OBELISK to the victims of the 1859 *Royal Charter* disaster (*see* Moelfre), of whom 140 are buried here.

FFYNNON ALLGO, 400 yds SW. A well of uncertain date. A small chamber of limestone blocks set on edge, with a stone bench on three sides and the pool in a rectangular conduit below.

PARADWYS CALVINISTIC METHODIST CHAPEL, ¼ m. NE, on the main road junction. Late C19 probably by *Richard Davies*. Uncommonly severe. Two tones of limestone, the gable with stepped corbelling and no fewer than ten openings, mostly square-headed.

PARCIAU (or BRYN DDIOL) PROMONTORY FORT, ½ m. SW (SH 495 847). A small inland fort. The flat hilltop is defended by naturally steep slopes except on the SW, where three ramparts and ditches cut off the neck of the promontory. The outer ramparts are now very low but the large stone construction of the central one can still be seen. The inner rampart, much higher and thicker, continues around the top of the plateau, where some large upright stones can be seen. Entrance is on the S with a causeway coming through the second rampart and over the ditch to the inner rampart, which is slightly inturned at this point. Inside, foundations of many round stone huts, most clearly seen in the E half as circular depressions. In a dry summer the walls, too, can be traced. Excavations in three huts dated them to the C3–C4, no doubt a reoccupation of an earlier defensive site.

LLANBABO

NW of the large Llŷn Alaw reservoir, 1966, and with the Llŷn Alaw WIND FARM of thirty-four turbines, installed 1997, along the ridge to the N.

ST PABO (SH 378 868). In a circular *llan*. Small unicameral
church of C12 origin, partly rebuilt in the C14. The eight
chevron-carved stones re-set over the S doorway indicate the
removal of the chancel arch and apse (as at other Anglesey
churches) to allow for a larger chancel. In the S wall a small,
round-headed window in a splay. The W wall is a puzzle: its
steep gable corresponds to the pitch of the oldest parts of the
roof, yet it stands higher and has no copings, so seems to be
older again. C12, or are they late medieval? The E wall C14,
from the enlargement planned for the shrine of King Pabo. In
it a one-light window of the local type with mouchette tracery
forming an ogee arch. Original copings and base of the gable
cross. The W bellcote of this date too? One high C15 window,
S. The roof is clearly one of the earliest on the island: three
pairs of jointed crucks set low in the walls (the E couple the
least altered), with simple arch braces and no chamfers. Could
these too be C12? The chancel has a single arch-braced truss
relating to the lower pitch of the E gable. That so much remains
legible reflects the absence of restorations, except that by
Harold Hughes, 1906–9. – FONT. C12, shallow, circular, tapering. – CARVED HEADS. Three in low relief beside the S doorway
outside and above it inside, of ancient but unknown origin
(cf. Llanfachraeth). – RELIEF OF KING PABO. Pabo was king
in C6 North Britain, who on expulsion was granted land in
Anglesey by Cadwallon Lawhir. The stone is late C14, carved
by the same workshop as the images of Iestyn at Llaniestyn
(Llanddona) and Eva in Bangor Cathedral. This use of the fine
pale Flintshire sandstone (*see* p. 146) connects it with the
patronage of Wenllian ferch Madoc and Gruffudd ap Gwilym.
Originally it formed part of a shrine set on a chest tomb in the
chancel, as at Llaniestyn. The low-relief figure is set in a broad
trefoiled canopy rising to an ogee, with flat leaf forms in the
spandrels. The king, in a long pleated robe, wears a crown
ornamented with fleurs-de-lys and quatrefoil leaves; his
knopped sceptre also ends in a fleur-de-lys. The head is
bearded, the eyes closed, long wavy hair to either side. It is
inscribed on the r. HIC IACET PA[BO] POST PRIDD CO . . . O
. . . EL . . . MA. The ends were obliterated in its recovery from
the churchyard in the later C17.

16

3895

LLANBADRIG

NE of Cemaes, the church beautifully set on the cliffs above the
cave where Saint Patrick, shipwrecked here, is said to have
worshipped.

ST PATRICK. Tucked into its windy site. The W parts of a
rebuilding of *c.* 1300; arched W bellcote, short nave and chancel
arch, S porch with big pointed entrance. The long chancel looks
like a replacement of *c.* 1840, to judge by the unusual elliptical-arched sandstone windows. The original chancel arch is

two-centred, on crude responds. Perp E window reused, three lancets under a four-centred arch. On the inner wall beside it a C15 niche with tall shafts supporting a nodding cusped canopy. After a fire, the church was much restored in 1884, including the unusually designed roof timbers, by its patron the 3rd Lord Stanley †1905. His profession of Islam is held to explain the orientalism, which appears in the decorative elements, by an unidentified architect (perhaps the patron himself). – Glazed TILES, lining the sanctuary. With paterae, olive-sprig motifs and sea-blue glazes suggestive of the Middle East. By *Powells*. MOSAIC PANEL in the niche of the Good Shepherd, 1884, also by *Powells*. – GLASS. With attractive slightly Islamic geometrical motifs. – FONT. C12, cylindrical. Continuous Romanesque arcading. A whorl motif in each arch. – INCISED STONES, C9–C11, one with a wheel-cross and Latin cross, another with a fish symbol. – MONUMENTS. C14 slab carved with serpents and ballflower.

To the N is FFYNNON BADRIG, a holy well.

DINAS GYNFOR, 1 m. E (SH 390 950). The rocky headland is defended by two probably late prehistoric ramparts on the landward crest. The inner rampart, looking like a grassy bank but revealing a stone face at the E end, runs along the top, curving around a flat terraced area, W. The entrance through this rampart is approached by a sloping track protected by the much slighter outer rampart, probably an earthen bank rather than a wall.

The track leads down to PORTH GYNFOR, or Porth Llanlleiana (SH 388 951), used for exporting the china stone (altered felspar) quarried here in the C19 (damaging the interior of the fort). Ruined buildings of a CHINA CLAY WORKS and chimney. On the E headland, the most northerly point of the island, a ruined TOWER built to commemorate the 1901 Coronation.

PORTH WEN, 2 m. E. On the W side of the bay, in an extraordinary setting, the ruins of a BRICKWORKS operational 1889–1924, with three large circular kilns. 97

LLANBEDRGOCH 5181

A scattered settlement 2 m. SW of Benllech. In the centre some buildings with stonework not yet coated in pebbledash, which has reduced too many Anglesey villages to architectural illegibility. Examples include a late C19 terrace in finely jointed squared masonry, and a former chapel of *c.* 1825 of coloured random stonework with tall pointed windows. Prominent on the main road, ½ m. E, a house by *Harry Bannister & Partners*, 1959, in the form of a tapering tower like a windmill (actually the round wall on the site was a limekiln). Bold cantilevered balcony with a view of Red Wharf Bay.

ST PETER (SH 509 799). On a hill, S, within a circular *llan*
enlarged to the S. Short chancel, nave made cruciform by the
addition of long C17 transepts lit by mullioned windows. Perp
N doorway, with latest Gothic circled motifs in the spandrels.
Either side of this two medieval heads in low relief: bishop with
mitre, a man's face. Of the pre-restoration fabric the slight C18
roof trusses, halved together. Restorations 1840, 1885. – FONT.
Octagonal, scalloped back to a narrow octagonal base. – Two
late medieval panelled BENCH ENDS brought from Llaneilian,
one carved with a mermaid, form the reading desk and seat. –
MONUMENTS. Armorial brass to Anne Morgan †1675, wife of
the bishop of Bangor, below an inscription to Dr William Lloyd
†1661, rector of Llaneilian. – Slab with relief inscription to
Roger and Catherine Roberts †1704.

(GLYN, ½ m. NE of the village. C17. W part with a N wing for the
dog-leg stair, dated 1613 on the plaster; E part added 1644 by
John Bold. Some unusual plasterwork here. In the ground-
floor room, a frieze with cannon, crossed muskets and other
military trophies, and heraldry over the fireplace; in the upper
room (once entered through a five-sided porch) moulded
plaster with drops on a beam, and an accomplished overmantel with a scene in high relief of a man seated in a hall receiving a standing figure, another scene, and palm trees either end;
in the attic a corner fireplace with a shield of arms with two
supporters, more plainly done.)

Excavations after 1994 revealed traces of a C7 farmstead,
apparently made defensible against the Vikings but with a
Viking-style C10 house within and graves suggesting violent
deaths.

3776   LLANBEULAN

Just the church, down a track 1½ m. SW of Gwalchmai.

ST PEULAN (SH 373 754). Preserved by the Friends of Friendless Churches. A memorable sight, approached across a
causeway by a green lane. Raised *llan* of unusual elongated-
rectangular plan. Well-proportioned nave with S chapel, W bellcote, and chancel; entry through the E doorway of the chapel.
The nave probably C12, but its W doorway is plastered over;
the E window of the chapel, its round head formed of a single
stone, is perhaps reused from it. Next to it a re-set C14 two-
centred doorway, its jambs old, the arch replaced. The adjacent datestone 1657 appears to be *ex situ*, unless it refers to the
larger window. Two-light trefoiled chancel window with deep
label and headstops; its S window square-headed, its N window
blocked. The lofty chancel arch (albeit rebuilt) and the S chapel
arch seem to confirm a C14 reconstruction; the former with a
round but subsiding arch with two orders of continuous chamfers, the latter also with two orders but with a pointed arch.
Late Victorian restorations include the arch-braced roofs, the

gable crosses and the upper part of the bellcote. – FONT. The best of Anglesey's remarkable Romanesque series. Peter 15 Lord suggests that it began as an altar of the first half of the CII, but Malcolm Thurlby sees the ornament as typically Norman, CI2. Rectangular. The E end carved with an expanded-arm cross on a ring, with two half-spheres at the base, all framed with plain and chevron or rope bands in such a way as to allow a shaft or roll moulding to form the angle above the base. The W end has chequerwork and a Greek fret. On the long side a shallow relief of blank arcading with stilted arches above a lozenge pattern. Its motifs and style connect it with one of the high crosses at Penmon Priory, and with the fonts at Heneglwys and Llaniestyn. – Painted Arts and Crafts COMMANDMENT BOARDS, W wall.

LLANDDANIEL FAB   5070

A substantial village SE of Gaerwen. At the centre cross-roads, CLOTH HALL, mid- to later CI9 with arched windows on two floors. To the W, Y NEUADD, converted early C20 hall with offset battered-sided gabled porch. To the S, PRESWYLFA, former chapel of 1907 by *Richard Davies & Son*, stucco with eyebrow hood over the main window, and then Cana chapel (*see* below).

ST DEINIOL. In a circular *llan* extended to the S. All but rebuilt in 1873 by *Kennedy* with steep roofs, bellcote and S porch. Vestry doorway with re-set medieval moulded jambs and a carved face for the keystone. – STAINED GLASS. N window †1897. – In the porch a well-carved grave-slab with heraldry. Timber LYCHGATE, the steep roof facing the path.

CANA INDEPENDENT CHAPEL, at the SW end of the village. 1862, by the *Rev. Thomas Thomas* of Swansea, but with fussy cement dressings of 1906. Original the Palladian window and outer doors. Interior without galleries. Coved ceiling. Behind the pulpit a corniced arch. Attached schoolroom behind, with the 1862 plaque, unusually naming architect and builder.

CEFN BACH CALVINISTIC METHODIST CHAPEL, I½ m. SE. 1863. Attractively simple. Long small-paned cambered windows, two to the front, three to each side. The two doors have slate lintels.

(RHOSBOTHAN, I m NE. Early CI7. T-shaped, or nearly cruciform, plan with an axial corridor, the entrance in a two-storey but lower wing on the N. The other three gables full-height and step-gabled, a conceit of Jacobean design. To allow for the chimneys on all three gables (now of brick) the fireplaces are in the corners of the rooms.)

BRYN CELLI DDU, I m. E (SH 508 702). The best-known burial 7 chamber in Anglesey, restored and accessible to the public for many years. The passage grave is built over the remains of a henge monument, defined by a bank and inner ditch surrounding a level space containing a circle of upright stones.

The ditch and some stones can still be seen. These henges, which seem to belong to a system of religious thinking less closely allied to the cult of the dead, are found most frequently in the South of England; that the henge was subsequently covered and obliterated by the passage grave and its large round cairn suggests a return to the older traditions of the island.

Before this second monument was built a deep pit was dug in the centre of the henge and a single human earbone buried in it. Beside this pit lay a decorated stone, now in replica, which may have stood upright as the focus of some ceremony perhaps 'rededicating' the site. The lightly pocked spirals and meanders run over its top, demonstrating that it was never the walling stone of a chamber. The restored chamber is covered by a mound about half the size of the original, which would have come out to the kerbstones set in the bottom of the older ditch. The approach, by a long narrow passage with an unusual low 'bench' along one side. In the chamber a tall stone dressed to a circular shape, interpreted as the guardian spirit of the tomb; it certainly frightened the farmers who first entered in 1799.

8

LLANDDEUSANT

3586

A scattered settlement in farmland 3 m. NE of Llanfachraeth.

SS MARCELLUS AND MARCELLINUS. Rebuilt 1868 by a local amateur architect, *Goronwy Roberts*. Greenish stone with trefoiled windows. Chancel, nave and SW porch-tower, a big church by Anglesey standards. – FONT. C12 circular bowl with slight taper, decorated with blank arcading. With holes arranged geometrically in each arch, possibly for inset metal or stone ornament.

Opposite the church, the altered SCHOOL dated 1817.

HOWELL MILL, ¾ m. SSE (SH 351 844). Water-powered corn mill on the Alaw river. The mill of Howell ap Rhys was mentioned in 1335. The present mill is early C19, rebuilt 1850 and restored in the 1960s, remarkably intact. An overshot iron wheel drives three pairs of stones.

LLYNON HALL, 1 m. SW. Facing W, a small but internally complete mid-C18 Anglesey *plas* of six bays, built for a naval surgeon, Herbert Jones. The ampler E front, added for his nephew Humphrey, has two long canted bays. Small apsidal stair of *c.* 1800 in the earlier range. To the E the designed landscape embracing the road also reflects two phases, the drives being a second, less formal stage. In the outbuildings, a restored MILL with new 9-ft (2.75-metre) wheel.

LLYNON MILL, ¾ m. W. A stone tower windmill, about 30 ft (9 metres) high, built in 1775–6 for Herbert Jones of Llynon Hall. The sails, with a span of nearly 70 ft (21.5 metres), were restored by Anglesey Borough Council and the mill reopened in 1984.

BEDD BRANWEN, 1¼ m. W, by the Alaw river (SH 361 849). The
legendary grave of Branwen, daughter of Llŷr, whose tragedy
is recorded in the *Mabinogion*. The mound is much earlier but
the setting is sad and peaceful, suitable to the mood of the
story. The stone which protrudes through the centre stood as
a monument in its own right perhaps for some centuries
(radiocarbon dates obtained on excavation, 1967). Then a low
ring of stones was built around it, covering several cremation
burials in urns. Some were accompanied by smaller pots
containing charcoal and infant earbones, a peculiarity found
at other Bronze Age barrows. The ring was carefully built, with
large boulders forming an inner and outer face and smaller
stones between. Unlike ring cairns in Caernarvonshire, this
ring was immediately covered by a mound of turves and earth,
bounded by a kerb of upright stones still visible around the
perimeter. The central area was filled with large stones sloping
up towards the central stone. Amongst these stones was a
second series of burials. In all about eight people were buried
in the mound.

STANDING STONE (SH 368 857). Much larger than the one which
became the focus of Bedd Branwen. There is no evidence for
any connection between them.

LLANDDONA   5780

Modern village on the high ground NE of Beaumaris, the church
much below at the E end of Red Wharf Bay. Nearby are the
isolated churches of Llaniestyn, E, and Llanfihangel Din Silwy on
the headland, NE.

ST DONA (SH 574 809). In the circular *llan*. Drably rebuilt in
1873, by the *Rev. Peter Jones*. Nave, transepts, chancel, and W
bellcote. Re-set as the S doorway, a substantial casement-
moulded frame in yellow sandstone with a segmental arch,
and, in the spandrels, a cherub, dog, bird etc. of
c. 1500? Reset above the E window, a stone dated [1]566, upside
down. – FONT. Octagonal, C14? – STAINED GLASS. E window
by *Celtic Studios*, 1963.
    Pleasant RECTORY complex of *c.* 1800 opposite.

WERN-Y-WYLAN, 1 m. W. A group of Arts and Crafts houses
overlooking the bay, built *c.* 1934 by *Gordon Jackson* for the
Verney family (cf. Rhianfa, Llandegfan) as a kind of artistic
colony equipped with concert hall, petrol station, shop and
hotel. Rendered and timber-clad, with a profusion of gables
and hips. A prominent Germanic tower at the centre.

LLANIESTYN, ½ m. E. Just the church of ST IESTYN (SH 585
796) in a partly circular churchyard. Nave and chancel in one,
with added S transept, the broad opening spanned by a beam.
S porch with a barn-like entrance, its exposed truss carved with
running ornament. Of the late C14, to judge by the crisp late

Dec three-light E window (*see* Llanfihangel Din Silwy, below), with hoodmould and geometrical stops. The E gable cross and terminal gablets, and the narrow W doorway, are much eroded. Elliptical S doorway of *c.* 1500 in a deep casement-moulded frame with square head. S window in the transept restored as three trefoiled lancets. Tactful restoration in 1865 by *David Roberts* of Beaumaris. – ALTAR RAILS. Turned, of Laudian height. – FONT. C12. A squarish cylinder, its whole surface carved with bands of ornament. Blind arcading below, zigzag, and in the top band a variety: interlace, a straight-sided spiral and chequerwork, a Maltese cross in one corner.

RELIEF OF ST IESTYN. One of the three late C14 reliefs from the same workshop (cf. St Pabo at Llanbabo and Eva in Bangor Cathedral). The inscription names the donors, Wenllian ferch Madoc (sister-in-law of Eva) and her nephew Gruffudd ap Gwilym †1405, ancestor of the Penrhyn family. The fine grey sandstone came from Englefield, Flintshire, where Gruffudd had land as well as at Llaniestyn. This points to him also being the patron of the rebuilding. A surprisingly accomplished low relief of the saint, represented as a hermit with pilgrim's staff. He wears a full-length cloak, parted but held by a round brooch, and lies in a delicate cinquefoiled niche, its interior enriched with four-petalled flowers. He holds a scroll inscribed in debased Lombardic lettering which continues round the head of the slab and the cushion. The church was the last founded by Iestyn, and perhaps this was originally set in the S transept as a shrine. It was recorded in the C18 as on a tomb-chest in front of the altar.

LLANFIHANGEL DIN SILWY, 1 m. E of Llanddona church. On the headland, below the Bwrdd Arthur hill-fort, the church of ST MICHAEL (SH 588 815) in a circular *llan*. Short but wideish nave and chancel *c.* 1400. Nave rebuilt by *Kennedy* in 1854. A cross on the gabled E finial. The pointed E window is late Dec, three lights with wavy foiling, like the straight-headed two-light chancel S window. Hoodmould over the E window with stops carved with a head and a stag. Blocked S priest's door. Chancel arch of C14 profile, with the simplest continuous hollow moulding which on the chancel side dies into the wall. Shallow arch-braced roof. – FONT. C14, octagonal. – FURNISHINGS. Plain, wooden, of the best local kind, especially the PULPIT, 1628, a pair with that at Llangoed. Four sides of a hexagon, tapering towards the floor. The stiles carved with foliage and dolphins, the main panels with frets like plasterwork patterns.

BWRDD ARTHUR or DIN SILWY (SH 585 815). The most accessible of the Anglesey hill-forts. The single rampart might be mistaken for a recent field wall were it not for its thickness, well over 6 ft (2 metres). It ran all around the flat hilltop set back a little from the crest of the steep slope. On the E side it has been largely destroyed. Two original entrances, the more important, S, with a wide path leading up to it; that near the NW corner so narrow that only one man might enter at a time.

Midway along the NW side the suggestion of another small blocked entrance or sally-port. Some badly damaged features, possibly buildings, are set against the main rampart wall. In the E half of the fort some low rectangular mounds which may be modern 'pillow mounds' (artificial rabbit warrens). Casual finds of Roman coins suggest that the fort was occupied, probably reoccupied, in the first few centuries A.D.

LLANDDWYN ISLAND

3863

The island 3 m. SW of Newborough, at the W entrance to the Menai Strait, is reached by a causeway made in 1838. At the far end, TAI PEILOT, a row of earlier C19 pilots' houses, one refurnished as original. There was a lifeboat station here 1826–1907. TŴR MAWR, a whitewashed conical lighthouse tower of 35 ft (11 metres), was built for the Caernarvon Harbour Trustees in 1824, with a lantern of 1846. It superseded a smaller one of 1800. DAY-MARK to aid navigation, built 1823 by *John Lloyd*.

ST DWYNWEN. In a small circular *llan*. Little remains of this rare cruciform church, once 77 ft (24 metres) long but abandoned since the C17, apart from its chancel which had a wide, casement-moulded window of the C16. In 1906 enough remained for *Clough Williams-Ellis* to propose re-roofing it for the Hon. Frederick Wynne, adding a narrow tower at the SE angle as a sea-mark, but nothing was done.

LLANDDYFNAN

5079

The church and the standing stone 1½ m. W of Pentraeth on the Llangefni road.

ST DYFNAN (SH 503 787). In a round raised *llan*, extended to the E. A strange plan: chancel wider than nave, nave wider than W narthex, porch and bellcote added to the narthex. The nave is C14 and has arches at the E and W; the chancel arch is two-centred with continuous hollow chamfer, as is that to the narthex, which is thus of the original build; but the latter arch is taller, like a tower's. C14 N doorway, its two-centred under-cut label having as stops carved naked figures, one attacked by a beast. A carved stone of a head with hands supporting a drip-stone is re-set above. The chancel was rebuilt wider and almost square on plan in the C15. Fine Perpendicular E window with continuous mullions, three ogee lights and panel tracery, under a two-centred arch. Other windows two-light, cusped, under hoodmoulds with carved stops. The C15 devotional S doorway, grandiose for the island in being carved in yellow freestone, was inserted in the narthex. The stones of its frame are integral with the corbels over the doorway, so it is all of one date. Round-arched with carved keystone and spandrels in a handsome square-headed frame. Slightly unrelated at spandrel level, and on top, are three niches with crocketed finials, the lateral two with trefoil heads, the upper one with an ogee. These are treated not in the round as usual in the C15 but in low relief, not unlike the earlier local school of stone-carving. The lateral figures represent (w) the Virgin and (e) St John, both holding books. The Virgin's pleated garment appears beneath the outer robe and a veil reaches from her head to her feet. Inscribed round the niche ORATE P AIA JEM AP DIC AP IORW FFILII DIE MESERERE MIE. St John has curled hair and a pleated gown, and the inscription ORATE PO AIA LL AP IVOR AP DD AP EGN FFILII DIE MESERERE MIE. The third panel represents the Trinity, the twisting figure of Christ Crucified appearing below the head of God the Father to a larger scale. The interior still with two-decker pulpit, box pews and a w gallery apparently of *c.* 1846–7. – Two STOUPS. One by the s doorway, C14, with a pointed cusped opening.

STANDING STONE by the church (SH 502 786). It stands at the end of a line of five round barrows (of which only two can now be recognized) and is Anglesey's only large stone which has this close relationship to a Bronze Age cemetery. It was straightened some thirty years ago, but unfortunately no excavation took place. Two surviving BARROWS (SH 509 784), the largest in the group; excavated at the beginning of the C20. The e one covered a single inhumation grave, the body placed in a carefully constructed boat-shaped cist. The second barrow, only 650 ft (200 metres) w, contained eight cremation burials, all placed as the mound was being built. These people seem to have been prosperous, with several buried bronze ornaments or weapons. The goods, and the styles of pottery favoured, suggest trading contacts with Scotland, Ireland and the South of England. A much later burial, probably C6–C7, was in the top of the mound.

MARIAN, ¾ m. sw. On the s wall a massive lateral chimney with two flues paired under a quarter-round moulded cap. Handsome segmental fireplace arch of Tudor type too, but maybe reused. The n side renewed as a two-storey, five-bay front of very small Queen Anne windows.

PLAS LLANDDYFNAN, 1 m. wsw. Gentry house, built by John Griffith in 1709 (date over n door) and incorporating a late C16 house. Nearly symmetrical e front (formerly stuccoed) of five bays, raised above a cellar. Sashes, hipped dormers and a C19 limestone slab porch with steps. Three gabled wings behind (w), the n extending to a service wing. Between this and the main house, a late C16 cellar doorway with segmental head. Two-storey STABLE RANGE extending n from the service wing, with datestones 1803 and 1825. At the n end, a higher bay for carts, with wide segmental doorway and a pyramidal roof with timber cupola.

LLANDEGFAN

Parish bordering the Menai Strait just NE of Menai Bridge. The old village, Hen Bentref Llandegfan, is on high ground E of the church, with BARACHIA CALVINISTIC METHODIST CHAPEL, rebuilt 1900, and the VILLAGE HALL, 1904, by *Harold Hughes* with lobby library and caretaker's cottage. The NATIONAL SCHOOL of 1832 in dark ashlar is next to the SCHOOL of 1890 by *R. G. Thomas*, behind a fine Arts and Crafts WELL HOUSE, 1899.

ST TEGFAN (SH 564 744). W tower, unicameral chancel and nave, transepts and deep S porch. The simple Wyattish tower was built by Viscount Bulkeley in 1811 (inscription in Welsh and Latin). Much of the rough walling stone looks original, but the windows are Cheshire red sandstone replacements of 1901–3 by *P. S. Gregory*, apart from those on the transepts, of 1847. The reused porch doorway and peaked gable copings, of gritstone, look C14; and the elliptical-headed S doorway C15. Nave roof with trusses of the local C15 cruck-like type, and near-semicircular arch bracing. The slightly wider transepts have similar roofs, but the arches more elliptical and the feet of the trusses cut back instead of dying into the wall. An addition to the N transept, opening by a Tudor arch, not in alignment, was possibly a schoolroom. It has a similar roof, a type which continued after 1600. – FONT. Octagonal, outside the porch. – STOUP, on a swelling octagonal pillar. – SANCTUARY PANELLING, of alabaster, early C20. With fields of flowers. – STAINED GLASS. E, Crucifixion, by *Kempe*, 1902. – S transept E, Christ the Healer, 1908. – S transept S, delicate floral quarries of 1847. – Nave N, Noah and Moses, *Kempe*, 1902. – MONUMENTS. E wall. Thomas Davis †1649, 'servant to ye two most illustrious Princes Henry and Charles both Princes of Wales, and now to King Charles ye first Messenger in Ordinary'. Half-length, the Stuart arms on his doublet, in an oval niche. *Memento mori* above, princes' feathers below. – William Owen †1712, framed by a Baroque open pediment and volutes, erected by his friend Richard Viscount Bulkeley. – N transept, Owen Williams of Craig-y-don †1832. Fine Rickmanesque canopied wall tomb, replica of an original of *c.* 1500, taken to Bisham church, Berks, as the memorial for Owen Williams's sister Jane Wheatley. No effigy in the recess. The quatrefoil-enriched chest of stone, the slighter upper parts of *Coade* stone? – Brass tablet to Edward Bickersteth, surgeon, of Craig-y-don and Liverpool, who paid for the 1903 restoration. Thomas Williams †1802, the developer of Parys Mountain (q.v.) is buried here, his remains brought from Llanidan in 1812.

COUNTY PRIMARY SCHOOL, *Norman Squire Johnson* and *D. Gray-Williams*, 1972. Brick with slate roofs, facing the Snowdonia view. Based on the Inner London Educational Authority's Vittoria School, Islington, of 1967, an experiment in more informal grouping.

The COAST ROAD from Menai Bridge to Beaumaris was laid out
as a private road to Baron Hill, Beaumaris (*see* p. 111) in 1805
by Viscount Bulkeley. Improved into a turnpike in 1828. Along
this picturesque coastal road substantial villas and houses (*see*
below).

CADNANT. The coast road now by-passes the single-arched
PONT CADNANT. By the bridge, pretty stuccoed bargeboarded
LODGE to Plas Cadnant, a villa of 1803. Above the bridge,
two much altered later C19 WOOLLEN MILLS. Above Plas
Cadnant, the flat-topped rocky promontory (SH 552 734) is
occupied by a group of round huts and rectangular buildings.
The entrance through the broad E bank passes through a
rectangular building. Excavations at similar homesteads
suggest this may have been a threshing barn. The W section of
the plateau, naturally defended by low cliffs, is badly overgrown.

CRAIG-Y-DON, ½ m. NE of Cadnant. Tudorish, of *c.* 1830, built
for the descendants of Thomas Williams of the Parys copper
mine. Much altered in the Late Victorian period with a ballroom and three-storey tower. The lodge, stables and boathouse
are more intact.

92 RHIANFA, I m. NE. A fairytale castle as seen from across the
water. Built 1849–50 by *Lady Sarah Hay Williams* of
Bodelwyddan, Flintshire, for her two daughters. Having been
trained to draw by Peter de Wint, Lady Hay Williams had
sketched the castles of the Loire valley, subsequently commis-
sioning the Liverpool architect *Charles Verelst* to design a house
on those lines (anticipating Henry Clutton's influential
Remarks . . . on the Domestic Architecture of France by three
years). A forest of steep French roofs covered in fish-scale
slates, and a skyline fretted with curved and straight pitches
and spires, which are level with the road on the back. On the
seaward front, narrow drum towers with conical roofs at the
corners, and a galleried upper floor running between. The
centre projects in a style not easily described. Entrance passage
of exemplary craftsmanship in iron, the doorway with a quotation from Psalm 90. Hall with steep beamed coving and flat
centre with roundels where the beams cross. Doors with over-
scaled S-scrolls, fireplaces of rich materials. The terraced
garden, entered by a gate-tower and sloping S to the shore,
is of equal quality.

GLYN GARTH COURT, 1½ m. NE. The only high-rise building
on the Strait: a ten-storey slab by *Percy Thomas & Partners* of
Cardiff, 1971. The seaward side enlivened by triangular oriels
for the view, the landward by two lift towers in hammered
concrete. It replaced GLYN GARTH, a Neo-Elizabethan
mansion built for a Swiss businessman, S. Schwabe, *c.* 1850 by
J.E. Gregan of Manchester.

GRAND LODGE, 2 m. NE. At the foot of the disused graded drive
to the Bulkeley seat at Baron Hill, Beaumaris (*see* p. 113). The
particularly opulent white Tijou-style wrought-iron gate screen
with heraldry, of superb workmanship, is said without evidence

to have been exhibited at a Paris Exhibition. The small
François I-style lodge is by *R. G. Thomas*.

BRYN MÊL, ¼ m. E. 1899, by *P. S. Gregory*, Kennedy's successor
as Diocesan Surveyor, for the Platt family of Llanfairfechan.
Large and baronial. Two storeys and attic, over a semi-
basement. The walls of pebbles pressed into mortar, with
yellow sandstone dressings; the basement of darker, snecked
rubble. Octagonal bays at each end and a collection of stepped
gabled bays between. Twin-gabled porch and steps leading to
garden, l., an upper veranda, r.

LLEIFIOR, ⅓ m. E. 1897, by *P. S. Gregory* for himself while he
designed Bryn Mêl. Rubble, with bright red terracotta
dressings and finial copings. A big mullion-and-transom
window to the staircase, next to an oriel above the front door.
The remainder with idiosyncratic dropped heads.

LLANDRYGARN   3879

ST TRYGARN (SH 383 796). Isolated down a lane off the
Llangefni–Bodedern road, the old road to Holyhead, in a large,
partly round churchyard. The medieval nave, with a w bellcote, had its two-centred E window re-set at the w in 1872,
when the chancel was added by *Kennedy*. Also re-set, as the
priest's door in the chancel, the former nave N doorway, with
quarter-round mouldings of c. 1300. Perp S doorway, the
semicircular arch in a rectangular frame with trefoils in the
spandrels. Also of the C15 the cinquefoiled window in the SE
corner. Kennedy proposed to replace the nave roof, but its late
medieval collar-trusses survive.

Y GWYNDY, 1 m. E. Ruins of a substantial later C18 coaching
inn, replaced by that at Mona, Heneglwys, on Telford's new
road. J. M. W. Turner stayed here. The outbuildings include
cartsheds with stone voussoirs to elliptical arches, of c. 1777
and a barn with dove holes in the gable.

LLANDYFRYDOG   4586

Scattered parish to the NE of Llanerchymedd. The birthplace of
Hugh Davies †1821 who catalogued the plants of Anglesey in
1813. The poet Huw ap Huw (1693–1776) 'Y Bardd Coch o Fôn',
lived at Llwydiarth Esgob, 1 m. SW.

ST DYFRYDOG (SH 444 853). In a circular *llan* among farms.
A handsomely proportioned church. Chancel, rebuilt in the
late C15 or early C16, with big E window with wave-moulded
jambs, four-centred arch under a hood with beast-stops, and
three lancets. The nave, c. 1400, is broad, almost a square, its
chancel arch with two orders of hollow chamfers dying
into the responds. Paired trefoiled S window, the others
plain; S doorway with quarter-round mouldings, N doorway

two-centred and blocked. The high w bellcote, s porch, n vestry and s window above the pulpit of the 1862 restoration by *Kennedy & Rogers*. Roofs of the same date. Early C19 painted box pews throughout, perhaps from the restoration of 1823.

To the s, the former NATIONAL SCHOOL of 1816.

CARREG LEIDR, I m. SE (SH 446 843). A small standing stone, one of the few Anglesey stones about which there is a folk tale. It is said to be a thief who stole the Bible from the church and was turned to stone as he ran away with it. Clorach, nearby, is the site of the HOLY WELL where legendarily SS Cybi and Seiriol met, having journeyed from opposite ends of the island.

LLANDYSILIO *see* MENAI BRIDGE

LLANEDWEN

The parish borders the Menai Strait, and though dominated by the Plas Newydd estate contains several ancient houses. The church is within the park, the entrance by a charming pyramid-roofed roughcast LODGE of 1914. MOEL-Y-DON, beyond, was an important ferry point. The sturdy house overlooking, dated 1717, was the OLD CUTTER INN.

ST EDWEN (SH 517 683). Within the park, in an ancient church-yard. 1854–6, by *Kennedy*, replacing a rebuild by *John Welch*, *c.* 1840. An estate church with a broach spire on a NW tower. The Incorporated Church Building Society found the design 'inconsistent with the gravity of feeling which pervades the ancient churches of Wales'. Unplastered interior lit by candles. Some nave roof timbers could be reused medieval. Woodwork fragments include the doorhead of a C15 SCREEN; spandrels with a lion and a wyvern in front, lions passant and a shield-bearing angel behind. Also a classical frieze on the Victorian pulpit. – STAINED GLASS. E, 1853. Nave N, early C20, by *Shrigley & Hunt*. – MONUMENTS. Robert Hughes of Plas Coch, †1764. White urn on a grey pyramid. Earlier C19 slate tablet in a white aedicule to Sir Nicholas Bayly, †1782.

In the churchyard, w of the door, the Rev. Henry Rowlands †1723, author of *Mona Antiqua Restaurata*, is buried under a worn Latin inscription: 'All things are nought save what he gave to needy ones. These have force when arts perish and writings fall to pieces.'

PLAS NEWYDD, I m. N. The pale stone house overlooking the Menai Strait is of Late Georgian regularity, but has late medieval if not earlier origins as one of the houses of the Griffiths of Penrhyn. It is one of at least five on the Strait where the medieval complex included a great hall and a chapel. Moses Griffith's view of 1776 and surveys of 1784 show how much of this house then survived. The hall was at right angles to a chapel to the N, the chapel dividing the hall court from the kitchen court. Only the hall end walls and an enigmatic

spiral staircase descending to cellars (where a stone doorway
of *c.* 1470 suggests an undercroft) survived the late C18
rebuilding.

The Griffith heiress married Sir Nicholas Bagenal †1590,
notorious mercenary and commander in Ulster, and the
Bagenal heiress married Bishop Bayly of Bangor †1631,
eminent author of *The Practice of Piety* (seventy-one editions
by 1792). Sir Nicholas Bayly †1782 made a double pile of the
house in 1751–3 by an addition to the E side with a saloon
facing over the Strait and a SE elongated-octagon corner tower.
He had Gothic interests, making elaborate battlemented walls
and low towers on the landward side and bastions on the
seaward. His saloon, of equal length to the hall, classical in
plan with a central bow, was disguised as a castle with pointed
windows, arrow crosses and battlements. It is exceptionally
early for the Gothic taste, and it seems that Bayly himself
designed it.

Bayly married the heiress of the Pagets of Beaudesert, Staffs,
and for their son Henry (†1812), 9th Baron Paget from 1769,
the Paget earldom of Uxbridge was revived in 1784. Wealthy
from coal in Staffordshire, copper in Anglesey, and 100,000
acres, he transformed Plas Newydd over thirty years, using
James Wyatt, having employed him at Beaudesert in 1771–2,
Wyatt's earliest major Gothic work. Lord Uxbridge's first
phase, 1783–6, used not Wyatt but the builder-architect *John
Cooper* of Beaumaris, with advice from Col. William Peacock
of Plas Llanfair. Cooper balanced the E front with a canted-
fronted NE bay equivalent to the SE tower. Its smooth grey
Moelfre limestone became the consistent material for refacing
the whole house. The E front was refaced as a three-storey,
thirteen-window range. The central 1751 block gained spired
corner pinnacles; single-bay links connect it to the canted-
fronted outer bays, the l. one the SE tower. Bayly's Gothic was
much reduced: two pinnacles, battlements, hoodmoulds over
sash windows, and two four-centred garden doors. The plainer
s end has three close-spaced bays l. of the SE tower.

The second phase, 1793–9, remodelling the W front and 76
refitting the interior, was directed by *James Wyatt* but with such
close participation by *Joseph Potter* of Lichfield that the contributions are hard to disentangle. Potter had worked for Wyatt
at Lichfield and Hereford cathedrals from 1788 and emerges
as a designer in the 1790s; indeed, early C19 guidebooks credit
him with Plas Newydd. Wyatt signs surviving drawings for the
classical refitting of the mid-C18 saloon and ante-rooms, and
Potter those for the more remarkable Gothick hall and dining
room, while those for the classical stair hall are in an unidentified hand. But the two Gothick interiors relate so closely to
Wyatt's development that his must be the guiding spirit.

Lord Uxbridge decided to replace the medieval hall with a
taller and much deeper version to serve as a dining room,
bringing the front wall forward to align with the wings. Three
tall pointed windows with wooden traceries and three similar

windows above form a two-storey Gothick centrepiece, originally embattled, with slim octagonal angle turrets, between
plain three-storey wings with matching corner turrets. The
wings were shown in 1802 with three-bay fenestration but are
now sparsely windowed, enhancing the centre. Symmetry
required a porch either side of the hall, the l. one, since
removed, entered under the resited stairs.

INTERIORS. The r. PORCH is the main entry; shallow with a big
four-centred arch, canted sides and delicate Gothic vaulting.
The GOTHICK HALL, 1796–8, is a *tour de force* of Georgian
medievalism. The elaborate plaster vaults incorporate three
oval traceried domelets, the middle one once glazed. Four
canopied niches on the side walls have gone. The end bay,
traversed by a triple-arched gallery, foreshadows Wyatt's
similar feature at Ashridge, Herts, 1811. Clustered piers,
traceried spandrels and cusped lozenge railing; the slender
delicacy revealing it as carpentry. Double Gothic doors l. into
the MUSIC ROOM, enlarged from the medieval hall. The vault
of 1796–8, of huge span, so resembles Wyatt's destroyed vault
at Magdalen College chapel, Oxford, 1792, and his Great
Room at Bishop Auckland, 1795, that the conception must be
his. But Potter signed the drawings and supplied the timber
shafts, ribs, bosses and medievalizing chimneypiece. The
vaulting is preceded each end by a narrow band of blind
tracery, and the fans of the vault are traceried. Crocketed ogee
doorcases were removed in the 1930s, when stone-coloured
paint was applied to the Gothic interiors and as false ashlar in
the stair hall.

Along the E front *Wyatt*'s Neoclassical hand prevails. Friezes
of draped roundels in the ANTE-ROOM and the SE OCTAGON
ROOM to his design. Reeded chimneypiece by *Richard
Westmacott Sen.*, 1796. The SALOON of 1753 has an elaborate
garland frieze by *Wyatt*, 1795, fine chimneypiece by *Westmacott*,
1796, and mahogany doors made by *Potter* in 1798. Adamesque
doorcases and a huge overmantel mirror were removed in the
1930s. The BREAKFAST ROOM and former BILLIARD ROOM
beyond both have Wyatt's roundel frieze. The Billiard Room
has two niches in the back wall and canted corners, the
windows of 1783 too tall for the frieze of 1795. The Breakfast
Room has five matching sets of double doors. One opens W
into the square STAIR HALL, a classical space with twin fluted
scagliola columns both on the landing and in the opposite
window embrasure. The gently rising broad cantilevered stone
stair has elegant iron and brass anthemion balusters. *Potter*
made the columns in 1798 and supplied the balustrade.
Upstairs the two S end BEDROOMS have Neoclassical friezes
and marble chimneypieces, the coloured one in the SW
bedroom perhaps by *Benjamin Bromfield*. Descending to the
Gothick Hall is an exceptionally tight spiral STAIR, cantilevered
stone with thin iron balusters.

It was probably in 1793 that the medieval chapel
disappeared. The 1798 map shows the house complete.

The last phase, in which *Potter* was principally involved, was
the replacement of the service buildings N of the house with a
range running N to a three-sided small court, and containing
next to the house the new chapel with three traceried E
windows. This seems to have been fitted in 1806-7 with
elaborate Gothick fan vaulting by *Francis Bernasconi*. The surviving drawing is by *Potter*, though Wyatt must have been
involved, as the arrangement, with altar on the long wall and
stalls opposite, was as in Wyatt's chapel refitting of 1796 for the
Bishop of Durham at Bishop Auckland.

After the 2nd Earl inherited in 1812, becoming 1st Marquess
of Anglesey for heroism at Waterloo, the family lived mostly
at Beaudesert. The chapel was converted into the 'Gaiety
Theatre' in the 1890s by the spendthrift 5th Marquess
(1875-1905), but was removed altogether by the 6th Marquess
as part of his modifications. In 1922-31, under *Owen Carey
Little*, the house was overhauled, a plethora of bathrooms
inserted and the service court roofed over as a staff recreation
room. Then in 1935-6 *H. S. Goodhart-Rendel* made far-reaching
external changes, reducing the embattled skyline to plain
parapets with shortened turrets. He changed the uniform sash
windows for a variation each floor: thick-barred sashes, long
casements, and top-floor cross-windows. The theatre was
eliminated for a bedroom storey on the N wing, bringing it up
to a uniform nine-bay plain end stop to the accented E front.
On the W the N range is more severe, Georgian sashes giving
way at the l. to a grid of smaller windows. A wall at right angles
to screen car parking impairs the main front symmetry, though
with two good sandstone classical gateways, suggested by *Rex
Whistler*.

Two new rooms were formed in place of the chapel: a first-
floor library over a dining room. This was decorated by *Rex
Whistler*, 1936-7, his most important commission. A great
architectural seascape on a canvas 58 ft (18 metres) long was
fixed to the long wall, the opposite wall lined in mirror glass
between the windows. On the end walls, *trompe l'œil*
architecture; receding arcades extend the painted quayside.
Trompe l'œil grisaille ceiling panels with classical motifs. The
Octagon Room and bedroom above preserve decorations by
Sybil Colefax.

GROUNDS. The works of 1798-9 coincided with *Humphry Repton*
preparing a Red Book on the landscape, but there must have
been earlier designers under whom the Nicholas Bayly bastions
were swept away. The grading of the land between the house
and the water had already been eliminated for a simple sloping
lawn, and Repton alludes to over-hasty clearances – probably
those in 1791 by Lord Uxbridge, assisted by Col. Peacock.
Repton's main recommendations were for screening the house
from the new stables, improving the approach, and thickening
the existing woodland. He re-routed the drive for scenic effect,
bringing it out at the extreme NW corner, the GRAND LODGE,
with Gothic gate screen of thin stonework, by *Potter*, 1805.

The STABLES N of the house are of 1797 by *Potter*, perhaps with *Wyatt*. Symmetrical, part Gothick folly, part toy fort, everything at different heights and widths. Central false attic with blank Gothic window in a turret-clasped gable, otherwise a high single storey with round turrets framing both the three-bay centre and square outer pavilions, which each have a huge timber traceried window. Utilitarian behind, with short hipped wings. On the lawn in front, the much-illustrated Neolithic CROMLECH, an asset to any aristocratic parkland, with its enormous capstone. Difficult to place in any archaeological category, it appears to have consisted of two adjoining chambers without obvious access between, which makes it difficult to guess at the original plan. In the 1930s an underground reservoir was constructed here, and the greensward used for golf, then cricket. W of the cromlech, plain three-sided DAIRY, in rock-faced stone with iron lattice windows, mid-C19. The front wall has four octagonal piers as if some ornament was planned.*

N of the stables, the former H.M.S. CONWAY, a large naval training centre of 1962–4 by *Gornall & Kelly* of Liverpool. Formally symmetrical apart from the detached chapel, l., a broad and spreading hall block in front of a long five-storey dormitory block; modernized Neo-Georgian.

Along the water's edge is a broad terrace walk on a stone SEA WALL, *c.* 1796. Three semicircular bastions; between them two battered square projections, the N one with a room each side of an arch onto a jetty, the S one a plunge bath. Just S, a little HARBOUR, 1790s, with hipped-roofed building and decaying 1930s sea-water swimming pool. Italianate TERRACE GARDENS NE of the house of the 1920s, the top level the base of a late C19 conservatory.

Within the demesne, BRYN YR HEN BOBL, ⅓ m. SSW (SH 519 690), is a small but exceptional Neolithic burial chamber. It is the only tomb still covered by its original cairn, which survives to a considerable height. The front of the small rectangular chamber is closed by a stone (now broken) with two holes in it. A long, narrow, carefully built and contemporary 'terrace' ran S from the cairn, still just recognizable, its purpose unknown. It retained a certain sanctity for a Bronze Age cremation had been buried beside its end wall. Excavation in the 1920s found little in the ransacked chamber, but the forecourt provided evidence of ceremonial fires and the building of elaborate walls to seal the entrance. C18 records of skeletons with blue glass beads found in the top of the mound may be instances of Iron Age reuse, an increasingly recognized phenomenon. The cairn was built on the site of an earlier settlement, though no houses were recognized. Pottery finds suggested contacts with the South of England, contacts possibly reflected in the neat dry-stone walling which outlined the kidney-shaped cairn.

*Potter designed an octagonal dairy *c.* 1794.

PLAS NEWYDD HOME FARM, ⅓ m. SW of the house. Drum-shaped gatepiers on its drive. The buildings around a large courtyard are of *c.* 1800–10, by *Potter.* On the E and W sides, pyramid-roofed gate-towers with square lanterns between lofted ranges, linked by a long single-storey S range. Behind, a large late C18 brick-lined WALLED GARDEN with pyramid-roofed DOVECOTE W, and, in a smaller walled area W, a half-hipped brick APPLE STORE.

PLAS LLANEDWEN, ¼ m. NW of the church. Within the demesne, approached past Wyattish gatepiers and the early C20 FOREST LODGE, a pair with the lodge of 1914 by the church. Six-window, two-storey stone front typical of the Queen Anne wings added to older Anglesey houses. The rear wing and five chimneys confirm such an evolution.

CHARITY SCHOOL, on the main road SW of Grand Lodge. Founded 1818 for twenty-four poor girls. Low stone range with dominant hipped-roofed end pavilions.

PLAS COCH, ¼ m. NW. Dafydd Llwyd, an Anglesey lawyer in London, erected in 1569, a smallish Tudor house, incorporated in the S end of the present E-facing red gritstone, three-storey building. Its showy step-gabled Flemish exterior is partly the work of his son, Hugh Hughes, attorney general for North Wales from 1587, and partly skilful C19 enlargement. On the central projection, an elliptical-headed doorway and an oriel, the inner doorway confusingly inscribed '1569 DH MAD THYS HOU'. Until the mid C19 the long E range, one room deep, had just two projections, the porch tower and the one at the SE. Stepped gables and matching end gables, with polyhedron finials, and dormers between the towers similar with acorn finials. Pedimented mullion-and-transom windows generally of three lights, the shallow pediments without a frieze, as at Plas Mawr, Conwy. Behind many tall, plain chimneys the square-plan stair tower with a modillion cornice, added with the NW kitchen wing *c.* 1600.

The present symmetry, achieved by adding a matching NE projection, is from a skilful remodelling of 1846 for William Bulkeley Hughes M.P. The Elizabethan N walls were taken down and their red stonework reused for the third tower etc. on the front. Every window light was fitted with a small-paned Gothick casement; the stair-tower dome was replaced with a striking square-plan bell roof. These works, by an un-named Chester architect, represent a stage between Wyatt and the Ruskin approaches to restoring historic buildings. All earlier fittings inside then replaced, in a weak Tudor style. Imperial neo-Jacobean stair and eclectic upstairs dining room with inter-lace ceiling, perhaps by *Kennedy.* Under restoration 2008–9 with very large rear additions, by *Donald Insall Associates.*

To the W, a C17 BARN with stepped gables, opposed doorways and pigeon-holes in one gable. Queen-post trusses. The ruined COACH HOUSE is an addition by *Kennedy* of 1864; perhaps also by him the LODGE, matching the house but with shaped gables. Below the house the drive crosses an overgrown

lake by a BRIDGE of many small arches and past decorative
walling.

ABERBRAINT, 1 m. NW of the church. Rebuilt *c.* 1820 for the
Plas Newydd agent. A Gothick porch was removed in 1971.
Some older panelling re-set, together with two misericords,
perhaps from Bangor Cathedral. LODGE of 1825.

PLAS LLWYN ONN, 1 m. NNW of the church. Formerly
Plas Gwyn. Mid-to-later C19, Neo-Elizabethan, for Lady
Willoughby de Broke, apparently by *W. E. Jones* of Llanfairp-
wllgwyn. Three gables with two-storey stone bays. Extensive
service and stable ranges with verandas and battlements.
Inside, a Palladian chimneypiece from Plas Newydd.

PLAS PORTHAMEL, ¾ m. W of the church. The tall centre represents a mid-C16 house built by Rowland Bulkeley with a S
façade of highly coloured gritstone: reds, greys and oranges.
Did it originally have ornate gables? Its four-centred doorway,
with four-centred head and Bulkeley's initials in the spandrels,
is reused, widened, in the porch. Several rebuildings, principally a five-bay, two-storey C18 stage with sash windows. A re-
set first-floor datestone marked RI and PE 1630. Staircase of
c. 1700 with turned balusters. Later C18 W enlargement with a
small octagonal bay. In the mid C19 the house was enlarged
again for Lord Boston, using red stone for the E wing, and
given three S gables and slate hoodmoulds. On the parapet of
the porch were gathered elaborate heraldic stones, two dated
1653.

4694
LLANEILIAN

Parish at the NE corner of the island, E of Amlwch.

ST EILIAN. Architecturally one of the most distinguished
churches on Anglesey. In origin a *clas* church like Llanfechell,
and similarly given a Romanesque W tower. The tower's steep
stone pyramidal roof links it with the Romanesque work at
Penmon and Puffin Island/Ynys Seiriol. In the C13 Llaneilian
is referred to as 'abadaeth', perhaps indicating its evolution
into a house of Augustinian canons. The mature Perpendicular of the nave and chancel relate to contemporary work at
Holyhead; and the detached chapel of St Eilian is a reminder
of an ancient practice of venerating local saints revived in the
late C15, mostly at *clas* churches, e.g. at Clynnog Fawr.

13   The tower, externally harled and limewashed in 2002, is in
three stages, each slightly set back. Tall Romanesque slit N
window in the second stage. Three of the four similar slits in
the bell-stage have round-headed rere-arches. The vault seamlessly corbelled inwards above this. At the base the jambs and
capitals of the arch to the nave are C12, the pointed arch C13.

The C15 church has a splendour which exceeds its size.
Tudur Aled the poet attributed this to the rector Nicholas ab
Ellis, archdeacon of Anglesey in 1474. The nave is broad and

high with windows, roofs and screen on a noble scale; the chancel, as broad as it is long, has a complete set of medieval stalls. The fruit of wise restorations – in 1812, in 1873 by *Kennedy*, in 1913 and 1929 by *Harold Hughes*, and in 2002 by *Adam & Frances Voelcker* – is self-evident. St Eilian's chapel was rebuilt a century earlier than the church. A passage connecting it with the chancel is dated 1614.

Exterior articulated with angle and wall buttresses (s ones with the dates 1480 and 1481, though the style of many elements seems early C15). These turn diagonal and rise above the embattled parapet to support finials. E window with a steep triangular head – inside of almost ogee profile – and three lancets (an echo of its predecessor?). The nave of only two bays: three-light cusped windows in the E half; S doorway with multiple continuous wavy mouldings, the N one narrower and simpler. S porch with benches of the same period. Stonework in the mixed colours of the local quarries, on the nave red sandstone is used for parapets and pinnacles. Bold chancel arch with two orders of continuous chamfers. Shallow cambered chancel roof of noble Early Tudor type with foliate bosses; the nave roof renewed but the porch roof similar, resting on head corbels. Against the corbel posts eight demi-figures of angels, those in the chancel playing musical instruments like the recorder and bagpipes, those in the nave holding books; all are repainted. The main floors laid with small tiles in harmonious ochres. Like the S door with its fine metalwork these may be Hughes's work.

FITTINGS. SCREEN. A rare survival of a C15 screen in 36 Anglesey. The lower part plain, though with much-moulded rails and narrow buttresses at the doorway. Four lights either side, the doors with six lancet panels each. Lower cornice of running leaf and pomegranate ornament, then trefoil crestings, on both sides. The loft coved far forward on the W, less on the E. In the central W bay over the door, a painted skeleton with the inscription COLYN ANGAU YW PECHOD (Sin is the sting of Death), other images are defaced. Plain bressumers, then richer bands of carving with the same motifs, two on the W, one on the E. Parapets with plain muntins. – STALLS. The ends with geometrical panelling and crosses with paterae and roses; one with a cruciform design. Desks including on the returns, with panelled fronts and frieze of sub-panels. Secondary benches with ends with paterae, dated 1690. – ALTAR with date 1634.

SHRINE CHAPEL OF ST EILIAN. A distinct building, rebuilt *c.* 1400(?). Late Dec cusped tracery in the E window, W bell-cote with pointed arch. W doorway almost round-headed, N doorway two-centred. The plain parapet and cambered roof with carved foliage bosses again of the late C15 like the church. The W doorway is displaced from axiality by a recess in the N wall, perhaps for a shrine. The existing SHRINE BASE may derive from the C15 reordering. It is of wood, the front segmental in plan. Its panelled base has moulded muntins each

with a buttress (as on the screen). The wooden top retains
fixing holes for a lost superstructure, two square sockets either
side and two round ones in the middle. – FONT. Damaged
medieval round bowl cut to an octagon below.

CHURCHYARD CROSS. Octagonal shaft with a knop, on
three steps; the head of another cross on the lychgate beside.

SHILOH CALVINISTIC METHODIST CHAPEL, Pengorffwysfa,
½ m. s. 1835, altered in the 1890s. Rendered, with large sashes.
Roof hipped and grouted against the weather. Old-fashioned
plan with the pulpit backing on the entrance lobby.

POINT LYNAS, ¾ m. NE. An Act of 1762 granted authority for a
LIGHTHOUSE to the town council of Liverpool: a pilot station
was sited here from 1766 and there was an oil-fired beacon
from 1779. In 1835 the Mersey Docks and Harbour Board
moved the station to the top of the headland, which made a
tower unnecessary. The design by the Board's famous surveyor
Jesse Hartley had the lantern in a low semicircular building
projecting from an embattled walled courtyard. This sector
light was replaced by a square tower in 1874, and the s wall of
the enclosure was replaced by *George Lyster* with a gabled
gateway and pointed arch in 1879. The keeper's house is still
in the Neo-Tudor of 1835, flanked by a pair of Continental-
looking cottages of 1935.

On the hill above is a SEMAPHORE TOWER, part of the chain
from Holyhead to Liverpool set up in 1828. On MYNYDD
EILIAN, 1½ m. SW, was a TELEGRAPH STATION of 1841, part
of a subsequent signal chain.

LLANERCHYMEDD

The market town, which serves the N interior of the island, is
now on hard times. The rising Victorian main street is generously
laid out including the mid-C19 POLICE STATION in contrasting
stones; at the top, a house of *c.* 1840 in two limestones in bands.
A tighter pattern below the Market Square; a cartshed arch dated
1767. Little remains of the railway station on the branch to
Amlwch, opened 1866.

ST MARY. A large town church rebuilt in Dec style by *Kennedy*
in the 1850s. Nave and long chancel. W tower, the lower stage
probably C12 (cf. Llaneilian), suggesting origins as a *clas*
church; Victorian upper stages, with embattled parapet and,
strangely, a gabled bellcote on the E parapet. Round-headed E
doorway in tower, heavily plastered. – LYCHGATE. Neo-Tudor
with a bellcote on the N side, but the s side dated 1755, with a
brick basket arch and blocked *œil-de-boeuf* window.

(LLWYDIARTH ESGOB FARM, 1 m. E. Large gentry house,
C18 or early C19, extended to form a double-pile plan in the
mid C19. Two-storey with attic. Rendered. Triple-stack brick
chimneys.

Extensive FARM buildings, a good example of progressive farming in the C19. Early C19 corn barn with paired threshing doors. Cowhouse, stable, hammels etc. of the same date, with stone voussoir-head doorways. Mid to late C19 additions, with brick-arched openings: further stables, a slaughterhouse, cartsheds etc.)

GALLT-Y-BENDDU WINDMILL, ½ m. E. 1737. Thought to be the oldest windmill tower on the island, now a house.

At RHODOGEIDIO, I m. NNW, ST CEIDIO, a tiny church in a raised *llan* in a hilltop circle of trees – the epitome of ancient siting. Rebuilt using the old stones in 1845. The E window is C14, one light with ogee profile beneath mouchettes as at Tregaean. Two-centre hoodmould over. The N doorway, away from the wind, with an almost round arch and hollow chamfer, may be C17. Other windows and the W bellcote are Victorian and the fittings follow Early Victorian convention. – FONT. Octagonal, C15.

(ST MARY, in the fields ¾ m. W of ST CEIDIO. A very small unicameral church, 30 by 12 ft (9 by 3.7 metres), in a raised churchyard. The single-light trefoiled E window and the four-bay roof of arch-braced trusses suggest the late C15. – FONT. C12, circular and undecorated.)

LLANEUGRAD *see* MARIANGLAS

LLANFACHRAETH

3283

The village on the main road has good buildings of stone, including Victorian terraces and the SCHOOL near the church at the N end, but all are losing their quality to pebbledash. Just W, a water-powered WOOLLEN MILL.

ST MACHRAETH. In a largely circular raised *llan*, with a stable for the parson's horse at the W. Chancel and nave with W bellcote all rebuilt after 1878 by an unknown architect. To judge by the remaining fragments much was lost; Lewis's *Topographical Dictionary*, 1833, records a medieval church with a good E window. – Two STONES re-set in the W wall, carved with human faces, of unknown date, cf. Llanbabo. Part of the head of a WHEEL-CROSS, C10, expanded-arm cross framing a Crucifixion on one side, and interlacing on the other. The spandrels between the arms are pierced through. – FONT. Circular gritstone bowl, probably the medieval one re-dressed. – Heraldic carving from a C17 PEW, with the arms of the Bulkeley family and of descendants of Ednyfed Fychan. – BRASS PLATE to the Rev. Thomas Vincent †1738 and wife Jane. – (STAINED GLASS. By *Powells*. E window 1900, S window 1892, another of 1910, Faith, Hope and Charity.)

Tudor-style VICARAGE, 1838, by *Thomas Jones*, just to the N.

LLANYNGHENEDL, 1 m. s. In the village the partly circular *llan* of the church of ST CENEDL. The church of 1862 by *Kennedy & Rogers* has gone, re-erected as an extension to the base church of R.A.F. Valley at Llanfihangel yn Nhowyn (q.v.).

LLANFAELOG

3473

Mostly modern settlement on the main road, inland from Rhosneigr, the church prominent at the junction. Former RECTORY to the N, a long five-bay roughcast front with centre gable and hoodmoulded lower windows, by *Thomas Jones*, 1835. To the S, the former NATIONAL SCHOOL, gabled, two-storey, in stone, 1849, the recessed centre now filled in.

ST MAELOG. Rebuilt in 1847 by *Kennedy*, within the old *llan*. Steep-roofed nave and chancel with W bellcote, Dec style. The vestry N doorway is Perp, rescued from the old church. The character within comes from the reordering of 2000 by *Adam & Frances Voelcker*. The W end separated as a lobby with meeting room above, but a glazed upper screen maintains the scale of the church. It is finely etched by *Bill Swann* of Porthmadog. Remarkable carved wood FITTINGS by *Colin Pearce* to the Tree of Life theme, altar, rails, pulpit, and even the small branched clasp which holds the C12 FONT brought from St Mary, Talyllyn (q.v.), with a raised Maltese cross on one face and chevrons on another. – STAINED GLASS. E window, Last Supper, 1881. Small lancet *c.* 2000 in chancel S by *Stephanie Tate*, choir member. Nave N lancet, St Cecilia, later C19 in silver and gold, and a two-light *c.* 1902 by *E. Frampton*. W window, St Paul, 1902, *H. Seward & Co.* – MONUMENT. Plaque to Margaret Roberts, drowned in 1785 with fifty-six others crossing the Menai Strait. – John Roberts of Neuadd †1824, marble drapery.

PLAS LLANFAELOG, ½ m. NW. Substantial Edwardian house around a broad roughcast entrance tower with sandstone windows, the rest gabled and formless. The ground floor faced in tiny stones, like knapped flint. In the forecourt a little stone and timber GAME LARDER. Behind, MODEL FARM with brick details, grey slates and swept-up turret.

TŶ NEWYDD BURIAL CHAMBER 1 m. NNE (SH 344 738). Now badly ruined, it was once covered by a small circular cairn and had a short passage into the polygonal chamber from the E. Only the chamber survives, half covered by the capstone which split in the C18 when a celebratory bonfire was lit on top. Excavation in the 1930s found pieces of Late Neolithic Beaker pottery. The tomb is probably much earlier, since it belongs to an early style.

INSCRIBED STONE, beside the A4080 road (SH 356 746). At first glance like a prehistoric standing stone, but on the N side a vertically written Latin inscription CUNOGUSI HIC IACET reveals that it marks a C6 Christian grave. It is thought that the name of this chieftain survives in the place name Pencarnisiog, less than a mile away.

BARCLODIAD-Y-GAWRES, 1½ m. S (SH 329 707). 'The Apronful of the Giantess' is one of the most complete and interesting megalithic burial chambers in Anglesey. The covering cairn has been restored and a torch is needed to see the decorated stones properly. The tomb is a cruciform passage grave akin to the famous tombs in the Boyne valley, Ireland, built in the fourth millennium B.C. A long narrow passage (one side almost destroyed) leads into a central chamber which would have had a high corbelled vault (one roof stone survives). Off this chamber open three side chambers used for cremation burials,

Llanfaelog, Barclodiad-y-gawres, burial chamber.
Drawing of stone carving.

the western one with an annexe beyond (walling stones collapsed) and cut off from the central area by elaborate blocking. The central chamber rituals involved a fire quenched by
throwing over it a stew whose ingredients, frogs, toads, snakes
etc. recall Macbeth's witches' brew. The most notable feature
of tombs of this type is the abstract carving on the wall stones,
here found on five stones, including those of the passage as it
enters the central chamber. That on the w side is most easily
seen. Oblique light is needed to pick out the spirals, lozenges
and zigzags on the others. A series of spirals can be seen on
the back of the E chamber, a single small spiral in a similar
position in the w chamber. The large flat stone E of the
entrance to the central chamber is very lightly decorated in the
bottom right-hand corner.

On the neighbouring headland, Mynydd Bach (sh 328 708)
is a small ruined CAIRN covering a large empty cist grave, probably of the Beaker period (*c*. 2000 B.C.)

6177

LLANFAES

The chief town and port of pre-conquest Anglesey. It had 120
burgages on the English model. Llywelyn the Great founded a
Franciscan friary in 1237 on land directly back from the shore
on the death of his wife, Princess Joan of England. The friary
church, consecrated in 1245, with its triple lancet E windows,
survived as a barn till demolition in 1819, on the site of the house
called Fryars (*see* below). The town was suppressed in favour of
the post-conquest borough of Beaumaris chartered in 1296, and
the inhabitants moved to the Welsh town of Newborough.
Despite these troubles Llanfaes Friary continued as a burial place
(*see* the effigies of the Tudor family removed to Penmynydd
church). The medieval parish church further inland was largely
rebuilt in the C19. More recently Friars Bay was the site of the
Saunders-Roe seaplane works, moved here for safety in 1940,
where American Catalina flying-boats were modified for service.
Two large HANGARS survive just N of Fryars and a small concrete
slipway.

St Catherine (sh 605 778). In character a Victorian estate
church although there is a C13 nave, C14 chancel and a w tower
of 1811. The tower, built for Lord Bulkeley, was altered when
the spire was added in *Weightman & Hadfield*'s restoration of
1845. Ornate, cross-gabled Bulkeley chapel, N, 1885, by
R. G. Thomas, s aisle in C13 style by *Kennedy*, 1890. The effect
is completely Victorian within apart from some fine older
memorials. – STAINED GLASS (much commissioned by the
Williams-Bulkeley family of Baron Hill). E, Resurrection, by
Ward & Hughes, *c*. 1870–80; chancel N, 1845; s aisle s by *Gibbs
& Howard*; s aisle w, two angels with glorious wings, perhaps
Burlison & Grylls; N chapel, Crucifixion, *Ward & Hughes*, 1884.

- MONUMENTS. Distinguished low-relief memorial in an eccentric Baroque to Henry Whyte of Fryars †1728, with his bust in high relief above. – Chancel, Jane Whyte †1749, chastely Baroque. – Sir Robert Williams of Fryars †1830 and his wife Anne †1837, an overwhelmingly scaled Gothic canopied niche. – Anne Williams †1858 in a floral marble frame.

Churchyard. Fragments of broken C14 grave-slabs with incised Lombardic inscriptions. – Slab with indent of the brass to an archdeacon of Anglesey, c. 1310. – Pedestal memorial with urn and white marble panels, one in Welsh, one in English, to the Rev. John Elias †1841, the preacher – Grecian pillar to the Rev. John Williams †1921.

FRYARS, ½ m. SE. At the Dissolution the friary site was sold to the Wynn or Whyte family, whose house, with the last C15 monastic fragments, was demolished in 1866. This had a two-storey centre between tall wings with lateral chimneys. In the late C18 Sir Hugh Williams, stepfather of the last Viscount Bulkeley, commissioned alterations from *John Cooper*. The present house of 1866, in rubble stone, is gabled, Victorian Tudor.

HENLLYS, ½ m. WSW. A substantial Victorian Tudor mansion in fine grey ashlar, 1852–3 by *Charles Hansom*. Built for the Hampton family, owners from the mid C15 when William Hampton, Deputy Constable of Beaumaris, built a house on the probable site of Llywelyn's court or *llys*. Two ranges partly enclose a court, with mullion-and-transom windows and a two-storey gabled porch, the upper floor an open loggia. A service range runs back from one end. It has a tall four-storey clock tower with a corniced top, and originally an ogee dome.

ALMSHOUSES, 2 m. W of Beaumaris on the Llangefni road. Dated 1613 with the initials of David Hughes. A substantial single-storey layout around a square court with a well. There were originally seven tenements and a chapel in the centre of the E range (of which the E window of three arched lights survives), entered asymmetrically from the S by a cobbled passage. Its doorway has a segmental arch with shields in the spandrels, a dropped keystone with a diamond boss, and a hoodmould. Remodelled in 1937 but no longer in the intended use.

CARTREF, ½ m. E. Low-spreading house in Baronial style, built c. 1900 reputedly for the Vernon family of Liverpool. Red brick, red roof tiles etc. in the style of John Douglas. Red sandstone mullion-and-transom bay window to the hall, with embattled parapet. Octagonal corner bay, corbelled out, with blind tracery panels and spire. The hall has a minstrels' gallery.

LLANFAETHLU

Compact village inland from the w coast. John Davies (Sion
Dafydd Rhys), Renaissance scholar, was born here in 1534.
In the village, TŶ COFFI GRIFFITH-READE, 1892, one of the
three Temperance coffee houses built by Lady Reade of
Carreglwyd. Modest Arts and Crafts. TANFFYNNON, just S, is of
the 1830s, Tudor with a two-bay loggia between wings.

ST MAETHLU. Unusually sited down a steep hillside, and within
sight of the sea below. A single-cell church of c. 1425 with S
porch and W bellcote; chancel added 1874 by *Kennedy*. The
nave S windows have paired cinquefoiled lights under square
heads; the re-set E window is a refined late Dec design with a
cusped-mandorla light. Porch with rubble outer doorway,
benches and plaster vault. The nave ceiling also with a plaster
vault, a rarity in Anglesey, probably fixed to the camber of the
medieval arch-braced roof. – Late C19 BOARDS with the Lord's
Prayer and Creed, either side of the altar. – ALTAR RAILS. With
C18 balusters. – PULPIT. An Art Nouveau design c. 1925. –
PEWS. Fragments of Caroline classical woodwork from the
box pews of the Griffith family of Carreglwyd. On the dossal
of the made-up pew is carved a colonnade with depressed
arches, the arms of William Griffith (i.e. the three severed
heads of Ednyfed Fychan) and the date 1635. – FONT.
Octagonal; inscribed 'the gift of Richard Griffith 1640'. –
MONUMENTS. Mostly to the Griffith family of Carreglwyd
and their relations and servants, associated since 1544
when William Griffith of Penrhyn became rector. – BRASS
to this William Griffith, †1587. – William Griffith †1718,
John Griffith †1776 and others, a sophisticated Baroque wall
monument lettered as if a legal document. Inscribed apron
and two angels' heads supporting, on a gadrooned shelf, an
aedicule with fluted pilasters, open frieze and broken pediment. On top a floral vase between the family arms (Ednyfed
Fychan and Hwfa). – Mary Vickers †1772 and William Vickers
†1792, marble sarcophagus with oval relief of a putto extin-
guishing a torch, against a pyramid of slate. – Rice Jones
and his wife Jane, both †1786, damaged memorial in slate cut
as fabric folds; 'she nursed William, John, Robert, Hugh,
Francis, Magdalen and Mary, sons and daughters to John Griffith of Carreglwyd'. – Holland Griffith †1839. Chaste and
refined Grecian stele signed by *William Theed Jun.* at 'Roma'.
Female mourner in profile in high relief wiping tears away, on
a Greek Revival stool; she faces a garlanded pillar. – Rev.
William Lloyd of Blaenyglyn †1844, Gothic Revival, unusually
in carved and painted slate. – BRASS to his son †1888. – Pair
of trefoil-headed slabs to John Jones †1868, butler to the Griffiths 1820–66; and to Owen Thomas †1863, 'He had worked
for the Griffiths of Carreglwyd for over 80 years' and his son
Owen Thomas †1895. – Sir Chandos Reade †1890. Fine
Gothic carving in alabaster and green-veined limestone by
J. Forsyth Sen.

TABLE TOMBS against the S external wall. Richard Griffith
†1640, slab on six square balusters, its sandstone segmental
hood, of the North Wales type (cf. the Wynn tomb, Conwy). –
Katherin Griffith †1644, with roundels between pilasters.

EBENEZER CALVINISTIC METHODIST CHAPEL, W of Tŷ Coffi.
Remodelled 1908, by *Joseph Owen*. Pebbledashed. Polygonal-
end with gable; more gables to porch and transepts, all with
Tudor windows and finials. Art Nouveau glazing.

CARREGLWYD, ½ m. NW. The senior surviving seat of descendants of Ednyfed Fychan's second son Gruffudd. The Rev.
William Griffith †1597 settled here as rector in 1544, the house
was rebuilt in 1634 by his grandson Dr William Griffith
(†1648), Master of the Rolls. In 1755 the estate was joined with
Plas Berw, Pentre Berw, the house remodelled possibly in 1763
for Mary Griffith, the date on a rainwater head, with further
work for her son Holland (†1839). Of the Anglesey Georgian
gentry type, low and long with sash windows on two storeys,
and a hipped roof with several sturdy chimneys. L-plan, eight
bays by five, added to the earlier C17 core. Modest interiors of
the early to late C18. Only the design of the Regency dining
room has ambitions: its buffet end is a gentle crescent, pilaster
strips dividing the central section with an elliptical arch over
the sideboard from two narrower niches, one fitted with a
curved jib door on a kick hinge.

Entered undemonstratively at the top of undulating bare
greensward in the C18 taste, the demesne is hidden in thickets
of sycamore below. The internal landscape largely remodelled
c. 1880 in the Victorian taste for evergreen trees and heavy
stonework by Frederick Stanley Carpenter (a Deputy
Governor of Hong Kong), with the drive keeping low and
crossing a bridge to leave the house concealed. All hugs the
low ground as protection on this exposed headland in NW
Anglesey. The valley site was redesigned as a view from the
house with a long Victorian lake and wooded slopes. Indications of the older layout include the miniature roofless DOVE-
COTE of *c.* 1600 to one side, with its four gables, alighting shelf
and nesting holes. To the W behind the house the high C18 walls
of a one-acre WALLED GARDEN with curving corners. The
ESTATE BUILDINGS are grouped away from the house to the
N in the loosely spaced relationship characteristic of the island.
An C18 barn and other structures like a laundry house of 1871
form a service yard, and behind these a long stable and coachhouse range of largely early C19 Tudor character.

TREFADOG, 2 m. SW at Porth Trefadog. A hall-house mentioned
in a lease of 1419. Three bays of crucks with arch braces, the
walls now of stone. S of the bay, a small, very defensible
promontory FORT, excavated 1984. Probably *c.* C12, it may be
Welsh, Norman or even Viking in origin. Possibly built on an
earlier defensive site, it enclosed a rectangular building,
perhaps a hall.

STANDING STONE, ½ m. SE, by Capel Soar (SH 319 863).
Standing about 10 ft (3 metres) high.

5283

LLANFAIR MATHAFARN EITHAF

On the high ground inland from Benllech.

ST MARY (SH 507 829). The chancel medieval, with an early
C15 three-light E window with cusped flowing tracery. Nave
also early C15; two-centred N doorway, later round-arched S
doorway, both with quarter-round mouldings. Restored 1848
by *Kennedy*, who added Perp-style windows and the S porch.
His plans show that he installed the pews, removed the W
gallery, and replaced the Laudian altar rails. – PULPIT. 1969,
in memory of Goronwy Owen (1723–69) poet, born in the
parish and briefly curate here. – MONUMENT. David son of
William Daniel †1724, slate. – FRAGMENTS of two C12–C13
GRAVESTONES, one with four circles as a cross-head, joined
by hands, the other with an expanded-arm cross. – CHURCH-
YARD CROSS, C11. A wheel-cross with arms extending beyond
the circle.

PANT-Y-SAER BURIAL CHAMBER (SH 509 824). Now sadly
crumbling, but notable mainly for the number of people (over
fifty) originally buried in this small square box. C19 excavations
found a Beaker burial cist dug into the earlier burial layer.
Re-excavation in 1932 found communal Neolithic burials, with
pottery sherds and flint arrowheads. The chamber was always
blocked in front, but the funnel-shaped forecourt was the scene
of ceremonies, including the offering of an almost complete
pot at the foot of the solid 'door'. It is built into a large pit
from which the building blocks may have been prised, so that
the height inside is greater than appears externally. Surrounded by the remains of a kidney-shaped cairn which may
originally have extended further SW.

PANT-Y-SAER HUT GROUP (SH 513 824). Somewhat overgrown.
Excavation in the 1930s demonstrated occupation from the
Iron Age to the C6.

GLYN BURIAL CHAMBER (SH 514 817). Difficult to locate
among gorse bushes as it makes good use of the character of
limestone and involves little actual building. A slab was lifted,
propped at an angle, and the resultant hole deepened. C19
excavation found human bone.

5373

LLANFAIRPWLL

A village on the Strait, where Telford's road to Holyhead turns
inland. TOLL HOUSE at its S end, known as Llanfair Gate. A two-
storey octagon with an iron-railed veranda around, the finest of
five designed for the Anglesey stretch by *Thomas Telford c.* 1818.
The board of charges says that a horse and cart paid 3d., a horse
on its own 1d., cattle 10d. per score and sheep 5d. per score.
These were the last turnpike tolls in Britain, lifted in 1895.

Holyhead Street, the A5 road, is lined with low late C19 and
C20 houses. TREGARNE, S, is a villa of before 1914, as also TŶ
COCH opposite, brick and half-timber, built for Sir John Morris,

the Welsh language scholar. On the S, small First World War memorial CLOCK TOWER, *c.* 1920, Cubist with a touch of Gothic, in white ashlar. The STATION beyond, of 1848, red brick, like a mid-Victorian villa, has pretty wheel-pattern latticework on the footbridge. The famous C19 long form of the station name has generated a tourist shopping complex just W.

In the older village N of the main road, on Lôn Graig, a single-storey COTTAGE with octagonal brick chimneys. At Y GRAIG was held the first ever Women's Institute meeting in Britain, in 1915, the movement having begun in Canada in 1897; the meeting moved to the corrugated-iron hall by the toll house in 1921.

ST MARY, ½ m. S, close by the Strait (SH 537 712). 1853, by *Henry Kennedy*. Green stone. Dec Gothic. Nave and chancel, S porch under a thin and heavily buttressed tower and spire. Arch-braced trusses with high collars; wagon-ceiling to chancel. High chancel arch. – STAINED GLASS. E and W windows, 1876. In the churchyard, OBELISK on a granite plinth to fifteen men who died of injuries received during the erection of the Britannia Bridge.

BRITANNIA BRIDGE, ¾ m. SE. From its completion in 1850 to its irreparable damage by fire in 1970, *Robert Stephenson*'s Britannia Bridge was one of the world's engineering wonders. The rigid wrought-iron tubes of its two main spans carried the Chester–Holyhead railway unseen across the Menai Strait at a height of 104 ft (32 metres) above high water. New engineering techniques were invented both for the design and function of these horizontal members, and for raising them from water level to the tops of the towers by manpower and hydraulics

Llanfairpwll, Britannia Bridge.
Engraving, mid-C19

only. The stone towers survive, but their starkly original appearance was compromised by the steel arches erected in 1972–3; the tubes were distorted by the fire, which obliged their removal.* The arches supported the tubes during dismantling, then served to carry the rail and road decks which replaced them. To understand the grandeur of the concept, recourse to celebratory prints or old photographs is needed. To understand the magnificence of its realization, a scramble up to the railway portals, flanked by colossal lions carved by *John Thomas* (each 25 ft (8 metres) long and weighing 80 tons, sadly now obscured by the road deck), lets them speak for themselves. Robert Stephenson was appointed engineer-in-chief to the Chester & Holyhead Railway in June 1845.

p. 62

Through experiments he became satisfied 'that a wrought iron tube is the most economical structure that can be devised for a railway bridge across the Menai Strait'. The visual directness of the solution was matched by the feat of its construction; the engineers *William Fairbairn* and *Eaton Hodgkinson*, the railway's architect *Francis Thompson*, and *Edwin Clark*, resident engineer, played a part. Some figures: the height of the towers from their foundations is 221 ft 3 in. (68 metres), the centre or Britannia tower (built on a rock in the middle of the Strait) is 198 ft 9 in. (61 metres) above high water, the two land towers each 180 ft 6 in. (55.5 metres). Some 1,500,000 tons of masonry were erected, red Runcorn sandstone being used for core work and limestone quarries being opened especially at Penmon (q.v.) for the facings; some blocks were up to 20 ft (6 metres) long, some weighed 12–14 tons. The first stone was laid on 21 September 1846; Stephenson himself laid the stone completing the cornice on 22 June 1849. The towers to an extent follow Telford's Egyptian precedent at his suspension bridge; the pylons are taken up well above the tubes and pierced with openings for suspension chains which, in the end, were considered unnecessary. They are also carved with a portcullis motif, possibly reflecting Thomas's work on the new Houses of Parliament. A large figure of Britannia was proposed for the central pier, but cost too much.

Whereas Telford employed arches to lift his carriageway to the main span, Stephenson sprung his necessarily level deck from masonry causeways in the wooded hills either side. The two water spans and the two land spans together made a bridge 1,834 ft 9 in. (565 metres) long, the length of the water spans being 460 ft (142 metres) and the land spans 230 ft (71 metres). The four 1,800-ton tubes were assembled from wrought-iron plates on quays either side by the contractors *Mare & Co.* and *W. J. & J. Garforth*. They were floated out (it took 56 minutes each with 685 men working winches etc.),

*A length of tube survives as an exhibit on the mainland side of the bridge – *see* p. 258.

then raised vertically by hydraulic presses built by *Easton &*
Amos. Each operation took seventeen days. (The tracks for this
assembling on the inner faces of the towers are now obscured
by the supporting struts devised by the engineer for the C20
reconstruction, *Sir Charles Husband*.) The bridge opened in
1850, having cost over £600,000.

ANGLESEY COLUMN, ¼ m. E, on Cerrig-y-borth, a bluff
overlooking the Strait. A notably tall Greek Doric column by
Thomas Harrison, 1816–17, 112 ft (34 metres) high. Erected by
public subscription to Henry William Paget, Earl of Uxbridge
and later 1st Marquess of Anglesey, of Plas Newydd. He com-
manded the cavalry at Waterloo, where he was second-in-
command to the Duke of Wellington. The tower is of Moelfre
limestone, inscribed in English, Latin and Welsh on the plinth
above three great steps. The shaft is polygonal below, then
fluted. From its platform, reached by a wooden spiral stair
round a pine newel said to be of two masts end-to-end, the
panorama of the Menai Strait can be viewed. The bronze figure
was made in 1860 by *Matthew Noble*. This statue, 12 ft 4 in.
(4 metres) high and weighing 2½ tons, was erected by a
remarkable scaffolding technique using timber and ropes
invented by the Plas Newydd agent *John Haslam*. At its foot
the mid-C19 COTTAGE for the column-keeper.

ADMIRAL NELSON STATUE, ½ m. ESE, just offshore below the
church. 1873–5. A colossal figure, 19 ft (6 metres) high with its
base, on a pedestal and basement tower 22 ft (7 metres) high,
the work of Admiral *Lord Clarence Paget*, son of the 1st
Marquess of Anglesey. Sited looking w towards Plas Newydd,
the family home, it was intended as a warning mark of the tidal
rapids known as the Swellies. It is made of limestone and
Portland cement modelled round an iron core. A late instance
of the Nelson cult, apparently inspired by the Trafalgar Square
figure.

PLAS LLANFAIR, ¼ m. S. The medieval core has gone; there is a
re-set coat of arms with the initials LB and the date 1616. In
the late C18 this was the home of Col. William Peacock, one
of Lord Uxbridge's advisers in the embellishment of Plas
Newydd when *John Cooper* was the executant architect: so it is
reasonable to suppose that the colonel and architect were
responsible for the twin three-storey half-round towers like a
castle gateway, facing s over the Strait. Flat arches with keystones to the windows. To the w a three-bay wing with Gothick
windows on the upper floor in the Plas Newydd style, perhaps
part of Lord Clarence Paget's works of 1853, together with the
grotesque heads on it. Both of these are in the local gritstone
and have castellations. To the s, Italianate terraces, to the N a
walled garden, both of this period but obscured by recent
alterations. The present appearance and size is otherwise owed
to substantial late C19 remodelling for the Clegg family.
Architect and materials both seem to have come on the train
from Liverpool.

Battlemented LODGE. Late Georgian Tudor. Gates of Gothic Revival ironwork.

YNYS GORAD GOCH, 1 m. E. An island between the bridges. Immemorial fish weirs exist, in their early C19 form with iron traps (replaced on the Anglesey side in 1924, in experimental concrete form by *G. H. Hodgson*), together with a smoke tower of after 1811. The cottage on the island is C18; the gazebo was built in 1808 for John Randolph, Bishop of Bangor.

LLANFAIRYNGHORNWY

A small village 4 m. WSW of Cemaes, close to Carmel Head, the NW point of the island. The Thomas family of bone-setters lived here, descendants of a shipwreck survivor of the 1740s.

ST MARY (SH 327 908). The most important church of NW Anglesey, with an unusual plan. The rounded chancel arch suggests that the nave is C12, though the S door and two-light trefoiled window are C14 and the N window, of three rounded-headed lights below a label, typically C16. The chancel, longer than the nave and hardly narrower, was added in the late C15, dated by the two-centred E window and the arch-braced collar-beam roof. Early in the C16, a chapel was added S of the chancel, of the same length and divided by a three-bay arcade of four-centred arches of two hollow-chamfered orders. Lastly, the plain W tower, added *c.* 1660. A N chapel was proposed by the Baron Hill estate, *c.* 1847, with *Weightman & Hadfield* as architects. If carried out, the church plan would have been extraordinary. *Weightman & Hadfield* may have carried out restoration work at this time; *Harold Hughes* did further work in 1931.

The church is ringed with great trees, like the neighbouring former RECTORY, a substantial Tudor house with mullioned and transomed windows, of 1824.

CAERAU, ¾ m. NW. Once one of the most complete examples of a small Anglesey estate house, now derelict. Two wings at right angles, one late C17, the other dated 1730 on the joinery, possibly originating as a unit plan since both parts are nearly contemporary and of equivalent high standard as regards fittings. The older house, W, is a fragment with a massive lateral chimney. One downstairs room was handsomely wainscoted with fielded panels below and above dado height, and bolection mouldings round the fireplace and an overmantel feature. Staircase with heavy turned balusters. The block facing N, built for Thomas Rowlands, has a two-storey front six windows long with sash windows instructively larger. Its plan is complex. Chimneys on the end gables and one asymmetrically placed behind the entrance. On the S are asymmetrical gables. There was a remarkable Early Georgian fitted kitchen divided by dressers as partitions, and the bedrooms had overmantels decorated with landscape paintings. S of the transverse block, a walled COURTYARD entered by an early C18 classical gateway with the piers once carrying stone balls. This is not aligned with the C19 (?) entrance avenue. To the N a large walled garden. To the E an unusual broad-gabled building serving multiple purposes, a stable and barn below and a loft reached by an outside stair and lit by stone dormers, either granary or sleeping loft for the farm. Over the stream a four-seat privy.

CASTELL CRWN, ½ m. E (SH 332 908). Low-lying, almost hidden. A small, very precisely circular enclosure with a sharply defined bank and ditch. Likely to be early medieval or medieval rather than prehistoric.

STANDING STONES. Two at SH 334 906 and 333 903. A record of a third stone and two round barrows suggests there was a significant group of Bronze Age monuments here.

MYNACHDY, 1½ m. NW. A substantial late C17 harled house on the site of a grange of Aberconwy Abbey. The plan, typical of its date, consists of an entrance hall with parlour to the l., kitchen to the r., and axial dog-leg staircase projecting behind; so it is neither double-pile nor quite symmetrical. E front originally of eight bays (one now blocked) on two storeys. Chimneys on the end gables, and one more at the fourth bay from the r. where the doorway now is (the blocked bay was the entrance bay). Hall with double doors to the parlour, which has good bolection moulding round the fireplace; stair with panelled newels and turned balusters. At the W a large walled garden. To its W a group of small farm buildings with C18–early C19 segmental archways.

To the W, two rendered and limewashed rubblestone NAVIGATION MARKERS, 21 ft (6.5 metres) high, set up by Trinity House in the 1830s for navigation into Holyhead Harbour.

LLANFAIR YN NEUBWLL 3177

The area of dunes and bog S of Caergeiliog, the two pools of the parish name being Llyn Penrhyn and Llyn Dinam. The S part of the parish is now covered by R.A.F. Valley, established on land reclaimed from Traeth Cleifiog in 1776.

ST MARY (SH 297 778). Small, low church among the hummocks of rock by the tidal sands which form the sound separating Holy Island from the main island. Rebuilt *c.* 1300, to go by the E window of two lancets with plain image light above, the trefoiled lancet in the S chancel wall, and the N doorway. In the N of the chancel a C15 cinquefoiled window. Arch-braced roof trusses, sprung so low that they resemble crucks. Sensitively restored in 1857 by *Henry Kennedy*, albeit with the loss of C15 stained glass, C17 pulpit and a coffin-lid with a circled cross.

LLYN CERRIG BACH, SH 306 765. One of the best-known Iron Age sites in Britain. In the lake was found a wealth of arms, chariots, horse harness and other valued possessions of Celtic chieftains, offered to the water gods in the manner described by classical writers who had seen such ceremonies on the

Continent. Judging from the style of the swords and bronze-work this lake received offerings from *c.* 200 B.C. till the coming of the Romans in A.D. 60. Amongst the latest offerings were slave chains of Belgic origin, emphasizing the role of Anglesey as a retreat westwards from the Roman menace.

LLANFAIR-YN-Y-CWMWD *see* DWYRAN

LLANFECHELL

3692

Nucleated villages such as this are rare on the island. The core is the almost complete Early Christian circular *llan* in which the church stands. To its SE a small square with the war memorial CLOCK TOWER, 1920, crowned by a soldier standing guard, by *John Griffiths* of Llangefni, mason. Miniature streets to the E and S with cottages in terraces of *c.* 1800 and after. NE of the church-yard the lateral chimney of the former RECTORY suggests a late medieval or Tudor origin. Hall with cross-passage, the first-floor room above originally with an open roof.

ST MECHELL. Nave and chancel in one unusually narrow range, short transepts, S porch, and later W tower with stumpy octagonal stone spire. Under the ochre limewash of 2001 the vestiges of a Romanesque church are visible. These, the Royal Commission suggests, are enough to suggest that the C12 plan consisted of the present nave with to its E a crossing tower and short chancel, enlarged in the C13. Does this plan indicate a mother church for this part of the island? In the S wall the C12 elements are the doorway and low priest's doorway, both with crude imposts and thin voussoirs set almost vertically, and a blocked window E of that. In the N wall a blocked window high at the W, and a small round-arched window head re-set in the chancel when it was lengthened. Substantial alterations, characterized by flowing Dec traceries: E window with bold pre-Perp casement mouldings and renewed tracery, likewise the S and N transept windows. Other windows of Victorian plate-traceried type with paired lancets, set in round-headed reveals; of *c.* 1870, like the N transept? The tower, datable to the C16 by its Tudor window, is without other architectural features apart from three set-offs and crude battlements. The short spire (a rarity on Anglesey), its octagonal form resting on a circular stone vault, was added in the C18. Roof of close-set arch-braced trusses consistent with the late Dec, incorporating old timbers. The S porch roof of similar construction. The S transept arch is low, hollow-chamfered, with broach stops dying into the wall, the N arch a C19 copy.

FONT. C12, square, with recessed panels carved with coupled arches like the doorways. – ORGAN. Of *c.* 1900, Gothic by *W. Rushworth & Son.* – STAINED GLASS. E window †1869, by

C. E. Clutterbuck Jun. Two s windows, 1880s, and N window
†1907, Scottish figures, by *Shrigley & Hunt.* – N transept, C15
silver-stain fragments set as a sexfoil. – MONUMENTS. Rev.
William Meyrick †1819 and family, Neoclassical half-urn and
pyramid. – In the porch, a CROSS-SLAB with big floriations,
possibly C13. Also a stele with inscription to the Rev. Thomas
Jones †1830.

LIBANUS CALVINISTIC METHODIST CHAPEL. Hipped chapel
of 1832, altered 1850 by *Hugh Jones* of Llanfechell. Pedimented frontispiece 1903, of two storeys uncomfortably
squeezed. Interior of 1903 with icing-sugar plasterwork
around pierced wood circular ventilators, the pulpit with three
large high-relief plant carvings. – MONUMENT. Elizabeth, wife
of the Rev. John Elias †1841. He founded the first teetotal
society in Britain here in 1835. Adjacent SUNDAY SCHOOL,
1914, also pedimented. The two make a good show to the
square.

BRYNDDU, ½ m. s. The marriage of Arthur Bulkeley to Anne
the heiress of Brynddu, *c.* 1565, gives a date indication for
the Tudor E wing. To this a broad three-bay cross-range
was added later in the C16. A third wing built to its w by
William Bulkeley in the late C17 (now partly demolished)
formed the near-symmetrical w front drawn by Lewis Morris
c. 1742. Dark render outside and sub-classical refitting
inside, for General Robert Hughes *c.* 1850, including replacing window joinery, panelling and stairs, impede further
interpretation.

Next to the house at the sw the vestige of the late C17 entry
yard, in the tall stonework of the WALLED GARDEN – one of
the earliest to survive on Anglesey.

MAES MAWR FARM, ½ m. sw. George Bullock, a Liverpool
sculptor, bought a quarry here *c.* 1806, for the green and red
serpentinite or 'Mona Marble' used decoratively in mansions
(e.g. Penrhyn Castle) and churches (eg. Betws-y-coed). There
were also quarries on Holy Island.

STANDING STONES. The group of three on the top of low hill
just NW (SH 365 917) is unique and the arrangement cannot
be explained without excavation. Another single one about ½
m. away (SH 370 917).

BURIAL CHAMBER, ¾ m. NW (SH 359 919). A sketch made before
it collapsed shows an impressive monument, perhaps belonging to the class of portal dolmens.

PEN-Y-MORWYDD BARROW, I m. W (SH 384 913). The hilltop
is crowned by a Bronze Age barrow, quite small in area but
still high (because never ploughed over). In the C19 a Beaker
cist burial was found in the farmyard at Rhosbeirio to the E.
On the s slopes of the hill are remains of six pillow mounds
(artificial rabbit warrens), and a five-sided enclosure, now
badly ploughed down. Its date is not known though it can be
compared to the probably Romano-British five-sided
enclosure at Hendrefor, Llansadwrn.

LLANFFINAN see TALWRN

LLANFFLEWIN see MYNYDD MECHELL

3383
LLANFIGAEL

Isolated church on the N side of the Alaw river, 1 m. ENE of
Llanfachraeth.

ST FIGAEL (Friends of Friendless Churches). Small. Rebuilt
using old stonework in 1841, after being in ruins for forty years.
Now the image of a Late Georgian country church – see the
Regency Tudor E window. But the roof with its three collar-
beam trusses appears to be of the C18. The simple interior
jostles with box pews, humble benches with shaped ends and
a two-decker pulpit, so that there is hardly room for the altar,
screened in by short turned balusters. Standing and hanging
fittings for candles. – FONT. C14. Octagonal. A round fillet at
each angle.

   PLAS LLANFIGAEL, N of the church. The former vicarage,
Late Georgian, stone, with a shallow hipped roof. Built by *John
Cooper* of Beaumaris *c.* 1780. Front with two tripartite windows
in recessed arches, flanking the entrance in a brick canted bay.

   Former CORN BARN, S of the church. Large stone barn with
threshing-floor arches in brick, now a house.

LLANFIHANGEL DIN SILWY see LLANDDONA

4684
LLANFIHANGEL TRE'R BEIRDD

The church in a place with far views, beween Maenaddwyn and
Capel Coch, 4 m. ESE of Llanerchymedd.

ST MICHAEL (SH 459 837). W bellcote, nave, chancel, all with
pierced crosses: the work of *Henry Kennedy*, 1888,
following another reconstruction in 1811. However, the N
doorway with continuous chamfer and broaches is C14; there
is a C14 trefoiled window and a C15 cinquefoiled one in the
chancel. Wide, low chancel arch. – FONT. Medieval, octagonal,
re-cut. – GRAVE-SLABS. With early medieval ring crosses cut
at the head and foot and in the centre. – C13 incised cross with
trefoil terminals. – The church is the burial place of Morris
Prichard †1763, father of Lewis Morris and his brothers (*see*
Rhos Lligwy).

MAEN ADDWYN, ¼ m. S (SH 461 833). A large and imposing
stone, probably Bronze Age, just beside the road. It has given
its name to the village.

CAPEL COCH, 1 m. S. A good group of rural farm buildings. On
the E a farm dated 1750 and MELIN LLIDIART, a mid-C18
windmill tower, one of the oldest on the island. TŶ MAWR
CALVINISTIC METHODIST CHAPEL, founded 1785, was
rebuilt 1812, 1865 and 1898; the hipped form probably of 1865.

TRE-YSGAWEN HALL, 1 m. SW of Capel Coch. Victorian Italianate mansion in very Victorian grounds, rebuilt in 1882 for G. Pritchard-Rayner, by *R. G. Thomas* of Menai Bridge, on the site of the Pritchard family house. Fine sandstone ashlar, the compact façade in a series of planes: central triple window over a large balustraded porch with rusticated columns, outer bays stepped forward with angle pilasters and full-height canted bays. All the parapets balustraded.

LLANFIHANGEL YN NHOWYN

3377

Dominated by housing for nearby R.A.F. Valley. The parish name means St Michael in the dunes.

ST MICHAEL. In a rectangular raised churchyard. Unicameral nave and chancel, in part of medieval masonry; W bellcote and all windows of 1862, by *Kennedy & Rogers*. In 1988 the church was extended W and at right angles to serve as the church for R.A.F. Valley. For this the redundant church of Llanynghenedl, by *Kennedy & Rogers* of 1862, was dismantled and faithfully reassembled (it is a little loftier than Llanfihangel), but with the peculiarity that the W ends of the churches touch, so Llanynghenedl's W bellcote comes in the middle of the new plan and its E window now looks W. The two churches link through a low Neo-Norman arcade of three arches. The architect was *T. Baker* of *D. of E. Property Services Agency*. – FONT, rectangular, old but re-cut.

LLANFIHANGEL YSGEIFIOG *see* GAERWEN

LLANFWROG

3084

A scattered village 2 m. NW of Llanfachraeth.

ST MWROG. In a circular *llan*. Disused. The old stones entirely reassembled in 1864 by *Kennedy & Rogers* to conform to Kennedy's view of a traditional Anglesey church. Chancel, taller nave with W bellcote and unusually elaborate Neo-Dec window traceries. – FONT. Octagonal. Medieval but re-dressed?

LLANGADWALADR

3869

A hamlet at a junction of roads. The secluded churchyard is separated from the main road by the stuccoed Late Georgian VICARAGE, three-bay and hipped, extended by one bay r. Across the road, the former SCHOOL, in green stone, two-storey and steep-roofed. Two back wings, one with bellcote, later C19, but the front fenestration earlier C20.

St Cadwaladr or Eglwys Ael (sh 383 693). In a raised, enlarged, rectangular churchyard. The gabled and sub-gabled arch of the Gothic LYCHGATE of 1856, with the heads of some Victorians as stops, is the prelude to an already unusual Anglesey country church on which C19 money was spent. Chancel and nave with unbroken roof-line; the chancel with a N transeptal chapel and separately gabled s chapel, the nave with a large s porch and two-tier w bellcote. Much rebuilding under *Kennedy* in 1857–9 and later, for the Fuller-Meyrick family of Bodorgan. Blocked C13 N doorway, the pointed arch with multiple roll mouldings (cf. Llangristiolus). Kennedy's windows as so often have much cusping; externally at the E much carving of gargoyle beasts. The Victorian E window, with its Neo-Dec traceries, looks hard and agitated beside the C17 Gothic of the Bodowen Chapel. C15 chancel arch, nearly elliptical, with continuous chamfers; the arch of the N or MEYRICK CHAPEL, dated 1640 but much rebuilt in 1811 and 1856, follows that form. This chapel's N window, combining recess, tomb for Augustus Fuller †1857 and Sara Fuller †1856, and altar, all richly carved in grey limestone, is almost too Gothic Revival for the context.

64   BODOWEN CHAPEL. Added in 1659–61, in a fascinating combination of classical and Gothic, by the Royalist Col. Hugh Owen, and after his death by his wife Ann Williams of Llys Dulas. The chapel's founder, 'most firm to Monarchy', must have employed an Oxford stonemason, the outcome being like some of the mid-C17 college architecture, or Juxon's rebuilding of the Great Hall at Lambeth. On an E–W axis, with the dedicatory inscription over the w doorway. The s façade is a courtly design: central gable projecting, but not enough to justify the diagonal buttressing there and at the gables. The four-light s and E windows are pure Perp, set low, with two tiers of trefoiled lights. No upper transom, panel tracery. The ceiling paintings with the heavens and the words 'Holy, Holy, Holy' etc. and the depiction of Charles I in the E window have gone. Bold and low single arch to the crossing. – MONUMENT to the founders, Hugh and Ann Owen, over the s chapel w doorway. They kneel confronted at a prie-dieu within a double aedicule framed by Ionic columns; painted arms above.

39   STAINED GLASS. E, late C15, the Crucifixion with four angels; on the l., Saints Mary and John, above a panel with the donors of the window, Meuric ap Llywelyn of Bodowen and his wife Marged; on the r., their son Owain ap Meuric and his wife Elen Meredith of Glynllifon, in a scene of battle. It seems that the parents gave the window in thankfulness for their son's return from fighting for Henry Tudor at the battle of Bosworth, and the date is therefore *c.* 1485. – MONUMENTS. Owen Putland Meyrick †1825, the builder of the present Bodorgan Hall. Tall Grecian sarcophagus and draped urn, by *M. W. Johnson*, London. – N wall of nave, long C7 INSCRIBED STONE once marking the grave of Cadfan, grandfather of Cadwaladr, reigned 634–64, the last Welshman to assume the title of chief

sovereign of Britain. The inscription reads, CATAMUS REX
SAPIENTISIMUS OPINATISIMUS OMNIUM REGUM ('. . .
wisest and most illustrious of all kings'). – In the churchyard,
N, a good late C19 Celtic CROSS erected by the Meyrick family.

BODORGAN STATION, I m. N. One of *Francis Thompson*'s 'small
country stations'. A three-bay, two-storey faintly Italianate
house with deep eaves and three ornate chimneys, rising from
a longer one-storey range. This provides a covered shelter
between two offices of coursed green rubble. Taller GOODS
SHED beside it, in yellow stone, 1851.

LLANGAFFO   4568

ST CAFFO. Once known as Merthyr Caffo (the martyrium of
Caffo), later an Augustinian house. Of Early Christian origin,
in view of the exceptional number of inscribed fragments
found in C15 walls at the demolition of the old unicameral
church, which stood on the hillock above. A Perp doorway
from this church is reused as a LYCHGATE. The iron sunburst
gate is one of *Telford*'s, strayed from the Menai Bridge. The
larger replacement is an unlovely church in lancet style by
Weightman & Hadfield of Sheffield, 1846. Chancel, nave, w
tower and spire, a landmark E of the Malltraeth marsh. – FONT,
C12, with a saltire pattern, but completely re-cut. – PULPIT,
octagonal, with C17 carving. – REREDOS. Arts and Crafts
Gothic. – STAINED GLASS. E by *Mayer*, 1890. – MONUMENT.
Parts of an alabaster wall monument, *c.* 1660, including
Baroque pediments and cherubs. – INSCRIBED STONES. Six
cross-inscribed SLABS, C7–C11, and fragment of the head of a
standing WHEEL-CROSS with interlace. The shaft is in the
churchyard, with another. – INSCRIBED PILLAR, C7–C9, in the
vestry. It reads: IUS [ ] NIN FILIU[S] CUURI [S] EREXIT HUNC
LAPIDEM.

DINAM, ½ m E. Small late C17 estate house enlarged *c.* 1715 and
again in the 1920s. It passed to the Prichard family, the Rev.
R. Prichard instigating the church rebuilding in the C19. Late
C17 hall range with a sash-windowed E range added *c.* 1715.
This contains a handsome stair with turned balusters and
enriched newels, and a parlour with contemporary panelling
designed with pilasters and a frieze. Adjoining at the SE a mid-
C18 WALLED GARDEN with a gateway with a straight lintel, and
a small but complete contemporary STABLEYARD with stables,
cartshed, granary etc. Also next to the house at the SW a
pyramidal-roofed DOVECOTE, later a nine-hole privy. In a field
wall to the SW a C16 Perp doorway, apparently from the
medieval church. On the road a pair of early C19 monolith
gatepiers and cast-iron gates.

BODOWYR BURIAL CHAMBER, I m. E (SH 463 682). On a high
ridge with wide views, the ideal 'dolmen', however, badly
ruined. It has lost its circular cairn and its passage, which must
have been on the E side where the chamber is entered over a

high sillstone. The chamber is polygonal (one stone fallen) with
a neat mushroom-shaped capstone. The monument has not
been excavated, but this style of tomb is likely to be early
Neolithic (*c.* 4000 B.C.)

LLANGEFNI

4676

A minor market town from the C18, and a focus of increasing significance for the first free churches and their preachers, Llangefni
became the county town of Anglesey in the 1880s, succeeding the
less central Beaumaris. The new Holyhead expressway is con-
tributing to its industrial possibilities, and the new county offices
to its standing, but architecturally the town relies on a handful
of lively Late Victorian buildings round Bulkeley Square. The
church is set apart under the hill N of the Cefni.

CHURCHES AND CHAPELS

ST CYNGAR. Wholly rebuilt in 1824, an early instance of C19
church replacement, promoted by Viscount Bulkeley who paid
for the tower. Georgian Gothic in squared sandstone and
conglomerate. Typically repetitive detail, indeed some of the
tracery of cast-iron. Battlemented w tower with angle buttresses and Y-tracery bell-lights. The broad nave, entered from
the tower, has three-light traceried windows in iron and two-
light in stone. Little remains of the ancient church other than
a doorway reused at the w of the vestry. Some work by *Henry
Kennedy* in 1857–8. Short Perp chancel added in 1889. w organ
gallery. Shallow plastered vault compartmented by ribs, the
one between the nave and the former chancel enriched with
cusped tracery. – FONT, disused in the tower. C12 elongated
bowl with chevron rim. – STAINED GLASS. E window, Good
Shepherd with SS James and John, 1890? Nave windows, one
of the Redeemer and the Light of the World, another of the
child Jesus, 1890. – MONUMENTS. Richard Poole †1799 and
family. – Anne Poole †1815, by *Franceys & Spence* of Liverpool.
– Owen Poole †1823, by *W. Spence* of Liverpool. – By the w
door an INSCRIBED STONE of the C5, reading CULIDORI
IACIT ET ORVVITE MVLIERI SECUNDI. In the churchyard, a
HOLY WELL and a LYCHGATE, stone, Perp style, by *R. Grierson*, 1890.
CAPEL CILDWRN, Ffordd Cildwrn, up the hill to the w. The
first Baptist chapel in North Wales, founded 1750 and
renowned for the ministry of the preacher and hymnodist
Christmas Evans (1766–1838), minister here 1791–1826. The
chapel was built in 1781, altered in 1810, 1818, remodelled in
1846–9 when the walls were raised, and altered in 1866 and
1878. What we see is probably a late C18 envelope raised and
re-fitted in the mid-C19, but the deep plan looks early C19
rather than C18. Plain rendered long-wall front with five sash
windows, three lighting the gallery, two below. Outer doors.

Llangefni, Capel Cildwrn.
Engraving, C19

Small chapel house, l. Deep interior with five-sided gallery on
chamfered timber posts. Box pews face a pulpit with single
stairs up, the angles fluted. In the graveyard, MEMORIAL to
Catherine, wife of Christmas Evans †1823.

MOREIA CALVINISTIC METHODIST CHAPEL, Glanhwfa   103
Road. One of the most ambitious and successful Anglesey
chapels, built to replace that founded in 1794 by John Elias
(†1841) and as a memorial to him, to some extent in competition with the Baptist commemoration of Christmas Evans at
Penuel (*see* below). A porticoed design of 1894 by *R. G. Thomas*
was estimated at £5,005, far more than the £3,500 available,
so was simplified by *O. Morris Roberts* and built in 1896–8 at a
cost of £5,500. A serious façade of 1–1–3–1–1 bays in
contrasting squared rubble and grey ashlar. Outer balustraded
porches with roundels over curved-pedimented doors flank the
main chapel with short balustraded flanks to the pedimented
centrepiece. This has paired arched windows between Composite pilasters on the upper level. The detail is Italianate,
crowded in a late C19 way, with just a touch of the emergent
Queen Anne in the outer bays. Lobbies with gallery stairs lead
into the rectangular interior with seating arranged concentrically at the sides. Lovely figuring in the pine panels of the
curved galleries, which continue round for the organ. Fine
ceiling in plaster and pierced timber, designed with circles

within circles. The most elaborate *sêt-fawr* and pulpit on many
levels, and a large organ by *Wadsworth* of Manchester, 1928.
Behind, this complex building houses a large Sunday School,
deacons' room and caretaker's house.

PENUEL BAPTIST CHAPEL, Ffordd Glandŵr. 1897, by *Evan
Evans* of Caernarfon. Built as the Christmas Evans Memorial
Chapel to replace Capel Cildwrn (*see* above). Fussy two-storey
front in green and grey stone. Three parts, divided by clumsy
buttresses. All the openings arched. A little blind arcading in
the gable.

SMYRNA INDEPENDENT CHAPEL, Glanhwfa Road. 1903 by
Richard Davies. A competent giant-arched façade derived from
the Rev. Thomas Thomas's chapels of the 1860s. Snecked
rubble with grey ashlar Tuscan pilasters and arched windows.
No galleries. Corinthian pilasters to an arched aedicule, and
floriated ceiling plasterwork around timber ventilators.
Adjacent HALL in similar style.

CIVIC BUILDINGS

SHIRE HALL, Glanhwfa Road. 1899, by *R. Lloyd Williams* of
Denbigh, erected by *O. Morris Roberts & Son*, the r. wing added
in the same style by *Joseph Owen*, 1912. Green stone with grey
dressings. Three gables separated by narrow gabled bays, presumably all designed together as wholly symmetrical, though
unimposing. In front, the WAR MEMORIAL, a flat-topped
obelisk.

TOWN HALL and MARKET, Bulkeley Square. 1882–4. Tall Civic
Gothic structure commissioned by Sir Richard Williams-
Bulkeley from *R. G. Thomas*. Grandiose – even rhetorical – grey
stone façade in a C13 idiom, of three bays, its centre pinnacled
and gabled with a balcony in front of a lofty plate-traceried
window. The big two-storey range behind has the market hall
below. Its C18 predecessor was hipped with a bell-turret and
Gothic arches to the market.

COUNTY COURT, Glanhwfa Road, opposite the Shire Hall.
A handsome Neoclassical building of the 1860s, by an
unknown architect, with a reminiscence of Newgate Prison,
London. Five bays and just one storey with a very distinctive
use of massive rock-faced stone blocks, for the plinth, outer
entrance bays and pilasters of the central bay, contrasted with
smooth ashlar for the centre and intermediate bays. Arched
windows, a triplet in the centre, heavy cornice and low parapet.
The courtroom projects symmetrically behind.

COLEG MENAI and YSGOL GYFUN LLANGEFNI, Cildwrn
Road. Two successive secondary schools. Overlooking a lawn
with the school WAR MEMORIAL, the former COUNTY
SCHOOL, now Coleg Menai, 1900, by *Harry Teather* of Cardiff.
A long range in brown stone, two-storey in the centre, then
single-storey, with various shaped gables. Behind, extensive
buildings of the modern SECONDARY SCHOOL, by *N. Squire
Johnson*, County Architect.

PERAMBULATION

BULKELEY SQUARE is the formal space created by setting back
the Town Hall (p. 182). In front, grey limestone CLOCK TOWER,
1902 by *Douglas & Minshull* of Chester, in memory of George
Pritchard-Rayner †1900 in South Africa. A subtle design with
convex angles, gabled clock faces and a short spire. To the W,
the BULL HOTEL, a successful attempt of *c.* 1852 at a characteristic historic-town hotel in the gabled C16–C17 manner, also
of grey limestone. Mullion-and-transom windows, a twin-
gabled E front and good asymmetrical grouping on the rear,
W, with an attractive rubble stone stable range running back
along GLANHWFA ROAD. Further along, on the l. a very pretty
Arts and Crafts house, DOLDIR, 1913 by *Joseph Owen* of Menai
Bridge, green slates, roughcast and a tiny oriel window. After
this the civic and religious group of Capel Moreia, Shire Hall,
war memorial, Court House and Capel Smyrna.

Returning to the centre, High Street runs W. On the N side,
LLOYDS BANK on the corner of Field Street, early C20 in matt
green ceramic and roughcast, and a good later Victorian house
now ALLPORT OPTICIANS, with heavy bay windows and nat-
uralistic carving to the capitals. On the S side, the neglected
INSTITUTE AND READING ROOM, an essay in John Douglas's
Cheshire half-timber style, by *Richard Hall* of Bangor, 1907.
An excursion uphill to the W passes the disused early C20 railway
station, then the former NATIONAL SCHOOL, 1851–2, by
Kennedy, steep-roofed Tudor Gothic in rubble stone, then
Coleg Menai, l., and Capel Cildwrn, r.

Otherwise, FIELD STREET runs N with Penuel Chapel
prominent at the end, then turns E down Glandwr Road to
join CHURCH STREET. N, over the bridge and on the l. is the
parish church. Further on, ORIEL YNYS MÔN, the island's
museum and gallery, utilitarian buildings of 1991 and 2005,
with more likeable timber-clad addition of 2008 by *Russell-
Hughes Associates* of Llangefni. Turning S we return to Bulkeley Square. Little on BRIDGE STREET, the main road E. Off
to the N, in NEW ROAD, the CEMETERY with a pair of
lancet-style chapels, each at a different angle to the slope.
Prominent on the hill to the E the tower of the FELIN GRAIG
windmill, 1828, now a house. On the main road again, by
the R.C. church, THEATR FACH, housed in a C19 Gothic
barn, converted 1955. Beyond the cricket ground a lane runs
S to LLWYN EDNYFED, a moated site some 100 yds
square, reputedly the site of the house of Ednyfed Fychan
in the C13.

At RHOSMEIRCH, 1¼ m. N, EBENEZER INDEPENDENT
CHAPEL, 1869, a rebuilding of the island's first Nonconformist
chapel of 1749. Striking stuccoed façade with pilasters and a
giant arch. Granite centennial memorial to the founder,
William Williams †1773. Just W is the LLYN CEFNI
reservoir, 1947–9, crossed by the now disused Central
Anglesey Railway.

LLANGEINWEN *see* DWYRAN

LLANGOED

A large village with the built-up terraced street dropping down to the Lleinion stream, N. The village continues more informally N of the bridge, up towards Glan-yr-afon and the church.

ST CAWRDAF, ½ m. N. In a large near-circular churchyard. Cruciform, with S porch, rebuilt in 1881 by *Kennedy* apart from the N transept, dated 1612, and the N vestry of 1910, probably by *Harold Hughes*. Re-set C14 three-light E window, with flowing tracery for its image light. In the N transept, a segmental-headed E doorway with an inscribed keystone, and round-headed triplet N and E windows which gave the pattern to the vestry window and internal doorway. Lancets with purple brick surrounds, untypical of Kennedy, made in West Bromwich. – PULPIT. Dated 1622, octagonal and tapered like that at Llanfihangel Din Silwy (Llanddona). Four sides are original, the uprights carved with vines intertwining with serpents, the panels with flowers and lozenges. The rest carefully renewed 1911. – FONT. Plain, octagonal, C14? – Under the floor, a total-immersion BAPTISTERY. – STAINED GLASS. E window by *Powells*, warrior prophets, 1919. N window, three saints, 1907, Kempe-style. – MONUMENTS. A C13 carved foliate slab, cut down. – Elegant armorial tablet to the Tros-y-marian family, early C17–C18 slate memorials to other members of the Hughes family. – Neoclassical memorial to the Rev. Hugh Hughes of Plas yn Llangoed †1804.

TŷY RHYS CALVINISTIC METHODIST CHAPEL, E of the church. Nearly square, pebbledashed with hipped roof, perhaps the original of 1822 with front windows altered 1878 and the parapeted porch between lobbies added 1908.

BOARD SCHOOL, S of the church, now a house. A very eccentric design of 1896 by *R. Glynne Davies* of Bangor. T-plan, with a classical bellcote on the front and two octagonal porches on the rear corners.

HAULFRE, N of the river bridge. Long cottage-style mid-C19 villa, said to have been built for a doctor retired from India, which may explain the colonial array of bargeboards and the veranda (now enclosed) on rustic posts. Six bays; canted-sided gables project in the second and fifth with oriels opening onto heavy balconies set into the veranda roof. STABLES in three parallel ranges. They have an elaborate entrance tower with blind-arched triplet to the upper floor under a pyramid roof with clock stage capped by a double-pyramid bellcote with a railed platform around. The stable fittings survive.

TROS-Y-GORS, ¼ m. E of the centre. Two bays of a medieval timber-framed house (probably its storeyed cross-wing), within an C18 reconstruction. The N wall timber studs incorporate a small two-light window with pointed heads. If the recess next to the big fireplace contained the staircase, it is a rare occurrence in Anglesey.

PLAS YN LLANGOED, N of the river bridge. A datestone of 1604
in the SE gable, but the stone above, 1803, probably dates the
present house, now derelict. Eroding roughcast reveals brick
where the three-bay front was raised in the later C19, when
three big hipped dormers and rear extensions were added.
Wide full-height openings with stone voussoirs each side of the
front door. The lower service wing, l., has brick cambered
window heads.

CORNELYN, ¼ m. NW of Haulfre. 1861. An imposing villa with
an entrance lodge, built for William Massey. Grey limestone
with smooth dressings. Basically with gables and long mullioned windows, but made busy. The entrance feature has
canted sides, an arched doorway with blocked pilasters and a
Jacobean gable; the garden front has two-storey bays, one
square with a similar gable, the other round and conical-
roofed, set against the r. gable.

GERLLEINIOG-WEN, ¼ m. E. A former BBC transmitter
station, now a house, in 1930s International Style. Flat roof,
white rendered walls, corner windows and concrete hoods.

LLEINIOG, ¼ m. E. Probably late C16. Lobby-entry plan. Long
two-storey five-bay front, undergoing repair at the time of
writing. To the r. an incongruous tall C19 stuccoed addition
with a polygonal front and segmental-pointed windows.

CASTELL ABERLLEINIOG, ¼ m. E. Large MOTTE with a bailey
to the S, built by the Normans c. 1088–90, and captured by the
Welsh under Gruffudd ap Cynan in 1094 after a stiff siege. It
is a mysterious site, whose history has only just begun to be
unravelled. A square masonry structure of uncertain date
surmounting the motte may be an C18 or C19 folly. Limited
recent archaeological work suggests that it was added to a pre-
existing earth bank which may be the structure referred to as
Lady Cheadle's Fort in the 1640s. Entrance on the S, and a
small round tower set at each corner, each with small rectangular slits, although one has collapsed; the one to the N has
been restored in modern times. This restoration may be associated with use as a defensive position in the Second World
War. The curtain walls are buttressed on the exterior; evidence
for a latrine on the NW side. Further E at LLEINIOG, on the
edge of the beach, a possible MOTTE scarped from a natural
mound.

TROS-Y-MARIAN WINDMILL, 1 m. N. Built by Henry Williams
in 1741, one of the earliest wind-powered corn mills in Anglesey. Now a house, with part of the top storey cut away to form
a glazed belvedere.

TROS-Y-MARIAN, 1 m. NNE. C17 gentry house with walled
gardens and outbuildings, a remarkable example of Renaissance ideas reaching this far-flung corner. The double-pile plan
must be of two periods (straight joint between the parallel
ranges). The N range with three gables and square pavilions
each end looks late C17, the S range, of seven bays with centre
gable, looks mid-C18, when the whole must have been re-
windowed. The handsome Palladian windows inserted in the

central N gable and in the end gable of the E pavilion are later
C18, of a date with the inserted staircase and pedimented front
doorcase. The beauty of the house derives from proportions
rather than detail. Walls of roughly coursed limestone and gritstone, of better quality on the s front where the keyed lintels
form continuous bands above the windows. The central gable
has a short chimney on moulded coping with finials on the
kneelers, and a crude triangular-headed gable panel. The N
gables front three roofs running back to the s roof, so presumably altered, the outer ones with ridge chimneys. The
gables are not quite equal, the symmetry further thrown by the
offset Palladian window.

Inside, the s range has rooms each side of a three-bay hall.
This has a rear fireplace and an arched opening to a staircase
in the N range, lit by the Palladian window. The hall has a nine-
panel beamed ceiling, plaster heraldry over the fireplace and
moulded doorcases, all C18. The E room has reused C17 panelling and later C18 cupboards; the w room has painted C18
panelling with cornice and dado rail. In the earlier N range, the
E part was long ruinous. The centre has the inserted stair, with
a continuous rail and thin balusters, under a barrel ceiling.
Adjoining to the l. is a late C17 stair with thick turned balusters and square newels, used as a service stair. Beyond, w, the
kitchen with a segmental-arched fireplace and panelled door,
both C17 though the door inscribed RR 1769. The upstairs
rooms panelled, four in the s range and one over the kitchen.
The two over the hall with bolection mouldings of early C18
type, the other three of C17 type similar to the w room below.

The s front faces a long walled PLEASANCE, roughly 20 by
100 yds (18 by 90 metres). Straddling the far end wall, a small
SUMMERHOUSE, with a tripartite pedimental front and acroterion blocks, its doorway and window bays with remnants of
plaster decoration. Each side of the walk, further walled enclosures: downhill E, a one-acre orchard; uphill w, a larger tree-
planted area which meets the stepped formal approach to the
s front of the house. Further w, the farm buildings. BAKE-
HOUSE; cross-gabled C17 DOVECOTE (now roofless); next to
it, CORN BARN dated 1678 with the initials W/HA (perhaps for
Williams); early C19 range of seven CARTSHEDS; and STABLE,
dated 1735 and with the initials W/HA again.

ERIANALLT, ¾ m. NNW. Small late C17 three-bay house with a
lobby-entry plan, a type rare in Anglesey. Massive projecting
window lintels below, the upper floor raised in the C19.

LLANGRISTIOLUS

The modern village is about a mile w of the church, which is on
a hillock just s of the A55, overlooking the Malltraeth marshes.

ST CRISTIOLUS (SH 450 736). In a partly circular *llan*. The nave
perhaps C12 but rebuilt with the old stones; the chancel C13,

wider and higher; the porch perhaps later C16, with rounded head and unusual double concave moulding. The rebuilding by *Kennedy* in 1852 was thorough. He rebuilt the chancel, but retained the E wall, the big E window, of five uncusped lights and a deep hollow moulding, early C16, and the two-light N and S windows. He inserted the Dec windows, the chancel ones awkwardly proportioned with more height above the springing line than below, and added the cross-gabled bellcote. The surprise is the elaboration of the late C13 chancel arch, which Sir J. E. Lloyd associated with Einion ap Gwalchmai, 'a church-builder on an ample scale'. A pier placed against responds, with a further order on the E side. Shafts in triplets on the angles and similar plain rolls above the capitals. The arch mouldings, of two-centred profile, have simpler but bolder rolls. – FONT. Romanesque, circular, the decoration of its drum divided into six panels under sub-arches. Four panels with plaits, two with knots. – MONUMENT to John Roberts †1845 by *Seddon & MacBride* of Liverpool. White marble on black, done as a Tudor rather than classical aedicule.

HENBLAS, 1 m. SW. One of the old estates, belonging to the Morgan family but of uncertain history. The building history starts in the early C17 (a beam with the date 1572 not being *in situ*). At the N is a two-room house with its original (but blocked) entrance opposite the immense chimneystack; back-to-back fireplaces with elliptical arches. Stones now on the W wing, dated 1625 and 1626 with the initials HM, may relate to this. This small W front has five bays with small C18 sash windows. Close beside on the E another C17 block, later incorporated into the C18 house and providing it with a broad dog-leg staircase. Abutting these two unit-like wings is a long Anglesey gentry range of *c.* 1700 facing S, added to the older house at right angles for Chancellor William Morgan. Front of fine masonry with eight irregularly spaced windows under flat arches; cyclopean doorway in the third bay from the r. Hall with diagonally laid paving, a bolection-moulded doorway to a parlour and, facing the entrance, a portal with fluted pilasters and segmental head, leading to the staircase with turned balusters.

The well-preserved manorial group is now entered not from the drive to the S front, but from the N where the Picturesque LODGE stands across the road from the gate. Circular plan, one storey of Gothick windows; handsome conical roof of fish-scale slating which rises to a stepped central chimney. The drive enters through a stable yard. Late C18 lofted COACH-HOUSE with three segmental arches in ashlar. Opposite, a lower late C17 range with dormer gablets. Behind this the house itself, and close to its W two partly WALLED GARDENS.

GREAT BARN, isolated in fields and long roofless. One of a p. 188 group of large C18 corn barns (cf. Llanidan etc.). Opposed openings with segmental arches, ventilation slits in two tiers all round. Dated 1776 on a heraldic stone with the initials HEM over one threshing door.

Llangristiolus, Henblas, great barn.
Conjectural reconstruction

Equally isolated from the mansion house at Henblas
Country Park, the unusual STABLE COURTYARD of the later
C18. The plan is half a hexagon, 175 ft (54 metres) in diameter.
Single-storey ranges of rubble stone with elliptical arched
openings. Paired elliptical arches at the terminations of the end
pavilions.

CEFN-LLWYN, 1 m. SW of the village. Two-storey Arts and Crafts
house by *Joseph Owen*, 1906. Between the two gables (deliberately not matching), the roof sweeps down over the entrance.
Stepped base to the chimney, reminiscent of H.L. North.
Elegant staircase, with heart-shaped baluster cut-outs and
tapering, capped newels. Decorative glass to the stair window.

LLANGWYFAN

The medieval church on an imperilled islet in the sea WSW of
Aberffraw is one of the more extraordinary sights of Anglesey. Its

survival is remarkable seeing that it was replaced by a new church on dry land in 1870, by *Kennedy & O'Donoghue.*

St Cwyfan (SH 336 683). The dedication is thought to be to the Irish saint Kevin whose centre is at Glendalough. Originally the church was on a promontory between two bays; erosion made it necessary to make a causeway of boulders in the C17 or C18 but this was slowly washed away in the later C19, till the remnant rising 12 ft above high tide was protected by a sea wall *c.* 1890. Nave and chancel in one with a w bellcote. In the s wall, elements of the small rectangular C12 church: a string course, the former arched doorway and, inside, the stone seat benches. The church seems to have been lengthened in the C14 (see the bellcote with its pointed arched and gableted finial, and the E window which originally had two trefoiled lights under its two-centred arch); and then doubled in plan in the early C16 by a full-length N arcade of three bays, the aisle and a s porch being removed *c.* 1840. The early C16 remodelling gave the church two windows, of one broad cinquefoiled light under hoodmoulds, the s doorway and its roof of arch-braced trusses. The arcade visibly survives, the arches typically very flat; as in other such C16 designs it has octagonal piers and two orders of chamfers, one hollow. In 1891 the young *Harold Hughes* made a survey preparatory to the careful restoration in collaboration with *Arthur Baker* of 1893. Restored again in 2006 by *Adam & Frances Voelcker.*

Llangwyfan Isaf, ¾ m. N. Pedimental doorway dated 1589, with the initials OW MW for the Wood family. During the C18 and C19 services were held here when tides did not permit access to the church. The Tŷ Croes Camp nearby was an artillery training establishment in the Second World War, using airborne targets. Now a motor-racing circuit.

LLANGWYLLOG

4580

NW of Llangefni, the small church down a track off the road to Llanerchymedd.

St Cwyllog. A plain rectangle of about 15 by 45 ft (4.5 by 14 metres), perhaps datable to the C15 by the three trefoiled lights of the four-centred E window, the N doorway under a square label and the base of the E gable cross. w bellcote. Massive quoin stones at the angles. At the w a low room, added for a school perhaps, with a C16 arched doorway at the NW. Tactful restoration of 1854 by *D. Roberts* of Beaumaris. Rare surviving Georgian FITTINGS mostly of 1769: the ALTAR RAILS look Laudian with their turned balusters and finials on the newels, but are C18; BENCHES to their s and N; two large BOX PEWS, one C18 and one C19; three-decker PULPIT and READING DESK dated 1769 on its back panel beneath a scrolly pediment. – FONT. C12, circular. A broad band of carving (one piece apparently unfinished), with a quatrefoil and a run of thick

interlocking foliate pattern. Rope moulding below. – STAINED
GLASS. E, 1882, by *Henry Holiday* for *Powells*. – MEMORIALS.
Richard Hughes †1762 and William Hughes †1793, of Bryn-
gola; and William Prichard †1763 and Henry Prichard †1801,
of Trescawen, together showing the evolution of the Late Geor-
gian slate tablet. – George Pritchard-Rayner, †1900 in South
Africa, with repoussé lettering in bronze, by *John Williams* of
London, 1901.

4967   LLANIDAN

The ruined church is in woods near the Menai Strait, in the
private grounds of Plas Llanidan Hall.

ST NIDAN (SH 489 674). Partly demolished in 1844 including
the chancel, an act condemned by the new Cambrian Archaeological Association in 1846, especially since the new church
at Brynsiencyn (q.v.) cost twice what was needed to repair the
old. Another grievous reflection is that its vicar from 1676 to
1723 was Anglesey's greatest historian, the Rev. Henry Rowlands, author of *Mona Antiqua Restaurata* (1723).
    Early Christian circular *llan*. By tradition founded in 616; in
the C13 annexed to the Augustinian Priory of Beddgelert. A
C14 church (see the re-set two-centred N doorway and Dec
trefoil-headed tracery), rebuilt as a double-naved church
c. 1500 in connection with local pilgrimages, with a S porch
with two elliptical arches, and S chapel. Six bays of this Perp
arcade remain with two hollow-chamfered, four-centred arches
on octagonal piers, but only four bays of the arch-braced roof,
and the W wall with double bellcote. Over the N doorway a
painted text in Welsh (from Psalm 84) alone survives from
many others. By the S door two crudely carved heads and the
miraculous STOUP that was said never to run dry. Some fittings
were removed to the new church at Brynsiencyn.
LLANIDAN HALL. The proximity of the house to the church once
belonging to the Augustinian Order makes it likely that this
began as a grange, and that the medieval vaulted cellars
originate in a residence for the Prior of Beddgelert. In 1605 it
was bought by Richard ap Rhydderch (1576–1652), M.P. for
Beaumaris and Sheriff of Anglesey. The house he built, marked
by a datestone for 1631 now on the NW wall, seems to form
the core of the C18 house built round it. The three-storeyed
Jacobean house seems to have had a double-pile plan, and
the stone four-centred fireplaces on the ground floor may be
in their original places. Some bolection panelling may date
from a C17 remodelling for ap Rhydderch's granddaughter's
husband Pierce Lloyd. From 1772 to 1802 the tenant was
Thomas Williams, who from 1775 was Lord Uxbridge's chief
agent and then partner at the copper mine on Parys mountain
– the likely explanation for the use of copper glazing bars in

the windows. It was he, probably with the architectural help of *John Cooper* of Beaumaris, who gave the house its Late Georgian appearance, particularly with additions on the SE including the projecting canted bay, and the library shelving. Considerable alterations in the C19 were followed by demolition of a SW wing in the 1920s.

The STABLES were apparently built by ap Rhydderch in the early C17. Rectangular with elliptical-headed stone doorway. No original fittings. Later used as the vicarage; perhaps the C18 storeyed rear wing belongs to this phase.

A WALLED GARDEN W of the house dates from the early C17. Its walls and gates contain stonework reused from medieval buildings on the site. This and the stone-walled DEERPARK on the ground sloping S to the Strait were formed by Richard ap Rhydderch and are comparable with the contemporary layout at Baron Hill above Beaumaris. Henry Rowlands says he planted within it 'shady beech trees, pines, chestnuts, ash trees and sycamores in the direction of the sea with beautiful and pleasant avenues'. In the late C18, Thomas Williams planted an avenue N of the house and a grove of sycamores leading to it – apparently the trees still existing – and made a HA-HA round the E and S sides of the garden.

YSGUBOR DEGWM, 430 yds N of Llanidan Hall, in a group of agricultural buildings. A gritstone corn barn, one of the largest on the island. It has opposed doorways with cambered voussoir heads, a course of dove holes and a quarter-round eaves moulding; details of *c.* 1700(?).

LLANIESTYN *see* LLANDDONA

LLANNERCH-Y-MEDD *see* LLANERCHYMEDD

LLANRHUDDLAD

3389

The village is 2 m. inland from the church, which overlooks Porth Swtan or Church Bay on the NW coast. Three clusters of houses, the chapel at the NE, the school at the SW.

ST RHUDDLAD. The old lychgate and mounting block, from which Holyhead can be seen across the bay, create a very different impression from the church spikily rebuilt by *Kennedy* in a new position in 1858. Chancel and nave with Y-traceries in hard limestone, S porch with tower and stone broached spire. – FONT, cylindrical, medieval. – STAINED GLASS, E, by *Forrest & Bromley* of Liverpool.

BETHEL HEN CALVINISTIC METHODIST CHAPEL. 1904–5, a complex almost on a collegiate scale in the free Perp Gothic of the period by *Joseph Owen*. A bold traceried window in the rendered gable is flanked by canted-ended porches, the r. one taken up as a stone octagonal tower with slated spire, a typical asymmetry. To the r. lower Neo-Jacobean gables of the chapel house and Sunday School. Gothic detail to the *sêt-fawr*, pulpit and pulpit recess. – STAINED GLASS of biblical scenes, *c.* 1906.

BOARD SCHOOL (former), 1901, possibly by *Joseph Owen*. Pebbledashed, with a profusion of busy gables, one containing the name and date, another a bellcote.

At PORTH SWTAN, SWTAN (National Trust), a charming reconstructed single-storey cottage, whitewashed with a tiny window each side of the door and a thatched roof of wheat straw on gorse underthatch, i.e. the type of the Celtic coasts. On the ridge SE, the tower of MELIN CAERAU windmill, burnt 1914.

LLANRHWYDRYS *see* CEMLYN

LLANSADWRN

On the high ground N of Menai Bridge, the church SW of the modern village.

ST SADWRN. In a circular churchyard. Basically a small unicameral nave and chancel and N transept idiosyncratically rebuilt in 1881 with a new N porch and W bellcote by *Kennedy*. Reused elements include the C15 N doorway with an elliptical arch and hollow chamfer; the six C15 arch-braced trusses of the nave roof spanning only 14 ft (4.3 metres), and two shallower C16 ones over the transept. On the N transept gable two C16 gargoyles, carved as a man in a Tudor leather cap, and his bear. The chancel refitted in 1895 by *Demaine & Brierley* of York, for George McCorquodale of Gadlys. – FONT. A small classical pillar of Penmon limestone dated 1737. – ALTAR CANOPY. 1895, with excellent Tudor-style gilded carving, the fields painted in subdued colours with the Instruments of the Passion, and REREDOS with the Crucifixion and four saints, on the diminutive scale of the chancel. Both made by *Shrigley & Hunt* of Lancaster. – STAINED GLASS. E, the Risen Christ, 1880, by *Powells*, the design by *Henry Holiday*. S, Christ blessing children, 1895, and N, SS Aaron and Albion, 1900, both *Shrigley & Hunt*. S, SS Luke and John, and the chapel windows, all possibly by *Wailes*. – INSCRIBED STONE. On the chancel N wall a small stone of *c.* 600 to St Sadwrn himself and his wife: HIC BEAT(US) SATURNINUS SE(PULTUS) . . . IACIT ET SUA SA(NCTA) CONIUX PA(X). – MONUMENTS. John Roberts †1711, oval panel in a Baroque surround. – Elizabeth Wynne †1714, on a simple fictive cloth of marble. – George McCorquodale †1895, floriated Gothic like the altar canopy, but in alabaster.

CHURCHYARD. A CROSS to Lt H.S. McCorquodale, killed at Spion Kop, 1900. The design by *Harold Hughes* is loosely

based on St Martin's Cross, Iona, with Christian imagery on
one side, and African snakes and lions interwoven on the other.
Carved by *R. Bridgeman* of Lichfield. – Sir Andrew Crombie
Ramsay †1891, Director-General of the Geological Survey, and
pioneer of the study of glaciation, commemorated by a glacial
boulder.

HAFOTY, 2 m. NNE (SH 563 783). One of Anglesey's classic small
medieval houses, repaired in 1973 and again more recently by
Garner Southall Partnership. H-plan. The central hall and
narrow uphill E wing probably built by Thomas Norres, captain
of the guard at Beaumaris Castle in 1439; originally box-
framed, with a central hearth and one cruck-like truss with a
boss, later encased in rubble. Pointed doorways connect the
hall to the rooms in the wing, probably across a former screens
passage. In 1511 Hafoty passed from Norres's great-grandson
Henry to Richard Bulkeley who added the downhill W wing
(tree-ring-dated 1509–53) and replaced the central hearth with
the low Tudor-arched lateral fireplace, topped by a hipped
gable supporting the tall diagonal chimney. Inscribed over the
fireplace Si Deus Nobiscum Quis Contra Nos and emblems of
the Bulkeley family, and traces of red paint. Three-light round-
headed window opposite, and similar windows in the W wing,
reconstructed (two in timber) from C16 stone remnants. The
latrine towers attached at the NW and SE corners do not
survive. The adjoining STABLE has the date 1827 and Bulkeley
initials.

HENDREFOR BURIAL CHAMBER, 1 m. NNW (SH 551 773).
Deliberately knocked over in the C19. One large stone remains
standing, with fallen stones immediately behind it, and another
fallen group about 16 ft (5 metres) to the W. It is likely that the
tall stone was a portal stone, but excavations at Trefignath
(Holyhead) and Din Dryfol (Trefdraeth) have shown that
confident interpretations of the original structure would be
unwise.

EARTHWORK, S of Hendrefor (SH 545 765). An almost
rectangular enclosure, set in a marsh so that the ditch is almost
always flooded. The precise rectilinear plan probably reflects
Roman influence, but this was a native settlement, for at least
one round hut survives in the interior. One of several homesteads in the island which suggest that their native owners and
designers were much impressed by Roman work, but did not
abandon their traditional domestic architecture.

BRYN ERYR EARTHWORK, 1 m. W (SH 540 757). A much eroded
square-ditched enclosure, visible in the field S of the driveway
to Bryn Eryr. Excavation in 1985–7 produced good evidence
for the longevity of early farms on good land. Founded before
150 B.C. as a single clay-walled round-house within a fenced
enclosure, it was impressively remodelled in the late Iron Age;
a new house was built alongside and granaries were
constructed in the yard, now enclosed by a very substantial
bank and ditch. Pollen, seeds, bones etc. suggest a prosperous

mixed farm, believed to have continued into the C4. During the Roman period a new stone round-house was built, but the surrounding ditch was allowed to silt up. The excavation also showed that round-houses, so familiar in stone, were contemporary with similar buildings of clay and wood, a conclusion that has been confirmed at three farms excavated under the path of the new A55 road. The late prehistoric and Roman population of the island is therefore likely to have been much larger than the visible stone remains would suggest.

CREMLYN STANDING STONES, 1½ m. NE. Two large stones about 325 yds (300 metres) apart, the s one conspicuously set on the top of the ridge, the N one in a hollow. The s stone fell over in 1977. Excavations before it was set upright again revealed that the stone had replaced a wooden post, but gave no indication of dates or why this spot should have been marked in this way. Excavations in Cornwall have revealed a similar sequence of markers on one spot.

LLANTRISANT

3685

The old church is isolated by Tŷ Mawr Farm, SSE of Llanddeusant, the new church is 1 m. ESE. The C6 Llantrisant stone now in the Gwynedd Museum, Bangor, was found at Capel Bronwen. It is inscribed in Latin: 'Ina, a most holy lady, lies here, who was the very beloved wife of Bivatig[irnus], servant of God, a bishop, and a disciple of Paulinus, by race a ..udocian, and an example to all his fellow citizens and relations both in character, rule of life, and in (that) wisdom which is better than gold and gems.'

SS AFRAN, IEUAN AND SANNAN (SH 349 841). In a partly round *llan*, roofless cottages round it. Rescued in 1968 by Cadw's predecessor after the W end of the roof fell in, and by its guardians since 1978, the Friends of Friendless Churches. Unicameral nave and transept with W bellcote. Its Dec E window with two trefoiled lights with a shield-shaped light above tells that it is C14. S transept almost as big as the church, added to the chancel; this has C18 roof trusses, the nave copies of the late medieval ones. – FONT. *c.* 1200. Large round bowl with three rings at the rim and two below. – C17 ALTAR RAIL of Laudian height. – Early C19 BOX PEWS. – MONUMENTS. John Wynn of Bodewryd †1669. Baroque arms and foliage above, winged *memento mori* below. – Hugo Williams of Nantanog †1670, Doctor of Theology, a fine Baroque marble cartouche with floral festoons, volutes, cherubs and arms. – Rev. Morgan Ellis †1789, Neoclassical, carved in slate.

LLANTRISANT NEW CHURCH (SH 364 836). 1899, by *P. S. Gregory*. Plain E.E. with red sandstone dressings.

TREGWHELYDD STANDING STONE, 1 m. SW of the old church, (SH 340 831). An impressive stone, broken but mended by a stout bronze band.

LLANWENLLWYFO see DULAS

LLANYNGHENEDL see LLANFACHRAETH

LLECHGYNFARWY

3881

On the high ridge SW of Llanerchymedd, with views to the sea, and to the mountains far to the S. The *llech* or stone of Cynfarwy near Trefor was removed in the C19.

ST CYNFARWY. Nave and chancel in one. S transeptal chapel added 1664, the datestone with the initials of William Bold of Tre'r Ddôl. Rebuilt in 1867 by *Kennedy & O'Donoghue* almost from the foundations, with big traceried windows, new roofs and a porch. – FONT. C12. Small roundish bowl with four saltire crosses. – STAINED GLASS. E, geometrical of *c.* 1860. – MONUMENT, S chapel. Helen Bold †1631 aged 84, 'uxor Rheasi Bold, nobilis' of Bold Hall, Lancashire; erected by her son Sir William Bold. Very large brass plate with a long Latin inscription, explaining the descent of the Bolds from the Tudor family, which they Romanized as Theodore. Low-relief Baroque frame with heraldry in the tympanum and four *memento mori*s.

CARMEL CALVINISTIC METHODIST CHAPEL, Carmel, 1 m. NE. 1854–5 by *Hugh Jones* of Llanerchymedd. A good group. Simple Gothic chapel, with a three-arch porch in yellow brick, *c.* 1885. A railed court with chapel house and a Sunday School with outside steps to the gable entry and a Gothic window in the other gable.

TRE'R DDÔL, 1 m. E. The main Anglesey seat of the Bold family. Tall C17 T-plan house, surprisingly small and old-fashioned in view of its status. Two and a half storeys, all harled, with dormer gablets. Many internal features lost in recent years. Stairs dated 1655 leading to an upstairs parlour with an over-mantel dated 1662, both with the initials WFB. On the upper floor the arch-braced timber construction, dated 1888, seems to be a Victorian reproduction of the original following a fire. The setting, though much degraded, is the remains of a park (recorded by Lewis Morris in the 1720s). Apart from the sycamore avenue on the N approach there is little to be seen.

LLECHYLCHED see BRYNGWRAN

LLIGWY see RHOS LLIGWY

MALLTRAETH

4169

A tightly built village at the head of Malltraeth Sands, the estuary of the Cefni. Running S towards Newborough, a mile-long SEA WALL begun after Acts of Parliament of 1788 and 1790, completed after vicissitudes in 1812 to reclaim 3,000 acres of

Malltraeth Marsh or Cors Ddyga to the NE. The river became a straight-cut drainage channel, rebuilt after storm damage in 1826 with Cornish zigzag masonry to protect the banks.

In the village, SARDIS CALVINISTIC METHODIST CHAPEL, 1860. Simple rectangle with hipped roof and minimal Palladian window, possibly an alteration of 1896. Further on, a mid-C19 POLICE HOUSE with arched double chimney on the hipped roof. EGLWYS CRIST-Y-BRENIN is a late C19 mission church, tiny with bellcote and porch.

RAILWAY VIADUCT, N of the village. Eighteen low arches, part of *Robert Stephenson*'s line to Holyhead, opened 1848. By the railway embankment a STANDING STONE, SH 408 693. Strangely sited on such low ground, but its bulk and height suggest that it is prehistoric and not simply a cattle-rubbing stone.

MARIANGLAS

The modern village, 1½ m. NE of Benllech, is loosely built around a village green, a rarity on the island. The older sites are 1 m. W. The cliffs at TRAETH BYCHAN, 1 m. E, were quarried for fine limestone, known as Anglesey marble, and for a conglomerate stone used for millstones.

ST EUGRAD, Llaneugrad (SH 495 842). Very small – small enough to have preserved its plan from the Early Christian church – in a large circular *llan*. Nave and chancel joined by a Romanesque arch now plastered over; one small Romanesque window in the nave S wall, blocked. C16 N transept to the chancel, once separately entered by a Tudor W doorway. The exterior rendered, so little is visible; the C15 round-arched S doorway and the C14 pointed N doorway are obscured by a clumsily battlemented C19 porch and vestry. Some windows also replaced in the late C19 (fragments reused in the vestry). W bellcote with C17 arch. The high nave roof C18, the chancel roof with C15 arch braces, the transept roof C16 with arch-braced trusses and small wind-braces. – FONT. C12. Plain tapered bowl with band at base. – Two STOUPS. – CARVING of the Crucifixion, from above the S doorway to the nave. The figure set against a wheel-cross. C13? – Panel from the Jacobean pulpit dated 1644.

PARCIAU, ½ m. W. Asymmetrical stone house of the 1830s. The landscaped valley below is the setting for the cross-gabled DOVECOTE, dated 160? with the initials IEE. This John Thorpe-like tower, square on plan, has two storeys, entered by a shallow pointed doorway and with mural stairs to the upper floor. Externally that level is marked by an alighting shelf with a lozenge-shaped opening above on each side. The cupola, also cross-gabled and with finials, rests on plain corner piers with miniature Doric columns between.

PARCIAU HILL-FORT. *See* Llanallgo.

MENAI BRIDGE/PORTHAETHWY 5573

This was the most important of the historic crossings of the Menai Strait. It had the merit of being the shortest passage, despite proximity to the Swellies, where the twice-daily tide race through the rocks leaves the surface seldom still and safe enough for boats. Some early warehouses and alehouses survive from the port days crowded near the Anglesey shore, but most of the quays have been rebuilt. The stupendous scale of the Menai Suspension Bridge (and of the Britannia Bridge further w) requires appreciation from sea level as well as from its deck. The town is at the fulcrum of roads to Beaumaris, Llangefni and Holyhead, along which a small new Victorian town developed, with substantial, and sometimes spectacular, private houses on the coasts to the e and w. Menai Bridge and Llangefni are to some extent complementary in expressing Anglesey's c19 aspirations, and in a manner distinct from the development of Bangor on the opposite shore.

St Mary, Mona Road. By *Kennedy*, 1858, set picturesquely but not conveniently on a rocky knoll above Telford's road. It replaces the old church of Llandysilio (*see* below). A respectable Dec church with nave, chancel and w tower, all in green stone with grey limestone dressings. It shows what Kennedy could do with a little more money, £1,450 from the Marquess of Anglesey. The reticulated windows, porch doorway and tower bell-stage show an urbane quality rare in his work. New rooms and gallery at w end by *Adam & Frances Voelcker*, 2007. – Stone reredos, Last Supper, by *Mayer & Co.*, 1885. – stained glass. e, 1869, big five-light composition, possibly by *Mayer*. s, two windows of *c.* 1876, probably *Shrigley & Hunt*. n, three lights, Incarnation of Christ, 1882.

St Tysilio, Llandysilio. On Church Island in the Strait (sh 552 717). Linked to the shore by a causeway among the shallow bays, wooded islands and traces of medieval fish weirs that comprise the edges of the town here. Small. Rebuilt in the c13, on a double-square plan, with a w bellcote. The e window with flowing tracery is a copy of 1897. n doorway in oak, cut to a pointed arch and chamfered. Roof of three pairs of crucks, forming with their braces nearly semicircular arches like a medieval domestic hall in miniature. – font. Octagonal, c13. – panelling in sanctuary, of the restoration by *R. G. Thomas* of 1871. – stained glass. e, Resurrection, by *Jones & Willis*, 1896. – In the churchyard, a Celtic cross by *Harold Hughes* (who is buried on the island).

Capel Mawr (Calvinistic Methodist), New Street. Dated 1856, altered 1904. Unusually handsome pedimented chapel in Caernarfon yellow brick, with stucco dressings. Two doorways and three long windows, all with curved pediments. The striking glazing must date from 1904, but were the original windows so long? Balustraded five-sided rear addition of 1904, for a choir. Elaborate interior of the later c19 and early c20, suggesting a major re-fit after 1856. Pews and gallery both on a U-plan; the pews of 1904, the panelled gallery front looking earlier. Rich *sêt-fawr* and pulpit of 1871, the seat arcaded, the pulpit with arched panels. Elaborate five-bay ceiling in quatrefoil and square panels. Organ of 1913, replacing the choir pews.

ENGLISH PRESBYTERIAN CHURCH, Telford Road. 1888, the major work of the local architect *R. G. Thomas*, paid for by Richard Davies M.P., of Treborth Hall, Bangor, and built by Davies's brother Robert. The only example on the island of that full-blown ecclesiastical Gothic preferred in general by English Nonconformists. Large, raised on a full basement, and cruciform. A distinct chancel, and a canted-ended chapel nestling alongside. The porch in the nave angle rises with some elaboration to an octagonal spirelet, so often the Non-conformist substitute for a tower. Dec tracery, the chancel window with a rose over four lights. The interior richly ecclesiastical, with wall-shafts and marble shafting to the chancel arch and pulpit. – STAINED GLASS. Big chancel window, to Robert Davies †1905, by *Powells*, 1906, biblical scenes. – MONUMENTS. Marble tablets to the patron family and to the architect †1909.

MOREIA BAPTIST CHAPEL, Dale Street. 1885. Green stone and yellow brick Romanesque façade with wings and wheel window, all done economically. Derelict 2009.

TABERNACL INDEPENDENT CHAPEL, St George's Road/Ffordd Cynan. 1867, by the *Rev. Thomas Thomas*. Green-ish rubble stone with grey dressings, in Thomas's typically minimal Gothic, i.e. plain lancets, triple in the centre and paired each side.

86   MENAI SUSPENSION BRIDGE, 1818–26, by *Thomas Telford* for the new road completed in 1832. The bridge coincidentally transformed life on Anglesey and in particular made the old port village beneath it obsolete.

Telford's bridge was a development of his proposal of 1815 for a bridge over the Mersey, and one by Captain Brown for a bridge over the Tweed. The completed Menai Bridge had the world's longest span, 579 ft (178 metres) between the towers. Its total length is 1,388 ft (427 metres), its height above the water is 100 ft (100 metres) and to the top of the towers 138 ft (42 metres). But such figures do not describe the sublime contribution the bridge makes to the landscape of the Strait. It still looks miraculously right, and also shockingly bold, in its crowded site on the curving narrows. Reached by three rusticated masonry arches from a bluff on the s side and four from a steep embankment raised on the N, it is surprisingly unsymmetrical. Its harmony partly results from the piers of these arches and the towers themselves having a strongly battered profile, as though sections taken from a stone embankment – an engineering solution Telford had already used at the Pontcysyllte canal viaduct over the Dee completed in 1805. The batter continues up to the tops of the stone pylons, through which the roadway passes in paired arches.

Menai Suspension Bridge.
Lithograph, 1849

The stone was quarried at Penmon for the contractor *James Wilson* (*see* the Conwy Suspension Bridge, p. 340). The cost was £165,000.

The original effect was more startling still, since the platform and chains were slighter than now and the footway ran along the centre. Telford's ironwork, despite strengthening after storms in 1840 (by *W. A. Provis*, engineer 1818–50) and in 1893, was calculated to carry much less weight than the C20 has required. The chains were made, as with the Conwy bridge, at *William Hazledine*'s works in Shropshire. Once raised they were anchored into the N embankment in an elegant catenary arch, but at the S they had to end more abruptly, and higher above the carriageway, in a brutal mass of stone so as not to obstruct the coastal road. A wooden toll house stood beneath that section of chains. At this end Telford's lattice design for 5-ft (1.5-metre) safety fencing along the bridge can be seen surviving at the turn of the road, and also one of his sunburst gates. A short length of the same design remains round the chain anchor point on the N embankment.

The significant change to the bridge's aesthetics, as well as engineering principle, came with works carried out in 1938–40 by the engineer *Sir Alexander Gibb* and the contractor *Dorman Long*. The chains were moved apart to the sides from their position in the centre, their wrought iron replaced with steel, the hangers shortened, the deck modified and widened by 2 ft (60 cm.) either side; and – most obtrusively – the main span modified as a lattice girder design. The loss of elegance can be judged from early photographs.

The irregular crossing at the centre of the town is UXBRIDGE
SQUARE, overlooked by the triangular NATWEST BANK, an
undisciplined mix of red brick, terracotta and roughcast with
an oriel over a Baroque doorcase, by *Joseph Owen* of Menai
Bridge, *c.* 1902. TELFORD ROAD climbs the hill up to the
church and the bridge. On the l., the VICTORIA HOTEL of
c. 1852, intended for the Irish trade. Three-storey front of three
bays between two-storey wings of one bay, in limestone rubble
between squared flush quoins, with a Doric porch. It has steps
down to the quays. Past the English Presbyterian Church
(p. 198), Chapel Street runs l. to New Street, with Capel Mawr
(p. 197), and down to the foreshore and the huddle of buildings under the bridge. Turning S, in PORTH YR WRACH, one
of the few surviving stone WAREHOUSES, with deep eaves. The
site was a timber yard of the Davies family of Treborth from
1828 and of William Roberts & Co. from the 1860s to 2005;
converted to houses 2006. On BEACH ROAD, the former
POLICE STATION, *c.* 1845, and MAGISTRATES' COURT, 1868,
each preserving internal fittings. Also an early C19 FOUNDRY
of two storeys with cambered brick window heads and a hipped
roof. In CAMBRIA ROAD above, THE CAMBRIA, the former
ferry inn, T-plan, C17 and C18. The promenade under the
Menai Bridge leads to the causeway to Church Island and the
church of St Tysilio (*see* above).

Returning N, the foreshore road passes around the inlet
called PORTH DANIEL, with a small C18 QUAY where the ferry
landed. By iron gates, a tiny stone building of 1904, which
served as the booking office for the Liverpool steam packet.
A waterside walk leads to ST GEORGE'S PIER, once one of
four for the steamers. Originally 250 ft (77 metres) long,
designed by *J. J. Webster* (cf. Bangor Pier). Replaced by a
shorter concrete version in 1967.

Further N on St GEORGE'S ROAD, the delightfully named
MENAI VILLE, a big later C19 terrace of stucco villas with
outsize Gothic ballflower ornament. Then the road climbs
past Tabernacl chapel to the N end of the HIGH STREET.
Here modest stuccoed houses, rising to three-storey with
HAWTHORN HOUSE, on the E, Late Georgian with a trellis
porch.

At the top of Dale Street, PENTRAETH ROAD runs N. On the
l., CARREG LWYD, one of two pebbledash and render houses
(cf. Doldir, Llangefni) by *Joseph Owen*, 1913, displaying the
disposition of traditional elements such as canted bays, oriels,
gable lunettes etc. in the relaxed Arts and Crafts way.

At the E end of the High Street a granite MILESTONE marks the
start of the private road built along the Strait in 1805 by
Viscount Bulkeley, which in 1828 was improved as the four-
mile turnpike between Menai Bridge and Beaumaris. Along
this picturesque coastal road many villas and houses were
subsequently built (*see* Llandegfan), best seen from the Bangor
side. Among the islets in the muddy bays just E of the town,
on YNYS GAINT, a small terrace garden laid out by *Clough
Williams-Ellis c.* 1935.

MOELFRE   5287

The small fishing village was built round a beach harbour, Porth Lydan, in the lee of a headland on the E coast. It was a dangerous coast, notorious for the wreck of the steam clipper *Royal Charter* in 1859, with the loss of 459 lives (*see* Llanallgo). The lifeboat was established here in 1830, the present LIFEBOAT HOUSE by *W. T. Douglass*, of 1909. The core of little streets has low stone houses with few architectural features. Moelfre was long known also for its high-quality building stone, from the limestone quarries inland at Penrhyn, in use from at least the mid C18. Adopted as a seaside resort around 1900, it has continued to grow without architectural order, apart from a nicely composed gabled stone TERRACE of *c.* 1900 at the bottom of Pen Lôn. Proposals by *Clough Williams-Ellis* to build a disciplined layout at Nant Bychan round two quadrants came to nothing.

MONA *see* HENEGLWYS

MYNYDD MECHELL   3690

Rocky piece of upland SW of Llanfechell. In Mynydd Mechell, MELIN MECHELL, the tower of a C19 former windmill and two chapels, JERUSALEM CALVINISTIC METHODIST CHAPEL, 1865, and CALFARIA BAPTIST CHAPEL, 1897.

ST FFLEWIN, Llanfflewin, ¾ m. SW (SH 350 891). In a circular raised *llan*. Entered by a voussoir-arched lychgate, the centre of its round coped top rising again, perhaps C17? Small rectangular church with W bellcote, judiciously partly rebuilt in 1864. – FONT. Roughly dressed, nine-sided, C14? – GRAVESTONE on the E window sill. A fragment of after 1300, inscribed HIC IACET MADOCUS.

NEWBOROUGH/NIWBWRCH   4366

After the Conquest of 1283 the old Welsh centre of Llanfaes was suppressed. In compensation, the town of Newborough was founded at the far SW corner of the island in 1303, near the former seat of the princes of Wales at Rhosyr, and the people of Llanfaes were transferred to it. Dafydd ap Gwilym wrote in the C14 of 'Tref Niwbwrch, tref llawn obaith' (Newborough town, town full of hope). Privileges were conferred on it up to the reign of Henry VII when the assizes were moved there and it became the county town. The town never flourished notwithstanding, and its decline to insignificance dates from the mid C16. The *plas* fell down in the 1920s.

ST PETER, just SW of the village (SH 420 655). Covered in roughcast and of uncertain history; it may be older than the borough and possibly its original dedication was to St Anno.

A C14 poem of Dafydd ap Gwilym mentions a 'grey tower' for which there is no evidence. Unusually long. Chancel and nave E of the blocked N doorway apparently early C14; the W part of the nave and S porch with elliptical arch and double bell-cote added in the late C15. The reticulated three-light E window, and the N and S chancel windows with circles and tre-foils follow patterns used at Beaumaris church. Repairs, new windows, a new chancel arch and new roof in 1850 by *Kennedy*; more restoration by him in 1886 for the 3rd Lord Stanley, when glass similar to that at Llanbadrig was inserted. – FONT. The C12 cylindrical bowl crudely carved with an interlace cross with knot terminations, and other knot patterns including a Maltese cross, left unfinished. – At the W, fragment of a C9–C11 CROSS, and fragments of a cross-slab. – STAINED GLASS. E and a N single light, 1885–6 by *Powells*, the E window design by *H. E. Wooldridge*. – Two C14 MEMORIALS to priests. David Barker. A tapered sandstone slab with a circular cross-head from which sixteen stems with palmettes radiate. A running leaf pattern down the stem, inscribed in Lombardic capitals X HIC IACET DD BARKER CU AIE PPICIET DEUS. – Matheus ap Elye, in a niche, chancel S side. Effigy, the head and shoulders in high relief, the rest flat. The head rests on a cushion in an ogee arch; he holds a chalice and has a maniple over his left arm. Round the edge is written HIC IACET DNS MATHEUS AP EL[Y]E CAPELLANUS BEATE MARIE NOVORBURGI P CUIUS AIA QCIESCVO DIXERIT P[AT ET] AVE MARIA HABERI QUIQUE CENTUM ET XX [D]IES IDULGE CIA DE ROMA. – Broken C14 SLAB with a floriated cross, inscribed HIC IACET ELLENA QUONDAM UXOR IEWAN T.

EBENESER WESLEYAN METHODIST CHAPEL. Rebuilt in 1861 and 1881, the latter by *Richard Davies*. Stuccoed. Shouldered gable and four arched windows above a hipped porch with big balustraded centre arch. The porch must date from 1881, also the interior with a U-plan gallery, the front with an inset band of pierced cast iron. In the *sêt-fawr*, a brass reading-desk of c. 1900. The platform pulpit has pierced fretwork panels and the big plaster aedicule unusually incorporates two stained-glass windows of c. 1912 by *J. Dudley Forsyth*. Ornate ceiling rose.

PRICHARD JONES INSTITUTE and COTTAGES, Pendref Street. 1902–5, by *Rowland Lloyd Jones* of Caernarfon. Given by Sir John Prichard Jones, a local man, chairman of the Dickens & Jones department store in Regent Street, London.* Both in amplitude and generosity this is the prominent structure in a village of low two-storey terraces. The idiom is that of an irregular Tudorbethan mansion, with its off-centre, internal entrance porch and three-storey clock tower with a lead cupola. Façade of grey stone below, half-timber with red Ruabon stone windows above, composed as two wings.

---

*The other benefaction bearing his name is the main hall of the University in Bangor.

The larger, l., houses a library and assembly room above, each with huge mullion-and-transom windows. That on the r. has three storeys and again over-scaled windows; attached to it the caretaker's wing. Art Nouveau fittings, especially the library with its shelves and cupboards and glazed screen of floral glasswork, and the reading room with its plaster coving and tiled fireplace. In the Library a BUST of the donor by *W. Goscombe John*, 1909. Other rooms include the public hall with an open roof upstairs, a coffee room and smoking room. The concept included a forecourt of six COTTAGES, three each side, also of stone with timber gables and moulded brick chimneys set on a gablet, but one-storeyed. A WAR MEMORIAL at the centre.

LLYS RHOSYR, w of the church (SH 419 653). Rectangular enclosure of the Welsh princes, where Llywelyn the Great signed a charter in 1237. Partial excavations have revealed stone foundations of halls and other structures of timber.

PARYS MOUNTAIN/MYNYDD PARYS

4490

Parys Mountain, a ridge 478 ft (147 metres) high to the s of Amlwch is dominated by copper workings and multicoloured waste tips. The mine was worked both opencast and underground. Charcoal and hammer stones, found in spoil thrown into Oxen Quarry (SH 443 906) and *in situ* in some galleries, have been dated to the Early Bronze Age, and there is circumstantial evidence for Roman working.

During the C15 the mountain was given to an English official, Robert Parys, involved in the collection of fines after the Glyndŵr uprising. But the mines are only recorded as active again with a lease to Roe & Co. of Macclesfield in 1765 and the rediscovery of low-grade copper ore near the surface three years later on the site of the Mona Mine. The use of copper to clad the hulls of naval vessels made the metal extremely valuable both to the owners, the Pagets of Plas Newydd, and their lessees and agents. The Parys Mine, discovered in 1775 and exploited by Thomas Williams †1802, local lawyer, became the most productive in the world, forcing the established Cornish copper mines to sink deeper shafts and invest in more sophisticated machinery, with profound consequences for mining technology. Williams also took over the Mona Mine, and employed some 1,200 workers.

After 1815 competition increased and, with the discoveries in Chile, Anglesey ceased to be a world centre for the industry. Mining continued through the C19 as evidenced by the mining villages around the mountain, Rhosybol and Penysarn, but deep mining effectively ceased in the 1880s. Some exploration continues; a head-frame stands over a shaft sunk in 1988.

The two great QUARRIES near the summit of the ridge, from the closing years of the C18, result from deliberate collapse of the underground workings opened since 1768. The need to follow the veins deeper underground led to the construction of the two most prominent standing buildings, both of which operated underground pumps. The ENGINE HOUSE near the NE limit of the site (SH 447 907), of 1819, is believed to be the oldest surviving example in Wales to be built for a Cornish beam engine. The WINDMILL at the summit was installed in 1878 as an auxiliary to a steam pump engine, for which the twisted holding-down bolts can be seen nearby. It is a stone-built conical tower mill, 26 ft (8 metres) across the base and approximately 65 ft (20 metres) high. Uniquely for Anglesey, it was a five-sailed mill. Cap and machinery are missing.

An unusual feature of the mine was the practice of precipitating copper-rich water (which had permeated through the mine or over the tips) with scrap iron in large purpose-built ponds, yielding ore which could be dried and used to pigment paint. This process outlasted the end of conventional mining and continued until 1958. The vast PONDS survive all over the mountain, many still holding water. The best surviving examples are at DYFFRYN ADDA (SH 438 915), together with an ochre-drying floor and a kiln building dating to 1815–19. This area is undergoing restoration by the Amlwch Industrial Heritage Trust.

The quadrangular MONA MINE YARD (office) was in existence by 1786. Now extremely dilapidated, it contained a smithy, lime store, wagon shed, furnace, carpenter's shops, assay office, stables, a turnery and a place for the bier. The PARYS MINE YARD is shown on a map of 1815; very little remains, but it seems to have been laid out in a similar way.

The sites of CALCINING KILNS are also evident at a number of locations. Calcination removes and preserves the sulphur dioxide from the ore by burning it in heaps. The sulphur fumes were collected in flues running over the smouldering heap and condensed into a fine yellow powder in stone-built condensation chambers running parallel to the heap, for sale to the chemical industry and to gunpowder manufacturers. The kilns are now visible as vivid pink craters, the condensation chambers as parallel stone walls a few feet apart, in between which is a profuse growth of heather.

6781

PENMON

Penmon is the easternmost headland or tip of Anglesey at which the sea-routes between the Irish Sea, the Strait and the coasts of North Wales and NW England meet. The terraces of limestone pavement inland from the cliffs have been occupied from early times. The promontory behind the Priory, preserved as a deer-park, retains small terraced fields of early date in many parts, especially the W sector. The lynchets, sloping banks at the edge of the fields, are due to the gradual build-up of soil against a fence or wall as the result of centuries of ploughing. Some twenty small round stone huts of Romano-British type, scattered amongst these fields, may be contemporary with the Early Christian settlement of St Seiriol. His monastery island lasted a millennium and after the property passed at the Reformation to the Bulkeley family, their buildings did not diminish the sense of Penmon as a domain of archaeological and spiritual importance. None of its dispersed structures is large, and the stone roofs of the pyramidal church tower and domed dovecote in the central group add visual fantasy.

PRIORY OF ST SEIRIOL. A site with unsurpassed views to the 18
mountains s of the Strait. The founder, King Einion, great-grandson of Cunedda, installed his relative Seiriol as prior in the early c6. The Celtic *clas* was re-founded as an Augustinian priory by the 1220s. The cruciform church is the one notable example of Romanesque architecture in NW Wales. Dating it has been a matter of debate, between the whole work being of the time of Prior Idwal *c.* 1130 or of the early years of the reign of his brother Owain Gwynedd *c.* 1140–50, or whether the crossing tower and s transept were added *c.* 1160–70. Crucial in this debate is the relationship of the central tower with its arms. It sits inboard of the arms' walls, which gives the tower, Thurlby argues, a pre-conquest date, thus pre-dating the nave and transepts. He suggests the sanctuary was in the tower, with the nave to its w. However, more recent research* has shown that the original nave may have been E of the tower (that is, where the chancel now is) and that this became the chancel when the present NAVE was added to the w in the early to mid C12. Shallow buttresses on the N and s, a small round-headed window in each wall, not quite opposite, and one in the w gable which was made steeper in the C19 when the roof was renewed. s doorway with an outer order of a pilaster and column with paired capitals supporting a semicircular arch with billet, hollow and roll mouldings. Within, plain jambs carry a mono-lithic tympanum, carved in low relief with a crouching dragon within a border of knots. The N doorway is C13, with a Caernarfon arch. The s TRANSEPT added a little later, its E wall and window rebuilt in 1855 by *Weightman & Hadfield*. They also rebuilt the N TRANSEPT in its entirety, and the big CHANCEL on the foundations of the C13 one, itself a bigger rebuild outside the walls of the previous one. Drawing-board Dec windows and s timber porch. The crossing TOWER has the plainest possible pair of round-headed openings on the E and N faces and clumsy substitutes on the s and w. Pyramidal roof of coursed squared limestone blocks.

* By David Longley, Gwynedd Archaeological Trust.

INTERIOR. The chancel is a Victorian parish church to the letter: sanctuary with *Minton* tiles, stained glass, and oddly high sanctuary steps of the local mottled limestone. Steps lead up to the crossing, replacing the sloping floor which originally continued from far end to far end. At this higher level a display of the best Romanesque architectural carving in NW Wales, as well as late Celtic carving on two standing crosses. Under the crossing tower the E arch to the chancel is low and unadorned, the N one is rebuilt. The W side of the W arch, on the other hand, is richly carved. Of two orders, the inner of multiple shafts and one octagon, the outer with columns. Capitals crudely cut with grotesque figures. Inner arch with multiple rolls, the outer worked with zigzag under a hood of billet ornament. The surprise is in the S transept. Archway with single shafts and scalloped capitals, the E shaft octagonal and with chevron mouldings. Within, wall arcading (re-set?) on the W and S; the colonnettes variously round, and one with shaft-rings and one carved in a spiral, or octagonal and chevron-patterned. The capitals mostly cushion-type, carrying arches all with chevron patterns. Was this elaborate little space used as the chapter house? – Two re-set CARVINGS in the S transept, one a bearded head, the other a sheila-na-gig. – FONT. CIO–CII, square and tapering towards the top, on a CI9 base, carved on three sides with fret or labyrinth designs. –

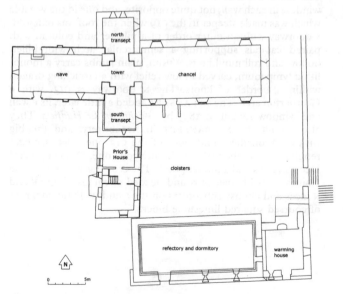

Penmon, Priory of St Seiriol.
Plan

PILLAR PISCINA. Late C12. The bowl cut like the C12 capitals of the crossing. – CROSSES. LATIN CROSS, set in the N chancel wall E of its W window. In the nave a C10–C11 CROSS, moved in 1977 from the deerpark NW of the church. Carved base, much eroded; rectangular-section shaft carved on all four sides. On the front, St Anthony tempted by demons and The Flight into Egypt (?); interlace and knots elsewhere, with a ring-chain on the back. The missing head replaced by that from another cross, of Celtic type with a cross in the middle, thought to be made by the Manx school of carvers. In the S transept a nearly complete C10–C11 CROSS found reused in the refectory. The shaft patterned with frets etc. like the font. The head a nearly complete Celtic wheel-cross, its expanded-arm cross carved between interlaced triquetras. The whole group exhibits motifs common to Scandinavian carvings in northern sites (and cf. Meifod in Powys). – STAINED GLASS. E window 1912. – Chancel N, Jesus and Mary Magdalene in the Garden, by *Celtic Studios*, 1984. – S transept, fragments from the C15 E window, St Christopher and St Seiriol, carefully set in York-type glass, probably by *David Evans*, c. 1855.

S of the chancel the monastic buildings, forming a raised courtyard (the former cloister), open to the E and reached by a gently Baroque stair dated 1709 with the initials of R. B. Bulkeley. The PRIOR'S HOUSE, attached to the S transept, is of uncertain date, but perhaps rebuilt in the early C16 with a hall, a lateral W fireplace and a cross-passage. Later, a second W chimney added, and perhaps an E oriel. In the parlour, r., early C18 oak panelling with moulded cornice and dado. Much altered in 1923 and again, by *Adam & Frances Voelcker*, 2005, when the W and S elevations were lime-rendered.

REFECTORY and DORMITORY. A roofless three-storey, C13 rectangular block, forming the S side of the former cloister. The undercroft or cellar within its battered plinth below, the refectory above at cloister level. The main floor is lit by square-headed lancets but the doorway in the N wall is pointed. The dormitory was up in the roof, lit by a very tall lancet in the W gable, with stepped chamfers and hoodmould, and by a smaller one in the E gable. Abutting to the E the C16 WARMING HOUSE, more domestic in character, containing a kitchen, warming-room above lit by a two-light S window, and pigeonholes in the gable. Single-room structure, of uncertain date, added behind, approached from cloister level.

Remains of the EARLY CHRISTIAN SETTLEMENT lie just E of the monastery. ST SEIRIOL'S WELL is set back among the limestone cliffs which fringe the valley. Scant traces of stonework evoke the doubtless much larger group of structures founded by Seiriol c. 500 A.D. Outer rectangular cell or chapel with benches either side of the doorway. Within, a square of paving also with benches on two sides frames the spring chamber; of uncertain date though the vaulting is dated 1710. Beside this, the footings of an oval HOUSE for the early community. Below the well a FISH POND retained by a dam.

The C16 and C17 squires adopted the Penmon land for lay purposes, but unusually the church continued in use while little was made of the monastic buildings, the opposite architectural development of so many *plasau* or manor houses.

57   DOVECOTE, E of the church. A pantheon for pigeons to lay in, of noble appearance. On a square plan, the sides 25 ft (8 metres) long with a masonry dome also square in plan. Profile of French Renaissance character so perhaps of soon after 1600, with projecting courses of limestone suggesting an entablature, then the lofty vault and on top an octagonal cupola with open sides, also vaulted. Inside, the many tiers of nesting holes are built in pairs: in the middle the round pillar to support a revolving potence for gathering eggs. Abutting to it a slightly later CORN BARN, now roofless.

DEERPARK. Stone walls 2½ m. long run from the flats by the shore to the W up to the skyline and on to the E. This very large C18 sporting enclave corresponds with areas settled by much older cultures, a coexistence hard to read now as a result of C19 stone quarrying and scrub growth since its abandonment.

PENMON QUARRIES. The grey limestone found at Penmon is among the best in Wales, seen in most of the C19 buildings on the island and many on the adjacent North Wales coast.* The extent of C19 extraction may be judged by its use for the piers of Telford's Menai Bridge and Stephenson's Britannia Bridge, and for the Manchester Ship Canal (from Dinmor quarry). On the coast below, structures dating from the limestone quarries, expanded on an industrial scale in the late C19 and early C20.

The FLAGSTAFF QUARRY was a source of building stone and of burned lime, expanded between 1885 and 1916. The inclines from the quarries lead past CRUSHER HOUSES, a steam-powered MILL and STABLES to GRADERS and the OFFICE on the quay. To the S a pair of gigantic LIMEKILNS with circular mouths. Other quarry structures not requiring specific mention stand abandoned all over the headland.

TRWYN DU LIGHTHOUSE, 1 m. NE. Built in 1835–8 by Trinity House to mark the entrance to the Menai Strait; on an innovative stepped base, close to the shore. This 96-ft (30-metre) tower designed by *James Walker* has a crenellated parapet and a cast-iron lantern holding the original fixed lens. Doorway above the plinth with Trinity House arms over, rooms on five levels still with early C19 fittings. The light was automated in 1922. A pair of Neo-Tudor COTTAGES for the lighthouse keepers remain near the shore, dated 1839, together with their allotment garden walls with bastions.

---

*The stone, often known as 'Anglesey marble', can take a fine polish. It must, however, be distinguished from 'Mona marble', a red or green serpentinite quarried elsewhere on the island, and exploited by *George Bullock* of Liverpool to decorate rooms in Penrhyn Castle and no doubt elsewhere.

PENMYNYDD   5174

Midway between Menai Bridge and Llangefni, the *Plas*
associated with the Tudor family. The church is isolated to
the NE.

ST GREDIFAEL (SH 517 749). A generously proportioned C14
country church, its rebuilding marked by the Tudor family
arms on the chancel. Nave with W double bellcote, the S porch
and N chapel rather later. The style late Dec to early Perp, with
cusped side windows under straight heads, and E and W
windows under pointed arches with continuous mullions and
less cusping. S doorway with continuous quarter-round mouldings. Fragments of Romanesque carving such as chevrons in
the outer chancel walls, from the C12 church. Windows and
priest's doorway with hollow-moulded rere-arches, as also on
the arch of the sedile. Chancel arch two-centred, with two
chamfered orders on faceted capitals. Low arch to the N chapel
with two hollow orders dying into the responds; on its axis on
the S side a Perp recess for an Easter Sepulchre (?), adorned
with a low ogee overarch and finials at the sides. One-light
E window to light an altar. The roofs have slender C16 arch-
braced trusses. Long S porch with steps and seats, and doorway
under a hoodmould. The church underwent exemplary
restoration in 1848 by *Henry Kennedy,* directed by the learned
vicar of Llanfaes, the *Rev. Henry Longueville Jones.*

   STALLS and PEWS of 1848, with hefty fleur-de-lys ends as
unmissable reminders of the Tudor family's descent from the
Valois kings of France. – BEAM carved with running ornament
(from the rood screen?), re-set in the chancel. – FONT. C15,
octagonal with chamfered base. – STAINED GLASS of *c.* 1853,
E window, Crucifixion and N chapel E with Tudor emblems,
possibly by *David Evans.* – TOMB-CHEST of Gronw Fychan of   42
Penmynydd (†1382) and his wife Myfanwy, in the N chapel. Its
lustre for the history of Wales lies in his having been
great-uncle of Owain Tudor and ancestor of the later Tudor
families in Anglesey – who confusingly changed their name
first to the classicizing form Theodore and then to Bold.
The RCAHMW suggests *c.* 1385, so coeval with the church, but
Peter Lord attributes to it a later date, *c.* 1490, because of its
similarity with the Bulkeley tomb at Beaumaris (q.v.). Of
alabaster, and so probably from the sculpture workshops of
Derbyshire or Notts. Five shields on each side and two on each
end, those on the sides hung in cusped panels alternating with
canopied niches for statues of equal width, those on the ends
hung in two-light panels. He, very robust, is in armour with a
surcoat, his head in chain-mail with his moustaches spread on
top of it, his feet on a lion. She has more delicately detailed
clothing and ornaments, her head in a wimple embraced by
two winged angels, her feet under a hem where two lapdogs
also nestle.

PLAS PENMYNYDD, 1½ m. W. A bank defending this
promontory site above the Ceint river and Neolithic finds

suggest this was a significant place from early times. Penmynydd enters written history with Llywelyn the Great's gift to his seneschal Ednyfed Fychan in the 1220s. His heir, Owain, born here in 1410, became the progenitor of the Tudor dynasty (he was also the last of that line to live at this house). Penmynydd passed through a second branch of the family, who, judged by their buildings, hardly flourished as Anglesey squires and died out here in the C18. No doubt medieval Penmynydd consisted partly of timber structures, substantially larger than those now occupying the plateau; so the reductions could be partly explained by decay or fire. The date of the house is taken as 1576, the year on an *ex situ* stone with the initials of Richard Owen Tudor, and also carved on a charred beam long ago removed; but this could relate to a hall-house, replaced not long after by the existing small storeyed house. That would explain the Elizabethan design of the elliptical doorhead and surviving stone fireplace, both more suitable for a larger house, and the absence of contemporary timber within the house's plainly rebuilt walls. Doorway label with the arms of Ednyfed (a severed head) and the Tudors as stops. On the front wall, the squared stones at the base give way to random masonry, so any stone-framed windows were enlarged for the sashes of a little Queen Anne *plas*. The steep gables for a modest thatch roof visible at the ends were evidently raised *c.* 1700 for the slate roof carried on the present trusses with cambered collars of that period. While originally open, the hall has long been storeyed; its lateral fireplace has double roll mouldings; one head corbel for the original roof remains. Tiny C17 service range behind, NE. Regency alterations include a dining-room wing at the NW with a tripartite window; and a stylish miniature first-floor landing formed by a Wyattish curved partition painted with fictive ashlar – a spin-off from Plas Newydd? Other inscribed stones assembled here later as Penmynydd's historical standing grew.

ALMSHOUSES, ½ m. SW. A miniature row of ten one-room units under a continuous roof, built down the hill for Lewis Rogers in 1620. The central one has a porch with a round-arched doorway with a dropped keystone and the donor panel above; the next two have LR over Tudor doorheads; the outer two with tiny projecting wings. Small mullioned windows throughout. Later outhouse range opposite.

PENRHOS

The NE corner of Holy Island is now dominated by the ALUMINIUM SMELTING WORKS of 1969 (*see* p. 57) and the Penrhos Coastal Park annexed to it, set up in 1972.

PENRHOS was the home of the Owen family of Holyhead from the C16. In 1731 a five-bay double-pile house was added for William Owen. This was shortly to acquire two more bays, a full third storey and two flanking wings with Venetian windows, all carried out for his niece Margaret on her marriage to Sir John Stanley in 1763. Further additions for 1st Lord Stanley by *John Cooper*. These ranges are roofless ruins, together with the remnants of three-storey castellated corner towers and the Neo-Jacobean wings of the Late Victorian years. The end came when the house was requisitioned by the army in 1939 and vandalized; after the war Penrhos was sold to the planner Patrick Abercrombie, who died before he had time to rescue it.

The 1st Lord Stanley planted great numbers of trees in this exposed site and in *c*. 1802–9 developed the Home Farm, opposite the ruined house. In the FARM COURTYARD the circular, crenellated Candle Tower remains, and a cartshed with four elliptical arches in the local green stone. SE of the walled garden stood the four-storey water tower, made like a church tower with diagonal buttresses. Further S on the edge of the park was a mid-C18 betting stand built by Margaret Owen to watch horse-racing on the flat ground.

The STANLEY EMBANKMENT was built across the sands of Beddmanarch Bay to form a more direct link from the main island to the port of Holyhead than the route across Four Mile Bridge, as part of Telford's new transport system, in 1822–3. It was 14 ft (4.3 metres) wide at the base, 34 ft (10.5 metres) at the top and 1,250 yards long. In the 1840s it was widened for the railway and the new A55 road now also runs parallel. At its W, the octagonal STANLEY GATE TOLL HOUSE of 1826, taken down in 1969 and re-erected in 1974.

PENRHOS LLIGWY *see* RHOS LLIGWY

PENTRAETH

5378

Main road village 4 m. NNW of Menai Bridge. The name ('head of the beach') refers to Red Wharf Bay down the valley to the NW.

ST MARY. Nave and chancel of medieval origin, with late C16 S chapel. Restored in 1821, then heavily rebuilt with red sandstone dressings in 1882 by *Kennedy*. He extended (or rebuilt?) the chancel, defining the sanctuary with an arch, and added the S porch. Reset E window of *c*. 1400, of three cinquefoiled lights and flowing tracery. Chapel E and chancel N windows also re-set, late C16 or early C17. Reused roof trusses. A barrel-shaped font re-set in the porch as a STOUP, under a piece of C17 window tracery. – STAINED GLASS. E, 1890 by *Powells*, Crucifixion with SS Mary and John. – MONUMENTS. John Jones of Plas Gwyn †1727, Dean of Bangor, scholar, educationist, philanthropist. – William Jones (the builder of Plas Gwyn) †1755, simple Baroque memorial with *memento mori*. – Jane Panton, daughter of William Jones †1764, with open triangular pediment. – Paul Panton of Plas Gwyn †1822, husband of Jane Jones; 'his knowledge of books, the sciences and the arts was solid and extensive'. – James Panton Jun. †1830, Grecian sarcophagus. – Constance Vivian †1905, alabaster oval in laurel wreath. – In the churchyard. Elen Verch Hugh, wife of John Rees ap William †1653, and William Jones †16.., both on Jacobean shaped-baluster legs. – A group of C19 Celtic CROSSES to members of the Vivian family of Plas Gwyn.

75   (PLAS GWYN. The handsome red brick villa commissioned by William Jones (1688–1755) was scarcely finished at the time of his death; he was a barrister, and it passed to his daughter who in 1756 married a barrister who *could* have finished it – Paul Panton (†1797) from Flintshire, later an outstanding Anglesey scholar and authority on Welsh literature. However, the architect of a house clearly related to Robert Taylor's early English Palladian villa designs has not yet been identified. The concept is advanced for *c.* 1750; the client had the chance to meet the leading architects of houses for professional London men; and its component parts, though outlandish in Anglesey, could have been shipped from Liverpool. All the same, a documented explanation has not been found, save that gradual changes could have been made by Panton's son (†1822), who was more consistently resident here.

Plas Gwyn stands at the foot of the escarpment of Mynydd Llwydiarth in a landscaped park, a mile from the sea, with a substantial older group of stone farm buildings to its E. Unique in the island in its assertion of classical architecture, its exterior has a reticent simplicity. N front of two and a half storeys to the parapets, the three centre bays evenly grouped in a slight forward projection under a pediment, the pair of side bays more widely spaced in the astylar façade. The E side not unlike, but with a half-octagon bay in the centre. Main (N) doorway with two three-quarter Doric columns carrying a full Doric frieze with triglyphs and guttae and a triangular pediment. In the hall, a plain lugged doorcase again with triangular pediment, and two either side of the staircase with depressed arches with key blocks. Three architectural chimneypieces: the drawing room with a scrolly pediment, the dining room with Ionic pilasters not related to the modillion cornice, the library with a chaste open pediment.)

LIMEKILNS, 2 m. N, on the old NW side of the estuary of Traeth Coch.

TŶ FRY, 1¼ m. SSW. Built by Owen Williams in 1679. A long single-pile plan with the staircase in a wing beyond the hall. Two-storey façade of eight bays, the five to the l. original, the three to the r. of the early C18; the sash windows of twenty-four small panes under flat arches with ashlar keystones belong to the later period. Two further bays at the w were added with the same roof-line in the Regency, but as a single storey with tall window and dormers in the roof. In the hall a stone fireplace of almost Jonesian nobility: Ionic pilasters supporting a segmental pediment touching the ceiling, within which is a carved coat of arms.

Nearby FARM, of the same dates as the house, two ranges of cartsheds with depressed arches, of seven and four bays, one with a loft.

PENTRE BERW   4773

Linear village on the Holyhead road, just W of Gaerwen, on the NE edge of the Malltraeth Marsh. There was a small coal pit here from the C15 to mid C19. Two chapels, BEREA INDEPENDENT CHAPEL, 1860, gabled, and PENSARN BERW CALVINISTIC METHODIST CHAPEL, 1867, plain Gothic.

ST MICHAEL, Llanfihangel Ysgeifiog. *See* Gaerwen.
PLAS BERW, ½ m. SW. Two houses, one of the late C15 and one   50
of 1615, standing corner to corner in a walled forecourt, within a medieval deerpark, on the S side of Malltraeth Marsh. The hall-house, one of the few to survive in Anglesey, has been a ruin at least since the early C19, possibly since a fire in the C18. Before that, however, it continued in conjunction with the new storeyed house for several generations: an illustration of how the 'unit system' flourished among the gentry as well as at the yeoman farms.

An archway at the N of the court leads across to the house probably built *c.* 1480 for Ithel ap Howel, one of the descendants of the C12 lord of Menai, Llywarch ap Bran; and to the the Renaissance one, r., built for Ithel's descendant, Sir Thomas Holland. It has a stepped upper profile like the noble vanished gateway of *c.* 1612 to the Jacobean garden at Baron Hill, Beaumaris, which perhaps it copied. Wide segmental, chamfered arch. The N wall of the hall is comparatively complete up to the first storey, and explains much of its history. An elliptical arch with a roll moulding led into the screens passage. The service wing lay to the W and its small rectangular window to the yard is original, part of it later incorporated into the C17 house. The hall window, l. of the doorway, is blocked. It retains in fragmentary state three trefoiled lights under a square head and label. On the opposite wall the hall fireplace. The tall cross-wall crowned by a bellcote to the W of this is a late insertion, possibly *c.* 1700, and divides the house that developed at the solar end from the (by then) storeyed hall. The plan was therefore comparable with Cochwillan's. The history given by the Royal Commission is that the hall was given an upper storey and had its walls raised *c.* 1536; at its SW corner the putative solar stair next to the lateral chimney was replaced *c.* 1600 by a three-storey tower, presumably containing another stair, though this part too is full-height but ruinous. Its many openings indicate the rooms served in the vanished solar wing; one early C17 window that remains in the ground floor of the hall shows that the old house was modernized when the new one was built.

Thomas Holland's house combines a number of the characteristics of C16–C17 Gwynedd houses, e.g. Plas

Talhenbont, Llanystumdwy (q.v.). The entrance, with the builder's heraldry in a stone panel above it, is l. of centre, the kitchen being one side of the hall and the parlour the other. Beyond the entrance hall is the pyramid-roofed staircase tower, rising three storeys to form a belvedere higher than the roof, and looking over the marshy estuary. The stairs are not original, but of modest C18 design, re-set. Plas Coch, Llanedwen (q.v.), has a similar plan and tower. The E front has five bays of three-light mullion-and-transom windows, the lower ones taller than the upper. The gable-end chimneystacks, square in section and unusually tall, frame the most complete example of an elevation of this Gwynedd house type. Inside, re-set panelling of various C17 periods, and a corbel with the initials OJH, for Sir Thomas's nephew. Exemplary restoration by *Robert Heaton*, c. 1990.

ESTATE BUILDINGS. The 'village' of lesser structures around, including stone garden gatepiers, is a significant if decayed and altered survival. Small early roofless BARN on the cliff N of the house, one of its arches in red stone; of the date of the second house? COACHHOUSE, with mid-C19 brick dressings.

DEERPARK, on the former seaward slope SW of the house. Of around the date of the first house, i.e. the first surviving in this island of huntsmen, and bounded by walls as thick as hedges. The drive skirts one of its inner divisions and is lined with C18 beech trees. Unexpectedly it then plunges under the disused line of the Amlwch branch railway, which overshadows the courtyard. The E stretch of the deerpark wall was removed in the 1980s for road widening, but the section turning S is still intact.

PENYSARN
4692

Large linear village just E of Parys Mountain (q.v.), developed largely for the copper-mine workers.

BOZRAH CALVINISTIC METHODIST CHAPEL. 1864. The archetypal layout, the chapel at the top of a little railed yard, house and school facing each other across it. Hipped with arched doorway and two arched windows, all quoined. No galleries.

PLAS NEWYDD *see* LLANEDWEN

PUFFIN ISLAND/YNYS SEIRIOL
6583

An uninhabited island of some 78 acres about ½ m. off the E corner of the island, restricted of access. Having the earlier name Ynys Lannog or Glannauc, this monastic island came to be named for the church, with the same dedication as the more important Early Christian monastery at Penmon, across the sound. The remains, though very ruinous, are perhaps the most telling for the first Christian age in the whole area, since they are protected by or attached to a large irregular oval enclosure like an Irish cashel.

MONASTERY OF ST SEIRIOL. All that remains of the CHURCH is the mid-C12 crossing tower, narrow and with a pyramidal vault, which stands like a seamark high on the island. Excavations in 1901 showed that the first chancel, with a barrel vault and steep roof, was just 5 ft (1.5 metres) square, perhaps a mortuary shrine.* Above its round W arch, the higher creasing on

Puffin Island, Monastery of St Seiriol.
Drawing by Harold Hughes, c. 1900

*A skeleton was found here at the time of excavation.

the E face of the tower is that of its larger C13 successor. The tower measures 8 ft 9 in. (2.7 metres) square, and has Romanesque E and W arches and traces of a S window splay. Above the string course is an upper stage with round-headed windows set high on each face. The nave, about 18 ft (5.5 metres) by 12 ft (3.7 metres), has disappeared. A transept was added and the S tower wall broken through for it, replaced later by a small cottage, now ruined.

(MONASTIC BUILDINGS. Earlier than all, perhaps, but the primitive chancel. The oval walled enclosure is surprisingly large. Main entrance at its narrow W end, a gap in its D-plan E end. At an early stage a cross-wall was built E of the church. The remains of the cells are attached to either side of the N wall W of that, quite near but not directly related to the church. Walls of three rectangular early small fields are attached to the W end of the enclosure wall.)

SEMAPHORE STATION, NE corner of the island. One of eleven semaphore stations linking Holyhead to Liverpool, built by the Mersey Docks and Harbour Board in 1827. It operated as a one-mast, three-arm system (upgraded in 1841). The record time for a message to be sent was 23 seconds. A brick dwelling with attached signal room with a semicircular window facing the next stations at Llaneilian and the Great Orme.

RHODOGEIDIO see LLANERCHYMEDD

2675

RHOSCOLYN

Parish of scattered farms at the S end of Holy Island, formerly quarried for the 'Mona Marble'. The church stands on a rocky outcrop by PLAS RHOSCOLYN, an C18 house enlarged into a strange Victorian folly for E. H. Verney (of Rhianfa, Llandegfan), with added wings of 1874 and 1895. Beside it a stone-walled viewing platform. The lane winds down to Borthwen Bay. The LIFEBOAT STATION here, closed 1929, was the fourth since 1830.

ST GWENFAEN (SH 268 757). In a rectangular raised church-yard, with spectacular views S to distant mountains over the sea; but victim of a tough rebuilding of 1875 and 1879 by R. G. Thomas of Menai Bridge. From the decayed medieval church the S doorway was salvaged, an elliptical arch with crude late Gothic spandrels in a deep casement-moulded square frame. – GLAZED TILES probably by Powells, cf. Llanbadrig. – FONT. C15, octagonal, and unusually covered in decoration. The sides of the bowl have fluting and saltires, the undercut facets have blank arcading with round arches, and the base which tapers out again has a tiny cusped panel on each side. – STAINED GLASS. E, Christ on the Sea of Galilee, by *Powells*, 1912. – Nave E windows, by *Kempe*, 1892 and 1896. – SW window, SS George and Michael, 1919, by *Morris & Co.* to *Burne-Jones* designs. By the firm also six single-light nave windows, 1920–2. – NW window, 1907, possibly *Burlison & Grylls*. – MONUMENTS. A group for the Owen family of Bodior, including a provincial Baroque one to John Owen of Bodior †1709. Heraldic achievement between flaming vases; the whole shallowly carved so that it lies rather flat against the wall.

CALVINISTIC METHODIST CHAPEL. 1906. In a railed yard. Entertaining façade in cement and pebbledash with corner piers topped with flaming vases and a parapet, echoing the line of the arched triplet window, with name panel and an urn. On the l. TŶ CAPEL, an early C19 farmhouse used as a chapel and later as schoolroom and stable, and on the r. TŶ RHOS, the cottage where the cause began.

ST GWENFAEN'S WELL, ½ m. W (SH 259 754). Impressive lining of large stones around the pool, of unknown date. Lewis Morris tells of drinking the water for inspiration in the C18. An outer square chamber at the E is entered by three steps down, and has stone seats across each corner. The adjoining inner pool chamber has a rectangular plan with a stone seat in a recess on either side; to its W a second, outer pool with steps down on each side; thence the water flows into a channel lined by slabs and over the cliff edge.

CHURCH HALL. Plain Arts and Crafts hall by *Harold Hughes*, c. 1912, with oak windows and sweeping buttresses on its gable-end porch.

(BODIOR, 1 m. NE. The house was founded by descendants of Llywelyn Aurdorchog of Iâl, who changed their name to Owen. A re-set stone has the date 1529, but the known history suggests a late C16 low house of two wings ending in crowstepped gables, that on the l. entered by a two-storey porch with a crowstepped gable. Enlargements in the C18, and especially in 1848 for the Hampton Lewis family (cf. Henllys, Llanfaes), produced a much larger Tudorish house based on the r. wing, with the old house on the l. as the service wing.)

YNYSOEDD GWYLANOD, ½ m. offshore. On the main island, RHOSCOLYN BEACON, a C19 day-mark, though it has internal stairs; tall round tapering tower, round top.

RHOS LLIGWY

4987

The modern settlement is on high ground above Lligwy Bay, 2 m. W of Moelfre.

ST MICHAEL, Penrhos Lligwy, ½ m. SW at Tŷ Mawr. In a circular *llan*, enlarged to the N. Chancel with two-light late Dec traceried window, nave with a continuous-chamfered pointed N doorway, both indicative of rebuilding c. 1400. Otherwise much renewed in 1865 by *Henry Kennedy* with over-elaborate Perp windows, N porch, W bellcote. The wide chancel arch has two continuous hollow chamfers, and dies into the chamfered responds. The roofs look late medieval, much restored. – INSCRIBED STONE. A C6 stone set in the chancel is inscribed HIC IACIT MACCUDECCETI. – COMMUNION TABLE. Turned front legs, arched apron at front and sides. Mid-C17. – MONUMENTS. Plaques to Margaret Prichard, mother of the Morris brothers (*see* below) and her youngest son, Sion †1740.

CAPEL LLIGWY, 1 m. ESE of the village. Tiny rectangular C12 church, now roofless. Round-headed S doorway, blocked E window, the W bellcote perhaps C14. S chapel with blocked Tudor windows, added in the C16. It has steps down to a vault roofed with limestone slabs that form the floor above.

MORRIS MONUMENT, NW of Brynrefail (SH 478 873). A Celtic cross of 1910 with a relief of a sailing ship, by *Harold Hughes*, to the famous Morris brothers from Pentre Eirianell farm below. Inscription by Sir Goronwy Owen. Lewis Morris †1765 surveyed the Welsh coasts 1737–48 and was a polymath scholar, antiquarian and promoter of Welsh literature; Richard †1779, chief clerk in the Navy Office in London, with similar interests, founded the Honourable Society of Cymmrodorion in 1751; William †1763 also collected manuscripts and was a founder of Welsh botany; and John †1740, naval officer, died young.

10 DIN LLIGWY ROMANO-BRITISH HOMESTEAD, ½ m. ESE of the village (SH 496 862). One of the finest such homesteads in Gwynedd. It is spaciously designed, with huts and working buildings around an open courtyard enclosed by an imposing wall, on a fine site with splendid sea views. It is likely to have been the headquarters of a prosperous estate, the equivalent of the southern English *villa*, which flourished in the C3–C4.

The owner was undoubtedly non-Roman, for the main living hut is a very well built version of the native round hut, here given slightly higher walls, imposing door jambs and a carefully dressed threshold slab. Finds from this hut included pottery from the South of England, part of a glass jug, and an ingot of silver, signs of high living which sit rather uneasily with iron slag from the same floor. In the SE corner another round hut, much less imposing, possibly a later addition. This compound wall on the N side, where it fronts a low cliff is 5 ft (1.5 metres) wide and built of huge upright slabs of limestone; on the S where there is an easy, level approach, the wall is much slighter, which suggests that it was designed to impress rather than to defend.

Five rectangular buildings are built against the wall. The entrance passes through one of them, which may have been a threshing barn. Two long buildings to N and S contained hearths with evidence for iron working. The square building on the ledge above the main living hut showed signs of

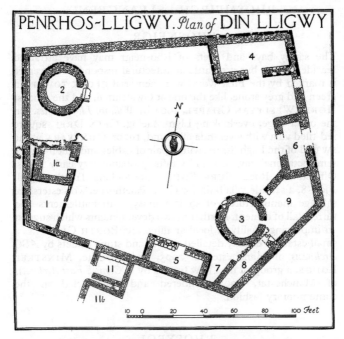

Rhos Lligwy, Din Lligwy Romano-British homestead.
Plan

occupation but it is unlikely that the enclosure beside it was
ever roofed. Just outside the enclosure, s, is a small building,
purpose unknown. At a late stage rubbish was dumped in it.

This well-ordered settlement superseded a much less formal
group of huts, of which only a few curved walls survive in the
surrounding wood. These earlier huts also produced Roman
material, but prehistoric flint implements found during excavations in 1907 suggest that occupation began in the Neolithic.

LLIGWY BURIAL CHAMBER, 1 m. ESE (SH 501 860). Famous for
the enormous capstone, a massive limestone block some
18 by 16 ft (5.5 by 4.8 metres), on variously shaped supporters. The height of the chamber beneath was mainly obtained
by digging out the easily quarried limestone. When the tomb
was excavated in 1908 it was found that a man could stand
upright under the capstone. The floor was covered with human
bones, about thirty people in all, mixed with pottery sherds
and flint tools, but divided into two layers by a paving of flat
stones. There is no record of any cairn. The structure lacks any
formal plan, the chamber merely reflects the shape of the capstone, and it is likely that this simple but impressive tomb
belongs to the later Neolithic, when architectural traditions
were weakened.

RHOSMEIRCH see LLANGEFNI

3274   ## RHOSNEIGR

The sandy bays and islets of Rhosneigr may have attracted
seaside homes, but very little architectural response. The centre
is marked by the First World War memorial CLOCK TOWER, in
green and grey stone, like the one at Gwalchmai, and the modest
HOREB WESLEYAN CHAPEL, 1904 by *William Lloyd Jones*. On
the outer edge, overlooking Llyn Maelog, CEFN DREF, square
red-tiled villa with a veranda all round, 1920s. OONAVARA, at the
SW end of the High Street, with a pair of gables and an off-centre
semi-octagonal bay. Arts and Crafts, probably very early 1900s.
Off Station Road, SURF POINT, overlooking Traeth Cigyll.
1906–8, a seaside villa built for C. H. Palethorpe, Worcestershire
sausage manufacturer, of some fantasy, with battlements and
turrets, all of cement. Further N, two developments which suggest
an improving quality in local architecture: PORTH CRIGYLL, a
small estate of cleanly detailed timber and stone chalets by *ABC
Architects* of Manchester, *c.* 2005, and opposite, MINSTREL
LODGE, a group of nine new houses by *O'Connell East Architects*
of Manchester, 2008, rendered and timber-clad in the
contemporary fashion.

4388   ## RHOSYBOL

One of the miners' villages for the Parys Mountain workings. To
the E, the large Trysglwyn WIND FARM, 1996.

CHRIST CHURCH. 1875, by *Kennedy*. Divided nave and chancel,
N porch, S vestry. E window with plate tracery. – STAINED
GLASS by *Celtic Studios*, 1977.
At the top of the village, BETHANIA INDEPENDENT CHAPEL,
1884, with pretty windows, but swamped in pebbledash. Oppo-
site, war memorial CLOCK TOWER. Below, GORSLWYD
CALVINISTIC METHODIST CHAPEL, a rather formidable
group, two hipped-roofed blocks, the chapel of 1867 by *R. G.
Thomas*, the school early C20, within a big, iron-railed yard.
Chapel front of four tall windows and two doors.

2795   ## THE SKERRIES/YNYSOEDD-Y-MOELRHONIAID

Rocky island amid treacherous rocks 2 m. off Carmel Head. The
first beacon was built on the island in 1716 by William Trench of
London. As drawn by Lewis Morris in 1748 it was circular with
a coal-fired brazier on top. Trench died penniless but passed the
lighthouse to his relations the Morgans of Cilwendeg, Capel
Colman, Pembs, who were finally bought out by Trinity House
in 1841 for the astonishing sum of £444,984 11s. 3d.,
representing twenty-two times the revenue in 1820. This
represents a payment from every boat that passed, collected on

shore in the various ports, principally Liverpool. The recently renovated crowstepped keeper's cottage of 1716 adjacent is the oldest such dwelling in the British Isles. A tower was built c. 1759, with a coal brazier on top, and in 1814 this was heightened and given an oil-burning lantern glazed all round. In c. 1848 this was enlarged again by Trinity House with a cast-iron lantern, by *James Walker*. Low circular tower for a sector light, 1888 or 1903.

SOUTH STACK *see* HOLYHEAD

TALWRN 4977

Village 3 m. NE of Llangefni with the church of ST DEINIOL, 1891, small and pebbledashed, and two chapels. SILOAM INDEPENDENT CHAPEL, 1880, is sub-Norman round-arched. To the W the CALVINISTIC METHODIST CHAPEL, 1880, by *Richard Davies*.

BODEILIO, ¼ m. NE. Dated 1602 and 1618 on the big central storeyed porch, which has a tall capped gable chimney. Rounded doorway and hooded upper window.

ST FFINAN, Llanffinan, 1 m. SSE (SH 496 755). In the remnant of a round *llan* above the Cefni river. Rectangular and harsh Neo-Norman rebuild of 1841, by *John Welch*. Low BOX PEWS; W gallery. The C12 circular FONT has its sides crudely decorated with continuous interlace.

HIRDRE-FAIG. 2 m. SSW. Demolished 1967. A long wing was added c. 1710 to an earlier house. Added parapets without cornices made it one of the longest and strangest of Anglesey Queen Anne houses. There remain the WALLED GARDEN of c. 1710, some BARNS and a four-arch CARTSHED. In the PARK, a well-placed clump of trees and one of Telford's latticed iron gates.

TALYLLYN 3774

Isolated church 2½ m. SW of Gwalchmai, its village entirely vanished. Before the Black Death there were twenty-two houses.

ST MARY or ST TUDUR (SH 367 728). (Friends of Friendless Churches). A chapel of ease to Llanbeulan, in a largely round *llan* with a small stable at the N. Almost double-square nave (23 by 12 ft, 7 by 4 metres) with a round-headed W doorway under a relieving arch, chancel and S chapel in line with the chancel wall. This church has the vernacular character of Anglesey's country buildings, which survives scarcely at all in the churches. The nave could be C12; the gabled W bellcote also has a round opening. The chancel gable is irregular, appearing to follow the deformation of the roof structure within; its three-light window of three round-headed lights is, however, placed centrally. The chancel has dressed quoins, the chapel simply boulders; both still have Tudor moulded copings and fleur-de-lys gable finials. Other windows at the E and W have replacement stone dressings. Stone-flagged nave with stone benches along the S and N walls, as at Llangwyfan. Two of its three late medieval arch-braced trusses survive (that at the W is C17), perhaps corresponding to the dates of the two additions. Irregular four-centred chancel arch apparently cut into the nave E wall – yet it has C13 chamfered jambs and cushion stops on the W. The chancel roof has one arch-braced cruck truss, suggesting early origins (cf. Llanrhwydrys and Llanbabo) and one of the C17. The C17 family chapel, also with stone benches, opens through a similar arch. The furnishings of this limewashed interior are C18 and of the simplest. Tiny island sanctuary raised on one step and enclosed by panelling painted blue-grey; the front with turned COMMUNION RAILS, dated 1764. – BENCHES. A rare and admired backless design, one dated 1786; one end rests on the wall benches, the other on continuous stretchers. Reproduced from what remained after the rest were stolen. – FONTS. The C12 one is now in Llanfaelog church. The other font is C15, octagonal with a roll moulding above the octagonal base, on a sophisticated Perp pillar.

TAL-Y-LLYN, ¼ m. NW. One wing of a house with Renaissance pedimented windows (one dated 1597 with the initials HW and HW, for Wood), mullioned and transomed, of four lights and eight lights. One has Gothick iron opening casements similar to those at Plas Coch, Llanedwen.

TREARDDUR

2579

At the narrow centre of Holy Island, with a lovely rocky shore to the Atlantic, a series of bays between Porth Dafarch and Porth Diana (originally Porth Dwna). Trearddur, like Rhoscolyn and Rhosneigr, has sadly provoked little in the way of architectural response to its beauties. The remoteness of this area ended when the main route to Holyhead came through, over Four Mile Bridge, superseded by Telford's Stanley Embankment (Penrhos) of 1815–22. *Thomas Telford* was one of the first outsiders to have a house here, reputedly the four-bay TOWYN LODGE in Ravenspoint Road, possibly 1820s.

BONT METHODIST CHAPEL, Four Mile Bridge, 1½ m. E. 1874, by *Richard Davies*. Disused 2006. Characterful High Victorian Gothic with a small rose window.

TYWYN-Y-CAPEL, on the beach (SH 256 790). A truncated mound of sand between the promenade and the car park associated with St Bridget. Until the late C18 a small ruined chapel stood on top, surrounded by a cemetery. C19 erosion exposed a series of cist burials, recorded by W. O. Stanley. Erosion has continued, and further excavations took place during 2002–3.

These revealed a series of dug graves, separated by a period of agricultural use from a lower series in stone cists, likely to pre-date the C7. The rapid accumulation of wind-blown sand pre-served the original above-ground grave markers, a low mound of earth surrounded by a ring of boulders, never previously recorded at these early cemeteries.

The Late Victorian start of the holiday town was along the main road, LÔN SANT FFRAID. Here the Stanley family of Penrhos had built MELIN-Y-GOF, a windmill of 1826, which worked until 1936. On this road is CAE GRUGOG, a twin-gabled Arts and Crafts house perhaps of the 1920s; its long garden front has a recessed porch, panoramic windows with long horizon-tal panes, and an overhanging slated roof – a Voysey borrowing. More recent houses, e.g. *Gilbert Fraser*'s Y NYTH, a studiedly irregular, white roughcast house, which sums up the taste of so many seaside homes in North Wales. Except that the small-paned cottage window had been replaced by the new sheet glass picture window, little had changed by the time houses by such architects as *B. Hallwood Lingard* were being built in the 1960s. On the w of Lôn Sant Ffraid, in the grounds of Trearddur House, one of three circular PILLBOXES of the Anglesey type, of two storeys and disguised as garden structures. There is no coherent seafront, the *sine qua non* of the Victorian resort.

Behind the Trearddur Bay Hotel two more PILLBOXES sited together on a rocky point, their circular wall-heads disguised with stones set on edge, their entrances masked by screen walls. On a promontory further on, CRAIG Y MÔR, by *F. G. Hicks* of Dublin. Begun 1911, completed 1922. L-plan Neo-Georgian, the wings of five and four bays respectively. Its boldest feature is the full-height canted bay overlooking the sea. Of snecked rubble masonry with freestone dressings, the roof covered with small green slates. Further w, the CLIFF HOTEL, 1947, by *Lloyd & T. H. Lloyd Jones* of Caernarfon, on another poem of a rock, an intrusion of baffling disharmony with its surroundings. Finally at PORTH DAFARCH, 2 m. w, the little harbour completed in 1819 to allow mail and pas-sengers to land on Holy Island when N winds made landing at Holyhead impossible. The single-storey, brick barrel-vaulted building was the Customs Post.

RAVENSPOINT ROAD runs sw past PORTH DIANA, a concentration of Arts and Crafts houses, revealing the early and best side of the development of Trearddur Bay. PORTH-Y-CASTELL, by *H. L. North*, 1923, is typical, with pebbledash walls and green slate roofs enlivened by asymmetrical oriels and dormers. One of the more striking, up the hill, is AVILION, of *c.* 1910 by *Richard Hall* of Bangor, symmetrical, with sweeping roofs and conical-roofed round turrets at the sides, in homage to Rhianfa, Llandegfan, and preserving its internal decorative features. A few others make a substantial mark, even if poorly related to the bays and islets whose beauty provoked their construction; the best are three-storeyed, white-roofed and ornamented with Arts and Crafts bays and battered chimneys. Their failing is not to relate to each other: a defect which, after the First World War, was perhaps part of Clough Williams-Ellis's critique and inspiration for his holiday village at Portmeirion (q.v.).

PORTH DAFARCH ROUND BARROWS (SH 234 801). Close to the shore and now almost overridden by roads was a complex group excavated in the C19 by W. O. Stanley. The earliest were three round barrows of Beaker and Early Bronze Age date. The easternmost one was disturbed and built over in the Roman period when a group of round stone huts and rectangular rooms extended over it. This settlement was similar to the larger village a few miles away at Tŷ Mawr, Holyhead (p. 137). The level of prosperity would seem to have been quite high, for a fine carved intaglio was found. One of the round huts can still be seen in the corner of the field. When the huts were abandoned the area was used for burial and several long cist graves of C6–C7 type were dug into the remains. On the peninsula to the SW, a PROMONTORY FORT (SH 223 794).

TREFDRAETH

4271

On the N slope of the Malltraeth marshes near the mouth of the Cefni, where in post-Napoleonic times about 1,000 acres were reclaimed from the sea. The change is commemorated in the new river crossing at PONT MARQUIS, a single arch with flood arches over the Cefni, of c. 1820. The modern settlement is at Bethel, ½ m. W.

ST BEUNO (SH 408 704). In a partly circular *llan*. Low, unicameral nave and chancel, but these are confusingly rearranged. C14 W bellcote. Porch, with roof dated 1728 and doorway with continuous hollow chamfer. Similar doorway to the S transept. E window of Dec flowing tracery with mouchettes. A window on the N of the chancel is late C15, under a straight label with stops. C15 S doorway with continuous hollow chamfer. Repaired for once, rather than replaced, by *Kennedy* in 1854, following repairs in the 1840s; the vestry added then, outside the late C15 N doorway. Strangely the chancel arch, a large two-centred arch with continuous quarter-round mouldings, is re-set in the transept just S of its original opening, which has short responds with quarter-round mouldings to the nave, hollow chamfers to the chapel. Nave roofs of unusual construction, close-set collar-trusses with every third one being arch-braced with cusped apex strutting, perhaps C15; chancel roof hidden by a Victorian painted celure. – ALTAR RAILS. Turned, early C18. – PULPIT, Arts and Crafts, dated 1920, in the style of *Harold Hughes*, with pierced Gothic motifs. – FONT. Small, cylindrical, C12, with six panels round the bowl, four with saltires and one with a knotwork cross. – STAINED GLASS. E,

the Crucifixion, by *Kempe*, 1904. – Fragments of *c.* 1500 in the
s sanctuary window. – N, Mary and Simeon, in the Kempe
style, 1902. – MONUMENTS. Repainted inscriptions to
Chancellor Robert Lewis of Bangor †1766, and to Hugh Lewis
†1666 and Owen Williams †1723 of Marian, of slate with arms
below in lowest relief.

(TREFEILIR, ⅔ m. NW. The range built *c.* 1725 for William
Evans, agent to the Vaynol estate, Y Felinheli, and approached
past an C18 gateway, was added to a five-bay C16 house with
a finialled gable at the centre; of this a finely moulded, four-
centred fireplace arch survives in the wing to the l. Within the
later wing a Chinese Chippendale staircase.)

DIN DRYFOL BURIAL CHAMBER (SH 396 725) stands on a
narrow shelf on the w side of an impressive knob of rock which
is called 'Dinas' but is not artifically defended. The tomb is
badly ruined and only one high portal stone and the collapsed
remains of the second and third chambers survive. Excavation
revealed that it has been built in stages like Trefignath.
The earliest chamber is at the far end and is reasonably
complete. Only one fallen sidestone of the second remains;
excavation showed that, very unusually, it had a wooden portal,
but that the low façade fronting a long narrow cairn set
between the rock outcrops was of stone. At a later date the
tomb was extended eastwards. Nothing remains of the
final chamber except one enormous portal stone. Pottery
suggests that it had a relatively short history and dates from
the Early Neolithic.

TREFOR 3780

Cross-roads settlement 2½ m. E of Bodedern, with EBENEZER
WESLEYAN CHAPEL, simple Gothic, mid-C19.

TRE IORWERTH BARROW (SH 354 805). Excavated in the 1960s,
it proved to be a simple cairn capped with a thick layer of
yellow clay. Dug into in the C19, when Bronze Age cremations
were found; seven more of these burials found in 1967 show
that the barrow was a 'cemetery mound' like so many in
Anglesey. In the C6–C7 a number of Christian burials in long
stone cists were dug into the upper levels.

TREGAEAN 4681

Isolated church 3 m. NNW of Llangefni.

ST CAEAN. A low church of the C14 which, partly because its
walls lean, gives an impression of what the Anglesey parish
churches were like before so many were reassembled in the
C19. E window of one light in a deep reveal, the main panel
made ogee-headed by using two mouchettes as tracery. The w

bellcote also rises to an ogee, and has sub-gables either side. Bold Perp s doorway of the local kind, with trefoils in the spandrels. The arch-braced trusses are of *c.* 1600, with one tier of wind-braces under the low purlins, renewed. – FONT. C12, carved with a band of chevrons. – STAINED GLASS. E, by *Curtis, Ward & Hughes*, 1916.

TREWALCHMAI *see* GWALCHMAI

VALLEY/Y FALI

2879

An A5 village, unusual in being laid out as a cross-roads, the historic land access to Holyhead being to the SW by Four Mile Bridge. So the houses are away from the Telford axis for once. In the street, TABOR CALVINISTIC METHODIST CHAPEL, 1881, by *R. G. Thomas*, with a giant-arched pilastered cement front. Next to it, BEECROFT, a small villa of 1908 possibly by *Richard Davies*, in yellow brick (ruined), and the Edwardian former POLICE COURT, so lettered in terracotta, with a shaped gable. At the S end the RAILWAY STATION, one of the two original station buildings of 1849 on the Chester to Holyhead railway (the other is at Bodorgan). The stone building, of two storeys of scribed stucco below and rubble with freestone dressings above, is one of *Francis Thompson*'s small country station designs, with Italianate details and eaves. GOODS SHED beside of 1851.

ST MICHAEL. Sited diagonally to the A5. Cruciform, with Neo-Tudor windows; without crossing arches. The architect was the 3rd *Lord Stanley*, 1887, with his agent Mr Elliott. The tall vicarage house beside it.

FOUR MILE BRIDGE, 1½ m. SW. Stone embankment with battered sides, probably of the last quarter of the C18, with one narrow arch. Built to carry the mail coaches across the sands to the packet harbour on Holy Island.

CAERNARVONSHIRE

ABERCONWY ABBEY *see* MAENAN

ABERDARON

ST HYWYN (old church). The sister church to that of the abbey of Enlli on Bardsey Island, standing in the centre of the broad sandy bay – an archetypal Welsh Early Christian situation. This was the most important church in Llŷn, the embarkation point for pilgrims, and its *clas* or monastery was a place of sanctuary.

Two large naves of equal length. The N is older, largely late C12. Fine W doorway: three eroded orders of chamfered mouldings, semicircular arches, simply moulded capitals. Above the set-off, the W gable is perhaps C14, its stark bellcote flat-topped like the Conwy valley ones and perforated by a lancet. In the N wall, a blocked priests' doorway, late C12. Chamfered semicircular arch on plain imposts. The E gable has a relieving arch of tall C14 profile. Inserted beneath is a renewed early Perp three-light window. In the S nave E gable, a fine renewed Perp window: tracery lights grouped two-one-two, cusped ogee heads beneath the transom. In the S wall, two early C16 windows, Tudor-arched with three short uncusped lancets. Near the W end, a similar two-light window in a former doorway. No windows in the N wall; oak window inserted in an opening in the SW gable, 2006.

Spacious INTERIOR, refurbished 2006, by *Tim Ratcliffe,* in earshot of the waves. The rere-arches of the Romanesque doorways are unadorned. The arcade, its arches four-centred, is a distinguished one of *c.* 1500. Warm pale gritstone. Five richly moulded arches with hoodmoulds to the early nave, slender octagonal piers with moulded capitals and bases. Restored hammerbeam roof, the trusses with decoration in spandrels and apexes. N nave roof of *Kennedy*'s restoration 1868. – FONT. Perp, plain octagonal. – STOUP. Plain oblong stone bowl, medieval. – PULPIT. 1911. Elaborately detailed with buttresses, tracery panels and canopies of crocketed gables. – INSCRIBED STONES. Two water-worn boulders, both 3 ft (90 cm.) high, with Roman capitals in horizontal lines, to Veracius and Senacus, priests. C5–C6.

ST HYWYN (new church), ½ m. N. Built 1841, because the old church became dilapidated, but the Neo-Romanesque design, by *John Welch,* provoked so much criticism that the old one was repaired. Large nave, tiny chancel. Two thin W towers, with a gabled porch between. They look gauche in relation to the bulky nave, but there is something endearing about the W end – the belvedere-like tower tops (now blocked), the twin lights within a single overarch high on the gable, the powerful sparsely dentilated verges and the serrated head of the W doorway, all reminiscent of North Italy. Large interior roofed with queenpost trusses braced on wall-posts. W gallery removed. Interesting BOX PEWS, with curious finial bench ends and an unusual mixture of forward and side orientation.

The treeless VILLAGE, at the bottom of a steep combe in a S-facing cove, has an end-of-peninsula feel. A sheltered cluster of whitened houses and stone bridges. The old church is almost on the beach, its churchyard rising steeply behind. S of the Pont Fawr, CEGIN FAWR, C17, whitewashed, with stone dormers. Next to it, set back and providing a successful stop-end to the street, the old POST OFFICE, 1950, by *Clough Williams-Ellis*. Whitewashed rubble, the central gable containing an arched window. Just below the road climbing NE, the old CORN MILL. ½ m. further, the new church (*see* above). To its W, BODERNABWY, an earlier C18 farmhouse of colour-washed rubble. SE of the church, the slate-clad PLAS YR WYLAN, the former vicarage and home of the Rev. R. S. Thomas, poet and vicar of Aberdaron, 1967–78.

PENRHYN-MAWR, I m. E. A Nanhoron estate farmhouse, probably early C19. Three-storey central bay, its gable running through from front to back. A chimney at mid-point. Two-storey parallel side outshuts, the roofs continuing the slope of the central gable, but stepped down. A further step down over a later extension to the N. A highly unusual arrangement, seen at Port Penrhyn, Bangor.

BODWRDDA, I m. ENE. Keeping a low profile in the Daron valley, this minor mansion is perhaps the most important house in Llŷn. Owned by the Bodwrdda family from the early C16 (their fortune reputedly made from piracy), then by the Edwards of Nanhoron from the mid C18. Long S block running E–W, with two gabled N wings. The W end of the S block, of rubble, is early C16. Now of two storeys and attic, but originally lower, probably with opposed central doorways N and S. Of the earlier date, two windows in the S elevation, and a blocked one in the W gable, all slightly pointed. Hugh Bodwrdda, Cambridge-educated and High Sheriff of Caernarvonshire in 1606, extended the house in 1621, adding the N wings and refacing the centre of the S block to form a grand symmetrical entrance front. The style of the wings, totally alien in this remote part of North Wales, and the very early use of brick, are both significant. Which buildings provided the inspiration, and where did the bricks come from? Whether the E end of the S block was built at the same time is uncertain; it seems unlikely that extending the house on this scale in one go should have been carried out so many years after Hugh Bodwrdda was at his peak (and just a year before he died). The lateral chimney in

the s wall may be coeval with the wings. The stone windows
certainly are: of two lights, with elliptical heads and quarter-
rounded mullions and jambs, all ovolo-moulded, below flat
Tudor hoods. Above the attic windows in the wing gables,
lozenge plaques with the painted inscription 'HB/1621'.
Central doorway, with stop-chamfered moulded jambs and a
depressed four-centred head. Central dormer and matching
dormers (now blocked) to the wings. Some C16 post-and-panel
partitions survive, and fine arch-braced collar-beam trusses in
the w end of the s block. Their quality indicates that they were
to be seen from the main rooms below, so one must assume
all were re-set at a higher level when the house was enlarged.
C17 panelling in the lower room of the NW wing, with ovolo
mouldings and a frieze of intersecting foliated semicircles, and
door frames with ovolo mouldings at the E end. Early C19
central staircase, with curved winders and handrails, and plain
square balusters, Shaker-like in its simplicity.

PENCAE, 1 m. E. Typical *croglofft* cottage, with in-line byre, r.
Later N extension at right angles. Not so typical the rather
good C20 hipped extension further N. The big timber corner
windows offer lovely views over the valley.

CAE-CRIN, Uwchmynydd, 2 m. SW. Typical hillside encroach-
ment cottage. *Croglofft* plan; byre to l. Whitewashed rubble.
Many similar cottages dot the hillside here, and further N on
Mynydd Anelog (1½ m. WNW).

CWRT, 1 m. W. Substantial Newborough estate farm, mid-C19.
Two-storey three-bay farm-house with rear wing. Rubble, now
rendered. FARM BUILDINGS to the SW, including a big
L-plan PIG RANGE: sty wing, incorporating two latrines
for the farm workers, front wing with chimney, for making
swill.

CARMEL BAPTIST CHAPEL, 1½ m. NNW. Only 18 ft
(5.5 metres) square. Early C19 chapel. Unassuming outside,
but a remarkably intact interior. Panelled box pews on three
sides, stepped on the E wall, facing the five-sided pulpit in front
of the w window. Attractive balusters around the simple
sêt-fawr. Whitewashed walls, timber rail at window-head height.
One truss, painted timber-boarded ceiling. Oil lamps, two
suspended and two on standards. Chapel house, to the same
roof-line.

CARREG, 1¾ m. NNW. Large house of two storeys, cellar and
attic, owned by the Carreg family who were first recorded in
1396. Probably two houses, joined in line but facing opposite
ways. The older SE block, perhaps later C17, with a C20
projecting gabled SW extension. The NW block probably later
C18, extended to the rear (NE) with a gabled wing which was
doubled up in the C19. Whitewashed rubble to the SW side,
rendered elsewhere. Hipped dormers. The tiny windows at the
far end of the SW front indicate closets next to the large
fireplace.

CASTELL ODO, 1½ m. NNE (SH 187 284), tops a low but
dominant hill. Two eroded ramparts enclose eight round stone

houses, as well as a post-medieval 'pillow mound' or artificial rabbit warren. Excavation in 1959 demonstrated that the outer rampart was the earlier and more complex. Initially the settlement was undefended, a group of round wooden houses of probable Late Bronze Age date, subsequently surrounded by a palisade burnt down before completion. This settlement may have been abandoned. The decayed palisade was later covered by a wide earthen bank, afterwards heightened and given a stone revetment. The inner rampart, also stone-revetted, may also have been built then. This seems to have been deliberately slighted, perhaps by Romans removing the native population from defensible positions. However, they returned later, for one stone house is built over the dismantled gateway.

ABERERCH

4037

Attractive village of stone houses on a single street, the church at the top (w) end, the BRIDGE at the bottom, *c.* 1800, its three segmental arches taking the narrow road over the Erch river. Opposite Capel Ebenezer, a short cobbled lane to the church. TŶ UCHAF on the s side, with gabled semi-dormers, probably C18. Tiny CHURCH HALL, N side, early to mid-C19, formerly the parson's gig house. On the N side of the street: SCHOOL TERRACE, mid–later C19, opposite TŶ GWYN, an C18 village farmhouse similar to Tŷ Uchaf. The steeply roofed SCHOOL, *c.* 1875, is by *Kennedy*. On the s side, BRYN AFON and MORAWEL, a distinctive C19 cottage pair with half-hipped roofs and entrances at the gable-ends. Opposite, the gateway to Capel Isaf. Further E, NEW ROW and POST OFFICE TERRACE, probably built for Broom Hall estate workers, early to mid-C19. A few surviving horizontally sliding windows, and some very long lintels.

ST CAWRDAF. In a large, partly round churchyard. Nave and chancel in one, with a shorter N aisle. Of roughly coursed bouldery stone, considerably repaired by *Kennedy* in 1850. The blocked N doorway to the nave suggests a pre-C15 date, since the pointed w doorway looks C15. This C15 church was extended E, its traceried three-light E window later moved to the N aisle. The present big Tudor-shaped E window, also restored, has five lights of typical Llŷn pattern. The N aisle, probably contemporary with this big window, was built in two halves: first the E, *c.* 1520 with the reused Perp sanctuary window mentioned above and a N doorway with four-centred head, then the w end *c.* 1530. The roofs tell the same story. Six trusses to the original nave, with arch-braced collars and cusped struts, formerly with wind-braces and a canopy over the sanctuary bay. The four later E bays are less ornate; their canopy also removed. Shallow N aisle roofs, with plain V-struts in the apex. Arcade of four four-centred hollow-chamfered arches, the piers with quirk mouldings on the diagonals. A former screen divided the N aisle, indicated by the slot in the elongated central pier. Corbels, one dated 1615, are evidence for a screen, as is the short piece of wall between the second and third aisles.

Of the elaborate late medieval FITTINGS, only the STALLS remain. Winged heads are carved on the hand-rests, water-lilies and roses on the four MISERICORDS. Desk in front with blank tracery, one finial carved with two standing figures. – FONT. Plain, octagonal, medieval. – STAINED GLASS. Chancel s, *Morris & Co.*, 1935. – MONUMENTS. A C13 slab with shield, sword and spear in relief, in the sanctuary. – William Jones †1857 and Rowland Jones †1856, both by *W. T. Hale*. Similar Grecian tablets.

EBENEZER INDEPENDENT CHAPEL, w of the church. A pair of tall round-headed windows with margin-light sashes, between a pair of round-headed doorways. Plain surrounds, with keystones and imposts. A tiny roundel above, and the date 1868 in a plaque at the top of the pebbledashed gable. To the s, CHAPEL HOUSE of 1886, its roofs steeper, and the window surrounds more ornate.

CAPEL ISAF (Calvinistic Methodist). Set back, with an attached house, w, and lower vestry extension, NE, mid-C19. A pair of entrances at the *sêt-fawr* end. Large sash windows between. Gallery on three sides, on fluted Corinthian iron columns coloured to look like marble, probably 1876 by *Richard Owens*.

YOKE HOUSE, 1 m. w. Mid-C19 house built by Griffith Jones, Pwllheli solicitor and agent of the Glynllifon estate. Three-bay garden front (SE), with a veranda on timber columns. Hoodmouldings with stiff-leaf stops. A long rear wing, NW, forms a separate unit. Service buildings, NE: two-storey STABLE and GIG HOUSE, with a gabled bellcote, CART HOUSE and PIG-SWILL HOUSE, with tall cylindrical chimney. The most remarkable, an OTTER HOUSE used in the training of otter hounds. Circular, about 6 ft (1.8 metres) in diameter, with a conical roof. The brick base contains a zinc-lined pool, a raised timber house at the centre. Iron railings surround the drum, below an upper section of latticed battens. A rarity indeed.

PLAS HENDRE, ½ m. E. Probably C17 or early C18, remodelled in the late C18 and again in the 1830s. Two storeys, attic and cellar. Roughly coursed rubble and wide eaves, the roofs projecting on brackets at the N and S gables. Three wide bays to the entrance (W) front. Twelve-pane sashes above sixteen. Plain central porch with shallow slate-slab roof. Blind windows to the r. The garden elevation (s) also three-bayed, but much tighter. Large sashes, the lower ones set within larger, semicircular-headed openings, the space between opening and window filled with slabs of slate, suggesting an arcade. Fine staircase at centre rear, a large window at the half-landing. Good panelling to the doors and window shutters, and elegant marble and slate fireplaces. Cobbled floor to the cellar, king-post trusses in the attic.

To the rear (E), L-plan OUTBUILDINGS forming a service yard. Attached to these, facing S, a parabolic CONSERVATORY, probably early C20. Further E, the two-storey STABLE. External steps to the upper level, an elliptical stone lintel in two pieces over the upper (S) doorway, perhaps from the old house. Attached PIGSTY. Single-storey COACHHOUSE of coursed rubble. N, a WALLED GARDEN with box hedges, bays and yews.

BRYN BERYL HOSPITAL, ¾ m. NNW. The main building formerly a house, Bryngoleu, by *Robert Williams*. Dated 1929. Neo-Georgian, Clough Williams-Ellis style but lacking the wit. Steep hipped roof with swept eaves. Eight-bay pebbledashed garden front (SE), pilasters framing three radial-head French doors. Another, smaller feature to the entrance side (SW), with large window above.

TAN-Y-GRAIG, Llwynhudol, ½ m. NW. In an elevated position overlooking Abererch and Cardigan Bay. L-plan, of two storeys, the NE wing half a level below, and possibly pre-dating, the mid-C19 SW one. Outbuildings to the NE, including a large converted pig barn. Remodelled and extended 2004–6 by *Dobson:Owen*, in a clean modern manner using lots of glass and chunky unpainted oak. A conservatory, with wide sliding glass doors, added to the SW wing. A slate-roofed GARDEN ROOM added, at a slight angle, to the NE wing, and continued N as a glazed link to the piggery. A successful scheme architecturally, in which the new, transparent elements are nicely contrasted with the existing stone buildings.

CLOGWYN TOWER, ¾ m. WNW. 6 ft (1.8 metres) in diameter by about 7 ft 6 in. (2.3 metres) high, rubble-built. Probably by the Jones family of Yoke House.

6673   ABERGWYNGREGYN

ST BODFAN. Rebuilt in 1878 by *Pugin, Ashlin & Pugin*, in early Dec style. A welcome break from the ubiquitous Kennedy. The *Building News* thought it one of the most perfect specimens of ecclesiastical architecture in Bangor diocese. Divided chancel and nave, a vestry and organ chamber at the SE. Slim NW tower, with embattled parapet, dragon gargoyles, slated pyramidal roof. Squared granite with yellow dressings. Red Mansfield stone columns to the arcade between chancel and vestry. – STAINED GLASS. E and W windows perhaps contemporary with the church. Two N by *Curtis, Ward & Hughes*. – MONUMENTS. From the old church. Mary Hughes †1741 and John Hughes †1752. – Lady Dorothy Bond †1738, and Sir Thomas †1734. Arms in an early Rococo cartouche. – Rev. Williams Griffith †1773, a handsome aedicule with triangular pediment in white marble. – Richard Jones †1720 and Lumley Owen †1784, horizontal white oval plaque on a shaped coloured ground. – Rev. Richard Owen †1788, and wife; upright oval in a marble frame. – John Crawley, R.N. †1815. White circular marble tablet on grey, the border bound with ribbons.

CALVINISTIC METHODIST CHAPEL. Possibly 1896, by *Richard Davies*. Snecked granite, with red sandstone window surrounds. Side windows are paired lights with ogee heads; the end window facing the street, a five-light window with ogee heads and round-headed tracery above, all below a three-centred arch. NE porch, partly open with oak framing.

Small VILLAGE, 'most pleasingly situated at the entrance into a charming romantick little Valley' (Fenton, 1810). Church and rectory are set apart to the w, Pen-y-bryn (*see* below), the old mansion, to the E. PEN-Y-MWD, a 22-ft (7-metre)-high motte between the river and the lane leading s, was perhaps built in the CII by the Earl of Chester. In the CI3 buildings adjoining it served as a *llys* of the princes of Gwynedd. In the mid CI9 the Penrhyn estate created a Picturesque village here. COTTAGES, of the 1860s and 1890s, some perhaps by *George Benmore*. Mostly in pairs with gables, overhanging verges and projecting porch roofs. All built in the local granite, the later ones with slate-hung upper storeys.

OLD RECTORY. E of the church, in a large garden. The cross-wing is of the 1630s with a cross-passage partition and heavy upper-floor beams. The rest is stuccoed Tudor for the Penrhyn estate, *c.* 1840. Cusped windows, dripmoulds, ornate circular chimneys. Fine staircase, with quatrefoil decoration to the strings, turned balusters, carved newels, and clusters of slim shafts supporting a Tudor arch above the stair foot.

PEN-Y-BRYN, ½ m. E. A puzzling site associated with the *llys* of Llywelyn the Great. A rectangular layout of enclosures to the E seems to relate to the existing house but does not suggest a medieval one, and excavation to the N proved inconclusive. From the CI6 the home of the Thomas family; the small BARN of *c.* 1700 with a queenpost roof among the enclosures to the NE may be the site of their first house and incorporate stonework from it. A small early Jacobean house replaced it. The range along the contour has mullion-and-transom windows of two and three lights, the upper two in dormer gablets. Porch placed symmetrically, its apparently *ex situ* sandstone doorway elliptical-headed and carved with classical pilasters. Attached to its E just later is a four-storey round tower with a conical roof, reached from the house by a dog-leg stair of *c.* 1700. Windows larger with each ascending floor. Viewing room at the top with three mullion-and-transom windows together.

WIG, 1½ m. w. A Penrhyn estate farmhouse, *c.* 1860, probably by *George Benmore*, possibly incorporating parts of an earlier house here. Gabled cross-wing, central porch and smaller bay with half-hipped dormer roof. Lower W wing, with dormers at eaves level. Elaborate chimneystacks. Hipped OUTBUILDINGS behind.

MADRYN FARM, I m. ENE. Built in the 1880s as a model farm for Gorddinog, the home of the Platt family (cf. Llanfairfechan). A range of farm buildings, partly surrounded by a crenellated wall. GATEWAY with Tudor archway, clock, battlemented parapet and lead cupola.

MAES-Y-GAER, ½ m. E. A substantial stone rampart encircling the summit of this prominent spur which overlooks the village. Inturned entrance at the SE corner; no identifiable house platforms inside.

HAFOD-Y-GELYN, 1¾ m. SE. (SH 676 715) A rectangular farmstead enclosure containing one very large round-house, with others outside to the N, overlain by a later long hut. On the slope above, a large oval enclosure containing two conjoined circular houses and associated with cleared and levelled fields to the N. In the corner of one field, a small rectangular house foundation, likely to be medieval. Towards the top of the ridge, several small stone cairns, including CARNEDD-Y-SAESON (SH 678 717), with concentric rings of kerbstones surrounding a burial cist from which the capstone has been dislodged. Other groups of late prehistoric round-houses, some enclosed in the surrounding fields.

FARMSTEAD (SH 668 704), close to the path near the foot of the Falls. Oval enclosure with a blocked gate, overlaid by a round hut and, probably later, by a rectangular building. Other single round-houses further down the valley witness to considerable occupation in earlier periods. On the ridge above, remains of a BRONZE AGE BURIAL CAIRN (SH 671 709), placed to command a striking view down the valley to the sea.

3228   ABERSOCH

Popular seaside VILLAGE in a sheltered cove at the mouth of the Soch river.

Y GRAIG CALVINISTIC METHODIST CHAPEL, Lôn Engan. 1904. Pedimented gable, with parapets concealing the returned hips of the roof. Venetian window below a keyed roundel. Tall round-headed margin sashes below and to the sides, all with moulded heads, keystones and pilasters. Drab cement render. The porch looks later.

INDEPENDENT CHAPEL. 1873, remodelled 1922. Gable-fronted, with quoined angles. At the centre a projecting Venetian window below a pediment, the base arching segmentally over the elongated keystone. Another pediment above the entrance porch. A pair of small-paned windows each side. Schoolroom added behind, 1906.

As at Aberdaron, the road drops down, crosses a bridge and climbs up again, twisting and turning as it goes. A MOTTE existed N of the harbour; the E and S scarps remain. The parish church is at Llangian, 1 m. W (q.v.).

The main street, STRYD-Y-HARBWR, winds gently towards the harbour but turns its back to it. STRYD PENLAN leading down to the water contains the few old buildings, single-storey fishermen's cottages, just on one side. At the main cross-roads, opposite the Independent Chapel (*see* above), the NATWEST

BANK, 1930, by *R. D. Jones*. Three white-rendered gables above
a stone base and mullion-and-transom leaded windows. Below
the chapel, PUBLIC CONVENIENCES, an imaginative building
in contemporary style partly jettied out over the harbour
like a medieval latrine. By *Dobson:Owen*, 2000. The tame
LIFEBOAT STATION, seen across the river, misses an
opportunity, but CILGERAINT, a new house on LÔN PONT
MORGAN, again by *Dobson:Owen*, 2007, is more inspiring. The
curved sedum roof is a welcome change from the ubiquitous
slate. LÔN GARMON leads NW off Lôn Pont Morgan. On the
corner, PENYGRAIG, an unremarkable white L-plan cottage
extended by *Clough Williams-Ellis* for his father, *c.* 1906.

LÔN ENGAN climbs W from the bridge. On the l.,
GLANDWR, a three-bay mid-C19 house with sash windows, still
unrendered. LÔN GWYDRYN leads back to the centre, past
Capel-y-graig (*see* above), r., and the crazy-paving-rubble
VILLAGE HALL of 1914, l. Between them, l., tiny wooden
SCHOOL built *c.* 1924 by Frank Minoprio of Haulfryn, who
thought Abersoch deserved better than the corrugated-sheet
building proposed. Might the architect have been his son
(*see* Haulfryn, below)?

PENBENAR, the promontory E of the main street, is the most
rewarding area for quality houses. Off Lôn Traeth,
BENARFRYN, a large gabled house with an octagonal stair-
tower at the rear and modern glazed balcony extensions at
each end. Mildly Tudor detailing, late C19 or early C20.
Immaculately white, like an iced cake. To the N, small and
symmetrical, PEN-Y-BENAR, *c.* 1913, by *R. T. Beckett* of
Chester. Parallel to Lôn Traeth, a drive leads to two houses
which seem to encapsulate the cosmopolitan (and un-Welsh)
character of this holiday village. On the r., GARTH, built *c.* 1913
for the village doctor, Dr O. J. Evans, by *William Wands*, a pupil
of Lutyens. House and surgery combined, Neo-Georgian with
a hint of France. Two storeys, looking like one, with the upper
floor in a mansard of strident red tile, with steep hipped
dormers all round. Tall sash windows, with red brick rustication continuing up to blind panels. Broken pediment over the
front door, and blank pebbledash panels each side. On the
garden side, a recessed three-bay loggia, now glazed in.

Further W, HAULFRYN. Built 1911 as a holiday home for
Frank Charles Minoprio. Enlarged *c.* 1920 and later, the post-
1922 work by his son *Anthony Minoprio*, pupil of Sir Charles
Reilly at the Liverpool School of Architecture. Stylistically
another English import, in a relaxed Arts and Crafts manner.
Yellow and grey stone, green slate roof. Small-pane casement
windows, shouldered and coped gables. The real joy is the
GARDEN. From a far corner of the front (E) garden, steps lead
N, doubling back to a paved and planted TERRACE surrounded
by a pergola, extending the full frontage of the house. Up a
few steps to a second terrace at house level, with a stone
GAZEBO at one end. In the more formal W garden, a hexagonal
PIGEON TOWER. Red brick, leaded roof. Next to it, the tennis

court with two wooden PAVILIONS. Near the Baillie-Scott-ish LODGE (*c.* 1911), the eccentric SQUASH COURT, its hard cubic form disguised by a rustic viewing gallery built of waney-edge boarding and a felt roof.

In Lôn Sarn Bach, opposite the Fire Station, MADRYN, 1936, by *F. E. Bromilow* of Birmingham. A white-rendered holiday bungalow with a sensible if quirky plan: main house facing the garden, a curvy tail (containing the kitchen) attached to the garage (now a bedroom).

CASTELLMARCH, 1 m. N. Gentry house, built 1625–9 for Sir William Jones, Chief Justice of Ireland. Tall, two storeys and attic, raised above a cellar. Main E-facing wing and S cross-wing, forming an L-plan. Pedimented porch on Doric columns, approached up a stately flight of steps. In the pediment, a shield with the date 1628. The off-centre location of the entrance suggests a matching N cross-wing was planned, but apart from the absence of a plinth along the N wall, there is no further evidence for a larger house. Mullion-and-transom windows, ovolo-moulded and with plain hoods. Interior much altered, but with a fine staircase in the S wing, with tall moulded newels and carved balusters. Plaster overmantel relief, dated 1629, also in the S wing; another dated 1628.

RHANDIR, 1 m. NNW. In the farmyard, an unusual C19 animal building, part of the Vaynol estate. Small, with two rooms for pigs and poultry, the latter with slate nesting boxes. On the roof, a tall brick stack, set diagonally and perforated with dove holes, each with a tiny slate balcony. In the yard to the S, a row of brick-arched geese enclosures.

BANGOR

INTRODUCTION

Unlike the other Gwynedd coastal towns, Bangor stands not directly on the sea but in a hollow parallel to the Menai Strait, a cathedral site analogous to that chosen by St David in SW Wales. The view that best displays this small cathedral and university city is from the terrace of the Edwardian university buildings; from there, the way the buildings of these two leading institutions dominate the narrow valley of the Adda is most apparent. Bangor became the ecclesiastical centre when St Deiniol became bishop of Gwynedd *c.* 546, presumably protected by Maelgwn the ruler (which may make this the oldest episcopate in Wales or England). The Celtic Christian complex lay along the banks of the stream; its elliptical plan can be traced in the curving frontage of the shops on the N of the High Street at its W end. Of the Dominican Friary founded in 1251 further down the valley there is no trace, and little of the C13 earthwork castle high on the ridge above it, or of post-conquest fortifications.

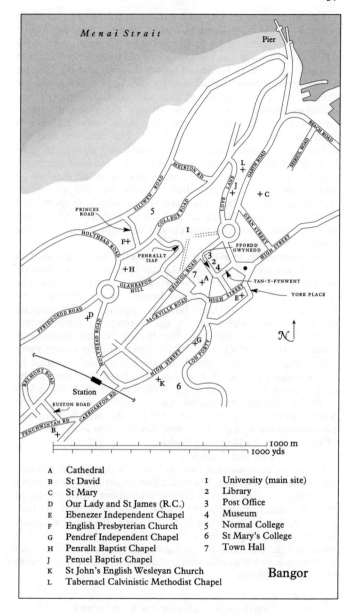

A   Cathedral
B   St David
C   St Mary
D   Our Lady and St James (R.C.)
E   Ebenezer Independent Chapel
F   English Presbyterian Church
G   Pendref Independent Chapel
H   Penrallt Baptist Chapel
J   Penuel Baptist Chapel
K   St John's English Wesleyan Church
L   Tabernacl Calvinistic Methodist Chapel

1   University (main site)
2   Library
3   Post Office
4   Museum
5   Normal College
6   St Mary's College
7   Town Hall

Bangor

The town came into its own late, by accident of its strategic position on the C19 London–Dublin route across the Menai Strait to Holyhead, close to the Snowdonian slate quarries for which Port Penrhyn was built NE of the old town centre. Thomas Telford's A5 road to Holyhead passes through and the Chester to Holyhead Railway (which crosses the Adda valley at the SW somewhat surreally, vanishing into tunnels either side). These transport links eventually made Bangor the regional capital, rather than Caernarfon or Conwy. It was the patriotic choice in 1884 for a university for North Wales. The cathedral and the university (a non-denominational foundation) now seem symbolic of NW Wales, institutional rivalries reflected in architectural paradox. For it is Hare's university tower on its hill that can be seen from afar; the cathedral's towers are disappointingly unemphatic. Its setting is encroached by commercial sprawl and on the N by Deiniol Road, cut through the bishop's park in 1905 as part of the university project, and undoubtedly more to the latter's advantage.

The limitations to Bangor's opportunities were embodied in the narrow streets of inadequate houses in the valley, significantly smaller than those in the more prosperous quarry villages. The cramped core contrasts with the breadth of the Victorian and Edwardian suburbs of Upper Bangor, especially in the university district. A move was made by the Borough to replace them between the wars, starting with *Herbert North*'s picturesque p. 83 cottage terraces of 1927 in Seiriol Road, and spreading more widely with the larger, brick-built 'Bangor houses' designed by the Borough Engineer *B. Price Davies*, erected after 1929 in the centre, around Friddoedd Road to the NW and at Maesgeirchen to the SE. C20 housing extends SW to Penrhosgarnedd, and the town continues to grow in linear fashion. An extra-urban shopping area to the W, and commercial development in the parkland of Vaynol, S of the Britannia Bridge, are on a scale to serve both Caernarvonshire and Anglesey.

Cathedral and university apart, Bangor's most striking buildings lie outside the town. Just to the E on its parkland promontory is Penrhyn Castle (p. 398) a fantasy monument on an important medieval site. Jutting into the Menai Strait to the N is the Late Victorian Garth Pier; while Telford's Menai Bridge to Anglesey is 2 m. W and Stephenson's Britannia Bridge for the railway is another 2 m. W. These frame the beautiful shores of the Strait with their wooded knolls, which Bangor has wisely not tried to turn into a seafront.

CATHEDRAL CHURCH OF ST DEINIOL

The oval fenced enclosure of the mid-C6 Bangor Fawr yn Arfon (Great Bangor in Arfon) is still represented by the largely open space in the valley bottom. By the C12 the site of the cathedral church had moved up the S slope. Its lack of height may result partly from unstable ground, partly from repeated sackings (twice in the C7, in 1073, in a raid by King John's men in 1211,

and in the Glyndŵr troubles in 1402). Its present form is
determined by the cruciform church begun *c*. 1120 by Bishop
David, under the princely patronage of Gruffudd ap Cynan †1137
and his son Owain Gwynedd †1170, both of whom were buried
near the High Altar. Some 130 ft (40 metres) long, its nave was
aisleless and two bays shorter than now, the transepts were
shorter, and the chancel was apsed.

A Gothic reconstruction began *c*. 1220, at the E as usual, with
the replacement of the apse with a longer choir, probably under
the patronage of Llywelyn the Great. Work continued W under
Bishop Anian I (celebrated for his Pontifical, now in the
University Library) between 1267 and 1307, and Bishop Anian
II between 1307 and 1328. First came the S transept, then, after
the Edwardian conquest, the N transept, both with E chapels; and
the E end of the nave, together with a belfry or crossing tower,
which was damaged by fire in 1309 and never rebuilt. These
works were lost to history by subsequent alterations, until
G. G. Scott's re-creation of them following his report of 1866.
The crossing tower reached its present modest height only in
1966. The aisle windows seem to date the outer walls to the early
C14, but these could have been reused in widening an aisleless
nave. Campaigns of *c*. 1480–1500 brought the fine E window, roof
and E end battlements. Less refined Tudor work in the 1520s–30s
left the nave with its present arcade and clerestory apart from its
battlements. The strangely abbreviated W tower was added in
1532, and maybe the big chancel S window.

Scott removed all traces of post-Reformation and C18 work.
The extent of this transformation can be seen from prints of the
late C18. Low Gothick E ranges, whether library or chapter house
or the crenellations dressing up the whole E end, had evolved in
a fashionable variation on medieval church design. The library of
the 1720s was rebuilt by *James Wyatt* in 1778 with the addition
of a chapter house. *John Cooper*'s works of the 1780s included an
organ screen. At this period the medieval stained glass perished.
John Hall's battlements of 1824 and *John Foster*'s contemporary
(and lowly) replacement of the crossing arches in 1824–8 and
even *Kennedy*'s choir roof of 1857 all no longer exist.

EXTERIOR. Of the mid-C12 church with its three apses, only the
double pilaster and a blocked window on the outside of its
main apse are visible, embedded in the S presbytery wall. The
C13 rebuilding of the entire E end with a long, rectangular presbytery and longer transepts has had such thoroughgoing (if
faithful) Victorian restoration that almost the only untouched
parts, inside or out, are the E angle buttresses. Bangor is *George
Gilbert Scott*'s cathedral E of the nave, begun in 1868 and completed in 1884 under *John Oldrid Scott*; that it now has a cathedral scale at all is due to him. Excavation told him the C13 plan
and the sections of its piers and so of its arches. His reconstruction was scrupulously confined to what was missing structurally; so he reused later features like the E window of *c*. 1500
with five cusped lights divided by a transom, and the early C16

Bangor Cathedral.
Engraving by S and N. Buck, 1742

s window, elliptical, uncusped and with no transom. Scott's work can be described as in the latest phase of E.E. before the Decorated. Apart from the elimination of Georgian Gothick, the other chief aim was to stabilize the medieval structure, with a view to erecting a tall crossing tower and spire. However the foundations have never allowed that, so the church lies low to this day. Scott's work stopped just above roof level, and it was only in the 1966–71 restoration that *Alban Caröe* added the deep parapet with its massive merlons, behind which rises a low pyramidal slated roof.

Scott reused much stonework in re-creating the TRANSEPTS. He restored the offsets at the base of the walls, the angle buttresses with their angle shafts and rings (and some foliate capitals, maybe recarved). The corbel tables and battlements are new, in Anglesey limestone. A C15 stair-turret remains in the NE angle. Fine plate tracery: in the S transept, big paired lancets and a cusped circle; in the N transept four lights framed by shafts and dogtooth; as high a standard of Gothic design as anywhere in Gwynedd. The large storeyed vestry N of the presbytery was added in the old position, with plate traceries and buttresses.

The W PARTS were rebuilt using local sandstone and quartz conglomerate in the early and mid C14, on a larger plan of seven external bays – but less ambitiously than the E parts, in fact more in the character of a market town church. Extensive work was required in the C15 and C16 to make good damage in the Glyndŵr uprising in 1402. The N aisle is an interesting project in Decorated design: three-light windows with cusped circles as tracery and a doorway having multiple roll mouldings, between buttresses without offsets capped with small niches, closed with cusped and crocketed ogee heads. The doorway is plain with many continuous mouldings. The S aisle is similar, but its windows have three quatrefoils as tracery. Its doorway has an ornate crocketed and finialled niche above, and the buttresses have offsets and no niches. The aisles have plain parapets, the later clerestory has battlements.

The repairs begun by Bishop Deane (1496–1500) were

mostly internal. The arms of Bishop Skevington (1509–33) appear on the W TOWER added in 1532 as if to a parish church; appropriately since the nave served the Welsh congregation. This is a curious design, rising to much less than the height suggested by the scale and breadth of its base, and seeming to suffer from the elision of at least two intermediate stages; was it again unstable soil or little money that led to its hugging the ground, or was its construction disrupted by the Reformation? Perp, with diagonal buttresses, and of ashlar, red sandstone from Cheshire mixed with buff from Flintshire. w window with uncusped flowing tracery. It is worth noting how the buttresses step abruptly back at the bell-stage, placed without intervening rises over the w window. It contains a re-set late C13 three-light window with typical local details.

INTERIOR. No features of the Romanesque church are visible, but the C13 crossing piers were found in the Victorian excavation to encase the C12 ones, so the spans of the four arms of the C13 church are almost those of the C12. Almost all the E parts visible date from the *Scott* restoration. They are in a pinkish brown stone. The chancel E and S windows have original Perp traceries. The chancel has a fine stellar lierne vault by *Scott* in painted wood on stone trefoiled wall-shafts. The medieval roof survives above. The decorative painting of the roof, by *Clayton & Bell*, 1873, was extended to the presbytery walls c. 1880, since removed. The piers of three crossing arches have multiple shafts and mouldings typical of the early C14, the w piers have big half-columns. The first stage of the tower has a (surely conjectural?) blank triforium with two pairs of openings on each side, then a flat roof. The transepts have hammerbeam roofs. In the S transept *Scott* restored the large E arch, formerly to the Lady Chapel, destroyed in 1402.

The architecture of the NAVE reflects the vicissitudes of its history; it lacked a paved floor and was little used or maintained till the late C18. The arcades inserted by Skevington in 1527 corrected the misalignment of the C14 nave in relation to the aisle walls, but the new six-bay division (presumably for stylistic reasons) created a discrepancy with the seven-bay aisle walls, and the new alignment made the w end of the nave off-centre to the W tower arch. While the aisle walls are of moderate height, courage failed with the insertion of the arcade and clerestory, which simply look too low. The Tudor four-centred arches emphasize this lowness, as does the shortness of the clerestory and the shallow pitch of the roof. Appropriate scale only returns with the full-height W arch with its continuous mouldings, which relates anomalously to the nave and the tower as built.

FURNISHINGS. Oak REREDOS with many carved figures and angel finials, 1881, by *J. O. Scott*, gilded 1984. – BISHOP'S THRONE, CHOIR STALLS and CLERGY STALLS, by *J. O. Scott*, to his father's designs, 1879–80. The stalls with elaborate canopies. – C15 MISERICORD. One survives (exhibited at the w). – Delicate oak SCREEN by *J. O. Scott*, 1908. –

35

SCREENS in crossing and S transept. – REREDOS, 1950, by *Alban Caröe*. – HANGING ROOD, 1950, by *Caröe*, carved by *Harold Youngman*. – Carved PULPIT of Caen stone, after Italian prototypes, designed by *G. G. Scott*. – FONT, early C15, octagonal, and thickly carved. Moulded base; stem with heraldic shields in cusped panels on each face, the bowl with a crude frieze of circled quatrefoils. – BOUND ROOD (The Mostyn Christ). A wooden late C15 sculpture of rare iconography, removed from Llanrwst church to Gloddaeth, but possibly the figure described in a poem of 1518 as at the Dominican Friary at Rhuddlan. Near life-size wooden figure (missing the arms) of Christ, seated and bound, in the last moments before and with the emblems of his Crucifixion. Carvings of this devotional kind are now so rare in Britain that stylistic comparisons for the Northern realism of the exhausted face and torso are not easily made. – FIGURES. Five woodcarvings of saints, perhaps Flemish, early C16. Another two, mid-C17 or later, Madonna and Child, and Christ the King holding an orb. – TRIPTYCH. Flemish, early C16, from Penmachno church. – PAINTINGS by *Brian Thomas*, Dean of Bangor 1903–34. S transept lunette, 1953, Invitation to the Supper at Emmaus, set in Wales. W end of nave, two 'lectures in paint' on the life and history of the Welsh church, installed at St Mary's College in 1955, moved to the cathedral in 1976. In the S aisle, 'Why?', 2000, by *J. G. Gregory*, after Caravaggio. – Re-set in the floor in the SW angle, the remaining C14 FLOOR TILES from presbytery and choir. Of a type known to have been made in Cheshire, with finely drawn designs impressed into the clay and tinted black. The subjects include heraldic and symbolic birds, animals from a bestiary, and vine and fleur-de-lys patterns. C19 copies are in the presbytery floor.

STAINED GLASS. E, 1873, by *Clayton & Bell*, in the original Perp tracery. Ten scenes from the Life and Passion of Christ. Two rows of saints above. – Presbytery S, also *Clayton & Bell*. Scenes from the Acts of the Apostles. – N transept N, by *Burlison & Grylls*. – S transept E, *Mayer*, 1885. – Three S aisle windows of North Wales saints, by *Burlison & Grylls*, 1905–29. – Five N aisle windows by *Powells*, 1911. – The W and two adjoining aisle windows have early revived glass, 1838, by *David Evans* of Shrewsbury, originally in the E window. Nine painterly figures of prophets, Evangelists and saints.

MONUMENTS. S transept. A segmental-pointed tomb-recess, late C13, lacking an effigy; thought to have been made for Ednyfed Fychan †1246. C20 memorial to the Rev. Edmund Prys †1623, author of the much-reprinted *Salmau Cân*, metrical psalms.* – Nave S. Double Baroque memorial to the families of Bishop Morgan †1673 and Bishop Humphrey †1701. Three Ionic columns placed incorrectly under a segmental pediment, the inscribed tablets transposed when it was moved. – N aisle E. Two *ex situ* half-length figures of

*The Vaynol family vaults are to the E, the Penrhyn family vaults to the W of the W crossing piers.

divines, lacking the heads: to Bishop Vaughan, 1607, and to Bishop Rowland, 1616. – Doric aedicule in grey marble to Charles Allanson †1729, of Renaissance serenity. – N aisle sw (but found in the N transept). Beautifully carved low-relief TOMB-SLAB of a lady identified as Eva, one of three such C14 effigies probably by the same hand, the other two to local saints in Anglesey at Llanbabo and Llaniestyn (*see* p. 140). Dressed in a simple folded robe, with the head-cloth closely framing the face and a rectangular wimple, she holds a rosary and raises both hands, palms outwards. Elegant cinquefoiled canopy and the surfaces enriched with leaves and flowers. Several small fragments of (?) grave stones/architectural elements with C10–C11 decoration.

CATHEDRAL PRECINCT

The PRECINCT is the visible remnant of the c6 'Bangor Fawr', which continued as the garden and park of the Bishop's Palace. It deserves a master plan for long-term re-evocation, because the scatter of diocesan and secular structures since the Bishop's Palace was given up in 1899 has made it hard to read. Excavations have disclosed buildings on the N slope typical of early monasteries which remained in use at least till the late C13, when the *clas* was transformed into a secular chapter of canons serving the cathedral. In the enclosure were at least one small Celtic church (Llanfair Garth Brenan), buildings for the three ancient Archdeaconries of Bangor, Anglesey and Merioneth, and a little palace for the bishop (does the *ex situ* embattled chimney of *c.* 1400 (?) on the corner of Lôn Pobty come from one of these?). The parish church of Llanfair Erw Nant, demolished 1539, stood at the foot of the N slope opposite the cathedral.

DEANERY, by the w tower. 1863, by *George Benmore*. Stucco with a helm-like half-hip squeezed between outer gables. It may incorporate some of the original deanery of *c.* 1685.

TOWN HALL (formerly BISHOP'S PALACE), N of the cathedral. Low U-plan rendered ranges making little impression, but structurally a timber house of *c.* 1500 for Bishop Deane, doubled in size before 1533 for Bishop Skevington. If the hall, measuring 22 by 33 ft (7 by 10 metres), is Deane's and was built as a lower and an upper hall, it may be the first of the type in Gwynedd. Added on the N for Bishop Pearce is a modestly grand mid-Georgian stair hall, floored in square flagstones with diagonal black marble inserts and under an elliptical shallow dome, dated 1753. The wooden stairs have carved step-ends and column balusters. Bishop Majendie added the NW wing of 1810 with Gothick glazing, containing a drawing room with a coved and enriched plaster ceiling. He put the segmental plaster vault in the former upper hall (the present Council Chamber) with fields edged with husk garland. The building was remodelled in 1962, and the curved end of the l. wing rebuilt flat.

Majendie also built the Tudor-style red sandstone GATEWAY, 1812, below the cathedral E end, at the former entrance to his garden. Iron gates from the *Mersey Foundry*, Liverpool.

Inappropriately sited beside the palace, the new POLICE STATION, 2005, by *Ainsley Gommon Architects*, replacing a building by *John Thomas*, 1882.

GWYNEDD MUSEUM AND ART GALLERY, the former CANONRY, N of the chancel. An attractively asymmetrical High Victorian villa of 1862 in snecked stone with a variety of Gothic windows. Was *Kennedy* the architect? The Museum has some late C13 slabs from the Dominican Friary.

DIOCESAN CENTRE, E of the cathedral. Two-storey pebbledashed vicarage of 1815, extended N with an Arts and Crafts hall reticently detailed with stepped lancets in a recessed arch, by *Harold Hughes*, 1911.

BISHOP ROWLANDS' ALMSHOUSES, on the SE edge of the graveyard. 1805. Originally Bangor Hospital, eight almshouses, now four. Two-storeyed, with a pair of advanced gabled entrance bays. Pointed doorways with ogee lights.

CHURCHES AND CHAPELS

ST DAVID, Caernarfon Road. 1888, by *A. W. Blomfield*. Commissioned by a wealthy resident for the expanding town. A major town church, expensively built in unlovable dark rubble with red sandstone dressings, E.E. style. Tall SW porch-tower, nearly detached and baldly finished with battlements, but originally with a pyramid roof. Nave, transepts and chancel raised high on a basement, impressively tall on the N, where a NE vestry runs parallel. Tall E lancets with blind lancets between, all with ringed shafts, and carved gable panels. The interior is one of the best of its era in North Wales, lined in red brick, powerful and controlled. Sturdy and unusual nave roof, with braces off the purlins to cusps on the heavy trusses. Ashlar crossing arches, taller for the chancel with a low screen wall. Iron RAILS of 1936. The chancel is appropriately richer, under a boarded panelled roof, with marble-shafted triple lancets over a carved stone REREDOS, the Last Supper, in Gothic arcading. A good oak columned screen with shield cresting, *c.* 1923, S, to the Lady Chapel. – FONT. Round, on marble columns, *c.* 1889. – PULPIT. 1889. Gothic, with intricate scenes in relief panels, constructed, steps included, in terracotta. – ORGAN. 1906 by *William Hill*. – STAINED GLASS. A complete set by *Mayer*, *c.* 1890, giving the opportunity to judge the strengths and weaknesses of the firm. Rich colours, boldly used, the drawing style not medieval and very detailed. The floral W window, if theirs, is very good. In the Lady Chapel, E, two saints in opaque Arts and Crafts glass, 1923, by *N. D. Spooner*; two S lancets, 1922, by *Powells*, flanking a Christ figure by *Mayer*. Chancel N, 1923, and S, 1925, both by *Powells*.

ST MARY, Garth Road. Set back down an overgrown yew drive.

1864, by *H. P. Horner* of Liverpool, in that spiky Gothic associated with the low or Evangelical wing of the Church. Rubble
with grey limestone. Nave with low clerestory lit by trefoil
windows, spreading aisles, and an octagonal SE pencil spire.
Broad interior with skeletal nave roof on long wall-posts; Bath
stone arcades without capitals, but tiny foliage let into the pier-
heads. The chancel ceiling is unorthodoxly pierced to borrow
light. W end enclosed, 1997, by *Graham Holland*. – PULPIT.
Very solid, painted stone with blind tracery. – RAILS. Brass
with passion-flowers. – STAINED GLASS. E window, 1894,
Nativity. S aisle, Resurrection, *c.* 1920, by *Shrigley & Hunt*,
deep greens; and St John the Baptist, 1864. N aisle, Virgin and
Child, 1981, *Celtic Studios*.

EGLWYS-Y-GROES, Maesgeirchen. 1958, by *S. Colwyn Foulkes*.
T-plan, with hall etc. for the large housing estate of Maesgeirchen, built in the 1930s by the City Council under *B. Price
Davies*. Drab pebbledash. Understated, but a big cross inset in
the E gable and an eyebrow of slating over the entrance.

OUR LADY AND ST JAMES (R.C.), Holyhead Road. Originally
Anglican, St James's, by *Kennedy & Rogers*, 1864–6, with S
chapel of 1884 by *Kennedy*, and vestry, 1894, by *Harold Hughes*.
Brown rubble with grey limestone, in Kennedy's spiky light-
weight manner, with much flowing tracery. SW tower with a
limestone spire, detached from the aisle. Six-bay nave with
arcades of round columns with elaborate capitals. – STAINED
GLASS. E and W windows by *Pilkington*, 1864. Lady Chapel,
Crucifixion, by *Alexander Gibbs*, *c.* 1875.

EBENEZER INDEPENDENT CHAPEL, York Place. Disused. 1858,
by the *Rev. Thomas Thomas*, 1858. Italianate, in stucco with
Ionic pilasters and pediment.

ENGLISH PRESBYTERIAN CHURCH, Princes Road. 1882, by
Richard Davies. Churchy Gothic. Nave, transepts and chancel.
Plate tracery.

PENDREF INDEPENDENT CHAPEL, High Street. 1881–2, by
Owen Williams of Bangor. An assured façade in dark Penmaenmawr granite with careful detail in grey limestone. Pedimented centre and hipped wings, pedimented outer windows
and doors. Italianate, but the central feature marries an arched
triplet and a quatrefoil roundel. Intense short interior, with
panelled galleries, curved pulpit of almost Austrian profusion
with biblical carvings and sweeping stairs, set against a domed
apse that accommodates the choir.

PENRALLT BAPTIST CHAPEL, Holyhead Road. Built as
Twrgwyn Calvinistic Methodist Chapel in 1854, but the handsome Italian two-storey façade is of 1865 by *Kennedy & Rogers*,
in strong contrast with their St James's church nearby. Pedimented centre and balustraded wings, the detail unusually
good. Rich interior of 1865 with panelled gallery and ribbed
ceiling. Later arched organ recess.

PENUEL BAPTIST CHAPEL, Garth Road. 1950, by *B. Price
Davies*, designer of the 'Bangor houses' (*see* p. 238). A
large chapel in the streamlined-traditional of the 1930s.

Thin-coursed rock-faced yellow sandstone, on a grey stone plinth. The long front has arched upper windows each side of a broad canted-sided tower with tapered parapet, the narrow arched stair light with Art Deco glazing.

ST JOHN'S ENGLISH WESLEYAN CHURCH, High Street. 1875, by *Richard Davies*. Gothic, nave and chancel. Churchy SCHOOLROOM, r., with a canted apse. 1908, by *W. G. Williams*.

TABERNACL CALVINISTIC METHODIST CHAPEL, Garth Road. Now flats. 1902–5, by *James Cubitt*, but totally different to his massive Union Chapel, Islington, of 1876. Soft Arts and Crafts Gothic, in grey rubble, with mottled pink sandstone dressings. Church-like aisled nave, with transept and chancel, the detail Late Gothic. At the apparent crossing a saddleback tower, with a witches-hat stair-turret; but the chancel is actually the hall, aisled with a timber clerestory. At the back, hipped house with chamfered corners. The interior was of red brick with round-arched arcade.

PUBLIC BUILDINGS

TOWN HALL. *See* Cathedral Precinct.

GWYNEDD MUSEUM. *See* Cathedral Precinct.

PUBLIC LIBRARY, Ffordd Gwynedd. 1907, by *Albert E. Dixon* of *Dixon & Potter* of Manchester. Small-scale but colourful and busy Baroque exterior of red Ruabon brick with sandstone dressings, blue slate roofs and a lead dome. Gabled wings with Venetian windows. Recessed entry to the domed entrance hall. Surprisingly large reading room with segmental vaults.

POST OFFICE, Deiniol Road. 1909, by *W. Pott*, architect to the P.O. Northern Division. Bright red Ruabon brick on a Portland stone base. It accommodated the Inland Revenue and the County Court offices also, establishing Deiniol Road as a second pole in the emerging civic centre of Bangor, and setting a scale later taken up by university buildings.

RAILWAY STATION. The Chester to Holyhead line reaches Bangor from both sides through tunnels; Neo-Egyptian PORTAL, E, 1847; W, plain, 1881. The long thin original station, p. 74 1848, by *Francis Thompson*, of red brick above stone, with quoins and Grecian windows, is engulfed in additions. An intelligent Early Modern station was added to the E for the new LMSR in 1924. Canopy over the pavement to stairs between the offices, up through an arch to the platform bridge, on narrow brick towers (cf. Llandudno Junction).

YSBYTY GWYNEDD HOSPITAL. *See* p. 257.

98 GARTH PIER, at the end of Garth Road. 1896, by *J. J. Webster*, engineer. Surely Wales's least-known pier and at 1,550 ft (477 metres) its longest. Built for landing from pleasure steamers, it had no amusement buildings. Closed 1971, rescued with public money 1987. Entrance ironwork profuse, with barley-sugar twists between Hindu kiosks. The deck widens four times for octagonal kiosks with tent and onion-dome roofs before an

ampler widening and an ornate pavilion once serving the
landing stage.

EDUCATIONAL BUILDINGS

UNIVERSITY OF WALES, BANGOR. The University Colleges of [108]
North and South Wales, at Bangor and Cardiff, followed the
University College of Wales, opened at Aberystwyth in 1872.
Bangor was founded in 1884. Temporarily housed in the
Penrhyn Arms Hotel (*see* p. 254) and with about 150 students,
the university started building in Upper Bangor: chemistry and
physics laboratories, a lecture hall, a gymnasium, etc., 1885–95,
by *Richard Davies*. When the skyline site was donated in 1903,
the university commission determined on an ideal three-
courtyard plan. A limited competition held in 1905, between
J. Francis Doyle, *A. Marshall Mackenzie*, *Arnold Mitchell* and
H. T. Hare, was assessed by Aston Webb.

The winning design of 1906 by *Henry T. Hare* drew on his
Beaux-Arts experience as a student in Paris. It proposed a very
large quadrangle with big pavilions in the centre of each side:
arts and administration on the long side overlooking the valley,
two sciences opposite, and a library and museum on the short
side with a day training department opposite. Hare completely
revised the plan in 1907 in part because the original budget of
£250,000 was halved. In the new project the library and
museum, 130 ft (40 metres) long, were to be placed overlooking the cathedral at the s side of a great quadrangle of buildings for chemistry and physics, with hemicyclical lecture
theatres, and a N gateway range onto College Road.
At its E the library was to abut a massive TOWER, giving
the city the landmark that its cathedral could not provide.

Bangor, University of Wales.
Lithograph by Raffles Davison, 1907

Standing forward from the lip of the scarp, there was to be a long arts and administration range at the lower side of a small quadrangle rising up the slope, closed at the upper end by a great hall 149 ft (46 metres) long having its main entrance at its end in the first court. N of the hall, space was left for a small irregular quadrangle, which has, however, remained open to College Road.

This second design was marked by substantial advances. Hare was familiar with the variety of Oxford's stone quadrangles and as a North of England man he brought a feeling for heroic effects in masonry. Possibly this led him to scale up the college for landscape reasons a little too much, spurred on by innovations in very wide steel spans. The outcome is nonetheless a triumph of Picturesque planning and of the Northern Renaissance style – historicism which Hare treated with a free Arts and Crafts approach. The whole complex was erected in only four years. In view of the quality achieved in the sandstone facing, the pale Preseli slates and the floors and stairs of Hopton Wood stone, that was a feat worthy of the donations from all over North Wales. The Drapers' Company sponsored the library and museum range (as at Cardiff), and the great hall was named after its donor John Prichard Jones. The stone carving, of exceptional quality was by *Lawrence Turner*; the fittings, all designed by *Hare*, were made by *Elliots* or *Bartholomew & Fletcher*. To assert that Bangor has the finest university buildings in Wales reflects not only their siting, inspired by prototypes like the medieval grouping at Durham, but also their character as a citadel of learning, serious and cheering at the same time.

The TOWER is the fulcrum, encouraged to soar by the batter which gives elegance to this formidably monumental feature. Its style is more that of abbey than castle, having a bell-stage with on each face two tall traceried windows with a statue in a niche between: St David, Owain Gwynedd, Llywelyn ap Gruffudd and Owain Glyndŵr. Simplified forms, especially the parapet with scarcely divided merlons. Around its base, on all sides press the collegiate buildings, their detail overlapping between medieval and Renaissance.

The LIBRARY range suggests a long gallery above a cloister, the central doorway evoking the confused C17 classical architecture of Oxford and Cambridge. Ultimately the effect is more Bess of Hardwick, with deep first-floor oriels and W stair-tower with projecting buttressed gables with two more statues, Bishop William Morgan and Goronwy Owen. Royal arms over the doorways, handsomely carved directly on the ashlar. The Museum at ground level became a library in 1921; low shallow elliptical vault. The main SHANKLAND LIBRARY above has bare stone walls and a shallow timber barrel vault with plaster panels. High and deep bookcases project inwards between the windows, linked across the aisle by archways in carved wood under luxurious scrolled pediments. Later C20 bust of John Morris-Owen by *R. L. Gapper*.

III

The E side of the GREAT QUADRANGLE, two storeys, with mullion-and-transom windows, the lower with eyebrow pediments, the upper with flat ones. On the upper floor, the Principal's rooms, evoking panelled Jacobean parlours. At the end of the corridor the COUNCIL CHAMBER, 50 ft (15 metres) long, with oak panelling and furniture and a stately limestone end chimneypiece with the arms of the North Wales counties. Segmental plaster barrel ceiling set with painted heraldry of the princes. – Busts of William Cadwaladr Davies and Sir Isambard Owen, key figures respectively in the 1884 establishment, and the 1906–11 building programme, by *W. Goscombe John*.

The centrepiece is the gable-end of the PRICHARD JONES HALL. Its slightly recessed façade is more markedly Arts and Crafts. A transverse antechamber and a Crush Hall of three bays with a groined vault before the hall, which has a fully semicircular plaster barrel vault springing from below the window heads, its span the most spectacular outcome of Hare's use of new techniques and materials. Roof trusses stamped Glengarnock, Ayrshire.

The great hall also forms the N side of the INNER QUADRANGLE, an enclosure of considerable architectural inventiveness. On a S gable, a niche with the figure of Lewis Morris. The hall's Free Tudor windows fill the entire side. A central timber flèche picks up the axis of steps rising by three grass terraces from the taller lower range, a surprising landscape design by *Hare*. The model for the other façades is that of Cotswold manor houses as interpreted by Arts and Crafts architects, with oriels, arches and gables in a near-symmetrical jumble, a deliberate contrast with the external S front to the town. Superimposed corridors lined with stone, paved with green and white marble, and with groin-vaulted ceilings. They were healthily open to the air, but were glazed later. The principal corridors running N and S are the main survivors of the 1906 plan, their grand classical design linking either end to stone staircases. In the upper lobby opposite the library, STAINED GLASS by *J. Dudley Forsyth*, of Painting, Humanity, Music, Science, and in the lobby below, Architecture (with a Greek temple) given by Hare. On the E side of the court, the POWIS HALL, with wainscot panels and a ribbed barrel-vault ceiling. Big mural, The Hall of Illusions, 1992–3, by *Edward Povey*.

The S FRONT has most prominence from the town since it is placed in front of the tower. Ten bays, between gabled wings, an attic behind a parapet, and chimneys every two bays. Elliptical arches below with buttresses between, of which the middle four are open; first-floor mullion-and-transom windows with broken pediments too small for them, then plain ones above. It gives onto the grandest terrace in Gwynedd: very broad, the retaining walls over-sturdy for their job, and entered from the S by noble Baroque-style wrought-iron gates made by *William Bainbridge Reynolds*.

Hare's uncompleted outer quadrangle received the missing W and N sides in the Robbins expansion of 1966, but they scarcely do it justice. Additional LIBRARIES of little note on the W, and the ARTS BUILDING completed in 1974 on the N, both by the *Percy Thomas Partnership*. The latter seems to stand the test of time better than the former: raised on pilotis to allow free access to the quadrangle, its tall undulating façades of bush-hammered concrete are handled as a single storey of very tall and narrow windows.

For later university buildings *see* Perambulations.

YR HEN GOLEG, Siliwen Road. Originally the Normal College, for training schoolteachers. 1858–62, by *J. Barnett* of London. Grandly collegiate E-plan façade, in grey limestone with Jacobean shaped gables. Oddly gawky proportions. Entrance bay with an oriel backed against a high square tower over the stair hall.

COLEG MENAI. Two sites on Friddoedd Road. The first was built as the Friars School, 1899–1901, to an 1888 design by *Douglas & Fordham*. Low and carefully irregular like a Jacobean manor house with an off-centre squat tower. Mullion-and-transom windows, alternate upper ones rising through the eaves. The second was the Caernarvonshire Technical College, 1955, by the County Architect (*H. Williams*). Canted barrel-vaulted roofs over the workshops and a four-storey curtain-walled block with an oval water tank on the roof. Slate wall inscribed with the tools of the building trade.

NORMAL COLLEGE (George Site), Holyhead Road. The original house *c.* 1770, later the Bangor Ferry Inn that served the main crossing before the Menai Bridge was built. Enlarged *c.* 1850 to become the George Hotel, with additions by *Lloyd-Williams & Underwood*, 1867. Used as the Normal College from 1919; now University halls.

ST MARY'S COLLEGE (North Wales Training College), Lôn Pobty. High above the town. 1893–4, by *R. Grierson*, completed by *Frank Bellis*. Late Tudor collegiate Gothic, in drab roughcast. The quadrangle has a polygonal-ended chapel E, the principal's residence, W, and a tower behind. To the S, early C20 block in the style of Hare's Normal College halls. *Richard Hall* added a wing *c.* 1930; further halls of the 1960s.

YSGOL FRIARS, Lôn y Bryn. 1997–9, by *Gwynedd County Architects* (job architect, *Graeme Hughes*).[*] A relaxed grouping of two-storey blocks in domestic style, its slate roofs stepping, sliding and cascading in the manner of Bowen Dann Davies.

YSGOL TRYFAN, Lôn Powys. 1937, by the County Architect, *Westbury Lloyd Jones*. The former County School for Girls, moved from College Road to a hillside site and serving the new housing estate of Maestryfan. Brown brick and green slate hipped roofs; E-plan, two-storey, and utilitarian, except for the heroically tall entrance.

---

[*] The latest manifestation of the original Friars School, endowed by Geoffrey Glyn at the Reformation, rebuilt 1557, moved out of the centre in 1899 (*see* Coleg Menai).

PERAMBULATIONS

1. The Town Centre

From the cathedral, paths lead up to a minor widening for markets, part way along the narrow HIGH STREET. Largely of Late Victorian character and with no buildings of great merit, this long, primary road links the town's older buildings. Proposals in the 1930s to widen the street were never fulfilled. Going NE, on the l., the low limestone front of the MARKET HALL (now W. H. Smith's) of 1831. Next, a BURTON'S shop of 1930, by *N. Martin*, their architect, taller than its neighbours. Classical-Deco front boasting half-columns *in antis* on the upper storeys. Further on the l., NATWEST BANK, 1860 by *Kennedy*, a sumptuous Florentine Gothic façade which shows what could be done with a larger budget and finer Penmon stone than churches could afford. Ground floor lined with polished limestone, window colonnettes of turned limestone. BANK PLACE has as its modest focus a red Ruabon brick CLOCK TOWER of 1887, by *A. Neill* of Leeds. On its SE side another two less expensive BANKS. LLOYDS TSB (formerly Williams & Co.), Jacobean, by *Weightman, Hadfield & Goldie* of Sheffield, *c.* 1849, the other built as three premises in 1850, then the North and South Wales Bank from 1905. W of the clock tower, the 1980s DEINIOL CENTRE encroaches on the cathedral's space; E, the more bulky MENAI CENTRE (by *Leach Rhodes Walker* of Manchester, 2008) with curving curtain walls of glass and slate, replacing a 1960s development. The former WOOLWORTHS store of 1939, r.

Further E, DEAN STREET, the limit of pre-industrial Bangor, runs N past pleasing variants on the 'Bangor houses' built in 1939 by the Council, part of a larger scheme never completed. In GARTH ROAD, LLAIN DEINIOL, 1980s housing by *Bowen Dann Davies* skilfully incorporates parts of *Kennedy*'s St Mary's Church School of 1868. To the SW, at the Post Office, FFORDD GWYNEDD leads l. back to the centre, past the Library and the Museum, l., and the Police Station and Town Hall, r. TAN-Y-FYNWENT joins from the l., past LLYS GWYNEDD, a three-storey stucco house with a nice Adam doorway; the Italianate, vermiculated PENRHYN HALL, built *c.* 1857 by Lord Penrhyn as a concert hall; and the former DIOCESAN REGISTRY, 1866, modern Gothic, with sashes and more pointed windows, possibly by *Kennedy*. A return to the cathedral can be made past the Diocesan Centre.

2. The University: Deiniol Road and College Road; Holyhead Road and Glanrafon Hill

DEINIOL ROAD, the link along the valley between the station and Garth, was made through the cathedral land in 1905 on the University's behalf. As well as achieving its romantic vision in Upper Bangor, the university needed science buildings. Hare's proposal to link the University and Deiniol Road with monumental ramps and steps, and to start a second symmetrical park of faculty buildings at the lower site, was unrealized. This axial approach has since been replaced with a linear arrangement along Deiniol Road, more recently using the hillside between as well. This leaves the connection between the two levels unresolved and architecturally muddled, so it is to be hoped that the proposals to redevelop this area (involving the replacement of Theatr Gwynedd and the Students' Union and Refectory with a new Arts building) will give some sensible structure to the area.

DEINIOL ROAD leads NE from the railway station, past C20 terraces, to the first of the University buildings, the BRAMBELL BUILDING (Zoology). Brutalist concrete, by *Sir Percy Thomas & Partners*, 1969. Set back in a new square, the environmentally conscious ENVIRONMENT CENTRE WALES, by *Fairhursts Design Group*, 2007, its gently swelling front of slatted timber contrasting with the more static dark slate block to the l. Next, the MEMORIAL BUILDING (Biological Sciences), the Wrenaissance brick and stone frontispiece to a (partly demolished) group of SCIENCE BUILDINGS, 1927, by *Alan E. Munby*. The DEINIOL BUILDING, opposite, was the Central County School, 1935, by *Westbury Lloyd Jones*. Next, MENTEC, 1986–94, by *Gwynedd County Architects*, project architect *Graeme Hughes*, of neatly detailed brown brick. The THODAY BUILDING opposite, by *Sir Percy Thomas & Son*, 1954, has a long, brown brick, half-windowless front, Dudok in derivation. At the cross-roads a weak, Tudorish gateway, the NORTH WALES HEROES MEMORIAL, by *D. Wynne Thomas*, 1923. His original design, a distinguished circular mausoleum, was judged too Greek. Sited askew to Glanrafon Hill, the gateway addresses one of the climbs to the university, passing between the REFECTORY and STUDENTS' UNION buildings of 1963, by *Sir Percy Thomas & Son*. These are linked above the path by a glazed walkway in the form of an exedra, kept low to enhance the ascent to the main site.

The approach from below makes clear Hare's majestic vision for this citadel of learning. The W quadrangle was not completed by him, however, but by the *Percy Thomas Partnership*. Their Library wing extends N to College Road, facing across Penrallt to new buildings by *Nicholas Hare Architects* (project architect *Jayne Bird*), the BRIGANTIA BUILDING of 1996, and behind, the DEPARTMENT OF PSYCHOLOGY, 2003. Using the materials of the area, plastered walls and slate roofs, they mediate between the bland flat-roofed Library and the terraces of Upper Bangor, and set a standard for courtyard spaces and simple handling of large volumes. The impact from the main town below is well considered, too.

Opposite the unrealized N range of Hare's university, in College Road, the self-effacing low building with black-and-white gables is *Richard Davies*'s SCIENCE BUILDING and GYMNASIUM, late C19. Above the car park, l., BRYN AFON,

1885, by *O. Williams* of Bangor, a flamboyant villa in red brick, terracotta and fish-scale roof tiles. Big cusped arches to the verandas. Beyond Hare's main buildings, the Ruabon red brick MUSIC DEPARTMENT was the County School for Girls, 1897, by *J. H. Phillips* of Cardiff. The BUSINESS SCHOOL MANAGEMENT CENTRE, opposite, was built as hostels for the Normal College, 1910, by *Hare*. Axial layout, on two levels; four T-plan blocks form an H-plan with a refectory set transversely at the centre. A much freer Arts and Crafts than Hare found appropriate for the University, with rendered walls, overhanging eaves and curvy Voyseyish gutter brackets. Around the stepped open courts, the ranges are of varying heights, gabled, with tapering buttresses; sitting above the entrance drive, ATHROLYS, a matching house for the Principal. Further along College Road, r., NEUADD RATHBONE, originally the university hall for women, 1897, by *Frank Bellis* of Bangor. In the Queen Anne deemed suitable for women after Champneys's Newnham College, Cambridge; enlarged 1955–9 by *Sir Percy Thomas & Son*. Next, NEUADD JOHN MORRIS JONES, the present women's hall, by *S. Colwyn Foulkes*, 1965. Brick and shallow copper roofs, Swedish in feel.

FFORDD MEIRION leads uphill NW, past BODALWEN and WINDOVER, two roughcast houses by *H. L. North*, then down to SILIWEN ROAD, lined with substantial villas overlooking the Strait. After the Normal College buildings, l., BELVEDERE and its counterpart TAWELAN, r., by *Richard Davies, c.* 1907, noteworthy for their sub-Voysey composition of gables, battered buttresses and careful windows. PRINCE'S ROAD leads back past the UNIVERSITY ANGLICAN CHAPLAINCY, a Victorian house re-founded as the Church Hostel and School of Divinity by Dean Edwards in 1886. *H. L. North* added the small CHAPEL in 1933, one of his surviving minor masterpieces. Approached by a delicately scaled passageway. Nave with tall lancets and gabled buttresses, chancel with four-gabled pyramidal roof, set diagonally. Interior recalling E. S. Prior's St Andrew, Roker, with full-height pointed arches like brick crucks. The painted decoration in the chancel vault, as rich as that of his master Henry Wilson, is all that survives of North's interior. His memorial stone, moved from Llanfairfechan. E window by *F. C. Eden*, 1933. In the garden *North*'s little ALICE WILLIAMS LIBRARY, 1938, with a double gable and tall triplet windows. Students' block added by *P. M. Padmore*, 1953.

From College Road, HOLYHEAD ROAD leads W to the bridges, passing MENAI VIEW, 1851, a stucco terrace of sixteen boarding houses with enjoyable details, especially on Nos. 1–6, and on the proto-Grecian gateway at the E end. Then, set back in a garden, l., past a two-storey lodge, BRYN-Y-MÔR, perhaps 1847, stuccoed with trellised veranda and Tuscan portico.

In the other direction, Holyhead Road leads back to the centre, past Penrallt Chapel, l. Just before St James, GLANRAFON HILL leads steeply downhill, l., past ELDON TERRACE and FRONDIRION TERRACE, handsome two-storey stucco rows of

c. 1851, with rich detailing. Set back further down, BRYN TEG
TERRACE, plainer and of three storeys. At the bottom of the
hill, r., TANRALLT, a small house of 1755 for Archdeacon John
Ellis, sadly boarded up at the time of writing. A Chinese
Chippendale stair may survive. A late C18 painting by Moses
Griffith shows a Baroque garden extending below the house.

Across Deiniol Road, Nos. 39–41 GLANRAFON, simple early
C19 terrace houses facing a square which links to the Bible
Garden just N of the cathedral.

3. *Garth Road, leading to Garth*

Dean Street meets Garth Road opposite Penuel chapel (*see*
above). After Tabernacl chapel (*see* above), r., Nos. 1–5 ERW
FAIR. Anglesey limestone, mid-C19 classical, with an added
front bay at No. 4. Further E, the Edwardian GAMBIER,
GARFIELD and GORDON TERRACES, three terraces of eight,
with fronts of yellow Caernarfon brick. Covered SWIMMING
POOL of 1966 opposite. At the junction to Garth, the former
BRITISH SCHOOL of 1848, in limestone, with gables and
entrances for boys and girls and a tablet stating there were 500
pupils. A short detour SE of the junction, along the waterfront,
leads to SEIRIOL ROAD, r., lined with terraced cottages by
H. L. North. Built in 1927 for the Bangor Copec housing
group, to replace insanitary industrial rows and proving that
local need could be met at about £400 per house. Gables in
pairs in North's way, the chimneys between, simple metal
windows in pebbledash walls and porches slated like the roofs.
The small peninsula of Garth retains aspects of the ferry and
coastal settlement before the Telford period and its subsequent
integration with the town. The sight of the Anglesey shore and
Garth Pier (p. 246) is rewarding. Just to its E the stone GARTH
JETTY, no later than the early C19 and over 300 ft (92 metres)
long, for one of Bangor's pre-Menai Bridge crossings to Anglesey. On the NE shore a second minor port (now a boatyard).
On the hill, W, EARTHWORK of unknown date, perhaps the site
of the medieval castle.

4. *North-east to Port Penrhyn*

From Dean Street, the High Street leads NE, past FRIARS
TERRACE, a fine three-storey seven-bay terrace, *c.* 1820, raised
above the street, with an elegant segmental-headed doorway
and fanlight. PENYBRYN ROAD, r., cuts through on a level
from the High Street, part of the *Telford* works of 1817. TAN-
Y-COED, r., commissioned from *Benjamin Wyatt* in 1810 by
Dean Warren, as the Caernarvonshire & Anglesey Dispensary.
Slate slab porch with the name handsomely inscribed above
the doorway. Midway along the cutting, the stone BRIDGE
provided a formal approach to the Penrhyn Arms Hotel of
1799, now vanished except for the entrance PORTICO.
Opposite, PENRHYN FARMHOUSE, of five bays, the end two

advanced and gabled. Later C18. The three-bay PENYBRYN HOUSE, l., with its central pedimental gable, is of 1779, perhaps by *Samuel Wyatt*. The old road was by-passed *c.* 1934. The hotel was demolished and 'Bangor houses', MAES ISALAW, designed to present a fitting approach to the town, were built near its gardens.

PORT PENRHYN became a far more successful Menai Shore port than Garth. A long-established landing place at the mouth of the Cegin, then a Georgian estate harbour which grew with the slate industry in the first half of the C19, Port Penrhyn is still a working harbour on a limited scale. By 1786 Richard Pennant, Baron Penrhyn, had decided on this as the principal harbour for exporting slate from his quarry in the Ogwen valley, building a road to connect the two. His agent was *Benjamin Wyatt*. The 1793 tax on slate slowed down business, but redundant workers were put to constructing a six-mile horse-drawn RAILROAD from the quarry, opened 1801 and built under the canal engineer *Thomas Dadford*, who considered it more practical than a canal. Of this early period, the first QUAY built by *Thomas Knowles* of Pentir along the E bank of the Cegin, extended N to form a pier in 1803. W of the stream, a stone and red brick U-plan WAREHOUSE with a lower storey of cambered arches (now converted). W range and part of the E built 1803, extended N and S in the 1830s when it was linked to the quay by a cast-iron bridge (replaced in concrete).

PONT PENRHYN was rebuilt in 1820 by George Hay Dawkins-Pennant. Segmental arch, with decorative balustrade and niches at each end. It provided a dignified entrance to the developing port, l., and Lime Grove, r., the agent's residence (*see* p. 256). On axis is the Port Lodge (p. 404), presumably built at the same time in preparation for the greatly expanding Penrhyn Castle to the SE. The railroad passed under the road beyond the E end of the bridge, and continued past PORT HOUSE, the office from which the port was run. Handsome Neoclassical villa, built *c.* 1840, perhaps by *James Wyatt II*.* Three bays, in limestone ashlar. Big windows with segmental heads, porch with monolithic Doric columns. A clock in the pediment of the projecting centre.

p. 256

By 1855 a third and more extensive reconstruction had taken place in the boom years of slate quarrying. The quay was lengthened and faced in Anglesey limestone, and a second pier or breakwater was constructed E of the first, for the spacious NEW DOCK. Along the quays either side ran the sidings of the Chester & Holyhead Railway (branch to Port Penrhyn made 1852). Of this period perhaps the small round tide-flushed PRIVY, with conical slate roof and wooden finial. A complex of RAILWAY BUILDINGS was built *c.* 1878–80: a locomotive shed with two distinctive round-arched doorways, a carriage shed and small workshops. E of the Port House, the single-storey but lavish Italianate ESTATE OFFICE, *c.* 1860, faces the

---

*Not the famous James †1813, Benjamin's brother, but Benjamin's son James 1795–1882, who succeeded him as estate agent.

Bangor, Lime Grove, Port Penrhyn.
Engraving by Lewis Wyatt, 1801

estate walls and the Port Lodge. To the s is the later C19 LODGE
to PLAS-Y-COED, a large gabled pile built 1865 and extended
1878, for the estate agent. It replaced (or encased?) Lime
Grove, a Neoclassical villa by *Samuel Wyatt*, 1790s. This had
a Doric porch with paired columns *in antis* between large
windows in arched recesses, a motif continued on barely projecting pedimental side pavilions. U-plan STABLES, W, C19.

CEGIN VIADUCT, ¼ m. s. Railroad bridge over the Cegin. Three
segmental arches with voussoirs, *c.* 1800. One of the oldest
multi-arch railway bridges to survive. Further up, INCLINE
COTTAGE, on the quarry tramway. Attributed to *Benjamin
Wyatt*. Twin cottage wings divided by the winding house at the
top of the incline; arched recesses on their N gables. Lengths
of smooth slate crudely used to form the broken-based pediments, blind arches and window heads. The park wall of the
1820s skirts round this preceding estate building.

5. *South-west from the Cathedral to Caernarfon Road*

SW from the cathedral, little of interest in the High Street as it
runs out to the Caernarfon and Holyhead roads. A detour up
Lôn Pobty passes BODIFYR, l., mid-C19 stucco with dentil
cornice and a steep central gable, and BRYN KINALLT, r., of
similar date, but with an elaborate late C19 or early C20 porch.
Further uphill the former St Mary's College (p. 250).

Back on the High Street, an impressive late C19 TERRACE of
shops below flats, r., of red brick with yellow brick details, and
a variety of window heads, named Josiah Hughes in the gable.

The BLACK BULL INN, r., was the former R.C. church of 1835 by *J. J. Scoles*, stripped of its stucco Neo-Norman detail outside and in, but the underlying stone arcades remain. Capel Pendref (p. 245), l., and, at the junction with Farrar Road, the former BRITISH HOTEL, built as the railway hotel, 1851. Brick, Italianate, so possibly by *Francis Thompson*.

Beyond the railway bridge, CAERNARFON ROAD runs sw through areas of housing dating from the 1930s and later. Above Penchwintan Road and close to the former railway marshalling yards, BELMONT STREET, a tight enclave of railway workers' terraces, *c.* 1898, and in EUSTON ROAD, the London & North Western Railway INSTITUTE, by the resident engineer *W. Dawson*, 1898. St David's church (*see* p. 244) is further along Caernarfon Road.

6. Penrhosgarnedd

An older settlement sw of Bangor, with its own church and chapel but continuous with the city along Penrhos Road.

ST PETER. 1956, by *P. M. Padmore*. Severe lancet style, clearly influenced by his partner, Herbert North. Drab pebbledash with steep slated roof and copper flèche. Windows single and in threes in projecting bays alternating with buttresses. W porch with arched windows and door below a flat pediment. Painted brick interior, with big pointed arches in brick, springing from low down. Double row of corbelled arcading each side of the E window. – FITTINGS. Octagonal PULPIT, READING DESK and a low SANCTUARY ENCLOSURE all of brick. Riddel-post ALTAR, under a painted celure.

GRAIG CALVINISTIC METHODIST CHAPEL. 1872, by *R. G. Thomas*. Disused. Rock-faced grey limestone, in a mixed round-arched-to-Gothic style. Main window gathering a triplet and three roundels within a giant arch, the voussoirs increasing to give a Moorish outer arch.

YSBYTY GWYNEDD HOSPITAL. 1977–80, by the *S. W. Milburn Partnership* with *W. S. Atkins & Partners* as engineers. A 540-bed District General Hospital, in very long four-storey ward blocks linked to a lower centre. It was to be erected as quickly as possible on a very exposed site, so a reinforced concrete flat-plate structure of brown hammered concrete panels, on pre-cast columns, was adopted. The HERGEST UNIT, 1994, in a much softer manner by *Mari Withecombe*, is one of many later clustering round it. New entrance and administration block *c.* 2000.

MAES-Y-FFYNNON, Penrhos Road. 1980, by *Brian Lingard & Partners*. Large T-plan complex of offices built for Welsh Water (now the DVLA offices). Buff brick. Strips of dark metal windows below wide overhanging roofs.

HAFOD ELFYN, Penrhos Road. An unassuming L-plan office by *S. Colwyn Foulkes*, 1959. Roughcast with metal windows. Pink sandstone entrance.

TROS-Y-CANOL, No. 198 Penrhos Road. Early C19, probably by the Penrhyn estate. Stuccoed. Deep eaves and three half-hipped gables. Picturesque detail. Gothick panes to the sash windows, hoodmoulds below. The centre first-floor door was to a balcony over the latticed porch.

7. Treborth and the Britannia Bridge approach

On the outskirts w of Bangor, one of the great might-have-beens of North Wales. As conceived by the Chester & Holyhead Railway and designed by *Joseph Paxton*, *c.* 1850, BRITANNIA PARK was to be a residential suburb of Bangor and the setting for a grand hotel serving travellers using the recently completed railway bridge. The vast HOTEL, its principal front over 500 ft (150 metres) long, would have had 500 beds. It was planned to link to the station via a glass arcade filled with exotic plants. The design was by *Charles Verelst* of Liverpool. Work began in 1851 but was soon suspended, and eventually abandoned, as the company had overstretched itself with building the bridge. However, the pleasure grounds, now the UNIVERSITY BOTANIC GARDENS, were developed. A tunnel bringing water below the railway to the waterfall survives.

In 1867, the park and the adjoining Treborth Isaf estate to the w were bought by Richard Davies, ship-owner and M.P. for Anglesey. He built himself a big and dull Italianate mansion, TREBORTH HALL (now a school and much altered), by *R. G. Thomas* of Menai Bridge, 1871–2. The GROUNDS were laid out a few years later by *Edward Milner* of London. Linking mansion and park across the railway, a BRIDGE of five segmental arches on battered piers, stepping down. At the E end of the park, a semicircular GATEWAY and single storey LODGE with embattled porch, by *R. G. Thomas*, 1871.

BRONWYDD, ¾ m. w of Penrhosgarnedd church. 1905, by *Richard Hall*, for H. Vincent, solicitor. Squarish plan, with a lower gabled cross-wing to NE and a single-storey service wing and yard beyond. Pinkish rock-faced stone, the upper storey white-rendered. Veranda to the garden (SE), its hipped l. end supported on a canted bay. Above, a large window extending above the eaves and with a flat leaded roof; a lower window tucked under the eaves, r. Cambered heads to the ground-floor windows. Extended at both ends in 1922 for Sir William Vincent, presumably by *Hall*. Good fittings: inglenook seats, copper fireplace hoods and lustre tiled surrounds, patterned lead glazing etc.

p. 62   BRITANNIA BRIDGE (*see* Llanfairpwll, Anglesey, p. 169, for full description). Down a lane N of Bronwydd, a surviving length of the original box bridge, erected as an exhibit. In the undergrowth, a pair of huge amiable stone LIONS guarding the entrance to the original rail bridge, now below the modern road.

PARC MENAI. A large business park off the A487 road, in the grounds of the Vaynol Estate. Two buildings stand out. TECH-NIUM CAST, by *TACP* of Wrexham, 2004. High-Tech aesthetic, white metal cladding below a glazed upper storey with continuous balcony and sunshade. INTEC, by *Gwynedd County Architects*, job architect, *Graeme Hughes*, 1999. Red brick divided by paired piers. Cranked L-plan, with oversailing roofs above the escape stairs at the ends.

PENRHYN CASTLE. *See* Llandegai.

BARDSEY ISLAND/YNYS ENLLI

0822

About 2 m. s of the extreme w tip of the Llŷn peninsula. Only 450 acres, a grid of small walled fields w of a central track, Mynydd Enlli (500 ft) to the E, and a spit of flat land beyond the bay to the s. Gerald of Wales noted a settlement of Culdees (celibate monks), later Augustinian. Throughout the Middle Ages, an important place of pilgrimage, the end-point of a string of pilgrimage churches along the Llŷn. A dozen houses sheltered the small fishing community in the late C18 and early C19. The 3rd Baron Newborough developed the island *c.* 1870–5, but by the 1960s only seven permanent residents remained. Owned by the Bardsey Island Trust since 1979.

ABBEY OF ST MARY. The ruined tower of the C13 Augustinian monastery remains, in the NW corner of a walled enclosure. Three late C19 CELTIC CROSSES, one commemorating the 20,000 saints reputedly buried on the island, another with wheel-cross head, of 1891, designed by *Evan Evans* of Caernarfon.

WESLEYAN CHAPEL. Built 1875 by Lord Newborough. Rubble, with sandstone quoins and yellow brick dressings. s porch with excessively tall brick bellcote. Central pulpit, five canted sides made up of C17 and C19 bits, the date 1875 prominent in a Baroque frame on the front. CHAPEL HOUSE, N. Gabled and rendered, with a central porch, also gabled.

OLD SCHOOL. Built by Lord Newborough, probably mid-C19. Simple rubble rectangle. One room.

CARREG-BACH is the only pre-1870s domestic survivor, an early C19 *croglofft* cottage of whitewashed rubble. The remaining houses were built by the Newborough estate, 1872–5, as tiny MODEL FARMS, with steep gables and timber mullion-and-transom windows suggesting involvement by *Henry Kennedy* or *George Benmore*. Four pairs and three detached, all with separate walled enclosures containing the farm buildings. The pairs s and NE of the Abbey ruin share a double enclosure, with paired brick-arched entrances, L-plan barns etc. and back-to-back pigsties. CARREG, also detached, has murals of island life by the artist *Brenda Chamberlain*, who lived here in the 1950s.

LIGHTHOUSE. By *Joseph Nelson*, 1821. Tall (98 ft, 30 metres) and square, slightly tapering. Painted red and white, with an octagonal lantern.

5948 # BEDDGELERT

ST MARY. On the site of a presumed C6 Celtic *clas*. Still an independent monastic community when Gerald of Wales visited in 1188, but soon afterwards brought into line as an Augustinian priory. Nothing survives of the conventual buildings, which probably lay to the s. Despite fires *c.* 1282 and *c.* 1432, there remains C12 (?) stonework at the NW angle of the church and a relieving arch above the w window, early C13. The very tall triple E lancet, *c.* 1230, was considered by Hughes and North to be 'possibly the finest architectural feature in the whole of Snowdonia'. The reveals splayed inside, of two chamfered orders outside, in Anglesey gritstone. Also of this date the chancel N doorway and the sophisticated two-bay arcade between nave and N transept. The octagonal pier and responds have clustered shafts, with capitals linked by ring mouldings and deeply cut rolls to the two-centred arches. The present appearance is due to C19 alterations. In 1830 the nave s wall was rebuilt, possibly the chancel wall too. A full-length N aisle, its roof a continuation of the nave roof, was demolished and the arcade was blocked. *Kennedy* unblocked it and added the present Lady Chapel, *c.* 1880. The bellcote and chancel arch are his too, the porch and s windows probably from the earlier C19 phase. The queenpost roof could be of either. – REREDOS, ROOD SCREEN and PARCLOSE SCREEN. Finely carved oak, elaborate mixed Dec-Perp style, 1921. On top of the chancel screen, a tripartite canopy niche, and rood group above. ALTAR and CANDLE-STAND, in similar style. – FONT. Dated 1882, but possibly older. A curious hollowed-out polished stone, just 1 ft (30 cm.) across, incised in Iolo Morganwg's Bardic characters, on a base inscribed with the late C8 Nennius alphabet. – STAINED GLASS. E window in memory of James Wyatt †1882, agent to Lord Penrhyn. – Good chancel s window, by *Dunstan Powell* of *John Hardman & Co.*, 1920. – MONUMENTS. Evan Lloyd of Hafod Lwyfog †1678. Carved oak panel, with the arms of Owain Gwynedd.

The VILLAGE is picturesquely sited at the confluence of the Colwyn and Glaslyn. This Y-plan defined the early ownership pattern: Cistercian land to the N, Augustinian to the w, secular farms to the E. Slate and copper were worked here in a small way, but the tourist potential was recognized early (*c.* 1800) and remains the village's mainstay.

BRIDGE, at the centre. Two arches and a small flood arch. No doubt of ancient origin, but much rebuilt after a flood in 1799. On the N side, a row of substantial Regency houses,

mostly three-storeyed, built by the Sygun estate *c.* 1830.
Starting from the r., the PRINCE LLEWELYN HOTEL.
Three-bay main part, with Gothick-tracery windows. A later
two-bay wing, r., with a simple porch on cast-iron columns.
WATERLOO HOUSE (now Beddgelert Antiques), two storeys
and attic, raised above street level. Gabled wing projecting,
steps up to the r. bay porch in the angle. The COLWYN GUEST
HOUSE, three bays, nearly symmetrical, has windows which
sadly look out of place. PLAS GWYNANT has its gable to the
street; wavy bargeboards, deep verges. Lastly, PLAS COLWYN.
Two-storey three-bay villa, with hipped roof and wide bracketed eaves. Lower monopitch wings. All are built of good
coursed stone, stained the colour of rust. CAERNARFON ROAD
continues gently uphill to the w, following the Colwyn. A footbridge leads to the small COUNTY SCHOOL, dated 1911 above
a big round-headed window. VICARAGE, set back in gardens
above the road about ⅛ m. further w. Built *c.* 1851, plainly and
severely, with huge coursed blocks. Projecting gabled bays
flanking a three-bay centre with a small gable. Strangely, the
front door is not central.

Back at the bridge, SMITH STREET leads E. To the l., a handsome TERRACE following the bend, Tŷ Popty with a gable
above a canted bay. Opposite, also on the bend, Nos. 1–6, a
lower, less unified terrace. Smaller windows, some with
Gothick tracery. Glan Awen is the best-preserved. Round the
bend, the street becomes STRYD GWYNANT. On the N side,
three mid-C19 quarry-workers' terraces of well-coursed stone,
some with large lintels framed with slate hoods. No. 14, Hafan,
has a large window with timber surround and bracketed hood.
This house, and many others in the street, were once shops.
Opposite, Nos. 1–7 CLUB STREET, a terrace in two sections
built in 1841 by the 'Benefit Society of Eryri in Beddgelert'
(plaque on No. 6). Nos. 1–4, r., two-bay houses each side of a
three-bay pair. Nos. 5–7, more formal, with an advancing
gabled bay in the middle.

s of the bridge, CHURCH STREET, the first street to be
built, *c.* 1820 (Nos. 5–7 later). Nicely placed at the corner,
LLEWELYN COTTAGE (Tŷ Isaf), a sub-medieval two-storey
house, once the alehouse, altered and extended *c.* 1700. A lane
follows the river E, past the former NATIONAL SCHOOL
(1859), to a footbridge over the Glaslyn to SYGUN TERRACE,
an attractive row of ten quarry-workers' houses facing a green,
built *c.* 1860 by William Ormsby-Gore of the Brogyntyn estate.

The main street leads W from Llewelyn Cottage, past later
C19 and C20 detached houses, and the former CYSEGR
CONGREGATIONAL CHURCH, late C19 or early C20, towards
the ROYAL GOAT HOTEL, originally Beddgelert Hotel, built
by Thomas Jones in 1802 for the growing tourist trade.
Tall and imposing. E-facing stuccoed wing, with C20 ground-
floor loggia and front terrace; shorter s-facing wing, with a
two-storey canted bay. Hipped roofs with wide eaves.

On the hillside w of the hotel, OBERON WOOD, a 1970s housing estate by *Phillips Cutler Phillips Troy*. White render, with contrasting areas of stone. Relaxed and varied, in a sensible modern vernacular.

CWM CLOCH, ⅔ m. w. A pair of upland C18 farmhouses joined end-to-end. Both of three bays, the l. house slightly forward of the r. Lean-to additions behind. A very late example of the unit system.

DINAS EMRYS, 1 m. NE (SH 606 492), is the legendary strong-hold of Vortigern, the C5 prince who invited Saxon warriors to help him defend his kingdom, but was ousted by them and forced to flee westwards. The legend related by Nennius in the C9 states that Vortigern tried unsuccessfully to establish a fortress on this precipitous hill. The tower on the hill today is probably medieval, but the rather insignificant ramparts around the hilltop may be C5. Excavations have shown occupation in the C3–C4, and Mediterranean amphorae indicate a C5–C6 phase when occupants were wealthy enough to import wine. The entrance at the w end, flanked by three poorly built stone ramparts (not accessible) and the single rampart around the summit, also poorly built and incorporating a lot of crags and rock bosses, belong to a style thought to be characteristic of late forts. The rectangular keep on the summit is reduced to its clay-bonded footings. Excavation did not provide evidence of date, but the later C12 is likely.

5266
BETHEL

The village has no real focus. A back street of late C19 and early C20 terraces, otherwise C20 sprawl mostly along the main road.

BETHEL INDEPENDENT CHAPEL. 1856 and 1866, remodelled 1901. Snecked rubble, ashlar dressings. Raised pediment between flanking parapets, with a semicircular arch over three windows with their own pediment. Twin doorways, with deep entablatures. SUNDAY SCHOOL, l., set back behind an early C20 obelisk memorial.

ERW-PWLL-Y-GLO, 1 m. SW. A pretty two-storey Late Regency house, formerly stuccoed. Three-bayed, with single-storey extensions. Hipped roofs, wide eaves. Fine doorcase, with panelled pilasters, consoles and flat hood in purple slate, and a delicate fanlight.

6367
BETHESDA

CHRIST CHURCH, Glanogwen. Early Dec, aisled, of 1855–6, by *T. H. Wyatt*. Commissioned by Lord Penrhyn despite a competition between *G. E. Street*, *Henry Kennedy* and *Weightman, Hadfield & Goldie* (who sued the vicar). The sw tower is the memorable part. Three stages, gabled angle buttresses, semi-octagonal stair-turret. Short broach spire, perhaps too squat, with gabled lucarnes. A six-pointed star in the head of the big E window. Arch-braced trusses with large cusps and wall-posts on floriate stone corbels. Two-centred arcades, piers alternately round and octagonal. – STAINED GLASS. W windows, Annunciation and Visitation, by *Henry Dearle* of *Morris & Co.*, 1922.

BETHESDA INDEPENDENT CHAPEL (former), High Street. The first chapel, which gave the village its name, 1820; rebuilt by *Richard Owens*, 1872–5. A grand Italianate front of three bays, stuccoed. Pediment to the central bay, above a name panel with raised letters. Three-light rectangular window divided by Corinthian pilasters, and a recessed porch with Tuscan columns and Corinthian pilasters, all incorrectly applied. Pedimented windows to the outer bays, above round-headed ones with rusticated surrounds. Dentilated cornice to the entire façade; paired Corinthian pilasters at the angles, above rusticated quoins. Converted to flats in 1998 by *Geraint Efans*.

BETHANIA INDEPENDENT CHAPEL, Bangor Road. A late work, in Lombardic style, by the *Rev. Thomas Thomas*, 1885. Bright red Ruabon brick and sandstone dressings. Three bays divided by piers which terminate with stepped pyramidal caps. Big round-headed window, heavily recessed with angle shafts above twin gabled doorways. In the outer bays, Florentine windows above triple recessed slits. Stepped detailing to the gable verges. (Shallow elliptical-vaulted ceiling with tie-beams and queenpost trusses to centre, flat panels to side ceilings. Curved gallery on iron columns. Fluted pilasters, arches and pediment behind the pulpit.)

JERUSALEM CALVINISTIC METHODIST CHAPEL, Ogwen 101 Terrace. Built 1842 by *T. Evans* of Bangor, remodelled 1872–5 by *Richard Davies*. Set back behind a small park and the war memorial, it looks more town hall than chapel. Nearly square plan, with hipped roof and bracketed cornice. Five large upper windows with rope-moulded architraves and flat cornices on brackets. Monumental central porch, the large round-arched doorway with a heavily moulded surround. Vast horseshoe-plan interior, the gallery sweeping round like an amphitheatre. The curved wall has large windows, matching those of the front, but mostly internal, borrowing light from the outside. Raked seating throughout. In front of the *sêt-fawr*, a railed semicircular area for the orchestra. Curvaceous PULPIT, polished mahogany, with brass rails and steps each side. Above, huge ORGAN, bought from Huddersfield Town Hall in 1903, in a triple-arch gallery with balustrades and a Renaissance pilastered and corniced frame. Circular ceiling with radiating panels. Gilded pendant at the centre, its funnel lined with mirror glass, possibly a 'gas sunlight' by *Stroude & Co.* of London. Large two-storey SCHOOLROOM and VESTRY behind.

SS PIUS X AND RICHARD GWYN (R.C.), High Street. 1962, by *Weightman & Bullen*. A very steep slated roof, on two parallel grey brick walls which continue in front and contain the flat-roofed entrance hall. Slit windows, and a large skylight above the sanctuary area, which is at the w end. Light spacious interior. Laminated trusses like modern crucks.

ROBERTSON MEMORIAL CHAPEL, Coetmor, ¾ m. NW. Small Anglican chapel by *Orpen & Dickinson* of Dublin, 1911, a memorial to Dickinson's friend Donald Robertson who died in a climbing accident in Snowdonia. Nave and chancel under the same roof, divided internally by a chancel arch. Dark granite-type stone, the walls battered below the windows. w bellcote, set in from the gable end.

A large VILLAGE with an urban character, begun *c.* 1820 by quarrymen for themselves on land not belonging to the Penrhyn estate. Later, it developed in a more orderly manner along the winding High Street, Telford's road, following the Ogwen river. During the late 1860s the area had the largest chapel and church attendance in North Wales, with four churches and fifteen chapels.

Most of the noteworthy buildings are on the main street. At the s end, just off the lane leading w to Tregarth, No. 6 TŶ'N TŴR, the oldest building. The l. half modern, the r. half a much altered C15 hall-house, the reputed hiding place of Archbishop Williams of York during the Civil War. Diagonal C17 chimney, set back from the ridge. Small window openings, one pointed. (Large fireplace. C17 upper floor, with chamfered and ogee stops to the beams. Post-and-panel partition. Two cruck trusses, with large purlins and a surviving wind-brace.) BRAICHMELYN, lined with quarry-workers' cottages, winds uphill E of the main street. A less-altered row in a narrow cul-de-sac N of Braichmelyn, Nos. 1–12 CAE'R BERLLAN. Mid-C19, single-storey two-room houses. Over each front door a slate slab on timber brackets. Across the path, tiny outbuildings with slate slab roofs. Further N, l., the Roman Catholic church (*see* p. 263) and the DOUGLAS ARMS HOTEL, an early C19 coaching inn. Three-storey double-pile plan, with a large hipped roof lantern over the central valley. Doric porch with entablature and cornice, and pilaster responds. Nice railings. OGWEN TERRACE, *c.* 1830, follows the bend in the High Street. Three-storey houses many now pebbledashed. A few unaltered fronts. Nos. 1–2 are unusually faced in blocks of cut slate, presumably original. No. 2 has a Palladian upper window with sandstone lintels. Opposite No. 22, the gateway to Christ Church (*see* p. 262), leading to an avenue of yews. To the N and in front of Jerusalem Chapel, the surprisingly grand WAR MEMORIAL, by *R. J. Hughes* of Llanfairfechan, *c.* 1923. Low semicircular wall behind, iron railings to front. The memorial has flanking pedestals set diagonally, facing tall obelisks each end of the front railings. Grey limestone and rubble. Further N, JOHN STREET rises E, the narrow winding alley a remnant of the quarrymens' settlement. The High Street now becomes VICTORIA PLACE. On the l., the KING'S HEAD INN, mid-C19, white roughcast with eared window surrounds in black, the name in big letters in the frieze. Then the VICTORIA HOTEL, also mid-C19 but possibly incorporating earlier work. Three-bay central range, extending at both ends to form coach entrances. Rubble slate-stone below, roughcast above. Pilastered entrance with shallow canopy. Behind, the NEUADD OGWEN, which replaced the market hall. Further N, opposite the imposing Bethania chapel (see p. 263), GORDON TERRACE, early C20, follows the shallow bend of Bangor Road. A continuous veranda roof above bay windows, on decorative iron brackets.

BRYN MEURIG, ¼ m. SW. Built c. 1820 for the Penrhyn quarry doctor, and extended in the mid C19 by Dr Hamilton Roberts, the first in Wales to use ether as an anaesthetic. Of three bays, extended r. to form a full-height canted bay. Roughcast, hipped roof behind a parapet with moulded cornice. In the garden, some fine specimen trees planted by Dr Roberts.

BRYN DERWEN, ⅓ m. WSW. 'A beautiful Villa' according to Fenton, built c. 1810 for the Penrhyn quarry manager. Curious window levels, additions and an ungainly modern portico hide the original three-bay stuccoed front with pedimented centre and hipped ends. Coursed-rubble N range, with slate window voussoirs; roughcast elsewhere.

COETMOR FARM, Coetmor, ½ m. NNW. A good planned estate farm, c. 1870. HOUSE, S, L-plan with gabled cross-wing, r., and central timber porch. Slate-clad, above rubble. Tall narrow windows. To the N, BARN (earlier), PIGSTIES, STABLES etc. around a courtyard. Hipped and half-hipped roofs.

PENRHYN QUARRY, 1 m. SSW. Opened 1782 by Lord Penrhyn with profits from his West Indies sugar plantations. The huge pit, once one of the biggest man-made holes in the world, is stepped to form a series of near-vertical terraces 59 ft (18 metres) high, connected by inclines. The early inclines were operated by counterbalance, the full wagons pulling up the empty ones; but by 1810 they were powered by water wheel so that slate from the lower levels could be lifted to the processing areas. Water balances were also used to lift slate vertically up shafts, the SEBASTOPOL SHAFT using machinery by Ratcliffe's of Hawarden, 1856, the PRINCESS MAY SHAFT with machinery by DeWinton's Union Ironworks in Caernarfon, 1900. A railroad, completed in 1801, linked the quarry with Port Penrhyn, Bangor (p. 255). The main pit is no longer used but the purple Cambrian slate is still quarried and worked elsewhere in the vast site, mostly by machine.

MOEL FABAN (SH 636 678). On the summit three Bronze Age cairns (much disturbed); on the N slope a ruined ring cairn, and across the deep gorge, another large cairn. A small mound of burnt stone at SH 639 681 close to a C19 leat (Ffos Rhufeiniaid) and the ephemeral group of stone huts and paddocks in Cwm Ffrydlas (SH 644 684) may also belong to the Bronze Age, but the more substantial round huts and more systematically cleared fields probably date from the last centuries B.C. and the Roman period. The clearest of these farms is at SH 638 680 where the houses stand at the foot of the slope, approached along a walled lane up from the present trackway.*

BETWS GARMON

ST GARMON. 1841–2, by *George Alexander*. A replacement of the medieval church which lay to the E. Very small. Nave and chancel in one, small semicircular apse and W bellcote. Simplified Romanesque, eminently suitable in the dramatic Snowdonian landscape. – FONT. Circular bowl on octagonal column, dated 1614. – MONUMENT. John Rowlands of Nant †1703. Brass plaque with a shield between floral sprays.

Hardly a village: two tiny settlements a mile apart, with the former school midway. On the hillside to the E, the scars of mine shafts and zigzag quarry paths of the Garreg Fawr iron mines. BETWS INN, SE of the church, dated 1750. Three bays, two storeys, with a C19 extension, r. Roughcast, with plain window surrounds. NE of the church and bridging the Gwyrfai, PONT BETWS, built by 'Henry Pary 1777'. Four segmental arches, with cutwaters. Probably altered 1820 when the turnpike was formed.

PLAS-Y-NANT, 1¼ m. SE. In the grounds of the C19 house, a late C17 or early C18 BARN, converted for a private chapel in the late C19. Four-bay roof, with plain collared trusses (the lower collars cut off) and three tiers of purlins. Below the timber floor, the original stone one, of massive slabs on cyclopean corbels built into the walls.

LLWYN-BEDW, ½ m. NW. L-plan two-storey house, tree-ring dated 1585. Big primary and secondary beams in the three-bay W wing, remodelled in the late C18. A plaster shield with fleur-de-lys above the fireplace in the rear (E) wing.

FFRIDD-ISAF, Rhyd-ddu, 4 m. SE. Remote on the hillside SW of Snowdon. Three-bay front wing of c. 1800 added to the original house at right angles, tree-ring dated 1600. Large fireplace with segmental arch of slate-stone voussoirs, surprising in a small house. Original slotted beam to (modern) partition. BARN to the S, dated 1612 on a truss.

BETWS-Y-COED

An idyllic location, in a deep wooded valley just as it joins the wider Conwy valley.

ST MICHAEL, Old Church Road. The old church beside the Conwy river, in a big circular churchyard. A simple rectangle under one roof (of thick old slates). Partly rebuilt W bellcote. S doorway with two-centred head of short voussoirs. Large,

*There are similar remains on the W slope of Moel Faban, around Llanllechid, and in Cwm Caseg above Gerlan.

broad N transept added by Lord Willoughby de Eresby, 1843. One feature of architectural quality, the recess in the chancel N wall. Of typical mid-C14 profile, the arch has a continuous quarter-round moulding. Parts of the C14 or C15 arch-braced roof trusses show beneath the C19 plaster vault. Of the same date, the timber windows, with quirky little pointed centres. – Double-decker PULPIT and DESK, from older bits perhaps brought from Gwydir Castle. On the pulpit, some oddly geometricized pieces of C16 linenfold panelling. In the desk, carvings include a date, 1697. Both have reused twisted balusters. – FONT. c. 1200. Low and square. On each side an incised segmental arch with zigzag decoration, with two leaves in the 'tympanum'. The undersurface treated with a machicolation of pointed and round arches. – STAINED GLASS. E, fragments of Dutch Rococo, with merchants' marks. W, C16 heraldry etc. – SCULPTURE. Effigy of Dafydd ap Gruffydd Goch, c. 1385. An excellently preserved figure in armour, head on helmet, arms folded on chest, wearing a short tunic and detailed leg-pieces. The table slate is inscribed HIC IACET GRUFYD AP DAFYD GOCH AGNUS DEI MISERE ME. – LYCHGATE, W, dated 1756.

ST MARY. Built 1872–3 to replace the old church, too small for the growing number of visitors. It would be hard to praise too highly. The architects were *Paley & Austin* of Lancaster, the style adopted the noble Transitional between Romanesque and E.E. A monumental crossing tower, with blind arcading on the S and a stair-turret on the N. The clock stage was added in 1907, and instead of the steep pyramidal roof originally proposed, an invisible much shallower one behind the parapets. The catslide roof to the S transept is particularly successful. The E window has plate tracery, the W is a rose window. The nave aisled, with a clerestory. Arcades of circular piers, bold pointed arches without chamfers. The stones must be mentioned: Ancaster limestone varying from pinkish to buff is used for all the dressed work; externally and on the internal nave wall surfaces there is uncoursed rubble in the local, but pale, blue stone. The Ancaster stone takes carving very well, and the capitals, all dissimilar, have Normanesque waterleaf, scalloping etc. The crossing and sanctuary are vaulted and faced with the Ancaster stone, its warmth contrasting nicely with the austere lines of the many-ordered arches. The corbelling of their inner steps is imaginatively handled by bands of shallow ornament. The passage of light in the chancel is beautiful. Then the nave roof, again confidently detailed with kingposts in the tie-beams, spaced between close scissor-bracing. – REREDOS, of Italian alabaster, with scenes of Christ's life, 1929. – CHOIR STALLS. Discreetly Art Nouveau; on the bench ends and especially on the fronts and finials of the priests' desks are repoussé bronze panels, mostly fluent interweavings of hedgerow forms. – PULPIT, 1899, with columns of serpentine. – FONT, 1872, a massive unadorned tub of ruby serpentine on colonnettes of green, perhaps Mona Marble. –

105

STAINED GLASS. S aisle W and N aisle W, 1919, to designs by
Burne-Jones. Perhaps another by him, eastern most in N aisle.
– W, symbols of the Evangelists, *Shrigley & Hunt*. – S aisle, one
by *Jones & Willis*, another by *Shrigley & Hunt*.

At the W, a PARISH HALL has been tacked on to the porch
with good effect. Triangular in section, so its roofs are its walls
and its skylights the windows. The end walls of stone,
incorporating windows and a door from a nearby derelict
church. By *George Hedges*, 1978.

BRYNMAWR CALVINISTIC METHODIST CHAPEL. 1872, by
Richard Owens. One of his Lombard designs with triangular-
headed recesses, seen many times elsewhere (e.g. Dwyran).

Three rivers meet in the VILLAGE, and over each, a fine bridge.
The youngest, the Waterloo Bridge (*see* below), took Telford's
road over the Conwy river in 1815–16. The railway from
Llandudno Junction reached the town in 1868, marking the
real starting point of the tourist resort. By 1884 there were six
licensed hotels, five temperance hotels and thirty-four boarding houses. Examples line one side of the main street at the SE
end, none of great architectural worth but with good
stonework and attractive gables. OLD CHURCH ROAD leads N
to St Michael's church, past the OLD COURTHOUSE of 1872,
with bands of red brick and yellow brick chimneys contrasting
with the dark stone walls. E of the church, an elegant
SUSPENSION BRIDGE across the Conwy river. A pair of steel
latticed pylons each end, supporting a cambered timber
walkway hung from cables and hangers. By *David Rowell &
Co.*, Engineers, of Westminster, 1930. W of the church and
reached by a footbridge, the RAILWAY STATION, built by
O. Gethin Jones (who built St Mary), 1868. Its size and
grandeur indicate the popularity of the C19 resort.

Back on the main street, the ROYAL OAK HOTEL, a fine three-
storey building *c.* 1861, with shouldered stone gable copings
and huge lintels above the straight-arched windows. A touch
of Scottish Baronial. Before it was rebuilt, it was the centre of
the Betws-y-coed artists' colony, a coterie established by David
Cox (1783–1859). Further NW, the PONT-Y-PAIR dramatically
crosses the Llugwy river. Probably C17, but a bridge existed
here long before. Segmental arches in five spans, only the
central one over the river itself. On its NE side, BRYN-Y-BONT,
a Gwydir estate cottage, 1840s (*see* Trefriw), with the
characteristic circular chimney and heavy eaves corbels. Next
to it, the MEMORIAL HALL, opened 1929 on the site of a
former National School. The central upper window corbelled
out on stone brackets, with a flagpole above. Dark, coursed
granite, with lighter cut-ends at the quoins. Further down the
road, the former ALBERT MILL, now flats and without its
water wheel. Next to it, BODLONDEB, formerly the Miners'
Arms. Further NW along the main street, nearly opposite
Brynmawr Chapel (*see* above), the former TABERNACLE
CHAPEL, 1870, now a shop, with a huge dark-stained timber
and glass bay added in front, by *Bowen Dann Davies*, 1990s.

PENTRE DU forms almost a separate settlement at the W extremity of the village, built for the Hafodlas quarry workers *c.* 1900. SCHOOL by *Rowland Lloyd Jones*, County Architect. First designed in 1913 but not built until 1928. One of a number of open-air schools in the county. The 'marching corridor', with its folding windows facing S, and the folding partitions between the classrooms survive. The inclined wooden MINERS' BRIDGE crosses the Llugwy river here, possibly the oldest of the crossings. Used in the mid C19 by workmen to reach the lead mines N of Betws-y-coed (*see* below).

WATERLOO BRIDGE, ¼ m. SE. A handsome cast-iron bridge by *Thomas Telford*, taking his Shrewsbury to Holyhead (A5) road across the Conwy river. With a span of over 98 ft (30 metres), it is an impressive example of early iron technology, from the foundry of *William Hazledine*. Emblazoned on each side, following the line of the segmental arch, 'This arch was constructed in the same year the battle of Waterloo was fought', in fact completed 1816. The spandrels decorated with the national emblems: rose, thistle, shamrock and leek.

PONT YR AFANC, 1 m. S, beside the huge Beavers' Pool. Large single-span (98-ft, 30-metre) bridge across the Conwy river, *c.* 1805. Snecked, rock-faced stone.

PONT AR LLEDR, beautifully sited ¼ m. S of Pont yr Afanc. *c.* 1700 rubble stone bridge of two elliptical arches, the smaller a flood arch. Small cutwaters on upstream side.

TŶ'N-Y-COED, ¼ m. N, on the B-road to Trefriw. In a dramatic elevated position. Dated 1877. Dark granite rubble with red sandstone band and windows. Steep hipped slate roofs. The SE corner full-height bay has an octagonal spire. Next to it, the roof slides down over an open balcony with a zigzag timber balustrade and rolled sandstone corbels. At the rear, an octagonal tower, slate-clad and with tiny leaded windows.

PENCRAIG ISAF, 2 m. NW. A two-storey T-plan house, the uphill (N) stem early C17 with a projecting stair next to the fireplace, now timber but probably once of stone. The three-bay S-facing wing is later and may also have had, at its W gable, a large fireplace with a staircase next to it. The interior of this part is decidedly Georgian. Panelled doors and window reveals, egg-and-dart plaster cornices, Chinese Chippendale balustrades to the later C18 staircase. The small study upstairs has some fine re-set panelling with guilloche mouldings.

TŶ UCHA, Rhiwddolion, 1¾ m. W. Small whitewashed cottage, in a dispersed upland community serving the slate quarry. Single-storey, with a *croglofft*, and an attached barn in line. Small windows, one a Yorkshire sliding sash. Below, the small CHAPEL, built 1869 to function as a school too. Both now owned by the Landmark Trust.

LEAD MINES. The hills to the N were one of the main lead-mining areas in Wales worked until 1963. CYFFTY, 2 m. NW, originally Pencraig Mine was established in the 1850s, though there was mining here earlier. Two shafts, for pumping out water and for extracting the ore. Surviving buildings 1870s, including a crushing mill, a circular buddle pit and a row of cottages. At the LLANRWST LEAD MINE, Bwlch-yr-haiarn, 2½ m. N, the 59-ft (18-metre)-high chimney survives. Rubble with brick above.

3438

BODUAN

ST BUAN. An ample Romanesque church remodelled in 1894 for the Hon. F. G. Wynn by *Henry Kennedy*, or maybe his last partner, *P. S. Gregory*, from a cruciform Georgian church of 1765. Rendered, with red sandstone dressings. A tall, embattled tower is added at the crossing and the nave was extended W to provide an arcaded internal narthex between a N vestry and the S baptistery. The organ loft above, and to the W, a later porch. Round-headed windows, in equal triplets at the W gable and on all sides of the tower. Engaged shafts and cushion capitals, elaborated in the E window. Where the organ floor meets the N and S windows these are daringly divided into a roundel above a short semicircular light. Inside, a Renaissance-inspired space with Romanesque detailing, all in pinkish stone. Chevron-moulded arches on paired columns define the crossing, its flattish ceiling supported on spirally carved angle shafts, exuberantly foliated top and bottom. Shafts and florid capitals to the windows, one to each wall so the interior is bathed in daylight.

FURNISHINGS. COMMUNION RAILS. Low and arcaded, matching the front to the organ loft. – FONT. Shaped like a cushion capital, on a cylindrical base. – TABLETS in the sanctuary, incised with Lord's Prayer and Creed; of slate, with painted foliage margins. At the W, tablets inscribed with the Four Last Things (Death, Judgement, Hell and Heaven), each of a different marble: black for Hell, white for Heaven etc. – STAINED GLASS. Chancel, 1895 and 1905, by *Charles Hean*. S transept (St Cadfan) and N transept (St Buan), by *George J. Hunt*. – MONUMENTS. Sir William Wynn †1754. Chaste white marble urn. – Sir John Wynn †1773. White marble sarcophagus, decorated in relief with a garland encircling a vase, a mourning female, and a second vase. Both by *Nollekens*. – Griffith Wynn †1680. Coat of arms carved between flowers, above the inscription. – Baptistery, Sir William Wynn †1754, a second urn to him (from another church?). Very handsome; spirally fluted with carved foot and gilded flames.

PLAS BODUAN. Large stuccoed mansion in its park, close to the church. Home of the Wynn family from the C16. Seven-bay S elevation (extended E and W in the late C19) of 1736, for Thomas Wynn. According to Hyde Hall in 1809, 'a building of small pretension'. Large N extension, *c.* 1830 and a U-plan STABLE BLOCK of 1850, both for Spencer Wynn. CHAPEL, late C19 and extensively altered in the C20. In the grounds, two WALLED GARDENS and an octagonal GARDENER'S COTTAGE. Following a delightful (public) lane running along the

E boundary of the estate, a stream, waterfalls and small lakes. Near the junction with the B4354 road, a LODGE in *cottage orné* style – half-hip roofs, leaded windows, veranda on tree-trunk posts.

No village, but the scattered houses with ornamental bargeboards hint that this is estate country, first created by Lord Newborough in 1776. A cluster near the church and the main LODGE to the Plas. GARDEN COTTAGE, originally the smithy, has the pierced droplet motif used for the estate bargeboards. The LYCHGATE of 1912 (by *Harold Hughes*?) and a short avenue of yews frame a good view of the church. In the lay-by N of the cottage, a black and yellow AA TELEPHONE BOX, 1950s. Set back from the main road, W, THE OLD RECTORY. Mid-C19, stuccoed, unbalanced by the relocated front door and open porch. ¼ m. NW, another cluster of buildings around the small mid-C19 (former) SCHOOL. To the SE, BRYNTIRION, a miniature (but much extended) two-storey house with hipped roofs and open timber porch; to the NW, PENYGROES, the veranda on fluted tapering iron columns.

Below Garn Boduan (*see below*), 1¼ m. NW, a third group. First, Nos. 1–3, TAN-Y-FRON. A simple stone terrace, two bays to each house, their windows irregularly spaced. PEN STEP, a tiny *croglofft* cottage, and No. 3, BRYN HYFRYD, the last in the group, retain their original character. The latter is single-storeyed, with a gabled central bay abutted by an angled front door with its own little triangular roof.

BRYNIAU, ½ m. SW. Single-storey *croglofft* house, with outbuildings in line. Rubble, the house whitewashed. Small windows and stable door. Corrugated metal roof, in places over old thatch supported on thin pole rafters at very close centres. Unspoilt.

NANT, 1 m. WNW. Early C19, formerly part of the Newborough estate. A pretty two-storey HOUSE, of three bays. Rubble. In line to the S, a lower block with a small horizontal sliding sash above a large modern window. Further S, and lower again, the single-storey MILL ROOM, with water wheel, and the STABLE, for three horses. At right angles, and following the downward slope, COWHOUSE, CARTSHED, BREWHOUSE and PIGSTIES. A good example of an estate farm, carefully preserved.

PENHYDDGAN, 1½ m. WNW. Late C16 house of two storeys and three bays, with a gabled stair wing projecting on the NE. Access originally from the SW, the main doorway with rough voussoirs to the head. Later, access moved to the opposite (NE) side (perhaps as a result of the road improvements), and the stair wing became a front porch. Rounded walls contain the wooden spiral staircase, probably a replacement, and a tiny loft, with gable window and mini-truss. Large fireplace in the main room, with recesses on both sides. Central beam and fluted joists. A fine oak partition divides this room from two former service rooms to the NW. Low four-centred doorways to each (one now blocked), and guilloche mouldings to the uprights. Two roof trusses, the one in line with the screen finely cusped, indicating that it was to be seen from the main chamber. Recesses each side of the SE fireplace, each with a tiny window, so probably closets. OUTBUILDINGS to the S, one with a slate plaque: T. P. Jones Esq. 1790 (i.e. Thomas Parry Jones of Madryn, one of the chief promoters of the Tremadog to Porth Dinllaen turnpike).

GARN BODUAN, 1¼ m. NW (SH 310 393). A large hill-fort covering the 25-acre summit of an isolated and naturally defensible hill. The simple stone rampart with entrances on the S and N sides (the N one blocked in antiquity) was remodelled at least once. On the N side the later line is set a little further in; on the W the later one drops downhill to take in a projecting rock boss. The shelving interior is well filled with about 170 round stone houses. On the E side is a small citadel built against the highest cliff edge, cut off from the rest of the fort by a stone wall rather different in style from the main ramparts. There was a well-built gate in this wall, subsequently blocked. Excavation in the 1950s provided evidence of Iron Age and Late Roman occupation, but not a conclusive date for the citadel itself. This is generally thought to be late, possibly even post-Roman, as suggested by the name Boduan (i.e. residence of Buan, a quasi-legendary C7 figure).

BODYSGALLEN see LLANRHOS

BONTNEWYDD

4760

Linear main road settlement, the 'new bridge' taking the turnpike to Caernarfon across the Gwyrfai. Just N of the bridge, the NEWBOROUGH ARMS, an earlier C19 coaching inn, roughcast, two storeys, with central gable and Gothic casements. Uphill, S of the bridge, PENTRE UCHAF, a row of early C19 roadside single-storey cottages, possibly the 'Poor Cottages' of the 1839 tithe map. Next, CARTREF. A matching pair of houses built as an orphanage for Robert Bevan Ellis, draper, by *T. Taliesin Rees* of Birkenhead: for boys, 1902, and for girls, 1908. Cheerful Edwardian domestic. Similar colour stones to Siloam chapel (*see* below) but with half-timbered outer gables. Centre with swept roof and dormer over a timber veranda. PLAS-Y-BONT, opposite and down a short track, a C17 two-storey house with taller S cross-wing and square chimneystacks. (Fine dog-leg late C17 stair in four flights and an early C18 panelled room.)

SILOAM CALVINISTIC METHODIST CHAPEL. 1896, by *O. Morris Roberts & Son*, possibly remodelling his chapel of 1877. Striking both for colour and style. Italianate with a Baroque flavour, the front clasped by towers with octagonal tops and squat domes, the centre with an unconventional Palladian triplet over a porch, the doorway flanked by wavy parapets. Grey-pink granite neatly laid in squares and narrow levellers, like a woven place mat, and yellow sandstone dressings. Good interior with panelled plaster ceiling, curved gallery in long panels, and a rich ensemble of balustraded curved *sêt-fawr*, pulpit panelled in contrasted wood grains, and Ionic triple-arched corniced aedicule behind.

PLAS DINAS. ½ m. ssw. Roughly H-plan, the original part in the centre is early C17, added to in the mid C17 by Thomas Williams, son of Sir Thomas Williams of Vaynol, and then much extended in the C19. Later owned by the Armstrong-Jones family. Of the C17, a re-set tablet on the E elevation inscribed T.WI.W 1653, the camber-headed doorway with quarter-round mouldings and a large fireplace with a segmental arch.

FRON DINAS. ½ m. S. Built *c.* 1908 in a comfortable but not over-elaborate Edwardian style. Single and paired gables face the approach drive. Entrance porch to S, veranda-bay window to N. White roughcast, timber windows, red ridge tiles. Alterations and extensions to the E in 1998 by *Adam & Frances Voelcker* in pared-down Arts and Crafts manner. To NE, BRONANT, another Edwardian house in similar style, with its own lodge.

BRIDGES. The NANTLLE TRAMWAY BRIDGE, W of the road bridge. 1828, built for the tramway from Talysarn, for which *G. & R. Stephenson* were engineers. Further W, a triple-arched brick RAILWAY BRIDGE over the Gwyrfai, *c.* 1867, on the line from Afonwen. Another similar ROAD BRIDGE SE of the village.

BORTH-Y-GEST   5638

ST CYNGAR, Church Road. A dour church, by *Harold Hughes*, 1913. Small but upright, its height accentuated by the base-ment-level meeting room. Dark local stone, laid crazy-paving fashion. Pointed windows in singles, pairs and triplets, all with rectangular lead glazing. Nave and chancel in one with transepts, the N one heavily buttressed with a catslide roof. Slate-clad porch added 1964. An arch midway along the nave, curiously. Medieval-style arch-braced trusses and flat wide purlins W of the arch, a boarded ceiling to the E. Was the church planned to be longer?

EBENEZER CALVINISTIC METHODIST CHAPEL, Seaview Terrace. 1880. Tall gable front, stopped short of the angles by small returned hips. Round-headed margin sash windows either side of the centrepiece, a slightly projecting affair which contains the round-headed doorway and a Palladian window above. Glazed roundels in the window heads. Pebbledash, with rendered quoins etc. Possibly by *Richard Owens*.

A delightful VILLAGE curling around a small sheltered bay W of Porthmadog, the crossing point over the Traeth Mawr tidal sands before the Cob was built. Shipbuilding was the mainstay in the second half of the C19. At the top of MERSEY STREET, a steep road lined with stepped two-storey houses, the early C20 SCHOOL and attached SCHOOL HOUSE, by *O. Morris Roberts & Son*. Half-hipped roofs and dormers, and chamfered-head windows, ingredients unusual in the County Schools.

On the opposite (NE) side of the bay, up a footpath to Porthmadog, two C20 houses in GARTH ROAD rise above the level of domestic mediocrity. On the r., CROGLOFFT, by *Roger Harrison, c.* 1985. Unexciting on the road side, but on the garden side it becomes two-storeyed and opens up to the views with sliding doors, balconies etc. On the l., BROMEBYD, a square yellow brick bungalow by *Keith Garbett* of Cambridge, built in the 1970s for his parents. A shallow brick colonnade encircles the house, with a low pyramid roof tweaked up at the apex for a triangular lucarne. Small windows to the street, larger to the garden. A nice simple plan arranged around a full-height 'snug' at the centre. Unplastered brick inside.

SAETHON, ½ m. N. 1899, for David Breese, a Porthmadog solic-itor, by *Percival Currey* of London. Squarish plan, with a veranda on three sides. A single-storey service wing forms an L; in the angle, the porch, set back below the gabled upper storey. The lower storey of dark stone quarried nearby; the upper walls and roof of red clay tiles. More East Sussex than North Wales. In the LIBRARY, a good linenfold fireplace sur-round by *De Vynck*, 1920, originally made for Morfa Lodge (Gelli Faia), Porthmadog (q.v.).

LLWYN DERW, ½ m. N. An attractive and unassuming house of 1900. *O. Morris Roberts & Son* for Arthur Edwards. White painted pebbledash above dark rubble. The gable front half-timbered, and projecting over a sitting-out area which continues to the l. under a veranda on thin monolithic slate posts. Tall diagonal brick chimneys. Edwards collected oak furniture, so some fireplace surrounds are reconstructed from older parts, but the copper fire-hoods, with Arts and Crafts heart shapes, must be contemporary. Lovely staircase hall, with a big window and tall tapering Voysey-ish newels and moulded caps.

CLOGWYN ISA, *c.* 215 yds E of Llwyn Derw. Also by *O. Morris Roberts & Son*, of similar date. Two gables to the front, a mono-pitch dormer between. The roof continues down to form an arcaded veranda on slate posts.

BRYN GAUALLT, ½ m. NNE. Built 1896 for J. R. Prichard, a local banker. Rather heavy-looking, of dark granite, relieved by the round machicolated SW tower and the partly glazed veranda wrapping around it, and continuing around the large canted SE bay.

BOTWNNOG

ST BEUNO. 1885, replacing one of 1835 by *William Owen*, itself a rebuilding. Divided nave and chancel, with N porch. Late C20 S extension. The chancel stonework is different, the style suggesting two phases. Dec windows. Square W tower, slightly engaged, diminishing in three stages, then becoming octagonal at belfry level, with a stone spire. An awkward affair. Predictable interior containing little of importance. – STAINED GLASS. E window by *Clayton & Bell*, *c.* 1890. N by *Jones & Willis*.

Along the N side of the churchyard, the former GRAMMAR SCHOOL. 1616, founded under the will of Bishop Henry Rowlands, thus one of the earliest in Wales. Extended and heightened *c.* 1810. Now unrecognizable below pebbledash and new windows.

The small VILLAGE straddles the B4413 road, but church and school are on a side road which climbs N. Beyond the church, TŶRYSGOL, the former school house; probably the same date as the SCHOOL which was relocated S of the church in 1848. Just a steep gabled bay survives, with a spindly diagonal chimney. Engulfing it, later buildings by *Rowland Lloyd Jones*, *c.* 1899. Opposite the chapel, SURGERY, 1987, by *Bowen Dann Davies*. Roughcast, with a lively roofscape and strip windows (originally dark-stained timber). The recent (2005) extensions and alterations have diluted the crispness of the original.

BOD NITHOEDD, ½ m. W. Plain but handsome farmhouse dated 1845, of coursed grey and rusty rubble, with a long range of outbuildings stepping down in line, W. Perhaps one of these is the original house. Embattled porch with a round-headed doorway. Owain Llŷn, a local bard, lived here.

PLAS GELLIWIG, 1 m. S. Largish two-storey house with a complicated plan. Double-pile, facing W (entrance front) and E (garden front), with a lean-to N extension, a big cross-wing, S, and an L-plan block attached at the SE. Recorded from the early C17, but the oldest extant part is probably the C18 W block. Four-bay front, a fifth bay, belonging to the late C19 cross-wing, disguised to make it nearly symmetrical. The E-facing garden front probably late C18 or early C19, of four unequal bays and without a door. Both fronts have parapets. Their Georgian character is replaced in the S cross-wing by Gothic: Tudor-arched entrance with a projecting window on corbels above, stone mullion-and-transom windows, stepped gable parapets, a battlemented turret and an octagonal chimney. The L-plan wing, with stepped gables and lattice-glazed windows, has a (re-set?) carved stone plaque with a windmill and the date 1731. Some good detail inside, including a C19 Gothick landing and passage. S of the house, OUTBUILDINGS with Gothick doorways. Late C19 COACHHOUSE and STABLES, and a circular stone pond with central pillar (said to be part of a former dovecote). WALLED GARDEN, with box hedges etc. and an ornamental POND, E.

BRYN BRAS CASTLE *see* LLANRUG

BRYNCROES 2232

ST MARY. Small single-chamber church. Below window-sill level, the walls are probably medieval; the round-headed W and

N doors late C16. Of this date too the repaired trusses, with arch braces and cusped struts. *Harold Hughes* rebuilt from sill level up, 1906, and added the simple Romanesque W porch. Small lancets with round heads and deeply splayed internal reveals, replacing blocked former windows with square heads. Wide projecting eaves and gable bargeboards, functional but not pretty. An unusual, if dark, interior: the walls faced with small chunks of granite pressed into wet mortar, and the roof structure (renewed, apart from the trusses) stained dark green. – PULPIT. Wood-panelled, on a red sandstone base which divides nave from chancel. – FONT. Large hollowed-out boulder on a rectangular base. Probably medieval. – STAINED GLASS. E window by *Morris & Co.*, 1935. – MONUMENTS. Two framed oak boards to members of the Trygarn family, †1666 and †1687.

TŶ MAWR CALVINISTIC METHODIST CHAPEL, ½ m. N. Built c. 1840. A rare example of the long-wall façade plan, with chapel house attached, r., under the same roof. Large sash windows either side of the slate tablet, projecting porches at each end and above them, smaller sashes to the former galleries. Drab render.

The small undistinguished village lies just off the B4413 road. Opposite the churchyard gate, LETTY, a pair of late C18 or early C19 *croglofft* cottages, now one. Whitewashed rubble, old thick slates. S of the church, FFYNNON FAIR, a small square holy well.

5663   BRYNREFAIL

BRYNREFAIL CALVINISTIC METHODIST CHAPEL. Dated 1873. Grey-green rubble, grey dressings. Round-headed Florentine windows. Schoolroom and vestry at right angles. On a sloping site, so basements below both.

SNOWDONIA DESIGN AND ENTERPRISE CENTRE. 2003, by *Gwynedd County Architects*, project architect *Graeme Hughes*, on the site of the large County School of 1900. A group of fifteen workshops/offices, with café and an organic vegetable garden, run by a co-operative. L-plan, on two storeys. Large café upstairs at the faceted external corner, its big horizontally glazed windows slightly cantilevered out over the white roughcast walls of the lower floor. The café's radiating roof sweeps up to the ridge to provide a tiny diamond-shaped window.

CAE MABON, Fachwen, 1 m. SE. A rural retreat, on a sloping wooded site overlooking Llyn Padarn, started by *Eric Maddern* in 1990. A dozen tiny cabins surround the thatched, pole-constructed round-house. Some are rectangular and shed-like; others are circular or polygonal, with turf roofs and lime-rendered cob or straw-bale walls. Doors in all sorts of shapes and sizes, and hardly a window with a right angle. The character is similar to Menter y Felin Uchaf (*see* Rhoshirwaun) by Dafydd Davies Hughes, who helped the volunteer workforce here. But if there is a philosophical underpinning, it is to Maddern's native Australia that one must turn rather than to Rudolf Steiner, and more particularly to the aboriginal ideas of Sacred Land etc.

CAEATHRO

5062

Tiny settlement just E of Caernarfon, dwarfed by the big caravan park in the grounds of Glangwna Hall.

WERN, ⅓ m. SE. L-plan house, mostly early C17, but incorporating a C16 house at cellar level at the NE corner. Of the earlier C17 the wide deep fireplace with bread oven, a segmental-arched SE doorway and the NW and SW chimneys. Gabled porch and dormers added probably in the 1870s, for the Glynllifon estate. Timber transom-and-mullion windows with a horizontally sliding lower quadrant, similar to those in the estate houses on Bardsey Island. Fine Jacobean staircase with tall shaped finials and slat balusters. Overshot WATER WHEEL to the NW wing. To the W, a late C17 barn converted in the C19 to STABLES. To the E, C19 PIGSTIES.

BRYN EGLWYS, ⅓ m. SW. Stuccoed mid-C19 house. Lower rear extensions, SE. Twin-gabled NE entrance front, with gabled porch and off-centre window above. Full-height canted bays to the garden front. STABLES and COACHHOUSE, W, white-washed rubble. Catslide dormer.

PENRHOS, ⅓ m. SW. Three-storey mid-C19 house of some distinction. T-plan. Stuccoed, with a slate-clad rear wing. Two full-height canted bays to the NW front, with a veranda roof between, and single-storey hipped wings. Wide bracketed eaves. Rendered quoins and window surrounds. Sir William Henry Preece (1834–1913) lived here, and Marconi stayed here, both carrying out pioneering work on wireless telegraphy in the early C20. The stone TOWER in the garden was used to transmit messages to the tower in the grounds of Coed Helen, Caernarfon, seen in the distance.

GLANGWNA HALL, ¼ m. N. A house of ample proportions, built in Elizabethan style in 1893 by *Douglas & Fordham* for J. E. Greaves, slate magnate and Lord Lieutenant of Caernarvon. It replaced a 'much admired villa' of Thomas Lloyd Esq., c. 1815. Grey limestone ground floor under jettied half-timber, the panels in herringbone, lozenge and quatrefoil patterns. Westmorland-slated roof, and tall terracotta chimneys, some octagonal, others twisted. Mullion-and-transom windows, some projecting on curly brackets. A nearly symmetrical entrance front to SW: the battlemented and buttressed porch is off-centre and the pair of main gables to the r. advance more than the l. pair. The other elevations less regular. At the NE, the rectangular plan is broken by a projecting service wing, with a turret in the N angle. Octagonal copper cupola and weathervane.

p. 71

The huge central HALL extends up to the arch-braced roof and lantern. Jacobean-style STAIR, with carved newels, finials, pendants and elaborate fretwork balustrades. It rises then divides before reaching the large landing with three arcaded sides. DINING ROOM r. of the hall, former schoolroom and servants' hall beyond. DRAWING ROOM to the l., with small octagonal bay at the N corner. The splendid LIBRARY beyond, with Jacobean-style ceiling, panelling and full-height bookcases crowned with gabled canopies. Other surviving fittings include fireplaces, water closets and wash stands, servants' bells etc.

Stone-balustraded TERRACES to NW and SW. A courtyard of single-storey OUTBUILDINGS, SE, with tall spirelet and hipped dormers. Approx. 160 yds E, a large STABLE BLOCK around a courtyard. The entrance is through a giant round-headed archway, with clock and leaded cupola above. LODGES at the former entrances to NE and SW, the latter with a hipped veranda on rustic timber posts.

7763

CAERHUN

Hardly a village. *H. L. North*'s lovely church design of 1898 was never built, nor any of its subsequent reworkings. Only the church hall was built.

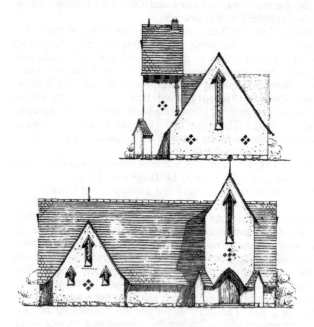

Undated church design.
Drawing by Herbert North

St Mary. In a square churchyard above the NE quadrant of the Roman fort Canovium. Nave and chancel in one, the latter added in the C15. At the same time, the w wall probably rebuilt, with a slightly corbelled double bellcote, its top straight as at Llanbedr-y-cennin, but here with a small central gablet. On its w face, a carved crucifix, and below it, a doorway with a rounded head. s porch of the same date, later converted to a vestry. s chapel added 1591 by Edward Williams of Maes-y-castell, dated on a wooden board above the E window. As with most of the Conwy valley churches, the E wall of the chapel is in line with the chancel gable. The junction between the spaces formed by a wide bressumer, supported on a re-set capital, perhaps C13. A triplet of arched lights to the chancel E window, a flat head outside, a rounded rere-arch inside; perhaps reused from the earlier E wall. Next to it, a pointed niche. The chapel windows, cusped with square heads, must pre-date the chapel; probably reused. Nave windows all C18. An arch-braced truss and a queenpost truss to the chapel roof, supporting purlins and rafters; but to the nave and chancel, close-spaced rafters with high, arched collars, interspersed with secondary rafters when the thatched roof was slated. The valleys are slated in the old manner. Gently repaired by *Kennedy* in 1851, including much rebuilding of porch and chapel. – FONT. Round and tapering, early medieval. Next to it, a C16 STOUP. – MONUMENTS. Hugh Davies of Caerhun †1721. White marble. – Katherine Roberts †1739. Brass plaque, with unusual spelling. – Hester Davies Griffith †1829. White marble, with pedimental top. – LYCHGATE. Early C18. Slated roof and rubble walls containing reused Roman material.

The former CHURCH HALL, ¼ m. s, c. 1904, by *Herbert L. North*. To the front, his familiar paired gables, but elaborated so that, further back, the roofs extend above the centre of the hall to support a small gabled ventilator. Purple slates, with zigzag rows of green. 'A little extreme, my dear fellow, a little extreme', North confessed to a friend. Gable windows with faceted heads; small octagonal window lower down on the r. side. Interior subdivided (now a house), but sympathetically. In the garden, a charming triangular COAL HOUSE. Rubble walls, pyramidal slate roof.

CAERHUN HALL, ¼ m. w. A large mansion in extensive grounds, on the site of a C17 house of medieval origins, built in 1895 for Major-General Hugh Sutlej Gough. The Jacobethan style is reminiscent of John Douglas, drawing inspiration from Plas Mawr, Conwy, but the architect may be *T. M. Lockwood*, who had designed a different house for the same site in 1892. Main N–S wing, with L-plan service wing, w. A restless design, of light grey limestone and grey-green slates contrasting with red Runcorn dressings. Stepped gables with ball finials, some corbelling in above canted bays in Douglas's manner. Mullion-and-transom leaded windows; heads straight, cusped or rounded. Oriels to the N entrance gable and an octagonal service stair-turret with belvedere as at Plas Mawr. Octagonal chimneys. Jacobean styling to the ample interior, with strapwork and barley-twist balusters to the staircase, large fireplaces with Tudor-arch niches, and reused C17 panelling from the old house.

FARCHWEL, ½ m. NE. An imposing two-storey house in an elevated location, its upright proportions in contrast to the local vernacular. But these belie an older structure, a substantial mid-C16 storeyed house of three structural bays: the two bays to the S accommodating the *cegin fawr* (big kitchen) below a solar, the N bay a service room (or two) below a chamber. E wing added in the C19, masking the N end bay of the C17 front elevation, and tall sashes inserted. A mural staircase in the SW corner is probable, and the RCAHMW suggests a lateral fireplace in the solar. If so, an unusual arrangement. The house underwent modernization in the late C17. (A central staircase inserted on the W, its half-landing partly within the lateral fireplace, and the original rooms subdivided with little relationship to the earlier structure. Raised-and-fielded panelling fitted in an upstairs room and the windows enlarged.)

MAES-Y-CASTELL, ¾ m. W. Extensively rebuilt in 1886, but dated 1582 on a reset plaque with the initials EW GW. The particularly fine moulded ceiling in the W wing indicates a house of high status. The ceiling, of three bays, with main and secondary beams carrying the joists, all intricately moulded, is one of the finest in Gwynedd. Some late C16 panelling survives in one of the E rooms, and to the E front, a puzzling timber-framed wall jetties out above the lower storey.

CANOVIUM ROMAN FORT. The fort commands the crossing at the upper reach of the Conwy, a very strategic position in the road network. Excavated in the 1920s. It is likely to have been founded by Agricola in A.D. 77 with a broad clay rampart and timber buildings. In the mid C2 the defences and internal buildings were rebuilt in stone but the new narrow gateways suggest that the garrison may have been reduced. Occupation, particularly of the large civil settlement (*vicus*) to the S, continued into the early C4. The remains of the rampart can be clearly seen, especially where the road to the church crosses it, as can the confused remains of the *vicus* and the bath-house between church and river.

4863   CAERNARFON

Arfon, the fertile land looking over the Menai Strait towards Anglesey, is a well-defined landscape. Its fortified place, Caernarfon, has been seen as its capital since Roman times. The Roman fort of Segontium (occupied from A.D. 77 to A.D. 393) is on the plateau above the Seiont river; the medieval castle to the W, on a small peninsula between the Cadnant and Seiont rivers. Llanbeblig church just outside the Roman fort is still Caernarfon's parish church, left isolated from the Roman withdrawal till the later C20, since the town developed around the castle.

The potent myth of Caernarfon was its association with the Roman imperium (*see* Castle, p. 288 and St Peblig, below). This imperial aura was given form at the castle for the new English rule by reference to the banded walls and angled towers of Roman remains. The town was also to accommodate the government of NW Wales, as well as for the county of Caernarfon.* Part county town, part Welsh borough, it became in Pennant's pithy observation a place of lawyers, and rich in timber houses. It also became a focus for cultural life (an *eisteddfod* was held in the castle in 1821) and for early tourism after the Napoleonic Wars. The plateau E of the walled town provided both the superb public space of Castle Square and the imitative grid layout of the 1820s, reinforcing the character of a town of urban views, and views of the walls and castle from outside especially, rather than of individually fine buildings. This growth was interrupted by mid-C19 cholera outbreaks, prompting the building of new suburbs to the E and S. Then in a generation Caernarfon changed into an industrial town – albeit short-lived – with a thriving seaport. Railways into NW Snowdonia brought slate and metals down to new quays round the estuary and the new Victoria Dock.

A planning disaster struck in the 1970s. The inner relief road blasted away the W side of the Twthill to form a 50-ft (15-metre) cliff, then bridged over the Cadnant valley with a huge viaduct, inflicting a cruel wound, visually, historically and spatially.† A few terraced streets and villas survive round the look-out crest of the Twthill now accessed by vertiginous footbridges. One minor post-war success is the public housing around the ancient Christian site of Llanbeblig, low layouts in modest greys which leave its setting open enough. Overtaken by Bangor as a university town and transport hub, Caernarfon had few other reasons to build in the C20. But the C21 has begun with some optimism, though the risk is of excessive scale, already evident in the mixed-use development at Victoria Dock.

CHURCHES AND CHAPELS

St Peblig or Publicius, Llanbeblig. In a sense the mother church of Arfon, and still Caernarfon's parish church, though well outside the town walls, by the Roman fort. Peblig or Publicius, reputed son of the emperor Maxentius, founded the church after the expulsion of the Irish in 433. Another Early Christian site was near the river below; a chapel and well

---

*In the event Chester and Ludlow proved more convenient in the medieval period in respect of government of Wales, and the Act of Union of 1536 rendered such considerations void.
†Not for the first time was a road driven through historic fabric: Llanbeblig Road had done the same, through the site of Segontium.

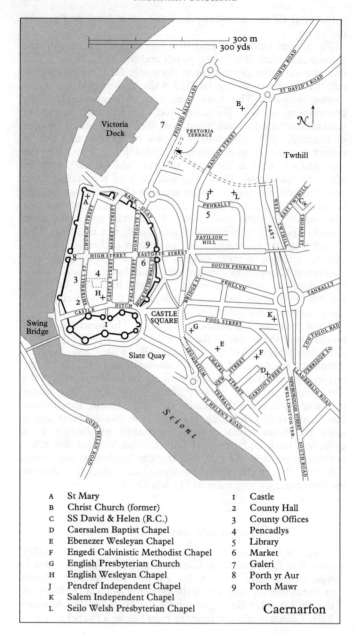

A	St Mary	I	Castle
B	Christ Church (former)	2	County Hall
C	SS David & Helen (R.C.)	3	County Offices
D	Caersalem Baptist Chapel	4	Pencadlys
E	Ebenezer Wesleyan Chapel	5	Library
F	Engedi Calvinistic Methodist Chapel	6	Market
G	English Presbyterian Church	7	Galeri
H	English Wesleyan Chapel	8	Porth yr Aur
J	Pendref Independent Chapel	9	Porth Mawr
K	Salem Independent Chapel		
L	Seilo Welsh Presbyterian Chapel		

Caernarfon

dedicated to Helen, probably Elen, wife of Maxentius, transmuted into St Helen, wife of Constantine. The very large churchyard is thought to have been the Roman, pre-Christian, cemetery. It looks as if the NW section is part of the raised round *llan*.

A cruciform church of some size with transeptal N chapel (the Vaynol Chapel), N porch and tall W tower. Of multiple building dates and of stone of various kinds and colours, among which one looks in vain for reused Roman material.* The various parts are loosely and confusingly joined, nave and chancel not aligned and the transepts roofed continuously N–S, across the crossing (cf. Clynnog Fawr). Chancel and s transept share a deep stepped plinth that looks late C14. Of the same date the s transept diagonal buttresses. The fine five-light s window cannot be earlier than *c.* 1400: ogee-headed lights, the wider middle one with continuous mullions framing four tracery lights; the others paired under tracery. This is of much higher quality than the two late Perp chancel windows (one s, and the former E window moved to the N transept), which have deep-coved surrounds, probably inserted at the same time as the chancel battlements. Was the s transept raised at the same time? The nave s has some ogee tracery in a two-light window, but with a late flat head (the matching window to the r. is a copy of 1840), but its walling may be the oldest, of the later C13 when Llywelyn the Last granted the church as a royal chapel to Aberconwy Abbey. Significant work must have been done in the C14 as indicated by a very good window re-set in the Vaynol Chapel N wall. Also two, mostly C19, two-light windows, one in the chancel s and one in the C19 N vestry, of a simpler C14 design; the chancel one may be original, the other a copy. The tower is probably C15 in its main part, with sw stair, but the bell-stage with bell-lights under flat hood-moulds is later, late C15 or early C16, as is the W window. The Irish stepped battlements, much eroded now, were finely done in sandstone. The Vaynol Chapel was presumably added to house the pompous table tomb of William Griffith and his wife, whose arms in the C16 four-light E window are dated 1593. But the entrance arch and roof within look late C15, so it may be a remodelling. Its C14 N window, moved from the chancel N presumably, is Dec, rare in the region, of two trefoiled lights with a trefoil interlaced with a concave-sided triangle in the head. Fine-featured heads to the hoodmould. The W door looks C16, now concealed by the infill vestry. This has a neat battlemented gable formed in 1894. The adjoining N transept has the re-set late C15 E window, but its brown stonework represents a rebuilding of 1775, which had two storeys of arched end windows, the upper lighting a gallery. C18 arched doorway, re-set to the l. as a vestry entry. The nave N wall is windowless,

---

*A Roman altar stone was found in the footings of the nave s wall in 1894.

the N door plain C15 hollow-moulded. N porch mostly of 1894, with some C16 timbers.

The work in 1894 by *R. G. Thomas* of Menai Bridge was one of the last thorough-going Victorian restorations of the region. Photographs record the previous interior, refitted in 1785 and 1840: plaster barrel ceilings, all-embracing galleries, an organ loft, a Gothick three-decker pulpit and box pews. Thomas confused a great deal. Externally his worst feature is the E window, for which unaccountably he moved the existing one. But he did reveal the C15 roofs in the nave, transepts and Vaynol Chapel. He built new the chancel roof, and his are the arches to the chancel, organ chamber, nave E, and tower; the chancel arch pierced for access to a stone pulpit. The broad C15 segmental pointed arch to the Vaynol Chapel has half-octagonal piers narrower than the walls in which they stand, which led the RCAHMW to suggest that this too was moved, in the late C16 when the chapel was built, but this seems a move too many.

The roof timbers which Thomas exposed are C15 and quite rich with embattled purlins, wind-braces and arch-braced collar-trusses. The transepts have a single roof from N to S, giving a strange dominance over chancel and nave. The S end has close-spaced arch-braced trusses (mostly renewed) as if for a celure, making a kind of nave and chancel facing the S wall. In this wall an eroded but ornate C14 TOMB-RECESS with a broad cinquefoiled arch with crockets, flanked by two pinnacles. To the l. a PISCINA in an ogee niche, the crockets hacked off the arch. All this may be coeval with the S window, *c.* 1400; but who, at this period, would all this commemorate? In the sanctuary, a CREDENCE TABLE, r., a C14 trefoiled niche over a moulded shelf. By the N door a three-sided STOUP. The Vaynol Chapel has two wide bays of arch-braced trusses and cusped wind-braces, more C15 than 1593.

FURNISHINGS. FONT. Octagonal, C15, re-dressed. – Good later C19 STALLS in the chancel and S transept. – In the S transept relics of the 1840 Gothick fittings: the former altar rails, around an altar made up of panels from the pulpit. – ORGAN. 1894, by *F. W. Ebrall*. – STAINED GLASS. E window, 1893, in the rich colours of *Mayer* of Munich. Chancel S windows: 1912, by *John Hall & Sons*, finely drawn; and 1894, with small C16-style scenes. – S transept S, 'Come unto me', crowded and colourful, with manacled slave, by *Mayer*, 1892. – N transept, 1894, *Lavers & Westlake*, deep colours. – Nave S, good Arts and Crafts glass, *c.* 1920, two figures in opaque blues and purples, l., and, r., Christ stilling storm, *c.* 1896. – MONUMENTS. – Vaynol Chapel. Alabaster tomb of William Griffith †1587, son of Sir William Griffith of Penrhyn, and his wife Margaret †1593. He is the likely builder of Plas Mawr, the town's lost Elizabethan mansion. They lie facing E, he in armour, she in Tudor finery with a lion at her feet, both on woven mattresses, his rolled under his head. The chest has a robustly secular character with egg-and-dart moulding and stumpy tapered fluted pilasters, each carrying a shield. Fifteen children are carved and named on the N and S; and on the W end is their son John, the donor, with wife and ten children. In the window jamb, a fine alabaster shield, with WG 1593. – Above the W door (visible from the vestry) a small relief of a surcoated figure, possibly a knight, C14. – Plaques. N, Frances Rowlands †1718, chastely Baroque with encomium; and four under the window, the l. one, Margaret Jones †1716, with incised winged head and bones. E wall, Capt. John Lloyd †1741, crude pediment, recording service to three monarchs, and William Williams †1769, with well-carved consoles. – Chancel, several brass plates, one S one a rarity: Richard Foxwist †1500, depicted bed-ridden holding a shield with the Five Wounds. Also Richard Rowland †1719, armorial; and Margaret Oliver of Massachusetts Bay †1796, 'Like other tyrants death delights to smite . . .' – N, Lewis Meyrick of Ucheldref, Corwen, †1690, and William Wynne †1760. – N transept, Richard Garnons †1841, tapering neo-grec, and William Bold †1609, armorial. – S transept, Margaret Griffiths †1784, slate-framed, the base fluted. – Nave S, two coffin-lids with carved crosses, and some fragments, C13–C14.

Crowded churchyard; some carved C17 TOMB-SLABS in the SE angle of the church. C19 stone piers and iron GATES, by a derelict SCHOOLROOM, of grey limestone, with pedimental gables, 1825.

ST MARY. From outside the church can be recognized by its bell-cote above the postern to the quay, which it blocks. Although the town church, this is still a chapel of ease to Llanbeblig, no new church having been planned for Caernarfon (unlike Conwy, where the abbey was adapted). It began as the garrison chapel, designed by the deputy master mason *Henry de Ellerton*, who obtained the licence for a chantry chapel in 1307. It occupies the burgage plot in the NW angle of the town walls, so the corner drum tower could accommodate the chaplain, his room reached by a mural stair from the vestry. The church's N and W walls are *Master James of St George*'s massive limestone masonry of 1284–90, incongruously pierced in 1809–11 by deep windows.* The buttressed S and E walls facing the town were rebuilt at the same time, with cusped two-light S windows and E window of intersecting tracery. The architect was *Benjamin Wyatt*, agent at the Penrhyn estate. He also re-set the E window at the W end. This has Dec tracery, its three cusped lancets grouped by intersecting ogee overarches, and the space formed below the pointed head makes an image-light.

The church has an unusual plan for its early date, the chancel and nave flanked by aisles of equal length, all arcaded and of one design. Nave piers of square section set diagonally, all chamfered, carry two-centred arches with dripmoulds and

---

* A guide of 1911 says that the N windows were opened about eighty years previously by an architect called *Dale*.

carved headstops. Chancel arch and its lateral arches of the same height, with similar details. Plaster barrel vaults of 1809–11. – PISCINA, C14 ogee style. – STAINED GLASS. E window, the style of *Percy Bacon Bros*, *c*. 1907. N aisle E, *Kempe & Co.*, 1933. S aisle E, probably *Lavers & Westlake*, *c*. 1910. – ORGAN, originally in the w gallery, 1813. – HATCHMENT with the arms of Rice Thomas of Coed Helen †1814.

CHRIST CHURCH, Bangor Street. Converted to a play centre, 1999. A large but lifeless church at the N entrance to the town, designed 1855 by *Anthony Salvin*, and built 1861–4. Penmaenmawr stone with Ruabon sandstone. Aisled clerestoried nave and tall chancel with a large traceried E window. The landmark SE tower, 1885–6, by *Arthur Ingleton* of Caernarfon, is more interesting, tinged with Early French in the double bell-lights and the lucarnes of the octagonal spire. Little discernible inside apart from the Bath stone chancel arch, the pulpit, and attractive glass of *c*. 1870 in the E window head.

SS DAVID AND HELEN (R.C.), Twthill East. Built as St David's for the Anglicans, 1873. Wide nave with a little plate-traceried rose over short W lancets. Polygonal apse. The NW tower has an octagonal spire entirely in yellow brick. Yellow brick interior banded in red.

CAERSALEM BAPTIST CHAPEL, Garnon Street. 1869, by *John Thomas*. Stuccoed, stylistically incoherent, the main window of two arched lights with Florentine tracery under a big quatrefoil roundel, a hoodmould curving around. Twin porches with front windows under Neo-Norman notched arches on

NEW BAPTIST CHAPEL, CARNARVON.

Caernarfon, Caersalem Baptist Chapel.
Engraving by John Thomas, 1869

columns. Galleries with panelled fronts; coved and ribbed plaster ceiling. Behind the pulpit a shallow apse with Corinthian arch.

EBENEZER WESLEYAN CHAPEL, Chapel Street. 1826, by *John Lloyd*. One of the first buildings in the new E suburb, and one of the first chapels in Wales to the new confident scale of urban Nonconformity. Broad ashlar two-storey front raised on a basement, approached by a ramp and steps. Three Regency Gothic upper windows, the tracery in iron, angle turrets and finials. Elaborate High Victorian Gothic porch with pinnacles, 1875–6, by *Richard Davies*, by whom the interior with curved-ended gallery with pierced iron panels, stepped down in front of the organ, was added in 1893. Curved balustraded pulpit. – STAINED GLASS. Lower front window, SS Martin and Michael, *c.* 1914, by *Jones & Willis*.

ENGEDI CALVINISTIC METHODIST CHAPEL, New Street. Disused. 1867, by *Richard Owens*. A stately and untypical Italianate work with a broad five-bay front and fine three-bay balustraded Tuscan portico sheltering three large arched doorways. Five arched upper windows; outer bays with quoin strips. The masonry contrasts crazed granite rubble with grey Anglesey limestone, the side gutters improbably of stone. Inside, ornate coffered ceiling with plaster roses. Curved-ended gallery with panelled front and octagonal pulpit in front of a pilastered organ recess (of 1890?).

ENGLISH PRESBYTERIAN CHURCH, Castle Square. 1882–3, by *Richard Owens*. An uncompromisingly Gothic intrusion into the square, and one of Owens's most serious efforts in the E.E. style. Yellow rock-faced Cefn sandstone in thin courses, with grey limestone. The main gable has strong verticals: a roundel above a tall triplet of multi-shafted lancets on a basement row of four low ring-shafted ones. Asymmetric wings, the l. one hipped with the stair-line marked by stepped windows and the r. one taken up as a tower and spire. Here the weakness of the design, the tower too thin for the scale. Focused interior: the boarded roof framing a Gothic organ recess.

ENGLISH WESLEYAN CHAPEL, Castle Street. 1877. Gothic with sandstone dressings, lancet-style. Stepped five-light main window, seriously detailed. But the tower, l., must always have been odd, even with its lost spirelet – steeply shaved on top to an octagonal flowerpot. Now the Masonic Hall.

PENDREF INDEPENDENT CHAPEL, Bangor Street. The chapel of 1791 was replaced in 1839 and altered in 1881. High box-like stucco front with a parapet and small pediment above four upper windows in late C19 pedimented surrounds. Below, an inset porch with Tuscan columns between channelled piers, 1839 perhaps, but the cornice looks cut short. The interior late C19 with boarding in the ceiling, and gallery with ornamented panels, on iron brackets. Balustraded *sêt-fawr* around a pulpit with arched panels, and a big arched pilastered pulpit-back.

Salem Independent Chapel, Pool Lane. A florid Venetian
Renaissance front achieved in two stages. Initially of 1862 by
the *Rev. Thomas Thomas*, his typical giant-arched front was
extended with pyramid-roofed corner towers framing a lean-
to porch in 1890–91 by *O. Morris Roberts*. Thomas's outer bays
have giant pilasters carrying lettered friezes and the central
arch is strongly voussoired. The additions have more wayward
detail: red granite window shafts, bi-colour slate roofs. Handsome interior of 1862 with Thomas's panelled pilasters to the
gallery fronts and a good plaster ceiling. *Sêt-fawr* of 1877–78
by *Richard Owens,* who did other alterations, including the
stained glass in the lobby; arcaded pulpit probably of 1890–91
when the organ loft was added.

CAERNARFON CASTLE*

Introduction

26, 31   Edward I's mighty stronghold, still the property of the Crown,
had a humble predecessor, an earth-and-timber motte and bailey
built as part of the Normans' short-lived territorial gains in NW
Wales. The motte, which remained until the late C19, dictated the
layout of the Upper Ward of the Edwardian castle, with the bailey
in the area now occupied by Castle Square to the E. The castle
was sited by the water, in common with many other Norman
castles in Wales. Its position across the S end of a peninsula that
jutted into the Menai Strait gave it its elongated figure-of-eight
plan. The river Seiont laps the S castle, while the river
Cadnant lay to the N and E, beyond the later town walls.

p. 290   The present castle and town defences, along with those at
Conwy and Harlech, were begun in 1283 following Edward I's
victory in the second Welsh war. A fortress-palace of great
proportions, there is nothing comparable to Caernarfon in
terms of design and the symbolism with which it is imbued.
At Caernarfon the symbolism is twofold, because not only
Edward's castle is on the site of its Norman predecessor, but also
because of the association of the area with Imperial Rome. The
nearby Roman fort of Segontium has long been associated with
the legends of the *Mabinogion*, most notably with Macsen Wledig
or the Emperor Magnus Maximus, the reputed father of
Constantine, and his visit to a far-off land and finding of a city
with towers of differing colours. It cannot be coincidence that
the imperial context of Caernarfon was carried into its design,
with its polygonal towers and bands of different-coloured
masonry, perhaps intended to mirror Roman walls that were still
standing in such places as York. Macsen also saw an ivory throne
with two golden eagles, and eagles, albeit in stone but possibly
painted, crested the greatest tower in the castle, the magnificent

---

*Not all features of the castle are visible, due to such attractions as the theatre and
museum occupying several of the chambers in the towers; thus, much use has been
made of the RCAHMW survey of 1960.

Eagle Tower at the W end of the site. Thus Caernarfon was a fitting capital of Edwardian North Wales, the administrative centre of the king's new shires of Anglesey, Caernarvon and Merioneth, and it remained the governmental centre of North Wales until the C17.

The initial phase of construction, overseen by *Master James of St George*, continued to 1292. This seems to have begun in summer 1283, when a large quantity of timber was shipped to the site, but the plan and design must have been drawn up earlier that year. The later sacking and partial destruction in the uprising of autumn 1294, when Caernarfon was lost to the Welsh for six months, led to the destruction of many records, so that we do not have a detailed picture of expenditure. However, it has been calculated that of the £9,414 spent on the castles in Wales in 1282–4, some £5,000 or more must have been on Caernarfon, the total for both castle and town wall being approximately £12,000 by 1292.

The ditch or moat on the N and E sides was begun in June 1283, with a timber palisade for protection. Houses in the way were cleared, and an earth bank was revetted with turf in the spring of 1284. Timber-framed buildings were erected within the planned enceinte, notably for the visit of the king and queen, and by the late summer masons were on site. The town defences to the N were begun in late 1284 and were virtually complete a year later, at a cost of just over £2,000. At the same time a quay was constructed on the N side of the town, with a pond (The King's Pool) to the E, serving the royal mill. Much of the workforce involved with the town walls was taken from the castle, so by late 1284 enough of the castle walls, at least on the S side, must have been built to what was deemed a secure height, with every effort during the following thirteen months being made to secure the perimeter to the N. So by 1292 it is thought that the exterior of the S and E façade, from the Eagle Tower to the North-East Tower, stood some 33 ft (10 metres) above the ground, with the Eagle Tower, then consisting of a basement with two storeys above, roofed temporarily by 1285. On the N side, the walls, including the King's Gate, may not have stood much above the ditch (by early 1296 their height varied from 11 ft to 24 ft, 3.5 metres to 7.5 metres). The extent of construction in 1284 can be gauged from the stone that projects from the NW face of the North-East Tower, which provided a line of sight for the alignment of the town defences with the castle on this side.

The regaining of town and castle early in 1295, following the Madog ap Llywelyn uprising, led to considerable expenditure. The rear walls of some of the towers were added at this time, e.g. the North-East and Black towers. *Walter of Hereford*, in charge of the building programme, and *Hugh of Leominster*, clerk of works, reported in early 1296 on progress. The town walls, which had virtually been razed, had been repaired ahead of schedule at a charge of over £1,000, more than half the original sum. Between 1295 and 1299 repairs cost over £4,400, but soon after there was a lull whilst efforts were concentrated on

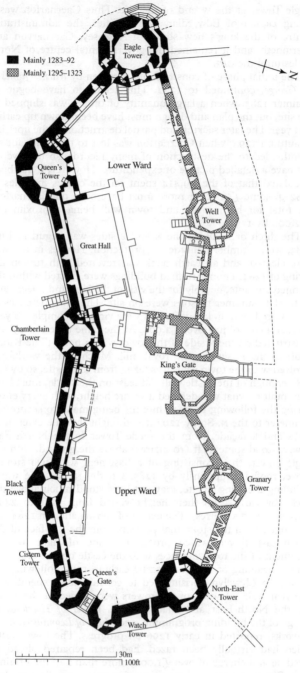

Mainly 1283–92

Mainly 1295–1323

Eagle
Tower

N

Queen's
Tower

Lower Ward

Well
Tower

Great Hall

Chamberlain
Tower

King's Gate

Black
Tower

Upper Ward

Granary
Tower

Cistern
Tower

Queen's Gate

North-East
Tower

Watch
Tower

30m
100ft

Caernarfon Castle.
Plan

Scotland. The pace and amount of work from late 1304 cannot be compared to the early years. Detailed records stop *c.* 1330, and by then the cost of all the king's works, including the quay, was over £25,000. In 1305 the inner faces of the s towers (Black, Chamberlain and Queen's) were completed, presumably with the towers being roofed at the same time. It is known that the Eagle Tower was raised a further storey, and that, together with the turrets, this was finished in or soon after 1317. The year before, a timber-framed building from Conwy, known as the hall of Llywelyn ap Gruffudd, was re-erected inside the castle to store supplies. In the early C14, prior to its removal, this hall became the core of the private residence intended for Edward I's son as Prince of Wales, the future Edward II. By 1320 the front half of the King's Gate was almost complete, with the statue of Edward II being set in its niche, and timber purchased for the gate's hall. In 1347, if not earlier, it was ordered that the timber bridges that enabled the wall-walk of the town walls to pass across the backs of the towers were to be replaced in masonry, and two survive today.

It is evident from the interior of the castle, even to the untrained eye, that the original plan was never finished, particularly in the Upper Ward, and we learn as much from William de Emeldon's survey of 1343. Much of the rear of the King's and Queen's gates was never realized, toothings for planned walls can be seen against the North-East and Granary towers, whilst the Upper Ward itself was meant to have been divided from the Lower Ward to the w by a thick curtain wall extending from the King's Gate to the s curtain by the Black Tower.

In terms of building work, the castle remained as it stood in the early C14 until the C19. It, and the town, were strong enough to hold out with a tiny garrison against the Welsh under Owain Glyndŵr in 1403–4, even with the French supporting the Welsh. By the early C16, although the walls were considered sound, many floors had collapsed in the towers owing to lack of repair. The Eagle Tower was re-roofed at this time, and repairs made to the town walls, with further repairs undertaken, including to the quay, in 1538. In 1595 the King's Gate was reported to contain two prisons, for debtors and for felons. By 1620 only the King's Gate and the Eagle Tower were still roofed, whilst most of the internal, probably timber-framed, structures had collapsed. Caernarfon surrendered to Parliament in 1646; in spite of an order in 1660, on the Restoration, to demolish both castle and town walls, little or nothing was carried out.

It was at the time of increasing prosperity through the growth of the C19 slate industry, with goods shipped from the new quay to the s, that increasing attention was paid to the castle. In the 1840s *Anthony Salvin* undertook repairs, and much was done during the deputy-constableship of Sir Llewelyn Turner in the closing decades of the C19, comparable to the work initiated by the 3rd Marquess of Bute at Caerphilly and Castell Coch in the later C19. The final storey of the Well Tower and the turret were

Caernarfon Castle.
Engraving by S. and N. Buck, 1742

added in 1891–2, staircases in the towers and battlements were renewed, the Queen's Tower was floored and roofed, whilst the N ditch was cleared, although not to its original width. Further work was undertaken in time for the 1911 Investiture of the Prince of Wales, and afterwards, up to 1914, notably re-flooring and roofing the Eagle and Queen's towers. Maintenance has continued ever since, the last major project being the clearance of the remaining buildings from the exterior of the town walls, completed in 1963. Not all the rooms in the castle are accessible to the public, for example in the King's Gate, whilst others are given over to exhibitions and to the museum of the Royal Welch Fusiliers.

The Exterior

Most visitors' first experience of the castle is the view of the S front, overlooking the main car park, for in spite of the re-creation of the N ditch, the town buildings on this side still hem in the approach to the King's Gate. The architectural drama of this fortress-palace is best appreciated by walking E from the Eagle Tower, past the Queen's, Chamberlain and Black towers and the Queen's Gate, and so round the NE corner and up into the King's Gate. Beyond the gatehouse is the Well Tower, with its basement doorway on the W side, placed as it was envisaged that small ships would enter a moat through a watergate to unload alongside the tower. Turner's late C19 restoration is evident from the crispness of the upper masonry, particularly the battlements, and through the use of granite and a buff-coloured sandstone that was quarried in NE Wales. The arch of the gate in the lee of the Chamberlain Tower and the steps down from it are modern. Arrowslits occur throughout the walls, with those in the NE curtain served by triple embrasures. Bands of brown Aberpwll sandstone ashlar from quarries on the Menai Strait contrast with the Carboniferous limestone, the main building stone, probably quarried from Penmon on Anglesey, creating a polychrome effect. However, the Aberpwll stone does not appear on the main N front, nor on the upper parts of the s front. That it was planned to have this effect on the N front, so that the banding ran all round, is clear from the lower courses on the North-East Tower, and to the E of the Eagle Tower, where sandstone continues into the curtain wall, but then comes to a stop. The lack of the courses of Aberpwll stone on the N is evidence for the two main construction periods, the banding being dropped when every effort was concentrated upon completing the castle after the destruction of 1294.

The s curtain is distinguished from that on the N by having two levels of continuous wall passages, and at the SE side there is a prominent glacis at the foot of the curtain which revetted the late CII Norman motte. Traces of a glacis exist on the N, but much is still buried.

The King's Gate

The tour of the interior starts with the main entrance, then examines the main features, moving anti-clockwise round the Lower Ward and from there to the Upper Ward.

The main entrance is through the KING'S GATE. Access now is up and over modern steps and a bridge, although originally the intention would have been for the royal household to enter the Inner Ward through the Queen's Gate on the E side, which would have been reached from a ramp up from what was the Prince's Garden, the area that is now Castle Square; a similar arrangement survives at Conwy. Arrowslits are visible in the ground and first floors of the King's Gate, with mullioned-and-transomed windows in the upper storeys, each with trefoiled lights set below a quatrefoil. Above the entrance arch, rising from a moulded string course, is a niche that houses a statue of Edward II, set below a crocketed canopy. Framing the niche are crocketed pinnacles and arrowslits.

In terms of its defences, the King's Gate, even in its very incomplete state, is one of the most impressive examples of medieval military architecture in Europe. Having crossed a drawbridge, the sockets and counterpoise pit for which still remain, the entrance passage in front passes between the two polygonal towers, and is defended by arrowslits, doorways, murder holes and four portcullises. This passage was intended to lead into a lobby, but now just takes the visitor into an open courtyard. Originally, from this lobby the passage continued w around the rear of the gatehouse and into the Lower Ward, and possibly another ran E into the Upper Ward. Whilst there is no evidence for the E passage, the remains of the vaulting for the w passage is visible on the external wall of that part of the gatehouse that is sometimes referred to as the Prison Tower, i.e. the tower that sits behind the main w tower of the gatehouse, and now housing the shop. Here too there is evidence for two further portcullises, giving the complex a total of six. The gate consists of a basement with three upper storeys, the topmost never completed. The basement chambers in the E and W towers, lit by slits, must have been entered from ground-floor trap doors, while the rectangular basement of the Prison Tower on the W could be entered from above, down a mural staircase, or at basement level through the W doorway, with drawbar and portcullis. The ground-floor chambers of the main towers are entered through passages, protected by murder holes, towards the rear of the main entrance passage. Both rooms contain fireplaces and doorways leading to latrines at the end of mural passages; opposite the passage in the E tower is a small chamber with fireplace set in a corner. Further along the main gate passage, now in the open, is the doorway into the Prison Tower, the one part of the castle which did not have a polygonal-shaped chamber, but a rectangular one.

The upper floors were reached from the staircase in the Prison Tower. There would also have been first-floor access along a passage within the incomplete curtain to the E, the stub of which projects from the SE corner of the gatehouse. The first floor consists of a chamber in each tower and a chapel. Both chambers contain hooded fireplaces and are well lit, and a doorway in the E room leads into a latrine. The mural passage to the latrine in the outer face of the W tower is entered just beyond the chapel; the passage and its equivalent on the E contain multiple arrowslits of a form enabling more than one archer to fire through the embrasure to a single external slit. That the room over the gate passage was a chapel is shown by the double piscina with trefoil head; it also housed two of the gate's portcullises and murder slots. To the rear of the gates, mural staircases led down from the main chambers to mezzanine rooms above the gate passage.

The second storey was to contain the principal chamber or hall, and is now reached only from the wall-walk, although the staircase in the Prison Tower must have been intended to provide the main access. Three two-light windows noted earlier, with seats in the embrasures, lit the hall, and it can be seen in this outer wall that the two arrowslits in the centre are both served by three embrasures, as on the floor below. On the E side a mural passage leads to a latrine.

The Lower Ward

To the W of the King's Gate is the LOWER WARD, dominated by the Eagle Tower at the far end. The CURTAIN WALL on the N side, connecting the King's Gate with the Well Tower, contains a mural passage at ground level leading to a latrine in the NW face of the W tower of the gatehouse. Built against the curtain between the gatehouse and the Well Tower is the KITCHEN range. This is a surprisingly small structure for such a great castle, but the springing for a large arch, set in the middle of the N wall, indicates that a greater building was planned originally. On the E side stood a two-storey accommodation block, while to the w, against the Well Tower, is the setting for two cauldrons, heated by fires below, the toothing for the chimney set in the N curtain; this has been interpreted as a boiling house. Behind the cauldron settings is a channel for piped water from a tank in the tower, as well as a wall cavity for storing foodstuffs. Between the boiling house and the accommodation block by the King's Gate block lay the kitchen itself, marked by further toothings running up from the floor that were for a wall that may have housed the main fireplace; a mural passage linked the boiling house with the main kitchen. Other features include a recess that housed a sink, a sluice, and a rubbish disposal shaft in the wall thickness, whilst the line of the water pipe from the Well Tower is still evident in the mural passage.

The WELL TOWER is one of the most interesting features of the castle in terms of household organization. It was intended that goods should be received directly into its basement from the moat, a vessel having entered through a watergate that abutted the Eagle Tower, but this scheme was never completed. A portcullis protected this basement entrance, and there were also two murder holes and two doorways; this room also had its own access down steps from within the Lower Ward and through a doorway with a drawbar. Above the basement are three storeys, the topmost largely C19 restoration. Corbels and settings for the main beams that carried the floor joists mark the floor levels. The rooms were well appointed, with fireplaces and latrines set within mural passages, and single and two-light windows, as well as slits. The ground-floor entrance leads to the stair to the upper levels, and on the r. is the well chamber itself; opposite the well is the setting for a tank or cistern from which water was piped to the kitchen. To the l. of the main entrance a doorway with drawbar opened into a small lobby, giving access both to the main chamber on the ground floor and to the latrine passage. From the w window in the chamber steps lead down to a small chamber from which the portcullis and murder holes, protecting the basement entrance from the moat, were controlled. On the first floor a small chamber with fireplace, above the well-head, may have served as a kitchen to the main chamber at this level. A recent re-examination has led to the suggestion that the tower's ground-floor chamber was designed to act as the counting house, the centre for the management of the royal household's finances and the issuing of daily foodstuffs.

In the CURTAIN WALL to the w, whose wall-walk communicates with the Eagle and Well towers, are a number of arrowslits, as well as evidence for buildings erected against the curtain: a restored fireplace adjacent to a two-light window, corbels for the roof and toothing for return walls. A mural passage houses a latrine. At the w end of the basement of this range there was access to the basement of the Eagle Tower. The flimsy evidence for the range built here implies that most of these walls were timber-framed, even if the original intention had been stone throughout.

31   The EAGLE TOWER, with its walls 18 ft (5.5 metres) thick, is one of the great buildings of the Middle Ages, a fitting residence for Edward's justiciar in North Wales, Otto de Grandison. Originally it consisted of two floors over a basement, with ten-sided chambers. A moulded string course marks the point where the upper storey, with its turrets, was added in the early C14; another string course runs below the battlements and around the turrets. The main entrances to the basement, besides the one noted above, lie to the E, from the Lower Ward, and to the W, from the quay. Steps down from the Lower Ward lead to the E entrance. Open doors and the arrowslit in the deep embrasure on the S side would have provided the only natural light for the chamber beyond, the room through which anyone arriving by sea would have entered the castle. Although no fireplace was provided, some domestic comfort was intended with the provision of a latrine at the end of a passage off the S embrasure. The passage on the W has two doorways and a portcullis. Just before the inner doorway another passage led up to the upper part of the planned Water Gate; although never built, the responds for the gate and the chase for a portcullis are visible on the exterior of the tower.

Another doorway in the tower opens into a lobby or passage, connecting the Lower Ward with the ground-floor chamber; the doorway was secured by a drawbar. Off the S side of the lobby itself is a passage to the staircase to the upper floors, whilst at the foot of the stair a doorway leads into a small octagonal groin-vaulted wall chamber; it may have been a chapel as there is evidence for what may have been a piscina. On the N side of the lobby a doorway, also with drawbar, leads into the mural passage round the E and N sides of the tower, with two mural chambers, a doorway into the main room and also one to the former N range in the lower ward; the passage continues to a doorway up to the abandoned watergate, and adjacent arrowslit. In the chamber itself, which is lit by two-light windows, is a large hooded fireplace. A doorway to the NE leads into the mural passage noted above, whilst on the W another passage leads to the portcullis chamber over the external entrance. The doorway on the S opens into a passage running E and W. At the E end of this passage is a rectangular chamber housing a latrine with a ventilation shaft, whilst the hexagonal room at the W end is lit by an arrowslit.

The first floor was the main chamber of the tower until it was raised a further storey. Here the mural passages, with chambers, are almost continuous, and there is a latrine chamber and octagonal chapel on the S side; in the chapel a trefoil-headed piscina. The rectangular mural chamber on the N side has a fireplace and a window with seats; to the E a small chamber containing a window with the arms of the future King Edward VII as Prince of Wales. Two-light windows to the NW and NE, set in large embrasures, light the main room, now occupied by the theatre, although the NE window was altered to take a doorway to the N curtain wall. On the S side, a fire-place with its lintel flush with the wall.

The topmost floor is entered directly from the staircase, lit by a two-light window at this point, the doorway into the chamber having a drawbar. Two-light windows set in stepped embrasures and provided with window seats lie to the NW and NE. Fireplace on the W side, with a flush lintel like that on the floor below. A mural passage to the S leads to a latrine, whilst the rectangular chamber to the N of the stair may have been a kitchen, and is lit by a two-light window. A further chamber is entered from the NE window embrasure. The stair continues to the roof, and on up into the one of the three turrets. The battlements have not been restored. Arrowslits are set in alternate merlons, and on the copings of the merlons and those of the turrets are the remains of stone figures. The more substantial remains of an eagle surmount the W turret.

The curtain wall between the Eagle and Queen's towers has three embrasures for arrowslits; the wall passage here is open to the elements, but was to have been roofed. It runs contin-uously along the S front and originally on through the Queen's Gate to the N side of the North-East Tower, although wooden doors could block access. The wall-walk above is restored. Foundations of a building are to be seen at this point. The QUEEN'S TOWER, once the Banner Tower, is now occupied by a museum. In the NW corner a staircase leads to the first and second floors, and on to the roof with its hexagonal turret, also connecting with the mural passages within the thickness of the external face of the upper floors. A doorway with drawbar enters a lobby and so on to the ground-floor chamber; a passage off the lobby leads to a latrine. The room has arrowslits in three of the five outer faces, with a lighting slit high up between two of them, and two windows on the N, whilst the upper floors are mainly lit on the N side with two-light tran-somed windows. All the main chambers have fireplaces, and in each a doorway on the NE leads into a small rectangular chamber, that on the second floor entered through one side of a window embrasure. All three small chambers may have been chapels, for which the trefoil-headed stoup and piscina in the uppermost provide the most unequivocal evidence. The mural passages have arrowslits, and give access to latrines in the SW corner. The turret houses a small chamber at half-height, and a narrow flight of stairs continues to the summit. Above the steps the lintel contains a round hole for the base of a pole from which the banner flew.

The curtain wall to the E contains upper and lower wall passages with embrasures, which, along with the wall-walk, link the Queen's and Chamberlain towers. The roof of the lower passage, consisting of slabs on corbels, is medieval, that of the upper passage is of 1901. The gateway to the quay lies to the E, and between the two towers are the foundations of the hall. The remains of the moulded plinth at the W, dais, end of the hall is the sole indication of the former quality of this building.

The hall's screens passage communicated directly with the CHAMBERLAIN TOWER by a doorway on the NW side of the tower, via a passage that led to a doorway into the ground-floor chamber and on to the staircase to the upper floors. The W end of the passage also gave access to steps up to the curtain, and so on into a latrine; a latrine also lies at this point on the two upper levels. The main stair could also be reached from another doorway, set in the NE corner of the tower where it faced the Upper Ward, and there is a further doorway into a rectangular chamber on the NE side, and so on through to the main room. The ground and first floors with their adjacent NE chambers are now museum and offices, the first-floor NE chamber formerly being a chapel. The main rooms all contained fireplaces, and the upper floors were lit from the N; the ground floor has an embrasure on the SW and SE sides. The upper floors have a chamber on the NW through which there was access to the continuous wall passages round the tower. The main stair leads up to the original medieval battlements and to the turret, against the foot of which sits the only surviving medieval chimney in the castle.

The Upper Ward

32 The curtain running E to the Black Tower has two wall passages, the upper never roofed as intended. Midway the curtain makes an adjustment in its alignment to account for the now destroyed motte and its ditch. The foundations for internal buildings run across the back of the curtain and adjacent towers. The BLACK TOWER only contains two floors, the lower equating with the first floor of the other towers. Its rear wall was completed in a later phase. On the W side the wall passage enters the lower chamber and continues from a doorway on the opposite side; the passage on the W also leads on the N to the stair to the upper floor, and to a latrine on the S. The lobby of the stair opens to the chamber on the N side of the tower. There is no fireplace in the main chamber, and three embrasures light the room. The floor above has a fireplace. Slits on to the mural passage provide some light, as does a two-light window overlooking the NE chamber. This room was a chapel, with an ante-chapel to the W. The mural passage passes round the S front and contains slits and embrasures, as well as a latrine on the SW side. The stairs continue to the tower's battlements and turret. At roof level steps on either side take the wall-walk across the tower; it is possible that a third storey was planned, with the present steps giving access to another wall passage rather than an open wall-walk.

The lower level of the small CISTERN TOWER or turret is entered from the wall passage in the curtain, the groin-vaulted chamber having three arrowslits. The upper storey originally contained a cistern to collect rainwater, channelled by duct to a latrine shaft in the Queen's Gate. A section of this stone duct can be seen running across an arrowslit in the curtain to the E. A drain at the bottom of the cistern fed into this duct, enabling the cistern to be emptied totally.

The QUEEN'S GATE, like the King's, lies unfinished to the rear. Originally a stepped ramp led up to the gate, a turning bridge giving access to the gate passage that was framed by the two polygonal towers. The sockets for the axle on which the bridge pivoted are visible below the modern wooden platform. The passage was defended by door and portcullis, as well as several murder holes. On either side of the passage lay a porter's lodge or guard chamber, each with an arrowslit. The lower wall passage from the Cistern Tower provided access to the S tower, and a latrine is situated by the entrance. As the rear wall of the N tower was never built, the entrance arrangement is uncertain; a latrine is situated at the end of a passage that is entered from one side of the embrasure. There is evidence for an inner portcullis and doorway on the NW side of the gate's S tower, again never completed, but, as in the King's Gate, the main passage may have led into a lobby from which access to the Upper Ward was gained, through this inner doorway. It must have been intended to light the first-floor chambers from windows overlooking the Upper Ward, as the outer face of the towers contains the continuation of a mural passage that ends on the N side of the first floor of the North-East Tower; mural passages were omitted from the second phase to which the N front largely belongs. It was intended that the second floor of the gatehouse would contain a hall, similar to that in the King's Gate, lit by three arrowslits in the outer wall, although as with the floor below the main windows must have been intended to be in the inner wall. At this level the wall-walk led to the Watch Tower to the N. Latrines were located N and S of the hall.

A short passage and stairs lead to the top of the WATCH TOWER. The crenellations retain their medieval form, with grooves to take shutters in order to close off the crenels, and the coping stones on the merlons retaining the bases of finials. Those on duty on the tower were afforded a measure of shelter by a pent roof. Beyond lies the octagonal NORTH-EAST TOWER, another of only two main storeys; an exhibition occupies the ground floor. The outer half of the tower belongs to the initial phase, the rear forming part of the later build associated with the N front, as the wall butts against the inner face of the E curtain. Toothing on the exterior, either side of the main entrance, is evidence that walls were planned, one to meet the Granary Tower to the W, the other to meet the SE curtain by the Queen's Gate. Above the toothing of the N example is a doorway to a proposed wall passage. The ground-floor chamber is entered through a passage secured by a doorway with drawbar and also by murder holes; the room itself has a fireplace and a latrine at the end of a passage in the N wall, and is lit from two two-light windows set high up. The principal chamber on the first floor has a hooded fireplace, a two-light window in an embrasure with seats, and slits leading to one opening on the outer face of the N wall. On the S side a doorway leads to the usual first-phase mural passage, at one end of which is a latrine. Above the restored battlements is the usual turret, with a difference in that it has loops set below the crenellations.

Set into the curtain between the North-East and Granary towers is a remarkable range of arrowslits, with a variant form in the wall that links the Granary Tower with the King's Gate, at both ground and upper levels. They are similar to those already seen in the top floor of the King's Gate, for each arrowslit on the external face is served by three openings set in the inner wall, allowing more than one archer to discharge his bow. Buildings were planned against the curtains here, as indicated by the corbels, roof creasing and two-light windows, set below quatrefoil openings.

The GRANARY TOWER, of four storeys, is the least accessible tower, for only the upper, roofless chamber can be visited. A doorway from the Upper Ward leads into a lobby, with a passage running round the tower on either side. Opposite the entrance is the modern door into the ground-floor chamber; the original doorway lies on the W side, at the end of the passage. There is also a latrine at this point, and access to the stair to the upper floors. The room is lit by slits and has a fireplace; the basement was entered through a trap door in the floor. The E passage leads to a well in the NE corner of the tower. A window similar to those in the adjacent curtain walls lights the heated first-floor chamber, and in the embrasure a passage leads into a latrine. A square chamber to the NE can only be reached from a window embrasure in the curtain wall to the E. The topmost storey has a fireplace with hood, and a two-light window, as well as a loop overlooking the Upper Ward, and set in the N wall is the middle of three slits leading to a single external loop; the slit on the W is reached from the latrine mural passage, whilst that to the E is set into the window embrasure. Doorways lead out to the adjacent wall-walks, and the remains of finials can be seen on the battlements, above which is the usual turret.

TOWN WALLS.* The borough's defences include eight towers, seven of which are semicircular, whilst the northernmost is circular. There are two main gatehouses, on the E and on the W, and at least two postern entrances, with perhaps a third by the Chapel of St Mary. The towers, which may have had timber-framed rear walls, consist of two storeys with battle-ments, the upper storeys having arrowslits, the lower floors being unlit except probably from the rear. The remains of finials can still be seen on some crenellations.

---

*The numbering of towers and gates around the wall follows that in the current Cadw guidebook.

On leaving the castle by the King's Gate and turning r., Hole in the Wall Street takes one behind the circuit of walls, whilst Greengate Street skirts the outside. On the castle side of the first tower there is the first postern or Green Gate, with evidence for a portcullis and doorway with drawbar; the passage passes through a thickening of the town wall that carried a flight of steps up to the wall-walk and the top of TOWER ONE, the upper treads of which still remain. Most of the facing masonry within this tower (and TOWER SIX) has been robbed. Much of the curtain adjacent to TOWER TWO and the Exchequer Gate has been rebuilt in regular courses of masonry with a pink hue. A feature seen best here is the remains of the masonry revetment to the earthen bank. The EXCHEQUER GATE (TOWER THREE) was the main entrance to the medieval town, and was also the administrative head-quarters of NW Wales; it is also known as the Great or East Gate. In spite of much rebuilding in the C18 and C19, and some C20 reconstruction, the medieval form is still evident, with twin rounded towers framing a central passage. Evidence for a latrine corbelled out on the N side. The original bridge to the gate was replaced by a five-arched stone structure c. 1301–2, although the innermost arch must be no earlier than the mid C16, as a timber drawbridge here was under repair in 1520. The gate originally had a barbican, similar to that which survives in front of the West Gate.

TOWER FOUR and the curtain wall beyond it to TOWER FIVE represent the best-preserved section. The tower stands to full height, with the bridge carrying the wall-walk behind it, while the town wall beyond has traces of the arrowslits at bat-tlement level. Three streets pass through modern entrances in the N section of the circuit. TOWER SIX also retains its wall-walk bridge. At the NW corner is the circular TOWER SEVEN, which in the early C14 became part of the Chapel of St Mary (see p. 285), and the interior has been adapted for ecclesiasti-cal use. The first floor, reached from a mural stair into a lobby with a two-light window, was residential, with a hooded fire-place. Steps led up to the battlements on one side of the room, and a passage led off to what must have been a latrine. A blocked doorway is visible in the town wall immediately S of Tower Seven, originally forming the W entrance into the chapel and replacing an earlier postern, the evidence for which is adja-cent. Much of TOWER EIGHT is modern, forming part of a later house (Landmark Trust). Beyond, the much altered WEST GATE or Porth-yr-Aur (Golden Gate; Tower Nine), with a small barbican projecting from it, which gave access to the medieval quay. The Royal Welsh Yacht Club occupies this twin-towered gatehouse (see p. 305), and the windows and battle-ments are C19. There is evidence for the portcullis in the gate passage, and on the N side at first-floor level is a corbelled latrine. The N and S walls of the gate are medieval, but the chambers within may have been enclosed at the rear with a timber-framed wall, perhaps later.

From the gatehouse the town wall runs to the castle, with one further mural tower (TOWER TEN) in which an original arrowslit is visible. A modern entrance into Castle Ditch is on the site of another postern, possibly that built in the C15 to replace a smaller doorway close by. From here the town wall runs to meet the castle, this section dating from 1326 after the plans for a large watergate at this point had been abandoned (*see* Eagle Tower, p. 296).

PUBLIC BUILDINGS

COUNTY HALL, Castle Ditch. 1863. An exemplary civic building, by *John Thomas*, County Surveyor, on the site of the medieval court house and Justiciar's lodging. Classical, of blue-grey rock-faced squared rubble, with dressings of large pieces of creamy-grey Anglesey limestone. Seven bays. Central Doric portico of four columns supporting a pediment enriched with a blindfold figure of Justice. Blind projecting outer bays with pilasters. Overscaled new entrance to the Crown Court, in Shire Hall Street, by *Dan Mitchell* of *PSA Wales*, 1989. (Council chamber to the r., with coved ceiling, domed lantern and apsidal recess with Tuscan archway.)

COUNTY OFFICES, Shirehall Street. Originally the County Gaol, 1867–9, by *John Thomas*, replacing one of 1793 by *Joseph Turner*. Converted to county offices 1928–30 with most of the prison windows enlarged and a council chamber inserted. Then, *c.* 1985, another council chamber was added by *Dilwyn Gray-Williams* of *Gwynedd County Architects*, with a towered entry in a chocolate-box approximation of Dewi-Prys Thomas's Pencadlys across the street. T-plan, three-storey gaol, with simplified Gothic detail of a serious kind. The front office range is hipped with segmental arches over paired and triple sash windows. The rear range has impressive giant arched end windows to light the full-height galleried cell block. On the back, some original barred windows at basement level, and a canted centre projection to overlook exercise yards. Detached outlying houses for officials on Shirehall Street, with banded stonework, the N one enveloped in the 1985 additions, with the blank slate walls of the council chamber beyond. Inside, the cell block retains in part the spine corridor and has some cells in the basement. New stairs give access to the 1928 council chamber, with plaster shallow barrel vault, oak furnishings padded in blue leather, and on the end walls large and gloomy lunette paintings: Hywel Dda lawgiving behind the dais, signed *S. Agnew Mercer & Sons*; Snowdon opposite. The 1985 chamber is an elongated octagon with steeply raked seating. The over-dominant ceiling, a large roughcast upturned bathtub, is suspended to allow very diffuse light around the perimeter.

COUNTY OFFICES (Swyddfa Arfon), Penrallt. 1990, by *Pritchard Owen Davies Partnership*. Crowning the Penrallt site, in loud brown-red brick. Wide eaves with strip windows below. Council chamber, l., with chamfered corners and cut roofs.

The green patent-glazed entrance is on the diagonal, up a flight of steps.

WELSH ASSEMBLY OFFICES, Penrallt. 1974, by *PSA* with *Brian Lingard & Partners*. Big four-storey block, the top floor behind large dormers. Continuous strips of window alternate with bands of pre-cast concrete, punctuated with full-height rubble stair-towers.

ROYAL TOWN COUNCIL OFFICE, Pavilion Hill. Built 1884, by *Richard Owens*, as a workmen's institute, with library, lecture room and an art room with roof glazing. A bold sandstone Civic Gothic building with big traceried windows, typical of the improvements of the mayoralty of Sir Llewelyn Turner. Windows stacked on four levels to Bridge Street, the top ones gabled. The grand entrance on Pavilion Hill, with a gabled hood over the doorway and shafted windows above. Extended, l., 1912, by *Rowland Lloyd Jones*, for the Royal Borough Council. Chamber with ribbed barrel ceiling and panelled dado. In the basement, the public baths, with some surviving bath cubicles and glazed tiling.

GWYNEDD COUNTY HALL (PENCADLYS CYNGOR GWYNEDD), 1982–6, by *Merfyn Roberts* and *Terry Potter* of *Gwynedd County Architects*, with a historian's overview for the elevations supplied by *Dewi-Prys Thomas*. The large county office squeezed into Castle Street and Shirehall Street adopts a strategy of fragmented planning to reconcile it with the historic Caernarfon townscape. It always risked architectural over-ambition – an unconvincing relationship with the castle, an over-mighty relationship with the town. And the self-conscious urbanism of opening secondary spaces in the medieval street grid and forming quasi-collegiate connections seems only partially successful, particularly at the price of the six-storey office-block at its centre. The project's weakness lies perhaps more in the style than the brief, since anything other than a rigorous discipline and high-quality materials (as at the Victorian County Hall) is destined to look insubstantial just where the opposite is needed. Today it looks a case of the budget having driven the conservationist architectural approach of its time beyond what it can sustain, so that it relies on pastiche instead of eloquent restraint.

The larger part of the OFFICES is grouped between Castle Street and Shirehall Street, with a courtyard between, facing a new square in Castle Street. Smooth rendered walls painted a greenish colour, strips of small-paned windows below the eaves or grouped singly elsewhere, with coloured render surrounds, and at street level, low arcades on stubby concrete piers with over-sized capitals. A two-storey range E of the new square, with mansard roof and a covered way on paired steel columns. At the corner with Castle Ditch, a tall TOWER, symbolic of the revival of Welsh local government and *Dewi-Prys Thomas*'s own creation. Stone base, rising to a timber *bretèche*, in the loose, Postmodern relationship with historic building which does not quite carry visual conviction.

POLICE STATION (former), Castle Ditch. Built in 1853 as the first County Hall, by *John Lloyd*. Classical, in limestone ashlar. Three storeys and three bays, the advanced centre rusticated below and pedimented above. Lower windows and door set back within semicircular recesses.

PUBLIC LIBRARY, Penrallt. 1982, by *Gwynedd County Architects* (project architect *Terry Potter*), on the platform of the 1877 Eisteddfod Pavilion. The most satisfying of the Penrallt buildings. Three limestone pavilions stepping up the hill, linked by lower blocks which are glazed or rendered.

ERYRI HOSPITAL, 1 m. s. Stark workhouse range of *c.* 1840, with pedimented centre, since entirely slate-hung on the s front. Additions include the Infirmary, 1881, by *Thomas & Ingleton* and a large stuccoed complex, 1911, by *Rowland Lloyd Jones*.

YSGOL SYR HUGH OWEN, Bethel Road. The earliest block, sw, by the County Architect, *Rowland Lloyd Jones*, 1898. Bright red brick, coped gables, sandstone dressings. Mid-C20 T-plan addition, NE, with a shallow glazed bow above the entrance. The latest buildings, by *Gwynedd County Architects* (*Graeme Hughes*), in four phases 1988–2002, continue the red brick and the gables of the first building but have a convincing vocabulary of their own, substituting brick for stone dressings.

YSGOL PENDALAR, off Bethel Road. By *Gwynedd County Architects* (*Graeme Hughes*), 2007. Special needs school in the relaxed style of the recent County Schools.

CAERNARFON YOUTH CENTRE, South Penrallt. Former British School of 1858, later the Board School, by *John Lloyd*. Tall single storey with shaped gables, a frontispiece with slender turrets, and the schoolmaster's house behind (s).

GALERI, Victoria Dock, 2005, by *Richard Murphy Architects* of Edinburgh. Conceived to bring together creative enterprise businesses and performance activities. In plan, three parallel strips, with the long sides SE and NW. Outer strips accommodate offices with a ground-level restaurant and second-floor music school, while the taller, wider centre has the auditorium at one end and two levels of studio at the other, divided by a full-height foyer lit from a clerestory, with a bar below a minstrels' gallery. Painted steel frame, expressed inside and out, with horizontal boarding and dark-painted windows, typical of Murphy. Immaculately detailed and entirely at ease in the dockland setting. Inside, wood and steel again, and shiny polished plaster coloured dark red, purple and pale green. The magic of the place lies in the transparency between the internal galleries and the glazed offices, and the clever circulation pattern, which leads from one end of the foyer to the other to reach the top floor.

SEGONTIUM ROMAN FORT, Llanbeblig Road, ½ m. SE. The main Roman base in North Wales from the Conquest till the end of the C4. It was garrisoned for longer than any other fort in the region, which suggests that it had become an economic and administrative base as well as a military one. The fort was founded by Agricola in A.D. 77 or 78. In the early C2 the defences were rebuilt in stone. The internal buildings, too, were gradually replaced in stone. There was major rebuilding activity around A.D. 140, 200, 300 and 350. The site has been extensively excavated, revealing the traditional arrangement of barracks, granaries, garrison headquarters, commander's offices and gateways whose foundations have been laid out for visitors. The bath building was in the S sector. A small museum on site displays the finds from the fort and from other sites in the vicinity, such as the Mithraeum discovered E of the fort and the Roman cemetery on the site of the new cemetery across the road from St Peblig's church. The civil settlement (*vicus*) is covered by the streets of the modern town S and W of the fort, but there is one surprising survival: a substantial walled enclosure (Hen Waliau, *see* Perambulation 6). The fort features as Caer Aber Seint, 'the many-towered fort at the mouth of the Seiont', in the *Dream of Macsen Wledig*.

PERAMBULATIONS

1. The Walled Town

The WALLED TOWN is still more than half surrounded by water, its walls liberated outside in the 1960s from houses built against them since the C18, its ditches and quays still legible. Its interconnection with the commercial and industrial extension of the town after 1800 is modestly but effectively handled. Within, most of its oldest buildings were replaced in the same era, but it possesses urban qualities which so far have maintained balance between residence, shops and administration. The evident risks are pressures from the latter and from tourism; Caernarfon's walled centre is too precious to lose as a functioning town.

CASTLE DITCH, a mid-C19 street created by *Salvin,* connects Castle Square through the gap in the medieval circuit of the walls left for the castle's ditch, and continues N of the castle to the quay W of the Water Gate. PALACE VAULTS, mid-C19, four stuccoed bays, central pediment and paired Ionic columns at street level. Then more stucco, three-storey shops with flats above, in a variety of colours, and from here a view past the County Hall (*see* p. 302) to the water beyond the arch in the ragged and never-completed wall closing off the ditch. Just outside, r., the ANGLESEY HOTEL replaces the early to mid-C18 CUSTOM HOUSE. The quay along the Menai Strait, originally of wood, now the PROMENADE, was rebuilt in stone after the rising of 1291. Disused after the Slate Quay and Victoria Dock were made, the whole has an incomparable role as a westerly walk, the view excelled only by that of the walled citadel from the sea itself. Midway along, PORTH YR AUR gateway, the upper storey rebuilt *c.* 1870 as the ROYAL WELSH YACHT CLUB by Sir Llewelyn Turner, of the slate-owning family, responsible for much later C19 civic improvement. Caernarfon windows in brown freestone, a balcony on the

small barbican. Next, the BATH TOWER, so-called after Lord
Anglesey established a public bath house here in 1823, with
sea-water baths in the lowest floor and a billiard room above.
The concert room at the top, with big Neo-Elizabethan
windows, was used as a chapel when St Mary's Training
College took over in 1856. Restored by the Landmark Trust.
Round the angle tower, the town can be entered from BANK
QUAY through the break at Church Street, the first of three
breaches made in the N wall by the Corporation, before 1777.
CHURCH STREET is residential in character. Opposite St Mary's
church, TAN-Y-MUR, flats for the elderly by *Brian Lingard &
Partners*, 1963, followed by a red brick Victorian terrace with
bay windows. Opposite, CAE'R MENAI, r. (and backing onto
the Bath Tower), established as St Mary's Training College in
1856; it then became the first County School in 1894. Nos. 9,
7 and 1, r., Late Georgian, with pleasing proportions and nice
doorways. On the l., part of Plas Bowman (*see* High Street,
p. 307). SHIREHALL STREET continues s, curving towards the
castle's inner front. On the r., the canted slate wall of the new
council chamber, then the former gaol with its two detached
wings (*see* p. 302). On the l., the arcaded façade of Pencadlys,
finishing with Dewi-Prys Thomas's Portmeirion-like tower.
The parallel and central N–S axis is CASTLE STREET. On the l.,
the Wesleyan chapel (p. 287). In the new square formed to face
Pencadlys, a tall riven slab SCULPTURE, of purple slate
surmounted with the Gwynedd eagle, commemorating the
defeat of 1282, by *Glen Hellman*, 1982. On the N side of the
square, PLAS LLANWNDA, an early C19 ashlared stone front
with, on Castle Street, the shallowest bay imaginable. The
square, more than any other part of the Pencadlys scheme, is
imbued with the spirit of Clough Williams-Ellis: the little iron
balcony on the Neo-Georgian s block (salvaged by Dewi-Prys
Thomas from a building in Liverpool) and the veranda-like
double columns of the low E range, repeated again in the
Pencadlys courtyard. Nos. 6–12, l., a mid-C19 stucco terrace,
with attached Ionic colonnade and pediment. No. 4 has in a
reused Gothic niche, an angelic choirboy holding the Foxwist
arms, dated 1628. Opposite, No. 1, early red brick.
  On the corner of Market Street, the arcade of the former
meat market survives as the ground floor of the very tall
stuccoed WORKING MEN'S CONSERVATIVE CLUB, 1886.
In MARKET STREET, stucco terraces, l., No. 3 dated 1760.
No. 12, r., a large Victorian Italianate town house in tuck-
pointed red brick with lavish sandstone dressings. At the end,
TOWER HOUSE, r., the town house of the Glynne family of
Glynllifon. Large, earlier C19, a stark façade of triple sashes
without a door. NORTHGATE STREET returns s from Bank
Quay, with the much altered C17 BLACK BOY INN, r., then
C19 stucco houses, l.
On PALACE STREET, running s, the MARKET, by *John Lloyd*,
1832. Minimal Late Georgian ashlar detail; iron gates and a
pivoting crane. A fine galleried interior, remodelled in the

later C19, with big kingpost trusses above a clerestory. The building is on the site of Plas Mawr, Caernarfon's outstanding Elizabethan town house (and similar to its namesake in Conwy). Opposite, a four-storey warehouse of *c.* 1880 in decorative yellow brickwork. No. 6, r., a small medieval timber house rebuilt in stone, formerly the Vaynol Arms. Further on, the mid-C18 three-bay No. 14, stuccoed and symmetrical. Full-height canted bays and a good staircase. HOLE-IN-THE-WALL STREET, squeezed between Palace Street and the Town Wall, returns to High Street, past the GREEN GATE, r., so called because it opened towards the Green, once the 'Prince's Garden'. On the l., the identical rear wall of the Market.

HIGH STREET runs w from PORTH MAWR or East (or Exchequer) Gate, the main entrance to the medieval town and also the administrative headquarters of North Wales. Two towers face E; all the other detail of 1873 when *John Thomas* rebuilt it as the Guildhall, his upper storey and tower since removed. No. 42, l., tall and narrow, mid-C19 Italianate, with fluted columns to the shopfront. No. 38 is earlier C18, with three big dormer gables. Inside, a turned-baluster staircase. No. 28 has a bowed Regency shopfront. No. 20, Late Georgian and red brick, turns the corner of Castle Street. On the r., PLAS BOWMAN, four-bay brown stone front, 1808, the stuccoed return in Church Street dated 1652. At the end, Porth-yr-aur (*see* p. 301) and the former CUSTOM HOUSE, r. Gabled and with big windows like an Amsterdam house. Opposite, PLAS PORTH-YR-AUR, mid-C19, of grey stone.

2. Castle Square and South-east

CASTLE SQUARE (Y MAES) is probably the outer bailey of the motte built by Hugh of Chester in the 1080s, and urbanized in the early C19. In some ways the most satisfactory urban space in Gwynedd, Castle Square is formed of three terraces converging on the twin towers of the Queen's Gate. That was, however, only made part of the space in 1911 by the removal of the three end houses on the S side for the Investiture of the Prince of Wales. This belvedere, now occupied by *W. Goscombe John*'s STATUE of David Lloyd George, 1921, created also the wonderful view to the Coed Helen tower. Nos. 32–37, the long TERRACE on the S side, is handsomely built of brown-red local brick with burned headers, with a stuccoed pedimented centrepiece, the CASTLE HOTEL, early C19. The six E bays are poor-quality 1990s reinstatement. At the SE corner, COFI ROC, by the *Aegis Consultancy Group*, *c.* 2002. Deep eaves with a strong rounded-edge profile. But as a key element of urban fabric at a critical location, it fails to contain the square's space.

The finer façades are on the E side. First, the stuccoed POST OFFICE of 1880, its sorting office lantern visible. Then, l. of the English Presbyterian Church (*see* p. 287), the early C19 HSBC BANK, with a three-bay three-storey limestone front and paired monolith porch columns, and turning the corner into

Pool Street, the florid Edwardian NatWest Bank, probably
by *W.W. Gwyther*. Along the N side, a long stuccoed TERRACE,
mostly Victorianized, the taller PATERNOSTER BUILDINGS on
the r.

In the Square on the E side, the WAR MEMORIAL, 1922, by
Rowland Lloyd Jones. A tapering sandstone pillar with delicate
Gothic detail and a dragon. In the centre, a bronze STATUE of
Sir Hugh Owen, promoter of the University of Wales, by
J. Milo Griffith, 1887.

Running SE from the square is an early C19 grid-plan suburb of
two- and three-storey terraces, called TRE'R GOF (i.e. Smith
Town), for those employed in the slate and engineering
industries. The chapels are the main features. On Chapel
Street, Ebenezer (p. 287). On New Street, Engedi (p. 287). At
the top, in Pool Street, a FOUNTAIN with a monolithic basin,
dated 1868, commemorating the water supply that followed the
disastrous cholera outbreaks of 1832, 1849 and 1854.
Just behind is Salem chapel (p. 288), next to the relief road.
Returning down GARNON STREET, a simple Ionic doorcase
on No. 28 and Caersalem chapel (p. 287) r.

Parallel to Chapel Street, SEGONTIUM TERRACE is impressively
placed on the tall stone revetment for the railway and the slate
quay. Stuccoed houses with delicate fanlights, iron balconies
and lattice porches. A flight of steps down to ST HELEN'S
ROAD which affords a fine view of the castle's towers and
banded walls at the turn of the river, complemented by the
Coed Helen landscape on the l. SE of the steps, the late C19
UNION IRONWORKS, its assembly shop, l., with a front of big
round arches in moulded brickwork, and the Venetian Gothic
offices and showroom, r. The area between here and the castle
had copper-ore yards, from the C18, then coal yards, and now
serves the small fishing fleet. Some warehouses remain, mostly
dating from the expansion of the railway *c.* 1870. Facing the
quay S of the castle, the HARBOUR OFFICE, 1840, sub-
classical, stone, with a narrow two-storey centre between low
wings, each with its own entrance. The massive SLATE QUAY
originated in an Act of 1793 for improving the harbour, and
was constructed on the marshy N shore in 1803, but designed
so that incoming ships could unload the ballast for enlarging
it. The Nantlle Railway, a horse-drawn line from the Nantlle
slate quarries, engineered by *R. & G. Stephenson*, opened in
1828. A pier and slipway for shipbuilding followed in 1830, and
in 1867 a tunnel under Castle Square was engineered by
William Baker, linking the 1852 branch of the Bangor &
Caernarfon Railway (which previously terminated at the
station N of the town centre) to the new line S (to connect to
the Cambrian Railway between Criccieth and Pwllheli).

The wharf deprived future generations of seeing the sea-girt
castle walls reflected in views across the little estuary, but it is
still well worth crossing the 1960s SWING BRIDGE by *Redpath
Dorman Long* to consider the Constantinian myth of the castle
and its realization in stone. The far side of the tidal river is

admirably preserved as parkland, the diminutive FERRY
HOUSE of 1822 serving to shelter the ferryman, and the
castellated SUMMERHOUSE (see Coed Helen, p. 311) at the
summit of the hill.

3. Bridge Street, Penrallt, Twthill, to Victoria Dock

BRIDGE STREET leads N from Castle Square, named for a bridge
over the Cadnant, at the head of the mill pond on the site of
the Penllyn shopping centre. On the l., a late C19 painted-
stucco row with a sharp prow and steep turret at Nos. 11–15,
then a lively skyline as far as No. 25. EASTGATE, l., bridges
over the dismantled railway (now a road) just before the former
Lloyds Bank, exaggerated Jacobethan in buff terracotta,
c. 1900. Then over Bank Quay, which follows the outer E and
N sides of the walls. Bridge Street becomes BANGOR STREET,
the last component in the staged remodelling of the C19.
On the corner of Pavilion Hill, r., the former Free Library
(see Royal Town Council office, p. 303). Pavilion Hill led to the
Eisteddfod Pavilion of 1877, designed to hold 8,000 people
under a galvanized iron and timber structure, now the site of
the Public Library (p. 304). Above, in Penrallt, the local government offices and SEILO CHAPEL 1976, by Colwyn Foulkes
& Partners. Little on Bangor Street apart from the tall four-
storey mid-C19 block, l., once housing the Liberal Club but
built as the Queen's Hotel, and Pendref chapel, r. (p. 287).
Next, the CELTIC ROYAL HOTEL. Early C19, built as the p. 51
Uxbridge Arms Hotel for the 1st Marquess of Anglesey, probably by Robert Jones. It belongs to the start of comfortable
tourism in Snowdonia after the Napoleonic Wars, comparable
with the Penrhyn estate developments designed by Benjamin
Wyatt. The five-bay front, of three storeys with architrave and
cornice, is of a finely jointed pale brown ashlar, with a
projecting porch on four paired Doric columns, very elegant
monoliths of Wyattish slimness. Four-bay stucco wings. Bland
modern additions.

A footpath, r. just before the hotel, runs up to TWTHILL, crossing
the 1970s chasm. Modest mid-C19 villas and terraces in WEST
and EAST TWTHILL. THOMAS STREET has a Doric-porched
public house on the corner and three-storey terraces. From the
bottom of East Twthill a path leads to the summit. Here it is
instructive to compare the townscape with that in the 1750
John Boydell engraving.

Back on Bangor Street, a footpath leads W towards Victoria Dock
past PRETORIA TERRACE, 1900; ten houses linked by a
veranda between gabled ends, showing how this housing type
should be done.

4. Victoria Dock

Immediately N of the walled town is the new harbour and
VICTORIA DOCK of 1868–75, promoted by Sir Llewelyn

Turner and designed by the engineer *Frederick Jackson*. The large rectangular basin is fed by the conduited Cadnant river, and has a rising gate between it and the Strait. A slipway for the shipbuilders faces it on the E, and to the S and E, a number of WAREHOUSES, serving the dock and the London & North Western Railway. Two low stone buildings, the former drill battery, on a canted plan, 1890s, and the MARITIME MUSEUM. Additional larger structures: the economical CAERNARFON RECORD OFFICE, 1982, the GALERI ARTS CENTRE (*see* p. 304) and finally the monstrously huge DOC FICTORIA development, 2008, by the *Watkin Jones Group*. Fifty waterside apartments rise to seven storeys, with shopping, leisure and office/commercial accommodation at the centre of the site. The materials and forms take their cue from nearby buildings but the restless design is little more than a random jumble, and from the distance (particularly from the Anglesey shore), it competes with the World Heritage Site castle and town wall.

5. The North Road Suburb

North Road begins with MENAI TERRACE which faced the former railway station, then some chunky turn-of-the-C20 villas in the local yellow brick. In ST DAVID's ROAD, r., an unusual three-storey crescent in the same brick. Up Sydney Road, in Y CLOGWYN, TÝ NEWYDD, by and for *Maredudd ab Iestyn*, 2000, is end-on to road, monopitched with a single-storey lean-to and staircase tower. A rich palette: grey-stained boarding, corrugated steel sheet, blue-painted brickwork, smooth render and steel balconies on slanting legs. Light and airy Scandinavian interior. Further along NORTH ROAD, LLYS MEIRION, a 1930s row of white semi-detached houses (like one at Holyhead), originally with curved glass in the bays. On the NW side, mid- and late C19 villas, CAE SYNAMON the best. Further out, two Late Regency villas in larger grounds. PLAS TÝ COCH, behind a high wall and with a veranda; then PLAS BRERETON, of pinkish ashlar and pyramid-roofed.

6. East and South Suburbs

Pool Street leads uphill to the relief road (A487). On the far side, UXBRIDGE SQUARE, a small Georgian cul de sac with a gateway. Built by the Vaynol estate, which also built HOLYWELL TERRACE, a row of six early C19 single-fronted houses to the N, in Lôn Ysgol Rad (formerly Llanberis Road). The CHURCH HALL, r. of the terrace, was an infants' school, probably by *John Lloyd*, 1836. In the pediment, a roundel painted with 'Feed my Lambs'. Further up Lôn Ysgol Rad, r., the BARRACKS, built by *John Lloyd* for the Royal Welch Fusiliers, 1855. Brown stone, Georgian windows. $4\frac{1}{2}$–4–$4\frac{1}{2}$ bay front, with a deep parapet apparently for muskets. CWELLYN, further on and across Llanberis Road, a Regency house with shallow gabled ends and a veranda.

NEWBOROUGH STREET leads S from Uxbridge Square, past WELLINGTON TERRACE, r., six stucco VILLAS, some paired, with enjoyable Late Regency detailing, a surviving length of Caernarfon's urbanism. Further on (now SOUTH ROAD), the diminutive former Carnarvon Grammar and Collegiate SCHOOL (known as the Ysgol Jones Bach). Mid-C19 Tudor, single-storey with basement. Opposite, HEN WALIAU, a detached length of high ROMAN WALL, probably part of a C3 warehouse for stores brought up from ships. Then BRON HENDRE (now a health clinic), mid-C19. Symmetrical, in ashlared limestone, with a segmental bow to the view, a canted bay and pedimented side porch. Further S, r., BRYN HELEN, a deep-eaved stuccoed 1840s house with a veranda to the panorama over the Seiont, the quay and the castle.

7. *Outliers*

COED HELEN, ½ m. W. Small C18 mansion of Rice Thomas, much altered but with some C17 and C18 internal features. Its park ran down to the Seiont estuary. The white Gothick TOWER at its apex acts as a foil to many views. The designer is unknown.

ANTUR WAUNFAWR, Cibyn Industrial Estate, Llanberis Road. 2005, by *Selwyn Jones*. Offices and retail space, for a social enterprise organization. Environmentally conscious, steel-framed with steel-sheet roof and teak cladding. Projecting entrance wing with generous overhang supported on tall steel columns. Elegant and crisply detailed, a welcome break from the usual quality of industrial park design.

CAPEL CURIG

7358

A junction of mountain routes and a tourist resort of long standing. Thomas Johnson, the botanist, was here in 1639, J. M. W. Turner at a later date. The village was renowned for harp-making in the C17.

ST JULITTA (formerly ST CURIG). In a raised, rectangular p. 312 churchyard beside the Llugwy river. Small, of double-square plan with a S chapel in line with the E wall, thus forming an L. Hughes and North noted that it is the only church in the area not subsequently lengthened. The main body probably C13–C14, the chapel *c.* 1500. A blocked slit window in the chapel gable and a blocked door at the W end of the N wall, with a huge lintel, are original openings; all the others were formed in *Mr Baxter*'s restoration of 1837 which presumably also removed the chapel arcade that Cotman saw. Barrel-vaulted plastered ceiling, with plaster arches concealing the roof trusses. – C19 BOX PEWS in the nave, double-decker PULPIT and DESK on the E wall, S of the chancel window.

ST CURIG (new church), ¼ m. E. 1883, by *Goronwy Owen*, architect to the Penrhyn estate. Plain Romanesque, with

Capel Curig, St Julitta (formerly St Curig), before 1837.
Etching by J. S. Cotman

s porch and apsidal sanctuary. Internal walls lined with red brick, and a pair of chancel arches, each on polished grey shafts. The apse ceiling tiled with mosaic work by *Salviati* to designs by *Clayton & Bell*, a memorial to Georgina Sackville-West. Two small s windows by *Morris & Co.*, 1936. Imaginatively converted to a guesthouse.

ROYAL FARM, across the road from St Julitta (old church). Probably built to serve the Royal Hotel (*see* below), so *c.* 1800. Its formality suggests an estate architect was involved, perhaps *Benjamin Wyatt*. A long, nearly symmetrical range, starting with single-storey wings, rising to hipped two-storey blocks and a higher, gabled central bay.

PLAS Y BRENIN, 200 yds w. Formerly the Capel Curig Inn, later the Royal Hotel. By *Benjamin Wyatt*. Opened *c.* 1800 by Richard Pennant of Penrhyn, to accommodate the growing number of tourists. Hyde Hall described it, in 1809, as 'a sort of pivot on which the intercourse between London and Dublin is constantly turning'.* By 1854, when George Borrow stayed there, it was 'a very magnificent edifice'. Much enlarged and altered since, with late C20 work by *Bowen Dann Davies*; now the National Mountain Centre.

YSGUBOR-Y-GLYN, 2 m. E, in the M.o.D. training camp. A rare cruck barn, of two building dates. Six bays to the w, probably C15, the crucks of varied shape. To the E, a C16 extension of three bays, of box-frame construction. Both parts clad in stone, with a modern slated roof. A cowshed lean-to to the N.

TÝ-HYLL (Ugly House), 2½ m. E. A leprous version of the standard estate cottage built *c.* 1840 by Lord Willoughby de Eresby on the Gwydir estate. But this was probably built

---

*Facing the lake, it had a two-storey canted bay, with Gothick windows and an embattled parapet.

c. 1820 when Telford's road was formed, so it may have provided the inspiration. Built of exceedingly rough boulders without mortar, with massive corbels at the eaves and a projecting conical chimney at the E gable.

DYFFRYN MYMBYR, 1½ m. W. Small two-storey house, with lower, attached barn to the NE. Probably late C16. Over the S doorway, a cyclopean head with the hint of a Tudor arch. Modern Yorkshire sliding windows.

ROMAN FORT of Caer Llugwy, or Bryn y Gefeiliau, on flat land close to the river (SH 745 572). The ramparts can just be recognized, and stone buildings, possibly part of a *mansio* or guesthouse, are visible beneath trees. Excavations in 1920–2 revealed occupation and industrial activity (lead working) in the C1–C2 A.D. Many broken wine amphorae were found near the guesthouse.

CARNGUWCH *see* LLITHFAEN

CEIDIO *see* LLANDUDWEN

CHWILOG 4538

A small linear village on the 1808 turnpike, halfway between Tremadog and Porth Dinllaen (Madocks's proposed packet port for Ireland). On the S side, the MADRYN ARMS, of 1868; the original inn was built by Jones-Parry of Madryn on another site E of the river.

CAPEL UCHAF CALVINISTIC METHODIST CHAPEL. 1882. Yellow brick, divided by bands of red and blue. Above the projecting doorway a triplet of round-headed windows. To each side, taller single windows. All with brick voussoirs and keystones.

SILOH CHAPEL. A competently designed classical gable front, dated 1869 and 1897. Stucco, with raised quoins and mouldings, and a plain rusticated base. Single windows each side of the doorway, a smaller pair above, all with fluted Corinthian pilasters. Paired pilasters each side of the entrance. Pebbledashed gable.

CLYNNOG FAWR 4250

ST BEUNO. Cathedral-like in scale compared with the other 33 churches in Llŷn, the great collegiate church of Beuno – one of the Early Christian fathers of North Wales – was rebuilt from the late C15 with outstanding consistency in a noble Perp style. It has a chancel, transepts, unaisled nave, W tower and a chapel to the SW over the saint's grave, linked by a passage (cf. Llaneilian, Anglesey). The previous buildings leave no trace, but foundations connected with the old Celtic *clas* were discovered below the chapel floor in 1913.

Construction began *c.* 1480 with the chancel and transepts. The splendidly rich and broad E window has seven lights, grouped 3:1:3 and alternately two-centred and ogee. Other windows are three-light, except for the five-light transept N and s windows. Octagonal rood-stair-turret in the angle of s transept and chancel. Nave, of *c.* 1500, with windows more fully cusped. The parapets are all embattled, with pinnacles on the angles, and the roofs are of very shallow pitch. Two-storey N PORCH, of the same date. Doorways here and elsewhere all of conventional, hooded shapes. The W TOWER dates from the early C16. Its full-height diagonal buttresses with many set-offs give an indecisive profile. Fine W doorway in a deep square recess. The hoodmould on bishops' headstops; shields and tracery in the doorway spandrels. The W window is uncusped but repeats the pattern in the transepts. Of this third build also the three-storey VESTRY N of the chancel, with a cross-vaulted lower storey.

Bright, spacious INTERIOR. In the chancel, three SEDILIA, with ogee heads and leafy finials, and with pinnacles between. A plain octagonal PISCINA in a two-centred chamfered opening. The transepts run right across the crossing, strangely, with a continuous transverse roof (cf. Llanbeblig). Two-centred chancel arch, responds composed of filleted shafts set against one concave and one convex stage; the grand nave E arch is similar, and both have ogee and wavy mouldings above continuous capitals. The tower arch is more elaborate: two concave and two convex stages behind the shaft, a profile vigorously repeated in the capitals and in the arch as well. The nave rejoices in a lovely Perp roof. Its shallow main beams rest alternately on wall-posts and hammerbeams, the latter supporting little traceried arcades with bosses on the ends. The other chief carpentry decoration is the star-like leaf and flower bosses on the joins of the secondary frame. Other roofs replaced by *Kennedy*, 1856, not unalike.

The early C16 CAPEL-Y-BEDD is approached through a passageway from the tower, probably C17 despite its slab-vaulted roof, Tudor doorways at each end. The chapel's style is much weaker than that of the church – the W doorway, probably inserted later, has spandrel tracery but the odd label mould, resting on animal stops, is too narrow. The small window above, of two trefoiled lights. Big five-light E window, of two intersecting groups of three, without cusping. Repairs by *Basil Stallybrass*, 1913–14, and again by *Harold Hughes*, 1926–37.

FURNISHINGS. A fine range of fourteen STALLS, six against the screen and eight returning to the E. Heads on the arm-rests. – MISERICORDS with vaulting and mostly with vine leaves. Handsome desks with linenfold fronts. Their finials are well carved with poppyheads and with double-headed eagles on the sides facing the aisle. – Two SCREENS. Chancel. Three bays of much-moulded uprights either side of the doorway and two above its straight head, dated 1531(?). The remainder, and the loft, renewed *c.* 1940. – Beneath the tower. Late C17, massive, with heavy balusters on top. – PULPIT. Hexagonal, *c.* 1700(?), with serpent motifs on four sides. – FONT. Perp. The bowl, of wood, has trefoil panels on the sides, as on the stone stem.

MONUMENTS. Chancel, table tomb to William Glyn †1609, with shields on the panelled sides as well as on the slab. He is represented kneeling, with twelve children, on a tablet above. – George Twisleton †1714, with open pediment. – Rev. Hugh Williams †1833. Grecian, by *W. Spence.* – Transept. Small brass to William Glynne †1633. The figure is a woman's. – Armorial slab to William Wynne †1660. – Altar tomb of George Twisleton †1667. Lettering and arms recessed in relief in a slab with guilloche border. Rectangular baluster legs. – BOULDER, the Maen Beuno, with a Latin cross incised. C8?

In the churchyard, a granite SUNDIAL, Irish Celtic type, probably C10–C12. – Victorian Gothic TOMB to the bard, Ebenezer Thomas (Eben Fardd) †1883.

A neat VILLAGE at the foot of Bwlch Mawr, once the starting place of pilgrimages to Bardsey Island. The BEUNO INN dominates a raised green above the road recently by-passed. Late C18, though with earlier origins, remodelled in the early C19 and extended r. in 1912. Imposing front gable, with gabled porch on paired timber columns. Roughcast, white. STABLES etc., l. Leading w to the church, the POST OFFICE, with a mid-C19 shopfront, and a row of mid- to later C19 cottages continuing SW along the main road. Ebenezer Thomas (Eben Fardd), bard and school teacher, lived at BOD CYBI. The lychgate, opposite, leads to the church and to COURT COTTAGE, 60 overlooking the N vestry. Late C17, probably the former vicarage. Whitewashed rubble, with three gabled half-dormers. More gabled dormers at BODFASARN, SW of the church. Built in the early C17 as an inn, rear wing added in the late C17. The front dormers altered, but the rear ones, with projecting slate heads and coped gables, look original. Large slate slab over the rear entrance. Further SW, MAES-GLAS, a pretty, early to mid-C19 three-bay house with margin sashes and a glazed timber porch; and beyond, FFYNNON BEUNO, a holy well within a walled enclosure, probably coeval with the church.

NE of the inn the lane leads to the EBENEZER CALVINISTIC METHODIST CHAPEL, 1843, rebuilt 1907. Set back to the r., behind a garden, TŶ CAPEL, the manse. Probably 1843. Pebbledashed, rendered dressings. To the l., the SCHOOL and the SCHOOL HOUSE, of the same date and forming a good group, now a museum, the Canolfan Hanes Uwchgwyrfai.

HAFOD-Y-WERN, ⅓ m. SE. Substantial upland farmstead, arranged round a large courtyard approached from the SW along a short avenue. L-plan house, NE, the rear wing the earlier part, probably C17, with fireplace and mural staircase; two-storey front wing added by the Glynllifon estate *c.* 1860, with sash windows arranged symmetrically about the doorway.

Long ranges of OUTBUILDINGS, SE and SW: stables, barns, cowhouses etc. PIGGERY, NW, with sties and yards attached to the higher pig-swill building with chimney. Feeding troughs, hearths etc. inside.

TAN-Y-BWLCH, 1 m. ESE. In the garden, a stone HOVEL, a rare example of a *hafod*, or summer dwelling associated with pastoral transhumance. Minimal, like a quarry-workers' *caban*, just 6 ft (1.8 metres) high, the same across and 8 ft (2.5 metres) long. Fireplace in one corner, little niches in the walls and huge boulders for the roof. To the r., a tiny pigsty. Exact dating is difficult, but probably C18 or early C19.

GYRN GOCH, 1 m. SW. Small hamlet on the A499 road. SPORTSMAN'S ROW, formerly an inn. Two-storeyed to l., with small sash windows, the upper ones set well below the eaves. Single-storey cottages, r. Further SW, SEION CHAPEL, 1875, with a cottage, l., and chapel house, r. On the hill behind, PANT-Y-FFYNNON, a whitewashed rubble farmhouse with projecting gabled wings either side of the central bay, its rear roof curiously stopping just beyond the ridge. Diagonal chimneys, plain Tudor-style window hoods. Mid-C19, maybe earlier, perhaps part of the Glynllifon estate.

BACHWEN BURIAL CHAMBER (SH 407 495), in the middle of a field 750 yds WSW of the church. Best known for its capstone decorated with 110 cup marks. These marks most frequently appear in association with tombs of the portal dolmen family.

Clynnog Fawr, Bachwen burial chamber.
Engraving, 1878

Their purpose and meaning is unknown. This chamber is denuded of cairn and the surviving supporters are widely spaced (at least one was moved during uninformative excavations in 1876), so any classification is uncertain, though the rectangularity of the chamber and the wedge-shaped capstone suggest a portal dolmen. Another burial chamber at SH 430 510 is even more badly ruined. Together with other completely lost tombs, it demonstrates that this coastal plain was well occupied during the Neolithic period.

CONWY   7878

The Conwy is the noble river of NW Wales, rising in mountains thirty miles S, flowing through a grand and pastoral valley before its wide estuary between Conwy and Deganwy. The C12 princes sited their castle to defend Gwynedd against the English on the E side, on the crags of Deganwy, and Llywelyn the Great endowed a Cistercian abbey on the W shore, where he built a princely hall in the early C13. The defeat of the princedom in 1283 and its incorporation into the English state were symbolized in the displacement of the abbey upstream to Maenan, and the reuse of its site for as tough a fortification as then existed in Europe. Conwy thus made a new start as a royal outpost for Edward I defining an important frontier, dominating the river mouth and the mountains of Snowdonia beyond.

The town attached to the castle was situated (as at Caernarfon) on the seashore and benefited from an inland pool and mill fed by the Gyffin river on the S. This settlement was formidably defended with twenty-one towers and three twin-towered gateways, the shortest flank being on the beach, and the rest of the walls rising in a right-angled triangle to a keep-like tower on a crag at the top. Brooding and dark, the castle and walls (albeit only for a small town) are one of the sights of Wales and indeed of Europe.

In economic terms Conwy is a river-port, shut off from the NW Wales coast by the headland of Penmaenmawr. The river was navigable for flat-bottomed boats as far upstream as Llanrwst and even Trefriw, where timber, lead and slate were exchanged. The borough, chartered in 1284, rapidly developed into an important place of trade. Two notable merchants' houses survive at the timber-built Aberconwy House, of c. 1420, and the Elizabethan palace of Plas Mawr. Meanwhile the abbey church site was reused for the parish church, enclosed in a rectangular churchyard defined by the grid of the burgage plots. The early houses were largely of stone with half-timber above, as C18 and C19 views show, but most were replaced just as antiquarian interest in them began.

The town, confined within the walls until the late C19, found new significance with the transport links along the North Wales coast, as the castle occupied the only practicable spot for one end of the vital estuary crossing. The rocky bluff has been so used

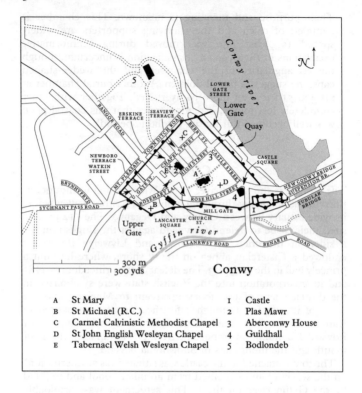

A	St Mary	1	Castle
B	St Michael (R.C.)	2	Plas Mawr
C	Carmel Calvinistic Methodist Chapel	3	Aberconwy House
D	St John English Wesleyan Chapel	4	Guildhall
E	Tabernacl Welsh Wesleyan Chapel	5	Bodlondeb

three times, twice imaginatively by pioneer engineers – *Thomas Telford*'s road bridge in 1825 and *Robert Stephenson*'s railway bridge in 1848 – and in 1958 more obtrusively, for the A55 road bridge. The latest transport link, the quasi-motorway of 1986–93 linking Ireland with Britain and the Continent, passes under the estuary (an engineering feat) and mercifully not on the overweening suspension bridge first proposed.

Within the walls, a variety of new functions have been ingeniously fitted since the mid C19 into a testing context, including the railway. The NW part of the grid is lined with small-scale terraces typical of the region. The last fifty years have enhanced the setting of the walls by clearing encroaching structures. Little has done the town more good than removing the heavy road traffic and, at least on the W shore, the landscape cost of the new road is low. The town is the administrative centre of the new local authority of Conwy, carved out of the historic counties of Caernarvonshire and Denbighshire.

PLACES OF WORSHIP

ST MARY. In origin the church of Aberconwy Abbey, founded by Cistercian monks sent out in 1186 from Strata Florida,

Ceredigion (where building had only begun in 1184). They went first near Caernarfon, but Gerald of Wales mentions them here in 1188, apparently under the patronage of Llywelyn the Great. Aberconwy became the burial place of Llywelyn and three of his family, and was where Llywelyn the Last signed the humiliating Treaty of Aberconwy, 1277. The abbey church was built by 1200, but damaged in an English raid, 1245, and, presumably, in the conquest of 1283. Its length, as represented by the present church, is equivalent to just the nave at Cymer or Strata Florida. In 1283 Aberconwy Abbey was removed upstream to Maenan to free the site for the English town.

The C13 monastery is little known, as archaeology has proved disappointing. The SE corner of the town must represent the precinct, as distinctly apart from the 1284 grid-plan. The near-rectangular churchyard with four entry alleys is hidden by the burgage plots of the new townsfolk. It seems likely that the town church does incorporate the outline and some walling of the abbey church, but so rebuilt as to suggest severe damage in 1283. Harold Hughes's suggested history is that the abbey church, of aisled nave, transepts and chancel, was remodelled in stages to the mid C14. A tower was inserted in the W bay of the nave incorporating the abbey W wall, the N transept removed, the S transept reconstructed to high quality and the nave altered with new arcades under a quatrefoil-windowed clerestory. An alternative would be that the abbey had just a nave, aisled in the W half, that the S transept is added, and that the N one may have come and gone, or never have existed. The C15 to early C16 saw the raising of the tower and roofs (losing the clerestory); also the Perp E window, screen, and possibly the N porch. C16–C17 mullioned windows in the aisles have gone. From 1872 *Sir George Gilbert Scott* reinstated the clerestory, renewed the roofs and restored windows. *John Oldrid Scott* did work after 1878. *Harold Hughes* furnished the N aisle chapel, 1919–21, and probably added to the vestry, 1925.

EXTERIOR. The W front has a long chamfered offset above the door that extends across the N aisle, showing that the abbey church was aisled (there are signs of a lost matching SW corner). Triple lancets and doorway in red sandstone, as also the tower S quoins. The lancets resemble the earlier C13 ones at Llaniestyn (C) and Llanfrothen. The doorway is particularly good: half-octagonal piers with fine early Gothic foliage but no separating band, and multiple arch mouldings. Oddly it was not made to hold a door – Hughes thought it the chapter-house entry reused. Above, a good foliage-carved early C13 stone. In the N aisle, two tiny windows may be early, but are too rough to date. The tower is distinctly rectangular, with earlier C14 trefoiled small lights at the original bell-stage,* below the late C15 embattled top. The crease of the C14 roof is visible on the E. The clerestory was raised by *Scott*, having been from the

---

*Hughes posits two C14 phases from the form of the stair-turret doors within.

early C16 concealed under a single-pitch roof, with the quatrefoils reinstated but set higher. N door with eroded C14 mouldings, in a porch with massive oak front: moulded pointed arch within a full cruck, presumably C15. C14 cross-slab and fragments within.

The possible N transept site is framed by buttresses, but its existence remains unconfirmed. Between, set high, a C14 pointed three-light of uncusped lancets in brown stone. The N chancel window, set low, matches, but in red stone and with voussoirs; Hughes thought it a C17 copy. The lean-to vestry may be C14 from the renewed E window; the 1925 N addition reuses its C16 N window.

The abbey E end is marked by the string course below the big Perp E window (C15 with C19 tracery) and buttresses with rough red stone quoins. The SE buttress is not aligned with the S wall assumed by Hughes to be rebuilt after the 1245 raid as there are two mid-C13 two-light windows, the r. one with a quatrefoil head, the l. one plain. An alternative is that the windows are reused in a mid-C14 wall, datable from the low S door. In the angle, narrow lights, for the C15 rood screen. The S transept is mid-C14 with angle buttresses and some high-quality textbook Dec tracery in the E windows, intersecting, l., reticulated, r. The big S five-light is *Scott*'s, based on a little evidence. The walls have been raised. The lean-to on the W accommodates the discomfort of a high transept arch and low S aisle. The distorted round arch of the S porch proves to be reused C13; roll-moulded, but all but the inner moulding hacked off. S door with C14 shallow wave mouldings; studded plank door.

INTERIOR. Wide nave of three bays; arcades of C14 octagonal piers with perfunctory capitals and arches of two orders of concave mouldings, the hoodmoulds with large and crude mask-stops. But before the S transept arch, a finely moulded cusped niche introduces a higher order of C14 work that includes the S arch and the transept W arch. These have two continuous wave mouldings, an outer chamfer, hoodmould and delicate carved headstops. The E respond of the S arcade matches, which suggests a grand scheme halted before the arcades were started, then done simpler, very like Beaumaris, where the clerestory also has quatrefoils.* The transept has a cusped S PISCINA. In the S aisle, two tomb-recesses with segmental-pointed arches, and a simpler piscina. The roofs appear entirely *Scott*'s, shallow wagon-type with wind-braces forming lozenges, and cusping over the screen.

FURNISHINGS. SCREEN. A spectacular example of the Devon Perp type, every surface carved, marked with the badge of Sir Richard Pole, Constable 1488–1504. Five bays, four pointed traceried lights above a dado with perforated bands. Deep fan-vaulting on both sides to support the rood loft, with pendants. Above, two rows of undercut mouldings, the motifs

---

*Hughes thought the sequence reversed: aisle piers first, then the transept, but the nave arches C16.

including a wyvern, birds, beasts and a fish. The loft front has
gone, as has a successor C17 balustrade. Rood stair in the S
wall, emerging high in the S transept. The STALLS are contemporary, two rows on each side, returned behind the screen.
Richly panelled ends with a wealth of detail including pomegranate and Tudor rose, with large poppyhead terminals.
Plain wall benching. The eastern stalls have reused C16 bench
ends, one lettered 'Gloriosa passioni . . .', and the DESK has a
carved owl and traceried panels with heraldry. Frontal of C17
turned rails, from the screen balustrade. – FONT. C15. Unusually ornate, though eroding. Octagonal with tracery, the base
with pierced buttressing. – TILES. Re-set on the sanctuary S
wall, C14, with incised patterns. The floor tiles are C19 copies.
– ORGAN. 1906, by *William Hill & Son*. – Oak Gothic fittings
in the N aisle, 1919–21, by *Hughes*. – Earlier C20 oak PULPIT
and REREDOS. – ALTAR RAILS. 1960, by *Thompson* of Kilburn.
– HYMN-BOOK STORE. An elaborate Gothic enclosure, 1939.
– STAINED GLASS. Chancel E, Ascension, 1870, in the bright
colours of the 1850s, the angelic host above. Chancel N, Last
Supper, 1882, by *Mayer*; similar nave N, 1886, adjoining. N aisle
E, 1854, by *Holland* of Warwick, bright. S transept, E, l., the
Empty Tomb, 1870, by *Cox & Sons*, painterly; r., grisaille frag-
ment in the tracery, C15? W, c. 1936, Bible translators. S aisle,
two sad Burne-Jones saints, by *Morris & Co.*, c. 1915; W, signed
A. L. Moore & Son, 1912.

MONUMENTS. Chancel, Robert Wynn, builder of Plas
Mawr, †1598. Sandstone tomb-chest with semicircular hood,
possibly the first in a series of similar tombs seen elsewhere in
Gwynedd and Clwyd. Its outer and under surfaces moulded
like the rims of wheels, and enriched with the heraldry of which
Wynn was so proud. – John Wynn †1637, armorial; E wall, small
Baroque monument to Margaret Coytmor †1684; Anne
Apthorpe †1788, tablet placed by her American husband. – S
wall, five C16–C17 slabs: Edward Williams †1601, with heraldry;
the Rev. John Brickdall †1607, with skull and bones; one 1666;
Dorothy Wynn †1586, with skull and bones in stalks of wheat;
the last C16, obscured. Cadwaleder Wynn †1752, pilastered,
with marble cherub. – N wall, Margaret Owen †1837, plaque
by *Gaffin*; painted plaque to Jane Fletcher †1708. – S transept,
two tomb-chests in the corners, one 'Edward Holland placed
it 1584' with arms, the other Robert Williams †1760. – E wall,
Johannes Hooke †1600, eroded plaque, he and children kneeling, in a guilloche border; Robert Howard †1776, entertaining
Neoclassical with coloured marble inlay, by *Benjamin Bromfield*
of Liverpool. – S aisle. In the l. tomb recess, Maria Williams
†1585, still medieval, low-relief effigy, with hands clasped. In
the other, C14 coffin-shaped slab with foliate cross. John
Gibson †1866, 'one of the first sculptors in Europe', born the
son of a gardener at Benarth, Gyffin, 1790. Marble bust by
William Theed, 1866. – N aisle. John Williams †1706, black
polished slab on six pillars; C14 coffin-shaped floor slab with
floriated cross; C16–C17 ledger slabs. Plaques to Sir David

Erskine of Cambo †1841, and Silence Holland †1812, by *Franceys*. – Nave N, Margaret Coytmore †1757, Neoclassical in coloured marbles, but the heraldic stag's head still Rococo, by *B. Bromfield;* Hephzibah Williams †1832, thick drapery, by *W. Spence.*

St Michael (R.C.), Rosemary Lane. 1915. Roughcast, minimal Gothic. stained glass, Crucifixion, *c.* 1950. Outside a remarkable white marble Calvary and set of large white marble plaques of the Stations of the Cross, affixed to the town walls, all of 1934, presumably Italian. The architect, *Giuseppe Rinvolucri*, was involved.

Bethesda Baptist Chapel, Church Street. Disused. 1875. Stuccoed. Presumably by *Richard Owens*, from the tall triplet and the outer triangular-headed recesses.

Carmel Calvinistic Methodist Chapel, Chapel Street. 1875, by *Richard Owens*. An imposing winged façade in stucco, the centre gathered in a triangular-headed recess and the triplet of arched windows each with a roundel in the head, typical Owens motifs, and the wings balustraded. Panelled gallery fronts with leaf ornament. Behind the pulpit, a later arch to the organ recess. The vestry to the r. looks older, the gable stuccoed to match the chapel.

St John English Wesleyan Chapel, Rose Hill Street. 1880–1, by *Robert Curwen*, small, Domestic Gothic with a little half-timber. Careful new entrance in the angle to a set-back schoolroom. The original angle porch had a timber octagonal spirelet.

Tabernacl Welsh Wesleyan Chapel, York Place. Remodelled in 1885, by *Richard Davies*, the previous front at the other end, to Chapel Street. Davies's work in rock-faced grey stone is strong, with stepped coursing under the gable and plain square-headed windows, the centre triplet with stepped dripmould to encompass the plaque. The rear, of 1864, faced in broken stone pieces with sandstone dressings, is round-arched. Interior of 1885, the galleries with cast-iron pierced panels, balustraded *sêt-fawr* and arched-panelled polygonal pulpit.

CONWY CASTLE AND TOWN WALLS

From mid March 1283 until early May King Edward himself was at Conwy, the Conwy valley having been secured following the capture of Dolwyddelan that January. Accounts for the construction of castle and town defences begin from March, running up to 1292, the total cost being *c.* £14,500. By late 1284 over £5,800 had been expended, and the peak in the summer of 1285 about 1,500 men were employed. To all intents and purposes the design had been completed by the end of 1287. This was all undertaken under the control and supervision of *Master James of St George*, whilst others were responsible for certain aspects, e.g. *Henry of Oxford*, master carpenter, and *Richard of Chester*, the engineer charged with recruiting masons and others. One *John Flauner*, who had been involved in other royal projects, was paid for 142 arrowslits in the town walls and castle, and also prepared ashlar dressings for various doorways and windows.

Placing castle and borough here was as symbolic as the construction of Caernarfon with its imperial Roman associations; for not only was the abbey the burial place of Llywelyn the Great, grandfather of the late Llywelyn, Prince of Wales, but near the abbey lay the residence of the princes of North Wales, the so-called Llywelyn's Hall. It was also at Conwy that the administration of the construction of the king's works in North Wales was based.

The castle is admirably located on a great boss of rock that overlooks the confluence of the Gyffin and Conwy. The rivers provided castle and town with a natural defence to the S and NE, whilst on the N and NW a ditch enveloped the town walls. Detailed accounts survive only for 1285–6, when a further £3,313 was spent, and it is clear that amongst the works undertaken were the N and NW sections of the town wall, i.e. that part of the circuit where the natural defences of the rivers offered no protection. The construction of the remainder of the town walls followed in 1286–7. In the castle, the bulk of the walls and towers must have reached almost their full height by 1285, when the internal 'houses' against the walls had been built, as had the chapel in the NE or Chapel Tower; an inspection of the hall and Inner Ward ranges on the S side shows that their walls butt against the curtain wall. The accounts for 1286 specify such finishing touches as limewashing the battlements of the town wall and the construction of the truly remarkable line of twelve latrines W of the Mill Gate for £15. Two towers at the ends of spur walls were also built in 1286, one extending SE from the castle's East Barbican, the other at the N end of the quay on the E side of the borough. In 1287, with works costing just over £1,990, the main building period came to an end; to this year can be assigned the town wall that fronted the quay, including the Lower Gate and probably the turrets of the Inner Ward's four towers. Thereafter in Edward I's reign expenditure amounts to only a few hundred pounds. There is little surviving evidence that the king stayed at Conwy, apart from Christmas 1294–5, during the Welsh uprising, although his son, Prince Edward, received homage from Welsh lords here in 1301.

In the early C14 repairs were undertaken on the town defences because of flood damage, whilst a murage grant in 1305 may indicate that part of the walled circuit had not been completely finished. It is worth noting that two towers at the E end of the N circuit are finished in a different stone and have cross-slit arrowslits, whilst all the other towers originally had plain vertical slits. In 1316 a timber-framed building against the town walls, known as the hall of Llywelyn ap Gruffudd, was re-erected inside Caernarfon Castle to store supplies. Prior to its removal, this hall had become the core of the private residence intended for Edward I's son as Prince of Wales, the future Edward II.

In 1325–6 £139 was spent on an unspecified project: it has been suggested that the upper part of the spur wall protecting the quay, marked by a clear horizontal break in the masonry which runs the length of this wall, might date from this period.

By the 1330s, however, the castle was considered unfit for royal habitation; as early as 1321 much of the timberwork in the towers and hall had decayed. By 1347 the castle's roofs were being re-leaded for Edward, the Black Prince, and in the hall range eight stone arches were built to take the weight of a new roof. There is evidence that similar work was planned in the Inner Ward, although this may never have been fully implemented. The work was the last major piece of expenditure; thereafter, small sums were spent on basic maintenance.* A small number of men appear to have been employed for routine work, one of whom, a Welsh carpenter, enabled the supporters of Owain Glyndŵr to seize the castle for a short period in 1401, during which time houses were set on fire and bridges at the gates burnt. Instructions were issued for the repair of various royal castles and town walls under Henry VIII, when work was undertaken on the well-house and the drawbridge between the Inner and Outer wards. Almost a century later, in 1627, a detailed survey revealed a castle in a dire state. In that year the Crown sold it to Edward, Lord Conway of Ragley, Secretary of State to the king.

In the Civil War the redoubtable Conwy-born John Williams, Archbishop of York, held town and castle for the king until 1646. Parliament then garrisoned Conwy, and various works were undertaken including platforms for ordnance and iron window bars to keep prisoners secure. Although instructions were issued in 1655 for the slighting of Conwy's castle and town walls, along with those at Caernarfon, nothing appears to have been done, unless the collapse at the base of the Bakehouse Tower dates from this period. Ten years later anything salvageable was sold by the 3rd Lord Conway, predominantly lead and timber, leaving the castle open to the elements. The Bakehouse Tower had certainly collapsed by 1742, the date of the Bucks' engraving (repaired in the later C19).

The road and rail networks created across North Wales in the C19, and the growth of tourism, led to some improvements, notably when J. H. Parker of the Ashmolean Museum in Oxford restored the tower at the highest point of the town walls (Tower Thirteen) at his own expense. But Telford's suspension bridge destroyed some outworks on the E side in the 1820s, and the construction of the Chester & Holyhead Railway in 1847 pierced the walls, and affected their southern aspect. In the second half of the C19 the castle came under the control of the mayor of Conwy; the castle and town walls passed in 1953 into the care of the Ministry of Works and its successors. The remains of the path to the dock on the NE side of the castle, which survived Telford, were lost when the new road bridge was constructed. Post-war

---

*Although an unknown project cost over £70 in 1437–8.

conservation, in particular the opening up of views of the walls, has been well chronicled by the late Arnold Taylor, the driving force behind this work.

Exterior

The castle rises from a ridge of Silurian gritstone, used to   29 construct much of the castle and town walls. This greyish stone contrasts with the locally quarried rusty-coloured rhyolite, mainly used in the N section of the town walls. Ashlar dressings for arrowslits, doorways, windows and other fine architectural features had to be brought from further afield. Much of this sandstone came from across the river, opposite the castle to the N, but we know that the stone for the new works for the Black Prince in the 1340s was quarried near Chester.

Eight great circular towers enclose the rock on which the castle sits, rising up from masonry that has an almost imperceptible batter. The towers are almost identical in plan, but the four that frame the Inner Ward at the E end, the residence of the royal household, have turrets (the Stockhouse, Chapel, King's and Bakehouse towers). Of the other four, those on the W (the North-West and South-West towers) would have been occupied by the Constable, with other household staff in the main chambers of the Kitchen and Prison towers. To the E and W are barbicans protecting the land (W) and water (E) entrances. The curtain walls run straight across the rock, but on the S, to take advantage of the topography, the curtain is bowed outwards, with the Prison Tower as the central feature.

Examination of the towers shows that the main rooms were lit by rectangular two-light windows, originally barred and glazed, and that the towers also contained long arrowslits. Smaller slit windows lit the stairs and latrine chambers. At battlement level the merlons contained arrowslits; they were capped with finials. Running round the towers, below the crenellations, are sockets for an overhanging timber hourd or gallery from which the garrison would defend the bases of the towers. When Conwy was built the walls were whitened, and traces of limewash remain, some of the best evidence being visible on the N turret of the E barbican. The use of the French or Savoyard practice of inclined or helicoidal scaffolding is best seen on the North-West Tower, and also on Tower Thirteen at the highest point of the town walls, where putlog holes spiral up and around the walls. Along the curtains are a number of latrines, four on the S and six on the N. Those on the S are corbelled out above the rock, one in the lee of each of the four towers, serving the upper floors. The latrines on the N side are contained in the thickness of the curtain wall, and open out where the masonry meets the natural rock. The exterior of the westernmost latrine on the N side is the best-preserved; here we see that the base is enveloped in a curving wall of masonry to prevent access via the chute.

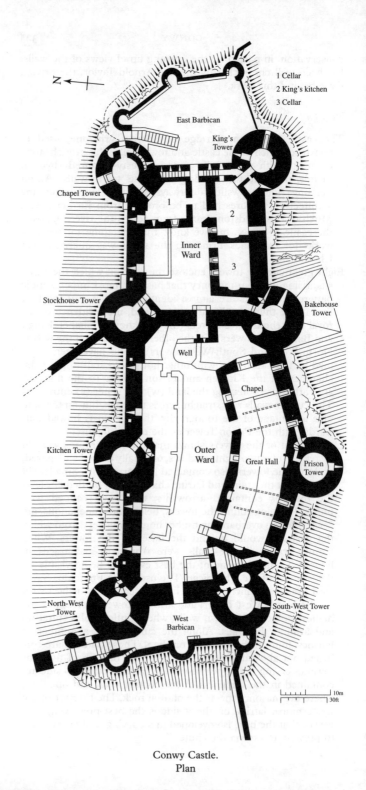

1 Cellar
2 King's kitchen
3 Cellar

N

East Barbican

King's Tower

Chapel Tower

1

2

Inner Ward

3

Stockhouse Tower

Bakehouse Tower

Well

Chapel

Kitchen Tower

Outer Ward

Great Hall

Prison Tower

North-West Tower

West Barbican

South-West Tower

10m
30ft

Conwy Castle.
Plan

The West Entrance and the Outer Ward

The main entrance to the castle lies on the W side, within the
town. Originally the BARBICAN gateway to the N was entered
from a stepped ramp, part of which remains, and over a
wooden drawbridge; the W socket for the bridge axle is still
extant. The modern entrance is through the E side of the barbican, which consists of two solid turrets, the tops of which
were reached by stairs. A wooden door and a portcullis secured
the entrance to the passage, which was originally roofed, with
a further two-leaved door at the inner end, opening onto the
barbican itself.

The barbican curtain has three rounded turrets with arrowslits,
overlooking the ditch on the W side; the northernmost contains
a guard chamber that was reached by a flight of steps, and it
has an arrowslit overlooking the entrance passage. The town
wall runs W from the S turret. Unlike the main entrances to
the other great Edwardian castles, the OUTER GATE within
the barbican was not a gatehouse, simply a passage through
the curtain wall, overlooked by two of the great towers. A line
of battlemented machicolations, the corbels for which remain,
overlooked the immediate approach to the gate. A portcullis
and a two-leaved door with drawbars protected the passage.
Further drawbars were set in the outer part of the passage to
hold two large timbers to obstruct the passage, one above the
other. A flight of steps on the S side of the W wall-walk led
down to the room from where the portcullis was operated. Just
within the Outer Ward, slight foundations on either side mark
the site of a building across the rear of the gateway, the inner
walls of which had collapsed by 1627, corbels marking the line
of the roof. Similar foundations remain on the N side of the
ward where, according to the 1627 survey, the kitchen was
situated, with stables adjoining its E side.

The length of the S side of the ward is occupied by a substantial
building originally subdivided by timber partitions, two of
which formed a cross-passage; it was lit in the N and S walls
by windows with seats in their embrasures. One of the great
arches built as part of the 1340s re-roofing remains, renewed
in 1923, as do the stumps of several of the remaining seven.
Stubs of corbels are the only evidence for the timber trusses
of the roof of the 1280s. The range housed the garrison
CHAPEL on the E, the cross-passage dividing it from the
GREAT HALL in the centre, with an ANTE-ROOM and a
CHAMBER or LESSER HALL on the W. Part of the ground floor
of this range is set on the natural rock; the remainder was
floored over as a basement or CELLAR, entered from the W
down a flight of steps from the Outer Ward and through a
passage, and lit by narrow windows in the S, N and E walls. The
main entrance to this range was through a porch into the cross-
passage between the Great Hall and the chapel; opposing doorways led in to these rooms, with an additional doorway into
the hall at the S end of the passage. The E window, the

embrasure of which contained the altar, dominates the chapel. This window was originally of three lights. Fragments of tracery remain. A two-light traceried window in the N wall and two smaller windows to the S also lit the chapel. Another two-light traceried window in the N wall lit the Great Hall, with a narrow window in the SE corner of the original room, through one side of which lies a passage to the Prison Tower. A hooded fireplace in the centre of the S wall heated the hall; the jambs and much of its hood remain, with corbelled lamp brackets on either side. The ante-room, lit by a solitary window, has a fire-place in the N wall that has lost most of its dressed stonework. In the adjoining lesser hall or chamber fragments of the fire-place hood remain, whilst the lamp brackets are set on ornate corbels. This room is lit by the third of the two-light traceried windows in the N wall, with two smaller windows in the opposing wall.

The MURAL TOWERS consisted of two upper storeys over a base-ment, except for the Prison Tower, which has three floors over a deep basement, clearly the castle's prison. The SOUTH-WEST TOWER is approached through a small enclosed area reached by a flight of steps from the Outer Ward, and entered through a restored doorway. The upper rooms, reached from a restored newel stair, each have a fireplace as well as single- and two-light windows with window seats. Each floor had access to latrines; that on the first floor in a mural chamber, that on the upper floor at the end of a passage. The basement contains an arrowslit opening to the S, and an oven is set into the E wall. The NORTH-WEST TOWER is furnished in a similar manner, although the basement has two slits and there is no oven; the room, with a lockable doorway, was probably used for storage. Off the renewed staircase, between the two floors, a passage to a small chamber housing a latrine.

The newel staircase in the KITCHEN TOWER has not been renewed, so the upper rooms are best seen from the wall-walk. The tower was entered from the kitchen itself. A passage and some steps led down to its basement, possibly another store-room, or perhaps a larder. The upper rooms have particularly fine fireplaces, and are lit in the usual manner; there is a latrine passage off the first floor, with another reached from the stair-case. The PRISON TOWER on the opposite side of the court-yard is entered from the passage off the SE window in the Great Hall, a newel stair leading to the upper chambers. The basement or dungeon is lit and ventilated by a narrow slit in the S wall. The floor above, the level of which is shown by a ring of joist holes, was a plain room lit by a solitary slit, probably also a room of confinement. It must have had a trap door through which the basement was entered. The doorway to this ground-floor room is set well above floor level, a trap for the unwary. The first- and second-floor chambers are similar to those in the other towers, with fireplaces and single- and two-light windows. A latrine off the newel stairs serves both rooms.

At the E end of the Outer Ward is the entrance to the Inner Ward, an enclosure designed for royal residence. A quarried cleft in the rock not only created a ditch between the wards, but also enabled a well to be located here, in front of the small MIDDLE GATE. A chasm, infilled in 1532, formed a drawbridge pit in front of the projecting gate.

The Inner Ward and East Entrance*

A doorway with drawbar socket led from the Middle Gate into the INNER WARD. This is a small courtyard here, on the S and E sides of which lay a suite of rooms. Those on the first floor were devised for the personal use of King Edward and Queen Eleanor, and entered from external timber staircases. The alternative entrance to this area was from a watergate, now destroyed, up into the EAST BARBICAN with its three rounded turrets, and through a gateway, covered by machicolations similar to those over the W entrance, into the Inner Ward. The gateway and steps up into the barbican area are covered by one of the barbican turrets and the Chapel Tower, the original arrangement being best appreciated from a Buck brothers' engraving of 1742. The barbican area itself was planned as a garden, and therefore the area enclosed by the defences here is greater than that at the opposite end.

The rooms on the E and S of the Inner Ward are regarded as the finest examples of medieval royal apartments to survive

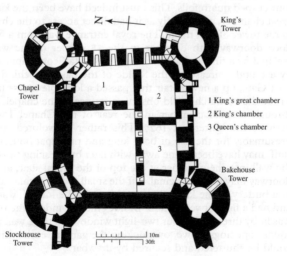

King's Tower

Chapel Tower

1 King's great chamber
2 King's chamber
3 Queen's chamber

Bakehouse Tower

Stockhouse Tower

10m
30ft

Conwy Castle, Inner Ward.
Plan

*John Kenyon is indebted to Jeremy Ashbee for sharing with him his results of an examination of the domestic arrangements in the Inner Ward, and allowing him to make use of his work.

virtually unaltered. The detailed survey of the castle in 1627 assigns names and functions to the chambers, although one must be wary of such documentation 300 years after the ward was planned and built, and with little royal use ever made of them. On the ground floor on the NE side is a room used as a cellar in 1627, with a rebuilt fireplace, two-light window with seat and also a slit in the W wall, the wall itself built partly against an arrowslit in the N curtain. The main entrance, with drawbar, into this 'cellar' is in the S wall, in the passage between the E and S ranges that runs behind the East Gate, and there is also a doorway into the Chapel Tower from within it. W of the cellar are traces of a building against the N curtain, incorporating another arrowslit; this may have been the granary, which is of uncertain date.

The ground-floor rooms in the S range were a kitchen, E, and a parlour, W, with a passage to the Bakehouse Tower beyond. The doorway into the kitchen has a drawbar, but that to the parlour has not on present evidence. Corroboration of the 1627 identification of the E room as a kitchen is borne out by the fireplace in its W wall, the largest in the castle, whilst the doorway in its S wall would have led to an outlet for kitchen refuse. The window details have largely been robbed.

The royal apartments lay on the first floor, and the Chapel and King's towers formed an integral part of the arrangement. The 1627 survey names the E range room as the Great Chamber. Its handsome traceried window in the W wall, of which fragments remain, originally had two lights set below four cusped quatrefoils. This must indeed have been the king's great chamber, particularly as it had direct access to the chapel in the tower of that name. The royal entrance was from a first-floor doorway with drawbar in the SE corner of the ward, reached by a timber staircase. Household staff could approach by a mural staircase on the N side of the passage behind the East Gate, up a newel stair that passed a lockable recess from where the monarch could observe a service in the chapel, and through a small chamber in the rear of the Chapel Tower, perhaps the buttery of 1627. This rather convoluted route, presumably for the use of both king and principal household staff, may have been done away with later by breaking through the wall into the chamber at the top of the mural stair, as this doorway may not be original. Off the small room, perhaps used as a buttery, is the king's latrine; this could be locked, was lit, and had a flue for ventilation. Besides the W window, the room was lit by three of the four two-light windows in the E wall with square openings above, overlooking the garden; each window could be shuttered and secured by drawbar.

A doorway in the SE corner of the Great Chamber led into the S range, consisting of the Presence Chamber on the E and Privy Chamber to the W, according to the 1627 survey, now interpreted as the king's and queen's chambers respectively. Three two-light windows that overlooked the Inner Ward lit these rooms; all three had lights under traceried heads of three trefoils. The Presence Chamber also received light from the southernmost of four windows in the E curtain wall, set below the machicolations. There is a fireplace in each room, as well as access to latrines on the S side. In the SW corner of the ward a timber stair led up to the first-floor doorway into a lobby and so through to the W chamber, which may have been the queen's equivalent to the king's Great Chamber; the Presence Chamber may have been used as a communal dining area by the royal household, whilst staff occupied the adjoining rooms in the King's and Bakehouse towers. The wall dividing the main chambers on the first floor has two doorways, the southernmost of which, likely to be the original, is blocked. The 1627 survey mentions a pair of handsome withdrawing rooms by the Privy Chamber; the only place for these, however unlikely, is the passage or lobby to the W, between the S range and the W curtain of the Inner Ward, into which the external timber stair led.

There is evidence that these buildings were re-roofed at the same time as the Great Hall, in the 1340s, and one arch does survive in the W chamber, as does evidence for others. However, in places the springing for the arches in one wall is not matched in the opposing masonry, and it may be that the work was abandoned unfinished. Evidence for the original, C13, roofs survives, with a corbel for a roof truss in the Great Chamber and marks set in the plasterwork left by wooden posts on the S wall of the Presence Chamber.

The towers on the W side are the STOCKHOUSE (NW) and the BAKEHOUSE TOWERS (SW). The former consists of two floors over a basement; the newel stair is unrestored. The doorways from the Inner Ward and that which opened into the basement were secured by drawbars. The basement has a solitary arrowslit; in both upper floors is a two-light window with seats and a simple slit opening, as well as a fireplace. On the first floor a passage leads from the slit window embrasure to a latrine. A second latrine is at the end of a passage off the staircase. The outer face of the Bakehouse Tower was largely restored in the C19, following collapse or demolition. It is so named from the large oven set into the basement wall. The upper floors were similarly appointed as the Stockhouse Tower, the only original section of the outer wall of the tower being at second-floor level.

The towers at the SE and NE corners are not identical. The KING'S TOWER consists of four floors. The lowest, entered by trap door in the floor of the ground-floor chamber, was lit by a single slit. The ground floor was entered by a passage from the kitchen or via the S mural stair from the East Gate, which connected with this passage to the kitchen. The chamber has a two-light E window, with an arrowslit overlooking the barbican, and a hooded fireplace in the S wall. Also at this level, and accessed from the passage, is a small barrel-vaulted chamber with a slit window, from which steps lead up to a latrine also accessible from the Presence Chamber. The newel stair continues to the upper floors. At first-floor level, a short passage leads from the stair into one side of the embrasure of a two-light window in the main chamber. As with most rooms in the towers, there was an arrowslit and a hooded fireplace. The room above also had a two-light window, but was unheated, unless a brazier was utilized.

One of the glories of Conwy is the CHAPEL TOWER. The lower chamber, currently housing an exhibition, has an arrowslit flanking the N curtain, and the usual two-light window, with seats, in the N wall. In the E wall, reached via a mural passage, is a doorway overlooking the steps into the barbican, possibly to allow goods to be hoisted directly into the tower. Just beyond this feature, to the N, is evidence for a newel stair in the face of the tower which was never completed. The chapel itself lies on the floor above, and is undoubtedly one of the finest castle chapels in the country. The circular chamber forms the nave, with the semi-hexagonal rib-vaulted chancel set into the E wall of the tower. High in the opposing wall is the rectangular opening from the watching chamber through which the king could observe Mass. Lancet windows, grooved for glass, are set in three of the chancel's seven bays. Each bay contains a trefoil-headed arch up to the levels of the sills, forming a blind arcade running round the chancel. This arcade extends as brackets into the nave for a rood beam. There is a piscina on the S side of the chancel, and on both sides a small window opens from side chambers. A lockable doorway off the nave enters the sacristy on the N. This room has a two-light window with seat. To the r. of the window is an embrasure of the aumbry facing onto the chancel, accessible from both chancel and sacristy. The mural chamber to the S lies off both the staircase and a doorway in the main room of the chapel; this room may have been the vestry. The floor above the chapel has the usual fireplace, window and slit, as well as evidence from a series of joist holes for the original roof being lower. The internal plastering at this level and in the chapel survives to a considerable degree, confirming the statement in 1627 that the tower was 'in the best repare'.

The Wall-walks

The remarkable state of preservation of much of the tower battlements can be best seen from the WALL-WALK, and so too can the internal arrangements of the towers. Although the wall-walk allowed access all round the perimeter, sections could be closed off, probably more to preserve the privacy of the Inner Ward than for defensive reasons. The best example of this lies to the rear of the Stockhouse Tower, where there is a rebate for a wooden door to prevent access from Outer Ward to inner; a similar feature can be seen at the Bakehouse Tower. In order to take the wall-walk around the rear of the Kitchen Tower the wall here is supported by corbels. The creasing cut into the battlements and towers originally took lead flashing to

waterproof the masonry. Given that the creasing cuts such
features as the door rebate on the back of the Stockhouse
Tower, this work must have been undertaken later, probably
as part of the roof alterations undertaken in 1347. The
staggered arrangement of the arrowslits in the merlons, the
stumps of finials on the merlons, and the sockets for timber
hourds below the crenellations are all best appreciated from
the wall-walk.

TOWN WALLS.* The town walls, with twenty-one extant towers   28, 30
and three gatehouses, run NW from the castle's Stockhouse
Tower, along the quay by the river Conwy, SW along Town
Ditch Road and Mount Pleasant, and then turn to form the
southern perimeter, to link up with the castle's west barbican.
The length of the circuit is about ¾ m. The defences are
remarkably complete, with towers at regular intervals, ideally
placed to enfilade an assault on the intervening sections of
curtain, and three twin-towered gatehouses controlling access
to the town. The predominant form of the towers is
D-shaped, although Tower Thirteen is circular, and apart from
this tower and Tower Sixteen all were open at the back. The
towers were floored at wall-walk level and provided with three
arrowslits, and may well have been unroofed, apart from Tower
Sixteen. Both towers and wall-walks had provision for hourd-
ing, as in the castle. Originally, in order to pass behind each
tower one would have had to cross over a wooden bridge
behind it, something that could have been removed easily
during an assault. From the ground, the wall-walk would have
been reached by stairs distributed around the inner face, and
the battlements of the towers had steps up to them.

The modern road has removed a section of the wall beyond the
Stockhouse Tower, but thereafter it is continuous, although
with modern sections inserted for roads and railway. The
section along the quay, which consists of four towers and a
gatehouse, is the hardest to appreciate. Later buildings are set
against the defences here, the towers lack crenellations, and
windows replace their arrowslits. A thin screen wall runs NW
from the castle, originally crossing the ditch and then meeting
the thicker and crenellated town wall itself in the area of
Telford's mock medieval tower of 1826 across the road from
the castle. This thinner wall, and its equivalent on the S side,
lacked a wall-walk for reasons of security, so that an enemy
who gained a foothold on the town walls would not have been
able to use the wall to try to force a way into the castle.

TOWER ONE, at the S end of the quay, overlooks a simple
POSTERN in its lee, without a portcullis. Beyond it are two
further towers. Next is the LOWER GATE, the smallest of the
three gatehouses, which has also suffered modern depreda-
tions. The gate consists of twin D-shaped towers flanking a

*The numbering of the towers around the town wall follows that in the current
Cadw guidebook.

passage with a portcullis at the end. Rectangular chambers inside.

A SPUR WALL extends into the water from runs from TOWER FIVE and protects the N end of the quay. At the end was a round tower, long since collapsed. This wall shows evidence of two phases: a clear horizontal masonry break runs the length of it, and the upper part does not bond with Tower Five. The heightening also caused an arrowslit in the tower to be altered to allow access to the spur's wall-walk. The spur wall has a crenellated parapet on both sides of this wall-walk. Close to Tower Five a small GATEWAY, enlarged in more recent times, provided access to the quay from outside the walls. One groove remains for a portcullis and a shaft for the counterweight.

The N SECTION of the walls was cleared of gardens and build-ings against it in the second half of the C20. Now with the bank reconstructed and part of the ditch opened, it is one of the most imposing medieval town defences in Europe. The wall runs from Tower Five to Tower Thirteen at the highest point of the circuit and originally did not contain any GATEWAYS at all. A number have been inserted since, although the only one marring the appearance is that of 1827 through Tower Ten. Most of the towers have lost their battlements, and TOWER ELEVEN subsided and cracked following construction of the railway tunnel. TOWER SIX provides the best idea of the original form, with slits in the crenellations, as well as three in the upper floor. On the W side of several of these towers is, or was, a projecting stone from which a plumb-bob may have been suspended. This would have given the masons the correct alignment for raising the walls, the construction of the towers generally having preceded by a short period. In the circular TOWER THIRTEEN, and in the town wall to its E, there is evidence from the putlogs of the use of inclined scaffolding during construction; the holes spiralling around the tower are unmistakable. The walls either side of the tower are canted, and this places it beyond the line of the walls, providing a line of sight all the way down to the water on one side and along the southern section on the other, including the Upper Gate, the main entrance into the medieval town.

The wall from towers Thirteen to Fifteen includes the UPPER GATE. In front of the twin D-shaped towers was a BARBICAN, one wall of which survives with four slits. It defended the approach to the drawbridge over the rock-cut ditch; the bridge when raised would have sat in the rectangular recess in the outer arch of the gate passage. The modern road through the gate is much lower than the medieval arrangement; note the level of the stone setting in the passage wall for the draw-bridge axle. The bridge was worked from a timber platform reached from the gate's S tower, the joist holes for the flooring of which are evident. The passage was protected by a portcullis, as well as by a two-leaved door and drawbar. Guard chambers occupied the ground floor of both towers, entered from door-ways flanked by narrow slits in the rear walls, and secured by drawbars. Slits in the chambers covered the gate passage, as well as the town wall to the N and S; this level in the N tower is divided by a cross wall. Those lodged in the gatehouse occupied the first-floor chamber across the back and utilized the S tower; the rear wall at this level was timber-framed. The main entrance to this part of the gate was up an external flight of steps, which also connected with the town wall to the S, to Tower Fourteen, and to a latrine for the garrison. A separate room in the N tower was reached from the adjacent wall-walk and stairs. The latrine appears to be the only domestic provision, as, surprisingly for a great gate, there are no fireplaces; any heating would have had to have come from braziers. The archway S of the gate is a modern insertion for pedestrians.

One of the best-preserved sections of town wall runs S from the Upper Gate, and includes TOWERS FOURTEEN and FIFTEEN. Here the battlements remain almost intact. On the inside can be seen a section of three lines of corbelling, built to enable the wall-walk to have the desired width. Just E of Tower Fifteen is a clear vertical break, where the main section of town wall, built 1283–4, met the wall of 1286 that ran to the castle. E of the break is a row of three rectangular windows with seats in the embrasures. The town wall at this point was built against, or close to, Llywelyn's Hall (*see* p. 323). TOWER SIXTEEN differed from the others by being D-shaped. Originally open at the rear and unroofed, in 1305 the tower was heightened and the roof and two floors added. The ground floor was entered from the N, the chamber having a single loop. The rectangular first floor, with two rectangular windows and hooded fireplace, was the main chamber, with a small with-drawing room or solar on the floor above.

Between Tower Sixteen and the castle are three modern ARCHES cut through the walls. The largest, pushed through in 1847 for the railway between towers Seventeen and Eighteen, has mock battlements. TOWER EIGHTEEN retains its battlements. Ranged along the wall between it and the Mill Gate is one of the most remarkable features of Conwy, a line of twelve corbelled-out LATRINES built in 1286, some of which retain [30] grooves for wooden seats. The latrines must have discharged into the river Gyffin, or even the leat serving the adjacent mill, and were located here to serve the staff of the king's wardrobe or the royal secretariat. The hall of the Wardrobe, a timber building erected as early as June 1283, was located in this area, and utilized the S tower of the Mill Gate.

The MILL GATE is set at an angle to the town wall on either side of it for a reason that is unclear, unless a pre-existing road or gateway in the abbey precinct dictated the layout. The gate-house is also unusual in that one tower (N) is D-shaped, with polygonal chambers, whilst the other (S) is rounded, the chambers likewise. A portcullis and two-leaved door barred the passage; there was no drawbridge. The ground-floor guard chambers were entered from doorways, with drawbars, in the rear walls. Both contain a single arrowslit in the front of the towers, the N room having a further loop in its N wall; no loops opened on to the gate passage. The upper chambers, whose rear walls, like the Upper Gate, were timber-framed, were both well appointed, with a fireplace, window and slit in each room. A doorway in the N tower led to the wall-walk to the E, whilst the most easterly of the twelve latrines is reached from a doorway on the SW side of the S tower. The main point of entrance to the first floor of the gatehouse must have been from the now lost building to its W.

From the Mill Gate the town wall with TOWERS NINETEEN TO TWENTY-ONE runs E to meet the castle. It crosses the site of the ditch, now the road out of the town to Llanrwst and Betws-y-coed, which passes through a C19 archway. The section nearest the castle is simply a screen wall without battlements and wall-walk, like that on the N side.

PLAS MAWR

Built for Robert Wynn, a younger son of the Wynns of Gwydir Castle who had seen foreign service both diplomatic and military in the 1530s–40s. Plas Mawr, begun 1576, is half palazzo and half manor house. Astonishingly large for a house in such a town, it represents the revival of Welsh fortunes in the Tudor era, the arrival of Renaissance culture and, in the heraldic plasterwork within, the North Welsh sense of family status. The classicism is of course not straight from the source, but it is more than skin-deep: pedimental window heads apparently derived from the 1550 work at Somerset House in London; a gatehouse on the kind of near-cruciform plan later popularized by John Thorpe; and the Italian taste for plasterwork friezes carried out with unconvincing female caryatids and heraldic motifs.

As a house type, Plas Mawr follows a group of villa-like merchants' houses evolved on the Thames estuary in the third quarter of the C16, including Eastbury Manor, Barking and Valence House, Dagenham. Eastbury is regarded as the first of these, completed in 1576 but perhaps begun more than ten years earlier. Plas Mawr is likewise almost symmetrical, with classical display on its elevations and a skyline rich in stair-turrets and chimneys, but it occupies a most awkward urban site and its construction plainly came in three phases.

Little used after the first two generations, so little altered despite becoming tenements, Plas Mawr was let in 1885 by the Mostyn estate to the Royal Cambrian Academy, for art exhibitions. *Arthur Baker* and his nephew *Herbert Baker* made adaptations, and *Baker & Hughes* in 1895 added a gallery at the back (since demolished). Repairs for the Academy from the 1950s replaced most of the dressed stonework, but resources were inadequate. The Academy moved to the converted Seion chapel in 1993, allowing thorough restoration in 1993–7 by the *Building Design Partnership* (project architects *Ken Moth* and *Alan Davies*), for Cadw. This dramatically changed the exterior by lime-

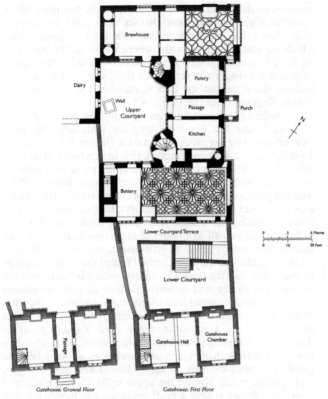

Conwy, Plas Mawr.
Plan

rendering all the external stonework, and the interior by, controversially, picking out in colour the motifs of the plasterwork.

The three building phases between 1576 and 1585 were determined as much by the availability of space as by architectural
ambition. First the rectangular N wing on one burgage plot at the
top of Crown Lane, distinguished by more extravagant details;
then the central block facing the lane and matching S wing in
1580, to form a symmetrical courtyard house entered by a central
doorway and passage; and lastly the achievement of a new
entrance and second courtyard by erecting a gatehouse to the S,
on High Street.

The NORTH WING, dated 1576, set the style for the rest, and
though entered at the S by passing through the hall, it is best
described first. Robert Wynn (c. 1520–98) had only minor connections with the Tudor court and no country house in Snowdonia, but even this first section would have stood out in
Elizabethan North Wales. Elaborate windows of Deganwy

stone on its show end to the lane, those on the two main floors
corbelled slightly forward; each has six lights and is transomed,
with a low pediment. Semicircular attic oriel. Stepped gables
which became the motif of the whole house, at the ends and
on the dormers, the lowest step corbelled sideways, the highest
supporting a diagonally set square finial capped with a polyhedron; these suggest the Low Countries, but were fashionable in England from the mid C16.*

A vanished porch opened from the s into the present BREW-
HOUSE, l., the big freestone fireplace with elliptical arch.
Beyond a service room, the PARLOUR (facing the street) has
a plaster ceiling with intersecting ribs in lozenge and quatrefoil patterns. The plan repeats above in the main apartment of
two rooms with a lobby and servant's room divided off by
wooden partitions between. The CHAMBER OVER THE BREW-
HOUSE (as named in a 1665 inventory), limewashed white, has
a just-projecting overmantel with a huge shield and RG 1577
in outsize figures, all in low-relief plasterwork. To either side
stumpy columns, reeded to half-height, on corbels. Bold if
coarse heraldic decoration is carried round the room, so tall as
to use nearly half the wall. The ribbed ceiling is finer, with the
intersecting circles and squares, Serlian designs circulating
since the 1550s, scattered with motifs from the shields. Wooden
screen with guilloche and arch ornament. Similar but richer
decoration in the CHAMBER OVER THE PARLOUR, again
dated 1577. Chimneypiece with slender moulded jambs supporting a shelf with Renaissance mouldings, above a bravura
lintel of stones locked like a jigsaw. Shield and initials above,
and heraldic motifs around the upper walls. Ceiling pattern of
a four-leaf flower against a grid, miniature leaf bosses on each
intersection. Placed among them the signs of the Zodiac etc.
– as a whole, the most refined craftsmanship in the house.

The addition of 1580 turned this first phase into a
substantial E-plan house, levelled with the N wing despite the
falling ground by cellars at the s beneath the hall. The
CENTRAL RANGE has a shallow timber entrance tower facing
the lane, replaced in the C18. Both this and the s wing have
simpler stone-framed windows, flush with the walls and
without pediments. On the ground floor, a cross-passage
between kitchen and pantry, the former with a handsome elliptical fire-arch and hoodmould and old plaster surfaces decorated in red and black patterns. In the angles of the courtyard
are two polygonal stair-turrets, their ascending spirals lit by
windows stepping up, a belvedere at the top of the s stair. They
give access to both N and s apartments and to the GREAT
CHAMBER across the centre. The wall treatment here shows
how Elizabethan great chambers derive from Italian prototypes: original wooden benching all round, then a band of plain
plaster for hangings. An upper band is articulated with what

*The gable detail reappeared on Plas Mawr, Caernarfon, of 1591.

Thomas Pennant called 'rude stucco' – puzzlingly proportioned caryatids not quite doing their job of supporting the
cornice. Fireplace on the back wall, repainted as fictive marble,
with, above, the royal monogram and Garter encircling the
Tudor rose. Flat ribbed ceiling of star patterns radiating from
heraldic circles. Inserting this ceiling was plainly a late decision, since the Great Chamber as built has its ornamental open
timber roof intact above it: four shallow cambered arch-braced
trusses spring from stone corbels, three of these having apex
trusses with quatrefoils between two small circles.

The SOUTH WING has the same plan at upper levels as the N
one, with a similar attic oriel, but the ground floor contains the
HALL, originally entered from the upper courtyard but after   52
1585 adapted to be entered on the gatehouse side by an internal porch. Wooden screens with two doorways, and buttery
below it. Fireplace of the familiar design with kneeler corbels,
painted as black marble. Wildly extravagant overmantel plasterwork dated 1580, with more caryatids and misused architectural motifs, as well as emblems of Welsh princehood and
Tudor sovereignty. The plaster ceiling, as big as the Great
Chamber's, similarly based on bosses with radiating ribs, here
has frets arranged diamond-wise, and not designed to fit. On
the floor above the hall, two rooms with studio between but
without plaster ornament.

The new entrance having replaced that halfway up the
steeply sloping Crown Lane, the drop in level was overcome,
with Renaissance ingenuity, by making a terrace outside the
hall on its S with dog-leg steps up and cellars beneath.
The terrace level continues on a three-arch bridge on the W of
the new courtyard to provide access directly between the hall
and the first floor of the gatehouse.

This GATEHOUSE of 1585 is the most perfect design in the
complex. It has a porch projecting into High Street on the axis
of the central passage, which is flanked by two equal rooms
with lateral chimneys at the rear. On the first floor the
Gatehouse Hall, entered by stairs on the gable wall, which uses
the porch as an oriel, and has a smaller chamber beyond; on
the second floor, one large unheated space, reminiscent of the
top-floor look-out rooms at hunting lodges, but here treated
as a gallery with three bays of arch-braced trusses with diagonal apex braces. Exterior with pedimented windows aligned
vertically (though still without pilasters or architraves), and
dormer windows set on the corbel tables at the eaves. They and
the main gables have stepping and polyhedron finials as on the
earlier work.

PUBLIC BUILDINGS

ROYAL CAMBRIAN ACADEMY OF ART, Crown Street. After
vacating Plas Mawr, the Academy converted the adjacent
former Seion Independent Chapel of 1858 and 1876 into new

galleries, 1992–3, by *Bowen Dann Davies*. Stucco original, with a big glazed piece angled out of the side wall.

GUILDHALL, Rose Hill Street. Facing down Castle Street. 1863. A hard Gothic structure of purple stone dressed with sandstone. Two narrow two-light gable windows and a squat tower to the r. with an indefinable ashlar cornice. The low parapeted structure on the l. corner, with a square turret, was the porch, replaced as part of large rear additions of 1925, by *C. H. Minshull* of John Douglas's firm. The new entrance is in a softer Gothic with relief carving, the Council Chamber (l.) has a canted gable end. The original part has a Gothic hall and fireplace; the 1925 chamber has a hammerbeam roof with brightly coloured plaster panels.

BODLONDEB, ¼ m. NW. Aberconwy Council Offices. On an idyllic hill overlooking the estuary, a substantial Victorian mansion built for Albert Wood, of Henry Wood & Co., anchor-makers of Saltney, mayor of Conwy.* 1877, by *T. M. Lockwood*, replacing a Regency villa. Gothic softened by Nesfield and Shaw's Domestic Revival of the previous decade. Grey limestone with plain tile roofs, rising in the middle to a Germanic steep hip with lead finials. The windows are mostly modern sashes, the Gothic confined to gables and oriels. Some pretty woodwork, and in the centre a full-height galleried hall with coloured glass in the lantern, the staircase, also top-lit, to one side. Borough Council Offices since 1937. A long wing was added NW, in 1991, with gablets nodding to the late C19, by *Eaton, Manning, Wilson* of Shrewsbury. – LODGES by *Lockwood* to SW and SE with a little half-timbering.

CIVIC HALL, Castle Street. Built as municipal offices and assembly hall on the site of the market, 1897, by *T. B. Farrington*, Borough Surveyor, with help from *Richard Davies*. Gatehouse-like small front with an iron-crested pyramid roof and angle turret, facing up the High Street. The hall was burnt in 1967 and poorly replaced, its flat roof ugly from the Quay.

88   SUSPENSION BRIDGE. Built by *Thomas Telford* in 1822–6 with a span of 327 feet (101 metres). Land traffic to Ireland having long been restricted by the ferry, about which there were many complaints, government support for a bridge was obtained in 1822, four years after the Menai Strait project. A previous scheme for a high bridge by *John Rennie*, 1802, would have demolished much of the castle, but Telford resolved to build a 600-ft (185-metre) embankment from the E bank to a rocky islet, and then a suspension bridge only 16 ft (5 metres) above high water. The superimposed drums of Telford's paired towers, immensely strong despite their flimsy parkland-Gothic appearance, were built from 1822 by *John Wilson*, with narrow machicolated arches between. Originally darkened, their pale Penmon limestone contrasts with the un-rendered walls of the castle. The cast-iron chains were made, as for the

---

*Wood's art collection here included Millais's *Blind Girl*.

Menai bridge, by *William Hazledine* of Shrewsbury, and assembled by *William Provis*, who was forced by river currents to fit them link-by-link from a rope bridge instead of floating the chains out complete. This is the only major early suspension bridge still to have its original chains; they have always been painted white. Strengthened in 1903-4 by *J. J. Webster*, who added a footway (removed in 1966), heavier decking (removed in 1988) and a steel cable above the four chains. Restored for foot traffic, the deck hangs from its suspension rods nearly as when opened, the roadway having three layers of fir planking. On the w, Telford's adaptation of the castle footings and watergate etc. is visible. At the e his TOLL HOUSE, a miniature Scottish Baronial design. Uncluttered by the later bridges, Telford's work would reveal itself as a masterpiece of landscape art.

RAILWAY BRIDGE. Two tubular girder spans of 400 ft (123 metres), erected in 1846-8 to designs by *Robert Stephenson*, and used as a test structure for his much more ambitious Britannia Bridge over the Menai Strait; since the 1970 fire there the principal surviving example in Britain of the type. The consultants for the ironwork were *William Fairbairn* and *Eaton Hodgkinson*. Unlike on the Strait, the Chester–Holyhead line was placed next to Telford's road, using the same embankment. After the bridge, it skirts the castle to the s. In such close proximity, the bridge's bulk is not a harmonious match with Telford's, nor with the castle. The line passes through massive square limestone gate-towers, embattled, with lower drum towers on the outside flanking the paired arches, and little pepperpot turrets on the inside flanking the iron tubes. The towers may be designs of *Francis Thompson*. The attempt to be in keeping is less successful than the bolder pylons of the Britannia Bridge. The vast tubes, wrought-iron box girders weighing over 1,000 tons each, were assembled on the river bank by William Evans, then floated out and hoisted into position. Two tubular piers added at the sides of the main span in 1899. A QUAY, SE, was built in 1852 for transhipment of river-borne goods.

ROAD BRIDGE. 1958, by *H. W. Fitzsimmons*. An over-high steel arch, from abutments suggesting bastions.

ROAD TUNNEL. 1986-91, by *Travers Morgan & Partners* with *Christiani & Nielsen*. The first immersed tube tunnel in Britain, the prefabricated box segments in 384-ft (118-metre) lengths floated out and dropped into the underwater trench, appropriately the mirror image of Stephenson's technique in 1848.

PERAMBULATION

As a true fortress town, Conwy can be well viewed from outside its walls, which from inside are often invisible. From the wall-walk, the two come into focus together. Conwy's origin rested on access to the sea, so the QUAY below the walls is the place to begin. The little tidal port was protected by the castle and a spur from the town walls. The quay was built in 1833, by *William Provis*, engineer for Telford's bridge, of grey limestone. The walls here are screened by a variety of boathouses, but at the NW end, LOWER GATE STREET, a short row of houses backs onto the wall, including No. 10, a tourist attraction since 1900 as 'the Smallest House'. Once C19 infill in a longer row, its tiny upper floor was reached by ladder. Through the Lower Gate, the Civic Hall (p. 340), l., faces CASTLE STREET, opposite ABERCONWY HOUSE (National Trust), the one survivor of the houses-cum-warehouses of the English merchants. Tree-ring-dated to *c.* 1420, it was a Temperance hotel in the later C19 and came in 1934 to the National Trust, which restored it in 1976. Very few of these modestly scaled buildings, once common in trading towns and ports across northern Europe, remain. Narrow stone-walled cellar, entered by the small Gothic doorway at the SE corner; the heavy beams and corner fireplace inserted with the low intermediate storey above, probably in the late C16, with a corbelled oriel to the l. of external stone stairs. Above this the mark of prosperity: a timber-framed upper storey jettied to the E and N on deep curved wooden brackets set on corbel stones. Kentish-style curved braces in large panels, both plaster and timber limewashed. Impressive gabled roof, probably once stone-tiled. The inserted first-floor hall has a timber-framed partition and heavy beams and the upper floor has inserted partitions, tie-beam-and-collar trusses and wind-bracing, but there is evidence for the attic being floored.

Beyond, typical C19 stucco up to the churchyard entry. Opposite, Nos. 7–9, later C19, with oriels enriched with egg-and-dart moulding, rears above low neighbours. No. 11, dated 1589, has the initials of the Rev. J. Birchdall, vicar. Heavily altered with upper windows in small gables. The BLUE BELL, mid-C20, in brewers' Old English fails to fit in.

The CHURCHYARD, r., is a space apart, though the largest in the town, backed onto by surrounding houses. The W exit leads into CHURCH STREET with an altered C18 row, Nos. 4–8, opposite the Baptist chapel (p. 322). LANCASTER SQUARE, an accidental public space, is presided over by the step-gabled POLICE STATION, 1859, by *John Lloyd*, roughcast with limestone dressings, and has at the centre a small stone FOUNTAIN, 1895, by *Grayson & Ould*, with a painted bronze of Llywelyn the Great, by *E. O. Griffith* of Liverpool, on a column. On the lower side, two early C20 banks: BANK HOUSE, l., in buff sandstone is Free Tudor, and the small HSBC BANK, r., has 1920s Georgian detail. Off York Place, before the Tabernacl chapel (p. 322), set back, is a rare early C19 COCKPIT, circular with conical roof; in the late C19 the studio of the artist J. D. Dawson.

The HIGH STREET runs downhill to the Lower Gate. On the l., Nos. 20–22, much altered, with mock timber, is C16 or early C17 within. The gatehouse to Plas Mawr (p. 339) then projects. On the r., a three-storey C19 stucco row; two well-mannered 1930s red sandstone commercial buildings; and the contrasting strident CASTLE HOTEL, Neo-Jacobean by *Douglas & Fordham*, 1885. Green stone in broken pieces, with dressings and shaped gables of orange brick and terracotta, and a manorial centrepiece in purple sandstone. By the standards of Douglas's best work, a coarse assemblage, but it is a refacing of earlier C19 houses, as shown by the w staircase within. Opposite, the most thoughtful C20 addition to Conwy's streetscape, the PALACE CINEMA, by *S. Colwyn Foulkes*, 1935. Dark rubble dressed with red-brown sandstone. Moderne simplifications of historical forms; proto-lancets in groups separated by reeded piers. Stepped gables in homage to Plas Mawr, the l. one with a slender full-height window infilled with lovely branching ironwork. Below, stuccoed C19 buildings both sides, those on the r. with steep gables to suggest the C17. BERRY STREET runs NW parallel to the quay towards the Porth-yr-aden break in the walls. Stucco and roughcast terraces, those on the r. backing onto the walls. No. 2 on the lower corner with High Street, five bays with Late Georgian sashes, has an earlier lateral chimney behind. CHAPEL STREET climbs SW into the area of small C19 housing. Carmel chapel (p. 322) faces down Llewelyn Street. SEAVIEW TERRACE and ERSKINE TERRACE at right angles are blind alleys derived from the medieval plan, with miniature terraces, in Erskine Street a stone row with gabled upper windows. On the l. the original façade of the Tabernacl chapel (p. 322), the Royal Cambrian Academy (p. 339), and the garden gate to Plas Mawr. Scant remains, r., of PARLWR MAWR, birthplace in 1582 of John Williams †1650, Archbishop of York.

At the end, BANGOR ROAD is crossed. A brief glance r. shows the gateway widened by Telford for the main road, with the former POST OFFICE, 1907, by *T. B. Farrington*, r. On the corner of UPPER GATE STREET, the ALBION, 1930s brown brick and half-timber. The street climbs over the 1845 railway tunnel, past low terraced houses, r., in the blind NEWBOROUGH TERRACE and WATKIN STREET, to the Upper Gate. Around the corner from the topmost tower, a good view down MOUNT PLEASANT of the line of the NW wall. Two mid-C19 stone villas l., LLYS LLEWELYN and CASTLE BANK, with cramped Plas Mawr gables. A short detour w up Sychnant Pass Road reveals Nos. 2–4 BRYNHYFRYD, a good roughcast pair with asymmetrical outer gables, by *H. L. North*, 1919, their coachhouses a little N. Returning to the Upper Gate, another good view of walls, down the steep S flank, wonderfully with a field in front.

Back inside the defences, ROSEMARY LANE runs past the R.C. church (p. 322) and its marble Calvary. The low porches r. are bridge-entrances to TŴR LLYWELYN, an ingenious informal grouping of flats and houses by *Bowen Dann Davies*, 1985, stepped down to the level of the STATION. The station building by *Francis Thompson*, 1845, has gone; it had stepped gables, inevitably. The surreal course of the line from Stephenson's bridge to the tunnel under the upper town is surprisingly inoffensive. A bold Tudor arch of red sandstone pierces the medieval wall. ROSE HILL STREET curves round. The MALT-LOAF, l., was the Erskine Family Hotel when Charlotte Brontë stayed in 1859. Enlarged and extended in the later C19 to three storeys and five bays. The NATIONAL SCHOOL, r., 1838, of dark squared stone has gables and deep-chamfered triple windows. Beyond, the medieval Mill Gate (p. 335) that led to the pool in the Gyffin valley has been ingeniously adopted to provide a footpath from the valley car park up to the town. It also leads s to the finest view back to the whole, from the slopes of Benarth Hill. Small Late Victorian buildings on the l. include ST MARY'S HALL, 1887, of almost Arts and Crafts simplicity, of grey limestone and St John's Wesleyan Chapel (p. 322).

On the corner of CASTLE SQUARE is the Guildhall (p. 340). Behind, the Castle VISITOR CENTRE, by *Bowen Dann Davies*, 1985, project architect *Jonathan Knox*. Opposite, only the l. flank remains of the gateway designed by *Thomas Telford* in 1826, an arch with a lodge in the old stone, unlike the towers of his bridge. On the N, PLAS FARDRE, earlier C19, three-storey stucco, with three bargeboarded gables and a fourth set back l. Behind, BODREINALLT, of similar date, also gabled, faces over CASTLE STREET. On the l., NatWEST BANK, 1867, High Victorian Gothic, for the National Provincial Bank. Of the muscular Seddon or Burges type, in banded stone, the arches with inset circles for ornament. The former MUNICIPAL OFFICES was a Post Office by *Kennedy*, *c.* 1879, clumsily refronted in 1907–8 in a weak Gothic, by *F. D. Cheers* of Liverpool. The ground floor looks earlier. No. 20, YR HEN GOLEG, is the sad remnant of a C15–C16 timber-framed house, which when drawn in 1811 had a remarkable double-cylinder oriel on an oak base shaped as twin fan vaults. The base survives, barely recognizable, with a heraldic shield. Opposite, Nos. 23–25 were called new in 1835, two-storey, with large sashes. Finally, by the churchyard entry again, Nos. 14–16, a tall mid-C19 four-bay pair with four bargeboarded gables and exceptionally large stucco-framed main windows.
See also Gyffin.

CRAIGSIDE

8282

The N-facing bay of Llandudno (q.v.) has rocky promontories at each end. Craigside is a select residential suburb, nestling beneath the E one, Little Orme.

Facing the sea on COLWYN ROAD, detached late C19 houses with tiny octagonal towers and battlemented parapets. Just one lead spire remains. On the end houses, the date 1896 in a little terracotta aedicule above the front door. Further E,

VILLA MARINA, a *tour de force* of Modernist confidence totally appropriate in its seaside location. Built *c.* 1936 for Harry Scribbans, by the cinema specialist *Harry W. Weedon*. L-plan, the two arms radiating from a glazed entrance hall facing SW. Wide balconies, rounded window bays and nautical handrails. White-painted walls, with bands of brickwork. The vast slabs containing the chimneys and the stair-tower extend up above the roof terrace, like ship's funnels. Service and maids' rooms and a garage for four cars in the S wing. A large living room in the W wing, facing the sea and connecting to a round dining room adjacent to the hall. Above these, sumptuous bedroom suites. The double-height terrazzo-finished ENTRANCE HALL is the showpiece, with a spiral cantilevered staircase rising across the curved glazing. In the garden, a circular GAZEBO above a drum containing changing rooms. From here, a long curving ramp down to the beach. All stone-clad, with decorative bands of glass block, grey stone and black faience.

Further up Colwyn Road, LONGLEAT AVENUE leads N towards the sea. Two houses stand out. EDGECLIFFE, *c.* 1930, by *Baron C. S. Underhill*. Tiled gambrel roofs above a rendered ground storey, a big waney-edge boarded gable above the front door. More Kent or Sussex than Wales. To the W, TŶR CRAIG, a playful composition of white-and-black render, red tiles and pebbledash. A battlemented stair-tower with stepped windows and a circular bay with a conical roof. Not great architecture, but fun nevertheless. Also off Colwyn Road, to the S, BRYN-Y-BIA ROAD. At the top of a short cul-de-sac (Bryn-y-bia Place), SHERATON, *c.* 1933, possibly by *Clough Williams-Ellis* and similar to Coed-y-Castell, Deganwy (q.v.) with its pair of bowed wings. But here there is a central balcony, and at the back, a cantilevered bow overlooking an ornamental pool with waterfalls, surely a Clough mark. Further up Bryn-y-bia Road, CHEVRONS. 1930s International Style.

CRICCIETH/CRICIETH

5038

A quiet unspoilt seaside town on a gentle slope facing S towards Harlech and Cardigan Bay. The castle dominates a promontory which subdivides the beach. Built in the 1230s by Llewelyn the Great, it was conquered in 1282 by Edward I, whose garrison town, probably unwalled, was created to the N side and granted its charter two years later. Further N, arable land provided food for the castle, and the *maes* originated as commons land. The church is at some distance from the castle, perhaps on the site of a Celtic foundation. Most of present-day Criccieth developed after 1809, when the turnpike road, now the High Street, replaced the old track past the Castle. The railway came in 1867, after which the peaceful little fishing village expanded with boarding houses and villas. It remains a popular coastal resort.

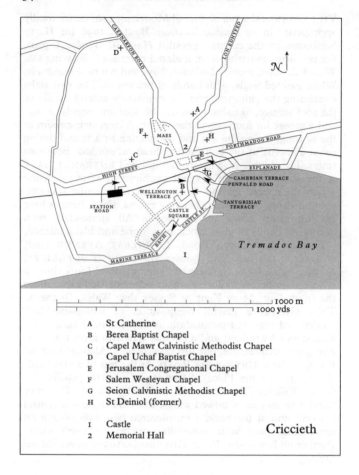

CAERNARFON ROAD
LÔN EIFNYD
D
N
A
F MAES H
C PORTHMADOG ROAD
2 E ESPLANADE
HIGH STREET G CAMBRIAN TERRACE
PENPALED ROAD
B WELLINGTON
TERRACE TANYGRISIAU
STATION TERRACE
ROAD CASTLE
SQUARE
LÔN
BACH
I Tremadoc Bay
MARINE TERRACE

| | 1000 m |
| | 1000 yds |

A   St Catherine
B   Berea Baptist Chapel
C   Capel Mawr Calvinistic Methodist Chapel
D   Capel Uchaf Baptist Chapel
E   Jerusalem Congregational Chapel
F   Salem Wesleyan Chapel
G   Seion Calvinistic Methodist Chapel
H   St Deiniol (former)

I   Castle
2   Memorial Hall   Criccieth

CRICCIETH CASTLE

p. 349

23

Criccieth is one of the finest native Welsh castles, its twin-towered gatehouse unique amongst the castles of the Welsh princes, apart from the much slighter example at Dinas Brân, Denbighshire. Set on its great rock and dominating the surrounding area, with clear views of the adjacent coast, it is no wonder that Edward I made use of it following his conquest in 1282–3; the king's new castle of Harlech is clearly visible from Criccieth.

Arguably, more has been written about the phasing of this castle than any other in Wales. Nevertheless, there is now general agreement over the dating of the key stages, up to the early C14: the Inner Ward was built first, followed by the Outer Ward.★

★ Some have argued that the castle is all of the first half of the C13, with the Inner Ward and gatehouse built after the Outer Ward.

The first reference to a castle is in 1239, when Llywelyn the Great imprisoned members of his family here. This early C13 castle consists of what is now the Inner Ward, a polygonal enclosure with the gatehouse and a rectangular tower, built using local stone. The gatehouse has been compared to that of a similar date at Beeston Castle, Cheshire, built by Ranulph de Blundeville, whose nephew and heir, John le Scot, had married a daughter of Llywelyn.

Llywelyn the Last extended the castle considerably from the later 1250s, with a curtain wall and two further rectangular towers. A gateway on the s side of the new curtain wall became the new main entrance. This phase is distinguished by the use of a different mortar, and of stone brought from further away, laid in less regular coursing. From 1283 some £500 was spent on the castle by Edward I, which was no mean sum, but the accounts do not itemize what was done. Again, masonry and mortar help to distinguish this phase, as shown by the heightening of the gatehouse, with a new stair to its upper levels at the rear, the major reconstruction of the SE tower, largely encasing the earlier masonry, and modifications to part of the SW tower, as well as small-scale works to the outer gate to form a barbican, and the new staircase built against the N tower.

Further work under Edward II (1307–27) cost over £250, the gatehouse being heightened again, as well as repairs to the towers and internal buildings. About 1404, the castle was surrendered to Owain Glyndŵr, and was burnt and destroyed. C20 excavations found evidence of the destruction, and fire-damaged masonry can still be seen in the SW and SE towers.

The approach to the castle from the visitor centre, to the W of which are the remains of the OUTER BANK, passes over the OUTER DITCH and INNER BANK, all created to augment the landward defences. Originally a path must have led to what is now the Inner Gatehouse, but with the construction of the Outer Gate c. 1260, the approach led along the s or main seaward side of the castle, now quarried away. The modern route leads through the remains of the OUTER CURTAIN WALL, equipped with arrowslits, which connected the SW and N towers. The main part of the OUTER WARD, with its thin CURTAIN WALL, lies on the W side, at the s end of which are the scant remains of the OUTER GATE. E of this gate, tucked against the SE tower and s doorway to the Inner Ward, is the setting for a cistern, the channel for a lead pipe still evident. The main building in the Outer Ward is the rectangular SOUTH-WEST TOWER, to one side of which are the remains of the late C13 staircase, as well as foundations of a building of unknown date. The SW tower as built by the Welsh consisted of a first-floor hall over a basement, but it may have been heightened by Edward I with a second storey. Also dating from c. 1283–92 is the entrance to the basement, flanked by slit windows; one side of the doorway has a decorated doorstop,

similar stops being used at the foot of the new stair to the upper
floor. A drain runs from the outside of the basement entrance
to the curtain wall.

A narrow passage leads from the Outer Ward on the N side
of the Inner Ward to the enclosed area in front of the main
gatehouse; that the passage was covered with a pent roof can
be seen from the sockets in the inner curtain. The outfall of
the latrine chute of the gatehouse is a prominent feature. The
INNER GATEHOUSE and, opposite, the NORTH or ENGINE
TOWER dominate this part of the outer enclosure. The walls
of the North Tower now stop at basement level, but there
would have been an upper storey, on the roof of which was
positioned the piece of artillery that led to the name Engine
Tower. Four chutes visible on the outer face of the NW side
served a pair of latrines on the first-floor and battlement level.
Evidence for the entrance to the first floor in the Welsh phase
must have been on the site of the later, Edwardian, staircase.
A partly blocked arrowslit can be seen in the outer wall S of
the tower, a drain running through the blocking.

Three phases of the INNER GATEHOUSE are evident from
the Outer Ward. Most of the masonry represents Llywelyn the
Great's gate, up to the line of horizontal sockets for a hourd
or projecting timber gallery, whilst the crenellations of battlements added by Edward I were blocked by the final early C14
phase. The ground floor has three arrowslits in both D-shaped
towers. The passage is entered under a modern arch, just
beyond which are grooves for the portcullis. The passage floor
is modern, although the spring-fed medieval cistern survives.
To one side is the entrance to the guardroom or porter's lodge
in the E tower; a similar room in the W tower. The timbering
of the first floor would have covered the rear of the passage.
A suite of chambers, one possibly a chapel, was provided on
the first and second floors, both levels having access to latrines
on the W side. The gatehouse now lacks its inner wall; from the
remains of chimneys found when the castle came into state
care, it seems that this would have contained fireplaces. At the
rear are remains of three phases of staircases to the upper floors
and battlements.

There are some undated foundations, including those of a
possible oven, on the S side of the Inner Ward, but the main
feature here is the SOUTH-EAST TOWER. Its basement was
originally entered via a staircase from the floor above, but
c. 1260 ground-floor access was achieved through a pair of two-
leaf doors, the outer being secured by a drawbar. The upper
storey in the later C13 was reached from the curtain wall, and
possibly, an external staircase from the Inner Ward. A single
Edwardian latrine chute is visible on the NE side, adjacent to
four early C13 latrines reached by two stairs from the Inner
Ward.

The CURTAIN WALL on the W and NW sides of the Inner
Ward stands to battlement level, with evidence for arrowslits,
as well as drains from the roofs of the timber buildings that
would have been arranged around the courtyard. To the S is

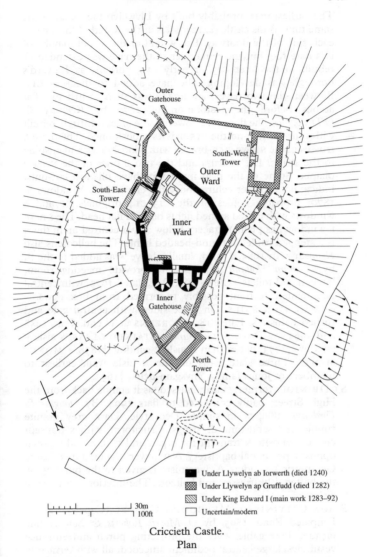

Under Llywelyn ab Iorwerth (died 1240)
Under Llywelyn ap Gruffudd (died 1282)
Under King Edward I (main work 1283–92)
Uncertain/modern

30m
100ft

Criccieth Castle.
Plan

the small doorway or postern, a back door into the first castle,
but one that would have given access to the Outer Ward in the
later C13; slots for the door frame survive, and holes for the
drawbar. The buildings represented by the adjacent undated
foundations would have made use of this doorway impossible.

CHURCHES, CHAPELS AND PUBLIC BUILDINGS

ST CATHERINE, Lôn Ednyfed. Its distance from the castle, and
its partly curvilinear graveyard, suggest that it may stand on
the site of an earlier church dedicated to a Celtic saint.

The earliest part, probably built by Llywelyn the Great at the same time as his castle (*c.* 1230s), is at the W end of the S nave, each side of the doorway. The W end of the S wall may be of this date too, but the remainder of the nave was extended or rebuilt in the later C13 or early C14, perhaps as Edward's borough was developing. The nave added to the N is C15. Between the two naves, an arcade was then of just two flat arches before the restoration of 1870 by *Kennedy & O'Donoghue*. The floor level lowered, the arcade entirely rebuilt with four arches and the C15 trusses repositioned. The three E trusses in the S nave arch-braced with wind-braces and cusping to the struts. The W truss and the two E ones in the N nave plainer. Some of the principal soffits have filled-in cut-outs, indicating a former celure above the chancel (S). Windows of 1870, probably copies of the C13–C14 originals. N and S windows with paired arched lights below a flat head. The S nave E window has plain Y-tracery below a two-centred arch; the N is a stepped triplet of round-headed lights. The bellcote is also *Kennedy*'s. In 1983, a third, smaller 'nave' was added to the N, by *Graham Holland Associates*, to provide meeting room, kitchen and toilets. – REREDOS. Oak, dated 1679, with central pedimented section; possibly re-formed from box pews. – COMMUNION RAILS. On three sides, with central gate and turned balusters. Late C18. – SCREENS at W end. Oak, 1958 and 1963, by *Dr C. A. Gresham*. – STAINED GLASS. S aisle E window †1873, better than N aisle E window †1878. – MONU-MENTS. Three slate slabs on the N aisle wall, earliest to members of Jones family, Ynysgain-ucha, †1692.

ST DEINIOL (former). Easily missed, as it stands back from the High Street; badly converted to flats 1994. By *Douglas & Fordham*, 1884–7, in simple Dec style. Dark grey granite rubble, red sandstone dressings. Cruciform, with S transept chapel opposite N transept for organ and vestry, and S porch opposite polygonal baptistery. A W tower was intended. Large Geometric E window. A dynamism is given to the building by the battered buttresses and bellcote. The interior had passage aisles.

SEION CALVINISTIC METHODIST CHAPEL (Capel-y-traeth), Penpaled Road. 1895, by *O. Morris Roberts & Son*. A fine façade: three gables over the projecting porch and entrance vestibules, large central pediment stuccoed, all with terracotta tile insert panels. Balustrade and urns on the skyline. A fine interior too. The side pews are arranged concentrically so each has its own curve – always a mark of superiority over the humbler straight arrangement.

CAPEL MAWR CALVINISTIC METHODIST CHAPEL (former), High Street. 1878, by *O. Morris Roberts*. Snecked granite with limestone and render dressings. Roundel within the gable ped-iment. Below, an arcade of six round-headed windows with pink polished granite shafts and Corinthian capitals. Basket-headed lower windows each side of a weak-looking central buttress and projecting doorways with curious tiny pyramids perched along the entablatures. (Interior with gallery on fluted Doric iron columns. Ceiling with multiple circle motifs round the ventilator.)

BEREA BAPTIST CHAPEL, Tanygrisiau Terrace. 1886. The most elegant of the town's chapel façades. Rendered walls painted primrose. A triplet of round-headed lights above a central porch, and longer single lights each side, all with pilasters, imposts and keystones. The windows have delicate margin lights, and circular glazing at the heads. Simple interior.

JERUSALEM CONGREGATIONAL CHAPEL, Cambrian Terrace. Almost within sight of Capel Berea (above), same date and same colours. Here, the central triplet lights are not of equal size, and the mouldings run continuously without imposts or keystones. Gallery on three sides on slender iron columns, with organ at rear. Ceiling of five rectangular panels.

SALEM WESLEYAN CHAPEL (former), W side of the Maes. Rebuilt or refaced 1901, North Italian Gothic. Snecked granite with sandstone dressings. Gabled tripartite façade divided by tall buttresses and adorned with an array of pinnacles, pepperpots, gablets etc.

CAPEL UCHAF BAPTIST CHAPEL (former), Caernarfon Road. The first purpose-built Baptist chapel in the district, built c. 1791 but converted to a house c. 1980; till then it had its low box pews and pulpit on the N gable-end.

MEMORIAL HALL. Lôn Ednyfed. Dated 1922 and built as a First World War memorial. By O. Morris Roberts & Son of Porthmadog in Arts and Crafts style (swept eaves with generous overhangs, fluidly shaped windows to the main doors, battered buttresses, roughcast finish). Central tower heightened later to incorporate a clock. Extensions by Adam & Frances Voelcker on the W, 1996, and on the N, 1998–9. Impressive auditorium with barrel-vaulted ceiling and gallery. Inside the central front doors, a circular Hall of Memory.

PERAMBULATION

The view of the town from the CASTLE mound makes this the obvious place to start. CASTLE SQUARE, below, is the heart of the old town, a small intimate space attractive before the fashion for pebbledash and replacement windows. Leading downhill to the E, Nos. 21–27 CASTLE STREET, an early C18 row with a cobbled pavement. No. 23 has a wide gable with a round-headed window. Further downhill on the S side, TŶ MAWR (No. 2) and No. 4 next door, now a single dwelling. Tŷ Mawr, probably late C16, has a fine voussoir head to the doorway, and a similar one to the cellar window, now blocked. At the bottom of the hill, TŶ'R FELIN, a white-painted C17 cottage with tiny slated raking dormer, named from the nearby converted mill. Just before the latter, the LIFEBOAT STATION. Gabled, the walls of stone below and pebbledashed within red painted render bands above. Built in 1893 to replace the old station of 1853, and carefully extended by Clive Moore in 1993.

PENPALED ROAD leads l. uphill, past PENPALED, a small early
C19 house dwarfed by Seion chapel (*see* p. 350) and surrounded
by late C19 terraces. Before crossing the railway, WELLINGTON
TERRACE leads l. back towards the castle, past Nos. 5 and 6,
a pair of stone cottages with axial chimney stacks, central
doors, stone dormers and modern replacement windows.
Probably late C17. Across the railway and l., CAFÉ CWRT,
which housed the Court of Petty Sessions until it moved to
Tremadog in 1825. Originally a one-and-a-half-storey C17
dwelling, but the gable stonework shows later heightening.
LÔN EDNYFED leads N uphill past the Memorial Hall on the
l. and up to St Catherine's. Opposite the lychgate, HAFOD-Y-
BRYN, *c.* 1913, perhaps by *T. Taliesin Rees,* and showing Arts
and Crafts influence. White roughcast walls, partly inset
dormers and upper balcony below a central gambrel gable.
Veranda along most of the front. At the rear, miniature garage
to match. Some original details inside (e.g. heart-shaped cut-
outs in the window seats). Delightful and eminently suitable for
seaside architecture. E of the church, BRYN HENLLAN, a Free
Style house in a spacious garden, dated 1884, and probably by
Douglas & Fordham. Knapped granite, the upper storey in
diaper pattern using contrasting colours. Ground-floor
windows with flat ogee heads, often used by Douglas. Further
up the lane, hidden in trees on the l., BRYN HIR, a large
rambling house of many periods. Single-room cottage behind,
built in the early C17 and extended later in the same century.
Main range added to give a formal front: pebbledashed, sash
windows with shutters and a later glazed-roof veranda. Early
C19 STABLE block, E, with an archway containing stonework
perhaps from the original arcade in St Catherine's church.
Back to the High Street and W to the MAES, which has a
picturesque group of three houses (Berth, Garth and Maes
Glas) on its NE side, built after 1922. Pebbledash alternating
with smooth rendered and slate-hung bays, and hipped roofs.
An octagonal bay turns the corner of the L-shaped ensemble
particularly successfully. N of the Maes and close to Holywell
Terrace is the well-proportioned former RECTORY, 1828–31,
as a glebe house to the rectory (then at Mynydd Ednyfed, *see*
below). Coursed stone walls, wide projecting eaves. On the
Maes, some walls remain of the former police station and
pound. At the SW corner, the LION HOTEL, an enlargement
of an C18 house called Tŷ'n-y-maes.
On the HIGH STREET, and E of St Deiniol's church (*see* p. 350),
NANT Y FELIN, built *c.* 1890 by *Douglas & Fordham.*
Symmetrical front, canted bays with hipped roofs at each end,
central veranda with wide dormer gable above. Some nice
details, e.g. the stonework to the side porch doorway and the
lead finials to the hipped roofs. W along the High Street, the
former NATIONAL PROVINCIAL BANK, r., 1923, by *Palmer &*
Holden. A gem of a building. Crowstepped parapets and
gables, very steep roofs of diminishing green slates, leaded
glazing. Inside, head-height panelling all round, a fireplace

with Delft tiles, and barn-like roof trusses. Further W, the GEORGE IV HOTEL, by *Douglas & Fordham*, c. 1890. Jacobethan style, knapped granite with sandstone dressings. Full-height projecting bays, each slightly different, continued up to roof level as gables. The canted one corbels out at eaves level. The main bay has ball finials, a three-centred arch to the entrance, and a pedimented four-light window above it. Windows progressively shorter as they go up, mullioned and transomed below, simpler above. The interior modernized, but the staircase and arcaded landings are typical of Douglas. On the l., the BRYNHIR ARMS, built c. 1840. The archway leads through to former stables. Further to the W is the LIBRARY by *Rowland Lloyd Jones*, 1905. Ruabon brick, Talacre stone dressings, roughcast and half-timber to the gables. Further W on the r., the HEALTH CENTRE, by *Ap Thomas, Jones & Evans*, 1978. Two wing linked with a flat-roofed area. Slate roofs split at the ridge. White painted render walls and plain square windows. Of its time.

The perambulation can be completed by returning to the castle via STATION ROAD, over the railway and through the park to LÔN BACH, part of the original town where some old cottages still stand. MARINE TERRACE (1880s) stretches W, along the promenade built for H. J. Nanney of Gwynfryn, Llanystumdwy in 1883–9. Imposing in its length and unexpected after the small scale of the old town. Uphill to the E, the MARINE HOTEL which must have seen better days. Its Voysey-ish tower set on the diagonal for the view and the wide projecting eaves on brackets are attractive. The CHAPEL OF ART (formerly English Presbyterian and a branch of Capel y Traeth) has an interesting forecourt paved in 2000 with tiles made by potters from around the world.

OTHER BUILDINGS

MORANNEDD CAFÉ, at the very E end of the esplanade. By *Clough Williams-Ellis*, c. 1948. Modernist style. Boomerang-shaped plan, flat roofs with wide overhanging eaves, rendered concrete block walls, steel and glass-block windows.

MYNYDD EDNYFED FAWR. ¾ m. N, at the top end of Lôn Ednyfed. Late C18 farmhouse of three storeys, rear extension of two, all rendered and painted white. Central slate plaque 'Built by the Rev Wm Evans AD 1796 / Heb Dduw Heb Ddim / Dduw a digon' (Without God, nothing; With God, enough).

GWYNT Y MÔR, ¾ m. E. Almost the last house on Porthmadog Road, a picturesque toy-town house with green slate roof, rebuilt by Mr Lane (who also built Morannedd Café, *see* above) after seeing it exhibited at the Daily Mail Ideal Homes Exhibition c. 1945–6.

BRAICH Y SAINT. 2 m. NNE. Two separate but attached 'unit' houses. E house almost entirely late C16. Corbelled chimneystack on E gable, voussoir arch to doorway. W house partly of the same date, but extended S in the late C18.

HAY BARN at Parciau Mawr, Lôn Fel (very w end of High Street). Particularly good example of a Snowdonian open barn. Tall stone piers with stepped-out bases, and kingpost trusses.

CAER DYNI (SH 511 382). A possible Neolithic burial chamber or large Bronze Age cist grave, within a low stone cairn on land overlooking the mouth of the Cedron. The rectangular chamber is not exceptionally large, 5 ft by 2 ft 9 in. (1.5 by 0.85 metres), but the dislodged capstone is bigger than would be expected to cover a Bronze Age grave.

CEFN ISAF BURIAL CHAMBER, Rhoslan (SH 484 408) has lost all evidence of its covering cairn but the chamber, with a huge capstone, is virtually intact, lacking only a side stone on the s. The blocking stone, projecting NW side stone and NE supporter form a fairly characteristic portal.

YSTUM CEGID ISAF BURIAL CHAMBER (SH 498 413) is now incorporated into a field wall. This all but conceals the uprights of a curving passage to the N of the big polygonal chamber with its large thin capstone. Early records of the monument (which was partially reconstructed in the C19) are confusing. The most likely classification is as an outlier of the Cotswold–Severn Group, comparable in size and eccentric design to Arthur's Stone on Dorstone Hill, Herefordshire.

CWM PENMACHNO

7548

RHYDYMEIRCH CALVINISTIC METHODIST CHAPEL, Rhydymeirch. 1898, by the *Rev. Thomas Parry* of Colwyn Bay. Away from the village, between the two bridges. Quite large and severe, with attached vestry and schoolroom, and a detached house to the w. Round-headed windows with broad recessed surrounds, flanking a Venetian window, also recessed under an arch. Above, a flat band containing round motifs and a quatrefoil at the top of the gable. Square battlemented porch.

SILOH WESLEYAN CHAPEL. 1864, rebuilt 1895. Segmental window heads and keystones; the central one with pilasters and plain capitals. Large segmental arch with infill of slate piers and lintels framing three rectangular windows and a swept fanlight above. Central gabled porch.

CARMEL WESLEYAN CHAPEL, Glasfryn Terrace. Built 1882, for the elderly and very young, for whom Siloh was too far away. Small. Gabled front, with the quoins at the angles and around the windows picked out in black against white. Three triangular-headed windows with straight intersecting tracery, the central one above the door.

VILLAGE at the head of the Machno valley, to serve the slate quarries, the nearest of which, Rhiw Fachno, it overlooks to the s. The earliest dwellings are probably Nos. 1–6 RHOS GOCH, early to mid-C19 single-storey cottages of rubble. Projecting slate mouldings above the openings provide the only adornment. w of these, a little T-plan settlement of two-storey houses, GLASFRYN TERRACE and RHIW FACH TERRACE.

All of stone, with margin-light sash windows; many now rendered. Little gardens, with slate fences between. At the E end
of the village street, TREVALLEN, formerly the National
School. Snecked granite/slate, with yellow brick surrounds to
the paired, pointed windows. *Herbert L. North* converted the
National School to a small church room when the County
School was built, *c.* 1921. He added the tall slate tower at the
hinge of its L-plan, his intention, perhaps, to give the village
the church it never had.

FFYNNON EIDDA, 2½ m. S of Carrog (SH 762 437). A drovers'
well. The plaque reads 'Ffynnon eidda yf a bydd ddiolchgar',
drink and be thankful. Rebuilt 1846.

CWM Y GLO 5463

A small village, now by-passed, probably once connected with
charcoal burning and the smelting of copper mined at Llanberis.
Just one street, but tiny paths and lanes wind steeply uphill, past
groups of cottages, to a maze of small, walled fields at the top of
Bwlch.

ST GABRIEL. Tiny C19 mission church hidden behind the street.
Three pointed lancets to the gabled front, sashes to the sides.
Small stone bellcote above the entrance.

TABERNACLE INDEPENDENT CHAPEL. 1867. Stucco, with
raised strips continuing up the gable verges. Pointed Y-tracery
windows, central door with elliptical head and raised quoins.

CWM Y GLO CALVINISTIC METHODIST CHAPEL. 1904.
Prominent on the hill, now disused. A central pediment, excessively raised, above a group of three pilastered flat-headed
windows below a segmental pediment. Two doorways below,
with matching pediments, and fluted pilasters. Giant fluted
pilasters at the angles. Stucco front, pebbledashed sides.

DEGANWY 7880

Suburban in character and continuous with Llandudno Junction
to the SE, Deganwy faces W and SW across the Conwy, with the
remains of its castle perched on the twin hills of the Vardre
behind, and the church at the foot, to the S.

DEGANWY CASTLE. The W of the twin hills was the site of the
early medieval Welsh centre, the residence of Maelgwn
Gwynedd in the C6. Robert of Rhuddlan established a castle
here in the late C11, a stronghold much disputed between
Norman and Welsh in the C12. The Welsh destroyed the castle
in the early C13 before King John could take it. Llywelyn the
Great rebuilt the stronghold from 1213. Little survives of this
castle, or of that built in 1244–54 after the castle had been
surrendered to Henry III, the king himself attending its

construction in 1245; although unfinished, Henry's works cost about £10,000. The new work on the w hill was built in 1247–9. In 1250 Mansell's Tower was ordered to be raised by 12 ft (4 metres) and roofed, with the bailey between the hills walled in stone, with two twin-towered gatehouses, although this was only completed on the s. In 1263 Llywelyn the Last took and destroyed the castle in an impressively systematic way, leaving little to see today. A fine early C13 corbel, excavated in the 1960s and now in the National Museum of Wales, possibly carved to represent Llywelyn the Great himself, is the only indication of the quality of the Welsh stronghold.

The core of the castle, known as the DONJON, occupied the summit of the w hill, the BAILEY lying between it and the e hill on which stood the rounded MANSELL'S TOWER. Most of the fragmentary remains belong to Henry III's castle. The main entrance lay on the s, with slight traces of a twin-towered GATEHOUSE, close to which stands a mass of fallen masonry from the demolition period. A gap and a stub of masonry mark the site of a N entrance, and on this side is a prominent BANK and DITCH, possibly never defended by a stone wall. At the SE corner of the polygonal enclosure of the donjon are traces of a ROUND TOWER overlooking the e inner entrance; adjoining the tower lay the hall. A further gateway lay on the SW side of this hill. Traces of the CURTAIN WALL are evident on the w and N sides of the hill, the revetment on the N side being part of Llywelyn's castle. Earthworks to the N may represent traces of the mid-C13 English borough.

ALL SAINTS, All Saints Avenue. A very fine church, built 1897–9 for Lady Augusta Mostyn (*see* Llandudno and Llanrhos) by *Douglas & Minshull*. Pinkish sandstone, rough outside, smooth

Deganwy, All Saints.
Engraving after E. Hodkinson, 1897

and more buff inside. Distinctive W tower with a squat,
Germanic spire. Tiny hipped lucarnes, and broaches which
develop on the S side into hipped roofs above a pair of
buttresses, one becoming a stair-turret lower down. Aisles, and
SW porch. The chancel is wider and taller than the nave. Arch-
headed Perp windows to the chancel, flat-ogee-head windows
to the nave and aisles. Inside, very good timber roof structure,
as always with Douglas – bold and functional in the nave and
aisles, more feminine in the chancel, with barley-twisting to
the queenposts. – REREDOS. High-relief work in stone, dated
1905. Christ as a shepherd, in the central panel, below an elaborate canopy. – FONT in baptistery at W end below tower.
Round bowl on octagonal base, white marble with Purbeck
marble shafts. 1899. – WAR MEMORIAL, a Gothic reredos by
J. H. Hutchings, a local art teacher. – STAINED GLASS.
Most of the original glass is by *Lavers & Westlake*. Later glass
less good.

A row of late C19 shops along STATION ROAD, some sharing
a cast-iron veranda over the pavement. Opposite, the CASTLE
HOTEL, C19 and later, on a commanding site but pinched
between the road and the branch line to Llandudno.
Below the hill, leafy residential streets and comfortable houses
with English names. GANNOCK PARK is the best street.
Directly W of the castle, BRACKENRIGG, built in the 1930s,
for Sidney Aston, a furniture retailer. In Gannock Park West,
COED-Y-CASTELL, a plainer house of the same date, for
Dr and Mrs Talbot, by *Clough Williams-Ellis*. Almost Modernist
with its pair of semicircular bays, were it not for the pitched
conical roofs and shaped chimneys. N along DEGANWY ROAD,
a close of five small houses in echelon, Nos. 30–38, and further
N, Nos. 54–58 – all by *North & Padmore*, 1933. In toy-town
style, with busy roofs in coloured slates and brick chimneys
with stepped tops. Between road and railway, C20 luxury apartments. These continue SE of the station along Glan-y-môr,
forming DEGANWY QUAY and MARINA, once the site of a
slate quay serving Blaenau Ffestiniog. Parallel to Glan-y-môr,
in Tŷ Mawr Road, No. 40, MINAFON, an attractive two-storey
mid-C19 house of three bays, end-on to the road. A slightly
projecting central bay, with a gable and curly bargeboards.
Later timber porch, of elaborate Gothic design. At the SW end,
facing the marina, an exemplary modern extension designed
c. 2000 by *Clive Hardman*. A hipped slated roof with wide overhangs and exposed rafter ends all round, cedar boarding, steel
balustrading and big retractable windows. The garden gate
from the street opens on to a pergola-covered bridge above a
pool, Japanese in feel. Vardre Park leads uphill NE into
Tan-y-fron, where PARK LODGE sits hidden in trees above the
new houses. A large white roughcast house of *c.* 1926, showing
Arts and Crafts influence, with hints of Voysey, but twenty
years behind the times. By *Longden & Venables*, for Maj.
W. H. Lovatt, a Manchester businessman, whose wife took an
instant dislike to it.

DEINIOLEN

CHRIST CHURCH (Llandinorwic). Built 1857, 'at the sole expence of Thomas Assheton Smith Esquire', by *Kennedy*, in remote moorland, set apart from the village. A grandiose but not large Dec church, its height exaggerated by the w approach, which leads up from the gateway and then circles the church, as at Christ Church, Llanfairfechan. The nave entirely hidden by the separately roofed aisles, chancel and the tall w tower and spire. Windows with differing tracery. Lofty aisles and nave, the latter with trusses forming huge ogees, and multiple verticals linking braces, collar and principals. Cusped braces to the chancel roof, on stone corbels of angel musicians. Good contemporary FITTINGS.

CEFN Y WAUN CALVINISTIC METHODIST CHAPEL. 1868, by *Richard Davies*. In competition with the nearby church but, without a spire, the inevitable loser. However, a fine wheel window in the w gable. Below it, a pair of Neo-Romanesque doorways. Stepped Lombardic gables, with oculi. Two more oculi in the outer bays, below Florentine-headed windows. Snecked, rock-faced rubble with ashlar dressings. Unexceptional interior.

EBENEZER INDEPENDENT CHAPEL, High Street. By the *Rev. Thomas Thomas*, 1858. Three-bay pilastered gable front, much altered.

LIBANUS BAPTIST CHAPEL, Gwaun Gynfi. 1877, by *Richard Owens* of Liverpool. Tall and upright, with wings below hipped roofs. Rubble, with orange and yellow brick dressings. Three windows at the centre, with a large oculus above and a slightly projecting porch below, its gable crashing through the window sill.

An upland VILLAGE, now joined to Clwt-y-bont to the s; mid-C18 squatter settlements which evolved into nucleated villages in defiance of the surrounding Vaynol estate land won through enclosure. Church and chapel are well outside the village to the E. The HIGH STREET is the old slate road from the quarry to Port Dinorwic, perhaps 1811, lined with two-storey stone terraces now mostly pebbledashed. Faintly classical CARNEGIE LIBRARY (1913), w of Ebenezer chapel. It overlooks YSGOL GWAUN GYNFI, the primary school, with the recessed bay windows characteristic of the County's early C20 'open-air' schools. From here, HAFOD OLEU curves downhill towards Clwt-y-Bont. On the l., stepped groups of early C20 COUNCIL HOUSES, in Garden Suburb style, with bracketed porch roofs and central passages to the rear gardens. NEW STREET, parallel with Hafod Oleu to the E, leads steeply down past RHES FAWR on the l., a terrace of two-room houses built in the 1830s by *David Griffith* of Caernarfon.

DINORWIC/DINORWIG

DINORWIC SLATE QUARRY, Gilfach Ddu. Established in 1787 by Thomas Assheton-Smith of Vaynol, taking over quarries which had developed sporadically since the early C18. The first incline was built in 1789, tramways served each terrace by the 1830s, and a new railroad linked the quarry with Y Felinheli/Port Dinorwic (q.v.) in 1843 (replacing an earlier tramway). Production reached c. 100,000 tons annually in the later 1890s. The quarry closed in 1969. In addition to a few quarry-working buildings on the terraces, a large workshop complex and a hospital survive, both on the NE shore of Llyn Padarn.

QUARRY WORKSHOPS (The National Slate Museum). Huge and impressive quadrangle around a courtyard, like a fort or a large estate farmyard. Built 1870, for saw-sheds, pattern-making shops, foundries, blacksmiths' and fitting shops, canteen, chief engineer's house etc., on a scale intended to impress (i.e. the competition at Penrhyn). All the machinery is powered by a 50-ft (15-metre)-diameter WATER WHEEL by *de Winton* of Caernarfon, the largest in mainland Britain. Imposing front (N) elevation, but with something of the Stalag about it. A tower at each front corner, with pyramidal slate roof crowned with a tall cupola. Forbidding walls of dark snecked granite connect them to the hipped central GATEHOUSE, with a smaller cupola and a clock above the round-headed entrance. The windows all round-headed, most with very narrow lozenge panes in cast-iron frames from the workshop foundry. The W elevation has no fewer than fourteen chimneys, for the forges. Huge trusses in the two-storey S block. Circular SHOP built in the courtyard, and to the S, a CAFÉ with wave-form roof and a LIFT to the water wheel. All by *Ap Thomas Partnership*, c. 1998. Clad in slate (surprisingly, grey slate from Blaenau Ffestiniog rather than matching purple slate from nearer quarries), with large areas of glass, in a clean style which contrasts with the old buildings. S of the lift, a TERRACE of four quarry-workers' houses from Fron Haul, Tanygrisiau, re-erected in 1998 to illustrate changing ways of life. Above the workshops to the E, the quarry OFFICE, with a slate-roof veranda to protect quarrymen as they queued for their wages. The HOSPITAL sits high above the lake, N of the workshops. An attractive building of 1860, for employees and their families, replacing the earlier one perhaps at Bron Elidir (*see* below). Two-storey three-bay block with gabled middle bay, single-storey three-bay wings. Snecked rubble, with dressed quoins and window surrounds of a lighter colour. Octagonal chimneys in groups of four. Built into the hillside to the NW, the MORTUARY, 1906. On the steep hillside S of the hospital, some restored quarry structures, including INCLINES and DRUM HOUSES. In the Vivian Quarry, a BLONDIN CABLE-WAY, one of a number installed in the 1920s (named after the tightrope-walker over the Niagara Falls). Near the summit, the ANGLESEY BARRACKS, built c. 1870 for Anglesey quarry workers who camped in the quarry during the week. Two rows of two-room single-storey dwellings across a yard, with privies beyond. All of slate and little else.

On the steep hillside NE of the workshops, managers' houses. BRON ELIDIR, a pretty stucco house, was perhaps once the first quarry hospital. Two gables and a flat-roofed porch. A grand round-headed gateway leads from the garden to the quarry, via a steep winding slate stairway. HAFODTY, to the SE, another manager's house, larger and altered. Further N, along the track to Dinorwic village, TANYBRYN, a good example of quarry-workers' houses. Granite rubble, with slate quoins and garden walls. The nice simple slate porches, with just a touch of decoration to the cornices, suggest company officials lived here.

DINORWIG POWER STATION. A pumped-storage hydro-electric plant mostly buried within the slate mountain on the NE side of Llyn Peris. During the day, six turbines located in a vast chamber 585 by 75 by 163 ft (180 by 23 by 50 metres) high supply energy to the National Grid, generated by water falling 1,640 ft (500 metres) between the Marchlyn Mawr reservoir and the lower lake; at night, the turbines are reversed to replenish the upper lake, using off-peak electricity. Started in the early 1970s, commissioned 1984. *James Williamson & Partners* were the civil engineers, with *Frederick Gibberd, Coombes & Partners* as landscape architects. Constructed by *MBZ*, a consortium led by Sir Robert McAlpine.

DOLBADARN CASTLE *see* LLANBERIS

DOLBENMAEN

5144

A small nucleated settlement consisting of motte, church, rectory and manor. Mentioned in the Mabinogion, it may have been the *maerdref* or administrative centre of Eifionydd. Its MOTTE (now hidden in trees near the Plas) guarded the ford across the Dwyfor. Here too would have been the prince's hall and the associated village of bondmen. The court moved to Criccieth *c.* 1230. Garndolbenmaen, about 1 m. NW, developed in the latter part of the C18 on the common land of Dolbenmaen. A glance at the O.S. map will make clear that the area is a dense maze of smallholdings. The buildings, small *croglofft* cottages for the most part, are basic and without architectural aspiration.

The parish is a large one and takes in Cwm Pennant and Cwm Ystradllyn, to NNE and ENE respectively. Many small quarries (slate and minerals) punctuate the former; the larger Gorsedda Quarry (*see* below) is at the head of the latter. The area is thick with stone-hut groups, remains of platform houses and enclosures. Eifion Wyn, a local bard, lamented: 'Why, Lord, didst Thou make Cwm Pennant so beautiful, and the life of an old shepherd so short?'

ST MARY. Tiny C15 single-cell church, with arch-braced collar-trusses with cusped kingposts, pairs of purlins each side with wind-braces, and exposed rafters. Stub ends of former gallery

beams at the w end; the present reredos is probably the early
c19 gallery front. Unusual LYCHGATE with a storeroom on
each side of the central passage.

PLAS DOLBENMAEN, SE of church. Late c18 house with rear
wing. The roof to the latter continues as a catslide over a later
extension. Chimneystacks at each gable. Extensive farm
buildings to the w, adjacent to the motte.

PLAS HOLLAND, w of church. Formerly the rectory. Front part
built in 1786 by the Rev. Jeffrey Holland, onto an earlier
(c. 1700?) house behind. Sash windows, and two Gothick
windows to the w side. Front rooms largely unchanged.

TŷNEWYDD, ½ m. NW. Unspoilt farmhouse set back behind a
gateway with inset slate name plaque. Early c19 front of three
bays containing sixteen-pane sash windows, built onto a c17
rear wing.

YSTUMCEGID, 1 m. SW. Late c17 or early c18 farmhouse of two
storeys. A hint of Renaissance formality about the central front
gable, with small attic window. Tall chimneys each end. A good
range of PIGSTIES behind.

BRIDGE, 1 m. E. Built for Sir Joseph Huddart of the Brynkir
estate, 1819. Two segmental arches, with a pilaster pier at the
centre. Built near to the bridge and at the former entrance to
Brynkir Hall, a large c19 mansion built by Sir Joseph Huddart
(now derelict), an early c19 LODGE. Hipped roof with wide
eaves, central chimney, attractive Gothick cast-iron windows.

TŵR BRYNKIR (Tŵr Gwynllan), the six-storey stone tower on
a stone platform, at the end of a tree-lined track, was built by
Sir Joseph Huddart as a folly. Built in two stages: lower half
1821, upper 1859. This is corroborated by changes in stone and
in window type (timber below, cast iron above, all Gothick).
Crenellated parapet. All four corners chamfered and pierced
with dummy cruciform loopholes (cf. St Mary, Tremadog).
The staircase winds round within the thickness of the wall.
Refurbished by *Adam & Frances Voelcker*, 1994.

SCHOOL, 2 m. NE. Tiny converted c19 school with school house
next to it. Attractive and unspoilt ensemble.

ST MICHAEL, Llanfihangel y Pennant, 1½ m. NW. Rebuilt
c. 1850 in Pre-Ecclesiological style. Continuous nave and
chancel, entrance at w end, bellcote above. Many c18 grave-
slabs in churchyard.

ISALLT-FAWR, 2 m. ENE. Late c17 house on an earlier site.
Possibly the earlier house forms the base, since a change in
stonework is visible in front. Central doorway with slightly
curved voussoir head and dripstone above. Upper windows at
eaves level with stone gables to each. Originally four windows
in the w gable, all but one blocked. Main room, E end, with
large fireplace and mural staircase lit by a small window in the
s wall.

CLENENNAU, 1½ m. ESE. Once one of the most important
estates in Caernarvonshire. Home of Sir John Owen, well-
known Royalist leader in North Wales, †1666 (*see* Penmorfa
church). The westernmost building on the site, now in ruins,

may be mid-C16. The large barn to the NE, with a moulded and mortised beam still in place, may stand on the original C15 hall-house, plundered in 1648. Sir John probably then built a new house, which was taxed on seven hearths in 1662. Part is visible in the rear wing, but it must have been L-plan, the front wing altered *c.* 1880 (early C16 arch-braced collar-trusses survive in the front roof). In all buildings, high-quality (undressed) stonework. Unusually, sandstone voussoirs to the flat-headed windows in the rear wing ('. . . not a single doorway even arched', complained Fenton in 1810). At some distance NE of the house, a range of FARM BUILDINGS. A tall hay barn with hipped roof, flanked by single-storey buildings with stone-walled enclosures in front.

EREINIOG, 3 m. E. Farmhouse of two storeys, the main E-facing part late C16 or early C17, the rear wing later. Mural staircase next to the fireplace, lit by a small window in gable. Ceiling beams in the main room moulded and chamfered, with floral decorations carved on the underside.

CEFN COCH ISAF, 2½ m. E. Probably early C19, with later short service wing to rear (NE). Two storeys, with attic. Three-bay front to garden (SW). SE entrance, with central upper windows. Good coursed rubble, wide eaves with slate soffits. Fine staircase. Attached at the NW, the original house, probably C17 (but perhaps earlier). Single-storeyed, with loft. Monolithic slabs each side of the fireplace. Carriage house to SE, with elliptical head to doorway lofted carriage.

99   YNYSPANDY SLATE MILL, 3 m. E. Superb structure, a veritable cathedral of the local slate industry. Built in 1856–7 by Evan Jones of Garndolbenmaen and probably designed by *James Brunlees*. It specialized in the production of slate slabs for floors, dairies, troughs, urinals etc. At its heyday in 1860, it was producing over 2,000 tons, but seven years later, production was down to 25 tons (due to poor quality of the quarried slate) and the business went into liquidation in 1871. The building provided a venue for *eisteddfodau* until the roof was removed *c.* 1906. Ingeniously planned so that the natural fall of the site assisted the manufacturing process. Grand, round-headed openings, closely spaced like a Roman aqueduct. At the E end, some decoration is allowed to adorn the openings; otherwise, the construction is bold and plain, but none the less impressive. A deep trench inside accommodated a large overshot water wheel (26 ft (8 m.) in diameter), and on the S side, a long curving ramp brought the tramway from Gorsedda Quarry.

GORSEDDA SLATE QUARRY, 4½ m. ENE, at the head of Cwmystradllyn. Classic 'gallery' quarry, worked until 1865–6. Four galleries, each with its weighbridge house and slate-makers' hut. At the bottom, a corbelled WALL over the tramway, intended to form a tunnel below the tips as they extended, but never completed. To the W, TREFORYS, a development of thirty-six *croglofft* cottages in three parallel rows, built 1857. Below, in the trees but now demolished, Plas-yn-llyn, the quarry manager's house. The tramway ran through the garden, on its way down to the slate mill at Ynys-pandy (*see* above).

COPPER MINE, Gilfach and Cwm Ciprwth. Typical of mineral enterprises in Cwm Pennant, in sporadic and largely futile operation in the C19. The lower workings (SH 531 478) include a long adit, a water-powered crushing house and settling tanks. The upper workings (SH 525 478) boast a water wheel by *Dingey & Sons* of Truro, installed *c.* 1890 to pump a shaft 145 ft (45 metres) away. The wooden flat-rods which trans-ferred the power are a rare survival, painstakingly restored by the Snowdonia National Park in 1987.*

CASTELL CAERAU, set high above Dolbenmaen on a projecting boss of rock. Small, only 65 ft (20 metres) across but heavily defended with an encircling wall 11 ft (3.5 metres) thick. It is likely to belong to the centuries after the withdrawal of the Romans. The site is much encumbered with later walls and sheep pens.

DOLGARROG   7667

The Snowdonia National Park boundary makes a polite detour to exclude Dolgarrog, an industrial village connected with the production of aluminium, its power supplied by water from large lakes in the hills W of the village. The WORKS, established in the early C20, between the main road and the river. Suburban-looking HOUSING strung along the road, built for the Abdon Clee Stone Quarry Co. between 1911 and 1926. Concrete frame and infill, with some half-timbering for effect, and red-tiled roofs, similar to estates in Neasden and Wolverhampton.

SCHOOL, by *Westbury Lloyd Jones*, County Architect, *c.* 1932. Long N elevation facing the playing field, two-storey gabled block at the centre, single-storey wings. Sash windows alter-nating in height, the tall ones extending up to form dormers. Wings at right angles, S, linked by a low corridor with the sliding-folding recessed bay windows characteristic of the 'open-air' schools which Rowland Lloyd Jones (his father) had developed a decade or two earlier.

DOLWYDDELAN   7453

The junction of many tracks at the beginning of the C19, but without a proper road to the outside world. It was part of the Gwydir estate in the mid C19, Lord Willoughby de Eresby adding to castle and church, and providing cottages for the slate quarry villagers. The Conwy valley branch of the LNWR was cut

*This entry is by Dr M. J. T. Lewis.

through in 1879, its station at Pentre-bont, the old village s of the river.

22   DOLWYDDELAN CASTLE. Llywelyn the Great replaced Tomen Castell with a new castle some time after 1210. Set on the SE slope of Moel Siabod, it overlooks the Lledr valley to the E and the original road that lay to the W of the castle. Unlike at Dolbadarn, the main tower or keep came first. The construction of the curtain wall must be seen as part of the same plan, even though it butts against the tower. There is no evidence of any courtyard building from this phase, although at the N end of the later C13 W tower is a latrine chamber that may have served an earlier block.

The castle was captured during Edward I's Welsh war of 1282–3, garrisoned under the constableship of a Welshman, Gruffudd ap Tudor, and equipped with stone-throwing artillery and shot. The only reference to building works relates to the construction of a *camera* or lodging, and this has been taken to be the W tower, work on which commenced as soon as the castle was taken. It may have been at this time that the keep was heightened. In 1284 repairs were made to various

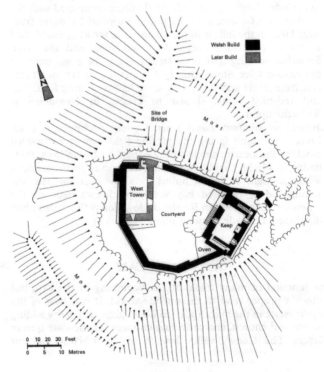

Dolwyddelan Castle.
Plan.

chambers, with further work undertaken in 1290–2; part of the masonry at the bottom of the flight of steps to the keep's roof dates from this time.

The castle may have been abandoned by the early C14, but in the late C15 it was leased to Maredudd ab Ieuan ap Robert (cf. Gwydir Castle), and it is to this period that the external staircase against the W tower belongs, leading up to the curtain wall. Between 1848 and 1850 the keep was restored by Lord Willoughby de Eresby; the battlements and the drains that project below them belonging to this final phase, as does much of the N and S walls. The C19 masonry is largely regularly laid shale, the medieval stonework from a variety of sources.

Where the natural precipitous slopes did not protect the castle, ditches were cut into the rock, to the E and W. The castle was entered through a simple doorway, adjacent to the W tower, a bridge having spanned the ditch at this point. A further doorway is situated in the same stretch of curtain wall, and a POSTERN is set in a short section of curtain wall NE of the keep, dating from the late C13.

The two-storey WEST TOWER was built abutting the earlier curtain, the ground-floor chamber utilizing the early C13 LATRINES at the N end, whilst a new set of latrines was built against the NW corner of the curtain wall, to serve the first-floor chamber. The surviving dressed stonework in the ground-floor doorway and S window is sandstone, possibly from the Chester area, which would suggest that the tower is indeed the *camera* of 1283. The large fireplace on the first floor confirms that this was the main chamber; an internal timber stair must have reached this level. To one side of the one window that remains on this floor steps led up to the roof level and battlements. The late C15 external staircase butts the S side of the tower.

The only other feature of the courtyard, besides the curtain wall, is the remains of an OVEN of uncertain date, in the angle of the curtain and the SW side of the keep.

The KEEP as built by Llywelyn the Great is the best surviving tower of its type. Before the C19 restoration, drawings show that the building stood to its upper walls, albeit roofless. The largely C19 S wall includes a projection that houses a passage to the latrine, and against the W wall a flight of steps leads to the first-floor entrance. The landing outside the keep's doorway was covered by a porch or forebuilding, itself with doorway and drawbar, whilst a pit within the porch provided an added defence, with a bridge that could be moved or raised to prevent access.

Entry to the basement, a room lit by three small slits, must have been through a first-floor trap-door. As first built, the main room on this level would have been lower than it is now, but the wide windows in the E and W walls are original, and were provided with seats. Although the tower was heightened in the Middle Ages, there is no evidence that a second floor was intended. The fireplace, restored in the C19, is in the E wall, the window above and to one side of it being a C19 addition, as is that in the upper W wall. A doorway in the SW corner opens into a passage that has a latrine at the end. The line of the original roof is marked by an offset, whilst the creasing of one gable can be made out in the S wall. The N window in the E wall has a doorway to one side of the embrasure, and this leads to a staircase to the C19 roof and battlements.

St Gwyddelan. Rebuilt 300 yds NE of the ancient site by Maredudd ab Ieuan, *c.* 1500. Nave and chancel in a single, very small rectangle, and a S transept built *c.* 1590 by Robert Wynn, of Plas Mawr, Conwy.

Well-dressed stone throughout. Cyclopean heads of Tudor profile to the N doorway and to the E windows of nave and transept. W bellcote, N porch and new windows (including one in the partly blocked S doorway) of *c.* 1850. The roof has just five bays of arch-braced trusses, with two tiers of small wind-braces. Over the sanctuary, a celure with a grid of ribs and bosses; carved on its N wall-plate, an elongated dragon-like creature. In contrast to the late medieval stonework is the S arcade of two segmental arches, on a re-set monolithic Doric column that Frances Lynch suggests may be Roman.

Dark oak FURNISHINGS, unusual and remarkably complete. – ALTAR RAILS. Turned, with graceful balusters, C18. – PULPIT. Like a small box pew on legs, with candlesticks and finials. Dated 1711. – DESK. C17. The back of the seat with finials. – BENCHES. Yoked in threes or fours, like those at Rûg Chapel, Rhug (M) without carving, but one inscribed MAINGC IR DYLA I CLYW (for the hard of hearing). The backs and arm supports with splats of wavy profile, *c.* 1700? – COLLECTION BOX in a wooden pillar. – SCREEN. Of three bays either side of the broad doorway. In the small lights, heavily carved foliate heads. The doorhead has long stylized leaves in solid spandrels. Sturdy Tudor-moulded muntins on a massive dado rail. On the head beam, a parapet with wavy balusters like the pews', perhaps from the W gallery. – FONT. Square, post-Reformation. – STAINED GLASS. E, fragments of a yellow-stained window. 1512? – N, a small C16 window, to St Christopher. – MONUMENTS. Members of the Wynn family, beginning with Maredudd ab Ieuan †1525. A rustic Elizabethan design of plaster, repainted. Five shields in strapwork and other heraldry. Divided in three by colonnettes, with cherub-head capitals and acorn finials.

St Elizabeth (former). 1886, in lancet style. The original architect was *E. B. Ferrey*, but the Incorporated Church Building Society disliked his scheme. Plans by *G. T. Ewing*, Lady Willoughby's architect, were accepted after more objections, but by then he had retired and Ferrey saw them through. So both architects can claim credit, for a dull building.

Capel Isaf Independent Chapel, Church Street (Pentre-bont). Attractive, lateral façade of 1860. A pair of tall

1. Landscape, the Bala fault and Llyn Tegid, M, aerial view (p. 545)

7. Llanddaniel Fab, A,
   Bryn Celli Ddu,
   burial chamber,
   Neolithic (p. 143)
8. Llanddaniel Fab, A,
   Bryn Celli Ddu,
   burial chamber,
   interior (p. 144)
9. Llanaelhaearn, C,
   Tre'r Ceiri, hill-fort,
   Bronze Age and
   Iron Age, aerial
   view (p. 385)
10. Rhos Lligwy, A,
    Din Lligwy,
    Romano-British
    homestead, c3–c4
    (p. 218)

29. Conwy Castle, C, 1284–7, from the south (p. 325)
30. Conwy, C, town walls, with the Mill Gate and line of latrines, 1285–7 (p. 335)

58   Pant Glas, C, Pant Glas Uchaf, 1570s (p. 480)
59.   Llan Ffestiniog, M, Bryn-yr-odyn, mid- to late C16 (p. 648)

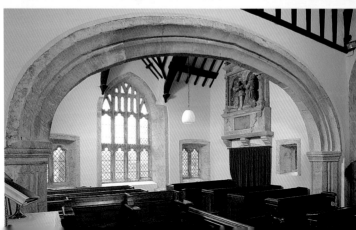

74. Llanegryn, M, Peniarth, north-west front, 1730s (p. 632)
75. Pentraeth, A, Plas Gwyn, *c.* 1754, north front (p. 212)

76. Llanedwen, A, Plas Newydd, entrance front, by James Wyatt and Joseph Potter, 1793–9 (p. 153)
77. Llandwrog, C, Glynllifon, by Edward Haycock, 1836–46, south front (p. 427)

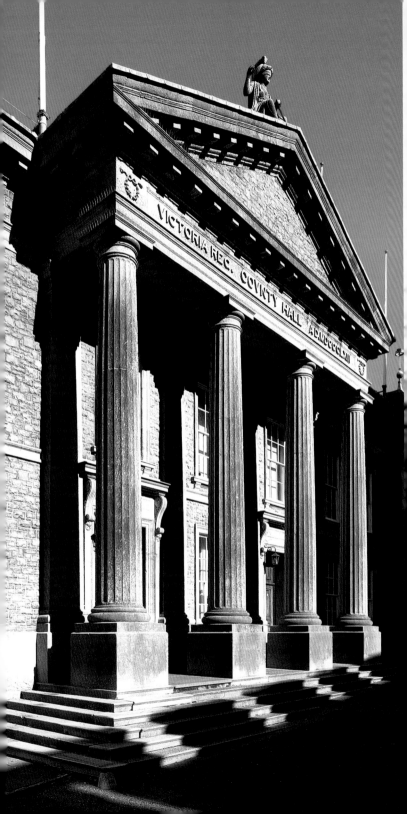

93   Caernarfon, C, County Hall, by John Thomas, 1863, portico (p. 302)
94. Llandderfel, M, Palé Hall, by S. Pountney Smith, 1869–71 (p. 625)
95. Arthog, M, Tŷ'n-y-coed, by William Parry James, *c.* 1875, hall (p. 544)

119. Caernarfon, C, Galeri, by Richard Murphy Architects, 2005 (p. 304)
120. Llanberis, C, Snowdon, Hafod Eryri, by Ray Hole Architects, 2008–9
   (p. 395)

round-headed windows in the centre, and round-headed doors each side, all with fanlights. Margin-light sashes. Half-hipped roofs. A MINISTER'S HOUSE attached at the S end. To the E, HEN GAPEL, the former Methodist chapel, later Assembly Rooms, dated 1835. Both chapels are now dwellings.

MORIAH CALVINISTIC METHODIST CHAPEL. A large imposing chapel, built for 600. Italian classical style, 1880, by *Richard Davies*. Tripartite front facing S, with a wide pedimented central bay framed with plain pilasters. At the upper level, a group of three round-headed windows, a projecting pediment on consoles above the central one. Below, the inscription band with the name and the date. Paired round-headed doorways, with pilasters and keystones, and an entablature adorned with three acroteria. Tall windows to the narrow flanking bays, with lugged architraves. The fine interior has been altered to form a huge dwelling on many levels. Attached at the N end, the manse.

SCHOOL, near the station, by *Westbury Lloyd Jones*, County Architect, *c.* 1934. Gambrel roofs, big sliding partitions between the classrooms and (former) sliding windows to the S bay windows.

BRYN MOEL, 1 m. NE. L-plan, dated 1563, perhaps two unit-system houses, as both arms are close in date but have separate access. The S wing has a fireplace and a former mural stair in the N wall (the date 1563 inscribed above its blocked window). Extended N and connected by a way-through on the opposite side of the fireplace. To the E, the second house, with a lateral chimney and an external doorway W of it. Crude voussoir relieving arches above wooden lintels to the E wing windows.

TAN-Y-CASTELL, ¾ m. W. C17 farmhouse, once single-storey; raised and extended, later C19. Projecting shouldered chimney at the E gable. On its r., a big slate plaque bearing the names of three ministers and a deacon, all Jones brothers, who lived here in the late C19 and are commemorated on the nearby MONUMENT.

PONT SARN-DDU, 1½ m. WSW. Called the 'Roman' Bridge because this was on the Roman road from Ffestiniog to Dolwyddelan. A long clapper bridge of eight spans, with rectangular rubble piers, huge slate lintels and a modern roadway. Medieval or earlier.

PONT-Y-LLAN, the village bridge. Dated 1808. An arch each side of a larger central one.

PONT GETHIN, 3½ m. ENE. A dramatic viaduct, taking the LNWR railway over the river and the A470 road. 1,060 ft (326 metres) long, one main arch and six smaller ones. Machicolated parapet, arrow slits above the arches, semicircular turrets etc. Built in 1879 by *O. Gethin Jones* of Penmachno.

TAI PENAMNEN, Cwm Penamnen, ¾ m. S. The traces of a row of buildings, of various dates. Maredudd ab Ieuan lived here, late C15.

TOMEN CASTELL. A rocky knoll with ditch, set in the valley E of the main castle, was the site of the first castle here. It may

have been the birthplace of Llywelyn the Great. The base of a
sub-rectangular tower on an artificial platform was excavated
on the summit in 1964.

DWYGYFYLCHI see PENMAENMAWR

EDERN

ST EDERN. In a circular raised churchyard, now extended.
Rebuilt as a cruciform church, mostly on old foundations,
in 1868 by *Richard Coad*. Lancets and plate tracery. Some
roof timbers reused; two of *c.* 1500 in the N transept, recorded
there in 1847 by Glynne, are ornamented on the soffit,
one with a continuous roll with two bosses, the other with
nailhead studding in the mouldings and floral bosses near
the bottom. A third, now in the C19 S transept, is of the
same cusped, arch-braced type. The much steeper pair of old
trusses in the nave raises a problem; with their pointed arches
and simpler cusping (an upright quatrefoil between two
circles), can they belong to a nave of *c.* 1400? – FONT. C19,
round with shallow decoration. – STAINED GLASS. E by *Clayton
& Bell*, *c.* 1865.

CALVINISTIC METHODIST CHAPEL, Groesffordd, ⅓ m. W.
1875, by *Richard Owens*, altered 1898. Grand pedimented
centrepiece rising above hipped wings, forming a rusticated
arch. The name and date in raised letters in the frieze, and a
keyed roundel in the pediment. Within the archway, three
round-headed windows above a wide central doorway and
small flanking windows. All with plain pilasters, moulded arch-
heads and keystones. Paired round-headed windows to the
hipped wings, above paired rectangular ones.

Three parts to the VILLAGE. The old nucleus at the bottom of
the hill, where the single-arch early C19 BRIDGE crosses the
Geirch. Altered MILL buildings etc. E of the bridge. On the N
side of the main road, GLAN AFON. C18, gabled half-dormers,
whitewashed rubble. Further up (SW), RHIANFA, with a
moulded hood above the lower window, and fluted pilasters
and a dentilated entablature to the door, unceremoniously cut
in half by improvements to the next-door house. A little way
up Lôn Fawr (towards the church), FACTORY COTTAGE on
the l. Early C19, perhaps connected with the mill. Humble,
built into the hill one end. Further S along Lôn Fawr, the
second group, near the church. The former NATIONAL
SCHOOL of 1845, with a Tudor porch and a tiny W bellcote.
To the S, the school house. The third part of the village at
GROESFFORDD, consists of the chapel (*see* above) and stone
terraces, mostly modernized.

PEN-Y-BRYN, ¼ m. SW. Farmhouse, dated as late as 1790, with
three gabled, coped half-dormers irregularly spaced and
modern lower windows.

FELINHELI/PORT DINORWIC   5268

Known nowadays by its original name (also Y Felinheli), after the tide mill (literally 'salt mill'), the village expanded hugely in the mid C19 as the port for the Dinorwic slate quarries. In the late C20 the docks were converted to yacht marinas.

St Mary. 1865, a late work by *J. G. Weightman*. Grey rubble with yellow sandstone dressings. Poor ground conditions precluded the w spire. Unfussy E.E. s transept added by *Montagu Hepworth*, 1890, so now cruciform. Trussed rafters forming an open wagon roof. Between crossing and transepts arcades with polished grey Aberdeen granite piers and pierced quatrefoils in the spandrels. – Pulpit. Octagonal, with tracery and ornate cornice. Polished grey granite shafts around the base. – Stained glass. e window by *O'Connor* of London. – s transept and nave s by *Jones & Willis*. – n transept by *Percy Bacon Bros*.

Bethania Calvinistic Methodist Chapel. 1913, by *L. Wynne Williams* of Birkenhead. Dark grey snecked rubble contrasted with fiery red terracotta dressings and window surrounds – the result is like an excess of lipstick. A wide eight-light window, with segmental arch, continuous transom and cusped heads to the lights. Two- and three-light transom-and-mullion windows each side.

The village, 1½ m. long, has little of interest sw of its centre along the main street, Caernarfon Road. St Mary's Church is at the far sw end and the two 1860s chapels, Bryn Menai and Salim, have been converted to houses. A perambulation starts conveniently where Snowdon Street drops from the main street, now Bangor Street, towards the water and Beach Road. From here, the Moel-y-don Ferry operated until the Menai bridges were built, bringing Anglesey workers to the Dinorwic Quarry. A footpath leads ne, through late C20 luxury apartments facing the South Dock, built 1839–41 for slate. The tapering slate chimneystack remains from the dock boiler house.

Back on Bangor Street, Arvonia on the r. A large emporium with warehouse, later C19, in yellow brick with red and black details, an original shopfront and the name emblazoned in raised letters on red brick. Further ne, the war memorial clock tower. 1925, by *Segar Owen* of Warrington (architect of Port Sunlight, Cheshire). Square, with chamfered corners. Rock-faced Anglesey limestone and dressed stone to the clock stage which has a pediment on each face, and an ogee-shaped roof of fish-scale slates. Nicely placed diagonally at the corner, facing the pebbledashed and mildly Arts and Crafts Church Hall; behind, up a short lane, the railway station, surprisingly big even when built in 1874. It replaced a station near Halfway House Inn, built when the railway was extended from Bangor in 1852. Yellow brick, with red brick patterns, like

Arvonia. Two gables each side of the centre, then wider bays each end. The diaper-work and half-hips suggest a country station in Germany rather than Wales.

Bangor Street takes on an estate feel from this point. TERFYN TERRACE on the l., 1862. On the r., a pair of detached houses of c. 1870, CAE GWYN and FFINFA. Pink stone with canted timber bays, gables, ornate bargeboards, hipped roofs etc. Next, Nos. 1–2 BODARBORTH, plainer and earlier (c. 1850). Elliptical heads to the window and doorway in the projecting bay, lozenge-shape window panes, diagonal brick chimneys. Opposite, No. 1 FRON HELI, with three projecting gabled bays, the middle one larger with a cruciform loop. Octagonal brick chimneys in clusters of four. Further E, the longish HALFWAY HOUSE INN, midway between Caernarfon and Bangor on the early C19 turnpike. Next l., Y FRON, a pretty mid-C19 stucco house on its own, with a nice trellised porch, then Nos. 1–5 CAE GLAS, r., c. 1863 estate cottages. Plain and simple, with steep dormer and porch roofs, and wavy barge-boards. ABERPWLL, beyond, is an interesting planned estate. U-plan, with a lane encircling a group of four estate houses, one in each quadrant. The one facing Bangor Street, PORT CHURCH HOUSE, is the showpiece. Picturesque cottage style, with a large gable between wings set back behind verandas with rustic tree-trunk posts. Only the small bellcote at the r. gable hints that this was an estate church, built c. 1863 to replace the Seaman's Mission.

Opposite Halfway House Inn, a lane leads down to the MARINA. To the r., the DOCK of 1900–2 on the site of the original mill and tidal inlet. LOCK GATES and BOLLARDS by *Cleghorn & Wilkinson* of Northwich. SWING BRIDGE. Red-brick dock walls, stepped in the DRY DOCK. Facing the bridge, the DOCK OFFICE: fish-scale slates of purple, grey and green to the walls and roofs. On the s side, late C20 OFFICES and yachting facilities. Pillared slate; the three-storey tower end projecting on tall steel posts. Further E, early C21 HOUSING of two and three storeys, the ground floor recessed behind steel posts. The bridge leads to a large area of HOUSING beautifully positioned on the sw tip of the Vaynol promontory. Built c. 1979 by *Phillips Cutler Phillips Troy*. Two- and three-storeyed, smooth light-coloured render, flat-roofed dormers, balconies etc. Restless in its striving for variety, and rather dated, but the landscaping is now well established.

VAYNOL/Y FAENOL

VAYNOL/Y FAENOL, 2 m. NE. The township or Maenol of the bishops of Bangor until the Reformation. The early features, including the Old Hall, were built by the Williams family; the new house etc. from the mid C18 to 1859 by the Smith/Assheton-Smith family, who after the Napoleonic Wars made the deerpark and began the harbour at Port Dinorwic, w, to serve especially the immense Dinorwic slate quarries at Llanberis; Late Victorian

and Edwardian buildings by the Duff family, heirs of the
Assheton-Smiths and owners till 1984.

The C16 OLD HALL, its garden, and its chapel on a terrace above
and askew, cluster together at the centre of the park. The Old
Hall is a jumble of low C16 blocks, adding up to an
E-shaped front which faces N. Of red and grey gritstone with
yellow freestone for the windows etc. The porch wing and
narrow l. wing were early additions to the hall. The porch wing
has a four-centred arch, mouldings without capitals, and
cusping and blank shields in the spandrels; diminutive window
of three rounded-headed lights to its upper room. Within, the
porch is wide and has stone benches either side. Inner doorway
with Tudor roses in the spandrels. The narrow l. (E) projection
has windows with four lights below and three above; lateral
chimney to the hall between. The more ornate r. wing, added
for Sir Griffith Williams perhaps in the 1660s, projects further
after a section of wall in plane. Stepped gable, windows with
four round heads below and two lights with a transom above.
The E side faces a sunk walled garden; it has three storeys and
no primary doorway. Restored Tudor four-light windows with
dripmoulds on the first floor and a transomed five-light one
on the second; its S chimney is set diagonally. The S side forms
one side of the stableyard. Of four storeys with ovolo-
moulded, mullioned-and-transomed windows and cavetto-
moulded gable copings. Here the house appears as a downhill-
sited hall with additions. W front with lateral chimneys.
The interior structure has been revealed after removal of the
    Victorian finishes. The HALL is wainscoted with small-field
    panelling and a frieze, brought down from the room above in
    the early C20; the showy low ceiling is divided crosswise into
    four compartments, each subdivided into four, with the joists
    with their enriched chamfers all set parallel. The chimneys at
    either end of this wing seem to have jointed, perhaps reused,
    fireplace lintels: on the ground floor, the N one hidden by the
    panelling, the S one on corbels and reassembled; on the first
    floor, the Great Chamber's of three stones with joggled joints,
    a yellow one between purple ones, the S fireplace lintel just
    jointed and chamfered. Roof with raking struts over the Great
    Chamber. Reset Jacobean staircase with big square newels,
    shaped finials and pendants, and turned balusters.
The STABLEYARD, S, is entered by a gateway with an iron over-
    throw. Elaborately re-fitted for racehorses in 1913, with stalls
    by *Young & Co.* On the W the house stands at the margin of
    the vista to the Edwardian clock tower on the barn (*see* below).
    Broad segmental archway beside it, rebated for gates.
The CHAPEL OF ST MARY stands at an angle to the W inner
    garden wall above this archway. The family chapels at Plas
    Newydd and Penrhyn having been destroyed, Vaynol's is all the
    more valuable to illustrate the type. A simple small rectangle,
    dated 1596 with the initials of William Williams in the porch.
    Standard mid-Tudor details apart from the drop-keystone in

the porch doorway. E window of four round-arched lights under a dripmould, the S and restored N windows of three. Eaves with roll mouldings. The porch doorway with an elliptical arch and hollow-moulded under a gable with moulded coping; inner doorway of yellow gritstone, with an elliptical arch and wave-moulded. The interior was remodelled as a mausoleum in an Italian style in 1910 by Sir Charles (Duff) Assheton-Smith and his wife (and became his memorial in 1914); it is paved and lined with marble and has two kneeling marble angels on the altar.

The GARDEN of the Old Hall seems substantially late C16–early C17. The ground in front of the house rises by low grass terraces to the level adjoining the chapel, but is not well related to either. E of the house the sunk garden, with an axis of semicircular steps from the terraces to the basin placed in it. In the upper terrace also an Edwardian exedra and round pond. Here the historic high outer walls survive at the NE and NW, with two Jacobean doorways, perhaps re-set. One is dated 1633 with the initials of Sir Thomas and Katherine Williams; elliptical-arched with a keystone and stepped dripmould. The inscription ('Ye mystic garden Fold me close I love thee well Beloved Vaynol') is apparently of the period of the chapel interior, c. 1910. The other doorway with casement mouldings of red sandstone, facing N. Detached to the E, the WALLED GARDEN, confused by Victorian additions.

The historic site is linked by the grand Edwardian vista to the ESTATE YARDS, the most extensive in Gwynedd. This broad way passes the model DAIRY (now an office) on the r., dated 1911 with the initials CAS, a stone Neo-Elizabethan building with a bold veranda along the front, and rises towards the cupola added asymmetrically in 1899 to the GREAT BARN. This was erected for William and Dorothy Williams in 1605; at 100 ft (31 metres) long, the largest in Gwynedd. Roof with eight bays of collar-trusses with king- and queenpost struts. Two rows of vent slits beside the segmental arches; the W addition of c. 1660 looks as if it was storeyed once, perhaps in adaptation as a coachhouse.

The barn is enclosed by much more recent yards of model farm buildings, aligned transversely. Long ranges on the N, of stone and single-storeyed. Further scattered buildings beyond and in other directions, mostly for animals – whether for the many needs of sport in the early C19, or keeping exotic menageries c. 1900, or just the Vaynol herd of White Park Cattle. To the W, Victorian brick outbuildings once reaching almost to the New Hall. Of particular architectural note the NEW CHAPEL of c. 1845 near the barn, in a somewhat mechanical Decorated style, with W porch and bellcote. This substitute place of worship for the estate employees, sited almost among the working yards to its S and much larger than the Tudor chapel as well as more public in conception, is another feature unique to Vaynol. Pews with fleur-de-lys finials. The eight stall backs either side of the W door could be from the old chapel.

New VAYNOL HALL (now offices), 300 yds SE of the old one. The reversion of the Vaynol estate was left to the Crown; King William III granted it to John Gore in 1699 in trust for the Smith family. In 1774 his grandson Thomas Assheton inherited Vaynol. His son and grandson, both called Thomas Assheton-Smith (†1828 and 1858) laid the industrial foundations of the estate. The evidence for the new house, designed in 1793 by *James Defferd* of Bangor, is confusing.* This core, a three-storey stuccoed house with a semi-octagonal S bay and two bays either side, looks like the mid-C18 house of the Smith family. The central hall and room to its r. have mid-C18 plaster ceilings, and the upper l. room retains raised-field panelling. E of this core a large drawing room with canted corners, of the kind added elsewhere by *John Cooper* of Beaumaris, perhaps of 1793 and marked by larger windows; the balancing W wing does not survive. Large additions to the W and N included the staircase of c. 1900. The plasterwork generally was by *Jacksons* of Hammersmith, c. 1933. After the demolitions to the N c. 1960 a new circular hall in simplified Late Georgian was devised by *Sir Michael Duff (Assheton-Smith)* (architect *John Penn*). This has eight Doric columns in terracotta scagliola supporting a circular architrave silhouetted against a shallow dome, and landscape wall paintings by *Martin Newall*. To the E of the new approach a long descent of EDWARDIAN GARDENS with yew hedges, pools and flower borders, designer unknown.

The New Hall faced the Snowdonian panorama across the Vaynol plateau, well back from the Menai Strait. Its remarkable setting was redesigned as a DEERPARK with iron fencing in the early C19, for the first Thomas Assheton-Smith. The smoothing of the flattish ground, leaving a few old Spanish chestnuts and forming a shallow lake, was in character and planting English, understated and sporting. A few other buildings. Gothic MAUSOLEUM by *Henry Kennedy*, 1878, hidden in the wood at the N of the park; of limestone rubble, lined with Bath stone with Mansfield stone columns. – On the shore of the Strait (now National Trust), a BOATHOUSE and small DOCK opposite Plas Newydd. – On the slopes to its S a round eyecatcher TOWER, now hidden in trees.

The enormous PARK WALL, well over two miles long, was built for George William Duff c. 1860 during a recession in the slate industry. Seamlessly constructed of Moelfre stone in random squared ashlar, with chunky purple slate-on-edge coping. GATEWAYS at the W with tall pylon piers like those of the Menai bridges. The grandiloquent main gateway is evidently later than the wall. A screen recessed between convex quadrants pierced by upright oval windows, all in rusticated stonework, with pylon piers capped with depressed pyramids. The designer is unknown.

---

*The archives were burnt at the other Assheton-Smith estate at Tidworth, Hants.

GLASINFRYN

ST ELIZABETH. 1871, by *Sir G. G. Scott*. Small E.E. nave and
chancel in one, and S porch. Round multi-lobe W window. Now
a dwelling.

BETHMAACA INDEPENDENT CHAPEL. 1895, by *Richard Davies*.
Shallow porches either side of a tall Venetian window. A smaller
rectangular one above. Pebbledash, with rendered quoins and
surrounds. Witch-hat roof ventilators.

A small compact VILLAGE, just one street gently falling S towards
the Cegin. Mostly workers' houses, with nice cobbled
pavements. Behind the church, the former SCHOOL, 1869, with
yellow brick surrounds and chimneys. N of the church, Nos.
1–4 ELIZABETH TERRACE, early C19, with half-dormers, the
stone exposed or roughcast. Opposite, Nos. 8–9, the former
Post Office to the r., with an open porch. Further N, r.,
BODLONDEB. In its gabled elevation facing the street, a slate
plaque with the date 1836. Attached on the E, and stepping
downhill, Nos. 1–6 HOWE STREET, a pretty terrace of tiny
white-rendered cottages facing a sloping lawn across a cobbled
path. Possibly once a back-to-back row.

BRYN-Y-MEDDYG, ¼ m. NNE. An L-plan two-storey house, built
by the Penrhyn estate *c.* 1880, probably for the village doctor.
Three-bay E front, with full-width veranda and a latticed
timber porch. Slate-clad upper storey. Ornate bargeboards.

GLODDAETH *see* LLANRHOS

GLYNLLIFON *see* LLANDWROG

GWYDIR

GWYDIR CASTLE, ½ m. W of Llanrwst. The centre of the most
powerful estate in NW Wales in the C16 and earlier C17. Maredudd
ab Ieuan ap Robert †1525 reoccupied the C13 castle at
Dolwyddelan *c.* 1489 and bought Gwydir before 1500. A military
man who fought at Tournai in 1513 (commemorated in full
armour in his brass at Dolwyddelan church), he is said to have
travelled twice to Rome on pilgrimage, so his cultural links were
wide. The next three generations completed his house. John Wyn
ap Maredudd †1559, Morys Wynn †1580, and Sir John Wynn first
Baronet †1627 were public figures as High Sheriffs and M.P.s.
The second was older brother of Robert, the builder of Plas
Mawr, Conwy, and married Katheryn of Berain, known as the
'mother of Wales' for her husbands and progeny. The last, an
intriguingly modern figure promoting industry and trade, built
the private retreat at Gwydir Uchaf in 1604. He wrote a history
of the family. His elder son, Sir John †1614, died at Lucca. His
next, the second Baronet, Sir Richard †1649, was groom of the
bedchamber to Charles I and treasurer to Henrietta Maria, an
intimate of the Stuart court. He built the family chapel in
Llanrwst church, 1633–4, and probably commissioned Llanrwst

Bridge, 1634–6. The third son, Sir Owen †1660 was known for
alchemy. Their caution in the Civil War and Protectorate
preserved the estate, though Owen's son, Richard, was briefly
imprisoned. As fourth Baronet, Sir Richard †1674 began the
chapel at Gwydir Uchaf in 1673. He was comptroller of the
household of Catherine of Braganza, and his chapel hints at
Catholicism. His daughter married Lord Willoughby de Eresby,
later 1st Duke of Ancaster, adding 100,000 acres to the Ancaster
estates, and the house became dormant. A fire affected part of
the courtyards in the 1720s.

Sir Peter Burrell †1827 married a Willoughby heiress and made
Gwydir his seat (becoming Lord Gwydyr in 1796), and adding
the Castle appellation. He greatly reduced the house
in 1816–20 clearing the timber-framed ranges, fortunately
recorded by Buckler just before, and fitting out interiors in an
antique manner. His son, Lord Willoughby de Eresby, had
Charles Barry tidy the remains, 1828, and make gardens in C17
style, with *Lewis Kennedy*, agent to Lady Willoughby's family at
Drummond Castle, and designer of the famous parterres there.
Rooms were modernized *c.* 1838 for his invalid daughter Elizabeth; others were apparently coloured to give 'antique splendours'. In 1896 Gwydir with little land was sold to a cousin, Lord
Carrington, later first Marquess of Lincolnshire. After he sold in
1920 to the art-dealer Duveen, the interior was plundered for
saleable fittings, the dining room going for £10,000 to William
R. Hearst, and the oak parlour apparently also. Refitted for
Countess Tankerville, the Solar Tower and the dining room wing
burnt in 1922, and the SW corner burnt in 1924. G. H. Kenrick,
barrister, began repairs under *John Swarbrick*, but the Solar
Tower was only reinstated after 1950 for Arthur Clegg †1964.
Since 1994 Peter and Judy Welford, with *Graham Holland*, have
recovered the early Tudor character, and most unexpectedly the
dining room sold to Hearst.

The C16 house, exceptionally for the region, was around court-
    yards, their extent and number uncertain, but is now reduced
    basically to two ranges at right angles, the long low W range
    incorporating the two-storey Hall of Meredith and at the N end
    the remarkably tall house called the Solar Tower. The W range
    also has two wings to the rear. Mostly of fine dressed slate-
    stone, it incorporates pink Deganwy stone from Aberconwy
    Abbey at Maenan nearby, dissolved in 1537, the reuse datable
    to the time of John Wynn ap Maredudd.
From the road, the modest Tudor-arched GATEWAY dated 1555
    had until 1820 a timber-framed upper storey. Original doors
    (the wicket tellingly small). The arch leads the eye gently down   51
    a continuous range on the l. of which the further half is the
    early C16 Hall of Meredith, to the four-storey Solar Tower at
    right angles. There were stables SE of the gatehouse, of which
    the base of the roadside wall survives, but the layout of the
    courtyards is impossible to unravel. The gatehouse timber
    storey was matched with timber-framed ranges on at least two

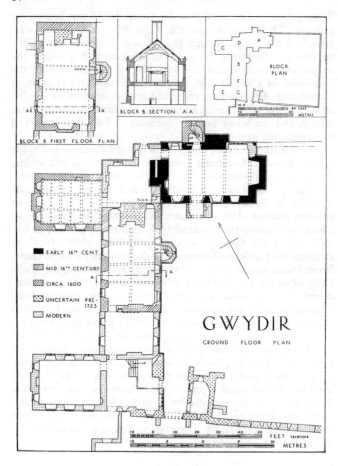

Gwydir Castle.
Ground-floor plan

sides of the court, as illustrated by Buckler. A low square-framed w range l. of the Hall of Meredith was replaced in stone by *Barry*. A NE range set back running r. of the Solar Tower had ornate lozenge and quatrefoil framing. Apparently dated 1558, it was extended 70 ft (22 metres) probably for a Long Gallery. The courtyard wall may be part of it, now with trefoil finials from elsewhere, the E wall on the site of ranges shown on a 1723 map linked to the stables. This has a Tudor archway, two-sided, possibly moved.

46, 51 The Hall of Meredith and the Solar Tower may both be of *c.* 1500 for Maredudd ab Ieuan, large enough to operate separately, so precursors of the Gwynedd unit-system. But the stonework does not match, so the two were not of one build; the hall could be earlier, late C15. The massive rectangular SOLAR TOWER is a puzzle, inadequately studied before the fire. Four storeys, four bays with ornate porch-tower added at the front and stair-tower behind. If of Maredudd's time, there is no parallel for such a house with principal rooms on the two upper floors and top attic storey, unless an analogy for the Gwydir arrangement is the medieval keep and detached hall at Dolwyddelan, Mare-dudd's previous residence. Small rectangular windows with modern leaded glazing, two bays r. of the porch, one to the l. In the early C20 the upper windows had ogee tracery and the first floor had Tudor mullions as on the hall block, but these were C19; Buckler shows them unadorned. They are said to have had the earliest domestic glass in Wales, supported Italian-style by ironwork (*ferramenta*). In the angle l., a small blocked pointed doorway to the inserted room between the primary ranges. Very high chimneys each end, diagonal, l., and a massive square, r.; similar lateral chimney behind. The big r. one served the ground floor, the l. one the attic, the apparent chimney-breast actually the latrine shafts for the two middle floors which were warmed from the lateral chimney. The romantic crenellated chimney-tops, so characteristic of Gwydir, are late C16 as also the upper floors of the porch-tower. The hoodmoulded tower door reuses roll mouldings from Maenan, so after 1537. Its acentrality suggests the tower was slightly widened in the 1590s when the elegant four-light window above was put in to become the oriel to Sir John Wynn's Great Chamber. There is evidence for a plaster vault inside, characterizing it as an attempt at a loggia, an Italian-ism seen also in the oversailing hipped roof on long stone con-soles. Under the eaves, a heroic eagle cartouche for Sir John Wynn, and on the side, the Gerrard arms of his wife.

The rear has the chimney-breast central and added narrow gabled stair-tower, r. The upper parts of the former and all the latter contain material from Maenan, mostly later C15 (though some possibly late C13–C14). The stones are squared or orna-mented with quatrefoils and there are ogee two-light traceries as stair windows. The reuse of the spiral stairs, widened to fit, and also of slightly cambered arches for doorheads witness ongoing demolition at Maenan. This overlap between anti-quarian and pragmatic is characteristic of the Wynns. The suspicion that the windows are earlier C19 insertions like those formerly on the front is dispelled by the masonry.

The INTERIORS lost in the sale and fire were fortunately recorded. The ground floor now stripped to the stone, revealing the 12-ft (3.7-metre) flat voussoired fireplace, was the 'Oak Parlour'. It had heavily moulded three-tier beams of *c.* 1500, linenfold panelling of the 1530s, and overmantel (from the gatehouse) with two moustachioed Caesars flanking splen-did heraldry, dated 1597, and C17 leather wall-covering. The room was sold, so not burnt, but its pieces have disappeared. The first-floor beamed ceiling was removed (possibly to the dining-room wing) so that the upper Elizabethan plaster ceiling could serve a double-height space. This Great Chamber was a miniature of Hardwick Hall with classical tapestries above the wainscot and a huge C17 overmantel with heraldry on a field of fine acanthus carving. It was probably done for Sir John Wynn, *c.* 1600. The burnt-out shell was reinstated in the 1950s, and the upper parts remodelled since, respecting implied early partitioning.

The adjoining HALL, with that of Bishop Deane at Bangor, is the earliest first-floor hall surviving in Gwynedd. It could even pre-date Maredudd to the C15 owner, Hywel Coetmor. Low-built, four bays, the windows, tidied in 1828, now match those on the 1828 addition to the l. Chimneys as on the Solar Tower, diagonal l., and massive square r., the crenellated tops late C16. The half-octagonal stair-tower originally gave external access to the upper hall (exchanged in the late C16 for an inside entry). At the top, under a five-sided hipped roof, each facet has a window of pink stone, an ogee light with two panels above, all cusped, and a corbel table above. This comes from Maenan, and the stonework suggests that the whole tower was re-erected in the mid-C16 with precision, its oak roof with the Wynn arms and ribbed upper door of that date. The parapet finials are earlier C19 ornament, apparently reused from C17 garden walls.

The rear is plain: off-centre doorway and two-light windows, possibly some from Maenan, the two upper ones lengthened in 1828. Low wings project either side. The NW one containing the dining room is C16, the upper floor added in the late C16. It burnt in 1922. The SW one, by *Barry*, contained the kitchen, reusing masonry from demolished parts. It burnt in 1924. The early wing has a leaning end wall with more elliptical-arched windows and the N side has reused trefoiled single lights of *c.* 1300 and two gargoyle heads. Near the road, an 1820s COACH HOUSE perhaps on the site of a pigeon house of 1597.

Inside, the ground floor is now one space with a low ceiling of noble construction, its beams and joists in three tiers. An oak frame from the smoke-bay in front of the NE fireplace has in the panels plaster lion heads, roses and fleurs-de-lys, among the little surviving C16 plasterwork at Gwydir, and like 1580s work at Maenan Hall and Plas Mawr, Conwy. Incomplete post-and-panel partition at the other end, moved here *c.* 1950. The upper HALL OF MEREDITH was scraped of plaster including a flat Elizabethan ceiling in the 1950s. The compensation was reincorporating the open roof into the hall. The fireplace is at the other end to that below: simple timber lintel, and so meant for plaster. At the NE is the oak-framed smoke-bay. The roof looks early, shallow-pitched, arched-braced collar-trusses with apex struts, and short cusped wind-braces. Could it be C15 and of the Coetmor period? Three main bays, then a half-bay at the SW, which indicates a dais canopy. The first-floor room beyond, in the 1828 addition, was re-formed in 2000 and given C16 panelling, *ex situ*. In Barry's SW kitchen, a panelled library designed by the owner, *Peter Welford*,

1999. In the angle to the Solar Tower, a room called the HALL
OF JUSTICE, not large, panelled, with a corbelled chimney-
breast and stairs to cellars.

In the NW wing is the DINING ROOM, reinstated in 1998
after the carved woodwork and wall-coverings removed in 1921
and bequeathed by Hearst to the Metropolitan Museum,
New York, were generously returned, a restitution equally
generously funded by Cadw. Gwydir thus reacquired one of
the courtly interiors for which it was celebrated, a seemingly
authentic but heterodox example of a Stuart eating parlour,
since at least a century separates the main carved components.
The extent of C19 rearrangement is unknown. Small-field
wainscot above a dado of bold geometric patterns; painted and
gilded leather above, of C17 London manufacture. At either
end are outstanding carved architectural features, the doorway
and the chimneypiece. Of high quality, possibly London, workmanship, they may be repositioned, as the doorway seems to
have been made for a room with a lower ceiling. Presumably
Carolean, it has giant spiral columns in pairs of opposed twist
with shallow foliage following the spirals, as though cast in
bronze and Corinthian capitals. Fluted frieze and cornice with
delicate relief-carved putti and plant-scroll, broken forward
over the columns. C17 acanthus-carved tall bolection doorcase,
the door a C19 assemblage of C17 carved woodwork. The cresting, a segmental piece of Jonesian frond carving is also reused,
between crude C19 Jacobean finials. The chimneypiece around
a plain C17 fireplace is acanthus-carved under an intricately
carved overmantel. The centre has the Wynn arms, carved
locally, but the flanking panels are of fine and tight Low
Countries style, and the framing uprights have C16 motifs. Its
main feature is the Flemish bracketed cornice on exaggeratedly
spiral columns deeply carved with vines in limewood. These
are set on high plinths, each with an idealized low-relief profile
portrait in the Italian or 'Romaine' manner. Probably of the
1530s, possibly John Wynn ap Maredudd, his son Morys and
their wives, illuminating the Renaissance culture in which
the family moved more than any other surviving piece. The
columns could be mid-C17; they are of less than architectural
scale, and may have had a different purpose.*

The GARDENS are an amalgam of early layouts rationalized in
the 1830s. In the court the eight-lobed parterre, by *Barry* with
Lewis Kennedy. On the slope to the E, cedars planted for the
accession of Charles I indicate, with large yews, formal gardens
later overlaid with Victorian parterres. Along the NE a raised
terrace with steps down at the NW by a late C16 stone ARCH
built by Sir John Wynn. Serlian arch under a gable, robustly

*This room contained the earlier C16 Wynn Sideboard, a canopied buffet, now in
the Burrell Collection, Glasgow. The coffered plaster ceiling is modern. Before the
1922 fire the room had a beamed ceiling like that under the Hall of Meredith, possibly moved from the Solar Tower in the late C16.

detailed with raised roundels, and carrying three obelisk finials
– the sole example of this language in Wales. The NW vista or
Dutch Garden, one of several in mid-C17 North Wales, is
notable for the length and breadth of the double line of yews
clipped to umbrella forms. The single-jet fountain at the house
end is fed by a late C16 system from the hill above.

Gwydir was linked to Llanrwst by Gwydir Avenue, a straight
C17 road, and on foot by a narrow C16 causeway from the
garden. It began at a lost summerhouse that Colt Hoare noted
as dated 1592. This curved to the river bank (where it now
dwindles away) in such a way that it could have also been
meant to deflect flood. If so it was typical of Gwydir in combining several things, and it is a unique piece of masonry, with
a slab-paved walkway for hundreds of yards.

GWYDIR UCHAF. A second place, distinct but not fully separate,
built by Sir John Wynn in 1604 as a retreat, and mostly
demolished in the late C18. It became the favoured residence,
and the private chapel was built here in 1673. There was a
shallow artificial MOUNT or ziggurat, a great rarity in Wales,
ascended by a spiral path edged with holly, and, at some
distance, there was a bowling green. The wide zigzag Lady
Mary's Walk, down to Gwydir, Thomas Dineley in 1684 called
'a pleasant melancholy descent under trees'. The whole could
be seen as echoing the Continental villa or *lustschloss*, the
exchange of the formal for the cultured life. The HOUSE, as
drawn with uncertain accuracy by Dineley, was a Renaissance
five-bay hipped villa, of one main storey, with basement and
attic. A strange pyramid porch on columns was approached by
balustraded steps with obelisks at the feet. After its vicissitudes,
the limestone Doric porch columns are all that is externally
recognizable, and a heraldic overmantel of 1622 must have
come from Gwydir.

CHAPEL OF THE HOLY TRINITY, Gwydir Uchaf. Begun 1673
for Sir Richard Wynn †1674. Detached from both houses yet
very much a country-house chapel. Squared yellow sandstone
apart from local slate in the plinth and W wall. Large roofing
slates, and simple bellcote with schematic pediment, the bell
dated 1752. The last-built of the six or seven Gwynedd private
chapels, it resembles closely Colonel Salusbury's 1637 chapel
at Rhug before its Victorian re-casing. Pointed E window of
four lights, minimally Perp, with no cusping, and all in wood.
The side windows, still less Gothic, have segmental heads and
straight mullions. Arched N doorway with Perp-survival
mouldings; dated above SRWB 1673.

Within, the ambivalence is between religion and politics.
The painted ceiling (for all the artist's lack of training) sets out
Christian doctrine in imagery more Counter-Reformation
than Protestant while the Royal Arms affirm in confident
Baroque brushwork loyalty to Charles II. Sir Richard flew
close to Catholicism, consulting the Jesuit, Fr Edward
Petre, over 'procuring a Cross' – a stained-glass Crucifixion.

The sanctuary has Laudian ALTAR RAILS on two shallow steps, paved in front with interlaced octagons. The main part is handsomely panelled to two-thirds height with painted grained panelling, cornice and some applied winged angel heads. Matching PEWS on a collegiate plan returned at the W ends, the SW return a reading desk. The tall PULPIT central on the S side has two resited small C17 carved putti. At the W, a slate-paved congregational area with benches is under a brightly painted GALLERY with stout balusters over a slightly Jacobean frieze. The stair is more Jacobean, perhaps reused, with pendant finial. On the W wall, a wooden C17 cartouche. The chapel's glory is its painted CEILING on boards fixed in four cants, between the arch-braced trusses. The scheme runs from the E wall: Creation (Heaven and Earth; Night and Day), then the three parts of the Trinity in the three main ceiling compartments (God in red, Christ and the Holy Spirit symbolized), and finally angels trumpeting the Last Judgement in the W one. On a blue-grey sky with clouds; gilded winged angel heads frame the main motifs, and below angels gesture appropriately off clouds amid gold stars or Pentecostal fires. The painting is delightfully naïve but recognizably of the European Baroque. Fixed to truss ends, cut-out angels on clouds stiffly hold inscriptions (as at Rhug).

LLANRWST BRIDGE (Y Bont Fawr). Steeply cambered and very graceful. Three segmental arches with full-height cutwaters and parapets; 1636 and the royal arms on plaques. The contract of 1634 names four Lancashire masons, *Barnard Wood* of Sharples, *James Stott* of Benthouse, *Thomas Crompton* of Boulton and *John Mellor* of Rochdale. The traditional connection with *Inigo Jones* is given strength from Sir Richard Wynn's position as Treasurer to the Queen. He would have paid Jones and his master mason Nicholas Stone (from whom Wynn

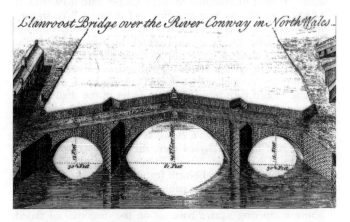

Gwydir, Llanrwst Bridge.
Engraving, 1753

commissioned a plaque for Llanrwst church, 1634). So Palladio's not-dissimilar design for a three-arch bridge of 60 ft (18 metres) main span and 48 ft (15 metres) outer ones may be behind Llanrwst's 60 ft and 40 ft (12 metres).

TU HWNT I'R BONT. Low dormered house on the bridge approach. Early C17, altered in the C18.

7877

GYFFIN

A small village s of Conwy, now its suburb. A battle took place nearby at Cymryd, in 880, when Anarawd, prince of North Wales, defeated Edred, Earl of Mercia.

ST BENEDICT. In a large partly round churchyard. Long nave, s porch, chancel with two transeptal chapels. Breaks in the nave walls indicate that the E part, a double square, is the earlier. The separately roofed chancel had, before restoration in 1866 by *Kennedy & Rogers*, a s doorway with a three-order E.E. doorway. Only the jambs are *in situ* now. The w end of the nave is probably early C16; it has a segmental, chamfered N doorway with its original criss-cross-braced door, and a timber porch with two plain trusses and a wind-brace; the outer arch is a shaped box frame. Datestone for 1694 beneath the C19 bellcote. The nave and chancel have similar late medieval roofs, of slight, close-set collar-trusses. In the chancel, the barrel profile begins at the low wall-plate, which is enriched over the altar as a panelled canopy of honour. The rails are moulded, with bosses, headstops and embattling. The sixteen panels are
38   covered with faded PAINTINGS of saints, full-length, in red, olive and grey, against a foliage background. They are the only comprehensible C15 church paintings in Gwynedd, and though not of high quality, are worth seeing. The E end received enlargements: Elizabethan-roofed s chapel with a PARCLOSE SCREEN which has long muntins and debased Perp tracery, and a C17 N chapel with a three-bay timber arcade. This was partitioned for the vestry and rebuilt by *Kennedy*, who also reused the chancel arch and replaced all the windows. – COMMUNION RAILS. Mid-C17, with sturdy turned balusters. – FONT. C13. A small goblet-shaped bowl; beneath the rim, an arcaded motif with inserted fleurs-de-lys in the shallow relief adopted in North Wales. – COFFIN LIDS. C13 and C14, re-set in the porch. – STAINED GLASS. E, *c.* 1858, showing Christ as the Good Shepherd. By *T. Baillie & Co., c.* 1858.

Opposite the churchyard gate, the former SCHOOL. Built 1903 by *H. L. North*, to ease overcrowding in the Conwy and Hendre schools. Typical North features: roughcast walls (with some slate cladding to the gables), steep roofs with patterned slates, metal windows. A candlesnuffer roof to the flèche, above a tapering square base set on the diagonal, all slated. Further s up Henryd Road, the OLD RECTORY, L-plan and quite large, probably later C19. Gabled open porch to the NW, a later canted bay to the SW. The main, three-bay elevation faces SE, the centre a full-height canted bay with polygonal roof.

TYDDYN-CYNAL, I m. SE. L-plan house, dated 1826. Rubble, with brick voussoirs and hoodmoulds. A longish three-unit range of FARM BUILDINGS, W, containing a sub-medieval house and attached barn. To the r. unit, a slated roof and two chimneys, the l. chimney serving the middle unit, which has two crucks and a small louvre-truss. The chimney was probably inserted into an earlier cruck-framed, thatched house of three bays, later clad in stone, and then extended at both ends and fitted with lofts at the l. end, where the falling ground provided more height. To the N, a small COWSHED, PIGSTIES and an open byre.

CYMRYD, I m. ESE, close to the Conwy. Small hall-house of c. 1500, the W parlour bay later replaced by a two-storey wing at right angles, dated 1696 but possibly much earlier. C18 (?) S wing altered c. 1890 and extended c. 1965. Post-and-panel partition with two Tudor-head doorways at E end of the old house. Projecting N lateral fireplace, its stack rebuilt, with re-set linenfold panelling in the ingle. Central truss (hidden by the later attic floor) of jointed cruck principals, cusped struts and wind-braces. W wing staircase of 1696, steep, with flat shaped balusters and wattle-and-daub partition. L-plan Tudor-style STABLE RANGE, S, dated 1826. Mid-C19 BARN, E, with two rows of ventilation slits on each side.

BENARTH HALL, ¾ m. E. An elegant stucco mansion, probably built for Samuel Price c. 1790, in a raised position overlooking the Conwy estuary. Sir George Beaumont, painter and connoisseur, stayed here regularly between 1799 and 1806. Grand aspirations are evident, but the result falls short. Of three storeys, with canted full-height bays too tightly squeezing the pilastered and open-pedimented centre. Below, a bowed Doric colonnade, with a balustraded terrace, c. 1900. Single-storey pedimented wings. Plain entrance front with a big Diocletian window, above a Doric porch – both c. 1900. Interior modernized. To each side, big circular pavilions with domed lead roofs and glazed lanterns, the music room, l., and the kitchen, r. GARDENS, originally with hothouse, greenhouse, pinery, melon pit and peachery, and a red brick domed ice house. Brick SUMMERHOUSE, c. 1900, with conical slate roof and lead ball finial.

HENRYD

A tiny village, its BRIDGE built 1849 by *Thomas Lloyd*, replacing the old ford across the Gyffin. CHAPEL (Independent), built 1822 and restored 1866. Long S side to the road, central W door facing a small walled graveyard. Large sash windows to s and w, with plain rendered surrounds and bracketed sills. White-painted box pews, stepping down to the *sêt-fawr* at the w end, backing onto the entrance lobby. To the w, HENRYD COTTAGES. Mostly modernized, but No. 2 still has small-pane sash windows and exposed stone walls. To the E, HENRYD FARMHOUSE, early C17, of one storey and attic. Half-dormers to the s and a chimney at each end, larger on the l. The E gable has an upper window (now blocked), noted by Hughes and North as a rarity in North Wales. Inside, a spiral stone stair next to the large fireplace, and an oak post-and-panel partition. Tudor-headed doorways at the head of the staircase and to the later N wing. Further E, YSGOL LLANGELYNIN, a National School built 1844. The hand of *H. L. North* is surely visible in the panels of slate cladding on the gables, and, above the windows, the projecting stone lintels, canted to form a triangular head.

ST CELYNIN, ¾ m. s. 1840, by *Thomas Jones* of Chester, as Llangelynin new church. Rubble, even around the arched and chamfered lancets, and brick w doorway. w tower which becomes octagonal, a crenellated parapet crowning the top. The original design had a tall stone spire, without the parapet. *H. L. North* reordered the interior in 1903, replacing box pews and paired pulpits with benches, and providing a ceremonial raised altar. Little remains of his work, except the roof colours (white timber, blue ceiling) and patterned floor tiling. – STAINED GLASS. Two N windows by *Jones & Willis* (†1893 and †1914).

TABERNACL INDEPENDENT CHAPEL, Hen Dŷ, Llechwedd. ⅔ m. NW. Probably 1860s. Gable to front. A pair of round-headed doorways, and between them, a pair of tall round-headed sash windows with Georgian-style radial glazing at the heads. Attached behind, a large Sunday School room and the chapel house. Tiered pine pews, the outer rows slightly angled, then turned in at right angles at the front.

PLAS CELYNIN, ¼ m. E. An elegant Regency villa, possibly built as the rectory. Stuccoed, three-bay w front, the central bay projecting and gabled, a bay window. Shallow hipped roofs with wide eaves.

PLAS IOLYN, ⅓ m. N. Late Regency. Hipped roofs, with wide bracketed eaves. Stuccoed, rusticated quoins. Three upper windows with shutters. Below, a Late Victorian enclosed veranda, its roof on alternating piers and Tuscan columns. The rear (E) extension wraps around a small service yard, forming a U-plan.

GWENDDAR MILL, ½ m. W. Mid-C18 water mill, with early C19 cross-wing. Of random rubble, with voussoirs to the cambered openings. Some machinery survives, including the water wheel behind (N).

TŶ GOBAITH, Tremorfa Lane, 1 m. SE. A children's hospice, in a superb location overlooking the Conwy, by *ISP Architects*, 2004. A modern vernacular: white roughcast walls, square

metal windows, slated roofs with stone or concrete verge
copings. To give variety, areas of cedar cladding, with shallow
metal roofs. A jaunty red-tiled GAZEBO in the garden.

TYDDYN GRASOD, 1¾ m. W. A multi-cellular group of stone
sheepfolds, typical of the area.

LLANAELHAEARN

3845

The old part of the village on a winding lane between the A 499
and the scenic B4417. The hill-fort of Tre'r Ceiri (*see* below)
looms over it. The drab CAPEL BABELL of 1876 and the BOARD
SCHOOL (*c.* 1873) on one side of the lane, the church on the
other. ST AELHAEARN'S WELL, just within the village on the
B4417 road, is little more than a dark square pool inside a
modern stone shed.

ST AELHAEARN. Small, cruciform and low. The W end of the
nave has a blocked S doorway, *c.* 1200. Tall and pointed, W
doorway, C15 perhaps. Tall bellcote, in dressed stone, above.
On the S transept, the date 1622. In the transept and nave, on
the S, paired elliptical-headed lights of this date. N transept C16.
The chancel was lengthened in 1892, retaining the E window;
three round-headed C14 lancets of equal height, deeply splayed
either side (cf. Llaniestyn). Restoration by *Kennedy* in 1848 and
1892, especially to the roofs. Three arch-braced principals
survive in the nave. – SCREEN. C16. Three bays either side of
the doorway. Uprights with Tudor mouldings set in a continuous horizontal rail carved with crude paterae – bird, flowers.
Renewed trefoil traceries with leaves (cf. Llanbedrog and
Llanengan). – PULPIT. Incorporating C18 fielded panels, two
incised with stars. – PEWS. *c.* 1800. Of box type throughout,
with open turned rails in the fronts, doors and backs (cf. Llanfrothen). – MONUMENTS. A c6 pillar-stone immured in the N
transept, inscribed ALIORTUS ELMETIACO(S) / HIC IACET, or
Aliortus, a man of Elmet (i.e. the C5 British kingdom around
the Leeds area, Yorks), lies here (cf. Penmachno stones). –
Catherine Glyn of Elernion †1702. The elaborate achievement
of arms and the inscription in relief on slate. Outside the W
doorway, a STONE PILLAR with an early medieval cross
incised, C7–C9.

TRE'R CEIRI (Town of the Giants), ¾ m. W (SH 373 446). The
most spectacular and best-known hill-fort in North Wales,
crowning one of the sharp peaks of the Eifl range, with
ramparts surviving over 10 ft (3 metres) high and enclosing
some 150 round stone houses, many with walls still more than
3 ft (1 metre) high. The fort occupies the long narrow summit
which rises to a peak at the E end. Here there is a large round
cairn covering an Early Bronze Age cremation burial which
pre-dated the defences. Excavation has shown occupation
during the Roman period, but the site was probably built much
earlier, perhaps even during the Late Bronze Age, though most

p. 386

9

Llanaelhaearn, Tre'r Ceiri hill-fort.
Engraving, 1878

of the visible structures are likely to belong to the first centuries A.D. and it is difficult to know how many houses would have been occupied at any one time. The main rampart is impressive in scale but simple in concept. It surrounds the top of the hill with a narrow entrance flanked by bastions at the W end, a wider and more convenient one on the N side, and a postern gate at the NE corner overlooking a spring. An outer rampart on the gentler N side, clearly a late addition, blocks off a well-established path to another spring. The steep W entrance also has extra protection, probably more for display than defence. To either side are enigmatic enclosed plots. The rampart at the NE end retains evidence of a walk and the ramps by which access was gained to the top. The houses are closely packed into four or five bands across the width of the fort. They vary in size (10–26 ft, 3–8 metres) and shape: most are circular, but some larger ones have been subdivided and some are D-shaped. Larger rectangular buildings abut the rampart.

CARNGUWCH (SH 375 428). An exceptionally fine hilltop cairn (visible from a distance) 20 ft (6 metres) high and 100 ft (30 metres) across, founded on a boss of natural rock and the added stone revetted with a well-built wall. There has been no excavation and debate continues about whether it is a burial cairn or a motte.

An astonishingly complete record of occupation since late prehistoric times survives on the s-facing slopes of the mountain mass between Llanaelhaearn and the marshy valley of the Dwyfach. At the E end is the HILL-FORT of Pen y Gaer (SH 428 455). A good rampart on the W side preserves evidence of a double wall, perhaps evidence of refacing, perhaps a structural device to prevent collapse. Early records suggest that this double-walling was common at Llŷn hill-forts, but the evidence has not survived so well elsewhere. Below the fort is a very large kidney-shaped MOUND OF BURNT STONE, a boiling place of Bronze Age date. On the lower slopes all the way along towards Llanaelhaearn are ENCLOSED FARM-STEADS within areas of terraced fields. These sites, with three or four round buildings set around a yard and enclosed with a rectilinear or curvilinear wall, are likely to belong to the last few centuries B.C. and may have continued to the middle of the first millennium A.D. The modern farms and more recent ruins echo their distribution on this band of good soil. At CWM CORYN (SH 406 454) the continuity is particularly striking. In the fields around the farm are round huts of likely prehistoric/Roman date, overlain by rectangular buildings which may be medieval. Just beyond the farmyard are the ruins of a stone farm building of 1663, almost certainly an addition to a late medieval timber hall which was replaced by a stone house in 1723. The farmhouse on the other side of the yard appears to be early C20.

LLANARMON

No village as such, but some substantial houses. This compara-tively remote area was a centre of recusancy in the late C16, then in Puritan times. Later still, the Methodists became the object of religious intolerance.

ST GARMON. Double-naved church. Most of the present build-ing is c. 1500, but older fabric at the NW suggests the N aisle predates the S. This was added c. 1500 by means of a four-bay arcade of four-centred arches of two hollow-chamfered orders, on octagonal piers with moulded caps and splayed bases. Windows at E and SE of the S aisle are c. 1500, but the N aisle E window is likely to be late C16. Other windows are Victorian, by *Kennedy*, who also added the porch, renewed the roofs, re-floored and pewed the interior, 1858–62. – SCREEN, N aisle. Early C16, with reed-moulded standards and incorporating stall ends carved with grotesque beasts. – FONT. C15, octago-nal, stone. – MEMORIALS. Slate tablet dated 1763, others late C17 and early to mid-C18. – Also inscribed slate notices in the porch, recording parish charities. – COLLECTING BOX, by the S door. Reputedly placed here in 1166 by command of Henry II; probably C17. In the churchyard, CHEST TOMB to John Vaughan of Glasfryn, 1665, and the former SCHOOL, c. 1800. A single-room building, established for the poor.

PLAS-DU, 1 m. NW. Small but substantial house, early C16, one of the earliest storeyed houses in Gwynedd, with C19 additions and alterations. Very tall square chimneys, projecting stone eaves, monolithic arched lintel to front doorway. Small slit windows in E gable, to mural stairs and upper closet. (Fine oak trusses to roof, with cusped apex braces.) Home of the recusant Thomas Owen, High Sheriff 1569.

PENARTH FAWR. 1 m. s. An important medieval hall-house. Its chief feature is the spere-truss, unique in Caernarvonshire and unusual outside NE Wales (but see Egryn, Talybont (M)). The original late C15 house faces W. The service end to the S and the cross-passage remain, but not the solar at the N end (beyond the present N wall). A louvre-truss indicates an open hearth, but this was replaced c. 1600 by Hugh Gwyn, High Sheriff, with a lateral fireplace on the E wall, with shield of arms. Enlarged c. 1650 to form a grand U-plan, with E wings. The SE wing remains, with an addition of c. 1680; the NE wing was demolished c. 1843. Restored in 1936, when the lateral stack to the SE wing was removed.

BROOM HALL, 1½ m. SSW. Impressive, late C18 stuccoed house in extensive parkland, once the largest estate in Eifionydd. Built by Rowland Jones Jun. and the grandest of three Llŷn houses attributed to *Joseph Bromfield*, the plasterer-turned-architect from Shrewsbury (Nanhoron (q.v.) and Plas Bodegroes (p. 449) are the others). Main three-storey block facing SE, with an attractive veranda on three sides. Originally it had very slim iron columns, but in the late C19 or early C20 they were replaced with more substantial Tuscan ones. At the same time, a segmental pediment on brackets was added to the central first-floor window, and the sash windows had remarkably thin brass glazing bars fitted. Late C19 extensions and alterations at the rear (NW), and further work carried out sympathetically in 2000–3. Axial entrance hall, stair behind and rooms symmetrically disposed each side. Towards the rear, a modern atrium for use as a kitchen, dining area and upper gallery. To the NW, a walled kitchen GARDEN, with laundry, game larder, potting shed, apple store etc. To the E, FARM BUILDINGS including a fine stone towered GATEHOUSE, dated 1850. Four rooms, one above each other, over the archway. The tower steps in as it ascends to a pyramidal slated roof carrying a weathervane. Round-headed main windows and clock faces to SE and NW at third-floor level. Unusual and most attractive.

LLANBEBLIG see CAERNARFON

7669

LLANBEDR-Y-CENNIN

A village in two parts, on the E slope of Pen-y-gaer (q.v). The lower part clusters around the chapel. More memorable is the older, upper village near the church. On the l., the BULL INN. Late C17 or early C18, of two storeys, with sash windows and some original timbers inside. Opposite, CHURCH HOUSE (dated 1754 internally) and CHURCH COTTAGE, with a rare C19 oat kiln in the basement of the C19 E wing. All of rubble, painted white. A lane leads N to the church. Below the E end of the churchyard, a TROUGH and WATER TAP in memory of William

Gaskell Holland and his wife (†1910 and †1918) of Gell-y-vorwyn (q.v.).

ST PETER. Of the usual local type in a near-circular churchyard. Restored 1842 by *Henry Kennedy,* his first recorded church job in North Wales. Short nave and chancel in one, the chancel C15 but the nave earlier. C16 transeptal N chapel. The S porch has a shallow C16 roof and seats; the S doorway, almost round-headed and of the same date as the nave, is unmoulded. W bellcote on medieval corbels (cf. Caerhun) and similarly with a small relief of the Crucifixion. The roof over the nave is a C15 Conwy valley arch-braced rafter one, of shallow profile; that over the transept has arch-braced principals with purlins, very wide rafters and two tiers of wind-braces. Apart from a C17 or C18 timber window in the transept, the windows and the two-bay arcade are *Kennedy*'s; Neo-Norman E window, with round head, roll mouldings, shafts and foliated capitals. Inside, tiered seating W of the doorway, replacing a former gallery above. – COMMUNION RAILS, *c.* 1700, with turned balusters and a detachable funeral collection box. – BOX PEWS, re-set on each side of the altar, of the C18, and in the nave, some numbered pews of the C19. – CREED and COMMANDMENTS BOARD, apparently of 1842. – Handsome TWO-DECKER PULPIT as rarely extant in the county, with the date 1724 on the reading desk. – FONT. Small, C13 tub, much retooled. – Unattractive STAINED GLASS in E window, 1908, by *Henry Gustave Hiller* of Liverpool.

SALEM INDEPENDENT CHAPEL. 1871–2. Gable front. Round-headed windows within triangular-headed recesses, and a central triplet of round-headed windows below a rounded hoodmould.

BRYNIAU, ½ m. N. A sub-medieval storeyed house, with end chimney, typical of Snowdonia. THRESHING BARN, N, with good-quality C16 trusses, perhaps re-set.

GELL-Y-FORWYN, ¼ m. NNE. Stone, early C19, and perhaps originally a pair. Enlarged *c.* 1900 for William Gaskell Holland, Merseyside businessman, in a loose Arts and Crafts manner. E extension, with a slate-roof veranda added to the garden (S) front, and an arcaded loggia (now glazed) at the SE corner, under a pair of canted oriel windows, below twin gables. Inside, much of the upper storey of the original house removed to provide a double-height hall, with a fireplace and an L-plan staircase leading to a balustered gallery. Lots of dark timber-boarded panelling. There must have been an architect. But who?

FFYNNON BEDR, ⅓ m. SSE. An early site associated with the nearby ST PETER'S WELL, of which little remains. The very thick walls of the COTTAGE suggest an early date, but altered in the C18–C19, so no significant features inside. To the SW, a large BARN, late C17 or early C18. To the W, a two-storey STABLE and CARTSHED, early C19, with segmental doorway arches. Traces of early FOUNDATIONS on the site. Herbert North claimed an old dovecote with a centre column existed (cf. Penmon, Anglesey), and a small chapel associated with the well.

PEN-Y-GAER HILL-FORT (SH 750 693) overlooks the valley on a steep spur but access from the W is easy. This multivallate hill-fort has complex defences, including the unusual protective device of *chevaux de frise*, small upright stones set into the ground to trip attackers; house sites cut into the hillside can be easily seen on the S side, and on the N side the defences are overlain by a medieval farmstead. The path from the W comes out below the main entrance, the outer gate of which is protected by an area of *chevaux de frise*. Another patch protects a secondary entrance on the S, where a third, earthen rampart has been added to the two stone and earth ramparts which encircle most of the hill. *Chevaux de frise* are very rare in Britain but relatively common in northern Spain, a product of contacts which existed along the Atlantic seaboard in later prehistory. The date of Pen-y-gaer is unknown because there has been no excavation, but it is likely that occupation behind slighter defences began in the Late Bronze Age and continued until the arrival of the Romans.

LLANBEDROG

3333

The village is divided by the main A499 road to Abersoch. The lower part, attractively sheltered by its rocky headland, is the older. At the bend opposite the church (q.v.), THE COTTAGE, the early home of Elizabeth Caldecot, later Lady Jones-Parry. C17 or early C18, built by the Madryn estate (*see* Llandudwen). Two-storeyed each end, single in the middle, but under the same roof-line. W gable bellcote, tall diagonal brick chimneys. A larger, Regency house of 1806 above the cottages to the rear. Very few windows and no proper façades. Next to the lattice porch, part of a slate coat of arms of the Love Parry family. This, and the open-well stair, brought from Wern Fawr. LÔN NANT IAGO leads down to the beach. Here, colourful beach HUTS, l., and FOXHOLE, r., fishermen's cottages Gothicized in the C19 as part of the Plas Glyn-y-weddw estate.

The upper part of the village is of less interest. The COUNTY SCHOOL of 1908 above the road on the r. and the chapels (*see* below) further along on the l., in LÔN PENBRYN. A few terraces at the W end, but all modernized.

ST PEDROG. Nave and chancel in one, the nave perhaps mid-C13, the chancel early C16. A Perp cusped recess in the E wall outside. Restored 1865 for Lady Jones-Parry, by *Kennedy*. Tower added 1895. – SCREEN. Early C16. Three bays either side of the doorway, with continuous posts. Trefoil traceries with vine leaves growing between each cusp, and spandrel panels. The dado has an openwork frieze of quatrefoils, leaves and panels, between rails studded with fleurons. – FONT. Tudor-style, re-tooled. The sides of the octagonal bowl carved with sunk lancet, criss-cross and quatrefoil designs; the under-surfaces the same but with a fleur-de-lys and Tudor 'window'. – STAINED GLASS. E, Nativity, Crucifixion and Resurrection, *c.* 1853, with architectural canopies and tracery. – Chancel, S and N, Parable and Miracle scenes against a floral background, *c.* 1864. – N window (l.), a war scene. Lovely colour and design, *c.* 1920 – w, a jumble of *c.* 1500 glass, re-set *c.* 1850. Trumpeting angel and other heads. – Two C19 Jones-Parry HATCHMENTS. – MONUMENTS. Anne Parry †1730 with arms and cherub. – Martha Grant Calder †1839, Grecian with a lily spray, by *M. W. Johnson*, London. – Henry Jones-Parry †1849, in a Gothic stone frame with angels and ballflower. By *Brown*, London. – Robert Jones-Parry †1870. Trefoil brass tablet within a coarse cable-moulded marble roundel, by *Chapman* of Frome. – In the external niche below the E window, a slate panel in beautiful raised lettering, to Love Parry †1707. The armorial panel above copied from the original now at The Cottage. – Table tombs in the churchyard, to Margaret Hughes †1661, and Mary and Assurance Parry, sisters †1658.

PENIEL CALVINISTIC METHODIST CHAPEL, Lôn Penbryn. 1866, coursed rubble. Two round-headed windows with intersecting tracery, within a recessed archway, flanked by doorways with similar fanlights.

PLAS GLYN-Y-WEDDW, off Lôn Nant Iago. A large mansion in High Gothic style by *Kennedy*, 1856. Now an arts centre. The 'widow's glen', it was the dower house for Elizabeth (Caldecot), widow of Sir Love Jones-Parry of Madryn Castle (*see* Llandudwen). She never slept here, but it housed the family art collection. In 1896, Solomon Andrews, the Cardiff entrepreneur who built much of late C19 Pwllheli, developed the house as a public gallery, with tearoom and ornamental gardens, and a horse tramway along the beach from Pwllheli. Squarish plan, with three gabled bays to the front (E), each different. At the centre, a leaded lantern lighting a splendid baronial hall. The staircase divides at a half-landing, then continues up to serve a gallery on three sides. Stained glass. Hammerbeam roof. To the S, a big CONSERVATORY. To N and w, service quarters, stables etc.

WERN FAWR, 1½ m. NNW. Largish two-storey house, late C16 or early C17. C19 wing to the rear. Tall stone chimneys each end, the r. stack diagonally set. A fine doorway to the front, with four-centred head and hoodmould, and wavy mouldings. Tall sash windows, the one above the doorway, C20. Small upper windows at far l. and r., probably to closets. Post-and-panel partition in the N room, late C17.

LLANBERIS

C18 copper-mining and C19 slate-quarrying village, popular with tourists after 1896 as the embarkation point for trains to

Snowdon's peak. The original Llanberis (Nant Peris) is about
2 m. SE, beyond Llyn Peris; modern Llanberis lies on the SW side
of Llyn Padarn. Dolbadarn Castle, immortalized by Richard
Wilson and Turner, sits between the two lakes.

2, 21   DOLBADARN CASTLE. One of the C13 strongholds of Llywelyn
the Great, controlling access into Llanberis Pass. As with
Criccieth, the design of the key feature, in this case the round
keep, indicates Llywelyn's links through marriage with
prominent Welsh Marcher families. Three Welsh phases of
development can be seen. The low drystone wall enclosing this
promontory that juts above the two lakes, Llyn Peris and Llyn
Padarn, dates from the beginning of the C13, although butt
joints may suggest a sub-phase. The keep, with its mortared
walls, was added c. 1230. The E curtain also dates from this
time, but after the great tower had been constructed. A fourth,
English, phase, C13 or early C14, is represented by the
E building. Slate is the main building stone.

The foundations representing S and W towers are of the first
period, as was the hall at the promontory end. Later in C13 the
castle was considered strong enough for Llywelyn ap Gruffudd
to confine his brother Owain in the main tower. The castle fell
to the armies of Edward I by summer 1283, and the Crown
accounts reveal that timber was removed in 1284 for the new
works at Caernarfon. Nevertheless, the castle remained occupied as a royal centre, and repairs were undertaken in the early
C14. The rectangular building NE of the keep is clearly later,
and dates from the English occupation. Thereafter nothing is
known of the castle's history. Its artistic claim to fame dates
from the later C18 when it became the subject of some fine
landscape paintings.

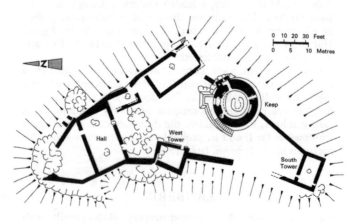

Llanberis, Dolbadarn Castle.
Plan.

The ENTRANCE today must mark the site of the original gateway, flanked by the W and S buildings or towers, as the ground here is less precipitous than elsewhere. They can never have stood particularly high, and both may simply have had a ground-floor chamber and a battlemented wall-walk. The HALL would have dominated the enclosed courtyard, lying across the spur E–W, with opposing doorways signifying a cross-passage at the E end. A latrine lay outside to the NE. In the E curtain a small GATEWAY is evident, next to the footings of a small rectangular structure. A further entrance, reached externally by a short flight of steps, lies further S, against which the late C13 or early C14 building was constructed, utilizing the original curtain for its external wall.

The round KEEP, its lowest courses battered, is approached by external steps of uncertain date, which appear on C18 views; the original access may have been up a timber staircase, and then through a porch. On the NE side a projecting pent-roofed structure houses the latrines. The tower consisted of two storeys over a basement, a rare feature in a castle of the Welsh princes, where most towers had only one main floor. Also unusual is the setting for a portcullis, unique in the round keeps of the English Marcher and other Welsh lords. The doorway, rebuilt in the C20, which leads into the first floor was secured by a drawbar, the socket for which remains. Sockets for the joists, as well as an offset on the N, mark the setting of the first floor, through which access to the basement would have been gained. The only opening in this chamber was a ventilation shaft on the E side, and the function and date of the clay and rubble structure in the middle of the basement floor remain a mystery. On the first floor a doorway leads into the latrine block, a small slit window providing some light, and on the SE side of the chamber is a window with a recessed seat on each side of the embrasure. Adjacent to this is the fireplace, the top of the flue of which is a slit in the external face. The doorway on the NW leads to the spiral stair up to the upper storey, spiralling anti-clockwise, and then on up clockwise to a landing at roof level, and then so on up to the battlements; the stairs are lit by small slit windows.

The upper floor was the main chamber, a well-appointed room with four windows and a fireplace. To one side of the E window a vaulted passage leads down to the latrine block. The only window without seating is that on the N, in which the raised portcullis rested. The roof of the keep, set well below the wall-walk and battlements, is marked by a groove all the way round the inner face, sockets and corbels taking the main and secondary timbers. The crenellations have long since disappeared.

ST PADARN. An impressive cruciform church with crossing p. 65 tower, by *Arthur Baker*, c. 1884; the nave completed, and the Lady Chapel (N aisle) added by Baker's son-in-law, *Harold Hughes*, 1914–15. Snecked rubble with Runcorn dressings.

Battlemented tower with plain corbel table and louvred and shafted paired bell-lights. Three broad stepped lancets to the E and W gables, four stepped lancets with roundels between the heads to the S transept, and, facing the town in the N transept, a row of seven stepped lancets below a semicircular arch. A spacious and well-proportioned interior, with panelled wagon roof. Pink sandstone contrasting to good effect with grey slate in horizontal bands. Slate relieving arches, which dive down from the crossing and land uncomfortably on the lower transept arches, having made a brief external sortie on the way. – FONT. Late medieval, dark granite octagonal bowl on lighter-coloured pedestal, from the old church at Nant Peris.

CAPEL COCH CALVINISTIC METHODIST CHAPEL. Large and impressive, Italianate, 1893 by *Rowland Lloyd Jones*. Snecked rubble, with lighter stone for the dressings and rock-faced quoins. Tall pedimented central bay divided into three between the broad angle piers. Two-storey triple arrangement, arched windows between Doric columns over arched doors between Doric pilasters. Wings set back, with tall paired windows at two levels. Fine interior. The sumptuously plastered ceiling is the showpiece, with pendant ventilators and light fittings integrated in the richly decorated panels and ribs. Gallery on three sides, on fluted cast-iron columns. Intricate *sêt-fawr* with Jacobean detailing.

SUNDAY SCHOOL, 1909, behind, with half-timbered gables, like his County Schools. The slightly bowed entrance bay is a playful touch.

SNOWDON MOUNTAIN RAILWAY. The idea had been resisted by the landowner, Thomas Assheton-Smith, but the threat of possible competition changed his mind. Founded as the Snowdon Mountain Tramroad and Hotels Co. in 1894 and opened in 1896. Swiss rack-and-pinion system, engineered by *Sir Douglas Fox*. At Llanberis Station, the ENGINE SHED, long and rectangular, of green-painted weatherboarding and a slate roof. Aisled construction of I-section cast-iron columns supporting king- and queenpost trusses. A Swiss feel to this and the other station buildings. The steeply sloping LOWER VIADUCT takes the 800 mm.-gauge track across Church Road, launching it on the 4 m. journey to the summit over thirteen skewed round-headed arches which rapidly increase in height. Further up, the WATERFALL VIADUCT above the Afon Hwch falls, of four tall skewed arches. Three passing loops at Hebron, Halfway and Clogwyn, with stations originally designed as mountain chalets. The Summit Station is at 3,526 ft (1,085 metres).

There was a hotel here, 'Roberts Hotel', in the mid C19, before the railway was built. A new Modernist concrete structure was proposed by *Clough Williams-Ellis* in 1934; but within six months the big windows of the partially built scheme had been blown in and the building became progressively more like a bunker. Demolished in 2007 and replaced with a new,

Llanberis, Snowdon Summit Station.
Design drawing by Clough Williams-Ellis, 1934

aerodynamic building HAFOD ERYRI, by *Ray Hole Architects*. 120
Steel structure, curved walls and roof clad in granite to lessen
the impact, and angled glazing to reduce reflections and to
guide views through to the peak behind, its white fabric ceiling
like billowing clouds.

PERAMBULATION. The castle provides a good starting point,
with views of the lakes, the new and old villages to NW and
SE, the Dinorwig Power Station (*see* Dinorwic) at the head of
Llyn Peris, and, towering above, the formidable slate quarries.
The main road leads W, past JERUSALEM CHAPEL, 1881,
simple classical, and an early C19 single-storey quarrymen's
TERRACE. On the bend down to the village, the large ROYAL
VICTORIA HOTEL, built for the early C19 tourist trade. Of
stucco, in the style of Haycock. The least spoilt elevation faces
SW: three storeys and 1–3–1 bays, the outer ones projecting
slightly and the hipped roof continuing over the central bay as
a deep overhang. Loggia with paired Doric columns. The
station for the Snowdon railway is on the l. The main road
by-passes the village, continuing NW along the old railway
line next to the lake, and the HIGH STREET forks l. Here,
MAES PADARN, an estate of Swedish prefabs built by the District Council in 1947. Opposite, the SURGERY, with a yellow
cupola lighting the circular waiting room and a round bay
window facing Snowdon. 1994, by *Adam & Frances Voelcker*.
On the l., DOLAFON, a large boarding house probably built
1880s, stone with red tile cladding to the gables, a rarity in
these parts. The former STATION can be seen down Station
Road, r. Just past Church Road, l., a good view of St Padarn
(*see* p. 393). CAPEL COCH ROAD leads l. to the Capel
Coch Chapel (*see* above), the large but undistinguished
SCHOOL and, on the corner of Fron Goch, BRYN EIRIN, a
pretty hipped stone villa, *c.* 1860, but looking earlier.

Along the High Street, more boarding houses on the l.: DOLPERIS, and beyond the mutilated SPAR building, ERW FAIR and MOUNT PLEASANT, substantial, of rubble, with steep gables and bay windows, very much in the late C19 guesthouse style (cf. Betws-y-coed). The High Street becomes colourful at this point, with buildings taking on rainbow hues in contrast to the predominantly purple of the slate quarries. MEIFOD and GARTH MAELOG a stuccoed pair with gabled wings and a porch roof between.

WELSH SLATE MUSEUM. *See* Dinorwic.

5566   LLANDDEINIOLEN

ST DEINIOL. 1843, an early work by *Weightman & Hadfield* of Sheffield. One of the first Ecclesiologically correct churches in the diocese, but dull. Nave, very short chancel, transepts, N vestry, N porch, W bellcote. Dreary interior. – FONT. Octagonal, inscribed IHC 1665 WS:WP. – STAINED GLASS. E, very dark, probably by *Charles Clutterbuck*. – Nave, S. Two windows, the r. by *C. C. Powell*. – MONUMENTS. Elizabeth and Jane (†1688), daughter and wife of Robert Wynne, Rector of Llanddeiniolen. Square brass plaque with a border of naively drawn skulls and skeletons. – Above, a slate plaque to the Rector †1720, with hourglass, skull etc. – William Thomas of Coed Helen †1763 – Capt. John Browning Edwards of Nanhoron †1813. White and mottled green marble, dated 1817, with an urn on top. Similar, with a plain pediment. – CHURCHYARD. A group of yews, some reputedly over 2,000 years old.

DINAS DINORWIG (SH 550 653). A hill-fort which was radically remodelled, from a simple stone-walled enclosure to a multi-vallate fort with massive banks and ditches. The remains of the early stone wall 11 ft (3.3 metres) thick (overlain by a thinner modern wall) can be seen just inside the later inner bank. It had a simple entrance on the E, ignored by the later bank builders, and another on the W which was maintained when the site was remodelled. The work added two massive banks and ditches with a final counterscarp bank, producing a glacis defence with a height from ditch to rampart-top of 29 ft (9 metres) and an overall width of 195 ft (60 metres). This style of rampart, best seen at Maiden Castle, Dorset, is very rare in North Wales. An impressive entranceway comes through the new defences at an angle towards the narrow gate through the original stone wall. An annexe on the N, now occupied by the farm, was probably added when the fort was remodelled. On the surface of the outer rampart S of the entrance is a large boulder later used as a 'rock cannon', drilled with linked holes for powder and fuse and used for celebratory salvoes in the C19.

LLANDEGAI/LLANDYGAI   *6072*

The estate village for Penrhyn Castle.

ST TEGAI. Approached from the w along an avenue lined with railings and yews. Cruciform. Chancel and transepts added in the c16 to the perhaps late c14 nave. Little survives from the earlier date: parts of the N and S walls w of the crossing, perhaps, and the bases of the chancel arch responds. Chancel and transept windows of three pointed lights (the E window of five) below four-centred heads, with casement-moulded jambs. According to H. L. North, the church was colour-washed in 1780, to match the yellow tiles of Penrhyn Castle. In 1853 *Kennedy* enlarged the church in late Perp style with a distinct estate character. He lengthened and refenestrated the nave, built the dominant crossing tower, rebuilt the embattled parapets and added the w porch and N vestry. A fine interior. Shallow tie-beam trusses filled with multi-foiled openwork, on four-centred arch braces. w gallery, with a busily arcaded timber balustrade on a three-bay arcade. – Elaborate alabaster REREDOS, partly obscuring the window. Late C19. – PULPIT, of slate, with free Perp detail. Late C19. – PEWS, with traceried ends. – ORGAN CASE, in the gallery. Neo-Norman, made for the chapel in Penrhyn Castle so perhaps by *Hopper*. – STAINED GLASS. E, Last Judgment, 1887. – Nave, s, S S Tegai, David and Deiniol, by *Kempe*, 1890.

An outstanding collection of MONUMENTS. Below the gallery, Late Gothic alabaster TABLE TOMB perhaps of Sir William Griffith (†c. 1506) and his wife. Life-size figures, he in armour with a lion at his feet, she very slender, in a long gown. Shallowly modelled angels under crocketed and pinnacled canopies on the tomb-chest. – John Williams, Archbishop of York and owner of the Penrhyn estate †1650. His half-life-size effigy kneels at a prie-dieu, in an aedicule of black marble and alabaster with an open segmental pediment on Corinthian columns. His achievement of arms with a mitre above, his regalia in the spandrels but his helm and spurs now missing. – George Hay Dawkins-Pennant †1840. Dark slate, Neo-Romanesque, perhaps by *Hopper*. – Juliana Douglas Pennant †1842 in Pisa. White marble, with a pediment. – Large Neoclassical monument to Richard Pennant, 1st Lord Penrhyn of Penrhyn, and his wife (†1808 and 1816) by *Sir Richard Westmacott*, 1820. Life-size figures of idealized peasants. On the plinth, four pastoral scenes in high relief of cherubs playing pan pipes to goats; chiselling slate; learning to read; dancing and harvesting. The inscription records that 'he opened the first carriage road through the valley of Nant Ffrancon, formed the quay of Port Penrhyn, enriched and adorned the demesne and the country around it with buildings, agriculture and plantations'. – In the churchyard, SE of the chancel, a fine pyramidal slate TOMB to Benjamin Wyatt †1818, agent to the Penrhyn estate; and to other members of this huge family. –

(SW of the church was the big octagonal Neo-Norman MAUSOLEUM of the Lords Penrhyn, c. 1840, demolished c. 1940.)

The walled VILLAGE was laid out in the mid C19 by the 1st Baron Penrhyn. Lanes radiate from the church gateway, low walls and hedges half-screening Picturesque Tudor-style cottages with steep gables and diagonal brick chimneys. The architect was probably *James Wyatt* (1795–1882), son of Benjamin Wyatt, both in turn agents to the estate. Immediately N of the church, TALGAI HALL, the former school, built 1813 by Baroness Penrhyn for the village girls and their teacher. Hipped reverse (i.e. mullioned-and-transomed) Tudor windows. The present SCHOOL, formerly for the boys and their teacher, is SW of the churchyard. Built 1843 in Anglesey limestone. Deep mullioned windows, Tudor hoodmoulds; the schoolroom windows in two tiers. W of the church gateway, THE ANCHORAGE, built for the head forester probably by *George Benmore* in his usual style, seen in Llanfairfechan and Abergwyngregyn: a large gabled bay projecting r., a porch nestling in the angle and a gabled dormer, l. Below the village, along the turnpike to the E, a Neo-Norman HORSE TROUGH and FOUNTAIN, set into the estate wall, dated 1834. Opposite, a lane leads S to Nos. 1–8 TRE FELIN, four long semi-detached cottages arranged in a gentle curve, and the MANAGER'S HOUSE, for the workers of the former sawmill. The cottages have raised brick window surrounds and hipped porches facing the gardens. To the S, fourteen-arch RAILWAY VIADUCT, of rock-faced red sandstone, built by *Robert Stephenson* and his assistant *Francis Forster* c. 1848 on the Chester to Holyhead line.

The village expanded with more estate houses, S along Telford's road to Capel Curig. BODEILIAN and LYRIC COTTAGE at the road junction, a pair of side-entry cottages with slate cladding above snecked stone. Further S, HAULFRE, c. 1870, probably by *Benmore*, the porch two-storeyed here. Next, TAN-Y-GRAIG, with a catslide dormer next to a gabled one, c. 1860. More slate cladding at Nos. 1–3 TAN-Y-BRYN, similar to Bodeilian, but a third unit inserted between the two gabled ones. PEN LAN, ¼ m. S, a simple three-bay house, probably early C19. A dummy window above the hipped porch.

PENRHYN CASTLE

Very extensive fantasy castle by *Thomas Hopper*, largely built from the early 1820s to 1837 for George Hay Dawkins-Pennant. Keep,

p. 400
corps de logis, entrance yard, kitchen and outer yards, stable yards,

79 all composing a country house in a single mass of building and, as we shall see, one largely unified by architectural style. Before that is considered, however, Penrhyn's historic context and sequence of construction need explaining.

The promontory site at the E mouth of the Menai Strait just E of Bangor, between the Cegin and Ogwen rivers, was granted in the mid C13 by Llywelyn the Great to Goronwy, son of his powerful steward Ednyfed Fychan. It remained the seat of his heirs the Gruffydd family till the early C17, the estate becoming united with that of their cousins the Tudor family of Penmynydd, Anglesey. An early C15 HALL-HOUSE with its two end wings was built for Gwilym ap Gruffydd between 1410 and his death in 1431, according to a note written by his son. Moses Griffith drew this in the late C18 as a ground-floor great hall with two early Perp traceried windows on the long wall facing W, a pointed doorway at the screens end (N) and a turret to its l. This was largely rebuilt by *Samuel Wyatt* from 1782 for the heir, the entrepreneur Richard Pennant, who developed the slate industry at Bethesda and the related Port Penrhyn (qq.v.). Another Griffith drawing shows how thoroughly Wyatt did away with its medieval character in replanning the hall as the entrance vestibule of a Late Georgian castellated mansion, with a central doorway between symmetrical Gothic windows, and irregular crenellated wings added at either end.

With Penrhyn, the Cochwillan estate at Talybont also descended to Pennant, who had a second fortune from sugar estates in Jamaica. Both passed to a nephew, George Hay Dawkins-Pennant (1764–1840), who thus had more than enough means to build. As complicated as any of the vastest High Victorian mansions, the house was complete enough for its patron to move in before his death; and after further alterations it had reached its present state by the time of W. G. Haslam's survey of 1871. Next the estate passed to the Douglas-Pennant family; and finally, 40,000 acres of mountain estate and the castle itself passed to the National Trust via the Land Fund in 1951.

Penrhyn is one of the most enormous houses in Britain, and one of the most unusual since it is so wholeheartedly Romanesque. That this is also a serious work of architecture is easily overlooked. The dauntingly fine masonry rises sheer out of the woods. The sombre walls meet the natural slopes like a medieval castle's, without intermediary structures or gardens, all other elements being contained within or sited at a distance. The castle's irregularity and size mean that the whole is never seen together, an effect which disguises some disunity of date and style. While the bulk of the work took some fifteen years from *c.* 1820, substantial dismantling and rearranging, using both existing stonework and new, continued in the 1840s–50s and after. Even within the main phase, the re-cladding of the Wyatt stableyard at the N with mock C14 towers, as though it were defences for an outer bailey, followed the primary Neo-Romanesque domestic core. Wyatt's version of the house proper vanished, apart from influencing the S part of the *corps de logis* plan. The resulting sky-lines were surely designed to outpace other modern castle-making especially Rickman's castellated scenery at Gwrych in Den-bighshire, completed 1816. The heroic mood suggests that Hopper and Dawkins-Pennant drew inspiration partly from ancient Mediterranean ruins (the latter's uncle James Dawkins led the expedition which rediscovered Balbec and Palmyra) as well as from the vocabulary of C11 and C12 castles or churches.

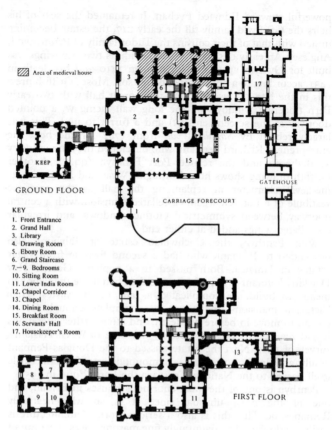

Llandegai, Penrhyn Castle.
Ground- and first-floor plans

KEY
1. Front Entrance
2. Grand Hall
3. Library
4. Drawing Room
5. Ebony Room
6. Grand Staircase
7.–9. Bedrooms
10. Sitting Room
11. Lower India Room
12. Chapel Corridor
13. Chapel
14. Dining Room
15. Breakfast Room
16. Servants' Hall
17. Housekeeper's Room

The House

79   The PLAN of Penrhyn Castle was largely ready by 1820. It bears no
relation to medieval precedent. The notably few best rooms – as
distinct from circulation spaces – are gathered on the W, round
the core of the C15 house as enlarged for Richard Pennant in the
C18, with a new great hall as the fulcrum. The house is entered
from the opposite side, E, and visually much of its great extent
is formed by the outer walls of three service courts to the N.
There is evidence that the unimaginable gaunt spaces of the
carcase were completed some time before being fitted and decorated in the mid 1830s. These internal finishes seem to have
been sourced from further afield, including from London.

  Hopper's greatest successes were the silhouettes his castle
creates, combined with the masonry with which these effects
are achieved. The contractor and masons were employed

directly. The names of a few are known: *Griff Jones, D. McFar-lane, William Prichard, Nathan Ryan, Hugh Williams*. The design and geometrical simplicity of the carved stones, following observable medieval practice translated to suit the quality of the grey Penmon and Moelfre limestone from Anglesey, underlie Penrhyn's extraordinary three-dimensional quality. The sense of mass is negated by the paper-like surfaces, tempering the great size with a sense that this is a model of a castle (as reason says it is).

Seen from outside, the hall has far less impact than the KEEP, built in 1827–30 as family accommodation. This is detached from the *corps de logis* except for a two-storey link with, inside, a broad corridor stepping up towards it. The impact of the full-height clasping buttresses and the sheer-surfaced stonework deeply perforated by round-headed windows is hard to parallel in English architecture at this date. Part of the inspiration could be the taste for huge fortified houses in Scotland.

The keep on its eminence is seen from the drive below, which passes it by so that the whole length of the E side is revealed on the main approach. The drive then climbs and turns back through the GATEHOUSE or barbican into the FORECOURT of 1828. The carriage-turning space by the door, cantilevered by machicolations over the sloping ground to the E, is a mid-Victorian enlargement. This side, including the flank of the stables and the tall square blocks of the house as it rises towards the front door, is better resolved than the W flank, where some incoherence has resulted from significant changes of plan. The small wind porch at the S end is the least of many modifications, typically less sure-handed than the original work. Further N was another addition to the original plan, apparently taken down unfinished before 1836, but potentially as dramatic as the keep: a broad square fortress-like block with round towers at three corners. At the fourth it was to have joined the main house beside the Ebony Room; and here was the central doorway to a reception room intended to be almost as big as the hall, with five big windows on the S. One tower was reused as the ice tower at the NW angle of the outer court. The result is a muddle, more satisfying seen from inside the court. It also reduces the sense of a defensible castle which is sustained round the rest of the exterior.

At the N end of the castle fortifications are again on a magnificent scale. The machicolated gateway to the service yards faces away from the W lawn and groups with the outside of the STABLE COURTYARD and its two entrances, built 1831–3. As left by *Samuel Wyatt* this was already a very large block, with stables for over forty horses and, to its E, a covered ride 136 ft (42 metres) long. Hopper treats it on three sides as a cross between an outer bailey and a town wall, with stones cut in massive broaches, and abstractions of castle design elsewhere (e.g. Warwick Castle); the internal yard elevations were also refaced.

INTERIORS. Hopper's irregular, low-vaulted ENTRANCE
GALLERY was being built in 1830. It closes the external
approach, and forms a preface to the far higher vaults of the
GRAND HALL. This dramatic substitute for the late medieval
prototype seems regular at first glance, but axial corridors pass
through it on two levels by means of arcaded galleries: on the
E side the long spine from the keep, S, to the N parts, including the upstairs chapel linking at right angles with the entrance
passage; on the N side linking with the parallel E–W gallery
connecting to the main stairs. The hall is a strikingly inventive
piece of architecture, having a certain antique quality as
though discovered half-buried in desert sands and camped in
by nomads. Complex piers support two bays of cross-vaulting,
with, on either side of the central intersection bosses, window
perforations perversely filled with stained glass. These and the
big 'early' coloured-glass N windows are by *Thomas Willement*.
All the stonework is buff – including the two huge enriched
luminaires in a composition material – and the floor is flagged
with huge York stone slabs (since stained dark green to imitate
slate). Ascending flights on the S axis lead to the keep, where
bedrooms are partitioned among huge arching vault ribs,
evoking the idea of an ancient structure put to modern use.

The main receiving rooms, structurally almost complete by
1828, are unexpectedly hidden W of the hall. A perversely nar-
rowed and asymmetrical doorway opens into the LIBRARY, an
early instance of the *beau idéal* for the masculine rooms of mil-
lionaires ever since: subdivided by internal piers but low, and
lined with oak panelling fitted round the architectural bookcases. Their gilt brass grilles were made in 1834. All is restlessly
plastic, even the polished Anglesey limestone fireplaces carved
by *Thomas Crisp* with mummers taken from a Flemish manu-
script (published in Joseph Strutt's *Sports and Pastimes of the
People of England*, 1810). The ceiling plaster design is a recurring
feature, derived perhaps by scaling up the running ornament on
church screens, so that interlacing bands wriggle in a not undisciplined way across the fields between ribs like those of a flat
vault. In the S wall, stained-glass shields by *David Evans* explain
the family's descent; in the corner turret or BOUDOIR three
more images in *Evans*'s stained glass of Hywel Dda, his daughter pregnant by her husband Tudor Trefor and their descendant
Richard Pennant, Abbot of Basingwerk in Flintshire.

Every room having a different character, the DRAWING
ROOM – once the great hall of the C15 manor house – is given
the dignity of vaulting, like the hall but not as colossal. Again
the architectural framework, clustered piers, is of oak, and the
arches are depressed. Some steps from the spiral stair inside
the stair-turret of the C15 hall survive behind panelling in the
NW corner. Chimneypiece of Mona marble. The rest of the
former footprint is now occupied by the N half of the library,
and by the EBONY ROOM next door. This closet-like space has
jet-black architecture made of Jamaican ebony; and polished
black limestone. E of the GRAND HALL is the vast rectangular

p. 48

80

DINING ROOM, lit by a quintuple C12-style window and with medievalizing stencilling on its walls, but still a Late Georgian room. Beyond that the smaller BREAKFAST ROOM, like the Dining Room with a fictive under-ceiling of canted beams, seemingly carved but actually in fire-resisting iron and plaster, like those in Wyatville's work at Windsor Castle.

Connecting the main levels is the *tour de force* of the building, the GRAND STAIRCASE. Square-well stair of exceptionally finely carved grey stonework. Its plan is Renaissance, not medieval, with a flight to each side, and the space is lit only from the top. Its architectural character is Oriental, and above all Indian, with stilted arches, intricate fretted surfaces and running drop ornament below each flight. Upper parts and vault in pale plasterwork, the intersecting star-plan vault suggesting a memory of Piedmontese architecture. Like the Grand Hall, the Grand Staircase is at the same time antiquarian and anarchic, and seems intended to play on the emotions produced by fantasy and antiquity as novels and poems were doing in words. As built at Penrhyn they are, in practical terms, beyond normal description, but the prolific grotesque heads in plaster speak for themselves, just as they do on genuine medieval buildings. Upstairs, the CHAPEL, dedicated to St Anne and complete by 1830. One of the largest rooms in the house, including the deep family gallery by which it is entered, and in the simplicity of its architectural decoration and broad barrel vault one of Hopper's best designs.

At 440 ft (135 metres) long Penrhyn exceeds even the palace-castle of a medieval king at Caernarfon along the coast, a building it asks to be compared with. Seen at the time simply as Picturesque scenery, the style of the castle can also be interpreted as representing, however pretentiously or even mischievously, the Pennant family's descent from the founder princes of Welsh nationhood. However, the published sources for Norman architecture, such as the antiquary John Carter's *Ancient Architecture of England* (1795–1814), hardly touch on domestic design and so fall far short as source material for the decoration of the stairs, ceilings and furniture, which one can only approach with stupefied admiration. But like Hopper's contemporary Gosford Castle in Ireland, Penrhyn did not spring from nothing. Among the possible sources is the English love of the 'castle air' in building, which had inspired Vanbrugh and Adam in the C18. Enlightenment thinking and distant travel also encouraged an interest in the primitive, as in Soane's speculative lectures and elsewhere. Hopper, with his office in London and a track record in eclecticism, was well placed to elaborate these concepts in his finest surviving work. Perhaps the castle's nearest peer is Wyatville's enlargement of Windsor Castle, begun in 1824 for George IV, with which Penrhyn's client may have been familiar; certainly, Continental travellers along the Holyhead road marvelled at the British and their political economy, which enabled a commoner to erect a palace fit for a king.

Park and Grounds

On the level ground to the W of the castle were the pre-Wyatt service yards, the stables being moved to their present position N of the mansion by Wyatt in 1791 (the date on the clock; for these, *see* above). The CHAPEL, in a range facing the house as with the Tudor chapel at Vaynol, was also removed for Pennant and re-erected as a Picturesque landscape fragment beyond the lawn on the W. Fine pale ashlared Anglesey gritstone like the local churches, with Perp window traceries, supported on Wyatt's red brick and of course roofless. Further W again the fashionably designed WALLED GARDEN, in brick with curved upper corners, with early C20 improvements.

The C19 project seems to have begun by *c.* 1819 with the park wall and the Port Lodge at Port Penrhyn (cf. p. 255), where the approach bridge is dated 1820, i.e. before the remodelling of the house. The WALL was the first major early C19 wall to enclose a Gwynedd demesne; it is 8 ft (2.5 metres) high, built in 2-ft (60-cm.) courses of limestone rubble with a coping of broken Bethesda slate. PORT LODGE is a stylistically indecisive, medievalizing composition. Taken with a contemporary sketch for rebuilding the house as an expanded C12 keep, this suggests that another unidentified architect was tried shortly before *Hopper*, whose GRAND LODGE, built directly on the new A5 road, is already in the uncompromising manner adopted for the new house. Telford's Holyhead Road also gave the opportunity to enlarge Penrhyn's park westward, which made redundant the approach of the 1790s created for Richard Pennant.[*] His extraordinary stone PIER survives, damaged beyond repair. It was built out from the shallow N shore to permit boating, and provided with a seven-bay, temple-fronted banqueting house on the T-plan widening at the sea end.

HOME FARM, ½ m. SW of the castle. Model farm of mid-C19 limestone buildings. It is impossible to recognize in them the *Benjamin Wyatt* model farm described *c.* 1800. Two main yards, on a smaller scale than the nearby estate farms. On the road through, cartsheds and stables on the l., a Victorian cottage and dairy with veranda, r. On the l. of the side access, two fire-engine houses and a big arch tapering up to a bellcote; on the r., a barn and a threshing-engine house. This barn divides the yard. Walls of coursed, then squared, rubble.

7883

LLANDUDNO

Llandudno is a place of superlatives. Not just Wales's pre-eminent Victorian seaside resort, nor just its pre-eminent planned town, it is a C19 watering-place of European ambition, and results from

[*] A Neoclassical arch over this drive, probably by *Samuel Wyatt* and perhaps sited near Llandegai church, was removed.

a single idea being pursued by its owners and authorities for three generations.

The bay between the limestone headlands of the Great Orme and Little Orme has natural splendours comparable with Mediterranean resorts like Menton or Palermo, and enjoys a sunny microclimate despite facing N. Thomas Pennant noted 'the beautiful half-moon bay of Llandudno' in the 1770s, now known as the North Shore (to distinguish it from the w-facing West Shore). Stucco terraces follow this curve behind an esplanade made to conform unostentatiously with the lie of the land – a curve which is repeated in the principal street set one block back. Its chief drawback has been the great width of the bay (over two miles), which means that the project remains incomplete. What was achieved in the C19, however, is strikingly homogeneous architecturally, and the addition in the 1890s of iron arcading on wide pavements to the shops around Mostyn Street adds another unifying element. Later additions lost the initial élan; the suburban housing of Craig-y-don and elsewhere is not greatly different from elsewhere along the coast, and the development of the second seafront, the West Shore (never part of the Mostyn estate) has been notably uninspired.

The plain largely belonged, as it still does, to the Mostyn family of Gloddaeth, just inland. It is not clear whether the idea for a town on the dunes was theirs or was stimulated by wider opinion, particularly by a Liverpool surveyor, *Owen Williams*, who saw the possibilities in 1846 on landing from one of the new coastal steamers. The evolution of the town deserves tracing. The earlier settlement was a village for copper-miners sheltered on the SE slope of the Great Orme and named after the ancient church of St Tudno up on the N cliffs. The mine lessees built a new church, closer to the miners' settlement, in 1841. Villas began to appear on the slopes around it by the late 1840s, the road significantly named Church Walks and by 1854 the first baths were built under the E cliffs. The vehicle of development was a private Enclosure Act obtained by the Hon. E. M. Lloyd Mostyn in 1848, making 955 acres available adjoining his own estate. He and his agent, John Williams, took up the idea of a planned town with a Promenade and grid of wide streets, launched in 1849 with offers of leasehold plots without architectural specification. An Improvement Act in 1854 set up a Board of Town Commissioners, which Mostyn chaired until 1861. A link to the main railway came in 1858, the year that the first pier was built, destroyed the next year in a storm. Its replacement was only completed in 1878, so till then passengers from Liverpool were disembarked onto small boats.

The 'Building Regulations for the Projected New Town' were probably drawn up by the architects *Wehnert & Ashdown* who exhibited a view of the new town in 1855 at the Royal Academy, published as an engraving in 1857. This shows the town basically as subsequently developed, with villas on the hill slope, terraces lining the North Shore broken by cross-axes, and a funnel-shaped main opening from the town centre (with a sunken railway that was never built). No house was to be built higher than the width of the street, nor within 15 ft (4.5 metres) of the street line, and there were to be no court houses. There was to be uniformity of frontage and elevation. Identified buildings by *Wehnert & Ashdown* are oddly few: a bath house on the rocky side of the Great Orme, a demolished market hall, and very probably St George's Crescent on the seafront (shown in the engraving). They may have designed some other early terraces and villas but no evidence survives.

The Italianate is elaborated from the more Regency stucco of Brighton, Cheltenham and Leamington, only the first row, St George's Crescent, showing giant pilasters. The other terraces tend in a mid-Victorian way to ornate window surrounds and stylistically mixed motifs.

Plans for the drainage were made in 1857 by *T. M. Smith*, a London engineer, and in the same year *George Felton* was appointed architect and surveyor to the estate, suggesting that *Wehnert & Ashdown* had left.* Felton, according to Williams' *Complete Guide to Llandudno* (1865), was 'in sole charge of the Architectural Department of the estate', and his 'judicious and refined taste' may have underlain the realization of the core stucco-faced buildings. His street plans were issued in 1859, but apart from Holy Trinity church of 1865 and St George's Hotel, little again is identified, and indeed the name of the distinguished Birmingham architect *J. A. Chatwin* has been suggested for Gloddaeth Crescent. The role of Town Surveyor is more clearly identified; *T. T. Marks* (1876–91) and

Llandudno, Gloddaeth Crescent.
Engraving, C19

*In 1857 they were exhibiting plans for another new town at Milford Haven.

E. P. Stephenson (1891–1910) planned major works, such as the water supply and sea defences.

The town supported various architects, *Abraham Foulkes* and *B. Nelson* in the 1870s–80s, and *Edwin Turner* from the 1880s. Foulkes acted for the estate from 1876 to 1889, succeeded by his nephew, *George Alfred Humphreys*, who remained in post until he died in 1948. Humphreys took the town stylistically from seaside stucco to the richer colours of brick and terracotta. It seems likely that the prevalent brick and half-timbered villas are largely his, as are the larger blocks with shaped Jacobean gables. He even went on to design the Happy Valley colonnades in Thirties Concrete Classical.

The 'Design for laying out a further portion of the Estate . . . for building purposes', to the S and E, was drawn up in 1894 by *H. & P. Currey* of London.* The fifty-year-old concept of seafront terraces broken by cross-axes was kept, with lesser ones on the road behind and then detached suburban houses. Gloddaeth Street was to be extended at its original width to the West Shore, a SE axis was to be formed along the Conway Road, and four more streets roughly parallel to Gloddaeth Avenue were designated for lesser terraces and detached houses. Only the N section, Lloyd Street and the Recreation Ground, was soon realized. This project is recognizable in the streets off Lloyd Street by the informal character of the housing, much of it probably designed by *Humphreys*. It enlarged the area of the town about four times – yet the first stage of development remains the prevailing image of Llandudno.

By the Edwardian era Llandudno had reached a peak, complete with theatres and concert halls, and shortly picture palaces. Its winter population has increased since to over twenty thousand but its summer population was already three times that. Electric light came in 1898 and a tramway system opened all the way from the West Shore to Colwyn Bay in 1907, since dismantled. Edwardian suburban houses spread S, from the West Shore in an arc to Craig-y-don in the E, and the hope was to expand further eastwards, by the Mostyn Estate acquiring the smaller Bodafon and Craigside estates between the Nant-y-gamar Road and the Little Orme.† While inter-war houses infill and expand the Edwardian area, little of note was added to the town centre after 1914 apart from the war memorial, the National Provincial Bank and the Palladium Theatre.

Llandudno stands as a model of Victorian and Edwardian eclecticism and its main task is now to preserve itself. Post-war buildings look too light and shallow and too suggestive of pastiche, whether blocks of flats in the E of the town or the newly completed Parc Llandudno shopping zone in the centre.

*Henry Currey had laid out the Duke of Devonshire's estate at Eastbourne.
†The former, known as Bodafon Fields, is still unbuilt on; the latter was developed separately as Craigside.

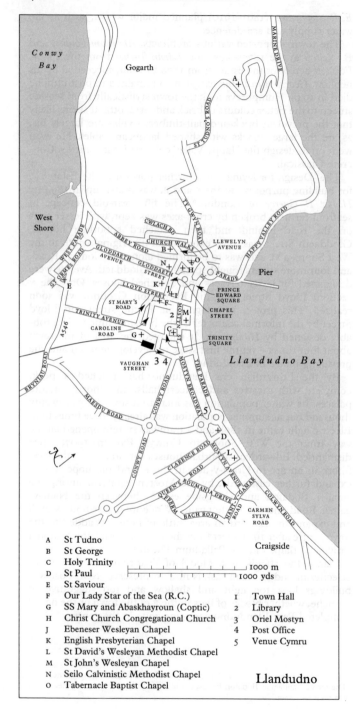

Conwy Bay

Gogarth

MARINE DRIVE

A

ST TUDNO'S ROAD

West
Shore

TY GWYN ROAD

HAPPY VALLEY ROAD

CWLACH RD.

ABBEY ROAD

CHURCH WALKS

LLEWELYN
AVENUE

WEST PARADE

GT. ORME'S ROAD

GLODDAETH AVENUE

GLODDAETH STREET

B

N

O

H

PARADE

Pier

K

LLOYD STREET

ST MARY'S
ROAD

MOSTYN ST.

1

PRINCE
EDWARD
SQUARE

TRINITY AVENUE

F

CAROLINE
ROAD

2

M

CHAPEL
STREET

A546

G

C

TRINITY
SQUARE

BRYNIAU ROAD

VAUGHAN
STREET

3 4

Llandudno Bay

MAESDU ROAD

CONWY ROAD

MOSTYN BROADWAY

THE PARADE

5

D

CLARENCE ROAD

L

MOSTYN AVENUE

QUEEN'S ROAD

ROUMANIA DRIVE

NANT-Y-GAMAR ROAD

COLWYN ROAD

QUEEN'S
BACH ROAD

CARMEN
SYLVA
ROAD

A   St Tudno
B   St George
C   Holy Trinity   Craigside
D   St Paul
E   St Saviour   ⊢───────────┤ 1000 m
F   Our Lady Star of the Sea (R.C.)   ⊢───────────┤ 1000 yds
G   SS Mary and Abaskhayroun (Coptic)   1   Town Hall
H   Christ Church Congregational Church   2   Library
J   Ebeneser Wesleyan Chapel   3   Oriel Mostyn
K   English Presbyterian Chapel   4   Post Office
L   St David's Wesleyan Methodist Chapel   5   Venue Cymru
M   St John's Wesleyan Chapel
N   Seilo Calvinistic Methodist Chapel
O   Tabernacle Baptist Chapel   Llandudno

CHURCHES AND CHAPELS

ST TUDNO, St Tudno's Road. Isolated on the Great Orme, in the remnant of a rounded churchyard. Unicameral nave and chancel with W bellcote. The walls oldest at the NW angle, but otherwise largely C15. Arch-braced roof of eight bays, and moulded chancel wall-plate. W and N doorways with pointed rubble arches. N porch with C16 roof and E chamber. Victorian Dec E window and lancets. Abandoned in the 1830s, it was restored in 1855 by *J. A. Cossins* of Birmingham, and further in 1906–7. – Fragment of C15 BEAM carved with vine trail, from the rood screen. – Early C20 oak SCREEN. – FONT. Circular, of moulded profile, the rim with a sort of billet motif, and in the sides a run of ten foliate motifs, transitional between Romanesque and Gothic, so of *c.* 1200. – Two early C13 GRAVE-SLABS, built into the SW wall. Both have incised crosses, the heads of four circle motifs linked in a square pattern, then shafts decorated with scrolls. One has foliage of Romanesque type at the base.

In the churchyard, an OUTSIDE PULPIT with stone arched hood, 1912, made for large outdoor services, a feature of Llandudno summers. The old church is dwarfed by three CEMETERY enclosures in the shallow treeless valley, each with its own LYCHGATE, the lowest, Gothic, dated 1887. Why did this remote place become the town cemetery, when so much space was more conveniently available below? MORTUARY CHAPEL, 1903(?), Arts and Crafts with wooden verandas.

ST GEORGE, Church Walks. 1841, by *John Welch*, built for the copper-miners by the lessees of the Old Mine. Cruciform with lancets, tripled in the gables, and a low tower with a kind of saddleback, similar to Welch's church at Brynsiencyn, Anglesey (q.v.). Additions to the chancel 1883 and NE vestry 1903 by *Edwin Turner*. Bald interior, now used for architectural salvage. – STAINED GLASS. E window by *O'Connor*, 1860s, Christ and the Apostles. N transept N, three-light of *c.* 1916 and E lancet of 1885. S transept S, Faith, Hope and Charity, *c.* 1896. One nave S window signed *Davies* of Shrewsbury, *c.* 1895.

HOLY TRINITY, Trinity Square. 1865–74 by *George Felton*. An ungainly church for so good an urban space, the only square in the new resort, and alongside the main avenue. Designed to seat 1,200, it is reminiscent of large London suburban churches; broad and cruciform in rubble stone, Dec Gothic, with cross-gabled aisles and canted apse. NW tower added 1892 by *Edwin Turner*. NE chapel 1924, and chancel altered 1932 by *R. T. Beckett*. The tower is harsh, with large paired bell-lights and thin pinnacles. Quintessentially Victorian interior, the nave and transepts with yellow brick walls banded in black, and Bath stone arcades with thickly carved foliate capitals on mottled grey monolith columns of Anglesey marble. The chancel has ashlar lining and *Minton* tile paving, partly overlaid by marble in 1932. The War Memorial Chapel, NE, has close-spaced triple lancets and a scissor-truss roof. – STALLS.

1882, by *Jones & Willis*. – REREDOS, 1939, and carved wood PULPIT, 1951. – STAINED GLASS. Apse, five good windows of *c.* 1880 by *Hardman*; early life of Jesus. NE chapel, 1925–39, one signed by *C. C. Powell*. N transept, a dramatically coloured and crowded three-light of Christ in Majesty, 1891; S transept, Miracles of Christ, in deep mid-Victorian colours. S aisle, one of 1913, Martha and Mary, *Hardman*, another, Baptism and Christ Blessing, 1887, *A. L. Moore*. – CARVING. At the NW end a single giant piece of mahogany, intricately carved tiny scenes on a winged form with angel's head, by *Handel Edwards*, 1970s.

Attached to the SW, a large Gothic group of VESTRIES and CHURCH HALL.

ST PAUL, Mostyn Broadway, Craig-y-don. Built as a memorial to Queen Victoria's eldest grandson, the Duke of Clarence, in 1895–1901, by *John Oldrid Scott*. A fine work, despite not having the intended SW tower and spire, showing Scott in the vein of J. L. Pearson, a master of C13 Gothic. Tall and elegant in grey limestone with buff Bromsgrove stone dressings. Clerestory of cusped roundels, aisles, tall E and W windows, the gables chequered and a bellcote with flèche between nave and chancel. Rich interior of Bath stone ashlar banded with pink sandstone, the arcade columns of black Frosterley marble. The clerestory windows are linked by blind lancets, and the chancel arch has ringed shafts of black marble. – Alabaster octagonal PULPIT and green marble FONT. – REREDOS. 1920s by *C. M. Scott* – Very large brass eagle LECTERN, 1897. – STAINED GLASS. E window by *Powells*, 1913. – ORGAN. 1910 by *William Hill*.

ST SAVIOUR, Great Ormes Road, West Shore. Now Llandudno Baptist Chapel. The nave only of an elegant Late Gothic work by *R. T. Beckett* of Chester, 1911 won in competition against H. L. North and others. Red Runcorn sandstone, with low passage aisles stopped at twin porches. It was to have had a tower with a flèche over the chancel. The alabaster FONT is a memorial to Lewis Carroll.

OUR LADY STAR OF THE SEA (R.C.), Lloyd Street. 1893, by *Edmund Kirby* of Liverpool. A tall aisled church in rock-faced Yorkshire stone with dressings of red Runcorn. Late Dec tracery, with the E window rising higher than the other apse windows, under a gable. A tower was intended. Inside, red stone arcades on columns of granite from Shap and Mull. The chancel has a timber groined vault.

SS MARY AND ABASKHAYROUN (Coptic), Trinity Avenue. The former Rehoboth Calvinistic Methodist chapel of 1893. Stucco with a cheerful mix of Northern Renaissance detail and standard arched windows.

CHRIST CHURCH (Congregational), Abbey Road. On a prominent corner site of the upper town. 1857–8, by *Joseph James* of London. C14 Gothic, a very early example of correct Gothic for a Nonconformist congregation in Wales. Enlarged with transepts in 1863 by *James*; the cross-gabled side tower added in 1867, originally with a spire.

EBENESER WESLEYAN CHAPEL, Lloyd Street. One of the most notable chapel designs in Wales, of 1908–9, by *W. Beddoe Rees* of Cardiff. Planned in dignified relation to the neighbouring Town Hall, the chapel could itself be an Edwardian Baroque public building. Square plan with a shallow lead dome and cupola and elevations of very red Ruabon brick with copious sandstone enrichment. Lively elevation, the projecting pedimented Ionic frontispiece echoed in minor key by recessed centres on the side façades, all held in balance by corner pavilions with parapets and the openings gathered in giant arches. The detail plays freely with motifs from Wren and late C17 artisan design.

The remarkable circular interior echoes the late C18 St Chad at Shrewsbury, but without galleries. Tall iron columns carry a ribbed dome with round windows around the base. A broad shallow arch on paired columns frames the pulpit and organ recess and the pews radiated from this. The corners of the square plan house porches and vestries. – STAINED GLASS. One window by *Jones & Willis*, 1908.

ENGLISH PRESBYTERIAN CHAPEL, Chapel Street. Now Gloddaith United Church. Prominently sited on a corner, across Gloddaeth Street from Seilo chapel (*see* below). 1891, by *T. G. Williams* of Liverpool, specialist in unusual chapel plans (cf. his chapel at Ruthin, Denbs). Serious C14 Gothic, in local limestone with Cefn sandstone. There is a suggestion of a conventional nave-and-transepts design with corner tower and spire, but closer inspection shows that the 'nave' bellies out between the gables and the plan is actually a large oval, a single undivided space with a conical pitch-pine roof and curved raking seating.

ST DAVID'S WESLEYAN METHODIST CHAPEL, Mostyn Avenue, Craig-y-don. 1924, by *A. Brocklehurst* of Manchester. Suburban Late Gothic.

ST JOHN'S WESLEYAN CHAPEL, Mostyn Street. 1865–6 by *George Felton*. Ecclesiastical Gothic, built like the other two towered and spired chapels for an English congregation. Dec Gothic in dark green rubble with sandstone dressings. Complex tracery to the main window. The tower is buttressed with a recessed spire. Hammerbeam roof. – STAINED GLASS. Transept windows, 1960s by *Halkyn Studios*.

SEILO CALVINISTIC METHODIST CHAPEL, Arfon Avenue. 1905 by *G. A. Humphreys*. A striking, and at £8,779, an expensive church in grey and purple ashlar. Two storeys with ground floor of purple Cheshire sandstone, the upper floor of grey limestone with extensive purple dressings, and, on the outer bays, large purple cupolas with igloo masonry domes articulated with detached columns – almost a Borrominian effect. Inside, curved-ended gallery on iron columns, curved seating, and *sêt-fawr* and pulpit backed on an ORGAN by *P. Conacher*.

TABERNACLE BAPTIST CHAPEL, Llewelyn Avenue. 1875 by *Richard Owens*, Italianate stucco with an open-pedimented centrepiece and detail that proves Gothic on a closer look. Interesting Edwardian classical addition down the r. side, 1902, by *G. A. Humphreys*, the Ionic colonnade on the corner hiding a doll's house porch.

PUBLIC BUILDINGS

TOWN HALL, Lloyd Street. A competition victory of 1894, by *T. B. Silcock*, but not built until 1899–1901. This was an early success for the Wren revival, significantly by an architect from Bath, where J. M. Brydon's Neo-Baroque design had won the 1891 competition for additions to the Guildhall. The contrasting red brick and white stone was an economy, though it echoes Brydon's Chelsea Town Hall of 1885–7 that initiated the revival. The long façade appears finicky, in an architectural language more suited to an ampler scale, although the details are pretty. Hipped three-bay centre with a roof lantern, linked by lower two-bay wings to hipped single-bay end pavilions. The sober ground floor is of channelled Portland stone with a half-round columned porch under a stone centrepiece with double-curved pediment and Palladian window. The rest of the upper floor is red brick with much stone detail: curved pediments, eaves balustrades, pilasters and quoins. Inside, a stair hall on the l. leads up to the Council Chamber with early C18 detail. To the rear, a large public hall.

WAR MEMORIAL, Prince Edward Square. 1922 by *S. Colwyn Foulkes*. A 50-ft (15-metre) obelisk of Cornish granite, superbly silhouetted on the seafront at the head of the main cross-axis. The obelisk with its gilded mortar also marks the transition from the sloping part of the town to the Promenade, and by the brave placing of four ornate columnar lamps in line reconciles this lateral flow along the curve of the bay with its formal axial function.

LLANDUDNO PIER. 1876–8 by *James Brunlees & McKerrow*. Projecting from the foot of the Great Orme cliffs, it once served the steamers plying in Liverpool Bay and as far as the Isle of Man. The first pier of 1858 was destroyed in the great storm of 1859. Relatively unencumbered with buildings, the pier offers a notable vista of the long seafront and the mountains beyond. It cost some £26,000 and stands on cast-iron piles with wrought-iron girders and bracing. Following widening and lengthening in 1908, the deck has ornate cast-iron parapets and six pairs of hipped iron kiosks along the length of 1,234 ft (380 metres) before the pierhead, which has an octagonal pavilion with zinc roofs and an ogee dome. The cast-iron walkway S from the pier along the cliff face was added in 1883 to link to the Pier Pavilion, 1886, (by *B. Nelson*), a large iron and glass theatre over a sea-water swimming bath sited just l. of the Grand Hotel, destroyed by fire in 1994.

Public Library, Mostyn Street. 1908–10, by *G. A. Humphreys*. Built with a donation of £4,000 from Andrew Carnegie. An animated Edwardian Baroque front in Cefn sandstone with concave corners, echoing the outer pavilions at Cardiff City Hall, and columns on two storeys. Inside, a circular vestibule open to a domed colonnaded gallery above. The front reading room has a plaster vault.

Oriel Mostyn, Vaughan Street. 1901–2 by *G. A. Humphreys*. Built by Lady Augusta Mostyn to encourage the development of the arts and crafts, it closed in 1914 and reopened in 1984. Red brick and orange terracotta, an undisciplined mixture of turn-of-the-century motifs over five bays, the centre with a slated spire. Plans for extensions in 2009 by *Ellis Williams Architects*.

Post Office, Vaughan Street. 1904 by *G. A. Humphreys*. By contrast with Oriel Mostyn next door, a careful design, in the same red brick and orange terracotta, but the motifs more concentrated. The upper floors are united in a recessed Ionic colonnade clasped by outer bays crowned with little domed cupolas, flanking a gable.

Venue Cymru (North Wales Theatre), The Parade. 1994. Large and originally architecturally null. The twin towers may suggest seaside gaiety. To each side, additional circulation spaces and conference rooms, 2006, by *SMC Hickton Madeley* of Telford. Glazed and white outside, light and airy within, in a Modern Movement idiom, emphatically horizontal against the grain of the seafront.

railway station, Vaughan Street. The messy remnant of a large brick station of 1891, for the LNWR. Four gables, three of brick, one a glazed carriageway. The platform roofs have all gone.

John Bright School, Maesdu Road, 2004, by *Clive Hodgman*. A large secondary school and leisure centre complex planned as a series of five curved-roofed buildings, their end walls following a shallow curve, the main school entry marked by a portico of steel columns. Cladding in broad bands of colour: red brick, then white render then dark grey, the overall form and aesthetic industrial.

North Wales Medical Centre, Queens Road. Built as the Lady Forester Convalescent Home in 1902–4 by *E. B. I'Anson* of London; closed in 2006 and converted to flats. A very large and generous benefaction for families from industrial Staffordshire, the architecture trying for a homely touch over an impossible scale. White stone with purple sandstone dressings, symmetrical with canted wings and arcaded sun-catching loggias. A multiplicity of mullion-and-transom windows and a roof-line of gables culminate in a tall hipped centrepiece with a copper flèche and a purple porch-bay rising the full four storeys. This centre housed the staff; the patients were segregated in the wings, meeting in a large communal dining hall. Of the same date, two lodges and the laundry.

PERAMBULATIONS

1. The Centre from the War Memorial via Church Walks,
The Parade, Vaughan Street and Mostyn Street

The War Memorial on THE PROMENADE is the natural starting
point, with the great curve of the bay running away to the SE
and curving up to the N to the rocky edge of the Great Orme.
From here the stucco terraces seem broadly uniform, which
they are in height, but not in detail. Their architecture broadly
parallels contemporary developments such as Bayswater in
London. Those of the 1850s have Italian detail soberly applied;
in the 1860s this inflates with large brackets to cornices, more
complex grouped windows and bays; in the later 1860s and
1870s come ever larger bay windows, and the detail becomes
eclectic with borrowings from other round-arched styles and
from the Gothic. Eclecticism of a Northern Renaissance sort
appears at the end of the C19, with shaped gables breaking
up the skyline. The cast-iron verandas, so much a feature of
the commercial centre, seem to be late C19 and early C20
additions.

The view N from the Memorial takes in the HAPPY VALLEY
ROAD curving around the edge of the Great Orme (*see* p. 420).
Massively present is the GRAND HOTEL, 1898–1902, by
J. F. Doyle of Liverpool, for many years the largest in Wales.
Stuccoed but scraped of detail apart from the pyramid roofs.
It is on the site of the Italianate baths and reading room of
1855 by *Wehnert & Ashdown*, typically one of the first amenities
of the new resort. NORTH PARADE has stepped stuccoed
houses of the early 1860s curving to the end of Church Walks,
the terraces giving way to villas. On the E the gatepiers of a
former mews. No. 17, OSBORNE HOUSE, was refaced in stone
in the later C19; No. 18 is bargeboarded and slightly Gothic, a
villa type restricted to the early resort here on the slope. Prominent on the steep hillside above, the late C19 HEADLANDS
HOTEL, stuccoed with a shaped gable and spired bay. Above
again, and very prominent, ARDWY ORME and GLAN ORME,
two good villas of 1895 and 1897 by *G. A. Humphreys* in the
style of Norman Shaw or J. J. Stevenson, the l. one for himself,
with shaped gable in red sandstone, the r. one with tile-hung
upper parts.

CHURCH WALKS runs W and then SW along the slope. This was
the fashionable street of the transition from hillside mining
village to planned resort from the late 1840s until the early
1860s, when the focus shifted down Mostyn Street. Facing S
down Mostyn Street is the EMPIRE HOTEL, built in 1854 as
the Italian Warehouse, a department store for the new town,
Italianate, four storeys and eight bays. There are some terraced
rows of a modest sort before the pattern of building turns to
villas, detached or semi-detached.

After VICTORIA STATION, the bottom station of the Great Orme
Tramway, 1902 (*see* Great Orme, p. 421), the most spectacular

of the villas, BODLONDEB, 1890s, a sandstone castle with the
stepped gables of Plas Mawr, Conwy, and an octagonal corner
turret ringed with grotesque heads. Rich interiors with marble
balustrades and baronial fireplace. Above and running SW are
slight remains of pre-resort Llandudno, the small cottages in
CWLACH STREET, and above again, in CWLACH ROAD,
detached stuccoed villas under the cliff. TOWER HOUSE,
triple-gabled with bargeboards, surprises with a large glazed
octagon on the roof; CWLACH, c. 1860, is Italianate with a
belvedere tower, oddly the only one of this mid-Victorian type
so popular in e.g. Torquay; finally HAULFRE is gabled and
bargeboarded, with gardens stepping up the rock behind. From
the end of Cwlach Street a path drops SE to Church Walks
opposite the NATIONAL SCHOOLS of the 1840s, built in two
parts, the low l. part rubble stone and the taller r. part added,
stuccoed with ashlar mullion-and-transom windows and tall
chimneys.

Returning up Church Walks past St George's church (p. 409).
Llewelyn Avenue runs E past the Congregational chapel and
Tabernacle chapel (pp. 410, 411) to UPPER MOSTYN STREET.
Here it is helpful to pause and look eastwards along this main
avenue, 80 ft (25 metres) wide which follows the curve, a deep
block back from the Promenade, and so have a sense of the
whole town. This upper end has stuccoed stepped terraces of
the late 1850s on the l., but the r. side, exceptionally, is in
yellow sandstone, in the mixed styles of the early 1860s: first
round-arched Italianate, then a triplet of tall Gothic windows
with pentangles for the MASONIC HALL, 1867, by *Lloyd-
Williams & Underwood*, then a stepped three-storey terrace
curving into Gloddaeth Street, the first-floor windows divided
by piers in a continuous Gothic arcade. Here we first meet the
iron awnings or verandas typical of Llandudno, as they are of
Southport. The awnings are rarely consistent, not apparently
part of the original design, with a variety of columns, occasionally stamped with a maker, such as *Macfarlane* of Glasgow.
Most date from the early C20, some of the Art Nouveau
designs being by *Edwin Turner*.

At the foot of the hill Mostyn Street crosses the principal E–W
axis of the planned town, Gloddaeth Street runs SW to the West
Shore, and Prince Edward Square runs NE for the short distance back to the seafront. The one broad avenue that runs
from the War Memorial on the North Shore right across to the
West Shore is a grandiose concept but the architecture fails a
short distance down Gloddaeth Street (*see* below). It is better
to return to the War Memorial through PRINCE EDWARD
SQUARE, the funnel-shaped centrepiece of the *Wehnert &
Ashdown* plan. Grand four-storey terraces on each side of the
later 1860s, North and South Parades. The CARLTON on the
right-hand corner to Mostyn Street has a good pub front of
c. 1900, sheltered by a fine veranda.

SOUTH PARADE curves around onto THE PARADE. The houses
to Prince Edward Square have triple-arched windows on the

third floor, of the 1860s, but the design changes on the slightly earlier curve to the seafront, where outsize console brackets frame the top-floor windows. The next terrace is GLAN-Y-MÔR PARADE, five houses with the canted bays of the 1860s, and a taller E end stop with a return down St George's Place, 1870s, the bays uneasily pedimented, and arched windows above.

4   ST GEORGE'S CRESCENT is probably by *Wehnert & Ashdown*, the only terrace to resemble their 1857 engraving. It can be dated by the twin end hotels with giant Corinthian pilasters, the ST GEORGE'S HOTEL (W) opened 1854 and the QUEEN'S HOTEL (E), of 1855. The terrace has a measured rhythm different from later work, partly due to the absence of bay windows and partly to the generous five-bay width of each house. The effect is Early Victorian, more Belgravia than Bayswater. Note the very rich ironwork on the St George's Hotel balcony, a particularly rich and fleshy scroll, and at the other end, the delicate trellis on the White House Hotel, both early C20 additions from respectively the *Macfarlane* and *Coalbrookdale* catalogues. Less attractive is the agitated skyline added in 1892 to the centre and r. part.

The longest terrace of the whole seafront, GLODDAETH CRESCENT, by contrast, is already mid-Victorian, *c.* 1865, attributed to *J. A. Chatwin* of Birmingham. It shows the weakness of later Llandudno terrace design, effective from afar, but not quite achieving cohesion. A formality is attempted with taller end stops and a four-house centrepiece cleverly divided to a 4–4–4 rhythm. The detail is Italianate, but with the boldness of the 1860s evident – as on Neville Crescent further E – in big rounded arcaded bays, and also on the initial CHATSWORTH HOTEL and terminal HOWARD HOTEL in an eaves gallery of squat pilasters under a steep mansard. Beyond the Howard Hotel is the very large IMPERIAL HOTEL to the corner of Vaughan Street, the lower three floors of 1865, the top two of *c.* 1905 with shallow gables. The interior is said to incorporate doors from *Norman Shaw*'s Dawpool, Cheshire, of 1882–6, dem. 1926.

VAUGHAN STREET runs back to cross Mostyn Street at the TUDNO CASTLE HOTEL. A large stuccoed Italianate block facing down the street, not quite designed for so prominent a role, as it was built as two hotels and lacks a centre. The iron porch is particularly good. The S half of Vaughan Street is aligned on the station (p. 413); the l. side, on the site of the 1896 Eisteddfod, is all by *G. A. Humphreys*, displaying his versatility in generally Northern Renaissance styles. The date sequence runs in reverse from the Post Office of 1904 to No. 1 of 1897. No. 7, IMPERIAL BUILDINGS, 1898, has the orange terracotta of the Post Office and Oriel Mostyn (p. 413). Several good iron verandas.

MOSTYN STREET returns NW to the centre, the scale building up steadily, and mostly stuccoed without particular accents before TRINITY SQUARE on the l. Here the opportunity for a

grand display of the Bayswater or Hove type was not taken up,
rather there are semi-detached stucco villas of no particular
character. CLONMEL STREET runs back to The Parade, the r.
side detailed like Gloddaeth Crescent. In the next stretch of
Mostyn Street, St John's Wesleyan Church on the r. and the
Library on the l. Then a main cross-axis has Lloyd Street
running inland and ST GEORGE'S PLACE running back to the
sea, the pyramid-roofed tower of the late C19 addition to
the ST GEORGE'S HOTEL (*see* above) dominant on the r. On
the l., the corner block has giant pilasters, a C20 modification
for BURTONS. Next, Nos. 7–9 is late C19, stuccoed with shaped
gables, and then a lower eleven-bay row is the return of the
end block of Glan-y-môr Parade, 1870s.

LLOYD STREET begins with a show of early C20 wealth and
assurance on the r., the sequence of bank, Town Hall and
Ebeneser chapel (*see* pp. 412, 411). The NATWEST BANK far
outscales the Town Hall, a lofty Portland stone pile of 1920
built for the National Provincial Bank by *F. C. R. Palmer*, their
architect, a bravura display worthy of the City of London.
A monumental arcaded ground floor with two storeys above,
the short façade to Mostyn Street with a triumphal porch and
top pediment. The style is less individual than Lutyens, more
the heroic Neo-Georgian of Edwin Cooper. The banking hall
has a rich coffered ceiling.

The show fades quickly thereafter, but there is a suburban excursion to be made by continuing. On the l. two villas, PLAS
MAELGWYN, 1900, with ornate half-timber gables and the
R.C. PRESBYTERY, presumably by *Kirby*, *c.* 1895, a nicely
sober Tudor design behind his R.C. church (*see* p. 410). Across
St Mary's Road, three more villas of *c.* 1900, a digest of
Llandudno suburban building materials: red brick and red
sandstone on STELLA MARIS; red brick, brown sandstone and
half-timber on the extravagant Nos. 37–39 (which have slated
spikes over Gothic porches); dust-pressed brick and roughcast
on Nos. 41–43. Next, the BOARD SCHOOL in grey rubble
stone, Gothic and picturesquely varied, 1881–2, by *A. Foulkes*,
and the LIFEBOAT STATION, 1903, marooned here equidis-
tant from North and West shores. Returning, ST MARYS ROAD
is one of the most consistent suburban streets, the houses of
red brick and half-timber, *c.* 1900, the 1893 chapel, now the
Coptic church, nicely closing the view. In TRINITY AVENUE,
a large early C20 school, YSGOL TUDNO, roughcast with five
timbered gables typical of *R. Lloyd Jones*, and returning on
CAROLINE ROAD, Nos. 28–30, on the corner, a semi-detached
pair with particularly fancy scrollwork in the gables, and more
half-timbered brick villas, one dated 1899.

Returning to MOSTYN STREET, the stretch from Lloyd Street
to the main crossing with Gloddaeth Street has interesting
early C20 interlopers. On the N side the scale drops between
the stuccoed corner buildings, Burtons at the E and the
Carlton at the W. No. 85 is a narrow and lively Edwardian
Baroque piece, *c.* 1905, the façade gathered under an open

pediment, No. 97, CLARE'S, is Art Deco classical with upper
columns, No. 103 has an added two-storey front with Free
Renaissance detail and No. 111 is Baroque again, dated 1913.
The verandas are continuous though different in detail. On the
other side, Nos. 64–80, a stuccoed row of 1864 with eclectic
detail, has a centrepiece of 1–3–1 bays with twin pavilion roofs
and corbelling. This was built as the St George's Hall and
became the Prince's Theatre. BARCLAYS BANK in Portland
stone is Neo-Georgian of the 1930s. Then a stuccoed row of
the 1860s turns the corner into Gloddaeth Street.

In GLODDAETH STREET little to match the grand scale of the
Avenue. On the r. the stone buildings on the corner of Upper
Mostyn Street (see p. 415), with some Art Deco shopfronts.
Good iron verandas on both sides. THE PALLADIUM, by
Arthur Hewitt, 1920, is to the right scale, a late example of the
Edwardian music hall, now a pub. The tall stucco façade has
a giant open-pedimented aedicule flanked by narrower ones
with curved pediments capped by octagonal domes, and a
great deal of detail in between. Inside, a saucer-domed foyer
and an auditorium with two balconies and boxes, and profuse
plasterwork. The English Presbyterian Chapel and Seilo chapel
(see p. 411) stand on opposite sides. Behind Seilo is its CHAPEL
HOUSE of 1884 and a handsome turn-of-the-century block
with Northern Renaissance detail in red brick and stucco.
Architectural interest ends with Nos. 29–31, on the l. on the
corner of Maelgwyn Road, a very red suburban pair with
shaped gables and octagonal angle tower, *c.* 1900.

2. The West Shore

GLODDAETH AVENUE continues Gloddaeth Street straight to
the West Shore, with complete loss of architectural interest. At
the far end a delightful SHELTER at the tramway terminus,
1928, circular, of iron and glass with a copper roof and little
dome. Sheltered seating alcoves outside interlock with similar
alcoves inside. A stone STORM PUMPING STATION nearby of
1996 by *Colwyn Foulkes & Partners*. Little of note otherwise.
On a small green to the s, the former St Saviour's church
(see above). To the N, against the Great Orme, LORETO
CONVENT, Abbey Road, with a big pebbledashed school of
1912.

3. From Vaughan Street, east to Craig-y-don

From Vaughan Street THE PARADE continues E in large stucco
blocks. First, MOSTYN CRESCENT of the 1860s with big
hipped end accents. The MARINE HOTEL at the W has pavilion roofs to Vaughan Street, an up-to-date Second Empire
touch, but the rest of the terrace is more soberly Italianate with
two-storey bays. NEVILLE CRESCENT shows a mid-Victorian
mix as on Gloddaeth Crescent further W, the bays curved with
a vaguely Gothic notching and a minimal polychromy in
encaustic tile bands and stone and brick dormers. The ends

rise a storey with hipped roofs. Just before the l. end a four-bay block, part of the HYDRO HOTEL, jumps higher still with late C19 detail, the skyline climbing to a pavilion roof capped with a feature like an upturned bath. This must be late C19 rebuilding. The hotel is said to date from 1860, which seems too early for the terrace. PENRHYN CRESCENT beyond is a short four-storey row of six by *Edwin Turner*, 1886, with two-storey bays. Then the big theatre complex, Venue Cymru (*see* 413). Across Clarence Avenue, CWRT SANT TUDNO, 2004, flats with weakly classical centrepieces.

Clarence Road marks the beginning of Craig-y-don, a separate estate sold for development in 1884. On the corner, the surprising WASHINGTON HOTEL, 1924, by *T. Jenkins* of Burton on Trent, like a Latin American bank, in white stucco with an arcaded first-floor loggia and a round corner entry with a Palladian first-floor feature and copper dome. The rest of EAST PARADE is a long terrace of two-bay houses with brackets at the eaves and gabled dormers. CRAIG-Y-DON PARADE, the last stuccoed terrace block, is similar, presumably all late 1880s. Finally, the DORCHESTER, a block of modern flats imitating the theme in stucco and cast stone, *c.* 2002, brings us to the abrupt end of the town at the green fields of Bodafon Farm.

Nant-y-gamar Road skirts the field, and MOSTYN AVENUE running w is the end of the long avenue that began at Upper Mostyn Street above the town centre. Suburban houses here and in the streets to the N, named after Marie, Queen of Romania, the novelist Carmen Sylva, who visited for five weeks in 1890, most of the houses of after 1900. For the dedicated, CARMEN SYLVA DRIVE runs s up to ROUMANIA CRESCENT crossing ROUMANIA DRIVE, revealing a number of brick villas with half-timber or roughcast. The best, at the top of the slope, is RAPALLO HOUSE, on FFERM BACH ROAD, with a great deal of half-timber and a turret. It was built *c.* 1900 for F. E. Chardon who left the house and his art collections to the town in 1927. Queen's Road returns to the seafront.

If one stays on Mostyn Avenue, St David's Wesleyan Church is on the r. The housing varies from two- to four-storey. Nos. 35–39 on the l. dated 1896 are four-storey, as is the former DUNPHY'S store, on the corner of Queen's Road, with domed turrets and shaped stuccoed gables. w on the Broadway, St Paul's church on the r. and then the former GRAND THEATRE of 1901, by *G. A. Humphreys* with the theatre architect *Edwin Sachs*, externally plain in red brick with a gable grid of yellow terracotta, but the interior delicately enriched with two balconies and boxes, and a shallow dome with a plaster sunburst. The l. side is given over to modern shopping, notably the brick-clad PARC LLANDUDNO complex, 2002. A long detour up Conway Road offers only the incongruous LINKS HOTEL, a confection of 1898 playing on an inflated scale with the Llandudno suburban themes: roughcast, half-timber, red brick and tile-hanging. The municipal golf links have gone.

HEN DŴR, Nant-y-gamar. On the crest of the rocky ridge s of Craig-y-don. A windmill recorded from the earlier C17, and already a house by 1840. Conical roughcast tower with a pointed roof.

GLODDAETH HALL. *See* Llanrhos.

4. Great Orme's Head

The limestone promontory of the Great Orme (Pen-y-gogarth) projects into Liverpool Bay, isolated from the Creuddyn peninsula by the coastal flats that form the site for the modern town. Its sheer sides define it as a former island relating to Puffin Island (Ynys Seiriol) and the Penmon headland on Anglesey.

ST TUDNO. *See* p. 409.

COPPER MINES. The dome of Carboniferous Limestone has productive lodes of copper ore and also malachite and copper pyrites. Copper working from very ancient times was confirmed by exploration, which suggested that this was the largest area of prehistoric subterranean mining known in Europe, covering some six acres on the surface, descending some 200 ft (60 metres) and with some three miles of passages. Finds of stone hammers and tools of bone and wood, and radiocarbon dating suggest working between 1900 and 600 B.C., though the actual operations at any one time may have been small. The opencast GREAT ORME MINE (SH 771 831) at the top of Tŷ Gwyn Road may be a collapsed underground chamber, and is the entrance to underground galleries where early workings are still distinguishable from C19 shafts.

There are three principal later sites, the OLD MINE and the NEW MINE close to each other on the ancient workings and TŶ GWYN MINE (SH 778 828), just above the North Shore. The whole 700 acres of the Old and New Mine sites was leased in 1824 to Samuel Worthington but waterlogged conditions made mining difficult until a half-mile adit was driven in at sea level from the West Shore in 1834–42 to drain workings 400 ft (120 metres) below the surface. An 18-inch (46-cm.) Cornish engine was installed at the Old Mine in 1835, that drove a crusher and winding apparatus. Despite management from 1853 by the experienced firm of John Taylor & Sons, yields declined, the Old Mine closing in 1861 and the New Mine by 1880. Tŷ Gwyn mine was successful into the 1840s, but although a Cornish engine was installed at great expense in 1842, it also declined and was closed in 1856 after sea water entered the workings.

Settlement on the Head long preceded the foundation of the town, named from the church site on the Great Orme, (*see* burial chamber, p. 422). From the modern town TŶ GWYN ROAD leads steeply up to a zone of quite different character, with random terraces of small houses for the miners. Mostly stuccoed, they look C19, suggesting replacement or enlargement of earlier structures. The Great Orme was adopted for tourism experiences by the Marine Drive of 1875–8 that encircled the headland and then by the funicular railway of 1902.

GREAT ORME TRAMWAY, Church Walks. 1898–1904. A cable railway climbing steeply from the edge of the Victorian resort and through the earlier village, to the summit. It passes a rebuilt HALFWAY STATION (1999) and terminates at the SUMMIT HOTEL (1909 on the site of a telegraph station of 1826) just below the top. More recently still this was joined by the aerial CABLE CAR rising from Happy Valley.

GOGARTH ABBEY, below the w end of Marine Drive. The once extensive palace of the Bishops of Bangor seems to have been burned in the Glyndŵr disturbances, and later mostly eroded by the sea. The site was adopted in 1894 for an Italianate VILLA with an octagonal tower on the seaward angle. The palace is thought to have been built by Bishop Anian I (1267–1305). The most recognizable part is the low walls of the GREAT HALL, entered from the SE beside a projecting oriel. Three original window openings in the NW wall, and some moulded stonework, including a double lancet, contemporary with Anian's work at Bangor Cathedral. Further fragmentary early structures entered by the hall's SW doorway. Slots at the mid-point in its walls suggest that a cruck-truss spanning 30 ft (9 metres) supported the roof.

MARINE DRIVE. The Drive must have afforded a stranger landscape experience originally, seeing that its patrons made the circuit in horse-drawn vehicles. The six-mile horseshoe of road, by the engineer *Hedworth Lee* and *George Felton*, engineered with difficulty in 1872–8 is perched halfway down the limestone cliffs, replacing a far more exposed path, that terrified Gladstone. From Llandudno Pier, HAPPY VALLEY ROAD curves around the first headland, the concrete COLONNADE on the l. of 1932 by *G. A. Humphreys*, designed as a shelter with upper walkway to enjoy the views. In Happy Valley, the JUBILEE FOUNTAIN, 1889, by *A. B. Deakin*, a bust of Queen Victoria under a domed canopy of sandstone, marble and granite. At both ends of the Drive are castellated TOLL HOUSES of 1878 by *A. Foulkes*, engineer to the scheme. At the furthest N end, the GREAT ORME'S HEAD LIGHTHOUSE, a castellated two-storey building and cottages by *G. F. Lyster*, engineer to the Mersey Docks and Harbour Board, of 1862. As at Point Lynas, Llaneilian, Anglesey, the cliff site (325 ft above the sea) made a tower unnecessary. Disused in 1985. Down the w side, the remains of Gogarth Abbey (*see* above) are below LLYS HELIG DRIVE, which runs N at a lower level to some of the last Arts and Crafts houses of Llandudno. First the ground-hugging PLAS BARDD, then BRONYMOR, *c.* 1939, by *H. L. North* for Frank Tyldesley, his favourite builder,* with two gabled wings fanning out to embrace the view.

* North gave him the plans as a wedding present.

Much altered, but North's massing is still clear. Then PLAS LAFAN, 1941, also looking over the sands, by North's partner *P. M. Padmore*, similar but to a tighter geometry. The arched loggia openings would probably not appeal to North.

OGOF LLECH. The Victorians were not the first to relish frissons on this vertiginous promontory. A little summerhouse or fishing retreat (now inaccessible due to rockfall), was formed in a natural cave on the W side by Sir Roger Mostyn of Gloddaeth, *c.* 1680. Celebrated in a poem of 1683, its chamber is lined in ashlar with an egg-and-dart frieze and cornice mouldings.

KENDRICK'S CAVE, Tŷ Gwyn Road. Named for its finder in 1880. Inside were bones with incised zigzags and notches, the earliest portable art found in Wales, of the Upper Palaeolithic period, *c.* 10,000 B.C.

LLETY'R FILIAST BURIAL CHAMBER (SH 772 829), on the W side of the Pwllau valley, indicates occupation on the headland during the Neolithic. The tomb has been damaged and the original shape of chamber and cairn (which is partly a natural outcrop) are uncertain, but it was probably a square closed chamber. No finds are recorded from it.

LLANDUDNO JUNCTION

The town has a superb site at the mouth of the Conwy estuary, which it totally ignores. Its *raison d'être* is the junction of the Holyhead railway with the Llandudno Town and Blaenau Ffestiniog branches, opened in 1858 and 1863–79 respectively. The STATION was rebuilt on a new site in 1897 for the London & North Western Railway. Opposite, the OLD STATION HOTEL, 1898, by *Edwin Turner* of Llandudno, a Tudorbethan extravaganza of half-timbering above red brick. Three-storey gabled wings, three-bay entrance, with bracketed oriel windows above splayed terracotta bays; the brick corner piers added later, replacing carved brackets. CONWY ROAD, the main thoroughfare, leads E. Mostly late C19 flats above shops, frilly bargeboards and half-timber surviving in places. On the corner of Glyn-y-marl Road, the former NATIONAL PROVINCIAL BANK, with its logo inscribed in stone on the side wall, by *F. C. R. Palmer*, 1928. N of Conwy Road, indifferent housing estates, but some 1920s examples clearly inspired by Garden City ideals – relaxed layout, trees, houses grouped and placed at strategic locations, roughcast cottage aesthetic. ST DAVID'S AVENUE and MARL CRESCENT, N of the station, are the best examples. In MARL DRIVE, Nos. 45 and 69 preserve their original character, with small-paned windows, a lattice light in the front door and a simple flat canopy above.

ST MICHAEL AND ALL ANGELS, Glyn-y-marl Road. 1929, by *R. T. Beckett*, in a style so plain and unfussy that it lacks life. Nave and chancel in one, with a slightly shorter S aisle and a modern W extension. Projecting and cantilevered timber bell-cote, W. Rock-faced limestone outside, smooth ashlar inside. Simply detailed arcade. – FONT. Octagonal, slightly tapering, with Dec blind tracery. C19? – STAINED GLASS. Good modern glass in both E windows, by *Goddard & Gibbs*. Crucifixion, chancel, 1966; Ruth, S aisle, 1973.

MOST HOLY FAMILY (R.C.), Bryn Eglwys. 1969, by *Weightman & Bullen*. Cruciform, with a squat tower at the crossing. Panels of light-brown brick, with narrow full-height strips of glazing recessed rhythmically between. A shallow pyramid roof set back behind the tower parapet, supported on four slim steel columns which demarcate the sanctuary. Simple altar, font and ambo, in white Sicilian marble, disposed symmetrically on the black marble platform.

ENGLISH PRESBYTERIAN CHURCH, S end of Victoria Drive. 1898, by *A. W. Smith* of Manchester, in Arts and Crafts Tudor. Red brick and half-timbering.

PRESWYLFA WESLEYAN CHAPEL, Conwy Road and Queen's Road. Dated 1909, by *Arthur Hewitt* of Llandudno. Gable-fronted, in rock-faced limestone. Porch with triplet above and a single louvred light at the top. Behind, a detached school-room, vestry and chapel house.

MEMORIAL HALL, Penrhos Avenue. 1927, by *B. de Helsby* of Llandudno Junction. War memorial plaque set between the entrance doors. Sloping curved walls continue each side, implying a forecourt. Nice lettering to the side entrance, above a semicircular head of three brick orders.

YSGOL MAELGWYN, Broad Street. 1907, by *Rowland Lloyd Jones*, County Architect. E-plan school, with hall wing behind. Half-timbered gables above red brick. Forecourt wall, with iron railings and stone gatepier cappings. Inside, a pleasant airy passage runs the length of the building, passing the hall which is entered through a triple arcade clad in light-blue glazed tiles. A fireplace in the hall, also tiled. One of many similar schools, functionally planned and soundly built.

PLAS BLODWEL, Broad Street. By *S. Colwyn Foulkes*, c. 1924. Neo-Regency, in dark brown brick, originally the workhouse children's home. Central entrance with an upper-floor balcony on thin paired steel columns, with an openwork balustrade. Intersecting tracery to the central upper windows.

MANWEB SHOWROOM (former), Glan-y-môr Road. By *S. Colwyn Foulkes*, c. 1938. A round brick drum with offices above the showroom, and single-storey wings radiating to N and E. Big curved windows, with sunshade incorporating the Manweb logo. Decorative brick cornices, almost Dutch in their busy detail, and a tall columned cupola.

MARL HALL, Marl Lane. ½ m. NNE, just beyond the A470 road. A beam dated 1661 is all that survives from the early house, enlarged considerably in the early C18. Imposing three-storey limestone front (W), two storeys and dormered attic, with slightly advancing three-storey wings. Small-paned sashes with thick glazing bars. Repaired and extended in the early C20 by

Crouch & Butler of Birmingham. The entrance hall and stair-case retain their Edwardian character, with finely detailed Arts and Crafts features to the newel posts and glazed doors.

LLANDUDWEN

2737

ST TUDWEN (SH 274 368). In a square walled churchyard in a field, reached along a walled path. A C16–C17 rebuilding on the medieval site. T-plan. Off-centre W doorway with arched voussoir head and bellcote. Three steps down into the nave, which gently slopes down eastwards. Only the S transept windows are original, early C17. The ovolo-moulded jambs and mullions resemble those at Madryn Gatehouse (*see* below). – FONT. Medieval octagonal gritstone bowl on a modern base. – MONUMENTS. Slate and stone ledgers in the transept floors, to members of the Griffiths family of Nyffryn (*see* below), †1670 to †1774. – LYCHGATE. Probably C17.

DINAS CALVINISTIC METHODIST CHAPEL, Dinas, ½ m. SW. 1860s, altered 1906. Set back, with the schoolroom to one side. Standard gable front, with a pair of round-headed windows below a bigger arch.

MADRYN GATEHOUSE, ¾ m. ESE. Madryn Castle was occupied by the Madryn family from the C16, and the Jones-Parry family from *c.* 1740. The two-storey gatehouse was originally on axis with the former mansion, one of the most substantial and sig-nificant gentry houses in Caernarvonshire. Rubble (formerly rendered); embattled parapet of dressed stone. Ovolo-moulded window jambs and mullions, with C19 cast-iron latticed case-ments, and flush voussoirs to the opposed arched doorways. Derelict.

NYFFRYN (now Nyffryn Bella), 1 m. W. Stone end-chimney house, of the Griffiths family from the mid C17. Two storeys and attic, with a full-height staircase bay behind (W). The tiny windows on each level to the l., in line with the fireplace and chimney, are probably for closets rather than a former staircase.

CAERAU, ¾ m. WSW. A plain but pretty house, part of the Cefnamwlch estate. Roughly coursed rubble, brick chimneys and small-pane sashes. The surprising date 1903 on a stone just below the central upper window.

ST CEIDIO, 1 m. NE. In a small raised and circular churchyard, in the former parish of Ceidio. The undivided nave and chancel only 29 by 15 ft (9 by 4.5 metres), surely one of the smallest in Wales. The W wall, with its multi-cusped double bellcote, the cusped lancets with rere-arches, and the Perp E window date from a sensitive restoration in 1897. The roof, perhaps early C16, has two trusses with much apex cusping over the nave, and a plain arch-braced one at the E. – FURNISHINGS. A slate tablet with biblical inscription behind the altar, 1744. Some simple C18 benches with owners' names. In the SW window sill, a basin hollowed out of the oblong boulder.

STAINED GLASS. E window, the Adoration of Christ crucified, movingly leaded in clear glass.

LLANDWROG

The estate village of Glynllifon, seat of the lords Newborough.

St Twrog. In a partly round raised churchyard. On this ancient site is an ornate cruciform church of 1858–64 by *Kennedy*. Very fancy SW tower and steeple, with the entry beneath. The interior, clad in Bath stone, is eccentric, beginning with a sort of jubilee, an organ loft supported on two free-standing arcades E and W, the stone arches busily cusped. Nave and transepts are lined with stalls under canopies, no doubt required by the patron, the 3rd Lord Newborough, to suggest a family chapel. The canopies become more elaborate in the transepts, with crocketed pinnacles to those on the E walls. The parapeted Glynllifon Chapel S of the chancel, looks like an addition, but is of the same date.

FONTS. Disused octagonal one in the porch, 1703; *Kennedy*'s on four columns at the W. – PULPIT, stone with staircase guarded by mastiffs. – READING DESK. Two carved panels of the Crucifixion, representing the driving in of the nails, and the Maries and the centurion beneath the crosses, both full of figures and realism and perhaps C16 German. – The ironwork SCREEN, *c.* 1863, is quite rare. Lavishly foliated circled panels with integral stalls on the E, and on the pinnacles sprout ivy, passion flowers, wheat, chestnuts and their leaves etc. – STAINED GLASS. Good windows in the transepts: S, by *Hardman*, dated 1920. N, an early very fine *Clayton & Bell* window, *c.* 1860. – MONUMENTS. In the Glynllifon Chapel some of the best C18 memorials in the country. Ellen Glyn †1711 and Lady Frances Glyn †1709, tablet with flaming vases. – Thomas Wynn †1749. An Augustan bust, white marble, and a sarcophagus and pyramid of grey. Lively Rococo ornament, appearing early here, including flaming vases, wave-like volutes and garlands needing repair. Possibly by *Henry Cheere*. – Frances Wynn, spinster, †1784, a green marble demi-urn with a lady perched on the lip. – Thomas, 1st Lord Newborough †1807. Seated figure of Faith above the fabric and inscription, by *W. Spence* of Liverpool. – Thomas, 2nd Lord Newborough, †1832, with a mourning dame by the urn. – Maria, Lady Newborough, †1843, by *W. Spence*. – At the W end of the nave, the 'worthy and respectable' Bodvel family of Bodfan (*see* p. 431), †1731–60. Seated female reading, in an Ionic surround, with biographies below, by *Joseph Nollekens*. – In the churchyard, a grand LYCHGATE and a baluster SUNDIAL dated 1746.

ESTATE VILLAGE. Laid out by the 3rd Lord Newborough close to his mansion, *c.* 1830–60, in Picturesque Gothic style, the single street following the wall around the churchyard.

Starting at the Glynllifon (s) end, Nos. 1–6 CAE'R LLWYN
on the l., a long row of single-storey L-plan houses in joined
pairs, the end ones gabled and the double-bay inner ones
hipped. Between each of the four projecting wings, continuous
porch verandas on rustic timber posts. Gothic windows
below slightly swept brick heads and Tudor hoods. Set back
on the r., the SCHOOL, by *Kennedy*, c. 1853. Gabled wings, a
steep bellcote above the middle window. Next on the l., Nos.
1–3 TAI'R YSGOL, a projecting gable for the middle house.
Just beyond, a classical HORSE TROUGH, of Anglesey limestone. ROSE COTTAGE, opposite is dated 1835 above the
arched stone porch doorway. Across the narrow lane leading
to the walled CEMETERY beyond the school, CAE'R EGLWYS.
The 1774 datestone must be re-set as all the houses S of the
church date from the 1830s. W of the church, the HARP INN,
also 1830s but possibly incorporating an earlier building. U-
plan, with semi-octagonal wings and entrance veranda. Blind
central windows to the wings, a slate plaque in the lower r.
opening. Brick jambs to most and tall brick chimneys, some
now rendered. Nos. 1–5 CILGANT (The Crescent), c. 1850–60,
nicely follows the rounded wall N of the church, then another
TROUGH. Opposite, VESTRY COTTAGE, built into the raised
churchyard and formerly with a connecting door and staircase.
Beyond, a short row of three taller houses, c. 1860, all with
steep gables and now unsympathetically rendered. Perhaps
Kennedy had a hand.

GLYNLLIFON

½ m. SE, in the valley of the Llifon river. Acquired by the Wynn
family soon after 1700. Sir Thomas Wynn (†1749), who held
court appointments for George II in London, started the formal
gardens. These became by stages up to the late C19 the best
artificial water gardens North Wales has produced; but the
dominance of the huge, cement-rendered house (which as rebuilt
extends to twenty-five windows) and of the Victorian arboretum
of exotic evergreens, compounded since the 1950s by forestry
plantations, makes their earlier qualities hard to capture. In 1954
the main house became the centre of the Caernarvonshire Agricultural Institute, now Coleg Meirion Dwyfor and based in the
stable court, which uses the kitchen garden and farmlands for
training; the house awaits reuse as a hotel. After the sale in 1947,
the historic park timber was largely replaced by Forestry
Commission conifers, but the extensive gardens and remarkable
Estate Yard were adopted as a country park, Parc Glynllifon, in
the mid 1980s. Despite the various public and private
ownerships, Glynllifon is treated here as a single landscape.

The predecessor of Glynllifon was mostly destroyed in a fire
in 1836. It was built in 1751 by Sir John Wynn (†1773), son of Sir
Thomas, apparently next to the house of 1609 built by Sir
William Glynne. The survey by John Reynolds dated 1751 shows
this to the E of two other blocks, with stables nearby to the SE.

This seems to have been a large three-storey version of the Gibbsian, mid-C18 brick villa used at Plas Gwyn, Vaynol etc., the garden side with a central semi-octagonal bay and the entrance side, E, with two-bay wings at the ends.

The present MANSION was commissioned from *Edward Haycock*   77
of Shrewsbury, to stand on the cellars of the 1751 house. It was completed and fully furnished by 1846. All that remained of its entrance front was incorporated in the new E side, again of three storeys and with a five-bay centre recessed between two-bay projections, and with a string course above the lower storey. The new house faces S. It has a palatial thirteen-bay façade, once limewashed (?), with a giant hexastyle Ionic portico and noble pediment raised on five linked arches, all of Anglesey limestone. Apart from the stone centre, the facing is a hard, seemingly original, render detailed on the architrave with Greek key etc. The balustraded loggia in the portico opens from the main drawing room, looking back to C18 Palladian precedents like James Paine's Wardour, Wilts (the s slope of the valley obstructs distant views from windows below first-floor level). The sides are articulated by pilaster strips supporting plain parapets. The long W wing of ten bays and two storeys, rising to three at the terminating two-bay pavilion, is a clever addition for Frederick Wynn after he inherited in 1888, raising Glynllifon towards the image of a great house; his designers are not known. Similar detail, the windows grouped 2–3–3–2 by pilaster strips carrying vases. The triangular pediments on the lateral *piano nobile* windows, the glazed three-bay entrance canopy, and the conservatory and its natural rock grottoes added to the first floor on rising ground to the NE are all also of after 1888. Also the cement statuary: in the loggia, four figures of the Seasons; on the apex of the pediment, Mercury, his foot poised on a ball; on the parapet plinths, four female deities.

INTERIORS. The ENTRANCE HALL, as wide as the portico, has a screen of four Ionic columns in dark grey marble with responding pilasters, the central spacing the widest. Branching stair behind with cast-iron balusters decorated with bay leaves, a frieze of acanthus leaves and lions' heads alternating; Doric guttae on the ceiling. On the first landing, Doric columns *in antis* in a pedimented window, all in grey marble, and decorative stained glass probably by *David Evans, c.* 1848. Similar details on the second stairs. To the r. of the hall a MORNING ROOM with a marble fireplace with an allegorical panel and cornucopiae; gilded cornice with consoles. Other Neoclassical rooms opening off a spine corridor. LIBRARY with a cornice decorated with trefoil brackets and scallops between. DINING ROOM with a carved doorcase, screen of two Ionic columns of grey marble, a gilded frieze and the ceiling painted with cartouches and a foliage centre. Upstairs, the ORGAN ROOM behind the loggia is in a lighter, more French taste. Gilded frieze with high-relief anthemion and honeysuckle motifs and

acanthus brackets. The ceiling with a flat-domed centre, the
square frame and centre circle decorated with acanthus, the
octagonal field between these decorated with tulips.

Service Buildings

In the SERVICE YARD behind, parts of the N walls and the paired
Doric columns at the kitchen doorway are thought to come
from the 1751 house. Remains of an early ice house, since
incorporated; a laundry with machinery like that at Erddig; the
L-plan servants' hall is an addition. Dramatic W exterior at the
1889 entrance gate.

The STABLES (Coleg Meirion Dwyfor) were re-sited W of
the new house and below it, separated by a sunk court overlooked by their main façade. By *Edward Haycock*, 1843. Large
quadrangle, now made to face W with additions for the college.
On the E side, central arch dated 1849 with a clock in the attic
and a copper cupola on Ionic columns. End pavilions with
paired pilasters and an attic storey.

The ESTATE YARD (Parc Glynllifon Visitor Centre) was
assembled in the early C19, partly in response to the rebuilding after the fire of 1836. Entrance arch under a gable and bellcote to the paved yard, now free of buildings. One- and
two-storey workshops in coloured stones with shallow brick-
arched openings, and the steward's office, all in the W range.
On the W the STEAM ENGINE HOUSE and its brick chimney,
containing the 1850s engine by *de Winton* of Caernarfon who
installed the GAS WORKS in 1857. Just below, on the Llifon,
GLANYRAFON MILL, which worked to saw timber or mill
flour; converted to electricity *c.* 1914. Standard Glynllifon
estate-building details of the mid C19.

Further W, either side of a wide roadway leading N beside
the estate yard, the very large KITCHEN GARDENS (Coleg
Meirion Dwyfor), that to the W having two gardens. Stone
walls apparently of the early C19 and so part of the 2nd Lord
Newborough's agricultural improvements. The N walls
especially high, and lined with brick.

Gardens and park

The house of 1751 looked E up the valley along a large formal
vista or *allée*, a level lawn edged with lime trees, on whose
centre line the river had been made to flow, perhaps *c.* 1740,
in a straight canal. To the N and S were early C18 grids of
enclosed gardens and paths, comparable with those at Gloddaeth (p. 451), and linking to a high terrace walk along the N
side of the valley; further S was a trapezoidal walled enclosure
with paths through trees meeting at a *rond-point*, and a kitchen
garden beside it. The next generations concentrated on larger
layouts, so by stages the gardens round the house changed
towards informality. The river was moved to a canalized course

s of the house, in place before 1836. The general character of
Glynllifon is now of two C19 periods, not easily distinguished.
The principal period is Late Georgian, for the park improvements of the 2nd Lord Newborough (†1832) soon followed by
the reconstructions of his brother the 3rd Lord. This included
further levelling either side of the river on the s, the Llifon itself
being widened as a small lake as it passes the house. It is
crossed at either end by paired drives over flat BRIDGES kept
level with the grass, with minimal parapets ending in twists of
stone. Secondarily, Late Victorian and Edwardian improvements, including the flamboyant embellishments of the 3rd
Lord's grandson the Hon. Frederick Wynn (†1932). There is
also Thomas, later Lord Newborough's not-quite-serious Fort
Williamsburg in the park, of 1761.

The PLEASURE GARDENS (Parc Glynllifon) extend
upstream from the mill for over a mile. Some of their stone
features no doubt originated as water mills. The artificial
CASCADES of the Llifon and its streams make the water fall
from level weirs and lips in the Roman fashion. They may have
begun with Sir Thomas Wynn in the early C18; stonework less
old may be attributable to any of the three C19 owners most
interested in the garden, the 2nd and 3rd lords Newborough
and Frederick Wynn, and to more recent repairs. Above the
stables where the river is impounded for the mill, a miniature
mid-C19 BOATHOUSE and BELL-TOWER in coloured brick, for
children. In the defile of the valley the s bank was enlivened
with a MILL or grotto for children, while on the N the terrace
walk was formalized with STATUARY, perhaps by Frederick
Wynn. The great feature, perhaps of the Haycock period but
more characteristic of Wynn's extravagance, was a row of three
FOUNTAINS in the valley lawn, on the line of the suppressed
canal. The basin nearest the house, now ruined, had a sculptural group of Neptune with dolphins; the end basin, with
water gushing down three circular dishes, is still *in situ*. Higher
up, at the confluence of the small stream from the E, an octagonal HERMITAGE in Reptonian Gothic of *c.* 1825. The island
made by the 2nd Lord Newborough in the river beyond was
redesigned in the late 1980s as an open-air theatre by *Howard
Bowcott* and *Meic Watts*, one of three sites forming a SCULP-
TURE PARK conceived by *Peter Lord* and based on themes in
Welsh literature. *Denys Short, Ian Hunter* and *Robert Camlin*
designed 'Plu'r Gweinydd', a hollowed-out slate mound and
story-telling area for children.

PARK. The chief monument of the Georgian park is FORT
WILLIAMSBURG, ½ m. SE of the house, above the Llifon
valley. A low earthwork with angle bastions of Continental type
in a place without relevance for actual defence, made in 1761
by *Thomas Wynn*, later 1st Lord Newborough, for training his
militia (cf. his Fort Belan, p. 431, an entirely serious shore
defence at the w mouth of the Menai Strait, 4 m. N). Entered
by a small decorative gatehouse, with a square headquarters
building at the s and barracks buildings in the bastion beyond,

and shaped to them. On a mound in the opposite corner a hexagonal TOWER with a projecting stair-turret, now burned out, of two slender storeys and all rendered. Slight batters at the base, the upper floor with large round-headed windows. Crenellated lookout platform. While this could be the addition recorded in the 1770s, it is more Regency in character and so perhaps a work of the 2nd Lord Newborough.

After 1825 the 2nd Lord Newborough began the high rubble PARK WALL, nearly seven miles long, with six gates and lodges set round it. His park had a huge rectangular nursery to the S to raise seedlings. The original main GATE pre-dated this wall, in a simpler Neoclassical version of 1797. As now, this had two lodges with a wide gate screen between, with stone lintels carried on columns and shapely Wynn twin-headed eagles on Wyattish piers with niches either side. The present Italianate, stuccoed TRIUMPHAL ARCH must be due to Frederick Wynn, c. 1890. With sculptures of a large maned lion over the centre and two eagles displaying their wings at the sides, it has magnificence combined with a measure of hyperbole. High and broad carriageway arch and two footway arches, separated by pilasters on high plinths detailed like those added at the house. Inside, a pair of COTTAGES behind triple-arched loggias.

PLAS NEWYDD. In the park 1 m. SW, in a small rectangular garden moat. Tall stone house for Thomas Glyn, dated 1632 on a rainwater head and 1639 on two heraldic overmantels. Rectangular plan with lateral and end chimneys, a two-storey porch wing on the E and a two-and-a-half-storey stair wing on the W. It was incorporated into the park as a Picturesque *ferme ornée*, with a drive arriving from the N at a diminutive cottage-cum-gate-lodge with a bellcote. A miniature yard is formed by one-and-a-half-storey ranges with steep dormer gablets and Tudor and pointed voussoir arches, including for a porch to the house. Are they too part of Frederick Wynn's works in the 1890s?

(MAUSOLEUM, 1 m. SE. Unfinished and never used. Begun in 1826 by the 2nd Lord Newborough, and continued by his son till the fire at the house. Circular tower, of massive masonry, with dressed stone openings. Cruciform chambers at ground and first floor, with a vaulted octagonal chamber above, intended for a chapel.)

GLASFRYN and RHANDIR, ½ m. NE. Built 1850 as the rectory, perhaps by *Henry Kennedy*. A slightly projecting central gabled bay with off-centre Tudor-arched door. Stalky octagonal chimney or finial (?) at the apex. Rubble, with ashlar dressings. Mullion-and-transom timber windows.

TAI ELEN GLYN, ½ m. NNE. Built c. 1890 under an endowment by Elen Glyn as almshouses for destitute spinsters. The gabled colour-washed exterior looks unexciting, but through the Gothic archway at the centre, a glimpse of round-headed openings promises more. Inside, one is suddenly in a Spanish *patio*, with an arcaded walkway on all sides and on two levels, and a richly planted garden in the middle.

MOUNT HAZEL, I m. NE. Largish early C19 house, now entirely pebbledashed. Three storeys and three bays. The front half-dormers are gabled in the centre and hipped each side, the latter added in the early C20 to replace sliding sashes tucked below the eaves. A two-storey N wing of 1904, also of three bays but smaller, and a single-storey extension beyond, both Georgian in style, by *Deakin & Howard Jones*.

BODFAN, ⅔ m. WSW. A group of three substantial houses, perhaps for related households, so an example of the 'unit' system. The earliest, to the W, is C17 and though much altered shows evidence of a big end fireplace with (former) mural stair next to it. Attached to the E via a link and a yard, a three-bay late C18 block, with a central dog-leg staircase, and connected to a gabled cross-wing to the S, perhaps *c*. 1800. (Fireplace with pilastered bolection-moulded surround and overmantel with oil painting on a raised panel.) At right angles to the NE, linked by a stone wall, the third house dated by the plaque above the front door 'B/L+A/1710' (Lloyd and Anne Bodvel). Front (S) elevation of five bays, with a steep roof and tall chimneys at both gables.

FORT BELAN, 3 m. N. Every child's dream fort, complete with cannon, ramparts, look-out towers, drawbridge etc. On a sandy spit almost touching the S tip of Anglesey, where the Menai Strait is at its narrowest and the tide its strongest. Built *c*. 1775 by *Thomas Wynn*, later the 1st Lord Newborough, as new accommodation for his Caernarvonshire Militia (previously garrisoned at Fort Williamsburg – *see* p. 429) and in answer to the threat posed by the American War of Independence. Garrisoned again twenty years later, against Napoleon. 82

Rectangular FORT. Battered, stone-revetted ramparts all round, 12 ft (3.7 metres) high, topped with a walkway. Salients in the shorter sides: to the N, a gun battery platform, with cannon dated 1846–7; the main S entrance, with drawbridge. Postern tunnel at the NE. Circular sentry towers, SE and SW. Inside the ramparts, a crenellated inner wall as second line of defence; monopitch (former) barracks leaning against it, around a grassed courtyard. Gatehouse to N, with sundial dated 1898 over the archway and timber look-out tower above and to the S, with mock cross-loops and the Wynn double-headed eagle emblem over the archway. To the E, the DOCK, built 1824–6. Narrow basin with battered stone walls, surrounded on three sides by the dock buildings: forge, stores, chain furnace (with circular brick chimney) and Dock Cottage. Rubble, with red brick dressings.

MAEN LLWYD (SH 445 541) at the SW corner of Glynllifon Park. A large pointed stone, excavated in 1875 by the Hon. F. G. Wynn who found cremated human bones and the remains of a small food vessel about 3 ft (1 metre) from its foot. The association of a standing stone with human bones is surprisingly rare.

DINAS DINLLE HILL-FORT (SH 437 565). Originally surrounded by two earthen ramparts with a deep ditch between, but the fort and its isolated hill of glacial drift are being eroded by the sea and the whole w circuit has been lost. Finds of Roman pottery suggest that the site was occupied, or re-occupied, in the C2–C3 A.D. A large mound in the interior may be an earlier Bronze Age barrow.

LLANDYGWNNING

2730

1 m. SSE of Botwnnog.

ST GWYNININ (also ST TEGONWY). In an old roundish churchyard. Rebuilt by *John Welch* in 1840, the church has the charm of the miniature. The leaning w tower is octagonal for two storeys, then goes circular for the belfry and the conical cap. Nave and chancel in one, with blank lancets to the w and wooden Y-tracery elsewhere. The interior is just as delightful – white paved floor, white walls and roof (apart from the trusses), and green-stained woodwork. – DECALOGUE on two marble tablets. – PULPIT. Two-decker, N wall. – PEWS. In two rows, C19 reusing C18 panelling. – W GALLERY. Balustrade reusing C18 communion rails. – FONT. Low round cylindrical bowl with a roll moulding beneath and on the stem; the base heptagonal. Probably C14 – STOUP, hollowed in a square stone. – MONUMENTS. Armorial slate ledger to Jane Jones †1721. Next to it, two smaller slabs, to Margaret Williams †1727 (aged fourteen days) and Elizabeth Williams †1710. Restored 2004 and looked after by a local trust.

LLANENGAN

2927

ST ENGAN (EINION). One of the beautiful pilgrimage churches of Llŷn. Nave with continuous chancel, *c.* 1520, and slightly later s nave and chancel of the same length, *c.* 1530. s porch (formerly with an upper floor) and w tower (unusually with latrine in the s wall) added 1534. N chancel E window of five lights, ogee heads alternating with pointed, the middle three with transomed lights above (cf. Clynnog Fawr). s chancel E window similar but smaller. Three-light square-headed N and s windows mostly C19 renewals, presumably based on the orig-inals though the jamb profiles are not consistent. The tower with angle buttresses to half-height, battlemented parapet with pinnacles and a four-centred w doorway with continuous case-ment-moulded jambs and head, and a panelled hood. Above, two rows of raised lettering, very worn, recording the tower's date (1534) and the dedication to Einion, king of Wales. Four-centred arch to porch doorway, on semi-octagonal responds with moulded imposts.

Inside, it is possible that the eight roof trusses over the N nave, of heavier timbers than the others and of two-centred profiles, indicate the size of the C13 church mentioned in the

Norwich Taxation. The roof is of the universal arch-braced collar type, with quatrefoil and trefoil cusping above some of the collars. Big wind-braces, mostly cusped, in two rows. Between the two naves, an arcade of four Tudor arches. Piers nearly octagonal, with a recessed obtuse-angled moulding in the longer, diagonal sides. The arches have four sunk ovolo mouldings. The slightly later s roof seems all of one build, though the arch-braced trusses are not of consistent design. Within the same building period, the N and s chancels possess slightly different roof designs still in the Perp style. The four exposed trusses on the N have Tudor profiles and cusped apex struts; the sanctuary bay has a painted celure, its embattled wall-plate resting on corbels. The date is perhaps c. 1520, like the E window, with black-letter IHS monograms on its splays. The s arcade, of early Perp type, has two continuous hollow chamfers; the E bay, probably altered, is narrowest, with a semicircular arch. Fine tower arch, richly moulded with a hood; Tudor doorway to the internal SE stair-turret, and a basket rere-arch to the w doorway. *Henry Kennedy* was architect for a restoration in 1847; another by *Harold Hughes*, c. 1911.

The dark oak FITTINGS equal the quality of the fabric. Two ALTAR TABLES, C19 and c. 1700. – Stout turned COMMUNION RAILS, late C17, re-set across both aisles. – SCREENS. Extraordinarily fine Early Tudor work, one in each chancel. Richly moulded continuous posts, head beams exuberantly carved with interlacing vines and waterleaf trail. A LOFT over the s screen, with flat ribbed coving in the Welsh fashion and open-work panels in the parapet, carved with the Instruments of the Passion, a coiled snake, a tree etc. – STALLS against the E side of both screens, with carved finials. – READING DESK. Gothic Revival, with canopied front. – LECTERN. An eagle with a snake in its talons, on a double-spiral stem. – FONT. Late Perp, with quatrefoil and tracery panels on the octagonal bowl and some rosettes on the stem. – GLASS. E windows, *Kempe* glass, c. 1900, re-set in leadwork designed by *Donald Buttress*, c. 1980. – LYCHGATE. Of uncertain date, but containing C16 timbers.

The quiet VILLAGE is centred on the church and the cross-roads. Lead mines were worked near here in the C17; the stone and brick CHIMNEY of the Porth Neigwl mine survives E of the village, 1870s. To the N, the former NATIONAL SCHOOL, c. 1845, by *Hugh Jones*. Big Jacobean gables to the front and two ends, the wild curves and the central finial exaggerated by the thick coating of cement render. Further N on the r., the OLD RECTORY. Built c. 1805 by the Rev. William Lloyd, originally as a three-bay house with pedimented gable and set-back wings. Altered, and extended to the r., by *H. Kennedy*, 1860. Not an enhancement, but the full-width veranda is attractive. The upper part of the l. wing removed after a later C20 fire. GORPHWYSFA, just N of the Sun Inn, may have been the vicarage. Early to mid-C18, gabled half-dormers, now pebbledashed. Set back to the E, THE ROCK (formerly Belle-vue, for good reason). Possibly 1816, for the manager of the

Llanengan lead mine. Two-storey, four windows but no front door. A wall joint suggests the r. half was added later. At the l. end, a handsome doorway with thin fluted columns and fanlight, and a radial oval window above. Tall window to the corner staircase. Up the hill towards Abersoch, MINFFORDD on the l. Unspoilt whitewashed cottage, probably originally single-storey with *croglofft*, later heightened to two storeys. FFYNNON ENGAN, W of the houses W of the church. Holy well, about 6 ft (2 metres) square and stepped all round in rough stone, like a miniature Indian step-well.

LLANFAELRHYS

2127

2½ m. E. of Aberdaron.

ST MAELRHYS. Tiny, with a chancel added to the medieval nave and a rebuilt W gable, but little to date any part firmly. Much irregularity, e.g. the internal set-back in the N wall, and the non-parallel N and S walls. Blocked N and S doorways, with rough voussoir heads. – FONT. C15. Octagonal bowl, with cross incised on one face. – Mid-C19 BOX PEWS, and an area of plain open BENCHES on the N side. – Mid- to late C19 brass COFFIN PLATES to the families of Ysgo and Meillionydd, both local gentry houses now much altered.

BLAWDTY. Two-storey farmhouse, earlier C19. Long and low, extended E as a service range. Tiny lower windows at both ends of the S front, to closets or mural stairs.

LLANFAGLAN

4760

A small parish S of Caernarfon, with no real core. The old church is idyllically located amongst fields overlooking the Menai Strait, about 1 m. W of the cross-roads. Across the water, Fort Belan and its dock – *see* Llandwrog.

ST BAGLAN (Friends of Friendless Churches). Single-cell C13 (possibly C12) church with late C16 or early C17 S chapel; chancel rebuilt *c.* 1800, and N porch added, incorporating a truss from the earlier chancel. Rough slate slab floors; lime-washed walls and roof timbers. Plaster celure to chancel. – PEWS. Generally C18, most with date inscriptions; some open benches, some box pews, the best in oak, with carved top rail. – PULPIT. Double-decker, with sounding-board above. – MONUMENTS. Mostly of slate and C18, some charmingly naïve. The sill and head of the porch window are reused C13 gravestones, with inscribed crosses (also a ship on the sill stone). Above the door, a reused C6 pillar-stone which reads FILI LOVERNII / ANATEMORI. – LYCHGATE dated 1722.

ST MARY. 1871, typical routine *Kennedy*, in E.E. Divided nave and chancel, N porch and NE vestry, W bellcote. Serviceable but uninspired.

Cefn-y-coed, ½ m. NNW. Built for Col. Richard Jones in the early C19. Approached up a tree-lined drive, past a gate and lodge. A stucco villa with a central bow containing curved sash windows. A tall sash window lights the stair hall behind. Hipped slated roofs, red-tiled ridges with scroll finials. To the NNW, Cefn-y-coed-uchaf, the estate farm. The largely unspoilt farmhouse has a pretty elevation; stone wall left unpebbledashed, small sash windows, four-pane light above the door.

Glanrafon Fawr, ⅓ m. SSE. Late Georgian, of three storeys. Altered on the rear (approach) elevation, but the well-proportioned stucco front still has its sash windows and central doorway.

LLANFAIRFECHAN

6875

Mountains to the s and e, sea to the N. Llanfairfechan remained quiet and rural until the roads (Sylvester's in 1772, Telford's in 1830) and later the railway (1848, station 1860) connected it to the outside world. Two English businessmen settled here in the late 1850s: John Platt, industrialist, from Oldham, and Richard Luck, solicitor, from Leicester. The village expanded as a result of the holiday trade, but has declined since the A55 expressway diverted passing trade and effectively cut it off from the sea. Of special interest is the work of the local architect, *Herbert Luck North*. The greatest concentration of his work, spanning from 1898 to *c.* 1940, is in and around the village.

St Mary (former). In a formerly round raised churchyard at the top of the village. The rebuilding of 1849, by *Kennedy*, produced a cruciform Dec church like the preceding one. Corbelled w bellcote, with arches on glum figureheads. Chancel rebuilt, and cross-gabled vestry and chancel s aisle added, 1875, also *Kennedy*. N aisle added by Fanny North in 1884 in memory of Thomas North, perhaps by *Arthur Baker*. Inside, nothing specially accomplished, except for *H. L. North*'s delicate war memorial SCREEN of 1925, painted white, red, blue, green and gold with tracery simplified to a lozenge pattern and a flat-panelled canopy with rood. Also the RIDDEL-POSTS, typical of the English Altar so beloved by *North*, and the skylight he inserted in the chancel roof. – STAINED GLASS. s transept, by *Clayton & Bell*. Other windows by *Powells* and *Ward & Hughes*. – MONUMENTS. A tablet to John Roberts †1728, the coat of arms nicely engraved. – Catherine and Dorothy Roberts †1763 and 1767, with arms in an open pediment.

Christ Church. Brazenly English. Built 1864 for John Platt of Bryn-y-neuadd by *George Shaw*, of Saddleworth in Platt's Lancashire homeland. Also from Lancashire, the yellow stone. The incumbent was a Ritualist chosen to minister to the Platt and Luck families, the increasing English holidaymakers and to stem the tide of Nonconformity (eight chapels between 1863 and 1900). Dec style, with SW tower and tall stone spire. N aisle 1874, in memory of John Platt (†1872), chancel rebuilt 1892, with vestry. Lavish FITTINGS, all intact. – Alabaster REREDOS with stone figure flanking the E window, designed by *Edmund Ferrey* and made by *Forsyth*. – Wooden traceried war memorial ALTAR and REREDOS in the Lady Chapel, *c.* 1921, by *H. L. North.* – STENCIL PAINTING on the chancel celure and vestry door, also by *North*, possibly *c.* 1912. – Ironwork SCREEN of 1894, by *Hart, Son, Peard & Co.* – In the S aisle, four Platt family PEWS, longitudinally disposed as in college chapels, with canopies and panelled backs and fronts. Most unusual of all, the ceiling is carved with quatrefoil panels and bosses. – FONT, over-ornamented, with a tall, much simplified wooden cover by *North*. – STAINED GLASS. E, *Clayton & Bell*. – Sanctuary S, *Kempe*, 1900. – W, by *Hardman*, 1872. – N aisle W (Presentation in the Temple) and N, *Kempe*, 1902. – Next to the font, another by *Kempe*, 1905. – Lady Chapel, pleasant traditional glazing of 1936.

HOREB CALVINISTIC METHODIST CHAPEL, Bryn Road. 1912. Ungainly, in a style hard to pin down, but a hint of Tudor in its mullioned-and-transomed windows. Snecked granite, with limestone surrounds and pronounced string courses. Single-storey wing to the l. and a full-height stair-tower to the r., with a window high up, originally with a steep pyramidal slated roof.

CAERSALEM CALVINISTIC METHODIST CHAPEL (former), Penmaenmawr Road. 1880. Gabled, with a small Venetian window above a big one. Projecting side doorways in yellow brick with segmental heads.

INDEPENDENT CHAPEL (formerly BRONDON ENGLISH PRESBYTERIAN CHAPEL), Penmaenmawr Road. 1873 by *Richard Davies*, in Gothic style, for English visitors. Snecked granite, yellow brick and limestone dressings. Steep roof. Central wheel window in a two-centred arch.

LIBANUS BAPTIST CHURCH, Penmaenmawr Road. 1878. Again, snecked granite and yellow brick, but the style less clear. A gable elevation divided into panels, some with windows, some blind. Zigzag brickwork at the verges. A large canted porch, all three faces gabled.

WERN ISAF, Penmaen Park. Originally 'Rosebriers'. By *H. L. North*, 1900 (date above the front door), and one of North's first houses. Ingenious plan, with the living rooms (and bedrooms above) wrapped around three sides of the octagonal staircase hall, facing the views, and the recessed entrance, cloaks etc. in the SE angle. Single-storey scullery wing tagged on at the SW. The three main bays expressed externally by steep gables, each with a pair of tall windows upstairs and shorter squarer windows below. Pebbledashed walls, vertical slating above the entrance, small-paned timber windows, steep slated roofs. Front door made from a single plank of elm, with an inset star-like prism of glass. Delightful INTERIOR. The main rooms connect through big glazed doors and have shuttered

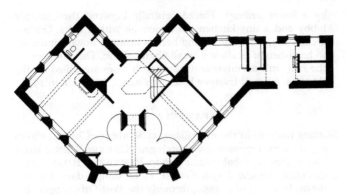

Llanfairfechan, Wern Isaf.
Plan

windows, each with a differently shaped cut-out. The living room fireplace faced with a lattice of blue glazed tiles interspersed with strips of mother-of-pearl, silvered glass and stone, and a timber mantelpiece extending upwards to form a cove. The staircase winds up on three sides of the hall, extending as a window seat above the front door and becoming a gallery on the remaining sides. The GARDEN designed integrally with the house – with terraces continuing the geometry of the house plan, contrasting areas of lawn and shrubs, and a turning circle at the entrance, with an oak tree in the centre.

To the E, WERN ISAF BACH, a small cottage built in 1925 for the cook and gardener. Timber weatherboarding, asbestos roof tiles laid diagonally, very low eaves lifted for the dormer windows. Originally with integral garage (lit by replacing roof tiles with glass diamonds), now filled in. Construction based on North's 'Merton Abbey' plans, commissioned by Morris & Co. around the same date, for 'an inexpensive scheme of construction suited to small or poor parishes, but far superior to that employed in temporary building'.

CHURCH INSTITUTE, Park Road. 1912, by *H. L. North*. A large [109] lofty hall with off-centre gable, splayed single-storey entrance wings. Stage and meeting room with cellar below at one end; hall with Buckley brick fireplace at the other, with a kitchen extending behind. Steep roofs of diminishing green slates from the Gallt-y-llan quarry (below Snowdon), hipped dormers and a conical ventilator flèche at the intersection of the gables. Timber leaded windows and North's characteristic canted downpipes. North gave his services free and for a while tended the garden. A keen amateur dramatist, he often performed in pageants here.

Behind is the CHURCHMEN'S CLUB, 1927, like a shy sister, but a no lesser building. *North* gave the land and his services free to the Church of England Men's Society social club. Large hall, with a high roof on modern cruck-trusses (now concealed by a lower ceiling). Placed centrally between the entrance lobby and a tiny kitchen, an inglenook with a brick Gothic-arched fireplace. The ceiling here is brought down intimately to head-height to allow a small library above. This connects to the hall with an internal window with roses stencilled on the shutters. A small lavatory block was added by *North* in 1935.

PERAMBULATION

Starting high up in the old village, at St Mary's Church, allows a good view. Opposite the church gate, CARREG WEN, a stone house, 1860s, probably once a shop. PENYBRYN ROAD curves downhill, passing FRON GOCH, r., of similar date. Further down, l., SHOP of *c.* 1850, formerly the Post Office, opposite, the LLANFAIR ARMS, built 1863 by *Hugh Davies* of Erw Gron. The PONT-Y-PENTRE, 1849, also by *Davies*, crosses the small river here. A handsome *c.* 1870s house, BODAFON, can be seen up Mill Road. Beyond the bridge, BRYN ROAD leads r. uphill, past Nos. 1–4 BRYN HAUL, two semi-detached pairs by *H. L. North*, backing onto similar houses in the Close. Further up, Horeb chapel (*see* p. 436). VALLEY ROAD, built 1880, continues uphill, with comfortable houses facing the river.

VILLAGE ROAD, from Pont-y-pentre down to the main cross-roads, is the centre of the village. Former police and fire stations to r., the B & H STORES to l., an imposing mid-Victorian house and shop of three storeys. Then the surprisingly large TOWN HALL, 1901, in classical style by *Richard Davies* of Bangor (son of Hugh Davies) for a local consortium. Three bays divided by pilasters, with a shop each side of the entrance. A clumsy gable replaces the original, more flamboyant curved one, and balustraded parapets with finials have also been removed. More mid- and late C19 shops and houses further downhill. At the junction with Park Road, PLAS NEWYDD, a gabled house of *c.* 1860, probably by *George Benmore*, architect to the Penrhyn estate. Also by *Benmore*, PLAS LLANFAIR COTTAGE, r., 1857 for North's grandparents. Here we see both Benmore and *North* (rear extension *c.* 1900) using the same elements in different ways.

PARK ROAD, off Village Road, winds round NE, past NORTH-COT, one of *North*'s earliest houses, 1899. On a triangular site, with a stone gateway at its prow, this house is noteworthy for elements which later disappear from North's vocabulary, e.g. timber bargeboards and exposed stone walls. BOLNHURST, first on the l., 1899, also with elements rarely repeated, e.g. eyebrow dormers, bull's-eye and round-headed windows. These give a looser, quainter feel than the more angular Gothic style which emerges at THE CLOSE, a remarkable planned development built further uphill between 1923 and 1940. The houses, variations on a few themes, are of two basic types: the lower houses double-fronted, with a central entrance, and facing each other across front gardens; the higher houses with a s corridor so the rooms face the view. At the top of the site, bigger houses. (North planned an extension to be called Upper Close, but this was never built.) Though varied to suit their owners' requirements, the houses are homogeneous in character and sit well on the site. Building materials are consistent: steep roofs slated from the Gallt-y-llan quarry, concrete brick cavity walls under painted roughcast, metal windows from Henry Hope & Sons (with whom North collaborated in determining the size and proportion of the panes, even producing their catalogue illustrated with buildings by himself, Lutyens and Detmar Blow), cast-iron gutters and canted downpipes, and always enchanting chimneys. The target was £1,000 per house, which allowed downstairs lavatories, linen cupboards, inglenook fireplaces and verandas. All have gardens, some have tiny hipped-roof garages behind. Between the gardens, traditional slate fences or beech hedges. Despite UPVC windows and filled-in verandas, the estate retains its magical quality. A perambulation can follow the lane which circles The Close, returning from the E end along Park Road, past modern housing on the site of the former St Winifred's School for Girls, tragically demolished in 1970. Here, North had done much building, including one of his masterpieces, the school chapel. Further W, PLAS FARM, part of which is early C18, and opposite, the Churchmen's Club and the Church Institute (see p. 437).

STATION ROAD was built c. 1866 down from the cross-roads towards the seafront. On the l., a varied Edwardian three-storey shop terrace, by *Richard Hall* of Bangor, c. 1905–8. A delightful variety of forms and materials. Roughcast, timber, red brick, terracotta. Half-timbered gables next to curved semi-dormers. No. 6 has shop windows with curved glass above a plinth of green glazed tiles, and a mosaic floor to the recessed entrance. Beyond, the buildings drop to two storeys, using many of the same elements. No. 10, introduces Art Nouveau details. The strangest of all, No. 15, is a low row of three shops with flats above, of terracotta, squeezed between river and street, the end elevation little more than a narrow curved bay window. Stepped gables, curiously linked with arcading. On the E side of the street is the former CASTLE HOTEL, 1883. Three storeys with an attic lit by gabled dormers. Rounded corner with Plas Gwyn Road, with steep conical roof and tiny corbelled balcony.

Station Road continues under the A55 road and the railway, terminating at the PROMENADE, built c. 1876. Here, the unassuming PAVILION (1910), and THE TOWERS (formerly Morannedd), built c. 1870 by John Platt of Bryn-y-neuadd as part of a proposed marina. A picturesque ensemble, built of rubble granite laid to courses, and limestone dressings. Gables and pointed windows. Most memorable is the cylindrical tower, with a conical roof of blue and purple slates, and windows all round for a lantern to guide in the boats. Along the Promenade to the E, boarding houses, the first in 1859. To the W, a boating pond, tennis courts etc. and further along the shore, TALFOR and GORSEFIELD, a semi-detached pair built by *North*, *c*. 1905, and WHITE FRIARS, by *North & Padmore*, 1933.

ABER ROAD leads w from the main cross-roads. At the driveway to Christ Church, a tapering, octagonal WAR MEMORIAL by *North*, 1920. Along the drive, CHURCH COTTAGES, 1860s, a pair with timber porches and raking dormers. On the N side of Aber Road, the former estate of BRYN-Y-NEUADD, home of the Platt family, demolished in 1967. Some of the fine agricultural buildings remain. The FARMHOUSE has an attached ornamental DAIRY (containing marble tables with baluster legs, walls with Delft tiles, and coved panelled ceilings with polychrome painted decoration in Renaissance style). The LODGES also still stand. The architect was probably *George Shaw* (cf. Christ Church).

PENMAENMAWR ROAD leads E from the cross-roads. No fewer than four chapels here, a school and numerous late C19 detached houses. The land slopes steeply, so most of the buildings have basements. The largest is the former CONVALESCENT HOME, 1896, by *Thomas Bower* of Nantwich, for Robert and Arthur Heath in memory of their father. Local granite and Cefn stone dressings. YSGOL PANT-Y-RHEDYN. 1908, by *Rowland Lloyd Jones*. Five half-timbered gables, the three main ones with the entrances. Small-paned tripled windows, the central light taller and wider.

LODGE, Plas Heulog, 1 m. E. 1906, by *North*. Octagonal, with steep slated roof and a complicated brickwork flourish of a chimney, almost a building in itself: a cruciform cluster of four gabled shafts supporting a fifth, set diagonally. Before the charming little building was extended, the kitchen, living room and bedroom all backed onto a central fireplace core, with a second bedroom upstairs, lit by dormer windows on the four cardinal points.

5066

LLANFAIRISGAER

No village, as Port Dinorwic, 1 m. NE (*see* Felinheli), developed in the mid C19.

ST MARY. Beautifully sited looking NW towards Anglesey. Very small nave and chancel. The w bellcote might date the church to the C14. The chancel roof has two arch-braced trusses, the nave one, all C18 or earlier. Restorations by *G. G. Scott* and *J. O. Scott*, 1865 and 1874–5. – SCREEN. 1928. Three-bay, with vine-leaf decoration to the beam. – FONT. C14 or C15. Octagonal, with two raised ornaments, a Gothic niche and a circled triskele, and an incised floral disc. – STAINED GLASS. E, by *O'Connor & Taylor*, 1874. – W, *Mayer & Co.*, Munich, 1903. – N, two by *Jones & Willis*, 1883 and 1890. – MONUMENTS. Re-set stone, inscribed 1644 RD LL, the 4s backward. – A carved stone with the arms of Sir John Wynn of Gwydir and an eagle displayed, c. 1600. – Engraved brass plaque to Catherine, daughter of Hugh Morgans of Rustrad, †1733. – Members of the Wynn family of Llanfair, †1730, 1745 and 1764. Slate plaque within white marble frame, winged cherub head below, arms in lozenge above. – John Griffith of Llanfair †1830. White marble on slate, anthemia at the corners, a shield above.

PLAS LLANFAIR, ½ m. ENE. Victorian Italianate villa of older origins. SE wing of c. 1830, r. of the porch. To the l., the side of the gabled SW wing, c. 1860–70, facing the TERRACED GARDEN. Three-bay enclosed portico, with giant pilasters and hipped roof. Large flat-headed windows above keyed round-headed ones. To the l., a recessed single bay, then a four-storey belvedere tower, stuccoed with an iron balustrade to the roof terrace.

BARN, on a knoll to l. of drive to Plas Llanfair. C17, partly rebuilt in the C18. Rubble, with stone verge copings. Voussoir-headed doorway and ventilation slits each side. At the NE gable, a C14 re-set window with Anglesey-style tracery, perhaps from the church.

PLAS MENAI (NATIONAL WATERSPORTS CENTRE), NE of the churchyard. A good work by *Bowen Dann Davies*. Built 1982 as a centre for outdoor pursuits, in a superb location on the S side of the Menai Strait overlooking Anglesey. The accommodation (boat stores, teaching rooms, pool, dining room, bedrooms etc.) arranged loosely around sheltered courtyards, stepping back and forth on plan, the purple slate roofscape sliding and cascading in sympathy with the hills of Snowdonia to the S. A tight, well-controlled palette of materials: white roughcast and granite walls (with areas of slate cladding) and dark-stained timber windows, usually arranged as long strips beneath the wide overhanging roofs. The interior less skilfully handled, perhaps too dark and the flow of space restricted. S of the main complex, a courtyard of STAFF HOUSES, intimate and civilized, an example too rarely followed by today's house-builders. Good landscaping completes the scheme, making it perhaps the best C20 building in Gwynedd.

LLANFIHANGEL BACHELLAETH
see RHYDYCLAFDY

LLANFIHANGEL Y PENNANT (C)
see DOLBENMAEN

LLANGELYNIN (C)

7773

ST CELYNIN, 1½ m. WSW of Henryd (SH 776 740). On a small remote plateau almost 1,000 ft above the Conwy valley, in an irregular and hilly, sheep-grazed churchyard surrounded by high dry-stone walls. Small C15 or C14 nave and chancel in one, S porch, N transept and W bellcote. C15 S doorway, of oak, the jambs continuing to form a round head with a high threshold; the door itself *c.* 1800. Stone porch with a C15 truss, stone seats and a peephole facing the churchyard gate. Post-Reformation s windows. C16 straight-headed E window with three cusped lights. The N transept (Capel y Meibion, the Men's Chapel) has a red sandstone, ogee-headed E lancet of *c.* 1400, and a N window. Sensitively conserved by *H. L. North* and *Harold Hughes* at different times in the early C20.

The interior is one of Caernarvonshire's least disturbed. Slab floors, rough plaster, open-backed benches. In the N reveal of the E window, half of a well-moulded Perp niche destroyed for the larger embrasure. Over the chancel, close-set arch-braced trusses (cf. Gyffin), perhaps once boarded as a celure (which North wanted to replicate); over the nave, C17 trusses. The N part of the rude dado of the SCREEN survives, with evidence for the rood loft in the beams and doorway on the s. At the w, the beam which supported the gallery of *c.* 1800. The N chapel, up two steps, has the usual broad Elizabethan roof and part of a PARCLOSE SCREEN. – PAINTINGS round the E window. 'Fear God and honour the king' in a border above. Jacobean? – REREDOS, *c.* 1700, with the IHS monogram in one fielded panel. – COMMUNION RAILS. Tall and handsome, later C17, with twisted balusters. – READING DESK incorporating Elizabethan panels. – Parts of a box pew and the C18 two-decker PULPIT, disused. – FONT. Octagonal, tapering upwards. C14? – In the s corner of the CHURCHYARD, ST CELYNIN'S WELL, with seats round. In the field beyond, foundations of a CIRCULAR HUT 30 ft (9 metres) across, perhaps associated with Early Christian occupation (RCAHMW).

MAEN PENDU, an impressive prehistoric standing stone, about ½ m w of the old church (SH 739 735). A low stone circle, almost overwhelmed by peat and heather, lies just across the track from the stone.

CAER BACH. A small hill-fort near a track leading SW from the old church (SH 744 730). A substantial bank and ditch seem to have replaced a more traditional stone-wall rampart, remains of which can be seen in the interior. Both defences have their entrances on the E. A round-house can be recognized abutting the earlier rampart. A longhouse, probably medieval, has been built over the ditch on the s side.

2929   LLANGIAN

ST CIAN. In a pretty churchyard next to a tiny tributary of the Soch river. A long single-chamber church of which the w two-thirds may be the church mentioned in 1254. The E part probably added in the late C15. Ten arch-braced collar-trusses, with two tiers of cusped wind-braces. All except three at the E (which were no doubt above a celure) and two at the w have cusped apex braces. Much restoration in 1858 by *Kennedy*, including all the lancets, and the cusped arch inserted to mark the chancel. His wheel window in the w wall and a pointed doorway were removed *c.* 1906 when the timber porch was built. – SCREEN. 1886, with rood. – PEWS. Poppyhead ends, probably by *Kennedy.* – FONT. Octagonal, 1638. – HATCHMENTS. Early C19, of the Edwards of Nanhoron (q.v.). – MONUMENTS. Timothy Edwards †1780. A fine urn, surrounded by a nautical trophy including his man-of-war *Valeur,* placed on an Ionic entablature. Green-veined marble background. By *C. Harris* of London. – Catharine Edwards †1811, with a flaming vase. – Richard Edwards †1830, by *B. Baker* of Liverpool. Big Grecian stele. – Richard Edwards †1855, with two swords on top of an inscribed scroll, by *W. T. Hale.* – Grecian tablet to Richard Edwards and others, by *Hale.* – INSCRIBED STONE, S of the church. 3-ft (1-metre)-high pillar of granite, reading downwards MELI MEDICI/FILI MARTINI/IACIT, a rare reference to a profession (doctor). Probably C5 or early C6. – LYCHGATE. 1863. Attractive, with slatted timber gables supported by curved timber brackets on stone corbels.

A delightful VILLAGE nestling below the hill, with a complement of community buildings and only a handful of houses. SMYRNA CHAPEL, 1878, and the CHURCH HALL, 1911, both small and unassuming. Opposite the hall, TŶ'N LLAN, the former parsonage. Late Georgian, with a later timber column porch and tall brick chimneys set on the diagonal, characteristic of the Nanhoron estate. At the road junction, SIOP LLANGIAN, the shop house on the corner, the former doorway at the canted angle now blocked. Further up towards the lychgate, FFRAINC on the l. with a slate plaque recording date (1850), owner and, unusually for such a simple building, the architect, *J. Owens.* The pair of houses above the church, NANT-Y-CELYN and PLAS-Y-BONT, share a blind window. Diagonal brick stacks.

LLAWR-DREF, ⅓ m. WSW. Late C16 or early C17, its external features mostly hidden by pebbledash and the windows renewed. But the original roof trusses survive. Two are splendidly cusped, and must have been seen from the chamber below.

LLANGWNNADL

ST GWYNHOEDL. Built on the burial place of a C6 saint, beside the Pen-y-graig river. The *cell-y-bedd* (burial chamber) was possibly where part of the N aisle now is. The Early Tudor church has an extraordinary plan – three naves of equal length, the overall width greater than the length. The older, central section, approximately a double-square plan, has a Perp E window, a blocked w doorway and above it, a neo-Perp window of 1850. The N nave E window is of three lights, the central one ogee-arched, with cusping and narrow panel lights similar to Llanengan. Hoodmould with headstops. Blocked narrow w

window. Three-bay N arcade, the diagonal faces of its octagonal piers being the broadest. No capitals, and only a crude
incision in its four-centred arches to create a double chamfer.
The E respond has a beautifully executed inscription in raised
lettering in countersunk panels. A second inscription round the
E pier, giving the date 1520. In the W face an ogee-headed
niche. The S arcade is less debased in style; again of three bays
and with octagonal piers with a double-recessed moulding in
the diagonals (cf. Llanengan, Abererch, Llaniestyn), capitals,
and two hollow chamfers. E window with three ogee-headed
lights; small straight-headed S window. The S doorway has big
Tudor mouldings. The date of all this work is *c.* 1530. The roofs
are simple arch-braced collared trusses, except for two with
foiled struts and two with plain ones at the N. They were
rebuilt, and the excessively cusped aisle windows inserted, by
Kennedy in 1850. – FONT. Early C16. Eight sides, with two
heads, flowers and the sacred monogram. – STAINED GLASS.
Fragments of *c.* 1500 glass in the E window traceries. – MON-
UMENTS. Upright slate slabs against the E wall of each aisle:
John Lloyd †1667, S, Catherine Owen †1717, N. – Built into
the E wall inside the S aisle, a granite boulder incised with a
circled cross, C6.

PENYGRAIG CALVINISTIC METHODIST CHAPEL. 1901. Three
round-headed upper windows, with raised lettering above,
within an arch which breaks through the base of the pediment.
Side-entry porches, linked by a slate roof.

CILYRADWY, Rhydlos, 2 m. SW. *Croglofft* cottage, partly built of
cob (earth), once typical of the locality. A change in texture
suggests the walls have been heightened. Two fields away to the
S, another cob COTTAGE, attached to a stone outbuilding. Now
derelict.

STANDING STONE (SH 208 325) in a field next to the road.
A fine example of a prehistoric marker stone. There used to be
more in western Llŷn, but such monuments are easily lost.

LLANGWSTENIN

A rural parish in the heart of the Creuddyn peninsula. No village
as such, though Bryn Pydew forms a small hamlet to the W. The
church is said to be on the site of the first Christian church in
Wales, founded by Constantine (Cystenyn in Welsh). From the
OBELISK on Bryn Pydew hill (*see* Bodysgallen, Llanrhos), a stunning panorama of the peninsula.

ST GWSTENIN. 1843 by *Thomas Jones* of Chester. Undivided
nave and chancel. Slightly projecting central bay, W, containing a three-light Perp window, extending up to a pedimented
bellcote. Curious tracery in the upper W window. At the W end
of both sides, a tall Perp window in a projecting gabled bay. W
gallery. – STAINED GLASS. Fragments of *c.* 1500, representing
the Resurrection, St Nicholas, St George, St Peter and St

Catherine. – MONUMENTS. Marble tablet, with moulded cornice and draped urn, to Catherine Lloyd of Llangwstenin Hall, †1799, by *C. Regnart.*

PABO HALL, ¾ m. WSW. A largish house of 1885 (date on a fireplace later moved to the Castle Hotel, Deganwy). The architect cannot be traced. Open veranda along the S front (formerly with a heavy timber balustrade above), with French windows and bays, one bay with stained glass carrying the name Brooke. A coved cornice to the shallow hipped roof, four gabled dormers and tall brick chimneys. A curiously uncomfortable front elevation: three bays each side of the central tablet, the l. windows more widely spaced. To the NE, the asymmetry looks more intentional, helped by a handsome tower with ogee-slate roof and lead cupola. Detached at the NW (but formerly joined by a rear extension), an elegant CLOCK TOWER of pinkish stone with yellow dressings, dated 1886 and a steep ogee slated roof. Downhill, to the SW, the former STABLE BUILDINGS, with fancy gateways, one dated 1885.

LLANGYBI   *4341*

Small clusters of houses: the oldest centred on the church, the newest about ½ m. W, comprising drab pebbledashed houses and a primary school.

ST CYBI. Single-cell building with yew-lined approach. Nave probably C14, chancel late C15, much restored by *Kennedy* in 1879. All openings apart from the plain two-centred W doorway and the big early Perp E window are his; so are the porch, bellcote and vestry chimney. He also raised the roof to its present height, reusing two original trusses at the E end. – COMMUNION TABLE. Oak, with drawers at front and side, and turned legs inscribed WP RT 1736. – FONT. C15 octagonal gritstone on modern base. – MONUMENTS. Carved oak memorial by *Jonah Jones* to John Clough Williams-Ellis (Sion Pentyrch) of Glasfryn and Brondanw, †1913, probably designed by his son *Clough Williams-Ellis.* – Marble tablet on slate, to John Lloyd of Trallwyn †1855, by *Seddon* of Liverpool. – Alabaster aedicule to Roger Williams-Ellis, RWF, †1900 at Krugersdorp aged 19. – White marble tablet on slate, to Owen Rowland of Ynys-legi, †1927. – CHURCHYARD. Inscribed stone with Celtic cross, standing upright on church-side of lychgate, C7–C9.

FFYNNON GYBI/ST CYBI'S WELL. In a delightful hidden dingle behind the church (through the churchyard and across a stone causeway). Two well-chambers of uncertain date. The larger may have had a vaulted stone roof. Attached cottage for pilgrims, provided *c.* 1750 by William Price of Rhiwlas (*see* Llanfor (M)), and at a discreet distance a privy. Cures used to be sought here for eye and skin complaints and rheumatism; the waters were also bottled.

ALMSHOUSES, E of the church. E-plan, the two wings enclosing a small yard, with a central archway under a pediment and semi-dormers. Built (or rebuilt?) by William Price in 1760, but restored in the C19 and more recently. An attractive ensemble.

GLASFRYN. 1 m. NNE of Pencaenewydd. Asymmetrical C19 house of many parts, including a clock tower, built by the Williams-Ellis family, probably incorporating an older house. Influence of Clough Williams-Ellis (who spent his early childhood here) seen at the rear.

CARN PENTYRCH. Hill-fort on the rounded hill above St Cybi's Well. It may have been occupied in the C6–C7 by the saint's protector or patron since the innermost circuit of defence is a very thick wall surrounding a small space, more like a tower than a hill-fort and comparable to a number of other citadels added to earlier defended sites, possibly in that period. The two outer ramparts, probably late prehistoric in origin, enclose a larger area. They are themselves quite complex and may have been modified, especially the middle stone rampart which has been replaced by a ditch and bank on the NW.

LLANIESTYN (C)

2734

ST IESTYN. A downhill-sited C13 church given a second nave perhaps in the late C15. The W part of the N nave is the earliest, with a N lancet and a blocked S lancet. The W doorway probably late medieval, the paired W lancets probably later again. The N chancel E window, of three lancets, looks c. 1300; similar E window in the S chancel, C15. The S nave, a bay shorter than N one, has a small blocked S doorway and a fine, low gritstone arcade. Quasi-octagonal piers with strangely tall and richly moulded bases, and moulded capitals also; E respond carved with a small head. The arches four-centred with two broad hollow mouldings, later C15. Their mitred stops either side form a plain block, perhaps meant for carving. The rest of the lancets are early C19, the likely date of the kingpost roofs. – FONT. C15. The octagonal bowl has its vertical and sloping facets carved with tracery and paterae in sunk panels. Base with deeply sunk panels. – GALLERY, half a level up at the W end of the N nave, early C19, probably for musicians. – STAINED GLASS. N chancel E, by *Moore & Son*, c. 1900. – MONUMENTS. Crude armorial slab to Evanus Saethon †1639. – Rev. Ellis Anwil †1724. A pretty slate tablet with gilded flying children in relief. – Rev. Owen Owen †1765. A simple tablet.

A tiny VILLAGE. W of the church, TŶ'N LLAN and TŶ'N LLAN BACH, a pair of whitewashed cottages, late C17, formerly the rectory. Very low upper storey, each with an attached outbuilding, the l. one at an angle. Whitewashed rubble. W, along the road and snuggling below the hill, the surprisingly large OLD RECTORY. Three-bay l. half of 1724, heightened to three storeys and extended by two bays to the r. probably in the early C19. Partitions of straw-rope under plaster survive inside.

Attached at the l., RECTORY COTTAGE. Perhaps also 1724, with alterations.

GARN FADRYN, 1 m. NE (SH 280 352). Stone-walled hill-fort with round stone houses, mainly tucked in under the rocks which form the largely natural defences on the W. A large annexe on the NE slope contains relatively few houses. Several more on the lower slopes further N, not within any defensive enclosure. On the craggy summit a small dry-stone-walled enclosure or citadel, considered to be one of the castles referred to by Gerald of Wales in 1188 as Carn Madryn. So this is one of the earliest Welsh castles, but very prehistoric in style.

LLANLLECHID   6768

ST LLECHID. Approached down a tunnel of yews. 1844, by *Kennedy*, one of his earliest churches, Neo-Norman, condemned by the Ecclesiologists: 'The western bellcote is Italian, not Norman. This comes of the same architects essaying church architecture who deal in the revived-pagan.' A monumental and clumsy church, with over-scaled detail but not devoid of charm.

Nave and chancel, with shallow buttresses, clasped and shafted at the angles. Roll mouldings to the eaves cornices, and big rounded kneelers. Windows with shafts and decorated block capitals. The large S porch doorway similar. E and W windows of three and four lights respectively, arches intersecting, the W one not convincingly resolved. Above it, the large Lombardic bellcote housing a tiny bell. The interior is very wide. Arch-braced trusses alternate with plainer ones, and rest on idiosyncratic corbels. Curved staircase to the W gallery on columns with capitals. Round chancel arch of two orders, scalloped capitals and half-octagonal responds, with a small doorway through to the panelled slate PULPIT. – REREDOS and ALTAR RAILS of intersecting Neo-Norman tracery and blind arcading. – FONT. Octagonal, with C18 cover. – LECTERN. A gilt eagle on a stone shaft with cable decoration. – STAINED GLASS. E, early glass of 1844, probably by *Charles Clutterbuck*.

PANDY NEWYDD, ¾ m. W. Large ungainly former rectory built 1865, perhaps by *Kennedy*. Steep gabled central bay, slightly advanced. Square timber mullion-and-transom windows, the two upper central ones sharing a simple hood. Curved kneelers to coped verges, and dentilated eaves.

No village, but ½ m. S the small quarrying village of RACHUB. It extends E uphill, with short single-aspect terraces at right angles, stepping one above the other off the HIGH STREET. To the l. of the High Street, at the bottom, the ROYAL OAK INN, late C19 or early C20, roughcast, gabled, a projecting bay window on brackets above the entrance; r., the former SCHOOL, dark stone with some yellow brick in the r. wing. The former CARMEL INDEPENDENT CHAPEL, High Street, by the

Rev. Thomas Thomas, 1860. Tripartite front divided by fluted Corinthian pilasters. A plethora of brackets below the cornices, windows etc., later C19.

LLANLLYFNI

4752

St Rhedyw. A cruciform church with s porch and w bellcote, on a knoll at the bottom end of the village. Of the C14 nave there is the w end with very big dressed quoins and a N voussoir-head doorway. C15 chancel, and slightly unequal transepts, both with fine quoins. Tracery from *Kennedy*'s restoration of 1879. Rearranged roof trusses of two distinct types: five bays of pointed arch-braced trusses on wall-posts over the nave, very plain yet with two tiers of basic wind-bracing and curved struts (which have a C14 look?); in the chancel and transepts, rather more rounded C15–C16 arch-braced principals, with or without straight struts. – FONT. A rough octagonal granite bowl on a cut-down sandstone block, which, like the base, has C15 mouldings. – The armorial end of a TABLE TOMB, dated 1603.
Salem Calvinistic Methodist Chapel, Ffordd Rhedyw. 1871, by *Richard Davies*. Three pointed windows. Y-tracery in the tall outer ones, more elaborate in the wider central one.
Ebeneser Baptist Chapel, Felin Gerrig. Elaborately panelled pediment, though the date 1826 must refer to an earlier building. Pilasters at the angles, a pair of square-headed windows each side of the porch.
village. A single street leading downhill past the church to the Llyfni river, which separates it from Penygroes to the N. Mostly two-storey quarry-workers' houses. Opposite the church, Bryn Eglwys, a mid-C19 L-plan house with a projecting gabled wing at the centre and Gothic window heads. s of the bridge, set back on the r., Plas Felingerrig, a substantial quarry-manager's house, with generous sash windows and a pair of gables.
Lleuar-fawr, 1 m. w. L-plan, two-storey house built by the Glynllifon estate in the early to mid C19. Fine porch doorway and coat of arms inscribed G 1675 T, remnants of a house built by Col. George Twisleton.

LLANNOR

3537

Holy Cross. In a squarish churchyard. Undivided nave and chancel, C13 but largely rebuilt in 1855 by *Kennedy*. Tall w tower: the lower storey late C15 or early C16; the upper storey rebuilt, with a saddleback roof and stepped gables. s transept of 1905, by *Harold Hughes*, slightly w of the earlier, Bodvel chapel demolished in 1855. The windows are all Victorian; the w tower door has a C15–C16 head, and replaces a former window. An unremarkable interior. – ALTAR. A polished grey limestone slab on six cylindrical legs on a green base, the shells wonderfully lucid. Presumably 1855. – REREDOS, incorporating metal panels painted with the Lord's Prayer etc. – FONT. Low, octagonal. Probably C15–C16 base and lower stem. – STAINED GLASS. E window probably by *Wailes*. – MONUMENTS. William White †1811, by *J. & M. Whitehead*. A weeping cherub drying its eyes with the urn's drape. – Sarah Gaven †1832, by *Pistell* of London. Draped urn above, shield of arms below. – In the porch, a small tablet inscribed 'Bodvel', for Huw Gwyn and Thomas Bodfel, the initials either side of the shield of arms. Early C17. – Above the porch entrance, a slate slab to John Owens, Chancellor of Bangor and vicar of Llannor 1723–37. Naïvely carved angels in low relief. – INSCRIBED STONE. In the porch, a rough vertical pillar inscribed at the bottom to Figulinus, son of Loculitus. C6. – The LYCHGATE must be by *Harold Hughes*.

LLANNERCH, ¾ m. NNE. A tall late C17 gentry house, built by Richard Madryn, High Sheriff, 1695. Of three bays and two storeys, with attic (and cellars, now filled in). A large service wing, and centrally to the rear of the house, a stair-tower for a stately dog-leg staircase, very shallow in pitch and with its own catslide roof. Carved on a beam over the foot of the staircase, 'RM KM 1687' and a fleur-de-lys, the badge of Collwyn ap Tangno. Early use of brick, for the upper gables and the chimneys.

BODFEL, ¾ m. WSW. A tall upright house of three storeys and attic, perhaps intended to be the gatehouse to a large mansion. But the probable builder, Sir John Bodvel, died prematurely. In the late C17 it was licensed for Dissenting worship, and in 1741 it was the birthplace of Hester Lynch Salusbury, later Mrs Thrale (later still Mrs Piozzi), authoress and friend of Dr Samuel Johnson. Cruciform, with the staircase wing added centrally at the rear. Three-bay front, central projecting gable. A crude portico of engaged Tuscan columns and a plain architrave frames the archway to the original passage. The windows above have hoodmoulds, with curiously angled returns. Drab cement render. (Dog-leg staircase with finely turned balusters. Painted panelling to upper rooms, some with tropical scenes, perhaps the Barbados sugar plantations owned by Samuel Hanson of Bodfel, C17.)

CEFN MINE, 1¼ m. SW. A substantial double-pile house originally with the late C17 rear staircase projection. The main block extends to the S, but it is unclear if this part is a slightly later extension or an earlier building (its large N fireplace and probable winding stone stair imply a late C16 or early C17 date). The long E block was added to, along its W side, *c*. 1800, and the original staircase block was extended to the W too, in the C19. Rendered and painted white, with sash windows. Small slate-clad dormers with raking roofs.

PLAS BODEGROES, 1¼ m. S. Small stuccoed mansion perhaps by *Joseph Bromfield* of Shrewsbury (cf. Nanhoron and Broom Hall, Llanarmon). The date 1780 on the rainwater heads; built for William Griffith, High Sheriff in 1809, perhaps incorporating an earlier house. Five-bay s front. The upper windows with segmental hoods without brackets. French windows below, with central glazed door and fanlight. Veranda, on iron columns, on three sides, with a shallow vaulted ceiling. Yorkshire sashes in the gables. The main entrance on the E, perhaps moved from the original s location (the circular sweep of the entrance drive just discernible below the lawn). Facing W, a two-storey bow, with flat roof. Grand open-well staircase, formerly leading from the vaulted s passage.

TŶ NEWYDD, ¾ m. NNW. Damaged MOTTE with wet ditch; slight traces of the bailey.

LLANRHOS

Tiny estate village s of Llandudno, originally at the entrance to the Gloddaeth estate, also called Eglwys-Rhos as the church is here.

ST HILARY. Cruciform, in a raised square churchyard. The nave without datable features, after restorations in the early C19, and by *G. Felton* in Dec style in 1861. The N transept w window has twin trefoiled ogee heads cut from one stone; this implies that the transepts are C14, so the nave is perhaps C13. s porch with early C19 elliptical arch. Internally, one or two roof timbers and bosses of *c.* 1500.

FURNISHINGS. FONTS. C13, goblet-shaped, but re-tooled. – A font with zigzag, C12(?), loose by the pulpit. – STAINED GLASS. E, figures with well-coloured borders, *c.* 1861. – s transept, early C19 grisaille panels, borders of *c.* 1861. – w, by *Ward & Hughes*, 1881. – MONUMENTS. Roger Mostyn †1652. – Mary Mostyn †1675. – Large tripartite Gothic memorial to the Mostyn family, detailing deaths from the C18. – INSCRIBED STONE, C5 or early C6 (?), SANCT/INVS/SACER/I [N]P. – LYCHGATE with a mounting block, and a drinking fountain dated 1889 and inscribed '[to] everyone that thirsteth come ye to the waters' and, more prosaically, 'This water supply is from the Llandudno main'. In the churchyard, NE, a burial ground to the Mostyn family of Gloddaeth.

N of the church, LLANDUDNO LODGE, dated 1881, and SSE, CONWAY LODGE, dated 1894, at the original entrances to Gloddaeth before the A470 road was built. Picturesque cottage-style, grey limestone with red sandstone dressings, red tiled roofs and half-timbered gables. Opposite the church, the OLD POST OFFICE, in similar style, built by Lady Augusta Mostyn as a cocoa house, to replace two village inns which she had demolished. Large, with a big central gable and corbelled gablets at both ends. Curly half-timbering at high level, above random limestone with red brick quoins and window surrounds. Heavy black-and-white timber posts to the open porch. SSW of the church, also on Conway Road, the former NATIONAL SCHOOL of 1822, endowed by Miss Frances

Mostyn of Bodysgallen. Rubble, and hipped roofs. Single-storey gabled centre with bellcote and clock face. Two-storey wings, with central porches and small-pane sashes. Further s, at the roundabout, more Gloddaeth estate houses, EDEN-HURST and WOODVILLE, a pair with fancy timber gateways like lychgates. Next door, THE NOOK, similar, dated 1897, has a small lead-domed tower over the entrance. Perhaps all by *G. A. Humphreys*, agent to the Mostyn Estate.

GLODDAETH (ST DAVID'S COLLEGE), ½ m. E. By 1500 the land in the sheltered heart of the Creuddyn peninsula was held by branches of the Mostyn family, of Mostyn Hall in Flintshire, as two estates. The respective late medieval houses, Gloddaeth and Bodysgallen, faced each other across the vale.* A smallish family seat of local importance in the C16 and C17, Gloddaeth's second heyday came in the later C19, when it was greatly enlarged (as was Bodysgallen) by Lady Augusta Mostyn till it had forty bedrooms; in this C19 boom too Gloddaeth was the powerhouse for the Mostyns' creation of the resort of Llandudno (q.v.). After a sale of contents, the estate let the house and park from 1935 as Gloddaeth School for girls, and from 1965 as St David's College.

The historic core, originally approached from the s through a gatehouse, is the GREAT HALL, raised on a paved terrace and with an external seat running the length of its s wall. As with the Great Hall at Mostyn, this is nothing if not ancestral, both in being in the medieval tradition yet made well into the reign of Henry VIII. The original design of hall and two-storey

Llanrhos, Gloddaeth, pre-Nesfield.
Engraving, mid-C19

*The Gloddaeth part came to the family shortly before 1460 by the marriage of Hywel ap Ieuan Fychan of Mostyn to Margaret, the great-granddaughter of Madoc Gloddaeth. Their current directions are marked by Gloddaeth's array of recent school buildings and by Bodysgallen's new skyline obelisk.

solar wing remains intact as built for Thomas Mostyn, a unique case for NW Wales. The hall has a rubble wall, the original elliptical-headed doorway and door, and two traceried windows. These are of three lights of ogee-headed main and upper panels and without cusping, so of similar looped design to (e.g.) the early Tudor s window in the choir of Bangor Cathedral. The SOLAR WING and the larger wing soon added to its E are of squared white limestone with continuous plinths, their respective mullion-and-sash windows replaced with Victorian stone ones. Both ranges have lateral chimneys. The LOWER END was altered inside and out by *W. E. Nesfield* from 1876, as described below. The W RANGE added by *John Douglas* in 1889 almost doubles the size of the house. In his institutional-domestic Elizabethan manner, in limestone with red sandstone dressings, it could almost have been designed for a school, yet Lady Augusta Mostyn's monogram appears on the leadwork. Asymmetrical grouping in bays of ascending height till the pair of fourth-floor timbered gables.

INTERIOR. The HALL is stone-flagged and has a dais; segmental-arched fireplace with shallow Perp mouldings and the Mostyn motto carved round the arch in raised Renaissance lettering. At the upper end oak panelling made with tall posts with beaded mouldings and shaped as trefoiled heads. Above this a deep coved canopy in lath and plaster, curving forward to meet the bressumer and the plain vertical posts of the timber frame above it. This canopy is wholly painted; the visible layer is late C19 but may follow original work likely to have been done in the 1580s. The ground in black-on-grey arabesque work; against this a field like an embroidered cloth with the arms of Elizabeth I and other heraldry, between classical colonnettes. At the lower end, a post-Restoration gallery with a balustrade of twisted balusters, resting on a bressumer carved with bay-leaf garland. On the wall behind, a second large panel of grey arabesque painting of the Elizabethan stage (?), removed in the late C19 by an Italian by the *strappo* method from on top of earlier wall paintings in the Solar. The hammerbeam roof is exceptionally ornamental. Four arch-braced trusses with foiling in the apexes; firring struts support the lower purlins, then two more tiers of purlins with short cusped wind-braces. All these elements and the rafters are richly moulded.

The SOLAR WING has its original dimensions, but the use of the parlour below as the family dining room in the C18, the apparent use of the Solar as a chapel, and some later C19 remodelling including fine doors, Gothic Revival door furniture and staircase modifications, make the rooms less easy to understand. The PARLOUR (now Headmaster's study) has its full length, with a blocked mullion-and-transom, ovolo-moulded window at the N, three beams, and small-field wainscot. Fireplace with segmental arch inscribed Thomas Mostyn Armiger, with the arms of Tudor Trevor and Madoc Gloddaeth in the spandrels; rectangular Perp-moulded frame

with more arms in the label ends. Copper hood with the head
of Medusa, by *Douglas & Fordham*, 1894. The broad STAIRS
have twisted balusters and low handrails and look adapted
from a well to a dog-leg plan, with an odd length of older cut-
out balustrade above. They lead past evidence of the Georgian
house to the ANTECHAMBER and Solar, seemingly the original plan. Over the partition doorway a gilded plaster Renaissance cartouche inscribed T(homas) B(ridget) M 1673. The
three-bay SOLAR is wainscoted. Its gable walls and that of the
antechamber are painted in ochres with a floral or tendril
design, apparently C19 but over another. Again a hammerbeam
roof, but slighter than the hall's and with plain apex struts; one
of the angels on the hammerbeams could be original. On the
inner gable wall are crudely painted angels with the symbols
of Christ's Passion. Was this always a chapel? Or was it converted after the Restoration, like the chapel of the family's
Wynn cousins at Gwydir Uchaf? The taller E WING could
perhaps be associated with the reused staircase, and with an
account for 'the new parlour' dated 1664.

The LOWER END was shown in a drawing of 1831 still to
have its historic form and large lateral kitchen chimneys. What
is visible is its S wall, again of squared white limestone, and a
well stair at the N giving access to three floors including the
hall gallery, their baluster types being the same. *W. E. Nesfield*
was engaged by Lady Augusta Mostyn in 1876 for some
admirable alterations. First a small STUDY in the irregular
space W of the hall, where his nicely proportioned bay window
clad in lead and slates fits well with the hall. In it, heraldic glass
of not later than 1586. Off here, a new full-height DRAWING
ROOM, expressed externally in a canted, thrice-mullioned bay
window under a half-timbered gable. A subtle link with the
long C18 bedroom range behind was created by Nesfield with
his ingenious STAIRCASE, which passes other spaces also. The
bottom level is a wainscoted room where the stair starts with
a carved lion newel; it rises only one storey to galleried spaces
decorated with dark wallpaper and stained glass and landings
with benching, beneath a gilded ribbed ceiling. Perhaps the tall
brick chimneystacks throughout were part of his overhaul.

SCHOOL AND SERVICE BUILDINGS. E of the mansion on the
same level, Neoclassical STABLES of *c.* 1820 with pedimental
centre and taller wings, all with segmental windows, and later
C19 loose boxes. Then a long barn, converted as a service wing
in 1897 and again as an ASSEMBLY ROOM. On the opposite
side a tall C16 DOVECOTE, square on plan, with four stepped
gables and alighting shelf.

W of the mansion, additional buildings in a Gloddaethian
manner by *T. Griffith* of *Griffith & Williams*: TRYFAN, 1987, a
large boarding house disguised by stepping it down the hill;
CHELSEY HOUSE, 1997 and more vernacular; AYRTON
HOUSE, 2000. Further buildings are planned at the W.

GARDENS. The small box-hedged KNOT GARDEN in front of the
great hall dates from Lady Augusta Mostyn's Arts and Crafts

phase. The TERRACED GARDEN and wider landscape of Gloddaeth contain significant features from the C16 on. The wooded framework and outer walks are attributed by Pennant to Sir Roger Mostyn (†1739); within are earlier layouts. The car park in front of the house covers the former courtyard, recorded by William Williams (?) in the late C18; the parapet may be C17. Below, a broad grass terrace (where a lead version of the Farnese Hercules is re-sited) with another C17 (?) parapet. E of this, fragments of walls including a cyclopean doorway dated 1658. Below that a high retaining wall for fruit trees, and a long level terrace, below which again were sloping kitchen garden beds. On the flat ground a straight canal, with semicircular masonry ends. The great meadow or Lawn was defined by planting in the early C18, these trees being, Pennant says of Sir Roger's works, 'laid out, according to the taste of his time, in straight walks, intersecting each other, or radiating from a centre, distinguished by a statue'. While some of this can still be traced, the enormous maze laid out in the early C17 on the hilltop of the Gaer W of the house, and recorded on Thomas Badeslade's survey of 1742, cannot.

LODGE. Set back beyond the drive entrance. In similar style to the other two lodges (*see* p. 450), dated 1884 and with Lady Augusta Mostyn's monogram.

BODYSGALLEN, ¾ m. SSE. A four-square gabled house of complex plan and evolution, unified by its red stone and its vernacular, mullion-windowed style. The residence of the Wynn family, and then their Mostyn heirs from 1776 to 1967. The harmonious appearance derives partly from Arts and Crafts consolidation by Lady Augusta Mostyn (cf. her stewardship of the sister Mostyn seat of Gloddaeth across the vale to the N) and her son Henry Lloyd Mostyn, the owners from 1878 to 1938 – unlike at most such accretive *plasau*, which were replaced in the C19. Falling ground all round, formed into gardens *c.* 1600 and largely completed before the present house was begun, makes it loom like a castle.

The W RANGE with the tall gabled SW end dated 1620 is the oldest existing part. Large enough to stand as an independent hall-and-great-chamber house, it resembles local C17 solar towers too. On its r. an original full-height oriel tower, and at its centre a full-height porch-tower of 1915. Its SW wall has a basement with a voussoir doorway and two windows; the first floor a four-light window; the second again a four-light window but with a full hoodmould and label, rising at the centre for the datestone with the initials of Robert and Katherine Wynn who built it; the third storey has two two-light windows and the attic floor one of these. This end gable and the two small NW ones have plain copings, as does the CROSS-WING added not long after at the NE of the NW front; three storeys of windows placed in the local way either side of the flues for its high and stark gable-end chimney. This wing has late C19 mullion-and-transom windows for the library in the N angle, and a step-gabled projection dated 1884 to light the staircase.

Against the SE wall of the Jacobean block, tall chimneystacks of complex plan.

Attached to the 1620 range NE of the chimneys, a narrow six-storey TOWER occupies the place beyond the cross-passage where a domestic stair-tower would be expected. Its well stairs have been rebuilt using early C17 oak balustrades; from the third floor up, however, the steps are part of a newel stair of c. 1300, set anti-clockwise. Since Robert Wynn, from the Salusbury house of Berthddu further up the Conwy valley, was a descendant of the Wynns of Gwydir who bought the site of Maenan Abbey after the Dissolution, and since the steps are faintly red like the Deganwy stonework from the abbey surviving elsewhere, this spiral stair could well have been shipped downriver to Bodysgallen in the second half of the C16, and then re-erected a second time (the rainwater head is dated 1752) as a romantic look-out.

This leaves open whether the Bodysgallen of before 1620 had a medieval or Tudor hall like Gloddaeth, or whether it was a learned Renaissance building made for Richard Mostyn (grandfather of Robert Wynn's wife Katherine), a classical scholar and collector of Welsh manuscripts. It is frustrating to know so little of the preceding buildings, whether they were of timber, and whether burned down. The obvious site for this early house would be on the SE, above the first terrace garden. In its place are two further WINGS or 'units' common to Gwynedd *plas* complexes, a three-storey block (perhaps of the C17) with four-light upper windows in its gable on the W, and a narrow two-storey wing dated 1730 between its gable-end windows on the NE, added to the older E range. In the C18 these formed a seven-bay front with sash or mullion-and-transom windows, since obscured by more irregular Neo-Jacobean enlargements on the upper terrace, the largest dated 1905. The SE front became a service side as a result, and the SW became the garden front, with the addition in a space next to the 1620 hall of a single-storey WING for a drawing room, dated 1894 with the initials H L M and P G M. Almost central and projecting from the older mass, this consists of a bay with a five-light, twice-transomed window under a gable with balls on the kneelers, boldly set against a wider, step-gabled block. The architect is not known, and nor is the date for the general replacement of the Georgian sash windows with stone frames.

The INTERIOR of the 1620 range is uncommonly intact, both the hall and the great chamber above it having small-field wainscot and fireplace lintels on moulded brackets rather as at the Elizabethan Plas Mawr at Conwy. In the chamber, as well as Neo-Renaissance iconography, there is a painted overmantel perhaps of the C18 with a pair of shields with many quarterings, between still-life panels of flowers. The Plas Mawr chimneypiece design taken up also in the Victorian drawing room. The wide staircase of 1884 is a copy of the late C17 dog-leg stair at Gloddaeth, with twisting balusters.

The OUTBUILDINGS were converted to hotel use *c.* 1980–5 by *Bowen Dann Davies*, in a continuing but modern use of the vernacular. E of the house, the former STABLEYARD, largely C18–C19, with a rectangular dovecote tower on its W; to the NW the scattered former SERVICE STRUCTURES. Further NW and below, BODYSGALLEN FARM, with C18 barns tactfully converted for a swimming pool etc. by *Eric Throssell*, 1991. The present drive replaced an older one to the S in the C19; it has an early C20 LODGE.

GARDENS. The Renaissance garden formed *c.* 1600 is a significant survival by any measure, but was oddly little mentioned by visitors whose eyes were taken by the picturesque scenery. With the formal LANDSCAPE around, the garden continued little changed till Lady Augusta Mostyn's revival in the late C19, and Historic House Hotels' restoration of the whole in the late C20.

On the sheltered SE slope a series of four terraces with high walls starts a hierarchy of classical garden designs. The top one is without historic features, except that the terraced upper level N and E of the house retains part of the 1860s layout. The second S terrace is a *hortus conclusus* with a Gothick cottage at the NE and the remnant of a gazebo (?) at the SW. The third level is a subtle SUNK TERRACED GARDEN, inspired by Tuscan gardens on declivities and very rarely surviving from such an early date in Britain. It is a rectangle measuring 90 by 60 ft (28 by 18 metres), overlooked at the upper long side from a narrow VIEWING GALLERY with a parapet of thin limestone slabs, placed upright, with chamfered edges. It is entered from this level by ramps of steps with similar parapets down the short sides, the NE one *in situ*, the SW one turned round parallel with the gallery to ease access from the parts of the SW terraces rearranged *c.* 1900. The geometrical box parterre on the central plot is probably of the late 1880s. A final level outside the lower margin, formed by a COPED WALL of limestone 110 yds (100 metres) long and plainly intended for fruit trees, links the shelter of this pleasure garden with the larger enclosures for production to the W. At the NE of this vista an arched ARBOUR with pyramidal roof by *Bowen Dann Davies* spans the path; beside this a Victorian GREENHOUSE moved from Gorddinog near Llanfairfechan.

The plan of the terraces cut from the rock SW of the house platform is less orderly. Its chief feature is now the stone STAIRWAY leading down from near the drawing room to an intermediate level with a rectangular pool on axis, which together with topiary compose the ideal of the Edwardian garden recorded in *Country Life*.

Paired WALLED GARDENS lie below the house to the SW, in a dingle seemingly filled and levelled for them. Brick enclosing walls of mixed bond, *c.* 1600. The first garden measures 51 by 57 yds (47 by 53 metres), the second less, because of the rocky site. Four dividing paths meeting at a central well, the paths now linked to Victorian doorways in the walls and lined with box, and the four compartments laid out as rose gardens after *William Goldring*'s plans for Bodysgallen of 1904–5.

Around this broadly rectangular historic core to the N, E and S are parkland and old woods, with an abandoned late C18 drive leading N to Gloddaeth. To the W, however, planned irregular wilderness paths lead to two further instances of Renaissance gardening, still on this unexpectedly generous scale. Along the lip of the valley to the W the PANORAMA TERRACE and the MOUNT offer views of the Conwy River, Deganwy Castle and the sea. The terrace, some 15 ft (4.5 metres) wide, runs for 130 yds (120 metres) between a bank and a retaining wall. To its N the path leads on to the sophisticated and apparently original design of a zigzag path up the natural rocky viewing mount; its summit now given a focus by the folly castle ruin in pink stone designed by *Eric Throssell*, 1991. Visible from the mount, an OBELISK (by *E. Throssell*, 1992–3), of ochre stone from the site, on the rounded summit of Ffrith Hill at Pydew, ½ m. S. The 64-ft (20-metre)-high silhouette does much for the quarry scar on the N of the hill, and appears also as a component in a surprising number of far views.

TŶN-Y-COED, ½ m. S. Large Gothic pile, built in 1878 for a Liverpool timber merchant, by *G. Felton*. The pointed blind relieving arch in the original central part reminiscent of Waterhouse. Extensions both ends, 1899 and 1927, in a plainer, Tudor style. Now a long rambling front, with no clear balance. Snecked rock-faced limestone, with yellow stone dressings.

BRYNIAU TOWER, Bryniau Hill, ½ m. W. A round rubble tower, about 20 ft (6 metres) high. A look-out tower or windmill, probably medieval.

LLANRHYCHWYN

ST RHYCHWYN, 1 m. SSW of Trefriw (SH 774 616). In remote farmland, about 1,000 ft above the Conwy valley. The churchyard is square, with old yews and a LYCHGATE dated 1762. Two parallel naves. The S nave, of coursed boulders, may be the church founded by Llywelyn the Great, *c.* 1200. The RCAHMW inventory suggests the W and battered S walls may be of this date, with the chancel end added in the C15. S doorway with a shallow voussoir arch, perhaps more of the C15 kind. The C16–C17(?) door, hung Roman-wise on a post hinge, has bevelled panels. Much re-detailing in the C17, but the E window head, of two cusped lights, is C15, though re-set beneath a datestone for 1753. Rough angle-braced close-rafter roof, with C19(?) boarded celure. The N nave, of equal length, was probably built by Maredudd ap Madog, *c.* 1520. E window with a Tudor monolithic head, and W bellcote with a C14 bell. Both roofs are covered with thick graded slates. The internal division is formed by three square piers with similar responds, carrying horizontal timbers. The C16 roof of the N aisle is a curious one: the principals are set further apart as they go E, and at the W their cusped wind-braces, in two tiers, have notches in the point of the cusp. The dark INTERIOR is flagged with slate, a step higher at the W. – On the S nave COMMU-NION RAILS, the very early date of 1636. Tall and sturdy turned balusters, tapering slightly towards the base. – FONT, square, tapering downwards, with bevelled angles. On two steps against the W pier. Of C12 type. – At the W, a HORSE BIER. – In the N nave, a two-decker PULPIT and DESK. The former is octagonal and dated 1691 in a nicely cut shield, the latter is early C18. – STAINED GLASS. N nave E, the Crucifixion in the upper part, probably 1533. – S nave E, beautifully drawn York-type glass, probably c. 1460. – N windows, a variety of frag-ments, C16–C19.

LLANRUG

ST MICHAEL. The uneven and battered walls of the low nave and tiny chancel look medieval, but no stonework shows beneath the dreary obliterating restoration of 1856 by *Kennedy*. Two strangely shallow transepts. Dec fenestration, the trefoil-headed chancel N window possibly copying the old one. W bell-cote, perhaps 1767, the date of the bell. Before 1856, the appearance must have been charming – Lewis's *Topographical Dictionary* records it as 'whitewashed all over, not even except-ing the roof'. N porch and C16(?) timber N doorway with an elliptical-headed frame. Roof trusses mostly C16–C17, and plain, except the fourth from the W which has hammerbeams on well-moulded wall-posts (renewed above). What did this elaboration mark? – PULPIT, mid-C19. Fixed to the front, a carved wheatsheaf, the emblem of Duncan Alves of Bryn Bras Castle, early C20. – STAINED GLASS. Late C19–early C20, mostly (all?) by *Jones & Willis*. – Big stone LYCHGATE, of 1714.

LLANRUG CALVINISTIC METHODIST CHAPEL, N of the Post Office. 1867. The pediment broken by an arch, with a wooden rose window clumsily elongated to form a flat sill. Dark crazy-paving-style granite, raised quoins and window surrounds in a lighter colour.

CAPEL-Y-RHOS CALVINISTIC METHODIST CHAPEL, ½ m. ENE of the Post Office. Late C19. Central pediment with hipped side roofs. Segmental arch containing a triplet. Mono-pitch porch, with its own pediment. Smooth render, raised quoins and stepped Lombardic verges.

TANYCOED CALVINISTIC METHODIST CHAPEL, ½ m. SSE of the Post Office. 1901, by *Rowland Lloyd Jones*. Three-bay front. Pedimented, with recessed arch containing a two-light window above the door, all with plain pilasters, capitals and entabla-ture. The side bays lower, with panelled parapets hiding the hipped side roofs. Elegant pilastered windows, margin sashes. SUNDAY SCHOOL to S.

The VILLAGE has no real centre and too much pebbledash. The church out on a limb to the w, the former railway station to the E, serving the former Caernarfon to Llanberis branch line opened in 1869. Here, the PONT RHYTHALLT bridges over the Seiont, the railway and the Padarn slate railroad (1843) which ran between the Dinorwic quarry and Port Dinorwic. W of the Post Office, HAFAN ELAN. A relaxed group of twenty-four single-storey dwellings for elderly people, with community room and warden's house, by *Bowen Dann Davies*, *c.* 1981. Short terraces arranged around two well-landscaped court-yards. Conventional slated roofs on one side of each terrace; on the access sides, the very steep roofs sweep down to nearly waist-height, with small skylights for the windows and cut-back recesses for the doors.

PLAS TIRION, ¼ m. SW of the church. *c.* 1800, said to incorporate a C16 house in the central block. At each end, a projecting bay with shouldered gables, the r. one with a blind loop. Veranda on cast-iron columns between the wings facing the garden (W). Gothick windows with Y-tracery. Tudor-arched front door. Sober without its former stucco. Cantilevered open-well stair cutting across a tall latticed window. WALLED GARDEN to E, STABLES and COACHHOUSE to SW, all early C19. Another STABLE BLOCK to the NE, late C19.

LLWYN-Y-BRAIN, abandoned in the grounds of the Seiont Manor Hotel, ½ m. N of the church. In a superb raised location overlooking the Seiont river, with lawns to NW and SW. An abandoned early C19 country house, small but with grand aspirations. Three-bay NW front with pleasing proportions, but unbalanced by the single-bay mid-C19 addition to the l. Porch, with very shallow slate-slab roof and fanlight to doorway. Stuccoed (removed from NW front). C20 hotel to the NE.

RAILWAY CARRIAGE SHED, ½ m. SE of Pont Rhythallt. Very long (140 yds, 130 metres) and very thin (10 ft, 3 metres). Built 1895 by the Padarn slate railroad. Roughly coursed slatey stone. Louvred timber windows. Slender iron kingpost trusses at close centres. Damaged by fire *c.* 2005.

PRYSGOL, 1 m. SW of the church. A house of some stature, rare in the hinterland E of Caernarfon, but much altered. Part of the Vaynol estate in the later C16, but the former cruck base in the E wall indicates an earlier hall-house. Very thick N and S walls at ground level, thinner walls above, suggesting the house was enlarged in the late C16. Stepped W gable, probably C17.

BRYN BRAS CASTLE, 1 m. ESE of the Post Office. A Romantic folly on a scale that aspires to the solid defensiveness of Caernarfon Castle and the more picturesque Neo-Norman of Penrhyn Castle but somehow fails to deliver on both counts, the result of later accretions and the drab grey pebbledash which covers the entire building.

At its heart – and on the fork of two old roads connecting Llanberis to Caernarfon – is a mid-C18 farmhouse. In 1828 Thomas Williams married into the Panton family of Plas

Gwyn, Pentraeth (A) and put his newly acquired wealth into
converting the house to a castle, *c.* 1830–2. *Samuel Beazley* or
William Provis, Telford's engineer for his two bridges, have been
suggested as possible architects. Williams attached a three-bay
wing to the E side, facing the gardens. Of two storeys but
looking one, the bedrooms hidden behind a tall embattled
parapet, perhaps with open loggias E and W. Dividing the three
E bays, four embattled turrets, exceedingly tall perhaps to
counteract the thrust of the three big arches to the lower
French windows. Three further towers added beyond the
original house, W, one at the centre, the other two at the
corners of walled service yards.

A second phase of work was begun *c.* 1832, extending the E
front to the N with a D-plan tower (later the library, then a
chapel) and to the S with the FLAG TOWER, bigger and with
an attached stair-turret. Squeezed between the Flag Tower and
the main E wing, the main entrance leading to a big Neo-
Norman hall. From this, a wide passage runs along the rear of
the E wing, first through a small ante-hall, then through the
stair hall before reaching the Dining Room and Library. The
triangular site was later filled in up to its W prow by successive
owners, both J.Ps. and High Sheriffs: F. S. Barnard, 1897–1917,
then D. E. Alves, an oil magnate from New Zealand, 1920–40.

But to return to the second phase which is undeniably the
most significant. Here the aspirations of Penrhyn Castle (built
1827–40) were perhaps met, if on a much reduced scale;
indeed, *Thomas Hopper* was probably the architect. The big
slate fireplaces in the Hall and main rooms are virtually identical to some at the grander castle, and the heavy Neo-Norman
detailing of the openings and ceilings bears his hand. Particularly fine is the main room in the Flag Tower, approached up
a wide circular stair. Round-headed arcading encircles the
room, each capital different. Above doorhead height, a deep
band of blind intersecting tracery, then a decorative plaster
ceiling. Four round-headed windows, deeply set and narrow.

Hopper's hand begins to peter out N of the Hall, and Alves
takes over from 1920, stamping his initials, his motto 'Deo
Favente' and his wheatsheaf wherever he could. He enlarged
the ante-hall with a three-sided bay filled with decorative glass
windows and inserted the chunky Jacobean-style staircase,
with barley-twist balusters and an elaborate landing arcade, all
madly emblazoned. The Dining Room is a curious collection
of re-set panelling, dated 1680 and 1709, and a Jacobean fire
surround and overmantel. The Library is the work of Barnard,
c. 1907, after a fire in the 1880s. More Jacobean woodwork,
with naturalistic vines, acorns, oak leaves etc. An ornate fire
surround, with overmantel carried by cherubs and a
decorated-glass window immediately above. E window, of plain
intersecting lancets and containing late C19 glass perhaps by
Heaton, Butler & Bayne. The upper rooms contain less of
interest. The former E loggias now contained within the
bedrooms, the crenellated parapets having been heightened

and sash windows inserted, presumably before 1897. One other curiosity to note: a bathroom lined with large green Vitrolite tiles, a mirror ceiling, and 1920s fittings.

Across the lane to the s, a big complex of former OUTBUILDINGS, including the Head Gardener's house (now Fernlea), all turreted and embattled. Alves converted the stables to a ballroom, and connected the two sites with a castellated BRIDGE over the lane. On the turret at the castle end, a complicated iron beacon with heraldic dragons and the crown of Richard II, by *D. J. Williams & Son* of Caernarfon, 1925.

The GARDENS are uphill E of the main front, either side of the entrance drive which sweeps down from the SE. Created between 1837–87, with stream, pools, waterfalls, ornamental bridges, lawns, woodland walks, a rosary and a walled garden. Improvements carried out in the 1920s by *Alves*, including the castellated SUMMERHOUSE, two stone statues of gladiators and the walled 'knot' garden.

LLANWNDA

ST GWYNDAF. Rebuilt by *George Alexander* in 1847 as a cruci-form Neo-Norman church with an apse. Coursed rubble, with ashlar windows. Double bellcote. A spacious interior. Plain arches to the chancel and transepts, and rounded arch braces to the trusses. – MONUMENTS. Fixed to the w wall, two sides of the table tomb of Owen Meredith †1612. Each is carved with three arches on pilasters, with shields either side; the kneeling family of three generations occupies four recesses. – Thomas Bulkeley M.P. †1708, a handsome wall monument, perhaps by *Robert Wynne* of Ruthin. Drapery bearing inscription held up by three putti; sprays of lilies etc. above and two more flying putti holding the Bulkeley shield. – Anne Quellyn †1730 and Hugh Quellyn †1749, with a Baroque shield above. – Lady Elinor Williams †17?9 and the Hon. Mrs Lumley Bulkeley †1718, a pair of slightly inept Early Georgian memorials, one dated 1733, with segmental architraves on pilasters and carved marble garlands. – Catherina Quellyn †1746 aged seven months, in an oval frame. – Nicely lettered tablets to Robert Armstrong-Jones †1943 and Ronald Armstrong-Jones †1966. (In the churchyard, a showy sarcophagus to R. W. Jones †1896.)

VILLAGE. A curious settlement pattern, with the church to the N, near the junction of the former Caernarfon to Afonwen branch line with the Welsh Highland Railway, and the village ¾ m. S, consisting of a much altered INN and a TERRACE with gabled ends and lean-to veranda to the six houses between. Along the main road, mostly C20 buildings, but TAFARN HEN, an early C19 former tavern, stands on the corner of the road to the church.

MAENGWYN, ½ m. S. A pretty, early C19 two-storey house with single-storey wings. Hipped roofs, blind central window.

VORYD LIMEKILN and COTTAGE, 1½ m. W. A rare example beside a tidal mud estuary. Slightly battered walls to the kiln, and crudely embattled parapets.

PLAS DOLYDD, Dolydd, 1 m. S. Behind the house, an C18 COTTAGE of roughly coursed rubble. Pigeon holes in the N gable. Facing the house, a catslide roof over the upper doorway which is approached by a flight of steps.

4739

LLANYSTUMDWY

A pretty little village straddling the Dwyfor, now by-passed by the main Porthmadog–Pwllheli road. Knitted together as a cultural landscape by two factors. David Lloyd George (1863–1946) was reared at HIGHGATE on the main street, lived his last years at Tŷ Newydd, N, and is buried at its heart, near a museum devoted to his political achievements. The architectural expression of these components is largely due to his neighbour *Clough Williams-Ellis*, whose response is a complex work of high landscape and emotional qualities.

ST JOHN THE BAPTIST. In a partly round churchyard, with no certain remnants of the original church, nor of one built in 1819. Present church by *Kennedy & Rogers*, 1862. Stubby little chancel. W bellcote continuing down as a pair of buttresses on a wide battered base. Unusually wide and spacious nave, roofed with simple trussed rafters. Tiered seating at rear. High Victorian stone and marble PULPIT, 1878. – STAINED GLASS. E, 1863, by *T. Baillie & Co*.

MORIAH CALVINISTIC METHODIST CHAPEL. A distinguished and original essay in this building type by *Clough Williams-Ellis*, 1936. In a colonial Palladian style, chastely coloured, and placed long-side-on to the village street. Rectangular hipped-roofed centre with semicircular bows at each end, the rectangular element in the local pale dressed granite, the apses in fine grey render. Deep eaves and architrave combined, painted white; small-slate roofs following the plan; tall square open cupola with ogival roof painted copper green. The central feature, on axis more-or-less with the first of the memorial gateways, is three round-headed windows under a pedimental gable, with the elliptical slate giving the chapel name and date of the preceding building (1866) and this one, under a white garland. This centre is framed by a pair of Clough's signature Irish yews; axial gateway from the road, with slender urns.

LLOYD GEORGE MUSEUM. Entered by a tall recessed gateway opposite the chapel, a commemorative walk bends gently westwards up the slope to Lloyd George's grave. The concept of using spare sites in the village to link the two expresses the fascination of *Clough Williams-Ellis* in small-scale village centres. Wrought-iron GATES of expensively florid design compared to the rest of the project, so perhaps bought-in and then enlivened with Clough motifs. The original MUSEUM building of 1960 is

a modest, one-storey building: six sash windows with an elliptical slate placed centrally, to give its purpose and date in the
architect's cursive writing. The bronze head of Lloyd George
is by *K. Scott.* This stands on the r. of the walk; attached is a
larger GALLERY and LECTURE THEATRE of 1990, by *Dilwyn
Gray-Williams,* of *Gwynedd County Architects,* bolder in scale,
still classical but distinguished by Postmodern freedom, the
theatre expressed by its tall piers and quadrant plan. The upper
GATEWAY is more reticent than the lower. Again with tall stone
piers and flaming vases, and black iron gates with plain verticals curving down to an LG monogram finial; a pair of elephants and castles confronted at the sides (why?). This opens
across a double-apsed space to the public lane and then to the
grave itself.

GRAVE OF DAVID LLOYD GEORGE. A hero's burying-place and a
consummate work of small-scale landscape design, by *Clough
Williams-Ellis, c.* 1945. Narrow platforms of pitched stone lead
down between low walls to a stone arch in profile with walls
swept up to a little gable. This screen lacks a third dimension
apart from that suggested by the false perspective in its fixed iron
gate, and the open *œil de bœuf* with the LG monogram again. The
life commemorated was intimately linked with this place: in old
age, Lloyd George would sit on the boulder now used to mark
his grave, within hearing of the river below this wooded slope.
The elliptical plan, sunk and raised along the contour above the
river, recalls the watery aesthetic of the Villa d'Este gardens at
Tivoli; the classicism being contained in a structure where the
visitor follows the fall and rise of the steps around the grassy
platform but is denied access to it, and a Welsh voice being
expressed in the ellipse of pitched stones under the boulder, and
the closeness of the beech wood around.

TŶ NEWYDD (The National Writers' Centre for Wales), ½ m. N.
Imposing mid-C18 house built around a much older core. The
approach is along a tree-lined drive, then through fine iron
gates and a path paved with sea-pebbles on edge. The main
C18 façade was embellished by *Clough Williams-Ellis* in the early
1940s. Much of the inside was altered by him, and he formed
the first-floor library with coved ceiling and semicircular bay
window facing the S garden. Medieval features include a length
of oak partition in the dining room (possibly brought from
elsewhere) and remnants of a roof truss at the rear; from the
C18 house, some window shutters in the front rooms and a
Chinese Chippendale balustrade to the main staircase. The
house and nearby range to the NE were extensively refurbished,
and a new staircase/conservatory added, in 2005–6 by *Adam
& Frances Voelcker* (E range by *Maredudd ab Iestyn*). Glass art
work by *Bill Swann* and *Catrin Jones.* TŶ NEWYDD COTTAGE,
E of entrance is a whitewashed bailiff's cottage by *Clough
Williams-Ellis,* in a Dutch style, with rounded corners and an
eyebrowed porch.

TŶ CANTON, to E of Highgate, and Nos. 1–4 TAI
NEWYDDION, to W of Highgate. Late C18 or early C19, simple

village vernacular. So too TAFARN-Y-PLU (The Feathers Inn) on the main village, and set back on the same side, the former TABERNACL chapel, now a dwelling.

YSGUBOR-HEN, 1¼ m. W. A pretty country house in miniature, *c.* 1700, of the local character adopted by Clough Williams-Ellis. Tall chimneys at each end, and a wide central pediment with roundel. Kitchen with large exposed bressumer in the rear wing. A pair of timber arches at the foot of the staircase in the NW corner of the front wing.

TALARFOR. ½ m. E. 1851, for John Williams, surgeon. Hipped two storeys, central porch with columns. Sash windows with margin lights.

PLAS TALHENBONT, 1 m. NW. A large Renaissance house, originally known as Plas Hen, rebuilt in 1606–7 by William Vaughan of Corsygedol on his marriage to the heiress Anne Vaughan. It occupies a wooded reach of the Dwyfach valley. Hall wing with a lateral fireplace and W cross-wing, handsomely designed with mullioned-and-transomed, ovolo-moulded windows on two storeys; four lights for the hall and three on the upper floor, two on the gable-end of the wing. Tall plain square chimneys on the gables. The main doorway at the angle, of Elizabethan type, has an elliptical arch with continuous mouldings beneath an elaborate rectangular hoodmould; above it, a heraldic panel, somewhat crudely carved in relief with the arms of Collwyn ap Tangno, Osbwrn Wyddel and Ednyfed Fychan. The interior is greatly altered; a small stair wing opposite the entrance preserves the mid-C18 staircase, which has two turned balusters to each tread, a handrail swept up to the newels, and carved scroll decoration on each of the risers.

PLAS GWYNFRYN, ¾ m. NW. Burnt *c.* 1982, this must have been an impressive if architecturally uninspired pile, beautifully

Llanystumdwy, Plas Gwynfryn.
Engraving, 1877

placed in parkland with the mountains of Snowdonia in the distance. Designed by *George Williams* of Liverpool for Hugh Ellis Nanney and completed in 1876, reputedly for £70,000. Castellated style, with battlemented parapets and mullioned windows. Pinnacled *porte cochère*.

TREFAN, ¾ m. N. Five-bay, three-storey house faced in scribed stucco; the windows respectively five, four and three panes tall. A rainwater head at the rear has the date 1774 and the initials of Zaccaeus Hughes of Nanhoron, but the house seems to have been rebuilt in the early C19. In the hall, a three-bay screen of idiosyncratic columns; stairs of *c.* 1830 in a full-height well.

LÔN GOED. A 4½-m. tree-lined avenue running roughly N between Afon Wen (SE of Chwilog) to Hendre Cennin (W of Brynkir). Created by *John Maughan*, who became agent to the Talhenbont estate in 1817, to link various farms.

YNYSGAIN FAWR. ½ m. SSE. Farmstead consisting of house, stable, cartshed with granary above, cowhouses, pigsty and boatshed. The house (facing NW) is C18, with attached barn, and C19 rear wing. All carefully restored by the National Trust.

BRON-EIFION. ¾ m. E. Large stone house (now a hotel) in extensive gardens, designed and built by *J. E. Greaves* (owner of Llechwedd slate quarries in Blaenau Ffestiniog), *c.* 1885. It stands on an extensive terrace bounded by roaming parapets of mini-monoliths. The core is a galleried hall of two-and-a-half storeys, featuring Neo-Norman paired granite arches on the ground floor and enriched with polished panels of figured maple on the doors. Very broad gallery round all four sides, its parapet having a Norman colonnade in miniature. These exposed bedroom passages are lit both at this level and by the continuous lantern at the sides at the half-level above. The roof construction is of double arch braces in Oregon pine. Service courtyard with the buildings in humbler black-and-white. LODGE in the same style. Good planned FARMSTEAD behind, showing progressive principles of farm management, but now largely converted to other uses.

PONT BONTFECHAN, 1 m. SSW. Four low arches over the Dwyfach, perhaps *c.* 1617, widened on the downstream side in 1780.

TOMEN FAWR. 1½ m. W, near the junction of A497 and B4354 roads. Castle ringwork with substantial rampart and ditch.

LLITHFAEN 3544

A small, linear village on a shallow escarpment looking S towards Pwllheli. The tiny Victorian CHURCH, built in 1882 by *Kennedy*, is now a house.

LLITHFAEN CALVINISTIC METHODIST CHAPEL. 1905, by *O. Morris Roberts & Son*. Pedimented W gable, broken by an arch. Three equal round-headed lights above a single doorway, all with moulded heads and fluted Corinthian pilasters. Similar outer windows, at both levels.

NANT GWRTHEYRN, 1 m. NNW. The lane leads steeply uphill N
of the village, then descends dramatically through conifers,
following the precipitous side of Vortigern's Valley. At the
bottom, but on a shelf still well above the sea, PORTH-Y-NANT,
a planned settlement of c. 1878 for the granite quarry workers.
The quarry closed in 1914, the last inhabitant left in 1959.
Then in 1978 Dr Carl Clowes established the National
Language Centre here.

Two terraces at right angles around a large green: TREM-Y-
MYNYDD (Mountain View) facing S and TREM-Y-MÔR (Bay
View) facing W, both with small walled gardens in front. W of
Trem-y-mynydd, Y PLAS, the manager's house, c. 1880, with
its own walled driveway but surprisingly near the workers'
houses. The S end of Trem-y-môr turns to face S; it contained
the village shop and quarry office. All in local stone, roughly
coursed. The slate roofs step and fall with the slope. Dour,
dark-stained modern windows and doors. But the mood
lightens with the former CHAPEL, built 1878, converted to a
visitor centre in 2003 by *Maredudd ab Iestyn*. Boldly detailed E
extension, using local stone, slate, oak and stainless steel to
form a ramped and covered entrance. At the W end, a brave
all-glass conservatory which looks too narrow to be useful.

ST BEUNO, Carnguwch, 1½ m. SE. In an isolated partly round
churchyard below Mynydd Carnguwch, and on the pilgrimage
route from Clynnog Fawr to Bardsey Island. The Norwich taxation records a church in 1254, and Hyde Hall (c. 1810) a cruciform church 'in a condition utterly disgraceful to a Christian
community'. The present church, small but surprisingly wide,
appears to be of 1828 except for the re-set Perp E window.
Undivided nave and chancel, with N door. W tower, about 6 ft
(2 metres) square, rising well above the nave roof, with a
shallow roof, coped verges and a small aperture for the bell.
Kingpost trusses, plastered walls with remnants of a stencilled
dado. – ALTAR RAILS. Plain, three-sided. Square balusters,
turned gateposts. – PULPIT. Two-decker, panelled sides, a
shallow staircase with brass handrail. – PEWS. Open benches,
back rails inscribed 'Ld N' for Lord Newborough. One large
box pew for the Lloyd family of Trallwyn (Y Ffôr). All early
C19. Closed, in the care of a local trust.

An exceptionally fine hilltop CAIRN (SH 375 428, visible from a
distance), 20 ft (6 metres) high and 98 ft (30 metres) across.
On a boss of natural rock, the added stone revetted with a well-
built wall. There has been no excavation and debate continues
about whether it is a burial cairn or a motte.

MAENAN

ABERCONWY ABBEY. The Cistercian abbey of Aberconwy,
founded just before 1200 on the site now occupied by Conwy
church, was moved here after the conquest of 1283 by Edward
I, who endowed it with the flat fields E of the Conwy river and

gave money for its rebuilding. After the Dissolution of 1538 much material was reused at Gwydir Castle (q.v.). Since then, perverse Victorian mansion-building and the mysterious affinity between caravan parks and Cistercian sites in Wales have done their worst. Nonetheless the abbey complex and the *plas* of the Wynne family of Melai, of *c.* 1600 and after, can to a limited extent be discerned around them.

The ABBEY CHURCH was cruciform and its chancel and nave are thought to have been aisled. The High Altar was near the present gate from the main road, the cedar tree stands in what was the crossing; footings of the NW angle of the transept and nave were excavated in 1924, and the SW angle may be represented in the angle of the C18(?) slab-coped WALLED GARDEN. W of the church site an early C15 pointed doorway with roll and hollow mouldings is re-set in a wall; near it a hexagonal moulded plinth from Barry and Pugin's House of Commons. The MONASTIC BUILDINGS extended N from the transept and the W of the church to the Nant Llechog stream; the remaining fragments of red Deganwy stone, reused at Bodysgallen (q.v.) and at Gwydir Castle (q.v.), indicate buildings of high quality both in the late C13 and in the C15. These stood round a cloister whose site is roughly occupied by the present steep-gabled Neo-Elizabethan MAENAN ABBEY, *c.* 1850, by *Henry Kennedy*. Embattled tower at the S, then a cross-wing with the main rooms, but the porch is on the E in the angle of the inner range linking to the larger N service wing. Within this range the flying, galleried staircase with Jacobean ornaments. By the N garden wall a gable with a cross on it. To its W an arch of re-set C17 voussoirs forming a garden bower with an *ex situ* datestone for 1654; within this the studded double doors with a wicket which could have been part of the Renaissance gatehouse recorded in 1599. In the NW angle another garden arch of *c.* 1600, cambered and unchamfered.

MAENAN HALL. A low stone house of gently classical character containing the rarest of small medieval halls, and set in an outstanding garden designed in the late 1950s by *Lady Aberconway*. For centuries the home of the Kyffin family, descending from the lords of Cynllaith. Their hall, built after 1400, is in the downhill stroke of the T-plan. It sets the scale for a house kept close to the ground, as in Anglesey, though it occupies a shelf above the Conwy valley. The last Kyffin added an upper-end wing soon after 1700; his granddaughter's son William Kyffin Lenthall completed this as a new NW entrance front of seven bays *c.* 1820; and *S. Colwyn Foulkes* followed the same idiom in 1952. Maenan was part of the Victorian view of North Wales, drawn by J. T. Steadman and well described in Bezant Lowe's *The Heart of Northern Wales* (1912), but it dwindled to a meagre farm in the C20.

The Regency entrance façade has a central doorway, deep sash windows under flat arches and a stone cornice. It was made more regular by *S. Colwyn Foulkes*, when it became a garden front and the entrance reverted to the post-medieval passage. Elsewhere the windows continue the Queen Anne scale. A cross-passage formed by oak-post partitions divides the medieval storeyed 'lower' (albeit uphill) end, with a small parlour with three-tier joinery in its ceiling, from the PLASTER ROOM or GREAT HALL. This is of one-and-a-half bays (maybe once more?), which means that its cruck-truss is not central to the space. Nothing can be said of the structure of this unique soaring Gothic arch since it is covered in lime plaster, but its two tiers of purlins have deep cusped wind-braces, an indication that this hall roof is as early as any in North West Wales.* The hall's second glory is its plasterwork, dated 1582. This has two surprisingly different components, a profession of loyalty to Elizabeth I at the upper end and a mysterious tapestry of tendrils everywhere else. At the dais end, a post-and-panel partition with two doorways. Above, a pair of rusticated pilasters frame a field of foliage. In the centre the royal arms and monogram, with royal badges beside it. Higher again, acorns and Tudor heads; below, heraldic beasts, lions' heads etc., all in a fairly sophisticated Renaissance manner. On the s wall the Kyffin arms appear, self-effacingly small, near a peep window from the 'chamber over the hall'. All around, and over the blades of the crucks, loop intertwining tendrils in raised plasterwork; not quite the spiral forms of c13–c14 vine decoration in churches, not quite the formal intricacy of Elizabethan ceilings (despite the fleur-de-lys and pomegranate finials), but a sort of labyrinth without straight lines. This must date to Maurice Kyffin, High Sheriff of Caernarvonshire in 1579 and of Anglesey in 1585. On the upper floor at the 'lower' end, the exposed timber structure has queenposts with curved braces below. The solar, to the s again, has its ceiling plastered like a vault, also dated 1582 and with the Kyffin arms in a panel. Its more conventional motifs include vines, sunflowers and leaping heraldic beasts. Outsize bolection panelling. At the 'upper' end the original plan has been replaced by the ingeniously designed staircase of *c.* 1820. The geometric floor paving is said to have come from Maenan Abbey; the c16 stone fireplace is from Parlwr Mawr in Conwy.

On the N terrace the CRYSTAL ROOM, a tiny tent-like summerhouse of glass by *Clough Williams-Ellis*, 1961; on the W terrace its larger successor of 1991. The clean pastoral slope of the hill allowed *Lady Aberconway* a free hand in making a garden; the succession of geometrical forms is a visual response to the place and to the flow of water. Beside the house a massive ring of stonework retains a circular pool; in front, a generously scaled lawn is terraced forward in response to the grand vista of the lower Conwy valley. High on the ridge, an earlier feature: a circular two-storey tower with curved brick-framed Serlian windows in its upper storey. Made for William

* A Kyffin was later abbot of Maenan Abbey, but there is no reason to connect this use of crucks with monastic building.

John Lenthall in the late C18, this became the TOWER OF
HELIOS when restored by *S. Colwyn Foulkes* in 1959, with the
surreal addition of an external spiral stair.

MORFA NEFYN

ST MARY, Lôn-yr-eglwys. By *W. Pritchard* of Nanhoron. A
mission church, *c.* 1870. Nave and chancel, W porch. On the
roof, a slated bellcote on timber legs. Lancet windows between
buttresses. E window by *Powells*, 1924. Vestry by *Harold Hughes*,
1933.

CAERSALEM BAPTIST CHAPEL, Lôn Terfyn (B4417 road). 1853.
Unusually, a long-wall plan. Squarish, two windows to each
elevation except on the W where the CHAPEL HOUSE is
attached. Modern porch.

MORIAH CALVINISTIC METHODIST CHAPEL, Lôn Uchaf
(B4412 road). An accomplished design by *O. Morris Roberts*,
1882. Three bays, of white render, the centre porch projecting
with a low balustrade. Big pediment, the corners as tiny hips.
The central bay breaks through the pediment. Round heads to
the three upper windows and entrance, segmental to the front
lower windows. All with raised surrounds and keystones.
Margin-light sashes.

Along LÔN ISAF (B4417 road to Nefyn), at right angles to the
road, ARDD WEN. Three-bay house, with lower N extension.
Hipped roof, white roughcast, sash windows. Mid-to late C19.
Set back N from Lôn Isaf, up a track, GLAN-DWR. Mid- to late
C19 stucco house of three bays, not quite symmetrical. Sensibly
replanned and extended to the rear (N) and side by *Maredudd
ab Iestyn*, 2004, using a modern vernacular. Further up the
track, BRYN BRAS. Two gabled dormers. Dated 1789,
surprisingly late.

On LÔN UCHAF, E of Moriah chapel (*see* above), OAKFIELD.
Late C19, with moulded surrounds to margin-light sashes and
a fine classical doorway.

LÔN PEN RHOS leads WNW towards the golf links. At the junction with LÔN LAS, a monstrous block of luxury apartments,
quite out of scale with the village. LÔN BRIDIN leads downhill, N, to the beach. On the l., a few houses which merit a
glance. SWN-Y-MÔR, probably 1930s, pebbledashed with
canted bays and swept eaves. Next, BWLCH, 1903, extended
sympathetically, 1990. A touch of the Colonial style at
BRENDON, next door. Relaxed seaside vernacular at its
humblest best. At the beach, a group of houses on the r.,
probably late C18 or early C19. TŶ NEWYDD, a tall house of
three storeys with a tall, thin round-headed central window,
spanning two storeys, between sixteen-pane sashes. Just a hint
of Clough Williams-Ellis. To the E, a three-bay two-storey
house, extended to the W. Lastly, a lower house, its upper
storey half in the roof and lit by raking dormers. All whitewashed rubble, with four-pane sashes. A pleasant ensemble.

BRYNCYNAN INN, ¾ m. SE, at the roundabout of B4412 and A497. On the Pwllheli to Porth Dinllaen turnpike, so early C19. U-plan, the wings enclosing a small court, now filled with a projecting porch. Simple returned hoodmoulds above small paned windows. Coped verges with moulded kneelers. L-plan STABLES behind.

PORTH DINLLAEN, 1 m. NW. The great 'might-have-been' of North Wales, had Holyhead not been chosen as the port for Ireland. Most of Madocks's work in the Porthmadog area, and indeed the road network between there, Pwllheli and the port, assumed this protected cove would become the conduit for traffic to Dublin. But the little port remained small, just serving the herring trade and steamers carrying local produce to Liverpool in return for coal. Now a popular holiday spot and owned by the National Trust.

A number of old houses, including the TŶ COCH INN, but mostly altered. S of the inn, WHITE HALL, a parallel group of earlier C19 houses linked at the upper level to form a bridge over the sandy street. Rubble, sash windows.

PORTH DINLLAEN PROMONTORY FORT (SH 275 416) is a classic example of the type. The only defence necessary is across the isthmus, where there are two lines, a rampart with a ditch and counterscarp bank (now badly damaged by the road to the Tŷ Coch Inn), and a larger inner rampart without any ditch. These cut off an 18-acre length of the narrow promontory. No visible evidence of prehistoric houses; rectangular foundations at the very tip were for barracks for the workmen brought in for the proposed port installations in the early C19.

6066   MYNYDD LLANDYGAI

1½ m. SW of Bethesda.

ST ANN, Bryn Eglwys. 1865, by *Goronwy Owen*, replacing a church of 1813 noted by Fenton for its simplicity and elegance, probably by *Benjamin Wyatt*, but swallowed up by quarry workings. Nave and chancel, aisles, N porch and S vestry. Two-stage NE tower, with tall broach spire. Dark rubble, limestone dressings. Dull E.E. Disused.

On the bleak moorland above the Penrhyn quarries, a remarkable estate development of the 1860s, when the Penrhyn estate enclosed common land to accommodate its workers. Two parallel lanes run ⅓ m. SE to NW, LLWYBR MAIN and TAN-Y-BWLCH. To the SW side of each, single-storey two-room cottages in pairs, with privies, vegetable gardens and 110-yd (100-metre)-long livestock enclosures, all divided by stone walls or slate fences. The plots were leased to quarrymen for thirty years on condition that they build houses to the estate pattern, which Benjamin Wyatt had developed from the traditional *croglofft* cottage in the late C18.

NANHORON

CAPEL NEWYDD (Independent), ½ m. s (SH 285 309). 67
The oldest surviving and most important monument of
Nonconformity in Llŷn, 1770. Simple and barn-like, originally
entered by a door between two windows in the long N wall,
later blocked to provide for a pulpit. Whitewashed walls and
an earth floor. FITTINGS mostly of the same period, including
tiered seating and a box pew for Catherine, wife of Timothy
Edwards of Nanhoron. Restored in the 1950s by
T. Alwyn Lloyd & Alex Gordon of Cardiff with *M. T. Pritchard*
of Blaenau Ffestiniog.

No village, but a scattering of buildings connected with the
Nanhoron estate, in one of the prettiest spots in Llŷn. s of Pont
Llidiard-y-dŵr (Inkerman Bridge), THE FACTORY. House
and (former) woollen mill, 1860s. The house may have
incorporated a shop and knitting workshop; the mill produced
flannel blankets. Near the next bridge s, FELIN NEWYDD, the
mill house and corn mill. The latter of three storeys, the
entrance in a splayed wall with a plaque 'R.E.A. 1823 Na
ladratta' (i.e. Richard and Annabella Edwards. Do not steal).
Good coursed stone, voussoirs to the cambered openings. Two-
storey corn-drying kiln attached to s. Further s, at the junction of the B4413 and B4415 roads, RHYDGALED. Early C19
house with a strangely asymmetrical front and an attached
smithy. Nanhoron house and home farm (q.v.) to the w. The
B4413 makes a delightful double bend over a small bridge in
a wooded dell; a lane leads NE past the track to SIOP-Y-NANT.
Late C18 or early C19 house of whitewashed rubble, l., large
service wing, once the shop, r. Uphill, CAPEL NANT (Calvinistic Methodist), 1877, built of stone probably from the Nanhoron quarry. Below the B4413 to the E, BODLONDEB.
Attractive L-plan farmhouse, with gable finials, and small farm
buildings to the N, neatly contained within a wall. Probably
c. 1870.

NANHORON. Built *c.* 1803 by *Joseph Bromfield* of Shrewsbury, for 81
Richard Edwards, in a later C18 setting. Nanhoron Uchaf was
a typical T-plan C17 house, from which a datestone for 1677
survives, adjoining the stables and barns E of the present house.
Capt. Timothy Edwards R.N. (1731–80) began an ambitious
GARDEN and LANDSCAPE in relation to this C17 house, partly
derived from study of Philip Miller's *Gardeners' Dictionary* of
1763; a datestone for 1756 by the early site implies that his
uncle Richard Edwards started before this with the stone-
walled KITCHEN GARDEN. Timothy Edwards's landscaping
was confined to the curving wooded w flank of the Horon
valley, the wider view s becoming part of the estate only later.
A survey of 1777–8 records two WALLED GARDENS, the first
of stone lined with orange brick, the second of purple brick,
with a cobbled road between; their corners were made rounded
in the 1830s. The second garden is now laid out in an amalgam
of C20–C21 styles. The arm of woodland, with its contour

paths 5 ft (1.5 metres) wide as recommended in the *Gardeners'
Dictionary*, contains a small tufa GROTTO. It reaches round a
'lawn' which was to have a piece of 'water', to end in a somewhat picturesque site for a new house, permitting the park 'to
be seen from the parlour window'.

In the event Richard Edwards and his wife Annabella Lloyd
(of Hirdre-faig, Anglesey) built their new HOUSE nearer the
estate buildings and the road. He seems to have consulted
Joseph Bromfield in 1796, who proposed a sheer Neoclassical
house with a curved central bay, like that later built at
Rhug (M). A rather smaller version of five by four bays without
the bow was proposed in 1802, and built before 1809. This
evolved as a deep-eaved villa with sheer walls in the dark grey
granite of the place. Two secondary WINGS of 1834 of matching design, attaching the house to the second walled garden,
are by *Hansom & Welch*. Round the main house is an iron
veranda of before 1834, perhaps an afterthought to relieve its
plainness, and of such a bold scale as to suggest the hand of
Bromfield again. Its openwork supports with oversize
anthemion motifs are stamped at the *Victoria Foundry*,
Pwllheli.

Inside, the hall opens through a screen of Ionic columns to
the top-lit stairwell with cantilevered stairs. The drawing room
with the restrained Neoclassical (and repainted) frieze typical
of Bromfield was subsequently joined to the adjoining ante-
room. Dining-room frieze, of vine leaves. Fireplace with a rare
Mona marble surround. The library is part of the wing of 1834;
beyond it is a billiards room added in 1904 by *A. S. Manning*
of Newmarket.

SAETHON, 1 m. NE. Two houses facing across a courtyard, an
example of the 'unit system'. The most likely date is the later
C16, for Robert Saethon. A plaque above the W house entrance
records Evan Wynn Saethon, but the date 1666 is too late stylistically. The E house, perhaps slightly earlier, of typical
Snowdonian plan: two opposite doorways (now blocked), end
fireplace with mural stair next to it. Later converted to a barn,
with a small bellcote at the N gable. Of more interest is the
grander W house. Originally three main ground-floor rooms,
each with a fireplace, that in the central room with a lateral
chimney on the W wall. The staircase is next to it, within
the same thick mass of stone, an arrangement seen at
Hafod Garegog, Nantmor (q.v.).* Remains of post-and-panel
partitions on both floors; in the attic, wattle-and-daub
partitions and arch-braced trusses suggesting that the upper
rooms were originally open to the roof. In the S gable, a
blocked two-light window with the remains of cusping. To the
N, a STABLE RANGE, possibly early C19. To the W, a BARN
(C18 or earlier) and a range of COWHOUSES (mid-C19).

---

*Evan Saethon's wife was a daughter of Morris Williams of Nantmor.

NANT FFRANCON

The exceptionally beautiful Ogwen valley extends s from Bethesda to Llyn Ogwen. On the w side, the old road described by Pennant as 'the most dreadful horse-path in Wales', remade by *Lord Penrhyn c.* 1791. On the e side, *Telford*'s A5 (1815–30), which replaced the old turnpike of 1802–8, parts of which can still be seen below the road.

PLAS PENISARNANT, I m. SSE of Bethesda. A delightful late C18 house by *Benjamin Wyatt* for Lady Penrhyn, in 'one of the loveliest spots imaginable' (Fenton). Part house, part dairy and also showpiece for Penrhyn slate. Square plan, with a central chimney crowning the pyramidal roof. Veranda on four sides, on slender cast-iron columns. Pointed windows with Gothick tracery, cast-iron horizontal sliding sashes above. The walls faced with large slate slabs, painted cream. Two rooms each side of the central hall and staircase: dairy rooms to r., kitchen and Lady Penrhyn's sitting room to l., with green and orange glass in the window tracery and internal shutters. The wooded GARDEN steps w towards the Ogwen river. In the grounds were kitchen and fruit gardens, apiary, piggery, poultry yard with a fountain, furnaces for steaming potatoes etc. ¼ m. S, the estate farm, DOLAWEN. E-plan. Hipped roofs and cambered-head openings.

MAES CARADOC, 2½ m. S. Farm, probably Penrhyn estate. The COACHHOUSE and STABLES were used as a staging post on the old road. Cruciform plan, with lean-to aisles. The double HOUSE, one unit in line with another, is later, *c.* 1880. Rough-cast, with painted brick window surrounds. Also PIGSTIES and an L-plan COWHOUSE, with ventilation slits either side of the N door.

BETHEL METHODIST CHAPEL, 2 m. SSE. The elegant round-headed front windows with Gothick tracery and the hipped roof suggest the mid C19 or earlier. Boarded ceiling, (former) fittings, and front porch later, perhaps 1869 (inscribed over a rear door lintel). Attached house behind, with stable and hayloft.

NANT GWYNANT

One of the beautiful valleys of Snowdonia, stretching NE from Beddgelert to Pen-y-gwryd. The lakes Llyn Dinas and Llyn Gwynant lie midway, either side of two small groups of houses centred on Bethania chapel and the former school. Small-scale slate and copper mining were the chief activities; the Sygun copper mine (I m. ENE of Beddgelert) was worked in the mid C19 but has much older origins.

BETHANIA CALVINISTIC METHODIST CHAPEL. 1867. Prominent above the road, accentuating the height of the gabled front, already considerable because of the former schoolroom unusually placed in the attic. Round-headed

openings, big rounded lintels. Converted to a café in 2006 by
Dobson:Owen. A tea-terrace formed on the N side, with a fan-
shaped glazed canopy.

CRAFLWYN, 1¾ m. SW. The estate was owned *c.* 1200 by
Llywelyn the Great, later by the Cistercians. Home of
Humphrey Jones, High Sheriff, in the early C17. Of this date,
the core of the house, defined by its thick walls and large NW
fireplace. Extended *c.* 1873 by Llywelyn Parry, with gabled
wings, roughcast and colour-washed, and with ornate bargeboards and embattled canted bays. A curious three-storey
tower at the rear, with a steep roof and Jacobean-style coped
gables. At a higher level to the NW, a long row of OUTBUILD-
INGS, mostly single-storeyed, the centre adorned with a bellcote above a gable. Beyond the N end, a small BOTHY with
triangular oriels on brackets, with steep slate roofs. LODGE also
with a bay window, busily latticed. Substantially refurbished
and extended to the NE by the National Trust, 2004, as a base
for conservation work.

HAFOD-LWYFOG, 2 m. NE. C17 gentry house, home of Evan
Lloyd, High Sheriff in 1670, reusing material from a mid-C16
house on the site. Built into the hillside, so a dairy cellar at the
N end. Long plan, of the hall-and-parlour type seen first at Plas
Mawr, Conwy (early block of 1576): hall-kitchen to l., parlour
to r. and a small service room between, backing onto the
entrance lobby. The partitions to these, and the bedrooms, of
post-and-panel construction, with fluting to the posts and open
balustered sections at the top. Mural stair, l. of the parlour fireplace, closets to the r. on both storeys. Large main beams with
ovolo mouldings, and fluted joists. Axial parlour beam,
engraved 'ELL/E 1638'. Tall square chimneys, C19 windows.

HAFOD-RHISGL, 2¼ m. NE. Late C16 farmhouse on the site of
a grange of Aberconwy Abbey later owned by Sir John Wynn
of Gwydir. Used for Nonconformist gatherings in the early C19
(a removable pulpit survives inside). Cross-passage plan, with
opposing doors. Large fireplace, l., the possible site of a mural
stair now access to a S extension.

GWASTAD ANNAS, 2¾ m. NE. The remains of a cruck, tree-ring-
dated *c.* 1508, and a fireplace bressumer, tree-ring-dated
mid-C16, indicate that this was an oak-framed hall, later clad
in stone and provided with a central fireplace and chimney.
Lobby entrance W of the fireplace. C19 floor and (raised) roof.

PEN-Y-GWRYD ROMAN MARCHING CAMP (SH 660 557) Such
temporary camps to protect the advancing army overnight
must belong to the earliest period of campaigning in Wales
(A.D. 48–77) and are seldom recognizable as field monuments.
This one straddles the pass, a strategic position used later for
Second World War defences. The S side of the 10-acre enclosure
is easiest to see from the A498 road; on the W the Roman bank
is overlain by a modern wall, on the E it is unencumbered; the
NW corner can be seen above the A4086 road.

CWM DYLI FARMSTEADS (SH 655 541). At least three groups of
round-houses and fields radiating from them can be seen in

this patch of flat land at the head of the valley (two groups of four/five huts E of the river, one on the slope to the W). They are evidence of how intensively such small parcels of good land were used, in such a rocky and unforgiving landscape.

NANT PERIS

6058

A small village, the original Llanberis, at the SE end of Llyn Peris, and gateway to the steep Peris valley below Snowdon.

ST PERIS. Small, with an unusually complex plan for the area. Nave with N porch and W bellcote, transepts, and N and S chapels flanking the chancel, so that there are three E gables. The nave certainly came first, and the obscured two-centred N doorway probably dates it to the C14, but its original length is unclear. The transepts added, and the chancel too, probably in the later C15 or early C16, thus forming a cruciform plan. Later in the C16, or perhaps early C17, the quadrants N and S of the chancel were filled in as side chapels, with small flat-headed E windows. Octagonal piers and responds demarcate the chapels. Access is through oak archways facing W: four-centred to the N chapel, a flatter, later archway to the S. The screen (parts of it now at the W end) is of this date. It stood W of the crossing, with a loft above. Moulded and billeted wall-plate to the S chapel S wall. Arch-braced collar-beam trusses throughout, the braces of the nave trusses forming rounded arches, those to the re-set E roofs more pointed. Cusped wind-braces below the nave purlins. A barrel-vaulted celure above the chancel, cutting across the E window. This, and the remaining ones, by *Kennedy*, who restored the church in 1848. – PULPIT. High Victorian, in C14 style with carved alabaster enrichment etc. – SCREEN, *c.* 1500. With three lights with renewed tracery either side of the doorway. Heavily moulded upper and lower rails, into which the uprights are mortised; the embattled head beam perhaps belonged to the loft. – Brass TABLET on slate, to Mary Morgan †1779. – Robert Lloyd Williams †1870, Gothic, in painted slate. – In the churchyard, many C19 slate GRAVESTONES with the common motifs of clasped hands, weeping trees, flowers etc. in their shaped tops.

REHOBOTH CALVINISTIC METHODIST CHAPEL. 1876, by *O. Morris Roberts*. Full-frontal pedimented gable, above a tripartite composition of windows, all round-headed except for the main lower ones. A three-light upper central window, the lights deeply recessed and divided by polished Corinthian shafts. Projecting porch with a pair of doors either side of a window, all with round heads. Snecked granite, and dressed quoins and dressings.

NANTLLE

5254

Perhaps the earliest slate quarrying in North Wales was carried out in the Nantlle valley, as slate found at Roman Segontium may have come from Cilgwyn and the main source until the late C18. There was also copper-mining. The Nantlle Railway of 1828 was built to serve several slate quarries.

The VILLAGE is in two parts, on the N side of Llyn Nantlle Uchaf. The E part consists of a long terrace, TAI VICTORIA, built *c.* 1897 by *Rowland Lloyd Jones* for the Pen-yr-orsedd quarry. Facing, semi-detached houses for quarry officials. To the E, the small SCHOOL, 1873. Opposite, the fields are lined with SLATE FENCES, thin slabs held together with wire. The W part centres on CAPEL BALADEULYN, its Neo-Romanesque vestry the only surviving part. In the garden, a slate WAR MEMORIAL depicting quarry scenes, perhaps by *Mary Elizabeth Thompson*, an English artist who made her home in Bethesda in the late 1930s. To E, Nos. 1–5 TAI BALADEULYN, mid-C19 quarry-workers' houses. Projecting gabled bays with paired windows, decorative bargeboards, horizontal-paned windows and the tiniest of sliding sashes high up in the gables. Down a track at the end of the terrace, PLAS BALADEULYN, now the Trigonos Centre, largish and undistinguished. Built for the Pen-yr-orsedd quarry manager, *c.* 1863.

The oldest building is TŶ MAWR, S of the lane to the quarries. Early C16. Small windows and dormers, arched doorway with chamfered jambs and a Tudor hood. Projecting from the S gable, a garderobe at upper-floor level, possibly the only one of its kind in Caernarvonshire.

NW of Tŷ Mawr, two rows of quarrymens' BARRACKS, now workshops. Further W, BRYN DEULYN, built *c.* 1860 for the manager of the Dorothea quarry. A veranda above a pair of canted bays, the upper storey clad in two colours of slate.

DOROTHEA QUARRY, extending from Nantlle to Talysarn, about 1 m. long. Opened in 1829 by William Turner and John Morgan; owned by the Williams family, 1853–1970. Now a wilderness of purple slate tips and heroic remains of quarry buildings, largely overtaken by nature. In the dense undergrowth, the remains of earlier houses: PEN-Y-BRYN, a C17 (?) farmhouse, and TAL-Y-SARN HALL, a three-storeyed C18 mansion once in its own grounds with a grand gateway and exotic trees. Towards the W, the tall ENGINE HOUSE, for a Cornish beam engine built *c.* 1904 by *Holman Bros* of Camborne to provide power for haulage and pumping.

PEN-YR-ORSEDD QUARRY. Opened *c.* 1816 and worked by William Turner; in 1863, bought by W. A. Darbishire, Unitarian philanthropist, who also owned the Graig Lwyd quarry in Penmaenmawr (q.v.). Closed 1997, but still producing slate waste. Large SLATE MILL with vast kingpost trusses, late 1870s, next to the SLAB MILL of 1868. DRUM HOUSES to the inclines, their wooden drums still in place. QUARRY OFFICES, of *c.* 1863 and later; BARRACKS and the QUARRY HOSPITAL, all of relentless purple slate.

Numerous other small QUARRIES on the S side of the valley, including the TWLL LLWYD QUARRY, still producing multi-coloured rustic slates.

DRWS-Y-COED, 2 m. E. A tiny remote hamlet, serving the copper mine worked here from the 1760s. Two short rows of two-room COTTAGES, and the CHAPEL, probably of 1892. Pebbledashed, with rusticated surrounds and quoins.

NANTMOR 6047

A small village up a winding lane at the head of the Glaslyn estuary, on the resurrected Welsh Highland Railway.

PENIEL CALVINISTIC METHODIST CHAPEL. 1868. Snecked rubble. Two tall windows between the doors, all round-headed. An elaborate date-plaque above. A pair of mid-C19 COTTAGES behind, one of them the chapel house. A pleasing ensemble.

ABERGLASLYN BRIDGE, ⅓ m. W. C17, altered 1795–6, by *J. Defferd* spanning the Glaslyn with a single arch. On the w side, TŶ BONT, a mid-C19 house for the Aberglaslyn estate. Corbelled bays and hipped roofs.

BERTHLWYD, 2½ m. NE. Early C17 upland farmhouse, built end-on into the hillside. Stair wing projecting E, with a corbelled gable and a canted return to the S, just at the upper level. The original house, of three bays, was extended to S, later to N. Small windows, the openings mostly original and with stepped internal heads. The interior is largely restoration.

TŶ MAWR, ½ m. E. Early C16 hall-house. Five bays, originally with a pair of service rooms in each end bay (perhaps with a dais backing onto the E rooms) and a cross-passage next to the w pair. Large fireplace inserted in the middle bay, probably replacing a central hearth. The 1519 inscribed on the bres-sumer cannot be the date of this insertion; but tree-ring dating suggests that it was nevertheless done very early, maybe during building. Pegged collar-beam trusses, some with cusped wind-braces, elaborated as an arch-braced truss above the hall. A post-and-panel partition at the E end, with Tudor-arched door-ways. C20 oak windows with chunky chamfered mullions. Unpointed rubble slate-stone walls.

(DOLFRIOG, ¾ m. E. Built *c.* 1830 by George Holmes Jackson, extended in the late C19. Largish, two storeys with attic and basement, in Gothick style. Three-bay extended front wing with projecting central gable over Tudor arched doorway with overlight of intersecting tracery, and an oriel above. L-plan range behind, the stonework of larger blocks. Tall mullion-and-transom windows, some with straight Tudor hoods. Wide central hall with the principal rooms either side and a large richly decorated chimneypiece with seats each side. A fine can-tilevered staircase.)

CAE DAFYDD, I m. ESE. Largish house, built by John Priestley in 1852, on a site associated with the C15 bard Dafydd Nanmor. T-plan, two-storeyed. Three-bay front, extended NE with a long wing with a gabled projection facing NW. Well-built walls of coursed local rubble, wide eaves on carved brackets.

OERDDŴR UCHAF, ¾ m. wsw. In a remote upland location, perhaps an early encroachment. Late C18 two-storey house, extended in-line l. Whitewashed, small casement windows. Disused water wheel to r. gable. The home of the bard William Francis Hughes (1879–1966).

LLYNDU, ¾ m. s. The cedar-clad house, by *David Wilkinson*, 2006, sits on the edge of the woods, slightly raised, facing E over a small lake towards more woods, and mountains beyond. Longish single-aspect block, with cross-gabled wings, largely an overcladding of a timber 1930s bungalow. The s end is for daytime use, the N end for bedrooms, with service rooms behind, and a magical glazed corridor of huge sheets of frameless full-height glass facing the trees w. The sitting room and main bedroom open through French windows onto a terrace E. Upper-floor studies are tucked into the wings, the N one extending up as a delightful tower with windows on all sides and a pyramid roof. Staircase of thick cantilevered treads, the landing projecting as a semicircular bay; stone-clad at the base, glass blocks above.

HAFOD GAREGOG, I m. s. T-plan house, much altered. Dated 1622 on a small re-set plaque for Morris Williams, High Sheriff of Merioneth, on the site of the home of the early C15 bard Rhys Goch Eryri. A mural stair adjacent to the lateral fireplace, an unusual arrangement – but seen at Saethon, Nanhoron, home of Morris Williams' son-in-law. Re-set post-and-panel partition, probably originally fixed to the slotted cross-beam, r. Small C17 BARN, N, with coped verges and opposite voussoir-headed doorways. Steps to an upper doorway in the E gable.

3241

NEFYN

Set back from the sea and the harbour cove, PORTH NEFYN, perhaps used by the Romans. A small town under the Gwynedd princes, Edward I held tournament here in 1284, celebrating his conquest. Seventy years later, his great-grandson, the Black Prince, granted it borough status. Its trades naturally related to the sea: fishing and boat-building, and more recently, the holiday trade. The town failed to impress Fenton (1804) and Samuel Lewis (1849), and today it remains a disappointment. Too much pebbledash, too many UPVC windows.

ST DAVID. 1903, by *P. S. Gregory*, in the style of John Douglas. Nave and chancel, N aisle of four bays with four-centred arcades. Chancel arch, on a blocked pair of colonnettes holding an unfinished label stop. Blocked s archway in the chancel to a tower never built. Projecting bell canopy at the w gable. The half-timbered s porch is as memorable as Douglas's at Maentwrog (q.v.). Arch-braced trusses, in pine, with multi-verticals above the collars and cusped wind-braces. Snecked granite inside and out, Ancaster dressings. – E window by *Celtic Studios*, 1958.

ST MARY, Stryd-y-mynach. Late Georgian, c. 1825–7, on the site of a C13 church. Nave and chancel in one, embattled N porch added later. Thin w tower with louvred bell-lights, pinnacles on the steep raking parapet angles and an endearing sailing-ship weathervane. Pointed timber windows with Y-tracery. Arch-braced trusses in the medieval style. Now a maritime museum.

SOAR INDEPENDENT CHAPEL, Pen-y-bryn. 1880, by *O. Morris Roberts*. Painted render. The flanking windows within a tall rendered frame. The centre, a little higher, is more fanciful. A roundel above an unequal flat-headed triplet, a door with fanlight and decorated render panels each side. The name and date above the roundel, and a tiny blind arcade at the top.

MORIAH WESLEYAN CHAPEL, Stryd Moreia. 1881, by *O. Morris Roberts*. Tall thin round-headed lights flank an elaborate centrepiece of openings juxtaposed with blind panels. A rounded band of panels above the triple window containing a round light in its head. Below, a round-headed doorway, with wide panelled pilasters.

The TOWN formed around a cross-roads, Y GROES. STRYD-Y-FFYNNON leads N. On the l., ST MARY'S WELL. Built in 1868 by the Corporation of Nefyn. Square, with stone pyramidal roof and copper finial. On each side, a triangular dormer with inset inscription slab, and a recessed blind doorway below, with rusticated surround. STRYD-Y-MYNACH leads E to St Mary's Church (q.v.). STRYD-Y-PLAS leads SE from Y Groes, past SEION BAPTIST CHAPEL (1904), l., into Y FRON. On the r., TAN-Y-FRON, a small house dated 1829 on the slate plaque. Opposite, DERWEN, a large stucco rectory-style house in a big garden. Three bays, two storeys and attic, and a timber and glass porch.

STRYD FAWR, s, has little of interest, but it leads SE to STRYD MOREIA. On the r., a small unspoilt house owned by the Town Trust, with hoodmoulds. Moriah chapel (*see* above) is just beyond.

PEN-Y-BRYN leads w to Soar chapel and St David's Church. Just before the church, the small WATCH TOWER on the summit of the medieval MOTTE. Dates of both unknown, but the stone tower was perhaps connected with the herring industry, i.e. early C19. Further w, l., the GANOLFAN (Village Hall). Sub-Arts and Crafts, with its tapering buttresses and steep roof. Then the SCHOOL, the old British School, *c.* 1860, by *George Northcroft*, with tall upright SCHOOL HOUSE.

HEN DAFARN, Porth Nefyn. The oldest in a group of houses on the beach, perhaps late C16 or early C17. Whitewashed rubble, with two gabled half-dormers above two upright windows. Chimneys each end, and probably a mural staircase once within the l. gable. A hint of Scottish vernacular in the proportions.

PANT GLAS

4747

A hamlet on the A487 road once with its mill and inn on the *c.* 1823 turnpike and later a station on the 1867 branch line from

Caernarfon to Afon Wen. Its tiny river, the Nant Call, is mentioned in the Mabinogion as the scene of a mighty battle.

Former NATIONAL SCHOOL, 1 m. w. 1858, by *Kennedy*. F-plan
with attached school house. Three gables, the central one
larger. Coursed granite with brick dressings.

58 PANT GLAS UCHAF, ⅔ m. E. Two-bay house of two storeys, tree-
ring dated *c*. 1570s. Access to the upper room by a mural stair
with a slit window in the gable. Slightly lower, three-bay barn
attached at the N end, possibly earlier. Plain trusses, stop-
chamfered beams and floor joists, all in oak. Multicoloured
roof slates, gabled dormers of later date. C20 extension to SE.

DERWYN BACH, 1½ m. S. A mid-C16 storeyed house of three
bays, with opposing doors, a large fireplace with bread oven at
the N end, and a spiral stone stair next to it. Modern beams
and post-and-panel partition, in the original locations;
upstairs, the original trusses and purlins. Small square
windows, rough voussoirs above the E doorway.

PEN LLYSTYN ROMAN FORT, 1½ m. S (SH 480 448) has been
almost entirely removed by the gravel quarry in Bryncir; only
the N rampart remains above the pit. The recovery in the late
1950s of the plan and history of this early campaigning fort,
reduced in size in the C2, was a triumph of rescue archaeology
by the RCAHMW, at a time when no provision was officially
made for such work.

LLYSTYN GWYN OGAM STONE, 1¼ m. S (SH 482 455). Found
in 1901 close to Pen Llystyn fort and now built into the
garden wall at Llystyn Gwyn Farm, Bryncir. It is a large gravestone with an alphabetic inscription in the top r. corner and
the same information in Irish Ogam script up the r. side.
The inscription records ICORI(X) FILIUS / POTENT / INI
(Icorus son of Potentinus) in Roman capitals of C6 style. The
Ogam script (tally marks across the angle) reads upwards
ICORIGAS ([the stone] of Icorus). Such bilingual inscriptions
are common in SW Wales, but this is the only one in North
Wales.

EARLY FARMSTEADS AND FIELDS, ½ m. N (SH 469 488). The W-
facing slopes above the main road N of Caerau are covered with
terraced fields amongst which lie several enclosed farmsteads.
Two just N of Caerau were excavated in the 1930s; others, W
of the road on the gravel island of Graeanog, were excavated
more recently when the gravel pits were extended. The Caerau
sites are typical of two common types. The more northerly
(SH 469 489) is an oval enclosure containing two large round-
houses on either side of an open yard. It is thought that such
curvilinear enclosures may be slightly earlier than more tightly
planned rectilinear ones, like the southern site (SH 470 488).
This has round, oval and rectangular buildings ranged around
a smaller yard within a very thick wall, made up, to a large
extent, of stones cleared from surrounding fields. A later, possibly medieval longhouse has been built over the E side of this
enclosure.

Excavation of three such farmsteads at Graeanog revealed Bronze Age activity, settlement and exploitation in earnest from *c.* 200 B.C., reaching a peak with large enclosed farmyards during the Roman period, and continuing at one site into the post-Roman period. A group of three platform houses were dated to the C12 A.D. These excavations revealed that the 'hut groups' of North Wales, previously judged exclusively Roman, were occupied from the late Iron Age into the emergence of the early Welsh kingdoms.

CAIRNS AND STANDING STONE, 1½ m. NNE (SH 455 492). The only monuments remaining on the gravel island at Graeanog. Bronze Age. Extensive excavations to the S did not find any houses contemporary with them.

PENISARWAUN 5564

ST HELEN. 1883, by *Kennedy*, for George W. Duff Assheton-Smith, concerned that the villagers might lapse into indifference or Dissent. Nave, chancel, S porch. W bellcote, on a pair of buttresses, as at Llanystumdwy. Rubble, with red sandstone dressings. Uninspired. Interior walls unusually of brick: red to dado level, yellow above.

PRIMARY SCHOOL, ⅛ m. E. *c.* 1993, by *Gwynedd County Architects* (project architect *Dilwyn Gray-Williams*). Two arms extending from the central assembly hall, which is crowned with a cross-gabled cupola. Steep gabled portico, in line with the ornate gateway. White render with dark-stained windows and doors; slated roof. The formality of the design, is surprising for a modern primary school in a tiny village, and the detailing is quirky and overworked (e.g. triangular-headed windows, massive cruciform columns with giant capitals).

PENLLECH 2335

2 m. SW of Tudweiliog.

ST MARY. From the distance, only the bellcote distinguishes the small church from the farm buildings close by to the N. Rebuilt *c.* 1840 by *Samuel Jones*. Undivided nave and chancel. Three blocked lancets towards the E end; plain pointed windows with wooden Y-tracery. Unaltered interior. Passed to the Friends of Friendless Churches, 2008. – PULPIT. Octagonal, with reading desk. Sounding-board, with eight-ray sun on its soffit and an embattled cornice. – Open BENCHES, panelled and painted BOX PEWS, E. – FONT. Plain cylindrical bowl, probably medieval, on a later square base.

PLAS-YM-MHENLLECH. N of the church. Perhaps C17, with a late C18 NE wing; occupied by a branch of the Wynne family of Cefnamwlch in the C17–C18. Farm buildings across the lane, including a mill; duck pond. Much altered, but the ensemble with the church forms a manorial settlement more usually seen in England.

CUP-MARKED STONE (SH 224 345), 3 ft (1 metre) tall, against the hedge inside the first field on the l. on the road leading to the church. Seventeen to twenty shallow cup marks on the flat face. Its origin is unknown; it could have come from a Neolithic tomb or a Bronze Age cist. Such cup-marked stones are rare in Wales.

7850

PENMACHNO

The Machno valley extends from the A5 road, where the river joins the Conwy river, to its head at Cwm Penmachno (q.v.), almost 6 m. SW. Unusually numerous substantial houses and farms, many taken over by the Penrhyn estate in the mid C19. Penmachno lies halfway along. A quiet, unspoilt village straddling the river by a long, five-arched bridge, PONT LLAN, built 1785. The church and two chapels are on the W side, surrounded by small stone houses and a maze of tiny streets.

ST TUDCLUD. In a big churchyard between the confluence of the Machno and Glasgwm rivers, once the site of two churches. Dull, Dec style, by *Lloyd-Williams & Underwood* of Denbigh, 1859–63. Lord Penrhyn purchased the Ysbyty estate in 1856 and demolished the old church. Unplastered walls inside. Stripy chancel arch of alternating dark and pale voussoirs. The interior is flooded with light from an archway to the former S transept, now with a modern timber window. – REREDOS. Carved oak, early C20. – FONT. Simple bowl, square base. C12? – STAINED GLASS. Poor E window, 1867 by *Ballantine & Son* of Edinburgh. A better one to the N, by *Jones & Willis*, 1909. – INSCRIBED STONES. An important late C5 to mid-C6 collection exhibited in the chancel, and later ones at the W end. The Cantiorix stone reads CANTIORI(X) HIC IACIT / [V]ENEDOTIS CIVE(S) FVIT / [C]ONSOBRINO(S) / MA[G]LI / MAGISTRATI (Cantiorix lies here. He was a citizen of Venedos [i.e. Welsh Gwynedd] [and] cousin of Maglos the magistrate). The references to 'citizen' and 'magistrate', unique in an inscription of this date, suggest a continuation of Roman hierarchies long after they left Wales. – The Carausius stone reads CARAVSIVS / HIC IACIT / IN HOC CON / GERIES LA / PIDVM, intriguingly: Carausius lies here in this heap of stones. Before it, the Chi-Rho symbol, a rarity. – A split pillar, [ ]FILI AVITORI / IN TE(M)PO[RE] / IVSTI[NI] / CON[SULI(S)] ([The stone of . . .] son of Avitorius [set up] in the time of Justinius the consul).

BETHANIA CALVINISTIC METHODIST CHAPEL, White Street. Dated 1867 in the central cartouche. Enterprising front, higher than the chapel's roof. Two storeys, with three-quarter Corinthian columns at the angles and pilasters between.

Entablature with dentil cornice and ball finials. Very like the 1867 chapel in Penmaenmawr.

SALEM CALVINISTIC METHODIST CHAPEL. By *Richard Owens*, 1873 in his Lombard style. Snecked greenish granite and grey limestone dressings. Three round-headed lights below a round four-lobe window, and a door under a slightly projecting gable. Flanking triangular-headed panels, as at Dwyran (A).

NE of the church, CHURCH VIEW, a short row of mid-C19 cottages with tiny windows tucked under the eaves. Up the lane E of the village, ELUSENDY, former almshouses built *c.* 1740 through the gift of Richard Anwyl and Lewis Lloyd of Hafod-dwyryd. A tight U-plan, the original entrance between the arms, giving access to ten single-room units. Elliptical voussoir doorway, tall square chimneys on the gable ends. In Llewelyn Street, GLAN-Y-PWLL, an early C19 terrace, recently restored. Further N, r., the COUNTY SCHOOL, 1908.

WOOLLEN MILL, 1¾ m. NE. In existence by 1809, with a small group of houses and a chapel nearby.

PEN-Y-BONT, 1¼ m. SSW. A good example of a planned farm, *c.* 1870, for the Penrhyn estate. BARN with opposing central doors and ventilation slits; cowhouse; hay barn. Two-storey stable and cartshed, with granary above. Pigsties, with attached privy. The hipped roofs characteristic of the estate's buildings in the Penmachno and Ysbyty Ifan valleys. The house is of less interest.

HAFOD-DWYRYD, ½ m. S. A good vernacular group, of many parts. The original house is to the S, probably late C16, with a lateral fireplace and a doorway with a cyclopean lintel. Extended N, perhaps early C17. Two-storey gabled porch added to the W front, dated 1678 above the elliptical-headed doorway, with the initials of Richard Anwyl. Modern windows. Late C17 panelling and doors in the N room. To the N, a very fine BARN, probably built by the Anwyls. Large central doorways each side, with long narrow voussoirs below a slate hoodmould. Six bays, collar- and tie-beam trusses. Ventilation slits.

PENYBRYN, in an elevated position ½ m. SW. C17. Chimneys at each end, both rebuilt. Cyclopean heads to the doorways each side, unusually not opposite each other. Long quoin stones. C19 windows, probably in enlarged openings. Its length, the loftiness of the main rooms and the quality of the detailing indicate gentry status. Six bays, divided by heavy oak beams, some with slots for partitions, at least one of which survives. The fireplace at the N end has, unusually, large voussoirs rather than an oak bressumer. Fireplace in the room above. Next to it, a space once taking the staircase. Original trusses, with queenposts, collars and raking struts infilled with plaster. The S truss has arch braces and the ceiling each side was formerly coved and plastered.

Attached agricultural range to the W, incorporating a C17 STABLE. To the N, a five-bay BARN of exceptional quality, similar to that at Hafod-dwyryd. Segmental arches of long voussoirs. Straight hoodmould over the central doorways. The kneelers indicate former verge copings.

BENAR, ¾ m. NNE. Like a miniature mansion, commanding a fine view SE. T-plan, two storeys with large attics. C16 rear (NW) wing built into the hill, with large fireplace (perhaps with former mural stair) and oak partition. SE front dated 1693 (from a hinge on the cross-boarded front door), an imposing symmetrical five bays. Mid-C19 sash windows, with timber lintels (the lower ones faced with slate). Gabled porch on cylindrical rubble piers. Tall stone chimneys. Walled garden TERRACE in front, approached by a stone STAIRWAY with seat recesses halfway. To the S, a stone PRIVY, surprisingly large, with a double seat above the stream. Stone BARN, NE, probably stables with a former loft above. C17; C19 extensions and alterations.

DUGOED, 1½ m. NE. An early C17 upland house. The earlier, SE wing of c. 1600 is of three bays. The fireplace and shouldered chimney project. No mural stair, as in the N wing, so the original staircase was probably of timber and internal, unless it was a one-storey open-hall house. Double-chamfered, stopped beams. Slightly later N wing with a cyclopean lintel over the E doorway. The upper window openings facing SE look original.

DYLASAU ISAF, 2½ m. NE. The home of the Lloyd family, prominent in the C17. Two wings at right angles, meeting at a point, so probably a 'unit' house. The smaller, earlier wing at the SE, probably C16, has a very tall shouldered chimney projecting to the NW, and an external stone staircase. Good stonework, laid to rough courses. The main wing dated 1735 is an L-plan, with chimneys at all three gables, the NW one with a mural stair beside it, and 'T P Esqr 1735' on the bressumer. Post-and-panel partitions. The window l. of the present front door was the original doorway, with a shaped lintel. Facing, the STABLE, with stone steps to the loft, and the BARN and COWHOUSE. Good stonework again, laid to courses. Collar-and tie-beam trusses.

COED-Y-FFYNNON, 1¾ m. NNE. L-plan house, perhaps the home of the poet Huw Machno (†1637). The earliest part, facing E, is C16. Projecting shouldered chimney at the N end. The RCAHMW believes it may have been an open hall, the upper floor added shortly afterwards. The two-storey gabled porch wing added centrally on the E front, its doorway on one side, its head segmentally arched, and with a drawbar slot inside. The rear (W) wing added c. 1700. (Stop-chamfered beams, with slot for panel-and-post partition. Collar-beam trusses with cusped wind-braces to the purlins. A C16 plaster shield on the S wall of the upper storey, containing the arms of Gruffudd ap Dafydd Goch.)

PLAS GLASGWM, 1 m. W. A puzzling plan, due to many alterations. The main E-facing part probably early C18 but incorporating an earlier house. A projecting and stepped chimney at the N gable, an oven in the external angle between the house wall and the chimney, with its own rough stone roof. Another chimney at the centre. Three dormers to the E, with raking roofs. To the W, a dairy extension and a 6-ft (2-metre)-diameter water wheel. The house extended at the SW and the roof altered to hip form. Good FARM BUILDINGS, the oldest with queenpost trusses.

TŶ MAWR, Wybrnant, 2 m. NW. The reputed birthplace of Dr William Morgan (c. 1545–1604), Bishop of Llandaff (later of St Asaph) and the first translator of the complete Bible into Welsh (1588). Probably C17, but incorporating fragments of cruck blades. Large square chimney to the S. The N chimney corbels out at head-height, then reduces to a tall square shaft just below roof level. Heavily restored by the National Trust. in the late 1980s. To the W, a COTTAGE and attached BARN C18, rebuilt for the guardian and an exhibition space. To the NW, a small (new) BRIDGE across the Wybrnant river.

BWLCH-Y-MAEN, 2 m. NNW. Two-storeyed, probably C17. Extended SW in the C19 to provide a cartshed, with an external staircase to the room above. Five bays, the central one a former screens passage, indicated by partition slots in the beams, and the central opposed doorways (both now windows). At the NE end, a projecting fireplace and chimney, which turns diagonal just above the chimney shoulders. Large kneelers at the NE gable, but the verge copings removed.

FEDW DEG, 2 m. N. Part of a C16 storeyed house, now in the guardianship of Cadw. It may be an instance, fairly rare in NW Wales, of a lobby-entry house, or perhaps the central chimney was an insertion (cf. Tŷ Mawr, Nantmor). A fine cyclopean S doorway, just three massive stones. Renewed windows of oak, the mullions set on the diagonal. Oak lintels. Re-set internal partition, with a pair of double-ogee-headed doorways. Old thick slates on the renewed roof, just one curved principal surviving.

CONWY FALLS CAFÉ, 2¼ m. NNE at the B4406/A5 road junction. Neo-Georgian style, by *Clough Williams-Ellis*, c. 1955. Advanced central bay with a loggia to the upper-storey café, above three fanlight windows. Hipped roofs. The first design (1938) was far more exciting: a Modernist building dramatically perched on the rocks above a bend in the river. A glazed restaurant on three sides, sitting on a more solid base, and in front, a semicircular terrace following the prow of the rocky bank. Was Frank Lloyd Wright's Fallingwater (1936) influential?

BRIDGES. A number of small bridges, all of rubble stonework. The 'ROMAN' BRIDGE, in a picturesque setting near Penmachno Mill (SH 806 529), probably C17. Single arch. Nearby, the PONT-Y-PANDY, early C19. At the junction of the B4406 with the A5, the PONT CONWY or BONT NEWYDD, c. 1826. (SH 780 486), PONT PEN-Y-BEDW, single arch with two flat-headed flood openings each side, late C18 or early C19. Best of all, the steeply cambered PONT RHYD-LLANFAIR (SH 827 524), crossing the Conwy in a superb setting with a single high arch spanning about 88 ft (27 metres). By *Robert Griffiths*, dated MDCCLXXX on the E parapet.

7276 # PENMAENMAWR

Hemmed in to the S, E and W by mountains, and to the N by the sea, the old parish of Dwygyfylchi (in which the modern Penmaenmawr lies) remained isolated until the turnpike over the Sychnant Pass was built, *c.* 1772. The area is a collection of settlements rather than one centre. Capelulo, towards the W end of the Pass, developed as a travellers' halt, with three inns and a smithy. Development was swifter after 1830, when Telford constructed his road below the precipitous Penmaen-bach to the E. The export of cobblestones to Lancashire was succeeded at this time by the more organized manufacture of setts, necessitating accommodation for quarrymen on the slopes below Penmaen-mawr, to the W. The railway station opened in 1849, initiating a tourist surge. Boarding houses, villas, shops, churches and chapels sprang up, encouraged and often financed by the Darbishire family, owners of the Graig Lwyd quarry. An added attraction was the frequent holiday visits of W. E. Gladstone. Further development took place after the First World War in the area W of St Gwynin's church. In the early 1930s, a thousand men were employed in the quarry, but automation has replaced manual labour (now mostly for rail ballast) and the fortunes of the area have declined drastically.

ST SEIRIOL, Church Road. A bold church in E.E. style, by *Alfred Waterhouse*, 1867. Local granite with sandstone dressings, fish-scale slates and crested red ridges. Lady Chapel and vestry to the N, and a S aisle. The most distinctive feature is the detached SW tower, added in 1885, and connected by a short roofed passage. Angle buttresses meet at eaves level of its saddleback roof, extending upwards as octagonal pinnacles. Paired louvred bell-lights, interrupted at sill level by small pediments above clock faces. Plate tracery. Four-light E window with cinquefoil. Three-light W window with three cinquefoils, its sill interrupted by a fleur-de-lys crowning the huge trefoiled doorhead below. A lofty interior, with a wagon roof, boarded above the chancel. Red and yellow brick in bands, and alternately above the openings. The chancel and arcade openings have alternate bricks chamfered back to give a serrated edge, reminiscent of Romanesque chevron-work. – REREDOS. Last Supper, carved oak, designed by *W. D. Caröe*, 1907. Also by him, the delicate filigree ROOD SCREEN, 1925, and probably the PARCLOSE SCREEN too, with thin barley-twist verticals. – PULPIT. 1908, with traceried panels, the central one of deep relief, depicting the Ascension. – FONT. On a stepped tiled platform, a wide shallow bowl decorated with lilies, and an attached book-rest supported on a small pier. – ORGAN SCREEN, E end of S aisle.

Reputedly made by members of the congregation in 1902; if so, they must have been very talented. – STAINED GLASS. E window, 1880, and S aisle W, perhaps by *Clayton & Bell*. W window by *Ward & Hughes*, in commemoration of Queen Victoria. N nave, by *Joseph Bell & Son* of Bristol, 1914–18 war memorial. Lady Chapel, W of two, by *Mayer & Co*.

ST DAVID, Bangor Road. Built for Welsh-language services in 1893, by *Sir A. Blomfield*. Lancet style, in local stone with red brick around the openings. An economical exterior with a better interior, still in red brick and with sturdy roof timbers. Undivided nave and chancel, with N aisle and S porch. Pointed arcades, on round pink stone piers.

ST GWYNIN (GWYNAN), Dwygyfylchi. In a roundish raised churchyard. Rebuilt 1889 by *E. M. Bruce Vaughan* of Cardiff, using the walls of the 1760 church, itself a rebuild. Lancet-style, in the local snecked stone, with red sandstone dressings. Inset at the SW corner, a window head, probably C15 or C16. Shallow apsidal sanctuary, NE vestry under a catslide roof, and a twin-gabled organ/narthex wing to the S. Attractive slate and timber fleche. – FONT. 1899, with heraldic emblems inscribed. Eight faces, divided by short shafts. – STAINED GLASS. Good. Six Welsh saints in the nave; in the chancel, St Mary and St John each side of Christ, by *Heaton, Butler & Bayne*, 1889. – MONUMENTS. Tablet to Rhys Lloyd †1710. – Marble tablets to members of the Smith family of Pendyffryn. – Slate slab commemorating the 1760 rebuilding (vestry).

SALEM CALVINISTIC METHODIST CHAPEL, Bangor Road. 1862, by the *Rev. Thomas Thomas*. Three-bay gable front, divided by pilasters, with Venetian window and tall round-headed outer windows. Pebbledashed, with stucco dressings.

ST PAUL METHODIST AND UNITED REFORM CHURCH (formerly Wesleyan), Bangor Road. 'Planned with a view to make it a model sea-side place of worship', by *John Wills* of Derby, 1890–1. Granite crazy-paving walls, with limestone quoins and yellow sandstone dressings. L-plan, with S porch and lower storey below street level. Two-stage tower at the internal angle, with a curious pinnacle at one corner.

CHURCH OF THE LADY OF THE ROSARY (R.C.), Old Conwy Road. Built in 1867 as a Calvinistic Methodist chapel, now disused. Three-bay front, with Tuscan columns supporting a full entablature, very similar to Bethania chapel, Penmachno (q.v.). Ball finials above each column, central cartouche with date. The frieze inscribed 'Domus Dei et Porta Coeli'. Central doorway, with moulded architrave and bracketed entablature. Flanking windows with moulded architraves and pediments.

HOREB INDEPENDENT CHAPEL, Old Conwy Road, Dwygyfylchi. Dated 1813 on the porch, altered *c*. 1840. Three large sash windows. At the W end, an added porch. Hipped roof. (Grained pitch-pine box pews, stepped. Boarded ceiling with large plaster roundel ornamented with acanthus.)

N of the main cross-roads, a MONUMENT to W. E. Gladstone,
1899. A bronze bust on a polished granite base. PARADISE
ROAD leads downhill, past BRYN, a substantial turn-of-the-
century house of red brick and pebbledash. At the bottom of
the hill, the STATION, on the Chester to Holyhead railway
(1848). A slated veranda still covers one side of the platform,
on cast-iron columns and handsome brackets geometrically
pierced.

PANT-YR-AFON leads E from the cross-roads, past a glass-roofed
arcade in front of CAMBRIAN BUILDINGS, and into CONWY
ROAD. At the junction with Constitution Hill, the YOUNG
MENS INSTITUTE AND LIBRARY of 1923, by *R. J. Hughes*. A
stylish building with wide sprocketed eaves and hipped roofs.
Further E, towering above the road, the former CHURCH
HALL by *Harold Hughes*, 1913. Higher at the N end because
of the steep site, this elevation distinguishes between the
hall, with its lancet windows and central chimney, and
the accommodation below, with much smaller swept-head
windows and a central brick-lined doorway. The clumsy
composition lacks the finesse of Hughes's colleague, Herbert
North.

OLD CONWY ROAD forks r. beyond Pant-yr-afon and leads
uphill towards the Sychnant Pass, the old road before routes
were cut below the cliffs. This is the wealthy end of town, with
detached Victorian houses in spacious gardens stretching
uphill to the S. Past St Seiriol's church (*see* p. 486) in Church
Road, the R.C. church (*see* p. 487), on the r. at the junction
with Graiglwyd Road. Here also are substantial late C19 villas,
in particular GWYSFA and TREWEN, possibly part of an estate
by *William Dawes* of Manchester featured in *The Architect* in
1888. Red-tiled roofs and upper storeys, half-timbered gables,
Elizabethan-style windows with leaded glazing, granite with
red brick dressings. Little England at home in North Wales.
Further E, in a large park-like garden, r., NODDFA (formerly
Tan-y-foel). 1860s, by *Cornelius Sherlock* of Liverpool, for
Murray Gladstone, Manchester-based businessman and
cousin of the Prime Minister. A large Italianate villa in cement
render, with hipped roofs and wide bracketed eaves. A big
entrance tower, behind a glazed timber porch with a balcony.

BANGOR ROAD leads W from the cross-roads towards the
quarries, where the mountain looms above. BRYNMOR, r., is
the oldest building in the village. L-plan, probably early C17
and possibly belonging to John Williams, Archbishop of York.
Main three-bay range facing E, with central entrance and openwork timber porch. Late C19 W wing and, adjoining the N side,
BRYNMOR COTTAGE, also C19. Further W, just into Celyn
Street, r., MARETH HALL, *c.* 1900 with large shopfront, fluted
pilasters with bracketed stop-ends to the entablature, and a
half-timbered gable. All very grand, but just corrugated tin
sides. NEW YORK COTTAGES, on the S side of Bangor Road,

four mid-C19 single-storey dwellings recently restored and converted to offices. Further w, just before St David's church, a SCHOOL with gables, the w one dated 1875 and with a pair of thin iron columns supporting the lintel above the window. The OLD CO-OPERATIVE building opposite is stone and brick with half-timbered gables and oriel windows. 1887, by *R. Grierson*, of Bangor. Up St David's Lane, the MASONIC HALL is probably by the same architect. Next along Bangor Road, the former SEION CHAPEL, late C19. Three stepped windows above a porch, tall flanking windows, stone with wide red brick bands. Further along, in grounds which must have once been splendid, PLAS CELYN, a handsome mansion built *c.* 1830 by the Smiths of Pendyffryn. Roughly coursed rubble stone. Central block of three bays, with the upper windows taller. Symmetrical lower wings, L-plan, the N gables with large segmentally arched windows. The porch must be an addition. MAENAN CHAPEL, further along at the junction with St John's Park. From a distance, the battlemented tower with pyramidal slated roof looks enticing, but the rest is disappointing. Later C19. Now a dwelling.

Chapel Street leads uphill towards WATER STREET, one of many rows of late C19 quarrymen's houses at this end of town, particularly interesting because the steep site has pushed the upper side pavement well above the lane, with a strip of tiny gardens between. More rows at the top of St David's Road, opposite St David's church: DAVID STREET and ERASMUS STREET, narrow, rather forbidding, with rubble stone houses with lanes, yards and privies behind. 1890s, but looking older. Further downhill, ST DAVID'S TERRACE, 1924, houses for the managerial class. Red brick, tile-hung gables, and verandas between. For some good later housing, a long row of flats below the ESPLANADE, perhaps by *R. J. Hughes*, who worked for Herbert North for a time. Built for the Penmaenmawr & Welsh Granite Co. in the late 1930s, possibly in response to the 1937 legislation concerning overcrowding. Much care was taken to divide the fifty flats into a composition which avoids the tedious repetition of so many housing schemes. Four roughcast blocks, each with advancing and receding bays, and roofs which go up and down. The front doors, recessed for shelter, are reached by bridges on the uphill side.

GLAN-Y-COED, Dwygyfylchi. Large house built in 1882 for Vernon Darbishire. Yellow and red brick. Gothic windows and tall gables. A tower over the entrance, with a steep slated roof, French in feel. Symmetrical LODGES face each other at the entrance gateway, dated 1923 on their half-timbered gables. Each with a Voysey-ish tower above the door, bullseye windows and pyramidal roof. To the N, PENDYFFRYN HALL, *c.* 1700–10, for George Thomas Smith, enlarged in 1854 for S. Dukinfield Darbishire. Stuccoed, with Doric porches to S and E. Much altered and now surrounded by caravans.

The DRUID'S CIRCLE is the best-known of a group of Bronze Age monuments set on a high plateau. The monuments designed for ceremony are this impressive stone circle, with tall stones linked by a low stone bank with an entrance on the W side; a low ring cairn 160 yds (145 metres) to the SW, without uprights but with larger stones spaced regularly around the inner edge; a line of stones blocking the approach to the plateau from the W with a badly disturbed ring of boulders beside it; and a small ring of large boulders on the NE approach to the sanctuary. These open circular monuments were excavated in 1959 revealing pits filled with burnt earth and quartz and human cremation burials. These belonged to the final phases of activity in monuments likely to have been used for several centuries during the second millennium B.C. Gathered around the ceremonial circles are a number of BURIAL MOUNDS. The most impressive are on the col to the W.*

5542

PENMORFA

Before Tremadog, Porthmadog and the surrounding land were developed, Penmorfa was the first dry footfall for those crossing the muddy Traeth from the S.

ST BEUNO. Delightful setting, at the end of a lane WSW from the village. Small church with undivided nave and chancel. The battered internal walls of the nave suggest it is earlier than the chancel, probably C14. S doorway probably C16; C18 porch and vestry. W window in a blocked doorway, possibly C16, or much later; the upper W window indicates a former gallery. Other windows C19. The church was extensively restored and re-roofed by *John Douglas* in 1899 as a result of his involvement at Wern Manor (*see* below). Now owned by the Friends of Friendless Churches. – SCREEN. Jacobethan style and arcaded. – LECTERN, an oak angel with spreading wings, and FONT COVER, a winged eagle, both very late C19, carved by *Constance Mary Greaves*, an aunt of Clough Williams-Ellis. – STAINED GLASS. Early C16 fragments, w. – Chancel N by *Ward & Hughes*, 1896. – Chancel S, by *Mayer* of Munich, attractive. – MONUMENTS. Alabaster cartouche to Sir John Owen, Clenennau, (†1666), by *Robert Wynne* of Ruthin, *c.* 1700. – Three marble memorials to members of the Huddart family of Brynkir and Bath, *c.* 1840. – C17 tablets to William Maurice of Clenennau †1622, and Emanuel Annwyl †1646. – SE of the chancel, a large slate chest tomb again to William Maurice of

---

*In the centuries around 3000 B.C. Penmaenmawr was the third largest source of stone axe-heads in Britain. The geologically distinctive rock (Graig Lwyd, Group VII) can be shaped by controlled flaking, is exceptionally hard, and can take a good polish; many hundreds of axe-heads made from it have been found, mainly in North Wales but also in Wiltshire, the Thames estuary, Yorkshire and Scotland. Exploitation seems to have expanded through the third millennium B.C. until the use of metal made such stone tools redundant.

Clenennau, apparently of this size because he was buried with his horse. – LYCHGATE. Wonderfully organic, dated 1698.

ZION CALVINISTIC METHODIST CHAPEL. 1868, possibly by the *Rev. Thomas Thomas*. Rubble, with ashlar quoins and dressings. The outer lights of the central triplet neatly establish the height for the tall flanking lights. Florentine window heads.

GATEWAY, on main road just below Zion chapel. Stone gateway to village playing field (King George's Field), probably by *Clough Williams-Ellis*, on land given by Richard Greaves of Wern. A flight of steps leads to a platform above a semicircular archway through which a stream disgorges into a pool. From the platform, access to the field is through a second semicircular arched opening; above, a Dutch gable, with plaque 'George V A.D. 1910–1936'.

PLAS ISA. E of the chapel, on S side of the main road. A pair of early to mid-C19 semi-detached houses. No. 1, nearest the road, is largely unchanged. Of three bays. Blind upper window at centre. Veranda below. Wide eaves, with slated soffit and modillions.

WERN MANOR, ½ m. SW of Penmorfa (access is from the A497). Large country house remodelled in Jacobean style by *Douglas & Fordham* in 1892 for R. M. Greaves, of the Llechwedd slate quarry in Blaenau Ffestiniog and uncle to Clough Williams-Ellis. Imposing main front, composed asymmetrically, a three-storey central part with shaped gable, flanked on the r. by a two-storey semicircular bay to the drawing room, and on the l. by a single-storey porch busily decorated with obelisk finials and strapwork-carved pilasters. The E elevation is long and straggling, and changes in the stonework indicate the different builds. A few fine rooms, but most of the interior is altered. In the entrance hall, a ribbed ceiling, oak floor and Delft-tiled fireplace. To the E, the drawing room with ornate ceiling; to the W, the saloon, a vast room, with bay window and a grand Jacobean fireplace. The main staircase is behind the drawing room, with an open well and a three-arched screen at first-floor level. Greaves was an inventor of gadgets, and designed a miniature railway which ran between kitchen and dining room (sometimes delivering children if not food) within a duct incorporated in the boxed window sills; also, a chemical refrigerator (which exploded) in the cellar, a copper coat-dryer, water closets flushed with hot water in the winter and a complex fire extinguisher located behind the hall.

N of the main house, a fine COURTYARD RANGE, consisting of coachhouse, stables, turbine house, gun room and a two-storey clock tower with a pyramidal slated roof punctured by gabled windows on all four sides and surmounted by a timber bellcote containing the clock. E of the house (beyond a walled garden), substantial FARM BUILDINGS, including an open-sided barn. The GARDENS were laid out in 1891–2 by *Thomas Mawson*, an early example of his work, consisting of terraces, axial summerhouse and ornamental pool. Also of note are the LODGE and GATEWAY, probably pre-dating Douglas's work.

St Michael, Treflys, 1¼ m. sw. In a raised squarish churchyard on the headland E of Criccieth. A tiny church, perhaps
c13. Low nave and chancel, sturdy gabled w bellcote.
w doorway of two monolithic jambs and thin voussoirs.
Restored by *Kennedy* in 1888–9 rebuilding the chancel with a
new arch to replace the previous rough round opening, a new
roof and lancet windows. – FONT. Medieval, small round bowl
with chamfered rim, from St Catherine's church, Criccieth. –
INSCRIBED STONE. C6, found in the churchyard wall in 1904.
Originally set vertically, so that the inscription reads
downwards below the Chi-Rho symbol. IACONUS FILI(?)
MIN-/IACIT.

Cist Cerrig, Treflys. Only the three fine and well-matched tall
stones from the front of this portal dolmen survive, a satisfying sculptural group. The chamber and cairn have gone. On
the sloping surface of an outcrop s of the tomb is a group of
cupmarks.

PENRHOS

3434

1½ m. NE of Llanbedrog.

St Cynwyl. A small Neo-Norman church of 1842 by *George
Alexander*, replacing a thatched one. Round-headed w doorway
with plain shafts, tiny flanking windows. Triplet E window.
A tall MONUMENTAL PILLAR to Gruffudd ap John Wynn
†1613, carved with his arms, against the N wall. Now
redundant.

Bethel Calvinistic Methodist Chapel. 1863. Stuccoed,
an arch over two windows and an arched panel between.
Ornate ceiling rose.

PENRHOSGARNEDD *see* BANGOR

PENRHYN BAY

8482

The old village of Penrhyn-side, on the hill, overlooking the
sprawl of modern Penrhyn Bay. Winding streets and steep lanes,
some chapels converted to dwellings, a few early c19 houses
spoilt by pebbledash and plastic windows. Plas Coed, an
environmentally conscious house on the steep hillside above
Woodbine Terrace, puts the living rooms towards the sun and the
service rooms into the hill. 2007, by *Tarmaster Jones Architects* of
Deganwy. At the foot of the hill, Penrhyn Old Hall (*see* below).
Not much of note in the newer parts. Redlands, Penrhyn
Isaf Road, has a certain presence. Red brick, with some diaper
work, and green diminishing-course slates. Probably 1930s.
St David's Close, off St David's Road, is a quaint little
cul-de-sac of picturesque cottages, almost a village in itself.
Jettied upper floors, bay windows, half-timbering. By *G. A. Essex*,

a local builder, *c.* 1937. No. 63 LLANDUDNO ROAD, Art Deco. The usual rounded corners with curved windows, chevron glazing to the stairs, roof terrace etc.

ST DAVID, Glan-y-môr Road. 1963, by *Roiser & Whitestone* of Cheltenham. Set back from the road, with a tall free-standing brick and dark green granite campanile, w, and a church hall, E. Monopitch roof, much higher on the sunny side, supported on brick piers. Tall slightly pointed five-light windows between, each concrete mullion and strip of glazing set on the skew to prevent glare. Big curved laminated beams internally, and an E wall clad in granite slabs.

YSGOL Y CREUDDYN, Derwen Lane. The County School (now Ysgol Glanwydden) of 1910, was considerably expanded N in the 1980s by the *Gwynedd County Architects* (project architect *Graeme Hughes*). Now independent of the original school. The first phase a lopsided dual-pitch building extruded and bent to form a large C-plan around a courtyard. Roughcast ground storey, slated upper storey, very steep and with skylights on one side, shallower on the other. At each knuckle, the upper-floor passage bridges over a foyer. In a later phase, the courtyard filled in with more rooms and a large octagonal assembly hall. Additional blocks 2005. An imaginative and well-conceived scheme.

(PENRHYN OLD HALL, ¼ m. W. Largish C16 house, home of Robert Pugh, a Catholic related to the Bulkeleys of Beaumaris. H-plan, built into the hillside. The earliest part at the S corner, then gradually extended to the N, with a central cross-wing of *c.* 1570 and a NE wing of *c.* 1590. The SW wing, the Hall, is of three bays and has a lateral fireplace in the central bay, with a carved bressumer and a diagonal chimney. Fluted and roll-moulded beams in the NW bay. In the SE gable, a tall chimney partly projecting on three corbels. The cross-wing is in two parts: the earlier SW half of two bays, with a re-set C15 trefoil-head upper window and above, in the NE gable, a small wooden window with diagonal mullions. The NE half is of uncertain date and forms a link with the wider NE wing, the kitchen. Wide fireplace with a segmental arch of voussoirs and the date 1590 above. C18 built-in cupboard, r., with inscription 'Peace, quiet and good company'. Stepped SE gable. Much altered, now a pub.

To E, the former CHAPEL, probably C16. Now derelict.)

PENRHYN CASTLE *see* LLANDEGAI

PENTIR

ST CEDOL. An early church by *Kennedy*, built 1848 to replace the late C17 Llangedol chapel to the N. Very steep double bellcote, each narrow light with a quatrefoil above. Steep roofs. Rubble walls with grey limestone dressings, and gabled buttresses reaching the eaves. Pairs of lancets with roundel above, and carved headstops to the hoodmoulds. A nice three-light E window, stepped and with heavily moulded arch-heads. Attached shafts, detached inside, with floriate capitals. W gallery on cylindrical piers. Arch-braced trusses with high collars and curved struts. – PULPIT. Polished limestone, round and cantilevered from the chancel arch wall, with access from the S vestry. – Open BENCHES with tall fleur-de-lys finials. – FONT. Polished limestone, with fleurs-de-lys and cusped arcading on the bowl. C19. – MONUMENT. Hugh Williams †1754, his wife †1782, and other family. White marble tablet between enriched pilasters, a shield below and a weeping lady leaning on a big urn above.

S of the church, the tiny HAMLET on the old road, now by-passed. The heavily restored VAYNOL ARMS W of the 'square', and a terrace of three houses to the S. A former shop in the middle, and PLASTIRION on the r., with a lead-roofed veranda and bracketed eaves. Further E along the B4366 road, RHYD-Y-GROES, another collection of houses, and the Gothic-style converted CHAPEL, built 1868.

₅₃₄₀
PENTREFELIN

ST CYNHAEARN, Ynyscynhaearn, 1 m. S. (Friends of Friendless Churches). In a remote walled churchyard raised above marsh-land. By *John Williams* (?), *c.* 1832, slightly E of a previous church known as Ystumllyn chapel. Cruciform. Unpromising outside, but a good unspoilt pre-Ecclesiological interior, with W GALLERY, tiered BOX PEWS in the N transept, vestry in the S transept and shallow sanctuary with pews each side and Ten Commandments and Creed boards above the gilded REREDOS. – PULPIT. Three-decker; the plan shows direct access from the vestry, but the executed stair is an elegant curved one from the nave, as is the one to the gallery. – BENCHES AND PEWS. Simple design. Names of pew-holders painted on the ends. – ORGAN. Fine early C19 Gothic case, possibly made by *Flight & Robson*. Originally in Tremadog church, but moved to Ynyscynhaearn in 1854. – STAINED GLASS. E window 1899 and N transept window 1906, by *Powells*. – LYCH-GATE. Rough slate roof, rubble walls, cast-iron gate, with slate headstones inside; all C18. – CHURCHYARD. Two mid-C19 railed tombs to members of the Carreg and Pilkington families. – Gravestone (N side of path) to John Ystumllyn †1791, said to be the first black slave brought into Wales. – Pink late C19 granite tombstones outside the main N door, to John Williams (Ioan Madog) and Ellis Owen, bards. – Slate ledger tomb (W end of churchyard) to David Owen 1709–39, composer of 'Dafydd y Garreg Wen' and important figure of Welsh harp music.

CHURCH HALL. By *Clough Williams-Ellis*, 1937. An attempt at a convenient substitute for the old church, built in the vicarage garden. Stone, rectangular, with rounded corners. Sprocketed roofs of small slates ingeniously flowing round the corners. w doorway in a splayed recess, oval niche for the bell above, and a square-section Chinoiserie w cupola. The small sanctuary can be decorously shut off by folding doors.

LLYS CYNHAEARN. Built as the RECTORY by *Clough Williams-Ellis*, 1913. In the Philip Webb tradition; perhaps the most successful of Clough's Arts and Crafts houses. Stone, with generous slated roofs and tall chimneys of the historic Snowdonian type. Two wings meeting at a quadrant two-storey porch form the N entrance. The more substantial range, of eight small-paned windows on the s, externally has one storey with a central two-bay gable with an *œil de bœuf* window above and flanking semi-dormers, but two full floors internally. The semi-dormers are a repeating motif round the subtleties of the original massing. A recent addition to its w, albeit of stone and continuing the corbelled jetty of the porch wing, upsets the composition and shows up the refinement of the Edwardian work.

CARREG FELEN, ½ m. E. Two wings round a small formal garden. The r. wing is a medieval downhill-sited house rebuilt in the early C18 by Roger Price of Rhiwlas, Llanfor (M), High Sheriff in 1711. The l. wing is early C17; between them, a small C18 stair. Reticent alterations, additions and the paved garden by *Clough Williams-Ellis*, 1922.

YSTUMLLYN. 1 m. E of Criccieth. Elizabethan T-plan house, built by Ellis ap Cadwaladr, *c.* 1590, with an early C18 wing behind and many attached outbuildings of later date – all with tall chimneys. Main roof raised, with other alterations, in the early C19, then again in the mid C20. The old house follows the later medieval type with parlour and full upper floor. Cyclopean semicircular lintel to the main door. (Hall with a nine-compartment, three-tier beamed ceiling and a lateral fireplace. Flat timber lintel, and panels from a heraldic overmantel fixed beside it with the arms of Owain Gwynedd and Collwyn ap Tangno. The wing has initials and datestones for two prominent local clergymen, Ellis Wyn, 1729 and (in the garden?) Humphrey Wynn, 1720. The interior preserves the staircase with classical turned balusters, and an upper room with a wood pediment over the fireplace.)

BRON-Y-FOEL, in uplands 1¼ m. ESE. Roughly T-plan. The stem, of two storeys, probably late C16, with an end fireplace in the main (N) room and two service rooms to the s. A fine ceiling to the main room, of primary and secondary beams, all stop-chamfered. A spiral stair w of the fireplace. E of it, a doorway to the later cross-wing, of one storey with attic.

PENYGROES

4754

Penygroes developed in the early C19 as a result of quarrying in the Nantlle valley. A turnpike was formed *c.* 1820 and the Nantlle tramroad in 1828. The latter followed the route of the present FFORDD Y SIR (County Road) to Talysarn to the E, and LÔN PITAR and FFORDD HAEARN (Tram Road) to the NW. Small-scale workshops were established *c.* 1815 to produce quarry machinery.

CHRIST CHURCH. Small and low, in a churchyard without graves and surrounded by housing estates. Unremarkable E.E. design by *Kennedy*, 1890. S porch, S vestry. A proliferation of buttresses, surely for effect rather than necessity. Oversized stone crosses on the gables.

BETHEL CALVINISTIC METHODIST CHAPEL, off Stryd Fawr (NW). 1860, elaborated 1901. Balustraded two-bay Tuscan porch. Pedimented above Palladian window.

Next to the chapel, with a lane between, the SUNDAY SCHOOL, 1899. Also of three bays, but a single central door between paired pilasters and a two-light window above.

On STRYD FAWR (High Street), No. 17, a largish double-gabled building was the RED LION INN, by *Richard Hall*, *c.* 1900. The large doorway, r., led to stables behind. Sadly much altered since the fine illustration in *Building News*. Then, on the l., beyond the lane to Bethel chapel, TREDDAFYDD, a quarrymen's terrace built *c.* 1837 by *David Griffith* of Caernarfon. Original wide eaves, heavy slates and small window openings in some houses.

Along Heol Buddug, a small doctors' SURGERY, r., 1986, by *Adam & Frances Voelcker*. L-plan forming a little courtyard. Recessed entrance, a projecting bay window to the rear. At the junction of Heol Buddug with Ffordd y Sir, BOD OWEN and ARFON, a picturesque group of two tiny houses with colourful slated roofs, built in the early C20 as offices (and presumably showpiece) for the Dorothea slate quarry. Further E, another

Penygroes, The Red Lion Inn.
Engraving, 1901

decorative roof on TURNPIKE, a former toll house, c. 1840. Coursed rubble, with projecting pieces of slate in alternate courses.

YSGOL DYFFRYN NANTLLE, straddles FFORDD-Y-BRENIN. The first phase, r., built 1898 as the County Intermediate School, probably by *Rowland Lloyd Jones*. An attractive ensemble of rounded and triangular gables facing s. Later phases, l.: a meandering block, more roof than wall, by *Gwynedd County Architects c.* 1980s, and to the N, a largish block of 1939, by *Westbury Lloyd Jones*. Two-storeyed, with recessed canted bay windows at both levels, similar to those used in the 'open-air' schools earlier in the century.

PANT-DU, Hen Lôn, ½ m. E. Early C17 farmhouse, with a short W wing forming a T-plan. Tall N chimney, with moulded and corbelled capping; the lateral chimney to the W removed, but a plaster shield of arms surviving on the breast inside. Large fireplace, N, with mural stair. Much altered. Long BARN range, S, converted by *Adam & Frances Voelcker*, 2007–8.

PISTYLL 3343

ST BEUNO. By a stream, on a shelf 200 ft (60 metres) above the sea. A pilgrimage church, on the route from Clynnog Fawr to Bardsey Island. Nave and chancel in one, W bellcote. Blocked S doorway of a still smaller church, the E end being a late medieval addition (two slit windows to the sanctuary). W doorway with crude Tudor head. The roof, of unornamented arch-braced principals, has the shallow pitch of the C16 too. Rough wall-plate panelling. Renewed paving and pews. Walls scraped dark and bare, except for a text over the E window and a perished N wall painting of St Christopher. But the tradition of spreading the floor with rushes and sweet-smelling herbs is still maintained. – FONT. Late C10–C11*. Circular, but tapering inwards to the upper rim, which is scalloped. Carved all round with a Manx-style chain of overlapping ovals interwoven with a horizontal band, each of these forms being duplicated. Of buff gritstone.

CROSS-INSCRIBED STONE, 1 m. SSW (SH 319 418), re-set into the base of the S roadside wall between Pistyll and Nefyn (almost opposite a large lay-by). Small C8–C9 stone inscribed with a cross inside a circle. It is believed to have been a prayer stone connected with the pilgrim route to Bardsey.

PONTLLYFNI 4352

The BRIDGE, c. 1776, takes the Caernarfon to Pwllheli turnpike over the Llyfni. Hardly a village, but to the E, a small cluster

*The Royal Commission and Malcom Thurlby give a C12 date for this, and similar Anglesey fonts.

around BRYNAERAU CHAPEL. 1879. Plain round-headed windows with intersecting glazing bars, more handsome than those to the main frontage. Airy and spacious interior, surprisingly large for such a small place. CHAPEL HOUSE, W, and VESTRY, N. Up the lane to the SE, one of the first 'open air' SCHOOLS in the county, *c.* 1911, by *Rowland Lloyd Jones*, County Architect. The lane leads NE to PONT-Y-CIM, a charming little hogback bridge, only 9 ft (2.8 metres) wide, built 1612 by Catherine Buckley, whose fiancé drowned crossing the river here.

PORT DINORWIC *see* Y FELINHELI

PORTHMADOG

A busy town on the Glaslyn estuary. Once a port for shipbuilding and the export of slates, expanded to become the regional centre.

The first 'port' for shipping slates from Ffestiniog was 1½ m. SW, at Ynys Cyngar. But an unexpected result of Madocks's great embankment, the Cob (*see* p. 500), was that the Glaslyn scoured out a better harbour at the embankment's W end, not only deeper and more protected than Ynys Cyngar, but nearer to his new town of Tremadog (q.v.). The new harbour was formed 1820–5, facilitating imports of timber, coal and lime, and exports of copper ore and, of course, slates. These were hauled from the quarries on an arduous three-stage journey involving horseback, cart and boat. When a railroad was laid to avoid this inconvenience, the Cob was used for the final leg of the journey. The Festiniog (*sic*) Railway was completed 1836, and from this date Porthmadog grew rapidly. Initial development was in the Cornhill area, W and N of the dock. In the 1850s–70s, when shipbuilding became important, development shifted N towards Tremadog, the new part lozenge-shaped in plan. The non-maritime 'industrial sector' developed at the NE edge of the town. The Cambrian railway arrived 1868, its station at the N end. Today, the expansion is towards the W, in the form of business and light industrial units.

The town's buildings are mostly of stone and slate: the stone from the former quarries on Moel-y-gest, the mountain looming W of the town, and from the Minffordd quarries near Penrhyndeudraeth; the slate from Ffestiniog. A common alternative to stucco or bare stone is smallish pieces of granite pressed into mortar (see, for example, the NW side of Bank Place).

CHURCHES AND CHAPELS

ST JOHN, Penamser Road. Built 1873–6, more convenient location than the remote parish church at Ynyscynhaearn, Pentrefelin (q.v.) or St Mary, Tremadog (q.v.). The local architect, *Thomas Roberts*, was considered by the Incorporated Church

Building Society to be insufficiently experienced, so *Axmann & Perrott* were brought in from London. Aisled nave and chancel, with s vestry added 1897. Snecked rock-faced stone, yellow Bath stone dressings and pink sandstone bands. Two-light aisle windows with quatrefoils, alternating with stepped three-lighters, all cusped. The E and W windows hardly more elaborate. The three-stage NW tower, added 1898, stands detached from the nave. Angle buttresses and bold octagonal corner turrets. Surprisingly spacious interior, with a fine roof of arch-braced trusses alternating with kingpost trusses with tie, collar and semicircular arch braces. The chancel converted to a meeting room.

COMMUNION RAILS and PULPIT. By *H. Miller* of Norwich, the large octagonal oak pulpit carved by *Mrs Constance Greaves* and *A. G. Edwards*. 1912. – LECTERN. In similar style, with a carved figure, 1908. – FONT. Square with rounded corners and relief panels, on a round stem encircled with detached polished stone shafts. Late C19. – Good STAINED GLASS. E window, Parable scenes, probably by *Burlison & Grylls*, c. 1881. Chancel N and S, probably all *Lavers & Westlake*. S aisle, central two windows by *Lavers & Westlake*, c. 1893–4. S aisle, furthest W of four, *Percy Bacon Bros.*, c. 1907. S aisle W, *Powells*, c. 1911. S of W door, St Peter, possibly *Shrigley & Hunt*, c. 1914. – N of W door, semi-abstract Baptism by *Celtic Studios*, 1974. – N aisle w, Faith, Hope and Charity, *Powells*, 1913. – N aisle, l. of three, Sermon on the Mount, *Lavers & Westlake*, 1908. – Centre, Annunciation, by *E. Frampton*, 1899.

THE MOST HOLY REDEEMER (R.C.), Borth Road. An ungainly church, of 1933, neither wholly traditional in style, nor in the more daring C20 style which its architect, *G. Rinvolucri*, employed at Amlwch (A). A concrete barrel-vault roof, concealed in the 1960s below a slated roof behind awkwardly extended gables. On the front, a large stone cross superimposed on a round window. The interior is more successful, with the barrel vault echoed in round-headed apses on three sides of the sanctuary. These are lined with mosaic, blue behind the altar, gold to the sides, designed by *Jonah Jones* in the early 1960s. By him, too, the altar and lectern plaques, and two sandstone statues in the side apses.

SALEM INDEPENDENT CHAPEL, High Street. 1860. A fine (and early) example of the trademark of the *Rev. Thomas Thomas*, the giant arch breaking through the gable pediment. Three bays, the central one recessed, with a big Florentine window above the balustraded balcony and Tuscan porch. Tall round-headed windows in the outer bays, with keystones and impost bands. Giant Tuscan pilasters supporting the pediment, resting on the rusticated plinth. The rather plain interior is disappointing after the grand façade. [102]

GARTH CALVINISTIC METHODIST CHAPEL, Bank Place. 1898, by *O. Morris Roberts & Son*. Raised above the road. Gable front with lower staircase wings, each with a balustraded parapet and two-light windows over segmental-pedimented entrances. The central keyed arch breaks through the pediment as at Salem chapel, but the pediment base continues as the sill of a small lunette. Plain Corinthian pilasters divide the top storey, which is almost an arcade of windows, 2–3–2, all with round moulded heads. Slender pink granite shafts between, and bracketed sills. Below, the same rhythm of windows, the outer pairs with joined pediments, the central triplet with keyed rounded heads. Big urn finials at roof level.

ZION BAPTIST CHAPEL, Avenue Road. 1867. Three pointed windows, with grey ashlar surrounds and quoins contrasting with the darker rubble. A depressed ogee head to the central doorway, and a ball finial above. Now converted.

PUBLIC BUILDINGS

THE COB. A mile-long stone embankment, built 1808–12 by *William Madocks*, and his agent *John Williams* to reclaim the Traeth Mawr for agricultural use, and to link his new town of Tremadog (q.v.) with England, and eventually Ireland. 'A gigantick undertaking', reported Fenton on his tour in 1810, 'which would have appalled any other genius than that of the Gentleman to whose enterprising spirit we owe it'. Madocks did not originally anticipate that the embankment would be used to take a slate railway from the Ffestiniog quarries to his port, but this took until 1836 to become a reality. The embankment was also widened to provide a toll road at a lower level on the N side. The toll of 5p was abolished in 2001, when the road was widened and a path and cycle-way provided at a lower level still.

MARITIME MUSEUM, Oakleys Wharf. The last survivor of the many slate warehouses which covered the wharf. Built in the mid C19 by Matthews & Son, of the Rhiwbryfdir Slate Co. Single-storey, with low roof of fish-scale slates. The fronts were formerly open.

BRITISH SCHOOL (former), Chapel Street. 1869, by *O. Morris Roberts*, his name unusually on the slate plaque. A gabled wing at each end, single-storey to l., two-storey r., each with a lean-to porch. Small bellcote to the l. wing.

PUBLIC LIBRARY, Chapel Street. 1988, by the *Gwynedd County Architects*, on the site of the Tabernacl chapel. A large gable, on a pair of columns and the flanking walls, provides a covered porch area.

CANOLFAN HAMDDEN GLASLYN (Leisure Centre), SW of the railway station. By the *Ap Thomas Partnership*, 1997. A small ornate front added to the larger main building, the volumetric contrast enhanced by a change from the buff brick of the main building to white roughcast and slate. The entrance, a sort of wedge-shaped prow, with a tall recessed chasm of glazing and a huge buttress of slate next to it.

BRYN COFFA (war memorial), Avenue Road. By *Griffith Morris*, early 1950s. On a tiny outcrop, Ynys Calch. A tall granite Celtic cross on a paved plateau, with memorial slabs diagonally at the corners. A flight of concentric steps to a trabeated portal of three huge lengths of granite, then a path spirals to the summit.

PERAMBULATION

The COB is the best starting point, with stunning views of Snowdonia across the Traeth Mawr. The first building, r., is TŶ MOELWYN (Inland Revenue Office), by *Colwyn Foulkes & Partners*, late 1970s, a miserable welcome with its end wall clad in stone as if to mitigate the feeble main elevation. The three-storey mid-C19 CUSTOM HOUSE next, joined to a late C19 terrace with a veranda on decorated cast-iron posts. Behind this, BRITANNIA PLACE, a row of mid-C19 cottages for the Britannia Foundry workers. Nos. 6–7 with attractive radial cast-iron glazing and pivoting opening lights, no doubt made in the foundry. To the r., the SAIL LOFT, mid-C19, with an upper loading door below a projecting beak of roof.

Across the main road, the Festiniog Railway STATION, on the site of the first slate wharf built by Samuel Holland in the 1830s. Beyond, SOUTH SNOWDON WHARF, on the former Rotten Tare where ocean-going sailing ships were built until the late C19. Redeveloped in the early 1970s by *Phillips Cutler Phillips Troy*. The best of this firm's housing schemes in NW Wales, a dense village of yacht-owners' flats planned around a long courtyard for cars. A sawtooth skyline of monopitch roofs, stepping from two-storey to three and back again; all rather 'fidgety', Clough Williams-Ellis felt. Rendered walls in pale pastel shades which would be better if stronger. The courtyard is hard, and lacks greenery, but the outward-facing elevations, with their nautical ladders and balconies, are successful. To the s, CEI BALLAST, an island made from ballast dumped from ships plying the world's oceans, a rich resource for geologists.

The BRITANNIA BRIDGE – 1809 but much altered – takes the road across the Glaslyn. On the r., BRIDGE COTTAGE, mid- to later C19, with almost every surface clad in slate, regular courses alternating with hexagonal, and interlocking ridge and hip tiles. Over the bridge, on the r., in Heol Madog, PLAS YNYS TYWYN, built *c.* 1808 for John Williams, Madocks's director of works for the Cob and the harbour, later extended r. Two-storeyed, with a full-length lean-to and a curious Tudor-arched porch, possibly moved from one of Madocks's turnpike gates. Behind, N, the COACHHOUSE (or possibly the school attached to the foundry), with a tiny bellcote. Nicely juxtaposed with the former CO-OP supermarket by *Bowen Dann Davies*, 1990.

A footpath leads SW along the N side of the harbour, past the C20 slate-clad GANOLFAN (Community Centre) and the Maritime Museum (*see* above). Beyond its N end, the OAKLEYS, a mid-C19 shipping manager's house, with canted bays, hipped roofs and an office to the l. The long low CWRT-Y-HARBWR, behind, built by J. W. Greaves & Son as a

warehouse and two dwellings, now flats. The former SLATE
WHARFS, and a railway, extended from here S towards Craig-
y-don.

The hub of the early town was PENCEI or CORNHILL,
a large open square W of Greaves Wharf. Now attractively
landscaped, but a far cry from the untidy bustle which must
have once prevailed, with its houses, shops, shipping offices,
a bank, workshops, sail-makers' shops, public houses etc.
On the SW side, tall four-storey houses, offices and warehouses.
TŶ TORONTO, with access doors and a former pulley to the
central gabled bay, had a sail loft and William Griffith's
Navigation School in the upper storeys and Casson's Bank,
later the North & South Wales Bank, at ground level. Between
it and the lower terrace to the r., a long flight of STEPS leads
up to Garth Road, where sea captains lived. Nos. 7–10,
PENCEI, drop to three storeys, Nos. 11–15 to two. Nos. 17–21
continue along the NW side in similar vein, all built of good-
quality local stone, the best laid to courses using huge blocks.
At the S corner, the MADOC YACHT CLUB, formerly a three-
storey three-bay house and office to l. and a seamen's news-
room and library upstairs in the r. block, built *c.* 1852 by David
Williams of Deudraeth Castle. To the S, HARBOURSIDE,
another manager's house and office, with a hipped roof and
wide eaves. The octagonal stuccoed house beyond the garden,
TILE WHARF, looks as if it belonged to the grandest of the
managers or captains – in fact it was built in 1988, by *Gruffydd
Price.*

N of Pencei, LOMBARD STREET with well-built mid-C19
houses, shops, inns etc. faces the PARK, once used for making
ropes. Nos. 20–21, the BEE-HIVE ESTABLISHMENT, altered
in the later C19 to form a shop, has hoodmoulds and round-
headed dormers. Opposite, ST DAVID'S BUILDINGS, by
Griffith Morris, c. 1935, a symmetrical office block in brown
brick, the detailing almost Dutch. At the corner with Bank
Place, the MASONIC HALL. Late C19. Snecked rock-faced
stone with darker quoins and raised platband, and a Tuscan
portico. Low railings in front, incorporating the Masonic
crossed dividers.

From here, Bank Place returns NE to the High Street, past Garth
chapel (*see* p. 499). Borth Road runs SW, towards Borth-y-gest
(q.v.). After the R.C. church TERRACE ROAD leads l. into
GARTH ROAD, past the former BEREA CHAPEL (Scotch
Baptist, 1853), l., and the former CHURCH ROOM (1899), r.
Stepping uphill l., Nos. 4–9 ROCHE TERRACE, stuccoed
L-plan houses with curly bargeboards, round-headed upper
windows and bracketed door hoods. Further up, r., GARTH
TERRACE, an elegant row built for master mariners, all mid-
C19 except the later No. 1, with canted full-height bays and
iron balcony between, and the front of No. 5, with its porch
on paired fluted posts. From here, stupendous views of the
harbour, the Cob, the Traeth Mawr and Snowdonia beyond.
On the top, Bron-y-garth and Gelli Faia (*see* p. 504).

The HIGH STREET leads NW from Britannia Bridge, past the
PARK. The HSBC BANK l., originally the North & South Wales
Bank, 1868, by *Kennedy*. Symmetrical Gothic, with Caernar-
fon-head windows. A short lane l. of it leads to BRECON
PLACE, a pair of substantial early C19 houses backing onto
Bank Place. Both stuccoed and of three bays, with paired
brackets to the wide eaves, dropped hoodmoulds to the upper
windows, and a continuous veranda, divided into alternate
small and big bays, with timber latticework above the Tudor-
headed openings. At the corner of Bank Place and the High
Street, (former) WOOLWORTHS, crude 1980s, of dark grey
brick, with silly bracketed window hoods. On this key site was
the Market and Town Hall, built 1846, an upper floor and clock
tower added in 1875, and a glass canopy on two sides added
in 1902. Here was a proper focus to the town, now sadly
lacking. The remainder of the High Street is un-noteworthy,
though not unattractive. Here and there, bits of original fabric
show through the modern alterations: wide bracketed eaves,
hoodmoulds with long drops and decorated stops, generous
sash windows etc. At the roundabout, where the High Street
cranks N, KERFOOTS, dated 1874, with round-headed
windows, has a fine spiral staircase rising through its three
storeys. Two hotels at this end of town, the ROYAL SPORTS-
MAN, 1862, on the r. and the QUEEN'S beyond the station.
Both are solid but dull. Of more character, the COLISEUM
CINEMA, r. 1931. Probably by *J. Egbert Griffiths* of *O. Morris
Roberts & Son*. A stuccoed front, almost Art Deco. The interior remarkably unaltered. Then the 1930s Neo-Georgian
TELEPHONE EXCHANGE, of greenish-grey snecked stone and
greenish slates, and round-headed windows with radial glazing.
Reminiscent of Clough Williams-Ellis, but lacking his wit.
Opposite the TESCO supermarket and its large car park replace
the primary school. Bifurcated steel columns support a full-
length overhang. Simple, clean-looking and architecturally
unobjectionable. Opposite Zion chapel (*see* p. 500), Y CYT, a
narrow water channel running NW. This was the canal cut by
Madocks to connect Tremadog with the port.

PENAMSER ROAD leads W from the roundabout towards
St John's church. GATWS, early to mid-C19, the lodge to Morfa
Lodge (*see* below). Fish-scale slates on the roof. Beyond,
TUDOR LODGE, a three-storey half-timbered guesthouse, late
C19. Extended at the rear by *David Lea*, 1996, when it was the
Catholic Centre for Healing and Marriage. The extension faces
the garden. A long low wing, the owners' flat, divided unequally
into two lengthways, and barrel-vaulted internally. Two-storeyed
nearer the house, with a library overlooking the garden through
a large window. The building curls snail-like round the top end
of the garden, with four tiny counselling rooms in a tight semicircle around a pool. Inward-sloping slate roof, and a glazed
roof to the passage wrapping round the drum. White roughcast, with joinery painted Wedgwood blue or left clear. A lovely,
thoughtful scheme, sadly no longer in use as intended.

BRON-Y-GARTH, Garth Road. Largish house overlooking the harbour, built in 1849 for Charles E. Spooner, manager of the Festiniog Railway. Picturesque LODGE, with ogee lintels and a polygonal open porch on rustic timber posts.

GELLI FAIA (formerly Morfa Lodge), Borth Road. Built by William Madocks, c. 1806. The original nearly square in plan, with a veranda on three sides (now filled in) and a hipped roof with wide eaves, similar to Tan-yr-allt, Tremadog (q.v.). Three-storey N wing added in the mid C19. Much altered.

PORT PENRHYN see BANGOR

5842

PRENTEG

Tiny village overlooking the Traeth Mawr, E of Tremadog. It extends steeply uphill to the NW.

ABERDUNANT HALL, ¼ m. NW. A house is recorded in the early C17, owned by Maurice Wynn. In the early C19, the home of Col. G. L. Wardle, High Sheriff in 1803, friend of Madocks and 'by far the most colourful and least respectable of the Reform party' (Elisabeth Beazley). Much enlarged in the later C19 by Robert Parry Jones-Parry. Long SE-facing range with gabled cross-wings at each end. Hipped entrance, r., with reset archway, probably from one of Madocks's toll gates. Dark slatey rubble, mullion-and-transom windows with slate Tudor hoods.

GORLLWYN-UCHAF, 4½ m. E. Single-storey house with upper floor in roof, in remote uplands. Inside, two cruck-trusses and part of a post-and-panel partition. The crucks may date from the first half of the C16, when the house was perhaps timber-framed and thatched. Later replaced with rough stone walls (and a full-height projecting chimney on the NW gable) and a slated roof.

ERW SURAN, 1 m. NW. Late C17 or early C18 farmhouse. Two bays, with SE extension in line. Rough rubble, the walls rebuilt above the ground floor. Voussoir-headed doorway with massive r. jamb. With its outbuildings opposite, a good ensemble.

3735

PWLLHELI

The principal town of the Llŷn. The commotal centre of Afloegion in the C12. Already a town before the Edwardian conquest, it was created a free borough by the Black Prince in 1355. Laid waste by Owain Glyndŵr in the early C15, it recovered to become an important port, a shipbuilding centre and a thriving market town. Tourism has been its mainstay since the late C19, when the S of the town was developed by Solomon Andrews, entrepreneur from Cardiff. He had visited the town on holiday and thought it suitable for development, like Llandudno.

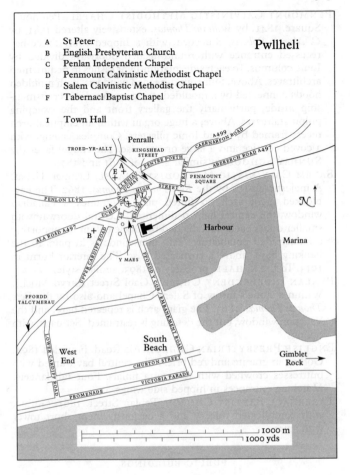

A   St Peter
B   English Presbyterian Church
C   Penlan Independent Chapel
D   Penmount Calvinistic Methodist Chapel
E   Salem Calvinistic Methodist Chapel
F   Tabernacl Baptist Chapel

I   Town Hall

Pwllheli

Penrallt

TROED-YR-ALLT
KINGSHEAD STREET
PENTRE POETH
Y FRATH
CAERNARFON ROAD A499
ABERERCH ROAD A497
PENMOUNT SQUARE
PENLON LLŶN
ALA UCHAF
LLEINIAU UCHAF
HIGH STREET
PENLAN ST.
GAOL ST.
ALA ROAD A497
FFORDD Y COB / EMBANKMENT ROAD
UPPER CARDIFF ROAD
Y MAES
B
N
Harbour
Marina
FFORDD TALCYMERAU
LOWER CARDIFF ROAD
South Beach
West End
Gimblet Rock
CHURTON STREET
PROMENADE
VICTORIA PARADE

1000 m
1000 yds

CHURCHES

ST PETER, Lleiniau Uchaf. An aisled church by *J. O. Scott*, 1887, succeeding the towered one of 1834, by *William Thomas*. Competent early C14 style, with windows of grouped quatrefoil lancets, in yellow and pink sandstone. Snecked rubble, grey and yellow stone in chequerboard pattern at the gable-tops. N aisle and vestry added *c.* 1908. The W tower never built. A spacious interior, the aisles surprisingly lofty. – FONTS. A deep heptagonal bowl – perhaps the medieval one from the demolished parish church, St Deneio. Also a flaring Dec design in red sandstone, of 1889, on an open-arcaded stem. – STAINED GLASS. Chancel and S aisle E windows by *Powells*, 1896 and 1889. Chancel N, by *George J. Hunt*. N aisle, three windows by *Kempe & Co.*, the central of the N windows, by *Powells*, 1913.

PENMOUNT CALVINISTIC METHODIST CHAPEL, Penmount Square. 1841, by *William Thomas*, extensively altered 1881, by *O. Morris Roberts*. Stuccoed, with a hipped roof. Three-bay recessed entrance with round-headed doorways divided by Ionic columns. To each side, margin-light sashes in pedimented architraves. Above, four round-headed windows, with moulded hoods connected by a moulded string course. Fine craftsmanship inside, particularly the gallery front and the sweeping pulpit staircases. Above, a huge organ within an elliptical-arch recess framed by fluted Ionic pilasters. Complex ceiling, with a coved cornice and a large ornate rose. The chapel faces the SUNDAY SCHOOL, in similar style, of 1861 and 1870.

SALEM CALVINISTIC METHODIST CHAPEL, Lleiniau Uchaf. A majestic design by the *Rev. Thomas Thomas*, 1862. The key-blocked giant arch on fluted pilasters frames a Palladian window, the central light pedimented. Central doorway with smaller doors each side, divided by Doric columns supporting a balustraded entablature. Tall, thin windows in pairs to the flanking bays, above a rusticated base. The interior burnt in 1913. To the N, HALL, probably of 1893, similar style.

PENLAN INDEPENDENT CHAPEL, Gaol Street (Stryd Moch). Within a stone's throw of Salem Chapel and also by the *Rev. Thomas Thomas*, 1863. The giant arch is repeated here, and the Venetian window, but the detailing is restrained. Set back, with railings.

ENGLISH PRESBYTERIAN CHURCH, Ala Road. Founded 1894. Gothic, in granite and red brick. The central bay framed with buttresses crowned with terracotta finials. Four tall lancets. Matching entrances in hipped side wings.

TABERNACL BAPTIST CHURCH, Penlan Street. 1861, Gothic, with complicated tracery and a curiously inept short tower with spire.

PUBLIC BUILDINGS

OLD TOWN HALL, Market Square and Penlan Street (now Rodney Adams Antiques). First mentioned in 1731 as a Guildhall. Rebuilt *c.* 1820 as a market hall, with council chambers above and a gaol in the cellar. Altered 1836, the louvred clock tower added 1866. Attractive ashlar building, with a cranked plan connecting the two streets. A broad pediment to each front, with a row of sash windows above segmental arcades.

TOWN HALL, Penlan Street. Built *c.* 1902 by *A. J. Dickinson*, Borough Surveyor, with a lack of finesse. Three storeys, very red Ruabon brick and terracotta. Large upper auditorium, with a three-sided gallery on cast-iron columns with foliate capitals.

COUNCIL OFFICES, Y Cob/Embankment Road. 1980, by *Lewis & Percival* of Wolverhampton, with *J. Arfon Hughes*, Dwyfor District Council Architect. L-plan, two storeys. Piers of grey brick with a brick parapet. In the foyer, a buff stone SCULPTURE by *Jonah Jones*, 1987, titled Etifeddiaeth (Inheritance), depicting an intimate family group.

BRITISH SCHOOL (former), Troed-yr-allt. 1856, by *Wehnert & Ashdown* of London and Llandudno. It was big and ambitious, Gothic style, but destroyed by fire in 1962, and rebuilt as flats incorporating a few original elements.

COLEG MEIRION-DWYFOR, Penrallt. Formerly the County School, *c.* 1903, by *Rowland Lloyd Jones*. Five gables, the outer ones wider and taller, and with odd, stepped copings. Classical porch with a guilloche-moulded parapet. Extensive c20 additions, N, by *Howard Jones, Gwynedd County Architects*.

FORMER COUNTY SCHOOL (YSGOL FRONDEG), Ala Uchaf. 1930, by *Westbury Lloyd Jones*, County Architect. An 'open-air' school, of two storeys. The entrances, are surprisingly ornate for 1930. The upper classrooms are grouped around a s-facing roof terrace intended for physical exercise. The original canted-recess windows all folded back. Now a community centre.

HOSPITAL, Ala Road. The former Pwllheli Union Workhouse, *c.* 1838–9, by *William Thomas*. Standard cruciform plan with a central octagonal block. The only front not covered in pebbledash faces the road. Three-bay wings each side of a slightly projecting pedimented bay. A large, recessed entrance subdivided with tall tapering piers.

RAILWAY STATION, Station Square. 1909, replacing a station of 1867 ½ m. E. Timber, with felted roof and brick chimneys. Three gables to the long front, and a lower gable to the porch. Concourse and platform canopies added *c.* 1920. Quaint and simple, just right for Edwardian visitors.

PERAMBULATION

The ASDA car park, at the NE of the town, makes a good start. It was the 'salt pool' which gave the town its name. The town developed around the haven it provided, particularly to the SW. Y TRAETH, which later closed off the haven from the E, leads S to PENMOUNT SQUARE, an attractive ensemble of mid-C19 stone terraces and chapel buildings (*see* Penmount chapel, above) around a paved courtyard with fine railings, perhaps the site of the medieval motte. The sea touched the chapel until a new SEA WALL was built *c.* 1802. The HIGH STREET leads W from here. On the l., No. 34, NATWEST BANK. An early C19 town house, with stables behind. Later segmental pediments to the upper windows. Next, No. 36, also stuccoed and perhaps two houses originally. No. 38, of four bays, has slender columns to the portico and blind attic windows. Gothic heads to the doorways of No. 40. Opposite, Nos. 33–35, a stuccoed pair with Corinthian pilasters and pediments busily dentilated like zips. Round the bend, l., No. 46, and the HSBC BANK, both *c.* 1899, by *Woolfall & Eccles* of Liverpool. The most sophisticated buildings in the town. Queen Anne, red brick and yellow stone dressings, competently handled. A shell-hood over the bank entrance, Gibbsian surrounds, and a cornice which sweeps up to a broad segmental arch on the side elevation.

Nos. 56–58, late C19, are slate-clad and would look more at home in Totnes. It is curious that slate cladding is not more common in the towns of North Wales. In MARKET SQUARE, a short cul-de-sac on the l., the Old Town Hall (see p. 506). Opposite, at No. 5, green-glazed Art Nouveau tiles around the otherwise altered shopfront. Nearly back on the High Street, an elegant side doorway to No. 60, 1839, with panelled door, fanlight and columns. No. 63, POLLECOFF'S, c. 1800, originally two houses. A good shopfront, with blind boxes. Further w, slightly set back, the large TOWER HOTEL, 1875. Five bays, stuccoed with paired windows on three floors. No. 76, late C19, is sheer fun at cornice level: a wild balustraded parapet adorned with urns and a rounded fanlight pediment.

At the junction with GAOL STREET (Stryd Moch),* PENLON LLŶN continues w along the former turnpike serving the Llŷn. No. 64 was the toll house, 1814. Nos. 39–45, four stuccoed two-storey houses attractively raised and set back behind railings and gardens. Further uphill, on the r., ARGRAIG, an Edwardian villa with half-timbered gable and lower octagonal bay, r., rendered, with idiosyncratic battlements. Timber balcony between.

Returning to the cross-roads, GAOL STREET leads s downhill. At the corner of Penlon Llŷn, the WHITEHALL, built 1818 as a hotel. Three-bay with deep eaves. The GAOL was built s of the junction with Ala Uchaf, 1829. Opposite, l. of Penlan chapel (see p. 506), Nos. 16–20, low two storeys with steep thick-slated roofs and overhanging eaves, mid- or later C18. STRYD LLYGOD, formerly Custom House Square, leads l. and on to PENLAN STREET, perhaps the town's most interesting and varied street. The car park behind, formerly called Gadlys, might be the site of the former royal court. On the r., CILCOED, classical stucco, built in 1831 by David Evans, timber merchant. Next, PENLAN FAWR, early C17, the oldest building in the town. At various times chapel, school, dental surgery, inn. Dr Johnson stayed here in 1774. Two-storey gabled porch extending over the pavement. The carriage entrance, l., leads to stables etc. behind. Further NE, Tabernacl church, l., then the new Town Hall and further on, the Old Town Hall (see p. 506). Nos. 6–10, r., are early C19. Three storeys, in coursed stone, No. 6 slightly raised at roof level. Unspoilt shopfronts.

KINGSHEAD STREET leads NW from the High Street, just E of the junction with Penlan Street, once called Caroline Square. Nos. 16–22 are mid-C18, with alterations. Half-dormers with raking roofs. PENTRE POETH leads NE, once the N edge of the 'pool'. On the r., LLAWR GORS, a cul-de-sac formerly known as Baptist Square. Photographic records of the (demolished) CHAPEL, built 1816, show a fine interior. Returning to Kingshead Street, the MAGISTRATES' COURT on the site of the Free Grammar School of 1656. Further uphill, parts of the British

*The Welsh name in recognition of the former pig market near the same junction.

School (*see* p. 507) are incorporated in the row of FLATS; above them, PICTON CASTLE, a cubic C19 house with slim corner towers. At the top of the hill, the Welsh Grammar School, now Coleg Meirion-Dwyfor (*see* p. 507).

LLEINIAU UCHAF leads SW from Pentre Poeth. On the l., ST PETER'S TERRACE, formerly Dearden Row, named after the builder. 1870s, steep stuccoed gables and arcaded windows above a continuous pentice roof. St Peter's church is opposite. Further W, Salem chapel. Up ALLT SALEM, l., a long block of pebbledashed flats. The shallow E-plan, gables and slate plaque are clues that this was the NATIONAL SCHOOL of 1843.

Returning downhill, Gaol Street leads into the MAES, reclaimed land later used as a cattle market. A mixture of uses developed, including smithy, slaughterhouse, gas works etc. On the E side, the BODAWEN HOTEL, the word 'Temperance' missing from the lettering – there were eight temperance hotels in 1880. E of the Maes, in STATION SQUARE, the station (*see* p. 507), l., and arcaded SHOPS of *c.* 1906, r.

FFORDD Y COB (Embankment Road) leads ½ m. S to SOUTH BEACH, on one of two embankments formed in 1813. There were two hotels and twenty-six houses here by 1893, and plans for a pier and a sanatorium. Some houses survive in VICTORIA PARADE and CHURTON STREET, but most are unrecognizable. To the E, MORFA'R GARREG, drab council housing of *c.* 1938, and the HARBOUR beyond. The small hill, CARREG-YR-IMBILL (Gimblet Rock), is the remains of a granite outcrop commercially quarried from 1857. To the N, across the narrow channel, GLAN-Y-DON, served by the second embankment of 1813, and now a large MARINA.

THE PROMENADE continues W from South Beach to the WEST END, an area developed by *Solomon Andrews* from 1894, but not united with South Beach until 1916. Very little survives of WEST END PARADE and the concrete-built hotel (demolished 2002), but further W, a late C19 three-storey TERRACE of pastel shades, the bays rippling in and out in harmony with the undulating arched window heads. All the details lost. Part of *Andrews*'s work, and probably built of the yellow Ruabon brick seen elsewhere. *Andrews* built a tramway along the front, initially to transport stone, and later enjoyed by holidaymakers. The track connected with a branch back to the town along UPPER CARDIFF ROAD. In this street, the ASSEMBLY ROOMS above the WEST END STORES, late 1890s, simple white stucco, with five tall upper windows following the shallow gable. Next, a yellow-brick building containing the POST OFFICE. 1900, of five bays, alternately gabled, the window heads of each floor different. Further N, FFORDD TALCYMERAU leads SW to the golf course. In Golf Road, TŶ'R BONT, reputed in 1982 to be the first Postmodern classical house in Wales. By *Oliver Richards* with *Paul James* under the aegis of Terry Farrell. Big pedimented gables front and back, broken by central windows, the S gable with a huge sunburst. Each side of the entrance, tall pillars with globe lights on top.

An awkward blunt-wedge plan, with living rooms above the bedrooms, and a double-height internal conservatory. It looks tired and dated, the fate of most PoMo buildings.

LOWER CARDIFF ROAD returns to the town, over PONT SOLOMON. Near the top end, a row of arcaded SHOPS (1897), r., and the POST OFFICE (1906), l. More yellow-brick TERRACES with curvy gables, built c. 1899 by *Andrews* in ALA ISAF, which runs W at the end of Cardiff Road, past the English Presbyterian church (*see* p. 506), l. and the POLICE STATION of 1874, r. Behind, in ALA UCHAF, Ysgol Frondeg (*see* p. 507) and W, just into ALA ROAD, the former Workhouse (*see* Hospital, p. 507).

BRYNHYFRYD, Abererch Road. Large stucco Italianate villa, built in the early 1840s for William Jones, master shipbuilder, and facing his shipyard before the land was reclaimed. Of two storeys, with substantial attic and cellar, and a lower wing set back on the r. Three bays to the front, with a glazed Ionic porch. Quoins and rustication to the lower storey. Margin-light sashes with moulded surrounds and hoods, the lower ones on brackets. Half-hipped roofs. Tall, grouped chimneystacks each end. Much mahogany used internally, as befits a master ship-builder. A fine grey marble fireplace in the dining room, elegant staircase, etc.

CAEAU GWYNION UCHAF, Deneio, ½ m. N. Late Victorian stuccoed farmhouse, replacing the original house still standing to the NW. A bargeboarded gabled bay each side of the narrow entrance bay. Veranda with hipped ends and fluted cast-iron columns, over two canted bays. Attached HORSE ENGINE HOUSE at the NE, for pumping water and operating the butter churn. A range of FARM BUILDINGS further NE: cowhouse, hen house, pigsties, cattle shed etc. Kingpost trusses, pointed brick doorway heads, impressive granite lintels from Carreg-yr-imbill.

GORPHWYSFA, ¾ m. NW. Stuccoed late C19 villa with two barge-boarded bays. So similar to Caeau Gwynion Uchaf that the builder/architect must be the same.

RHIW

ST AELRHIW. In a round, wind-swept churchyard. Mostly rebuilt, 1860–1. An interesting and unusual plan, for which the term 'cruciform' would be misleading as the chancel is so short. The nave, too, is surprisingly short and serves as the narthex and baptistery, leaving the transepts to accommodate the pews. These face towards the pulpit and reading desk, both reached from behind the sanctuary rails. One wonders why this pre-Ecclesiological layout was adopted as late as 1860.

The VILLAGE feels higher than its 600-ft (180-metre) elevation. The older part, above the wooded slopes surrounding Plas yn Rhiw (*see* below), is loosely centred on the church. The newer part lies sw, another loose scatter round NEBO CHAPEL (1876) and the school. Stupendous views SE towards Snowdonia and SW towards Ynys Enlli (Bardsey Island). Mynydd Rhiw, to the N, is the site of a Mesolithic axe factory, and in the early C20 the only deep manganese mine in Britain. The hillside is scattered with ancient mounds, enclosures, forts, cairns etc., most of them unrecognizable. More obvious are the numerous *croglofft* cottages, characteristic of the encroachment settlement of upland regions. The best collection NE of the church. TŶ'N-Y-MYNYDD, on the l. above the road, with attached byre, l. Tiny windows still, and rough stone copings to the gables. Below the road, TAN-Y-FFORDD, whitewashed, with small outbuildings attached to the N. A steep cobbled track leads downhill and then N, past similar cottages: FRON OLEU, sympathetically extended; FRONDEG, with rare corbelled domed pigsty, PICYPARC, and GWERNSAER.

N of the church, the OLD RECTORY. Long rear range *c.* 1775, squat two-bay front *c.* 1833. Well-coursed rubble stone, sash windows. Slate roof, replacing the 'meanly thatched' one seen by Hyde Hall in 1809. S of the church, on the lane to Plas yn Rhiw, TŶ'N-Y-GRAIG, the date 1762 and initials WWI on the E wall. One-and-a-half storeys, with gabled stair wing projecting at the front. Tallish square chimneys. Crude modern extension, r. SW of the church, FFYNNON AELRHIW, a holy well of uncertain date.

PLAS YN RHIW, ¼ m. SE. A stunning location midway up a steep hill overlooking Porth Neigl (Hell's Mouth). T-plan Regency house of three storeys and three unequal bays, surrounded by a lovely terraced garden. The original house, l., perhaps built by John Lewis in 1634, of two storeys and attic, with large S fireplace and mural stair. Extended r. in the late C18 (breaks in the stonework show more than one phase), then raised to three floors *c.* 1820 when the veranda was added, the front stuccoed and the windows enlarged. Stair wing added behind at the same date, then the adjacent kitchen wing in the mid C19. The three Keating sisters bought the ruinous house in 1939 and invited their friend *Clough Williams-Ellis* to repair it. He renewed the staircase and the posts supporting the double plaster arches in the hall, and generally removed plaster and stucco. The Gothick door between hall and rear wing is perhaps from Madryn Castle. To SW, at right angles, an early C18 *croglofft* COTTAGE, perhaps the dower house, later the bakehouse and laundry. Range of roofless OUTBUILDINGS, N, including the HEN GAPEL, of unknown date and purpose.

TŶ CROES BACH, I m. WSW. Two-storey stone house, extended to form an L-plan by *Dafydd Davies Hughes* for himself, *c.* 1995–2007. Just a few quirky details hint that the inside may offer surprises. Here, a carpenter and artist is at work, creating his version of a cruck house, within the stone walls, and roofed with old thick slates. Beams, joists, doors, floors, staircase, kitchen fittings – all hand-crafted using local wood. The result is a fusion of Ernest Gimson and American wood-butcher construction, with a touch of Rudolf Steiner as theoretical underpinning. Cruck OUTBUILDINGS, with thatched roofs, and one with straw-bale walls.

CREIGIAU GWINEU (SH 228 274) occupies a dramatic position overlooking the sea and making optimum use of natural defences. Only on the gently sloping E side is there a full stone rampart; on the W stone has simply been built up between the crags. The date is unknown.

TAN Y MURIAU BURIAL CHAMBER (SH 238 288). Ruined, but still impressive. The chamber at the W end of the long cairn is covered by an enormous wedge-shaped capstone. Beneath is a fine H-shaped portal indicative of the portal dolmen building tradition. A field wall built up against it makes it difficult to appreciate the original impact of the monument. Further down the slope, confused remains of a lateral chamber with a slipped capstone. It can be argued that this and the long cairn beyond it are later, built in a different tradition with connections to SE Wales and the Cotswolds.

AXE FACTORY on Mynydd Rhiw (SH 234 299). Now extremely difficult to find, but on the path over the N shoulder of the hill passes the area where pits (excavated in 1959) were dug to extract the axe-making material. Unlike Graig Lwyd at Penmaenmawr, the rock used here is not the volcanic dolerite, but the altered shale which has been fused to a fine, uniform, flint-like mass by contact with the volcano. The narrow band of suitable stone was mined in a series of pits, each one refilled when it became dangerously deep. The products, normally rather small but finely worked chisel-like axeheads, have been found in early contexts but it was never a major source; no more than twenty to thirty axes made here have been recovered and they were not widely distributed.

RHIWLAS

5866

The village on the NW-facing hillside was a quarry-workers' settlement. At the top, the former CHURCH, converted and with most of its features altered or removed. A stepped TERRACE of stone houses opposite. At right angles, the HIGH STREET, with a terrace on both sides; access to the N side is from a lower lane to the N. Here, TROS-Y-GAMFA, an C18 *croglofft* cottage painted in rainbow colours, and PISGAH CHAPEL of 1863. Most of the village below this is modern, but at the bottom of the hill WAEN PENTIR, later C19 hamlet, with the square pebbledashed PENIEL CHAPEL (1865), PENRHYN TERRACE, handsome dark stone houses with brick window surrounds and six-light sashes, and the Victorian SCHOOL and SCHOOL HOUSE, also of dark stone with bold yellow brick surrounds. Stepped five-light windows to the pair of gables, almost more window than wall.

RHOS ISAF

BETHEL CALVINISTIC METHODIST CHAPEL. An attractive
ensemble: gable-fronted chapel, house each side, both with
gabled half-dormers. Two round-headed windows and another
above the entrance, dated 1836 but probably late C19.

TRYFAN, ¾ m. SSE. Two houses. The earlier to the r., C17, of two
storeys and two bays. At right angles to the l., the late C18 or
early C19 house, stuccoed and with a full-width hipped
veranda. (Reset slate slab over back door, inscribed IG 1785.)

RHOSGADFAN

An upland settlement facing W, one of a number which grew up
on the Uwchgwryfai common during the latter half of the C19 as
a result of slate quarrying (cf. Rhostryfan, Carmel and Fron).
No churches, but each has a chapel, often giving its name to the
settlement. The area is distinctive for the numerous *tyddynnod*,
smallholdings consisting of a *croglofft* cottage and half a dozen
acres of walled land, built as encroachments on the common land
by those working in the quarries. *Tai moel*, houses with no land,
developed when available land became scarce, and these later
grew into villages. In the 1930s, bland local authority housing
estates were planted on the village outskirts in answer to poor
sanitary conditions in the traditional dwellings.

CAE'R-GORS. A typical *croglofft* cottage, built *c.* 1830, home of
the writer Kate Roberts. Kitchen with large fireplace to l.,
parlour-bedroom to r., with a sleeping loft above the latter.
In the lean-to behind, the dairy and a second bedroom.
Attached cowhouse, l., under the same roof-line. Now a
museum, giving a good idea of late C19 living conditions.
In the former hay barn to the N, toilets and a lecture room.
Black-stained weatherboarding to the side walls, originally
open. By *Maredudd ab Iestyn*, 2007.

RHOSHIRWAUN

MENTER-Y-FELIN UCHAF, ½ m. SE of the village. A 23-acre site
being developed (since 2005) as a centre to study the
environment and culture of the Llŷn, with an emphasis on sustainability. The vision of *Dafydd Davies Hughes*. A mid-C19
FARMHOUSE serves as the core, to be extended s as the Centre
for Living Arts and Science. In local stone, slate roofs and
Hobbit-like dormers. To the N, the ROUNDHOUSE.
Oak structure, mostly buried in the ground, with a circle of
posts supporting rafters which converge on a ring-beam below
an elegant conical thatched cap. S of the house, a kidney-
shaped SEED BUILDING is proposed, built of limewashed cob

walls, local oak and a turf roof. Next to it, covered with earth except for an oculus, the OBSERVATORY.

3336 RHYDYCLAFDY

ST MICHAEL, Llanfihangel Bachellaeth, 1½ m. WSW of Rhydy-clafdy. In a remote five-sided churchyard. Single-chamber, possibly C17. W bellcote and, unusually, external steps to a W gallery, added 1847. Three single lancets each side, two-light E window. Now a dwelling.

RHYDYCLAFDY CALVINISTIC METHODIST CHAPEL. 1881. An attractive gabled front. Tall paired lights, their round heads under a decorative arch above. Pedimented doorways. In huge recessed letters, the name of the village rather than the usual Biblical title. Plain interior, without a gallery. Howel Harris is said to have given his first Llŷn sermon, in 1742, on the mounting-stone in the front yard.

GALLT-Y-BEREN, ½ m. W. Late Georgian hipped farmhouse. Roughcast; with timber trellised porch (SW). Curious fenestration: the end elevation (SE) busy with big sash windows, three above three, but the front windowless r. of the porch.

NEUADD BODGADLE, 1 m. WNW. Early C19 roughcast front, three-bayed and two-storeyed, with a plain Doric porch. The offset façade and the big l. chimney hint at an earlier house, probably C17. Late C17 or early C18 single-storey N range, and a half-cellar to the r., where the ground drops away.

7673 ROWEN

SEION CALVINISTIC METHODIST CHAPEL, probably 1841 when the older chapel was re-dedicated. Gable front. Round-headed windows with radial glazing, margins to the entrance-front window glazing. Stone tablet 'Sion 1819' re-set l. of the l. door. Simple interior, with tiered seating.

A village of attractive stone houses, its street sloping W uphill parallel to the Roe river and following the probable route of the Roman road from Canovium (Caerhun) to Abergwyngregyn (see Maen y Bardd, below). At the bottom, l., the former SEION CHAPEL, 1819, now a dwelling. Rubble, half-hipped roof with central chimney, a pair of round-headed doorways with fanlights flanking a pair of similar windows, a date plaque between. Behind the inn on the r., a short lane leads to LLANNERCH-Y-FELIN, a double-fronted late Elizabethan Snowdonia-type house, of two storeys and attic, with an C18 single-storey extension behind. Rough rubble walls on large boulders, largish windows with oak lintels, chimney at S end. Well-preserved interior, with large fireplace, heavy oak beams and joists with ogee-stopped chamfering, oak window seats and post-and-panel partitions to both storeys.

Early C18 stair, with turned balusters and moulded newel caps, replacing the earlier (blocked) spiral stair next to the fire-place. This may have extended, probably in timber, up to the attic. If so, the house is an early example of one with a ceiled upper storey, the first being Plas Mawr, Conwy (q.v.). Sub-stantial roof trusses, with high collars and struts, and wattle-and-daub below. Some early C19 houses along the street: BODAFON and FRONFA, opposite the chapel. A pair of joined two-storey houses, with small-paned sashes. Further w, on the r., LLAIS AFON, a small stone cottage still with its old sash windows. Modern extensions to the w. At the E end of the village, near the Post Office, a charming bus shelter by *S. Colwyn Foulkes*. Stone walls, rounded each end, and rounded slated roof.

COED MAWR HALL, just N of the village. A substantial squarish three-bay house, with a former ballroom attached on the s. Probably mid-C19, gabled and bargeboarded. Large windows with hoodmoulds. Elliptical arch to tripartite doorway, intersecting tracery to fanlight, fluted columns. The original access from the E, along a drive with a lodge.

MAEN Y BARDD (SH 740 717). The earliest monument in an important archaeological landscape covering the s-facing slopes overlooking Rowen village. It is a burial chamber of the first farmers, now a free-standing stone box with a large cap-stone, but originally covered by a cairn, remains of which can be recognized in the field bank to either side. Of the family of portal dolmens, the dominant style built in the Conwy valley in the fourth millennium B.C., having a closed front facing uphill and a portal formed by projecting side stones. 100 yds NE, another large stone tomb, set into the ground, probably Bronze Age. To the w, two fine standing stones to either side of the track on the line of the Roman road, which must have been a well-travelled route long before the Romans formalized it. At the pass (Bwlch-y-ddeufaen), another two huge pre-historic stones, burial cairns, and a small but elegant stone circle (SH 724 713, just over the wall). Near the car park at the end of the road the modern track diverges from the Roman road whose original profile with flanking ditches can be recognized. Early field boundaries (lynchets) cover the slope on either side from SH 732 714 eastwards. Several late prehis-toric, Roman and medieval farmsteads amongst these fields.

SARN BACH   3026

A tiny lead-mining hamlet in the hinterland 1m. SSW of Abersoch. PLAS SARN, behind railings was the home of the manager of the Pant-gwyn lead mine. Modern render and plastic windows hide a handsome house. At right angles, BRYN BYCHAN, double-fronted with nice window surrounds. The round-headed windows in the former smithy came from the demolished Bwlch chapel, Llanengan. Opposite Plas Sarn, a pair of stone miners' COTTAGES. Mid-C19, single-storey and very small. Another row of workers' cottages to the S.

BETHLEHEM CHAPEL, 1 m. S. 1873. Stucco, added porches with fancy pedimented gables. Attached house, l.

CASTELL COTTAGE, Mynydd Gilan, 1¼ m. SSW. Simple, white-washed, single-storey cottage. With FAIRVIEW at right angles, and GARREG LWYD to the N, a good example of early C19 encroachment settlement on commons land.

PENRHYNMAWR, Machros, 1 m. ESE. Two-storey, probably late C17 or early C18. Altered in the C19, when it was the manager's office of the Penrhyndu lead mine. Of this date the puzzling brick insertions: a small roundel and a mid-level window, now blocked.

MACHROS FARM, Machros, ¾ m. E. Early C19 farmhouse on a downhill site. Double-fronted, whitewashed rubble. Slightly higher service wing, l., pebbledashed and with plain surrounds.

To the NE of Penrhynmawr, the ENGINE HOUSE of the Penrhyndu lead mine, built c. 1779 to house an early Boulton & Watt pump-engine. Rubble, now roofless. Lead mining here may go back to Roman times; in the Middle Ages, Cymer Abbey, Llanelltyd (M) (q.v.) may have owned the workings. Sporadic mining from the C17 to early C19, 1828–39 and 1869–92.

SARN MEYLLTEYRN

SALEM CALVINISTIC METHODIST CHAPEL. 1879. A common gable-front design like Penrhos and Pistyll: a pair of round-headed windows below a big arch on plain pilasters, and doors either side. Moulded hoods. Good plain interior.

The character of the pretty VILLAGE is due to the valley location rather than the buildings, most of them spoilt. The road climbs steeply and turns sharply each side of the bridge. An inn at each bend, a third inn, up the lane S of the village, the chapel beyond. The VILLAGE HALL, 2004, is S of the bridge. N of the village, remains of the CHURCH, St Peter ad Vincula, 1848, demolished in the 1990s. An early work by *Kennedy*, earning a compliment from *The Ecclesiologist*. In the churchyard, a granite STANDING STONE, 8 ft (2.5 metres).

TRYGARN, ½ m. SSE. Prominently overlooking the valley. Probably built c. 1730 by Robert Trygarn; the birthplace, in 1747, of Moses Griffith, Pennant's illustrator. Dignified front of five bays and two storeys, with dormered attic; the rear, just three window bays with stair lights. Unfortunately, all the sash windows renewed in plastic.

SYCHNANT PASS

The old route W from Conwy, when tides did not allow safe passage below Penmaen-bach. Above the Pass, a collection of houses designed by members of the Stott family, textile mill architects from Oldham. In 1847, Abraham Henthorn Stott, Sen. (1822–1904) set up practice in Oldham, later joined by two sons, Jesse and A.H. Stott, Jun. A third son, Philip Sidney (later Sir), also a mill architect, formed his own firm.

In 1871 *A. H. Stott, Sen.* bought a country estate at PENSYCHNANT, a two-storey late C17 house, which he extended with a large block to the S, *c.* 1877–82. A fairytale concoction of ideas and motifs. To the l., a tall gabled bay on three floors, its steep oversailing roof with a tiny hip at the top giving a Germanic flavour. To the r., a bowed bay, under a vast conical roof with a steep hipped dormer, in chateau-style. A grand Neo-Norman doorway l. of centre, with dogtooth carving and stubby pink granite shafts. To the N, the original house, dwarfed by the additions but adorned with fanciful bay windows and a small clock turret. In the drawing room, a heavily timbered ceiling with more dogtooth, and a large inglenook fireplace. E of the house, a group of farm buildings, the strangest of them a POWERHOUSE for generating electricity (also known as Stott's Folly). Stone, with bright red brick dressings. Heavily recessed windows, and moulded bricks around the doorway, above which perches a circular flue turret. The roof was originally domed, with turrets and pinnacles around its base.

NE of Pensychnant, PLAS DOLYDD, built *c.* 1922 by Stott's son, *A. H. Stott Jun.*, in Cotswold style. Gabled two-storey, with a square garage block to the NW. At the back a workshop under a hipped conservatory, with hints of Lancashire weavers' lofts in the rhythmic row of windows below the eaves. An eccentric essay in concrete construction, the walls made from chunks of local stone cast in moulds to form blocks, the pitched roofs of solid concrete covered with felt. Also of concrete, the mullions, the downpipes (cast integrally with the wall blocks), the staircase, the Neo-Norman doorways and the gargoyle faces of past owners and their workmen. Even the red-and-blue paving slabs are of coloured concrete.

To the S, along the lane to Llechwedd, CROW'S NEST HALL, by *Joseph Stott*, middle brother of Stott Sen.; RAVENSCRAIG, *c.* 1895, home of *James Stott*, youngest brother who was architect, then dentist, gas governor manufacturer, finally 'gent.'; and OAKWOOD VIEW built for John Lees of Oldham, possibly by *A. H. Stott Sen.* All have a certain presence, but are much altered.

OAKWOOD PARK, 1 m. E of Pensychnant. A huge black-and-white house built *c.* 1900 by *James Stott*, heated, ventilated and equipped by his firm. To the NE, PINEWOOD TOWERS has an odd French-looking slated spire capped with ornate ironwork, and an intriguing castellated gateway, but the house itself lacks interest and no records link it to the Stotts.

CASTELL CAER LLEION (SH 760 778). An impressive stone-walled hill-fort on the summit of Conwy Mountain, about 1 m. W. The main enclosure contains about fifty round-houses or house platforms, protected by a single stone rampart on the s and E (the N side is steep and needs no extra protection) and entered through a simple narrow gateway near the SW end. On the W nose of the ridge is a more heavily defended citadel cut off from the main fort by a stone rampart which clearly overlies the earlier wall just W of the entrance. This later citadel could only be entered from outside through an additional rampart on the S. This has a broad gateway, but it has been blocked and the rationale for the citadel design is difficult to understand. Its defence was further strengthened by an earthen rampart and ditch across the neck of the hill just outside the E wall. This is so different from the stone ramparts that it is tempting to suggest that it is a good deal later, perhaps connected with the C6 king Maelgwn, whom legend associates with the site. Limited excavations in 1951 failed to find datable remains. The lack of Roman material suggests that this is a rare example of a North Welsh hill-fort not reoccupied in the C3–C4.

6271

TAL-Y-BONT (C)
E of Bangor

A few Penrhyn estate houses in the mostly modern VILLAGE.

ST CROSS, ¼ m. E of the village. 1892, an early work by *T. D. Atkinson* of Cambridge. Austere Neo-Norman. Nave and chancel of equal width and height divided by a slightly battered two-light bellcote. N vestry and organ chamber, its gently tapering cylindrical NW chimney reminiscent of Pembrokeshire. Round-headed windows with the plainest of surrounds. Hoodmoulds above the four-light vestry window and the stepped three-light E window. The porch window jambs are roll-moulded, cut square at the leading corner. The interior simple and bold. White plastered walls, trussed rafters stained dark green forming a wagon roof, almost rounded rerearches to the paired nave windows. A hint of a point to the chancel arch, of two plain orders. Stepped SEDILIA with circular shafts, the fourth compartment the PISCINA, with a trefoiled head. – PULPIT, an extension of the low screen wall. – STAINED GLASS. E window, Crucifixion, the design by *Edward Burne-Jones* of *Morris & Co.*, 1908.

BETHLEHEM CALVINISTIC METHODIST CHAPEL. Rebuilt 1860. A voussoir arch rising through the pediment. Round-headed windows to the outer bays, Venetian window below a segmental head at the centre. Slate surround and bracketed door hood. SUNDAY SCHOOL behind, 1892.

COCHWILLAN, ¾ m. S. Part of the large medieval landholdings of the Gruffydd family of Penrhyn till separated away in the early C15; the present house seems to date from the late C15. Having survived as a barn and farm cottages till the 1960s, Cochwillan changed very little and is the most important complete medieval house in the area. Built by William ap Gruffydd (who fought for Henry VII at Bosworth), but was

sold by his heirs; it owes its early preservation to another
Penrhyn cousin, John Williams (Bishop of Lincoln, Keeper of
the Great Seal under Charles I and later Archbishop of York)
who bought it in the 1620s. The house was carefully studied
by Harold Hughes in the 1890s. Repairs c. 1970 brought it back
into use as a dwelling.

A cobbled lane from the N leads E past the house enclosed
in its two yards, turning to enter from the s where the original
entrance is ramped up at the site of a gatehouse, described by
Richard Fenton in 1810 as 'very plain and mean' and now completely replaced. This ceremonial approach from the direction
of the mountains is marked by the s side of the house having
richer architectural detail than the N side facing the private
yard or garden. This show front is faced with unusually
massive, but flush, masonry. Moulded doorway to the hall at
the w with four-centred arch; one fine trefoil-headed window
only to the body of the hall (the mullions renewed) under a
straight head, another to the upper room at the lower end.
The storeyed upper and lower ends were clearly taken down
and rebuilt in the C18 (see a N doorway dated 1759). On the N
the projecting lateral chimney to the hall is the main feature,
either side of this a three-light window lighting the dais, in a
casement-moulded reveal with a four-centred arch, its tall
trefoiled panels partly renewed; and a similar two-light
window next to the plain N doorway. The dimensions of the
hall (37 by 21 ft, 11 by 6.5 metres) are the original but
it is possible there were wings returning at the sides of the
courtyard.

Fenton peered through a gap in the w screen at the
hammerbeam-roofed space of the Great Hall while it was still   47
a barn. The dais-end screen had been moved forward under
the canopy projection, blocking the N window; but this hall has
never been floored and the fireplace with its chamfered stone
jambs and straight wooden lintel survives. This seems a telling
example of the taste for rich internal timber construction and
carved decoration which was perhaps widely followed in the
later Middle Ages, even when stone walls had replaced traditional timber ones, by noble owners continuing to evoke the
halls of the pre-conquest princes. The two screens are fascinatingly different one from the other, which suggests they were
meant to be seen as carpentry rather than be largely covered
with painted plaster. At the dais end, the lowest tier is designed
with very tall posts and two partial Tudor doorways. Then a
rank of wide panels, both of these elements being returned to
their place beyond the gable section in 1969. Above the latter
the dais canopy juts forward as a strip of ceiling parallel with
the floor, which implies that the tall plaster cove (as at
Gloddaeth) is missing. The bressumer below is moulded and
battlemented; above it, box framing. By contrast the service-
end screen has a conventional first tier consisting of a post-
and-panel screen, and two doorways, one nearly in the centre
with the low doorhead carved with the arms of Marchudd and
a second one to the N, all fitted to a moulded and embattled

bressumer. Above this, tall posts widely spaced up to the tie-beam, and short posts more closely spaced up to the collar; in the apex, two straight struts. The roof is of three bays, the hammerbeams resting on brackets with carved wall-posts; each has a shield dating from the restorations. The wall-plate is pierced with foliate running ornament, and all the roof members are moulded; both tiers of purlins are secured with short cusped wind-braces. Quatrefoil bracing in the apexes. The solution chosen for flooring the hall was a smooth wooden surface of narrow boards, an aesthetic employed also for the upper storeys at either end.

To the w two older farms with FARMHOUSES rebuilt by the Penrhyn estate c. 1880.

TAN-Y-MARIAN, ½ m. SSE. Built c. 1860 as a manse. Three-bay roughcast front, hipped roof, timber latticed porch, lattice fanlight.

TAI'R-MEIBION, 1¾ m. ENE. 1890s farmhouse, probably by *George Benmore*, one of the last farms built by the Penrhyn estate. His usual steep gables, nestling porch, upright windows etc. U-plan farm buildings, N, with a long open-fronted range in the centre.

TŶ'N-YR-HENDRE, 1 m. E. Large H-plan estate farmhouse of two storeys. Gabled dormer above a lean-to porch roof with chamfered posts; gabled wings. c. 1860, probably by *George Benmore*. Large quadrangular farmyard to the s, used primarily as the estate horse farm. Enclosed except for the entrance in the E side, and single-storeyed except on the s side (granary above stables) and part of the w (double-height barn). In the centre, a double-sided open-fronted shelter with pigsties attached. Segmental-head openings, cobbled floors, plain trusses. An exceptional ensemble.

PLAS HWFA, ½ m. ESE. Two-storey house, late C16 or early C17, with a c. 1700 extension behind. Largish fireplace next to the spiral stone stair. Small sliding sashes above.

TAL-Y-BONT-UCHAF, ⅓ m. ESE. Tallish C16 or C17 house, with a projecting chimney, l., and corbelled chimney, r. (hidden by an extension). Horizontal windows, probably the original shape, with sliding Yorkshire sashes. Long rear wing.

TAN-YR-ALLT COTTAGES, 1¼ m. ENE. Two pairs of estate cottages, single-storey, simply detailed, c. 1850. Four more pairs at TAN-Y-LÔN, ½ m ENE.

TAL-Y-BONT LODGE, ⅓ m. W. Neo-Norman lodge to Penrhyn Castle. Gabled centre with archway and shafts. Corner turrets with arrowslits.

TOLL COTTAGE, Lôn Isaf, ¾ m. S. On an unaltered stretch of Telford's A5 turnpike, now an access lane. T-plan toll-keeper's house, c. 1825. Pedimented gable to the projection, repeated symmetrically in the 8-ft (2.5-metre)-square WEIGHBRIDGE HOUSE across the road. Also repeated and facing each other, blind panels, once containing the toll charges.

GLAN-Y-MÔR-ISAF, 1¼ m. NNE. Penrhyn estate farm, close to the shore. 1846. Gabled dormers and tall brick chimneys.

Rubble, the upper storey clad in slate but perhaps not originally. Substantial FARM BUILDINGS, E, the courtyard now filled with barns.

TALYBONT
Conwy valley

Small village, where the Dulyn and Conwy rivers meet. The delightful SCHOOL sits back behind a semicircular garden and driveway, the house two-storey, l., and the school, r., single-storey but nearly as high. Chamfered window heads below half-hipped dormers, steep slated diagonal bell-turret.

CEUNANT, Perthi Lane. A tiny cottage deep in the woods, designed and built by the owners, *Vicky Buxton* and *Philip Owen*, as home and studio. Completed *c.* 1993. Just one room above another, with a lower wing. The cottage windows are sashes; the remainder, and the doors, are mostly round-headed, with thick tree-shaped mullions and glazing bars, all in light-stained softwood, with rounded corners and edges. Heavy fascia boards, decorated just at the bottom. Ceramic serpents around the chimney pots.

TALYSARN

ST JOHN. Its diminutive size and plainness leave no doubt about the religious allegiances of this village. Late C19. Nave and chancel in one, S porch and W bellcote. Rubble, with dressed stone lancets.

CAPEL MAWR CALVINISTIC METHODIST CHAPEL, Nantlle Road. 1884. Sitting majestically above the street, with a grand flight of steps up to the central entrance (bridging the old tramway). Paired round-headed windows each side, divided by slate shafts. At the centre, a magnificent wheel window, more like a *tour de force* of mechanical engineering than a window, its slate spokes radiating from the octagonal hub. Greenish rubble, with grey dressings.

SEION INDEPENDENT CHAPEL, Cavour Street. 1862, rebuilt 1886. A grand pilastered gable front of three bays. Tall round-headed windows, each side of a shallow segmentally headed window above the doorway, all with Corinthian pilasters, fluted just in the top half.

The VILLAGE developed in the mid C19 to serve the nearby slate quarries. A compact settlement to the E, near the Dorothea quarry; more linear to the W, following the former track of the Nantlle railways (the 1828 tramway and the 1872 railway). The community, largely Calvinist, was presided over by the Rev. John Jones, who managed the quarry and owned shops. E of Capel Mawr, No. 6 NANTLLE ROAD, a minuscule quarry-worker's house. Opposite, Nos. 15–21, more of the same, all

single-storey. No. 11 was the Gogerddan store, built 1877.
Above the shopfront, three pairs of round-headed windows,
with yellow brick surrounds and shafts between.

TREBORTH *see* BANGOR

TREFLYS *see* PENMORFA

3747   TREFOR (C)

ST GEORGE. Built *c.* 1880 for the quarry village by the Welsh
Granite Co. and designed by *George Farren*, the quarry
manager and engineer. Nave, apsidal sanctuary, W porch and
N vestry. At the SE corner, a slim unconvincing tower which
looked better when it had its steepish pyramidal slate roof.
Snecked granite with bands of red brick carried over wide
lancets, with deeply splayed reveals. Stepped corbels at the
eaves and W gable. Spacious interior. Large trusses, with kingposts on collars, and three trefoiled open panels below. Painted
corbels and chancel-arch imposts. – ALTAR. On five stone legs.
– FONT. Bowl with rounded lip, polished granite, 1901.
MAES-Y-NEUADD INDEPENDENT CHAPEL. Built *c.* 1880 to seat
600. Wide central bay with heavy dentilated pediment, paired
Corinthian pilasters and a rusticated base. Venetian upper
window above a pair of doors. Narrow flanking bays gabled to
the sides with plain angle pilasters. A fine panelled gallery on
cast-iron Corinthian columns painted like marble. Uphol-
stered seating to the elaborate *sêt-fawr*, and behind it, an arch
on paired pilasters supporting a pediment. In the centre of the
compartmented ceiling, a big faceted pearl light fitting.
Attached VESTRY behind, subdivided with a glazed partition.
GOSEN CALVINISTIC METHODIST CHAPEL. 1875, by
O. Morris Roberts. Pedimented gable. Squat, round-headed
central window with fanlight. Tall flanking windows, now
uPVC. A pair of doors in a slightly projecting porch. The
MANSE (now Goleufryn) is E of St George's church. Hipped
with veranda and bargeboards.
The VILLAGE snuggles below Yr Eifl, a granite mountain terraced
by Samuel Holland of Liverpool in the early C19 to produce
stone for the planned port at Porth Dinllaen. Paving setts
became its staple, reaching peak production in 1871. Known
originally as Pentre Trevor, after the quarry foreman Trevor
Jones. Its terraces of workers' houses are not regimented as at
Penmaenmawr (where a sister company ran the quarry), but
are delightfully informal, stepping down the slope. The best
rows, NEW STREET and LIME STREET, face each other across
a long relaxed space. Granite-paved footpaths serve the houses,
and small stone-walled gardens extend to the river which
meanders through. The incline to the quarry may be seen at
the W end of the village, extending N, past Morfa (*see* below),
to the stone PIER of 1883.

ELERNION, ¼ m. SE. Late C16 two-storey house, later irregularly extended, so now of three blocks and much altered. The earliest part, surprisingly square in plan, has a large lateral chimney, the pair of diagonal stacks with dentilated cornices.

LLWYN-YR-AETHNEN, ¼ m. N. The date 1718 on the W gable refers to later work as the house is probably C16. At the E gable, a projecting chimney, with a bread oven in the SW angle. Off-centre doorway with rough voussoir head. Rubble, with massive foundation boulders.

MORFA, ⅓ m. NW. Early C18 house on the Glynllifon estate, whitewashed with small upper windows. W of the house, a fine planned PIGGERY. E-plan with pigsties, back-to-back and each with its own yard. The end wings are larger, for swill preparation, storage, gig house etc. Linking them, a monopitch-roofed passageway against a high wall with cock-and-hen copings. In the passage, slate-slab feed troughs to the sty-yards.

TREFRIW   7863

On an E-facing slope, beside the Conwy river. In the early C19, slates from upland quarries were transported down to the quay, and thence to Conwy and beyond. By mid-century, a small spa resort, though the wells (q.v.) are a mile N of the village, and a manufacturing centre.

ST MARY. A double-nave church, like Llanrhychwyn, the S side early C15, the N early C16. Extensively restored c. 1850 by Lord Willoughby de Eresby of Gwydir. The exterior is all C19. Paired arched windows both sides, a triplet at the E end of the S nave. A curious pinnacled buttress between the two E gables. Heavily corbelled eaves, a feature used repeatedly in Willoughby's buildings. Both roofs are survivals: arch-braced collar-trusses, purlins and wind-braces to both, but the braces unusually long and straight in the S roof. Crenellated brattishing above the wall-plate on the N side. – PULPIT. Reconstructed, using C17 panelling carved with shells, leaves, grotesque human heads and cherubs. One panel dated 1653. – PEWS. Raised in front of the organ and containing more C17 panels. – FONT. C19, cylindrical, on four barley-twist shafts. – STAINED GLASS. S nave S window (r. of two) by *Lavers, Barraud & Westlake*, 1880. The other windows later (mostly c. 1932), probably by *Powells*. – MONUMENTS. Two oval marble plaques, to Thomas Jones, Rector †1759, and to Jane Hughes of Gomanog †1778. Large grey and white marble Gothic monument to the Rev. Evan Evans, the bard Ieuan Glan Geirionnydd †1855.

PENIEL CALVINISTIC METHODIST CHAPEL, W of the church. By *G. Dickens-Lewis* of Shrewsbury, 1907–10. Gothic, but Arts and Crafts in feel. A fine curvilinear window above a pair of two-centred arched doorways with foliate finials. Angled stair-case wings, with overhanging roofs. Dark snecked granite,

yellow Grinshill dressings. A fine interior. The gallery's iron
columns extend up to support the roof trusses. Large rolled
timber capitals at the lower level, and more delicate, foliate iron
ones above. Plain unvarnished pews in straight rows, the backs
inclined more than usual. A large organ, coving out above the
sêt-fawr, similar in detail to the pews and gallery front. Behind
the organ, a large SCHOOLROOM.

EBENESER INDEPENDENT CHAPEL, Crafnant Road. 1881 by
Richard Owens. Gable flanked by hipped bays. Triplet of
windows with larger, central light. Round heads to the upper
windows, flat segmental to the lower. Dark rock-faced granite,
lighter stone dressings and quoins. Dentil upper sill course,
machicolated cornices to the corner bays.

TREFRIW HALL, Gwydir Road. Mid-C19. Pedimented, with
heavy triple-stepped entablature all round. Rubble, with sandstone surrounds and keystones. A handsome building, spoilt
by the modern porch.

Opposite the church, on the E side of Gwydir Road, TAN-YR-
YW, a plain C17 house altered in the early C19. The birthplace
and home of Dafydd Jones (1708–85), bard, printer and collector of early Welsh manuscripts. On the W side, opposite the
short lane to Trefriw Hall, LLYS LLEWELYN. A slightly
awkward asymmetrical villa of the mid C19. A narrow canted
bay to the l. wing, and slim granite piers between the windows.
S of it, PLAS COCH, of the same date. Two parallel gabled
blocks, the front one shorter. Further up Crafnant Road,
Y GARREG LWYD, Arts and Crafts-style house of c. 1920, by
a local architect, W. H. Longbottom, for himself. Voyseyish
features such as the stone-framed leaded windows in roughcast walls, and the deep overhangs at eaves; and some less
so, such as the oval chimneys and the big stone corbels to the
front eaves, a nod to Lord Willoughby. The tiny windows
between the corbels offer views of the river from bed-height.
Over PONT TREFRIW, the modern TREFRIW WOOLLEN
MILLS, by Colwyn Foulkes & Partners, c. 1970. Of stone and
concrete, with the gables of three very shallow roofs oversailing the front elevation, like an Alpine hotel. Large and overpowering. More in keeping are the older mill buildings
upstream. SCHOOL HILL leads uphill just S of the school, to
the RECTORY, 1842, an early work by Kennedy. A pair of gables
with big lattice windows, in Tudor style. On the back lane S to
Llanrhychwyn, almost the last house in the village, BRYN
EDDA, a Gwydir estate cottage built by Lord Willoughby de
Eresby, c. 1840. Single-storey with attic. Rough stone walls,
heavy corbels to the eaves, a curved end wall and circular chimneystack above.

TREFRIW WELLS, 1¼ m. N. Two-chamber bath house built into
the hillside, with a pair of arched doors and a crenellated
parapet. Large slate slabs on the roof, sloping down each side
from the central wall. Of uncertain date, perhaps one of Lord
Willoughby de Eresby's follies, so early to mid-C19. Spa house
to E, 1874, with crow-stepped gables.

TREGARTH

ST MARY. A dull church, hiding behind a screen of yews. By *Thomas Jones*, 1869.* Nave and chancel, S porch, S vestry and N transept (organ). Dark rubble, grey limestone dressings. Scissor trusses in the chancel, insubstantial arch-braced ones in the nave, on floriate corbels and with high collars. – STAINED GLASS. N window by *Jones & Willis*. S, by *J. Wippell & Co*.

SHILOH WESLEYAN CHAPEL. 1896 in small raised numerals in the heavy pediment. An intricately dentilated entablature on stubby Corinthian pilasters. These divide the elevation into three almost equal bays containing cambered-head windows, three in the centre, two in both sides. The same below, the porch with rusticated pilasters and a shallow pediment.

The VILLAGE is bisected by two former railways, the old slate railroad between the Penrhyn quarries and Port Penrhyn, and the Bangor–Bethesda branch of the main railway. The latter tunnels beneath PENDINAS, the site of an Iron Age FORT E of the village. Both tracks can be seen to dramatic effect along the lane between Tal-y-cae and Braich Talog: the slate railroad bridging above, the railway in a deep cutting below.

The church is W of the village, forming part of an attractive group with GELLI, a single-storey worker's cottage, *c.* 1830; the former CHURCH HALL, originally a small mission chapel (1854), extended in 1926, perhaps by *Harold Hughes*, as a church school; LLWYN DERW, formerly St Mark's Orphanage, white roughcast, with pedimented half-dormers; and further E, HEN BERSONDY, the former parsonage, late C19 or early C20. Slate-clad above a rendered base, diagonal brick chimneys, heavily detailed stone porch.

E of Shiloh chapel along FFRWD GALED, more single-storey workers' cottages, in pairs. Later estate houses at Nos. 5–10 PENYGROES, with slate cladding above stone. Just into Braich Talog on the r., BRODAWEL, slate above stone again, with bracketed eaves and an ornate timber porch, so higher status. Further up Braich Talog on the r., FRON ELIDIR, a pretty house with a delicately carved slate porch, *c.* 1900.

A substantial development of quarry-workers' houses in FFORDD TANRHIW, N of the railway tracks. Once known as Blackleg Row, as it housed the workforce brought in by the Penrhyn estate to break the slate-workers' strike. Nos. 1–23 in terraces of four, Nos. 28–49 in asymmetrical terraces of five. Again, slate cladding, diagonal brick stacks etc.

TŶ'N-Y-CLWT, Tanysgafell, 1 m. SE. Longish two-storey house, *c.* 1830s. Six-window front (some formerly doorways), four chimneys: a former terrace of three, perhaps.

TANYSGAFELL, 1¼ m. SE. A planned group of three paired cottages, charmingly Picturesque. 1840–50. Clad in purple and green slates. Oriel windows, with hipped slate-slab roofs.

*Not Thomas Jones of Chester (*c.* 1794–1859).

FELIN FAWR SLATE WORKS, Coed-y-parc, 1½ m. SE, formerly
part of the Penrhyn quarries. FOUNDRY, WATER WHEELS, two
SLAB MILLS, WORKSHOPS etc. The earliest mill was built
c. 1803, but the present buildings date from c. 1832–c. 1907.
All of slate, granite and some brick, solidly built and plainly
detailed. Across the road, NEW MILL HOUSE, built c. 1880s
for the manager. Granite, green and purple slate cladding
above, and red brick dressings.

BRADITE PAINT WORKS, Coed-y-parc, 1½ m. SE. By *Jones Ap
Thomas*, c. 1947. A large steel-framed shed with a small
Modernist office block symmetrically in front. Above its
entrance, a complicated clock tower. Steel windows, the corner
ones wrapping round. Roughcast, painted green.

5641   TREMADOG

In 1798 William Alexander Madocks (1773–1828), romantic
visionary and by 1802 reformist M.P. (for Boston, Lincs), bought
land on the N side of the Traeth Mawr. The potential for land
reclamation and agricultural improvement was immense, and in
1800 he built an embankment (the first of two) which would win
him about 1,000 productive acres. The Act of Union (also of
1800) added impetus, for his land was strategically placed along
the southern of two proposed routes to Ireland, with a port at
Porth Dinllaen (*see* Morfa Nefyn). The need for a staging post
was obvious, so around 1805, Madocks began to develop his
model town, supposedly named after prince Madoc who in
legend set sail from nearby Ynys Fadog in the C12 to discover
America and whose name conveniently echoed his own.

Nestling beneath a dramatic cliff, the small town (which
Madocks liked to call a Borough) is planned around a square
with three streets forming a T. The buildings are well proportioned, simple without being fussy. Built of stone and slate, they
are very much rooted in the rugged Snowdonian landscape, but
they also have an atmosphere of civilized urbanity. No architect
is recorded. It is likely that *Madocks* himself, and his capable
agent *John Williams*, were responsible.

ST MARY. Completed around 1811, in Gothick style, one of the
earliest in Wales. On a rocky outcrop S of the square, its height
accentuated by the rendered brick W tower and spire. Cruciform, the transepts shallow, the original iron windows replaced
in stone. Closed in 1995 and converted to offices by *Arrol &
Snell* of Shrewsbury. – ALTAR and REREDOS, florid Renaissance
style, 1917. Designed by *C.R. Ashbee* and carved by *Emile de
Vynck*, a Belgian refugee living in Pentrefelin. – PULPIT, re-
sited above the new staircase. Carved in Jacobean style by
Constance Greaves of Wern Manor. – STAINED GLASS. E
window, Baptism of Christ above, Last Supper below. Perhaps
by *Shrigley & Hunt*, 1899. – MONUMENT. Tablet to John
Williams, Madocks's faithful agent, by *Spence & Son* of

Liverpool. – GATEWAY. A triumphal Gothic archway framing the approach to the church. Octagonal embattled piers, four-centred arch, wildly decorated with a menagerie of animals including dragons, monkeys, elephants and other elements of Gothick horror. Constructed in *c.* 1811 of *Coade* stone, rarely seen in North Wales but close stylistically to torchères at the Prince of Wales' Carlton House conservatory of 1813. A *tour de force* of wit, theatrical fancy and the exotic, so typical of Madocks.

PENIEL CALVINISTIC METHODIST CHAPEL. Built 1808–11. 100 The Bishop of Bangor disapproved of Madocks's welcome to Nonconformists, but was offered the reassurance that, whereas the chapel was built on sand, the church was on good hard rock. Much about the building's classical style would have been unfamiliar: its stucco Tuscan portico (added in 1849 though it was intended in the original conception), its size (large for a chapel congregation barely used to having its own building) and its orientation (most chapels up to this date presented a face on a long elevation.) The design lacks sophistication, e.g. the lack of entasis of the columns, but it has a naïve charm. Gallery on three sides (originally just at the entrance end), on fluted cast-iron posts. Numbered box pews, late C19 *sêt-fawr* and pulpit, ceiling renewed *c.* 1908. VESTRY and SCHOOL-ROOM behind, both later.

MARKET HALL, started *c.* 1807. This, rather than church or chapel, has pride of place in the town. Madocks planned it as an open market hall on the ground floor (now glazed) and a town hall cum assembly room above, with access from the next-door inn. The Market Hall was planned to double as an auditorium (Madocks loved theatre), its stage through the archway concealed behind the first house E along the High Street. Elegant façade: five arched openings with big windows above, each with a slate dripmould, and a shallow, widely projecting hipped roof. Strong platband, punctuated with medallions between the arch-heads and keystones cast with the faces of theatrical characters, all made of *Coade* stone.

ROYAL MADOC ARMS HOTEL. Built at the same time as the Market Hall as an inn for the passing coaches to Ireland. Symmetrical, with two-storey wings and a central block of three storeys with attic. The architraves and dormers are mid-C20.

TAN-YR-ALLT. ½ m. E. Madocks's first home in Tremadog. The original house extended s by *Madocks* in the early C19, later to the W. Low hipped roofs with widely overhanging eaves and a veranda on cast-iron columns. Shelley lived here for a spell in 1812–13, while writing *Queen Mab*. Below the house, a WALLED GARDEN; and at the bottom of the E drive, a pretty LODGE.

PERAMBULATION. The SQUARE, or Market Place, sets the scene: solid two-storey buildings of coursed squared stone from the nearby Moel-y-gest quarry, wide eaves, squarish sash windows. Two inns, the Golden Fleece and the Union, two shops at the SE and SW corners, and a former well at the SW corner.

Tremadog, Tan-yr-allt.
Engraving by J. Nixon, 1808

Madocks planned trees in the square, but changed his mind.
At the NE corner, the Cambrian Pill Depot, originally a shop
c. 1805, established as a dispensary in 1839 by Robert Isaac
Jones.

Leading w is DUBLIN STREET. The houses on the s side,
with catslide dormers, were probably the first to be built in the
town. Just one original Yorkshire horizontal sash type. Further
w, the old GRANARY sits back, now altered. On the N side, next
to the hotel, a stable block hidden by the modern warehouse.
A small lane leads N off Dublin Street, to attractive terraces
with names redolent of their raised position.

Back to the square and then E, the HIGH STREET, formerly
the old road from Merioneth. Terraces with cellars and outside
steps. Further E, Madocks's woollen manufactory: the
LOOMERY of five floors and five bays, with shallow hipped roof
and bracketed eaves, the walls and windows originally coloured
to Madocks's taste. Behind the open site to the E (formerly the
Woollen Mill), a high retaining wall containing a catchpool,
one of a series cascading down the hillside from Llyn Cwm
Bach (½ m. N), to provide water power. The CORN MILL and
MILLER'S HOUSE are now dwellings beside the lane to Tan-
yr-allt. Adjoining the loomery on the w side, BRONHAUL, and
next to it TŶ GWYN, both built for managerial use, handsome
houses containing some original features. Next, Nos. 9–13
FACTORY PLACE, a short row of one-and-a-half-storey houses
for the factory workers.

Back to the square again and now s along CHURCH STREET
(formerly London Street). At TŶ PAB, a break in the row
reveals an arcade in the s wall, probably part of another square
ambitiously planned by Madocks but never built. Further s,
later rows with attractive bay windows, gables and porches,
then, behind a stone wall and a row of trees, TŶ NANNEY,

built in the early C19 for David Ellis-Nanney, Attorney General for North Wales and friend of Madocks. Handsome, with lower wings, shallow hipped roofs, wide bracketed eaves and ornate chimneystacks. Elegant open porch added by *Clough Williams-Ellis*.

YSBYTY ALLTWEN, ¼ m. w. Small community hospital, 2008, combining primary health facilities and limited ward provision, on a rocky shelf overlooking reclaimed marshland NW of Porthmadog. The architects, *Nightingale Associates* of Cardiff (*Nick Durham* and *Tom Withecombe*) prove here, without doubt, that hospitals need not be dull (cf. Ysbyty Gwynedd, Bangor). The plan is like a partly open cranked hinge, the entrance at the open w end and the dining room at the pin. The s arm is two-storey, with the wards facing the view, above admin. and therapy rooms. The N arm and entrance are single-storey, at the same level as the wards. Between the two arms, a cranked atrium, the Winter Garden. This is divided longitudinally with a promenade at the upper level on the N side, looking down over a slate retaining wall to a slate-landscaped lower level serving the s wing lower rooms. The promenade has a low flat ceiling on columns, contrasting with the higher glazed winter-garden roof of alternating triangles of white and clear double-skin Teflon, supported by steel tubes which zigzag across the space. A bridge links the upper levels, with a lift tower and staircase, both clad in timber. Another, bigger timber-clad tower closes the space's open end. Its cladding continues externally, providing a contrast to the off-white render walls. Shallow metal sheet roofs N and S, with areas of flat sedum roofs between. Art works include fossil-pattern slate slabs built into the internal retaining wall, by *Alyosha Moeran & Guy Stevens*, and a steel balustrade to the dining-room terrace, by *Ann Catrin Evans*.

TUDWEILIOG

2337

ST CWYFAN. Rebuilt 1849 by *George Gilbert Scott* for Charles Wynne of Cefnamwlch (Scott also designed Pentrefoelas church for the Wynne family of Voelas, Clwyd). A world apart from the simpler Llŷn churches, but dull in its correctness and somehow out of place in its rural setting. Nave, chancel, s porch, N vestry, w bellcote. Dec throughout. Fittings by *Scott*. STAINED GLASS. Four by *Clayton & Bell*, 1906. – MONUMENTS. Neo-Jacobean plaque to Major J. S. Wynne-Finch †1906.

TUDWEILIOG CALVINISTIC METHODIST CHAPEL. 1885. Plain, cement-rendered. Round-head upper windows, arranged 1–3–1 with moulded heads.

Small and compact village. The chapel sits apart to the SW. In the centre, the POST OFFICE, 1909, built by the Cefnamwlch estate. Roughcast above snecked rubble, with slate cladding to the upper gables. ESTATE HOUSES around the

village, mostly 1907–11, all recognizable by their designed
appearance and the date plaques. The architects were *Grayson
& Ould* of Liverpool, employed by Mrs Wynne-Finch because
she admired their work in Port Sunlight. PORTHYSGADEN
(¾ m. W), an estate farmhouse of 1907, made slightly special
by hoods and granite lintels above the lower windows.
BEERSHEBA INDEPENDENT CHAPEL (¼ m. SE), 1828, much
altered.

BRYNODOL, ¾ m. E. A large and formal house for the region,
with C16 origins but mostly of 1743. Samuel Johnson and
James Boswell visited the owner, Hugh Griffith, in 1774 and
reported 'a small [i.e. by English standards] neat new built
house'. Two-storey with attics and cellar. Long main elevation
facing N, of seven bays with central doorway, minimally
decorated. Two stone cellar windows, r., *c.* 1600. Sash
windows, with thick glazing bars to front (cf. Tŷ Newydd,
Llanystumdwy). Stucco, with areas of painted and grouted
slate cladding. Gabled stair wing, S, also 1743, and kitchen
wing, SE, added mid to later C18. A fine interior of three rooms
above three in the main part with panelling, cornices, panelled
doors and shutters etc. Wide dog-leg stair with open strings
and spindly turned balusters. Service staircase similar.

CEFNAMWLCH, I m. S. The small, little-altered gatehouse is all
that remains of a C16–C17 house which stood on axis to it, E,
the home of the Griffith family, one of the most prominent in
Llŷn from the late C15 to the late C18. The house was demolished *c.* 1813, but a 1796 drawing by John Ingleby shows an
irregular two-storey front with a first-floor oriel. The GATE-
HOUSE, has low, cambered E and W archways, the voussoirs
flush with the rubble walls and a heraldic panel above, W, dated
1607. A pair of stone seats within, then the ogee-headed door
with a tiny wicket, then another pair of seats. Outside stair to
the upper room, heated by a chimney on the same side and lit
by two-light stone windows in gables above the archways.

The present HOUSE, of the late C17 or early C18, faces N
across the former forecourt between gatehouse and main
house, and forms the NE corner of a large courtyard of outbuildings extending S. Five bays, three storeys, with tall
moulded chimneys not unlike that to the gatehouse, and a
filled-in veranda extending S and also W along the lower range
W of the house. Pebbledash covers evidence of the raising of
the house in the early C19, before which dormers lit the top
floor. (Two large ground-floor rooms, extended at the same
time into the N veranda. Some bolection-moulded doors and
fireplaces, *c.* 1700.)

In the courtyard, former COACH HOUSE and STABLE in the
W block, and BAKE AND BREW HOUSE in the S, both early C19
and now converted. Parallel with the coach house, across a
yard, the BARN, also early C19, with brick jambs and small
loops. N of the house forecourt, a large expanse of lawn, then
the late C18 or early C19 WALLED GARDEN, with high brick
walls, splendid stone vases on the gate piers and a SUMMER-

HOUSE on the N side, of brick with stone quoins, and a pyramid slate roof.

BURIAL CHAMBER, on Mynydd Cefn Amwlch, 2 m. S (SH 229 345). An attractive monument with a gabled capstone on slender uprights. Removal of the covering cairn and of wall stones from the chamber makes it difficult to assign to any particular tomb-building tradition. A legend that it was once demolished, but that cows grazing in the field were so distressed by this vandalism that they bellowed without ceasing until it was restored, may suggest that it has been quite radically disturbed.

TŶN-Y-GROES

₇₇₇₂

A tiny village, straddling the cross-roads where the former Conwy to Tal-y-cafn turnpike of 1759 (the first in Caernarvonshire, extended S in 1777) intersects with a much older E–W route across the mountains. N of the cross-roads, the CHAPEL, gable to front and at right angles to the SCHOOL ROOM, sharing an entrance yard. Doorway with flanking windows and a smaller one above, all with pointed heads and intersecting Gothick tracery.

CEFN ISAF, ½ m. SW. By *H. L. North*, for John Nickson, a Lancashire businessman, as a holiday home. Built in two stages, the first in 1904. Advancing wing at the l. of a central range with two gables and a veranda, facing SE. The third gable and the r. wing added *c.* 1908. A sensible plan, with service rooms and passages along the rear (NE) and the main rooms facing the sun, the view and the terraced GARDEN, also designed by *North*. His usual palette of forms and materials, with a few features used less frequently, e.g. the curved-headed windows. A fine front door at the NE: a single plank of beautifully grained wood, punctured with iron studs and diamond-shaped glass prisms. But the chimney tops are disappointing. More interesting ones on CEFN COTTAGE, down the lane to the S, and a handsome roof of diminishing slates. Hipped dormers and diamond-leaded glazing, features which North tended to avoid.

BRYN CASTELL, ¾ m. E. Oval motte, on the W bank of the Conwy river near Tal-y-cafn bridge.

NE of Bryn Castell, in a field N of the farm Llwydfaen, a buried APSIDAL CHURCH, discovered by aerial photography by the RCAHMW in 2006. At the time of writing, no excavation has started.

VAYNOL *see* FELINHELI

WAUNFAWR

₅₃₅₉

One long street of pebbledashed late C19 and C20 houses, the chapel at the top end, the church at the bottom. E of the church, a denser network of lanes and modernized cottages.

ST JOHN. 1880. One of *Kennedy*'s dreariest churches. Nave and chancel in one, N vestry, glazed timber N porch. E.E. Paired lancets, simple plate tracery to the E window. Interior inaccessible and disused.

CROESYWAUN CALVINISTIC METHODIST CHAPEL. 1885, with Sunday School 1895, both by *Rowland Lloyd Jones*. Three-bay pedimented and pilastered front on a rusticated base, all in two-coloured render. Not without interest in this featureless village.

PLAS GLAN-YR-AFON, 1¼ m. WNW. Gentry house of the late C17, extended N, E and S in the early and mid C18, so a complex plan approximating to a T. The W stem is the earliest part, with a N lateral chimney as well as one at the W gable. Windows of vertical proportions, so C18, sadly replaced in UPVC. Fine mid-C18 panelled rooms, hall and landing in the W wing, and a balustered staircase rising through two floors. Above the upper-room fireplace, an oil-painted panel of Caernarfon. Late C17 BARN, S, and mid-C19 STABLE and BOTHY, SE.

4040

Y FFÔR/FOUR CROSSES

A small village at the junction of the Pwllheli to Caernarfon turn-pike (A499) with the 1808 turnpike (B4354) which linked Madocks's at Tremadog with Porth Dinllaen, his favoured port for Ireland. Inevitably, a large inn at the cross-roads, the (former) FOUR CROSSES INN, extending S as a terrace of well-built two-storey houses with grand pedimented doorways, and E as a row of lower, humbler houses. Sadly, lots of pebbledash and replacement windows. SALEM CHAPEL, to the E, 1863 with porch of 1913. An uncomfortable composition, its pair of upper windows pinched within a round-arched recess. To the W, YSGOLDY, the Calvinistic Methodist Sunday School. A round-headed doorway flanked by similar windows. Two schools N of the cross-roads. YSGOL HAFOD LÔN, for children with special needs, *c.* 1975 by *John Sam Williams*. Square plan. A flat roof hidden behind rounded, upturned eaves, and at each corner, a fat timber post. Set well back, and on a plinth, the external wall meanders in and out freely, the fluidity accen-tuated by the rounded corners. Next to it, YSGOL BRO PLENYDD, an 'open-air' school by *Rowland Lloyd Jones*, 1911. The characteristic folding partitions and the folding windows to the 'marching corridor' no longer exist.

PLAS GWYN, ½ m. S. The distinctive stepped gables and tall square chimneys, all C17, conceal an earlier, lower house, perhaps *c.* 1600. The change of the quoins at the upper sill level indicates that the house was raised, and a full upper storey thus provided. The original plan is clear: a wide fireplace and a mural stair (with C17 studded door and fittings in place) at the S end, and a cross-passage between the main S room and the N parlour. To the W, a later, dairy wing. Late C18 or early C19 FARM BUILDINGS, a stable and a cowhouse, and at a higher level, a hammel.

LLWYNDYRUS, 1½ m. NW. Early C17 two-storey house, in white painted rubble; possibly a two-unit house since there are two front doorways and large fireplaces each end. Perhaps the l. house pre-dates the r. The scratched inscription r. of the porch 'EV 1775' must refer to alterations. Voussoir-headed doorway to the l. house, opposite a blocked rear door. Blocked pigeon holes at eaves level. The upper part of the l. gable rebuilt, and small windows inserted. Projecting chimney to the r. gable. Both stacks rebuilt, and windows renewed. Remarkable internal features, indicating a more important history than the exterior suggests. In the l. house, a voussoir-headed doorway to the recess l. of the fireplace, probably a closet rather than a former stair since the ceiling is a huge stone boulder. A fine oven off the deep fireplace. Upstairs, remnants of straw-rope partition infill. In the r. house, a good panelled screen next to the front door. The middle rail carved with an intertwined red and white dragon, the door post with vine scroll and three linenfold panels within. In the N room, next to the small window r. of the fireplace, remnants of a plaster frieze, cornice and panelling, with moulded and gilded fleur-de-lys and Tudor rose emblems. Between the houses, the C19 staircase leads up to a half-landing from both sides, then continues up in a single, wide flight formerly partitioned down the middle.

TRALLWYN HALL, 1¾ m. NW. Imposing stucco house in its own parkland, home of the Lloyd family from the early C17. Double-pile plan facing E and W, the S side providing a third formal elevation facing the garden. The W front is the earlier, probably 1781 and on the site of a house of 1602 (removed datestones record both dates). Half-hipped roof, irregularly spaced windows, the top ones tucked tightly under the eaves. The building of the early C19 E wing may relate to the improving of the Caernarfon to Pwllheli turnpike, when a new entrance front was formed. Five bays, hipped roof, a doorway with radial fanlight, and a portico. Full-width S veranda, hipped each end, on slender Tuscan columns. Renewed c. 2006 by *Christopher Williams-Ellis*.

BURIAL CHAMBER, ⅓ m. S (SH 399 384). A small square chamber with a capstone, reconstructed in 1936, probably belonging to the portal dolmen tradition.

STANDING STONE (SH 400 390). An unimposing stone in front of the Canolfan y Gwystl, looking like a garden feature but in fact prehistoric.

YNYSCYNHAEARN see PENTREFELIN

YSBYTY IFAN   8448

This remote village is the highest in the Conwy valley. From 1856, it formed part of the Penrhyn estate. *George Benmore* was the estate's architect (cf. Abergwyngregyn). Now largely owned by the National Trust.

St John Baptist. As the place name attests, there was here a
hospice of the Knights Hospitallers (Knights of St John of
Jerusalem). Founded *c.* 1190; its endowments were increased
by Llywelyn the Great, 1221–4. The church demolished in
1858. Dull replacement by *George Benmore*, opened 1861. –
REREDOS. By *E. B. Ferrey*, 1882. – SEPULCHRAL SLABS.
Shield, with a hare below, from a shield and sword heraldic
slab, commemorating Cynwrig, son of Llywarch, *c.* 1330. –
Three fragments of a late C14 foliated cross-slab commemorating Maruret verch Hywel. Inscribed border. Vine trail. –
Fragment of a late C14 slab with base of cross and vine trail.
– MONUMENTS. Three mutilated early C16 effigies: torso fragment, female figure, headless ecclesiastic. Said to be respectively Rhys Fawr ap Meredydd, standard-bearer of Henry VII
at Bosworth; his wife Lowry; and their son Robert ap Rhys,
chaplain to Cardinal Wolsey. – Peter Price, 1792. Two winged
heads in a pediment and an urn on top. – BRASSES. Robert
Gethin and wife Anne, both †1598. Clasped hands. Below, a
shrouded infant and, kneeling, two sons and four daughters.
A further plate to Robert Gethin, their grandson, added above,
its inscription completed by the earlier one. Both are contained
in a crude stone frame.

The two parts of the VILLAGE are linked by a C17–C18 humped-
backed BRIDGE, of two arches, with small triangular refuges
above the cutwaters. On the Caernarvonshire (W) side,
PEN-Y-BONT, two attached buildings facing the bridge: the
former PENRHYN ARMS INN to the S, late C18 or early C19.
Three storeys and three bays, sash windows with brick arched
heads and a slate-slab porch. To the N, a mid-C19 FARMHOUSE,
of two high storeys but under the same roof-line, with farm
buildings to the W. Across the street, to the S, a picturesque
group of small buildings: the former CORN MILL, with a
restored water wheel. Symmetrical three-bay front, the lower
windows with recessed slate lintels. Next to it, the former
WHEELWRIGHT'S WORKSHOP, perhaps originally a house.
The road behind leads uphill, past FFYNNON PENRHYN, the
village water supply, dated 1866, to a row of former
almshouses, BRYN YSGOL. Founded (on another site) in the
early C18 for six poor men by Capt. Richard Vaughan of Pant
Glas. A new row was built here (this time for six poor women)
in 1885 by Mrs Catherine Vaughan. Uphill, the SCHOOL with
attached school house, 1857. Facing E across the river, Nos.
1–4 MILL STREET, with half-dormers and slightly arched
lintels to the lower windows, and their stone privies next to the
river. Next to them, BRYN FFYNNON, a group of three, the
central house gabled and advanced. Then, TŶ NEWYDD,
similar to Mill Street, but two larger units rather than four, and
with timber porches. More estate houses to the SE. On the
Denbighshire (E) side of the river, the HIGH STREET and
CHURCH VIEW, two terraces of two-storey houses, the best
BRYN CONWY, late C17 or early C18.

PANT GLAS, 1½ m. N. Seat of the Vaughan family from the early
C16, High Sheriffs for three generations. A large mansion stood
here until the end of the C18. The present house, on a site S of
the old house, is probably mid- to late C16 and may have been
the farmhouse, but much changed in the later C19. To the NE,
a symmetrical group of farm buildings around a courtyard,
built in 1883 by Lord Penrhyn, probably incorporating stone
from the old mansion.
TOLL HOUSE (Tŷ'r Peg), between Pant Glas and Hendre Isaf.
Early C19, on the 1813 Capel Curig turnpike, so pre-Telford.
L-plan, with an attractive veranda on timber posts. The gable
window was for collecting the tolls.
PONT EIDDA, 1 m. NNW, and PONT CALETWR, 1 m. ENE. Both
single-span rubble stone bridges, late C18 or early C19.

MERIONETH

ABERANGELL

The settlement straddles the Montgomeryshire boundary.

BETHANIA CALVINISTIC METHODIST CHAPEL. 1902, by
  G. T. *Bassett* of Aberystwyth. An assured design in dark tooled
  slate with orange terracotta confined to the door, three window
  heads, and a roundel plaque; exaggerated keystones. Chapel
  house in purple brick, 1925, by *Bassett*.
HOREB INDEPENDENT CHAPEL. 1899. Slate and yellow brick,
  the slate tooled like corduroy. Chapel house, 1900.

ABERDYFI

Aberdyfi, overlooking vast sands at low tide, began as a seaside
resort with the coast road from Pennal, 1827. But it was the probable site of the Council of Aberdyfi, 1216, where Llywelyn the
Great imposed his authority on the princes of Deheubarth and
Powys. Fenton saw extensive copper works behind the village in
1808, and mining of copper and lead were staples, with fishing,
until the early C19. The Custom House for the coast was here
until moved to Aberystwyth in 1763.

The early village ran inland up a narrow valley, but after 1827
lodging houses spread along the seafront, the plots cut back
into the rock. A hotel was built in 1829, the church in 1837.
The railway in 1863 aroused the same inflated expectations as
at Aberystwyth. The hotel was rebuilt by Thomas Savin, the
railway promoter, but like his hotels at Borth and Aberystwyth
it was not a success and was for sale by 1869. The railway
did stimulate the port as an outlet for Corris slate, for which
a wharf was built in 1882, but by the turn of the C20 the
future was clearly as a resort. Fortunately the railway was
tunnelled rather than taken along the seafront as at Barmouth,
a consequence apparently of the company secretary taking holidays here, and the steep rocky backdrop prevented disfiguring
sprawl. The seafront lodgings extended outward through the later
C19 and villas were built on the slopes behind, though not in
quantity before 1900. The resort was a pioneer in Wales of golf
and outdoor training. The anglicized name, Aberdovey, has fallen
into disuse.

ST PETER, Seaview Terrace. 1837. A neat Georgian Gothic box
with a W tower, of long blocks of slatey stone, on a rock-cut
terrace. Chancel of 1890, by *Henry Kennedy*, organ chamber,
1907. The nave has buttresses and acutely pointed windows,
the timber Y-tracery and delicate cast-iron glazing presumably
later. The tower has lancet bell-lights with hoodmoulds and
stepped battlements, and, inside, curving slate gallery stairs
with iron balusters grained as timber. Plaster Tudor-arched
nave ceiling; chancel lined in painted brick. – FONT, eight-
lobed, later C19. – FITTINGS. 1920s, e.g. the rails with Masonic
symbols, 1924. – STAINED GLASS. E window, 1873, by *Ward &
Hughes*, busy scenes. Chancel S, 1890 by *Powells*, with streaky
turquoise. Nave S, patterned glass, 1837, by *David Evans*. –
MONUMENTS. Susan Scott †1844, crocketed Gothic, by
Carline & Dodson of Shrewsbury. Baron Atkin of Aberdovey
†1944, brass of a judge, by *Peter Morton*.
   The terrace has cast-iron RAILINGS. Below, a pointed
LYCHGATE, the pretty metal leaves in the arch inserted 1953.
CHRIST THE KING (R.C.), Tywyn Road. 1974, by *Weightman
& Bullen*. Blockwork cube with low timber cross-gables,
attached to a flat-roofed hall.
CONGREGATIONAL CHAPEL, Seaview Terrace. 1880. Quite
small, Gothic, in green and grey stone, with five-light window.
Octagonal spire over a short porch tower, r.
ENGLISH PRESBYTERIAN CHURCH, Seaview Terrace. 1893, by
Richard Davies. Small, stuccoed, with an arched stone window
and a squat porch tower, r., under a slated pyramid. The detail
slightly Romanesque, the feeling American.
TABERNACL CALVINISTIC METHODIST CHAPEL, Seaview
Terrace. 1863–4. Now flats. At the head of a great flight of slate
steps with *Coalbrookdale* iron gates. Broad stuccoed front with
quoins, arched windows and paired doors.
BETHEL WELSH WESLEYAN CHAPEL, Chapel Square. 1868. A
broad front like Tabernacl, but Gothic, with plain lancets.
Unusually of brick, covered over in the 1920s.

PERAMBULATION

Central on SEAVIEW TERRACE, the DOVEY HOTEL, with late
C19 detail, is an earlier C19 rebuilding of the Ship Inn, from
which the 1729 datestone. COPPER HILL STREET runs
back to CHAPEL SQUARE, named not for the Wesleyan
chapel (E) but for the first Calvinistic Methodist chapel, 1828,
by the *Rev. Richard Humphreys*. Now DOVEY MARINE, it
is barely recognizable, but was substantial for the date.
The terracotta arch and gable plaque may remain from its
use as a market hall from 1864. Copper Hill Street continues
with two-storey houses on the W (No. 14 dated 1733,
altered), some three-storey on the E. Behind the W side,
EVANS TERRACE, 1827, a pretty row, one house with
horizontal-sliding sashes. Behind the E side, RAILWAY
COURT, mid-C19 tenements, arrestingly small. Beyond the

railway, TAI NEWYDDION, roughcast cottages of *c.* 1920, the upper block with eyebrow eaves.

From Chapel Square, CHURCH STREET runs up to the ABER-DOVEY HILLSIDE VILLAGE, holiday houses by *John Madin*, the Birmingham architect and planner of Telford New Town, who bought much of the upper hillside in 1965. Madin proposed a layout of houses and flats in pairs or short terraces, following the contours. Building has proceeded slowly over forty years, here and at ABERDOVEY HILLSIDE PARK, further up. The lower ones are pebbledashed with balconies, the first pair, EASTWARD and WESTWARD, 1967, with split-level interior and split roof, built by Madin for himself. The upper site, more exposed, has rendered houses cut into the slope.

Returning to the seafront, the QUAY of 1968–70 replaces the wharf of 1882. The long boathouse was nicely remodelled in 1995, with sets of large double doors. W of the Congregational chapel (*see* p. 537), GLANDOVEY TERRACE, stuccoed, three storeys and attic, but without unity, interrupted by a tall late C19 pair with square bays on green stone; Nos. 14–15, a good early C19 pair, three-storey with delicate two-storey curved bows. Paired columned and corniced doorcases. Then taller late terraces with canted three-storey bays to BODFOR TERRACE, 1890s, two blocks with red terracotta columns in the bays and doorways.

On SEAVIEW TERRACE, E of the Dovey Hotel, the altered OLD CUSTOM HOUSE, C18 with a large stone chimney. The Anglesey polymath Lewis Morris was Customs Officer here 1751–6. Three paired lodging houses are shown in early views: Nos. 15–16 altered with early C20 terracotta, but the two E of the church intact. Nos. 17–18, with a good Doric doorcase with triglyphs, and Nos. 19–20, with three-storey curved bows, and doorcase with spiral-fluted columns. These details can be found in Pier Street and Bridge Street, Aberystwyth. Past the Tabernacl chapel steps, Nos. 24–25, *c.* 1900, with bays and curved-topped upper windows. No. 26, BRYNAWEL, earlier C19, has a columned doorway with elliptical fanlight. Opposite the English Presbyterian church (*see* p. 537), in a tiny courtyard, the INSTITUTE, a reading room established 1882 in Bath House, a low stucco building for sea bathing. Festive timber veranda of 1897. On TERRACE ROAD, Nos. 1–3 CLIFFSIDE, *c.* 1885, stuccoed with Gothic columns to hefty bays; MERVINIA TERRACE, a mid-C19 small row of four, set back; and the LIFEBOAT HOUSE of 1887. Across the road, the former CHURCH HALL, 1922, prettily roughcast with a Gothic corner porch.

At PENHELIG there was small-scale shipbuilding in the C19. Under the railway bridge, NANTIESYN, a terrace of eight three-storey houses and the stone cottages beyond are both in a view of 1837. Between are the drives to the VICARAGE, later C19, stuccoed and gabled, and to PLAS PENHELIG, 1903–6. Large and roughcast with red-tiled roofs, double-gabled with an octagonal corner bay.

W of the town, beyond the railway bridge, the R.C. church, l., and PRIMARY SCHOOL, 1968, r. (on the site of the 1829 hotel). To the S, the STATION, *c.* 1865, red brick with sandstone windows. Early C20 villas on the hillside. HENDRE, r., *c.* 1910, is pretty with a tower diagonally set in the angle of an L-plan. Further l., GLASLYN, 1914, by *F. Howarth* of Tywyn, quirky, with different gables and undulating parapets. W again, MURMUR-Y-DON has similar motifs in miniature. Further W, the massive TREFEDDIAN HOTEL, later C20 recasting of a hotel of 1904, overlooks the GOLF COURSE in the dunes, the first in Wales, 1886–92.

OUTWARD BOUND CENTRE, 1 m. E. Established for wartime training, 1941, at Bryneithin, a gaunt later C19 gabled house. Stepped accommodation behind, 1989–90, by *Mitchell & Holden* of Pembroke, blockwork below painted roughcast.

TREFRI HALL, 1¼ m. E. Earlier C19 villa on a headland. Stone with roughcast above, three bays. Bargeboarded centre gable and tall ground-floor windows with hoodmoulds.

TREFRI FAWR, ¾ m N of Trefri Hall. Characterful early C18 farmhouse with three irregularly spaced gabled stone dormers and voussoired door. To the r., a small barn dated 1738.

FRONGOCH SLATE QUARRY, 2½ m. E. Worked 1864–84. The deep slate pit is connected by tunnel to a chapel-like engine-house with arched windows.

RHOWNIAR, 1½ m. NW. Hidden on a rocky outcrop, a small country house of 1911–12, built for William Kettle* by *Oswald Milne*. A good example of that relaxed rustic Georgian adopted by Arts and Crafts architects. Colour-washed with sash windows and steep roofs of small Preseli slates. Garden front between gables, the centre with slated gablets and a big sundial. To the r. a lower roof sweeps out over a garden room. The entrance side has a storeyed porch, between tall wall-face chimneys, with slated gablets each side. A rear addition of *c.* 1930 links to a near-detached billiard room.

Comfortable planning with the main rooms to the r. of an axial hall; stairs to the l. Shallow-curved plaster ceilings in the hall, garden room and billiard room, and much oak panelling. Stair with turned balusters and shaped finials. The bathrooms, one lilac, another turquoise, are lined in glassy streaked ceramic.

On the drive, CRUCK BARN was the original C16 hall-house. Low, the l. end raised but the r. end original. Two full cruck trusses here, and a massive stone fireplace, the lintel on corbels. Altered LODGE, dated 1911.

---

*Kettle's father, Sir Rupert, who encouraged John Corbett to buy the Ynysmaeng-wyn estate (Bryncrug) in 1879, had a house here.

ABERGEIRW

5 m. SE of Trawsfynydd.

Just the single-arched BRIDGE over the Mawddach (rebuilt wider, 2001) and the tiny CALVINISTIC METHODIST CHAPEL, 1834 and 1873, in a miniature forecourt. CWM SCHOOL to the SE, rebuilt 1934 by *Norman Jones*, was called 'probably more inaccessible than any in North Wales' in 1901.

BRYN-LLIN FAWR, ½ m. NE. C18, lobby-entry plan, with a cross-wing. The exceptionally large lintel stones must be deliberate display.

ABERGYNOLWYN

A slate-mining village, but without slate waste as the quarry was up the Nant Gwernol valley to the SE. Significant exploitation dates from 1864, when William McConnell, of the Manchester cotton firm McConnell & Kennedy, invested to offset the effect of the American Civil War on the cotton trade. His company also spent heavily on reservoirs and on the narrow-gauge Talyllyn Railway, 1865–6, to take the slate down to Tywyn. It built most of the village in 1865–75, seventy-one houses in three groups. The company secretary, the Manchester architect *James Stevens*, made designs for cottages in 1864 but the houses are much simpler than Stevens's village at Minllyn, Dinas Mawddwy (q.v.), so his actual involvement is uncertain. The company was wound up in 1882, but continued as a private business by McConnell. The local M.P., Haydn Jones of Tywyn, kept it open with difficulty from 1911 to 1946, it surviving just long enough to secure preservation of the railway in 1951 by a group led by the historian and engineer L. T. C. Rolt.

ST DAVID. 1879–80, by *Henry Kennedy*. Isolated to the W, built to counter the three new chapels. Nave and chancel with cusped lancets and a timbered porch. The bellcote on the vestry presumably replaces a W end one. Painted brick interior with open timber roofs.

From the main road, Llanegryn Street runs N down to the Dysynni bridge and a lane climbs S to the mine. Everything is built of slate, mostly rough-hewn discarded material. On the W side of LLANEGRYN STREET, two rows of single-storey cottages, twenty-four in all, of 1865–8. The former JERUSALEM CALVINISTIC METHODIST CHAPEL, 1878, has pairs of cusped lancets, and the former CWRT INDEPENDENT CHAPEL, 1878, a certain crude vigour with a Gothic rose. Parallel, W, separated by a back lane with paired outhouses, is WATER STREET (Heol y Dŵr), 1868–9, twenty-four two-storey houses in three rows, overlooking the Gwernol stream. Notably generous, with large upper windows. Back on the main road, PANDY SQUARE, a pretty L-plan whitewashed

row, pre-1864, runs diagonally to Y GANOLFAN, the community hall, 2004, by *Selwyn Jones* of Caernarfon. Laminated
cruck trusses.

Off the lane S, TANYBRYN STREET, two facing rows begun
1870, is the most urban composition, ending abruptly. Houses
vary from two to four bedrooms; the five largest, SW, with an
attic storey lit from the rear, contained a general store and the
Post Office. Late Georgian sashes and slate lintels. Again their
generous scale by contemporary standards is remarkable. The
lane joins the main road. Returning W, the former SARON
WESLEYAN CHAPEL, 1870, with sandstone arched window
heads; the slate-built SCHOOL, 1883; and, on the Llanegryn
Street corner, two single-storey cottages, MEIRION HOUSE,
rebuilt in slate, IVY COTTAGE, with original boulder-stones.

BRYN EGLWYS SLATE QUARRY, 1 m. SE. On the two superimposed slate beds that stretch from Dinas Mawddwy to the sea.
The Narrow Vein, 54 ft (16.5 metres) thick, produced the best
dark slate, the Broad Vein below it a grey slate of rougher character. As elsewhere in Merioneth, the slate was mined underground. The surface buildings have gone. The upper site, on
the Narrow Vein, had the Old Mill of 1847. The New Mill just
below was powered from the Boundary Reservoir and the
larger Llaeron Reservoir, ¼ m. SE, both 1864–5, now drained.
Above the latter, PONT LLAERON, a single-arch C18 bridge. It
marks the packhorse track over the hills to the Dyfi to which
slate was carried before the railway. The lower site, on the
Broad Vein, had an incline to the Lower Mill of 1881, a single
shed ultimately extended to 450 ft (138 metres) long, and three
further inclines dropping some 400 ft to the railhead.

ABERGYNOLWYN STATION (Talyllyn Railway), ½ m. W.
Successful Neo-Victorian, 1965, by *Douglas B. Thorpe*, reusing
iron columns from Tywyn Station.

ABERLLEFENNI
Corris

7710

Slate extraction is recorded in the C14, but the heyday was the
later C19, in the parallel valleys of the Llefenni and the Ceiswyn.
Col. R. Davies Pryce promoted an eight-mile horse-tramway in
1858 through Corris and Machynlleth to a quay on the Dyfi
beyond Derwenlas, converted to steam as the Corris Railway.

Hardly a village, just PENSARN, a terrace of fourteen houses
across from the large and crudely built DRESSING SHED. To
the N, a tiny derelict OFFICE with a bellcote. SW, the former
CALVINISTIC METHODIST CHAPEL, 1874, by the *Rev. David
Williams* of Mallwyd. Slate, Gothic, with a prolixity of
windows.

PLAS ABERLLEFENNI, just NE. The remnant of an important
gentry house owned in the earlier C17 by Sir John Lloyd. A
large C17 cross-wing to the r. of what remains was demolished

in the C20. This had massive lateral chimneys, mullion-and-transom windows and C17 plasterwork. What is left is not large, L-plan, the front range with a crowstepped l. chimney gable and rear lateral chimney, and a rear wing with another stepped gable. The façade spacing suggests the earlier C18, but inside are heavy C16–C17 chamfered beams with bar stops. Late C17 open-well staircase with turned balusters; post-and-panel partition to the E room. In the rear wing, a panelled first-floor room with early C18 bolection mouldings. The attics have regular collar-trusses.

ABERLLEFENNI QUARRY, ¼ m. NW. Huge waste tips loom over the road from both sides. One of the oldest worked sites in Wales, as the fine slate outcropped by the former route to Dolgellau. Developed by Col. R. D. Pryce from 1860, much of the working was underground, employing 169 in 1879. There were five inclines down to a slab mill, two water-balanced. A ruined DRUM HOUSE remains at the top of one. The long incline to the NW is from the CAMBERGI QUARRY, expensively begun in 1873, with seven levels and a mill on the s side of the road (SH 762 105); but little slate was produced.

HENGAE, I m. NW. A formal three-bay, three-storey house of *c.* 1800, isolated next to a tall conifer.

BRYNCOEDWIG MOUNTAIN CENTRE, ¼ m. E. The Council School, 1909, by *Deakin & Howard Jones*. Typical arched windows, the terracotta buff-coloured.

CWM RATGOED. The Nant Ceiswyn valley had no road. Slate was brought out by tramway (1863), the present access track. First, CYMERAU QUARRY, worked from 1869 by H. N. Hughes, its levels below the river. A TERRACE of four workers' houses remains. The track passes two further Cymerau workings and the ruined RATGOED COTTAGES, site of quarry cottages, shop, manager's house, chapel and manse. Then the ruins of the lower mills of RATGOED QUARRY, worked from the 1840s, the workings hidden in the hills (SH 787 119). Just beyond, in rhododendrons, is RATGOED HALL, built for Hughes in the 1860s. Grim, with rocky detail in slate off-cuts. It has lost an oriel and gabled dormers. ½ m. on, two small early houses: DOLGOED, C17, with voussoired doorway, and CEISWYN, a C16 hall-house with similar door and lateral chimney. Added late C19 front range. A cusped truss over the former hall, and post-and-panel partition. For all its tiny scale this was the home of a High Sheriff, Ieuan ap David Lloyd, in 1557–8.

ARTHOG

The village lines the main road at the base of a steep escarpment quarried for slate. The old route from Dolgellau to the coast, Ffordd Ddu, follows a fold behind the coastal ridge. Wealthy C19 owners built houses overlooking the Mawddach, and there was an attempt in 1900 to start a middle-class resort in the flat land around the junction of the three railways, from Machynlleth, Dolgellau and Porthmadog.

St Catherine. A chapel of ease to Llangelynin. Called new in 1808; tiny and charming with a w bellcote over a roundel, and a gabled porch joined to a miniature stair-tower. Arched windows; timber tracery with pretty leading of c. 1876. Inside, barn-like trusses and a simple gallery. – rails in turned oak, possibly early c18. – stained glass. e window, 1876, in muted colours. w roundel, 1952.

w from the church, a group associated with Arthog Hall (see below). The lodge, Efallon, 1835, has coarse Tudor detail – high gable parapets and triangular-headed lancets. Past the plain Gothic former Sion Calvinistic Methodist Chapel (1868), the dower house, Man Prydferth, 1837. Hipped, with a centre chimney. sw addition with bowed front wall and pretty Gothick glazing. Next, the home farm, now Arthog Barns, converted in 2007 by *Charles Mador* of London. A long hay barn dated 1833, and an earlier range, r., c. 1800, the stable loft with round pitching eyes; a cartshed beyond. Arthog Terrace has twelve well-built houses, each double-fronted with gables, the brick chimneys suggesting the later c19. The former school, 1883, has tall windows between outer gables. Up a track r., Garth-y-fog, 1796, two-storey with casements.

sw are scattered parts of a speculation by the Cardiff draper Solomon Andrews (see also Pwllheli). Three unrelated terraces were built 1900–3. Two are modest, stuccoed: Glasfryn Terrace, on the main road, and St Mary's Terrace, on the lane to the station. This stands under Ynys Gyffylog, an early c18 farmhouse on one of the characteristic rock outcrops. Behind the Ynys Fegla outcrop, on the waterside, Mawddach Crescent. Red brick and roughcast, like a London suburban terrace; intended for artistic clients.

ne from the church, Wesley Terrace, r., is mid-c19, but the r. pair earlier with a tiny disused Wesleyan chapel of 1833 attached. Beyond, the former National School, 1844, with bellcote and side chimney, and the derelict Salem Wesleyan Chapel, 1868, plain Gothic.

Arthog Hall, ¼ m. sw, on a rock terrace. Five bays, castellated, divided by two narrow half-round towers that rise no higher than the rest. Large sash windows with rough voussoirs, as if intended for stucco. Reginald Fowden, industrialist of Cheadle Hulme, probably built it after 1824; the chimneys look later still, but Fenton in 1808 mentions 'a pretty whimsical building' which William Roberts, surgeon, built 'to make the retreat more agreeable to a Mrs Pryce'. The long hipped rear range with massive stonework looks of c. 1800, as does a small two-bay lofted outbuilding with well-made arches.

Tŷ'n-y-coed, ¼ m. e, on the Cregennen lane. A superbly built Victorian villa on a terraced site. David Davis Jun., of the

Ferndale Collieries, Glamorgan, commissioned it *c.* 1875 from *William Parry James*, Cardiff contractor and architect. It seems too good for James alone, but *Edwin Seward*, the aesthetic architect of later C19 Cardiff, joined James in 1875, aged twenty-two. Green stone with grey dressings, symmetrical, with a spired lantern on the ridge. Canted-ended wings with fantastically bargeboarded dormers frame the centre behind an arcaded loggia with Ruskinian naturalistic capitals. Double-height hall with dining and drawing rooms, r., morning room and kitchen, l., and a basement servants' hall. The main rooms have panelled dados, pine-ribbed ceilings, and doors with brass fittings, but it is the polychromy of chimneypieces and stair-case that startles, showing very early the influence of William Burges's Cardiff Castle.

95   The HALL is spectacular. The ashlar stair walls have a stepped chequer of grey from the ends of the stair treads and are carried on pink marble arches. The balustrade opulently combines marble, wrought iron and Bath stone, the column newels topped by lustrous half-spheres of white marble.* This enthusiasm for materials characterizes the enormous fireplace and overmantel: coloured marbles and stone, with embossed glazed tiles under Gothic leaf carving. Similar unrestrained colour and materials in the dining-room chimneypiece and sideboard recess, and the drawing-room and morning-room chimneypieces. The splendid sideboard and other woodwork was apparently made in Manchester. Encaustic tiles in the landing panelling by *Minton*, two series, Shakespeare and naughty imps.

PANT PHYLIP, up a long drive above Tŷ'n-y-coed. 1731. Three-bay with big end chimneys and gabled dormers.

LLYS BRADWEN, ½ m. ESE of Tŷ'n-y-coed. Large boulder foun-dations of a medieval house of two rooms, one square, one rounded, associated with Ednowain ap Bradwen, founder of one of the fifteen tribes of North Wales.

GARTH ISAF, 1 m. NE. Down a track close to the water. The origi-nal Garthangharad (*see* below) before the Owens moved uphill in 1807. Earlier C17, stone, with dormers and good earlier C18 panelling and staircase. Behind, a two-storey late C17 second house with small windows under the eaves, and to the N a C17–C18 cottage with gabled upper windows. Further N, a C17 barn.

GARTHANGHARAD, 1½ m. NE. Another large Victorian holiday house, rebuilt *c.* 1880 for Sir Richard Wyatt, Clerk of the Peace of Surrey, incorporating the shell of the Owen house of 1807. Five bays, with gables on the first and last two, and broad canted bay windows. Crowstepped entrance tower. At the opposite end, a conservatory with Venetian windows hints at the transformation of 1911–12 by *Ralph Knott & E. S. Collins* that obliterated the Late Victorian interior for white-painted

* Very like those at Insole Court, Llandaff where Seward worked 1873–5.

rooms in a rich Edwardian version of Queen Anne. The more exotic CONSERVATORY has marble-clad octagonal columns, a sunken floor like a Roman bathhouse, and pretty lead glazing. Knott, winner of the 1908 competition for the London County Hall, did little other country-house work. The two pyramid-roofed LODGES are also by *Knott & Collins*. Early C20 Italian garden with half-round tank supplying three stepped *canals d'eau*.

HAFOD DYWYLL, 3 m. E. Uphill from Kings Youth Hostel. A well-preserved storeyed house of *c.* 1600. Five-light oak-mullion parlour window and a rear stair-tower contiguous with a lateral chimney. Good post-and-panel partitions, the triangular doorheads with incised crosses.

FFORDD DDU. Bronze Age monuments and later prehistoric and Romano-British settlements mark the line of this ancient trackway and its continuation towards Llwyngwril (q.v.). Near the Cregennen lakes are two or three small CAIRNS and CARREG-Y-BIG (SH 662 138), a large standing stone. Over the wall by the road junction (SH 665 135) is a large STONE RING, the base of a robbed cairn, which would have dominated the valley below. Further W by the old road (SH 652 133) is one of the most dramatic STANDING STONES in Merioneth, a tapering column fronting the crags of Cader Idris. Small CAIRNS may be seen on the hill-slope above Cyfanedd, 1¼ m. WSW, but the next group immediately beside the track is a pair of tall STANDING STONES (SH 626 117) and three CAIRNS a short distance W. A stone cist was found in the cairn at Goleuwern (SH 622 116), S of the track, in the C19. Remains of a double kerb around the edge. On the mountain shelf below Bryn Seward, a number of relict SETTLEMENT features including a very good round stone hut with its low walled enclosure. This 'concentric' type is judged to be Iron Age in date.

BALA/Y BALA

9336

The broad valley of the Bala lake, Llyn Tegid, is still the principal route from the NE to the coast as it was for the Romans. Penllyn district was a boundary between the princes of Powys and of Gwynedd, and the large earthen motte may be of Welsh rather than Norman construction. The linear town plan probably post-dates the Edwardian conquest, the charter dating from the early C14, but the parish remained Llanycil until the C19.

The town grew relatively wealthy in the early C19 from woollen goods, 'a vast trade in woollen stockings, gloves and caps, called Welsh wigs', according to the Rev. J. Evans in 1812. But the fame of Bala was as *de facto* centre of Nonconformist Wales from the time when the Rev. Thomas Charles married into a Bala family in 1783 to the 1960s. The Rev. Simon Lloyd, Charles's great supporter, was of the leading Bala family. In 1837 the Rev. Lewis Edwards came to open the school that became Bala College, for the training of Calvinistic Methodist ministers. His fifty-year tenure was followed from 1891 by that of his son, the Rev. Thomas Charles Edwards †1900. The Independent cause was served in Bala by the Rev. Michael Jones †1853, founder of the Independent College in 1842. His son and successor the Rev. Michael D. Jones (†1898) took the college into enormous controversy in 1879–85, resolved with his resignation and the college's re-establishment in Bangor. Michael D. Jones's radical nationalism made him a leading figure in the drive to establish Yr Wladfa, the Welsh settlement in Patagonia in 1865. The role of Bala in the dissemination of information began with Thomas Charles's printing office in Berwyn Street in 1802.

The long, wide High Street (Stryd Fawr), has parallel back streets, Mount Street (Heol y Domen) and Arenig Street (Heol Arenig), and is crossed by the old route from Montgomeryshire to Caernarvonshire – Tegid Street and Castle Street. The architecture is Late Georgian to Victorian, stone with some stucco and little brick before the railway brought the coloured bricks from Ruabon and Flint.

CHURCHES AND CHAPELS

CHRIST CHURCH, Ffrydan Road. 1853–4, by *Benjamin Ferrey*. Severe E.E., with tall aisled and clerestoried nave, chancel and a dominant w tower with broach spire. It has the serious detail of Pugin's Irish works, too spare for *The Ecclesiologist*, which preferred a later Gothic. Convincing interior, the detail Transitional – from round columns with scalloped caps in the pointed arcades, to waterleaf chancel arch capitals, to a fully Gothic shafted E triplet. A dramatic redesign, 2006–7, by *Roy Olsen*, swept away most fittings for a beige stone nave floor stepped as an apron under the chancel arch. Prow-like glazed parish room under a modern gallery that retains some C19 pews. The chancel feels empty, with chairs behind the boxy new ALTAR and READING DESK. – FONT. 1854, a shallow square on a shaft and four columns. – PULPIT. Late C19, carved sandstone. – ORGAN. 1887, by *Conacher*. – STAINED GLASS. E window, 1855, attractive patterned glass. – Three by *Burlison & Grylls*, c. 1923, C16 style, two S and one N. Also N, two saints, c. 1899 by *T. F. Curtis, Ward & Hughes*, and an interestingly coloured NE window, c. 1880.

OUR LADY OF FATIMA (R.C.), High Street. Converted in 1947–8 from the outbuilding behind a C17 house. Raised cruck trusses.

CAPEL TEGID (Calvinistic Methodist), Tegid Square. The successor to the chapel founded by the Rev. Thomas Charles (1755–1814). 1867, by *W. H. Spaull* of Oswestry. Unusually for the denomination, Gothic, with a thin stone tower and spire on the l. of the façade. Structural problems removed the original traceried window and in 2006 replaced the spire in metal. The spacious interior possesses the élan of good railway engineering – the structural members of iron and wood boldly exposed. Galleries with painted timber Gothic panels on iron columns. Above, a second layer of columns with florid capitals carry pointed arcades of timber. Elaborate pitch-pine *sêt-fawr* and pulpit, backed by an impressively large organ by *Conacher*, 1897.

Outside, within railings, eroding Sicilian marble STATUE of Thomas Charles, 1875, by *William Davies* of London, holding out the Bible. On the pedestal a sweet relief of a Sunday School class.

ENGLISH PRESBYTERIAN CHURCH, High Street. 1811. Built as the Anglican chapel of ease. A rustic tower topped by a steep pyramid in thin rubble courses. Tiny lunettes over arched windows flank the tower. To Mount Street, a canted projection with a minimally Palladian window. Curved plaster ceiling, otherwise Nonconformist fittings of 1904.

INDEPENDENT CHAPEL, Mount Street. 1866–7, by the *Rev. Thomas Thomas*. Italianate, the design reused at Newcastle Emlyn, Carms, 1868. A shallow gable with urn, between parapets. Good tooled-stone arched doorway and bracket cornice. Typical Thomas interior: gallery front with arch-panelled pilasters and timber ceiling boarding around big plaster roses. Octagonal pulpit with fretwork, in front of a large organ, 1914, by *James Binns*.

PUBLIC BUILDINGS

TOWN HALL, High Street. Late C18, perhaps originally an open market under an assembly room, but the lower floor used for the Court of Great Sessions by the early C19. Five bays. Arches with arched hoods under sashes with label hoods. Prominent moulded sandstone cornice. Central slate-hung clock turret, 1868, with a leaded ogee dome.

TOMEN-Y-BALA, Mount Street. Possibly the largest castle MOTTE in Wales after Cardiff. The ditch has been long infilled and any evidence for a bailey lost under later buildings. The size suggests a Norman rather than Welsh origin, but the only record is Welsh, in 1202 when Llywelyn the Great ousted Elise ap Madog, Lord of Penllyn.

PONT-Y-BALA. Four arches over the Tryweryn, probably C18. Widened on the s.

BALA COLLEGE, Ffrydan Road. Until 1967 the principal Calvinistic Methodist training college. 1865–7, by *W.H. Spaull*. Gothic, eleven bays, symmetrical about a central tower, with gables to frame the main seven bays. The outer two were staff houses, but students lodged in town. Spaull's tower, which had a slated wedge roof and two-storey traceried window, had to be rebuilt in 1898, to a duller battlemented design by *Richard Davies*. In front, the Rev. Lewis Edwards †1887, seated bronze STATUE, 1911, by *W. Goscombe John*.

YSGOL BEUNO SANT, Castle Street. 1872–3, by *Benjamin Ferrey*, built as the National School. Stone and Gothic with the boys' schoolroom gable, l., balanced by the master's house, r.

The girls' schoolroom was in the middle.

PENLLYN LEISURE CENTRE, by the lake. 1995–6, by *Alex Gordon & Partners*. Large complex in grey imitation stone with smooth bands. Pool and sports hall each under a big hipped roof. A lower range, r., with a throughway to the lake.

PERAMBULATION

The broad HIGH STREET runs straight, showing its Roman origin. The WHITE LION ROYAL HOTEL, diagonally opposite the Town Hall (*see* p. 547) is a stepped sequence of three ranges in whitewashed brick, dated 1759, with a little bow-fronted addition, r., of *c.* 1820, but overwhelmed by a mock-timbered gabled upper storey of *c.* 1890. Mid-C18 stair with turned balusters, decorated with C19 carving. NE of the Town Hall, HSBC BANK, 1880, by *E. Kirby* of Liverpool for the North & South Wales Bank. Ruabon brick and purple Runcorn sandstone, with gables and cross-mullioned windows. PLAS COCH, C18 house of the Anwyl family, was elaborately stuccoed *c.* 1870, by *Richard Owens*, but scraped in the C20. Some Late Georgian fragments inside. Opposite: Nos. 53–57, a postrailway row in buff brick banded in black; THE GOAT INN, *c.* 1910, brick and roughcast; and Nos. 37–39, Late Georgian three-storey, five bays, with narrow attic sashes. Nos. 31–33, similar, three bays, has a good mid-C19 draper's shopfront with Tudor-arched lights. Opposite, Nos. 48–52, earlier C19, formally grouped with a central open pediment, stuccoed apart from No. 52. No. 48 has a good fluted Doric doorcase. Nos. 40–42, very red Ruabon brick and terracotta, *c.* 1910, has lost two gables. BERWYN STREET nicely frames the Independent chapel (*see* p. 547).

Facing down the High Street is the lively bronze STATUE of T. E. (Tom) Ellis (1859–99), popular Liberal M.P., robed as the Warden of the Guild of Graduates of the University of Wales. 1903, by *W. Goscombe John*. Stone reliefs mark his life from home to Westminster, via Aberystwyth and Oxford. On the l., HEULWEN, mid-C19, stone, with cast-iron balcony and columned porch. Further up, PLAS-YN-Y-DRE, much altered with early C20 bays. The core may be late C18 for the Rev. Simon Lloyd †1836, supporter of Thomas Charles. Opposite, the former BRITISH SCHOOL, 1855, by *Ebenezer Thomas* of Bala, a steep-roofed classroom fronted by a storeyed gabled porch, and the English Presbyterian church (*see* p. 547). HENBLAS, Nos. 22–26, a handsome, deep-eaved, two-storey range, looks Late Georgian but is of the 1860s. In the front wall a mid-C17 roundel with a rampant rabbit, possibly the goat of the Caergai Vaughans. Generous floor-heights; contrast the three floors of No. 20 to the same height. Nos. 6–18 have deep flat eaves, slightly earlier, as also the row opposite rising to three storeys at Nos. 3–5.

A detour up FFRYDAN ROAD passes Nos. 4–20, a display of later C19 coloured brick, the first five black, patterned in red and buff, the last four buff with black. In ARENIG STREET, CHURCH HOUSE, 1911, by *Deakin & Howard Jones*, green stone with oriel and bays in terracotta. Nos. 1–15 is an improbably grand row for a back road. Edwardian Baroque of 1909, Ruabon brick with buff terracotta, divided by four pavilions, the middle two with big curved pediments and the outer two narrower and hipped.

The main street, now STATION ROAD, has a red brick late C19 row, l., opposite the Neo-Tudor GRAMMAR SCHOOL, built for Jesus College, Oxford, 1850–51, by *Wigg & Pownall* of London. Stone, collegiate, with the hall to the l. of the master's house, and a porch between with bellcote. Attractive iron glazing. Big two-storey range, r., added perhaps in 1887. Beyond is the Pont-y-bala (*see* p. 547). The riverside fields where the enormous revivalist meetings of Thomas Charles's day were held were taken for the railway in 1882, now car parking.

MOUNT STREET runs SW under the castle mound (*see* p. 547). After the Independent chapel (*see* p. 547), Nos. 48–52, mid-C19 cottages with tiny triangular-headed windows, and BERWYNFA, an 1870s villa faced in crazed sandstone. In TEGID STREET, running SE, No. 21, altered, has C18 stone-coped gables. Facing Tegid Square, Nos. 37–43, a handsome mid-C19 stone row, two mirrored pairs with big axial chimneys. In TEGID SQUARE, the Charles statue and Capel Tegid (*see* p. 546). The plain LLETY LODGE at the l. corner was the Methodist College in 1839–67, attached to the original chapel demolished for Nos. 34–40, a gabled later C19 stuccoed row. No. 46, opposite, is mid-C19 with bracket eaves and big lintels. Further out, set back, PLAS-YR-ACRE, an unusual earlier C19 house, has a steep hipped roof and tall panelled chimneys; subdivided. Returning NW, Nos. 3–11 have a sequence of C19 shopfronts from the simplest to the elaborately pilastered, at No. 5.

Back on the High Street, BARCLAYS BANK is a mid-C19 stucco facing of the house of the Rev. Thomas Charles. Behind, the schoolroom with arched iron windows was the Bala College of 1837. The OLDE BULL'S HEAD, a surprisingly large late C17 inn, has a big hipped roof, stuccoed nine-bay front and five gabled attic windows. The former WORKHOUSE, by *Thomas Jones* of Chester, 1838–41, abandoned in 1875 for a new one near the castle (by *Spaull*, since demolished), survived as militia barracks and pyjama factory. As at Corwen, the admissions block stands forward of a two-storey cross-range. But behind, a spine connects to a second, taller, cross-range with an octagonal centrepiece, allowing sight of four exercise yards. Prison-like arched iron windows, apart from the front block, which resembles a villa with deep eaves and shallow centre gable. The former BAPTIST CHAPEL, 1859, altered 1884, has an abundance of stucco hoodmoulds.

Further out, opposite fields, NEUADD BUDDUG, the Victoria Hall, 1891, refronted in the 1950s, and a well-designed early C20 stuccoed row with tower-like gabled features. Beyond is the leisure centre (*see* p. 548).

OUTLYING HOUSES. Opposite the leisure centre, ERYL ARAN is stone, gabled, with Tudor doorway, 1860s; BRYNYGROES, Stryd y Fron, is roughcast and gabled, dated 1902, extended 1914 by *Deakin & Howard Jones*. Uphill are BRYNFFYNNON and LLYS BEUNO, two good houses of 1971–2 by *I. Prys Edwards*. The one has two monopitch blocks separated by a paved approach, the other a single monopitch and a flat-roofed cube. Above, FRONDDERW was a Lloyd and Anwyl family house. The long hipped three-bay front is earlier C19, lined stucco suggested by whitewashed slabs of slate on battens. Inside, a stick-baluster stair, but two rooms behind have C17 beamed ceilings. Up Castle Street, GWYNFRYN, 1931, stuccoed and hipped, in an inventive Neo-Georgian with a festooned bullseye over an elaborate trellis loggia. On Ffrydan Road, BODIWAN, 1859, of good squared stonework with bargeboarded gables, for the Rev. Michael D. Jones.

6116   BARMOUTH/ABERMAW

Recorded as just a 'creek' in 1565, Barmouth developed as a port at the mouth of the Mawddach (from which the full Welsh name, Abermawddach). Improved after 1797, it was already the principal harbour for the export of woollen cloth, or webs, made in Dolgellau and Bala, and sold notably to clothe slaves in the Americas. Minerals and slate were also exported. Ships were built at Barmouth and along the estuary until the railway in 1867 completed a maritime decline begun after the Napoleonic wars. The wars and then the railway, however, encouraged Barmouth's new role as a holiday resort. Two main building types, the Late Georgian of the early resort in long blocks of slatey stone and the later C19 of the post-railway era, more mixed in materials and styles, exploiting notably the distinctive local green stones.

ST DAVID, Church Street. Originally a chapel of ease to Llanaber. 1830, by *Edward Haycock* of Shrewsbury, who designed similar resort churches at Aberystwyth and Aberaeron. In squared blocks of green stone, it is cruciform with a big hoodmoulded Perp window in each gable. Vestry 1886. Plain interior with deep-coved ceiling; diagonal beams span the crossing. – STAINED GLASS. E window, 1873, by *Alexander Gibbs*.*

106   ST JOHN, St John's Hill. One of the most splendid Victorian churches of Gwynedd. 1889–95, mostly at the expense of Mrs Perrins, widow of the Worcestershire Sauce manufacturer.

---

*All three Barmouth churches are not oriented E–W, but the text orientations are liturgical.

Her architects were *Douglas & Fordham*, who had built Plas Mynach in 1882 (*see* p. 554). The church was nearly complete when in 1891 the tower collapsed, taking much of the nave. Rebuilt with Mrs Perrins's generous help.

The cruciform church sits tightly on a rock shelf over the town, its colours, grey Minffordd granite with much red Runcorn sandstone, magnificent against the mountain. Early Perp. The long nave has aisles neatly framed by gables, of the transepts and the porches. The great crossing tower, set well E, against a short high chancel, has bold angle buttresses, paired bell lights, a parapet with finials, and a pyramidal roof. Big end windows, the E of seven lights, the W of five, the tracery here more Dec.

Inside, the red stone predominates. Five-bay arcades with angel-stops and octagonal piers under deep-set four-light clerestory windows. Chancel arch of many orders, the inner ones on foliate corbels. Douglas's roofs, with a hint of Arts and Crafts, never fail to delight: elongated shafts support crenellated tie-beams in the nave, and in the chancel, a higher wagon roof. – FONT. A marble angel holding a shell, after the much-copied Thorwaldsen font in Copenhagen, by *Davidson & Co.* of Inverness, 1894. – REREDOS. Large, in pink sandstone with canopied niches, the Crucifixion in the centre. – LECTERN. Wrought iron, with a repoussé copper panel of the Sower, by *Singer* of Frome. – PEWS. Simple benches, the ends arcaded. More elaborate STALLS, with fleur-de-lys finials. – STAINED GLASS. Mostly 1890s by *C. E. Kempe*; W window, 1910, by *Kempe & Co.*

ST TUDWAL (R.C.), King Edward Street. 1904–5, by *Alfred Gilbertson* of Liverpool. Grey granite with yellow Cefn sandstone lancets and a small, saddlebacked SW tower. Hammerbeam nave roof, short chancel, W organ gallery. – Elaborate oak FITTINGS by *Ferdinand Stuflesser* of Austria, 1909, especially the openwork spire over the tabernacle. Cusped framing to the flanking carved panels, and Last Supper panel on the altar. Also Stations of the Cross, pews, and panelling. Attached PRESBYTERY, twin-gabled with an oriel on a pier.

SILOAM INDEPENDENT CHAPEL, Beach Road. 1869–70, probably by the *Rev. Thomas Thomas*. Central triplet and tall single lights all with keyed arched heads, the door voussoirs brought to a Gothic point. This uncertainty of style also in the slim angle buttresses with pinnacles, and the corbel table following the gable.

CAERSALEM CALVINISTIC METHODIST CHAPEL, High Street. Disused but once very grand. Originally of 1865–6 by *W. H. Spaull*, rebuilt 1892 by *O. Morris Roberts* and altered in 1910, by his firm. Italianate. The pedimented centre, presumably of 1892, has a broad Florentine window with blind roundel. The handsome storeyed porches each side with matching cornices under balustrades may be of 1910. Keyed elliptical roundel over paired arched windows. Between, a double-arched loggia on black granite columns. Rich gallery with carved panels and enormous plaster rose of a multitude of roundels.

CHRIST CHURCH (English Presbyterian), High Street. 1878, by *Richard Owens* of Liverpool. Steep-roofed Gothic, with yellow sandstone dressings. Hipped stair wings flank the tall centre with paired windows, each with a big cinquefoil in the head. Above, a punched roundel.

EBENEZER WESLEYAN CHAPEL, High Street. Disused. 1855, by *John Evans* of Llanfair Caereinion, but the bold composition in green and buff ashlar presumably of 1881, the date on the porch. A broad recess with Romanesque corbelling frames a quintuplet, the centre light taller, above a big three-bay Romanesque porch. Gallery with boarded panels. Characterful MANSE, l., in green and pink blocks with a narrow gable front and two tall arched upper windows.

RAILWAY VIADUCT, over the Mawddach. 1867, by *Benjamin Piercy*. The largest timber viaduct still in use in Britain, 750 yds (685 metres), with 113 spans on diagonally braced piles. A steel SWING BRIDGE, 1899, replaces an earlier 'cock-and-draw' moveable section.

PERAMBULATION

The earliest part is the OLD TOWN stepping haphazardly up the steep cliff above St David's church like a Mediterranean hill-town. Alleys lead to a maze of unnamed stepped paths. Near the top, PENYGRAIG, late C17 T-plan, is three-storey to the front, two behind, with large end chimneys and small windows, the upper ones in stone dormers. ST GEORGE'S TERRACE and ROCK TERRACE, behind, forming a little village, were the famous settlement established *c.* 1874 by Ruskin for his utopian Guild of St George 'for the education of English peasantry', in practice a condominium with selected tenants and controlled rents. The thirteen cottages were donated by Mrs Fanny Talbot of Tŷ'n Ffynnon nearby, who also gave DINAS OLEU, the top of the cliff, as the first property of the National Trust in 1895.

The HARBOUR is cut off by the concrete railway viaduct. By the viaduct, 'The Last Haul', 2002, SCULPTURE by *Frank Cocksey*, carved from a wonderfully pitted block of Carrara marble recovered in the 1980s from a Genoese ship wrecked in 1709. Beyond the viaduct, the tin-clad SAILORS' INSTITUTE, 1890, with boarded reading room and billiard room. Beyond, the gable-fronted TŶ GWYN is a rare first-floor hall-house, built *c.* 1450 for Gruffudd Fychan of Corsygedol. Small basement and a ground storey with the entry, unusually, at one end and the fireplace at the other, cut into the rock. The hall above, also with end fireplace. It has an untypical roof with close-centred collar-trusses braced to the wall-plates, vertical joints where the principals meet, and threaded purlins. Behind, TŶ CRWN, 1833, a circular lock-up with conical roof and moulded stone stack.

From St David's church, a detour E down CHURCH STREET. On the l., ANCHOR COTTAGE, C18 with typical Merioneth hipped dormers, the cross-wing l. incorporating steps up. The road skirts the foot of Dinas Oleu past GRAIG FACH, an early C19 pair, to PORKINGTON TERRACE, ¼ m. out, 1870, a row of gabled boarding houses facing the estuary. GORONWY TERRACE, on the footpath to Gloddfa Road, is Late Georgian, with deep eaves and veranda. Finally, on the crest looking seaward, Nos. 1 and 2 BORTHWEN, an early C19 three-storey pair.

Behind St David's church, INGLENOOK, a low C18 two-storey pair. Tall mixed commercial buildings and houses line the long HIGH STREET running N. As in Dolgellau, turnings and widenings give unplanned hints of squares. The first part widens to frame ABER HOUSE, a good early C19 three-storey, three-bay house with fanlight. On the l., THE STEPS, its early C19 three storeys diminutive next to the later C19 compostion of the CROWN HOTEL, with arched-triplet upper windows, and flanking open-pedimented wings. Opposite, MIDLAND FLATS, in slatey stone like the earlier houses, but to a mid-C19 four-storey scale, with square and canted projections. Further on, Caersalem chapel, l., then TŶNYCOED, early C19, three bays, the fourth storey with two gables. Arched doorway with fanlight. Opposite, up the r. side of Ebenezer chapel, TŶNY-COED BUILDINGS, a two-storey backland terrace, early C19. The CAMBRIAN ESTABLISHMENT, l., a draper's shop of 1882, probably by *Thomas Roberts*, is richly Italianate like premises in Dolgellau, with pedimented and pilastered windows. The shop has iron columns, a helical gallery staircase and mahogany fittings. The four-storey proprietor's house, 1885, is attached behind. Next, much lower, PEN-Y-GRISIAU, colour-washed, late C17, has a tall gable chimney to the street and outside steps to the upper floor. On the E side, MEFYS-YR-HAF, a neat early C20 ironmonger's, has a mansard with dormers over a continuously glazed upper floor and a plate-glass shopfront. Next, set back, TANYFRON, a short early C19 three-storey terrace of three. The HSBC BANK occupies most of an early C19 four-bay terrace, the middle storey removed for an early C20 sandstone front for the North & South Wales Bank. WALTER LLOYD-JONES, similar four-bay Late Georgian, adjoins, with later C19 glazed iron canopy. Beyond, the former CORSYGEDOL HOTEL, 1869–70, has two blocks, four- and five-storey, with square hipped bays. Christ Church (*see* above) is opposite, on the corner of BEACH ROAD running W to the railway; Siloam chapel, r. The STATION, 1867, is stone with an outsize Gothic columned porch. JUBILEE ROAD following the railway S was never fully built-up; THEATR-Y-DDRAIG, l., occupies a much-altered Gothic Congregational chapel, 1896. A detour over the railway to the beach, where the PROMENADE has late C19 four-storey boarding houses and hotels. Back on the main road, ST ANNE'S SQUARE is an irregular widening. Set back E, ST ANNE HOUSE, a hotel or boarding house of *c*. 1800, three storeys and seven bays with a pediment, indicates the scale of the early tourist development. Adjoining r., MASONIC HALL, 1885, by *Thomas Roberts*, and further r., TANRALLT, early C19, three-storey, with later stucco. A late C19 terraced roadway, ST JOHN'S HILL, climbs up to St John's Church. Facing S, a strongly detailed green stone TERRACE of very large later C19 houses; big half-hipped gables over three-storey canted bays with ringed columns. Below the church (*see* p. 550), the CHURCH HALL, 1910, also built for Mrs Perrins, so perhaps by *Douglas*'s firm. Stepped gables, grey and red stone. The main road, now KING EDWARD STREET, runs N with typical late C19 terraces, r., with bays and gables; HANLITH TERRACE, 1890, is four-storey with sawtooth gables. Past the R.C. church (*see* p. 551), THE GABLES and GLENCAIRN in LLANABER ROAD introduce turn-of-the-century red tiles, half-timber and fancy glazing. CRAIG MYNACH and CIL MYNACH, of similar date, in roughcast with fiery red brick and terracotta, have canted hipped bays – each house with a smaller one beside a large outer one. The windows similar to Douglas's Castle Hotel, Conwy. Opposite, TŴR MYNACH, on a steep promontory, a villa overwhelmed by a three-storey tower with circular vice and corbelled parapet, 1885, by *Thomas Roberts*. In MYNACH ROAD, Y GARTH, has similar overblown colours and details as Craig Mynach and Cil Mynach. THE RECTORY, stone with terracotta mullioned windows in square bays, is contemporary, but less ostentatious.

PLAS MYNACH, Llanaber Road. On a rocky knoll, hidden by trees. Built for W. H. Jones by *Douglas & Fordham* in 1882–3, extended in 1886. Early C17 style, with stepped gables inspired by Dolaugwyn, Bryncrug, which Douglas knew. The *British Architect* praised its unostentatiousness: 'the idea of a perfect country house'. Grey snecked rubble with yellow dressings. The main block faces W, flanked by a big three-storey tower over the kitchen, l., and a crowstepped cross-wing, r., with crowstepped S gables. Flush mullion-and-transom windows and a simple corbel table between the floors, echoed under the tower parapet. Behind the tower, the 1886 gatehouse wing is also crowstepped with a broad pointed archway. Much panelling inside, and a landing arcade on turned posts. Terraced garden, W, with a square GAZEBO on the rock at the SW corner. Also a LODGE and PORTH MYNACH, opposite, with crowsteps and a lead cupola.

THE CLOCK HOUSE, ½ m. E, spectacularly set on a rocky promontory. Begun 1844, as Coesfaen. *Thomas Jones* of Chester, architect, died here in 1859. Could he have designed it? Extended impulsively through the later C19 to a festive ensemble of gabled and hipped parts around a tall slim clock tower with slated spire. The original cottage of just three bays has an outsized porch faced in dark green ashlar, the ogee door under a giant trefoil full of cusping, on gargoyle heads.

GLANYMAWDDACH, 1 m. E. Superbly set overlooking the estuary. A plain hipped earlier C19 stone villa, enlivened by a large arcaded C20 stone conservatory with radial fanlights. In front, a terracotta balustrade, 1910, with the initials of A. and J. Keighley, creators of the remarkable hillside GARDENS, extended after 1943 for Sir William Clayton Russon.

BETWS GWERFUL GOCH

0348

Named for a chantry in memory of Gwerful Goch, died *c.* 1200, granddaughter of Owain Gwynedd.

ST MARY (formerly St Elian). In a raised circular churchyard. Single-chamber, the surviving detail C15. The S doorway is formed of only three stones, the jambs stopped and chamfered, and the head of Tudor profile. Timber S porch dated 1606. Restored in 1880–81 by *John Douglas* who put paired cusped lights in arched C18 openings, but his extraordinary Arts and Crafts spirelet and broad-shouldered W wall have gone. Dark interior. The late medieval six-bay roof, arch-braced with cusped apexes, has carved heads and floral bosses. The celure has gone, but there are ornamental E wall-plates with a dragon etc. – REREDOS. Of late medieval panels presumably from a screen. Low reliefs of the Crucifixion, SS Mary and John, and the Instruments of the Passion. – PISCINA. C18. – FITTINGS. By *Douglas*, including the SCREEN, with varied tracery patterns, STALLS and PEWS. – CANDELABRA. C18, two tiers, on a turned wood shaft. – PULPIT. 1741. – STAINED GLASS. Of 1880, the E, Ascension, by *Heaton, Butler & Bayne*, and chancel S, by *Swaine Bourne*. – LYCHGATE. By *Douglas*.

PONT-Y-BETWS, ¼ m. SW. 1785, by *Joseph Turner*, the Denbighshire County Surveyor. Handsome triple-arched bridge over the Alwen, with pilasters between.

DINAS MELIN-Y-WIG, 1½ m. NE (SH 049 492). Beautifully situated hill-fort on a rocky promontory over the river Clwyd.* The promontory steep-sided, the defences almost entirely composed of scarped slopes rather than true banks and ditches. The original E entrance (partly damaged by a farm track) was defended by inturned ramparts – the only place where a strong rampart exists. On the N the remains of three lines of defence can be seen in the wood; the inner rampart is a low bank; the second one a broad sloping bank now faced on the upper side with a modern wall; the third line only a scarped shelf cut into the hillside. It is possible that there is a true ditch between the first and second, but on the W it becomes simply a shelf and the ramparts dwindle to two scarps between the high rocks. The sheltered N end of the 13-acre interior is likely to have been the area of settlement. Surviving remains suggest that a medieval farmstead occupied this

* Always in Denbighshire, but omitted from *The Buildings of Wales: Clwyd*.

favoured spot, replaced by the present, even more sheltered farm, Clegyr Mawr, tucked under the eastern rocks.

BLAENAU FFESTINIOG

The *blaenau*, or uplands, N of the old village of Ffestiniog, developed for slate-quarrying in the early C19, had become by the late C19 the slate capital of North Wales and the largest town in Merioneth. Excluded from the Snowdonia National Park, but with a special beauty of its own, from the ever-present backdrop of slate tips.

CHURCHES AND CHAPELS

St David. 1840–2, by *Thomas Jones* of Chester. Minimal Perp with w bellcote. The roof slides over short central projections each side. w porch and N vestry, 1907, by *Tapp, Jones & Son*. w gallery, and roof of long-raking braces to kingpost trusses. – stained glass. By *Powells*, the chancel N and S, 1948 and N transept E 1950.

Bethesda Calvinistic Methodist Chapel, Manod Road. Disused. 1848, by the *Rev. Richard Humphreys*. Crude but attractive, the rubble front divided by pilasters with a minimal entablature, and under a half-hip rather than a pediment. Arched openings. It outlasted a successor of 1870, by *Richard Owens*.

Bowydd Calvinistic Methodist Chapel, The Square. 1882, by *O. Morris Roberts*. Italianate, with hipped wings and pedimented centre. Idiosyncratic detail. The centre recess has a triangular head echoing the open main pediment. Pilasters just to the upper floor, and a Palladian window radiating spokes to an outer arch.

Calfaria Baptist Chapel, Towyn Road. 1881 and 1899. Another idiosyncratic façade. The giant arch and angles have quoins but no mouldings, and the windows have shouldered 'Caernarfon' heads instead of arches, amazingly uncomfortable in the centre Palladian triplet.

Carmel Independent Chapel, Tanygrisiau. In a railed forecourt. Probably by the *Rev. Thomas Thomas*, 1861–2, his basic giant arch design on pilasters with a broad entablature. The central triplet has wheel glazing to the main light. Columned porch.

Jerusalem Independent Chapel, Fourcrosses. 1867–8, probably by the *Rev. Thomas Thomas*, altered 1879. Sandstone voussoirs to the giant arch and quoins instead of pilasters. Moulded arched windows and door, the centre window a triplet.

Rhiw Calvinistic Methodist Chapel, Rhiwbryfdir. 1867–8. Backed against the slate tip. The largest surviving chapel. Pedimented, with acorn finials. Ample front, the centre deeply recessed in a giant arch. Arched windows, the centre three echoed in a triple-arched loggia. Converted to a studio by the sculptor David Nash. Schoolroom, 1889.

PUBLIC BUILDINGS

MARKET HALL, Market Square. Disused. 1883, by *O. Morris Roberts*, the plans modified by *Richard Davies*. Two storeys. Unadorned grey stone with bright red terracotta eaves. Polygonal w projection with narrow arched upper windows, and a smaller polygonal projection with an inaccessible balcony.

YSGOL-Y-MOELWYN, Wynne Road. The County School, 1899–1900, by *Willink & Thicknesse* of Liverpool. Originally of five bays, with a gable against a hipped roof. Extended in 1927 by *A. M. Howard Jones*. But the dark red terracotta entrance under a Jacobean gable looks earlier.

YSGOL GLANYPWLL, Glanypwll Road. Now workshops. A Board School for 500 on a rocky outcrop, 1880, rock-faced stone with grey dressings. Outer wings and small centre projection, each with a Palladian window. There were dormers and a central spire.

COMMUNITY CENTRE, Wynne Road. The former Central School, late C19, with large upper windows in threes under multiple gables. Extended skilfully in 1989 for a sports hall by *David Lea*. Local materials and traditional forms; roughcast, with stone on one side to integrate with the old. High Voysey-like window in the N gable. Elegant steel and timber trusses.

FFESTINIOG MEMORIAL HOSPITAL, Bron View. 1924, by *Clough Williams-Ellis*. Cottage-hospital sized, colonial in feel; superbly set, looking s. A small two-storey hipped core flanked by short hipped wings behind columned verandas. Only one veranda remains.

SLATE QUARRIES. Quarrying began *c.* 1765 in the bowl of hills to the NE at DIFFWYS (SH 712 463), the slates laboriously taken by packhorse to the Dwyryd river near Tanybwlch. Diffwys expanded from 1799 under William Turner and the Casson brothers from Cumbria, who may have introduced underground mining. The adjoining MANOD (SH 725 452) and Lord Newborough's BOWYDD (SH 708 464) developed in the early C19. Massive expansion then occurred on land owned by the Oakeleys of Tan-y-bwlch w of the Llanrwst road: Samuel Holland from Liverpool opened RHIWBRYFDIR (SH 693 473) from 1819, and after selling in 1825 to Rothschild interests in London, the Hollands opened CESAIL just behind, and GLODDFA GANOL (SH 694 470) adjoining, all these united as the Oakeley Quarries in the later C19. Bowydd was taken over by J. W. Greaves in 1834, who opened FOTTY (SH 706 465) adjoining and MAENOFFEREN (SH 714 465) behind Diffwys. Greaves started the huge LLECHWEDD enterprise (SH 700 470) E of the Llanrwst road in 1846. The Festiniog horse-drawn railway of 1836 to the new port at Porthmadog reduced costs hugely for those quarries that could connect to it. By 1873 Blaenau was producing some 150,000 tons a year. Over 3,500 were employed in 1901. The rapid collapse of the industry happened in the later C20. Only Gloddfa Ganol and Llechwedd still operate, combining quarrying with tourism. At LLECH-WEDD, the preserved quarry village, PENTRE LLECHWEDD, contains shops, workshops of 1852–3, offices, a smithy, the Miners' Arms inn, cottages with privies etc. The Greaves family house, PLAS WAENYDD, is at the entrance, half-timbered, with veranda, 1870.

FESTINIOG RAILWAY. The 2-ft (60-cm.)-gauge Festiniog (*sic*) Railway, *James Spooner* engineer, opened 1836, worked by horses and gravity. It was adapted to steam in 1863. Closed in 1946, it was reopened slowly by railway enthusiasts from 1955, not completely until 1982, as a deviation had to be made around the new Tanygrisiau Reservoir.

FFESTINIOG PUMPED STORAGE SCHEME, Tanygrisiau. 1957–63, the first of its kind in Britain, engineered by *Freeman, Fox & Partners*. Surplus electricity pumps water at night to a high reservoir, Llyn Stwlan, 1 m. w. Its DAM, 110 ft (34 metres) high, with massive concrete buttresses, is visible from afar. Daytime power is made by dropping the water 1,000 ft (300 metres) to a station by the Tanygrisiau reservoir. *S. Colwyn Foulkes*, the landscape consultant, designed the power station: coursed rubble in long stones and continuous glazing under a flat roof.

PERAMBULATION

The town is a linear collection of settlements in a horseshoe around Cwm Bowydd, which falls steeply to the S, the houses often dramatically against rock. CHURCH STREET at its head is the nucleus, curving round from the Market Hall W of St David's church. Opposite the church, TANYMAEN was the vicarage, 1845, of large blocks, with hoodmoulded sash windows. To the E, the CHURCH HALL, 1905, probably by *Tapp, Jones & Son*, and the RED DRAGON CLUB, built as Temperance cocoa rooms to an 1878 competition design by *C. Jenkins Jones* of London. Exuberantly inappropriate to a slate town: jettied half-timber over stone, the outer gables framing a long balcony under a higher centre gable.

S of the church is a network of low terraces. THE SQUARE comes as a surprise, grandly around the recreation grounds and bandstand with Bowydd chapel at the SE corner.

Back on CHURCH STREET, the rock of Garreg Ddu looms large over the former BRITISH SCHOOL, *c.* 1849. It follows the Rev. Hugh Owen's bleak plan of 1845 for a 'Rural British School', schoolroom and house under one hipped roof, the school windows set high. Around the rock, a valley opens NE towards the great slate-wastes of Fotty, Bowydd, Diffwys and Maenofferen. The landscaped urban space was created by the railways. DIFFWYS STATION, 1866, the final terminus of the Festiniog Railway, survives as public toilets. Small, with the railway's Prince of Wales feathers. Against the rock, W, in

DOL-GARREGDDU, the remarkable TAI UNCORN, a small square building incorporating four miniature dwellings around 89 a shared central stack. Built for Lord Newborough, 1825. Each cottage had a corner fireplace, tiny stairs and a loft room. The pyramid roof has rounded hips to save on ridge tiles. In Park Square, off l., the former COUNTY POLICE BUILDINGS, by *T. Taliesin Rees* of Birkenhead, 1902. Grey stone with red ashlar lettered band between the floors. Gables over the upper windows and a domed ventilator have gone. Church Street curves SE into HIGH STREET and continues S on a natural rock shelf, lined with attractive low stone terraces through FOURCROSSES, to become Manod Road at BETHANIA. PANT-YR-YNN MILL, NE of the main street, is probably pre-industrial, but was used as a slab mill for the Diffwys quarry in the earlier C19, as a school 1865–73, then from 1881 as a woollen mill. Single-storey, backed against the hill, with a water wheel, r. Returning to the centre, the A 470 climbs N through the most ravaged of slate landscapes: Rhiwbryfdir to l. and Llechwedd r. To the l. the three-mile railway TUNNEL, 1879, under the Crimea Pass. The pyramid-roofed building with short wings on HOSPITAL ROAD, l., was the former OAKELEY QUARRY HOSPITAL, 1848, before RHIWBRYFDIR village, along GLANYPWLL ROAD, with Rhiw chapel backed against slate tips. Glanypwll Road follows the Festiniog Railway SW. OAKELEY SQUARE, l., had grand aspirations but was barely begun. TANYGRISIAU, along the railway, has chapels, shops and terraces. SCHOOL, 1874, by *O. Morris Roberts*, similar to Llan Ffestiniog. MOELWYN MILL, by Pont Peithyll, was an early C18 fulling mill, with mid-C19 house (l.) and water wheel in front. The mill was re-equipped in the 1880s and closed in 1964.

CWM BOWYDD, Cwm Bowydd Road, ½ m. S. Deep in the valley below. Late C17, three-bay, with Georgian fenestration, a false window above the centre door. Byre, l., and taller Victorian house, r., for the Newborough estate. Gateway with acorn finials.

BONTDDU

On the Dolgellau to Barmouth road, the BONT DDU bridges a stream that descends in picturesque cataracts. E from the bridge, a former WESLEYAN CHAPEL, 1878, lancet Gothic with a cross-gabled porch. The HALFWAY HOUSE inn was remodelled by *A. B. Phipson*, 1881, for W. J. Beale of Bryntirion (*see* below) in the Old English manner of Norman Shaw, the roadside gable with a dramatic jettied timber oriel and the porch prettily barge-boarded. Next, YR EFAIL, a very low two storeys, raised from an C18 cottage and a smithy added, r. The former BETHANIA CALVINISTIC METHODIST CHAPEL, 1865, is round-arched, the gable roughcast *c.* 1900. Past Bryntirion, GRAIG FAWR, a mid-C19 short terrace, has fancy wooden eaves brackets.

BRYNTIRION (Bontddu Hall Hotel). Terraced above the road, a serious High Victorian Gothic house of 1874, by *A. B. Phipson* of Birmingham, for W. J. Beale, Lord Mayor of that city. Lavishly detailed with dressings and chimneys in gold sandstone. Three bays, the r. one a cross-wing with an ashlar two-storey canted bay, the rest with veranda and acute dormer gables. The mullioned windows differ on each floor: cusped, uncusped and finally with slim column shafts. The cross-wing has similar side detail and a rear NE entrance tower of four storeys with ponderous battlements.

The lane NW from Bryntirion was the ancient route over the mountains to Harlech. PEN NEBO, l., 1810, has a rounded front wall, like some Nannau estate cottages. FIGRA BRIDGE, below, l., a primitive mass of boulders, with a tapered opening. There was a mill for the gold ore on the other side. Further up, the footpath to the Clogau mine (*see* below), then DWYNANT, with a bellcote, built as a mission church, 1837, but never used. CAE HIR, off to the l., is C17, but shifted so that the present l. end was once the byre, and the r. end cart house was once a parlour. By the cart entry a C5 or C6 INSCRIBED STONE, marked 'Sylvanus'. C17 barn. About ¼ m. up the trackway an C18 MILESTONE marks the fork for Talybont and Harlech, the latter crossing the empty landscape to Pont Scethin (Dyffryn Ardudwy).

BORTHWNOG, ¾ m. E. Late C18, altered in the mid C19, the front stuccoed with veranda and five French windows each floor. Two chimneys each end are joined by theatrical parapets. An older house may be in the w range.*

TIBERIAS INDEPENDENT CHAPEL, 1 m. E. Perched between main road and estuary. 1889. Plain stone, arch-windowed, with house across the rear.

FARCHYNYS, 1 m. W. A small estate built up for T. Oliver, cotton manufacturer of Bollington, Cheshire. The house is gabled, stone, with grey dressings, dated 1876 on the entrance tower, which has similarities to the tower at Bryntirion. Across the hollow, FARCHYNYS FARM, much smaller, also with entrance tower, and a handsome BARN with five broad Tudor arches.

CLOGAU GOLD MINE, 2 m. N (SH 674 202). The most successful gold mine of the region. The workings on the bare crest yielded 77,500 ounces between 1861 and 1907. Copper was mined first, in the late C17 and in the 1840s, with a mill at Figra Bridge. Gold was found on the s side in 1853, but full exploitation from 1860 was on the St David's lode on the N. A tramway ran round the mountain to an incline from the sw and thence to Figra Bridge, later replaced by aerial ropeway. The heyday was from 1898 to 1907, when, refinanced and re-equipped, annual ore production exceeded 10,000 tons and the workforce rose to 253 in 1902. It closed in 1911, having exhausted

*The Borthwnog iron furnace, depicted by Paul Sandby in 1776, seems to have been by the Cwm Mynach river, a little E.

known reserves. VIGRA MINE, W of Figra Bridge, was mostly run with Clogau.

BRITHDIR

7718

ST MARK (Friends of Friendless Churches). Thickly encompassed by rhododendron, this is one of the pre-eminent churches of the Arts and Crafts Movement. 1895–8, by *Henry Wilson*, in memory of the Rev. Charles Tooth †1894, founder of the Anglican church in Florence. Sited here because his widow (they were married four months) had been married to R. M. Richards of Caerynwch †1873. Elemental and severe, intended to 'appear as if it had sprung out of the soil, instead of being planted down on it'. *H. L. North, Arthur Grove* and *C. H. B. Quennell* were the young architects whom Wilson employed, Grove as assistant, North to supervise the masonry, and Quennell to work the timber in true Arts and Crafts fashion. The walls rise sheer, with sparse windows under sweeping and lovely slate roofs. On the ridge a stepped two-tier bellcote, its shouldered profile the inspiration surely for North's stepped chimneys. A powerful geometry animates the structure. At the W end the wall continues into lean-to porches, in a great triangle accentuated at the apex by a stone hood on massive corbels that shelters a cross. The pair of windows closely flanking the cross and a second pair below are pushed to the centre, emphasizing wall. The transepts and E end give three further gables with varied relations of window to wall, the E without hint of the apse within. Superbly tooled stone, the windows square-sided with glazing grooved directly in. Delightful details abound: the varied window heads, the leaded glazing, the porch gates, the twisted iron gutter supports.

Tripartite INTERIOR in painted plaster, the spaces in 107 proportionate relation: nave with two bracketed rather Italian tie-beams and three-sided ceiling, tunnel-vaulted choir, sanctuary with quadripartite vault on arches to transepts and a shallow apse. Wilson refers to simple Italian Alpine churches 'where all the effect comes from the management of light and the proportions of the roof and walls'. The light is managed towards gloom: in the chancel dark paintwork makes the E window a pencil of light over the dull copper glow of the altar and all the other light sources are concealed. The colours, a rich, deep red for the chancel with a blue vault and a warm cream for the nave, although in precise reversal of those mentioned in a letter by Wilson, are surely the right ones, giving a progression towards a Byzantine richness. – FITTINGS. The most complete set of high-quality Arts and Crafts work in Wales, and one of the best in Britain. FONT. Circular lead bowl based on an 1889 design by W. R. Lethaby, modelled by *Grove* at Lethaby's newly opened Central School. Undulating trail of seaweed, with scattered shells, on a rough stone tapered base. Behind, the FOUNDATION STONE, 1895, in beaten metal, with the lion of St Mark. – ALTAR. Copper, cast by the lost wax process, a technical feat that gives remarkably fine detail to one of the outstanding works of its period. A single giant front panel of the Annunciation: the Virgin and dove to the l. faced by a kneeling angel-child and, to the extreme r., two sombre figures, Charles Tooth and his guardian angel. The drawing has the sweetness of Burne-Jones rather than the linearity of Mackintosh. The copper retable has embossed bluebells and a chalice on a central false tabernacle. This and the Ave Maria on the frontal hint at Anglo-Catholicism.* – PULPIT. Reached through the jamb of the adjacent arch. Beaten copper, three faces each with a wreath encircling grapes, over close-spaced lettering. Copper-sheathed base. – STALLS. Returned so that they form a low chancel screen. The ends have delightful animals carved by *Grove*, and the kneeler ends have SM for St Mark. – RAILS. Sturdy tapered outer posts with oval finials, perhaps the eggs of creation from Lethaby's *Architecture, Mysticism and Myth*, 1891, and centre post with grapevine. On the rails an inlaid chevron, looking forward to Art Deco. – LECTERN. A double book-rest on a column, designed by *Wilson* for the chapel at Welbeck Abbey, Notts, but ejected for a grander bronze one. – NAVE DOORS. As remarkable as anything in the church, oak and teak in chevrons subtly varied from straight to ogee forms, and the points with tiny sparkling crowns of mother-of-pearl. – ORGAN. 1901, by *Conacher*, commonplace. It replaces an experimental 'Vocalion' from Arthur Tooth's church, that never worked. Ironically, Wilson had written, 'So many otherwise beautiful churches are ruined by commonplace . . . organs.'

BRITHDIR INDEPENDENT CHAPEL. 1860. Minimal classicism in stone, with pediment, the enclosed full-width porch with pilasters and entablature. Sash-windowed sides; the five-sided apse actually a schoolroom.

PRIMARY SCHOOL, 1913, by *Deakin & Howard Jones*, with big arched windows, typical of the firm.

BRITHDIR ROMAN FORT (SH 772 189), ¾ m. E. A very small square Roman fort on the road from Bala. It can be seen as an earthwork, the top of the rampart at right angles to the lane opposite Nos. 5–7 Hengaer. When these houses were built, excavations revealed that the fort was originally larger but had been reduced, as were so many forts when the period of initial pacification was over. Small industrial ovens and a leather-tanning pit were then built on the site and there may have been a small bath house nearby, all suggesting a workshop and repair base for use by passing military units. (*See also* Gwanas, p. 564).

Y GOEDLAN, SE of the church. The former vicarage, 1902–3, by *Richard Hall* of Bangor, stone in an attractive Arts and Crafts

---

*The donor, Tooth's brother Arthur, was High Church, actually imprisoned for ritualism in 1874.

style. Balanced asymmetry: a cross-wing answered by a gable on the entrance front, the stair window and door between. On the garden front the roof flows over a veranda between unmatched gables. Compact stair hall, the newels with flat-topped urns.

BRAICH-Y-CEUNANT, ¼ m. s. Mostly of 1717, with remnants of an earlier house. Three bays with hipped stone dormers. Early C18 staircase with bobbin-turned balusters and fielded-panelled doors upstairs. The plank partition on the ground floor may be earlier, but those on the first floor are early C18.

CAERYNWCH, ½ m. s. Caerynwch's fortunes were made because Richard Richards, who married the Humphreys heiress in 1785, had by 1817 become Chief Baron of the Exchequer and Lord Chancellor Eldon's right-hand man. He commissioned the new house placed below the old on a better landscape site, built 1801–4, by *Joseph Bromfield* of Shrewsbury. The plan reveals Bromfield at his most free and ingenious. Two shallow full-height bows, faced in big blocks of the rare local silver-green stone, cut to radius, look W across to the first summit of Cader Idris. The entrance is not between these but on the plain five-bay SE front, again with deep sash windows. The porch with monolithic square piers looks like an afterthought (the house is otherwise astylar); it leads to a long narrow vestibule or wind lobby. Transversely to this a boldly connecting series of rooms, a central hall and staircase with plain iron balustrade one way, a second lobby connecting by two arches, originally open, to a drawing room the other; dining room in the space in the s angle. All have reticent plaster friezes typical of Brom-field. Elliptical arches, similarly used, to the upper spaces round the stairs. Long new drawing room in ashlared stone, added in 1867 to the N (plans signed *G. W. Owen* and *B. Camp-bell*); later chimneypiece made in Florence. A further N addition of the 1890s, intended as the chapel, became a billiard room when the project for the new church began. The new house was originally approached from the s and set on a small platform. A much larger platform and garden terracing were laid out in the late 1860s, probably when the Victorian drive was made up the Clywedog river from a new LODGE on the A470 road. This has bargeboarded gables, two little ones fan-like in the angle. (For the Torrent Walk, *see* Dolgellau.)

PLAS HEN, just E of Caerynwch. The original house of Caerynwch, a late medieval five-bay hall, externally early C18. Just one storey and attic, the attic with five large hipped dormers rising from the wall face, the long casement windows from the restoration by *Clough Williams-Ellis*, 1921. The plan of a narrow hall with parlour (r.) and upper end (l.) is remark-able for the double lateral stacks with mural stair between, serving hall and parlour. They are early, as the stair serves the room over the parlour, suggesting the hall was not then ceiled. Dais partition. The hall has *c.* 1700 large-field panelling and a bolection-moulded chimneypiece. Pretty balcony on the W end, and added SE service range of 1921, enclosing a tiny court.

DOLSERAU, 1 m. NW. 1864, for Charles Edwards. Very Victorian, in stone with a Gothic loggia and half-timbered gables, a significant early revival. The gables have a High Victorian sharpness, so not the 'Old English' pioneered by George Devey in Kent, nor the urban black-and-white revived by T. M. Penson in Chester. Compact interior without remarkable detail. Neo-Jacobean oak chimneypieces reusing old work. Armorial glass by *Thomas Baillie*. Robert Owen of Dolserau, a leading Cromwellian in North Wales, later persecuted as a Quaker, took his family to Pennsylvania in 1684.

DÔL-GAMEDD, 1 m. NE. On the escarpment above the river. Earlier C18 farmhouse with Merioneth hipped dormers. Staircase with turned balusters, the bobbin-turned form on the landing.

BONT NEWYDD, 1 m. NE. Single-span bridge over the Wnion, probably late C18.

GWANAS, 1 m. S. The A470 crosses the Clywedog E of the CROSS FOXES INN, 1859. Tall, three-bay with a storeyed porch. PONT GWANAS, the disused C18 twin-arched bridge, is next to the former Caerynwch main drive. GWANAS, just N, is a large estate farmhouse of 1838 with pediment and big clustered chimneys. The low range across the N end is late C17. The broad W porch has a C19 timbered gable but the walls are from a porch to a demolished late medieval chapel at Gwanas Fawr. Large plinth, chamfered sides and narrow sidelights. GWANAS FAWR, S of the road, was a medieval grange of the Knights Hospitaller. The farmhouse, heavily renovated, is dated 1722 within but has one C16 cruck-truss. The parallel BARN is later C16 with upper cruck-trusses. In 2007 aerial survey revealed a small ROMAN FORT near Gwanas Fawr and ground survey found the heavy boulder abutments of a bridge that could be Roman, an extension of the Roman road from Brithdir. The GWANAS SLATE QUARRY (SH 798 160), 2 m. E, was one of the most isolated of the region.

7921

BRYNCOEDIFOR

2½ m. ENE of Brithdir.

ST PAUL. 1850–51, an estate church to Caerynwch, Brithdir. Unused plans of 1846 by *Henry Kennedy* survive, and *R. K. Penson* made proposals in 1848–9, but the architect is uncertain. Neat Puginian Gothic of steep roofs and narrow lancets, the chancel and S porch appropriately enriched. Parallel-roofed NE vestry. Dark and richly turn-of-the-century interior embellished by the Owens of Hengwrt Uchaf, Rhydymain. Of 1851, the chancel arch on corbelled shafts and the FONT. In 1907 the chancel was floored in cream mosaic with pretty sanctuary motifs in green, and a very elaborate oak SCREEN was inserted. Free Gothic, the outer bays incorporating pulpit and reading

desk fronted in linenfold. Two angels thread their trumpets
through canopies. ROOD BEAM above. The designer of all this
is unknown. – STALLS. Early C20, a very nice minimal design
with pierced quatrefoils. – STAINED GLASS. A good set of
c. 1895 in C16 style. A painterly Crucifixion by *Powells*, 1850, is
re-set in the vestry. – MEMORIALS. – Lilla Bridgeman †1861,
brass, angel and child within a floriated octofoil, by *Hart &
Son*, based on the mid-C14 de Aumberdene brass at Taplow,
Bucks. – Rev. E. C. Owen, by *Joseph Edwards*, 1868, marble
relief, the ascending soul as an elongated female. – Ella Owen
†1923, plaster relief, Christ amid 1920s children, signed ED. –
Two crocketed Gothic plaques by *Bedford* to R. M. Richards
of Caerynwch †1873 and his wife †1852. – Marble BUST, probably the Rev. Owen, 1867, also by *Edwards*.

In the churchyard, slate-topped TOMBS of the Richards,
the largest to Harriett †1852. The LYCHGATE of 1906 still
eludes attribution; decorative work by the *Bromsgrove Guild*. A
pyramid roof with lovely angel finial and embossed lead gutters
caps a design of intricate subtlety. Concave-sided square plan,
the side walls of stone, the front and back implied by curved
thresholds and curved oak beams. A tiny plastered dome inside
with an intricately carved oak boss.

The church is flanked by the rambling, gabled VICARAGE,
1850s, and BRYNCOEDIFOR COTTAGE, altered, with Nannau
estate chimneys. At the junction, W, the former SCHOOL, 1872.
Altered by *H. L. North* 1928, when presumably he designed
BRYN ARAUL, the neat roughcast cottage opposite, the
windows unfortunately spoilt. Further N, the former SILOH
CHAPEL, 1874, with lunette plaque.

BRYNCRUG

6103

Mostly modern village, around the church. The marshland of the
Dysynni estuary, reclaimed in the C18 by the Owens of Ynysmaengwyn, forms the W end of the parish, which otherwise
follows the parallel valleys of the Dysynni and Fathew. The latter
was the turnpike route to Dolgellau and is followed by the 1865–6
Talyllyn Railway. Fenton in 1808 describes Owen's land reclamation as including straightening the Dysynni behind an
embankment and constructing drainage canals wide enough for
boats, in the expectation of finding coal in the foothills.

ST MATTHEW. Disused. 1880–2, by *E. B. Ferrey*. Plain in dark
green stone with Cefn sandstone lancets. Nave, chancel, S
porch, and bellcote. – FONT. Circular with carved marble
roundels.
BETHLEHEM CALVINISTIC METHODIST CHAPEL. 1883.
Large and stuccoed, raised on a basement. Two tall arched
windows and a little triplet over a hipped porch.
On the main road to the Dysynni bridge, the PENIARTH ARMS,
1901, by *G. T. Bassett*, green stone with some half-timber; an

early C19 single-storey cottage row, TŶ'N Y WINLLAN; and GWYNDY, earlier C19 shop with veranda. S of the village, on the Abergynolwyn road, BRONWYLFA, roughcast, L-plan with a three-sided slated porch in the angle, *c.* 1910.

PONT DYSYNNI, ¾ m. NW. The first Dysynni road bridge, late C18 or early C19. Four-arched, slightly curved, with raised piers.

YNYSMAENGWYN, I m. SW. The house was given to Towyn Council in 1948, neglected, and demolished in 1964, one of the greatest losses of the region. It was built in 1758 for Anne Owen †1760, heiress of the Corbets, though the Adam-style interiors must have been late C18. The estate included much of the SW corner of the county. Edward Maurice Corbet, noted agriculturalist, drained the marshes in the late C18 to create the flat landscape that extends from Bryncrug to Tywyn. In 1879 John Corbett of Chateau Impney, Droitwich, Worcs, bought the estate, attracted by the coincidence of surname, and developed Tywyn as a resort.

The house, 2–3–2 bays, overlooked a broad forecourt flanked by matching stone ranges, one dated 1733. What is left is depressing. A late C19 LODGE and gates give access to a caravan site. In a mess of broken garden walls and demolished outbuildings is a square later C18 DOVECOTE with two-tier pyramid roof, the interior lined in brick nesting holes, said to number 864.

DOLAUGWYN, I m. E. The best example in the county of the stepped-gabled C17 gentry house. Dated 1620 in the main range, with initials of Lewis Gwyn †1630, and 1656 in the cross-wing, with those of his son-in-law Griffith Nanney, but the uniformity of style may suggest continuous building. The porch has the Nanney lion. Two storeys and attic, the broad cross-wing, the tall storeyed porch and the attic windows all crowstepped, as also the two stair-towers. Quality coursed masonry; all the windows stone-mullioned, ovolo-moulded, transomed on the main floors with hoodmoulds. Hence it has

Bryncrug, Dolaugwyn.
Engraving by John Douglas, 1886

a severe regularity that impressed John Douglas, who based Plas Mynach, Barmouth, on it. The NE stair-tower is mid-C17, the original stair having been at the rear SE, by the hall fire-place. A datestone on the porch tower of 1820; *J. L. Randal* of Shrewsbury worked here before 1868; but the careful restoration of mullioned windows suggests work *c.* 1900. (C17 open-well stair; also parlour plaster ceiling divided by strips with relief foliage into panels with floral centrepieces. Heraldry over the fireplace, dated 1656. Plaster cartouche dated 1620 with mistletoe tendrils in the main bedroom.)

L-plan FARM BUILDINGS, a boulder-built C16 cruck-trussed barn with an early C19 cowhouse attached. The barn has raised gables and two layers of vents. The crucks had tie-beams and collars, the ties re-set higher.

CASTELL CYNFAL, 1 m. S. An earth motte set on a spur of rock, with rock-cut ditch, and traces of a bank on the summit. It is recorded briefly in the strife between the sons of Gruffudd ap Cynan, as having been fortified by Cadwaladr but almost immediately taken and demolished in 1147 by the sons of his brother Owain, after a stout defence by Morfran, lay abbot of Tywyn.

DOLGOCH VIADUCT, 3 m. E. Three-arch brick viaduct on the narrow-gauge Talyllyn Railway of 1865–6, by *J. S. Spooner*. The nearby Dolgoch Falls were a tourist attraction from the opening of the line.

On the road up the Dysynni valley: GWYDDELFYNYDD, three-bay, earlier C19, stone, with deep eaves; at GLANYMORFA, a boulder-stone C18 barn with raised gables and arched doorway, used as a chapel in the C19; then the later C19 brick LODGE to Peniarth (Llanegryn) with cast-iron glazing. Both drive and bridge across the Dysynni have gone. CILCEMAES is an attractive long stone house with an early C18 voussoired arched door, the windows and end bay early C19. PERFEDDNANT is dated 1711, but looks late C17. The gable to the road has dripmoulds, and there are lateral chimneys on the E. A low earlier C19 wing at right angles.

CAERDEON

ST PHILIP. Perched on the hillside above its steep graveyard and surrounded by woods, the church suggests a small monastery or farmhouse in Italy. Rough stone, with a loggia porch on the side and across the ridge a wall of bells. 1861–2, by the *Rev. J. L. Petit*, author of *Remarks on Church Architecture*, 1841, and *Architectural Studies in France*, 1854, which demonstrate an eclectic rather than archaeological enthusiasm. His brother-in-law, the Rev. W. E. Jelf, had retired to Wales to coach Oxford undergraduates at Caerdeon Hall and fallen out with the vicar of Llanaber over the lack of provision of services in English. Nave and chancel divided by a semicircular arch, S transept and N vestry. Not Gothic, but a kind of rustic vernacular:

arched E and S windows, round W window, and the nave ones
simply square-headed. The porch has two massive square
rubble piers supporting a deep rustic corbelled cornice, the
roof swept down from the nave. The bellcote above the chancel
arch has a long saddleback roof over four bell-apertures, the
bells rung by arms fixed to a long horizontal pole connected
to a wheel next to the vestry. The character is somehow upland.
The Ecclesiologist thought it derived from 'hillside chapels on
the flanks of the Southern Alps' and disliked it: 'something
between a large lodge gate and a lady's rustic dairy'. But it did
understand that Petit's aim was 'picturesque appropriateness'
– to integrate the church with the rocky landscape. – REREDOS.
Alabaster, with mosaic panels of musician angels, *c.* 1895. –
STAINED GLASS. E window by *Kempe*, 1894, to Samuel
Holland (*see* Plas Caerdon, below), Crucifixion, in a Renaissance style. – S transept, pretty floral glass. – LYCHGATE. 1927,
to Holland's widow. Appropriately simple, arched.

CUTIAU INDEPENDENT CHAPEL, 1¼ m. WSW. Early C19.
Small, of large, squared stones, with just two big sash windows
overlooking a tiny graveyard.

PLAS CAERDEON, W of the church. 1854, for the Rev. W. E. Jelf.
Charles Darwin leased it in 1869; sold before 1875 to Samuel
Holland M.P., slate-quarry owner. Rust-coloured squared
stone with advanced gabled wings, painted ashlar quoins and
mullion-and-transom windows. The r. side has a hipped three-
storey piece between chimney gables. STABLE COURT with a
complex pyramid-roofed entry.

TŶ'N-Y-COED, ¼ m. SW. 1756. Three-bay, Georgian, with a
pediment roundel like several in Dolgellau, but the steep coped
gables, tall end chimneys and asymmetry indicate a C17 house
remodelled.

GLANDŴR, 1 m. SW. Hipped stone villa of the 1840s, with additions marked by dressings in Barmouth green stone. Good
FARM BUILDINGS: a former C18 house with hipped half-
dormers and outside loft steps; a barn dated 1835; a big C19
range with a gabled archway between open bays. At the far end
an unusual arcaded hay barn, 1859, raised on a stable.

BODOWEN, 1½ m. WSW. Stuccoed pyramid-roofed villa of 1831,
altered and extended *c.* 1878. Victorian iron veranda on two
sides.

CARROG

The village and church are on the N bank of the Dee. The seat
of Owain Glyndŵr was probably on the S side near Llidiart y
Parc.

ST BRIDE (Llansantffraed Glyndyfrdwy). Rebuilt on a higher site
in 1610–11, and remodelled in 1867 by *G. E. Street* for Mrs
Lloyd of Rhagatt. He added the neat chancel with its cusped
intersecting E window, inserted the other windows and

replaced the bellcote. The old walls are of long sandstone blocks with chamfered eaves on the S, rougher on the N. C17 S porch and arched S doorway; the similar N doorway is dated 1610, both still with plank doors. Good C17 roof of seven bays of shallow arch-braced collar-trusses. Low ashlar screen walls connect to the octagonal oak PULPIT. The chancel roof echoes the nave one, but with more cusping and wind-braces. The SE window sill is lowered as a seat, with aumbry and piscina neatly in the l. jamb, and the E wall has ashlar cusped arcading with inset tiles, and a stone REREDOS with red and green marble quatrefoils, carved by *Thomas Earp*. – Good STALLS with fronts in small panels and high scrolled ends. – FONT. A tub ringed at rim and base, on a short shaft, possibly C12. – GARGOYLE HEAD. A detached carved head with the almond eyes and spade nose of medieval carving, perhaps also from the first church. – STAINED GLASS. Three nave windows, after 1848, painterly, possibly part of an E window of 1857 designed and painted by the 'Misses Lloyd of Rhagatt'. Two by *Clayton & Bell*, *c.* 1867: nave S, 'dewch attaf fi bawb' (Come unto me), with good Gothic drawing, and the lovely E window. The Crucifixion across three lights, the rich blue ground contrasted with the red of the three lower scenes. – Also three chancel windows, later C19 with saints, installed 1936 from the Lloyd family chapel at Berth, Denbighshire. – MONUMENT. Elizabeth Roberts †1798, sarcophagus tablet. By *Carline & Linell*.

SEION CALVINISTIC METHODIST CHAPEL. 1871–2, by *Richard Owens*. Lombard style, like Gwyddelwern and Llandderfel. Grey stone with brown sandstone. A punched rose over three arched lights; gabled doorcase.

BAPTIST CHAPEL. 1895. Similar to Bethel, Cynwyd. Roughcast and grey limestone. Quoined piers carry a central arch and the outer ball finials. The windows are arched, a triplet in the centre.

PONT CARROG. One of the series of good bridges over the upper Dee, of four elliptical arches and cutwaters carried up as pedestrian refuges. C17, dated 1661 on one parapet.

CARROG STATION, S of the bridge. 1863–4, probably by *S. Pountney Smith*. On the preserved section of the Llangollen–Corwen line. Immaculately kept. Gabled house with steep roof and a little oriel attached to a low ticket office with varied detail. Later platform building and signal box.

The settlement grew after the railway. The street climbs past the chapels with late C19 houses in a variety of materials. The tallest, PLAS BERWYN, *c.* 1900, stuccoed with a pyramid roof, has three-storey gabled bays facing every possible view. By the church, NEUADD CARROG, the National School, 1859, plain stone, altered as the village hall 1980–1, extended 2000. The PRIMARY SCHOOL, 1908, by *Deakin & Howard Jones*, typical in red brick and brown terracotta. On the NW edge, LLAN (roughcast, four-bay) looks early C19 but is older. The farm buildings opposite have a little C17 timber framing exposed.

St David, ¾ m. E. Built as Tir Llannerch, 1928–30, by *Edmund Kirby & Sons* of Liverpool, for J. P. Beausire, Liverpool sugar magnate. A large and late Arts and Crafts house, in roughcast with dressings of thin slatey stones and roofs of grey Preseli slate. Long symmetrical garden front broken by two big gables with broad canted bays. N entrance front of three gables, the centre one crowstepped. First-floor windows in timber galleries between the gables. The interior lacks the charm of earlier Arts and Crafts houses.

Rhagatt, 1 m. W. In a sloping park above the Dee. A Regency double-bowed house, built in 1819–20 for Edward Lloyd. Similar to Glan-llyn, Llanuwchllyn, with hipped low-pitched roofs and twin full-height bows, and small attic-like first-floor windows. The E side has a pedimented centre and recessed entry. The service wing has blocked openings and may be partly C17. Below the drive, a brick-lined ice house.

Owain Glyndŵr's Mount, ½ m E of Llidiart y Parc. Motte set on the end of a ridge overlooking the Dee valley to the N. Denudation has led to recent repairs to the structure. Perhaps the successor to a mutilated mound at Hendom (q.v.), ¾ m. to the E. This may, however, be of prehistoric origin; there is no evidence that it was ever a castle motte. Glyndŵr's residence, destroyed in 1403, may have been at the small moated site in the dip to the E of the Mount, but it is very small.

Carrog Uchaf, 1 m. ESE. The splendid tall gable that looks N over the valley is the main range of a T-plan C17 house, the cross-wing running along the slope. E side doorway with an arched monolith head; the small two-light stone mullion window to the l. marks an unheated parlour, over a basement. The hall has a lateral chimney on the W, in the angle to the wing, and a post-and-panel partition to the parlour.

Penarth Slate Mine, 1 m. SW of Llidiart y Parc. Worked in the later C19. Dressing sheds remain, and the incline with its drum house.

CASTELL Y BERE *see* LLANFIHANGEL Y PENNANT

CORRIS

Two villages a mile apart: Corris, at the confluence of the Dulas and the Nant Deri, and Upper Corris (Corris Uchaf) 1 m. NW. Corris barely existed before Sir John Edwards of Machynlleth, owner of the Braich Goch quarry, promoted the new main road up the W side of the Dulas valley and over the Talyllyn pass in the 1830s.* It became the principal quarrying area on the eighteen-

*The old road ran E to Aberllefenni and over the Bwlch y Waun pass.

mile slate vein that stretches from the coast to Dinas Mawddwy, the villages encircled by workings: Braich Goch, Gaewern, Tŷ'n-y-Ceunant and Tŷ'n-y-berth on the w, Abercorris and Abercwmeiddaw on the E, and with other sites to the S, mostly on the Montgomeryshire side. The quarries produced slab for flooring, window sills, fireplaces etc. more than roofing slates. Great piles of slate waste still enclose Upper Corris but the largest Corris site, Braich Goch, has been landscaped away.

Most of the buildings date from after the opening of the tramway to the shipment quay at Derwenlas in 1859. By 1875 some 20,000 tons left annually. Fortunes thereafter were cyclical, a downturn in the 1880s, an upturn in the 1890s, a major collapse in 1906, a revival in 1918–22 and final decline after 1945.

HOLY TRINITY. 1860. In a large sloping churchyard, a plain church built as a memorial to Sir John Edwards †1848. Slatey stone with buttressed nave and chancel. Lancet windows with iron lattice glazing, as at Aberdyfi. Tall interior, plastered, with arch-braced scissor trusses and a panelled chancel ceiling. – FONT. A massive block of pale stone, with cross-roundel each side. – PULPIT. Enamelled slate, octagonal. – REREDOS. Stone, with the Crucifixion against a modern battlefield in painted tile, c. 1920. – STAINED GLASS. E window, richly coloured Nativity, 1893, by *Alexander Gibbs & Co.* Nave s, 1955, SS Michael and David.

REHOBOTH CALVINISTIC METHODIST CHAPEL, Aberllefenni Road. Disused. 1923–4, to replace one wrecked by flood; the latest sizeable chapel of the county. By *O. Morris Roberts & Son*, in an unusual minimal Tudor, roughcast with dressings in grey terracotta. The rear looms high as the chapel is raised on a high schoolroom. The stepped N front disguises the bulk: a hipped porch, a broad window under a half-hip sloped back to a gablet. Tall mullion-and-transom side windows; alternate ones break the eaves under gables. Open timber roof but no galleries.

SALEM INDEPENDENT CHAPEL. 1868, apparently by *O. Morris Roberts*. Artisan classical in two colours of slate, with pale pilasters, the roof slopes curtailing the outer ones. The arched window heads bounce alternately high and low. Pews and panelled gallery of 1895.

CORRIS INSTITUTE. 1911, by *David Roberts* of *O. Morris Roberts & Son*. Consciously pretty in roughcast and half-timber, like the contemporary Glyndŵr Institute at Machynlleth, contrasting with the ubiquitous slate. Three unequal gables, the centre one jettied out twice, over the porch and an oriel. Panelled interiors: a public hall, l., and upstairs billiard room and library.

HUGHES MEMORIAL, by the A470 road. 1905. An elegant attenuated Celtic cross in pink granite with bronze portrait relief of Dr A. W. Hughes †1900, who organized the Welsh hospital in the Boer War. Designed and made by *W. Goscombe John*.

CORRIS CRAFTS CENTRE, ½ m. w. 1982, designed for the Mid-Wales Development Corporation by *G. Evans*, Head of

Construction, with *C. Williams* and *Malcolm Barmer*. A tight group of linked octagonal kiosks in pale brick around two courtyards with a central cluster for restaurant and offices. The effect is of a kraal. To the N an additional group, 2006, four square pavilions and boarded hipped workshops. The site is that of the BRAICH GOCH QUARRY, owned by Sir John Edwards and his daughter, the Marchioness of Londonderry. Developed from the later 1830s, it was largely underground. In 1864 the Birley family, Lancashire cotton merchants, took over, seeking to offset the effects of the American Civil War. By 1877–8 280 were employed and profits were good, but costs were high and the enterprise closed in 1906. It reopened fitfully from 1919 to 1970 and was finally cleared to realign the road. The site was landscaped in 1975–6, the waste spread up to 30 ft (9 metres) deep. Under the Crafts Centre, a part of the underground caverns is accessible as 'King Arthur's Labyrinth'. To the S, on the old road, BRAICH GOCH TERRACE, six later C19 houses and the former NODDFA BAPTIST SCHOOLROOM, 1898, slate with crowded red brick Gothic windows.

CORRIS RAILWAY. Built 1858–9 as the Corris, Machynlleth & River Dovey Tramroad, it ran from Aberllefenni through Corris to a quay on the Dyfi past Derwenlas. A branch from Upper Corris joined S of Corris, and there were branches to Montgomeryshire quarries. Horse-drawn until converted to steam in 1878–9, then renamed, it closed in 1948. A stone and brick ENGINE SHED, 1878, at Maespoeth, by the main road.

The village is tightly packed in the valley of the Nant Deri. Above, on the main road, BRAICH GOCH, stuccoed Tudor, an inn built with Sir John Edwards's new road in the 1830s. Three bays with pretty cast-iron glazing of the Plas Machynlleth estate type. Half-timbered top floor of *c.* 1905, oddly with the same iron glazing. BRIDGE STREET descends past the church (*see* p. 571); two detached villas on l. dated 1867 and 1873. Centre all of slate apart from the Institute, l. Two BRIDGES high over the stream; the lower one carried the tramway, 1858. Across the river, IDRIS HOUSE, with a later C19 shopfront, Salem chapel (*see* p. 571), and a row of three with the stuccoed SLATER'S ARMS.

At the cross-roads, a three-bay house on a terrace, the walls of field stone, so of before the slate era. MINFFORDD STREET descends SE to the Dulas. The irregular group at right angles apparently led to an older river crossing; TANYBRYN, painted stone, double-fronted, and GLANDŴR, overlooking the stream, three-storey. A long curved mixed terrace then runs down to the Dulas. YR EFAIL, l., was single-storey, raised a floor.

From the cross-roads the lane to Upper Corris climbs past the former SHILOH WESLEYAN CHAPEL, 1866, large and plain with arched windows. On r. the former BRITISH SCHOOL by *O. Morris Roberts*, 1872, Gothic with schoolroom

gable l. and teacher's house r. Further up, BRYNAWEL, tall
later C19 pair with gablets, BRONYGRAIG, a villa with bargeboards and two-tone brick window heads, and finally, BRYN-
HYFRYD, a hipped mid-C19 stucco villa with deep eaves.

UPPER CORRIS/CORRIS UCHAF, 1 m. NW. Slate waste of
GAEWERN QUARRY edges the main road. Exploited from the
1830s, it was combined with Braich Goch (*see* above) from
1880. In the village, after the later C19 IDRIS TERRACE, the
derelict BETHANIA CALVINISTIC METHODIST CHAPEL,
1867, of slate with dressings of the rough ends of blocks, and
BETHANIA TERRACE, 1880. E across the valley, later C19 three-
storey semi-detached houses and the disused BETHEL INDE-
PENDENT CHAPEL, 1885, raised on a high basement. The slate
waste on this side comes from ABERCWMEIDDAW (SH 746
093) to the NE, worked from the 1840s to 1905, largely as a
quarry but with some mining, and ABERCORRIS (SH 754 088)
to the SE, worked mainly underground from the later C19. The
tramway across the valley is still clear. On the main road,
HILLSBOROUGH TERRACE, l., is an unspoilt row of ten,
whitewashed, of 1853–4, built for G. H. Hills of the TŶ'N-Y-
BERTH QUARRY behind. The NEW STREET row above was the
former mill. PLAS TŶ'N-Y-BERTH, r., is mid-C19 stuccoed
and hipped, with Tudor chimneys. Further up, l., former
SCHOOL of 1873. Beyond, r., TŶ'N-Y-LLECHWEDD, a white-
painted C18 farmhouse with low gables.

PANTPERTHOG, 3 m. S. Roadside hamlet of a pair of cottages,
SCHOOL, 1902, by *Deakin & Howard Jones*, T-plan with arched
windows in orange terracotta and a pretty cupola, and the
CALVINISTIC METHODIST CHAPEL. This is later C19,
probably by *David Owen* of Machynlleth, the front a display of
tooled slate, the triple window and outer doors all with timber
octofoil heads. ¼ m. S, LLIWDY, a pretty bargeboarded Gothic
lodge with veranda, to ESGAIR, formerly Esgair Lleferin, a
mid-C19 house, roughcast with bargeboards and verandas.

PONT LLWYNGWERN, 3 m. S. 1853. High single arch over
the Dulas, with Gothic panels on the piers. Built for access
to Llwyngwern quarry (now the Centre for Alternative
Technology) and the owner's house (both in Montgomeryshire). To the S, remnant of the tramroad causeway to
the Corris Railway.

PONT FELIN-Y-FRIDD, 4 m. S. Bridge over the Dulas, of two
main arches and a third, all low. Probably C18. On the bank,
the earlier C19 MELIN-Y-FRIDD corn mill. Just above, below
the main road, TURNPIKE COTTAGE, the Fridd Gate toll
house, with canted front and cast-iron casements.

PONT-AR-DYFI, 5 m. S. 1804. Traffic-battered five-arched bridge
over the Dyfi. Pilasters over the cutwaters and a string course.
Upstream, the MILLENNIUM BRIDGE, 2000, by *Bruce
Pucknell* with the artist *Jon Mills*. Two uprights of white-painted
tubular steel, unsettlingly at opposing angles, carry the footbridge from steel stays.

CORSYGEDOL see TALYBONT

CORWEN

The town lines the A5, backed against the rock of Pen-y-pigyn, with the Dee below to the N. Long a place of transit, for drovers going E and coach traffic to Holyhead, its present character is largely later Victorian from after the arrival of the railway in 1864.

SS MAEL AND SULIEN. A large church in a large churchyard, and an interesting one despite heavy restoration of 1871–2 by *Benjamin Ferrey*. The cruciform C13 plan indicates its status as a *clas* church; five priests were recorded in 1291. The S transept was lost before *Ferrey* added the S aisle to which was added the SW vestry, 1898, and a SE organ chamber. The plain battlemented and undatable W tower has poor traceried bell-lights. Nave and chancel under one roof, large N transept. Traceries all by *Ferrey* apart from the three small E lancets which he uncovered, with tumbled voussoirs; they could be C13. The nave roof is remarkable: five main trusses with massive tie-beams, collars and crown-posts. In the three W bays almost vertical struts support the purlins. On the two E bays curved braces at a shallower angle; these bays are wider-spaced, with an intermediate broad arched truss. One truss is dated 1687 and the cheerfully crude traceries between the parts look C17, but the scale suggests medieval. C15 N transept roof with arch-braced collar-trusses and two tiers of cusped wind-bracing. *Ferrey*'s arcade and chancel arch have stiff-leaf capitals, as at Bala.

FONT. C12, thoroughly re-tooled, circular, with a roll mould at the rim and a cable at the base. – PULPIT. Ashlar, 1871. – N transept SCREEN, oak, 1938. – Medieval CHEST, hacked from a very large log. – REREDOS, with alabaster, marble and mosaic, 1871. – Hanging iron CORONA, 1871. – STAINED GLASS. Good glass by *Clayton & Bell*, 1871, in the E lancets, Nativity, Crucifixion and Resurrection. Chancel N, 1872. Nave N, 1920s, by *A. J. Davies*, Christ appearing to Mary Magdalen, Arts and Crafts glass of high quality, intensely worked.

MONUMENTS. In a chancel tomb-recess, the low relief effigy of Iorwerth Sulien, priest, mid-to-late C14. The head and shoulders are outlined in relief by the cutting in of the slightly ogee canopy, his hands holding a chalice. The lower part of his body is covered by a fictive rectangular cloth with a border inscription in Lombardic capitals like those on the Dolgellau effigy, HIC JACET IORWERTH SULIEN VICARIUS DE CORVAEN ORA PRO EO. His feet peep out at the end. – Maria Charlotte Lloyd of Rhug †1780. Very good, in three colours of marble, signed *van der Hagen*. Above a console-framed inscription, a winged cherub carved almost in the round points to a draped vase with an oval medallion carrying her portrait three-quarter-face. – Roger Jones of Cefn Rüg †1790, oval. – John Jones of Rhagatt †1797, a serene memorial in veined marble; a spirally fluted urn in a dark niche within a neo-grec frame.

– Margaret Parry †1800, oval, rustic, signed *Thomas Roberts* of Cefn Mawr. – Mary Williams †1829, plaque by *W. Spence* of Liverpool. – John Jones †1865, plaque by *J. Smith* of Liverpool. – Captain William Blake R.N. †1874 at Cape Coast Castle, with an engrossing account of his career, under a cross and anchor, by *Gaffin & Co.*

Outside, by the tower, a sandstone C9–C10 CROSS mounted through a big slate wheel. The 7-ft (2.2-metre) monolith has angle rolls and a raised dagger cross; the top swells as a kind of cushion capital, like the C9 Pillar of Eliseg at Valle Crucis nearby; the faces with eroded interlace. In the C18 it had an octagonal capstone. The crowded GRAVEYARD has numerous rough slate slabs of the C17 and C18 – one against the chancel s wall on bulbous sandstone legs. Also sandstone C19 table tombs and one rich neo-grec sarcophagus, to Jane Hill †1856.

On the s side is the COLLEGE (Coleg-y-groes), a range of six almshouses for the widows of clergymen, three on either side of an archway with pedimental gable and roundel. Each has a hipped dormer breaking the eaves. Endowed and probably built in 1750, but the charity was established in 1709, a date consistent with the carefully stopped and chamfered timbers within.

BETHESDA INDEPENDENT CHAPEL, Mill Street. 1888. A broad stuccoed front painted white and grey, a play of arches. Centre triplet and long outer ones, an arch in the pediment base, and in the apex, nine stepped arched flush panels.

ENGLISH CONGREGATIONAL CHAPEL, London Road. Now Oriel Corwen. 1879. Gothic, in red brick and sandstone, a little more considered than usual.

REHOBOTH WESLEYAN CHAPEL, London Road. 1879, by *Richard Davies*. Stone. Gothic of the basic lancet sort, the windows outlined in grey, but the gable and the porch with delightfully frilled bargeboards, the gable ones each with a giant cusp.

SEION CALVINISTIC METHODIST CHAPEL, Bridge Street. 1872–3, by *Richard Owens*. Set back behind good Gothic iron railings. Squared tooled slatey stone with limestone dressings. In Owens's Lombard style, like Rhyl and Dwyran (Anglesey), with triangular-headed outer recesses and a central arched frame to a rose above a triplet. Matching schoolroom behind.

THE OLD WORKHOUSE, London Road. 1838–40. Corwen's most imposing building. Like *Thomas Jones*'s Bala workhouse it has a villa-like forebuilding in long blocks of squared slate, but the plan is more concentrated, a single cruciform building with double roofs to get broad interior spaces. Behind the forebuilding, long wings extend l. and r. to end in pavilions, and a short wing runs back. All four angles of the crossing have the diagonal wall required for supervision of exercise yards; the crossing itself is capped by a jaunty spired lantern. The fenestration originally in small arched iron windows (as at Bala) has been much supplemented with late C19 sashes. The foreblock suggests a good architect: three bays with sandstone cornice and blocking course, the broad centre with pedimental gable and a Neoclassical inset porch of baseless Tuscan columns.

PONT CORWEN, ½ m. w. The longest bridge of the upper Dee. Supposedly of 1704, it has five main arches and outer flood arches, all segmental with rough voussoirs. Cutwaters between the main ones. Doubled in width in the early C19.

PERAMBULATION

THE SQUARE (Y Sgwar) is an elongated widening of the main road, made formal by a bronze STATUE of Owain Glyndŵr, aggressive on horseback, 2007, by *Colin Spofforth*. The buildings are mostly C18–C19, but on the w end the NATWEST BANK, 1928, by *F. C. R. Palmer*, is a *tour de force* of interwar historicism for the National Provincial Bank, timber-framed on the scale of a C17 market hall. The choice of black-and-white for Corwen seems arbitrary, but the conviction and quality overwhelm. Inside, oak posts and beams, C17-style plaster ceilings and oak panelling. Further back, facing E, the HSBC BANK was the North & South Wales Bank, stuccoed, later C19, the roof hipped, but with side gables, and terracotta eaves. The well-detailed sandstone classical bank front is early C20.

On the S, the well-crafted Neo-Georgian stone POST OFFICE front of 1936 spoils a substantial mid-C18 house with two full-height canted bays in careful squared slatey stone, and long axial chimneys. Behind, the sorting office has a glazed lantern. WATERLOO HOUSE, l., a draper's shop of *c.* 1880 with oriels and plate-glass, but the structure may be earlier. The centrepiece is the OWAIN GLYNDŴR HOTEL, formerly the New Inn. Mid-C18, hipped, of seven bays, in painted squared stone, it has sash windows above but cross-windows below. Broad arched doorway with a fanlight, in a C19 sandstone Corinthian porch. Later C19 large addition to the l. The mid-C18 staircase survives, and at the back are some heavy timbers possibly of an earlier building. Further l. a typical late C19 commercial group, all gabled, two in red brick, the middle one yellow with red terracotta; mostly with their plate-glass shopfronts.

The lower N side has a three-storey row E of the older, altered, HARP INN. Earlier C19 at the l., with the CENTRAL HOTEL in painted squared stone, and later at the r., with stucco and corniced sandstone chimneys. At the NE corner, a shorter stuccoed row with THE EAGLES, r., Late Georgian in style, the stucco rusticated.

E from The Square is LONDON ROAD (Heol Llundain). The library, l., is in the former TOWN HALL, built for Victoria's 1887 Jubilee, but economically. Roughcast, with a curved SE corner. CORWEN COURT was the police station and court house, mid-C19, in long slate blocks. Late Georgian sashes with hoodmoulds, single-storey courtroom to the l. and at the r. end some barred cell windows. Opposite, CHURCH HOUSE, 1930–1, a large roughcast church hall, has twin shouldered gables and interestingly disposed fenestration, spoilt by plastic. Next, the workhouse (*see* p. 575), set back. On the l., the Wesleyan chapel, a gaunt TERRACE of 1877 in black rock-faced slate with two-storey bays, and the former English Congregational chapel (*see* p. 575). A short lane runs N to the PAVILION, a very large corrugated-iron hall bought in Liverpool for the 1911 National Eisteddfod. It holds 4,000 people. Nearby, LLYS EDEYRNION, 2002, offices in roughcast wings set back each side of a schematic temple front in stone with tall square piers. Full-height entrance hall with unpainted steel stairs and landing. On the A5 again, a later C19 former SCHOOL group on the N, stone with brick, the school set back between a teacher's house and infants' schoolroom.

BRIDGE STREET (Stryd y Bont) runs W from The Square. On the S, the CROWN HOTEL, L-shaped, possibly C18 with C19 stucco and gables. On the N, the SPAR shop occupies a Late Georgian three-bay range with small square attic windows. Then, after Seion chapel, THE TERRACE, handsomely detailed, of the 1860s, to a standard exceptionally rare in terraced housing. Grey limestone with sandstone, composed as 1–3–10–3–1 bays, the largest houses in the hipped three-bay sections. On the S, COMMERCE HOUSE, a large half-hipped five-bay warehouse, earlier to mid-C19, with small-paned sashes on two floors, over shops; an unusual building type, sadly derelict (2008). At the W edge, the outer gables of the former STATION, 1863–4, survive, the centre replaced in plate glass. Further on, the large stone former GOODS STATION.

TŶ ISA, ½ m. E. 1876. Very Victorian, the broad gable front under a deep 'Swiss' roof, asymmetrically fenestrated, with cast-iron columns in the windows. Possibly the Tŷ Isa designed by *Henry Kennedy* for the Rhug estate in 1875.

PLAS DERWEN, ¾ m. E. The former rectory. Earlier C19, roughcast, with bargeboards to outer gables, porch and centre gablet. The windows mullioned and glazed in tiny panes. Inside, a cantilevered timber stair.

CAER DREWYN HILL-FORT and TREWYN FAWR. *See* Rhug.

CROESOR

6345

The village nucleus was formed by quarrymen in the mid C19, with later a school and a slate-hung chapel. CAE GLAS, W, is a much older house with a massive end chimney and a wind-braced roof tree-ring-dated *c.* 1547, with a coeval cruck barn beside it. Altered early houses to the NE in Cwm Croesor. BRYN, the early C20 home of Moses Kellow, the quarry engineer and pioneer of electric power, was said to be lit by electric light by 1906, supplied from his hydro-electric quarry installation 1½ m. NE.

PARC, ½ m. SSW. The principal home of the Anwyl family till 1746. Rebuilding here is attributed to Robert ap Morys in the mid C16. The collapse of his long HOUSE lies above a terrace garden, entered by steps in one corner beside a viewing platform, and flanked by the remains of a garden tower described by the C17 poet Huw Machno. A ruined early CROSS-WING to this house stands immediately SW, its lateral fireplace having a winding stair and a fine square chimney. At a right angle to this a further unit, of two full storeys with a round upper chimney and formerly upper crucks, and winding stair by the lower hearth. These were imaginatively turned into a farmhouse in 1951 by *Clough Williams-Ellis*, but another future is now needed for this middle house. They butt against a square POOL to the S with two tiers of slab seats and steps up to the N, seemingly related to the collapsed house preceding them.

Separated by a small yard is a slightly later and larger HOUSE, perhaps that built *c.* 1625, as lodgings for William Lewis Anwyl (in whose time Parc became noted for the poetry of the gentry bards), again of well-dressed masonry but of complex origin. The older part is downhill-sited, with blocked upper doorways in the N gable wall indicating a lost outside stairway. Front with two voussoir-headed doorways, one blocked, and two- and three-light sandstone mullioned windows to the first floor. The roof handsomely made, with cavetto eaves moulding, massive slate copings on moulded kneelers, and tall end chimneys of square section with moulded caps. In the centre a shallow pedimental gable. Wide voussoir-arched fireplace at the lower end. The upper floor has a queen-post roof with slightly cambered collar-beams which suggest a little long gallery duplicating as a granary. At the rear an added wing with an ample, square-plan stone stair and one room on each floor, and a further tall chimney. The datestone for 1671 on the NW angle, with the same initials as on the Beudy Newydd, appears to have been reset; tree-ring dates of the 1660s. The complex was first repaired by the author Richard Hughes in the 1930s.

To the NE, on the old drive up from the Maesgwm river, GATWS, a small building in a similar style but without the gated archway its name implies. Formerly with the entrance at first-floor level to a single heated room with chimney at the lower end; enlarged with a grass-roofed wing, 1990. This perfectly placed Picturesque building is not on the Mostyn estate survey of 1802, yet has tree-ring dates of 1618, the oldest on the site. So it could have been made of old material for Hugh Reveley of Bryn-y-gwin who bought Parc in the 1830s.

Immediately SW of the house group a large, square FARM-YARD. On its SW side a range 106 ft (32 metres) long, the

l. half a CORN BARN of C17 masonry coeval with the later
house; fine original N archway with dripmould above the voussoirs, two-light window above. The interior had a first floor and
has queen-post roof trusses. The r. half is an addition of *c.* 1700
for STABLES for horses etc., reusing the barn's gable copings.
On the NW side a long early C18 COWHOUSE. At an angle to
the farmyard a large square WALLED GARDEN for growing
food, originally divided axially into four by paths. Immediately
NE of the house group is a far more ambitious set of stone
structures, three unusual TERRACES some 150 yds (135
metres) long and each with retaining walls some 10 ft (3
metres) high, forming protected sloping areas. These appear to
have been orchards. The upper one, with older stonework, had
steps in the centre leading down to the second.

Almost everything on the estate mentioned so far is enclosed
in a high WALLED RECTANGLE, also apparently early C17. Its
SW line rises from the valley exactly on the outer side of the
corn barn (so excluding the square walled garden), and its NE
line rises on the boundary of the terraces where the Gatws is
sited. These meet at a wall at skyline level, with a double viewpoint seat near its NW angle. The oldest estate road slants down
above the terraces, crossing the Maesgwm river by an early
one-arch BRIDGE. It also intersects the SEA DRIVE, a very
wide engineered road from the historic shoreline to former
mine workings at Parc, 2 m. up. This enigmatic feature may
date from the C17 or the C18. Lastly, two massive PARK WALLS
span the peninsula between the Maesgwm and Croesor rivers.
One, at the top of the Sea Drive, allowed for a second bridge
of the C17/C18 over the Maesgwm at its corner; the other, well
below, bends round the BEUDY NEWYDD winter cowhouse of
1668 (enlarged *c.* 1960 for the artist Fred Uhlman by
C. Williams-Ellis). Far outside it, mills on the Croesor, and a
fine C17 LIME KILN on the former shore. Within it on a field
called Y Gaer, an Ossianic-looking MOUND at the panoramic
point for the estuary, with a stone seat and table later inscribed
'1851', very likely another pretence history contribution of the
Reveleys.

CROESOR TRAMWAY. Slate from the quarries W of Blaenau
Ffestiniog, particularly Rhosydd (SH 664 461), could not reach
railway lines over the mountain, and a joint tramway was built
in 1864 down the Croesor valley to cross the reclaimed Traeth
Mawr and so to Porthmadog. There were three inclines, one
at Blaen y Cwm, two at Parc. The section within the Parc estate
runs level on a causeway of stones robbed from the park wall
to a belvedere outcrop. Here the winding house for the next
two inclines was incorporated in 1962 in the DRUM HOUSE,
a single vaulted cruciform room to enjoy the panorama, by
Clough Williams-Ellis for Lady Christabel Aberconway.
Although always horse-drawn, the tramway served several large
operations apart from Rhosydd, including Croesor (SH 657
457), Pantmawr (SH 658 446) and Fronboeth (SH 646 447)
and small ones such as Parc (SH 626 436).

CYMER ABBEY *see* LLANELLTYD

CYNWYD

A settlement that grew in the C19 with small woollen mills by the Trystion river.

ALL SAINTS. 1855, by *Rhode Hawkins* of London. Routine lancet Gothic in slatey stone. Nave, chancel and bellcote. Remarkably massive blocks at the E end. Steep open roofs, the chancel ribs stencilled in a chevron pattern, remnant of a larger scheme. – STAINED GLASS. E window, Crucifixion, 1870, by *J.-B. Capronnier* of Brussels. Wholly painterly, showing how far Continental and British taste had diverged, but good of its kind. – FONT. Circular, C19. – MONUMENTS. All from Llangar church: Dorothy Maesmore of Maesmor †1710, a naïve version of Baroque drapery carving. – Edward Lloyd of Plymog †1742, marble cherub head on dark slate. – Major E. Salesbury Lloyd †1851 at 'Nakadah near Phillour on the right bank of the Suttledge'.

BETHEL CALVINISTIC METHODIST CHAPEL. 1896. Green stone, with thick detail in pink-grey ashlar. Paired arched doors in a corniced ashlar centre under a giant arch enclosing an arched triplet. Angle piers capped by ball finials.

The low C18 bridge, PONT TRYSTION, at the centre of the original settlement, was by-passed downstream by the very elegant PONT CYNWYD, a soaring single arch of good squared slate stone, mid-C19. Around the old bridge, some small mills: MINAFON, three floors to the water, with a later C19 gabled office across the end, and set back on the N, PRINCE'S YARD FACTORY, four bays of large windows, *c.* 1840. On the main road, at the modern centre, the long stone BLUE LION INN is mid-C19 with some iron lattice windows. N, after the church, a mid-C19 former SCHOOL with rendered gables for schoolroom and house; the 1970s brown brick PRIMARY SCHOOL is behind the church. Bethel chapel is at the N end.

PONT DYFRDWY, ¼ m. W. The best of the upper Dee bridges, said to date from 1612. Four broad arches with full-height cutwaters forming refuges. The parapets have extremely long coping stones.

TŶ'N-Y-BERTH, ¼ m. NE. Much altered C17, with tall paired diagonal chimneys on the side and E end.

TŶ'N-Y-LLWYN, behind Brynllwyn, ½ m. NE. Low, heavily rendered, but with lovely roofs of small thick slates. The tall ridge chimney marks a C17 inserted fireplace, when a late medieval cruck-framed hall was encased. The gabled projection with a two-storey slightly jettied bay may have been a C17 parlour, off the hall. Cruck-trusses with arched collars.

GWERCLAS, ½ m. N. Overlooking the Dee, the seat of the Hughes family from the C17. While Plas Uchaf (*see* below), the hall-house of *c.* 1435 just above, may be its predecessor, Gwerclas too has early origins; specifically, the tall slotted posts from a medieval screen, reused in a barn, seem to come from another hall-house. The C18 remodelling of the entire place, however, was so thorough that some C16 stone windows reused on the N and the NE angle of the tall block are among few earlier remains. A heraldic cartouche on the S front gives the date 1767 for these works, and the initials of Hugh and Margaret Lloyd. The replacement of the customary planning of houses in groups* and the use of red brick for their classicizing façade suggests a desire to emulate the modern houses of the English borders. The unity of small gentry seat, formal gardens and estate and farm courtyards was a rarity in the region in the C18 when the tide of its life had strangely ebbed away. Following one spendthrift generation Gwerclas passed as a farm to the Rhug estate, so survived little altered.

The tower-like central block of three storeys and three bays is set back between two-storey gabled wings like a great house in miniature. Of rubble apart from the Flemish-bond brick of the public façades. The centre is double-pile with parallel hipped roofs, and formerly had an eaves cornice. Pedimented Ionic porch between arched windows; two wide Palladian windows above with the cartouche between indicate a full-width room like the *piano nobile* of a town house. The plan repeats above giving an unusually high top storey but the façade returns to three windows. The exaggerated verticality and uncertain alignments suggest an amateur or untrained designer. The wings are gabled, too steep to suggest pediments, with blind lunettes. They have a Palladian window each, but on the ground floor, with two sashes above. A return range, r., closing the little service courtyard, echoes with blind windows the fenestration and lunette of the wings. The rear is as plain as a warehouse, in rubble, a continuous vertical stair light, r., seemingly cut in *c.* 1800.

Hall flagged diagonally with York stone, panelled and with lugged doorcases, and opening by a fine elliptical arch with English Baroque decoration to the wide stair, which climbs around a well to four storeys. Two narrow turned balusters per tread. This forms the link in an otherwise unresolved floor plan. Bedrooms with original fireplaces lined with rose and grey limestones, and simple vaulted plaster ceilings.

The FORMAL GARDEN on the steep slope behind, while having lost its centre to a rectangular lawn, is enclosed on the W by a brick-walled area, perhaps an orchard, on the N by a TERRACE with a two-storey C18 SUMMERHOUSE at the W, and on the E by another small structure given a brick front with Gothick windows. The complex of FARM BUILDINGS, all with trusses with inward-curving braces on which the purlins rest, are significant for the history of C18 agricultural organization.

PLAS UCHAF, 1¼ m. N. The seat of the lords of Edeirnion till they moved to Gwerclas in Elizabethan days. Late medieval hall-house, perhaps originally with timber walls, but now a

* Gwerclas, with seven hearths, was very likely comparable with the old house at Rhug, replaced a generation later.

single storey of stone with cyclopean doorways perhaps from
an Early Tudor rebuilding. It is cruck-framed but with an aisle
truss (ring-dated 1435) to screen the cross-passage from the
open hall. The end chimneys too replace a louvre over the hall,
perhaps *c.* 1600; the hall fireplace with an unusually wide oak
bressumer. Pre-glazing windows. Traces of four pairs of crucks
suggest the plan was of one (lost) inner room, and two outer
ones surviving at the E. In the reconstruction of *c.* 1600 an
upper storey was inserted with an elaborate beamed hall ceiling
(now at Fronfeuno, Llanycil). Restored for the Landmark
Trust in 1972–3, by *M. T. Pritchard.*

PLAS ISAF, 1½ m. N. On a bluff above the Alwen river.
A substantial Late Georgian stuccoed villa dated 1804, of some
ambition. Three broad bays, the outer ones advanced with
open pediments over arched attic windows in arched recesses.
Shallow arches over first-floor tripartite sashes, the centre one
more rounded, and the doorway similar, with sidelights. Blind
arches characterize the N wall, canted forward to read as a
single open-pedimented composition. A giant arch frames the
centre with an arched panel at each floor, and the outer bays
have tripartite sashes. Typical Regency stair with thin square
balusters.

HAFOD-Y-CALCH, 1 m. N. Late Georgian three-bay stone farmhouse, prominent from Llangar church. Square stone with
deep eaves. A secondary house added on the end of a rear wing.

DINAS MAWDDWY

8615

The tiny market town with a C14 charter did not prosper. The
small manor house at the head of the street was long held by the
Myttons of Shropshire; sold to Edmund Buckley of Manchester
in 1856 for his son Edmund Peck, renamed Buckley in 1864, a
baronet in 1868 and bankrupt in 1876. Buckley invested lavishly
and unwisely to create a model industrial and agricultural estate
of some 11,000 acres. He diverted the main road and built a Vic-
torian-Elizabethan mansion, PLAS YN DINAS, in 1864–7. Burnt
down in 1917, it had steep gables, mullion-and-transom windows
and a thin pavilion-roofed five-storey tower. Designed with the
estate buildings by *James Stevens* of Manchester.

Buckley built a model settlement at Minllyn, just S, with
housing, tourist hotel, slate mill, warehouse and railway terminus at the head of his seven-mile 'Mowddwy Railway' of 1866–8.
He planned a church and to extend the railway N to Bala. The
slate quarry was over-ambitious with its incline and fine storehouse, and failed in 1871, though restarted intermittently to 1915.
The last industrial use of the storehouse was from 1948 as a
woollen mill, Meirion Mill, to the 1980s. The railway closed in
1951.

The village street runs N with a mixture of stone and brick houses
and three chapels, all of the Buckley heyday. First, EBENEZER

INDEPENDENT CHAPEL, 1867, by the *Rev. Thomas Thomas*. Slate, with angle pilasters, tall outer windows and a central stepped triplet, all arched. Inside, a platform pulpit and galleries curved at the angles. The former WESLEYAN CHAPEL, 1868, by *William Thomas Jun.* of Dinas Mawddwy, also of slate, has grey stone quoins and rusticated Gothic window surrounds. At the upper end, the RED LION, C18, raised a storey in the earlier C19, whitewashed with end chimneys. Facing down the street, the entrance to Buckley's mansion, with slate Gothic LODGE by *Stevens*. On the road W, No. 1 WYLE COP, Late Georgian, three-storey and double-fronted, and BETHEL CALVINISTIC METHODIST CHAPEL, 1869, Gothic with grey dressings, like the Wesleyan one.

TANYBWLCH, ¼ m. E. Prominent across the valley. The Buckley estate farm. The FARM BUILDINGS, *c.* 1875 (incomplete in 1878), are of mass concrete, pioneered by *Stevens* (*see* below). Three ranges, with open cartsheds partly closing the fourth. Lofted stables, W, with five dormers; barn in the E range, cowhouse N. The FARMHOUSE, 1833, whitewashed with a centre gable, was built for the Nannau estate.

MINLLYN, ¼ m. S. The slate was brought down by incline to a SLATE MILL on the hillside past the former school; from here it was taken to a handsome storehouse in the railway yard, now MEIRION MILL, *c.* 1868, with broad end entries flanked by arched windows. The former STATION, 1867, has an L-plan house, with an oriel in the cross-wing, and handsome iron gates at the platform end. Just outside is a group of bridges. The modern road bridge by-passes PONT MINLLYN, 1845, single-arched with massive coping stones, and, much lower, the twin-arched PONT-Y-FFINANT that looks C17, but must itself have replaced the timber bridge on stone piers, built in 1635 by Dr John Davies of Mallwyd (q.v.). The superstructure has gone, leaving grassy arches of marvellous delicacy. Across the main road, the BUCKLEY PINES HOTEL, 1870–3 by *Stevens*, originally the Buckley Arms, a pioneer building in mass concrete, contemporary with F. P. Cockerell's Down Hall, Essex, and Lord Sudeley's buildings at Gregynog, Montgomeryshire. Lined and painted like stucco, with shallow pointed window heads and gables overhanging on brackets.

Beyond is the ESTATE VILLAGE, all by *Stevens*, but in stone. First the altered STABLES, then two opposed rows in a Picturesque aesthetic. MAWDDWY COTTAGES, 1868, opposed blocks of three, are designed like two single houses, gabled to the front and to each end, with overhanging bargeboards. Next, MAWDDWY TERRACES, 1870–6, has six houses facing eight, each row with a pair in the outer gables; similar gable detail.

CWM CYWARCH, 1 m. NW. Up this isolated valley, a small stone building at SARN NEWYDD with four pairs of full crucks, C16, and two miniature chapels, TARSUS CALVINISTIC METHODIST, 1877, and BETHLEHEM INDEPENDENT, 1876. They are here because of the COWARCH LEAD MINE (SH 854 194), worked in 1770 by the redoubtable Elizabeth

Baker before being ejected by the Myttons, and fitfully from the 1840s. Ruined C19 CRUSHER HOUSE. Utterly remote, amid bogs over the ridge NW (SH 844 205) are mine holes of uncertain date. Elizabeth Baker looked for copper here in 1770.

CWM CERIST. The A 470 runs NW past the stuccoed DOLHIR LODGE, to Plas yn Dinas, *c.* 1869, by *Stevens*. DOLOBRAN, ¾ m. NW, is a good later C17 farm group, the barn dated 1691, the house with upper crucks. Below is a stone PANDY (fulling mill) of *c.* 1800. Under forestry NW, the CRAIGWEN MINE, NW (SH 836 173), exploited for lead in the C18 and 1848–51, and, unsuccessfully, for gold, 1854–5.

7319   DOLGELLAU

The county town of Merioneth, between the Wnion river and the lower slopes of Cader Idris. The buildings are marvellously unified in their use of local STONE with little stucco or brick. A granite-like dolerite predominates, in shades of green to brown, often used in rough-hewn blocks that defy unaided lifting.* Mixed in, often for lintels, is a pitted slatey rock. Neither stone was easily dressed, but the slatey one is cut to even blocks in the early C18 parish church and the green successfully tooled and moulded on the Shire Hall in the earlier C19, both presumably at great effort. In the later C19 unity of tone was aimed for, the masonry now in smaller rock-faced squared blocks, even in colour, either a pale drab green or more commonly a dark green, almost black. Dressings were often in a grey limestone.

The town's PLAN is the most haphazard in Wales; *ad hoc* street widenings sometimes named as squares and streets that are rarely straight. But at the centre is Eldon Square, achieved by judicious clearance in the early C19, an urban heart that few Welsh towns achieve, spacious and varied. Queen's Square and Smithfield Square are more random meetings of numerous streets, Finsbury Square is just a widening and Meyrick Square a junction. Houses rise from roadways without pavements, and are rarely consistently aligned, gable-ends alternating with façades to picturesque effect.

Dolgellau was typically described as low and mean before the later C18, when it grew with the woollen trade, by 1833 employing 1,400. The basic cloth, called a web, was plain and white, and was shipped in quantity to the southern states of America before the Civil War. With wealth the low cottages with typical vernacular hipped or gabled dormers gave way to tall houses, this change first noted by tourists in the early C19. The woollen industry declined after the 1860s, tanning remaining significant into the mid C20. The town, always an important junction of roads at a river crossing, had a maritime link down the Mawddach to

* Fenton in 1808 describes 'an immense machine which takes above a day to erect' being used to lift stones.

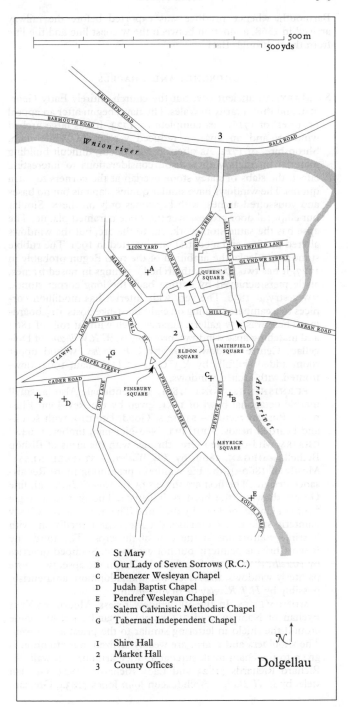

500 m
500 yds

FENYCEN ROAD
BARMOUTH ROAD
Wnion river
BALA ROAD

3

I
SMITHFIELD STREET
LION YARD
SMITHFIELD LANE
BRIDGE STREET
GLYNDWR STREET
MARIAN ROAD
LION STREET
QUEEN'S SQUARE
A

WELL ST
LOMBARD STREET
MILL ST
ARRAN ROAD
2
Arran river
ELDON SQUARE
SMITHFIELD SQUARE
Y LAWNT
G
CHAPEL STREET
CADER ROAD
C
FINSBURY SQUARE
F
D
LOVE LANE
SPRINGFIELD STREET
B
MEYRICK STREET
MEYRICK SQUARE
E
SOUTH STREET

A   St Mary
B   Our Lady of Seven Sorrows (R.C.)
C   Ebenezer Wesleyan Chapel
D   Judah Baptist Chapel
E   Pendref Wesleyan Chapel
F   Salem Calvinistic Methodist Chapel
G   Tabernacl Independent Chapel

I   Shire Hall
2   Market Hall
3   County Offices

N

Dolgellau

Barmouth, whence produce was exported before the railway arrived in 1868, a junction between the w coast line and the line from the e through Bala.

CHURCHES AND CHAPELS

66 ST MARY. An ancient site, but the church entirely Early Georgian and thus a rarity in Wales. The nave, begun after an appeal or 'brief' of 1716, was complete by 1723. It has large arched windows and an apse, a reduced version of Whitchurch, Shropshire, of 1712. As often in Merioneth, difficult building material interacts with stylistic considerations to interesting effect: the slabs of slatey stone overlap at the corners to form quoins. The windows have similar quoins, capitals but no bases and voussoired arches, with keystones only on the n. Similar but elliptical door arches, over the s one a framed plaque. The apse has the same stonework, cut to the arc, but the windows altered in 1864 and a central one inserted in 1901. The rubble stone tower lacks the ambition of the rest. Begun probably in 1727, it has two stages with arched openings in raised frames, angle piers achieved by cutting back the long corner stones. NW vestry, c. 1830. The very wide interior has modillion cornices to a cambered ceiling on eight mast-like posts. C19 boarding. There was a w gallery. Chancel arch with fat rolls of 1864 and matching apse windows, probably by *W. R. Williams* of Dolgellau. Centre window, 1901, by *G. F. Bodley*. w end upper room added skilfully by *Roy Olsen* of Dolgellau, 1992, bow-fronted with arched windows.

FURNISHINGS. FONT. 1861, conventional. Also a small marble octagonal bowl of 1651, given by the Rev. John Ellis, noted Puritan rector. – STALLS. Good, late C19, with scrolls and bearded heads. – PULPIT. Neo-Norman, timber, 1864. – CHAIRS. Mid-C19 Neo-Grec thrones with the arms of Bishop Bethell. – ORGAN. 1869, by *J. W. Walker*. – STAINED GLASS. Mostly of 1860–4, the big windows prompting more Renaissance designs. The best are three s by *Clayton & Bell*, with fine Gothic drawing, the borders Italianate. The first n, a single figure of Christ, perhaps by the same. The next is in the wholly painterly style that Gothicists despised: the Crucifixion, with horrible contortions at the foot of the cross. The third, the Risen Christ is painterly but not grotesque. Stamped quarries by *Powells*, 1863, in the fourth each side. In the apse, two more painterly windows, the Ascension and Adoration, amateurish, possibly by *H. J. Reveley* of Bryn-y-gwin.

MONUMENTS. In the NE window recess, Meurig ab Ynyr Fychan of Nannau, mid-C14 knight in sandstone, his name around the shield in lettering similar to the priest at Corwen. The shoulders and r. arm are weakly stylized, but attention is given to the chain mail, surcoat and leg armour. – N wall. Sir Richard Richards †1823 and Lady Richards †1825; Grecian stele, by *E. H. Baily*. – Archdeacon John Jones †1834, Grecian, making much of his Bampton Lecture given at Oxford in 1821. By *John Carline*. – NE corner. Jane Wynn †1726. Elegant segmental pediment and gadrooned vases, with cherubs below. – Two plaques with urns by the *Patent Works*, London, 1830s. – S wall, eastern bay. Robert Nanney †1751, and Lewis Nanney †1779, both open pedimented with cherub below, the later and finer one signed *van der Hagen*. Between, a fine armorial lead plaque to Ludovicus Nanney †1708. – S wall, central bay. Gothic alabaster plaque to the Rev. Edward Owen †1883. – Three enamelled slate plaques, notable product of the local slate industry, 1850s. – S wall, W bay: Lewis Williams †1879, inlaid with brass, by *Hardman*. – Later C19 brass to Thomas Payne, engineer, †1834, exaggerating his role building the Cob at Porthmadog. – Brass, nicely lettered, to Lowry †1645, mother of the Rev. John Ellis.

In the churchyard, a monolith baluster SUNDIAL, 1835. Some rough slate memorials raised on rustic classical legs of Egryn sandstone, one dated 1769. Iron GATES, by *Coalbrookdale*, 1881.

OUR LADY OF SEVEN SORROWS (R.C.), Meyrick Street. 1963–6, by *M. T. Pritchard* of Blaenau Ffestiniog, with Fr *Francis Scalpell* (born Joseph Scalpella in Malta), who insisted on a 'proper', i.e. traditional, building. Early Christian to Romanesque apsed basilica with a low NE campanile, in green to grey stone from four Merioneth and Caernarvonshire quarries. Stepped W portal, inspired by Cormac's Chapel, Cashel, under a naturalistic bronze CRUCIFIXION by *Giannino Castiglioni* (1884–1971) of Milan. Two bellied curves r.: the baptistery, W, and the Lady Chapel apse, S. Inside, stone dominates, mostly smooth but the arcade columns oddly rock-faced. Five-bay S arcade and two-bay N one, under an open single roof rounded at the apse. The Lady Chapel has a plastered vault and side arches into the baptistery and S aisle. – Rubble HIGH ALTAR with brass Crown of Thorns, under a roof-like hanging CANOPY. – Delicate brass SCREENS in the eastern arches. – Massive RAILS of polished slate. – ROOD. Painted by *Emmanuel Scalpella*, brother of Fr. Scalpell. – Fine wrought-iron hanging CORONAE. – STAINED GLASS. Five apse windows by *Hardman*, 1967, *dalle-de-verre*, fierce colours modified by the thick glass. – S aisle, single panel, 1970s, good kneeling figure.

EBENEZER WESLEYAN CHAPEL, Meyrick Street. 1880, by *Richard Davies*. Impressive two-storey Italianate, raised on a basement, in green and grey stone. Pedimented centre with three arched windows over two doors; outer bays with channelled corner piers. Inside, the gallery has ironwork in strips, arcaded *sêt-fawr* and panelled pulpit.

JUDAH BAPTIST CHAPEL, Bryn Teg. 1839, by the *Rev. Richard Humphreys*, altered 1875, the stuccoed front then covered by additions of 1928 by *O. Morris Roberts & Son*.

PENDREF WESLEYAN CHAPEL, South Street. 1905. Small, in green stone.

SALEM CALVINISTIC METHODIST CHAPEL, Cader Road. A large earlier C19 long-wall chapel disguised by the big pedimented centrepiece of 1893–4 by *Richard Davies*. Pebbledash and stucco, the centrepiece with arched windows above pedimented ones, the outer bays showing the deep eaves and porches of the original. The porches have columned doorcases facing in and pilastered fronts in tooled limestone. Remarkable D-plan interior of 1893 with deep-coved plaster ceiling. The woodwork is conventional enough: panelled gallery and a heavy carved pulpit fronting an organ, by *Wadsworth*. Matching VESTRY, l., 1904. Set back, r., a single-bay HOUSE of *c.* 1806 projects l. of a four-bay school range with an industrial-looking gallery of paired windows over two tall arches set to the l., one infilled, one a throughway.

TABERNACL INDEPENDENT CHAPEL, Chapel Street. 1868, probably by the *Rev. Thomas Thomas*. Grandly scaled, raised on a basement, the façade an unhappy mix of styles. Octagonal corner piers, formerly pinnacled, and a Tudor-arched centre recess over an Italianate triplet and broad pilastered doorcase. Panelled curved-cornered gallery, balustraded *sêt-fawr*, fretwork pulpit panels. In the ceiling a great plaster rose.

PUBLIC BUILDINGS

COUNTY OFFICES, Bala Road. The imposing site above the bridge was intended for an imposing building by *Sir Giles Gilbert Scott*, 1939, with a tower reminiscent of his New Bodleian Library, Oxford, fronting offices running back diagonally. The utilitarian post-war substitute by the County Architect, *Norman L. Jones*, 1953, has a small stone-faced cube with imitation-stone dressings between flat-roofed ranges – COUNCIL CHAMBER, l., offices, r., – pre-fabricated in alu-

Dolgellau, design for County Offices.
Drawing by Giles Gilbert Scott, 1939

minium by the *Bristol Aircraft Co.* The Council Chamber is a period piece in smooth pale wood with green leather Dunlopillo padding.

SHIRE HALL, Bridge Street. 1825, by *Edward Haycock*. Built for the Assizes: a courtroom flanked by side ranges for justices' rooms and cells. A neat triple composition in a strikingly green stone, the courtroom pediment repeated in miniature on the side ranges. The basis is the Palladian Tuscan temple that Inigo Jones used at Covent Garden with its rustic bracketed pediment: but Haycock takes rustic minimalism further, simplifying the mouldings until the pediment sails over the pilasters with the entablature left to the imagination. Segmental heads to three tall windows. The courtroom remains intact with a deep coved ceiling, simple grained woodwork and a square-pier aedicule behind the dais.

MARKET HALL, Eldon Square. 1870–1, by *W. H. Spaull* of Oswestry. A good building reliant on scale not ornament, its two floors higher than the three of Eldon Row adjoining. Arcaded under very large cambered-headed windows and deep timber eaves. Pale limestone dressings contrast with dark local stone. Four bays, the fourth wider as access to the assembly room, converted 2007 to Tŷ Siamas, the National Centre for Welsh Folk Music.

DOLGELLAU AND BARMOUTH DISTRICT COTTAGE HOSPITAL, Hospital Drive. 1927–9 by *North & Padmore* of Bangor. A loosely grouped complex in white roughcast with North's acute gables and simple Arts and Crafts detail. Mostly single-storey following the contour, but a tall entrance range projects N to a gable recessed between two more that are splayed diagonally. Minimal Gothic entrance arch in blue brick. Extensions of 1933 and 1938 by the same, the latter a wing, r., with a curious shouldered gable. On the ridges, some of North's stepped chimneys.

YSGOL-Y-GADER, Arran Road. The Jubilee County School of 1897–9, by *T.M. Lockwood* of Chester. Triple-gabled with big arched upper windows. E side entrance, curved-pedimented. To the W, TŶ'R YSGOL, *c.* 1905, a boarding house, Edwardian, roughcast, with open pediments. Behind, the 1962 secondary school by *Norman Jones*, roughcast with some tile panels.

PRIMARY SCHOOL, Penycefn Road. 1915. Formal, in dark stone with terracotta. A large mullion-and-transom window under the centre gable has two smaller echoes each side, then porches marked Bechgyn and Genethod mask the junction with splayed outer classrooms.

COLEG MEIRION-DWYFOR, Barmouth Road. The former Dr Williams' School, a girls' boarding school established in 1875, closed 1975. A linked range of buildings in dark stone with large sandstone windows; dated 1876, 1889, 1909 and 1937 sequentially from the l. Basically joyless; a shaped gable, lost behind a flat-roofed addition, marked the main entry. Architects, imprecisely recorded, include *S. Bull* of Llangollen, 1875, *William Jones* of Dolgellau, 1880, *T.M. Reade* before 1890, and *G. T. Bassett* of Aberystwyth, 1934. For Coleg Meirion-Dwyfor, a neat modern-traditional range to the W, *c.* 1990, by *Graeme Hughes* of *Gwynedd County Architects*, roughcast with a gabled piece in stone.

BONT FAWR, Bridge Street. Bridge over the Wnion of seven slightly pointed arches. Dated 1638, but doubled in width and the outer pairs of arches rebuilt before the roadway was ramped in 1868 to clear the railway (now the by-pass).

PERAMBULATIONS

1. Eldon Square to the Bridge and back via Smithfield Street

ELDON SQUARE (Stryd Fawr), large and irregular, is a real urban piazza, the Market Hall (*see* above) both suitably Italian with its arcade, and in scale suitably civic. Its two floors loom over the three of ELDON ROW, 1830, built by Sir R. W. Vaughan of Nannau and named in admiration of Lord Chancellor Eldon. The only formal terrace in Dolgellau, it presents a tidier version of the massive stonework of the town. Small-paned sashes, the glazing bars suggesting triple ones. Both ends of the square have a random quality. At the N, TÝ MEIRION, Late Georgian, four-storey with a triple sash each floor, is pushed to one side by the roadway. At the S, PLAS NEWYDD, low, with fat rounded bays. It looks Victorian but is of *c.* 1800, fronting an older house (beams within). To the r. a taller mid-C19 block with attic gables, the long lintel over the main window worth noting. On the E, CROSBY BUILDINGS, 1881 by *William Jones* of Dolgellau, a lumpish curved row with oriel bays, and the HSBC BANK, 1923–4, by *Woolfall & Eccles* of Liverpool, green with brown Grinshill ashlar, the corner entry mildly Georgian. Set back in Mill Street, the former FREE LIBRARY, 1910–11, by *E. A. Fermaud* of London. Designed to cost 'a very limited amount of money', and then simplified. Stucco with giant pilasters. Facing the long side of Tŷ Meirion, CENTRAL BUILDINGS was the Royal Welsh Woollen Warehouse, *c.* 1870, the first of a group of good Italianate commercial buildings. Four floors, with triple windows on the main floors and arched ones under a deep-eaved hipped roof. BOOTS, l., is older, with a pyramid roof against its neighbour and plain front to QUEEN'S SQUARE (Llys Owain). The square with six roads is haphazard, accentuated by the varied scale. The N side is well held by the ROYAL SHIP HOTEL, a big early C19 three-storey three-bay block with an added taller cross-wing. On the E, minor accents before PARLIAMENT HOUSE, a splendid Victorian ironmonger's emporium, 1882, again four-storey Italianate under a deep hipped roof. Two-storey shopfront set to the r. with much plate glass. Inside, the shelving, counters and mahogany manager's office remain. At the rear, cast-iron security windows. On the site was Cwrt Plas yn Dre, seat of Lewis Owen, Baron of the Exchequer, murdered by the Mawddwy bandits in 1555. This was timber-framed, C15 to C16, with a spere-truss. Bogus identification with Owain Glyndŵr at least secured a partial re-erection in Newtown. On the w, the OLD COURTHOUSE, reputedly of 1606, remodelled 1761. The upstairs courtroom has an infilled crude Palladian end window; massive unchamfered beams below.

On BRIDGE STREET (Heol-y-bont), GLYNDŴR, r., the third big Italianate block, c. 1880, with round-headed dormers and pilastered arcaded shopfront. It housed a music emporium, wine merchant and Temperance hotel. The view is closed by the NATWEST BANK, mid-C19, in imported grey limestone, three storeys, with the matching AGRICULTURE HOUSE, l. In LION YARD, l., PLAS ISA, mid-C18 with a hipped rear stair-tower. The former GOLDEN LION ROYAL HOTEL adjoining was the principal inn. Rebuilt in 1839, the three-bay centre with an arcade in the same green stone as the Shire Hall, between open-pedimented wings. Extensive outbuildings w and behind. In LION STREET, the COFFEE SHOP has a rare brick front, earlier C19.

Back on BRIDGE STREET, Nos. 1–2, l., six-gabled, rustic Geor-gian, 1773, has massive stonework. The STAG INN, 1771, was similar, since stuccoed. The nameless square before the bridge has the Shire Hall (see p. 589) and the late C19 BEECHWOOD HOUSE on opposite sides. Casually diagonal, facing the bridge, BRIDGE END, c. 1800, is rustic Georgian with tiny top sashes and a central attic gablet.

SMITHFIELD STREET (FFOS FELIN) runs to Smithfield Square through a grid plan of C19 commercial and industrial charac-ter. Much dark stone of the late C19. The diminutive earlier C19 GAS WORKS has windows in tall recessed arches, and had a tapering chimney. The tiny building, r., was a governor house. SMITHFIELD LANE (Cae Tanws Bach) and GLYNDŴR STREET, l., have small-scale housing for the tanneries and a simple Gothic Presbyterian chapel, 1877, by *Humphrey Jones*, now THEATR FACH. On Smithfield Street, r., the former BETHEL CALVINISTIC METHODIST CHAPEL, 1876, by *Richard Owens*, in his mixed round-arched to Gothic style, faces PLAS YN DRE, big, square, late C19, in dark stone. A mixed late C19 row, l., faces the twin-gabled TORRENT WALK HOTEL, of similar date, but incongruously attached to a low C18 range facing MILL STREET (Wtra'r Felin), an older back lane. Lovely stonework of massy irregularity here, con-tinued on the Late Georgian FORDEN HOUSE, raised a storey and re-windowed, and on the CROSS KEYS, long and low, C17 to early C18, with a row of hipped stone dormers.

SMITHFIELD SQUARE (Felin Isaf) is another irregular junction, the s end neatly filled by the three-storey Y MEIRIONNYDD, earlier C19 rebuilding of the gaol of 1716, rebuilt 1768 and closed 1813. Inside, a neat mid-C18 stair of four flights and the gaol cellar. To the l. a mixed three-storey row. To the r., the UNICORN INN and PLAS COCH, three-storey, apparently early C19, but Plas Coch has a good earlier C18 staircase with thick rail and turned balusters. UPPER SMITHFIELD returns to Eldon Square. Two commercial buildings, l.: THRESHERS, mid-C19, with small-paned sashes and a gabled cross-wing, and VICTORIA BUILDINGS, 1870s, taller and plain, on the corner of Meyrick Street.

2. Lombard Street, Cader Road, Love Lane, Finsbury Square

From Eldon Row, LOMBARD STREET winds W amid buildings of varied scales and angles. The COUNCIL OFFICES, l., early C20, pyramid-roofed, light green stone, have a corner capped with Prince of Wales feathers. On MARIAN ROAD, r., No. 1 was the Crown inn, earlier C19 with a good shop window; TAN-Y-FYNWENT, a good early C18 town house, has the Merioneth dormers and Georgian sashes, four bays, with a C19 trellis porch. Chimneys on the back wall flank a hipped stair-tower. Earlier C18 plaster in the hallway and a staircase with thick twisted balusters. At the end, in the cemetery, a Neoclassical pyramid MEMORIAL on a pedestal to the schoolteacher bard David Richards (Dafydd Ionawr) †1827, significantly inscribed in Welsh and Latin.

Back on Lombard Street, low C18 cottages and Late Georgian three-storey pairs. PLAS BRITH is an early C20 intrusion. HOPE HOUSE, r., was an early C19 woollen factory. Four uneven bays. Opposite, a row steps up to the OLD BANK, the Merionethshire Bank, established c. 1803. Entirely domestic, it backs onto the road with a long stair light. Y LAWNT (The Lawn) is a triangular space overlooked by a handsome mid-C19 former POLICE STATION. The careful squared stonework and arched windows in raised surrounds give an earlier character. Similar cell block behind. On the bank to the S, TANY-BRYN, c. 1830–40, Late Georgian, of massive stones. Further r., PENBRYN, a broad pair dated 1808, with large sashes and attic gables. They back onto Cader Road with long stair lights, one still with leaded glazing.

On CADER ROAD (Ffordd Cadair Idris), W of Salem chapel (see p. 588), Y TOLLDY was the toll house, the corner window for observation and the older toll-gate post built-in. E of Salem, IDRIS TERRACE is late C19 in dark stone apart from Nos. 1–2 of c. 1820. Five bays with three gables and two pretty doorcases. BRYN HOUSE is Late Georgian of three bays, hipped, with big ridge chimneys. The warehouse range to the l. suggests a commercial owner.

LOVE LANE (Tylau Mair) climbs the hillside behind, with a scattering of villas. BRYNFFYNNON, 1893, by *J. H. Swainson* of Wrexham, is typical of the later ones, dark stone with steep bargeboarded gables. BRYNTIRION is similar but symmetrical, but BRYN MAIR is possibly of 1831, early for an asymmetrical villa. Basement and three floors with deep eaves and clustered ashlar chimneys. BRYNBELLA, earlier C19, is conventionally three-bay with gablets. Down a track, FFYNNON FAIR, an ancient well, has a square pool of 1837 in ruined walls. After PEN BRYNBELLA, altered early C18, Penybryn

leads down to BRYNTEG. On a high terrace, TANYRALLT, Late
Georgian, three-storey, and BRYNTEG TERRACE, a looming
later C19 row of three, the centre gabled and uncomfortably
asymmetrical.

Back on CADER ROAD, the cruciform Gothic CONGREGA-
TIONAL CHURCH, 1878, now a dental surgery, and the back
of a mid-C18 house facing Tabernacl chapel (*see* p. 588) in
CHAPEL STREET (Heol-y-capel). Three bays, offset for a fire-
window each floor, the attic windows under hipped dormers.
Cader Road widens to become FINSBURY SQUARE (Porth
Canol). On the l. Nos. 7–8, a low C18 pair on a basement. They
had eyebrow eaves (as at Pandy'r Odyn, *see* p. 595), now
dormers. No. 6 is plain Late Georgian. All three have attractive
C19 trellis porches. Opposite, overlooking a small courtyard,
PLAS GWYN is mid-C18 with tall chimneys and gabled
dormers, the door early C19. Staircase with three slim balusters per tread, but other detail early C19. Facing the yard also,
ISFRYN, earlier C18 with hipped dormers, and ISFRYN
COTTAGE, late C19, both with trellis porches. The Square is
effectively defined by the five bargeboarded gables of IVY
HOUSE, *c.* 1830, at the E end. On the s, MAESGWYN HOUSE,
later C19, hipped, with grey quoins, and, across Springfield
Street, a bold earlier C19 three-storey canted bay. On the N, a
mixed group curves round to the s façade of the Market Hall.

3. Meyrick Street, South Street, Springfield Street

From the SW corner of Eldon Square, MEYRICK STREET (Heol
Feurig) runs S. On the l., VICTORIA BUILDINGS, later C19,
five bays and three storeys, with canted corner. MERVINIAN
HOUSE is detached, three-storey, earlier C19 with a later porch,
iron-columned and timber-balustraded. From 1868 the printing office of *Y Dydd*, the Calvinistic Methodist newspaper. The
widening overlooked by Ebenezer chapel (*see* p. 587) was Skin-
ners Square. STAR HOUSE, r., 1800, an ungainly four floors,
the upper two for weaving. Good late C19 shop. SPRINGFIELD
HOUSE, behind, is a later C19 bargeboarded villa. To the l.,
FRO AWEL, low and pretty, early C18, with three hipped
dormers and a fire-window. CEMLYN, opposite the R.C.
church (*see* p. 587) is also C18, painted stone. Next TŶ
MEURIG, earlier C19, has a square-piered porch in the green
stone of the Shire Hall. The rear wing has a curved wall, a local
type. TAN-Y-GADER, closing the view S, is one of a local Late
Georgian group with simple pediments and roundels, here
incongruously flanked by dormer gables. Early C19 staircase.

On MEYRICK SQUARE (Y Domen Fawr), another irregular
space, PLAS UCHA on the r. was an important C17 house,
rebuilt 1852 with big grey chimneys. The irregular street front
shows the more complicated history. The garden front has C19
gables and porch. SOUTH STREET (Maes-y-pandy) ascends
the Arran valley, a former industrial area with mills and tanneries. On the r. WESLEY PLACE, a short terrace, faces the

originalWesleyan chapel, HEN DŶ WESLEY, 1806. Large plain
lateral front with slab lintels. On l., GLANAFON, an earlier C19
villa with big ridge chimneys, and Pendref chapel, 1905. The
lane winds up to GLAN ARRAN, a good three-storey pedimented house, like Tan-y-gader, c. 1800. Attached, l., a pretty
cottage row with five dormer gables. Returning downhill,
FRON ARRAN, to the W, is three-storey in squared stone with
three bargeboarded gables, c. 1830. Y GRAIG and RHOSLYN,
behind HEN DŶ WESLEY, a mid-C19 pair with centre gablet
and big axial chimneys.

From Meyrick Square SPRINGFIELD STREET (Heol Plas
Uchaf) runs straight to Finsbury Square. Later C19 terraced
houses, the largest at the foot: a pair, GLENYDD and
WENALLT, and CAE'R FFYNNON, with cross-wing, 1872, by
Roberts & Morrow of Dolgellau.

4. Arran Road, east of the Centre

E of Smithfield Square, PONT-YR-ARRAN COTTAGE, l., is the
best of the town's small vernacular houses. Early C18, of lovely
stonework with a roof of small slates and three hipped
dormers. Nos. 5–6 opposite was a flannel warehouse, c. 1800,
five bays. Over the Arran bridge, ARRAN ROAD has artisan
housing: Nos. 1–7 BONT-YR-ARRAN facing the river, and, l.,
after an INFANT SCHOOL of 1884, MAES TALARRAN, three
rows of industrial cottages. On the S, Ysgol-y-gader with the
Hospital behind (*see* p. 589), then the former WORKHOUSE
(Llwyn View). Later and friendlier than the standard, built
c. 1855. Thirteen bays; the centre three, hipped with hoodmoulds, were the master's house, and the wings with arched
upper windows for the paupers. Cross-range and two yards
behind.

5. Cregennen Road and Tywyn Road, west of the Centre

First up CREGENNEN ROAD. BRYNHYFRYD in the junction
with Tywyn Road is a Late Georgian hipped villa in squared
stone, as late as c. 1840, with deep eaves and a veranda. The
stable has blind arcading above Tywyn Road. On the l., in Victorian grounds, CRAIG-Y-FFYNNON was a small earlier C19
villa, The Rock, enlarged 1872 with bargeboarded wings.
Above, BODLONDEB, a late C19 row of tall four-storey gabled
houses with big square bays, replaces a semicircular gaol of
1813, enlarged 1873 but closed 1878. Further on, CLOGWYN,
high above the road, is a villa enlarged from a downhill range
(dated 1726 inside) with mid-C19 additions each side of the
original gable-end: canted-fronted, l., and hipped, r. On the
roadside, r., BRON-Y-GADER, hipped, c. 1830, has a two-bay
front and a long three-bay side.

Returning to TYWYN ROAD, MAESCALED, l., is a cottage row
ornamented in Tudor style, 1832, as the lodge to Bryn-y-gwin

(*see* p. 596) with gable, stone oriel, hoodmoulded windows and bargeboarded porch. BRYNRODYN, on the drive is C18, given a bargeboarded gable and dormers by the estate. PANDY'R ODYN, further out on the Tywyn road, has an estate village feel with three groups of cottages. Nos. 1–3, r., has diagonal chimneys and tiny Tudor windows under eyebrow eaves, presumably early C19. Nos. 5–6, opposite, with four hipped dormers, may be late C18; and TALYBONT, by the bridge, a row of four with shouldered dormers, is earlier C19, spoilt by joining the windows vertically.

6. Bala and Barmouth Roads, north of the Centre

Overlooking the bridge are the County Offices (*see* p. 588). To the E, below the BALA ROAD, LLWYN has an unadorned three-storey seven-bay front of early C19 character but is in part later C16, built for a son of Baron Lewis Owen. The façade is clearly raised and the r. end has two blocked C16 stone cross-windows. Inside, early C19 doors and plasterwork, and a good mid-C18 stair, the best in the town, with column-on-vase balusters, ramped thick rails and carved tread ends. BWYTHYN LLWYN adjoining may be a remodelling of a C17 stable; two storeys, four bays. Beyond, a converted HAY BARN of 1820 with fabulous monolith slate piers.

From the County Offices, PENYCEFN ROAD climbs NW past the Primary School (*see* p. 589). TREM-YR-EGLWYS, 1872, by *John Prichard* of Llandaff, l., was the rectory. One of the best of the big late villas, in dark stone with steep roofs and a bargeboarded cross-wing. After Frondirion (*see* below), two villas prominent from across the valley: BRYNDERW, with cross-wing, 1880s, and, down a lane, PENYCOED, 1889, symmetrical with canted bays. An ambitious galleried stair hall inside.

On the BARMOUTH ROAD, w, a near-formal composition of *c.* 1880: two hipped villas, HEULFRYN and DOLYGADER, face across a driveway aimed at FRONDIRION, a lumbering twelve-bay terrace on the bank, actually reached from Penycefn Road. The four gables have big pointed attic windows over two-storey bays. After the POLICE STATION, 1978, by *M. H. Roberts*, are villas in sloping grounds, from steep-roofed later Victorian to Edwardian. COED CELYN, *c.* 1890, in green stone, has a good iron veranda and a cross-wing with a castellated bay. Then three of the 1880s with canted-hipped wings: at COED CYMER, two flank boat-shaped half-dormers, LLYSMYNACH has two, and BRYNDEDWYDD one. LLWYNCOED, *c.* 1902, intrudes an English suburban mix of half-timber roughcast and brick. Y BRYN, *c.* 1904, stone again, has a strong Edwardian character, a steep hipped roof and a cross-wing neatly combined. Beyond Coleg Meirion-Dwyfor (*see* p. 589), TREM HYFRYD, 1870s, has the steep helmet-like half-hips that Butterfield introduced.

BRYN-Y-GWIN UCHAF, ½ m. W. The small estate of the Owens
passed by marriage to Henry Reveley, who built the new Bryn-
y-gwin (*see* below), this, the old house, becoming a dower
house. Unpretentious: the low upper end is C17; the sequence
below C18 to early C19 – back-to-back ranges downhill to a
three-bay front across the lower end, with a veranda. Interiors
Gothicized by *H. J. Reveley* in the 1850s or earlier. The C17 end
has become an open hall with added braces and struts to the
roof truss. One rear room has plaster cherubs and dolphin over
a Gothic chimneypiece, and reused C16 panels on a cupboard.
The parlour has an early C18 chimneypiece. In the front, the
drawing room has a Regency cornice, the staircase is slightly
Jacobean of the 1840s, and the room above has false hammerbeams, bosses and a chimneypiece with finials and knightly
figures. Small lofted COACHHOUSE dated 1780.

BRYN-Y-GWIN ISAF, ½ m. W. 1803–6, for Hugh Reveley, who
married Jane Owen, heiress of Bryn-y-gwin, with additions
principally by their son *Hugh John Reveley*, to his own designs
after 1850. The motivation was to replace Bryn-y-gwin Uchaf
on a better site with an unobstructed view. But, with space for
only a narrow lane behind and no yards, the site is awkward.
However, each part thereby directly adjoins the gardens below,
so the concept could be called Reptonian on a miniature scale.

The main house has a curved l. end wall and five bays to the
front, the centre three bowed with a colonnade of Tuscan
columns of painted sandstone supporting an iron-railed
balcony. Very deep eaves with paired flat brackets. Stylistically
this has the hallmarks of *Joseph Bromfield*. Altered glazing, but
are such large windows original? On the rear, irregular enlargements to the hall for a new staircase, 1851–4, more Italianate,
but keeping the deep eaves as a unifying feature. Stair window,
Faith, Hope and Charity, by *David Evans*. The house is then
extended by two low recessed bays to a tall projecting cross-
range with a pediment. This is perhaps of the 1840s, but runs
back to a bowed rear wall that looks of the original early C19,
with a crude stone cornice under a low attic with deep eaves.
The Italianate bellcote may mark the joint. At the base of the
garden front an arched recess with a Victorian Neoclassical
tondo relief, unsigned, of two infant children of H. J. Reveley
carried to heaven by angels. After a gap, a line of outbuildings,
the near end with a pyramid roof composing well from the
garden.

GLYN MALDEN. *See* Penmaenpool.

DOLRHYD, Barmouth Road, 1 m. WNW (Cerrig Camu care
home). Of the house built by Griffith Nanney of Nannau in
1596 there is little evidence beyond the inscribed stones re-set
on a big E wall lateral chimney, one starting 'Viva Diva Eliza-
betha . . .' His great-granddaughter married William Vaughan
M.P. (†1775), of Corsygedol, who built the E-facing five-bay
house in the mid C18. A pedimental gable with lunette, and

four roundels over the outer bays, a clumsy hint of Baroque. The open-well staircase has thin turned balusters. A big canted-ended piece was added in 1835 to face the wonderful view, its lateral chimney inset with the C16 stones.

William Vaughan was Chief President of the Honourable Society of Cymmrodorion (Wales's first modern cultural body). For meetings of this learned circle he built c. 1770 the APOLLO, a small building on the front terrace. More library than temple perhaps, its cultural significance is greater than its modest physical expression. Squared stone with a lateral chimney and a simple gable pediment. The interior is Roman in miniature with an apse that may have accommodated Vaughan's presidential chair. Its glory is its barrel-vaulted and semi-domed ceiling exuberantly decorated with crowded Adamesque motifs, unique in Wales. Winged sphinxes and gryphons on pedestals, festoons, musical trophies, and symbols of other arts. This could be by *Joseph Bromfield*.

Uphill, the COACHHOUSE and STABLE, dated 1763. Eight bays with tiny loft windows, and two shallow voussoir arches in the pedimented centre. At right angles, an older BARN, with gable coping and a central shallow arch with dripmould.

GARTHMAELAN, 1½ m. NE. Earlier C18, with five hipped dormers, but the five bays below altered to three in the early C19. Modern glazing. Inside, a good double arch with fluted pilasters at the foot of a stair with turned balusters and a dog-gate. Panelled l. room with large raised panels and a bolection-moulded doorway, and r. room with big voussoired lateral fireplace. To the w, a ruined circular C19 BELVEDERE.

DOLGUN ISAF, 1 m. E. Late C16 or early C17 long low farmhouse with two C18 gabled dormers. Inside, plank partitions, and a large fireplace and winding stone stair at the l. end.

DOLGUN UCHAF, 1¼ m. E. An important surviving hall-house of c. 1500–20, altered, later C16. White-painted with a large lateral chimney marking the hall and a r. end one for the parlour. The hall chimney was inserted when the room was still open to the fine three-bay roof with cusped collar-trusses. Originally entry was to the l. of the chimney, altered when this end became a lofted cartshed. The present voussoired door, r. of the chimney, enters behind the dais partition which remains intact right up to the roof. Heavy planks and a single ogee-headed doorway. Quaker meetings were held in the cartshed loft in the later C17.

DOLGUN FORGE, 1½ m. E. Against a steep bank is a ruined blast furnace built for Abraham Darby I of Coalbrookdale, who died before completion in 1719. Intended to exploit local iron ore from Tir Stent and local charcoal, but by 1729 ore was being shipped from Lancashire; use ceased c. 1733. Below, in a caravan park, a wall with big Tudor-arched entry looks early C19, so probably outbuildings of the short-lived

Dolgun Hall.* The house site and walled garden are further w.

THE TORRENT WALK, 1½ m. E. Laid out in the early C19 by *Thomas Payne*, William Madocks's agent at Dolmelynllyn (Ganllwyd), and assistant on the Picturesque walk there. Here the clients were J. H. Lewis of Dolgun Hall and Baron Richards of Caerynwch, Brithdir, and it became one of the attractions of Picturesque Mid Wales, graded paths ascending the cascades of the Clywedog.

TABOR, 1½ m. ESE. A hillside hamlet around TABOR CHAPEL, a Quaker meeting house 1792–1845, sold to the Independents, and rebuilt *c.* 1851. Plain stone, chapel and house in line. The Quaker meeting began at TYDDYN GARREG, nearby, a small farmhouse with hipped dormers, the lower range probably the C17 house. Their BURIAL GROUND remains, across a field. TÝ NEWYDD, SW, is C18 with stone dormers. COED, NW of the chapel, is a charming house fashioned *c.* 1800 from a single range by adding a rounded end with triple sash each floor and a short parallel range with matching end, but not in line, giving an intriguing stepped profile. Sir Richard Richards of Caerynwch, Brithdir, was born here in 1752.

PLAS YN BRITHDIR, ¾ m. SE. C17–C18, with Merioneth dormers. In the 1830s the Nannau estate added a porch-tower like a diminutive windmill, and big octagonal chimneys.

BRYN MAWR, 1 m. S. High on an outcrop of Cader Idris. Formal Late Georgian with the pediment and roundel typical of the region. But it refronts the house from which Rowland Ellis fled persecution with a hundred of his Quaker neighbours in 1686 to the Welsh Tract in Pennsylvania, where the name is remembered in the famous women's college. Inside, heavy beams and two C17 roof trusses, one dated 1617. The low outbuilding in front has ceiling beams and a beamed fireplace. It may have been a secondary or dower house.

DYFFRYN ARDUDWY

A linear VILLAGE, largely mid-C19, along the turnpike between Barmouth and Harlech. Manganese was mined in the hills and woollen webs were manufactured in the village. The railway came through in 1867, with a station ¼ m. W near Llanenddwyn church. Ystumgwern, ½ m. NNW, was a royal *llys* at the centre of the Ardudwy commote with court buildings and chapel in the C13. The timber hall was moved to Harlech Castle in 1307 and nothing survives.

ST ENDDWYN, ¼ m. W. The parish church of Llanenddwyn. C13 origins, but C16, heavily restored by *Henry Kennedy* in 1883.

---

*H. J. Reveley in the 1850s says that this was an Italian villa designed by the London architect *James Lewis* †1820, for his son, but the villa was called eighteen years old when it burnt in 1844.

Cruciform; old masonry is visible on the chancel s and the nave N. N transept mostly rebuilt by Kennedy, and he raised the gables at the E and s steeper than their roofs. The windows are his except the s transept W and adjoining s nave window. These, of Egryn sandstone, curiously combine a semicircular hood over a pair of hollow-moulded lancets – C16? The s chancel window, of arched lights in a rectangular frame, may copy a C16 original. Re-set arch-braced collar-trusses; cusped struts in the chancel and s transept, so probably original early C16, the remainder plainer and later. – FONT. Plain octagonal, probably late C15. – STAINED GLASS. E window, 1883, by *Hardman*.

HOREB CALVINISTIC METHODIST CHAPEL, Ffordd Capel. 1863–4 by *O. Morris Roberts*, altered 1889. Imposing and severe stone front, on a railed terrace. Four tall arched windows with an impost band that arches over the outer windows and then lifts as a giant arch over the centre pair. Interior of 1889 with curved gallery on iron columns and elaborate ceiling in blue, red and buff. Patterned glass in the windows each side of a steeply pedimented stucco pulpit-back on four pilasters. Three-storey CHAPEL HOUSE, l., added to an earlier and lower Georgian house.

REHOBOTH INDEPENDENT CHAPEL. 1880. Snecked stone and rendered dressings. Characterful with arched doors flanking a tall narrow arched triplet with an outsized lunette plaque above and high gable shoulders with ball finials.

In the centre, TŶ CENNIN, three-storey Late Georgian in good coursed stone with small-paned upper windows; altered ground floor with veranda and bays. To the N, LIVERPOOL HOUSE, of large stones, with late C19 shop, then terraces to BRITISH TERRACE, mid-C19, on a high basement with stone steps up. At the s end the path up to the burial chambers (*see* p. 600) passes the SCHOOL, 1904, by *Deakin & Howard Jones*, five large arched windows under gables.

SARNLYS, ¼ m. N. Brick, 1950s, by *Griffith Morris*, influenced by Frank Lloyd Wright's Prairie houses. Upper rooms in a shallow hipped roof with big hipped dormers, one onto the flat roof of a large semicircular living-room projection. Symmetrical E front; the entrance recessed, under a wide dormer lighting the hall. Geometrical leading to the glazed doors, triangular oriels each side and the dormer.

DOLGAU, 1 m. N. Good example of a late C16 or early C17 storeyed house of the end-chimney type, with big tapering chimneys and cross-passage. Three bays, the narrow doorway with rough voussoirs offset to the r. and small windows above. Extended behind under a catslide roof.

BYR-LLYSG, ¾ m. NE. Reputed seat of Osbwrn Wyddel (Osborn Fitzgerald), C13 Irish ancestor of the families of Corsygedol, Glyn Cywarch and Peniarth. Small, altered late C16 end-chimneyed house with small dormer gables, one dated 1761. E of the house, a circular FORTIFIED SITE, nearly 200 ft (60 metres) in diameter.

BRONYFOEL ISAF, 1½ m. NE. Late C16, of some distinction, perhaps built by Rhys ap Tudor, son-in-law of Edward Stanley, mid-C16 Constable of Harlech Castle, then occupied by William Lewis, former Master of St Cross Hospital, Winchester. Two storeys and attic, steep-roofed with tall end chimneys, a mark of grandeur. Three bays, irregularly spaced; three tiers of tiny windows in the end gables. Remarkable two-storey end-wall latrine over a basement stream. The C15 lodgings at St Cross have one similar, so perhaps added by William Lewis. Service rooms N of the cross-passage; a two-bay hall, S, with big fireplace and winding stair. Lofty chamber above, with a panelled ceiling of stop-chamfered beams and joists, and N end fireplace. Unusually, the stone stair continues to the attic.

BRONYFOEL ISAF BURIAL CHAMBER, 1¾ m. NE (SH 608 247). Built into the roadside wall above Bronyfoel Isaf. A portal dolmen with a rather squat portal stone and two closing slabs (an unusual duplication) remaining, and a large capstone sloping to the ground behind them. The remains are set at the E end of a long cairn.

DYFFRYN ARDUDWY BURIAL CHAMBERS, E of the school (SH 588 229). Excavated in 1961–2 and since consolidated by Cadw, unfortunately ruining the appearance of the E chamber, one of two burial chambers. The W chamber is a small but classically designed portal dolmen which was surrounded by a circular cairn with a wide V-shaped forecourt. A single cup mark on the N portal stone. Remains of five Early Neolithic pots were found in a pit in the forecourt. This early chamber was superseded when the large E chamber was built in front of it and both chambers were covered by a long rectangular cairn. The E chamber is much less 'classic' in design, having no separate portals and a rather slight closing slab (now broken). The forecourt here was narrower, bounded by small upright stones and blocked by a stone bank, and contained pottery in Middle Neolithic style. The chamber was reused for burial in the Early Bronze Age. CULTIVATION TERRACES in the field to the N of the tomb. Likely to be contemporary with late prehistoric or Romano-British stone HUTS, once plentiful on these lower slopes. Some ruined ones survive in the wood just above the tomb.

FAIRBOURNE

6214

A holiday settlement on dune-land founded in 1895 by Arthur McDougall of the flour firm, the miniature RAILWAY laid down initially to transport materials. Nothing to recommend it architecturally. Some short rows of c. 1900 rise over the bungalows. Friog on the main road is the older village.

ST CYNON. On Ynys Faig, a rock outcrop. 1926–7, by *J. B. Mendham* of London. The very end of the Gothic Revival, with an Arts and Crafts feeling for materials. Slatey stone with a slate-clad bell-tower of Sussex type, apparently originally tiled. Central w buttress, pierced for a window; cross-gabled aisles. Inside, thickly pointed rough stone contrasts with pale ashlar piers, chamfered for the arcades, and shafted at the chancel arch. Open nave roof and painted panelled chancel ceiling. A sturdy oak frame carries the bell-turret, incorporating a pretty gallery. – STAINED GLASS. E window, 1927, by *William Morris, Westminster*, three saints. – Chancel s, by *Jones & Willis*, 1937. – w two-light, 1929, SS Margaret and Ann. – Also three attractive tiny lights, 1927, two w and one SE. – TILES. In the sanctuary, random Victorian encaustic tiles rescued from 'various college chapels of Oxford and Cambridge'.

FRIOG. On the main road, s, a derelict early C19 TOLL HOUSE. HEN-DDÔL, set back, small, late C17, whitewashed, has dormer gables. Large C17 barn and added hay barn in front. There were C19 SLATE QUARRIES at Henddôl (SH 619 122), worked underground, and Goleuwern (SH 621 122), open-pit, later a hydro-electric reservoir for McDougall.

FFESTINIOG *see* LLAN FFESTINIOG

FRONGOCH   9039

The church by *T. M. Penson*, 1857, has been demolished, as also the whisky distillery, 1887, set up by R. J. L. Price of Rhiwlas. The distillery became the FRONGOCH CAMP for prisoners of war, for eight months holding 1,863 Irish republicans arrested after the 1916 Rising, including Michael Collins and Terence MacSwiney. FRONGOCH, a large C18 farmhouse, has massive stonework and stone lintels.

CILTALGARTH, 1 m. NW. A large L-plan earlier C19 farm rebuilt for the Rhiwlas estate. Sashes and deep eaves with a cross-wing. Double service and farmyards behind, connected by a throughway.

TŶ UCHAF, 1¼ m. NW, below the road. The original Ciltalgarth, dated 1682. Huw Roberts, Quaker, left for Pennsylvania that year. Big off-centre storeyed porch, incorporating the stair, suggesting a late C17 enlargement of an earlier house. Lobby-entry; parlour to r. and hall to l., the parlour beam plastered. The BARN has five bays of full crucks, C16.

LLYN CELYN, 1½ m. NW. Reservoir controversially built by Liverpool Corporation in 1964–5 by damming the Tryweryn, flooding the several farms and the chapel of Cwm Celyn. Grass-covered gently graded dam. Silo-like VALVE TOWER rising from the waters, by *Frederick Gibberd & Partners*; engineering by *J. H. T. Stilgoe* for the Corporation, with *Binnie, Deacon & Gourley*. MEMORIAL CHAPEL at the NW end, 1964, by *R. L. Gapper*, below the resited gravestones of Capel Celyn. Sombrely modern, a monopitch in windowless rubble, the wall

curved around the end to a full-height glazed piece that
illuminates the memorial stones within.

GANLLWYD/Y GANLLWYD

7325

The turnpike road through the wooded valley of the Mawddach
and the Eden attracted visitors from the late C18. The young
William Madocks (see Tremadog) came to Dolmelynllyn in 1796,
attracted by the nearby waterfall, a pioneer of the Picturesque
appreciation of Mid Wales. Although Madocks began the great
enterprise of Tremadog (C) in 1798, he kept Dolmelynllyn and
visitors continued to come. A hotel on the main road followed,
and then Victorian fishing lodges.

In the village, the corrugated-iron COMMUNITY HALL was a
mission church of c. 1900, restored 2006 by the National Trust.
TŶ COCH and the PRIMARY SCHOOL, 1904–5, have striking
orange terracotta dressings, both by *Deakin & Howard Jones*,
Tŷ Coch with ornamental half-timber also. LIBANUS
INDEPENDENT CHAPEL, 1857, opposite, is stone with arched
openings.

DOLMELYNLLYN. Madocks's modest house of c. 1796, just
three rooms each floor, may have been an alteration of an
earlier house of the Vaughans. It survives shorn of its pretty
verandas between the Victorian house and a low W range that
is C17. The new house added in 1860 for C. R. Williams was
probably by his brother, *George Williams* of Liverpool, who certainly made alterations in 1873. It has crowstepped gables, one
central to the E front and one over the N entrance. A legacy
allowed injudicious additions in 1873: a harsh tower on the S
end (once with slated spire) and bits of timberwork. Further
additions included a loggia l. of the entrance; a curved arcaded
wall r. of the forecourt, and an oriel over the entrance, apparently of reused bedposts and oriental carved panels. Conventional interiors, the staircase with twisted balusters. Some
heraldic glass, in pressed quarries on the stair, and amid fragments of ancient glass in the SE room. SW of the house a rock-
faced stone GAME LARDER, c. 1870*. The LOWER LODGE,
c. 1870, toned down in white paint, mixes rock-faced stone
with brick arch-heads on the front and half-timber on the side.
Up the disused drive, a prominent FIELD BARN, c. 1800, well
restored. The UPPER LODGE, much extended, may date from
Madocks's time.

ABEREDEN, ¼ m. N. Green stone house of 1876, enlarged in the
1890s for W. Pritchard Morgan of the Gwynfynydd gold mine
(*see* below). Two front gables, one with a two-storey bay. The
S extension is friendlier with small-paned windows and SW

---

*Fenton in 1808 mentions a 'Gothick building made to imitate a ruin overgrown
with ivy, which Mr Maddox made a Ball room of'. The barn-like building at the
forecourt entrance shows older stonework but no mock-ruin.

corner porch with a shaped gable. In the older part, an arched stair light with floral glass.

TŶ'N-Y-GROES HOTEL, ¾ m. S. Early C19, altered. The hood-moulded ground-floor windows, with Gothic lights and the Gothic door, r., are original. The upper gables were half-timbered c. 1900.

BRYN CEMLYN, 1 m. S. On the road edge, a gaunt fishing villa in rock-faced stone with a little half-timber in the N end. Built for a brother-in-law of Williams of Dolmelynllyn, c. 1870.

GELLIGEMLYN, 1½ m. S. Originally a fishing lodge of c. 1870–80, in stone with detail similar to the Lower Lodge at Dolmelynllyn. Greatly extended in 1903 for H. W. Lee, in green stone with imitation half-timber. NE addition of 1912.

COED-Y-BRENIN. A very large area of mountainous Nannau estate land was given over to forestry in 1922 and renamed for the Silver Jubilee of 1935. VISITOR CENTRE, 2007, by *James Jenkins Thomas* of Aberystwyth, of forestry timber and heated with forest waste. Circular, boarded, with a balcony under a single conical shingled roof.

CEFNDEUDDWR, 1 m. N of Pont-ar-eden. On the saddle between the Eden and Mawddach valleys. C17 Nanney family house, altered in the early C18. Three bays, with sashes. Early C18 fielded panelling to door and window reveals; stair with panelled newels and turned balusters. First-floor post-and-panel screen, C17, and C18 wig-closet. The byre to the N was an early C17 subsidiary house with beamed ceiling. Late C17 barn, and, lower down, a smaller barn dated 1727.

GWYNFYNYDD GOLD MINE, 2 m. NNE of Pont-ar-eden. Gold was found in 1864. William Pritchard Morgan, called the Gold King, with experience in Australia, re-equipped it, 1887–8, and won gold worth £14,000 in the first year. At its peak it employed 250. It closed in 1916, and a reopening in 1934 failed when the new plant burnt down. The mill of 1888 was on the confluence of the Cain and the Mawddach, a site loved by early tourists, flanked on both sides by waterfalls. A giant water wheel was replaced in 1893 by a turbine, for which the iron pipes are still prominent. The mine at the top of the escarpment had an incline E to the Mawddach and a tramway to the mill. The approach passes a ruined manager's house and buildings associated with the TYDDYN GADLYS blasting powder works.

GARREG see LLANFROTHEN

GLAN-YR-AFON

9141

ST JAMES THE GREAT, Llawr-y-betws. 1863–4, to designs of 1860 by *George Gilbert Scott*, in memory of Sir Robert Vaughan of Nannau and Rhug †1859. Nave and chancel in one with N porch; sturdily detailed and in good proportions. Plate traceries in the nave, broad buttresses to support a bellcote over the chancel arch, and chancel lancets. Scissor-truss roofs. The nave, still with iron candelabra standards, is quite bare. The chancel by contrast is enriched with an outstanding display of *Minton* tiles: Welsh inscriptions in blue on the steps, dense patterns in the sanctuary floor, and sparkling on the E wall in embossed patterns on a ground of white, but at the centre a cross of plain blue of stark simplicity. Good E window, a broad pointed arch framing lancets with column shafts. A moulded sill course unites the chancel, carried over the vestry door and double sedilia. Tiny shafted piscina. – FONT, octagonal, with a garland of water-lily, Caen stone. – PULPIT. Delicate pierced timber on a stone base. – Simple well-designed STALLS. – STAINED GLASS. E window by *O'Connor*, 1860s. Crucifixion, St Mary Magdalene, and Jairus's daughter.

CALVINISTIC METHODIST CHAPEL. 1865. Red brick and sandstone with arched windows and outer doors. Inside, pitch-pine fittings, the pulpit backed by a plaster arch.

BETHEL INDEPENDENT CHAPEL, Bethel, 2½ m. WSW. Disused. Hipped; perhaps in part of 1816 with an enclosed pedimented porch. The classical detail in cement of 1909.

In the village, three contrasting SCHOOLS. Opposite the church, a late C19 Gothic Church School; up the lane, a mid-C19 British School, simple with roughly arched windows; past the chapel, the Primary School, 1908, by *Deakin & Howard Jones*, cheerful brick and terracotta with Palladian end windows.

CAER EUNI HILL-FORT, 2 m. WSW. Not excavated. The kink in the SE rampart indicates a great increase in size at some period. The present entrance is at the NE end in the earlier part, which has strong natural defences and therefore only one rampart, SE. When the fort was extended into a less well-defended part two ramparts were considered necessary. 'Vitrified' stones in the ditch near the W corner suggest that the rampart was strengthened by timber, subsequently burnt.

Several Bronze Age CAIRNS along the ridge to the W. The most interesting are the ring cairn and kerb circle at the N end (SH 993 410), close together on either side of the old track. The KERB CIRCLE, W, is a ring of contiguous boulders surrounding a low stone platform. On the SE side is a 'false portal', two stones projecting from the circle. Excavation in 1971 revealed that before the stone platform was laid there were two tall wooden pillars in the centre, at either end of a small rectangular platform, perhaps the setting for a grave. The smaller RING CAIRN was built around a projecting slab of rock. Opposite was a long narrow pit, filled with dark earth and quartz stones. The rectangular platform thus formed may also have been a grave. The ring is quite elaborate, with four concentric circles of boulders, many unfortunately removed. The site was occupied earlier; hearths and stake-holes were found, associated with a few pieces of Beaker pottery. To build the monuments, the site was 'tidied up' by covering it with a layer of clean clay.

GWERN BRAICHDWR, 1½ m. W, on the S side of Cwm Main. Dated 1611, with a tall ridge chimney and broad storeyed porch, it encases a late medieval cruck-framed hall with four pairs of crucks. Three-room lobby-entry plan, but also a rear parlour wing. Post-and-panel partitions in the hall – to one end and to the rear. C17 stable and barn, the latter with reused cruck blades.

RHYDYWERNEN, 3 m. W. Tiny INDEPENDENT CHAPEL, 1828, re-fitted in the late C19, charmingly simple without and within. Painted arched MEMORIAL to the Rev. John Griffith †1849. Opposite, RHYDYWERNEN, small late medieval cruck-framed hall, encased c. 1600, with inserted floor and chimney. The dais partition and hall truss with cusped apex survive.

GLYNDYFRDWY

1543

ST THOMAS. 1858–9, by T. H. Wyatt. Compact nave and chancel with plate tracery and a W bellcote. A spired NW tower was proposed. Inside, steep open roofs, the pulpit entered from the vestry. – STAINED GLASS. E window, Resurrection, 1895, in strong colours, by Mayer of Munich. – N second, the Risen Christ, 1924, by A. J. Davies, late Arts and Crafts in glowing colours, heavily worked. – N third, 1907, by J. A. Campbell & Co. of Dublin, slightly Pre-Raphaelite. – W, 1938, by Pearce & Cutler of Birmingham.

At the W end of the village, the BERWYN ARMS, three-storey Late Georgian, and SION WESLEYAN CHAPEL, 1903, roughcast with arched windows and a lunette. On the S, OWAIN GLYNDŴR MEMORIAL HALL, 1931, by Watling, Dickinson & Norman of Harrogate. Late Arts and Crafts with a Cotswolds feel, the steep roof carried low and a central gabled porch. Spoilt by attrition and addition. The r. bay carried a hipped dormer lighting a gallery. On the N, NEW INN FARM, with outbuildings against the road, the barn dated 1723. The pretty cruciform house, 1719, is whitewashed with painted voussoirs and central chimney behind a storeyed porch. Further E, the church (see above) and a disused BAPTIST CHAPEL, r., 1906, with a big pedimented frame to the doorway. Bare interior, a stretched temple front in timber behind the pulpit. Below, PRIMARY SCHOOL, 1914, by Deakin & Howard Jones; four gables with big arched windows; brick and terracotta. Detached teacher's house.

Down the lane to the Dee, a disused CALVINISTIC METHODIST CHAPEL, l., 1870, by Richard Owens, with Gothic triplet in sandstone, and, r., former SALEM INDEPENDENT CHAPEL, 1869, by S. Evans of Llandegla, red brick. The preserved STATION on the Llangollen–Corwen line, 1863, by S. Pountney Smith, has a gabled stone house and single-storey ticket office. Later timber SIGNAL BOX.

GLAS-Y-DŴR COTTAGE, 1½ m. NE, in a bend of the Dee. The cross-wing has heavy C16 box framing more typical of

East Wales. The long low hall range is rendered with a tall chimney serving both.

Y BWTHYN, 2 m. E. Early C19 toll house on the A5 road, with typical canted front.

SLATE QUARRIES. The DEESIDE SLAB QUARRY (SH 138 404), 1869, was linked by wooden-railed tramway to now-roofless SLAB WORKS (SH 148 417) and thence to the railway. Under the mountain ridge, derelict buildings and radiating spoil of the underground MOEL FFERNA MINE (SH 125 399), 1870s.

GWYDDELWERN

1647

ST BEUNO. In a large circular churchyard. Like Llandderfel, a Perp church related more to NE Wales than Merioneth. It was called new at the induction of the vicar Galfridus in 1538, which would fit the roofs, but some chancel windows are earlier. Segmental-pointed three-light nave windows, the lights simply cusped, and one small two-light N; also a blocked cyclopean N door. *Henry Kennedy* rebuilt the chancel with some accuracy in 1880, reusing two C14 Y-tracery windows and the narrow S priest's door, and renewing the broad Perp five-light E window. Unfortunately he added the SW tower covered in redundant tracery, with an alien spire. Broad arch-braced collar-truss nave roof with two tiers of short cusped wind-braces, carved central bosses and cusped apex struts. Inserted chancel arch; repaired two-bay chancel roof with wind-braces and celure with pierced quatrefoil bands. – FONT. C15. Octagonal bowl and stem together. – SCREEN, 1880, with C15 pieces in the dado; some pinnacles are attached to the PULPIT. – REREDOS, with C17 reliefs of funny birds and dragons; perhaps, like panels by the S door, from the Kyffin pew. Another panel is dated 1705. – STAINED GLASS. Chancel N, re-assembled glass of *c.* 1500, with two saints' heads. Nave N, *c.* 1915, probably by *Lavers & Westlake*. – MONUMENT. William Humffreys †1718 and his wife †1744, with arms and a cherub head.

In the churchyard, C18 headstones. TABLE TOMB, S of chancel, on four carved slabs, *c.* 1745, with rustic religious imagery. At the gateway, the former CHURCH SCHOOL, *c.* 1806.

MORIAH CALVINISTIC METHODIST CHAPEL. 1873 and later, by *James Hughes* of Denbigh. An unusual if clumsy T-plan in red brick, the front gable rendered. The rear cross-range has polygonal ends and wooden Gothic tracery.

WESLEYAN CHAPEL. 1870, by *Richard Owens*. Lombard style, like Carrog and Llandderfel, in dark rubble with grey limestone.

BOARD SCHOOL. 1873, by *Owens*. Red and yellow brick, Gothic.

ROSE AND CROWN INN (formerly Tŷ Mawr). The finest timber frame in old Merioneth, ring-dated 1572, extended to the N. The long façade has attractive lozenge-braced framing above a stone ground floor. The frame posts rise from ground level within, however, the restoration revealed no joints in the posts so the stone may be original. Re-created oak diamond-mullion windows. Fireplace probably inserted in the cross-passage or next to it. A service room was probably s of the passage, and a pair of long 'inner' rooms N of the hall, behind a post-and-panel partition, their dividing partition now lost. (Remains of a rare pre-glazing window with shutter grooves.)

HARLECH   *5832*

The castle high above the coastal plain is an unforgettable image of the Edwardian conquest. The little town behind grew beneath the walls, like Aberystwyth and Bala as a settlement within an older parish, here that of Llandanwg.

HARLECH CASTLE

The most compact and arguably the most visually pleasing of Edward I's Welsh castles. It stands on a rocky promontory that may have been lapped by the sea, which was certainly close enough for supply by water. The high inner walls were surrounded by a thin outer curtain, which gives Harlech its concentric plan, with the base of the rock also enclosed on the W and N by a thin wall with gates. Begun in April 1283 after the southern approaches to North Wales had been made safe with the capture of Castell y Bere. Overseen by the Savoyard *Master James of St George*, the construction here has the closest connection with Savoy, both in details, such as windows, and in actual workforce, various Savoyard names being recorded.

p. 33

25

The cost from 1283 to 1290, when the core was all but complete, can be estimated at around £9,500. Most of the castle is of local Harlech Grit, with freestone from Egryn, and slate to some extent in features such as arches. Metalwork was shipped from Chester. In June 1283 masons and quarriers were sent from Conwy, with carpenters and more masons following soon after. By summer 1286 the workforce peaked with 546 labourers, 227 masons and 115 quarriers, as well as carpenters and smiths. From autumn 1286 to November 1287 the total costs were almost equal to those at Caernarfon and Conwy.

Masonry evidence indicates clear phases. The earliest is represented by the first 15 ft (4.5 metres) of the curtain wall of the Inner Ward and the NE and SE towers, probably built in the opening season. A clear horizontal line indicates the later heightening; also parts of the curtain were not built at first to the planned thickness. A start must have been made on the gatehouse in 1284–5, as by the end of 1285 the masons had completed some rooms there. At about this time the much thinner outer curtain was begun. Accounts for 1289 show that the NW and SW turreted towers had been added, *William of Drogheda* coming over from Ireland specifically for this work, and that the curtain walls had

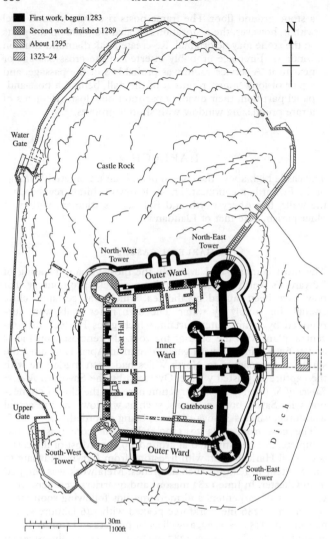

First work, begun 1283
Second work, finished 1289
About 1295
1323–24

N

Water Gate

Castle Rock

North-East Tower

North-West Tower

Outer Ward

Great Hall

Inner Ward

Upper Gate

Gatehouse

Ditch

South-West Tower

Outer Ward

South-East Tower

30m
100ft

Harlech Castle.
Plan

been raised and thickened, with internal buildings ranged around the Inner Ward, against the curtain. The two mural towers on the E side would also have been raised to full height. *William the Plumber* was paid for lead roofs on the gatehouse and the two w towers. Within the Inner Ward, the walls of hall, chapel, pantry and kitchen were built, with freestone for the windows, and the buildings were lead-roofed, again by William the Plumber. Two men were paid for dressing 171 corbels for the gatehouse turrets and the two seaward towers. At some stage the castle was rendered and limewashed, and much of this survived into the C19, as shown in artists' views.

The sea came much closer, with perhaps a channel to the base of the rock. To secure this area, a thin curtain wall was constructed from the SW corner of the Outer Ward round to a water gate; this 'way from the sea' included the Upper Gate. The N section of the wall around the rock, from the water gate round to the outer curtain at the NE point, was added *c.* 1295, after the scare of the 1294 Madog ap Llywelyn uprising, when Harlech had been cut off by land. Finally in 1323–4 the main approach was re-fortified with the addition of two small rectangular towers rising from the ditch, with a bridge connecting the two. A draw- or turning-bridge crossed to the first tower, with another between the second tower and the outer gate.

The most dramatic period was in the Owain Glyndŵr uprising. Reduced by disease, the garrison surrendered in 1404, and the castle became Owain's headquarters, and one of the two places where a parliament was held, with Machynlleth. The forces of Prince Henry, the future Henry V, under Gilbert Talbot, retook the castle in 1409, capturing Owain's wife and family. A massive cannon was probably responsible for the destruction of much of the outer curtain. Later, Harlech was the last Lancastrian fortress in Wales, falling to a Yorkist army in 1468.

C16 surveys, notably in 1564, stress decay and ruin: roofs gone, internal buildings uninhabitable, drawbridges replaced by planking. The gatehouse, however, was maintained as the location of the County Assizes. Harlech's final great siege came in the Civil War, when the last Royalist garrison to hold out surrendered in 1647. Only partly slighted, Harlech remained much as we see it today, conservation and some restoration beginning soon after the First World War.

The Gatehouse

A modern wooden bridge leads over the remains of the two p. 611 towers built in 1323–4, which originally had a central solid bridge and drawbridges at either end, and so through the OUTER GATE. This consists of two solid rounded turrets corbelled out from the curtain, the gate having lost its battlements. At this point, towering ahead stands one of the best examples of a medieval gatehouse at any castle. The GATEHOUSE, 24 fronted by twin, rounded towers, has three storeys. The battlements are virtually gone, although above the chamfered string course are remnants, one arrowslit surviving and bases of others. Narrow rectangular lights provide some illumination for the front ground-floor chambers, whilst larger rectangular windows light the upper floors; holes indicating metal grilles. Finer lancet windows over the passage between the towers, one above the other and each above a string course, are the E windows of two small chapels. On either side of both are narrow slits that run obliquely through the wall, lighting a small chamber on either side of each chapel, perhaps a vestry and a sacristy. Evidence for the use of Savoyard-style helicoidal scaffolding, as at Beaumaris and Conwy, is seen in the s tower, the putlogs spiralling up between the windows of the upper floors.

Two-leaved doors and portcullises secured the GATE PASSAGE, with an arrowslit overlooking from both towers; when raised, the two outer portcullises resided in the first-floor chapel. The first door, against the outer arch and secured by drawbar, opened outwards, from the way the towers are shaped to receive the curving door-tops. Beyond are the grooves for the first portcullis, then an arrowslit on each side. The site of the second portcullis next, then the second door, again with a drawbar socket. Towards the end, a doorway to a guard chamber or porters' room on each side. At the entrance to the Inner Ward are grooves of a third portcullis; and a socket or hole in the roof of the window seat on the floor above may have been for its pulley rope. If there was a third door here, all evidence has been lost. The floorboards of the main first-floor chamber could be lifted to create murder holes.

The rectangular GUARD CHAMBER, s, is plain with a slit window in the w wall, but lacking a fireplace; remains of a cross wall that separated it from the D-shaped interior of the round tower. In the sw corner is the doorway with drawbar socket to the turret housing the restored newel staircase. The equivalent CHAMBER on the N has in addition a corner fireplace and a slit window in the N and w walls. Thus this chamber could have been for the porter.

The UPPER ROOMS can be glimpsed from the stair-turrets and from the viewing platform on the w side, but looking up from the ground floor gives the best idea of their neat arrangements. The first- and second-floor rooms virtually mirror one another; it may be that originally the first served the constable and his family, whilst the more private upper floor was reserved for the king and queen, or visiting dignitaries. The w, rectangular, rooms may have been living rooms, with bedrooms in the gatehouse towers.

There were two rectangular rooms on each floor on the inner side. The ones to the s were larger, with two fine windows with seats in the w wall and one in the s wall; the N chamber on each floor has a single window in the N and w walls. These principal rooms and the small rooms to the N all had a hooded fireplace in the E wall. The main or great chamber on the first floor was entered through a round-headed doorway from the external staircase and platform built slightly later against the w wall of the gatehouse, the lowest string course on this side running over this doorway. Four other doorways in this room: to the adjacent chamber, N; to the chapel; to two latrines within the wall thickness (one at the end of a lit passage), and also to the chamber in the front of the gate; the fourth, secured by drawbar, to the stair-turret. The smaller chambers had doorways to the N stair-turret, each again with

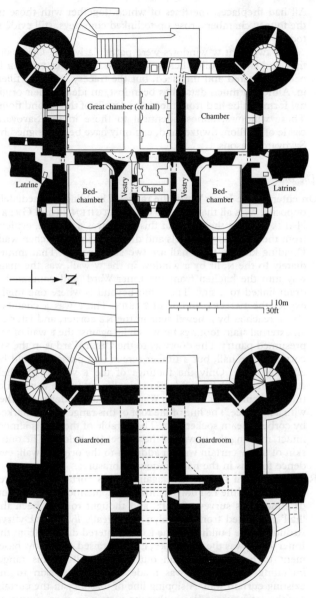

Harlech Castle, Gatehouse.
Plan

a drawbar, and there was also a doorway at both levels to the front chamber and also to a latrine. The wall-walk could also be reached from the second floor. The four rooms at the front of the gatehouse, two on each floor, each had two windows.

All had fireplaces, the flues of which, together with those in the four w chambers, rose up to linked chimneys, still evident today.

The two-light w windows were particularly fine. Originally they had twin-trefoiled heads with glass, the lower two-thirds being shuttered and unglazed, but the tracery was later filled in. Although much detail has been lost, an idea of their original form can be had from the N and S walls of the second floor. These windows, almost identical to those in the Savoyard castle of Chillon, Switzerland, can only have been designed by Savoyard masons.

The Inner Ward

On entering the Inner Ward, the range of buildings immediately opposite, w, is all that remains of the KITCHEN, l., and GREAT HALL, r. Along the E wall of this range was a pentise, evident from the three large corbels and dripstone in the kitchen wall. Dividing kitchen from hall are two small rooms. That immediately to the N, lit by a window in the w wall, was the main way into the kitchen from the Inner Ward, and contained a drain linked to a sink. The room beyond is where one might expect the PANTRY and/or BUTTERY. There was a chamber above reached by a newel stair in the NE corner, and later by an external stair, footings for which lie against the E wall of the presumed pantry. The doorway to the Outer Ward is in the SW corner of the hall, but a timber screen and passage would be expected here. Only the footings of the E wall of the hall survive, having three windows originally, but in the w wall, i.e. the outer curtain of the Inner Ward, are four windows, together with a fireplace. The line of the roof of this range is well marked by corbels, beam sockets, etc. The N gable of the hall is almost intact, meeting the w wall of the chapel (see below). The outer skin of the w curtain was an addition to the original wall; evidence for this in the hall window embrasures.

Running E from the kitchen, against the S curtain, is the presumed site of the YSTUMGWERN HALL, mentioned in William de Emeldon's survey of 1343, and thought to have been the 'hall' re-erected from Llywelyn the Great's llys near Dyffryn Ardudwy. The building to the E of it, entered directly from the Inner Ward, was the GRANARY, its floor raised over a low basement to help keep vermin out. The S wall of this range, including the kitchen, was made by adding a skin to the existing curtain wall. A sloping line of masonry in the curtain S of the gatehouse indicates that the curtain was not completed to the width originally envisaged.

The N range consists of the CHAPEL to the w and a building to its E that housed various services, including a bakehouse with its oven and a well; between the buildings is a doorway and passage into the Outer Ward. The chapel's walls still stand save on the S, with remains of the moulded jambs of the doorway in the SW corner. Beam sockets, corbels, a string course and the plastering line define the chapel's arched ceiling and the pent roof above it. A lancet window in the E wall. Three windows towards the Outer Ward lit the bakehouse range, which also had a pent roof.

The four CORNER TOWERS lack their floors. The NE and SE towers have seven-sided main rooms, over circular basements or dungeons, whilst those on the W are all pentagonal; the chambers in the North-East Tower are slightly larger than those in the SE one. Thus the interiors are comparable to those at Caernarfon. The NORTH-EAST TOWER is entered off the Inner Ward, a restored newel stair leading up to the first-floor chamber. This room must have contained a trap door, the only way that the basement could have been reached, a room with only a narrow slit sloping down from the NE side for light and ventilation. The first-floor chamber, and that above, each had a hooded fireplace; two barred and shuttered windows in the lower room, just one on the upper. Just outside the first-floor doorway a short passage leads to a latrine; another, small, latrine (or urinal) is at the top of the mural stair, just before the wall-walk. This stair runs up from the N reveal of the NE window in the first-floor chamber. The wall-walk running S from the North-East Tower leads to a doorway into the Gatehouse, with a second doorway close by that gave access to a latrine. The SOUTH-EAST TOWER is generally similar, but part way up the mural stair from the Inner Ward a second stair leads off to connect with the wall-walk on the S curtain wall, the main stair continuing to the first-floor chamber. Also, the stair leading up from the reveal of the SW window of this chamber passes a latrine. The second-floor chamber is somewhat larger than that below, but has a smaller fireplace. From the one window, a mural stair leads up past yet another latrine to the battlements.

The SOUTH-WEST and NORTH-WEST TOWERS differ from those either side of the Gatehouse in that they are four-storeyed, have turrets, and have pentagonal chambers. It was not possible to access the wall-walk from them, an unusual arrangement from a defensive point of view. The newel stair-cases to the upper floors and battlements have not been renewed, and with no floors the internal arrangements are not so easy to visualize. The South-West Tower is entered from the kitchen, the North-West Tower through a small courtyard created by the walls of the Great Hall and the chapel. Above the basements of both were two floors with fireplaces, with an upper storey with a single window and no fireplace. Most of the windows face seaward; the only chamber with two windows was on the first floor. At this level a passage led from the lobby outside the chamber doorway to a latrine; further down the stair another passage led to a lower latrine. The stump of one floor joist in the South-West Tower can still be seen within its socket. A section of crenellation with arrowslits survives above the string course on the SW side of the North-West Tower.

Little remains of the battlements at WALL-WALK level, and much
of what survives was raised for safety reasons in the C20.
A feature now lost is the look-out turret (*garrita*), a short
section of battlement built out from the W curtain in 1289 to
defend the doorway below the Outer Ward into the screens
passage. From surviving evidence, such a defence was used
around the inner curtain of Rhuddlan Castle, Flintshire
(1277–82).

The Outer Ward and Perimeter Defences

Most of the upper walling of the OUTER WARD has been lost,
although a section remains on either side of the outer gate,
and the bases of a number of arrowslits are still evident.
The horizontal break in the masonry of the curtain wall, the
result of a slight pause in construction, can best be seen from
the outer ward on both S and N sides. Other features to note
are the latrine chutes contained in the lee of the mural and
gatehouse towers. In the middle of the outer wall on the S is a
corbelled latrine turret, of Savoyard type, and beyond it, to the
W, a thin wall with a doorway cutting off the Outer Ward at
this point. The rock-cut ditch is best seen on this side and
round to the gatehouse. On the N side a small twin-towered
gatehouse controls access to the rock. E of it, in front of the
North-East Tower, a flight of steps leads down along the
curtain wall, built from this point round to the Water Gate
c. 1295, to a postern.

The 'way from the sea' led up to the Outer Ward from the WATER
GATE. Only part of this gate survives, although the drawbridge
pit can be seen. The steps led up to the UPPER GATE, where a
wooden ramp now occupies the space once covered by a drawbridge, and so on up, past a turret and some steps down to the
S ditch, into the Outer Ward. The seaward side of the castle
was probably protected by artillery, for on the rock below the
Outer Ward and over the 'way from the sea' are two rectangular
platforms on which small stone-throwing engines may have
been positioned, a function mentioned in the 1564 survey.
An alternative interpretation is that the platforms were to
support cranes to lift supplies and building materials.

THE TOWN

The characterful small TOWN, made a free borough by Edward
I in 1284,* was the county town before Dolgellau, but Fenton
found it 'the most forlorn, beggarly place imaginable'. Samuel
Holland, Blaenau Ffestiniog quarry-owner, developed it for
tourism from the 1860s and by the turn of the C20 it was a seaside
and golfing resort attracting an unusually artistic patronage.

---

*Harlech is named much earlier, in the Mabinogion, as the court of Harddlech to
which King Matholwch of Ireland came to ask for Branwen's hand.

ST TANWG, High Street. 1841, by *Thomas Jones* of Chester, replacing the church at Llandanwg (Llanfair). Pre-Ecclesiological Gothic in squared dark granite with large yellow sandstone lancets, a group of three at the W. The small chancel is added. A spacious interior with W gallery, the walls mostly stripped. – FONT. C15. Sandstone, octagonal, with blind tracery and quatrefoils; from the old church. – STAINED GLASS. S window, the Good Shepherd, 1965, by *Celtic Studios*.

S of the castle, a grim bronze SCULPTURE of the giant Bendigeidfran on horseback bearing the body of his nephew, 1984, by *Ivor Roberts-Jones*. The big twin-gabled CASTLE HOTEL, established 1876, is typical of Samuel Holland's buildings, with arched first-floor and attic windows, as also the arched TOILETS with drinking fountain opposite. In Ffordd Penllech, GWEITHDY SAER, set back, is late C17 or early C18, L-plan, with a beautifully laced slate roof-valley. Further down, TŶ'R FELIN, a C17 mill house, has a tall end chimney and a small raking dormer. From the cross-roads at the top of Twtil, the HIGH STREET leads SW past the R.C. CHURCH, formerly Seion chapel, 1872, by *O. Morris Roberts*, altered 1885. Around a cobbled courtyard, whitewashed stables of the former Blue Lion Inn, now the PLAS, built *c*. 1830 by Sir R.W. Vaughan of Nannau. Three-storey whitened rubble street front, but a better-built rear in squared stone with wide sashes and enclosed early C20 veranda. The SPAR shop, l., is two-storey of similar date. Down steps r., the HARLECH POTTERY, late C18, of squared rubble with sash windows. The street bends l. past the church (*see* above), the former TABERNACL BAPTIST CHAPEL, 1897, a winged façade with pedimented centre, and the INSTITUTE, 1908, possibly by *O. Morris Roberts & Son*, in rock-faced stone with shouldered gables.

CROWN LODGE, Ffordd Isaf. 1903, for W. H. More, Crown Receiver for Wales, the Crown emblem above the entrance. Slightly baronial in sombre stone with shouldered and kneelered gables awkwardly combined with small-paned sash windows. Older rear wing.

CAE BESI, at the junction of Ffordd Isaf and Ffordd Newydd. 1931, by *Griffith Morris* for Alvin Langdon Coburn, the American photographer. Interestingly detailed villa in rock-faced stone. Twin-hipped double dormer, and a recessed pair of upper windows like those on the Caernarvonshire 'open-air' schools. At the S end, a segmental-arched triple window onto a bedroom balcony.

COLEG HARLECH. Established in 1927 by Dr Thomas Jones, Cabinet Secretary to Lloyd George, as a residential college for adults, fortunate in being able to start with a bold building. PLAS WERN FAWR, a severe and idiosyncratically classical house of 1908, was built for George Davison, free-thinking director of Kodak in Europe, who had been attracted to Harlech as a school friend of W. H. More of Crown Lodge (*see* above). Davison had already employed his extremely radical architect, *George Walton* of Glasgow, to design exhibitions and shops. The dark rock-faced stone gives a Baronial flavour to the Georgian symmetry of a deep square plan, with pedimented faces E and W, and gables N and S carrying chimneys. The pediments are enormous, covering almost the full nine bays, and as tall as the gables. Minimal detail: sash windows with thick bars, the lower ones taller, roundels in the pediments. A semicircular W bay is asymmetrically placed. Walton's interiors are much altered: marble-paved hall, open-well stair with turned balusters in a stairwell with barrel vaults lit by roundels. On the N a single-storey arch-windowed library addition, 1910, formerly linked to the extraordinary Great Hall by *Walton*, burnt in 1968 and replaced by Theatr Harlech (*see* below). It was one of the outstanding interiors of its age, a lofty music room with massive stone arches at the groin-vaulted crossing, where Davison's 'Orchestrelle' organ dominated. Organ and fireplace showed Walton moving towards a pre-Art Deco geometrical aesthetic. Outside it was gauntly impressive, cruciform with gridded windows set high and each gable clasped by tall chimneys.

THEATR HARLECH, 1973, by *Colwyn Foulkes & Partners*, is unaccommodatingly different. In Brutalist brittle crustaceous materials, on legs spread crab-like around the body. The part-circular, part-hexagonal auditorium is clad in copper sheet, its underbelly and exposed staircases of fair-faced concrete, with meeting rooms sheltering beneath. Circular foyer, with terrazzo floor and a mushroom-like ceiling of radiating plywood. Attached on the other side is the college LIBRARY, by *Griffith Morris*, 1938, grandly scaled, American minimal classical, the windows in tall strips and a full-height apse at the S end. Shallow barrel vault and galleries on four sides. S of the house is the twelve-storey HALL OF RESIDENCE, 1968, by *Colwyn Foulkes & Partners*. Fortunately the scale is much diminished by the high cliff immediately behind, the entrance bridge being at mid-height. Precast concrete panels incorporating local stone, and horizontal windows in cast frames.

The GARDENS were laid out for Davison, the walls negotiating the difficult terrain like the outer walls of the castle and with a bridge over the road (rebuilt after road widening). The entrance arch has a pair of lovely wrought-iron gates with close-spaced verticals and Davison's initials. On the parapet, similar balustrades and two big copper lamps.

ST DAVID'S HOTEL. S of Coleg Harlech. 1908–11, by *George Walton*. A large hotel for golfers built by a syndicate in which George Davison (*see* p. 615) was involved, but altered and (2008) closed. The scale, five storeys and basement, was originally disguised by having the upper three in a giant mansard with rows of dormers. Rebuilt hurriedly after a fire in 1922 by *Griffith Morris*, the three-bay stone centre is now flanked by two storeys of stone, two of roughcast and the attic only mansarded. The centre too is altered on the top two floors and has a ground-floor addition.

TŶ CRWN, ½ m. NE. Circular summerhouse, *c.* 1922, with a conical roof, once thatched, and central chimney. Extended with curved hipped dormers by *Gruffydd Price, c.* 2001.

LASYNYS FAWR, 1½ m. NE. Late C16 irregular T-plan house, sheltered by a rocky knoll. Two storeys and attic, the main rooms unusually at first floor, reached from the NE, and service rooms below. Drastically remodelled in the early C18 with a large two-storey SE wing, and the platform extended NE as a long revetted garden terrace, for the Rev. Ellis Wynne †1734, author of the popular *Gweledigaethau y Bardd Cwsc (Visions of the Sleeping Bard)*, 1703. In the first-floor parlour, dentil cornice, large-field panelling and fluted pilasters to fireplace and doorways. Also, panelled window seats and an enclosed arched alcove with painted angels in the spandrels. In the main bedroom, a hinged truckle bed in an early C18 cupboard, and some small-field oak panelling. Raised cruck-trusses. Restored in the 1990s with considerable licence by the Project Office of the *Welsh School of Architecture* under *John Roberts*. Single-storey C19 BREWHOUSE, NE, extended.

MOEL GOEDOG, 2 m. ENE (SH 614 325). On the summit, a small later prehistoric HILL-FORT with relatively slight bivallate defences. Simple entrance on the SW side, just a narrow gap in the banks where a fold in the rock provides a natural path. The fort is divided into three parts by modern walls. The visitor approaching from the Bronze Age circles (cf. Llanfair, p. 645) and track below comes into the SW corner, but the circuit of defences can be best appreciated in the N half. Like Castell Odo, Aberdaron (C), in its small size and coastal position; here too there may have been palisades on the low banks.

On the S slopes, at the head of a sheltered valley, remains of HUTS and some terraced FIELDS of Romano-British and perhaps medieval date. The most easily recognized group is an enclosed HOMESTEAD (SH 616 322). Cut into the bottom of the slope are four round huts (or rooms) and a large rectangular building set around a courtyard with an entrance on the S. Attached to the SW corner is a small paddock. To the W is Erw Wen, an Iron Age SETTLEMENT (SH 606 323). The initial phases of the large central house were in wood, later replaced by the still visible stone-walled round-house. It is enclosed in a stone-walled circular yard. Cut into the slope, it provided a convenient site for a later settlement of three medieval houses.

LLANABER

6018

ST BODFAN AND ST MARY. On a windswept headland, in a crowded graveyard overlooking the sea. Little discloses the architectural gem inside. Externally Victorian from the 1858–9 restoration by the antiquarian W. W. E. Wynne of Peniarth, with *Philip Boyce* of Cheltenham. It may be that the little double-square chancel, so intimate in proportion and movingly stepped up the hill, is in plan the C6 or C7 cell of St Bodfan. Its high-quality early C13 rebuilding, the finest E.E. work in the region outside the monasteries, may have been for Llywelyn the Great.

Aisled nave with clerestory and lower chancel; C19 bellcote, S porch and NE vestry. There was a C17 porch with bellcote, like Llangelynin, and a large C17 or C18 NE addition. Dressings in Egryn sandstone. Chamfered lancets: reused in the rebuilt W gable, new in the chancel, but the late C13 S two-light with cusped heads was found in 1859. Original three-rolled rere-arch to the E window.

The nave floor is lower and off-axis with the CHANCEL, into which it opens through a noble pointed chancel arch with responds of one large half-column and four smaller ones, all with fillets. The arch itself has an inner chamfered step and two filleted rolls. The three-step capitals, of square section with square abaci, are carved with crossed stems and drooping leaf-heads, with a scalloped motif above.

This integration of Romanesque and E.E. is the style also of the NAVE, a tremendously solemn effect to have achieved within such small dimensions. It has five-bay arcades of ochre and greenish Egryn stone. The piers are round with splayed bases, the arches pointed with filleted outer rolls and plain inner chamfers. The capitals are consistent to a basic square section with the angles cut off, on piers and responds alike, except on the E where the capitals and responds themselves are two-step and chamfered. At the W end the responds follow the section of the capitals. So the earlier E end gives way to a no less monumental C13 fluency for the body of the nave. As for the decoration of the capitals, there are five different patterns, all basically of a single tier or garland of Transitional foliage in low relief. The most frequent type is of downward-turned fleur-de-lys, still rigidly conceived except on one S pier where the leaves hang down realistically. One N capital and the SE respond have shallow upturned leaf forms; the W responds have diamond-shaped leaves and those of the NE pier are similar but more deeply serrated. The NE respond has a frieze of upright acanthus leaves.

The splendid SOUTH DOOR is stylistically the latest part. Of no fewer than four orders of three shafts each, the middle shaft filleted and of strong projection. The capitals are treated as an undulating band of down-turned fleur-de-lys, sprouting leaf forms on top, a wholly E.E. treatment.

The lofty nave ROOF has tie-beams with curved struts and collars alternating with arch-braced collar-trusses. Two tiers of plain wind-braces. The earlier chancel roof has arch-braced principals with cusped apex strutting and two tiers of cusped wind-braces. Over the sanctuary a panelled celure, divided by three longitudinal bands of geometrical ornament, and with brattished wall-plates, similar to Llanddwywe, Talybont.

FONT. C14 Perp, octagonal. Uniquely in the county, each
face carved: a gargoyle face, a plant design, a rose, and quatrefoils, and shields in underside panels. – REREDOS. Arts and
Crafts, c. 1911, by *John Batten*, carved by *Mary Batten* and
others. A twisting central vine spreads over wheat-sheafs each
side. – SCREEN. Reconstructed from the medieval one, much
lower. – PEWS. 1890s, by *Douglas & Fordham*, from St John's,
Barmouth. – STAINED GLASS. Small and intimate pieces in
most windows, in a simple Gothic style, 1859. – MONUMENTS.
Rev. Robert Morgan †1811. A female figure – clasping an urn
on a diagonally placed tomb. By *S. & F. Franceys*. John Carson
†1877. Marble relief with female figure and anchor. –
INSCRIBED STONES, N aisle W. Two late C5 or early C6 pillars
with horizontal inscriptions in capitals, one to Aeturnus and
Aeturna, the other inscribed 'CALEXTI MONEDO RIGI'.
LLWYNDU, ¼ m. N. Late C16, ring-dated to 1592. Snowdonia
end-chimney house, with mural staircases both ends. Painted
render; three wide-spaced bays with tall chimneys, the r. one
with a fine moulded cap. Small square sashes upstairs, and a
tiny oak window, l., with a diamond mullion lights a closet.
Joists scribed to the sides as well as beneath. The outbuilding
with a tall chimney may be a contemporary dower house, the
stepped fireplace added later. WATER MILL, E, dated 1883.
PLAS CANOL, ¾ m. N. The Late Georgian three-storey, three-
bay front is the result of additions to a C16 downhill-sited
house perhaps built by Robert ap Morgan, former chaplain to
Henry VIII, rector in 1561. The lower end was replaced in the
early C18 with a two-storey range at right angles, a dog-leg stair
inserted in the original house. In the early C19 the eaves were
raised for the attic windows and later again first-floor oriels
were added.
    Refined but puzzling internal detailing. Two of the three
extant bays of the medieval house have an inserted ceiling with
massive moulded primary and secondary beams and counter-
changed joists forming four square sub-bays (one removed for
the early C18 staircase). This arrangement suggests one room
of some grandeur, yet a C17 post-and-panel partition with a
cusped doorhead divides the room centrally. Could it be re-set
from the E beam, which is grooved for a partition? The E
fireplace and bressumer look later than C16 and there is no
internal hint of the SE mural stair suggested by a blocked
window. In the attic, a fine cusped arch-braced truss and a
plainer E truss, suggesting a hall-like upper room. In the front
range, the SW room is panelled in large fields, with an earlier
C18 arched alcove and a late C18 chimneypiece; a moulded
plaster arch upstairs between front and rear. A former DOWER
HOUSE, E, is probably C17, one-and-a-half storeys, with a tall
S chimney.
TREMORA, ¼ m. N. Edwardian seaside villa, hipped, with ogee-
domed octagonal corner towers and centre loggia and balcony.
Panelled stair hall with twisted stair balusters and fluted
column newels.

LLANBEDR

The mild climate, the spectacular scenery of the Artro valley and Cwm Nantcol, and the railway encouraged later C19 and early C20 holiday and retirement houses.

St Peter. In a partly curvilinear, raised churchyard. Once a chapelry of Llandanwg. Nave and chancel with w bellcote. Mentioned in the C13, probably rebuilt C15–C16 but externally mostly of 1883 by *F. R. Wilson* of Alnwick. The interior, scraped of plaster, has unusually a chancel arch, of rough stone, probably post-medieval. Some reused C15 roof timbers. – FONT. Plain, octagonal, possibly post-medieval. – AUMBRY. Inlaid door with arms, inscribed SPES FALLACISSIMA RERUM. C18? – STAINED GLASS. E window, 1883. Crowded Passion scenes, Dürer style; similar s window. – INCISED STONE. A granite boulder spirally incised, found above Dyffryn Ardudwy, perhaps Neolithic. – Outside, an elongated pyramid MEMORIAL of polished slate, to Sir John Black †1965. – C18 LYCHGATE.

MORIAH CALVINISTIC METHODIST CHAPEL. 1913, by *O. Morris Roberts & Son*. Exuberant Edwardian Free Style, in honey-coloured terracotta. Hexagonal piers capped by little columned cupolas frame a scrolled gable with a roundel enveloped in scrolls and pediment. Coved ceiling bordered in timber. Tudor-style *sêt-fawr* and pulpit; arch behind.

SALEM BAPTIST CHAPEL, 1¼ m. E. In a lovely setting on a wooded hillside, over a sloping graveyard. Built 1850, by voluntary labour, extended *c.* 1860. Chapel, with house slightly set back, under one roof. Rubble; sash windows. Box pews at front, benches elsewhere, on a raking floor at the rear. Central raised pulpit with panelled sides. Continuous hook rail. The interior is depicted in S. C. Vosper's much-reproduced painting of 1908.

In the village, the mid-C19 BRIDGE over the Artro has a 1642 datestone with hammer and trowel in relief. Two- and three-storey C19 stone terraces with gables and bargeboards on the main road. Early C20 SCHOOL, typical of *Deakin & Howard Jones*, with big arched windows in red terracotta.

HAFOD-Y-BRYN, ½ m. S. Stone villa of *c.* 1870 for Samuel Pope Q.C., of Manchester. Bargeboarded gables to wings and centre, and timber oriels. Overlights painted with tiny comic animals. Beatrix Potter was here when her fiancé Norman Warne died in 1905. U-plan stable block, SW, with a clock turret. Across the main road, PLAS-Y-BRYN, half-timbered, was built on the tennis court, 1903, by *Rowland Lloyd Jones*. The HOME FARM, SW at Talwrn Fawr, *c.* 1870, has low buildings around a delightful octagonal DAIRY with veranda and louvred ventilator. Hay barn to the w.

TALTREUDDYN-FAWR, ¾ m. S. Late C16 N front, of four bays, offset, with voussoired door and tall end chimneys. Winding stair by the main fireplace. A fine post-and-panel partition with double-ogee doorheads survives re-set upstairs. A small two-light oak window at the sw corner is hidden behind a secondary stair. The E staircase must be later: stone, square and regular, with a good Jacobean balustrade with gate at the top. Early C17 rear wing with lateral W and s end chimneys, containing a square parlour with chamfered beams and counterchanging joists. In the SE angle, a last addition dated 1680 on panelling, with E chimney. Three-sided courtyard of FARM BUILDINGS to the N: barn with two rows of vents, perhaps C17, and early C19 hay barn, stables and cartshed.

CRAIG ARTRO, ½ m. ESE. 1939, by *Griffith Morris*. Rugged stone cottage, the upper floor in the roof; the deep eaves on exaggerated stepped corbels and an elongated catslide dormer with similar corbelling. The main house steps forward of small wings but all are nicely under one cascading roof behind.

ABERARTRO HALL, 1 m. E. 1907–12, by *C. E. Bateman* of Birmingham, for the Gamwell family, with South African diamond wealth. In splendid gardens above the confluence of the Artro and Nantcol rivers. Arts and Crafts house in dark rock-faced granite with leaded mullioned windows, flush and free of mouldings, Voysey-style, as also the flat dormers. The house faces sw with a NE entrance court. Built in two phases, as the former house of *c.* 1874 was kept at the NW end until replaced soon after 1910, with twin gables becoming the dominant accent of the whole front.

The approach is through an archway in the cranked L-plan stable and garage range. The porch-tower, l., has ashlar detail: in the deep corbelled parapet a balustraded panel above a pretty oriel, and that over an arched doorway, the detail C17 rustic classical. Glazed lobby screen with re-set *Morris & Co.* glass. To the l., a long line of service rooms to the courtyard, and kitchens etc. to the garden. To r. the hall, or 'sitting hall' is three-quarter panelled, with a broad Tudor arch to a deep inglenook and an enclosed panelled flight of stairs rising gently to a balustraded landing with square posts to the ceiling. Drawing and dining rooms to the garden side of the hall, a games room behind the ingle. In the terraced garden, the sw garden building reuses latticed windows from the C19 house.

PENTRE GWYNFRYN, ½ m. E. A pretty hamlet with front vegetable gardens sloping down to the lane and river. Two small chapels: GWYNFRYN CALVINISTIC METHODIST, 1861, rubble, with two sandstone arched windows and outer doors; and BESER WESLEYAN, 1890, with a basement below. The settlement, which included a woollen factory, was largely built by the Griffiths family in the early to mid C19.

PLAS GWYNFRYN, Pentre Gwynfryn. Another large Edwardian house, like Aberartro, in the Cotswold style, the architect unknown. Built *c.* 1910 for J. Henry Griffiths, Birmingham jeweller. Rock-faced dark granite with sandstone flush mullioned windows and Voysey-like steep slate roofs shot out on curved iron brackets. Two storeys, to an elongated courtyard plan, the entrance front with a gable, l., and a recessed cambered doorway. The garden front is more animated, the main roof sweeping down in a hipped catslide over a deep veranda on stout timber posts, between a gable to the r. and an asymmetrical pair to the l. The staircase is expressed as a gable behind the l. end chimney. Oak-panelled hall; drawing room with panelled plaster ceiling and inglenook with windows. Oak balustraded staircase with a window seat at the half-landing.

The GARDENS were laid out by Griffiths around rock outcrops before he built the house. Greenhouses, w, and walled garden, E, added *c*. 1922 for Sir Charles Phibbs, who began the incomplete MODEL FARM, by *Quick & Lee* of Leamington Spa, 1923.

PENRALLT HALL, ½ m. NE. 1865, for John Humphreys Jones, Caernarfon lawyer, perhaps by *Henry Kennedy*. Garden front recessed between gabled cross-wings, the side of the SE one having the entrance. Greenish squared stone with dressings in pale ashlar. Crowded detail: Caernarfon-arched lights, on the front all mullion-and-transom, the lower ones with blind trefoils above each light. The entrance side is calmer. Open-well stair with alternate twisted and ball-turned balusters. Single-storey FARM COURT with hipped ends and a storeyed gabled gatehouse. Simplified Caernarfon arches, of rubble.

DOLGWYNFRYN, Pentre Gwynfryn. 1995, by *Gruffydd Price* of Llanbedr. Inspired by 1930s houses by the German Organic architects Scharoun and Häring. Two storeys, with a single-storey w wing angled as a suntrap, its roof continued along the main house. Rubble, with windows in bands. A slope of glass continues the roof slope right down from solar panels almost to the ground. Recessed rear porch with a parabolic arch, repeated inside.

COED MAWR, 1½ m. ENE. Early C17 end-chimney house, double-fronted with centre door, and extended l. by one bay. A bakehouse and outbuilding, r., both have chimneys that copy the taller chimneys of the original. The stone half-dormers look rebuilt.

CRAFNANT, 2½ m. NE. Late C16 or early C17 altered, cross-passage plan with end fireplace and mural stair. Behind, a dower house, and linking the two, a C19 former dairy. The outbuildings form a good group around the house. To the s, the small hump-backed PONT CRAFNANT crosses the Artro to a former MILL, one of many in the valley, and an abandoned FIELD BARN.

CWM BYCHAN, 4½ m. ENE. At the head of the Artro valley beyond Llyn Cwm Bychan. Early C17 Lloyd family house with tiny square upper windows, widely spaced. Originally with a single chimney and winding stair, the w chimney added for an enlarged parlour. Mid-C18 single-storey rear range. Depicted in 1780 with a detached dower house, now gone. Collar-trusses, one grooved for a partition subdividing the upper floor. Bressumer inscribed 1770.

MAES-Y-GARNEDD, 3½ m. E. At the upper end of Cwm Nantcol. The birthplace *c*. 1597 of John Jones, the regicide.

The house is late C16, altered, of the lateral-chimney, cross-passage type. C19 outbuildings in-line to the r. A large Bronze Age CAIRN can be seen (SH 642 267) in the second field to the s of the house.

UWCHLAW'R COED, 1¼ m. SE. A stone house of two parts, 1585 and 1654, the latter for the regicide, John Jones. Altered windows. The original is dated on the monolith door lintel and on a slotted beam marking the former service rooms inside. The two-bay hall has a w fireplace and stair and ceiling of counter-changing joists. The two w squares are curtailed, indicating that the hall extended further, perhaps with a projecting chimney. It may have been altered in 1654 when the two-bay house to the E was added, dated on a huge main beam. Fireplace, stone stair and closet in the E gable. The new part is slightly higher, both parts have attics; collar-trusses with raking struts in the E roof. Dairy below catslide roof to SE, with water wheel. Beyond, the chaff-house, bakehouse to NW, a pigsty range and, further N, a group of farm buildings. All probably early C18, with later extensions to W.

STANDING STONES. Two stones on the flat land fronting the village (SH 584 270), the larger fully 11 ft (3.3 metres) high. Its low-lying site may be explained by the suggestion that it marks the start of the Bronze Age trackway over the hills of northern Ardudwy towards Trawsfynydd (see Llanfair). The smaller stone may not be ancient.

ROMAN STEPS, Cwm Bychan. A famous pathway over the Rhinogs, connecting Cwm Bychan with the Eden valley s of Trawsfynydd. Paved with large stone slabs, probably medieval.

LLANDANWG see LLANFAIR

LLANDDERFEL   9838

ST DERFEL. In a rounded churchyard. Unusually a single build of c. 1500, in squared slatey stone with large Perp windows, more typical of NE Wales. Hoodmoulds with lively carvings: grotesques and a ruffed beast among them. Restored in 1870 by *S. Pountney Smith*; his the big traceried w window and the undersized bellcote. Two porches said to date from 1639, the s one now a vestry. N door with deep Perp mouldings scarred by blade-sharpening. Arch-braced trusses of appropriate type but a little thin, possibly replaced after a fire in 1758; the two chancel bays are panelled, but only the wall-plates original.

Good medieval SCREEN, although only the frontal of the loft survives. Four lights either side. The posts, resting on broad dado beams, have oddly carved bases returning to a square. The dado beams, as at Llanfor, have slightly flattened blind arcs framing varied foiled circles and leaves, and spandrel rosettes. The main lights delicately cusped, and minutely pierced in the interstices and spandrel leaves. Twenty-three loft panels, with blind Perp tracery of a rather monotonous kind, under bands of pomegranate and vine. Other panels and some cresting are reused in the C19 REREDOS.

FITTINGS. Of 1870 the sandstone FONT and PULPIT, and heavy panelled STALLS. – An earlier C19 Gothic CHAIR reuses a 1665 panel. – STAINED GLASS. N window, 1890, by *Powells*, Adoration of the Magi, crowded. – MONUMENTS. Rev. S. Stoddard †1788, a well-carved Neoclassical half-urn. – Two of *c.* 1825 to the Williams of Bodwenni, grey and white with odd mixed detail. – In the vestry, John Lloyd of Pale †1742, painted wood. – In the porch, a large lobed stone BOWL. Also, ST DERFEL'S 'HORSE', a medieval relic of exceptional rarity. There was a pilgrimage associated with the saint; his effigy mounted on a stag was carried out and tethered to a staff in a nearby field. The village offered £40 to the despoiler Ellis Price to save the effigy, an enormous sum, but it was sent to London and burnt in 1538 with Friar John Forest, Catherine of Aragon's confessor, fulfilling a prophecy that St Derfel 'should set a whole forest on fire'. The stag was left but lost most of its head to a Rural Dean in 1730. What remains is a log, shaped as a stag's body with little legs folded under, and the defaced head pegged on. The detached short post was the saint's staff. – LYCHGATE. C18 stone walls. Two late medieval pieces reused as wall-plates.

SARON CALVINISTIC METHODIST CHAPEL, 1870, by *Richard Owens*. In his Lombard style, like Rhyl and Dwyran, the outer bays in triangular-headed recesses and a big centre rose over a triplet. A rich pitch-pine interior: the gallery front in long panels divided by squares; arcaded *sêt-fawr* and pulpit backing on a corniced plaster arch. MANSE. 1886.

The village street climbs from the Dee meadows. By the chapel (*see* above), an earlier C19 predecessor became the BOARD SCHOOL in 1872, altered 1910. Some original windows arched in stone, some in black brick. CHAPEL ROW, mid-C19 stone cottages, is the lower end of CHURCH STREET, lined by irregular terraced houses up to the lychgate. Two short streets run E; on the upper one, CROSS KEYS, a late C18 pair, was an inn from 1804. The outbuilding opposite may have been the previous inn, late C17. TRAFALGAR SQUARE was so named for holding the one-armed village pump, called Nelson. Tiny former NATIONAL SCHOOL, 1828, with Gothic windows renewed in the late C19. Uphill E, RAMA INDEPENDENT CHAPEL, disused. 1868, large, in the plain lancet Gothic of the *Rev. Thomas Thomas*.

TIRIONFA, opposite the churchyard. A very large rectory of 1826. Stone, cruciform, with deep eaves. Four projections from a hipped centre: service wings set back each side, a rear gable and a storeyed porch between pretty hipped verandas. Regency stair with square balusters.

PONT FAWR, ¼ m. S. Bridging the Dee elegantly on four arches, the centre pair larger; triangular cutwaters. Late C17 or early C18, widened later. The causeway SE, PONT-Y-BRYN, has a further five arches.

PALÉ HALL, ¼ m. S. 1869–71, for Henry Robertson, the railway
engineer. It stands out amid the Victorian mansions of North
Wales for the quality of its masonry and internal fittings.
Designed by *Samuel Pountney Smith* of Shrewsbury, for which
town Robertson became M.P. in 1862.* The previous house
was a smallish symmetrical Gothick structure with a canted
bay looking into the valley and thin corner towers – the existing plan of the three W rooms.

Of the finest Cefn sandstone, the house has an eclectic
Elizabethan exterior responding to the irregular plan. Entrance   94
by a porte cochère to a generous vestibule, and then a top-lit
galleried hall from which open the library, the central boudoir
and the drawing room with a new S bay, and a new dining room
entered beneath the ample stairwell. On the first floor were
eight bedrooms and a billiard room. The remaining third of
the house and the service ranges around a large yard, a huge
built volume, were just to make the Victorian Pale work.

Smith's elevations achieve a picturesque agglomeration of
parts. The body of the house has three storeys, the main W side
two, the tower over the vestibule four, united by strapwork
parapets concealing low roofs to leave the sky to tall chimneys.
The porte cochère is enriched with keystone heads, including
Robertson with a steam engine on the r. A loggia decorates the
garden side of the service court, which has a slim spired tower,
a Gothic accent in Renaissance dress, composing well in
distant views.

The internal sequence begins with the VESTIBULE paved
with polychrome *Minton* tiles, a marble fireplace by *Bennett* of
Liverpool, which rises by two sets of steps, and an engraved
glass screen to the heart of the house. The STAIRCASE of
carved and veneered woods by *Cox* of London. Exceptionally
rich fireplace in bronze, ormolu etc. The BOUDOIR has a
slightly domed ceiling on an elliptical plan and sumptuous
plasterwork with painted roundels of the Seasons and Elements. The DRAWING ROOM is mirrored for perspective effects
and also with a coved Neoclassical ceiling. The DINING ROOM
has a fitted buffet carved with fishes, fruits and birds, and a
compartmented plaster ceiling.

Lithographs of 1875 show mature trees from the Lloyd ownership, which formed the basis for a Victorian arboretum. The
latter reflects the head gardener, Thomas Ruddy, the nephew
of Pamplin who established Wales's first botanic garden at
Penyllan nearby. The ashlar lodge, TŶ BRYN, has bargeboards
and side verandas. Additions for Sir Henry Beyer Robertson
after 1888 included the red brick group by the upper entry, a
rock garden, and lost greenhouses in the walled garden in front
of the house.

FRONHEULOG, ½ m. SW. Prettily set on a rock terrace, a villa of
c. 1815, for John Davies, a leading Bala Calvinistic Methodist.

---

*Smith then designed Llantysilio Hall, further down the Dee, in Denbighshire, for
Robertson's business partner C. F. Beyer, 1872.

Stuccoed, five-bay with veranda and steep hipped roof.
TŶ'N-Y-DDOL below, his wife's family house, became the
home farm. The house looks early C19 but has an early C17
Tudor doorway and an immured cruck within. Simple early
C19 LODGE, w.

HENBLAS, ¾ m. NE. Altered and externally unremarkable, but
the attached barn contains two bays of a medieval hall
probably early C15. A full cruck-truss frames a partition with
three doors, two pointed and the centre one shouldered. The
birthplace of Edward Jones †1824, 'the King's Bard', harpist
to the Prince of Wales.

CROGEN, 2 m. E. A lovely site, occupied since the C12, backing
onto the Dee and sheltered by a rock outcrop. Right by the
house is a MOTTE set on a rock with no evidence of a bailey.
Recorded only in 1202 when Elise ap Madog, dispossessed of
his lands, was allowed to keep just this by Llywelyn the Great.
Scattered masonry on the summit. The house, owned in the
1640s by Maurice Wynn, Receiver General of North Wales, is
late medieval to C17, charmingly Gothicized in 1831. The E
cross-wing is the earliest part, marked by a good C14 window
head in the s gable. This surely is too ecclesiastical to be believ-
able here, but was illustrated in 1792, too early for antiquarian
insertion. A late medieval two-light window has been found
inside, on the w wall. The two lateral chimneys must be C16.
The character of the s front is of 1831, with a pretty and uncon-
strained variety of glazing. Added, in the angle, a storeyed
porch and on the w end a stone bay with Romantic Gothic
cross and loop. At the rear NW, a barely linked three-storey
block has Gothick glazing to a canted bay. Narrow open-well
stair with ogee iron balusters. To the NE, a late C19 steep-roofed
LODGE, half-timber over stone. On the w drive, a pair of well-
designed cottages of 1952.

LLANDDWYWE see TALYBONT

3864

LLANDECWYN

ST TECWYN. 1879–80, by *Thomas Roberts* of Porthmadog. Plain
lancet Gothic with porch and bellcote. – INSCRIBED STONE.
Latin, translated as '[the cross of] St Tecwyn, presbyter. To the
honour of God and the most illustrious servant of God, Heli,
deacon, made me'; with a cross. Perhaps C11. The church is
superbly sited high above the Dwyryd estuary, in a rounded
churchyard so raised that the C17 or C18 stone LYCHGATE
appears half-sunk. – TŶ'N-LLAN, adjoining, is single-storey,
dated 1672.

PLAS LLANDECWYN, ¼ m. S. Long early to mid-C17 house,
downhill-sited, the l. two bays a few steps above the lower four,
but under one roof. Irregular sash windows and tall end chimneys. Slate hoods on brackets above the two l. lower windows.
Outshut rear. A big l. end fireplace and mural stair with

window; smaller s fireplace. Altered, so unclear if of one build, or extended. The GARDEN has a stone gateway and terraced look-out, both C20, with a hint of Clough Williams-Ellis. OUT-BUILDINGS include a barn, C18 or early C19, and a C19 lofted stable with a round gable opening. Also a cottage s of the barn and a FIELD BARN by the drive, of wonderfully massive dry-stone, perhaps C18.

NANTPASGAN FAWR, 1½ m. ESE, in remote uplands. Early to mid-C16 cruck house, three bays but extended at both ends. Rough voussoired doorway, low raking dormers and tall end chimneys. The large N fireplace has a rough stone stair, l. Quite large first-floor s fireplace. The cruck-trusses have collars; the blades start low. s end addition with a chimney; N one with outside steps. Lean-to shelter on the w opposite stone animal pens built into the rock. Derelict field barns dot the landscape, evidence of previous prosperity despite the terrain.

LLANDRILLO
0437

ST TRILLO. 1876–7, by *S. Pountney Smith*. The old tower, without datable features, survives under an attractive octagonal bell-stage in pink sandstone, with recessed spire. The roofs inside are elaborately carpentered with opposed wind-braces and arch-braced collar-trusses. Tower and chancel arches in red sandstone. – Deep octagonal C14 FONT tapered and curved below; disused for a Victorian one. – Victorian pink stone PULPIT. – Caen stone REREDOS with two carved medallions. – ORGAN. By *Conacher*. – STAINED GLASS. E window, presumably 1877, by *Heaton, Butler & Bayne*, the Ascension across all the lights in beautiful colours with fine drawing. Two N windows, the Prodigal Son and the Brazen Serpent, also 1877. – Nave NE, three saints, 1936, by *Geoffrey Webb*. – MONUMENTS. Re-set in the organ chamber, some C18 plaques to the Lloyds of Hendwr.

In the churchyard numerous low and massive C18 slate slabs. Against the s wall, MONUMENT to Katherine Wynne of Branas †1706. A late example of the hooded tombs of North Wales (cf. Robert Wynn of Plas Mawr †1598, at Conwy). Sandstone chest tomb with guilloche edging, arcaded panels and fluted angle columns. The barrel arch or hood on top has cherub heads on the soffit.

MORIAH CALVINISTIC METHODIST CHAPEL, SW of the centre. 1881, by *Richard Owens*. A big painted stone front with stepped gable corbelling and arched windows, the central triplet with roundels in stilted heads.

The village has a proper street, passing round the churchyard with small C18–C19 houses down to the bridge. The terrace on the N begins with the former Bell Inn, 1748, and finishes with the DUDLEY ARMS, roughcast, dated 1776 inside. By the river, a late C19 Gothic CHURCH HALL. The bridge, PONT LLAN-DRILLO, has two arches and a flood arch, earlier C18, widened.

Up the E bank lane, the former vicarage, BERWYN HALL, later
C19, with sandstone and brick dressings.

TYDDYN LLAN, ¼ m. NW. C18, enlarged in the earlier C19 with
storeyed porch with arched doorway, and two attic gables.
Taller additions behind. C18 plasterwork and two Ionic
columns in the parlour. MAES TYDDYN, adjoining, was
the predecessor. C16 or early C17, marked by a very big lateral
chimney, gabled under a massive diagonal stack. Encased and
altered, but originally timber-framed. Hall and two outer
rooms with good beamed ceilings; four-bay wind-braced
roof, of tie-beam trusses with queenposts, or raking
struts, collars, and braces for the box frame. Was this a first-
floor hall?

PONT CILAN, 1 m. WNW. Early to mid-C18 bridge over the Dee,
two arches on cutwaters. Unwidened, the footways precari-
ously extended on iron supports with railings on particularly
long kerbstones.

LLAWR CILAN, 1 m. W. Prominent from the road, a big stuccoed
three-bay farmhouse remarkable for the brick axial chimney
with six diagonal shafts. This is Victorian, but the house looks
Late Georgian.

BRANAS LODGE, 1½ m. WNW. A miniature villa at the foot of a
waterfall. Although owned by the architect Joseph Bromfield
at his death in 1824 there is no evidence for his designing it or
living here. Toy-like two-bay front under a pyramid roof, with
minimally Gothic arched windows.

BRANAS UCHAF, 1½ m. W. An important C15 cruck-framed hall-
house, possibly always of stone, from the Tudor doorway. C16
or early C17 end wall and centre chimneys, the E one diagonally
set. The ground-floor windows have stone mullions, the
shallow ovolo moulding, long proportions and hoodmoulds
suggesting the mid to later C17. Five bays. Two three-light
windows l. of the door light the hall and parlour, and a three-
light and two-light, r., light outer rooms, the second a kitchen.
C18 upper wall and windows and also the NE wing. A rear NW
addition, not linked internally to the main house, has a Tudor
doorhead, presumably resited. Inserted chimney and passage
in the first bay of the two-bay hall, the chimney almost
obscuring the remnant of an aisled spere-truss, similar to that
at Plas Uchaf, Cynwyd. The W parlour has late C17 fielded
panelling. Two C17 OUTBUILDINGS flank the approach, a barn
and a lofted cowhouse dated 1607 on a tie-beam. Also a low
C18 hay barn.

HENDŴR, 1 m. N. An ancient site with a substantial mid-C19
house in C16 style with coped gables and latticed iron windows.
Central porch bay with an oriel over an arched doorway. By
the drive, a C17 FIELD BARN with raised cruck-trusses.

TAN-Y-COED MEGALITHIC TOMB, 2 m. NE, W of the main road
(SH 048 396). The capstone shows flat in a grassed mound.
Difficult to interpret because the shape of the cairn and the
approach to the chamber have been altered. One upright used
to be visible in the chamber beneath the capstone. There is a

hint of a passage to the edge of the cairn, which may be on an original line at that point. Cairn material survives around the chamber.

BLAEN-Y-CWM, 3 m. S. A large and remote farmhouse dated 1728. Three bays each side of a central door.

MOEL TŶ UCHAF, 1½ m. E (SJ 056 371). On the summit is a very beautiful KERB CIRCLE, a contiguous ring of upright boulders 39 ft (12 metres) in diameter. There are two gaps but otherwise the circle is perfect and most impressive. The central depression, the result of C18 disturbance, may have destroyed a burial cist. It is likely that there is a low platform of stones filling the centre, like that at Cefn Caer Euni I, Glan-yr-afon. On the slope to the S, a much less conspicuous PLATFORM CAIRN with a kerb of flat boulders and a good deal of quartz on the top. Around the base of the hill a number of small rectangular CISTS, some with slab sides, some with dry-stone walling. Their dates and origins are not known, though their size suggests that they may be graves of some sort.

MONUMENT. Just in front of the farmhouse at Tyfos (SH 028 388) is a rather enigmatic BRONZE AGE MONUMENT with a very large stone kerb. The mound within it has been disturbed and it is no longer certain whether it was originally a high solid mound, or some kind of ring with an open centre. The former is perhaps more likely.

LLANEGRYN

6005

A narrow strip of fertile land of the Peniarth estate borders the Dysynni river, backed by hills, with the village at the foot of the slope, the church isolated uphill.

ST MARY AND ST EGRYN. In an originally circular churchyard. A single chamber with W bellcote and S porch. It was dependent on Cymer Abbey and is recorded in 1253, but the surviving detail is late medieval. One Perp window is re-set on the N, and a Maltese cross is incised on the S chancel wall, but the exterior is otherwise Victorianized. *Henry Kennedy*'s restoration of 1846–9, halted owing to the 'age and imbecility of the incumbent', was restarted *c.* 1855 under *R. K. Penson* and finished under *E. B. Ferrey* in 1876. Kennedy rebuilt the porch and put in windows, the E tracery copied from Llandysilio, Anglesey. Penson replaced the bellcote and W window; Ferrey added the vestry. The porch has a fine roof of *c.* 1500 whose central arch-braced truss is studded with a boss and little dogteeth and has a trefoiled apex. Pointed S doorway of large slate blocks, simply chamfered. Inside, the roof is also good, with seven low-pitched arch-braced trusses with cusped apex struts and two-tier cusped wind-bracing. Over the sanctuary is a typical Merioneth celure, restored 1849. Bands of late Gothic quatrefoil and lozenge openwork separate the panels. Bosses, one carved with the instruments of the Passion.

37   The SCREEN is among the best in Wales. The story that it
     came from Cymer Abbey at the Dissolution is unproven. The
     date may be *c.* 1520; the carving is less wholly Gothic than that
     of the Mid Wales ones. There has been a great deal of repair,
     but oddly unrecorded. Three broad lights either side of the
     centre, each headed with a row of little open panels, except for
     an almond pattern on the r. The posts run continuously down
     to the sill (unlike Llandderfel). Original paired arches in the N
     dado and a band of perforated carving, typical of the county.
     The LOFT rests on a panelled coving with large carved bosses.
     The bands of running ornament above are remarkably intact:
     tightly packed waterleaf with characteristically entwined ten-
     drils and a regular vine pattern. The loft has thirteen panels
     with applied tracery divided by pairs of quite un-Gothic but-
     tresses that once framed statuettes. Above is a more undulat-
     ing waterleaf, without flowers, and delicate cresting. The E side
     is, surprisingly, still more intricate. The bosses include a stag,
     the serpent of eternity, and a wonderfully droll animal on the
     N. The lower bands of ornament on this side might be said to
     be confused in pattern but in the upper vine trails a sense of
     rhythm and differentiated form is re-established. The parapet
     is a gem and as fascinating a series of dissimilar openwork
     designs as exists. There are seventeen: net-like webs, whorls,
     almond shapes placed upright in ogee tracery or on their sides
     in intersected circles, and filled in with leaves, roses or grapes.
     Then there are more conventional geometrical panels, and
     finally four *reprises* of trail motifs. The best, for subtlety and
     inventiveness, has waterplant treated as sensitively as at
     Llananno, Radnorshire. The stairway mounts inward to the loft
     from the N vestry, suggesting that access was originally from
     outside. Panelled beneath with an openwork string.
        FONT. C12. Square and scalloped, the upper angles rounded
     so that the effect is almost Ionic. Cylindrical stem and square
     base. – PULPIT. 1858, panelled oak. – PEWS. 1850, some early
     C19 benches at the back. Around the font some reused C16
     or early C17 panels with arcading and guilloche moulding,
     perhaps from a pew. – STALLS and RAILS. 1850s, heavy oak. –
     Around the altar table, good encaustic TILES dated 1846. –
     STAINED GLASS. E window, by *H. Hughes*, Crucifixion, 1873,
     strident. Two by *Ward & Hughes*: W, the Empty Tomb, 1881,
     lurid colours, and N, 1882. S lancet, 1880, by *F. Holt* of Warwick,
     dull. One N window has eight reused medieval to C16 quarries.
     – MONUMENTS. Mostly to the owners of Peniarth: Richard
     Owen †1714, a handsome Baroque tabernacle with Corinthian
     pilasters supporting a curved hood and vases, and coloured
     arms. – Lewis Owen †1729, matching, but less well carved,
     with flaming vases. – Edward Williams †1763 and his wife Lady
     Bulkeley †1765, with arms on the plinth of a draped
     Neoclassical urn. – John Lloyd †1806 and his wife
     †1841. Grecian bronze plaque. – William Wynne †1834, neo-
     grec, by *J. Carline*. – Mary Wynne †1866, W. W. E. Wynne
     M.P. †1880, and W. R. M. Wynne †1909, brass crosses on

black slabs. – Owen Wynne †1908, attractive Edwardian Baroque.

In the churchyard, slate sarcophagus MEMORIAL with cast-iron urn, to Mary Jones †1847, signed *W. Rice*. Nearby, slate table tomb to Francis Williams of Peniarth Uchaf †1732. – LYCHGATE, stone and timber, moved in 1883, the timbers renewed. WAR MEMORIAL, *c.* 1920 of massive granite blocks.

BRIDGES. PONT DYSYNNI, 1 m. S, the lowest bridge over the Dysynni, has four elliptical arches on miniature cutwaters with piers above, *c.* 1800. PONT-Y-GARTH, 2 m. ENE, the next, was probably rebuilt 1797–8 when £103 was spent. Two arches.

DOMEN DREINIOG, 1 m. S. A damaged MOTTE, prominent by the river SW of Pont Dysynni. Possibly the Norman castle of *c.* 1090, but more probably Welsh in origin. TALYBONT, presumably the farm just N, was the site of a princely residence whence Llywelyn the Last wrote to the Archbishops of Canterbury and York in 1275 proposing peace. Edward I was there after the revolt of 1294.

The village street crosses the Nant Egryn stream. SE of the bridge, the charming pairing of two disused CHAPELS as end stops to a little row formed of identical late C19 vestries sharing a central gable. Bethel (Calvinistic Methodist) is dated 1867, and Ebenezer (Independent), 1879. Purple granite obelisk outside Ebenezer, a MEMORIAL, 1906, to the C17 minister, Hugh Owen of Bronclydwr. W of the bridge, l., BODEGRYN, a town house in scale, earlier C19, three storeys in large blocks of green stone, with unequal two-storey wings. E from the bridge: a former WESLEYAN CHAPEL, plain Gothic, 1878; PRESWYLFA, modernized in the C19 with eaves gables and sliding casements; and BRYNMEIRION and MAESYRHAF, a later C19 Peniarth estate pair with cast-iron windows.

TRYCHIAD, just E of the village. Built to the 'unit system', two farmhouses facing each other. Trychiad Uchaf, three-bay, stone, of C17 origins, looks N at the whitewashed Trychiad Isaf, probably early C19. Outbuildings attached, and behind Trychiad Uchaf, a two-bay hay barn.

CYNEFIN, W of the village. 2001–3, by *Christopher Day* with *Julian Bishop*. Of boulder stones and slate, the house is strikingly shaped under a complex hipped roof suggestive of folded hills. Hard angles are avoided for more organic shapes, as in the window- and doorheads, in the plan, and interior volumes. The strongest element, a stone bedroom gable, breaks through the roof on the SE. On the NW two arms frame a tight courtyard, enclosed further by a gateway and garage. Inside, the sense that this is a craftsman-built house is overwhelming. The woodwork must follow the unexpected planes and junctions of walls and ceilings. The ovoid entrance hall has a notably 'natural' staircase by *Dafydd Davies Hughes*, assembled as if from stripped branches. The same aesthetic extends to the door latches. Fine engraved glass by *Bill Swann*.

PENIARTH, ½ m. E. Mentioned in poetry of the C15, the estate grew to include the mountains seen over a ha-ha, an Arcadian

vista as fine as any borrowed for a Welsh park. The architectural history of the initially straightforward hipped three-storey
cube is not clear. On the l. side, the first two bays (of five),
rough rubble with blocked windows, may be C16–C17,* and a
stone cartouche of 1700 in the hall indicates work for Richard
Owen †1714. The transformation of the house and its
surroundings in an up-to-date Palladian style was due to Lewis
Owen †1729 and his heiress, Jane, who married in 1731 the 5th
Viscount Bulkeley (†1738) of Baron Hill, Beaumaris (A). The
remarkable red brick front of seven bays (the brickwork taken
down and rebuilt, 1999, by *Roger Clive-Powell*) has in the
pediment Lord Bulkeley's arms, so of the 1730s, and probably
the house was then enlarged to a double pile.

Lewis Owen built the FOLLY, a two-storey detached banqueting
house, in 1727 to the r. of the forecourt. This, in brick, with
handsome ashlar dressings, has a Queen Anne character distinctly earlier than the house façade. Pedimented, with quoins;
the three upper windows segmental-headed in eared stone
frames with double keystones. Corniced doorcase below with
a pulvinated frieze. The nice ogee-domed cupola is dated 1812
and the clock has the motto of C19 Wynne owners. To its l.,
also earlier C18, is a four-bay wing (the equivalent on the r. was
never built) with matching quoins, panelled parapet and brick
aprons under the upper windows. The bricks were apparently
made on the estate, and are of soft brownish red. A short return
behind to a low service court.

The facing of the MANSION brings it into the Palladian sphere:
the windows are square-headed without the frames, the quoins
are flush, and a fine redder brick is used for the voussoirs and
slim pilasters that frame the three-bay centre. Timber modillion cornice, and pediment completely filled by ashlar heraldry
and acanthus scrolls, carved to a metropolitan quality. Why
Lord Bulkeley's arms are so ostentatious on a house that was
not his principal seat remains a puzzle. The ground floor was
lost to an extension of 1858, but the doorcase with pulvinated
frieze was reused. The cartouche above has the crossed foxes
of Edward Williams, Lady Bulkeley's second husband.

The estate fell to the Wynnes of Wern, Penmorfa (C) and,
probably before 1834, the house was altered with early C19
wide sashes and French windows on the sides and rear.
W. W. E. Wynne †1880, the antiquary, added the single-storey
range placed like a blind colonnade across the main façade in
1858, possibly by *Benjamin Ferrey*. It enlarged the library in
time for his inheritance of the famous Hengwrt collection in
1859. The white-painted arched dormers may be of 1858 also.

INTERIORS. The ENTRANCE HALL has a Regency character,
including the slate and marble fireplace under the Baroque
cartouche of 1700. The STAIRCASE, beyond a simple shallow-
arched columnar screen, is open-well with early C19 alternate

---

*A similar straight joint at Nannau marks a tower engulfed in the later house.

iron-trellis and wood balusters. The LIBRARY, l., retains oak bolection panelling of *c.* 1700 and a marble fireplace. Behind, the large DRAWING ROOM has a good earlier C18 fireplace with a floral tablet and plaster overmantel framing a portrait of Lady Bulkeley.

The sweep of the drive and judicious planting disguise the missing r. wing of the Folly. C18 improvements included a WALLED GARDEN. A S drive crossed the Dysynni river by a bridge destroyed *c.* 1943, to an isolated Victorian lodge at Bryncrug (q.v.). Stone balls remain of gatepiers, the other stonework possibly reused in the present N entrance.

PENIARTH UCHAF, in a hidden valley above Pont-y-garth. Early C19, four bays, the fourth a cross-wing giving Picturesque asymmetry. Deep eaves, French windows and verandas typical of Regency North Wales. Opposite, low circular walls of a contemporary COCK-PIT, the roof probably on wooden posts, as on the octagonal GAME LARDER beyond the house. Further on, tall and formal stone STABLE BLOCK, 1–3–1 bays, the stables entered from a centre arch and lit with lunettes, and a coachhouse in each gabled wing. Five loft roundels.

ALLT-LWYD CAIRNS, 1 m. NNE. Two, on the summit, both badly damaged. In the centre of the N one a large burial cist, revealed at the bottom of a deep excavation. The S one, now scattered, appears to overlie a low stone ring. This may be a Ring Cairn, genuinely earlier than the cairn or some enclosure associated with a house built on the ruins. Features on the lower slopes include several PILLOW MOUNDS, artificial rabbit warrens of C17–C18 date.

LLANELLTYD

7220

CYMER ABBEY. Monks from Cwmhir in Radnorshire settled in 1198–9 in a meadow E of the Mawddach. The charters, p. 634 confirmed by Llywelyn the Great in 1209, record endowment by Maredudd ap Cynan †1212, Lord of Meirionnydd, of the Gwynedd princely family. The ruins belong to the unfinished building of the first half of the C13 with a rudimentary W tower of *c.* 1350. The church had an aisled nave whose E end was to serve as the monks' choir until the crossing, transepts and choir could be built. They never were.* The association with the house of Gwynedd was strong and sometimes dangerous: buildings were burnt in Henry III's incursion of 1241, and in 1282 royal officials removed possessions of Llywelyn the Last from here and from the Cymer grange that had been his headquarters. Edward I passed in 1283–4, giving £5 towards building, which suggests some late C13 work. It was the poorest of the Cistercian houses in Wales, always small, with just five monks by 1388, and correspondingly modest.

---

* David Robinson and Lawrence Butler feel that the monks would have begun with the E end, this perhaps destroyed and the E lancets reused in an inserted wall at the E of the nave.

19 The NAVE side walls survive in part. The eastern half of the nave
s wall, and the western half of the N wall with a three-bay
arcade, which if replicated on the s has left no trace. Also a
short eastern piece of the N wall. A surprising number of putlog
holes. The weather courses for lean-to aisles show on both sides
under scanty bases of clerestory lancets, and there are corbels
for aisle roof beams. Of the s aisle only foundations remain,
while the N one has a thick outer wall with little fenestration
detail apart from an E lancet. The E end was closed (with a
straight joint) by a wall containing three large stepped lancets
and small ones above them (shown more complete in the 1742
p. 21 Buck view). Externally there is a crude plinth and the lancets
have sandstone dressings with a slight chamfer.

The architectural detail that survives at the eastern end is
Transitional in character, the E lancets more fully Gothic,
consonant with a building period of 1200–40. The dressings
are in eroded sandstone, either red or a yellow one from Egryn,
Talybont. On the s wall a slightly pointed two-order doorway,
each step having a roll between hollows, with eroded triple
volute capitals and splayed triple bases. The side to the aisle is
taller with a double roll. Triple sedilia to the l. with a pointed
triple-roll arcade with clustered outer shafts and similar triple
volute capitals. The one surviving colonnette is reeded with fat
leafy capital volutes. E of this a segmental-pointed opening may
have contained a tomb; the sunk chamfered moulding C14 or
early C15. To the l. a broad pointed piscina, the mouldings

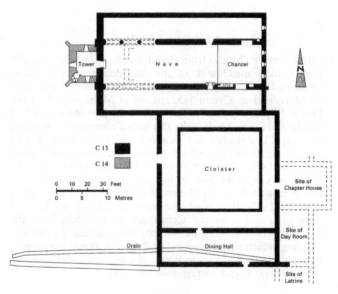

Cymer Abbey.
Plan

eroded. A big pointed tomb-recess in the N wall has two stepped hollow mouldings that may be C14. The E triplet has plain splayed outer lancets, but out-of-place capitals, designed for column shafts, with a keeled profile. The central lancet has a continuous roll broken only for crude triple capitals with keeled centre and horizontally reeded sides. On the r. jamb the roll mould forks into a single chevron and, though damaged, both rolls clearly forked into similar feet. Such chevron characterizes work at St Davids Cathedral, both of the late C12 and the post-1220 work.

If the central section was the monks' choir, the three-bay N arcade probably relates to a western end reserved for lay brothers. Tall twice-chamfered arches on octagonal piers with coved cap mouldings, late C13 to early C14, presumably after the Edwardian conquest but David Robinson points out that there is no sign of insertion. The added W tower is a poor thing, three walls each with an off-centre lancet, and two angle buttresses, but no architectural detail, nor any exterior door. SW spiral stair.

The plan of the MONASTERY has been partly uncovered. The cloister footings to the S of the church at a lower level; the W doorway fragment proves that it is contemporary with the church, and indicates that there was no W range (unless of wood). The monks' refectory lay alongside the S cloister walk, not at right angles to it, built over a stream. Evidence for the chapter house with its doorway and the day room S of this have been found at the E, but are covered by the farm.

Two separate W buildings, Tŷ FANNER and its outbuilding, may have been the abbot's house. Externally plain, three-bay with a broad plank door to the l. of two renewed timber cross-windows and two stone dormers added when the hall was floored c. 1900. End-passage plan with a W parlour wing entered through a Gothic doorway from the hall's upper end. It is assumed that a N cross-wing has gone. An inserted C17 lateral fireplace serves hall and parlour, now the kitchen. The hall roof, tree-ring-dated to 1441, is 25 ft (8 metres) wide, the widest medieval hall in the county. Five arch-braced collar-trusses and two tiers of cusped wind-braces. The trusses are ovolo-moulded apart from the central one, which has a roll between two hollows, and all with apex cusping. In the parlour wing, a similar solar roof truss, but without smoke-blackening, so presumably unheated, or with a fireplace from the beginning.

Across the yard a plain square block, lofted with outside stair and an oak-mullioned window each floor, possibly C16. The house with dormer gables attached to the W is C17.

ST ILLTYD. In a raised rounded churchyard, a single chamber with spectacularly massive stonework. The charming leaded arched windows and arched N porch probably date from 1834, the date on the flat-topped corbelled bellcote. But both N and S doors have medieval segmental-pointed heads, and the disused S porch is late medieval with close-spaced collar-trusses, and original oak with applied cusping. A N wall date of 1686 suggests work then; two sloping dormers on the s are later C18, and the E and W windows date from the restoration, 1900–1, by *C. Hodgson Fowler* of Durham. A good C15 six-bay roof of arch-braced collar-trusses with raked struts and small solid wind-braces. Its heavy timbers suggest the early C15. – FONTS. Octagonal, 1900; also a small stone bowl of 1689, like the marble one of 1651 at Dolgellau. – FITTINGS. Rearranged by *Fowler*. The PULPIT with a pretty domed tester includes late medieval panels pierced with miniature tracery and stars; similar pieces in the E end panelling, also two panels dated 1692. Twisted baluster RAILS, and PEWS with shapely bench ends by *Fowler*. – Panelled dado, earlier C19, preserving some brass pew plates. – Pretty Gothick domestic ORGAN by *William Allen* of London, 1812, from Bryn-y-gwin, Dolgellau. – STAINED GLASS. E window, 1900, and W lancet, 1901, both by *Burlison & Grylls*. MONUMENTS. – Sir Robert H. Vaughan †1792. Above the tablet, a single column falls, fractured at the base, an unattractive conceit. – Griffith H. Vaughan †1848, a brass cross, enamelled in colours. – John Roberts, electroplate of the Resurrection, *c.* 1901. – HATCHMENT. Sir Robert Vaughan †1859. – INSCRIBED STONE. A Latin inscription in C9–C10 Irish lettering records that the footprint of one Kenyric or Reuhic was inscribed on the stone before he left on pilgrimage. Some have discerned the outline.

In the churchyard, numerous rough slate C18 slabs, one by the s wall to Griffin Vaughan †1700, on supports of Egryn sandstone. The plate from this, apparently an early piece of cast iron, is inside the church.

84 PONT LLANELLTYD. Five arches over the Wnion. This is the most elegant bridge in the county, later C18, the arches broad and elliptical and the cutwaters finished as half-pyramids under pilasters.

CYMER CASTLE, 1 m. E. Hilltop MOTTE of the earliest surviving documented native Welsh castle, built 1116 by Uchdryd ab Edwin. A ruined late C18 or early C19 Nannau estate folly on the summit had fireplaces, chimney and timber-lintelled windows.

The village is harshly cut since 1974 by the A 470. Backing onto the churchyard, TŶ'N LLAN, T-plan, the range running s with two C16 cruck-trusses and a heavy beamed basement ceiling. Below, YSGOLDY was the church school, 1836, with hood-moulds and dormer gables. Beyond, TAN-LAN, a dower house to Hengwrt, in Victorian grounds. Mid-C18, with tall chimneys, and later C19 bays. Staircase with turned balusters and moulded tread ends. The little C18 stable is an early use of brick. W of the church, facing the old road up from the bridge, MINFFORDD, C18, was adapted as a toll house, with large porch. AWELON, T-plan, is earlier C18 and C19. To the W, by the bridge over the Wnion, PENIEL CALVINISTIC METHODIST CHAPEL, 1836, altered *c.* 1870, plain stone house and chapel in line. Further on, TŶ'N CELYN, 1773, three bays with a pediment like several in Dolgellau, and Tŷ'N-YR-ARDD, mid-C18 with sloping dormers.

HENGWRT, ½ m. S. Demolished in 1965. Celebrated for the collection of Welsh manuscripts assembled by Robert Vaughan †1667, the finest in post-Reformation Wales. It included the Red Book of Hergest and the Black Book of Carmarthen, now in the National Library. Vaughan's house was replaced in the mid C18: seven-bay, three-storey, with a pediment, but remodelled in the early C19 to two storeys with higher gabled outer bays. The surviving low SERVICE RANGE has earlier C19 coped gables and windows but some older stonework. The big BARN with high plinth and dove holes looks C17, altered when a long earlier C19 COACHHOUSE was added behind, gabled between pairs of Tudor-arched entries.

MINES. The hills above the Mawddach were mined for copper, lead and gold, MOEL ISPRI allegedly in ancient times. This was expensively re-equipped in 1898 for gold but failed by 1903. GLAN-Y-MORFA, on the A494 road, was the mill for the Prince of Wales mine, operational 1836–1903; the tall E block was the stamping mill. The CAMBRIAN MINE (SH 692 195), Taicynhaeaf, was re-equipped for gold after 1854 and large sums were lost by 1865.

CESAILGWM FAWR, 1 m. NNE of Taicynhaeaf. Late C17 long-house with exceptionally wide hall fireplace. There were mines just S. CESAILGWM BACH, NE, is later C17 with ovolo-moulded doorcase and four C18 hipped dormers.

DÔL-Y-CLOCHYDD, 1 m. NE of Cymer Abbey. In 1588 an ironworks was established here, by the Mawddach. Scant remains of a circular furnace have been noted.

LLANENDDWYN see DYFFRYN ARDUDWY

LLANFACHRETH   7524

Upland parish historically dominated by the Nannau estate, and characterized by the works of Sir Robert Williames Vaughan, the 2nd baronet. In his long tenure, 1792–1843, he changed the landscape by agricultural improvement, enclosing 10,000 acres in 1806, and laying out such roads and drives, fifty or seventy miles, that he (like Telford) was named the 'Colossus of Roads'. He also built great numbers of cottages and barns for his tenants. His lanes circle the contours of a landscape that rises through thick oak woods to bare rock. Nannau stands on the pass between Moel Cynwch and Moel Offrwm, Llanfachreth in the bowl of hills beyond. There was mining in the parish from at least the early C18, and a notable C19 copper mine at GLASDIR, 1 m. W., also exploited for gold.

ST MACHRETH. Tower and spire from the church rebuilt 1820–2 by Sir R. W. Vaughan in memory of George III. The tower has the rough-hewn quality of Vaughan's commissions. Chamfered corners, emphatic arched openings and a broach to octagonal below the spire. This is of neater masonry and is different in Gastineau's (possibly unreliable) engraving of 1830, but there is no other evidence of a later rebuilding. Outside gallery steps. The rest, nave, chancel and porch, is by *Benjamin Ferrey* (or possibly *E. B. Ferrey*), 1872–3, conventionally E.E. – FONT. 1873, circular. – Pink alabaster REREDOS, 1892, and PULPIT, *c.* 1902, elaborate Gothic. – STALLS. With traceried panels, *c.* 1918. – STAINED GLASS. E window by *Ward & Hughes*, 1887, like a steel engraving. Nave S, *Cox, Sons, Buckley & Co.*, 1888, colourful. Three chancel windows, *c.* 1874. Four nave ones, Kempe-style, *c.* 1900. – MEMORIALS. At the W end: Anne Nanney †1729. An early work of *Henry Cheere*. A billowing marble drape on which putti hold up the lady's portrait bust in an oval frame. Derived via the Hewer memorial in Clapham from Bernini's Maria Raggi memorial of 1643 in Santa Maria sopra Minerva, Rome. – Rice Jones †1801, poet and antiquary. Hope with her rock and anchor, signed *Franceys & Spence* of Liverpool, hence post-1819. – Griffith Price †1804, draped vase and abased torch, by *S. & F. Franceys*. – John Vaughan †1842, and Sir Robert Vaughan †1859, both 1861 by *Gaffin*, one Greek, one Gothic.

In the churchyard, NW, an intimidatingly large limestone slab, a Vaughan MEMORIAL of *c.* 1860. To the NE numerous headstones with the conventions of death and reunion – harps, doves, clasped hands etc. – astonishingly mostly C20. – LYCHGATE. Large and stone, probably of 1820, at the head of steep cobbled steps.

BETHEL CALVINISTIC METHODIST CHAPEL, E of the church. 1848, rebuilt 1868. The simple chapel and house in line, built against Vaughan opposition on one piece of ground not owned by the estate.

SILOH INDEPENDENT CHAPEL, Ffrwd, ½ m. W. 1875–9, in lovely isolation, also on a site not owned by the estate. Green stone with grey arched openings.

In the village, TŶ CANOL, by the churchyard, has a little veranda on brick columns, perhaps of a date with TAI NEWYDDION, to the NE, a short terrace of 1812 with similar veranda. Beyond is the SCHOOL, 1847, Tudor Gothic, in large stones. Additions by *E. B. Ferrey*, 1875.

MOEL OFFRWM HILL-FORT (SH 750 210). The most interesting fort in S Merioneth, probably Iron Age. It crowns a hill so steep on the N and W as to need very little extra defence. On the S, the remains of a stone rampart have collapsed downhill. There is a slight ditch and counterscarp bank below it. On the SE, the rampart is doubled as it approaches the entrance on the E. On this gentler slope the ramparts still stand as a formidable barrier, though the wall faces have collapsed. The ramparts curve in slightly towards the entrance where two semicircular guard chambers flank the gateway. Such chambers are characteristic of several large Iron Age hill-forts in NE Wales, but some doubt must attach to their exact form as they seem to have been partly rebuilt in recent times, perhaps when a beacon tower was built on the summit. Also remarkable are the twenty or more HUT PLATFORMS, both on the hilltop and cut into the shelving ground to the w. The platforms, the levelled sites of round wooden houses, indicate permanent settlement even on this windswept mountain. Attached to the SE side of the fort is a narrow annexe which encloses a flat-topped ridge within a low bank and ditch, seen best at the S end.

On a boss of rock projecting from the S slope, overlooked by the main fort, is a small FORT (SH 748 206), probably also Iron-Age. Its single stone rampart is fairly well preserved on the S, where diggings have revealed an impressive length of dry-built walling. The present entrance gap would seem to be a recent break, and the fort was probably originally entered by a more oblique track at this point. The relationship with the main fort is unknown.

NANNAU, 1¼ m. SSW on an extraordinary site at 700 ft (210 metres). The *plas* of the Nanney and Vaughan families and its park are wrecked, the downfall achieved in the second half of the C20. Nannau was a grand house *c*. 1600, when rebuilt for Hugh Nanney †1623, but disappears from the record in the Civil War, to be rebuilt in the 1690s as a plain three-storey five-bay house with a tower on the rear corner. The present rear wall incorporates a strong straight joint that could be the tower, and also carved stones including the arms of Elizabeth I, a date 1581, and an *englyn* in sub-Gothic letters.* The Nanney heiress married a Vaughan of Hengwrt in 1719; Hugh Vaughan (†1783) dissipated the estate, but his brother Robert H. Vaughan (1723–92), baronet in 1791, rescued it having married well.

The present HOUSE was probably begun after 1788 for Robert H. Vaughan, but possibly only after 1792, for his successor; completed 1795. *Joseph Bromfield* of Shrewsbury is the likely designer, the house typical of the school of Wyatt, a Neoclassical near-cube of squared stone with cornice, low parapet and hipped roof. Three storeys, five bays. The SE front has a centre bay in a dark slatey stone, contrasting with the lighter-coloured and bigger stones either side, odd but deliberate to give the effect of recession. Understated ashlar tripartite entry of Ionic columns *in antis*; triple window each floor above, all under shallow segmental arches; cornice and parapet with a raised balustraded panel. Plain sashes elsewhere and plain corniced four-bay side elevations. Enlarged in 1805 by *Joseph Bromfield* with wings (demolished 1971), set so far back as to leave the original block unencumbered.

The entrance hall had timber Ionic columns against the entrance wall, answered by an Ionic arched screen to the staircase, which has iron balusters with medallions. The screen being like the one at Nanhoron (C), and the ironwork being

---

*A stone with the names of Hugh and Ann Nanney is at Llanfendigaid, Llangelynin; one carved with Adam and Eve has been lost.

of Shrewsbury type, both indicate *Bromfield*'s involvement in the interior. All the plasterwork has been destroyed: the ceilings had oval garlands and in the drawing room also sprays of flowers.

The L-plan stables which ran back from the r. pavilion of the 1805 addition, survive altered. Also a WALLED GARDEN to the NW of the house, the lake and woods form the basis for designed parkland, but inevitably the further it spread into the landscape the more blurred the boundaries between natural and artificial become. The mood of landscape pleasure is more sharply expressed in PRECIPICE WALK, a level path delicately engineered round the rocks of Moel Cynwch. It has a sense of William Madocks (*see* Ganllwyd) and his friends exploring while the Continent was closed by war.

NANNAU ESTATE BUILDINGS. The 2nd baronet's cottages and farms dot the rocky landscape over five linear miles between Dolgellau and Drws-y-nant on the Bala road, many identified by the RWVAM initials of himself and his wife. The commitment to improved housing was prodigious and unequalled in the region, and to appearance too: most have a modicum of the Picturesque cottage style of contemporary pattern books. Four designs in P. F. Robinson's *Rural Architecture*, 1822, are named as having been built for Vaughan. As printed, they show typical cottage detail: bargeboards, leaded windows, Tudor chimneys, thatch. As built they have none of this prettiness, leaving just outlines and outsized chimneys, barely recognizable as a *Robinson* design. Vaughan also remodelled existing farmhouses, adding his chimneys, and scattered a standardized outbuilding, L-plan and lofted. Three routes are suggested: SW and SE from the village, and along the A494 road. *See also* Rhydymain, Bryncoedifor and Dolgellau.

1. South-west from Llanfachreth

Off the lane, drives to BOETHUOG, E, with eyebrow dormers over blank arches, and COED MAWR, W, an older farmhouse with added octagonal chimneys and a wing of 1838. Past the Precipice Walk r. (*see* above), the HOME FARM, r., with outbuildings dated 1834, screens the mansion. The longest of Vaughan's drives runs E over five miles almost to Rhydymain. A detour down it, l., ends now at a Tudor ARCH framing a superb view of the Aran range. The adjoining HYWEL SELE LODGE, *c.* 1820–30, is one of the most elaborate: a canted two-storey front with mock-ruin parapet and octagonal turret. The arch marks the DEERPARK, recorded in the early C15 when Hywel Sele treacherously attacked Owain Glyndŵr within it. Encircled by thick and curving walls; the ruined small TOWER on a hillock was probably a folly. Between the park and the road, a walled KITCHEN GARDEN below an overgrown area with ruins, with another Tudor ARCH, 1828.

Off r., MAES-Y-BRYNER has an archway on the drive and a barn dated 1838. Further on, the lane turns W in front of COED-Y-

MOCH LODGE, the principal lodge, *c.* 1830. Very coarse: gabled
upper floor over a big Tudor arch, and one bay to the r. The
clock permanently reading 4.55 apparently intimated that visitors would always be in time for dinner. Just sw, GARTH-
BLEIDDYN, early C18 with half-dormers, has an outsize
timbered porch dated 1831, and an octagonal chimney. A little
W, EFAIL FACH, one of the prettiest, has thin octagonal chimneys and a storeyed porch. It is, though barely recognizable,
Robinson's Design No. 6, without thatch or bargeboards, and
the half-timber translated into stone. CAE CLYD, W, is half-
hipped with massive paired chimneys.

2. South-east from Llanfachreth

CAE CRWTH, up a track l., a long farmhouse and barn, has two
eyebrow dormers, *c.* 1810–20. On the lane, r., TŶ'N-Y-LLWYN,
1812, a tiny D-plan cottage, has a bowed front with an incised
cross. BRYN-BLEW, uphill l., with catslide dormers, is dated
1747; an estate barn just below. A lane r. passes under GARREG
FAWR, a large boulder raised on 15-ft (4.5-metre) raking piers,
a rather grotesque folly, *c.* 1820. A drive joined here that gave
a level winter route to church. Further S, GALLT-Y-CARW,
whitewashed, C18, with hipped dormers, is extended with
arcaded stable and loft. GELLI, l., 1814, is a charming toy, the
end walls canted to make an octagon, but unresolved as the
roof is conventionally pitched. Porches, real or false, on four
sides. Up a track SW, BRON-Y-FOEL is early C18 with hipped
dormers. TAN-Y-FOEL, l., one of the larger estate houses,

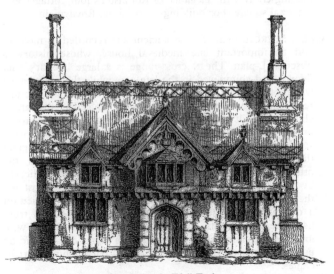

Llanfachreth, Efail Fach.
Engraving by P. F. Robinson, 1822

1830s, is hipped with an outrageously big double chimney. The outbuilding behind was a small late C16 hall-house with full crucks. The long E drive crosses just above OCHR-Y-FOEL ISAF, gable-ended with side lean-tos. Further round, PEN-ESGYNFA, r., is half-hipped with an arched door in a lean-to.

From Gelli, another lane drops SE. TŶ-HIR, up a drive N, is C18 with four dormer gables, and an estate barn. BRYN-COCH, r., 1812, is vernacular with dormer gables, only the diagonal chimney typical. TŶ'N TWLL, l., 1808, is gable-fronted with hoodmoulded window over an arched door. The road curves SE past Tŷ Cerrig (see below) to CAEGWYN, with a big square chimney. S from the cross-roads, TYDDYN ARTHUR, r., has a canted projection and a half-hip. The lane then winds through woods to the main road, past NANT-CNIDIW, C18, with hipped half-dormers; chimneys and additions of 1832.

3. Along the A494 road

First, 2 m. E of Dolgellau, BRYN-TEG, 1839, a determinedly architectural pair with a storeyed porch each side and two tall chimneys. The W front, improbably manorial, has outsize octagonal turrets in diminishing stages clasping the gable. The E is plainer but with some delicate leaded glazing. FFRWD GWYLLT, further on, has an octagonal chimney on a big square base and a W porch on stone pillars so thin as to suggest a perverse dislike of timber. Next, CARLEG is a pair to a strange V-plan: a hipped two-bay block with outsize apex chimney faces the road, and wings run back diagonally. It may be a crude and partial realization of *Robinson*'s Design No. 13, missing entirely the elegance of Robinson's four cottages in a diagonal square. For buildings beyond, *see* Rhydymain.

CAE'R MARCH, ¾ m. SE. An ancient site recorded as moated, and an important late medieval house, whose history is obscure. L-plan. The N cross-range is a large late C15 hall, floored and chimneyed in the late C16, while the other range was rebuilt in the C19 apart from the S end wall. Carefully restored in 2004 by *Morris Higham* of Dolgellau, the lateral chimney rebuilt and the end-passage doors reopened. Massive bressumer to the C16 lateral chimney and a post-and-panel screen, the two doorways with ogee heads. Primitive hinging: the inner door plank with stubs, one into a floor-hole, the other to a wooden bracket. The original open hall is indicated by full-height wall-posts carrying the dais-end truss. Upstairs, the hall truss has an arch-braced collar, the N side carried on a C16 wall-post inserted with the chimney. The dais truss has a heavy tie-beam, angled struts and collar. To the W, a low barn, possibly late C17 and with signs of a domestic use, perhaps a dower house. A C19 hay barn behind at right angles.

TŶ-CERRIG, 1½ m. SE. Early C17, altered 1790. Two gabled half-dormers; an outbuilding added as a cross-wing, r. Good interior with post-and-panel screens and stone fireplace stair.

LLANFAIR   *5829*

The parish extends NE from Llandanwg, once a harbour with its
ancient church in the dunes. In the uplands are substantial farmhouses with outbuildings and, often, an attached dower house,
evidence of C16 and C17 wealth.

ST MARY, Llanfair-juxta-Harlech. Mentioned in 1188. A long
and narrow single-cell in two builds. The E part is early C15.
Egryn sandstone E window of three cusped lights, the central
one with a tiny cusped light above a transom. Pointed hoodmould with carved stops. The W part is much rebuilt, but looks
added from the straight N joint. Arch-braced trusses off wall-
posts on corbels: the heavier E ones look earlier, the W ones
with cusped struts and wind-braces. A ruined N chapel was
removed in 1858 by *Henry Kennedy*, who replaced lancets, the
W door and the bellcote. – SCREEN. A muddle. Plain boards
below, turned posts that look late C17, and pierced bands in
the heads and cresting that look C19. – STOUP. N. Hollowed
boulder, perhaps a prehistoric mortar. – FONT. Perp, octagonal. – STAINED GLASS. E and S, 1858. – MONUMENT. Slate
plaque to the Owens of Crafnant.

ST TANWG, Llandanwg, ¾ m. SW. The old parish church of
Harlech in an ancient round churchyard half-buried in sand
dunes by the sea. Abandoned until saved by the Society for the
Protection of Ancient Buildings in 1884. Single-roofed, of
rough boulders, with a W bellcote. The W half is probably C13,
as suggested by the small blocked S door with voussoir head.
The church was doubled in length probably in the late C14,
the new E end with windows of Egryn sandstone: an
unusually high pointed E window with hood, carved stops, and
jambs of two hollow orders (partially blocked in the C17),
and N and S windows of two cusped lights. The W door with a
voussoired head is inserted, perhaps as late as 1685
(datestone above). Arch-braced trusses to the three E bays, with
two tiers of cusped wind-braces and an extra truss inserted
over the sanctuary for the celure, once richly painted.
Embattled eaves boarding each side. – SCREEN. Just the
beam survives, its mortices indicating the former
posts. – INSCRIBED STONES. An 8-ft (2.5-metre) pillar
lying on the sanctuary floor is inscribed INGENI and ENNB (?);
another inscribed stone and a cross-incised boulder
found 2008. C5–C6.

S of the lychgate, TŶ'N-LLAN, three-bay, late C18 former inn. TŶ
MAWR, N, is similar but later, the stonework more regular and
the chimneys less square. Further N, the MEMORIAL HALL,
1928, faced in small granite pieces. The name in an iron
overthrow. SE of the village, a SLATE QUARRY (SH 580 288),
active 1860–90.

LLANFAIR-ISAF, ¼ m. SW. T-plan ensemble, illustrating the
'unit' system. The oldest wing, oriented N–S, is a typical late
C16 storeyed end-chimney cross-passage house. The W wing,
not much later, is lower and of one storey, with a raised cruck
roof and possibly a former loft at the W end. The large size of

this wing suggests use by a son rather than a dowager. Voussoir-head doorways to both wings. Drawbar holes to the older house doorways. Post-and-panel partitions and substantial collar-beam trusses, some with wattle-and-daub infill. To w of the second house an attached two-storey stable, later converted to a dwelling, with an external stone staircase at the w gable. Late Georgian wing of coursed, squared stone added NE: three bays, two storeys, hipped roof. Polite detailing inside. At the same time, a lofted cartshed was added to the s end of the first house, also with a hipped roof, and a massive lintel above the two-bay cart opening. Outside loft steps. Open HAY BARN, SW, now partially closed in.

ARGOED, ½ m. SSE. Low limewashed C17 cross-passage house with attached barn. Half-dormers with stone copings and a small chimney at the r. corner. Immediately behind and half a level higher, a second 'unit', C19. Good OUTBUILDINGS, including a late C18 or early C19 BARK MILL, formerly with slate-lined tanning pits.

GARTH, ¾ m. SSE. Early C20, perhaps by *O. Morris Roberts & Son*. Rendered with a slate-hung gable to the tall l. block, and a broad hipped dormer on the low-swept roof to the r. Small-paned windows. In the garden, a COTTAGE, C17 or C18 with a wattle-and-daub chimney hood, rare N of Ceredigion.

LLWYN HWLCYN, ¾ m. SE. Two-storey late C16 or early C17 house with square chimneys at each end and roof of small grouted slates. Cross-passage, big fireplace with winding stair, slab floors. Late C19 HAY BARN, with tall rubble piers and a segmental-arched end opening.

TYDDYN-Y-FELIN, 1¾ m. E. Dated 1592 on the cross-passage partition. A stone two-storey house with very tall square end chimneys and a lateral stack at the rear, all with dentilated caps. The lateral chimney is rare; it projects with an angled side wall, probably for a former staircase. At right angles, the single-storey building is probably a C17 dower house. Small oak window to r.

GERDDI BLUOG, 2¾ m. ENE. Remote, on a shelf below Moel-y-gerddi. The home of Archdeacon Edmund Prys in the late C16. A surprising sight with huge mullion-and-transom windows, the result of a radical reworking in the 1960s by *Clough Williams-Ellis* for George Wiles. However alien, it does possess a confident boldness and is easily accommodated in the majestic landscape. The original late C17 house is now a cross-wing towards the s end. It has a projecting end chimney, the angles of which were filled in to form closets. The two-bay range to the l. may be C18, the cambered lintel inscribed MP 1667, for Morgan Prys, re-set. In the 1960s a dower house was demolished to make way for an overpowering addition to the r., consisting of a double-height dining room and a broader and higher second cross-wing, all with big stone or imitation-stone grid windows. Another such window fills the original gable, as this earliest part was gutted for a double-height great hall, with a balcony from the l. end range. It became a youth hostel in 1976. FARM BUILDINGS to the S, including a barn dated 1728.

GWERN EINION BURIAL CHAMBER, ¾ m. ESE (SH 587 286). A most impressive portal dolmen with high portal stones and closing slab and a large sloping capstone poised over a small square chamber. Walling against the closing slab, which had marred its impact, is now removed.

MURIAU GWYDDELOD, 1 m. NE (SH 586 302). Two late prehistoric or Romano-British farmsteads. At the S one a round hut can be recognized within a roughly circular enclosure wall, very massively built. The second group, some 33 ft (10 metres) to the N, is larger and better preserved, with three large round huts facing into a small courtyard. Abutting against the houses are the loosely built walls of small fields and paddocks. The name, 'Irishmen's huts', commonly used for such farmsteads in many parts of North Wales, is thought to reflect the memory of settlement by men from Leinster in the post-Roman period, but in fact the houses are several centuries earlier.

BEDD GURFAL, 2½ m. ENE (SH 613 312). A small Bronze Age ring cairn with impressive stones around its inner edge, very similar in design to the Lower Circle on Moel Goedog just N. Unfortunately a modern hole has been dug in the centre.

BRONZE AGE TRACKWAY. From the river creek just W of Llanbedr, the track went N through Pensarn, where two large stones mark its route, at SH 584 290 (a very fine stone now obscured by sheepfold walls) and SH 595 305. Above this point the modern road merges with the old route and several STANDING STONES may be seen on either side. The two most impressive are close beside the road at SH 599 309 (with a badly ruined cairn beside it) and SH 602 313. Two smaller ones may be seen on the flat ground before the modern road moves down the hill and the old track continues at the higher level along the slopes of Moel Goedog. Another stone is close to the track in the second field (SH 608 322), yet another just through the gate in the next field. Beyond is the Upper Circle, one of a pair of Bronze Age RING CAIRNS which form the climax to this group. The upper circle consists of a ring of boulders backed by a narrow stone bank, now covered in grass. The central space was free of stone and now appears to be slightly dished. The Lower Circle, just below the trackway, is rather more impressive, the inner edge being defined by slabs about 3 ft (1 metre) high. Excavation in 1978 restored missing stones and exposed the stone ring bank behind. The central space was used mainly for ceremonies involving the burial of charcoal in pits and the re-burial of small quantities of human bone; also one normal cremation burial, but without accompanying goods. The trackway continues N towards Bryn Cader Faner and Cwm Moch (*see* p. 706).

7243
LLAN FFESTINIOG

The old village of Ffestiniog, on a ridge high over the Vale of Ffestiniog, was the centre for the area before being eclipsed by Blaenau Ffestiniog in the mid C19.

ST MICHAEL. *Henry Kennedy*'s first church, 1843–5, in the briefly fashionable Neo-Norman. Although called 'one of the neatest and most commodious churches in North Wales', it is gawky with emphatic dressings in grey limestone. Arched windows, linked by a string course and shallow buttresses between; the three E lights under a big arched hood. The bellcote replaces an octagonal spirelet. Typically broad interior, the spindly trusses with open arcading. Short chancel, overdressed with a horseshoe chancel arch, roll moulded like a bicycle tube, on fat round columns. A side arch into the square timber PULPIT. Deep W GALLERY, on a central stone column. – FONT. Misunderstood Romanesque in silver granite, quite small, the bowl with scallops and flutes on a spiral-grooved stem. – STAINED GLASS. Good later C19 E window with scenes in roundels. – S window, by *C. C. Powell*, c. 1944. – N window by *Jones & Willis*, c. 1914.

PENIEL CALVINISTIC METHODIST CHAPEL. 1839, altered 1859, and in 1879, by *Richard Owens*. Chapel and house in line, under one half-hipped roof, tall as an urban terrace. Three-storey house to the l. of a six-bay chapel: four gallery windows; two tall central windows, low outer ones, separated by heavy square-piered porches. Stucco surrounds with keystones. Was the chapel raised in 1859 and remodelled with all the stucco in 1879?

VILLAGE. At the W end by CHURCH SQUARE, the churchyard overlooks the Vale. The rambling whitewashed PENGWERN ARMS HOTEL to the N has a two-bay centre dated 1728, with a large twin-gabled mid-C19 addition to the l., still with small-paned sashes. The projecting r. wing is early C19, a hipped three-bay square. The WAR MEMORIAL, E, by *W. P. Davies*, 1920, is corniced on slate pillars, the top stepped with a finial that spikes a polyhedron. At the SE corner, MEIRION HOUSE, 'established 1726' but with C19 shop windows. To r. the best building in the village, TŶ'R BANC and MELBOURNE HOUSE, three-storey in squared brown stone, c. 1830–40. Two three-bay houses joined by a gabled bay with blind windows on the party wall; the l. house was a bank, marked by a detached porch on thin columns. TEGANNEDD, Late Georgian, returns to the village scale and forms the SW corner of this unusually urban space.

PENGWERN, ¾ m. N. An important house, developed over at least four periods, three of which are clearly apparent. The original house is not obvious, a timber-framed storeyed T-plan building, probably built by Dafydd ap Ieuan ap Einion in the later C15. This consisted of a four-bay solar block, fairly narrow, with a wider SE-facing hall at right angles. In the late C16 this was encased with stone, perhaps by Maurice Lewis, High

Sheriff, 1596. The house was now a U-plan with the service wing to l., the parlour wing to r. and the hall at the centre, and the main chamber above. Of this date the immensely tall square chimneys, a true mark of nobility, the wings' stacks corbelling out from the SE-facing gables. A rear wing was added in the mid C17, and another at right angles, extending NE. The next period, *c.* 1693, concerned mostly internal alterations and the staircase wing added behind, perhaps for Owen Wynn. An armorial plaque in the NW wall commemorates John Lewis, his brother-in-law. The windows, pairs of leaded casements, probably date from after the house was sold to Lady Newborough in 1919.

The INTERIOR, altered, contains remnants of each phase. Of the medieval period, traces of the wall-posts embedded in the solar cross-wing walls, and more discovered in the central hall during repair work *c.* 2000. Arch-braced cusped trusses in the E roof, some darkened by smoke and indicative of the former hearth in the full-height solar. Of the Elizabethan phase, the huge lateral fireplace replacing the solar wing hearth, and the mural stair or closets next to the fireplace inserted between the hall and the W service wing. Post-and-panel partitions and plaster friezes survive in the cross-wing, and a cross-beamed ceiling in the hall. The fine panelling and bolection-moulded fireplace surround in the hall and chamber above date from the late C17 phase; also the two staircases with barley-twist balusters and panelled newels and strings. The doorway between the hall and the main staircase is especially splendid, with a segmentally arched head and slim fluted pilasters.

The former GARDENS extended E and S: walls, terraces and revetments formally laid out in the C17, with an orchard, perhaps, W.

CWM FARM, Cwm Cynfal, 2 m. ESE. Remote at the head of the Cynfal valley. Altered early C16 hall-house. The oak post-and-panel partition at the l. has holes for the dais bench and cut-outs in the head for upper room joists which probably projected to form a canopy. Blackening on the fine arch-braced central truss indicates that this was a two-bay open hall with a hearth. Later (but not much later) 'modernized' by inserting a central fireplace and chimney. Holes and rebates in the plainer, outer trusses for infill panels, so the single bays at each end had small rooms above the lower room(s), the solar at the l. end with its own fireplace. Later staircase wing at rear l.

HAFOD YSBYTY, Cwm Teigl, 1¾ m. ENE. A remote site, but on a medieval pilgrim route and in the C14 a grange of the Knights Hospitaller. Low single-storey house with attic, the front range of five bays, originally with two service rooms behind the post-and-panel partition in the N bay, an open hall of two bays, and a two-bay room to the S, probably a byre; thus a rare example in Gwynedd of the 'longhouse' plan. A fireplace was inserted in the central bay. An early date is likely, perhaps early C16, indicated by the arch-braced and cusped crucks (which stop

at waist height). The central truss is notable for the cusping at
the feet and the double rows of jointing pegs. Later rear wing
with large fireplace and mural stair.

CAE CANOL MAWR, Cwm Teigl, 1 ¾ m. NE. An upland location
at the foot of Manod Mawr. Probably C16. Hybrid plan, with
open hall at one end, passage and storeyed rooms at the other.
Post-and-panel partition, cusped wind-braces over hall.

59 BRYN-YR-ODYN, ¾ m. SE. Two-storey L-plan house, the tall
rubble main range mid to late C16, the lower rear wing C17.
The older part of three structural bays, but the central bay subdivided to provide a cross-passage with post-and-panel partitions each side. This, and the tall chimneys (now lowered),
point to a house of some distinction. Fine arch-braced trusses.
The main doorheads are typical of the Ffestiniog area – long
parallel voussoir stones wedged by a triangular keystone.

CYNFAL FAWR, ¾ m. S. A neat house of three close-spaced bays,
in coursed slatey stone, with square windows on each floor
including in the stone dormers. Is it mid-C18? The Gothic
glazing must be C19. At right angles, l., a low single-storey
house may be late C15. An arch-braced cruck survives. Morgan
Llwyd, noted Puritan and author of mystic verse, was
probably born here in 1619.

BODLOESYGAD, ¾ m. SE. Small C16 storeyed house typical of
the area. Opposite doorways front and back, the rear one low
and narrow, with rough voussoirs and block keystone.
Reed-moulded beams and chamfered main beams within.

PLAS BLAENDDOL, ¼ m. N. A large T-plan house of two storeys
and attic, at the end of a drive. Griffith Roberts of Blaenddol
was High Sheriff, 1729. The present character is C19, gabled
and bargeboarded, remodelled for William Casson, Blaenau
Ffestiniog slate-quarry owner. The original three-bay house
was raised and given a bargeboarded gable r. to match a big
added l. cross-wing with pierced bargeboards. The door was
moved, in a moulded slate surround; similar slate to the two
adjoining windows, and slate posts remaining from a slate-
paved veranda. Big C19 rear service wing. A small piece on the
r. end, of long Gelli Grin stones, is probably late C19. Later
C19 picturesque LODGE, with steep roofs, half-hipped and
canted.

BRYN-Y-CASTELL HILL-FORT, 2 m. ENE (SH 728 429). A small
defended hilltop, completely excavated in 1979–85, and
partially restored to show the simple stone rampart which
enclosed houses and workshops for the smelting and smithing
of iron. The discovery of wattle houses was a surprise in this
region. Their position is shown by a cobbled floor and the post-
holes of the door frames. The large stone building, NW, was a
conventional circular house, converted to a smithing workshop
by moving the wall to create the unusual offset entrance. This
provided a draught for ventilation and shade for a bank of
smelting hearths along the E wall. Other hearths and furnaces
were built in the lee of the rampart just outside the entrance.
Iron-making seems to have been the main occupation from

c. 300 B.C. to the coming of the Romans, when the site was abandoned. Manufacture began again when the garrisons had gone, within the large round building on the lower slopes, which was found to be filled with slag and surrounded by dumps.

The field behind the nearby Water Board station is the traditional site of the *Beddau Gwyr Ardudwy*, legendary graves of the men of Ardudwy, where the C6 Cantiorix stone now in Penmachno church may have been found.

LLANFIHANGEL Y PENNANT

ST MICHAEL. In an oval churchyard. A long single chamber with N transept, small W bellcote and small S porch. Mentioned in 1253, but without early detail. The transept has a small uncusped Tudor E window and a good C15 to C16 arched-braced roof with short cusped wind-braces. The nave is altered; S windows with C18 voussoired heads and 'long-and-short' stones to the jambs; similar masonry to an inserted transept N doorway. Was it used as a schoolroom? Restored 1871, with new E window and renewed nave roof, though the W trusses are possibly C18. At the W end some C17 panelling. – FONT. C12, scalloped, the base with crude scallops. – STAINED GLASS. E window, 1919, Christ with SS Michael and Gabriel. – MONUMENT. Anne Owen †1728, slate, simple Baroque. In the churchyard SE of the chancel, a slate slab on two stone drums, the inscription on the chancel wall to Mary Pugh †1704. – Arched stone LYCHGATE, possibly late C17.

The Dysynni valley narrows under Birds Rock and then opens into unexpected tranquil pastures ringed by hills. PONT YSTUMANNER preserves the ancient name for the SW corner of Merioneth. The fortress rock of Castell y Bere (*see* below) looms over the E side and the church is isolated further E. Beyond again, a cluster of houses by Pennant bridge. TŶ'N-Y-FACH, three bays extended to five, with gabled upper windows, has a voussoired door and a big E chimney. It was a C16 hall-house with two cruck-trusses, floored in the C18. Over the bridge, PENNANT is whitewashed, L-plan. The last house, GWASTAD-FRYN, with a big end chimney and flat hood-moulds, is C17, raised in the late C18.

CASTELL Y BERE. In 1221, having taken the *cantref* of Meirion-nydd from his son, Llywelyn the Great began a castle there, assumed to be Castell y Bere. Even in a land where castles occupy so many dramatic positions, few can match this site, with the castle on an island of rock in the Dysynni valley, in the foothills of Cadair Idris, commanding the route N from Tywyn to Dolgellau. In Edward I's second Welsh war (1282–3) its capture was one of the main aims, and it was garrisoned subsequently, with a borough being founded here when the king visited in 1284. In 1284–5 a new chamber was being built, with further works from 1286 to 1290. The revolt in South

Wales in 1287 appears to have been the spur for the strengthening in 1286–7, with over £200 expended, mainly to enclose an area of open ground and ditch between the Middle Tower and the South Tower. Both castle and borough appear to have been abandoned by the end of the C13, possibly after the uprising of 1294–5, when the castle was besieged.

The castle is very ruinous, and while masonry remains indicate full extent of the plan, few of the walls stand to any great height. It is difficult to assign phases, apart from the Edwardian build around the ditched yard. This presupposes that Llywelyn's castle is not of one build. Fine architectural fragments were found during clearance in 1851, now in the National Museum, datable to the first half of the C13.

The castle is surrounded by natural defences, supplemented at either end by a rock-cut ditch beyond the N and S towers. The main approach is from the SW, with an outer ditch, then the middle one, now spanned by a modern bridge but originally by a drawbridge, and so into the OUTER GATE-TOWER, the entrance to the BARBICAN. The foundations of this gate-tower can be seen under the inner end of the bridge, with the DRAWBRIDGE PIT. Wing walls connect the whole complex to the main body of the castle, that to the S being considerably thicker than the wall to the N. The passage up to the third ditch and the inner gate has what would have been a GUARD CHAMBER on the S side. With the ROUND TOWER to the N and the MIDDLE TOWER to the S, overlooking the entrance, this would be the most sophisticated gateway arrangement for a castle of the Welsh princes, even allowing for Criccieth, and it is unfortunate that there is no firm structural dating evidence – could some of it be Edward I's?

The INNER GATE, which retains some sandstone ashlar, a rare survival here, was entered over a drawbridge. A portcullis may have further defended the gate passage, although the grooves for this are uncommonly wide. The ROUND TOWER, with its battered base, lies N of the inner gate and across the W CURTAIN WALL, and further strengthened the entrance complex. The tower was originally of two storeys, and steps from within the courtyard gave access down into its basement. The upper storey may have been reached by an inner or outer timber stair, and even from the curtain wall. The doorway or POSTERN into the barbican, N of the round tower, is a later insertion, evident from the different style of masonry; the doorway was secured by a drawbar.

The shape of the rock on which the castle stands dictates the unevenness of the COURTYARD. Just inside the entrance is the CISTERN or well, placed to take account of a natural source of water. Ranged around the inner face of the curtain wall are a number of rectangular buildings of uncertain date, of which the northernmost butts onto the curtain; a narrow passage leads to an external flight of steps, suggesting that at least one of these buildings had an upper floor, the adjacent LATRINE serving both levels. The curtain wall here also contains another POSTERN, immediately W of the North Tower.

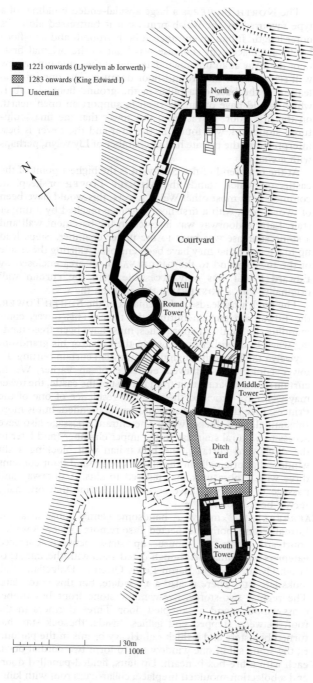

1221 onwards (Llywelyn ab Iorwerth)

1283 onwards (King Edward I)

Uncertain

North Tower

N

Courtyard

Well

Round Tower

Middle Tower

Ditch Yard

South Tower

30m
100ft

Castell y Bere.
Plan

The NORTH TOWER is a large apsidal-ended building, of a type favoured by the Welsh princes; it is buttressed along its outer length. It had an entrance at both ground- and first-floor levels; a replacement staircase was built to the original first-floor doorway at an unknown date, and at the same time a new wall screened off the ground-floor doorway. The one internal feature is the base of a pillar in the ground-floor chamber, which would have originally risen to support an open hearth on the first floor. It was from this tower that the fine sculptured stonework was found in the C19, and the tower is best interpreted as the private hall or chamber of Llywelyn, perhaps with a chapel.

At the other end of the courtyard is the highest point of the castle, on which stands the MIDDLE TOWER or keep. In common with most other Welsh towers, this would have been of two storeys, with a first-floor entrance reached by a timber stair. Later a doorway was inserted in the basement wall and a stone staircase was built to the upper chamber. Steps lead up to a terrace that may have been enclosed, skirting the N side of the tower round to the DITCH YARD, an area enclosed by Edward I that was only accessible from the curtain wall originally, with a POSTERN in the ditch on the S.

The ditch yard leads to the remains of the SOUTH TOWER, the Edwardian curtain butting the tower. This tower, commanding the southern approaches, must have been free-standing when built, either by Llywelyn the Great or his grandson, Llywelyn the Last (although the Edwardian curtain butting the tower could have removed evidence of an earlier, Welsh, curtain). As a separate unit from the rest of the castle, the tower may well have provided the personal residence of one of the Princes. Like the North Tower, it is apsidal-ended, but is more substantial, with thicker walls. The entrance passage also gave access to a mural staircase to the upper chamber (and later to the ditch yard curtain), the Edwardian wall blocking a slit window that originally lit the stairs. The ground floor contains three wide embrasures that tapered to slits. A doorway and passage in the S wall gave access to a latrine that originally served both floors.

CAERBERLLAN, ½ m. SW. A handsome gentry house in a fine formal setting, both unexpected in so remote a place. A walled courtyard fronts the house, up steps between corniced gatepiers with finials. Although dated 1590 with the initials of Hugh Owen, a son of Baron Lewis Owen of Dolgellau, it all looks late C17. There is also a 1755 date, but this is too late. The regular two-storey, five-window stone front has timber cross-windows and a canopied door. Three dormers in the roof, between stepped end gables. Inside, the oak stair has turned balusters and a thick rail. Heavy beams in the parlour, r., the stone sill of one window cut to form two cordial bowls each with a fire-box beneath. Upstairs, fielded-panelled doors and a bolection-moulded fireplace; collar-truss roof with king-posts and raking struts, reusing older timber. A cottage-like building set back to the r. may be an external kitchen (*cegin faes*) of the C18.

LLANFIHANGEL-Y-TRAETHAU *see* TALSARNAU

LLANFOR 9437

ST MOR. Disused. In a large rounded churchyard. 1874–5, by *E. B. Ferrey* ('the architect's aim has been to recall features of the old church, but with improved designs'). A low tower with crowstepped gables was replaced by a tall Victorian one with a steep saddleback. Single nave and chancel, the nave with a timber barrel ceiling divided by guilloche ribs, and a floor of thin bricks outlined in slate. – SCREEN. 1875, incorporating narrow two broad late medieval dado beams like those at Llandderfel (q.v.). Lively carving in the four blind arch-heads each side, with circled whorls and spandrel roses. – Bath stone cylindrical FONT, square PULPIT, and REREDOS, 1875. A good C13 FONT, octagonal with curved taper below stands outside. – STAINED GLASS. Beautifully coloured chancel glass by *Lavers, Barraud & Westlake*, 1875, with delicate Gothic drawing: eleven Gospel scenes E; the Apostles on rich red and blue in two S windows. – HATCHMENT. C19, probably R. J .L. Price †1842, whose grave-slab is in the chancel. – BELL. By the font, 1683. – MONUMENTS. Re-set in the tower and eroding. On the W wall an INCISED STONE inscribed 'Cavoseniargii' in C6 capitals, and dedication stones of 1599 from a demolished Rhiwlas chapel. – Large double monument of 1718 to Lady Sarah Bulkeley †1714 and her son; pilastered with coronets and trumpets in the friezes. – Helena Langford, high up, early C18, scrolled. – William and Elizabeth Price †1774 and 1778, an added panel to a pyramidal plaque with arms of Robert Price †1748. – Also two earlier C18 pilastered memorials with curved heads and heraldry: on the E wall, to Robert Price †1729 and his wife †1743, and high on the S.

In the churchyard, the bleak brick Price MAUSOLEUM, 1887, is inscribed: 'As to my latter end I go, to win my Jubilee, I thank my good horse Bendigo, who built this tomb for me', referring to R. L. Price's apparently spectacular winnings on the great racehorse in the 1887 Jubilee Cup at Kempton Park. – Nearby, a marble boy ascends stairs, lamp in hand, a poignant memorial to Ioan Price †1916, aged nine. – The LYCHGATE may be C18, the roof replaced.

An irregular square in front of the lychgate, with cobbled pavement outside ELLAND HOUSE, early C19. GLAN HAFESP, S, early C18, had five close-spaced windows, the outer ones blocked. Just W, PONT LLANFOR, two low arches, perhaps C18, widened. Facing the main road, PEN ISA'R LLAN, an unusually large stuccoed three-bay farmhouse, earlier to mid-C19, with a C17 barn in the yard behind. Across the main road W, the former RECTORY, three-bay, hipped, of 1814, by *Owen*

Owens of Llawr Cilan, Llandrillo. NW from the square, CHURCH ROW, C19 short row with gabled outer houses flanking a pair. Beyond, YSGOLDY, a little National School with the house in line, of large green stones, mid-C19.

PENUCHA'R LLAN, N of the church. A small medieval RING-WORK with prominent bank and evidence of a ditch.

ROMAN SITES (SH 936 365). Air photography and geophysical survey have revealed sites on the flat land to the S, including two early marching camps, a well-defended fort, probably the predecessor of Caergai (Llanuwchllyn), with its own *vicus* to the NW, and an unusual polygonal structure, possibly a stores depot.

TOMEN-Y-CASTELL, ¾ m. ENE. By the main road, an earth motte on an isolated rock at a junction of two streams.

RHIWLAS. ½ m. W. Rhiwlas and lands round it were given by Henry VII to his standard-bearer Sir Rhys ap Meredith (Rhys Fawr) after the victory of Bosworth in 1485, and have been held by the Price family ever since. Rhys Fawr came from Plas Iolyn in the Pentrefoelas uplands and the men he raised there were rewarded with the tenant farms. The present house is the third on this site, designed from scratch by *Clough Williams-Ellis* for Col. S. Price in 1951, its predecessor having fallen victim to wartime use and dry rot.

Rhys Fawr's grandson Cadwaladr and his wife Jane Wynn of Gwydir first moved to Rhiwlas and built a significant house in 1574. This is known from the roundel drawn by Thomas Dineley in 1684, a green and white painted screen now at St Fagans National History Museum, and, preserved in the present hall, the nine-compartment beamed ceiling with inscriptions in Welsh, Latin and English. The house stood on the present terrace approached from the S by steps, and had a pedimental doorway on axis on the main range and a return wing at the W. The front had mullion-and-transom windows; the wing had a cruciform end like a gatehouse; the roof-lines were lively with dormers and chimneys. In the C18 the return wing was much enlarged, and in 1809 the house was encased as a Georgian Gothick castle for R. W. Price. The symmetrical front rose to three storeys with three polygonal-fronted towers, the central one narrower and higher. The downstairs rooms were given plaster vaults. Some Gothick doors survive re-set.

The new house and garden, completed in 1954 with stones from the old (and modified in the 1970s) is one of *Clough Williams-Ellis*'s best, though its restraint makes it less recognizable than usual. To the C16 plan, but in his own Georgian with a quadrant porch and sense of ease with its surroundings. The PARK is the happy result of long planning with natural features. The first step was a project drawn by *William Emes* for R. T. Price in 1783. It extends along the river to the main road outside Bala, and includes two avenues. One, the Lovers' Walk to Llanfor, was to be planted with clumps in Emes's plan and there was to be an oval bowling green in trees, apparently not realized.

Llanfor, Rhiwlas.
Engraving by Thomas Dineley, 1684

The castellated GATE ARCH of 1813 next to Bala Bridge is
by *Thomas Rickman*, a more serious Gothic essay than the 1809
house, with corbelled battlements between slim octagonal
turrets. On the lane opposite the E drive, an enclosed STABLE-
YARD, dated 1869, with a toy-fort castellated entry and a
similar feature at the back. Uphill just N is a square pyramid-
roofed mid-C19 GAME LARDER. Further NE, a later C19 estate
FARMYARD, three-sided with half-hipped gables.

CYWAIN RURAL LIFE CENTRE, Rhiwlas. 2007–8, by
Dobson:Owen of Pwllheli. Reconstruction of Ysgubor Isaf barn
and hay barn, with likeable new linking buildings. The whole
fringes a grassed circle, the radius of which defines the curved
stone back wall of the new building, fronted in timber
boarding. This is linked to a turf-roofed boarded café.

COED-Y-FOEL ISAF, 1 m. N of Rhiwlas. Later C17 long farmhouse and barn range, the house four-bay with three gables.
The Quaker Ffoulkes family left for Pennsylvania from here in
1682. An early C19 brewhouse opposite and a lofted small
carthouse across the lane.

COED-Y-BEDO, 1 m. N of Cefnddwysarn. A whitewashed house
backed against rock, with a broad storeyed C17 porch. It
encases a five-bay late C15 cruck-framed timber hall associated

with the bard, Bedo Aeddren. A lost 1630s plaque would be right for the inserted chimney, floors and porch. The service end has a post-and-panel screen, repeated on the floor above, where are two visible cruck-trusses. Across the lane, a large STANDING STONE.

LLANFROTHEN

6242

Llanfrothen and the church are 1 m. SE of the principal settlement. Garreg, on the E of the Traeth Mawr, the point of departure for crossing the dangerous sands, reached by road over the hills from Tanybwlch. Its importance was lost once traffic took the new road to Porthmadog over the Cob after 1811. The landscape has undergone major changes. Part of the estuarial flatlands were reclaimed for farming in the 1750s by William Williams, the area vastly increased in 1811, over which the straight road from Penrhyndeudraeth was made *c.* 1860. The activities of the Williams family underlie the lifetime's work of *Clough Williams-Ellis* (1883–1978), native to this landscape and contributor to it for seventy years.

ST BROTHEN. (Friends of Friendless Churches). In an enlarged circular graveyard on the former shore. A rare, comparatively intact C13 church, of the period of the Princes. The dedication is C6 (Brothen was a disciple of St Beuno). Undivided nave and chancel, double W bellcote and S porch. The E gable is a study in vernacular masonry: dressed boulders and blocks of shale in random courses. Triple stepped lancets of equal width, with splays formed of thin dressed stones without freestone. The pointed arch of the blocked N doorway is of thin voussoirs set vertically, and the gable coping-stones are ingeniously keyed into the wall-heads. The roof is C15, of generously round arch-braced trusses, and covered with old thick random slates. One tall W lancet. The other windows are of 1844 by *William Hemming* of Maentwrog. The restoration of *c.* 1870 was also light: the sloping floor tiled, the pews repaired and rearranged. – FONT. C15. Octagonal. Conical COVER; 1840s? – Remains of a *c.* 1500 SCREEN of nine bays; on a base of horizontal planks, the top one pierced. The verticals are clusters of four shafts with plain capitals and bases, the l. doorpost with crude dogtooth, stiff-leaf and cable. The base panels are simply pierced. Later and damaged head beam. A primitive ROOD BEAM seems of different origin, perhaps part of a boarded tympanum. – PULPIT and READING DESK. Late C17, the latter dated 1671. – CHOIR STALLS with backs with short turned balusters, partly made from older pews. More of this pattern at the W. – C19 box PEWS, with parts of C17 to C18 ones reused at the W, with also turned balusters and ball finials, and C18 ones each side at the front. – REREDOS with a pair of C15 newel posts supporting a vine-carved beam. The late C17 RAILS now enclose the SW corner. – MEMORIALS. John

Isaak of Parc †1733 and John Edmunds of Parc †1800, both slate. Andrew Poynter †1802, slate in a fictive marble wooden frame. – Children of John Jones †1797–8, similar. – John Jones of Ynysfor †1901 by *Laurie Cribb* (Eric Gill's pupil).

Clustered minor houses and farm buildings either side of the church. By the lane NW, a ruined small Tudor RECTORY. Its successor, PLAS-Y-LLAN, *c.* 1840, possibly by *Hemming*, has four storeys on the S with a two-bay pedimental centre, but is entered at first-floor level from the N.

GARREG village grew at a rocky point on the former estuary, which preserves mooring rings for boats. On the axis from Penrhyndeudraeth, *Clough Williams-Ellis* placed a WAR MEMORIAL TOWER, 1922. In coursed local granite, its forced perspective and carefully judged voids make it at once an eye-catcher, a solemn memorial and a precursor of the architectural language of Portmeirion (q.v.; begun 1925). On the higher hill, beside the route of the Croesor Tramway, a second landscape intervention, the fragmentary rubble CASTLE viewpoint erected at the same time, as the architect's wedding present from others in the Welsh Guards in 1915. In the village, SIOP MENTER, by *David Lea*, 1988, is a low range, its stepped metal roof overhanging the glassy front. Late Victorian SCHOOL behind.

On the former coastal road, two terraces, the lower one mid-C19 (painted the Brondanw colours of white with green-blue), the upper late C19 and terminated by a precious dry-built domed GAZEBO, surely the work of *Clough*'s mason, *William Davies*. Further on, l., TŶ MAIN, once a coastal lofted cottage, was the penultimate home of the poet R. S. Thomas. The small Victorian CHURCH of St Catherine, 1867, below the village and CAPEL RAMOTH, above Plas Brondanw, are both now houses. At TANLAN, ½ m. N, a terrace of three-bay houses. One-arched bridge, PONT GWERNYDD, ½ m. W, of *c.* 1792. On the Croesor river above, the *croglofft* cottage GELLI has a tree-ring date of 1616.

PLAS BRONDANW. The home of the Williams family, and of *Clough Williams-Ellis* from 1908 to 1978, and taken with its garden and small landscape park, his masterpiece. [113]

The GATEHOUSE across the drive was erected in 1912. The curved-ended design with lateral chimney relates to a wildly Romantic village-hall project of 1911. The approach shaded by trees gives glimpses of the ancient house past Clough's embellishments of the chasm in the park and his garden enclosures. p. 658

The HOUSE predates the group of buildings of which it is at the core. The low downhill-sited block with a wide cambered fireplace arch of rough stone voussoirs at the upper end dates from the mid-C16 work of John ap Howel. Making an L with this is a three-storey parlour block, dated 1660 on its S gable, comparable with that at Dduallt, Maentwrog. This was apparently detached, since the link is dated 1690. Unframed Venetian window for the drawing room on the upper floor,

Llanfrothen, design for village hall.
Drawing by Clough Williams-Ellis, 1911

stone gable copings. After a fire in 1951, the library with drawing room above, were re-fitted with imported c18 panelling and a spreading stair of slate on concrete. The four-storey seven-bay w front is partly c18; buttressed by a porch-like tower of 1937. The tower arch over the walk in the lower garden keys garden and house together and shelters the entry to the cellar brewhouse.

N of the house is a broad stepped-gabled service block of c. 1880, and, forming a yard with it, *Williams-Ellis*'s bridge to the flat in the house attic, level with the road behind. S of the house, informal stables adapted by *Williams-Ellis*, a tightly planned structure with miniature cupola linking the public road and garden. Converted for a tearoom in 2008. PENSTEP, across the road, comprises two substantial c18 houses serving as extra domestic units.

The GARDEN is an outstanding and practically unaltered Arts and Crafts layout begun in 1908, and is entirely by *Williams-Ellis* apart from two apparently c18 grass terraces above the ancient ilex tree. Three stages: 1908–14; the inter-war years; and after 1951. Garden and park take every advantage of the mountain views, in a way both organic to the site and informed by historic Italian gardens. The architectural language is more restrained than at Portmeirion. Grey slate for façades and paving, clipped yews and pleached limes for spatial divisions, iron gates painted black and green-blue and statuary.

The yard gives N through downward-curving gates to the long walled garden next to the house, and w under an arch with a lower gate revealing the view above the double-

semicircle profile of its gate. Through this, a garden lobby with
spires of cypresses leads to the main features. The long paved
walk beside the base of the house ends in a circle, once
terminated with a small bronze of the St Petersburg Peter the
Great (since stolen), outlined against fields to baffle one's sense
of scale. Before this, r., a grove with a bust of Inigo Jones. Over
the lawn, NW, large iron gates with mermaids at the start of
the abandoned drive down to the Victorian NEW LODGE and
more gates. Along the W margin of the garden and a line of
fruit trees there is an intersection with a vista uphill, through
the levels of the garden, over the road and up 100 steps to
Penplas. The open garden is succeeded to its S by cheerful and
varied garden rooms, starting with that reached by broad steps
(up from the lawn, down from the cypress terrace) on which
the ORANGERY of 1912 now stands. Arched windows, outside   113
stair, sprocketed hipped roof, a quintessentially Clough
building. Embellished with the RIBA arms painted by *Bronwyn
Williams-Ellis* for their visit in 1976. To the S again the first
intersection with the transverse vista, with busts of Roman
emperors in a segmental-pointed aedicule at the E and its more
transparent reflection in yew at the valley end. The S margin is
formed as a raised terrace in the field, with a rampart and seats
at the essential viewpoint. Here the second vista can be seen
for the first time, the ultimate *coup de théâtre* since it is aligned
on the pyramidal peak of Cnicht, perched like a Picturesque
adornment above the broad *allée*.

The small PARK has a distinct character, not enclosed but
with far views like the garden. It is entered once more from
the yard, its lower margin enlivened with the rear side of the
garden features, and its own much nobler gateway. The
inclined avenue, relic of a slate quarry, is transformed with
lines of chestnuts grown from trees at Albury Park, Surrey. At
the top, past a formal spinney, the MONUMENT to the recovery of Plas Brondanw from the 1951 fire. The finely lettered
inscription at its base includes an *englyn* in Welsh and a tribute
to Clough's masons, led by *Henry Davies*. The circular railing
permits viewing overhanging a quarry chasm, gently formalized as a designed feature with a trickle of diverted water.*
Here too is a visual intersection, one way across the gulf to a
cut-out urn, another up the hill to the sham castle (*see* p. 657).
The upper entrance is marked by a wayside ARCH, placed to
catch the westerly light but also there to protect the house's
spring water supply, so inscribed 'Ffynnon Gwyfil'.

WERN, ¾ m. N. Two-and-a-half storeys, five bays, C18. Two
wings, that on the W of older masonry. In the early C17 a garden
was made here by a Sir John Wynn of Gwydir, who died at
Lucca, Tuscany in 1614.

OGORONWY, 1 m. N. Small late C19 or early C20 house linked
to an earlier cottage behind by a single-storey range, *c*. 1980,

*Christopher Hussey, in his book on the Picturesque, used the word appropriated
by C18 travellers to express a certain landscape emotion, 'horrid'.

by *David Lea*. Stone walls and low roofs in keeping, as also the modern glazed doors in the projecting bay.

YNYSFOR, 1 m. WNW, on a wooded former island. The altered end-chimney house of *c*. 1700 has Late Georgian windows and later C19 stepped gables. The new house built for the Jones family in 1889, higher up, has unusually steep gables. To the E, a high sea wall of the pre-Madocks period.

PARC. *See* Croesor.

LLANGAR

0642

1 m. NNE of Cynwyd.

ALL SAINTS. In the care of Cadw. Backed into the hill, down a track and across a field, in an arcadian stretch of the Vale of Edeirnion. The church happily survived after the new church was built at Cynwyd. Undivided nave and chancel with a broad s porch and small W bellcote. The fabric is a wonderful palimpsest from C15 to C18, spared the correcting hand of the Victorians. Dated stones, six of 1617, indicate work in the early C17. One is incised on the s porch, but the porch roof truss is dated 1702. Earlier C17 Perp-style three-light E window, the arched head showing the late date. The W end was probably again rebuilt in the early C18, because of subsidence. Stone-mullion windows: that to the s pulpit earlier C17, the N one and one high in the W wall earlier C18, the date of the gallery. Pointed chamfered s doorway; and a tiny C15 window to the sanctuary, s. Later C17 N doorway of cyclopean masonry. The church was taken into state care in 1967 largely to preserve

Llangar, All Saints.
Engraving, 1912

the wall paintings. In 1974 the chancel N wall was massively thickened for support and a late C18 coved plaster barrel ceiling was removed. More recent work has reinstated the exterior whitewash to excellent effect. New green Nantlle random slates cover the roof.

Sloping slate-paved interior. Late medieval arch-braced trusses with short cusped wind-braces survive to the three E bays; the easternmost bay is ceiled with moulded ribs and the two W bays were largely replaced in 1974. W GALLERY of 1715–16 reached by a broad winding stone stair, and supported on the l. on a tapering stone that may be part of the church-yard cross. The front is plastered and painted with texts in roundels dated 1764. The benches are early C18, with space for musicians or singers around a rare pyramid music stand. – FONT. Set into the wall, a crude tapering bowl, C12 or C13. – Three-decker PULPIT, early C19, with bits of C17 pews. – BOX PEWS mostly on the N and BENCHES along the S. The main, Gwerclas, pew is dated 1711 and has some C17 panels; two further E are dated 1759 and 1768. The rector's pew in the SE corner is dated 1841, with the C18 turned ALTAR RAILS butted against. – Pretty painted CUPBOARD door, C18 with winged cherub, in a blocked chancel N light. – COMMANDMENT BOARDS. C18, in Welsh, on the E wall. – WALL PAINTINGS. Restoration revealed no fewer than eight phases from the C14 to the C18. The N wall has a wonderfully robust C18 Death with pick and shovel,* a bishop, possibly C14, entering a church, and C15 scenes in panels. Similar panels on the S wall, part of a Seven Deadly Sins, each riding a beast. – Whitewashed LYCHGATE, 1731.

THE OLD RECTORY, just SE, above the main road. Two stone ranges at right angles, both with Georgian windows but big square central chimneys, suggesting C17 origins.

BRYNTIRION, ¼ m. E. Villa of 1852, in roughcast with pretty bargeboards to the centre gable. The back wall has two rows of decorative star-shaped brick chimneys

LLANGELYNIN 5707

A coastal parish, originally a twelve-mile strip from the Dysynni to the Mawddach, but Llwyngwril and Arthog since separated. The church is isolated above the sea and above the railway of 1861–3. A settlement at Rhoslefain, 1 m. inland.

ST CELYNIN. The church is approached from above, the low-pitched roof running out from the slope like a barn, overlook-ing the sweep of Cardigan Bay. The simplicity is moving, just a rectangle, the bellcote on the curious S porch. The base of

*Hanoverian Royal Arms from this wall have been detached for display at Rhug.

the w wall batters out and a single slit window with a Norman arch inside is set low. This gives a possible date of *c.* 1200. The gable was raised for the early C16 roof, the change in stonework clear on the side walls, which have string courses under the new eaves. Opposed N and S doors with low pointed heads; regular voussoirs exposed on the N one. One C16 two-light sanctuary window, S, with a hoodmould, its equivalent on the N robbed of tracery. Other windows later, with leaded casements. One set high on the N lit a W gallery, one on the S perhaps lit the pulpit. C18 arched E window with thin voussoirs. The porch is squat and sturdy, the broad arched entry with thin voussoirs and arched dripstones, capped by the rough bellcote with a segmental-arched lintel. Probably C17: the bell, exchanged with that from Llwyngwril, was dated 1660.

The peace and loveliness of the interior was preserved by neglect and then by careful restoration. In 1917 *Harold Hughes* brought the church back from disuse after the new church was built at Llwyngwril in 1842. Another restoration in 1970, and again in 2003, by *Adam & Frances Voelcker*. The whitened plaster walls, uneven floor slabs, and oak casements in old openings are foils to a magnificent Tudor roof, the oak felled between 1502 and 1530. Tie-beams rest on moulded wall-plates, supported by curved braces from wall-posts with a triple band at the feet, which stand on rough corbels. Each truss has a kingpost and vertical struts, the E ones with slotting for cusped boards between, as survives in the E truss. The sanctuary bay has C19 boarding, but a strip from the original celure, of pierced rosettes, down the centre. Repaired trusses at the W end, which had a gallery until 1917. In the sanctuary a blocked slit window and two arched tomb-recesses.

FONT. Discoloured, patched and bound in iron. Possibly C13, octagonal, deeply chamfered beneath; octagonal stem and base. – WALL PAINTINGS. Fragments of black-letter inscriptions on the N wall, restored 1917. At the W, found in 2003, a memorable skeleton figure of Death with scythe and spade, similar to the one at Llangar, but earlier, perhaps late C17, inscribed MEMENTO MORI. – The WOODWORK has much appeal, rustic and consistent; work is recorded in 1823 and most seems to fit this date. – A full set of Georgian BENCHES in raw pine, still with the names of their proprietors and their farms, painted in white. The back benches, for servants, just have farm names. – The SCREEN has some battered pierced medieval panels on the l. (ring-dated to 1497–1533) from the medieval screen. High Georgian rails fixed on top, Georgian gates with crude turned balusters. It is hard to imagine the liturgical purpose in 1823. – PULPIT. Late Georgian, corniced and panelled, some reeded detail. – COMMUNION TABLE. Very plain, on tall legs. The N DOOR is made in the medieval way with a post fitted into sockets at top and bottom to act as its hinge. – COMMANDMENT BOARD. 1796, in Welsh, the painted lettering beautifully irregular. – On the S wall a large C18 HORSE BIER. – CHANDELIER, dated 1843, presumably intended for Llwyngwril; another more florid affair is later. – MONUMENTS. – An obliterated mid-C18 cartouche with rustic Bible and winged cherub on a shield above. – Mary Thomas of Hendre †1785, marble plaque.

The CHURCHYARD is rectangular, steep and partly raised. LYCHGATE dated 1884 but perhaps only restored then, with seats and a livestock grid within.

LLANFENDIGAID, 1 m. SW of Rhoslefain. An ancient site: Foel Llanfendigaid, behind the house, has remains of a HILL-FORT, and there was a medieval chapel here. The house, of a branch of the Nanney family, was rebuilt in 1745–6. Stone in long blocks, seven bays, and typical of the Georgian houses of the region with three stone dormers and tall end chimneys. Rear wing largely of the 1920s. Inside, a fielded-panelled hall; staircase with turned balusters off to the l. The W room also has fielded panelling and the E room plain painted panelling. The size of the E chimney and some heavy beams suggest that an older house may be incorporated. In the attic, 1746 IN over a fireplace. Behind, a barn range dated 1863. In a garden wall, C17 stone from Nannau with the names of Hugh and Ann Nanney.

BRONCLYDWR, 1 m. S of Rhoslefain. The Rev. Hugh Owen, pioneer Nonconformist, was licensed to preach here in 1672. His house, dated 1688, has two storeys and attic with tall end chimneys. Three bays close-spaced in the centre, suggestive of deep fireplaces. C19 small sashes above and C19 enlarged windows below, and half-dormers apparently also C19. Inside, a fireplace lintel with Owen's initials and 1688; ogee stops to the beams. To the W, late C18 to early C19 OUTBUILDINGS including a barn, lofted cartshed and stable.

CASTELL MAWR HILL-FORT, ½ m. S of Rhoslefain (SH 581 048). On a narrow ridge of rock with good natural defences. On the W side is a deep ditch with a slight counterscarp bank. Only here and on the N end is there is any recognizable rampart. Though the artificial defences are slight, the cutting back of the rock ensures an impressive drop of 16 ft (5 metres) to the bottom of the rock-cut ditch. The entrance is on the S; only a very short stretch of ditch was dug on the E side (now becoming filled with rubbish). An annexe on the N tip of the ridge may represent a later addition.

TONFANNAU, Tonfannau, 2 m. S, across the railway. Ruins of a substantial C17 to C18 house of complex form, probably two separate units. The front of one-and-a-half storeys with raking dormers looks C18, but is joined to a long rear wing by a massive C17 chimney. Around, remnants of a 1939 anti-aircraft training base.

MYNYDD TAL-Y-GARREG HILL-FORT, Tonfannau (SH 574 036). The summit is strongly fortified, the banks and rock-cut ditches possibly early medieval rather than prehistoric. On the very top, with a shipping beacon placed on its wall, is a large circular house or tower. It is cut off from the rest of the narrow ridge to the S by two rock-cut ditches with a bank between.

The outer one appears unfinished, though still impressive. On the N and W the defences encircling the rocky plateau are less clearly defined; the banks no more than scarps and the ditch very slight. At the E end (over the modern wall) the banks can easily be seen where they end above the slope, so steep that it needs no further protection.

LLANGOWER/LLANGYWER

9033

ST CYWAIR. Disused small church, of medieval origins but mostly C18 and C19. Dated 1773 over a S window and at the SW corner; steep roof of bicolour slates of *c.* 1866 (date on the porch). Plain Victorian interior. – FONT. Circular, possibly C12, on a later octagonal shaft. – C19 HORSE BIER. – STAINED GLASS. E window, 1871. S window, St Margaret and Faith, 1878, by *Forrest & Son*.

E of the church, PONT GOWER. Single-arched, the soffit of well-cut stones, early C19. Above the church, the former rectory, PLAS GOWER, earlier C19. Hipped, square, with little gables on the garden side.

PONT MWNWGL-Y-LLYN, 2½ m. NE. Prettily distorted three-arched bridge, over the former outlet of the Dee, a minor inlet since the 1953–5 flood-relief scheme. Across the road, CASTELL GRONW, a small motte-and-bailey, associated with Goronwy ap Ednyfed Fychan †1268, seneschal to Llywelyn the Last.

FACH-DDEILIOG (Bala Lake Hotel), 2 m. NE. Holiday retreat built *c.* 1801 for Sir Richard Colt Hoare of Stourhead, Wiltshire. An enthusiast for the Picturesque, Hoare discovered the lake in 1796, spending two or three weeks a year here. His house is single-storey, the elongated octagonal central room flanked by two-bay wings with verandas. Modern end additions. It was a retreat, the services were separate in an older house behind (now gone). Hoare had been taken with 'the little retired villa' of Lord William Gordon on Derwentwater, Cumberland, also single-storey. On the lakeside, a small stone BOATHOUSE.

FFYNNON GOWER, ½ m. SW. Mid-C19, two-storey, three bays; the windows iron with tiny panes. Below, a painted brick railway cottage marks FLAG STATION whence the Williams-Wynns reached Glan-llyn, summoning a boat by flag.

PANT-YR-ONNEN, ½ m. E. Prominent on a shoulder of hill, a large earlier C19 Williams-Wynn estate farm. Hipped two-bay side-entry house and a tail of lofted outbuildings running E. Incorporated is a stone, R&S V 1656, and another, 'Row. Ellis'.

TŶ-CERRIG, ¼ m. S, on the hillside. L-plan, whitewashed. The N end cross-wing was a C16 hall-house with two ornate crucks, cusped above high collars. The house, of *c.* 1800, has small casement windows.

LLANSANTFFRAED GLYNDYFRDWY *see*
CARROG

LLANUWCHLLYN   8730

The upper end of the broad valley of Llyn Tegid, the Bala lake.
The source of the Dee (Afon Dyfrdwy) is in the mountains to
the NW. Two ancient and spectacular routes cross the mountains
out of the valley, NW to Trawsfynydd and S to Llanymawddwy.

ST DEINIOL. Disused. In an ancient rounded and raised churchyard. 1873, by *Edmund Ferrey*, in a bald E.E., elaborated a little
in the chancel. Parallel-roofed SE aisle divided by a two-bay
nave arcade and single arch from the chancel. – FONT. Octagonal with quatrefoils. Said to be C17; if so, wholly reworked. –
BAPTISTERY for total immersion; mid-C19 zinc-lined chest like
a coffin. – STAINED GLASS. E window, Ascension, 1867,
appalling and joyful, three free-kicking figures against a cloud-
and-sky background of primitive and primary colours. –
Chancel N, three lancets, one, the Good Shepherd, by *Ward &
Hughes*, 1885, by whom also the nave S, Crucifixion, 1913. –
MONUMENT. Ieuan ap Gruffydd ap Madog ap Iorwerth, of
Glan-llyn, a fine recumbent effigy dated 1370 or 1395. The
moustachioed head rests on a helmet, the hands joined at the
breast. The armour is decoratively treated – chain-mail, jupon
emblazoned with roses and boars' heads, and ornate arm- and
leg-pieces. Latin inscription in Lombardic letters along the
leading edge. – Ellis Lewis and family. Grey and white marble
with armorial cartouche and cherub head, *c.* 1720. – Stone
LYCHGATE with pointed arch, dated 1725.

AINON BAPTIST CHAPEL, 1 m. SW. 1840. A charming rural
chapel of massive field stones. Near-square with deep flat eaves
and domestic doors and windows. Simple panelled tall pulpit.
Some box pews l. of it, and raked to the back wall.

HEN GAPEL (Calvinistic Methodist), ½ m. NW. Founded 1746.
The present chapel of 1871, by the *Rev. Thomas Thomas*, with
typical giant arch on pilasters. The detail is particularly good,
sandstone ashlar on green stone, the pilasters daringly five.
Inside, pitch-pine pews and gallery with pierced ironwork. The
attached CHAPEL HOUSE looks uncomfortable now because
when built in 1810 it was continuous with a long-wall chapel.
Adjacent graves of the Rev. Michael Jones †1853, founder of
the Bala Independent College, and his son the Rev. Michael
D. Jones †1898, promoter of the Patagonia settlement.

The village is divided by the River Dee. N of the church, Nos.
1–6 CHURCH STREET, l., a later C19 row, No. 3 with original
iron casements. HENDŶ'R YSGOL, r., whitewashed stone
school of 1841, looks domestic apart from the large plaque
to the Watkins-Wynns, who gave it and also the iron
Coalbrookdale PUMP outside, 1891. ARADOL, opposite, much
altered, was the successor school, *c.* 1875, by *Benjamin Ferrey*.

The present SCHOOL, *c.* 1970, is set back before the MEMO-RIAL to the great educationist Sir Owen M. Edwards †1920 and his son, Ifan ab Owen Edwards †1970, founder of the youth league, Yr Urdd Gobaith Cymru. The two men, the older encouraging the younger, in bronze, 1972, by *Jonah Jones*, are set against a curving stone wall with rough reliefs that dates from the previous memorial to the father alone, *c.* 1960. The CEMETERY gateway has later C20 figurative iron gates, as at the Pandy graveyard (*see* below): Crucifixion with ascending doves and falling dragon. PONT LLIW, 1852, crosses the Lliw on two arches of squared and tooled stone with keel cutwaters.

S of the river, PLAS DEON, mid-C19, three-storey, stuccoed villa. The village here, PANDY, was devastated by flood in 1780, and mostly dates from after the railway, 1868. On the l., the MEMORIAL ARCHWAY to the chapel graveyard where Sir O. M. Edwards is buried, by *R. L. Gapper* of Aberystwyth, *c.* 1960. Silver granite, in six large pieces, monolith jambs, the arch inner ring in five cants. The gate pivots centrally, the intricate ironwork of an angel on a skull by *D. J. Williams* of Caernarfon. On STATION ROAD, E, two terraces, Nos. 1–4, 1870s, with slightly pointed brick doorheads, and Nos. 4–8, 1860s, in large squared stones with iron windows. Off l. is Neuadd Wen (q.v.). The former Pandy STATION, 1867, is well preserved by the Bala Lake Light Railway. Red brick, gabled. Gothic iron canopy (by *J. Morris* of Welshpool) reused from the Aberystwyth line. A small platform building and a signal box complete a neat railway group. At the top of the village, PONT-Y-PANDY leaps the Twrch in a single broad span, built 1781, after the flood.

CASTELL CARNDOCHAN, Dolhendre, 2 m. NW. Dramatically set on a mountain ridge above the Lliw valley, overlooking the lake and Bala. In the absence of evidence, the castle is interpreted as an early C13 stronghold of Llywelyn the Great. Fenton thought it 'the refuge of some ferocious chief who had lost all claim to society, and who lived by plunder and rapine'. The layout of this lofty shapeless mass of rubble and scree is best appreciated from the air. An apsidal tower commands the approach looking down the ridge. Access to the castle is over a ditch with counterscarp bank that divides the ridge from the building. A small square building is located in the centre of the courtyard, and to the NE are the remains of a D-shaped tower, possibly an addition, with a smaller semi-circular tower to the S. All the walls were originally mortared. The tower built with the greatest care is that to the SW, an apsidal tower, akin to those at Castell y Bere, and also Ewloe in Flintshire.

CAERGAI, 1 m. NE. C17, built within a C1 ROMAN FORT commanding the route from Corwen to Dolgellau (Brithdir fort), recognizable as a square platform surrounding the house. From the SW, the stone-walled rampart is easily seen, elsewhere the Roman features are partly buried beneath later walls.

Foundations of the E rampart cross the roadway at the farmyard entrance. Excavation revealed two periods of wooden
barracks and a later arrangement of buildings, which suggested
that the fort may have been reduced in size. Roman finds to
the W suggest a civil settlement (*vicus*) with a small cremation
cemetery. Geophysical survey revealed the plan of a possible
annexe to the S containing a substantial courtyard building,
and demonstrated the considerable size of the *vicus*.
An inscription named the first cohort of the Nervii, known to
be in Britain in 105.

Caergai was reputedly the place of Arthur's upbringing,
named for Cai Hir, or Kay, his foster-brother. The HOUSE is
mid-C17, rebuilt for the poet and Royalist Rowland Vaughan,
after being burnt by General Myddleton in 1645. Ten hearths
in 1662, probably the present house. Centre closely flanked by
gables, the r. one a cross-wing, and slightly broader. The
windows are C20 renewals and the openings may have been
regularized in the C19. Central C17 voussoired door between
windows, two above, under a two-window dormer gable. An
ancient avenue of trees to the rear, W.

GLAN-LLYN, 1½ m. ENE. On a platform overlooking the lake, a
shooting lodge of the Williams-Wynns of Wynnstay, at the
centre of an estate of some 35,000 acres, gained by marriage
with the Vaughan heiress. Fenton called the house new in 1804,
and 'a heavy gloomy building' by comparison with Fach-ddeiliog (Llangower). An occasional residence, its bedroom storey
is modest with narrow windows under the eaves. Square-plan.
The three-bay front has two broad flattened bows with French
windows opening to the view. Dividing stair within. Since 1950
the centre of a holiday complex run by the Urdd Gobaith
Cymru youth movement, and encumbered by modern
dormitories and sports halls, by *Ifan Prys Edwards*, or his
successor *Harry James*.

The estate passed for death duties to the government in
1946, and in 1951 was the focus of ambitious rural regeneration under the Welsh Land Commission. New houses and outbuildings were to be built and old ones renewed to remedy
decades of neglect. At LON, just NW, is a well-designed terrace
of five houses for estate workers in an appealing modern-
Georgian style, roughcast, the ends of stone with stuccoed
pediments and cartouches dated 1951. NE of Lon is the base
of a hilltop circular TOWER, an estate folly.

NEUADD WEN, Pandy. 1907–8, by *Samuel Evans*, County Surveyor of Flintshire, built for Owen M. Edwards (*see* p. 666) in
the year he returned to Wales as Chief Inspector of Schools.
A good Edwardian house, roughcast, with small-paned casements, bows and bays, under a deep hipped roof. Open-pedimented cross-wing, r. Remarkable two-storey porch in red
brick with the top chequered in sandstone; an up-to-the-
minute display. Well planned around a stair hall; the drawing
room with typical Edwardian inglenook arch springing from
little columns.

PANT-Y-CEUBREN, ½ m. ESE. Low farmhouse dated 1648, with fireplace stair.

PRYS MAWR, ¼ m. W. 1685, for a branch of the Vaughans of Caergai. Compact two-storey, four-bay front with C19 iron six-pane windows and a rear wing. Heavy framed ceilings; an embedded wall-post in the partition to the rear range may relate to an older timber frame.

DOLHENDRE, 1½ m. NW. Backing onto the road, a plain C19 two-storey ALMSHOUSE row, endowed, according to a plaque of 1731, for 'three decayed old men and three old women' by Maurice Vaughan, 'Cannon of Winsor'. Some Dolhendre farms were renovated in 1951 by the Welsh Land Commission (*see* Glan-llyn, p. 667), and a row built at FFRIDD HELYG in the same neat style as the Lon terrace. On Carndochan was a GOLD MINE, which produced enough for the Williams-Wynns to have made an ornate gold cup in 1870. DOLHENDRE ISAF, a long C19 two-storey range, has a porch on slate monoliths. CARMEL INDEPENDENT CHAPEL, 1893–4, isolated by forestry, has a simple gable front.

9236   LLANYCIL

A large parish N of the Bala lakeside, stretching to the two Arenig peaks and Llyn Celyn. The church, once the Bala parish church, is by the lake; settlements at Parc and Rhyd Uchaf inland.

ST BEUNO. In the care of the Bible Society. A single chamber of medieval origin, thoroughly restored in 1880. Both *Ferrey* and *Spaull* are named as architects, perhaps because the older Ferrey died that year. Very Victorian interior with good roofs, panelled over the sanctuary. – Gothic oak SCREEN and gabled REREDOS. – FONT. Over-wrought, with a different plant on each face. – RAILS. 1739, with turned balusters. – STAINED GLASS. E window, 1883, the Brazen Serpent, colourful and intensely detailed. N three-light former E window, patterned glass of 1855; two-light, 1880, C16 style. S window, later C19, muted colours. – MEMORIALS. Two plaques with small marble cherub heads on black-painted grounds: to Sarah Jones †1734 and Maurice Jones 1763. – Oval plaque to William Williams †1764. – Robert Lloyd †1768, a bulbous vase on grey. – Rev. Evan Lloyd †1776, who wrote satirical verses; marble flaming urn on a wreathed obelisk. His encomium by John Wilkes begins, 'Oh pleasing poet, Friend for ever dear . . .' – Rev. Rice Anwyl †1819, plain urn on grey, by *W. Jones* of Liverpool. – Rev. Simon Lloyd †1836, Methodist and friend of Thomas Charles, a deep-panelled neo-grec trapezium.

Large CHURCHYARD, the graveyard for Bala. By the S wall two sandstone TABLE TOMBS, to John Vaughan of Cefn Bodig †1671 and Catherine Lloyd of Rhagatt †1695, both highly ornamented. Vaughan's arms are set in the church wall above. E of the church, within railings, TABLE TOMB to the Rev.

Thomas Charles †1814, sandstone ashlar, with a plaque: 'North Wales . . . will probably retain traces of his various and strenuous exertions to promote the kingdom of Christ till time shall be no more'.

Opposite the church, LLANYCIL COTTAGE, 1838, a tiny church school, looking like an estate cottage. Hoodmoulded window each side of the porch, big central hexagonal chimney. The small r. room was the schoolroom for fifty or sixty, the rest the teacher's house. ABERCELYN was the vicarage, 1830s, three bays, hipped with a veranda, the r. cross-wing possibly added. Low BARN to the SE, dated 1774.

TALYBONT CALVINISTIC METHODIST CHAPEL, Rhyd Uchaf, 2 m. NW of Bala. 1870, by *Richard Owens* of Liverpool. Green stone with grey dressings, in Owens' Lombard style, like Carrog and Gwyddelwern.

FRONFEUNO, ¼ m. NE. Overlooking the lake, a house of unidentifiable original character lost in a remodelling c. 1960. Within is the very fine beamed C16 ceiling removed from Plas Uchaf, Cynwyd. Elaborate run-out mouldings to the beams and moulded joists. The staircase, with Islamic grid panels and newels with pretty roundels came, with other woodwork, from *Alfred Waterhouse*'s Eaton Hall, Cheshire, demolished in 1961 (*see also* Plas Moel-y-garnedd).

PLAS MOEL-Y-GARNEDD, ½ m. NW, overlooking the lake. A compact house of c. 1870, built for John Parry, Groom of the Great Chamber to Queen Victoria. Mullion-and-transom windows, the outer bays projecting with hipped roofs broached from square to canted – attractive and unusual. A hall fireplace is dated 1883. As at Fronfeuno, woodwork from Eaton Hall, Cheshire, principally panelling and doors. To the NE, a whitewashed COTTAGE with upper-cruck trusses.

CYFFDY, ½ m. E of Parc. Later C17, tall, L-plan, with a parlour wing at the l. The long section r. of the porch is probably C18, though a cart entry is dated 1881. Lobby-entry plan; an oak partition to the parlour. Early C18 stair with turned balusters and square newels in a rear tower.

LLANYMAWDDWY

9219

On the upper Dyfi, whose source is under Aran Mawddwy to the NW. A drovers' road runs N to Llanuwchllyn over the Bwlch-y-groes pass, still spectacularly remote, though the hills were mined for lead in the 1840s and for gold (unsuccessfully) in the 1850s.

ST TYDECHO. An ancient rounded churchyard, but the church rebuilt without flair in 1854 for the Rev. John Williams, co-founder of the Cambrian Archaeological Association, and himself an undisciplined antiquarian. Could he have designed it? Nave on the original footings; the chancel new. Single-roofed with bellcote and porch; cusped lancets in pairs and singles. – FITTINGS. 1939, by *Harold Hughes*. – FONT. A robust

C12 octagonal tapered bowl in ochre stone, each face a single scallop, and a band lower down. – STAINED GLASS. Good E window, 1864, Christ with St David and St Tydecho, by *Heaton, Butler & Bayne*. Two windows, nave N and S, *c.* 1900. – In the churchyard an eroded C17 TABLE TOMB. – Large stone LYCHGATE, 1958, by *P. M. Padmore*.

BRYN, ¼ m. NE. Remodelled in 1816 as a plain three-storey, three-bay stone house with deep eaves. Inside, an exceptional mahogany and oak dog-leg stair of *c.* 1700, with turned balusters on wreathed urns and ornate scrolled treads.

LLANERCH, 2 m. SW. Late C16 to early C17. Whitewashed L-plan house with a barn at the lower end. Remnants of cruck-trusses within, though the roof has been raised. The barn has a further pair and evidence that it was once timber framed, a far westerly example. Another timber frame, a small house, survives in the yard of TŶNYCOED, ½ m. W. Two-storey, two-bay, dated 1778, on a plaster partition but probably a little earlier. C16 or C17 crucks survive in the house and barn at TROEDYRHIW, across the valley from Llanerch.

LLAWR-Y-BETWS *see* GLAN-YR-AFON

5910

LLWYNGWRIL

ST CELYNIN. 1841–3, by *Thomas Jones* of Chester, to replace the isolated Llangelynin church (q.v.). Minimal Gothic in green stone with pink sandstone bellcote and triplet of W lancets. C20 W porch and vestry. Preaching-box interior with a panelled W gallery. – Chancel FITTINGS of 1931. – FONT. Overdone. 1914. – STAINED GLASS. E window, 1896, by *Hardman*; two chancel windows, 1915. Outside, a large granite Celtic cross WAR MEMORIAL.

The main road runs tightly between irregular terraces in greenish stone. S of the bridge, a row of four Late Georgian houses and one larger one, TŶ NEWYDD, behind. W of the road, BETHEL CALVINISTIC METHODIST CHAPEL, 1876, stucco, with a fancy curved-ended porch. N of the bridge, the GARTHANGHARAD ARMS, two whitewashed houses with gabled upper windows, the main part 1840, the r. similar but dated 1736. On the l. a severe late C19 TERRACE of four, green stone with buff dressings. FFORDD-Y-FELIN runs W past FELIN ISAF, an altered C19 corn mill, to TŶ NANT, a good Arts and Crafts house of 1908. Roughcast with slate-hung gables, careful asymmetries and Voysey-like plain stone mullions. Opposite, the former BOARD SCHOOL, *c.* 1872, and, on the other side, in a cottage row, TŶ'R EFAIL, dated 1732. On the main road, the blue-washed former SALEM WESLEYAN CHAPEL, 1871, Gothic, and ORIEL LLWYNGWRIL, the National School, 1834, extended 1923, also minimally Gothic. Hendre (*see* below) is beyond. Then, on the r., four detached or semi-detached VILLAS of *c.* 1910, green stone, with Edwardian asymmetries. After the last, a track runs E to LLWYN DU, two-storey, three-bay, dated 1708. The Quaker Humphreys left here for Pennsylvania in the 1680s. The later C17 Quaker BURIAL GROUND (incorrectly dated 1646) is down a lane W of the main road.

HENDRE, N of the centre. A regular five-bay stone front with Georgian sashes and five large stone dormers. Originally, three-bay, early C18, built for the Thomas family. Voussoirs mark the original door in the second bay, and the fireplace stair is indicated by windows with dripmoulds in the l. end. Extended r. and a three-bay C19 house added behind. The farm across the main road includes HENDRE UCHA, the house now part of the farm range. Attached late C18 cartshed with round loft lights, and a C19 water wheel. A cowhouse is dated 1769.

TŶ GWYN, on the S edge. Founded as a convalescent home by David Davies M.P. of Llandinam. 1928, by *A. S. Hill* of Newtown. Friendly Arts and Crafts style in white roughcast with greenish slates.

CASTELL-Y-GAER HILL-FORT, overlooking Llwyngwril from a spur, ½ m. SE (SH 592 090). The flat top was surrounded by a wide stone wall, badly robbed except on the S and E. Around the steep nose of the spur, no further defence. On the S side two deep ditches with a substantial rampart between. Entrance on the N side. A gap in the stone wall on the SE corner can still be recognized. The path from there curls round the N tip of the outer rampart, there raised for extra protection. The large, carefully built CLEARANCE CAIRNS in this district, some from modern field clearance, should be noted.

FFORDD DDU. From Llwyn Du a footpath ascends NE to Ffordd Ddu, the trackway that skirts Cader Idris (*see also* Arthog). Two small STANDING STONES above Parth-y-gwyddwch (SH 601 103) and just beyond, a late prehistoric or Romano-British FARMSTEAD terraced into the hillside. It consists of a stone wall, still over 3 ft (1 metre) high where the terrace has been built up. Inside it the site of a single large hut. About 1 m. NE towards the top (SH 616 113), an ALIGNMENT of five large stones. Three still stand, in a straight line of about 230 ft (70 metres), approximately SW–NE. The purpose of these alignments, shorter but employing taller stones than the famous 'stone rows' of Dartmoor, is unknown. They tend to occur in the vicinity of Bronze Age monuments with which they are likely to be contemporary.

MAENTWROG
6642

The parish, in the beautiful Vale of Ffestiniog, lies on both sides of the Dwyryd river, characterized by Tan-y-bwlch estate buildings. The heyday of the riverside quays SW of Maentwrog was between 1820 and 1836, when virtually all the slate from

Blaenau Ffestiniog was loaded here. A quarry at Gelli Grin produced the impressively long and regular blocks of brown slate-stone seen in many of the buildings.

ST TWROG. Below the village, down a delightful path part-lined with yews. A medieval church was replaced by a plain structure in 1814, transformed in 1896 by *Douglas & Fordham* of Chester, both for the Oakeleys of Tan-y-bwlch. Douglas added the chancel and windows, replaced the castellated bellcote with a W tower, and remodelled the interior. The tapering tower and splayed-foot spire, both slate-clad, are foreign to the region, yet lovable and in keeping in the estate village. Rubble, with Perp sandstone windows; half-timber S porch. Aisled interior, of cleverly inserted timber arcades, the plaster panels above decorated with stencilled motifs. – REREDOS. Finely carved in oak, with gold mosaic work, *c.* 1900 apparently by *Mary Oakeley*, wife of W. E. Oakeley, who according to her memorial did all the carving, so presumably also the SCREENS and the PULPIT. – STAINED GLASS. N aisle W, by *Edward Frampton*, *c.* 1896. N aisle third, by *C. C. Powell*, *c.* 1941. S aisle, *Celtic Studios*, 1964. – MONUMENTS. Anne Meyrick of Berthlwyd †1743. Stone Baroque cartouche with urn and cherub-head. – Robert Gruffydd of Tanybwlch †1750. Large and handsome. Above a sarcophagus plaque, a gadrooned urn and festooned flowers, and strange Rococo leaf-scroll ornaments beside. – Outside, against the SW corner, the MAEN TWROG – the stone hurled by St Twrog from the top of Moelwyn to crush a pagan altar. Picturesque LYCHGATE, 1897, by *Douglas & Fordham*. Half-timber with Gelli Grin stone; a little pyramid clock turret corbelled from the gable.

HOLY CROSS (R.C.), Gellilydan, 1½ m. ESE. A late C18 stone tannery, well converted in the 1960s for Irish workers building the Trawsfynydd nuclear power station. Round W window with stained glass.

CILGAL INDEPENDENT CHAPEL. Sturdy Gothic in rock-faced rubble with red sandstone, *c.* 1919. Buttresses, a triplet and three good quatrefoils – at the apex and over the outer windows.

MAENTWROG ISAF CALVINISTIC METHODIST CHAPEL. Prominent on the A487 road, now a house. 1873. An almost round-headed recess frames a nearly Tudor window above a Tudor door. The outer windows pointed.

PONT DOL-Y-MOCH, 1½ m. ENE. Probably late C17, over the Dwyryd. Segmental arches separated by cutwaters brought up as pedestrian refuges.

The pretty VILLAGE, picturesque at the foot of a W-facing bluff, was largely created by successive Oakeleys of Tan-y-bwlch. BULL STREET curves round the bluff. CEDRWYDD, l., was the toll house, late C18. To the r., the OLD RECTORY. Originally early C19, three-bay; it was grandly enlarged in the 1830s as Glan William, for an Oakeley cousin, William, son of Sir Charles Oakeley, Governor of Madras. Five bays with a deep-

eaved roof and pediment (as at Haycock's Shire Hall,
Dolgellau), and four great axial chimneys linked in Vanbrugh-
like pairs by arches. Hipped centre to the garden with verandas
each side. The stable blocks back onto the street. Next a handsome long TERRACE of *c.* 1834 up to the lychgate, with deep
eaves; squared blocks with huge lintels. Opposite, the tall four-
storey TANLAN, with a renewed two-storey timber veranda,
formerly the Oakeley Reading Room. From the war memorial,
a charming flight of slate steps divides into adjacent flights; the
better l. side to PENLAN, the rougher r. to its service building,
the four-storey sharp-cornered PENLAN FLATS. Penlan seems
to be two Late Georgian houses: one, three-bay, facing downhill with a lower two-storey bow to the r. linking to the other
at right angles, with stucco hoodmoulds. Higher, l. of the flats,
ARGRAIG, similar, completes the enchanting cluster.

Beyond the lychgate, forming a little square, PEN-Y-BRYN,
the former Rose and Crown, and BRON-Y-WERN, both with
gabled half-dormers. At right angles, LLYS TWROG, Late
Georgian style, with coped verges and rough roof slates. But
neither this nor CARTREF behind appear on the 1840 tithe
map. At Seion chapel, 1906, the road runs downhill past the
picturesque former SCHOOL, 1871, with a slated spire,
patterned roof slates, and big half-hipped dormers; Nos. 1–4
GLANDŴR, two pairs of semi-detached estate cottages, with
verandas and bargeboards. The lane, once called the Oakeley
Drive, leads on uphill to Gellilydan and the former Maentwrog
Road station, 2 m. E. Rows of TERRACES and Cilgal chapel
(*see* above) on the uphill side.

TAN-Y-BWLCH, ½ m. NW on the A487 road, is the estate village
to the Plas. It runs W from the splendid inn at the junction of
the old main route to Caernarfon over the hills to Llanfrothen
and the new one to the Cob at Porthmadog. The OAKELEY
ARMS, then the Tan-y-bwlch Inn, was a 'very neat small inn'
according to Pennant in 1784, recently improved by the Earl
of Radnor. Greatly enlarged by W. G. Oakeley before 1835 to
an exceptional scale. Three broad canted hipped wings
project, with wide eaves, separated by single-storey porches
against the earlier range, which is of rubble rather than Gelli
Grin slabs. Large earlier C19 COACHHOUSE, N. Gabled centre
block with roundel above a lunette over paired coach entries,
the lintels with quarter-round shoulders, neatly suggesting a
circle begun by the lunette. CILDERI, W, 1930s, single-storey
and hipped, was the estate manager's house and post office.
BUS SHELTER, *c.* 2001, by *Gwynedd County Architects*, carefully
in keeping. Stone, and braced oak posts. Downhill are estate
buildings: SMITHY, l., FLOUR MILL and KILN HOUSE, r., with
Gothic windows. Now dwellings. Behind is the SAWMILL.
Further SW, THE WHITE BARN, *c.* 1880, for the estate bailiff,
a long single-storey rather Indian bungalow, hipped with a
slate-pillared veranda. The HOME FARM is to the W: a long
open shelter on tall slate pillars, an octagonal dairy, stables,
pigsties, granary, sleeping lofts etc. Storeyed gateway with

a tall arch and a gabled bellcote. Louvred ventilators with pyramid-slated caps.

PLAS TAN-Y-BWLCH, ½ m. w. The estate was already large when William Oakeley (1750–1811), of the Shropshire family, married the Griffith heiress in 1789. He did much groundwork, draining the valley, embanking the river, laying roads etc. His son William Griffith Oakeley (1790–1835) altered the house and rebuilt much in Maentwrog, including the church, on the royalties of Blaenau Ffestiniog slate (£25,000 in 1824–5). On his early death, his wife Louisa Jane ran the estate until induced in 1869 to sign over to the heir, William Edward Oakeley (1823–1912), grandson of Sir Charles Oakeley. He rebuilt the house, church and school and did much to the landscape including creating the lake above (Llyn Mair). His swimming pool was filled by sea water brought by the Festiniog Railway to the private halt above the house. He rashly took direct control of the slate quarries in 1878, just as the industry faltered, and after his fortune failed he left the Plas in 1904, although the estate was only sold in 1962.

The HOUSE, on its terrace on the wooded N side of the Vale, was thought to originate *c.* 1748 for Robert Griffith, but a reused timber has been ring-dated 1536. Late C18 tourists' views show a tall L-plan house with a pediment and hipped dormers, typical of the region. The main part of the S front and the entrance front at right angles are the C18 house, given a battlemented attic and hoodmoulded windows before 1835, probably by W. G. Oakeley. Perhaps also for him the matching detached three-storey service range. Little more was done before 1868, but by 1872 the house was called 'newly-renovated and almost entirely rebuilt'. W. E. Oakeley's architect is not known; *John Douglas* may have been involved. A tower-like embattled block with a full-height canted bay was added, standing well forward l. of the earlier house, which was given mullion-and-transom windows and a projecting crowstepped central feature. On the entrance front the older sashes remain, though the Tudor porch looks added. To the r. an embattled Tudor-arched screen wall dated 1886 closes the service court. Mostly later C19 interiors, altered. A complex open-well stair has arcaded landings on two levels, and Oakeley heraldry in the window.

To E are earlier C19 STABLES, Tudor-style, of long stone blocks. Lofted, with central shouldered gable over coach entries and a door between to stables behind. Stables also each side, with leaded cross-windows. The Picturesque GARDENS to the S, begun by William Oakeley in the 1790s, were much extended through the C19, evolving to 70 acres of walks planted with specimen trees, overlooking the valley floor planted with clumps of Scots pines. The winding E drive begins at a later C19 LODGE, with ornamental bargeboards; similar but later S LODGE. The little TOP LODGE, by Llyn Mair, the lake formed to supply water, is a single-storey hipped cottage of *c.* 1881, by *John Douglas*. Stone to sill level, then, unusually, slate posts infilled with rust-coloured Gelli Grin stone. Similar chimneys. Leaded windows. Douglas had proposed a conventional timber frame.* HAFOD-Y-LLYN, high in the woods, was a C19 game-keeper's cottage. Single-storey, with a full-length veranda. Heated KENNELS below, now a dwelling.

TAFARN TRIP, ¾ m. NW. Two-storey, three-bay typical Snow- 61 donian end-chimney house, probably C17, once a tavern. Big roof, small windows.

RAILWAY BRIDGE, ½ m. NW of Tan-y-bwlch. A shallow segmental cast-iron arch carries the Festiniog Railway over the B4410 road. Gothic rails, the end posts with quatrefoil panels. Made at the railway's *Boston Lodge Foundry*, Minffordd, 1854.

BRON TURNOR MAWR, ½ m. ENE of Tan-y-bwlch. Large early C19 rectory. Stone, with hipped roofs. Four bays, the centre two advanced; the outer ones have large chimneys.

BRYN-Y-DDWYRYD, ¾ m. NE. A tiny mid-C19 Picturesque Gothic cottage. The central window and door, r., have steep pointed heads outlined in boulders. A similar attic window in the central gable.

DDUALLT, I m. ENE of Tan-y-bwlch. In oak woods, high on the 49 S side of the valley. Two parallel two-storey ranges linked by a shared storeyed lobby. The N range, with a later barn to N, is probably late C16; the near-square S range, on the downhill side – considerably taller because of the attic – is perhaps early C17. It served as the parlour, though the two ranges may have been independent at one time, thus an example of the 'unit system'. The parlour range has a rear mural stair, the other interiors and many windows are of a 1960s restoration from dereliction.

PLAS DOL-Y-MOCH, I½ m. ENE. Gentry house of 1643 for John Jones of Craflwyn, altered after 1910 by *Oswald P. Milne* for W. H. Jackson, London barrister. Four-bay centre between unequal cross-wings, the r. one dated 1643, with rendered attic gable, the slightly lower l. one apparently by Milne, carefully done. Oak mullion windows and dormers by Milne. In the main range, heavy beams and collar-trusses. Open-well stair in a rear tower, the steps of slate. Fine plaster frieze in the r. wing with arms of the fifteen tribes of North Wales and two good overmantels with plaster heraldry, one flanked by human heads, the other by figures. Three-sided STABLE, refurbished in 2006 by *Dobson:Owen* with an attractive glazed passage.

CAE'N-Y-COED ISAF, ¾ m. ENE. Apparently built by the Tan-y-bwlch estate *c.* 1830–40, as an inn. Squared Gelli Grin stone. Two parts united by exaggerated eaves and arched windows. The two-bay W block is pyramid-roofed with Gothick lower glazing. Then a piece with two windows over a door links to a gable with a large window on each floor.

TAFARN HELYG, Gellilydan. Late C18 or early C19 former inn. Late Georgian style. Stone offset three-bay front, with a lower range, r. Across a yard, FORGE and DAIRY, both with small chimneys.

---

* The Middle Lodge NE of the house is similar but simpler.

MELIN TYDDYN-DU, ½ m. E of Gellilydan. Late C18 oat-drying KILN with a perforated clay-tile floor on iron supports, all held up above the central hearth on a framework of slate beams and columns. The adjacent MILL, w, is dated 1775.

MALLWYD

The parish is associated with the Gwylliaid Cochion, the red brigands of Mawddwy, suppressed with eighty executions in the 1550s, not before killing the High Sheriff, Baron Lewis Owen of Dolgellau, near here in 1555.

ST TYDECHO. The medieval church, a chapelry of Llanymawd-dwy, was a thick-walled rectangle with a voussoired s priest's doorway: the w two-thirds of the present church. This is mainly now due to *Dr John Davies*, compiler of *The Welsh and Latin Dictionary*, biblical scholar and translator, vicar 1604–44. Davies added the chancel, 1624, and the timber bell-tower and timber porch in 1640–1. Minor works in 1764, 1791 and 1853, and a full restoration in 1915 by *Harold Hughes*.

Davies's chancel extends the nave on thinner walls. The E window sub-Perp, four-light, with a transom and no cusping; blocked s door.* The oak-boarded bell-tower (slate-hung in a 1798 view) has a pierced inscription SOLI DEO SACRUM ANNI CHRISTI MDCXL, a restoration by *Hughes* of one of three texts recorded by Fenton in 1808. Plain leaded windows carried through the eaves under gabled dormers. These are C18 and later. The w room lit by small N windows may be Dr Davies's schoolroom 'at the gable end' of the church. The porch dated

Mallwyd, St Tydecho.
Engraving after Harold Hughes, 1916

---

*Outside, against the S wall, a slate head of a crude three-light window, dated 1613. An E window preceding the chancel?

1641 has massive posts and braced beam giving a three-sided profile.

A dark low passage under the gallery separates the nave from the W room, under the massive jowled posts of the bell-tower. The nave has tiered BENCHES banked up against the gallery front. This extraordinary arrangement is late C18 or early C19, the gallery front beam dated 1764. Hughes thought the nave roof late medieval, as similar to that at Talyllyn. Tie-beam-and-collar trusses with struts, but most tie-beams and struts cut out as obscuring the view from the gallery. Two have cusping above the collars. The chancel is ceiled on close-spaced C17 ovolo-moulded trusses with massive collars. The celure is divided by transverse ribs from brackets, one with crude royal emblems: lion, unicorn and fleur-de-lys. Hughes repaired with an Arts and Crafts sensibility, introducing pews of solid simple design, keeping the textured plaster surfaces and the stepped arrangement (at the insistence of the parish and against the opinion of the ICBS).

FONT and ALTAR TABLE. 1734, gifts of John Mytton, lord of the manor. Black marble, the font small, octagonal, on a baluster stem. – PULPIT. C20, oak. – STAINED GLASS. E window, c. 1860, Evangelists on patterned quarries. S window, 1920s, sentimental. – MONUMENTS. Dr John Davies, a bicentenary Gothic plaque, 1844, by *Solomon Gibson* of Liverpool, brother of the more famous John. – Of similar date also by *Gibson*, the Rev. Robert Davies †1827, bizarre neo-grec. – Richard Williams †1805, slate plaque. – Mary Astley †1832, sarcophagus and urn, by *J. & H. Patteson* of Manchester. – CURIOSUM. On the porch two bones, variously described as the rib and patella of a whale or a fossilized mammoth tusk and epiphysis of a limb bone.

RECTORY, SW of the church. Built by *Dr Davies* in 1611 according to a terrier of 1730. Watcyn Clywedog's encomium of 1630 records a 'white tower', 'fair hall' and a 'white cross-wing' but the terrier more prosaically mentions two rooms below, two above, a closet and garrets over, also a buttery with cellar below and store above, which accords with the present three-bay house. Windows and stair late C18 to early C19, but the fireplace and beams may be early C17.

E of the church, GORPHWYSFA may be C17, divided into three in the C18. Whitewashed stone. PENUEL CALVINISTIC METHODIST CHAPEL, 1872, by the minister the *Rev. David Williams*, has a stuccoed Gothic front and brick sides. The BRIGANDS HOTEL, N, at the intersection of main roads was the Peniarth Arms. Stuccoed W façade to the A470 road. Three-storey, three-window centre between gabled wings, a formal Late Georgian composition. But the wings differ, the l. one blank, the r. one windowed, the l. one being the end of the original inn facing the A458. More vernacular, its four bays irregularly spaced, and raised a storey. Curious early C18 curved-cornered stone porch. Some heavy beams with late C17 scrolled stops and a timber-framed partition.

PONT MALLWYD, ¼ m. w. A single narrow stone arch over a gorge of the Dyfi, probably early C18, replacing the timber bridge of 1633 built by *Dr John Davies*.

PONT-Y-CLEIFION, ¼ m. N. A stone arch over the Cleifion, springing from rocks. '1637' picked out in white cobbles, but now grassed over, shows it to be the only survivor of three bridges built by *Dr John Davies*. Just N, the pretty mid-C19 bargeboarded LODGE with trellis porch, to the plain stuccoed Bryn Cleifion.

5938

MINFFORDD

A continuation of Penrhyndeudraeth, Minffordd was created after the Cob (*see* Porthmadog) of 1808–11 brought the main road from Porthmadog across what had been an isolated peninsula. The Festiniog Railway, 1836, then based its engineering works here. Little of a village; the late C19 vestry survives of the demolished 1879 chapel by *O. Morris Roberts*.

MINFFORDD STATION. The junction of the Festiniog Railway with the line from Barmouth, *c.* 1872. T-plan, house with ticket office and platform canopy. The toy-like boarded waiting room is a replica.

BRON-Y-GARTH HOSPITAL, ¼ m. E. Built *c.* 1838 as the Ffestiniog Workhouse, to the standard grid plan around a central octagonal block. Renewed front range, two-storey centre with single-storey wings. Three-storey connecting range to the octagon, two-storey rear wings. Additions, 1875, by *O. Morris Roberts*. Late C19 CASUAL WARD, SW, a dozen cells off a tall corridor, for vagrants who paid for their night by breaking stone.

By the Cob, 1 m. WSW, cruciform gabled TOLL HOUSE, built *c.* 1836, when the lower-level road was formed. Toll board from the Porthmadog toll house. BOSTON LODGE, adjoining, named for Madocks's Lincolnshire constituency, was one of two barracks built for the workforce constructing the Cob, 1808. Whitewashed, hipped, six bays. The Festiniog Railway stables of 1836 were enlarged, 1863, as the BOSTON LODGE WORKS when the tramway was converted to steam. The works contained all the engineering buildings for a remarkably self-suff'cient line, many surviving, if altered. They include an erecting shop of *c.* 1900; a two-storey machine shop; an iron foundry and smithy, with arched windows; a brass foundry; manager's office; etc.

PLAS NEWYDD, ¼ m. NE. Formerly of three linked units, a plan-form typical of the Anwyl family. The one surviving house is tall, with typical C17 slim square chimneys. Two storeys and an attic; stone dormers with copings on kneelers. The buttress, l., indicates the link with the middle house. Two rear dormers, the taller one a loft door, once reached by outside stairs. SW lofted stables.

P. 43

PLAS PENRHYN, ¼ m. sw. Overlooking the Cob. Double-pile two-storey villa, the front block added *c.* 1830 by Samuel Holland, slate-quarry owner, to an early C18 original. Deep eaves; veranda on trellised wrought-iron supports, returned in front of the end-wall entrance, with fanlight. The earlier house is lower, with near-square windows and a slate-slab open porch. Inside, some fireplaces below windows, like Madocks's Tan-yr-allt, Tremadog. In the older part an early hanging larder. Holland was Elizabeth Gaskell's uncle, and she visited. Bertrand Russell lived here 1955–70. Canted-fronted LODGE with ogee-headed windows.

BORTHWEN, ½ m. s. Long and low, of whitened rubble, with a gabled cross-wing and tall diagonal brick chimneys on the ridge. The late C16 or early C17 centre has a big end fireplace and heavy beams. It possibly had a winding stair, replaced by one in a rear stair gable. Extended beyond the big chimney for a second house. The l. cross-wing may be contemporary, as it has two lateral stacks. Oak staircase of *c.* 1700 with splat balusters. Part of an oak post-and-panel partition removed from Plas Newydd.

CAE CANOL, ½ m. wsw. Whitewashed. Prettily altered in the mid C19 with big sashes in half-dormers and trellis-gabled porch, but the façade offset, showing that it is late C17 or early C18. The diagonal end chimneys are also later. Additions each end, a stable to the r.

On the s side of the main road, a pair of widely spaced tall GATEPIERS unobtrusively suggest the nearby one-mile drive to Portmeiron (q.v.), as does the white iron SIGN with seagulls in profile on the N of the road, further E.

See also Penrhyndeudraeth.

NANNAU *see* LLANFACHRETH

PENMAENPOOL/LLYN PENMAEN
6918

A tidal quay on the Mawddach. The GEORGE III HOTEL occupies a pair of tall white-painted houses with stone dormers that may be late C17. In 1865 the Cambrian railways came up from the w, pushing on to Dolgellau in 1868. The STATION of chequered brick, 1879, now painted, was extended in 1981 for the hotel. Timber SIGNAL BOX. The picturesque timber TOLL BRIDGE dates from 1879, by *George Owen*, the Cambrian engineer; the centre span originally opened.

The village on the main road is the creation of the Penmaenuchaf estate after 1860. At the E end PENMAENUCHA FARM, 1868, by *W. R. Williams* of Dolgellau, a remarkable model farm around a long rectangular yard. The house in the centre of the N side faces a lofted steam-powered chaff-house with a timber flèche. Open-bay sheds each side and at the E. W entry between a lofted cart house and a hay barn. Beyond are seven ESTATE

COTTAGES in three blocks – stone, with gabled upper windows.

PENMAEN, ¼ m. W, beautifully set on a rock outcrop. The house of *c.* 1700 was remodelled *c.* 1900 with mullioned windows in red sandstone and red tiled roofs. Three shallow gables and a gabled timber porch. Big rear-wall chimney and SE rear wing. Original staircase with moulded rail and thick turned balusters. Earlier C19 plain COACHHOUSE with monolith stone lintels. S of the drive, beneath the main road, an attractive C18 COTTAGE with tall end chimneys.

PENMAENUCHAF HALL, ¼ m. E. Industrialist's retreat, terraced on the hillside. It was built in the early 1860s and named The Cliffe when sold in 1865 to C. R. Williams of Dolmelynllyn (Ganllwyd). Thomas Taylor (†1876), cotton manufacturer, of the Grecian Mills, Bolton, was then resident and the rebuilding may have been for him; it was certainly enlarged for his son. Loosely manorial, with gables and gabled dormers. In the hall, an overmantel of reused C17 woodwork.

ABERGWYNANT, 1¼ m. W. Another retreat on the Mawddach. 1839, by the amateur *H. J. Reveley* (*see* Dolgellau) for General Sir Henry Bunbury Bt, retired Under-Secretary for War; enlarged 1863. Reveley called it a 'small Gothic house'; now a large square united by ornate bargeboards. The N gable with a broad Tudor entrance arch may be original. Two of the three S gables have rock-faced stonework of the 1860s. Modernized; the galleried hall has Neo-Second-Empire fleshy ladies, the Seasons, by *C. Findlay*, later C20, painted around the lantern.

GLYN MALDEN, 1 m. E. Substantial five-bay house with coped gables and tall thin chimneys. It is probably mid-C18, though the corbelled eaves and the gabled stone dormers with dove holes have an uncommon solidity. The two big canted bays and the iron staircase balustrade are C19.

7001

PENNAL

Owain Glyndŵr called a parliament and synod here in 1406 from which the Pennal Letter was sent, expressing Welsh nationhood, and announcing his adherence to the Avignon papacy.

ST PETER AD VINCULA. An ancient rounded churchyard, but the broad single-chamber church with pyramid-roofed bell-turret probably of 1761 with porch of 1880 and vestry 1901. Large blocks of slaty stone, with straight-headed windows apart from the arched E one. The roof has arched braces in the medieval tradition, with kingposts above. Heavier W truss supporting the turret.

C18 FITTINGS. Supports of a dismantled W GALLERY, against the W wall; fielded-panelled PEWS; curving RAILS with slender pear-shaped balusters. – FONT. C18 goblet type in Bath stone, with cable-mould rim, the step with good C19 encaustic tiles. – PULPIT. 1872, timber. – CARVINGS. Four oak roundels of Saints Andrew, Jude, Paul and Mary Magdalene. Of unknown provenance, perhaps from the Low Countries, late C17 or early C18. – COMMANDMENT BOARDS. On metal, in Welsh, C19. – PAINTING. The 1406 Parliament, by *Aneurin Jones*, 1996, the present church ahistorically included. – STAINED GLASS. E window, Ascension, by *Holland & Holt* of Warwick, 1872. S, Suffer the children, by *Ward & Hughes*, 1893, and Heavenly City, 1923, by *Powells*, 'after Fra Angelico'.

MONUMENTS. Nave S. Matthews family, after 1849, by *Soward & Son* of London, tapered, Grecian. – Blanche, Emily and Parker Thruston, a fine brass by *Waller* of c. 1855, showing them Brontë-like around a day bed. – Richard Matthews †1824, white on black with an urn. – Rev. Lewis Hughes †1855, by *Dodson* of Shrewsbury, Grecian. – Maurice Anwyl †1832, marble by *Carline* of Shrewsbury. – Chancel S. Humphrey Edwards of Talgarth †1772. A touching work probably by *van der Hagen*. On a grey pyramid, four oval profiles in white marble, of Edwards, his wife, a young daughter and baby son. – Frances Thruston †1828, Grecian, by *W. Pistell* of London. – E wall. Lewis Edwards †1797 and Pryce Edwards †1809, grey and white marble; a matching one to Jonathan Anwyl of Llugwy †1852. – Chancel N. Captain Charles Thruston R.N. of Pennal Tower †1858, nautical, by *J. S. Westmacott*. – Hugh Vaughan †1717, tiny painted plaque. – In the churchyard an enormous slate slab to Lewis Vaughan of Penmaendyfi †1832.

CALVINISTIC METHODIST CHAPEL. 1908 refronting of a chapel of 1869, by *Richard Owens*. Rock-faced green stone with orange terracotta, free Jacobean style with long mullion-and-transom windows under keyed blind arches and a miniature pediment on the gable.

TO THE MEMORY OF BLANCHE, EMILY, AND PARKER. THRUSTON THIS MONUMENT IS PLACED AND INSCRIBED BY THEIR FATHER

LET THY MERCY O LORD BE UPON US ACCORDING AS WE HOPE IN THEE

Pennal, St Peter ad Vincula.
Brass. *c.* 1855

CARMEL INDEPENDENT CHAPEL. 1870–1. A nice contrast. Painted stone with grey limestone. The giant arch of the *Rev. Thomas Thomas* is here combined with a little Italian Gothic: a punched rose and the arches brought to a point on the extrados. The Gothic is not typical, but the big corner urns do suggest Thomas. Three-sided gallery, *sêt-fawr* and pulpit with pierced timber panels and a rich plaster pulpit arch.

w of the churchyard, the RIVERSIDE HOTEL, stucco and stone, three low storeys, early C19, and a single-arched BRIDGE with massive copings. Over the bridge, TŶ BONT with shop, Late Victorian, and the PRIMARY SCHOOL, *c.* 1870, with large arched windows in outer gables and additions, 1904, by *Deakin & Howard Jones*, with red terracotta. A lane runs NE past LLWYNTEG, roughcast with small-paned Tudor windows and bargeboards, and FELINDRE with triangular-headed iron casements in the back wall, both earlier C19. Further on was PENNAL TOWER, a mid-C19 Italianate villa with a big balustraded tower. A miniature Italian turret on the surviving stable. E of the church, YR HEN YSGOLDY, the Sunday School, 1889, pebbledash and red brick, with a tapered flèche.

CWM EBOL SLATE QUARRY, I m. NW (SH 689 017). Linked in 1868 by tramroad to a quay on the Dyfi at Llwyn Bwtri. Ruins of mills and traceable inclines.

ESGAIR WEDDAN, ¾ m. W. C17, altered for the Talgarth estate *c.* 1820, the new top-floor windows close above the main ones. Late C17 stair with splat balusters; first-floor post-and-panel partitions.

PLAS TALGARTH, ½ m. SW. Beautifully set overlooking the Dyfi, but encroached by holiday chalets. Begun in 1772 for Humphrey Edwards, the designer unknown. Three storeys, five-bay front and four-bay sides, in dark stone with sandstone quoins, dressings and, unusually, modillion cornice. Old-fashioned for the date, with hipped roofs behind parapets and a 2–1–2 division of the s front, the proportion of Nanteos, Ceredigion, built twenty years earlier. The window heads have a slight Baroque upsweep from voussoirs to fluted keystone. Those of the centre bay have shouldered surrounds with cornices, the attic cornice shorter than the surround, also a mannered device. Timber doorcase, open-pedimented but with narrow sidelights under short cornices. The interior is disappointing and altered. Open-well stair with close-spaced slender turned balusters. Attached at right angles, a much-altered earlier house.

By the drive, TOMEN LAS, an earth MOTTE, perhaps the castle of Aberdyfi built 1156 by Rhys ap Gruffudd of Deheubarth, but this is generally associated with the namesake on the Ceredigion shore.

PENMAENDYFI, I m. SW. Square Late Georgian house with a deep-eaved hipped roof and big chimneys, probably built for Lewis Vaughan †1832. Three storeys, on a slated platform with a rebuilt veranda.

CEFN CAER, ½ m. SE. Prominent on the hilltop, the farmhouse
is on the W corner of a ROMAN FORT. Very little can be seen
but geophysical surveys have revealed the extent of buildings
and of the informal civilian settlement (*vicus*) outside it. A
corner of the rampart was still visible when Fenton visited in
1804, and Roman material is said to have been seen in the
farmhouse, the church and the inn.

The HOUSE is a hall-house of 1525–6, floored in 1658–60
(dates established by dendrochronology) and re-windowed in
the earlier C19. Painted stone, five bays with a projecting gable
r. of a slightly arched centre door. One chimney on the ridge
just r. of the door (representing the inserted hall fireplace) and
a larger l. end chimney, also mid-C17. Dormer gables over the
centre and l. bays. C19 stone hoodmoulds. At the rear, outer
gables; outbuildings on both ends.

The central hall had, unusually, an oriel bay (in the gabled
projection). Ornate roof of cusped wind-braces and arch-
braced trusses with upper cusping. There were outer partitions
(the r. dais partition survives); chamfered posts and double-
curved doorheads, the l. one more fragmentary, also chamfered.
Similar doorhead to the cellar steps. C17 inserted fireplace, and
ceiling with bar-stopped joists and some gouged decoration.

LLUGWY, 1 m. SE, on the banks of the Dyfi. Owned by the Anwyl
family from the late C17. A C17 fragment seems to have been
the basis of a Neo-Jacobean rebuilding for R. C. Anwyl in the
1890s; grey stone with red sandstone mullion-and-transom
windows. The half-round gables with quarter-round shoulders
– two originally on the entrance front (one lost in the 1970s)
and three on the river front – are not the regional C17 type.
So, was everything rebuilt apart from the battlemented two-
storey porch? This has a Tudor-arched doorway under a
mullion-and-transom window with arched top lights. Neo-
Jacobean interiors. – Stuccoed L-plan later C19 LODGE, with a
tiny half-round oriel on one gable and a square bay on the
other, glazed in delicate cast iron.

PANT LLUDW, 2 m. E. A Late Georgian villa of the 1820s, well
set in wooded grounds. Of stone, with wide eaves, and a
veranda across the front, which is three-sided with single-bay
wings. Latticed French windows and an arched one above in
the centre.

PENRHYNDEUDRAETH   *6139*

A large village that began after 1862 was still 'a dismal village of
a few houses scattered among heaps of muck and cockleshells'.
The older upper part is on the rocky spine of the peninsula, the
newer part lines the main road. The Festiniog Railway of 1836
passes through the upper village, the Cambrian railway
skirts the bottom, both with small stations. Noted in the C20 for
the manufacture of explosives for the mining industries.

The wide High Street and connecting terraces were laid out for David Williams of Castell Deudraeth (Portmeirion).

BETHEL BAPTIST CHAPEL, Penlan Isaf. 1913. Pebbledash with brown terracotta. Gabled buttresses flank a broad Perp central window. Outer turrets with octagonal finials. Raised up over the schoolroom.

CARMEL INDEPENDENT CHAPEL, School Street. Now a house. 1859–60, probably by the *Rev. Thomas Thomas*, altered 1879–80. Rock-faced granite with slight limestone dressings. The impost of the giant arch connects all the window imposts – tall slim outer ones and a Palladian triplet.

GORFFWYSFA CALVINISTIC METHODIST CHAPEL, on the A487 road. 1880, by *Richard Owens*, similar to his Tabernacle, Aberystwyth, 1878–9, but better articulated and more consistently Italian. Projecting pedimented centre, balustraded outer bays. The centre has triple arched windows and angle piers above, broad corniced doorcase and quoins below. The outer bays repeat on the sides for greater effect.

HOLY TRINITY. 1858, by *T. M. Penson*, for Louisa Oakeley of Tan-y-bwlch (Maentwrog). Nave and chancel; cusped lancets and a slim octagonal spired turret over a spherical-triangle w window. The surprisingly large N porch has ballflower decoration and shafts with foliage capitals. – STAINED GLASS. E window, 1860s, stiff drawing, St Paul at Athens. Two lancets, 1906, s one by *Powells*, the N one possibly by *Jones & Willis*.

NAZARETH CALVINISTIC METHODIST CHAPEL, Nazareth Terrace. 1839, remodelled in 1879–80 by *Richard Owens*. A long-wall front given an imposing Italianate façade in rock-faced rubble and ashlar. Three bays, each with a pair of Florentine windows. Balustraded parapet with urns, solid to the centre with the name in big letters. Heavy corniced porches with square pillars. MANSE, r., with canted bays flanking a latticed porch.

TABERNACL WESLEYAN CHAPEL, High Street. 1862. Dark rubble with orangey sandstone. Giant arch and pilasters, suggesting the *Rev. Thomas Thomas*. The pilasters are thin channelled strips with urns on the outer shoulders.

CEFN COCH SCHOOL, School Street. 1907, by *Deakin & Howard Jones*. Stone with typical orange terracotta. Five bays. Three gables project with big windows, the central one Palladian, the others arched; the intermediate windows rectangular, with a gablet over just the middle light.

NATIONAL SCHOOL, on the A487 road. 1878, by *Thomas Roberts* of Porthmadog. Single-storey with a busy roof-line; slated central lantern, half-hipped roof pushed out at one end over the bell and a big arched window. Buttressed front with pairs of pointed windows. Now a house.

VICARAGE, SW of the church. 1858, perhaps by *T. M. Penson*. Rubble with slate lintels and hoodmoulds. The NE gable has a narrow two-storey bay with deep-mullioned lights. Big acorn finials to the staircase.

SNOWDONIA NATIONAL PARK AUTHORITY OFFICES, Trem-yr-wyddfa. 1995, by *Gwynedd County Architects*, project architect *Dylan Roberts*. A longish curved building overlooking a lake. Trefor granite with limestone dressings, stained timber windows, slate roofs – local materials *de rigueur* for a planning authority. Five linked blocks step up, two each side of the entrance atrium. After the hard entrance face, the sunny lake façade is softer, more glazed, the roofs cascading to almost head height. Much timber inside; particularly big laminated roof beams.

MARDIR, s of the church. 1926, by *Clough Williams-Ellis*. Stuccoed villa, with single-storey surgery attached. The approach, through a gateway and past the six-window surgery, leads to a Palladian loggia in the end wall. Neo-Georgian front of 2–3–2 bays, with a shallow pedimental gable and, under the hipped ends, bedroom balconies over the loggias. Sash windows.

MAES-Y-COED, ½ m. ENE. 1927. An early work by *Griffith Morris* of Porthmadog for C. F. Cooke of Cooke's Explosives. Small-ish stone villa. L-plan with half-hipped gables, the roof slid down over the porch in the angle. The gable to the l. has the recessed bay window of the contemporary Caernarvonshire 'open-air' schools and other Morris houses.

TŶ OBRY, ½ m. NW. Early to mid-C17 end-chimney house, the three bays offset. Big blocked E fireplace and mural stair with window. T-plan farm buildings, C17 to C19, to the W, with gable dove holes.

PLAS BRONDANW see LLANFROTHEN

PORTMEIRION 5938

Model resort village on the N side of the Dwyryd estuary, by *Clough Williams-Ellis*, 1925–75, with additions *c.* 1980–2006 by his daughter *Susan Williams-Ellis*. It was mostly conceived in two periods of reconstruction, after the 1914 and 1939 wars; the first period reflecting the architect's Arts and Crafts training, the second drawing more on classical imagery. The unique circumstances reflect the freedom of one artist, on his home ground, to act as owner, designer and developer. Williams-Ellis (1883–1978) was driven by a quest for a more cheerful public architectural language than the severities of local design since Late Victorian days, and had the prescience that tourist business could provide the opportunity. He was lucky also to leave a family who have followed that vision, and who through the Clough Williams-Ellis Foundation have steered it into the modern economy.

One of the most personal architectural statements of the C20, Portmeirion does not conform to the period's design movements as generally understood. Nikolaus Pevsner aptly remarked that Williams-Ellis was 'between traditional and modern'; put another way, visitors may see Portmeirion as expressing an edgy relationship to Modernist architecture – not least because Williams-Ellis did not accept all that was proposed by the architectural world of his lifetime. In its determination to communicate truths through architectural jesting, Portmeirion is disquietingly sophisticated as well as naïve.*

HISTORY

The wooded peninsula between Traeth Bach and Traeth Mawr was adopted in the mid C12 by Gruffydd and Maredudd, sons of Cynan ab Owain Gwynedd, prince of Gwynedd, as the site of a castle called Aber Iâ; its rocky knoll overlooks the village. This gave the name for the early Victorian villa of the Westmacott family (adopted as the hotel) in the bay below, with a fine stone quay to its w. The drive from Minffordd to an older house, Castell Deudraeth (*see* p. 697), was extended into the valley above, which was levelled to make a walled garden with a gardener's cottage, and with a stable range beside it to the N. The woods in the Gwyllt were planted with exotics by the late C19 owner, Caton Haigh, becoming the backdrop to a village always intimately associated with trees. These features were accepted with little change into the C20 layout, together with the matchless natural beauty of the site with its steep ascents and drops and rocks like cantilevers, all contrasting with the levels of the sea or the exposed estuarine sands below.

The abandoned estate was bought by Williams-Ellis in 1925. His existing idea of an architectural island, a cross between Italy's Lakes and Riviera landscapes and his Arts and Crafts training (for which he had failed to find a site sailing round the British coasts), was adapted for a citadel on the cliff above the hotel building. Its scale was kept small for economy; its bell-tower's perspective was forced; its coloured plaster surfaces were based on Claud Lovat Fraser's sets for *The Beggar's Opera* at the Lyric Theatre, Hammersmith. The genius in this siting was never exceeded, but it was the anchor for the experiment in town planning that followed.

The resort proved commercially viable as an early motel, based on accommodating motor cars as well as humans. It was also from the start a sociable place, dependent like the life of country houses on the charm and competence of owners – in this case the architect and his founder manager James Wyllie – and was recognized and welcomed as visual amusement by serious people. Williams-Ellis's experiments were measured against thoughtful and responsible contemporaries, with whom he had contacts through his London practice and his literary wife Amabel.† Public places need signage: he designed his own, in fine

*From the first the village had its guide-book, culminating in *Portmeirion, the Place and its Meaning*, 1963 and 1973, and now a fuller guidebook and the study *Portmeirion*, 2006.

†Others as diverse as Maxwell Fry, Christopher Hussey, Lewis Mumford and John Cornforth have been drawn to write seriously about Portmeirion.

italic lettering. Craftsmen and artists need work: he offered them
opportunities at some new project. There were curious artefacts
from the past on the market: he put them on show. Building is
an unending process: his village lives in a cycle of the old and the
new. These are attributes of the Arts and Crafts Movement,
which he fused with features of the classical and Mediterranean
worlds in a way particular to himself, and beyond imitation. The
whole eludes strict architectural analysis for the simple reason
that it is not architecturally strict.

Yet these paradoxes of whim and patriotism, of outrageous
artificiality and deep love of architecture, have consistently been
found hard to take both by the architectural profession and by
part of the public. The place may seem bafflingly ambitious for
a hobby, and worryingly insubstantial as architecture; the first
phases were lightly built for economy and speed (there were six
months for works each closed winter season), so plaster on wire
mesh on timber framing sometimes stood in for conventional
walling, a tribute to the skills of the master mason *Henry Davies*.
Portmeirion's irony is that what was made to be temporary has
now become permanent: with the substitution of the lasting for
the fragile, the fabric has become more architectural.

Did Clough Williams-Ellis get away with it? Thirty-five years
after his death, and over eighty years since the first realization, it
seems that he may have. While its improvising creator is no longer
in daily charge, its message of the need for gaiety in life and art
is unchanged. Strangest of all, some forty of its fifty main buildings were listed Grade II in 1971, one of the first cases of a living
architect's work being so recognized.

Portmeirion looks well when filled with the unbelievable
number of people attracted there in daytime; other moods
include very good floodlighting at night, and the mild and damp
solitudes of the Welsh coast out of season. Given its discursive
character – garden village, furnished outdoor space, commercial
exhibition, 'home for fallen buildings', demonstration of handi-
craft – it seems best to describe it mostly by means of short
perambulations. Areas private to the holiday tenants are so indicated on site, but the available roads and paths reveal almost (but
not quite) all that matters of a place that is not very large.

PUBLIC BUILDINGS

TOWN HALL, 1937–8. The largest building in the centre, and 114
visually the noblest. Being in a private village and so without
a council, it serves for social events. Its generic form follows
the Arts and Crafts village or college memorial halls that
Williams-Ellis designed in the 1920s, but its fabric has an air
of romance. It is composed of the stones – great thrice-
mullioned windows, doorways made up with Tudor fireplaces
– of the Jacobean part of Emral Hall in Flintshire, a house (says
Edward Hubbard, *The Buildings of Wales: Clwyd*) 'of strangely
haunting beauty'. At the demolition sale in 1936 Williams-Ellis

bought the great chamber ceiling with its reliefs of heroic
actions (£13), then had to acquire sufficient extra fabric to
re-erect it worthily, thereby saving one of the best Renaissance
works of art in Wales.

Very tall, asymmetrical upper storey with five-light oriel
windows, faced with carefully textured lime plaster with a red
ochre limewash, on a low basement of bare stonework. The
main entrance is by a porch-tower closing the cross-axis of the
piazza. This rises to a great height above tiers of old glass in
stone window frames, then via a tower as an attic tier with
inward-curving roof and square lantern in contrasting
materials, to a topknot confected from ready-made copper
objects. Its walls are enriched with old armorial carvings, new
hanging signs and an oval iron grille from Soane's Bank of
England. In its porch a bronze portrait BUST of Williams-Ellis
at eighty years by *Jonah Jones*, 1963.

The BALLROOM or HERCULES HALL, as reassembled,
has an oriel facing E and a nine-light window looking S. Its
oak wainscot dates from the reconstruction of Emral Hall
in the 1720s by *Richard Trubshaw* and *Joseph Evans*: fluted
Corinthian pilasters flanking double doors in semicircular-
headed frames, the fireplace with its plaster panel with
an allegorical figure, the walls otherwise with deep raised-
field panelling. At the entrance an ornate wooden sign
proudly announcing a charge to see 'the celebrated Hall of
Hercules'.

56   The early C17 plaster CEILING is a flat vault with curved
sides, designed to display scenes of the Exploits of Hercules
arranged in three rows of four, and installed here in 1938 by
the joiner, *R. O. Williams*. The articulating strapwork has an
air of early C17 Gothic, its motif (a finial shape with inward-
curving sides and triangular top) being arranged in interlocking patterns of four so that there are fourteen spaces for Zodiac
signs as well. The latter are incomplete and also seem to
include animals from the Hercules myths. The twelve scenes
are depicted on a larger scale, their sculptural quality not the
finest. Though based on classical iconography, they do not correspond exactly with the Twelve Labours. Starting at the NW
corner, side row: the infant Hercules strangling the snakes in
his bed (partly substituted after damage in removal); Hercules
with his club, carrying the boar of Erymanthus on his shoulders; Hercules fighting off the centaurs; Hercules mastering
Cerberus. Centre row, from the N: Hercules beheading the
Hydra; Hercules (dressed as a Jacobean gentleman) taking the
girdle of Hippolyte (?); Hercules and Atlas holding the globe
of the world; Hercules rescuing Hesione, chained to a rock
and about to be devoured by a sea dragon. Side row, from the
NE: Hercules and the Nemean lion; Diomedes punished
by Hercules to be devoured by his own carnivorous mares;
Hercules wrestling with Antaeus, with a moated house in the
background; Hercules taking a golden apple from the garden
of the Hesperides, which is guarded by a splendid dragon.

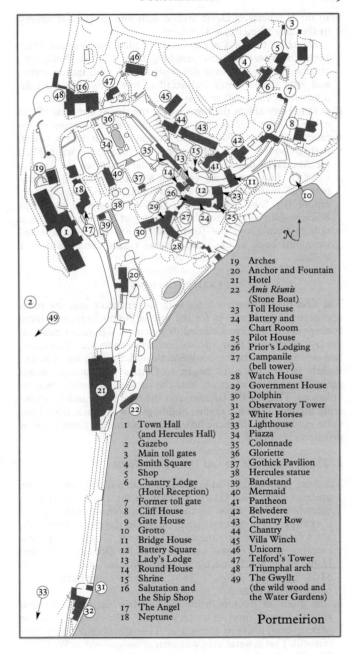

19 Arches
20 Anchor and Fountain
21 Hotel
22 *Amis Réunis*
   (Stone Boat)
23 Toll House
24 Battery and
   Chart Room
25 Pilot House
26 Prior's Lodging
27 Campanile
   (bell tower)
28 Watch House
29 Government House
30 Dolphin
31 Observatory Tower
32 White Horses
33 Lighthouse
34 Piazza
35 Colonnade
36 Gloriette
37 Gothick Pavilion
38 Hercules statue
39 Bandstand
40 Mermaid
41 Pantheon
42 Belvedere
43 Chantry Row
44 Chantry
45 Villa Winch
46 Unicorn
47 Telford's Tower
48 Triumphal arch
49 The Gwyllt
   (the wild wood and
   the Water Gardens)

1 Town Hall
   (and Hercules Hall)
2 Gazebo
3 Main toll gates
4 Smith Square
5 Shop
6 Chantry Lodge
   (Hotel Reception)
7 Former toll gate
8 Cliff House
9 Gate House
10 Grotto
11 Bridge House
12 Battery Square
13 Lady's Lodge
14 Round House
15 Shrine
16 Salutation and
   the Ship Shop
17 The Angel
18 Neptune

Portmeirion

In the N lunette, a Doric arcade with four allegorical figures; in the thin S lunette, a deer hunt.

Attached to the S a new HALL added by *Gruffydd Price*, 1998, incorporating C19 panelling from Castell Deudraeth; attached at the N a large flat-roofed CAFÉ with façade arches and over-scaled entry balustrades, by *Susan Williams-Ellis*, *c.* 1979–80. Both rather hem this fine building in.

CASTLE. High above the town hall is the site of the small Welsh castle of Aber Iâ. Now just a knoll of rock with a stone revetment added by *Williams-Ellis* in 1964. On it was a tower, perhaps built by the Welsh; a stone structure on top was robbed for Aberlâ House in the C19. On the E side of the knoll a GAZEBO, round, with a green tent roof and pierced iron parapets with mermaids, from a demolished sailors' home in Liverpool (by *John Cunningham*, 1846–8). Designed by *Susan Williams-Ellis* in 1983 for the centenary of her father's birth, it sails in trees above the Town Hall, providing an unexpected viewpoint back to the piazza in the village centre and its E skyline.

PERAMBULATIONS

The first perambulation deals with the entrance and the main approach to the hotel. As for the rest of Portmeirion, the initial concept seems to have included two zones, a significant mark on the landscape seen from the sea, culminating in the Campanile, and sketches for urban articulation behind. Before long, a belt of slightly larger structures began to form a new skyline inland again. These three zones are here the subjects of distinct perambulations. That for the Citadel, and the final perambulation covering the second-phase skyline buildings and the back drive, have to be in two parts since the little paths penetrating them are now private to residents.

1. The Entrance and the Old Drive to the Hotel

The drive from Minffordd introduces small buildings given some graceful detail, like CASTLE YARD on the l.: effects that are overwhelmed on the r. by the 1850s masonry pomposities of CASTELL DEUDRAETH (*see* p. 697). On the closer approach, a WAYSIDE SEAT; a glimpse of DORLAN GOCH (1934), the entrance to PORTH-Y-CASTELL (1965 for Donald and Isobel Hall), all on the l. and by *Williams-Ellis*; and the tiny COED MÔR by *Lionel Esher*, *c.* 1965, the one contribution by a national Modernist.

In the glade of trees in front of the main entrance, the free gravelled space survives which Williams-Ellis thought good for parking cars; it has its painted steel cut-out obelisk and yellow star still. This general area was seen as unresolved by Williams-Ellis. The key features in the 1950s and 1960s were the stone former TOLL GATE (early 1950s), and the painted timber workshops called SMITH SQUARE (1960s–71) outside on the

r. A later discrete area for coaches has thick GATEPIERS (1997) and iron gates reusing the Tremadog Market Hall design. The architect's last little structure is an outer miniature pillared TOLL GATE, of 1976 (with a taller companion, 1999). On the r. the SHOP. The inner former TOLL GATE evokes a stone castle ruin; within it a painted steel cut-out mermaid (made for the Observatory Tower, p. 694). Set back on either side, the start of domestic building again: CHANTRY LODGE (1969), r., now hotel reception, is in the older cottage manner with a curving bridge to the upper flat; CLIFF HOUSE, l., (also 1969) is light classical, with an eroded mid-C18 statue of a huntsman beside it.

The mid-Victorian drive to the house by the estuary (now pedestrianized) becomes a clear route at this point. It descends in a double loop, round the former walled garden (now Piazza) and former stables, and finally by steep gradient to the quay. At the top, GATE HOUSE (1954–5) has a crucial part to play: it spans the drive at the point where a defile in trees opens to a full view of the Dwyryd estuary. Random windows suggesting long evolution, the three main sides each in a different style and colour. The arch and tapering superstructure imitate a once-defended medieval village. A vertical band of symbolic and heraldic motifs is centred on the outward-facing arch: badges of royalty, honour, princehood, Wales. Neo-Baroque painted ceiling by *Hans Feibusch*, a composition of two couples of flying figures. On the r. beyond, a semicircular PILLBOX, combining Second World War defence with an eye for future embellishments. Beside it, across the road, BRIDGE HOUSE (1958); again three styles and colours: red ochre, ultramarine and a Venetian window the outer side, yellow with white pilasters and vases like a doll's house facing the square.

Emergence, still among gardened rocks, into the bright and busy BATTERY SQUARE is one of the village successes. On the l. a minute but ingenious booth for the 1920s toll-keeper. The principal ranges of building either side – broadly the first and final phases of development – are described in distinct perambulations, pp. 693, 696. The square is closed at the NW by the complicated little pairing of the LADY'S LODGE (1938–9) and the ROUND HOUSE (1959–60). The former evolved from a garage to a shop, acquiring Baroque gables, a lunette painting by *Feibusch*, etc. Steps descend between them to further perambulations; overhead is a bridge and walkway part-concealed in the arcade screen, which hides the apsidal shape of the second building, also a shop. The main descent follows the road past the wayside LOGGIA with its film-set Buddha (1963–4), and lesser architectural moments including the tantalizing walls screening the Piazza, to the mid-Victorian ex-stable courtyard. This was converted as SALUTATION or a tearoom in 1931, and later as a third set of shops including the SHIP SHOP. Original fabric with fish-scale roof slates and spiral-moulded yellow terracotta chimney pots, but 'Cloughed up' with outbreaks of ornament, lively domestic-commercial additions round a black-and-white paved court, and a garland mural by *Nigel Simmons* (restoring originals of *c.* 1956 by *Susan Williams-Ellis*).

A turn to the s reveals a streetscape between Arches (1963–4) and the Café and Town Hall (p. 687) on the r., and on the l., Trinity (1933–4), Neptune, and The Angel (both 1926), the latter two among the pioneer cottages on the site. THE ANGEL is a key building in two vistas, but in its own right an exemplary design. The plan is an S, walls and hipped roofs following its curves as on West Country cottages, with a slight overhang which, carried on pillars, becomes the feature of the s end. On the s side an angel, one of the early simple reliefs to explain a building. On NEPTUNE it is the roof which sports the wobbles, while the overhang is played up till it is neither horizontal nor, on the E, continuous since two windows break up through it. On the street side still more apparent additions and fantasy signs; shops fill both ground floors. The slightly battering front of ARCHES, opposite, was based on a design of 1954 for garages and staff flats, becoming in 1965 an antiques shop advertised by a fine elliptical panel by *Feibusch*. The Town Hall porch and gateway opposite close this little sloping street, one of the most brilliant of Portmeirion's miniature environments.

On the l. of the quickening slope down to the hotel, ANCHOR (1936, but designed 1930) and FOUNTAIN (1937) have three full storeys, hardly seen since they stand on the quay level, their backs to the cliff. The approach is by bridge to the top floors, protected by a small pagoda-roofed lodge with another mural by *Feibusch*, a marine couple. The circulation of visitors drawn towards the quay into the privacy of the hotel's immediate precinct was resolved in the original layout by a quite different route from the Gate House at the top to the shore further E. A set of STEPS descending to the quay on the l. outside the hotel forecourt, over which the other axes pass on bridges, was devised by *Richard Haslam* in 1987.

HOTEL. The Victorian villa of Aber Iâ stood above the sea on two stone terraces. Two single-bay wings looking E project from a rectangular house entered at the N. Fish-scale slate roofs, yellow terracotta spiral chimney pots. In the hall a big stone chimneypiece carved with the Westmacott bee emblem; in the drawing room facing the sea a chimneypiece carved with figures of medieval romances. Fire in 1981 damaged the library's carvings, especially the fine door panels of game by *John Rogers*, and destroyed the c18 staircase inserted *c.* 1850 (since reproduced). The architects for the restoration, 1988, were *John Ricardo Pearce* and *Gruffydd Price*.

This c19 house opened as the Portmeirion Hotel in 1926. A three-bay bedroom wing designed for the w end was eventually placed beyond a recessed block added to the villa. At ground-floor level the main rooms were extended: the swelling curve of the new restaurant (1930), where the roof was held up by sections of mast from a ketch wrecked in the bay; the smaller bow between the Victorian wings; and the similar bow for the manager's office outside the hall – the last destroyed by fire in 1981, together with the bar made from the timbers of HMS *Arethusa*, the last man-of-war to sail into action. Portmeirion's essential colours were established here: white walls, at least by the sea; shutters and other woodwork 'Portmeirion green'; the intermediate block of the hotel was pink, the little loggia ochre. On the l. of the main entrance, perhaps the best of *Feibusch*'s murals, 1950s.

Taken together, an element of Surrealism entered the designed landscape of the early 1930s in front: retained Victorian statues on the miniature parapet, steps curling round the Casino, a triple-arched loggia built in 1930, and mysterious steps and tunnels. On the quay, the ketch the *Amis Réunis*, wrecked in a storm, has an afterlife reconstructed from the deck upwards.

2. The Citadel, Battery Square, and the path from the Grotto to the Lighthouse

Williams-Ellis's resort began with a group of about ten buildings of 1925–34 on the crown of the cliff enclosing the village at its SW, linked to the hotel and the sea by a precarious composition of steps. Inspired by Portofino and Capri, these display a high degree of fantasy, at times approaching the treatment of buildings in Surrealist painting.

The short part of this walk starts by the E side of BATTERY SQUARE. Here is TOLL HOUSE, 1929, of black stained boarding jettied out twice under an eaves line with contrived wobbles. A little masonry structure is attached, with a balcony with a coloured wooden figure of a saint preaching from a scroll, and a hanging cut-out sign of a black sheep by *Susan Williams-Ellis*, 1957. The archways, steps and other devices by which Toll House turns W into the long side of the paved space and to the Round House are a tale in themselves. The highly irregular BATTERY, 1927, has white-painted Kentish horizontal boarding; CHART ROOM, 1927, adjoining, began as garages and became a house in 1953. The turn on the cliff behind is also managed with a timber building, PILOT HOUSE, 1930, which has the horizontal windows of the 1930s seaside. On the seaward terrace a cast-concrete relief of Sculpture, a slightly Eric-Gill-like work by *Gilbert Bayes*.

A second little square lies beyond these buildings. Placed on the high spot and treated with every contrivance of age, the CAMPANILE or Bell Tower, dated 1928. Thin like the North Italian church towers that inspired it, this has seven stages of surprisingly correct design – a quiet reminder that Williams-Ellis knew about architecture. The first four are of bare stone, the top three are plastered, with bells in the Serlian openings [112] on the fifth stage.* The NE side is formed by PRIOR'S LODGING, 1929. Tall laced windows on its upper floor facing the sea with blue shutters against pale red ochre plaster. On the SW side is WATCH HOUSE, 1926, small but telling: a white stone cottage, hugging the ground like the West Wales type, but bent in the middle, and with a round external Pembrokeshire chimney and a pillared, hipped-roofed veranda at the seaward end. It crouches on a crag, at the top of rough white steps and retaining walls.

Two further houses, to the w. GOVERNMENT HOUSE, 1928–9, painted in bleached colours, is three-storeyed and square, with a tall aedicule rising from its roof on which is a bronze seagull. The tall and narrow DOLPHIN, 1933–4, raised on arches over the final abyss, is long enough to be painted as two houses. Linking Dolphin and Government House, a covered bridge, from whose parapet leans a ceramic figure of Shakespeare.

The longer part of this perambulation starts above Battery Square, at the path leading, via a reset slate archway from one of Madock's toll gates, to the circular platform on the s of the road with its GROTTO, 1954, beneath. Blue interior with narrow windows for the view; sea shells set into the concrete ceiling and stone walls. From here a woodland path passes beneath the buildings just described, to connect with the steep picturesque descent by twisting steps to the quay; at the top a miniature version of the Watch House loggia. A walkway leads to the ornamented quay and steps made for the hotel, and via a tunnel to the long and level walk on the old terrace, passing covered seats originally made from upturned clinker-built boats, to a fine coloured-up STATUE of Nelson on the axis. Exquisitely sited at the turn of the stone revetting is the OBSERVATORY TOWER, 1936–7. Four limewashed stages, closely evoking the tower in the early 1920s model. Just beyond, a little sea dock and a house enlarged as WHITE HORSES, 1966, partly on arches over the path. Towards the sea a miniature folly LIGHTHOUSE, c. 1960: a metal white cylinder, green cupola, and parapet walk on a stone plinth. The views on the way back (which connects by underpass with the Victorian drive to the hotel) reveal Williams-Ellis's skill in composing buildings and ornament together.

3. The Piazza

The sunk centre of the village is surrounded by extraordinary buildings but is itself comparatively empty. Approximately

*The (unvisitable) inscription beside it deserves quotation: 'This tower, built in 1928 by Clough Williams-Ellis, architect and publican, embodies stones from the 12th century castle of his ancestor Gruffydd ap Cynan, King of North Wales, that stood on an eminence 150 yards to the west. It was finally razed c. 1869 by Sir William Fothergill Cook, inventor of the Electric Telegraph, "lest the ruins should become known and attract visitors to the place". This 19th century affront to the 12th is thus piously redressed in the 20th.'

square, it is defined on the N and E by the descending C19 drive, and on the W by the straight axis to the porch of the Town Hall, perhaps the first Williams-Ellis pegged out here (in 1936; as the architect and his wife joked, it was a case of 'the Early Curly and the Late Straight'). In this PIAZZA is a rectangular pool with segmental ends, an echoing fountain, and two gilded Burmese dancing figures on Wyatt Ionic columns towards the S.

Around the Piazza are three reconstructed C18 buildings, postwar presents to the village. Being of stone they blend with the outcropping rock above, together acting as a calm plinth to the riot of new form and colour being put in place on the skyline above. The visual effects and cross-axes are also developed in highly significant ways, both here and in front of the Town Hall to the SW.

First, at the head of the Piazza, the COLONNADE, re-erected 1959, once fronting the bath house of Arno's Court, E of Bristol. This was designed for William Reeve in the early 1760s; Pevsner in 1958 called it a 'charming whim'. The front is a colonnade of slender shafted columns, with a Gothic frieze and a balustrade with pierced motifs. The centre of the whole composition moves forward gently. The last bays l. and r. are solid and have doorways with four-centred heads. As re-erected the ogee dome on the raised centre is missing, and instead an attic wall with three vases stands behind, but the side bays now have small stone ogee domes which look original. It can be mounted as a viewing platform from the level of the C19 drive behind it.

To the N, the GLORIETTE, 1964–5, more Williams-Ellis than old work. It has a loggia of four unfluted Ionic columns salvaged from *Samuel Wyatt*'s Hooton Hall, Cheshire, 1778–88 – others are reused in the Piazza and elsewhere – with three of the favourite cast-iron mermaid panels (cf. the gazebo, p. 690) used as a balustrade between. The order stands on rusticated arches and carries an entablature, balustrade and impossibly attenuated vases. The building is dignified and cheerful in a Neo-Palladian way, with two miniature tiers of windows behind the giant portico, but the effect of solidity vanishes with the back wall falling away in fragments either side. The loggia doorway turns out to be level with the road behind, so that the passer-by moves theatrically from one world to another in a single step.

To the S is the GOTHICK PAVILION, re-erected 1965, or rather its rear porch with trefoil-headed doorway, where Williams-Ellis records his admiration for William Madocks of Porthmadog, 'who loved this region and strove mightily to increase its fame and its prosperity'. The pavilion was originally part of the transformation by *Benjamin Gummow* of Nerquis Hall, Flintshire, c. 1810. Columns of four shafts; frieze with trefoiled panels breaking forward over them, carrying very high pinnacles with crockets, obelisks and vases, between which run battlements rising pedimentally over the centre – the last a tweak by Portmeirion's architect.

To the W is a pre-existing N–S axis, with a cross-axis to the Town Hall. Coming up from below, the main axis crosses the road, passes through large Edwardian iron GATES dated 1908 beside The Angel's bow (see p. 692), then past the BAND-STAND, 1961, the arcaded loggia built on top of the village electricity substation; three arches by two, paterae between. On the axis, on a tall plinth, a bronze STATUE of Hercules in the pose of Atlas by the Edinburgh sculptor *William Brodie*, 1863, brought here in 1960. Below, a generous stairway on the line of the valley watercourse which descends only to a balustraded outlook point halfway down. A little space follows the statue to the N, with MERMAID, the former gardener's cottage of the 1840s with carved bargeboards, given an elegant S loggia and other ornament in 1926, and the dolphin FOUNTAIN of 1963. By the steps up to The Dolphin (see p. 694), a STATUE of Frix from among the Saxon deities carved by *Rysbrack* for Stowe, Bucks; a copy of the original, moved from Portmeirion to the Buckinghamshire Museum.

4. The inner skyline and back drive, and the Gwyllt

Perhaps a quarter of the village's houses stand slightly away from the original groupings, on the higher register of the cliff or otherwise N of the C19 drive. Though visually integrated with the earlier parts, this 'suburb' acquired its own character with a need for more privacy and car parking for residents as more day visitors came.

Steep steps from opposite Battery Square offer another little network of paths, converging on the viewpoint terrace of the accretive building called the PANTHEON. Here in 1957 was re-erected first a fragment of *Norman Shaw*'s Dawpool, Cheshire, a short-lived house of 1882–4: a vast late Perp chimneypiece in red sandstone now painted white, having two arches below and, above, an ornate oriel lit only by slit windows. Williams-Ellis wanted a dome for Portmeirion, so walls behind it on an octagonal plan followed two years later; finally the Pantheon was completed in 1961, with a timber cupola (joiner *Leslie Braund-Smith*). Full-height angle pilasters with unexpected pairings of tall narrow windows and upright *œils de bœuf* hard against them. The dome covering, originally plywood painted green, has been replaced with real copper. Made as an object to look towards, it is too high a vantage point for the village's own perspectives.

To the NE is BELVEDERE, 1960, quite restrained, as is the low CHANTRY ROW of 1962–3 behind the Pantheon, in effect a realization of Williams-Ellis's unbuilt council houses for Workington, Cumbria, of twenty years earlier. It seems to be a three-storey terrace but in fact is a single storey with a monopitch roof, its boiler chimney disguised by a green onion dome blatantly stopped at 180 degrees. It links to CHANTRY, 1937, an unusually large, prominent and four-square house in a style like that of Government House (*see* above), which, it was hoped, might become a studio for Augustus John. In front of Chantry another Ionic COLUMN from Hooton, with a weathervane on top. At an angle to it behind, another house for a private tenant, Henry Winch; called VILLA WINCH, 1966–7, this has a little classical dignity, belied as elsewhere in the final phase by a monopitch roof. Further w, UNICORN, 1964. A single storey with pilasters, pediment and a mermaid-parapet balcony, set on arches and filling the span of its little valley, like a model for a far greater mansion. To its l., on the bluff closing the inland view, TELFORD'S TOWER, 1958, named to celebrate Thomas Telford in his bicentenary year.

The backs of all these can be glimpsed from the second-period drive among trees. This enters the village through a TRIUMPHAL ARCH, 1962–3, the grandest entrance to the village and a work of uncharacteristic solidity. High main arch breaking through the architrave line of massive pilasters; segment-headed upper tier with volutes resting on these, and pierced by a niche containing a Neoclassical wooden caryatid painted a lead colour. Beside it, an evocative HALF-EXEDRA and its architectural hedge with terms in the arches (one by *Jonah Jones*), and other ornaments, including a filigree-iron-work Chinoiserie arch by one of the radiating paths which here enter the Gwyllt or wild wood. In the WATER GARDENS not far to the w, arbours and bridges, including FLORA'S PERGOLA, 2006, by *Susan Williams-Ellis*.

CASTELL DEUDRAETH, ½ m. SW. An ungainly castle-house of the 1850s for David Williams, the solicitor who promoted a logical plan for the enlargement of Penrhyndeudraeth nearby; whereas his own house, by an unknown architect, is fascinatingly illogical. A decade earlier he formed a smaller villa on the site called Bron Eryri, then added to it roughly in Lugar's (and the local) castellated manner, so that it has a four-square keep with a high octagonal NE tower, entered by a porte cochère, a lower embattled block and a square tower, all in differing stonework. Large S conservatory, rebuilt when stripped down and converted as a hotel by *John Ricardo Pearce* and *Gruffydd Price*, 2001. The Victorian garden layout survives, a project of 1909 by *Clough Williams-Ellis* not having been carried out.

RHOS-Y-GWALIAU

HOLY TRINITY. 1879–80, by *E. B. Ferrey*. Disused. Decent lancet Gothic, in green stone with sandstone dressings and bellcote. Cusped chancel lancets, and s porch with column shafts.

On a spit of land between two streams, the church stands between YR HEN YSGOLDY, T-plan former National School,

1839, and a mid-c19 former VICARAGE with gabled outer bays. The successor SCHOOL, NW, hipped, in purple brick, 1938, by *Norman Jones*, is now an outdoor pursuits centre. PONT RHIWAEDOG, over both streams, looks early c19.

RHIWAEDOG, ¼ m. E. Architecturally the most important historic house surviving in Penllyn, the Bala region, consisting of perhaps c16 but mostly c17 structures irregularly placed round a walled courtyard entered only through a gatehouse. Of millennial origin and associated with the c9 poet Llywarch Hen, Rhiwaedog was the home of the Lloyd family until the mid c18, and an important focus for c16 and c17 bards. It then survived as a farm on the Rhiwlas estate, then as a youth hostel; since 1997 abandoned.

The house is hard to understand; it is an accumulation of small domestic units in which timber elements may have been reused. Dug into the slope to the S is a possible early storeyed hall with moulded beams, and an upper-end oriel; but the slate-hung exterior and modernized interior defeat further analysis. At its N, a fine late c17 staircase with double doors, turned balusters and upper ogee doorhead. Running at right angles, a range of later dates, extended W as a lower hall. This is a two-storey wing with ovolo-mullioned windows with drip-moulds, including a three-light one to the hall. Parts of a roof with wind-braces, and an upper fireplace dated 1692. Two-storey porch with elliptical outer voussoir arch and original studded door, and the date 1664 and initials HLL. Its small upper room is wainscoted. Attached E is a broader, four-storey building with a lateral chimney, perhaps a solar tower, and of rougher masonry: segmental doorhead, cross-passage partitions and c17 stop-chamfered beams. At the W the main range abuts a barn, no later than the c17, with blocked dormers suggesting that it was another house unit.

The small polygonal front courtyard, enclosed as a garden with a high wall with flat copings, has the GATEHOUSE in the middle of its N wall, not aligned on the porch. Big enough for a small house, it is finely made of squared local stone. Gables over the passage, tall chimneys with hollow mouldings on the end walls. The N doorway is a poem of vernacular masonry, with a steep Tudor profile, unmoulded, the voussoirs cut to a level course above. Either side, a pair of mounting blocks.

The FARMHOUSE to the E is a secondary house of *c.* 1700, with a lateral chimney; closer to the SE farmyard with two long ranges, an 80-ft (25-metre) BARN with angle-braced wall-posts and queenpost trusses, and a long STABLE at right angles, both probably c17.

ABERHIRNANT, 2 m. SE. Single-storey earlier c19 house of Henry Richardson, inventor of the 'tubular' lifeboat, 1852. Stuccoed. The French windows on the l. and at the r. end are both prettily Gothick. Service ranges behind, reduced after a c20 fire.

RHUG/RÛG

Occupation here began very early. The large MOUND in the park (SH 055 439) is, in its present form, a motte, probably C11. Excavations have revealed, however, that it covers a Bronze Age barrow of some complexity.* When an ice house was constructed within in 1878 a stone cist containing cremated bone was found at the centre. This cist had been covered by a small cairn, in turn covered by an earthen mound with a kerb of laid stones. This central construction was eccentric to a much larger mound with a kerb of big stones, perhaps part of the MOTTE built during the first Norman incursion and mentioned in Domesday Book.

The estate descended from Owain Brogyntyn, Lord of Edeirnion in the later C12, to the Salusbury (later Salesbury) family of Bachymbyd, Denbighshire, in the late C15. Their home was immediately adjacent – a jumble of domestic blocks, which having fourteen hearths in 1662, may have been the largest vernacular *plas* in Gwynedd. There were two two-storey hall-and-parlour buildings each with its gallery. Humps of their masonry stretch along the site above the stream, abandoned when the new house was built for Edward, second son of R. H. Vaughan of Nannau (Llanfachreth), who inherited in 1780 and added Salesbury to his name.

RÛG CHAPEL (the Chapel of the Trinity in Edeyrnion). Built in 1637 by Col. William Salusbury at the E edge of Rhug park, on the road to Ruthin, so that exceptionally it functioned both as a country-house chapel and a public one, though neither consecrated nor licensed. The Salusburys had been recusants in the C16, yet its deed of endowment, 1641, stipulates the rites of the Church of England. The exterior was changed to pedestrian Decorated Revival for Sir Robert Vaughan in 1854–5, with a steep bellcote. Previously there were segmental-pointed windows with mullions but no tracery, two-light, and three-light at the E, and a smaller bellcote.

The INTERIOR has a courtly Laudian completeness, with   65 much original decoration and colouring. The frieze along the side walls shows the overlap of styles. The 'architrave' carving of fruits, leaves and tendrils could be late medieval running ornament; above it, in the frieze, panels of symmetrical Renaissance plasterwork, with animal motifs in the centre of acanthus leaves set diagonally, separated by console brackets, under a cornice. The hammerbeam roof harks back to late medieval examples, with cusped strutting in the apex. Alternate trusses have a broad-shouldered robed angel applied to the hammerbeam. The truss sides are painted with trails of roses, in green and red on white, with the feeling for pattern of William Morris. IHS and 1637 over the altar. The roof panels are decorated with abstract swirls; suns and moons over the sanctuary, and the moulded ribs have carved bosses at the

---

*Not far away on the river flats are two other mounds, at Glanalwen and Gwerclas, which may also be barrows.

intersections. The W GALLERY has turned balusters between rails painted in simple Jacobean ornament, the staircase enclosed in painted panelling. – WALL PAINTINGS. Nave, N. Within Corinthian pilasters in crude perspective, a *memento mori*: skeleton on a rolled mat under a slab with symbols of Time, a wreathed skull watching above. Four mottoes in Welsh, one quoting from the Catholic martyr Richard Gwyn †1584. Elsewhere, black-letter inscriptions, one in a fictive stone strapwork frame.

FURNISHINGS. Mostly C17, but did any of them come from nearby churches in the C19? Flanking the sanctuary, two painted CANOPIED PEWS, with carved friezes on turned balusters, marbled lower panels, and upper panels with arabesques. ALTAR RAILS between, painted and in keeping, but apparently from elsewhere; short turned balusters over wainscot. In the SE corner, triangular CREDENCE TABLE, dated 1632, made up of bits. Two rows of high C17 panelled PEWS. Behind, the BENCHES are linked down the aisle by two broad carved beams with a series of half-round dips between bench ends, like long sledges (cf. Dolwyddelan (C)). Running plant ornament below animal images from folk illustration. Originally there were no backs. PANELLING with a guilloche frieze on the walls. CANDELABRUM. Wooden, two-tier, a wonderful vernacular piece with winged cherubs' heads around the top.

The work of the C19 may be more extensive than is yet understood. Of the insertions, the floor tiles are insistent, but the SCREEN, 1854–5, is sensitive. The heads have straight pierced bands of Jacobean type, the base has strapwork and arabesque carving, and the incorporated PULPIT appropriate panels with painted inscriptions. The STAINED GLASS is partly 1850s, the busy E window, by *N. H. J. Westlake*, of 1896.

In the churchyard, a medieval CROSS said to have come from Denbigh Castle. A monolith base supports a chamfered shaft, but the cross itself may be the one shown in 1794 on the E gable.

RHUG. The astylar Neoclassical mansion in fine yellow Grinshill ashlar was erected after 1799 by *Joseph Bromfield*, following proposals by *Humphry Repton* in 1795, and then by *Joseph Bonomi*. Repton's Red Book proposed doubling the lake and carrying a drive across it to a new mansion 400 yds NE, set in open grazed slopes framed by tree belts. This was adopted, omitting the bridge and the turreted palace round two courtyards sketched by *William Wilkins Sen.* of Norwich.

Bromfield's exterior follows the Late Georgian pattern popularized by the Wyatts, while its plan is based on the long transverse passage of C17 classicism. N front of seven bays, the lower sashes very full, the upper ones shorter and on a plain string. Its surprising central feature is a giant Ionic portico that serves as a porte cochère. Columns and responds of exaggerated height support a flat entablature of which only the cornice is continued along the front. The same order is on the S front, but here the central feature is a full-height bow with three-quarter columns and there are nine windows not seven, so more closely spaced.

After Edward Salesbury died in 1807, the estate passed to his brother, then to his nephew Sir Robert Vaughan of Nannau †1859, then to Sir Robert's godson, Charles Wynn, a son of Lord Newborough. Wynn almost doubled the size of the house after he came of age, adding an ashlar E range with a broad pediment, c. 1880–5 by *Henry Kennedy*. The ground floor was a winter garden with two five-bay arcades, the front one open to a magnificent cast-iron conservatory and the back one to a ballroom with a billiard table engineered to rise and sink by hydraulic power. Of all this Late Victorian luxury just the arcades remain, roofless, with terracotta roundels of the Seasons and Ruskinian capitals. A service yard added on the w was also removed, the reductions by *Donald Insall Associates*, 1974–5, for the 7th Lord Newborough.

The interior is arranged as two sequences. Long transverse hall serving the arched axis along its inner side to the restricted stairs. Iron balusters by *William Hazledine* of Shrewsbury, typical of Bromfield, and reused panelling from the C17 painted heraldic parlour (one panel dated 1648). The suite on the S, entered by three unobtrusive doors from the hall, has spaces interconnecting by double doors. Also *Bromfield*'s excellent plaster friezes with wheat-ears, palmettes etc., painted and gilded, the dining room's being particularly fine. Internal adaptations of 1974–5 include the porch within the hall.

w of the house the pre-existing WALLED (or Kitchen and Fruit) GARDEN. Could this have been made for Edward Vaughan after 1780? Three of its four brick walls remain, and one of three summerhouses at its angles – hexagonal and two-storeyed and in the Renaissance tradition of horticulture. In the STABLE YARD to the N much of the masonry looks reused. A central pair of coachhouses with voussoir arches and a clock dated 1830 under the gable and bellcote. Lower ranges each side and opposite, that on the W with C16–C17 masonry parts.

At the main entrance, piers and a half-hipped LODGE, perhaps by *Kennedy*, but with fine C18 wrought-iron GATES, said to have been at Rhug since c. 1740. They are not like those of the famous Wrexham blacksmiths, Robert & John Davies. Opposite, CEFN-RÛG, the home farm, is dated 1732. Another half-hipped LODGE is on the Ruthin road.

PONT MELIN RÛG, ¼ m. w of the main gates. Handsome C18 bridge over the Alwen. Three segmental arches rising to the centre, with raised piers between.

BLAEN-Y-DDOL, 2 m. WNW. A C17 gentry house, in a remote site. The three-bay house set on a high terrace is earlier C17, altered. The l. cross-wing is raised on a basement, and dated 1727 with the initials of Griffith Roberts, High Sheriff in 1729. Cross-windows at the rear and a side chimney gable. Inside this part, a parlour ceiling with simple plaster roundels and motifs, birds, stars etc.

UCHELDREF, 1 m. N. Backing onto a lane, a whitened rendered
C17 house with corniced chimneys and irregular windows. Tall
square chimneys. Two wings enclose a small E courtyard, the
centre of the narrow E front slightly projected. The NE wing
has stonework evidence of being raised in the C18. It is suggested by Cadw that the SE wing may be the original house,
with a cross-wing, now the S end of the main range, earlier
than the good staircase dated 1686, which is against the centre
chimney. Flat balusters, reeded newels and carved finials.

CAER DREWYN HILL-FORT, 2 m. E (SH 088 444). The best-
known of the hill-forts in the Dee valley. On a sloping summit
at the western end of the Llangollen gorge overlooking Corwen
and the broad valley of the Dee where it joins the Alwen – a
strategic point in Welsh communications. The fort is large,
obviously altered at more than one period and employing a
number of construction techniques. Opinions have differed
about the sequence, in particular the relative date of the stone
fort and the bank and ditch outside it at the NE corner. The
best summary advances the following. First, a small, approximately triangular fort on the very top of the hill with a simple
entrance through its earthen bank and ditch on the E side. The
W half of this fort was then destroyed when a roughly rectangular fort with a thick stone wall was built across it. This wall
had a rampart walk behind the outer parapet (now visible only
on the N side), and clearance in the 1920s provided evidence
for at least one guard chamber in the inturned entrance
passage at the NE corner, a feature common in the major
Clwydian hill-forts to the N. The stone fort was then almost
doubled in size by dismantling the W wall, which would have
stood at the top of the scarp which cuts the present enclosure
in two, to build a thinner wall down the slope to the W. The
different scale of the two walls can be appreciated on the N
side, where a subsidiary entrance has been made at their junction. The enlarged enclosure has another inturned entrance
in the middle of the W side (now confused by the ruins of a
medieval hut built in the roadway). Finally, a small enclosure
on the summit with two round huts was contrived in the angle
between the stone fort and the original bank and ditch. This
small settlement, which may be post-Roman, involved the
refurbishment of the original entrance and the building of a
rough stone bank. The site is very exposed, and there is little
evidence of permanent settlement except in the last phase
when the huts were sheltered behind the earlier rampart.

MOEL FODIG HILL-FORT, 2 m. ENE (SH 096 457), just N of the
Rhug–Chester road. The small fort can be seen from the
summit of Caer Drewyn. The top of a low ridge, it is fortified
with a single bank and ditch at the E and W ends and with
a scarped slope where the contours are sufficiently steep.
The entrance to the enclosure – which can have been little
more than a farmstead – is at the E end, with indications
of two possible hut foundations. The W end damaged by
quarrying.

RHYDYMAIN

SALEM INDEPENDENT CHAPEL. 1868, in a large sloping grave-yard. Stuccoed, the front of stone with arched openings. Front plaque to Ieuan Gwynedd (the Rev. Evan Jones) †1852, defender of Nonconformity and the language after the 1847 Education Commission report. Raked box pews inside.

HENFAES, across the A494 road. Substantial house of the 1860s, in squared stone with rock-faced quoins and lintels. Four bays, the outer ones gabled.

HENGWRT UCHAF (Aran Hall School), ¼ m. SW, above the A494. A large Neo-Jacobean house, 1892, for C. E. J. Owen. Rock-faced stone with well-detailed sandstone dressings, the three steep gables with shoulders and kneelers. On the W entrance front a square porch-tower with Scottish ogee cap.

BLAENAU, 1 m. NW. Mid-C19, with bargeboarded gables, but the original house of c. 1700 behind. One room has C18 panelling. Rice Jones †1801, compiler of the verse anthology *Gorchestion Beirdd Cymru*, 1773, lived here.

Along the main road are Nannau estate buildings (see Llan-fachreth). FELIN NEWYDD LODGE, 1 m. SW, at the entry to the disused five-mile drive, is spoilt. The canted front with stone-pillared veranda survives, but raised, rendered and extended. Opposite, FELIN NEWYDD corn mill, earlier C19, has gable-end hoodmoulds and Gothic niche, and hipped side porch. Iron water wheel, and machinery with two pairs of stones. Mill house dated 1796, the cross-wing a converted hay barn. TROEDYRHIW, ¼ m. E, is T-plan with estate chimneys. ESGAIR GAWR, on the Drws-y-nant road, is dated 1830. The HYWEL DDA INN, dated 1789, was built to serve the new turn-pike road. Massive stonework, the pediment flanked by half-dormers. Across the road SE, the tiny SOAR CHAPEL, 1841 and 1924. DOL-FEILI, SW of the inn, 1836, has hoodmoulds and gables; a STANDING STONE is nearby, against the railway. Finally ½ m. NE of the inn, Y BWTHYN, an early C19 toll house, with a three-sided front like Gelli, Llanfachreth; tolls on a slate plaque. Opposite, neat HOUSING of 1953 around a green, built for a creamery, closed 1985.

TALSARNAU

CHRIST CHURCH, Talsarnau. Tiny, by *W. H. Spaull*, 1871. Steep patterned-slate roof, bellcote and canted apse.

ST MICHAEL, Llanfihangel-y-Traethau, 1 m. WSW. Single-roofed, with W porch and N vestry. A break in the N wall sug-gests the nave is older than the chancel. Much renewed, in 1845, in 1866 when the bellcote and vestry were added and a W gallery removed, and in 1884. Of 1884 the red stone Y-tracery windows and similar E window. Arch-braced trusses with heavy tie-beams, decorated with gilded verse. – STAINED GLASS. E window, the Risen Christ, bold and colourful, by

Joan Howson, 1958. – MONUMENTS. John Owen †1690. White
marble, inscribed in Latin. – In the vestry, slate and sandstone
memorials with nicely carved lettering. – STANDING STONE,
W of porch. A 5-ft (1.5-metre)-high schist shaft inscribed in
Latin, 'Here is the tomb of Wleder, mother of Odeleu, who
first built this church in the time of king Owain'.*

BETHEL CALVINISTIC METHODIST CHAPEL, Talsarnau.
Disused. 1864. Broad front in rubble with cement dressings.
Arched windows and doors alternating, all with moulded and
keyed heads. Florentine wooden tracery of 1887 uncomfortably doubled in the wider central window.

RHOSIGOR, ¾ m. SSW. Early C19, stuccoed with sash windows.
Below is a good vernacular group of FARM BUILDINGS in
rough stone: a barn, cowhouse, lofted stables, a hay barn with
tall stone piers, pigsty and brewhouse.

TŶ GWYN MAWR, Ynys, 1 m. WSW. Large mid-C19 warehouse
in well-coursed rubble, known as 'Y Warws'; for storing corn
for ferrying across the Traeth Bach. Also a local gathering
place. Three storeys with cellar; a house to the l., the warehouse with doors and hoist in the E gable.

TYDDYN EGLWYS, Ynys. On the lane to St Michael's church.
Earlier C19 rectory, hipped with a pair of axial chimneys and
a veranda.

EISINGRUG, 1 m. S. A hamlet in the hills serving Glyn Cywarch
and Maes-y-neuadd. EISINGRUG is vernacular, L-plan, the
wing with small-paned sashes and small old slates. Alterations
1889. BRYN-Y-FELIN, NW, Late Georgian style, with sashes,
was the house to the mill opposite, of rough rubble, the stones
shaped but not coped at the gable. YR YSGOL, W of Maes-y-
neuadd, was the school of 1757. Rubble, old thick slates.

GLYN CYWARCH, 1 m. S of Talsarnau. Stone house of several
wings, entered by a court closed by a gatehouse. The home of
a branch of the Wynns descending from the C13 Irishman
Osbwrn Wyddel (Osborn Fitzgerald), heraldry being much displayed inside. William Wynn and perhaps his son Owen seem
to have built and decorated most of the present house between
1616 and the latter's death in 1650. It passed by marriage to
Sir Robert Owen, of a courtier family already blessed with the
Morys properties of Clennenau, Brogyntyn (Porkington) and
Llanddyn, which, as a result, left Glyn to stand still until it
came to John Ormsby-Gore, 1st Lord Harlech, who added to
the house and gardens in the 1870s–80s.

Three ranges at right angles to each other but deliberately
not forming a court, which may indicate that the NW parts have
earlier origins. Another example of the unit system of separate
units of accommodation on one site. The low wing facing NW
is of finer masonry; semicircular oriel on two storeys, and an
upper room with inscriptions on the wall plaster, ascribed to
the early C18 poet Ellis Wynne of Lasynys, Harlech. At the S at
right angles is an intermediate wing with its own spiral stair,

*If 'winireg' is king Owain, this would be Owain Gwynedd, mid-C12.

part of a complex which Moses Griffith's drawing of 1805 suggests was more elaborate than now. To this again is abutted a handsome Renaissance house dated 1616, with initials of William and Katharine Wynn; its mullioned and transomed windows, asymmetry and dormer windows with finials topped with balls connect it with the new wing at Plas Berw in Anglesey, built the same year. Roof with queenpost trusses. In the hall at the E a plaster overmantel dated 1638, with heraldry between Adam and Eve, and the same initials. Early pilastered doorcase not *in situ*. Upstairs the main landing is panelled, with twin arches to the staircases. In the N room a heraldic plaster overmantel dated 1638, with strapwork. In the S room, similar arms, dated 1639, including those of the C12 Owain Brogyntyn, prince of Powys.

The house was enlarged at the N and E in the 1870s, for the 1st Lord Harlech, perhaps by *Benjamin Ferrey* whom he employed at Brogyntyn (Shropshire). Lightly remodelled, 1974, by *N. Johnston*.

The terrace originally related to WALLED GARDENS of which extensive traces remain at the SW among a C20 layout. Axially across the court is the GATEHOUSE, coeval with the SE wing, its four-storey tower with a four-gable roof between lower parts, reminiscent of the gatehouse at Corsygedol, Talybont. Low voussoir arches and hoodmoulds on the local pattern, mullion-and-transom windows. The OUTBUILDINGS abutting were raised a storey, made more Jacobean, and converted into stabling, library etc. by Lord Harlech, the S side in 1871, the N in 1877. Extensive modifications to the park followed, a new drive and LODGE in 1878, rebuilding at the FARM, much planting above the hidden valley, and a circular LOOKOUT TOWER in 1881.

MAES-Y-NEUADD, 1 m. SSE. Now a hotel. Seat of a branch of the Wynns of Glyn Cywarch. A complex plan, which perhaps began with the longish SE wing, now behind r. The N front, of two storeys and attic, four-plus-one bays, looks mid to later C17: bracketed window hoods, voussoired door, corbelled and roughly dentilated eaves, and tall square chimneys. The hipped Merioneth dormers may be later, or modernized. The wider r. bay may be added to link to the cross-wing. This is of similar style and date, suggesting two 'unit-system' houses. The second one, the cross-wing, is L-plan with a two-bay range at right angles in front of the SE original range, the court between now glazed over. Modern link to converted outbuildings, r., including a barn with bellcote. Inglenook fireplace with large bressumer in the oldest wing. Chinese Chippendale staircase in a stair-tower at the rear of the front range, leading from a plastered and panelled dining room, which also looks C18.*
WALLED GARDENS, W, probably C18. Across the lane, MAES-Y-MEILLION, the home farm, its half-round entrance with square piers and ball finials neatly opposite the similar

*Unidentified works in the 1860s by *J. L. Randal* of Shrewsbury.

entrance to Maes-y-neuadd, making a pleasing 'circus'. Late C18 cowhouse and barn of coursed large stonework of exceptional quality.

BRYN CADER FANER CAIRN CIRCLE, 2 m. E (SH 648 353), dramatically on the top of an isolated rocky ridge. A round cairn, robbed in the centre, with, emerging from its edge, a circle of tall thin slabs inclined outwards to give the monument its striking coronet effect. Several other cairn circles exist in Wales but none so dramatic, so simply designed, yet so subtly related to its setting as to force the attention and admiration of the traveller approaching from the S along the Bronze Age trackway. The N side was damaged in army manoeuvres in 1939. In the valley to the SW, a larger modern sheepfold overlying a small group of late Prehistoric or Romano-British HUTS (SH 645 352). Two circular huts may be recognized in opposite corners of a triangular enclosure, walls robbed to build the later fold.

Y GYRN CAIRNS (SH 640 358), NW of Bryn Cader Faner. Two BRONZE AGE CAIRNS on either side of the stream. The N one is a ring cairn, built with a rounded profile but without vertical stones. The central space is grass-grown, filled with earth rather than stone. On the S side of the stream is a burial cairn with a double kerb of large boulders and a central cist, now fully exposed. Another stony mound closer to the stream, composed of burnt stone, is the product of a system of cooking or water-heating by placing hot stones into a trough of water. Such mounds are characteristically horseshoe-shaped, surrounding the trough. Radiocarbon dates have shown that most belong to the Bronze Age. S of Caerwych, a small HUT GROUP. Probably three huts originally but only two can be easily recognized now, one above and one below the lower track. Over the brow of the hill to the SW, remains of MAES-Y-CAERAU, an exceptional 'concentric circle' Iron Age settlement: a large round house surrounded by two circular enclosures.

5922

TALYBONT

The modern settlement is around the bridge over the Ysgethin river, Llanddwywe church is just N at the foot of the long straight drive to Corsygedol, ancient seat of the Vaughans. The upland to the E and SE is one of the richest ancient landscapes in Britain. An orange sandstone, one of the very rare freestones of the region, was quarried E of Egryn Abbey from the C13. Manganese was mined in the C19, and briefly during the First World War.

ST DDWYWE, Llanddwywe, ¼ m. N. In a round churchyard enlarged to the E. A small single-cell church with S porch, W bellcote, and N chapel added for the Vaughans of Corsygedol. The nave may be C13, from the blocked N door with pointed voussoired head. Two paired trefoiled S windows of 1853 in a wall rebuilt in 1663. The porch also of 1853, with a 1593 date-stone above the shallow pointed door. The E three-light Perp window with hoodmould and headstops has narrow traceries probably inserted in the C19. The Vaughan Chapel was added in 1615, but no joint is visible in the E wall so perhaps the chancel gable was then rebuilt also. W door with a flattened three-centred head and a blocked high-level window, r. Two arched E windows, the jambs hollow-chamfered, and a similar three-light N window, with a fireplace built into the wall below (the flue pipe ingeniously divided to follow the two mullions, joining again above). The main roof, with arch-braced collar-trusses and two tiers of wind-braces, looks C16. Chancel celure with ornately enriched ribs and bosses, resting on a billetted wall-plate. The Vaughan Chapel has a single arch-braced truss with cusped struts, even at this late date, and moulded rafter soffits. In the vestry pieces of richly carved wall-plate are reused as a cornice.

REREDOS. Of at least two dates, the Georgian upper half with fielded panels, the later lower half perhaps from former pews. – STALLS. Panels matching the upper reredos. – RAILS. In front of the chancel, with late C17 tall turned balusters. Perhaps the three-sided altar rail which *C. Hodgson Fowler* of Durham moved in his restoration of 1901. – Between chancel and chapel, a fine SCREEN, added by William Vaughan in 1620 and carefully repaired by *Harold Hughes* in 1925. Richly moulded uprights with slim plain intermediates and transoms, all very close together, resting on a carved middle rail containing the date and WV.AV. – MONUMENTS. In the Vaughan Chapel. Griffith Vaughan †1616. Sandstone, with two arched recesses between outer columns, and a cornice with obelisks and heraldry. Griffith and two sons one side, Katherine and three daughters the other. – Richard Vaughan †1734. Ornate white marble on slate with floriate decoration. – Margaret Vaughan †1758. A large tablet in coloured marbles, with fluted frieze and flaming vase, by *van der Hagen*, 1772. – William Vaughan †1775. A shrouded urn in high relief, and hanging in front of it a medallion with his portrait in three-quarter-face and again in profile behind. The background is a pyramid of grey on pink marble. By *van der Hagen*, 1786. – Evan Lloyd Vaughan †1791. A broad vase set on a plinth on brackets. – Outside, under the N window, Elizabeth Jones †1751, faithful servant to the Vaughans for fifty years, her exceptionally large Rococo memorial ousted, however, for Vaughan tablets.

LLANDDWYWE, W of the church. First named in 1625, a drovers' inn until 1903. Under modern roughcast, a typical C16–C17 end-chimney house with hipped dormers. Farmyard with dairy, stable, pigsties, to N and W.

CORSYGEDOL, 1¼ m. NE. A dead-straight drive rising steadily up for a mile on axis from the church tells of the ambitions of the Vaughan family in the early C18 in this remote place; yet it leads to a seat which never grew to meet them. The DRIVE begun by Richard Vaughan M.P. †1734 appears on John Earle's survey of 1764.* C19 splay of walls and LODGES, then a lime avenue, with a coped wall behind as it passes through woods, and, after the Victorian UPPER LODGE, it passes a C16 to C17 cottage to arrive, not centrally but at an angle, at the forecourt framed by C18 GATEPIERS with pyramidal caps and balls.

p. 39
55

The forecourt is monumentally straddled by the GATE-HOUSE, its arch aligned on the Elizabethan porch of the house. Dated 1630, the gatehouse is exceptional, the best-preserved in Wales. Renaissance in spirit, and no later than Jacobean in form. A three-storey cross-gabled tower with depressed archways stands between short wings with stone dormers. The ogee-domed lantern and clock faces are both recorded by Earle. The first floor has a three-light stone mullion window under a crude pediment, echoed in the wing dormers. The arch is moulded, with on the keystone the date and the initials of William Vaughan (builder also of Talhenbont, Llanystumdwy, 1607).

The HOUSE is the most intact of Gwynedd's pre-classical gentry *plasau*, representative of ways of life and building before the compact, double-pile house made its appearance. At the core is a two-storey range built for Richard Vaughan, dated 1576 inside, that forms the centre and r. of the S front. This is of roughly six bays with tall end chimneys. The central gabled porch is dated 1593, with the initials of Griffith Vaughan (†1616) in a little classical aedicule above a depressed-arched doorway with diamond rustication over a hoodmould. Above that a three-light transomed window under a pediment (as at Plas Mawr, Conwy). To the r. the upper floor is lit by three Elizabethan windows with arched lights, like those at Gwydir Castle, of three, four and three lights, dated 1592 on the r. with the initials GV and KV. Similar windows below were replaced by sashes in the early C19 and then by the present stone cross-windows. The r. end chimney top is dated 1610. The two bays l. of the porch are dated 1660 with the initials of William Vaughan, but later C18 sash windows with octagonal panes, one each floor, light the stair hall, and a large semi-octagonal bow, l., is dated 1782, but altered.

The storeyed hall at the core has a grand lateral fireplace and a high-status compartmented ceiling, with three tiers of moulded beams and joists. The elliptical fireplace arch has a deep band around, SEQUERE IUSTITIAM ET INVENIAS VITAM ('seek justice and find life') in raised letters, presumably of 1576, except that the date panel above is architecturally unrelated. Could the fireplace also be of 1592? Under the arch an ashlar infill of plain arched recesses flanking a narrow fireplace. The room is lined in fine early C18 large-field panelling, part of a refitting for Richard Vaughan M.P., with a segmental

---

*The survey, made for William Vaughan then living at Dolrhyd, Dolgellau, has in the margin a proposed S front (a project of William Vaughan's?) of eleven bays and three storeys, including an old-fashioned porch-tower and slight two-bay wings.

doorway, l., and double doors in a bolection frame, r., in the partition to the parlour. This room, similarly panelled, has a strange small C16 or C17 chimneypiece with crude half-columns and diamond (or Vaughan saltire) decoration on the blocks and shelf. On the other side of the hall in a panelled stair hall are broad dog-leg stairs with fat Queen Anne turned balusters, also on the landing. The W end with the 1782 bay was re-fitted with shallow Adam-style plaster ceiling decoration. Upstairs, the long E room is again panelled, leaving exposed a plaster overmantel dated 1592, with helm, crest and motto over two many-quartered shields, showing original colour. It was a picture gallery when Fenton visited. The W room has a late C18 plaster musical trophy.

At the rear, a proliferation of later gabled wings at right angles. The C16 stair must have been here. Two wings possibly early C18, extend N and W with a staircase in the angle. In the W wing, elaborate later C19 woodwork of Restoration to Rococo style and plaster arms of Elizabeth I (reused or a copy?). This wing was extended W in the C19 and then with a long single-storey N range. Part of this may be the picture gallery inserted after 1858 by the Rev. H. Ker Cokburne †1866.

The GARDENS retain outlines of a layout perhaps largely of the second quarter of the C18. S of the drive, a levelled enclosure once divided in two, with C18 beech trees round, traces of straight walks, and a terrace at the top with niches in its walls. Above this a cobbled STABLEYARD of 1763. W of the house the design was altered in the C19, its stone-revetted pond made informal. N of the house, the remains of a large WALLED GARDEN, thought to have originated in the C16. It has a broad raised walk along its W wall of plain rubble. Is this coeval with the grander one at Aberglasney, Carms?

Uphill immediately NE, the FARMHOUSE, of six bays, with an armorial stone panel dated 1739. Just SE, the GREAT BARN, an ornate structure sited downhill. Dated 1685. Of coursed rubble, 72 ft (22 metres) long, with raised gables. Symmetrical front with ventilation slits framed in sandstone; the main N arch segmental, with quarter-round mouldings. Further stone farm buildings of the C19.

EGRYN ABBEY, 1 m. SSE. Never an abbey; so named only since the 1840s. A stone-built hall-house, ring-dated 1507–10, altered in the late C16 or early C17, and with a mid-C19 W addition. The hall had a pair of inner rooms E of the dais with a chamber above, behind the surviving full-height partition. On the W, there was another partition beyond the cross-passage; pieces survive reused as joists above the passage. A pair of rooms beyond and chamber above. An open hearth is certain because the small louvre-truss is visible just E of the main arch-braced truss. Defining the cross-passage is a remarkable box-framed spere-truss. The wide moulded posts rise until they meet the main cross-beam with a twin-bowtail flourish (cf. Penarth Fawr, where the posts extend up to the purlins). An arcade above the beam and cusped struts above the collar.

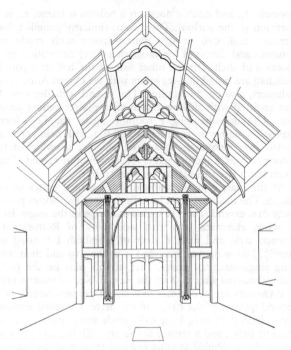

Talybont, Egryn Abbey, hall interior.
Reconstruction drawing

The two tiers of purlins, with wind-braces, are fully mortised
into the truss principals.

Of this first period, the s door with pointed louvre head and
the mullioned dais window, of ochre Egryn sandstone. The N
lateral chimney was added in the later C16, perhaps coinciding
with the provision of chambers above the hall and the upper s
windows – gabled dormers with coped verges and ovolo-
moulded jambs. Yet a part of the hall must have remained
open, because as late as 1830 a connecting bridge is recorded
between the E and W end chambers (probably along the N
side). After 1840 the W end was replaced by a small house at
right angles, facing the new turnpike road, with Late
Georgian sashes, the doorway oddly narrow and off-centre.
Parallel with the house, s, a second house was built 1615–18,
roughly contemporary with the main remodelling. Perhaps a
dower house. Rubble with end chimneys, and segmental-
arched doorhead of Egryn sandstone. Much altered for
agricultural use. A rare ROOT-STORE, probably C19, survives
SE, buried and roofed with large slate slabs covered with turf.

CORSYGEDOL BURIAL CHAMBER, I m. NE (SH 603 228).
A badly ruined Megalithic tomb, probably of the portal
dolmen tradition. Two upright stones survive. It is difficult to

decide whether they represent the front (portal) of the chamber, or the back. A large capstone slopes down behind the larger stone and there is evidence for a long stone cairn.

The open ground E of the road is covered with remains of two superimposed FIELD SYSTEMS, recognizable by low lynchet banks. The earlier system is likely to be contemporary with the enclosed HOMESTEAD (SH 604 230) on its N edge (near the modern water tank): two large round huts with a rectangular building between, which produced evidence for occupation in C2 A.D. Other single round huts may be seen amongst the fields. The later fields, outlined by low walls, may be associated with long huts of medieval type.

CRAIG-Y-DINAS HILL-FORT, 2¼ m. ENE (SH 624 230). Typical of many small fortifications in Merioneth, taking advantage of the natural defences of a rocky knoll. The dry-stone wall has tumbled down the slopes, but part of the original facing can be glimpsed around most of the circuit. The inside is obscured by a rough modern wall. Entrance on the NW side, a narrow passage running obliquely up the slope and protected by a projecting bastion. The N end has two further protecting walls, but they are weak by comparison with the inner rampart.

STONE CIRCLES. The LLECHEIDDIOR circle, 1½ m. E (SH 611 217) has a number of upright stones, none very high, backed by a wide, low bank of small stones. The HENGWM embanked stone circles to the SE (SH 616 214) have annular stone banks 104 ft (32 metres) and 169 ft (52 metres) in diameter with upright stones set at intervals around the inner edge. The smaller N circle was also surrounded by a shallow ditch. Excavation in 1920 revealed what may have been a grave in its centre, a 'fire pit' nearby, and a scatter of beaker sherds. No upright stones remain in position, the ditch is silted, and neither monument can now be easily recognized. On the same packhorse track are scattered remains of a large CAIRN strangely named the Hill of the Horns of Jove – Bryn Cornyn Jau. On the Bwlch y Rhiwgwr pass, remains of another CAIRN (SH 627 200) overlain by the modern wall built of its robbed stones.

CARNEDDAU HENGWM, 2 m. ESE (SH 614 205). A most important pair of long cairns, side by side on the moorland above Egryn Abbey. The S CAIRN is likely to be the older, almost certainly a two-period structure. At the E end (over the wall) is a ruined portal dolmen, still with two overlapping capstones when Thomas Pennant saw it in the late C18. Now only the S half of the chamber is standing, a high portal stone, the closing slab and a side stone; the capstones, backstone and N side slab lie nearby. This chamber stood at the E end of a rectangular cairn which has a length of unexplained walling exposed near its W end. The W half of the cairn was probably added to cover a small chamber built of dry-walling and a large capstone, entered by a passage from the N. A shepherd was living here when Pennant visited.

The N CAIRN is smaller and has many features – opposed lateral chambers at the E end, the use of dry-stone walling in the cairn (the high standard of work can be recognized in the NE chamber) and the smaller scale of the chambers – suggestive of the Cotswold–Severn tradition, probably built during the Middle Neolithic. The capstone at the W end appears to lie on cairn material, but one upright can just be recognized beneath it and it is likely that some other chamber has been removed from the hollow in the centre.

The moorland around the Carneddau Hengwm contains many monuments of interest. The path from Egryn Abbey passes through early fields with lynchets and low walls, probably medieval or C17 with several long huts and paddocks scattered among them. Visible from mid-slope, a characteristic Merioneth Iron Age SETTLEMENT at the foot of the hill, a 'concentric circle' with one large house central to a circular enclosure. On the higher shelf, above Carneddau Hengwm, an earlier HUT GROUP with three round huts, an oval paddock and clearance cairns. Close by is a Bronze Age RING CAIRN (SH 616 203), the outer edge marked by a circle of low slabs inclined outwards. Excavation in 1919 found nothing within the central area.

PEN-Y-DINAS HILL-FORT, 1¼ m. SE (SH 606 209), above the gorge of the Egryn river. A classic profile from the S; but closer examination reveals that the banks and ditches are not extensive, the main defence being produced by scarping the sides of a natural hillock. This strong-point was surrounded by a massive stone wall with an entrance on the W side, defended by outworks and a second, V-shaped ditch which may be a later addition. Partial excavation in 1919 found no dating evidence. The site may equally be post-Roman, or even medieval, but it must have been abandoned by the time a later medieval platform house was built across the entrance track.

PONT SCETHIN, 3 m. ENE. A single-span bridge over the Ysgethin, in wonderful isolation on the packhorse track between Harlech and Dolgellau, possibly late C17.

TALYLLYN

7210

A beautiful and sparsely settled parish under Cader Idris, the church at the foot of the natural lake (Llyn Mwyngil). The parish, originally Llanfair Bryn Muallt, extended from Abergynolwyn to Aberllefenni.

ST MARY. Disused. A single vessel like Llanfihangel y Pennant, probably C15. The W wall, of regular blocks with a small bellcote on a wall pier, must be C18. The long rendered S transept is perhaps C16, as also the broad porch, which has C19 roof timbers of a date with the mechanical Gothic windows, 1876, by *Henry Kennedy*. Careful repairs in 1914 by *Harold Hughes*. It is the ROOF that is the interest of the church, both as evidence for liturgical arrangements and for the painted celure, one of the delights of Merioneth. The roof divides into three parts over eight bays. The W four have arch-braced collar-trusses, sweeping low into the walls, and plain wind-bracing. The next three have cusped wind-braces and two low barn-like tie-beam trusses, one at the W and the other two bays on. The first tie-beam has big arched braces above, the second is grooved for a central doorway. Was the tympanum infilled too? The eastern bay was ceiled later, as there are stubs of a smaller E tie-beam, cut out presumably in Tudor times, for the celure is painted with the boldest Tudor roses, white on red and red on white. It is crudely ribbed into big squares subdivided by painted fictive ribs with painted bearded faces for bosses. The transept has two tie-beam-and-collar trusses. It is divided off as a vestry by reused panelling with plaster above, the panels said to come from a W gallery of 1765. – FONT. C12, square with the lower corners shaved. – Later C18 RAILS with turned balusters and COMMUNION TABLE with roughly shaped octagonal legs. – PULPIT. 1876, fretwork panels. – In the porch a slate CHARITIES BOARD, 1837. – STAINED GLASS. E window, c. 1876, the Good Samaritan, the inn sign a Welsh dragon. – MONUMENTS. Marble scroll to W. W. Kirkby †1864 in New South Wales. – Sarah Kirkby †1877, draped urn, by *Bovey & Co.* of Plymouth.

Two C18 LYCHGATES, the top one because the lakeside road from Corris was sometimes cut off by flood. Squared stone with arched entrances, the NW one with a lovely rustic angel above.

MAES-Y-PANDY, ½ m. WSW. Early C19 three-bay stone farmhouse with an older rear wing. On the lawn in front a two-storey hipped PRIVY dated 1743, the upper floor apparently the family schoolroom.

MINFFORDD HOTEL, 2 m. NE. Whitewashed C18 roadside inn, noted in 1808 by Fenton. Three bays with close-set stone dormers; flanking outbuildings.

TOWYN *see* TYWYN

TRAWSFYNYDD

7135

ST MADRYN. In a round churchyard. Two parallel naves (rare in Merioneth), the older to the N, extended far W of the C16 S one until, after a fire in 1978, the W gable and bellcote were rebuilt in line. S porch also C16, the wide door with rough voussoirs and a big keystone block. The naves are separated by a row of octagonal oak posts of uncertain date. The flat soffit lined with panelling from box pews before the fire. Restored by *Henry Kennedy*, 1853–4, when the windows were renewed and the roofs rebuilt reusing the medieval arch-braced trusses (those in the N nave, except the E one, destroyed in the fire). – PEWS. Mid-C19, panelled, with ogee-curved doors. – FONT. C19, octagonal. The COVER, a tall crocketed pinnacle intricately carved in oak, almost reaches the roof; more fit for a cathedral.

– STAINED GLASS. N nave E, the Charge to Peter, by *W. Warrington*, 1888. S nave E, by *Powells*, 1904.

MORIAH CALVINISTIC METHODIST CHAPEL. Imposing three-bay façade in rock-faced snecked green rubble with sandstone, 1885–7, by *Richard Davies*. The gable has stepped corbelling and the centre is advanced with paired arched doors under an arched triplet, all shafted with cushion capitals. A tiny Palladian vent above.

Quarrying VILLAGE cut in two by the A470 road. Disused slate quarries NE, near the former railway opened in 1882. Linear settlement W, mostly of two-storey terraces. In CHURCH SQUARE, W of the centre, the church and the OLD RECTORY, 1838, by *William Hemming* of Maentwrog. Three bays, squared stone, with hoodmoulded windows and columned porch. Similar three-bay side, tightly squeezed, most of the windows blind. The WHITE LION INN, Pen-y-garreg, is mid-C19, with wide eaves and an astoundingly long lintel (over 23 ft (7 metres)) over most of the lower openings. Next to Moriah chapel, a small bronze STATUE to Hedd Wyn (*see* Yr Ysgwrn below) by *Leonard Merrifield*, c. 1923, chosen after Goscombe John proved too expensive. To the S, YSGOL BRO HEDD WYN, the former British school by *O. Morris Roberts*, c. 1870, extended to the N. S again, incongruous Neo-Georgian HSBC BANK, 1960s. Hipped roof behind parapets, heavily quoined doorway and walls of stone pieces cast into blocks.

YR YSGWRN, 1 m. SE. 1830. Small farmhouse in rough squared blocks, with small-paned sashes; an outbuilding in-line. The home of the bard Hedd Wyn (Ellis Humphrey Evans), killed in Flanders only months before being declared winner of the chair at the 1917 National Eisteddfod. The chair, draped in black at the ceremony, is in the parlour. Elaborately carved by the Belgian *Eugeen Vanfleteren*, on the theme of 'The present-day Welshmen honouring the former Celtic art'.

RHIWGOCH, Bronaber, 2½ m. SSE. Now an inn. Dated 1610. L-plan, with rough dripstones and a good moulded sandstone doorway with a hoodmould. M R Ll 1610 in the spandrels, for Mary and Robert Lloyd; their shield above. Small angled upper window in the junction, and a tall square cornice chimney. Contemporary lower range, linked to the W range by a wall with slate bee-bole shelves. It has a through-passage with, above the N lintel, a C17 lettered slab with the arms of Llywarch ap Bran, C12 founder of the tribe from whom the Lloyds claimed descent. The birthplace in 1577 of St John Roberts, Catholic convert, first prior of the Benedictine college at Douai, executed in London 1610. Interior altered, but a first- floor C17 plaster overmantel survives.

RAILWAY VIADUCT, Cwm Prysor, 4 m. E. In wild country, carrying the 1882 Bala to Blaenau Ffestiniog line over the Nant y Lladron on ten tall arches.

118   TRAWSFYNYDD NUCLEAR POWER STATION, 2 m. NNE. Built 1959–63, on the N shore of Llyn Trawsfynydd, chosen as remote from human habitation. Designed by *Sir Basil Spence*, but as it was within the Snowdonia National Park a landscape

consultant, (*Dame*) *Sylvia Crowe*, was engaged to advise on how the large complex could best be treated in the wide open setting. She suggested the pair of reactor buildings, each *c*. 180 ft (55 metres) high and clad with pre-cast concrete made with local aggregate, should 'grow straight out of the landscape without an intervening zone of worried detail'. The station closed after just thirty years' operational life, with only sketchy plans for the 135 years required to make the site safe from radioactivity. A competition was organized in 1994 to explore alternatives (one entry recommended a covering of consolidated slate waste from Blaenau Ffestiniog) but Nuclear Electric's plans, to lower and re-clad the buildings, have prevailed.

CASTELL PRYSOR, Cwm Prysor, 3½ m. E. A castle mound consisting of a knoll of rock, heightened, and also revetted in masonry, commanding the W end of the valley; nothing quite like it anywhere else. It may be late C12, although the only date seemingly associated with it is 1284, when Edward I sent a letter from 'Pressor'. Thomas Pennant in the late C18 mentioned that, apart from traces of buildings about the castle, there was a wall around the mound's summit and a possible round tower. If the tower was circular, then a date in the first half of the C13 is likely. The masonry revetment, originally mortared, has some evidence of coursing. Traces of rectangular buildings lie to the NW and NE, and it has been argued that at Prysor we have a castle and a *llys*, a Welsh royal residence, with buildings comparable to those excavated at Abergwyngregyn and Rhosyr in 1993 and 1995 respectively.

CRAWCWELLT, 3 m. SSW. A partially restored Iron Age industrial settlement out on the moor (SH 686 308). Excavation revealed the manufacture of iron from bog ores. The houses, recognizable as levelled platforms, were originally light wicker structures rebuilt on many occasions to house small shaft furnaces and smithing hearths. Some were finally rebuilt in stone and are now easily visible, as is a medieval *hafod* and an Early Bronze Age cairn. The area around the buildings was covered in low slag dumps.

MAEN LLWYD, 1½ m. S (SH 707 330). A not very conspicuous standing stone, 4 ft 6 in. (1.4 metres) high, overshadowed by a hedge. Thought to have marked the ancient route from Harlech towards Bala. A smaller upright about 6 ft (2 metres) away may form a pair with it.

LLECH IDRIS, 3 m. SSE (SH 731 311). A fine Bronze Age standing stone, thin and pointed and over 10 ft (3 metres) high, dramatically sited beside an old trackway.

BEDD PORIUS, 3 m. SSE (SH 733 313). Inside a modern railing and stone enclosure lie two casts of the gravestone of Porius (C5–C6) who had been buried beneath a mound. He is described as 'Homo planus' – a plain man.* The original is in the National Museum, Cardiff.

---

*Also interpreted as a 'flat man', a leper who had lost his nose; a doubtful interpretation of a rare word.

TOMEN-Y-MUR ROMAN FORT, 2 m. N (SH 706 386). The auxiliary fort, high on bleak and windswept moorland, must have
been one of the most dreaded postings for any Roman soldier.
For all its remoteness it was then an important strategic post
commanding routes to N, S and E, and was originally quite
large, defended by exceptional double banks. This first Flavian
fort was reduced under Hadrian (117–28 A.D.) by abandoning
the W section, and new stone-walled defences were built. There
is no evidence for a garrison after 140 A.D., and many of the
external earthworks may have been left unfinished. In the CII
the site was reused and a huge MOTTE was built, perhaps by
William Rufus, over the W rampart of the reduced fort.

The external earthworks make this Roman station
particularly interesting, but they are difficult to identify on the
ground without a plan. An information board has been set up
in the farm ruin. N of the fort, at the end of the approach road,
is a small oval AMPHITHEATRE (damaged by a quarry
tramway across it), probably used for drill practice. To the S a
large flat area bounded by a low bank, interpreted as a parade
ground, a very rare survival, but paralleled at the equally
remote Hardknott fort, Cumbria. Across a small leat is an
unusual long mound, perhaps an observation or saluting base.

The FORT itself lies just S of the ruined farm. The square-
cut stones of the second-phase rampart contrast with the
rounded earthen banks of the original fort W of the medieval
motte, with its sharply cut ditch. Outside the E gate is evidence
for Roman buildings, perhaps a civil settlement. CI9 excavations suggested that the bath building was in this area, with

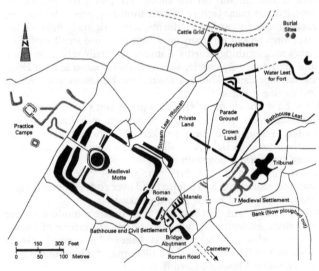

Trawsfynydd, Tomen-y-mur Roman fort.
Plan

water brought by the small leat from higher up the stream. A large courtyard building with stone foundations may have been a *mansio* or guesthouse. From here the road crossed the stream by a wooden bridge, the N abutment of which can be recognized. It carried on S past an enclosed cemetery, within which is a fine square-ditched barrow. Other smaller burial monuments can be recognized on the top of a low rise just E of the amphitheatre.

DOLDDINAS ROMAN PRACTICE CAMPS, 2¼ m. ENE (SH 735 378). There are five practice camps N of Dolddinas Farm on either side of the river; the three on the W side are better preserved. The smallest (72 ft (22 metres) square), closest to the farm, is the easiest to see but low vegetation and oblique light are needed. Such camps can be found close to military bases all over the Empire, but Britain contains more than most provinces, and this is judged to be the best-preserved British group. Others have been recognized from the air just W of Llyn Hiraethlyn just over ½ m. SE. The Roman road from Tomen-y-mur to Caergai (Llanuwchllyn) forms the E–W track beside Dolddinas Farm, and can be well seen in the W section, including the regular small quarry scoops from which the stone surfacing was obtained. A small mound close to the farm buildings may cover a Roman cremation burial.

TYWYN

Tywyn (the anglicized spelling Towyn has all but disappeared) is oddly shapeless considering its long history and the several attempts at creating a seaside resort. The site was settled in the C6 by St Cadfan. His monastery was the most significant in the county. The rebuilt C12 church is the major Romanesque church of the region. By the C18 a little town had gathered around the church, part of the estate of the Owens of Ynysmaengwyn (Bryncrug). The Owens and their successors the Corbets drained the marshes, and flat fields and marsh still back the High Street on the N. There was tourism in the early C19, the beach frequented 'by numerous genteel families . . . for the purpose of sea bathing' (1812). The grave of Cadfan in the churchyard was shown to Richard Fenton in 1808 and St Cadfan's Well still retained its healing powers. By 1833 the well had been enclosed with bathing facilities. Tourism was expected to grow after the Cambrian Railway came through in the 1860s, but the line mainly served to tranship slates brought down by narrow-gauge railway from Abergynolwyn. Although a scattering of lodging houses and hotels appeared, almost nothing was made of the seashore, ½ m. W, apart from a failed attempt at a pier in 1877–8.

The Corbet estate was bought in 1879 by the unrelated John Corbett (1817–1901), salt tycoon of Droitwich, Worcs. His investment in the town is clear to see: the hotel, the assembly rooms, the market hall, the school, the avenue to the sea and the seafront promenade; but urban unity is lacking. The promenade

Tywyn, seafront proposal.
Drawing by John Madin, 1961

was designed in 1889 by *F. J. Collingwood*, an engineer from Rhyl,
and a competition for laying out the town was won in 1891 by
W. Dunbar, another Rhyl engineer, but does not seem to have
translated into a great deal. In 1896–7 London engineers, *Tapp
& Jones* were building houses, probably the single seafront
terrace, but this stands in isolation. The area between the railway
and the sea remained basically undeveloped until the later C20.
In 1961 the Birmingham architect *John Madin* proposed a brave
plan for this area, with a twelve-storey hotel at right angles to the
seafront and a modern street plan with vehicle separation, but
the project was abandoned with almost nothing built. What has
filled the space since is depressing, a typical later C20 failure to
respond imaginatively to the seaside.

ST CADFAN. As remarkable a church as any in Wales, despite
the ravages of time. The *clas* monastery founded by Cadfan
survived unreformed into the C12. A eulogy of a lay abbot,
Morfran, by Llywelyn Fardd, written after 1147, compares the
church to Bangor and St Davids cathedrals, and praises the
miraculous relics of Cadfan. The impressive cruciform plan
with crossing tower is also found at Llanbadarn Fawr, Llanddewi Brefi and Llanfihangel y Creuddyn, ancient *clas* sites in
Ceredigion. But unlike those, the nave is aisled, which may
have inspired the cathedral comparison. The outline is greatly
reconstructed, for the tower collapsed in 1692 taking with it
most of the chancel and the s transept. The nave was kept in
use, the derelict w bay replaced in 1736 by a tower. This was
taken down in *John Prichard*'s ambitious restoration of 1881–4,
which reinstated the crossing tower.

One must start with the nave with its tiny arched clerestory [12] windows and aisles, quite without adornment. Another tiny arched light in the N aisle, so all C12. The S doorway with voussoired head looks C18. Prichard planned the overhaul of the nave and its extension to the W, but funds were insufficient, resulting in the survival almost unrestored of the C12 work, and in a temporary W wall that reuses three arched windows from the 1736 tower. For the eastern parts, Prichard chose early Gothic, mechanical in detail but effective in outline, the big tower with paired louvred bell-lights, Irish stepped battlements and a sheer SW stair-turret like an octagonal pipe. The transepts are plain, the stonework of the N one medieval with battered base, diagonal buttresses and an E lancet. Both have ugly C19 segmental-pointed windows. The chancel is mostly rebuilt, with a traceried S window and three E lancets. *Harold Hughes* added the S porch in dark green stone, 1919, to match his LYCHGATE of 1908, both in a strong and unadorned Romanesque. Cross-inscribed STONE built into the SW angle of the tower.

Inside, the nave is wonderfully luminous: piers, arcades, walls and even the aisle roof timbers whitewashed. Three bays of elemental Romanesque arcades survive of a presumed four, with stout cylindrical piers widening simply to an abacus no more pronounced than a lip, and carrying round arches that are wholly unarticulated. Square E responds are carried back to the crossing piers with a ledge. Clerestory windows in deep-splayed embrasures above the piers. Late C15 open roof of shallow pitch with arch-braced collar-trusses with apex cusping. Added thin tie-beams. The S aisle roof has three shaped blades supported on raking struts from the arcade abaci, and intermediate plain blades, but on the N thick buttresses are inserted across the aisle, perhaps C18. The crossing is all *Prichard*. Tall pointed arches, the deeply moulded and keeled inner order on corbelled piers. Beamed oak ceiling. The transepts have late C19 arches to the aisles and late C19 roofs. The chancel is not all C19; two medieval TOMB RECESSES in the N wall, and a deep-set N lancet that may be C13. C19 boarded ribbed ceiling.

FURNISHINGS. FONT. C13. Square monolith with chamfered angles, ogee-curved below to a short octagonal ringed shaft. Separate and inconsistent base with bold stops. Attractive oak cover, 1930. – ORGAN. Ill-sited in the S transept: 1897, housed in an extraordinarily elaborate oak case of 1911 by *C. E. Bateman*, derived from Late Gothic screens. – LECTERN. Oak, Gothic, 1883, by *Keith* of London. – REREDOS, 1908–10, by *Harold Hughes*; by him also the fussy Gothic panelling. – STAINED GLASS. E window, 1884, Christ and saints, by *W. F. Dixon*, very good in an intense German C15 style. – W window, 1883, by *S. Evans* of West Bromwich. Three large saints in busy colours. – N transept N, Kempe-style, 1909, by *H. W. Bryans*. – S transept S, c. 1900, C16 style, unusual dark colouring. – N aisle first, by *Geoffrey Webb*, 1943, sweet.

MONUMENTS. Two well-preserved recumbent effigies in the chancel recesses. One is of a priest in high relief, of the early C14. He wears full eucharistic robes and has his hands on his chest. Above his head a canopy with a nodding arch; the little angels beside it have been broken. The second is of a figure in armour, traditionally Gruffudd ap Adda †1331. It is well carved with the r. hand on the hilt of the sword while the l. hand holds the scabbard. The legs, beneath a short tunic, are uncrossed. – Nearby, Vincent Corbett †1723, very elegant Early Georgian, the curved head with arms, festoons and nautilus shells. – Rev. Pryce Maurice †1803, with curved cornice. – Chancel s wall. Lewis Vaughan †1832, a pious female figure in an eroding Gothic niche. – Athelstan Owen †1731, by *Henry Cheere*. Splendid Baroque pomp, with a top-piece of volutes flanking a cherub-headed vase set against a black medallion under a scrolled cornice with arms. – N transept. Edward Scott †1842, plaque by *Bedford*. – Earlier C19 tablet to the de Saumaise family of Belgium, the Welsh widow of the last having married Edward Scott. – Tiny brass to Ann Dafydd †1785. – S transept. Plain oval to Pryce Maurice †1818. – Crude marble plaque to the Edwards family, 1815; postscript, 1834, by *J. Carline*. – INSCRIBED STONE. A cross-incised pillar bearing on all four sides an inscription of *c.* 750, dated by the letters, big but lightly drawn half-uncials. They are barely visible, and, as deciphered, barely understandable, but the significance of the stone is that it is in Welsh, the earliest record of the language. – Outside the E end, fierce iron railings around two tombs of the 1860s with massive slate slabs.*

ST DAVID (R.C.), Pier Road. 1966–9 by *Weightman & Bullen*. A striking modern group. The church is a white roughcast hexagon with a metal-clad roof like an inverted six-sided funnel, glazed on the N and S. The flat roof, r., covers a hall that can be opened into the nave. A flat-roofed presbytery, l., completes the group.

BETHESDA INDEPENDENT CHAPEL, High Street. 1881–2. Stuccoed, presumably by *Richard Owens*. Pedimented with winged side bays and a stepped arched triplet.

EBENEZER WESLEYAN CHAPEL, High Street. 1882. Stucco and pebbledash. The façade in two storeys has a certain hefty character that suggests *Richard Davies*.

ENGLISH PRESBYTERIAN CHAPEL, College Green. 1871, by *W. H. Spaull* of Oswestry. Small, Gothic, in green stone with a spiky spirelet on the r.

MARKET HALL, College Green. A Diamond Jubilee gift of John Corbett, 1897–8. In a kind of Jacobean with an ogee-domed octagonal tower in the middle over five arches; two-storey cross-wing to the l. with shaped gable. Stone with yellow brick bands, sandstone arches, limestone quoins.

---

*Fenton in 1808 recorded a churchyard inscription by Nanney Wynn to the harpist Hugh Ellis, drowned in the Dysynni in 1774: 'The Nymphs of ye flood were rutting, plague rot'em/When the genius of musick went to the bottom/Their care and attention would else have supported/The child of the harp whom ye Muses all courted.'

Ysgol Tywyn, Station Road. Set back in ample grounds the cheerful County School of 1908 by *Deakin & Howard Jones*. Red brick and buff terracotta, the hall gable lit by a giant triple window and lunette, the low flanking wings with ornamented doors and lunettes in the end gables. Additions by the same firm of 1910 and 1925.

Tywyn Cottage Hospital, Aberdyfi Road. 1919–22, by *F. Howarth* of Tywyn. Altered, but keeping a little Arts and Crafts character. Whitewashed roughcast, single-storey with a big gabled porch and well-carved plaque. Sympathetic addition to the l. by *Howarth*, 1932, and presumably the mansard-roofed cottage beyond.

Wharf Station, Station Road. The terminus of the Talyllyn narrow-gauge railway, built in 1864–6 to bring slate from Abergynolwyn (q.v.) for transfer to main-line wagons. The engineer was *J. S. Swinton*. The line survived to become the world's first preserved railway in 1951. The present red brick station is based on a tiny C19 office, extended 1965 by *R. D. Butterell*, and again in 2002–5 by *Richard Leng*, when linked to a large Neo-Victorian office and museum.

PERAMBULATION

Corbet Square, e of the church, is an irregular space defined by the Corbett Arms Hotel on the e, an enlargement in 1900 of the earlier six-bay inn to ten bays, showing the aspirations of the Corbett era. Three storeys and attic, stuccoed, with coarse pediments over some windows and a central gable. In front, at right angles, the Assembly Rooms, 1893, cheerfully painted stucco with an arch breaking into a pediment, chapel-like apart from the cast-iron music-hall lettering and gable urns. The s side is a mixed three-storey row, one house lettered 'Bank'. This block, with Red Lion Street, e, and Church Street, w, is the heart of the old settlement. A mixture of C19 stone fronts. Set back facing the s end of Church Street, Tŷ Cadfan Sant, the former vicarage, early C19 of coursed boulders, raised on a basement with steps up to a Tuscan doorcase. Returning to the church, College Green runs w past the Market Hall (*see* above) to the High Street. Down a short lane N, St Cadfan's Well, a sad and utilitarian building of *c.* 1870, stone and brick, minimally Gothic. The well has been floored over.

At the top of the High Street, Neptune Road runs sw with a fat iron lamp stand on a stone pedestal, the Boer War Memorial, 1902. Further down, the Council Offices, *c.* 1925, dark slate stone and buff terracotta, tamed Edwardian with open-pedimented gables. The High Street is generally three-storey, later C19 to early C20, mixed in styles and materials. On the l., the former D. & J. Daniel hardware store, built in 1903 for H. Haydn Jones, M.P. for Merioneth 1910–45. Emphatically striped in brick and terracotta, the façade has more glass than structure, with big arched upper windows; capped by a tiny pediment. No. 24 is stuccoed Late Georgian style, probably mid-C19, Nos. 25–28, much taller, later C19. Opposite, beyond Bethesda chapel (*see* p. 720), the POLICE STATION, later C19 with a Neo-Georgian addition in brown brick with a pedimented entry, by *Norman Jones*, 1935. MAESGWYN is Edwardian, roughcast with open-pediment gables. On the S, No. 38, FRONDEG, *c.* 1870, is contrastingly Victorian with exaggerated acute gables, in red brick patterned in buff and black. Further down, in its own grounds, TREFEDDYN, an Italianate villa of *c.* 1870, green stone with grey dressings; curved dormers flanked by timber scrolls. The N side ends opposite Station Road with BRYNMAWR, a colourful three-storey terrace of eight, 1892, yellow brick, banded and chequered in red. On STATION ROAD, BRYN AWEL reverses the colours. PIER ROAD runs W to the sea. On the l., the R.C. church (*see* p. 720) and TRADYDDAN, the largest of a sparse scatter of late C19 villas. Brick with half-timber at the skyline. At the sea end, Corbett's PROMENADE, 1889, and just one seafront terrace, MARINE PARADE, 1896–7, probably by *Tapp & Jones*, not enough to compete with the tarmac roadway and car parks. Twelve houses in pairs. Dark green stone with wide two-storey bays linked by timber first-floor balconies and topped by longer attic balconies. The detail is being removed steadily. S is the muddle where the 1961 *Madin* development was planned (*see* p. 718). NEPTUNE ROAD runs back to the railway past RHIANVA, a gaunt pair of 1870s villas, with mansard roofs and three-sided window heads. Over the line, the Wharf Station (*see* p. 721) and STATION ROAD runs l. past Ysgol Tywyn (*see* p. 721).

CWM MAETHLON. This beautiful valley, termed Happy Valley, runs behind the coastal hills E over a watershed to Pennal. It was until 1827 the turnpike road from Machynlleth, marked by an altered early C19 TOLL HOUSE on the junction with the Aberdyfi road. On the l., BODTALOG, painted stone with canted bay and gables. Its character is later C19 but a mullion window in the r. gable and a lateral stack in the rear show C17 origins. On the main road, the three-storey BODTALOG MILL, 1860s, with arched windows. It was a flour mill, converted in the 1880s for enamelling slate. I m. E, the MELIN LLYNPAIR MINE site, the first of several in the valley. When Fenton passed in 1808 they were primarily copper mines but by the mid C19 were producing lead only. ½ m. SE is the drive to GWYDDGWION, a mid-C17 remodelling of an early C16 house. The elements are much encased and disguised but there is a roof with ornate close-spaced arch-braced collar-trusses, cusped above and with two tiers of cusped wind-braces. Although without smoke blackening, it is hard to see this as other than an open hall. At the E was a jettied upper chamber with similar three-bay roof, and the narrow W bay was the entrance passage. Inserted chimney and ceiling of massive beams. Mid-C17 rear wing with moulded beams and a reused cusped truss.

Beyond is the simple stuccoed Gothic CALVINISTIC
METHODIST CHAPEL, 1884, by *David Owen* of Machynlleth.
Opposite, BRYN-Y-BEDDAU, a grass-grown barrow. An
earthen monument in this stony landscape is unusual, as is a
mound surviving so well on the valley floor. Further E, S of the
road, DYFFRYN GWYN, 1640, low, of four bays with
Merioneth hipped dormers and end chimneys. The E end has
a tall square chimney and a stone verge at a steeper angle than
the roof, which may suggest thatch. The corner is dated 'Rice
Hughes hoc fecit anno domini 1772', but it is the W end that
looks later. Two ovolo-moulded stone windows, at front and
back, with dripmoulds. The front one, marked HP 1640, is l.
of a voussoired arched doorway. The outer windows were
similar, replaced with small sashes. Reused mouldings in one
E gable window and in the jambs of the three C18 dormers.
There was a mural stair in the E gable, but in the C18 a central
stair was inserted in the wide central bay. Post-and-panel
partitions each side, the posts reeded, as are the joists in the E
kitchen, which has a beam with ogee stops. Above, a similar
partition with a double-ogee doorhead, and corbelled E fireplace beam.

N of the road, CRUD-YR-AWEL, 1974, an A-frame triangular
timber house with 60-degree roof carried to the ground.
Behind, BRYN DINAS, plain roughcast with C19 dormers, but
substantially a C16 cruck-framed hall-house. There were outer
rooms and a two-bay hall with arched braces and a boss to the
centre truss. Inserted mid-C17 floor with bar stops to the spine
beam, and a massive chimney. Three parallel (and derelict)
farm buildings, the barn dated 1740, with a voussoired arch,
and 1762 on a cart-house addition. Just E, near the path to Llyn
Barfog, the 'bearded lake', are the spoil heaps of the BRYN
DINAS and TYDDYN Y BRIDELL MINES.

EGLWYS GWYDDELOD STONE CIRCLE (SH 663 002). A small
Bronze Age circle standing dramatically on a rocky ledge on a
trackway from Pennal to Bryncrug, overlooking the narrow
pass E of Cwm Maethlon. Five stones, the tallest only 29 in.
(75 cm.), in a circle 26 ft (8 metres) across. A block of quartz
in the centre may be original, but the large block on the N has
fallen from the crags above. On the floor of Cwn Maethlon
(SH 628 985) is an earthern barrow, unusual in this stony
environment.

ARCHITECTURAL GLOSSARY

Numbers and letters refer to the illustrations (by John Sambrook) on pp. 733–40.

ABACUS: flat slab forming the top of a capital (3a).

ACANTHUS: classical formalized leaf ornament (3b).

ACCUMULATOR TOWER: see Hydraulic power.

ACHIEVEMENT: a complete display of armorial bearings.

ACROTERION: plinth for a statue or ornament on the apex or ends of a pediment; more usually, both the plinth and what stands on it (4a).

AEDICULE (*lit.* little building): architectural surround, consisting usually of two columns or pilasters supporting a pediment.

AGGREGATE: see Concrete.

AISLE: subsidiary space alongside the body of a building, separated from it by columns, piers, or posts.

AMBULATORY (*lit.* walkway): aisle around the sanctuary (q.v.).

ANGLE ROLL: roll moulding in the angle between two planes (1a).

ANSE DE PANIER: see Arch.

ANTAE: simplified pilasters (4a), usually applied to the ends of the enclosing walls of a portico *in antis* (q.v.).

ANTEFIXAE: ornaments projecting at regular intervals above a Greek cornice, originally to conceal the ends of roof tiles (4a).

ANTHEMION: classical ornament like a honeysuckle flower (4b).

APRON: raised panel below a window or wall monument or tablet.

APSE: semicircular or polygonal end of an apartment, especially of a chancel or chapel. In classical architecture sometimes called an *exedra*.

ARABESQUE: non-figurative surface decoration consisting of flowing lines, foliage scrolls etc., based on geometrical patterns. Cf. Grotesque.

ARCADE: series of arches supported by piers or columns. *Blind arcade* or *arcading*: the same applied to the wall surface. *Wall arcade*: in medieval churches, a blind arcade forming a dado below windows. Also a covered shopping street.

ARCH: Shapes *see* 5c. *Basket arch* or *anse de panier* (basket handle): three-centred and depressed, or with a flat centre. *Nodding*: ogee arch curving forward from the wall face. *Parabolic*: shaped like a chain suspended from two level points, but inverted. Special purposes. *Chancel*: dividing chancel from nave or crossing. *Crossing*: spanning piers at a crossing (q.v.). *Relieving* or *discharging*: incorporated in a wall to relieve superimposed weight (5c). *Skew*: spanning responds not diametrically opposed. *Strainer*: inserted in an opening to resist inward pressure. *Transverse*: spanning a main axis (e.g. of a vaulted space). *See also* Jack arch, Triumphal arch.

ARCHITRAVE: formalized lintel, the lowest member of the classical entablature (3a). Also the moulded frame of a door or window (often borrowing the profile of a classical architrave). For *lugged* and *shouldered* architraves *see* 4b.

ARCUATED: dependent structurally on the arch principle. Cf. Trabeated.

ARK: chest or cupboard housing the

tables of Jewish law in a synagogue.

ARRIS: sharp edge where two surfaces meet at an angle (3a).

ASHLAR: masonry of large blocks wrought to even faces and square edges (6d).

ASTRAGAL: classical moulding of semicircular section (3f).

ASTYLAR: with no columns or similar vertical features.

ATLANTES: see Caryatids.

ATRIUM (plural: atria): inner court of a Roman or C20 house; in a multi-storey building, a toplit covered court rising through all storeys. Also an open court in front of a church.

ATTACHED COLUMN: see Engaged column.

ATTIC: small top storey within a roof. Also the storey above the main entablature of a classical façade.

AUMBRY: recess or cupboard to hold sacred vessels for the Mass.

BAILEY: see Motte-and-bailey.

BALANCE BEAM: see Canals.

BALDACCHINO: free-standing canopy, originally fabric, over an altar. Cf. Ciborium.

BALLFLOWER: globular flower of three petals enclosing a ball (1a). Typical of the Decorated style.

BALUSTER: pillar or pedestal of bellied form. Balusters: vertical supports of this or any other form, for a handrail or coping, the whole being called a balustrade (6c). Blind balustrade: the same applied to the wall surface.

BARBICAN: outwork defending the entrance to a castle.

BARGEBOARDS (corruption of 'vergeboards'): boards, often carved or fretted, fixed beneath the eaves of a gable to cover and protect the rafters.

BAROQUE: style originating in Rome c. 1600 and current in England c. 1680–1720, characterized by dramatic massing and silhouette and the use of the giant order.

BARROW: burial mound.

BARTIZAN: corbelled turret, square or round, frequently at an angle.

BASCULE: hinged part of a lifting (or bascule) bridge.

BASE: moulded foot of a column or pilaster . For Attic base see 3b.

BASEMENT: lowest, subordinate storey; hence the lowest part of a classical elevation, below the piano nobile (q.v.).

BASILICA: a Roman public hall; hence an aisled building with a clerestory.

BASTION: one of a series of defensive semicircular or polygonal projections from the main wall of a fortress or city.

BATTER: intentional inward inclination of a wall face.

BATTLEMENT: defensive parapet, composed of merlons (solid) and crenels (embrasures) through which archers could shoot; sometimes called crenellation. Also used decoratively.

BAY LEAF: classical ornament of overlapping bay leaves (3f).

BAY: division of an elevation or interior space as defined by regular vertical features such as arches, columns, windows, etc.

BAY WINDOW: window of one or more storeys projecting from the face of a building. Canted: with a straight front and angled sides. Bow window: curved. Oriel: rests on corbels or brackets and starts above ground level; also the bay window at the dais end of a medieval great hall.

BEAD-AND-REEL: see Enrichments.

BEAKHEAD: Norman ornament with a row of beaked bird or beast heads usually biting into a roll moulding (1a).

BELFRY: chamber or stage in a tower where bells are hung.

BELL CAPITAL: see 1b.

BELLCOTE: small gabled or roofed housing for the bell(s).

BERM: level area separating a ditch from a bank on a hill-fort or barrow.

BILLET: Norman ornament of small half-cyclindrical or rectangular blocks (1a).

BLIND: see Arcade, Baluster, Portico.

BLOCK CAPITAL: see 1a.

BLOCKED: columns, etc. interrupted by regular projecting blocks (*blocking*), as on a Gibbs surround (4b).

BLOCKING COURSE: course of stones, or equivalent, on top of a cornice and crowning the wall.

BOLECTION MOULDING: covering the joint between two different planes (6b).

BOND: the pattern of long sides (*stretchers*) and short ends (*headers*) produced on the face of a wall by laying bricks in a particular way (6e).

BOSS: knob or projection, e.g. at the intersection of ribs in a vault (2c).

BOW WINDOW: *see* Bay window.

BOX FRAME: timber-framed construction in which vertical and horizontal wall members support the roof (7). Also concrete construction where the loads are taken on cross walls; also called *cross-wall construction*.

BRACE: subsidiary member of a structural frame, curved or straight. *Bracing* is often arranged decoratively e.g. quatrefoil, herringbone (7). *See also* Roofs.

BRATTISHING: ornamental crest, usually formed of leaves, Tudor flowers or miniature battlements.

BRESSUMER (*lit.* breast-beam): big horizontal beam supporting the wall above, especially in a jettied building (7).

BRICK: *see* Bond, Cogging, Engineering, Gauged, Tumbling.

BRIDGE: *Bowstring*: with arches rising above the roadway which is suspended from them. *Clapper*: one long stone forms the roadway. *Roving*: *see* Canal. *Suspension*: roadway suspended from cables or chains slung between towers or pylons. *Stay-suspension* or *stay-cantilever*: supported by diagonal stays from towers or pylons. *See also* Bascule.

BRISES-SOLEIL: projecting fins or canopies which deflect direct sunlight from windows.

BROACH: *see* Spire and IC.

BUCRANIUM: ox skull used decoratively in classical friezes.

BULLSEYE WINDOW: small oval window, set horizontally (cf. Oculus). Also called *oeil de boeuf*.

BUTTRESS: vertical member projecting from a wall to stabilize it or to resist the lateral thrust of an arch, roof, or vault (IC, 2c). A *flying buttress* transmits the thrust to a heavy abutment by means of an arch or half-arch (IC).

CABLE or ROPE MOULDING: originally Norman, like twisted strands of a rope.

CAMES: *see* Quarries.

CAMPANILE: free-standing bell tower.

CANALS: *Flash lock*: removable weir or similar device through which boats pass on a flush of water. Predecessor of the *pound lock*: chamber with gates at each end allowing boats to float from one level to another. *Tidal gates*: single pair of lock gates allowing vessels to pass when the tide makes a level. *Balance beam*: beam projecting horizontally for opening and closing lock gates. *Roving bridge*: carrying a towing path from one bank to the other.

CANTILEVER: horizontal projection (e.g. step, canopy) supported by a downward force behind the fulcrum.

CAPITAL: head or crowning feature of a column or pilaster; for classical types *see* 3a; for medieval types *see* Ib.

CARREL: compartment designed for individual work or study.

CARTOUCHE: classical tablet with ornate frame (4b).

CARYATIDS: female figures supporting an entablature; their male counterparts are *Atlantes* (*lit*: Atlas figures).

CASEMATE: vaulted chamber, with embrasures for defence, within a castle wall or projecting from it.

CASEMENT: side-hinged window.

CASTELLATED: with battlements (q.v.).

CAST IRON: hard and brittle, cast in a mould to the required shape. *Wrought iron* is ductile, strong in tension, forged into decorative patterns or forged and rolled into e.g. bars, joists, boiler plates; *mild steel* is its modern equivalent, similar but stronger.

CATSLIDE: *See* 8a.

CAVETTO: concave classical moulding of quarter-round section (3f).

CELURE or CEILURE: enriched area of roof above rood or altar.

CEMENT: *see* Concrete.

CENOTAPH (*lit.* empty tomb): funerary monument which is not a burying place.

CENTRING: wooden support for the building of an arch or vault, removed after completion.

CHAMFER (*lit.* corner-break): surface formed by cutting off a square edge or corner. For types of chamfers and *chamfer stops see* 6a. *See also* Double chamfer.

CHANCEL: part of the E end of a church set apart for the use of the officiating clergy.

CHANTRY CHAPEL: often attached to or within a church, endowed for the celebration of Masses principally for the soul of the founder.

CHEVET (*lit.* head): French term for chancel with ambulatory and radiating chapels.

CHEVRON: V-shape used in series or double series (later) on a Norman moulding (1a). Also (especially when on a single plane) called *zigzag*.

CHOIR: the part of a cathedral, monastic or collegiate church where services are sung.

CIBORIUM: a fixed canopy over an altar, usually vaulted and supported on four columns; cf. Baldacchino. Also a canopied shrine for the reserved sacrament.

CINQUEFOIL: *see* Foil.

CIST: stone-lined or slab-built grave.

CLADDING: external covering or skin applied to a structure, especially a framed one.

CLERESTORY: uppermost storey of the nave of a church, pierced by windows. Also high-level windows in secular buildings.

CLOSER: a brick cut to complete a bond (6e).

CLUSTER BLOCK: *see* Multi-storey.

COADE STONE: ceramic artificial stone made in Lambeth 1769–

*c.*1840 by Eleanor Coade (†1821) and her associates.

COB: walling material of clay mixed with straw. Also called *pisé*.

COFFERING: arrangement of sunken panels (coffers), square or polygonal, decorating a ceiling, vault, or arch.

COGGING: a decorative course of bricks laid diagonally (6e). Cf. Dentilation.

COLLAR: *see* Roofs and 7.

COLLEGIATE CHURCH: endowed for the support of a college of priests.

COLONNADE: range of columns supporting an entablature. Cf. Arcade.

COLONNETTE: small medieval column or shaft.

COLOSSAL ORDER: *see* Giant order.

COLUMBARIUM: shelved, niched structure to house multiple burials.

COLUMN: a classical, upright structural member of round section with a shaft, a capital, and usually a base (3a, 4a).

COLUMN FIGURE: carved figure attached to a medieval column or shaft, usually flanking a doorway.

COMMUNION TABLE: unconsecrated table used in Protestant churches for the celebration of Holy Communion.

COMPOSITE: *see* Orders.

COMPOUND PIER: grouped shafts (q.v.), or a solid core surrounded by shafts.

CONCRETE: composition of *cement* (calcined lime and clay), *aggregate* (small stones or rock chippings), sand and water. It can be poured into *formwork* or *shuttering* (temporary frame of timber or metal) on site (*in-situ* concrete), or *pre-cast* as components before construction. *Reinforced*: incorporating steel rods to take the tensile force. *Pre-stressed*: with tensioned steel rods. Finishes include the impression of boards left by formwork (*board-marked* or *shuttered*), and texturing with steel brushes (*brushed*) or hammers (*hammer-dressed*). *See also* Shell.

CONSOLE: bracket of curved outline (4b).

COPING: protective course of masonry or brickwork capping a wall (6d).

CORBEL: projecting block supporting something above. *Corbel course*: continuous course of projecting stones or bricks fulfilling the same function. *Corbel table*: series of corbels to carry a parapet or a wall-plate or wall-post (7). *Corbelling*: brick or masonry courses built out beyond one another to support a chimney-stack, window, etc.

CORINTHIAN: *see* Orders and 3d.

CORNICE: flat-topped ledge with moulded underside, projecting along the top of a building or feature, especially as the highest member of the classical entablature (3a). Also the decorative moulding in the angle between wall and ceiling.

CORPS-DE-LOGIS: the main building(s) as distinct from the wings or pavilions.

COTTAGE ORNÉ: an artfully rustic small house associated with the Picturesque movement.

COUNTERCHANGING: of joists on a ceiling divided by beams into compartments, when placed in opposite directions in alternate squares.

COUR D HONNEUR: formal entrance court before a house in the French manner, usually with flanking wings and a screen wall or gates.

COURSE: continuous layer of stones, etc. in a wall (6e).

COVE: a broad concave moulding, e.g. to mask the eaves of a roof. *Coved ceiling*: with a pronounced cove joining the walls to a flat central panel smaller than the whole area of the ceiling.

CRADLE ROOF: *see* Wagon roof.

CREDENCE: a shelf within or beside a piscina (q.v.), or a table for the sacramental elements and vessels.

CRENELLATION: parapet with crenels (*see* Battlement).

CRINKLE-CRANKLE WALL: garden wall undulating in a series of serpentine curves.

CROCKETS: leafy hooks. *Crocket-ing* decorates the edges of Gothic features, such as pinnacles, canopies, etc. *Crocket capital*: *see* 1b.

CROSSING: central space at the junction of the nave, chancel, and transepts. *Crossing tower*: above a crossing.

CROSS-WINDOW: with one mullion and one transom (qq.v.).

CROWN-POST: *see* Roofs and 7.

CROWSTEPS: squared stones set like steps, e.g. on a gable (8a).

CRUCKS (*lit.* crooked): pairs of inclined timbers (*blades*), usually curved, set at bay-lengths; they support the roof timbers and, in timber buildings, also support the walls (8b). *Base*: blades rise from ground level to a tie- or collar-beam which supports the roof timbers. *Full*: blades rise from ground level to the apex of the roof, serving as the main members of a roof truss. *Jointed*: blades formed from more than one timber; the lower member may act as a wall-post; it is usually elbowed at wall-plate level and jointed just above. *Middle*: blades rise from halfway up the walls to a tie- or collar-beam. *Raised*: blades rise from halfway up the walls to the apex. *Upper*: blades supported on a tie-beam and rising to the apex.

CRYPT: underground or half-underground area, usually below the E end of a church. *Ring crypt*: corridor crypt surrounding the apse of an early medieval church, often associated with chambers for relics. Cf. Undercroft.

CUPOLA (*lit.* dome): especially a small dome on a circular or polygonal base crowning a larger dome, roof, or turret.

CURSUS: a long avenue defined by two parallel earthen banks with ditches outside.

CURTAIN WALL: a connecting wall between the towers of a castle. Also a non-load-bearing external wall applied to a C 20 framed structure.

CUSP: *see* Tracery and 2b.

CYCLOPEAN MASONRY: large irregular polygonal stones, smooth and finely jointed.

CYMA RECTA and CYMA REVERSA: classical mouldings with double curves (3f). Cf. Ogee.

DADO: the finishing (often with panelling) of the lower part of a wall in a classical interior; in origin a formalized continuous pedestal. *Dado rail*: the moulding along the top of the dado.

DAGGER: *see* Tracery and 2b.

DEC (DECORATED): English Gothic architecture *c.* 1290 to *c.* 1350. The name is derived from the type of window Tracery (q.v.) used during the period.

DEMI- or HALF-COLUMNS: engaged columns (q.v.) half of whose circumference projects from the wall.

DENTIL: small square block used in series in classical cornices (3c). *Dentilation* is produced by the projection of alternating headers along cornices or string courses.

DIAPER: repetitive surface decoration of lozenges or squares flat or in relief. Achieved in brickwork with bricks of two colours.

DIOCLETIAN or THERMAL WINDOW: semicircular with two mullions, as used in the Baths of Diocletian, Rome (4b).

DISTYLE: having two columns (4a).

DOGTOOTH: E.E. ornament, consisting of a series of small pyramids formed by four stylized canine teeth meeting at a point (1a).

DORIC: *see* Orders and 3a, 3b.

DORMER: window projecting from the slope of a roof (8a).

DOUBLE CHAMFER: a chamfer applied to each of two recessed arches (1a).

DOUBLE PILE: *see* Pile.

DRAGON BEAM: *see* Jetty.

DRESSINGS: the stone or brickwork worked to a finished face about an angle, opening, or other feature.

DRIPSTONE: moulded stone projecting from a wall to protect the lower parts from water. Cf. Hoodmould, Weathering.

DRUM: circular or polygonal stage supporting a dome or cupola. Also one of the stones forming the shaft of a column (3a).

DUTCH or FLEMISH GABLE: *see* 8a.

EASTER SEPULCHRE: tomb-chest used for Easter ceremonial, within or against the N wall of a chancel.

EAVES: overhanging edge of a roof; hence *eaves cornice* in this position.

ECHINUS: ovolo moulding (q.v.) below the abacus of a Greek Doric capital (3a).

EDGE RAIL: *see* Railways.

E. E. (EARLY ENGLISH): English Gothic architecture *c.* 1190–1250.

EGG-AND-DART: *see* Enrichments and 3f.

ELEVATION: any face of a building or side of a room. In a drawing, the same or any part of it, represented in two dimensions.

EMBATTLED: with battlements.

EMBRASURE: small splayed opening in a wall or battlement (q.v.).

ENCAUSTIC TILES: earthenware tiles fired with a pattern and glaze.

EN DELIT: stone cut against the bed.

ENFILADE: reception rooms in a formal series, usually with all doorways on axis.

ENGAGED or ATTACHED COLUMN: one that partly merges into a wall or pier.

ENGINEERING BRICKS: dense bricks, originally used mostly for railway viaducts etc.

ENRICHMENTS: the carved decoration of certain classical mouldings, e.g. the ovolo (qq.v.) with *egg-and-dart*, the cyma reversa with *waterleaf*, the astragal with *bead-and-reel* (3f).

ENTABLATURE: in classical architecture, collective name for the three horizontal members (architrave, frieze, and cornice) carried by a wall or a column (3a).

ENTASIS: very slight convex deviation from a straight line, used to prevent an optical illusion of concavity.

EPITAPH: inscription on a tomb.

EXEDRA: *see* Apse.

EXTRADOS: outer curved face of an arch or vault.

EYECATCHER: decorative building terminating a vista.

FASCIA: plain horizontal band, e.g. in an architrave (3c, 3d) or on a shopfront.

FENESTRATION: the arrangement of windows in a façade.

FERETORY: site of the chief shrine of a church, behind the high altar.

FESTOON: ornamental garland, suspended from both ends. Cf. Swag.

FIBREGLASS, or glass-reinforced polyester (GRP): synthetic resin reinforced with glass fibre. GRC: glass-reinforced concrete.

FIELD: see Panelling and 6b.

FILLET: a narrow flat band running down a medieval shaft or along a roll moulding (1a). It separates larger curved mouldings in classical cornices, fluting or bases (3c).

FLAMBOYANT: the latest phase of French Gothic architecture, with flowing tracery.

FLASH LOCK: see Canals.

FLÈCHE or SPIRELET (*lit.* arrow): slender spire on the centre of a roof.

FLEURON: medieval carved flower or leaf, often rectilinear (1a).

FLUSHWORK: knapped flint used with dressed stone to form patterns.

FLUTING: series of concave grooves (flutes), their common edges sharp (arris) or blunt (fillet) (3).

FOIL (*lit.* leaf): lobe formed by the cusping of a circular or other shape in tracery (2b). *Trefoil* (three), *quatrefoil* (four), *cinquefoil* (five), and multifoil express the number of lobes in a shape.

FOLIATE: decorated with leaves.

FORMWORK: see Concrete.

FRAMED BUILDING: where the structure is carried by a framework – e.g. of steel, reinforced concrete, timber – instead of by load-bearing walls.

FREESTONE: stone that is cut, or can be cut, in all directions.

FRESCO: *al fresco*: painting on wet plaster. *Fresco secco*: painting on dry plaster.

FRIEZE: the middle member of the classical entablature, sometimes ornamented (3a). *Pulvinated frieze* (*lit.* cushioned): of bold convex profile (3c). Also a horizontal band of ornament.

FRONTISPIECE: in C16 and C17 buildings the central feature of doorway and windows above linked in one composition.

GABLE: For types see 8a. *Gablet*: small gable. *Pedimental gable*: treated like a pediment.

GADROONING: classical ribbed ornament like inverted fluting that flows into a lobed edge.

GALILEE: chapel or vestibule usually at the w end of a church enclosing the main portal(s).

GALLERY: a long room or passage; an upper storey above the aisle of a church, looking through arches to the nave; a balcony or mezzanine overlooking the main interior space of a building; or an external walkway.

GALLETING: small stones set in a mortar course.

GAMBREL ROOF: see 8a.

GARDEROBE: medieval privy.

GARGOYLE: projecting water spout often carved into human or animal shape.

GAUGED or RUBBED BRICKWORK: soft brick sawn roughly, then rubbed to a precise (gauged) surface. Mostly used for door or window openings (5c).

GAZEBO (jocular Latin, 'I shall gaze'): ornamental lookout tower or raised summer house.

GEOMETRIC: English Gothic architecture *c.* 1250–1310. *See also* Tracery. For another meaning, *see* Stairs.

GIANT or COLOSSAL ORDER: classical order (q.v.) whose height is that of two or more storeys of the building to which it is applied.

GIBBS SURROUND: C18 treatment of an opening (4b), seen particularly in the work of James Gibbs (1682–1754).

GIRDER: a large beam. *Box*: of hollow-box section. *Bowed*: with its top rising in a curve. *Plate*: of I-section, made from iron or steel plates. *Lattice*: with braced framework.

GLAZING BARS: wooden or sometimes metal bars separating and supporting window panes.

GORSEDD CIRCLE: modern stone circle; one is erected annually at different Welsh sites in connection with the national Eisteddfod.

GRAFFITI: *see* Sgraffito.

GRANGE: farm owned and run by a religious order.

GRC: *see* Fibreglass.

GRISAILLE: monochrome painting on walls or glass.

GROIN: sharp edge at the meeting of two cells of a cross-vault; *see* Vault and 2b.

GROTESQUE (*lit.* grotto-esque): wall decoration adopted from Roman examples in the Renaissance. Its foliage scrolls incorporate figurative elements. Cf. Arabesque.

GROTTO: artificial cavern.

GRP: *see* Fibreglass.

GUILLOCHE: classical ornament of interlaced bands (4b).

GUNLOOP: opening for a firearm.

GUTTAE: stylized drops (3b).

HALF-TIMBERING: archaic term for timber-framing (q.v.). Sometimes used for non-structural decorative timberwork.

HALL CHURCH: medieval church with nave and aisles of approximately equal height.

HAMMERBEAM: *see* Roofs and 7.

HEADER: *see* Bond and 6e.

HEADSTOP: stop (q.v.) carved with a head (5b).

HELM ROOF: *see* 1c.

HENGE: ritual earthwork.

HERM (*lit.* the god Hermes): male head or bust on a pedestal.

HERRINGBONE WORK: *see* 6e (for brick bond). Cf. Pitched masonry.

HEXASTYLE: *see* Portico.

HILL-FORT: Iron Age earthwork enclosed by a ditch and bank system.

HIPPED ROOF: *see* 8a.

HOODMOULD: projecting moulding above an arch or lintel to throw off water (2b, 5b). When horizontal often called a *label*. For label stop *see* Stop.

HUSK GARLAND: festoon of stylized nutshells (4b).

HYDRAULIC POWER: use of water under high pressure to work machinery. *Accumulator tower*: houses a hydraulic accumulator which accommodates fluctuations in the flow through hydraulic mains.

HYPOCAUST (*lit.* underburning): Roman underfloor heating system.

IMPOST: horizontal moulding at the springing of an arch (5c).

IMPOST BLOCK: block between abacus and capital (1b).

IN ANTIS: *see* Antae, Portico and 4a.

INDENT: shape chiselled out of a stone to receive a brass.

INDUSTRIALIZED or SYSTEM BUILDING: system of manufactured units assembled on site.

INGLENOOK (*lit.* fire-corner): recess for a hearth with provision for seating.

INTERCOLUMNATION: interval between columns.

INTERLACE: decoration in relief simulating woven or entwined stems or bands.

INTRADOS: *see* Soffit.

IONIC: *see* Orders and 3c.

JACK ARCH: shallow segmental vault springing from beams, used for fireproof floors, bridge decks, etc.

JAMB (*lit.* leg): one of the vertical sides of an opening.

JETTY: in a timber-framed building, the projection of an upper storey beyond the storey below, made by the beams and joists of the lower storey oversailing the wall; on their outer ends is placed the sill of the walling for the storey above (7). Buildings can be jettied on several sides, in which case a *dragon beam* is set diagonally at the corner to carry the joists to either side.

JOGGLE: the joining of two stones to prevent them slipping by a notch in one and a projection in the other.

KEEL MOULDING: moulding used from the late C12, in section like the keel of a ship (1a).

KEEP: principal tower of a castle.

KENTISH CUSP: *see* Tracery and 2b.

KEY PATTERN: *see* 4b.

KEYSTONE: central stone in an arch or vault (4b, 5c).

KINGPOST: *see* Roofs and 7.

KNEELER: horizontal projecting stone at the base of each side of a gable to support the inclined coping stones (8a).

KNOTWORK: *see* Interlace. Used on early Christian monuments.

LABEL: *see* Hoodmould and 5b.

LABEL STOP: *see* Stop and 5b.

LACED BRICKWORK: vertical strips of brickwork, often in a contrasting colour, linking openings on different floors.

LACING COURSE: horizontal reinforcement in timber or brick to walls of flint, cobble, etc.

LADY CHAPEL: dedicated to the Virgin Mary (Our Lady).

LANCET: slender single-light, pointed-arched window (2a).

LANTERN: circular or polygonal windowed turret crowning a roof or a dome. Also the windowed stage of a crossing tower lighting the church interior.

LANTERN CROSS: churchyard cross with lantern-shaped top.

LAVATORIUM: in a religous house, a washing place adjacent to the refectory.

LEAN-TO: *see* Roofs.

LESENE (*lit.* a mean thing): pilaster without base or capital. Also called *pilaster strip*.

LIERNE: *see* Vault and 2c.

LIGHT: compartment of a window defined by the mullions.

LINENFOLD: Tudor panelling carbved with simulations of folded linen. *See also* Parchemin.

LINTEL: horizontal beam or stone bridging an opening.

LOGGIA: gallery, usually arcaded or colonnaded; sometimes freestanding.

LONG-AND-SHORT WORK: quoins consisting of stones placed with the long side alternately upright and horizontal, especially in Saxon building.

LONGHOUSE: house and byre in the same range with internal access between them.

LOUVRE: roof opening, often protected by a raised timber structure, to allow the smoke from a central hearth to escape.

LOWSIDE WINDOW: set lower than the others in a chancel side wall, usually towards its w end.

LUCARNE (*lit.* dormer): small gabled opening in a roof or spire.

LUGGED ARCHITRAVE: *see* 4b.

LUNETTE: semicircular window or blind panel.

LYCHGATE (*lit.* corpse-gate): roofed gateway entrance to a churchyard for the reception of a coffin.

LYNCHET: long terraced strip of soil on the downward side of prehistoric and medieval fields, accumulated because of continual ploughing along the contours.

MACHICOLATIONS (*lit.* mashing devices): series of openings between the corbels that support a projecting parapet through which missiles can be dropped. Used decoratively in post-medieval buildings.

MANOMETER or STANDPIPE TOWER: containing a column of water to regulate pressure in water mains.

MANSARD: *see* 8a.

MATHEMATICAL TILES: facing tiles with the appearance of brick, most often applied to timber-framed walls.

MAUSOLEUM: monumental building or chamber usually intended for the burial of members of one family.

MEGALITHIC TOMB: massive stone-built Neolithic burial chamber covered by an earth or stone mound.

MERLON: *see* Battlement.

METOPES: spaces between the triglyphs in a Doric frieze (3b).

MEZZANINE: low storey between two higher ones.

MILD STEEL: *see* Cast iron.

MISERICORD (*lit.* mercy): shelf on a carved bracket placed on the underside of a hinged choir stall seat to support an occupant when standing.

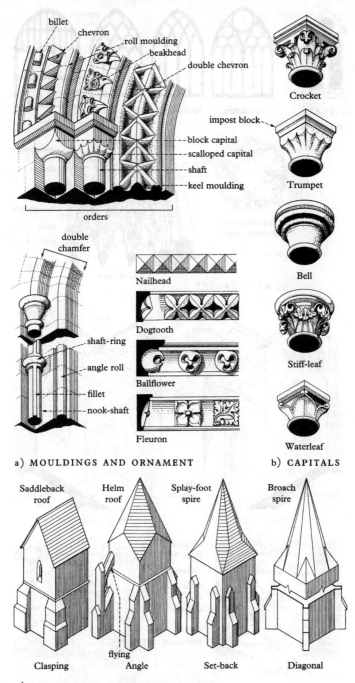

a) MOULDINGS AND ORNAMENT

b) CAPITALS

c) BUTTRESSES, ROOFS AND SPIRES

FIGURE 1: MEDIEVAL

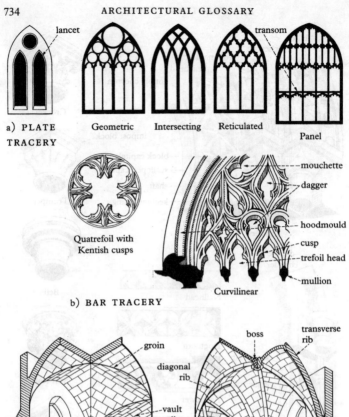

a) PLATE TRACERY

Geometric   Intersecting   Reticulated   Panel

Quatrefoil with Kentish cusps

Curvilinear

b) BAR TRACERY

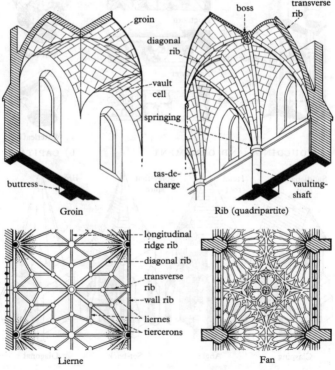

Groin

Rib (quadripartite)

Lierne   Fan

c) VAULTS

FIGURE 2: MEDIEVAL

ORDERS

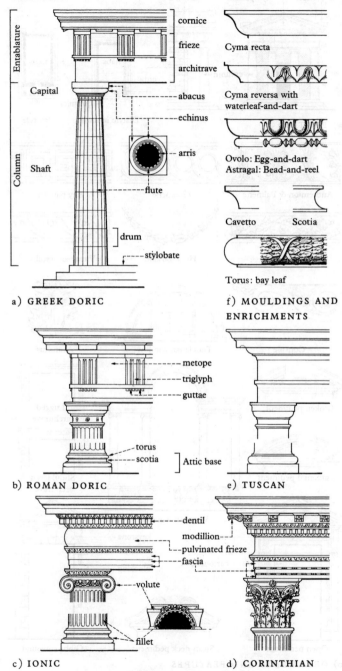

a) GREEK DORIC

cornice
frieze
architrave
abacus
echinus
arris
flute
drum
stylobate

f) MOULDINGS AND ENRICHMENTS

Cyma recta

Cyma reversa with waterleaf-and-dart

Ovolo: Egg-and-dart
Astragal: Bead-and-reel

Cavetto   Scotia

Torus: bay leaf

b) ROMAN DORIC

metope
triglyph
guttae
torus
scotia   Attic base

e) TUSCAN

c) IONIC

dentil
modillion
pulvinated frieze
fascia
volute
fillet

d) CORINTHIAN

FIGURE 3: CLASSICAL

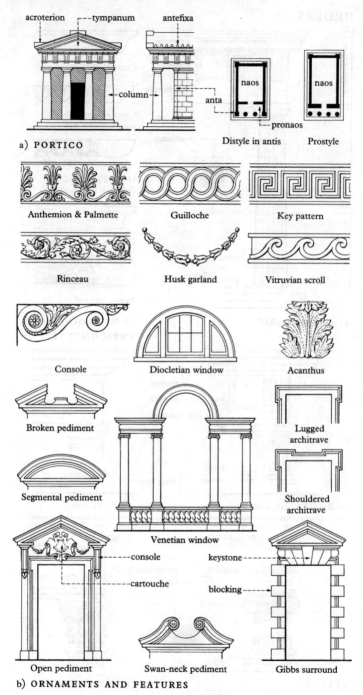

a) PORTICO

Anthemion & Palmette

Guilloche

Key pattern

Rinceau

Husk garland

Vitruvian scroll

Console

Diocletian window

Acanthus

Broken pediment

Segmental pediment

Venetian window

Lugged architrave

Shouldered architrave

Open pediment

Swan-neck pediment

Gibbs surround

b) ORNAMENTS AND FEATURES

FIGURE 4: CLASSICAL

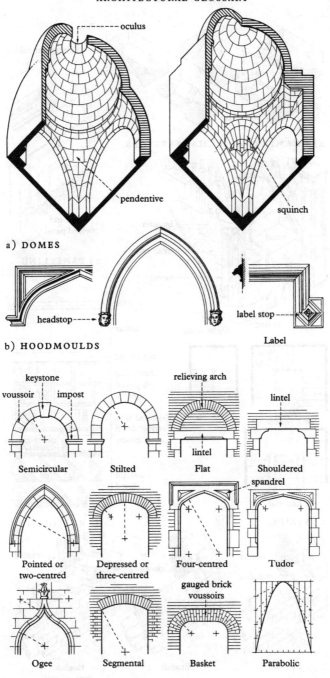

a) DOMES

b) HOODMOULDS

c) ARCHES

FIGURE 5: CONSTRUCTION

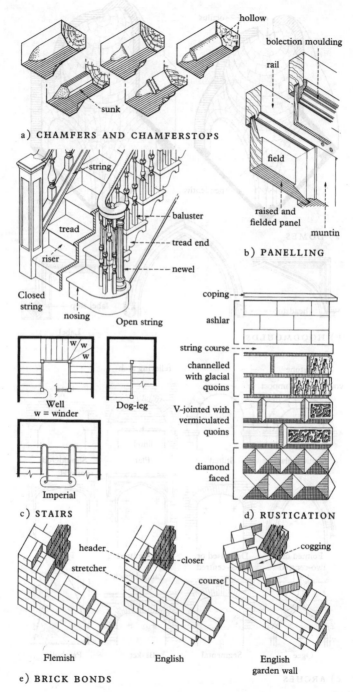

a) CHAMFERS AND CHAMFERSTOPS

b) PANELLING

c) STAIRS

d) RUSTICATION

e) BRICK BONDS

FIGURE 6: CONSTRUCTION

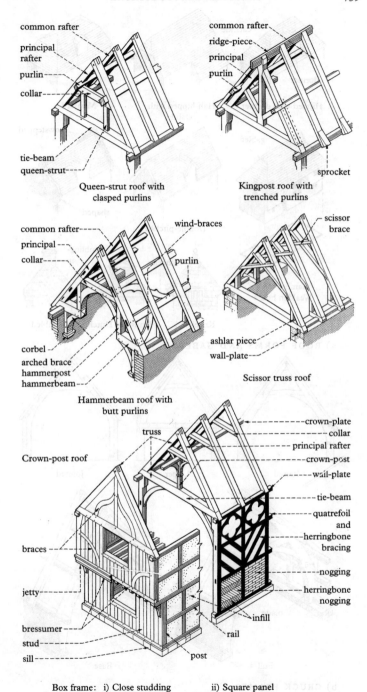

Queen-strut roof with clasped purlins

common rafter
principal rafter
purlin
collar
tie-beam
queen-strut

Kingpost roof with trenched purlins

common rafter
ridge-piece
principal
purlin
sprocket

common rafter
principal
collar
wind-braces
purlin
corbel
arched brace
hammerpost
hammerbeam

Hammerbeam roof with butt purlins

scissor brace
ashlar piece
wall-plate

Scissor truss roof

Crown-post roof

truss

crown-plate
collar
principal rafter
crown-post
wall-plate
tie-beam
quatrefoil and herringbone bracing
nogging
herringbone nogging
infill
rail

braces
jetty
bressumer
stud
sill
post

Box frame: i) Close studding   ii) Square panel

FIGURE 7: ROOFS AND TIMBER-FRAMING

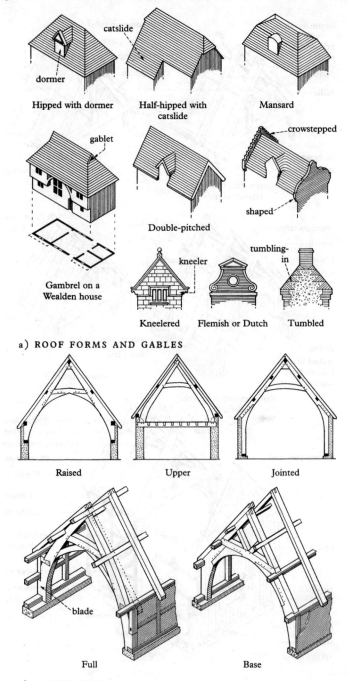

Hipped with dormer   Half-hipped with catslide   Mansard

gablet

Gambrel on a
Wealden house

Double-pitched

crowstepped

shaped

kneeler   tumbling-in

Kneelered   Flemish or Dutch   Tumbled

a) ROOF FORMS AND GABLES

Raised   Upper   Jointed

blade

Full   Base

b) CRUCK FRAMES

FIGURE 8: ROOFS AND TIMBER-FRAMING

MIXER-COURTS: forecourts to groups of houses shared by vehicles and pedestrians.

MODILLIONS: small consoles (q.v.) along the underside of a Corinthian or Composite cornice (3d). Often used along an eaves cornice.

MODULE: a predetermined standard size for co-ordinating the dimensions of components of a building.

MOTTE-AND-BAILEY: post-Roman and Norman defence consisting of an earthen mound (motte) topped by a wooden tower within a bailey, an enclosure defended by a ditch and palisade, and also, sometimes, by an internal bank.

MOUCHETTE: see Tracery and 2b.

MOULDING: shaped ornamental strip of continuous section; see Cavetto, Cyma, Ovolo, Roll.

MULLION: vertical member between window lights (2b).

MULTI-STOREY: five or more storeys. Multi-storey flats may form a *cluster block*, with individual blocks of flats grouped round a service core; a *point block*: with flats fanning out from a service core; or a *slab block*, with flats approached by corridors or galleries from service cores at intervals or towers at the ends (plan also used for offices, hotels etc.). *Tower block* is a generic term for any very high multi-storey building.

MUNTIN: see Panelling and 6b.

NAILHEAD: E.E. ornament consisting of small pyramids regularly repeated (1a).

NARTHEX: enclosed vestibule or covered porch at the main entrance to a church.

NAVE: the body of a church w of the crossing or chancel often flanked by aisles (q.v.).

NEWEL: central or corner post of a staircase (6c). Newel stair see Stairs.

NIGHT STAIR: stair by which religious entered the transept of their church from their dormitory to celebrate night services.

NOGGING: see Timber-framing (7).

NOOK-SHAFT: shaft set in the angle of a wall or opening (1a).

NORMAN: see Romanesque.

NOSING: projection of the tread of a step (6c).

NUTMEG: medieval ornament with a chain of tiny triangles placed obliquely.

OCULUS: circular opening.

OEIL DE BOEUF: see Bullseye window.

OGEE: double curve, bending first one way and then the other, as in an *ogee* or *ogival arch* (5c). Cf. Cyma recta and Cyma reversa.

OPUS SECTILE: decorative mosaic-like facing.

OPUS SIGNINUM: composition flooring of Roman origin.

ORATORY: a private chapel in a church or a house. Also a church of the Oratorian Order.

ORDER: one of a series of recessed arches and jambs forming a splayed medieval opening, e.g. a doorway or arcade arch (1a).

ORDERS: the formalized versions of the post-and-lintel system in classical architecture. The main orders are *Doric, Ionic*, and *Corinthian*. They are Greek in origin but occur in Roman versions. *Tuscan* is a simple version of Roman Doric. Though each order has its own conventions (3), there are many minor variations. The *Composite* capital combines Ionic volutes with Corinthian foliage. *Superimposed orders*: orders on successive levels, usually in the upward sequence of Tuscan, Doric, Ionic, Corinthian, Composite.

ORIEL: see Bay window.

OVERDOOR: painting or relief above an internal door. Also called a *sopraporta*.

OVERTHROW: decorative fixed arch between two gatepiers or above a wrought-iron gate.

OVOLO: wide convex moulding (3f).

PALIMPSEST: of a brass: where a metal plate has been reused by turning over the engraving on the back; of a wall-painting: where one overlaps and partly obscures an earlier one.

PALLADIAN: following the examples and principles of Andrea Palladio (1508–80).

PALMETTE: classical ornament like a palm shoot (4b).

PANELLING: wooden lining to interior walls, made up of vertical members (*muntins*) and horizontals (*rails*) framing panels: also called *wainscot*. *Raised-and-fielded*: with the central area of the panel (*field*) raised up (6b).

PANTILE: roof tile of S section.

PARAPET: wall for protection at any sudden drop, e.g. at the wall-head of a castle where it protects the *parapet walk* or wall-walk. Also used to conceal a roof.

PARCHEMIN PANEL:with a vertical central rib or moulding branching in ogee curves to meet the four corners of the panel; sometimes used with linenfold (q.v.).

PARCLOSE: *see* Screen.

PARGETTING (*lit.* plastering): exterior plaster decoration, either in relief or incised.

PARLOUR: in a religious house, a room where the religious could talk to visitors; in a medieval house, the semi-private living room below the solar (q.v.).

PARTERRE: level space in a garden laid out with low, formal beds.

PATERA (*lit.* plate): round or oval ornament in shallow relief.

PAVILION: ornamental building for occasional use; or projecting subdivision of a larger building, often at an angle or terminating a wing.

PEBBLEDASHING: *see* Rendering.

PEDESTAL: a tall block carrying a classical order, statue, vase, etc.

PEDIMENT: a formalized gable derived from that of a classical temple; also used over doors, windows, etc. For variations *see* 4b.

PENDENTIVE: spandrel between adjacent arches, supporting a drum, dome or vault and consequently formed as part of a hemisphere (5a).

PENTHOUSE: subsidiary structure with a lean-to roof. Also a separately roofed structure on top of a C20 multi-storey block.

PERIPTERAL: *see* Peristyle.

PERISTYLE: a colonnade all round the exterior of a classical building, as in a temple which is then said to be *peripteral*.

PERP (PERPENDICULAR): English Gothic architecture c. 1335–50 to c. 1530. The name is derived from the upright tracery panels then used (*see* Tracery and 2a).

PERRON: external stair to a doorway, usually of double-curved plan.

PEW: loosely, seating for the laity outside the chancel; strictly, an enclosed seat. *Box pew*: with equal high sides and a door.

PIANO NOBILE: principal floor of a classical building above a ground floor or basement and with a lesser storey overhead.

PIAZZA: formal urban open space surrounded by buildings.

PIER: large masonry or brick support, often for an arch. *See also* Compound pier.

PILASTER: flat representation of a classical column in shallow relief. *Pilaster strip*: *see* Lesene.

PILE: row of rooms. *Double pile*: two rows thick.

PILLAR: free-standing upright member of any section, not conforming to one of the orders (q.v.).

PILLAR PISCINA: *see* Piscina.

PILOTIS: C20 French term for pillars or stilts that support a building above an open ground floor.

PISCINA: basin for washing Mass vessels, provided with a drain; set in or against the wall to the S of an altar or free-standing (*pillar piscina*).

PISÉ: *see* Cob.

PITCHED MASONRY: laid on the diagonal, often alternately with opposing courses (*pitched and counterpitched* or herringbone).

PLATE RAIL: *see* Railways.

PLATEWAY: *see* Railways.

PLINTH: projecting courses at the

foot of a wall or column, generally chamfered or moulded at the top.

PODIUM: a continuous raised platform supporting a building; or a large block of two or three storeys beneath a multi-storey block of smaller area.

POINT BLOCK: *see* Multi-storey.

POINTING: exposed mortar jointing of masonry or brickwork. Types include *flush, recessed* and *tuck* (with a narrow channel filled with finer, whiter mortar).

POPPYHEAD: carved ornament of leaves and flowers as a finial for a bench end or stall.

PORTAL FRAME: C20 frame comprising two uprights rigidly connected to a beam or pair of rafters.

PORTCULLIS: gate constructed to rise and fall in vertical gooves at the entry to a castle.

PORTICO: a porch with the roof and frequently a pediment supported by a row of columns (4a). A portico *in antis* has columns on the same plane as the front of the building. A *prostyle* porch has columns standing free. Porticoes are described by the number of front columns, e.g. tetrastyle (four), hexastyle (six). The space within the temple is the *naos*, that within the portico the *pronaos*. *Blind portico*: the front features of a portico applied to a wall.

PORTICUS (plural: porticūs): subsidiary cell opening from the main body of a pre-Conquest church.

POST: upright support in a structure (7).

POSTERN: small gateway at the back of a building or to the side of a larger entrance door or gate.

POUND LOCK: *see* Canals.

PRESBYTERY: the part of a church lying E of the choir where the main altar is placed; or a priest's residence.

PRINCIPAL: *see* Roofs and 7.

PRONAOS: *see* Portico and 4a.

PROSTYLE: *see* Portico and 4a.

PULPIT: raised and enclosed platform for the preaching of sermons. *Three-decker*: with reading desk below and clerk's desk below that.]

Two-decker: as above, minus the clerk's desk.

PULPITUM: stone screen in a major church dividing choir from nave.

PULVINATED: *see* Frieze and 3c.

PURLIN: *see* Roofs and 7.

PUTHOLES or PUTLOG HOLES: in the wall to receive putlogs, the horizontal timbers which support scaffolding boards; sometimes not filled after construction is complete.

PUTTO (plural: putti): small naked boy.

QUARRIES: square (or diamond) panes of glass supported by lead strips (*cames*); square floor-slabs or tiles.

QUATREFOIL: *see* Foil and 2b.

QUEENSTRUT: *see* Roofs and 7.

QUIRK: sharp groove to one side of a convex medieval moulding.

QUOINS: dressed stones at the angles of a building (6d).

RADBURN SYSTEM: vehicle and pedestrian segregation in residential developments, based on that used at Radburn, New Jersey, U.S.A., by Wright and Stein, 1928–30.

RADIATING CHAPELS: projecting radially from an ambulatory or an apse (*see* Chevet).

RAFTER: *see* Roofs and 7.

RAGGLE: groove cut in masonry, especially to receive the edge of a roof-covering.

RAGULY: ragged (in heraldry). Also applied to funerary sculpture, e.g. *cross raguly*: with a notched outline.

RAIL: *see* Panelling and 6b; also 7.

RAILWAYS: *Edge rail:* on which flanged wheels can run. *Plate rail:* L-section rail for plain unflanged wheels. *Plateway:* early railway using plate rails.

RAISED-AND-FIELDED: *see* Panelling and 6b.

RAKE: slope or pitch.

RAMPART: defensive outer wall of stone or earth. *Rampart walk:* path along the inner face.

REBATE: rectangular section cut out of a masonry edge to receive a shutter, door, window, etc.

REBUS: a heraldic pun, e.g. a fiery cock for Cockburn.

REEDING: series of convex mouldings, the reverse of fluting (q.v.). Cf. Gadrooning.

RENDERING: the covering of outside walls with a uniform surface or skin for protection from the weather. *Lime-washing:* thin layer of lime plaster. *Pebble-dashing:* where aggregate is thrown at the wet plastered wall for a textured effect. *Roughcast:* plaster mixed with a coarse aggregate such as gravel. *Stucco:* fine lime plaster worked to a smooth surface. *Cement rendering:* a cheaper substitute for stucco, usually with a grainy texture.

REPOUSSÉ: relief designs in metalwork, formed by beating it from the back.

REREDORTER (*lit.* behind the dormitory): latrines in a medieval religious house.

REREDOS: painted and/or sculptured screen behind and above an altar. Cf. Retable.

RESPOND: half-pier or half-column bonded into a wall and carrying one end of an arch. It usually terminates an arcade.

RETABLE: painted or carved panel standing on or at the back of an altar, usually attached to it.

RETROCHOIR: in a major church, the area between the high altar and E chapel.

REVEAL: the plane of a jamb, between the wall and the frame of a door or window.

RIB-VAULT: *see* Vault and 2c.

RINCEAU: classical ornament of leafy scrolls (4b).

RISER: vertical face of a step (6c).

ROCK-FACED: masonry cleft to produce a rugged appearance.

ROCOCO: style current *c.* 1720 and *c.* 1760, characterized by a serpentine line and playful, scrolled decoration.

ROLL MOULDING: medieval moulding of part-circular section (1a).

ROMANESQUE: style current in the CII and CI2. In England often called Norman. *See also* Saxo-Norman.

ROOD: crucifix flanked by the Virgin and St John, usually over the entry into the chancel, on a beam (*rood beam*) or painted on the wall. The *rood screen* below often had a walkway (*rood loft*) along the top, reached by a *rood stair* in the side wall.

ROOFS: Shape. For the main external shapes (hipped, mansard etc.) *see* 8a. *Helm* and *Saddleback: see* 1c. *Lean-to:* single sloping roof built against a vertical wall; lean-to is also applied to the part of the building beneath.

Construction. *See* 7.

Single-framed roof: with no main trusses. The rafters may be fixed to the wall-plate or ridge, or longitudinal timber may be absent altogether.

Double-framed roof: with longitudinal members, such as purlins, and usually divided into bays by principals and principal rafters. Other types are named after their main structural components, e.g. *hammerbeam, crown-post (see* Elements below and 7).

Elements. *See* 7.

Ashlar piece: a short vertical timber connecting inner wall-plate or timber pad to a rafter.

Braces: subsidiary timbers set diagonally to strengthen the frame.]

Arched braces: curved pair forming an arch, connecting wall or post below tie- or collar-beam above. *Passing braces:* long straight braces passing across other members of the truss. *Scissor braces:* pair crossing diagonally between pairs of rafters or principals. *Wind-braces:* short, usually curved braces connecting side purlins with principals; sometimes decorated with cusping.

Collar or *collar-beam:* horizontal transverse timber connecting a pair of rafter or cruck blades (q.v.), set between apex and the wall-plate.

Crown-post: a vertical timber set centrally on a tie-beam and supporting a collar purlin braced to it longitudinally. In an open truss lateral braces may rise to the collar-beam; in a closed truss they may descend to the tie-beam.

Hammerbeams: horizontal brackets projecting at wall-plate level like an interrupted tie-beam; the inner ends carry *hammerposts*, vertical timbers which support a purlin and are braced to a collar-beam above.

Kingpost: vertical timber set centrally on a tie- or collar-beam, rising to the apex of the roof to support a ridge-piece (cf. Strut).

Plate: longitudinal timber set square to the ground. *Wall-plate:* plate along the top of a wall which receives the ends of the rafters; cf. Purlin.

Principals: pair of inclined lateral timbers of a truss. Usually they support side purlins and mark the main bay divisions.

Purlin: horizontal longitudinal timber. *Collar purlin* or *crown plate:* central timber which carries collar-beams and is supported by crown-posts. *Side purlins:* pairs of timbers placed some way up the slope of the roof, which carry common rafters. *Butt* or *tenoned purlins* are tenoned into either side of the principals. *Through purlins* pass through or past the principal; they include *clasped purlins*, which rest on queenposts or are carried in the angle between principals and collar, and *trenched purlins* trenched into the backs of principals.

Queen-strut: paired vertical, or near-vertical, timbers placed symmetrically on a tie-beam to support side purlins.

Rafters: inclined lateral timbers supporting the roof covering. *Common rafters:* regularly spaced uniform rafters placed along the length of a roof or between principals. *Principal rafters:* rafters which also act as principals.

Ridge, ridge-piece: horizontal longitudinal timber at the apex supporting the ends of the rafters.

Sprocket: short timber placed on the back and at the foot of a rafter to form projecting eaves.

Strut: vertical or oblique timber between two members of a truss, not directly supporting longitudinal timbers.

Tie-beam: main horizontal transverse timber which carries the feet of the principals at wall level.

Truss: rigid framework of timbers at bay intervals, carrying the longitudinal roof timbers which support the common rafters. *Closed truss:* with the spaces between the timbers filled, to form an internal partition.

See also Cruck, Wagon roof.

ROPE MOULDING: *see* Cable moulding.

ROSE WINDOW: circular window with tracery radiating from the centre. Cf. Wheel window.

ROTUNDA: building or room circular in plan.

ROUGHCAST: *see* Rendering.

ROVING BRIDGE: *see* Canals.

RUBBED BRICKWORK: *see* Gauged brickwork.

RUBBLE: masonry whose stones are wholly or partly in a rough state. *Coursed:* coursed stones with rough faces. *Random:* uncoursed stones in a random pattern. *Snecked:* with courses broken by smaller stones (snecks).

RUSTICATION: *see* 6d. Exaggerated treatment of masonry to give an effect of strength. The joints are usually recessed by V-section chamfering or square-section channelling (*channelled rustication*). *Banded rustication* has only the horizontal joints emphasized. The faces may be flat, but can be *diamond-faced*, like shallow pyramids, *vermiculated*, with a stylized texture like worm-casts, and *glacial* (frost-work), like icicles or stalactites.

SACRISTY: room in a church for sacred vessels and vestments.

SADDLEBACK ROOF: *see* 1C.

SALTIRE CROSS: with diagonal limbs.

SANCTUARY: area around the main altar of a church. Cf. Presbytery.

SANGHA: residence of Buddhist monks or nuns.

SARCOPHAGUS: coffin of stone or other durable material.

SAXO-NORMAN: transitional Romanesque style combining Anglo-Saxon and Norman features, current *c.* 1060–1100.

SCAGLIOLA: composition imitating marble.

SCALLOPED CAPITAL: *see* 1a.

SCOTIA: a hollow classical moulding, especially between tori (q.v.) on a column base (3b, 3f).

SCREEN: in a medieval church, usually at the entry to the chancel; *see* Rood (screen) and Pulpitum. A *parclose screen* separates a chapel from the rest of the church.

SCREENS or SCREENS PASSAGE: screened-off entrance passage between great hall and service rooms.

SECTION: two-dimensional representation of a building, moulding, etc., revealed by cutting across it.

SEDILIA (singular: sedile): seats for the priests (usually three) on the S side of the chancel.

SET-OFF: *see* Weathering.

SGRAFFITO: decoration scratched, often in plaster, to reveal a pattern in another colour beneath. *Graffiti*: scratched drawing or writing.

SHAFT: vertical member of round or polygonal section (1a, 3a). *Shaft-ring*: at the junction of shafts set *en delit* (q.v.) or attached to a pier or wall (1a).

SHEILA-NA-GIG: female fertility figure, usually with legs apart.

SHELL: thin, self-supporting roofing membrane of timber or concrete.

SHOULDERED ARCHITRAVE: *see* 4b.

SHUTTERING: *see* Concrete.

SILL: horizontal member at the bottom of a window or door frame; or at the base of a timber-framed wall into which posts and studs are tenoned (7).

SLAB BLOCK: *see* Multi-storey.

SLATE-HANGING: covering of overlapping slates on a wall. *Tile-hanging* is similar.

SLYPE: covered way or passage leading E from the cloisters between transept and chapter house.

SNECKED: *see* Rubble.

SOFFIT (*lit.* ceiling): underside of an arch (also called *intrados*), lintel, etc. *Soffit roll*: medieval roll moulding on a soffit.

SOLAR: private upper chamber in a medieval house, accessible from the high end of the great hall.

SOPRAPORTA: *see* Overdoor.

SOUNDING-BOARD: *see* Tester.

SPANDRELS: roughly triangular spaces between an arch and its containing rectangle, or between adjacent arches (5c). Also non-structural panels under the windows in a curtain-walled building.

SPERE: a fixed structure screening the lower end of the great hall from the screens passage. *Spere-truss*: roof truss incorporated in the spere.

SPIRE: tall pyramidal or conical feature crowning a tower or turret. *Broach*: starting from a square base, then carried into an octagonal section by means of triangular faces; and *splayed-foot*: variation of the broach form, found principally in the southeast, in which the four cardinal faces are splayed out near their base, to cover the corners, while oblique (or intermediate) faces taper away to a point (1c). *Needle spire*: thin spire rising from the centre of a tower roof, well inside the parapet: when of timber and lead often called a *spike*.

SPIRELET: *see* Flèche.

SPLAY: of an opening when it is wider on one face of a wall than the other.

SPRING OR SPRINGING: level at which an arch or vault rises from its supports. *Springers*: the first stones of an arch or vaulting rib above the spring (2c).

SQUINCH: arch or series of arches thrown across an interior angle of a square or rectangular structure to support a circular or polygonal superstructure, especially a dome or spire (5a).

SQUINT: an aperture in a wall or through a pier usually to allow a view of an altar.

STAIRS: *see* 6c. *Dog-leg stair*: parallel flights rising alternately in opposite directions, without an open well. *Flying stair:* cantilevered from the walls of a stairwell, without newels; sometimes called a *Geometric* stair when the inner edge describes a curve. *Newel stair:* ascending round a central supporting newel (q.v.); called a *spiral stair* or *vice* when in a circular shaft, a *winder* when in a rectangular compartment. (Winder also applies to the steps on the turn). *Well stair:* with flights round a square open well framed by newel posts. *See also* Perron.

STALL: fixed seat in the choir or chancel for the clergy or choir (cf. Pew). Usually with arm rests, and often framed together.

STANCHION: upright structural member, of iron, steel or reinforced concrete.

STANDPIPE TOWER: *see* Manometer.

STEAM ENGINES: *Atmospheric:* worked by the vacuum created when low-pressure steam is condensed in the cylinder, as developed by Thomas Newcomen. *Beam engine:* with a large pivoted beam moved in an oscillating fashion by the piston. It may drive a flywheel or be *non-rotative*. *Watt* and *Cornish:* single-cylinder; *compound:* two cylinders; *triple expansion:* three cylinders.

STEEPLE: tower together with a spire, lantern, or belfry.

STIFF-LEAF: type of E.E. foliage decoration. *Stiff-leaf capital see* 1b.

STOP: plain or decorated terminal to mouldings or chamfers, or at the end of hoodmoulds and labels (*label stop*), or string courses (5b, 6a); *see also* headstop.

STOUP: vessel for holy water, usually near a door.

STRAINER: *see* Arch.

STRAPWORK: late C16 and C17 decoration, like interlaced leather straps.

STRETCHER: *see* Bond and 6e.

STRING COURSE: horizontal course or moulding projecting from the surface of a wall (6d).

STRING: *see* 6c. Sloping member holding the ends of the treads and risers of a staircase. *Closed string:* a broad string covering the ends

of the treads and risers. *Open string:* cut into the shape of the treads and risers.

STUCCO: *see* Rendering.

STUDS: subsidiary vertical timbers of a timber-framed wall or partition (7).

STUPA: Buddhist shrine, circular in plan.

STYLOBATE: top of the solid platform on which a colonnade stands (3a).

SUSPENSION BRIDGE: *see* Bridge.

SWAG: like a festoon (q.v.), but representing cloth.

SYSTEM BUILDING: *see* Industrialized building.

TABERNACLE: canopied structure to contain the reserved sacrament or a relic; or architectural frame for an image or statue.

TABLE TOMB: memorial slab raised on free-standing legs.

TAS-DE-CHARGE: the lower courses of a vault or arch which are laid horizontally (2c).

TERM: pedestal or pilaster tapering downward, usually with the upper part of a human figure growing out of it.

TERRACOTTA: moulded and fired clay ornament or cladding.

TESSELLATED PAVEMENT: mosaic flooring, particularly Roman, made of *tesserae*, i.e. cubes of glass, stone, or brick.

TESTER: flat canopy over a tomb or pulpit, where it is also called a *sounding-board*.

TESTER TOMB: tomb-chest with effigies beneath a tester, either free-standing (tester with four or more columns), or attached to a wall (*half-tester*) with columns on one side only.

TETRASTYLE: *see* Portico.

THERMAL WINDOW: *see* Diocletian window.

THREE-DECKER PULPIT: *see* Pulpit.

TIDAL GATES: *see* Canals.

TIE-BEAM: *see* Roofs and 7.

TIERCERON: *see* Vault and 2c.

TILE-HANGING: *see* Slate-hanging.

TIMBER-FRAMING: *see* 7. Method of construction where the structural frame is built of interlocking timbers. The spaces are filled with non-structural material, e.g. *infill* of wattle and daub, lath and plaster, brickwork (known as *nogging*), etc. and may be covered by plaster, weatherboarding (q.v.), or tiles.

TOMB-CHEST: chest-shaped tomb, usually of stone. Cf. Table tomb, Tester tomb.

TORUS (plural: tori): large convex moulding usually used on a column base (3b, 3f).

TOUCH: soft black marble quarried near Tournai.

TOURELLE: turret corbelled out from the wall.

TOWER BLOCK: *see* Multi-storey.

TRABEATED: depends structurally on the use of the post and lintel. Cf. Arcuated.

TRACERY: openwork pattern of masonry or timber in the upper part of an opening. *Blind tracery* is tracery applied to a solid wall.

Plate tracery, introduced *c.* 1200, is the earliest form, in which shapes are cut through solid masonry (2a).

Bar tracery was introduced into England *c.* 1250. The pattern is formed by intersecting moulded ribwork continued from the mullions. It was especially elaborate during the Decorated period (q.v.). Tracery shapes can include circles, *daggers* (elongated ogee-ended lozenges), *mouchettes* (like daggers but with curved sides) and upright rectangular *panels*. They often have *cusps*, projecting points defining lobes or *foils* (q.v.) within the main shape: *Kentish* or *split-cusps* are forked (2b).

Types of bar tracery (*see* 2b) include *geometric(al)*: *c.* 1250–1310, chiefly circles, often foiled; *Y-tracery*: *c.* 1300, with mullions branching into a Y-shape; *intersecting*: *c.* 1300, formed by interlocking mullions; *reticulated*: early C14, net-like pattern of ogee-ended lozenges; *curvilinear*: C14, with uninterrupted flowing curves; *panel*: Perp, with straight-sided panels, often cusped at the top and bottom.

TRANSEPT: transverse portion of a church.

TRANSITIONAL: generally used for the phase between Romanesque and Early English (*c.* 1175–*c.* 120off).

TRANSOM: horizontal member separating window lights (2b).

TREAD: horizontal part of a step. The *tread end* may be carved on a staircase (6c).

TREFOIL: *see* Foil.

TRIFORIUM: middle storey of a church treated as an arcaded wall passage or blind arcade, its height corresponding to that of the aisle roof.

TRIGLYPHS (*lit.* three-grooved tablets): stylized beam-ends in the Doric frieze, with metopes between (3b).

TRIUMPHAL ARCH: influential type of Imperial Roman monument.

TROPHY: sculptured or painted group of arms or armour.

TRUMEAU: central stone mullion supporting the tympanum of a wide doorway. *Trumeau figure:* carved figure attached to it (cf. Column figure).

TRUMPET CAPITAL: *see* 1b.

TRUSS: braced framework, spanning between supports. *See also* Roofs and 7.

TUMBLING or TUMBLING-IN: courses of brickwork laid at right-angles to a slope, e.g. of a gable, forming triangles by tapering into horizontal courses (8a).

TUSCAN: *see* Orders and 3e.

TWO-DECKER PULPIT: *see* Pulpit.

TYMPANUM: the surface between a lintel and the arch above it or within a pediment (4a).

UNDERCROFT: usually describes the vaulted room(s), beneath the main room(s) of a medieval house. Cf. Crypt.

VAULT: arched stone roof (sometimes imitated in timber or plaster). For types *see* 2c.

Tunnel or *barrel vault:* continuous semicircular or pointed arch, often of rubble masonry.

Groin-vault: tunnel vaults intersecting at right angles. *Groins* are the curved lines of the intersections.

Rib-vault: masonry framework of intersecting arches (ribs) supporting *vault cells*, used in Gothic architecture. *Wall rib* or *wall arch:* between wall and vault cell. *Transverse rib:* spans between two walls to divide a vault into bays. *Quadripartite* rib-vault: each bay has two pairs of diagonal ribs dividing the vault into four triangular cells. *Sexpartite* rib-vault: most often used over paired bays, has an extra pair of ribs springing from between the bays. More elaborate vaults may include *ridge ribs* along the crown of a vault or bisecting the bays; *tiercerons:* extra decorative ribs springing from the corners of a bay; and *liernes:* short decorative ribs in the crown of a vault, not linked to any springing point. A *stellar* or *star* vault has liernes in star formation.

Fan-vault: form of barrel vault used in the Perp period, made up of halved concave masonry cones decorated with blind tracery.

VAULTING SHAFT: shaft leading up to the spring or springing (q.v.) of a vault (2c).

VENETIAN or SERLIAN WINDOW: derived from Serlio (4b). The motif is used for other openings.

VERMICULATION: *see* Rustication and 6d.

VESICA: oval with pointed ends.

VICE: *see* Stair.

VILLA: originally a Roman country house or farm. The term was revived in England in the C18 under the influence of Palladio and used especially for smaller, compact country houses. In the later C19 it was debased to describe any suburban house.

VITRIFIED: bricks or tiles fired to a darkened glassy surface.

VITRUVIAN SCROLL: classical running ornament of curly waves (4b).

VOLUTES: spiral scrolls. They occur on Ionic capitals (3c). *Angle volute:* pair of volutes, turned outwards to meet at the corner of a capital.

VOUSSOIRS: wedge-shaped stones forming an arch (5c).

WAGON ROOF: with the appearance of the inside of a wagon tilt; often ceiled. Also called *cradle roof.*

WAINSCOT: *see* Panelling.

WALL MONUMENT: attached to the wall and often standing on the floor. *Wall tablets* are smaller with the inscription as the major element.

WALL-PLATE: *see* Roofs and 7.

WALL-WALK: *see* Parapet.

WARMING ROOM: room in a religious house where a fire burned for comfort.

WATERHOLDING BASE: early Gothic base with upper and lower mouldings separated by a deep hollow.

WATERLEAF: *see* Enrichments and 3f.

WATERLEAF CAPITAL: Late Romanesque and Transitional type of capital (1b).

WATER WHEELS: described by the way water is fed on to the wheel. *Breastshot:* mid-height, falling and passing beneath. *Overshot:* over the top. *Pitchback:* on the top but falling backwards. *Undershot:* turned by the momentum of the water passing beneath. In a *water turbine*, water is fed under pressure through a vaned wheel within a casing.

WEALDEN HOUSE: type of medieval timber-framed house with a central open hall flanked by bays of two storeys, roofed in line; the end bays are jettied to the front, but the eaves are continuous (8a).

WEATHERBOARDING wall cladding of overlapping horizontal boards.

WEATHERING or SET-OFF: inclined, projecting surface to keep water away from the wall below.

WEEPERS: figures in niches along the sides of some medieval tombs. Also called *mourners.*

WHEEL WINDOW: circular, with radiating shafts like spokes. Cf. Rose window.

WROUGHT IRON: *see* Cast iron.

LANGUAGE GLOSSARY

Adapted, with omissions and a few augmentations, with the permission of the Director General of the Ordnance Survey, from the OS publication *Place Names on Maps of Scotland and Wales*. Crown copyright reserved.

a = adjective
ad = adverb
f = feminine
n = noun masculine

nf = noun feminine
np = noun plural
pl = plural
pr = preposition

abad, *n* abbot
abaty, *n* abbey
aber, *n & nf* estuary, confluence, stream
adeiladu, *verb* to build
aderyn, *pl* adar, *n* bird
ael, *nf* brow, edge
aelwyd, *nf* hearth
aethnen, *nf* aspen, poplar
afallen, *nf* apple tree
afon, *nf* river
ailadeiladu, *verb* to rebuild
allt, *pl* elltydd, alltau, *nf* hillside, cliff, wood
Annibynnol, *a* Independent
ar, *pr* on, upon, over
ardd, *n* hill, height
argoed, *nf* wood, grove

bach, *a* small, little, lesser
bach, *pl* bachau, *nf* nook, corner
bala, *n* outlet of a lake
banc, *pl* bencydd, *n* bank, slope
bangor, *nf* monastery originally constructed of wattle rods
banhadlog, *nf* broom patch
banw, *n* young pig
bar, *n* top, summit
bechan, *a see* bychan
bedd, *pl* beddau, *n* grave
Bedyddwyr, *a* Baptist
beidr, *nf* lane, path
beili, *pl* beiliau, *n* bailey, court before a house bailiff
bellaf, *a* far
bendigaid, *a* blessed
betws, *n* oratory, chapel

beudy, *n* cow-house
blaen, *pl* blaenau, *n* end, edge; source of river or stream; highland
bod, *n & nf* abode, dwelling
bôn, *n* stock, stump
bont, *nf see* pont
braich, *n & nf* ridge, arm
brân, *pl* brain, *nf* crow
bre, *nf* hill
brith, *f* braith, *a* speckled; coarse
bro, *nf* region; vale, lowland
bron, *pl* bronnydd, *nf* hillbreast (breast)
bryn, *pl* bryniau, *n* hill
bugail, *pl* bugelydd, bugeiliaid, *n* shepherd
bwla, *n* bull
bwlch, *pl* bylchau, *n* gap, pass
bwth, bwthyn, *n* cottage, booth
bychan, *f* bechan, *pl* bychain, *a* little, tiny

caban, *n* cottage, cabin
cader, cadair, *nf* seat, stronghold
cadlas, *nf* close, court of a house
cae, *pl* caeau, *n* field, enclosure
caer, *pl* caerau, *nf* stronghold, fort
cafn, *n* ferry-boat, trough
canol, *n* middle
cantref, *n* hundred (territorial division)
capel, *n* meeting house, chapel
carn, *pl* carnau, *nf* heap of stones, tumulus
carnedd, *pl* carneddau, carneddi, *nf* heap of stones, tumulus

carreg, *pl* cerrig, *nf* stone, rock
carrog, *nf* brook
carw, *n* stag
cas (in Casnewydd etc.), *n* castle
castell, *pl* cestyll, *n* castle; small
   stronghold; fortified residence;
   imposing natural position
cath, *nf* cat. (In some names it may
   be the Irish word cath meaning
   'battle'.)
cau, *a* hollow; enclosed
cawr, *pl* ceiri, cewri, *n* giant
cefn, *pl* cefnydd, *n* ridge
cegin, *nf* kitchen
ceiliog, *n* cock
ceiri, *np* *see* cawr
celli, *nf* grove
celynen, *pl* celyn, *nf* holly tree
celynog, clynnog, *nf* holly grove
cemais, *n from np* shallow bend in
   river, or coastline
cennin, *np* leeks
cerrig, *np* *see* carreg
cesail, *nf* hollow (arm- pit)
ceunant, *n* ravine, gorge
cewri, *np* *see* cawr
chwilog, *nf* land infested with
   beetles
cil, *pl* ciliau, *n* retreat, recess,
   corner
cilfach, *nf* nook
clas, *n* quasi-monastic system of
   the Celtic Church, existing in
   Wales, Cornwall and Ireland
   from the Dark Ages to *c.* 1200.
   Clasau comprised a body of
   secular canons
clawdd, *pl* cloddiau, *n* ditch,
   hedge
cloch, *nf* bell
clochydd, *n* sexton, parish clerk
cloddiau, *np* *see* clawdd
clog, *nf* crag, precipice
clogwyn, *n* precipice, steep rock
   hanging on one side
clwyd, *pl* clwydydd, *nf* hurdle, gate
clynnog, *nf* *see* celynog
coch, *a* red
coeden, *pl* coed, *nf* tree
collen, *pl* cyll, coll, *nf* hazel
colwyn, *n* whelp
comin, *pl* comins, *n* common
congl, *nf* corner
cornel, *nf* corner
cors, *pl* corsydd, *nf* bog
craf, *n* garlic
craig, *pl* creigiau, *nf* rock
crib, *n* crest, ridge, summit

crochan, *n* cauldron
croes, *nf* cross
croesffordd, croesheol, croeslon,
   nf cross-roads
crofft, *pl* crofftau, *nf* croft
croglofft, *nf* garret, low cottage
   with loft under the roof
crug, *pl* crugiau, *n* heap, tump
cwm, *pl* cymau, cymoedd,
   n valley, dale
cwmwd, *n* commote (territorial
   division)
cwrt, *n* court, yard
cyffin, *n* boundary, frontier
cyll, *np* *see* collen
cymer, *pl* cymerau, *n* confluence
Cynulleidfaol, *a* Congregational
cywarch, *n* hemp

dan, *pr* under, below
derwen, *pl* derw, *nf* oak
diffwys, *n* precipice, abyss
dinas, *n & nf* hill-fortress (city)
diserth, *n* hermitage
disgwylfa, *nf* place of observation,
   look-out point
dôl, *pl* dolau, dolydd, *nf* meadow
draw, *ad* yonder
du, *a* black, dark
dwfr, dŵr, *n* water
dyffryn, *n* valley

eglwys, *nf* church
(ei)singrug, *n* heap of bran or corn
   husks
eisteddfa, *nf* seat, resting place
eithinog, *nf* furze patch
elltyd, *np* *see* allt
ellyll, *n* elf, goblin
eos, *nf* nightingale
erw, *pl* erwau, *nf* acre
esgair, *nf* long ridge (leg)
esgob, *n* bishop
ewig, *nf* hind

-fa, *nf* *see* ma-
fach, *a* *see* bach
faenor, *nf* Vaynor. cf. maenor
fawr, *a* *see* mawr
felin, *nf* *see* melin
ffald, *pl* ffaldau, *nf* sheep-fold,
   pound, pen, run
ffawydden, *pl* ffawydd, *nf* beech
   tree
fferm, *nf* farm
ffin, *nf* boundary

ffordd, *nf*   way, road

fforest, *nf*   forest, park

ffridd, ffrith, *pl* ffriddoedd, *nf* wood; mountain enclosure, sheep walk

ffrwd, *nf*   stream, torrent

ffynnon, *pl* ffynhonnau, *nf*   spring, well

fron, *nf*   *see* bron

fry, *ad*   above

gaer, *nf*   *see* caer

ganol, *n*   *see* canol

gardd, *pl* gerddi, garddau, *nf*   garden; enclosure or fold into which calves were turned for first time

garreg, *nf*   *see* carreg

garth, *n*   promontory, hill enclosure

garw, *a*   coarse, rough

gefail, *nf*   smithy

(g)eirw, *np*   rush of waters

gelli, *nf*   *see* celli

glan, *nf*   river bank, hillock

glas, *a*   green

glas, glais (as in dulas, dulais), *n & nf*   brook

glo, *n*   charcoal, coal

glyn, *n*   deep valley, glen

gof, *n*   smith

gogof, *pl* gogofau, *nf*   cave

gorffwysfa, *nf*   resting place

gris, *pl* grisiau, *n*   step

grug, *n*   heath, heather

gwaelod, *n*   foot of hill (bottom)

gwastad, *n*   plain

gwaun, *pl* gweunydd, *nf*   moor, mountain meadow, moorland field

gwely, *n*   bed, resting place, family land

gwen, *a*   *see* gwyn

gwerdd, *a*   *see* gwyrdd

gwernen, *pl* gwern, *nf*   alder tree

gwersyll, *n*   encampment

gwrych, *n*   hedge, quickset hedge

gwryd, *n*   fathom

gwyddel, *pl* gwyddyl, gwyddelod, *n*   Irishman

gwyddrug, *nf*   mound, wooded knoll

gwyn, *f* gwen, *a*   white

gwynt, *n*   wind

gwyrdd, *f* gwerdd, *a*   green

hafn, *nf*   gorge, ravine

hafod, *nf*   shieling, upland summer dwelling

hafoty, *n*   summer dwelling

helygen, *pl* helyg, *nf*   willow

hen, *a*   old

hendref, *nf*   winter dwelling, old home, permanent abode

heol, hewl, *nf*   street, road

hir, *a*   long

is, *pr*   below, under

isaf, *a*   lower (lowest)

isel, *a*   low

iwrch, *pl* iyrchod, *n*   roebuck

lawnd, lawnt, *nf*   open space in woodland, glade

llaethdy, *n*   milkhouse, dairy

llan, *nf*   church, monastery; enclosure

Llanbedr   St Peter's church

Llanddewi   St David's church

Llanfair   St Mary's church

Llanfihangel   St Michael's church

llannerch, *nf*   clearing, glade

lle, *n*   place, position

llech, *pl* llechau, *nf*   slab, stone, rock

llechwedd, *nf*   hillside

llethr, *nf*   slope

llety, *n*   small abode, quarters

llidiard, llidiart, *pl* llidiardau, llidiartau, *n*   gate

llom, *a*   *see* llwm

lluest, *n*   shieling, cottage, hut

llumon, *n*   stack (chimney)

llwch, *n*   dust

llwch, *pl* llychau, *n*   lake

llwm, *f* llom, *a*   bare, exposed

llwyd, *a*   grey, brown

llwyn, *pl* llwyni, llwynau, *n*   grove, bush

llyn, *n & nf*   lake

llys, *n & nf*   court, hall

lôn, *nf*   lane, road

ma-, -fa, *nf*   plain, place

maen, *pl* meini, main, *n*   stone

maenol, maenor, *nf*   stone-built residence of chieftain of district, rich low-lying land surrounding same, vale

maerdref, *nf*   hamlet attached to chieftain's court, lord's demesne (maer, steward + tref, hamlet)

maerdy, *n*   steward's house, dairy

maes, *pl* meysydd, *n* open field, plain

march, *pl* meirch, *n* horse, stallion

marchog, *n* knight, horseman

marian, *n* holm, gravel, gravelly ground, rock debris

mawnog, *nf* peat-bog

mawr, *a* great, big

meillionen, *pl* meillion, *nf* clover

meini, *np* *see* maen

meirch, *np* *see* march

melin, *nf* mill

melyn, *f* melen, *a* yellow

menych, *np* *see* mynach

merthyr, *n* burial place, church

Methodistaidd, *a* Methodist

meysydd, *np* *see* maes

mochyn, *pl* moch, *n* pig

moel, *nf* bare hill

moel, *a* bare, bald

môr, *n* sea

morfa, *n* marsh, fen

mur, *pl* muriau, *n* wall

mwyalch, mwyalchen, *nf* blackbird

mynach, *pl* mynych, menych, myneich, *n* monk

mynachdy, *n* monastic grange

mynwent, *nf* churchyard

mynydd, *n* mountain, moorland

nant, *pl* nentydd, naint, nannau, *nf* brook

nant, *pl* nentydd, naint, nannau, *n* dingle, glen, ravine

neuadd, *nf* hall

newydd, *a* new

noddfa, *nf* hospice

nyth, *n & nf* nest, inaccessible position

oen, *pl* ŵyn, *n* lamb

offeiriad, *n* priest

onnen, *pl* onn, ynn, *nf* ash tree

pandy, *n* fulling mill

pant, *n* hollow, valley

parc, *pl* parciau, parcau, *n* park, field, enclosure

pen, *pl* pennau, *n* head, top; end, edge

penrhyn, *n* promontory

pensaer, *n* architect

pentref, *n* homestead, appendix to the real 'tref', village

person, *n* parson

pistyll, *n* spout, waterfall

plas, *n* gentleman's seat, hall, mansion

plwyf, *n* parish

poeth, *a* burnt (hot)

pont, *nf* bridge

porth, *n* gate, gateway

porth, *nf* ferry, harbour

pwll, *pl* pyllau, *n* pit, pool

rhaeadr, *nf* waterfall

rhandir, *n* allotment, fixed measure of land

rhiw, *nf & n* hill, slope

rhos, *pl* rhosydd, *nf* moor, promontory

rhyd, *nf & n* ford

saeth, *pl* saethau, *nf* arrow

sant, san, *pl* saint, *n* saint, monk

sarn, *pl* sarnau, *nf* causeway

simnai, simdde, *nf* chimney

siop, *nf* shop

sticil, sticill, *nf* stile

swydd, *nf* seat, lordship, office

sych, *a* dry

tafarn, *pl* tafarnau, *n & nf* tavern

tai, *np* *see* tŷ

tâl, *n* end (forehead)

talwrn, *pl* talyrni, tylyrni, *n* bare exposed hillside, open space, threshing floor, cockpit

tan, dan, *nf* under, beneath

teg, *a* fair

tir, *n* land, territory

tom, tomen, *nf* mound

ton, *pl* tonnau, *nf* wave

ton, tonnen, *pl* tonnau, *n & nf* grassland, lea

torglwyd, *nf* door-hurdle, gate

towyn, *n* *see* tywyn

traean, traen, *n* third part

traeth, *n* strand, shore

trallwng, trallwm, *n* wet bottom land

traws, *a & n* cross, transverse

tref, *nf* homestead, hamlet, town

tros, *pr* over

trwyn, *n* point, cape (nose)

twr, *n* tower

twyn, *pl* twyni, *n* hillock, knoll

tŷ, *pl* tai, *n* house

tyddyn, ty'n, *n* small farm, holding

tylyrni, *np* *see* talwrn

tywyn, towyn, *n* sea-shore, strand

uchaf, *a* higher, highest

uchel, *a* high

uwch, *pr* above, over

ŵyn, *np* *see* oen

y, yr, 'r (definite article) the
yn, *pr* in
ynn, *np* *see* onnen
ynys, *pl* ynysoedd, *nf* island; holm, river-meadow

ysbyty, *n* hospital, hospice
ysgol, *pl* ysgolion, *nf* school
ysgubor, *pl* ysguboriau, *nf* barn
ystafell, *nf* chamber, hiding place
ystrad, *n* valley, holm, river-meadow
ystum, *nf & n* bend shape

INDEX OF ARCHITECTS AND ARTISTS

Entries for partnerships and group practices are listed after entries for a single name.

INDEX OF PATRONS AND RESIDENTS

Indexed here are families and individuals (not bodies or commercial firms) recorded in this volume as having owned or visited property and/or commissioned architectural work in Gwynedd. The index includes monuments to members of such families and other individuals where they are of particular interest.

INDEX OF PLACES

Principal references are in **bold** type; demolished buildings are shown in *italic*.
'A' = Anglesey; 'C' = Caernarvonshire; 'M' = Merioneth